The SAGE
Handbook of

Tourism
Studies

The SAGE
Handbook of

Tourism
Studies

Edited by
Tazim Jamal and
Mike Robinson

Los Angeles | London | New Delhi
Singapore | Washington DC

SAGE Publications Ltd
1 Oliver's Yard
55 City Road
London EC1Y 1SP

SAGE Publications Inc.
2455 Teller Road
Thousand Oaks, California 91320

SAGE Publications India Pvt Ltd
B1/I 1, Mohan Cooperative Industrial Area
Mathura Road
New Delhi 110 044

SAGE Publications Asia-Pacific Pte Ltd
33 Pekin Street # 02-01
Far East Square, Singapore 048763

Library of Congress Control Number: 2008935470

British Library Cataloguing in Publication data

A catalogue record for this book is available from the British Library

ISBN 978-1-4129-2397-2

Typeset by CEPHA Imaging Pvt. Ltd., Bangalore, India
Printed in Great Britain by the MPG Books Group
Printed on paper from sustainable resources

Mixed Sources
Product group from well-managed forests and other controlled sources
www.fsc.org Cert no. SA-COC-1565
© 1996 Forest Stewardship Council
FSC

Contents

About the Editors and Authors

Editors

Tazim Jamal is an associate professor in the Department of Recreation, Park & Tourism Sciences at Texas A&M University, Texas, USA. She has a PhD in Management from the University of Calgary, Alberta, Canada, and an MBA from the University of British Columbia, Vancouver, Canada. Her main research interests lie in tourism planning, heritage tourism, collaborative processes and theoretical/methodological issues related to tourism and sustainability. Her current research areas include small mountain communities in Western Canada, rural communities in Texas, and the Riviera Maya, Mexico. She has published widely in various tourism-related journals.

Mike Robinson holds the Chair of Tourism and Culture at Leeds Metropolitan University. He is also Director of the Centre for Tourism and Cultural Change – an international research body that carries out work on the changing relationships between tourism and culture. Mike is founder and Editor-in-Chief of the *Journal of Tourism and Cultural Change*, an Associate Editor of the *Scandinavian Journal of Tourism* and is on the board of four other international journals. He is Series Editor of the Tourism and Cultural Change Book Series.

Authors

Cara Aitchison is Faculty Dean of Education and Sport at the University of Bedfordshire, UK and Professor in Leisure and Tourism Studies. Until 2008, she was Professor in Human Geography and Director of the Centre for Leisure, Tourism and Society (CeLTS) at the University of the West of England. Publications include *Gender, Sport and Identity* (Routledge, 2007), *Geographies of Muslim Identities: Diaspora, Gender and Belonging* (Ashgate, 2007), *Gender and Leisure: Social and Cultural Perspectives* (Routledge, 2003), *Leisure and Tourism Landscapes: Social and Cultural Geographies* (Routledge, 2001). Cara is a member of the UK Research Assessment Exercise Panel for Sport-Related Studies.

John Akama received his PhD in Geography from Southern Illinois University in 1994. Currently, he holds the position of Professor at Moi University, Kenya. Over the years, Professor Akama has taught both undergraduate and postgraduate courses in tourism policy and tourism planning, cultural tourism and destination management. His research interest is in the areas of tourism development in the Third World, tourism planning, and cultural tourism. He has widely published in those areas in journals and has made several chapter contributions. He recently coedited a book entitled, *Ethnography of the Gusii of Western Kenya: A Vanishing Cultural Heritage* (Edwin Mellen Press Ltd, 2006).

David Bell is senior lecturer in Critical Human Geography and leader of the Urban Cultures & Consumption research cluster in the School of Geography, University of Leeds, UK, where he is also a Deputy Director of the Centre for Interdisciplinary Gender Studies. David's research interests include urban cultural policy, lifestyles and consumption, geographies of sexualities, and science and technology studies. Recent articles have explored temporary outdoor ice rinks, the social impacts of the UK smoking ban, and "alcotourism."

A.P. Clevenger has carried out research during the last 12 years assessing the performance of mitigation measures designed to reduce habitat fragmentation on the Trans-Canada Highway (TCH) in Banff National Park, Alberta. Since 2002, he has been a research wildlife biologist for the Western Transportation Institute (WTI) at Montana State University. Tony is currently a member of the US National Academy of Sciences Committee on *Effects of Highways on Natural Communities and Ecosystems*. Since 1986, he has published over 40 articles in peer-reviewed scientific journals and has coauthored three books including *Road Ecology: Science and Solutions* (Island Press, 2003). His Banff research has resulted in 17 peer-reviewed publications since 2000. Tony is a graduate of the University of California, Berkeley, has a master's degree from the University of Tennessee, Knoxville and a doctoral degree in Zoology from the University of León, Spain.

David Crouch is Emeritus Professor of Cultural Geography and Senior Research Fellow at the University of Derby, UK. His research interests relate to tourism and leisure, nature, landscape, consumption, identity, visual culture, and performance. His relevant books include: *Leisure/ Tourism Geographies* (edited book, Routledge, 1999); *Visual Cultures and Tourism* (Berg publishers, 2003) (coedited with Nina Lubbren); and *Media and the Tourist Imagination* (Routledge, 2005) (coedited with Rhona Jackson and Felix Thompson). In addition David has published many articles and book chapters in cultural geography, tourism and leisure studies. David is a regular speaker at international conferences. He is also a part-professional artist, having staged several solo exhibitions of his work and made contributions to art-related publications and events.

Keith G. Debbage is a professor of urban development in the Department of Geography at the University of North Carolina at Greensboro, USA. His specific research interests include airline route networks and how they shape regional economies, and the economic geography of the tourist industry. Dr. Debbage is also the author of over 50 research publications in book chapters, contracted reports and various academic journals, including the *Annals of Tourism Research*, the *Journal of Air Transport Management*, the *Journal of Transport Geography*, *Policy Studies Review*, *Regional Studies*, *Tourism Management*, *Transportation Quarterly*, and *Urban Geography*. He was appointed in 2007 to the UNC Tomorrow Scholars Council by UNC System President Erskine Bowles and was selected as a GlaxoSmithKline Faculty Fellow with the Institute for Emerging Issues at North Carolina State University in 2008.

Tim Edensor teaches Human Geography at Manchester Metropolitan University. He is the author of *Tourists at the Taj* (Routledge, 1998), *National Identity, Popular Culture and Everyday Life* (Berg, 2002) and *Industrial Ruins: Space, Aesthetics and Materiality* (Berg, 2005). He has written widely on tourism and has also published articles and chapters on automobility, materiality, memory, mobility, national identity, urban regeneration, and global commodities. He is currently investigating the histories and geographies of building stone, the rhythms of tourism, and the class-oriented contestations over the display of Christmas lights on homes.

Nigel Evans joined the University of Teesside in 2005 as Deputy Dean Teesside Business School, following 15 years at The University of Northumbria in Newcastle, UK, which included periods leading the university's Tourism Department and travel and tourism degree programs. Prior to academia his commercial career included senior experience with a London based international tour operator. His research interests focus on structural and strategic changes in the international travel industry, the application of management tools, plus strategic alliances in the travel industry. He is the lead author of the book *Strategic Management for Travel and Tourism* (Butterworth-Heinemann, 2002, coedited with David Campbell and George Stonehouse).

Daniel R. Fesenmaier is a professor and Director of the National Laboratory for Tourism & eCommerce (NLTeC) for the School of Tourism and Hospitality Management at Temple University, USA. Dr. Fesenmaier is author of over 200 articles dealing with tourism marketing, advertising evaluation, and information technology. He has coauthored a monograph, coedited six books, and is co-founding editor of *Tourism Analysis*. Dr. Fesenmaier received his PhD in Geography from the University of Western Ontario, Canada.

John Fletcher is Director of the International Centre for Tourism and Hospitality Research and Head of Bournemouth University Graduate School, UK. As an economist he has developed an international reputation through his pioneering work in tourism impact and development research. He is the author of numerous articles and book chapters on tourism's economic impact and is coauthor of the leading textbook, *Tourism: Principles and Practice* (Edinburgh Gate, UK: Pearson Education, 2008), now in its fourth edition and Editor of the *International Journal of Tourism Research* and Special Adviser to *Tourism Economics*. He has undertaken economic and development research for international agencies, including the World Tourism Organization, the World Travel and Tourism Council, Development Banks, the EU, UNDP, and USAID.

Adam Ford, MSc Biology, is a wildlife research associate with seven years of experience working in conservation, ecology, and international community development. His work has taken him from the South Pacific to Eastern Africa, and from the temperate rainforests of western Vancouver Island to the native short-grass prairie of eastern Alberta. Currently, he is based in the Rocky Mountains of Banff National Park with research interests in the effects of roads on wildlife, mammal ecology and the effects of landscape structure on animal movement.

Robert C. Ford is a professor of Management at the University of Central Florida's College of Business Administration, USA. He joined UCF in 1993 as Chair of the Department of Hospitality Management and later became Associate Dean for Graduate and External Programs. He has authored or coauthored over 100 articles, books, and presentations on management and organizations focusing on human resources, services, and change management topics, especially on achieving service excellence in healthcare and hospitality. His published books include *Principles of Management* coauthored with Cherril Heaton (R.J. Brady, 1980); *Organization Theory* with Barry R. Armandi, and Cherrill P. Heaton, (Longman Higher Education. 1988); *Managing the Guest Experience in Hospitality* with Cheryl Heaton (Delmar Publishing, 2000) and *Achieving Service Excellence* with Myron Fottler and Cherril Heaton (Health Administration Press, 2002).

Adrian Franklin trained as a social anthropologist in the UK, and has held professorial positions at the University of Bristol, UK, the University of Oslo, Norway, and the University of Tasmania, Australia. His books include *Animal Nation: The True Story of Animals and Australia* (University of New South Wales Press Ltd, Sydney, 2006); *Animals and Modern Cultures* (Sage, 1999), *Nature and Social Theory* (Sage Publications Ltd, 2002) and *Tourism* (Sage Publications, London, 2003). *City Life* is due to be published in 2009. He is coeditor of *Tourist Studies* (with Mike Crang) and has written extensively on travel and tourism theory and the impact that modern mobilities have had on everyday life and the ordering of global modernity.

Suzanne Gallaway is a doctoral candidate in the Geography Department at the University of North Carolina at Greensboro, USA. She is currently working on her dissertation titled "The Geography of Industry Clusters: Tourism Development Strategies within the Appalachian Regional Commission area." Ms. Gallaway expects to graduate in 2009 and previously worked as an urban planner for the Winston-Salem/Forsyth County City Planning Department.

Yue Ge is an urban tourism planner with extensive experience in China. He has worked as an urban tourism planner for the China Academy of Urban Planning and Design for three years. He has consulted on various projects in China, on topics including urban and regional tourism planning, tourism development planning, urban master planning, and policymaking. He is presently working on his doctoral studies in the Urban and Regional Science program, College of Architecture, Texas A&M University, College Station, Texas, USA. His research interests currently focus on the impacts of natural hazards on coastal cities in America.

Nelson Graburn, educated at Cambridge, McGill, and University of Chicago, has taught Anthropology at U.C. Berkeley since 1964. He has held positions at Northwestern, University of Aix-en-Provence, National Museum of Ethnology, Osaka, the National University of Kyushu, Fukuoka, the Universidade Federal, Porto Alegre, Brazil, and since 2007 London Metropolitan University. He has carried out research among the Canadian Inuit since 1959, with excursions to Greenland and Alaska, focusing on kinship, social change, commercial arts and, recently, ethnic identity, tourism, and museums. He has studied Japanese domestic tourism since 1974 and more recently Japanese multiculturalism and tourism in, to and from China and Korea.

Ulrike Gretzel is an assistant professor at the Department of Recreation, Park & Tourism Sciences at Texas A&M University, USA and Director of the Laboratory for Intelligent Systems in Tourism. She received her PhD in Communication from the University of Illinois at Urbana-Champaign and holds a masters' degree in International Business from the Vienna University for Economics and Business Administration. Her research focuses on persuasion in human–technology interaction, the representation of sensory and emotional aspects of tourism experiences, and the development and use of intelligent systems in tourism to support travelers' information search, decision-making processes, and experiences.

Rich Harrill – author, lecturer, researcher, consultant, and traveler – is director of the International Tourism Research Institute at the University of South Carolina, School of Hotel, Restaurant and Tourism Management, USA. He also directs the university's Alfred P. Sloan Foundation Travel & Tourism Industry Center. The institute conducts local and international projects and research; the center focuses on US tourism industry competitiveness. His academic and professional experience combines tourism with economic development and urban planning. Dr. Harrill is editor of *Fundamentals of Destination Management and Marketing* (American Hotel & Lodging Association, 2005), the first comprehensive textbook for the destination management industry.

Andrew Holden is Professor of Environment and Tourism and also the Director for the Centre for Research into the Environment and Sustainable Tourism Development (CREST) at the University of Bedfordshire, UK. He is a Fellow of the Royal Geographical Society in London. His research focuses on the interaction between human behavior and the natural environment within the context of tourism.

Keith Hollinshead is an Anglo-Australian researcher of the representation of populations and their cherished inheritances. Once a student of Romano-British history, he now works via transdisciplinary/postdisciplinary approaches on the iconology of projected places and signified pasts. Having worked mainly at state government level in various regions of Australia – including a spell as Program Manager for the Yulara International Tourist Resort at Uluru in Centralia. Keith obtained his doctorate at Texas A&M University, USA where he specialized in the politics of tourism. He is currently Professor of Public Culture at the University of Bedfordshire, UK.

G.R. Jennings, PhD, is Associate Professor of Tourism Management, Department of Tourism, Leisure, Hotel and Sport Management, Griffith University, Gold Coast Campus, Australia. Her research agenda focuses on quality tourism experiences, sustainability, ethics and responsible practice, and the use of qualitative methodologies. She is a co-founder of Qualitative Research in Tourism and Hospitality Network, QUALNET[4RiTH]. Gayle has sole authored and edited a number of books, written book chapters, and journal articles across a range of topics relating to theoretical paradigms that inform research processes, water-based tourism, and quality tourism experiences.

Brian King is Making VU Program Director in the Office of the Pro Vice-Chancellor (Institutional Services) at Victoria University, Australia. He is also a professorial associate with the Centre for Tourism and Services Research. His research has focused on tourism in the Asia-Pacific region and he is founding and current Joint Editor-in-Chief of the journal *Tourism, Culture and Communication*. He is a Fellow of the International Academy for the Study of Tourism (IAST).

Bernard Lane is a consultant, writer, and lecturer specializing in sustainable rural tourism, heritage conservation, and rural development. He is an associate of Red Kite Environment (www.redkite-environment.co.uk), focusing on the management and sustainable development of heritage sites, protected areas, and rural regions. Clients have included the OECD, national and local governments, among others. With Bill Bramwell, he founded and is coeditor of the *Journal of Sustainable Tourism*, and is also an associate editor of the *Journal of Ecotourism*. He is a visiting research fellow at the universities of Bristol and Sheffield Hallam in the UK.

Naomi Leite is a doctoral candidate in anthropology at the University of California, Berkeley, USA. The co-founder of Berkeley's interdisciplinary Tourism Studies Working Group, her tourism-related publications have addressed cultural memory and constructions of heritage, museums, tourist identity and experience, materiality, and place. Her current research focuses on the implications of global interconnection for emergent identities, ethnic and spiritual "kinship," and belonging. She has conducted ethnographic fieldwork in Portugal, the USA, in online communities, and throughout the Portuguese diaspora.

Philip Long is Principal Research Fellow with the Centre for Tourism and Cultural Change at Leeds Metropolitan University, UK. He is also Course Director of the MA Cultural Tourism program. Phil is editor of books on royal tourism and on tourism and festivals. He is a Board member of the International Festivals and Events Association (Europe) and the UK Tourism Management Institute and is on the editorial board of the *Journal of Event Management*.

Mišela Mavrič is a doctoral candidate in Sociology at Lancaster University who has a BA in Tourism Studies (Turistica, Slovenia) and an MA in Tourism and Leisure (Lancaster University). Her research interests revolve around travel, tourism, mobilities, and cosmopolitanism. She is particularly focusing on "roots" and "routs" in mobile tourist performances and practices, and exploring "new" mobile research methods.

Joseph E. Mbaiwa is a senior research fellow in Tourism Studies at the Harry Oppenheimer Okavango Research Centre, University of Botswana. His research focus is on tourism development, rural livelihoods, and conservation in the Okavango Delta, Botswana. He has so far coauthored a book on tourism and the environment in the Okavango Delta, published over 20 journal articles, 10 book chapters and several conference papers on tourism development, livelihoods, and conservation in the Okavango Delta.

Robert Mugerauer, Professor and Dean Emeritus in the College of Architecture and Urban Planning, University of Washington, specializes in applying contemporary theory to the built environment. He is author of *Interpretations on Behalf of Place*, *Environmental Interpretations* (State University of New York Press, 1994), and, with David Seamon, coeditor of *Dwelling, Place, and Environment* (Springer, 1985). Recent essays on tourism include "The Tensed Embrace of Tourism and Traditional Environments: Exclusionary Practices in Cancun, Cuba, and South Florida," and with Monika Kaup, "Reconfiguring the Caribbean's Sense of Place: From Fixed Identity to Fluid Hybridity." Currently he is working on bio-technio-power in medical tourism.

Sanjay K. Nepal is an associate professor in the Department of Recreation, Park and Tourism Sciences at Texas A&M University, USA. He has a PhD in Geography from the University of Berne, Switzerland and a master's degree in regional and rural development planning. His research interests are on participatory conservation in developing countries, tourism and ecotourism impacts in remote locations, and in general aspects of tourism and change in mountainous regions. He has conducted fieldwork in Nepal, Thailand, Canada, and most recently in China, the majority of research locations are near or within national parks and protected areas.

Aylin Orbaşlı, PhD, trained as an architect and specializes in the conservation and management of historic buildings and places. She works as an independent consultant advising on heritage protection and management in the context of tourism development internationally. She is also a senior lecturer in the Department of Architecture at Oxford Brookes University and the author of two books, *Tourists in Historic Towns: urban conservation and visitor management* (Spon, 2000) and *Architectural Conservation* (Blackwell, 2008).

Stephen Page is the Scottish Enterprise Professor of Tourism at the University of Stirling, UK. He has worked in the UK, New Zealand, Australia, Ireland, and France and has written, edited or contributed to 20 leading books on tourism. He has worked with many private sector and public sector agencies on tourism consultancy in terms of tourism and leisure strategies, feasibility studies, problem-solving, including projects such as the Channel Tunnel and Auckland's Sky Tower in New Zealand. He is also an editor of *Tourism Management* and is a regular contributor to industry conferences and meetings as a speaker.

Michael Pearlman is a senior lecturer in the School of Hospitality, Tourism and Marketing at Victoria University, Australia. He is also a research associate with the Centre for Tourism and Services Research. The main focus of his research is the planning, development, and management of regional tourism. He is a member of the Executive Committee of the Network of Asia-Pacific Education and Training Institutes in Tourism (APETIT) with responsibility for fostering research and development activities.

William C. Peeper retired as President of the Orland/Orange County Convention & Visitors Bureau with over 35 years of service in the convention bureau business. He was the founding executive director of the not-for-profit Orlando/Orange County Convention and Visitors Bureau, Inc. in 1984. He oversaw the growth of the bureau's sales and marketing staff from two to its current 170 level with offices in five countries and convention sales offices in four US cities. Peeper has received numerous awards and is one of two inaugural inductees into the University of Central Florida's Rosen School of Hospitality Management's Hall of Fame.

Alison Phipps is Professor of Languages and Intercultural Studies at the University of Glasgow, UK, where she is Associate Dean in the Faculty of Education, and teaches modern languages, comparative literature, anthropology, and intercultural studies. Her books include *Modern Languages: Learning and Teaching in an Intercultural Field* (Sage Publications Ltd, 2004) with Mike Gonzalez, *Critical Pedagogy: Political Approaches to Languages and Intercultural Communication* (Multilingual Matters Ltd, 2004) with Manuela Guilherme, *Tourism and Intercultural Exchange* Channel View Publications, 2005 with Gavin Jack, and *Learning the Arts of Linguistic Survival: Tourism, Languaging, Life* Channel View Publications, 2007. She coedits the journals *Tourism and Cultural Change*, *Arts and Humanities in Higher Education*, and the book series *Languages, Intercultural Communication and Education*.

Jess Ponting is an assistant professor in sustainable tourism at San Diego State University, USA, recently relocated from the University of the South Pacific. He has consulted for both the private and public sector in Australia, Papua New Guinea, Indonesia and Fiji. Jess' research has empirically focused on various aspects of surfing tourism while theoretically helping to advance understanding of decommodified tourism practice and research; socially constructed tourist spaces; relationships between the media and tourism practice; humanistic psychology as it relates to the tourist experience; and the reorientation of surfing tourism in less developed countries to a sustainable trajectory.

Bernadette Quinn, PhD, is a geographer who lectures and researches in the Department of Tourism at the Dublin Institute of Technology, Republic of Ireland. Her research interests include festivals and events, tourism and cultural change and tourism mobilities. Her work has been published in such journals as *Urban Studies*, *Tourism Geographies*, *Social and Cultural Geography*, and the *Annals of Tourism Research*.

Kathleen Rettie has more than 30 years' experience working for Parks Canada in the mountain national parks. Currently, she is a social scientist with the Western and Northern Service Centre, Parks Canada Agency. She has a PhD in Social Anthropology from St. Andrews University, UK, and an MA in Resources and the Environment from the University of Calgary, Canada. She is an adjunct associate professor in Geography at the University of Calgary, a Fellow of the Royal Geographic Society and a Fellow of the Royal Anthropology Institute. Her research focuses on the human aspects of national parks.

Linda K. Richter is professor emerita of political science at Kansas State University where she taught public policy, ethics, and gender politics. Her primary research area is tourism politics about which she has written three books and over 60 monographs, chapters, and articles. She has done extensive field research in India, Pakistan, and the Philippines, and has lectured on tourism in 18 countries. She served on the US Travel and Tourism Advisory Board and as Associate editor of *Annals of Tourism Research* and the *Encyclopedia of Tourism*.

Tony Seaton is Professor of Tourism Behaviour at the University of Bedfordshire, UK. Educated in England and Scotland, he holds degrees in the Arts, Social Sciences, and Travel, including an MA in Literature from Oxford and a Tourism PhD from Strathclyde University. His main work has been in destination marketing, cultural tourism, and travel history. He has lectured, researched, and been visiting professor in over 60 countries, and been consultant to the UNTWO, European Union, USAID, and several governments on destination development. He has been researching thanatourism, a word he was first to use and theorize, since 1996.

Richard Sharpley is Professor of Tourism at the University of Lincoln, UK, and Head of the Department of Tourism and Recreation. His principal research interests include the sociol of tourism with a specific focus on tourist consumer behavior, tourism, and international development, tourism in island micro-states, and rural tourism. He has published in all of these areas, and has also written/edited a number of more general books including *The Management of Tourism* (Sage, 2005).

Mick Smith is Associate Professor and Queen's National Scholar in the Department of Philosophy and School of Environmental Studies at Queen's University, Kingston, Ontario. He is the author of *An Ethics of Place: Radical Ecology, Postmodernity and Social Theory* (SUNY, 2001) and coauthor, with Rosaleen Duffy, of *The Ethics of Tourism Development* (Routledge, 2005). His main interests are in environmental ethics; the ecological ramifications of political and social theory, and in different understandings, interpretations, and emotional responses to natural environments. He currently sits on the editorial boards of *Environmental Ethics* and *Environmental Values,* and is coeditor of *Emotion, Space and Society.*

Amanda L. Stronza is an environmental anthropologist and Assistant Professor in the Department of Recreation, Park, and Tourism Sciences at Texas A&M University, USA. She has a BA in International Affairs from the George Washington University, USA, an MA in Latin American Studies and PhD in Anthropology from the University of Florida, USA. She was a Lang Postdoctoral Fellow in Anthropological Sciences at Stanford. Her research focuses on community-based conservation and ecotourism in the tropics. She co-directs the Applied Biodiversity Science NSF-IGERT Program.

Peter E. Tarlow, PhD, founder and president of Tourism & More Inc. is an expert specializing in the impact of crime and terrorism on the tourism industry, and in event risk management. He lectures on tourism, crime, and terrorism to police forces and security and tourism professionals throughout the world. He also works with multiple US federal, state, and local government agencies and major universities. "Tourism Tidbits," an electronic newsletter on tourism and travel, is written by Peter Tarlow and is read by tourism and travel professionals around the world in English-, Spanish-, Portuguese-, and Turkish-language editions.

David J. Telfer is Associate Professor in the Department of Tourism and Environment at Brock University, Canada. His research interests include: links between tourism and development theory, backward economic linkages of tourism, and the relationships between tourism and agriculture. He is currently involved in an ongoing research project on rural tourism development in Japan. He is coauthor of *Tourism and Development in the Developing World* (Routledge, 2008) and coeditor of *Tourism and Development Concepts and Issues* (Channel View Publications, 2002) (both with Richard Sharpley).

Hazel Tucker is Senior Lecturer in Tourism at the University of Otago, New Zealand. She has a PhD in Social Anthropology from the University of Durham, UK, and is author of *Living With Tourism: Negotiating Identity in a Turkish Village* (Routledge, 2003) and coeditor of *Tourism and Postcolonialism* (Routledge, 2004). She has also published several journal articles and book chapters on tourism in Cappadocia, Turkey, on tourists' on-tour performances and on bed and breakfast business and host–guest relationships in New Zealand.

John Urry is a Professor of Sociology at Lancaster University, UK. His BA, MA Economics, PhD Sociology are all from University of Cambridge, UK. His honors and appointments include: Honorary Doctorate Roskilde University, Fellow, Royal Society of Arts, Chair RAE Panel 1996, 2001, Founding Academician and Member of Council, Academy of Social Sciences, Coeditor of *Mobilities,* and Editor *International Library of Sociology,* Routledge. He is the Director, Centre for Mobilities Research at Lancaster University, UK. Recent books include *Sociology beyond Societies* (2000), *The Tourist Gaze. Second Edition* (2002), *Global Complexity* (2003), *Tourism Mobilities. Places to Play, Places in Play* (authored with Mimi

Sheller 2004), *Performing Tourist Places* (with Joergen Ole Baerenholdt, Wolfgang Framke, Jonas Larsen, and Michael Haldrup – Ashgate, 2004), *Automobilities* (Sage, 2005) (edited with Mike Featherstone and Nigel Thrift), *Mobile Technologies of the City* (Routledge, 2006) (edited with Mimi Sheller), *Mobilities, Networks, Geographies* (authored with Jonas Larsen, and Kay Axhausen, 2006), *Mobilities* (Polity Press, 2007).

John Walton is Professor of Social History in the Institute of Northern Studies, Leeds Metropolitan University, UK. He was founding president of the International Commission for the History of Travel and Tourism and edits the *Journal of Tourism History*. His most recent books are *Riding on Rainbows: Blackpool Pleasure Beach and its Place in British Popular Culture* (Skelter, 2007) (with Gary Cross), *The Playful Crowd: Pleasure Places in the Twentieth Century* (Columbia University Press, 2005), and, as editor, *Histories of Tourism* (Channel View, 2005).

Stephen Wearing is an associate professor at the University of Technology, Sydney (UTS), Australia. He has been responsible for a variety of projects in the area of Leisure and Tourism Studies at an international and local level. He has directed a number of leisure and tourism community based projects in Papua New Guinea, Costa Rica, Solomon Islands, Guyana, and Australia, receiving a special citation from the Costa Rican Government for services towards community, conservation, and youth and an outstanding contribution award from Youth Challenge International in Canada. He has authored eight books and over 100 articles dealing with issues surrounding leisure and sustainable tourism. His practical experience as a town planner, environmental planner, and park planner at local, state, and international level have provided him with experiences that he brings to his teaching and research. He has been project director for a range of social sciences in natural resource management projects and research and a team leader for a variety of ecotourism, volunteer tourism, and outdoor education activities internationally.

R.E. Wood is Professor of Sociology at the Camden campus of Rutgers University, USA. He has been a resource editor for *Annals of Tourism Research* and was coeditor of *Tourism, Ethnicity and the State in Asian and Pacific Societies*. He is the author of *From Marshall Plan to Debt Crisis: Foreign Aid and Development Choices in the World Economy* (University of California Press, 1986) and numerous articles on tourism's relationship to culture, ethnicity, development, and globalization. His recent work has focused on the cruise ship industry as a paradigmatic case of neoliberal globalization.

Simon Woodward, PhD, is Senior Research Fellow at Leeds Metropolitan University specializing in the heritage and tourism sectors. He has worked in a wide range of destinations throughout Europe, Africa, and the Middle East, advising public sector clients and their partners on how to reconcile tourism development with asset protection.

Preface

This is the first *SAGE Handbook of Tourism Studies*. It has been a project in the making since we first embarked on it in Spring 2006. Our idea was to engage in cross-Atlantic collaboration that would bring academic perspectives from our respective continents into dialogue with scholars from other regions around the world. Our intention was to build a knowledge base illustrating how "tourism studies" was developing as a field of study and practice. In recent years there has been a sharp increase in the variety of academic genres and critical approaches relating to tourism, as new themes and issues have emerged. Our aim was to engage with academics as well as practitioners that were in a position to offer a benchmark statement on their particular field of interest. Clarifying the scope of tourism studies was the first important challenge, for that would determine what themes and topics should be considered for inclusion and which authors we could both agree upon to invite.

The spectrum of themes and topics selected for inclusion is, in itself, testimony to the multidisciplinary approach that has marked the evolving study of tourism. Of course, we are very much aware that there are omissions. In the reviewer's comments on our initial proposal for the *SAGE Handbook*, the most common line of critique revolved around our choosing of some topics and the exclusion of others. While the review process helped us as it should, it also reinforced that a handbook could never deliver a complete set of contents to appease all. In selecting what we have, we hope we have covered different approaches as well as accentuating emergent trends and inevitable overlaps. Importantly, the message from all of this supports the very idea of such a productive and lively field of enquiry. Also symptomatic of the health of tourism studies is the reality that for every topic or theme there are many fine scholars in the world. Therefore, our choices of whom to invite as contributors often turned on little more than the flip of a coin. We regret that we were unable to ask all of those we considered to contribute, but in the end, we were delighted with, and gratified by, the collection of authors we were able to enlist.

Organization of This Volume

The SAGE Handbook of Tourism Studies aims to provide academics across many disciplines with a definitive, critical, and indispensable resource and guide. It is not located in any one particular discipline, but seeks to reflect the wide-ranging conceptual approaches to the subject of tourism. Attention has been given to new perspectives on the core elements of the tourism sector and to recent emerging themes and issues. The overall thrust of the handbook is to provide much needed critical depth to tourism studies and to guide the reader through the central themes, conflicts, and problems in a clear and coherent manner. As shown, following a general introduction by the editors, the handbook is divided into three parts.

Part I—Approaches to Tourism Studies

This section addresses differing positions adopted across the disciplines and how these have advanced over recent years. Chapters in this section attempt to provide comprehensive and critical accounts of key disciplinary contributions to tourism studies, as well as approaches and critiques on specialized fields pertaining to tourism studies (e.g., hospitality studies and environmental studies). Cutting edge perspectives on the themes, issues, and problems surrounding the conceptualization of tourism and its study are to be found in these chapters.

Part II—Key Topics in Tourism

This section strives to provide state-of-the-art reviews of theory and research relating to central themes that preoccupy scholars of tourism. Chapters address tourism types, sectors, organization and planning, including conservation and sustainability topics and issues. Various chapters also help disseminate key empirical studies and frameworks that have enabled strong conceptual and research-related advance in the field.

Part III—Critical Issues and Emerging Perspectives

This section address recent learning and emerging themes that allow the reader to interpret tourism in more meaningful ways. A wide coverage is provided here that reflects a diversity of intellectual approaches to newer study areas such as postcolonialism and thanatourism (or dark tourism), theoretical/methodological insights and critiques (e.g., of global tourism operations, gender discourses), as well as emergent technologies of travel and new mobilities.

Chapter 39—Conclusion

The concluding chapter of *The SAGE Handbook of Tourism Studies* takes a look at past omissions and emergent futures for tourism studies. We attempt to summarize here some of the issues, conflicts and challenges that will face tourism scholars, as well as some new themes and topics.

Acknowledgements

Much has changed in the two years that have elapsed since we undertook this rather daunting task. New positions and responsibilities, the peaking of (in the UK at least), the Research Assessment Exercise, along with the ever-quickening pace and pressures of academic life, indeed, life in general, have all conspired to slow progress. For at least one author and one of the editors, this included the loss of a parent, which quickly turns all else into a *phantasmagoria*. This project would have remained unfinished were it not for the support, patience, and cooperation of chapter authors, students, friends, and family.

We would like to thank the following for assistance in the multitude of tasks involved, including reviewing and (copy)editing various chapters, providing helpful comments, suggestions, and references: Blanca Camargo, Michael Clement, Wesley Dean, Ulrike Gretzel, Christopher Menzel and Justin Taillon, all from Texas A&M University. Special thanks go to Justin Taillon for his assistance on various chapters, including conducting literature searches and reference checks where needed. Thanks to Xiangping "Coco" Gao for assistance in developing JPEG images from slides, as well as to Chris Rojek and Jai Seaman at SAGE Publications, the Department of Recreation, Park and Tourism, at Texas A&M University, and the Centre for Tourism and Cultural Change at Leeds Metropolitan University. We would also like to acknowledge the invaluable role played by Brian Smith, who created and maintained a database to keep track of author, chapter, and handbook information, did numerous reference checks, undertook with great efficiency and under heavy time constraints the multiple challenges of formatting and compiling chapters containing widely divergent formatting styles, language styles, and word processing idiosyncrasies, and also helped to ensure the final copy and index were as consistent and accurate as possible.

That there is now *The SAGE Handbook of Tourism Studies* is of practical and symbolic import—another marker of a growing field of study and a "community of scientists" whose research, voices, issues, and concerns are slowly transcending linguistic, cultural, and disciplinary barriers to find common spaces for knowledge sharing, discussion, and debate. It is hoped that this *SAGE Handbook* will provide libraries and researchers with an invaluable resource relating to the diversity and maturity of tourism as a field of study and will offer a comprehensive guide to the excellent work that we know is taking place from a variety of disciplinary perspectives.

Introduction: The Evolution and Contemporary Positioning of Tourism as a Focus of Study

Tazim Jamal and Mike Robinson

The Purpose of Tourism Studies

At first glance the idea of tourism as a focal point for serious academic enquiry does appear rather incongruous. Intellectualizing a seemingly frivolous leisure practice, rather feels like stretching things a little far. Studying people's vacations, from whatever perspective, sounds somewhat inconsequential, if not vaguely voyeuristic. And yet, here we are offering a *Handbook*. For while the idea of studying tourism can still conjure up concerns regarding its legitimacy, both among the tourism sector and the wider academy, it continues to flourish after a period of over 35 years; the very time when the patterns and processes of international tourism were being firmly established and enacted. However, as Hall and Page (2005) address, the study of tourism within the social sciences, in an Anglo-American context, can be traced back to the 1920s. More recently the emergence of tourism studies, and what Rojek and Urry (1997)

discuss as a process of institutionalization, has been tracked and discussed by the likes of Airey and Johnson (1999), Evans (2001) and Hall et al. (2004). Adjacent to such studies are a series of generally inconclusive "discussions," which have picked up on the issues surrounding the positioning of tourism studies and indeed, the questioning of its status and its relationships to other disciplines (see, for instance, Echtner and Jamal, 1997; Jafari, 1990; Jamal and Kim, 2005; Leiper, 1981; Ryan, 1997; Squire, 1994; Tribe, 1997, 2000) and the tourism sector itself (Ryan, 2001).

Semantics play a part here. The mobilization of the term "tourism studies" implies the status of a discipline or, at the very least, the aspiration to become a discipline. Such a position tends to invoke reactions from the traditional disciplines, ranging from wholesale appropriation, where the study of tourism is said to have always been a feature of inquiry and subsequently can never be "owned" outside of a particular methodological approach and must be interpreted via the accepted canonical literature of that discipline, to refusal to deal with tourism without selectively reconstructing in order that it can fit as an appendage of more salient and "worthy" phenomena. Tourism studies is of course not unique in this respect. The same debates have raged with regard to leisure, sports, management, cultural, environmental, and development studies. But interesting and important as such discussions are, they all generally fail to interrogate the very purpose of tourism studies, and bypass questions as to why study tourism and why there should be a handbook of tourism studies at all. Employing the idea of tourism as a *field* of study is perhaps a tactic of pragmatism rather than philosophical principle, for even without delving into the philosophical aspects, one can identify a number of good reasons for bringing tourism into the academic world. First, because tourism is, by any standard, a global phenomenon, with causes and consequences for populations that extend beyond the ranks of those which operate and practice it. Second, is that studying tourism allows the exploration of meaning from the experiences of *being* a tourist and *doing* tourism. Third, studying tourism allows us to engage with some of the key issues of globalization and modernity. The organization and doing of tourism, involving as it does transborder mobilities and structures problematizes notions of identity, nationalism and tradition and the variety of sociocultural and political processes that are bound up with such concepts. Fourth, studying tourism is increasingly necessary as, in theory at least, it should go to inform policy making at both national and international level (in addition to the local and regional level). These reasons for engaging with the study of tourism are now briefly discussed.

Global Importance of Tourism

The sheer scale of tourism as an organized activity and its global reach, coupled with its environmental and social impacts within and beyond the destinations and communities it focuses on, and its complexity demand, the attention of the academic community. MacCannell (1999: 46) notes that: "Taken together, tourist attractions and the behavior surrounding them are one of the most complex and orderly of the several universal codes that constitute modern society." Certainly, as an organized form of human activity, in its production and consumption, tourism is an immensely successful and truly global endeavor. Few places on the planet have escaped the curiosity of the tourist, or the ability of the tour operator to package even the most remote or dangerous location. Estimates from the World Tourism Organization (2005) anticipate that, by the year 2020 international arrivals are expected to reach over 1.56 billion. This figure will comprise 1.2 billion intraregional arrivals and 0.4 billion long-haul travelers. Europe is scheduled to be the top receiving region with 717 million tourists, followed by East Asia and the Pacific with 397 million, the Americas with 282 million, and Africa, the Middle East, and South Asia. Above average growth regions are predicted to be East Asia and the Pacific, South Asia, the Middle East and Africa.

However, while such statistics are useful, it is both difficult and unwise to consider tourism to be some unified economic sector or as a "catch-all" term for people's behavior while on holiday (Bruner, 2004). While Paul Fussell (1980: 49) definitively announced: "We are all tourists now, there is no escape," and Urry (1995) has suggested that we are all tourists all of the time, it has been increasingly revealed not to be the case and some qualification is required. Saying that tourism is global in its scope and influence does not take account of the fact that a significant majority of the world's population does not engage in tourism as tourists; despite this, communities are increasingly projected into the role of "hosts" *for* tourists. A further related point, which is not reflected in the notion of a "global tourism," is that it does not reflect the reality of a substantive imbalance in the benefits of tourism to the advantage of the developed over the developing world. Even within the context of extant asymmetry within global relations and against the background of the United Nation's Millennium Development Goals (United Nations, 2000) it is tourism that is widely heralded as a means to redress global economic and social imbalances. Hence, we have witnessed over recent years the rise of pro-poor tourism, not only as a practical mechanism through which disadvantaged and marginal communities with limited resources can participate in the development process, but also as a symbolic demonstration of the linkages that exist between environmental degradation, social injustice, and poverty, and the ways to tackle these. Several authors in this *Handbook* expand on the related issues of social and environmental injustices produced, accentuated, and, in some cases, addressed through tourism.

Finding Meaning Through Tourism

The world as known today exists as testimony to, and evidence of, the fact that people travel. The factors that shaped early patterns of travel were fundamentally directed by basic human needs (finding food and shelter), exchange (trade), relationships with natural phenomena (developing new settlements, escaping droughts or floods, etc.), and the result of conquest and conflict (occupation, expulsion, forced migration, and resettlement). Such factors still exert considerable influence on a large proportion of the world's population today, with contemporary pilgrimage routes relatively easy to identify, and tourism frequently building on established trading relationships and patterns of diaspora and relocation.

From the late seventeenth and well into the twentieth centuries, motivations such as curiosity education, and social betterment took over as "essential" travel evolved into discretionary, leisure travel, gradually moving from

a pursuit of the social elite of the developed world, to a widespread activity of the masses of the developed world, supported by a highly complex network of support structures and services. It is all too easy to dismiss contemporary international tourism as a leisure activity somehow separate and below more "worthy" social practices. As a leisure activity, tourism is carried out in "leisure time," as a temporary discretionary activity, and as a form of "reward" for, or counter to, daily work (Spode, 1994). However, the value of tourism cannot be solely judged in terms of the hedonistic recompense it brings to the individual. Nor can its value be solely expressed in relation to the economic benefits that it can undoubtedly generate. Tourism is centered on the fundamental principles of exchange between peoples and is both an expression and experience of culture (Appadurai, 2002). Tourism is cultural; its practices and structures are very much an extension of the normative cultural framing from which it emerges. As such it has a vital part to play in helping us understand ourselves and the multilayered relationships between humanity and the material and non-material world we occupy and journey through (Robinson and Phipps, 2004). Recognizing tourism as an intrinsically cultural phenomenon, and understanding how this plays out in everyday practices and through interconnected local to global economic and political structures is an important priority in tourism studies that a number of authors have taken up in this *Handbook*.

The business (large and small) dimension of international tourism can sometimes be seen as remote and impersonal; almost disconnected from the actual experience of "being" a tourist. For at its heart tourism is constructed around a series of very personal and intimate experiences as tourists encounter new and different cultures (Cohen, 2004). Tourists can be impressed and emotionally moved by a work of art, a festival, a musical performance, a building, or an object in a museum. These tangible and intangible expressions of culture act as triggers for interpreting the world past and present (Canestrini, 2001). But tourists also encounter "living" culture through a variety of other forms and media which express culture, and which embody both tradition and change, for example, experiencing varieties of "authentic" ethnic cuisine in different cities around the world, or traditional and religious ceremonies enacted around the world by the cultural groups practicing them, or experiencing them online through the Internet.

Being away from home—a necessity for a tourist—generates reflection on the meaning of home in relation the wider world (Harrison, 2003). Being among people who use a different language, eat different foods, and behave in different ways is at the very heart of tourism. Experiencing directly different "ways of life" can have a valuable educational function that stretches beyond tourism (Jack and Phipps, 2005), and despite advances in communicative and virtual reality technologies is difficult to emulate except through basic human contact, encounter, and exchange. In a world where much conflict is a product of cultural misunderstanding, miscommunication, and a basic lack of knowledge of the "hows and whys" cultures are different, exposure to, and experience of, a wide variety of cultures in the most ordinary of ways is essential. How these experiences are commodified (Cohen, 1998; Greenwood, 1989; Shepherd, 2002; Wang, 2000) or mediated by various intermediaries and providers (Boorstin, 1964; Dann, 1996; Strain, 2003), and how they change through their telling and retelling, and through various communicative mechanisms and information technologies, is taken up in the *Handbook*.

It would be a mistake to suggest that the search for different cultural experiences lies at the root of all international tourism, as Cohen's (1979) framework on the phenomenology of tourism experience sought to show. Clearly, there are a vast number of tourists that seek escape from some aspects of their own environments (Enzensberger, 1958), but not all, preferring instead to remain in the environmental "bubble" that is sometimes

associated with "mass tourism." This is not to say that the individuals that go to make up so-called "mass" tourism are somehow devoid of any interest in culture(s) (Wagner, 1977). But it does remind us that tourism reflects a certain degree of polarization between the persistence of culture as somehow elevated and special in society, and the culture of the ordinary and the everyday.

For a substantial percentage of tourists, experiences of different or "other" cultures in the settings of ordinary life presents its own challenges. As tourists, and as people, in a globalizing world, we are increasingly in contact with "other" cultures, able to experience the uniqueness of each and the commonalities of all. Tourism can be a powerful mechanism to understanding other places, peoples, and pasts, not through selective, high profile cultural sites and activities that may not necessarily be representative of the societies they operate in, but through a more democratic and ubiquitous approach to cultures (Bouchenaki, 2004). In these terms even mass tourism has important and forgotten cultural elements. Our first encounter with another culture is most likely to be through the food on the menu and the language of the waiter.

Tourism as an Entry Point to Understanding Globalization and Modernity

It is a trite but important point to remember that, as the practices of tourism have developed, so too has intellectual enquiry into these practices developed. When Hans Magnus Enzensberger published his *Theory of Tourism* in 1958, it was at a time of unprecedented movement of peoples for leisure purposes. While Enzensberger critiques tourism as a form of deception, importantly he was keen to highlight the inseparability of tourism from the wider globalizing processes of human development and modernity; tourism as a reflection of society. A number of chapters in this *Handbook* address this particular concern, situating tourism with wider global and cultural processes, while other chapters touch upon or elaborate on several of the above aspects.

Tourism is very much at the center of a substantive and increasingly rapid, transitory, but seemingly unending, process of transnational flows of peoples and cultures for leisure and business purposes, and is now one of the major outputs and driving forces for the complex and semantically slippery concept of globalization. Tourism operates at various levels and displays various paradoxes and tensions in the way it is organized and operates. It is a highly structured and globally interconnected industry, operating in a globalized world of flows of transnational capital, multinational organizations, and liberal movements of people, and ideas (Lanfant et al., 1995). Despite the apparent "de-territorialization" that would seem to underpin international tourism, the reality is still one of an industry built around the concept of the nation-state. Each country, with their own institutions and political systems, economic needs, and social/cultural capital, are all essentially competing with one another for the wealth and symbolic status that tourism can create. Against this inherent nationalist agenda can be contrasted the fact that tourists themselves are wonderfully bad at not recognizing boundaries and administrative divides. They work in the imprecise realm of "place" and loosely defined immediacy.

Understanding Tourism to Inform Policy

In Jafari's (2001) "four platform model" of the development of tourism studies, in which he identifies four positions taken by researchers,[1] it would be all to easy to see the "advocacy position," whereby research into the economic contribution of tourism is dominant and feeds the development of tourism as a thing of the past. Research around the measurement of tourism's economic impact remains very much a powerful feature of contemporary study and is both endorsed and mobilized by government agencies at various levels. Whatever the debate within the academy between the ethics and efficacy of quantitative or qualitative approaches to research, the reality is one of continuing research into the economic impacts of tourism so that policy decisions can be taken. However, over the years, approaches to *understanding* tourism as part of a much more complex and wide ranging cultural phenomena, have supplemented mere measurement approaches, to feed an emergent policy framework for tourism development and management at national, sub-national and international scales.

Tourism as a mode of development impinges directly upon issues of power relations, the ways in which external capital is accommodated in national contexts, the legitimacies of planning procedures, land rights, ownership, access, and the legacies of social inclusion and social exclusion. These interrelationships between tourism and substantive matters of development have become focal points for policy at regional, national, and international level. In policy and planning terms much has been done to "protect" culture, heritage resources and related natural environments from the excesses of unplanned and uncoordinated tourism development (Robinson and Boniface, 1999). Focus has very much been on attempting to alleviate the unwanted consequences of tourism (de Kadt, 1979). However, as our understandings on the complexities of culture have evolved, and the pace and extent of change has increased within the context of globalization, so too have new challenges emerged, and so new ways of addressing problems are required.

Since the landmark UNESCO (1972) "Convention Concerning the Protection of the World Cultural and Natural Heritage," we can broadly identify four key changes relating to the tourism–culture–environment interface and how these are being mobilized to shape policy. First, our understanding of culture as a concept and its fundamental importance for the construction of social identity has both broadened and deepened considerably. For instance, the definition of cultural heritage now also relates not only to material expressions such as sites and objects, but also to intangible expressions such as language and oral tradition, social practices, rituals, festive, and performative events. Culture is seen much more to refer to "ways of life" and everyday practice as well as being manifest in buildings, sites, and monuments. Moreover, the diversity of culture(s) is recognized to be fundamental to, and in line with, the principles of sustainable development and thus something which needs to be both "recognized and affirmed for future generations" (UNESCO, 2005).

Second, we understand better the close interrelationships between culture and natural environments and in protecting each we are helping to enable both to protect and re-create their resources. Cultural diversity relates strongly to the concept of biodiversity in that it shapes the landscapes in which genetic diversity, species diversity, and ecological diversity occur and interact. Indeed, there is a link between the social, economic, and health issues of indigenous peoples living in sites of significant biodiversity and the conservation and evolution of this biodiversity. This interrelationship, what Posey (1999) has termed the "inextricable link," is also at the center of the sustainable development concept. Tourists, in consuming the natural environment, may also be consuming culture in terms of the various local cultural values that may have been ascribed to a particular landscape or natural site. It is also important to recognize that tourists, in approaching natural sites, do so armed with their own sets of values and categories, which can conflict with those of the local community.

Third, in recognizing the fact that international tourism continues to expand, we also need to recognize that it is continually changing the ways in which it operates. While the global tourism sector is highly complex and fragmented in its operations, it has significantly changed its attitudes to the cultural resources and communities it depends upon. Clearly there is still substantive variation among the practices of the sector, but it is far more willing

to engage in the sustainable development agenda and this relates to its increasing ability to segment the market reflecting growth in sectors such as cultural, heritage, and ecologically based tourism. This ongoing process of market segmentation and product differentiation fits well with programs of developing cultural tourism and is especially important for less developed countries, whose infrastructure or environmental/cultural fragility may only support limited numbers of tourists.

Fourth, and importantly, policy and planning goals are shifting away from solely dealing with tourism's "impacts" on various aspects of culture and the environment towards a more proactive role, whereby tourism is integrated with other development aims and instruments to deliver key sustainable development outcomes (Rauschelbach et al., 2002). There is a growing network of stakeholders involved in tourism development, including local, national, and international organizations eager to assist in monitoring and ameliorating any detrimental impacts on culture and also in mobilizing tourism as a force for sustaining and developing culture and economy.

Such changes are symptomatic of policy agendas which are being driven in part by research, and at the same time require further research. A number of these changes are picked up in the chapters of this *Handbook*. The relationships between research communities, particularly those within universities, and policy makers, vary considerably across the world. Routeways between independent, rigorous scholarship, and the dynamics of policy and politics are frequently long, winding, opaque, and fraught with impediments cast from both sides, however, the need for a deeper and holistic understanding tourism continues to increase in line with the complexities and global extents of its development.

A Field of Fragmented Importance

As the importance of tourism continues to reveal itself across the disciplines, so do the latter continue to develop and experiment with ways of interrogating tourism and its routeways into multiplicitous other fields. It is wholly consistent with the very nature of tourism that it is addressed via different disciplines and differing methodologies. As tourism itself is labeled and thematized in practice so is this reflected in the emergence of new subfields or genres. Despite inevitable problems of definition, and the setting and overlapping of boundaries, there are now many different ways of breaking down tourism as a focus for study. These range from the highly specific, such as backpacker tourism (Hannam and Ateljevic, 2008), royal tourism (Long and Palmer, 2008), gay tourism (Waitt and Markwell, 2006), tourism in the Third Reich (Baranowski, 2004), sex tourism (Ryan and Hall, 2001), literary tourism (Robinson and Andersen, 2004), to more encompassing labels, such as cultural tourism (Richards, 2007; Smith and Robinson, 2006), niche tourism (Novelli, 2005), heritage tourism (Corsane, 2004; Timothy, 2007), and ecotourism (Fennell, 2007). At the same time tourism continues to be examined spatially, producing area studies of tourism and related development, such as, for example: Mediterranean tourism (Apostolopoulos et al., 2001), Asian tourism (Cochrane, 2008), tourism in China (Lew and Yu, 2002; Oakes, 1998), tourism in the Middle East (Daher, 2006), and tourism in the Caribbean (Daye et al., 2008; Ward, 2008).

The concept of genre in the world of tourism studies looks likely to prove particularly useful as even more subfields of interest emerge, closely tailing developments and trends in the tourism sector. It becomes too easy to see that in a handbook such as this, the selection of themes and topics and the categorization of chapters is problematic in the face of an extant and rapidly evolving range of categories, mirroring a similarly diverse disciplinary perspectives. Selectivity is inevitable. However, the overall issue of having such a long list of potential themes and topics only further illustrates the importance of the field.

Overview of the *Handbook*

The relationship between tourism and culture is one of the predominant lenses through which the study of tourism is studied by various authors in this handbook, regardless of the "disciplinary" orientation of the researcher/scholar. Some authors also add a critical lens to this, resulting in a critical cultural analysis of their topic. David Bell's Chapter 2 on *hospitality* commences Part I—Approaches to Tourism Studies and not only to addresses a valuable subject (hospitality) but also extends hospitality to the readers by familiarizing them with one of the more common approaches used by authors in this handbook. Bell's chapter in Part I and Hollinshead's Chapter 16 in Part II are illustrative of contributions that attempt to problematize common notions such as "hospitality" and pleasurable entertainment spaces such as "theme parks." Bell addresses aspects ranging from spaces of hospitality, foodscapes, drinkscapes, and restscapes, to theoretical discussion of philosopher Jacques Derrida's writings on hospitality which are perhaps less known to some in tourism studies.

Naomi Leite and Nelson Graburn (Chapter 3) provide a thorough and comprehensive review of "anthropological interventions" in Part I that illustrate not only the remarkable accomplishments made in the study of tourism, but also the interdisciplinarity of the topic. As they note, addressing the anthropology of tourism by way of reviewing the anthropological methods and approaches used may do better justice to the wide-ranging disciplines that draw upon them than focusing on contributions by anthropologists within the "anthropology of tourism." Their review spans the classic concerns that occupied the early decades of tourism research through to the present, and examines how recent changes to anthropological theory and practice have influenced emphases and emerging directions in tourism-related research. Their chapter is followed consecutively by two others that address tourism and culture from different orientations. Adrian Franklin (Chapter 4) on the sociology of tourism, charts how sociology came to tourism studies, followed by the principal sociological theories of tourism that dominated the field until a "new wave" brought much needed critiques, debates, and fresh insights into the complex phenomenon encapsulated by the single word "tourism." David Crouch (Chapter 5) goes on to show the valuable theoretical contributions that cultural studies can bring to conceptualizing the cultural processes and cultural politics in tourism, including issues of class, race, ethnicity, and gender.

Disciplinary perspectives to the study of tourism are addressed by many authors in Part I, though it should be noted that there are several chapters here that approach tourism from multidisciplinary viewpoints such as cultural studies (Chapter 5, David Crouch) and specializations such as that of development studies (Chapter 9, David Telfer). Philip Long and Mike Robinson (Chapter 6) interweave the study of popular culture with the role of the media as a communicative mechanism and as a form of entertainment and enjoyment. The idea of the popular, alternative understandings of media "effects," categories of media tourism, tourism's interrelations with various media forms (consider, for instance, film-induced tourism, popular cultural tourism) and research gaps are discussed. John Walton (Chapter 7) on the histories of tourism, presents a historical lens on the development and evolution of tourism, an examination of key debates and issues such as the ongoing and contentious relationship between history and the "heritage industry." He touches on numerous trends and themes (e.g., on literature, arts, transportation, modernization, national identity) to illustrate the importance of historical analysis and the work of historians to tourism studies. Sanjay Nepal (Chapter 8) reviews the contribution of geography, including perspectives from Anglo-American, German, French, and Chinese tourism geographies, as well as recent trends and challenges. David Telfer (Chapter 9) on development studies and tourism, discusses neoliberalism as one of four major paradigms, and also notes the recent focus of development on poverty alleviation as evident

in the UN Millennium Goals. John Fletcher (Chapter 10) on the economics of international tourism, reviews various approaches including tourism satellite accounts, multipliers, input–output models, as well as global and regional significances of international tourism, competitive and comparative advantage, and the associated economic and socioeconomic impacts of international tourism. Richter (Chapter 11) reviews power, stakeholders, the politicization of tourism, plus various inequities and issues ranging from health safety to medical travel. As Richter notes, many core issues of political science inquiry are relevant to tourism, but serious attention by political scientists to the politics of tourism continues to lag.

The two chapters towards the end of Part I are placed there in order to present some important topics that are picked up in different ways in Part II by various authors. The chapter on tourism and natural resources by Andrew Holden (Chapter 12) precedes that by Nigel Evans (Chapter 13) on strategic tourism business operations. Holden's chapter introduces the role of environmental studies and proceeds to trace the environmental problems over the last 50 years and responses to them, including the rise of environmental nongovernmental organizations (NGOs), key publications, and policy responses. Tourism's role as an agent of conservation, environmental ethic for tourism businesses and the consumer role are also discussed by Holden. Nigel Evan's chapter addresses the relationship between business studies and tourism studies, management challenges related to the nature of the tourism "product" and the local-global tourism system, trends and impacts, as well as human resources, strategic management approaches and strategic marketing issues. A number of issues and concerns raised by both Holden and Evans in their chapters are taken up in Part II—Key Topics in Tourism.

Part II begins by examining a few key types and sectors of tourism and moves on to consider issues of conservation, sustainability, planning, and organization/management. Readers will note that the critical perspectives, theoretical discussions, and critiques of tourism studies past and present are interspersed here with more applied chapters or chapters addressing practical issues. The first chapters in Part II continue the strong cultural theme evident in a number of chapters in Part I. The first chapter in Part II by Richard Sharpley (Chapter 14) explores the meaning-making potential of tourism and is situated adjacent to Wearing and Ponting's chapter (Chapter 15). It provides an in-depth look at forms of tourism that are religiously or spiritually motivated—a growing sector of the international tourism market and surprisingly under-researched as Sharpley notes. Secular religion/spirituality in relation to tourism is a key focus of the chapter, which addresses theological perspectives on tourism, spiritual dimensions of journeys, religious sites, and touristic places, and notes the lack of attention to situating "tourism as religion" discourses within contemporary theological perspectives on spirituality and religion, as well as the lack of empirical research here. Wearing and Ponting position volunteer tourism as a shift away from commodified, neoliberal approaches and provide examples of both commodified and decommodified (volunteer) forms of surfing tourism in the Mentawai Islands off the west coast of Sumatra to illustrate and explore the power relationships involved. Distinguishing deep and shallow types of volunteer tourism, their chapter draws upon Homi Bhaba's notion of "Third Space" to argue for the potential of volunteer tourism to resist and negotiate hegemonic constructions and dominant discourses, and enact self-reflexive, sharing, dialogue, and cultural interactions. Their chapter thus opens the possibility of exploring the spiritual potentiality of volunteer tourism spaces.

Keith Hollinshead (Chapter 16) on theme parks, addresses a popular topic from a critical cultural perspective. He targets his analysis to the design and management of theme parks, and provides a detailed examination of relations of culture and power, as well as the political consequences that theme parks are able to influence. His chapter calls upon not only those interested in cultural studies and tourism, but also upon management and development specialists (generally trained in noncritical traditions and often unaware of the above) to recognize theme parks as agents of a received symbolic order or preferred cultural change, as he presents it. Robert Mugerauer Jr. (Chapter 17) notes a different type of neglect; that between urban studies and urban tourism scholars. He provides what he calls an "effective history" of urban destinations, and discusses many different facilities, services, and attractions (retail, museums, special events, heritage sites, etc.). The latter part of his chapter addresses problems of distributive justice (segregated spaces, benefits, and burdens), theorization and methodological challenges and shortcomings, as well as future directions and issues. Mugerauer's chapter is followed by Aylin Orbaşlı and Simon Woodward's review and discussion of cultural heritage, conservation and tourism, focusing on the relationship between the built environment and tourism (Chapter 18). They address various aspects of heritage protection and management, as well as types of cultural heritage attractions, cultural tourism and heritage tourism (in the context of built cultural heritage), visitor impacts and authenticity issues. The cultural heritage and conservation theme of this chapter is complemented by Joseph Mbaiwa's and Amanda Stronza's chapter on sustainable tourism and ecotourism (Chapter 19) and are related to broader themes of environmental, social, and economic sustainability discussed elsewhere in the *Handbook*.

Mbaiwa and Stronza's chapter reviews sustainable tourism and ecotourism (including definitions, principles, impacts, management tools, certification, plus the notion of responsible tourism). They also discuss international tourism impacts and economic dependencies between developed and developing regions/ countries, and illustrate some key sustainability principles through an examination of international tourism impacts on developing countries and describe a community-based conservation program in Botswana. Bernard Lane (Chapter 20) on rural tourism, traces the evolution of rural tourism and the varied attempts at defining, and describing, a diverse activity that he suggests may be better viewed as an umbrella term encompassing a number of forms and types of tourism (these are summarized in the chapter). Lane also reviews impacts, supply side issues and demand side opportunities, transportation, organization and support (including various interest groups), as well as future uncertainties and challenges. The themes of integrated management, destination management organizations, and "green" holidays that he mentions under future considerations, are picked up by subsequent chapters in Part II.

Stephen Page and Yue Ge in Chapter 21 provide a comprehensive coverage of transportation and tourism. Relationships with leisure and recreation, conceptualization of the transportation–tourism relationship, trends, and different modes of transportation are covered, followed by a section on sustainability issues in transportation and tourism (ranging from environmental impacts to policy and planning issues). Four short examples are offered in relation to these sustainability issues: (1) integrated planning for urban tourism in Wuxi City located in Jiangsu Province, China; (2) sugar cane ethanol biofuels in Brazil; (3) heritage street cars in USA; and (4) cycling in Europe. Kathy Rettie, A.P. (Tony) Clevenger, and Adam Ford (Chapter 22) discuss environmental conservation and transportation issues in the context of national parks and protected areas. Their chapter traces the policy change and priority shift towards ecological integrity in the Canada National Parks Act, as well as the history of tourism growth and describes a unique initiative to bring the public together with scientific experts and park managers to address wildlife mortality on a major transportation corridor in Banff National Park (one of four mountain parks constituting a UNESCO World Heritage Site). Insights on methods and processes for visitor education and resident/stakeholder involvement, plus highway

mitigation and monitoring performance, are provided.

Planning, conservation, and sustainability are therefore addressed from multiple perspectives and form a significant theme in Part II. Brian King and Michael Pearlman (Chapter 23) present a review of tourism planning at the local and regional levels. Economic development and planning, physical/spatial planning, community planning, and integrated tourism planning are discussed. In addition, convergences in the planning domain, planning structures and frameworks, stakeholder management and implementation issues, indigenous representation, and other future issues are presented. Organizations involved in destination management are taken up from two different perspectives in the subsequent two chapters in Part II. In Chapter 24 Robert Ford and William Peeper review the historic evolution, activities, operations, and changing trends facing local destination marketing organizations. While their chapter focuses primarily on US Convention and Visitors Bureaus (a brief comparison with organizations providing tourism services outside of North America is provided), the challenges faced by these organizations point to the need for a more inclusive form of destination marketing organization that is grounded in destination management. This is the argument presented by Richard Harrill in his chapter on destination management (Chapter 25), which commences by summarizing some key characteristics and issues facing tourism destinations. His review of destination management issues and challenges, and his call for integrated destination management, builds on several existing arguments and research studies, and is further supported by two case examples he provides at the local and county level: the Juneau Convention and Visitors Bureau in Alaska; and the Queen Anne's County Office of Tourism in Maryland, USA. Noting various local to global issues facing tourism destinations, Harrill argues for the use the term destination management organization rather than destination marketing organization to indicate the more active management role being taken up by local and area-based tourism organizations. Peter Tarlow (Chapter 26) discusses safety and security in travel and tourism, and provides detailed "how to" management-oriented guidelines for implementing safety and security principles and measures at the destination level. Crime and terrorism, policing, various subfields of tourism security and safety (note the term *tourism surety* here), lodging, attractions, urban and rural security, port security, and cruise travel, are among the topics he covers.

Part III—Critical Issues and Emerging Perspectives—picks up themes from Parts I and II, as well as presenting several new perspectives. It contains a diverse range of topics, ranging from critical and theoretical perspectives to new emerging topics and methodological considerations. Bernadette Quinn (Chapter 27) on festivals and events in tourism, offers a detailed analysis of this study area. Commencing with the historical trajectory and a review of definitions, two dominant themes in festivals and events research are then laid out: (1) a synthesis of management perspectives (which includes a review of topics related to impacts, planning, evaluation, marketing, motivation, resident and stakeholder relationships); and (2) a critical review of social sciences and humanities perspectives related to festivals and events (including tradition and modernity: processes of cultural change, local and global: reproducing place, politics of identity and representation, relationships between leisure and tourism, production–consumption). Quinn's conclusions, which call for a multidisciplinary approach to research and improved linkages into contextual environments, reflect strong themes identified in many chapters.

Two other emerging areas in need of greater theoretical and empirical attention in tourism studies are situated in Part III: postcolonialism and thanatourism/dark tourism. Postcolonial theory and critique is a large robust inquiry that has seen surprisingly little engagement by tourism scholars until more recently, as Hazel Tucker and John Akama

note (Chapter 28). Their chapter draws upon postcolonial theory to illustrate the ways in which tourism relations may be embedded in colonial discourses and continue to reinforce them, and also how tourism research itself can perpetuate colonial processes and narratives. This leads the authors then to propose a move towards critical postcolonialism that offers counter-narratives of resistance to colonial relationships, including to "First World" representations of developing countries, and other discursive forms of power and control. This chapter points out the importance of postcolonial studies in understanding forms of cultural inequalities and domination. Chapter 29 examines the history and development of what appears to be another "dark" topic, Thanatourism. Tony Seaton discusses the debate over naming the phenomenon of dark tourism/thanatourism, supply side (site type) and demand side (visitor type/ motivation) characterizations, origins and transformations, as well as issues and directions for future research.

Issues of representation, performance, and embodiment, as discussed by David Crouch in Part I (Chapter 5), are elaborated on in other chapters, notably the theoretically oriented chapter on tourism and performance by Tim Edensor in Chapter 30, which also offers critique and analysis of spaces in tourism (*enclavic* and *heterogeneous* spaces, to use Edensor's terms). Ulrike Gretzel and Dan Fesenmaier (Chapter 31) on information technology and tourism, offer an in-depth understanding of the dramatically different spaces being shaped with respect to producer–consumer transactions, travel distribution, tourism marketing, and tourism experiences. Changes related to Internet-based technologies in the pre-consumption, consumption, and post-consumption process are detailed. As described in this chapter, the role of various information and communication technologies in increasingly mediating tourism experiences, changing and prolonging them, communicating and sharing then via consumer-generated media and new mobile technologies reveal new types of experiences in the making.

The "new" tourism consumers (as described by the authors), new technologies, new forms and characteristics of tourist experiences raise opportunities and challenges for researchers and providers, which are summarized by Gretzel and Fesenmaier.

The challenges posed by globalization, and the increasing dominance of global tourism businesses through neoliberalism and global free trade agreements, is a concern noticeable in several chapters. Fletcher's review (Chapter 10) of the economics of international tourism in Part I mentions the role of GATS (General Agreement on Trade in Services), of which a trenchant critique can be found in Wood's work (Chapter 33) on international tourism policy. Wood's critique of the neoliberal agenda, especially as demonstrated in his research on the international cruise industry, is drawn upon by a couple of other authors. Keith Debbage and Suzanne Gallaway (Chapter 32) review the trends in global tourist business operations, particularly in the airlines, hotel, and cruise industries, and raise neoFordism as a possible framework for understanding global production–consumption spaces of travel and tourism. The above authors discuss alternatives to neoliberalism in their chapters.

Mick Smith takes up the ethical perspectives and the ethical landscape of tourism in Chapter 34. He points out that ethics in tourism involves much more than normative and regulatory dimensions, and provides a strong critique of the moralization of tourism (as done by both researchers and organizations). Moral theories, rights, responsibilities and justice, environmental ethics and ecotourism, authenticity, and Heidegger's ethical ideas are among the topics discussed in this chapter, which offers other ways of understanding ethical tourism and the ethical body in relationship with others. Cara Aitchison, in Chapter 35 following, reviews theoretical contribution to tourism studies on feminist and gendered perspectives on the body. She chronologically traces gender and tourism research from the feminist empiricism of the 1970s through emancipatory Marxist and social feminism perspectives in the late 1980s

and early 1990s, to the fragmented poststructuralist critiques of the late 1990s and 2000s, leading to the "rematerialized" body in the latter part of the current decade. Her discussion of Foucault, poststructural feminism, and French feminist theory, and her use of sex tourism as an illustrative example to demonstrate the efficacy of particular feminist perspectives, offer useful directions for much needed theory building in this topic area.

The final three chapters in Part III engage with methodological issues and new ways of approaching the study of tourism. Mišela Mavrič and John Urry, Chapter 36, argue for a new mobilities paradigm. They provide a concise tracing of the history of tourism research, noting key problems, markers, and changes, including *sedetarist* and *nomadic* perspectives on place and space. This sets the ground for a theoretically structured presentation of the new mobilities paradigm and methodological approaches for studying new mobile tourism phenomena, relationships, performances, practices, and experiences. Alison Phipps, Chapter 37, engages with the body and embodied spaces differently through language; the discourse she uses attempts an "other" way to present the voice and work of tourism scholars. Gayle Jennings, Chapter 38, provides an overview of historical perspectives influencing the development of tourism studies and tourism research, along with a critique reflecting the domination of positivistic and post-positivistic approaches, and the marginalization of alternative culture and indigenous approaches. Jafari's (1990) four platforms of tourism research and scholarship are drawn upon by Jennings, as well as by Mavrič and Urry, and noted by Evans in his discussion of the multidisciplinary nature of tourism studies and its situation in business/management studies.

Charting this Moment in Tourism Studies

The range of critical, descriptive, and applied chapters in Parts I and II, plus the mix of theoretical, analytical, new/emergent topics, and methodological critique in Part III, call attention to the complex phenomenon called tourism, and the multifaceted, multidisciplinary perspectives needed to address the theoretical *and* applied demands of this field that is loosely referred to as "tourism studies." While some readers may grapple with the more theoretically dense chapters and appreciate the more applied chapters, others may question the lack of theoretical content in the more applied chapters. Arguably, this reflects the very nature of the field of tourism studies at present and indeed, its historical development. This *Handbook* reflects the contributions as well as the tensions and struggles of its "community of scholars" (noting Kuhn's [1970] discussion of how disciplines evolve). Holistically, the handbook charts the historical concerns of early scholars, the shift to the "cultural turn" and to new critical, theoretical explorations (bringing much needed attention to topics such as postcolonialism, and new approaches such as poststructuralism and feminist theories to study power relationships), but also marks out practical "real world" concerns, such as the impacts of globalization and GATS on tourism, destination management in the face of technological change and sustainability challenges, etc. In this sense, the *Handbook* documents a key moment in the development of the field—a moment where issues related to cultural critique and methodologies for cultural studies are preoccupying many scholars, and where global governance, neoliberal agendas, ethical and sustainability/conservation related issues are concerning many others. In the concluding chapter, we come back to some of these concerns and revisit the field of *tourism studies.*

Tourism Studies and Tourism Knowledge

The range of styles and structure contained in the chapters, together with the span between the theoretical and applied approaches, illustrates a diversity which brings us back to the question that we raised at the beginning of the chapter about the purpose of tourism studies: why study tourism and why should there be a handbook of tourism studies? In addition to the reasons cited earlier, a further one is worth considering in the light of the diversity contained within this Handbook. Tribe (2005) provides a valuable discussion of the tourism phenomenon in relation to tourism knowledge and curricula dealing with tourism. As Tribe argues, there is a flow from both knowledge and curriculum back to the phenomenon of tourism itself. The elaboration of theories and their transmission to the wider world through tourism education leads to the possibilities for change in the phenomenon itself. A similar argument was advanced by Jamal (2005) with respect to tourism pedagogy, specifically, teaching the theoretical constructs and principles of sustainable tourism in tourism curricula, facilitating learning via case studies and practical (field-based) experience, hence enabling the development of practical wisdom (Aristotelean *phronesis*) and *good* actions in tourism. In a similar vein, Jamal and Everett (2004) applied Habermas' notion on knowledge-constitutive interests to argue for greater attention to critical tourism research and critically reflexive *praxis* (change) oriented scholarship.

As "mainstream" tourism studies becomes increasingly informed by critical, reflexive research, and accepting of more traditional, mainstream as well as applied practitioners, the knowledge base will continue to change as should tourism curricula. Tribe (2005), noting the rise of new study approaches and methodologies (e.g., critical and interpretivist methodologies used by researchers working in areas like gender studies), identified two camps, one hosting the view of tourism as a business phenomenon (giving rise to curricula for vocational ends) and the other viewing tourism from a nonbusiness perspective, giving rise to liberal curricula. The current knowledge base presented in the *Handbook* reflects these changing moments and diverse perspectives, and the challenges facing tourism students and researchers to become familiar with the tensions and the trajectories of this area of study.

Of course, the coverage of the handbook is only partial. The power of editorial authority is limited by the practicalities of binding. The selection from the expansive knowledge base of tourism studies in the *Handbook* does exclude a number of topics and themes. We are aware for instance of omissions such as, for instance, specific topics such as retail tourism and sport tourism and, more explicit discussions of recreation, intercultural dialogue, and environmental justice, for example. However, we do hope the views of tourism studies provided in this *Handbook* offer a record of the field's theoretical and methodological evolutions, emerging cultural critiques, sustainability challenges being addressed, types of tourism that illustrate new theoretical insights and ethical criticisms, and hence a window into the future possibilities awaiting tourism studies.

Notes

1 Jafari discusses four perspectives/positions, broadly chronologically positioned as the "advocacy platform" of the 1950s and 1960s, the "cautionary platform" of the 1970s, the "adaptancy platform" of the 1980s and early 1990s, and the "knowledge platform" of the late 1990s and into the 21st century.

References

Airey, D. and Johnson, S. (1999). "The Content of Degree Courses in the UK." *Tourism Management*, 20(2): 229–235.

Apostolopoulas, Y., Leontidou, L. and Loukissas, P. (2000). *Mediterranean Tourism: Facets of Socioeconomic Development and Cultural Change*. London: Routledge.

Appadurai, A. (2002). "Cultural Diversity: A Conceptual Platform." In K. Stenou (Ed.), *UNESCO Universal Declaration on Cultural Diversity* (pp. 9–16). Paris: UNESCO.

Baranowski, S. (2004) *Strength Through Joy: Consumerism and Mass Tourism in the Third Reich*. Cambridge: Cambridge University Press.

Boorstin, D. (1964). *The Image: A Guide to Pseudo-Events in America*. New York: Harper & Row.

Bouchenaki, M. (2004). *Intervention de M. Bouchenaki Mounir, Sous Directeur général pour la culture at the Barcelona 2004 Universel Forum of Cultures*. Paris: UNESCO.

Bruner, E.M. (2004). *Culture on Tour: Ethnographies of Travel*. Chicago, IL: University of Chicago Press.

Canestrini D. (2001). *Travel Trophies: Anthropology of Souvenirs*. Turin: Bollati Boringhieri.

Cochrane, J. (2008). *Asian Tourism: Growth and Change*. London: Routledge.

Cohen, E. (1979). "A Phenomenology of Tourism Experiences." *Sociology*, 13: 179–201.

Cohen, E. (1998). "Authenticity and Commoditization in Tourism." *Annals of Tourism Research*, 15(3): 371–386.

Cohen, E. (2004). *Contemporary Tourism. Diversity and Change*. London: Elsevier.

Corsane, G. (2004). *Heritage, Museums and Galleries: An Introductory Reader*. London: Routledge.

Daher, R.F. (2006). *Tourism in the Middle East: Continuity, Change and Transformation*. Clevedon: Channel View Publications.

Dann, G. (1996). *The Language of Tourism: A Sociolinguistic Approach*. Wallingford: CAB International.

Daye, M., Chambers, D.P. and Roberts, S. (2008). *New Perspectives in Caribbean Tourism*. London: Routledge.

de Kadt, E. (1979). *Tourism: Passport to Development*. Oxford: Oxford University Press.

Echtner, C. and Jamal, T. (1997). "The Disciplinary Dilemma of Tourism Studies." *Annals of Tourism Research*, 24(4): 868–883.

Enzensberger, H.M. (1958). "A Theory of Tourism." *New German Critique*, 68: 117–135.

Evans, N. (2001). "The Development and Positioning of Business Related University Tourism Education: A UK Perspective." *Journal of Teaching in Travel and Tourism*, 1(1): 17–36.

Fennell, D. (2007). *Ecotourism*. London: Routledge.

Fussell, P. (1980). *Abroad: British Literary Travelling Between the Wars*. New York: Oxford University Press.

eacy...

nerI'llokay

Greenwood, D. (1989). "Culture by the Pound: An Anthropological Perspective on Tourism as Cultural Commoditization." In V. Smith (Ed.), *Hosts and Guests: The Anthropology of Tourism* (pp. 171–186). Philadelphia, PA: University of Pennsylvania Press.

Hall, C.M., Williams, A.M. and Lew, A.A. (2004). *A Companion to Tourism*. Oxford: Blackwell.

Hall, C.M. and Page, S.J. (2005). *The Geography of Tourism and Recreation: Environment, Place and Space*. London: Routledge.

Hannam, K. and Ateljevic, I. (2008). *Backpacker Tourism: Concepts and Profiles*. Clevedon: Channel View Publications.

Harrison, J. (2003). *Being a Tourist: Finding Meaning in Pleasure Travel*. Vancouver: University of British Columbia Press.

Jack, G. and Phipps, A. (2005). *Tourism and Intercultural Exchange: Why Tourism Matters*. Clevedon: Channel View Publications.

Jamal, T. (2005). "Virtue Ethics and Sustainable Tourism Pedagogy: Phronesis, Principles and Practice." *Journal of Sustainable Tourism*, 12(6): 530–545.

Jamal, T. and Everett, J. (2004). "Resisting Rationalization in the Natural and Academic Lifeworld: Critical Tourism Research or Hermeneutic Charity?" *Current Issues in Tourism*, 7(1): 1–19.

Jafari, J. (1990). "Research and Scholarship: The Basis of Tourism Education." *Journal of Tourism Studies*, 1(1): 33–41.

Jafari, J. (2001). "The Scientification of Tourism." In V. Smith and M. Brent (Eds.), *Hosts and Guests Revisited: Tourism Issues of the 21st Century* (pp. 28–41). New York: Cognizant Communication Corporation.

Jamal, T. and Kim, H. (2005). "Bridging the Interdisciplinary Divide: Towards an Integrated Framework for Heritage Tourism Research." *Tourist Studies*, 5(1): 55–83.

Kuhn, T. (1970). *The Structure of Scientific Revolutions*. Chicago: University of Chicago Press.

Lanfant, M.-F., Allcock, J.B. and Bruner, E. (1995). *International Tourism: Identity and Change*. London: Sage.

Leiper, N. (1981). "Towards a Cohesive Curriculum in Tourism: The Case for a Distinct Discipline." *Annals of Tourism Research*, 8(1): 69–84.

Lew, A.A. Yu, L., Ap, J. and Guangrui, Z. (2002). *Tourism in China*. Binghampton, NY: Haworth Press.

Long, P. and Palmer, N.J. (2008). *Royal Tourism: Excursions Around Monarchy*. Clevedon: Channel View Publications.

MacCannell, D. (1999). *The Tourist: A New Theory of the Leisure Class*. Berkeley: University of California Press.

Novelli, M. (2005). *Niche Tourism: Contemporary Issues, Trends and Cases: Contemporary Issues, Trends and Cases*. London: Butterworth-Heinemann.

Oakes, T. (1998). *Tourism and Modernity in China*. London: Routledge.

Posey, D.A. (1999). *Cultural and Spiritual Values of Biodiversity: A Complementary Contribution to the Global Biodiversity Assessment*. Nairobi: Intermediate Technology Publications.

Rauschelbach, B., Schäfer, A. and Steck, B. (2002). *Cooperating for Sustainable Tourism*. Kasparek: Heidelberg (for Gesellschaft für technische Zusammenarbeit—GTZ).

Richards, G. (2007). *Cultural Tourism: Global and Local Perspectives*. Binghampton, NY: Haworth Press Inc.

Robinson, M. and Boniface, P. (1999). *Tourism and Cultural Conflicts*. Wallingford: CABI.

Robinson, M. and Andersen, H.C. (2004). *Literature & Tourism: Essays in the Reading and Writing of Tourism*. London: International Thomson Press.

Robinson, M. and Phipps, A. (2004). "Worlds Passing By: Journeys of Culture and Cultural Journeys." *Journal of Tourism and Cultural Change*, 11(1): 1–9.

Rojek, C. and Urry, J. (1997). *Touring Cultures: Transformations of Travel and Theory*. London: Routledge.

Ryan, C. (1997). Tourism: A Mature Subject Discipline? *Pacific Tourism Review*, 1: 3–5.

Ryan, C. (2001). "Academia-Industry Tourism Research Links: States of Confusion." *Pacific Tourism Review*, 5(3): 83–96.

Ryan, C. and Hall, C.M. (2001). *Sex Tourism: Marginal People and Liminalities*. London: Routledge.

Shepherd, R. (2002). "Commodification, Culture and Tourism." *Tourist Studies*, 2(2): 183–201.

Smith, M.K. and Robinson, M. (2006). *Cultural Tourism in a Changing World: Politics,*

Participation and (Re)presentation. Clevedon: Channel View Publications.

Spode, H. (1994). "Reif für die Insel. Prolegomena zu einer historischen Anthropologie des Tourismus." In C. Cantauw (Ed.), *Arbeit, Freizeit, Reisen: Die feinen Unterschiede im Alltag* (pp. 105–123). New York: Waxmann Verlag.

Squire, S.J. (1994). "Accounting for Cultural Meanings: The Interface Between Geography and Tourism Studies Re-Examined." *Progress in Human Geography*, 18: 1–16.

Strain, E. (2003). *Public Places, Private Journeys: Ethnography, Entertainment, and the Tourist Gaze.* New Brunswick, NJ: Rutgers University Press.

Timothy, D.J. (2007). *The International Library of Essays in Tourism, Heritage and Culture: Volumes 1–3.* London: Ashgate.

Tribe, J. (1997). "The Indiscipline of Tourism." *Annals of Tourism Research*, 24(3): 638–657.

Tribe, J. (2000). "Indisciplined and Unsubstantiated." Annals of Tourism Research, 27(3): 809–813.

Tribe, J. (2005). "Tourism, Knowledge and the Curriculum." In David Airey and John Tribe (Eds.), *An International Handbook of Tourism Education* (pp. 47–60). Amsterdam: Elsevier.

UNESCO (1972). *Convention Concerning the Protection off the World Cultural and Natural Heritage.* Paris: UNESCO Publishing.

UNESCO (2005). *Sustainable Development and the Enhancement of Cultural Diversity.* Paris: UNESCO Publishing.

United Nations (2000). *United Nations Millennium Declaration,* Resolution adopted by the General Assembly, 55/2. New York: United Nations.

Urry, J. (1995). *Consuming Places.* London: Routledge.

Wagner, U. (1977). "Out of Time and Place: Mass Tourism and Charter Trips." *Ethnos*, 42: 38–52.

Waitt, G. and Markwell, K. (2006). *Gay Tourism: Culture and Context.* Binghampton, NY: Haworth Press Inc.

Wang, N. (2000). *Tourism and Modernity: A Sociological Analysis.* Amsterdam: Pergamon.

Ward, E.R. (2008). *Packaged Vacations: Tourism Development in the Spanish Caribbean.* Gainesville: University Press of Florida.

World Tourism Organization (2005). *Yearbook of Tourism Statistics 2005 (Data 1999–2003).* Madrid: World Tourism Organization.

PART I

Approaches to Tourism Studies

Tourist Boat on the Ill River in Strasbourg, France.

Tourism and Hospitality

David Bell

Definitions and Debates

Hospitality has been one of the most pervasive metaphors within tourism studies, referring in one sense to the commercial project of the tourist industry (such as hotels, catering, and tour operation) and in another sense to the social interactions between local people and tourists—that is, hosts and guests. (Germann Molz and Gibson, 2007: 6)

The last decade has seen a renewed interest in the concept of hospitality, in ways of researching and understanding hospitality, and in the intersections of hospitality, tourism and leisure (Jones, 2004). This renewal sits at the confluence of two intellectual trajectories: (1) a "critical turn" in hospitality studies, away from the solely functional, vocational emphasis of hospitality management or "hotel and catering" education and training, and towards a diverse, social science analysis; and (2) the take-up of the concept and practices of hospitality across a range of social science disciplines, where it is being used to critically explore key contemporary debates, such as those centered on immigration, asylum and refugees, and more broadly to understand diverse forms of "hospitable" interaction. The increasing commingling of these twin tracks means that hospitality is enjoying significant theoretical and empirical attention, and a

blossoming in publication and discussion (Morrison and O'Gorman, 2008). The aim of this chapter is to trace some contours of this commingling, and to connect it outwards to work on tourism by highlighting how debates about hospitality also shed light on some of the cornerstones of tourism studies—to trace, if you like, yet another commingling.

Hospitality studies and tourism studies share a significant number of key concerns and key concepts, especially in regard to ways of relating between "hosts" and "guests" and the problems brought about by the commodification of those ways of relating (Smith and Duffy, 2003). As bodies of knowledge, tourism studies and hospitality studies share that uneasy location between functional, vocational training for particular industries, and social science inquiry that draws on the conceptual and methodological resources of cognate disciplines (and the emerging traditions of hospitality and tourism studies themselves). As Morrison and O'Gorman (2008) show, hospitality studies has been enriched by the wider take-up of the concept across the social sciences and humanities—in history, sociology, cultural studies, anthropology, geography and history, to name but a few. Certainly, in my own adopted discipline of human geography, the concept has attracted significant attention as a lens for looking closely at key issues such as cosmopolitanism and multiculturalism, urban regeneration, relations between social groups, and feelings, experiences and spaces of inclusion and exclusion (see, among others, Barnett, 2005; Bell, 2007a, 2007b; Chan, 2005; McNeill, 2008b). This disciplinary location also inevitably shapes the version of the "hospitality story" that I present in this chapter—though a wider concern with the sites and spaces of hospitality has been one of the key characteristics of the "critical turn."

A central theme shared between tourism studies and hospitality studies explores encounters between people who are "strangers" to each other. This encounter involves the movement of a mobile actor (the guest) into the home territory of a static host. The host-guest encounter is also, of course, a power relation, though the dynamics of this relationship and the locus of power are complex issues, as we shall see. Moreover, the idea of hospitality has, like tourism, been used metaphorically as a symbol of broader social and cultural experiences and practices, and enactments of power between unequally situated social subjects. In philosophy, for example, notions of host and guest have been pondered, critiqued, and deconstructed (Derrida, 2001; Telfer, 2000).

While there has been growing cross-pollination between hospitality studies and its near (and some not-so-near) neighbors, it is still necessary to begin with some foundational work: the work of definition. And it should come as no surprise that the "critical turn" in hospitality studies has led to considerable scrutiny of the very object and subject of those studies—hospitality itself. As is commonly experienced when things turn "critical" or "cultural," nothing can be taken for granted any more, and a necessary "pause for thought" has to take place, to review the past, absorb cognate debates and new influences, before proceeding down a new path (Aitchison, 2006; Morrison, 2002). A certain amount of analysis of key concepts has to occur when things turn critical, and this has

indeed been largely welcomed by scholars in the field (though some are more cautious; see, for example, Ingram, 1999; Taylor and Edgar, 1996).

The hospitality management view of what constitutes hospitality tends to rest on the "holy trinity" of the provision of food and/or drink and/or accommodation—a simple enough starting point, though one that in itself has borne considerable reconsideration and deconstruction (Brotherton, 1999; Hemmington, 2007). Populating the term with actors gives us another troublesome definition, that of the hosts and guests, already flagged. At its simplest, hosts provide the "holy trinity" of hospitality for guests. Keep scratching at this seemingly simple, self-evident equation, and more questions than answers emerge: where does the act of hospitality take place, and when? Does it require the co-presence of host and guest? Do host and guest have to be human? Is the transaction voluntary on both sides? What compels the act of hospitality, and where does power lie?

Brotherton (1999: 165) provides a thoughtful discussion of this problem, asking whether hospitality should be considered "as a product, a process, an experience, or all three," before working his way through numerous preexisting definitions, both expansive and restrictive, of hospitality and hospitality management (see also Hemmington, 2007). He cites, among countless others, Hepple et al. (1990) who see hospitality as comprising four key characteristics:

1 It is conferred by a host on a guest who is away from home.
2 It is interactive, involving the coming together of a provider and receiver.
3 It is comprised of a blend of tangible and intangible factors.
4 The host provides for the guest's security, psychological and physiological comfort.
(Hepple et al., 1990, cited in Brotherton, 1999: 166–167).

As with the "holy trinity," here we have what seems at first glance a relatively commonsense and unproblematic conception, but which soon begins to come apart at the seams when we begin a critical interrogation: the guest must be traveling, the host at home—what counts as traveling, who gets to travel, where is home? Who carries the identities of "provider" and "receiver," are these interchangeable, must all moments of hospitality revolve around this couplet? What are the intangible factors invoked here—what does hospitality "feel like?" And must the host provide for the guest's security *and* psychological *and* physiological comfort? Who can judge what is comfortable?

As Brotherton (1999) acknowledges, every attempt at definition merely opens up new questions, new imprecisions, new ifs and buts. Even the "holy trinity" (food, drink, accommodation) is contestable, since the range of possibilities within each component defies easy categorization. This is perhaps especially true in terms of modern (and, indeed, postmodern) hospitality, where the proliferation of sites of hospitality and of means of giving and receiving it make any simple definition laughable. Exceptions and complications abound. Brotherton's own delineation of the "dimensions of hospitality" shows that, even having worked through all the problems of previous definitions, cloudiness remains. For him, hospitality can be thought of as "a human exchange characterized by being contemporaneous, voluntary and mutually beneficial, and by being based on specific products/services" (Brotherton, 1999: 169). To which we might ask: *Always* human? *Always* voluntary? *Always* mutually beneficial?

The question of definition still hangs over hospitality studies, though a careful invocation of the "holy trinity" might be cautiously used (as it is later in this chapter) to sidestep this seemingly endless problem. Considering the "spaces" of hospitality from a different angle, Lashley (2000) explores three "domains" of hospitality—social, private, and commercial—as a way of unpacking and tidying up some of the inherent complexity of the term. While still resting (albeit increasingly uneasily) on the "holy trinity," Lashley's focus on domains

allows him to split apart and make explicit some of the questions that dogged previous would-be definers. He sketches a Venn diagram of partially intersecting domains (private, social, and commercial) while acknowledging that hospitality studies has tended to cluster its attention around the commercial, fixing hospitality as an economic activity—and one in need of *management*. By pulling back the focus, however, he reintroduces broader conceptualizations of hospitality. So for Lashley, an historical view sheds light on the social domain of hospitality, on the development of shared social codes of giving and receiving, welcoming and graciously accepting—codes of civility and trust that sit outside of the commercial context. He is attuned to the ways in which hosting and guesting are embedded in the social order, and carry with them questions of status, obligation, reciprocity, and generosity. Here hospitality studies connects outwards not only to historical analysis, but to foundational work in sociology and anthropology, to explore the social processes of welcomes given and received, issues of reciprocity, rituals and taboos, and forms of exchange relationship such as gift giving. In this social domain, crossovers between hospitality and tourism research are very apparent, not least in their shared interest in sociological and anthropological lenses (Scott, 2006).

The private domain is, as Lashley shows, equally at the heart of understandings of hospitality, whether in terms of the literal hospitality offered by the host-at-home, or in broader, metaphorical terms through the evoking of "homeliness" as a key dimension of the constitution of hospitality. It is in the private or domestic domain, moreover, that Lashley ponders the relationship between hospitality and hospitableness—a pondering of the ways in which a sense of "welcome" is both given and received, and is understood "contractually" (in terms of not overstaying one's welcome, of knowing what it is acceptable to ask for or take, of knowing how "at home" one can be, and so on). The social bonds and social codes outlined above are equally apparent here at home. Looking into the private domain enriches the study of hospitality, even as it complicates its definition, not least since the homeliness of hospitality provision is a common benchmark used in the commercial sector. Indeed, areas of commercial hospitality provision trade on this association, as in the so-called "commercial home" sector (see Di Domenico Maria Laura and Lynch, Paul 2007; Lynch et al., 2007).

Finally, Lashley (2000) examines hospitality's commercial domain—the landscape of the hospitality industry. While on the one hand more straightforward, as we are now in the land of the "holy trinity" offered as an economic transaction, the very economics at work here complicate (and for some critics compromise or contaminate) the hospitality given and received, by making it into a service. The insertion of money into the heart of the hospitality equation thus stirs up questions about motive, about profit and exploitation, which muddy the generosity and reciprocity supposedly inherent in noneconomic definitions. Here we conjure the specter of "calculative hosting," the cynical performance of hospitality laid on for the sole purpose of getting paid (or getting rich). Here, too, we see "calculative guesting," whereby guests expect certain levels of service (and servility) simply because they are buying it, and the whole beauty of the pure, open, unquestioning hospitality relationship is sullied and spoiled by being bought and sold. Given the investment of many hospitality scholars in the training of workers and managers in the hospitality industry, such a bleak prognosis might seem counterproductive, and indeed a more nuanced picture of interactions in commercial settings is offered in "critical" hospitality studies. It is nevertheless important to remember the realities of the commercialization or industrialization of hospitality, and to keep a critical eye on topics such as labor relations, even as those at the sharp end of the industry provide evidence of ways of working with, round and against exploitative practice (see, for somewhat different examples, Collins, 2008; Tufts, 2006). The "calculative hosting" witnessed in the commercial domain seemingly fixes the identities of host and guest, and frames their encounter in particular ways. But one of the key moves of the "critical turn," already noted, has been to dissect or deconstruct these foundational roles.

From Host and Guest to Hostings and Guestings

As noted above, at the heart of understandings and ways of knowing hospitality, shared with tourism studies, is the seemingly simple but actually complex relationship of host and guest (Germann Molz and Gibson, 2007). This dyad frames the very possibility of a hospitality relation, and frames the polar-opposing actors whose co-presence is seen as necessary for a moment to be defined as one of hospitality. In the conventional formulation, the guest is a traveler, offered hospitality in the host's home. Expanded out and used metaphorically, the host's "home" can be scaled up to mean the home village or town, home region, home nation, and the "host" may be the person on the frontline of hospitality delivery, as in commercial settings, or a member of a broader "host community"—as in debates about asylum seekers and refugees, for example (see Gibson, 2007). Similarly, guests can be scaled up and away from the intersubjective, interpersonal encounter, and can be members of assorted groups of travelers, including migrants and tourists.

Germann Molz and Gibson explore the complex intertwinings and the equally complex unraveling of the host–guest couplet, noting that "host and guest [are] fluid, contested social roles that people move into, out of, and between as they negotiate extensive overlapping mobilities and social memberships" (2007: 7). Here they capture succinctly what is at stake—a decentering of fixed notions of who is host and who is guest, a flexible and fluid set of identifications that mean that any person can be both host and guest, changing roles as they move through social space. As Germann Molz and Gibson put it, a pertinent question to ask in this regard, is "*Where* is a host or guest?"—adding that they see a need to "dissociate stasis with hosts/homes and movement with guests/travel" (2007: 6–7; their emphasis). Inspired by the "new mobilities paradigm" in the social sciences (see Sheller and Urry, 2006), these discussions are more than word play, and require a rethink of the ways we conceptualize the comings-together that constitute hospitality (or for that matter tourism) encounters.

Other tourism and hospitality researchers have pursued the host–guest dyad's utility and its limitations, with Aramberri (2001) going so far as to state, provocatively, that the host should "get lost": given the total consumerization of tourism, he argues, it no longer makes sense to talk of "hosts" given what this might imply about choice, about generosity, about hospitableness. As with critics who deny the hospitableness of commercial hospitality, Aramberri suggests we need to talk instead of "service providers" and "customers," rather than using the freighted (but also idealized) terms "host" and "guest." Sherlock (2001) provides a different take on this. She notes that, while the terms lose their precision, given the mixing of categories (hosts may also be migrants, guests can settle and become hosts, and so on), the terms still have a commonsense usefulness and, moreover, are used reflexively and contestedly by those who might be labeled as host or guest. Instead of fixed identities, there are multiple hostings and guestings. Sherlock's study of the complex negotiations of "hostness" and "guestness" in Port Douglas, Australia, gives vivid empirical flesh to these arguments, with migrant workers and vacation workers performing "hostness" for guests but being construed as guests by other locals, and part-time residents (such as second-home owners) seeing themselves as sometimes locals and other times tourists (and sometimes in between, distinct from "local-locals").

A further insightful study, by McNaughton (2006), shows how migrant workers—in this case rural craft workers in India selling their wares at tourist sites—might be seen as

"hosts" by tourists, in that they constitute part of the tourist workforce, but that they may be seen nonetheless as guests—and in some cases as unwelcome guests—by other members of the host population. For McNaughton, a simplistic use of the host–guest dyad erases the politics and exploitation at work here: not all hosts or all guests are equal. Similarly, work by Parker (1994) shows how people constructed as "guests"—in his work, Chinese migrants to the UK—become "hosts" when taking up jobs in the hospitality industry, for example in Chinese restaurants and takeaways. In this case, their guests (customers) are at the same time members of the "host" (majority white British) population. (On the "guestness" of Chinese immigrant communities in the UK, see Chan [2005].) The "encounters across the counter" in the takeaway reveal for Parker the power dynamics that overwrite this commercial setting. Chan (2006) also complicates the power relations between host and guest in his work on Chinese tourists at the China–Vietnam border, where a "host gaze" meets the more familiar "tourist gaze," and Vietnamese hosts are seen to flex forms of cultural capital that disdain Chinese package tourists. Such encounters remind us of the complex vectors of power that overlay one another in any moment of hospitality.

Research by Lugosi (2007, 2008) complicates the host–guest dyad further still, by showing how "guests" perform hospitality in commercial settings—the experience of hospitableness in a bar or café may be in part (and sometimes in large part) the result of the "welcome" extended by other guests, rather than the formal host. As Lugosi observed in fieldwork in Budapest, spontaneous comings-together between guests (who are also strangers) can produce moments of hospitality in commercial venues (see also Laurier and Philo, 2006a, 2006b). Finally, there is the related issue of choice: some people freely choose to give their hospitality, while others are compelled to do so—especially frontline workers in the tourism and hospitality sectors, but increasingly too other members of "host communities" who are expected to extend a welcome to valued guests, as in cities that host so-called "mega-events" such as the Olympic Games (on sports, tourism, and hospitality, see Silk and Amis, 2005). Clearly, then, to talk uncritically of host and guest is highly problematic; but jettisoning the terms altogether seems equally foolish, given their conceptual and everyday utility. It might be better, therefore, to talk of hosting and guesting as *doings*, rather than host and guest as beings: this emphasizes shifting practices and performances, rather than fixed identities. But, to reiterate Germann Molz and Gibson's key question: *Where* is a host or guest? By turning, not without reservation, back to the "holy trinity" of food, drink, and accommodation, I now want to move to consider more fully some key sites of hospitality.

Spaces of Hospitality

In applying a spatial analysis, and mapping sites of hospitality through the lens of the "holy trinity," my aim is to illustrate some ways of understanding how the idea (and ideal) of hospitality is reshaping places. (I am mindful of Lugosi's [2008] comment that limiting analysis to this trinity ignores issues of entertainment and social intercourse at the heart of hospitality—I shall attempt to bring these vital elements in along the way.) My focus here will be on cities, though the arguments are not uniquely urban. In trying to further interrogate the relations of tourism and hospitality, I will be focusing on cities as tourism sites, but also more broadly understanding cities as nodes of assorted global flows, including flows of different sorts of people— migrants, tourists, and visitors. My analysis will sit within broader debates about the ways in which cities are struggling to position themselves relative to one another, and how they are engaged in various forms of inter-urban competitiveness in the context of post-industrialization. Key to this new way for cities to behave, short-handed by some

critics as "entrepreneurial governance" (Hall and Hubbard, 1998), is the ability of cities to draw in those global flows that have the highest value and to repel those of apparently low value. Positioning a city as a tourist attraction has been one important way of mobilizing these attraction/repulsion effects, though sometimes with unanticipated side effects and after shocks. As I will explore below, urban "foodscapes," "drinkscapes," and "restscapes" have been drawn in to the overall "hospitality offer" that packages cities (and neighborhoods) as attractive to certain kinds of guest. The increasingly complex "hospitality infrastructure" of cities, built up to service the needs and desires of valued guests, has reshaped the urban landscape, just as entrepreneurial governance has reshaped how cities behave, indeed what it means to be a city.

Hospitality Foodscapes

As cities jockey for position regionally, nationally, and globally, they seek to develop attractive "brands" and hospitality offerings to lure valued visitors, either as temporary guests or as new residents. The highest valued guests, members of the so-called transnational business class, to a large extent function as taste-makers able to define what counts as legitimate good taste, and to fashion markers of good taste into lifestyles (Featherstone, 1991). The urban landscape is reshaped to provide high-end consumption experiences for these taste-makers, including foodscapes. Of course, alternative city marketing strategies target different types of prospective visitor, including those whose palates seek familiarity rather than adventure: the choice of which market segment to aim for is part and parcel of the game of distinction played by city managers. Low-cost resorts provision their guests in ways amenable to their dietary requirements, just as high-end gastro-destinations tempt the taste buds of the culinary-cultural elites (Andrews, 2005).

Of course, for most traveler-diners, foodscapes are commercial hospitality venues—cafes, restaurants, delis, trattoria. While the fetish of home-cooked food means that gastronomic delights are available from "commercial home" settings, a more common way in which "home" is parlayed in foodscapes is through the deployment of signs of geographical distinctiveness and localness. Such a taste for the "local" has been critiqued as a depthless engagement with the broader "local" or "host" culture (Duruz, 2000; Hage, 1997); nevertheless, in terms of urban competitiveness, the marketing of locally distinct culinary cultures has considerable potency. Cities with iconic foodstuffs or foodscapes can center their tourist economy on this segment of the hospitality offer, and build a brand from it. At the same time, of course, foodscapes have been globalized (a better word might be "glocalized"), so that locally inflected variants of various national cuisines are routinely available no matter where one is visiting, as discussed in Jackson's (2004) work on Mumbai, for example.

However, as critical studies have shown, a fine balance must be achieved between trading on culinary cultures specific to place, and the threat to local culinary cultures brought about precisely by their successful co-option into urban imagineering schemes—the loss of authenticity which results in simulacral foodscapes. Nowhere is this anxiety (and the concomitant fetish of the local) more visible than in the Slow Food movement (Miele and Murdoch, 2002), which stipulates produce and processes with the aim of preserving local traditions and keeping the pace of hospitality *slow*. In terms of hospitality, the Slow Food movement favors the home-space and the local trattorie over the burger bar or the flashy restaurant, and the values it espouses emphasize not just food and cooking, but the conviviality of eating and drinking together, the pleasures of taking time. Slow Food recenters the pleasures of generous hosting, too—the giving of time. As Slow Food's ideas and ideologies spread beyond food to the broader Cittaslow (Slow Cities) movement, we can see

how a certain formulation of hospitable urbanism is being shaped by this emphasis on localness, authenticity, and conviviality (Knox, 2005).

Going Slow is not, of course, the only option for urban hospitality foodscapes—nor is it one universally available. The broader key point is to recognize the ways in which eating places are bundled into the tourism and hospitality offers of cities, and to explore how commercial hospitality venues such as restaurants and cafes are connected to larger narratives and processes of urban renewal. This theme is skillfully illustrated in Latham's (2003) study of one regenerating neighborhood in Auckland, New Zealand. By talking to bar and café owners as well as customers, Latham showed how foodscape entrepreneurs saw themselves as involved in a "sociocultural project" to reshape the neighborhood, and to contribute to the "feel" or "buzz" that rendered it attractive to certain types of customer (and in-migrant). Latham's work positions the food sector as a knowing and important player in urban regeneration, not merely as either a victim who will inevitably lose out to property speculation, nor as part of that speculation itself. Instead, Latham shows how "consumption has quite literally helped to build a new world" (2003: 1713) in this neighborhood, through the changes to the foodscape. Crucially, he emphasizes the mixing of new and old eating places, rather than the more familiar regeneration script whereby preexisting vernacular land uses are crowded out by gentrification, as Zukin (1982) described in SoHo, New York. Here a different version of "eating local" has been retained even as it has been reshaped, creating a convivial ecology whereby cafés and bars become the backdrop for other experiments in urban living.

To return to a point made earlier, borrowed from Lugosi (2008), eating places are sites of complex interrelations of hosts and guests, and of guests and guests. The conviviality Latham observed in Auckland is in part practiced or performed in encounters between customers, who signal a welcome (or not) through gestures and looks as much as through words. Lugosi et al. (2006a, 2006b) have looked closely at interpersonal interaction in eating and drinking places, and witnessed these micropractices that help create the overall ambience or "feel" of a hospitality venue. While previous work has delineated the way that staff are scripted into performances of hostness (e.g., Crang, 1994), studies such as those by Lugosi (2008) and Laurier and Philo (2006a, 2006b) refocus our attention on the "work" of hospitality willingly (and often spontaneously) performed by guests—the handing of napkins to mop up a spilt drink, an impromptu sing along, even just the clearing of space to allow a stranger to share a table. The choreography of hospitality in commercial foodscapes is dense with such detail—though with the corollary that diners can be made to feel out of place, perhaps especially if eating alone (since this re-reduces the dining experience to one of calculative refueling, maybe; Lukanuski [1998]). This focus on the "work" of customers should in no way overshadow the labor of hospitality workers such as chefs and waiters, washer-uppers and cleaners, whose work (sometimes ostentatiously visible, as in celebrity chefs, but frequently invisible) underpins the whole eating experience (Fine, 1996; Pritchard and Morgan, 2006). As Bourdain (2006) writes, we should also remember the global "ethnoscapes" that bring flows of migrant workers into restaurant kitchens. In the USA, he notes, these workers are likely to be from South America, and often work in nonunionized, informal, low-paid contexts. These workers should, Bourdain concludes, receive "the thanks of a grateful nation" of diners (2006: 46).

An important final point about performances of gastronomic hospitality is their *staging*: restaurant architecture and interior design serves to make some eating places tourist destinations, sometimes regardless of the quality of the food on offer (Franck, 2005). As part of its contribution to the hospitality offer, then, we must acknowledge the restaurant as spectacle, both in terms of its location

and design, and in terms of the experience and performance of eating there. Customers, it should be noted, are part of this spectacle, too. In other sectors of the hospitality industry, customers also make a spectacle of themselves, though not always in pre-scripted or desired ways—notably, perhaps, when alcohol is involved.

Hospitality Drinkscapes

My discussion of drinking places, hospitality and tourism will be limited to the consumption of alcoholic drinks in urban drinkscapes. This is not to deny that other kinds of drinking places, from coffee houses to tea rooms, juice bars to watering holes, are equally important components of the overall experience of drinking in the city—and, indeed, the country. It is, rather, in recognition of an emerging research agenda, concerned with alcohol consumption and the experience of place, or the ways in which drinking and place complexly commingle (Jayne et al., 2006, 2008). My discussion here draws on early stage research into "alcotourism" that seeks to explore the various ways that people travel to drink, drink while traveling, or even drink to travel (Bell, 2008).

This focus has to be set against the backdrop, in the UK, of concerns over the regulation of alcohol consumption, in relation to policies to manage the so-called "nighttime economy" (Bianchini, 1995). The drinkscape is part of the broader "urban nightscape" that Chatterton and Hollands (2003) describe as contributing a new "feel" to cities, a new sense of what urban experience might mean, and a new set of pleasures and problems for city dwellers and visitors. The "relaxation" of UK licensing laws in 2003 marked an attempt to "manage" a culture labeled as binge drinking, and to curb the antisocial behavior associated with "chucking out time" when pubs and bars close. This in itself was one of a raft of urban policy initiatives aimed at addressing various perceived problems in British cities—problems allegedly not observed in the city centers of the UK's European neighbors. Policymakers (and holidaymakers) had a sense that a "continental" café culture would inculcate British drinkers away from bingeing and towards "responsible drinking." Tourism experiences (and concerns from the tourism industry) certainly had a role to play in comparing UK pub culture with European café culture, in terms of both UK drinking habits when "at home" and those exhibited by "Brits abroad" in holiday resorts (Andrews, 2005).

The desire to promote a new "urban nightscape" was also part of a policy agenda to repopulate city centers, in order to address decades of movement out towards the suburbs. Again, the city centers of the UK were compared unfavorably with those of continental Europe, where a vibrant street culture and vital public realm were observed (Rogers, 1999). As Montgomery put it: "More and more people are inclined to use the cities and large towns at night; people are beginning to live more active social lives. They expect more from their cities. *They've been abroad and seen it working there. Why not here too?*" (1995: 104, emphasis added).

Of course, studies of "alcotourism" reveal more than the vital urban social lives that Montgomery highlights; they reveal a complicated set of practices and imaginings, whereby "local" drinking cultures are selectively appropriated, selectively transformed, and selectively ignored by tourists, while at the same time tourists' drinking tastes and habits remake "local" alco-cultures (Moore, 1995). For some travelers, drink is a taste of home-away-from-home (West, 2006), while for others, drinking "local" drinks is a way of experiencing the exotic. Some cities have traded on their local drinking cultures as symbols of the broader hospitality on offer to tourists—as in the growing phenomenon of "hen and stag party" tourism from the UK to cities of Eastern Europe such as Tallin, Prague, and Budapest (Bell, 2008). Entire national alco-cultures have been cemented to particular notions of conviviality and hospitality, then used to sell places—perhaps the

best known example being the Irish notion of the "craic," a kind of drink-fueled good time sold in images of Ireland itself as a tourism destination, and in the Irish theme pub (McGovern, 2002). Drink undoubtedly has a special place in the "holy trinity" of hospitality, for its ambivalent ability to oil the wheels of conviviality yet also to lead to antisocial and inhospitable behavior. Many cities have found themselves snagged on the horns of this dilemma, as they open up to new drinking venues as part of broadening out their nighttime economy offer, while simultaneously facing problems of regulation of the very consumption practices they have simultaneously promoted. Concerns over "binge drinking" in city centers have been framed in terms of a loss of the hospitality of "traditional" drinking cultures and places, and the ushering in of a new "inhospitable" alcoculture creating, in the words of Bianchini (2006), "alcoholic agoras."

Like restaurants, the story of bar architecture and design speaks volumes about the social codes of hospitality, from the historical moment of the insertion of the "bar" itself as a barrier between staff and customer as a way of framing "frontstage" and "backstage" regions, to the contemporary trend of "vertical drinking" venues which ease the transition from pub to nightclub, and which maximize drink consumption by foregoing chairs and tables and playing music too loud for conversation (Jayne et al., 2006). Detailed analyses of particular drinking places can provide rich ethnographic depictions of how venues are styled to attract certain types of clientele—vividly exemplified in Lugosi and Lugosi's (2008) work on informal, temporary "guerilla hospitality" spaces known as *romkert* (ruin bars) in Budapest, Hungary. Like Latham's (2003) cafés in a regenerating neighborhood of Auckland, the owners and patrons of these bars are engaged in a broader sociocultural project in the city, ambivalently located within broader "official" regeneration schemes. By self-consciously trading on images of urban decay, the *romkert* sell a particular way of relating to and drinking in the city.

In the UK, the proliferation and diversification of types of drinking venue in cities in the space of just a couple of decades has totally transformed the drinkscape, for better and for worse (Chatterton and Hollands, 2003). And in another echo of the foodscape, drinking venues marshal both staff and customers in collective performances of hospitality (and at times hostility). In the new nighttime economy of city centers this "welcome" is extended not only by bar staff but also by door staff, tasked with ensuring certain modes of hospitality between guests (Hobbs et al., 2003). The activities of the nighttime economy bring a different rhythm of hosting and guesting to cities, as drinkers are attracted in to the city center, performing certain modes of guestness—including those that clash with the lifestyles of unwitting hosts such as city-center residents (Roberts and Turner, 2005).

Drinking alcohol therefore has a strange location in ways of knowing and thinking about hospitality, and in ways of practicing it. At once central to the definition of hospitality, and firmly embedded in its history (see Walton, 2000), drinking is now stuck between continuing to deliver those hospitality benefits in cities, and bringing "new" problems (or new ways of seeing things as problems). While there have been significant studies of drinking venues as spaces of hospitality (such as Lugosi, 2007, 2008), less attention has been given to the role of alcohol itself (though see Latham and McCormack, 2004, on alcoholic urbanity). A turn towards the materiality of hospitality, and away from human–human interaction, might well serve to uncover the important (and contradictory) roles of drinking in the practices of hospitality in commercial, private, and social domains.

Hospitality Restscapes

As Walton (2000) shows in his short history of the hospitality trades, foodscapes, drinkscapes, and restscapes share a common heritage in terms of providing hospitality for travelers, and perhaps no institution better embodies the commercial provision of hospitality— usually offering the "holy trinity" under one roof—than the hotel. Moreover, hotels are stages for numerous other enactments of hospitality between host and guest and between guest and guest. Given the complexity of the services offered by hotels, their management has long been a core concern of hospitality training; yet, as Pritchard and Morgan (2006: 771) note, the hotel as a "cultural product" has been somewhat neglected in the emerging "critical" hospitality studies. As they add, hotels are emblematic of the key issues at the heart of hospitality as a concept, leading them to call upon scholars "to explore the spatiality of the hotel in order to analyze how interior and exterior hotel spaces are made through social relations and how social relations are in turn shaped by those self same spaces" (Pritchard and Morgan, 2006: 770). The focus of their analysis is the ludic and liminal "adventures" that guests may experience in these in-between spaces, which offer selective privacy and anonymity but plentiful opportunities for social intercourse (with friends and with strangers). Iconic in the architecture of the hotel in this regard is the lobby, where outside and inside meet, and the hotel bar, where particular modes of drinking and socializing are mobilized.

As McNeill (2008b) shows in his broad-ranging discussion of relations between the hotel and the city, this internal architecture of hotels delineates private and public in particular ways. Moreover, the diversification of hotels and their targeting of particular niche markets means that ever more attention has been afforded to the design of hotel spaces and the provision of tailored services, for example, the installation of now more-or-less ubiquitous en suite bathrooms, the availability of Wi-Fi not only in guestrooms and business centers but in "public" areas of hotels such as lobbies and coffee bars, and the offer of "pillow menus" and bespoke bedding to make the guest's stay perfect.

In his discussion of the "public" spaces of the hotel, McNeill (2008b) notes how lobbies and bars have opened out the hotel not only to paying guests but to other visitors, so "locals" can become "guests" and experience part of the spectacle of the hotel. As McNeill (2008b) adds, hotel lobbies and bars are often consciously styled as spectacles, as fantasy spaces that distil the "brand values" of the hotel, both to assure incoming guests that this is the right place for them, and to communicate more broadly the social and cultural positioning of the hotel on the increasingly crowded and competitive restscape. From themed hotels to boutique hotels, capsule hotels, business hotels, and apartment hotels, the differentiation of product in the hotel sector is matched by differentiation in design and in the hospitality offer. In a paper solely focused on airport hotels serving business clients, McNeill (2008a) traces how this particular niche has developed to meet the needs of the business traveler, providing a seamless business space where even the guest room is part of the "exoskeleton" of business-class connectivity. As well as hotel types serving distinct niche markets, distinctive local and national restscapes have developed, even while glocalized hotel brands have spread to new locations (McNeill, 2008b). In Japan, for example, novel forms such as the capsule hotel and the love hotel have appeared. The former offers minimal sleeping accommodation with none of the added extras familiar from standard hotel rooms and suites—"rooms" can be simply "pods" in which to sleep—while love hotels offer discretion via automation and hourly room rates for intimate liaisons (Foster, 2007). Elsewhere, local and national stereotypes and heritage are redeployed to give hotels and destinations a unique selling point, as in some former Eastern Bloc cities, where communism-themed restscapes offer nostalgic and kitsch touristic experiences (Light, 2000).

Indeed, iconic hotels have long been embedded in the place myths of particular cities, even as those myths change with time

(Wharton, 2007). So the exterior architecture also has symbolic importance in communicating certain values, hence the increasing call for "starchitects" to design restspaces (McNeill, 2008b). Moreover, the hotel reads as a microcosm of the city, a kind of distillation of the experience of urban living. This is both consciously achieved through the ways in which hotels relate to the cityspaces around them (the provision of certain vistas, the street-level interfaces, the images of the city used to market the hotel), but it is also revealed in "accidental" ways—in particular, through the composition of the hotel's labor force. McNeill (2008b: 390) writes that "hotels have always been poised uneasily at the frontline of social interactions between some very differently positioned groups and occupations . . . Hotels continue to house within one building extremes of wealth and exploited labor that eclipse conditions in many other service industries." This labor is frequently hidden (except for selective frontline tasks), and hotels have been described as hosting a particularly multicultural invisible labor force, often precariously employed and institutionally exploited (Gibson, 2006). Looking at one element of the hotel workforce, Seifert and Messing (2006) show how hotel cleaners have been subject to both work intensification and casualization, the former at least in part attributed to the "upscaling" of furnishings such as bedding and the latter a result of labor market restructuring and transnational migration. As their ergonomic analysis shows, the demands of this invisible aspect of hospitality provision have serious consequences for the health of workers.

Seifert and Messing (2006) discuss how forces of economic globalization have led to new patterns of migrant labor entering the hotel trades; as Steven Frears' film *Dirty Pretty Things* (2002) showed, the vast backstage regions of hotels are populated by workers from all over the world, producing hierarchies and stratifications within the workforce but also contributing to the host city's multiculturalism (see Gibson, 2006).

This theme has been picked up by hotel workers themselves, who in some cases have mobilized to make visible their contribution both to the hospitality offer of the city and to the cosmopolitan cultural life that acts as a draw to visitors. In Toronto, Canada, Tufts (2006) explores trade union organizing that has sought to reposition hotel employees as *cultural* workers:

> Immigrant workers employed in the hospitality sector of metropolitan centers not only provide services but also produce the cultural aspects of the city that attract visitors. For hotel workers' unions, promoting the cultural activities of workers as an entry point into debates of what constitutes a successful and authentic tourism industry. (Tufts, 2006: 343–344)

While this attempt to reposition hotel workers on the cultural landscape of Toronto has achieved some of its goals, Tufts acknowledges that the "alienating and seasonal" nature of employment limits workers' abilities and willingness to "attach any identity to the hospitality workplace" (2006: 358), limiting the transformative potential of this action. Moreover, in "packaging" hotel workers as standard-bearers of multiculturalism or cosmopolitanism, there is a danger of merely further commodifying and "exoticizing" employees in a sector already marked by employment hierarchies based on "race," class, and appearance. As McNeill (2008b: 393) concludes, "The hotel is a microcosm of the hidden processes of labor exploitation which are central to the consumption experience"—the hotel trades on offering certain experiences of urban heterogeneity and the "frisson of difference" while insulating guests from other encounters with difference, including those embodied by the "backstage" workforce. Such an analysis reiterates a key conceptual point: that hospitality invokes exclusions as well as inclusions, and that latent in the articulation of hospitality is hostility. These issues have been foregrounded in philosophical discussions of hospitality, which we shall encounter in the following section.

Hospitable Encounters

In a well-known series of meditations and discussions, the continental philosopher and deconstructionist Jacques Derrida has pondered the meanings of hospitality, taking as his starting point a critique of Kant's (1795/1996) treatise on global rights and citizenship (Derrida, 2001; Derrida and Dufourmantelle, 2000). While there is not time to provide detailed engagement with Derrida here—and this has occupied considerable space in the emerging literature already (see, among many others, Dikeç, 2002; Friese, 2004)—it is nevertheless important at least to *encounter* the Derridean perspective, which to my reading centers on the paradox between the impossible ideal of open, unconditional hospitality offered to anyone and everyone, unendingly and unquestioningly, and the various ways in which hospitality has in reality been made conditional, limited, and exclusive. Toying with the deconstructive possibilities inherent in the etymology and formulation of hospitality (and the hostility latent within it) and the relations of host and guest, Derrida asks us to think long and hard about the ways in which hospitality might be deployed conceptually and practically, and what is at stake in the mode of its deployment. Even the home as the site of "pure" hospitality comes under Derrida's scrutiny, for its doors may be closed as well as opened, and its walls mark the separation of inside from outside. The host who stands at the threshold becomes a gatekeeper, even a jailer, though by admitting the guest he may end up the prisoner, unable to reestablish the limits to the hospitality he offers to a guest who refuses to leave. The hospitable encounter is, for Derrida, fraught with complexity and ambiguity, which means that it is always already rendered conditional—for to offer absolute, unconditional hospitality would mean the host opening himself up unendingly, unquestioningly, asking nothing of the guest, not even his name (Derrida and Dufourmantelle, 2000).

Perhaps unsurprisingly, Derrida does not consider the commercial provision of hospitality; one can only imagine that such "calculative hosting" (and guesting) would for him show the epitome of conditionality. And he is not alone in dismissing commercial hospitality as the least "pure," most inhospitable form of "hospitality" (see, for example, Ritzer, 2007; for an alternative view, see Williams, 2000). Hospitality studies is poised at the fulcrum of this problematic, at once wedded to an analysis of hospitable encounters is commercial settings, yet also wanting to show the broader resonance of hospitality as a "social lens" to understand many ways of relating. The current "critical turn" in hospitality studies seems to be making productive use of this position, in opening out multiple ways of knowing hospitality. And, of course, in the realm of practice, there are countless examples of hospitality outside of its industrial manifestation; indeed, practitioners can be observed taking themselves out of what they see as narrowly economic exchange relations, reinserting the generosity and reciprocity of hospitality in their encounters. Germann Molz (2007) provides an interesting case study in this regard, in her work on "couch surfing" websites, whereby travelers exchange local knowledge and information on domestic accommodation with one another. We should also remember here work that highlights how, even in commercial settings, much of the "work" of hospitality goes on between guests—an idea we might extrapolate out to consider the broader network of hospitable encounters between strangers that constitute the experiences of everyday life (Bell, 2007b). Such a move also takes us away from the "holy trinity," as Lugosi (2008) suggests, to consider how hospitality is made up in all kinds of encounters in all kinds of spaces.

I want to end by considering another instance of hospitable encounter: the encounter between different disciplines and perspectives that share a common concern with thinking about hospitality. As Pritchard and Morgan (2006) rightly comment, research agendas have been overly compartmentalized, not least in the areas of leisure, tourism, and hospitality studies, each of which has a different theoretical and methodological biography. Yet for them, "the really interesting research problems are to be found when we combine these fields and their alternative research environments" (Pritchard and Morgan, 2006: 763). Opening out the study of hospitality, perhaps even unconditionally, offers the possibility for myriad hospitable encounters—encounters that stand to enrich both the emerging, multidisciplinary enterprise of critical hospitality studies and the broader intellectual and practical landscape of shared concerns with ways of knowing and doing hospitality.

Acknowledgements

I would like to thank Peter Lugosi, Donald McNeill and Mark Jayne for reading and commenting on drafts of this chapter, and for providing or pointing me towards additional sources.

References

Aitchison, Cara, C. (2006). "The Critical and the Cultural: Explaining the Divergent Paths of Leisure Studies and Tourism Studies." *Leisure Studies*, 25(4): 417–422.

Andrews, Hazel (2005). "Feeling at Home: Embodying Britishness in a Spanish Charter Tourist Resort." *Tourist Studies*, 5(3): 247–266.

Aramberri, Julio (2001). "The Host Should Get Lost: Paradigms in the Tourism Theory." *Annals of Tourism Research*, 28(3): 738–761.

Barnett, Clive (2005). "Ways of Relating: Hospitality and the Acknowledgement of Otherness." *Progress in Human Geography*, 29(1): 5–21.

Bell, David (2007a). "Moments of Hospitality." In Jennie Germann Molz and Sarah Gibson (Eds.), *Mobilizing Hospitality: The Ethics of Social Relations in a Mobile World* (pp. 29–46). Aldershot: Ashgate.

Bell, David (2007b). "The Hospitable City: Social Relations in Commercial Spaces." *Progress in Human Geography*, 31(1): 7–22.

Bell, David (2008). "Destination Drinking: Toward a Research Agenda on Alcotourism." *Drugs: Education, Prevention and Policy*, 15(3): 291–304.

Bianchini, Franco (1995). "Night Cultures, Night Economies." *Planning Practice and Research*, 10(2): 121–126.

Bianchini, Franco (2006). "Cultural Policy and City Development." Paper presented at the *International Conference on Cultural Policy Research*. Vienna.

Bourdain, Anthony (2006). *The Nasty Bits*. London: Bloomsbury.

Brotherton, Bob (1999). "Towards a Definitive View of the Nature of Hospitality and Hospitality Management." *International Journal of Contemporary Hospitality Management*, 11(4): 165–173.

Chan, Wun (2005). "A Gift of a Pagoda, the Presence of a Prominent Citizen, and the Possibilities of Hospitality." *Environment and Planning D: Society and Space*, 23(1): 11–28.

Chan, Yuk Wah (2006). "Coming of Age of the Chinese Tourists: The Emergence of Non-Western Tourism and Host-Guest Interactions in Vietnam's Border Tourism." *Tourist Studies*, 6(3): 187–213.

Chatterton, Paul and Hollands, Robert (2003). *Urban Nightscapes: Youth Cultures, Pleasure Spaces and Corporate Power*. London: Routledge.

Collins, Dana (2008). "When Sex Work Isn't 'Work': Hospitality, Gay Life, and the Production of Desiring Labor." *Tourist Studies*, 7(2): 115–139.

Crang, Phil (1994). "It's Showtime: On the Workplace Geographies of Display in a Restaurant in Southeast England." *Environment & Planning D: Society and Space*, 12(4): 675–704.

Derrida, Jacques (2001). *On Cosmopolitanism and Forgiveness*. London: Routledge.

Derrida, Jacques and Dufourmantelle, Anne (2000). *Of Hospitality*. Stanford, CA: Stanford University Press.

Di Domenico, MariaLaura, L. and Lynch, Paul (2007). "Commercial Home Enterprises: Identity, Space and Setting." In Conrad Lashley, Paul Lynch and Alison Morrison (Eds.), *Hospitality: A Social Lens* (pp. 117–126). London: Elsevier.

Dikeç, Mustafa (2002). "Pera Peras Poros: Longings for Spaces of Hospitality." *Theory, Culture and Society*, 19(1–2): 227–247.

Duruz, Jean (2000). "A Nice Baked Dinner . . . or Two Roast Ducks from Chinatown? Identity Grazing." *Continuum: Journal of Media and Cultural Studies*, 14(3): 289–301.

Featherstone, Mike (1991). *Consumer Culture and Postmodernism*. London: Sage.

Fine, Gary A. (1996). *Kitchens: the Culture of Restaurant Work*. Berkeley: University of California Press.

Foster, Derek (2007). "Love Hotels: Sex and the Rhetoric of Themed Spaces." In Scott A. Lukas (Ed.), *The Themed Space: Locating Culture, Nation, and Self* (pp. 167–181). Lanham, MD: Lexington Books.

Franck, Karen A. (Ed.) (2005). "Food and the City." Special Issue of *Architectural Design*, 75(3).

Frears, Stephen (2002). *Dirty Pretty Things*. London: BBC Films.

Friese, Heidrun (2004). "Spaces of Hospitality." *Angelaki: Journal of the Theorectical Humanities*, 9(2): 67–79.

Germann Molz, Jennie (2007). "Cosmopolitans on the Couch: Mobile Hospitality and the Internet." In Jennie Germann Molz and Sarah Gibson (Eds.), *Mobilizing Hospitality: The Ethics of Social Relations in a Mobile World* (pp. 65–82). Aldershot: Ashgate.

Germann Molz, Jennie and Gibson, Sarah (Eds.) (2007). *Mobilizing Hospitality: The Ethics of Social Relations in a Mobile World*. Aldershot: Ashgate.

Gibson, Sarah (2006). "The Hotel Business is About Strangers: Border Politics and Hospitable Spaces." In Stephen Frear's *Dirty Pretty Things, Third Text*, 20(6): 693–701.

Gibson, Sarah (2007). "Abusing our Hospitality: Inhospitableness and the Politics of Deterrence." In Jennie Germann Molz and Sarah Gibson (Eds.), *Mobilizing Hospitality: The Ethics of Social Relations in a Mobile World* (pp. 159–177). Aldershot: Ashgate.

Hage, Ghassan (1997). "At Home in the Entrails of the West: Multiculturalism, Ethnic Food and Migrant Home-Building." In Helen Grace, Ghassan Hage, Lesley Johnson, Julia Langsworth and Michael Symonds (Eds.), *Home/World: Space, Community and Marginality in Sydney's West* (pp. 99–153). Annandale, NSW: Pluto.

Hall, Tim and Hubbard, Phil (Eds.) (1998). *The Entrepreneurial City: Geographies of Politics, Regime and Representation*. Chichester: John Wiley.

Hemmington, Nigel (2007). "From Service to Experience: Understanding and Defining Hospitality." *Service Industries Journal*, 27(6): 747–755.

Hepple, J., Kipps, M. and Thomson, J. (1990). "The Concept of Hospitality and an Evaluation of its Applicability to the Experience of Hospital Patients." *International Journal of Hospitality Management*, 9(4): 305–317.

Hobbs, Dick, Hadfield, Philip, Lister, Stuart and Winlow, Simon (2003). *Bouncers: Violence and Governance in the Night-time Economy*. Oxford: Oxford University Press.

Ingram, Haydn (1999). "Hospitality: A Framework for a Millennial Review." *International Journal of Hospitality Management*, 11(4): 140–147.

Jackson, Peter (2004). "Local Consumption Cultures in a Globalizing World." *Transactions of the Institute of British Geographers*, 29(3): 165–178.

Jayne, Mark, Holloway, Sarah and Valentine, Gill (2006). "Drunk and Disorderly: Alcohol, Urban Life and Public Space." *Progress in Human Geography*, 30(4): 451–468.

Jayne, Mark, Holloway, Sarah and Valentine, Gill (2008). "Geographies of Alcohol, Drinking and Drunkenness: A Review of Progress." *Progress in Human Geography*, 32(2): 247–263.

Jones, Peter (2004). "Finding the Hospitality Industry? Or Finding Hospitality Schools of Thought?" *Journal of Hospitality, Leisure, Sport and Tourism Education*, 3(1): 33–45.

Kant, Immanuel (1795/1996). "Toward Perpetual Peace: A Philosophical Project." *Practical Philosophy: the Cambridge Edition of the Works of Immanuel Kant*. Cambridge: Cambridge University Press.

Knox, Paul L. (2005). "Creating Ordinary Places: Slow Cities in a Fast World." *Journal of Urban Design*, 10(1): 1–11.

Lashley, Conrad (2000). "Towards a Theoretical Understanding." In Conrad Lashley and Alison Morrison (Eds.), *In Search of Hospitality: Theoretical Perspectives and Debates* (pp. 1–17). London: Butterworth Heinemann.

Latham, Alan (2003). "Urbanity, Lifestyle and Making Sense of the New Urban Cultural Economy: Notes from Auckland, New Zealand." *Urban Studies*, 40(9): 1699–1724.

Latham, Alan and McCormack, Derek (2004). "Moving Cities: Rethinking the Materialities of Urban Geographies." *Progress in Human Geography*, 28(6): 701–724.

Laurier and Philo (2006a). "Cold Shoulders and Napkins Handed: Gestures of Responsibility." *Transactions of the Institute of British Geographers*, 31(2): 193–207.

Laurier and Philo (2006b). "Possible Geographies: A Passing Encounter in a Café." *Area*, 38(3): 353–364.

Light, Duncan (2000). "Gazing on Communism: Heritage Tourism and Post-Communist Identities in Germany, Hungary and Romania." *Tourism Geographies*, 2(2): 157–176.

Lugosi, Peter (2007). "Consumer Participation in Commercial Hospitality." *International Journal of Culture, Tourism and Hospitality Research*, 1(3): 227–236.

Lugosi, Peter (2008). "Hospitality Spaces, Hospitable Moments: Consumer Encounters and Affective Experiences in Commercial Settings." *Journal of Foodservice*, 19: 139–149.

Lugosi, Peter and Lugosi, Krisztina (2008). "The 'Ruin' Bars of Budapest: Urban Decay and the Development of a Genre of Hospitality." Paper presented at the *Council for Hospitality Management Education Research Conference*. Glasgow, May.

Lukanuski, Mary (1998). "A Place at the Counter: The Onus of Oneness." In Ron Scapp and Brian Seitz (Eds.), *Eating Culture* (pp. 112–120). New York: SUNY Press.

Lynch, Paul, Di Domenico, Maria L. and Sweeney, Majella (2007). "Resident Hosts and Mobile Strangers: Temporary Exchanges within the Topography of the Commercial Home." In Jennie Germann Molz and Sarah Gibson (Eds.), *Mobilizing Hospitality: The Ethics of Social Relations in a Mobile World* (pp. 121–144). Aldershot: Ashgate.

McGovern, Mark (2002). "The 'Craic' Market: Irish Theme Bars and the Commodification of Irishness in Contemporary Britain." *Irish Journal of Sociology*, 11(2): 77–98.

McNaughton, Darlene (2006). "The 'Host' as Uninvited 'Guest': Hospitality, Violence and Tourism." *Annals of Tourism Research*, 33(3): 645–665.

McNeill, Donald (2008a). "The Airport Hotel as Business Space." *Geografiska Annaler*, forthcoming.

McNeill, Donald (2008b). "The Hotel and the City." *Progress in Human Geography*, 32(3): 381–396.

Miele, Mara and Murdoch, Jonathan (2002). "The Practical Aesthetics of Traditional Cuisines: Slow Food in Tuscany." *Sociologica Ruralis*, 42(4): 312–328.

Montgomery, John (1995). "Urban Vitality and the Culture of Cities." *Planning Practice and Research*, 10(2): 101–109.

Moore, Roland S. (1995). "Gender and Alcohol use in a Greek Tourist Town." *Annals of Tourism Research*, 22(2): 300–313.

Morrison, Alison (2002). "Hospitality Research: A Pause for Reflection." *International Journal of Tourism Research*, 4(2): 161–169.

Morrison, Alison and O'Gorman, Kevin (2008). "Hospitality Studies and Hospitality Management: A Symbiotic Relationship." *International Journal of Hospitality Management*, 27(2): 214–221.

Parker, David (1994). "Encounters Across the Counter: Young Chinese People in Britain." *New Community*, 20(4): 621–634.

Pritchard and Morgan (2006). "Hotel Babylon? Exploring Hotels as Liminal Sites of Transition and Transgression." *Tourism Management*, 27(6): 762–772.

Ritzer, George (2007). "Inhospitable Hospitality?" In Conrad Lashley, Paul Lynch and Alison Morrison (Eds.), *Hospitality: a Social Lens* (pp. 129–140). London: Elsevier.

Roberts, Marion and Turner, Chris (2005). "Conflicts of Liveability in the 24-hour City: Learning from 48 Hours in the Life of London's Soho." *Journal of Urban Design*, 10(2): 171–193.

Rogers, Richard (1999). *Towards an Urban Renaissance*. London: E & FN Spon.

Scott, David G. (2006). "Socialising the Stranger: Hospitality as a Relational Reality." Unpublished MA thesis, University of Otago.

Seifert, A.M. and Messing, K. (2006). "Cleaning up after Globalization: An Ergonomic Analysis of Work Activity of Hotel Cleaners." *Antipode*, 38(4): 557–578.

Sherlock, Kirsty (2001). "Revisiting the Concept of Hosts and Guests." *Tourist Studies*, 1(3): 271–295.

Sheller, Mimi and Urry, John (2006). "The New Mobilities Paradigm." *Environment and Planning A*, 38(2): 207–226.

Silk, Michael and Amis, John (2005). "Sport Tourism, Cityscapes and Cultural Politics." *Sport in Society*, 8(2): 280–301.

Smith, Mick and Duffy, Rosaleen (2003). *The Ethics of Tourism Development*. London: Routledge.

Taylor, S. and Edgar, D. (1996). "Hospitality Research: The Emperor's New Clothes?" *International Journal of Hospitality Management*, 15(3): 211–227.

Telfer, Elizabeth (2000). "The Philosophy of Hospitality." In Conrad Lashley and Alison Morrison (Eds.), *In Search of Hospitality: Theoretical Perspectives and Debates* (pp. 44–52). London: Butterworth Heinemann.

Tufts (2006). "We Make It Work: The Cultural Transformation of Hotel Workers in the City." *Antipode*, 38(4): 350–373.

Walton, John, K. (2000). "The Hospitality Trades: A Social History." In Conrad Lashley and Alison Morrison (Eds.), *In Search of Hospitality: Theoretical Perspectives and Debates* (pp. 56–74). London: Butterworth Heinemann.

West, Brad (2006). "Consuming National Themed Environments Abroad: Australian Working Holidaymakers and Symbolic National Identity in 'Aussie' Theme Pubs." *Tourist Studies*, 6(2): 139–155.

Wharton, Annabel (2007). "Commodifying Space: Hotels and Pork Bellies." In Conrad Lashley, Paul Lynch and Alison Morrison (Eds.), *Hospitality: A Social Lens* (pp. 101–116). London: Elsevier.

Williams, Alistair (2000). "Consuming Hospitality: Learning From Post-Modernism?" In Conrad Lashley and Alison Morrison (Eds.), *In Search of Hospitality: Theoretical Perspectives and Debates* (pp. 217–234). London: Butterworth-Heinemann.

Zukin, Sharon (1982). *Loft Living: Culture and Capital in Urban Change*. New Brunswick, NJ: Rutgers University Press.

Anthropological Interventions in Tourism Studies

Naomi Leite and Nelson Graburn

Tourism is both more and less than an industry, more and less than a cultural phenomenon, more and less than a form of leisure. Its character is as quintessentially human as the faculty of language . . . (Ness, 2003: 9)

Introduction

We have titled this chapter "Anthropological Interventions," rather than "the Anthropology of Tourism," because despite the exponential growth of anthropological research on tourism over the past three decades, we find little evidence of a coherent subdiscipline, past or present, to which we could give that name. Both professionally and intellectually, most anthropologists conducting tourism-related research orient their work toward disciplinary audiences focused on other topics.[1] This is not necessarily negative. On the contrary, such a state of affairs is perfectly in keeping with anthropology's emphasis on viewing social and cultural phenomena holistically, within a richly described context, rather than in isolation. Anthropologists approach tourism in relation to a wide range of contemporary anthropological interests, among them ethnicity, identity, local and global politics, development, social inequality, gender, material culture, globalization, diaspora, lived experience, discourse, representation, and the objectification and commodification of culture. Nor is there a single theoretical perspective that unites anthropological research on tourism, though we do note a general trend toward more interpretivist than political-economic paradigms in recent years.[2]

Complicating our task further is the overall trend toward interdisciplinarity in tourism research. Given that anthropologists have long drawn upon sociology, geography, history, political science, critical theory, and cultural studies in making sense of their field materials, and given that tourism scholars from other disciplines routinely adopt anthropology's model of ethnographic research, how are we to distinguish who is or is not "an anthropologist" and how might we delimit "the anthropology of tourism"? By shifting focus instead to what we call *anthropological interventions*—characteristic methods, ways of formulating research problems, empirical contributions—this chapter clarifies the nature and breadth of contemporary anthropological research involving tourism and so provides more solid grounding for future interdisciplinary work.

Anthropology: The Study of Humankind

As the study of human life—its maintenance, structures, practices, expressions, and meanings—sociocultural anthropology offers a disciplinary framework for studying an enormous range of topics anywhere in the world.[3] Although originally developed in light of the colonial encounter with "exotic" and "primitive" peoples, for more than 50 years anthropology has also included research in Western societies, first among rural and inner-city populations, then increasingly in all levels of society. By the late 20th century, even New York stock traders, international journalists, global advertising agencies, development foundations, and European Union bureaucrats had come under anthropologists' ethnographic scrutiny. Research in postcolonial nations has continued apace. What unites and distinguishes contemporary anthropology is thus not a particular set of topics or peoples—in fact, there is substantial topical and geographical overlap between anthropology and the other social sciences—but a unique way of knowing, an overarching disciplinary perspective that foregrounds ethnographic research and holistic analysis. We address this general perspective below, then consider its implications for how anthropologists approach "tourism" as an object of study.

An Anthropological Approach to Tourism

For anthropologists, *ethnographic research* comprises a bundle of research practices that have been partially taken up by other disciplines under the rubric of "qualitative methods." Chief among these is participant-observation,

a method pioneered by anthropologists in the early years of the 20th century. Traditionally, the anthropologist spends an extended period of time (one or more years) participating in the daily life of the people studied, talking with them, joining in their activities, noting down observations, and in so doing gradually coming to understand their lived experience as "whole people" with multifaceted lives. The process is one of simultaneously joining in and holding back, "a continuous tacking between the 'inside' and the 'outside' of events: on the one hand grasping the sense of specific occurrences and gestures empathetically, on the other stepping back to situate these meanings in wider contexts" (Clifford, 1988: 34). Ultimately the goal is, in Bronislaw Malinowski's (1922: 25) famous phrase, "to grasp the native's point of view," to understand why it makes sense to participants to do things the way they do. Ethnographers typically supplement participant-observation with interviews, textual and visual analysis (of various media, locally produced texts, imagery, etc.), and occasionally open-ended questionnaires, all interpreted in light of what the anthropologist learns as a participant-observer. Whatever additional qualitative (and quantitative) methods might be utilized, however, an extended period of participant-observation is generally considered the defining element, the sine qua non, of anthropological research. This experiential immersion provides the basis for *holistic analysis*, an understanding of how the phenomenon under study fits into broader systems of meaning and action. It is a fundamental anthropological premise that all domains of human life—e.g., religion, gender, economics, leisure, politics, arts—influence and inform one another; to attempt analysis of one in isolation is to risk at best partial understanding. Importantly, the most relevant frame of analysis may not become apparent until well into the research period, when the ethnographer begins to build a complete, integrated picture.

While this approach is relatively easily applied in studies of "host" populations, ethnographic research among tourists, whose presence is by definition fleeting, is considerably more complex (Graburn, 2002).[4] Anthropologists have had to adapt their research methods to capture the transient tourist-as-native's point of view. Some researchers spend many months at a single tourist destination, slowly building up an understanding of visitors' motivation, behavior, and experience by talking with and moving among them on a daily basis (Edensor, 1998; Lehrer, 2007; Selänniemi, 2001; van den Berghe, 1994). Others accompany package tours as full participants (Ebron, 2000; Karam, 2007; Louie, 2001), even making the same journey repeatedly with a series of different groups (Feldman, 2008; Frey, 1998; Leite, 2007). Adopting the role of translator (Kim, 2003) or even academic guide (Bruner, 2005) during an international package tour offers additional complexity and insight to the participant-observer role.

In most cases, these scholars place their findings in a broader context by conducting extensive follow-up correspondence and even participant-observation at tour reunions or related gatherings (e.g., Basu, 2007; Frey, 1998; Karam, 2007; cf. Bruner, 2005: 26–27). Others rely on less orthodox methods, in combination with knowledge gained in previous participant-observation with the same general population, for example eliciting travel narratives through in-depth interviews at home, as Harrison (2003) did in her study of middle-class Canadian world travelers, or reading blog posts, as Graburn does in his current research on Japanese tourists' emotional experiences, building on his ongoing fieldwork in Japan (1983c, 1987, 1995b, 2008a). Some have tried additional techniques such as leaving comment books in hostels or asking tourists to keep diaries or take photos to share with them, all of which can be examined and discussed with the tourists afterward. Regardless of the specific methods or topic of study, anthropologists strive to participate in the most naturalistic settings possible as the primary means of gaining understanding.

It should be apparent from the foregoing that an anthropological approach precludes viewing tourism as a distinct entity in itself, to be defined everywhere in the same way.

It is, instead, "not one, but many sets of practices, with few clear boundaries but some central ideas" (Abram et al., 1997: 2), all embedded within broader social, political, and historical frameworks. As a cultural phenomenon, its significant components will shift depending on one's starting point. Thus "tourism" can refer to a category of experience counterposed to everyday life; a local, national, or global industry; an opportunity for employment; a source of strangers in one's home locality; a force for social change; a form of cultural representation and brokerage; an emblem and a medium of globalization; a venue for the construction and performance of national, ethnic, gendered, and other identities; or any combination of these and more. Tourism is thus most productively viewed not as an entity in its own right, but instead as a social field in which many actors engage in complex interactions across time and space, both physical and virtual. Accordingly, in the past two decades anthropologists have moved beyond debates over models and typologies of "the tourist" (Cohen, 1979; MacCannell, 1976) and of "tourism" (Cohen, 1992; Graburn, 1983a), and have begun to explore the ambiguities, contingencies, and slippages revealed in the particularities of each instance. The resulting body of scholarship attends to how actual people understand and conduct their involvement in the interrelated practices of traveling, encountering, guiding, producing, representing, talking, moving, hosting, and consuming.

Tourism and Anthropology at Large

The manifold practices subsumed under the heading "tourism" are not unique to travelers from the so-called Western nations (Graburn, 1983b; Nash, 1996), nor are postcolonial or developing countries the only tourist destinations that anthropologists study. In addition to research at a wide range of tourist sites throughout the USA and Europe, anthropologists have also conducted participant-observation among Chinese, Japanese, Korean, Laotian, Indonesian, Middle Eastern, Indian, Brazilian, and Mexican tourists, during both domestic and international travels, offering a global perspective on tourism behavior and experience. Moreover, this work is not conducted solely by Anglophone anthropologists: although space constraints preclude discussion of publications in other languages, ethnographic research on tourism is currently being conducted by Brazilian, Mexican, French, Spanish, Portuguese, Dutch, Japanese, Chinese, Indonesian, Jordanian, Saudi Arabian, Malaysian, and Indian scholars, among others, and Anglophone anthropologists routinely consult and collaborate with their counterparts in other countries.

For the most part, however, Anglophone anthropologists continue to do fieldwork in countries other than their own. In this they have had to face uncomfortable structural, historical, and epistemological linkages between international tourists and themselves: what qualitative difference is there between the kind of knowledge sought by ethnic/cultural tourists and that sought by anthropologists?[5] How is their social role different from that of tourists when they are in the field? This question, which has prompted some debate among anthropologists, arises both in interactions with tourists, who may wish to show off their own knowledge of local culture (sometimes competitively; see Errington and Gewertz, 1989), and with local populations, who have their own categories for and ways of dealing with outsiders that may not correspond with how anthropologists view themselves (Crick, 1985; Picard, 2007). Tourists and locals make sense of anthropologists based on their own perceptions of nationality, ethnicity, gender, sexuality, occupation, authority, and power, positioning scholars in ways that have profound implications for the kinds of knowledge attainable through participant-observation (Ness, 2003; Swain, 2004; cf. Graburn, 2002: 25–28). Anthropologists studying tourism have also had to reflect on their discipline's role as a type of cultural brokerage, like travel writing, tourism marketing, and tour guiding, all of which contribute representations of people and place that circulate widely and shape tourist expectations. While the association with cultural brokerage has not proved as disturbing to anthropologists as being mistaken for tourists, it reflects an additional way in which they are embedded in the very system they are studying and raises important ethical and epistemological issues (Adams, K., 2005a, 2005b, 2006; Adams, V., 1996; Bruner, 2005; Castaneda, 1996; Clifford, 1988; Picard, 2007).

Entering the Field

Anthropologists' historical resistance to acknowledging the presence of tourism in "their" field sites—and to being mistaken for tourists—is well documented, and it is widely acknowledged that many intentionally omitted tourists' presence in published accounts of their research (Boissevain, 1977; Bruner, 2005; Crick, 1985; Errington and Gewertz, 1989; Kottak, 1983). Rather than trace a history of early theoretical developments in the anthropological study of tourism, as has been done elsewhere (Crick, 1989; Graburn, 1983a; Michaud, 2001; Nash, 1996; Selwyn, 1994, 1996; Stronza, 2001), here we briefly outline how a handful of anthropologists first allowed tourism into the frame and mention a few of the classic social scientific models that underpinned their analyses.

The forefathers of the Western social sciences did not study tourism per se, but many of their concepts have proved foundational for anthropological studies of the subject. For example, the concept of alienation, which underpins influential early models of tourist motivation (Cohen, 1979; MacCannell, 1976), stems from the work of Marx (1999); the concepts of effervescence and communitas, key to understanding the experience of heightened energy and camaraderie in group contexts, come from Durkheim (1965); and the concept of conspicuous consumption, ultimately relevant to tourist consumption as a means of affirming status and identity, comes from Veblen (1934). Later "armchair" social scientists provided additional tools for analysis: Van Gennep (1960), on kinds of ritual, relevant for understanding the structure of journeys and the alternation between vacation and everyday life (Graburn, 1983a); Mauss (1954; see also James and Allen, 1998) on materiality, reciprocity, embodiment, and seasonal variation; Simmel (Wolff, 1950), on strangerhood; Goffman (1959), on "face-work"; and Huizinga (1950), on sociability in travel and sports. Although not themselves engaged in ethnographic research, these scholars offered a holistic view of the interconnections between different structures and events within society that has made their work particularly cogent for anthropologists.

Among social scientists, geographers were the first to explore tourism via field research in the 1950s and 1960s, focusing on economic and social impacts. A forerunner in envisioning tourism as a topic of study in its own right was Valene Smith (1953), a geographer-turned-anthropologist (and sometime travel agent, pilot, and tour leader). In 1974, Smith organized a path-breaking session on tourism at the American Anthropological Association (AAA) meetings in Mexico City; the collected papers, *Hosts and Guests: The Anthropology of Tourism* (Smith, 1977, 1989), remains a classic. The anthropologists who first gathered for that 1974 AAA session entered the study of tourism independently and for different reasons, as did others who began publishing on tourism around that time. Their paths into tourism research can be divided into four basic types: empirical discovery, work on adjacent topics, theoretical extension, and critical analysis.

Empirical discovery: In the 1960s, some anthropologists were struck by the intrusion of tourists into their field situations and began to document their impact (Nuñez, 1963). However, as Boissevain (1977) notes, tourism studies were only a by-product of their primary research; many anthropologists were initially embarrassed that tourists had appeared in "their" field sites and resisted interacting with them (cf. Kottak, 1983).

Work on adjacent topics: Some anthropologists wrote about phenomena that were only later recognized as contributing to the "anthropology of tourism," for example Graburn's (1967) "The Eskimo and Airport Art," on Inuit carvings exported for sale in southern Canada;

Nash's (1970) *Community in Limbo*, about expatriate Americans in Barcelona; and Cohen's (1971) "Arab Boys and Tourist Girls," a study of gender relations and dead-end prospects for young men in an Israeli town.

Theoretical extension: As anthropologists became aware of the global spread of tourism, some attempted to analyze it in terms of existing anthropological models. The view of tourism as analogous to traditional or religious ritual became common (MacCannell, 1976; Turner and Turner, 1978); Graburn (1983a) elaborated this model, drawing on Leach's (1961) writing on chronicity. Similarly, others adapted the concept of acculturation, which was initially developed to understand the cultural impact of ongoing colonial Native/white contacts (Redfield et al., 1936), for research on the impact of Southern "host"/Northern tourist interactions (Nuñez, 1963; Smith, 1977, 1989).

Critical analysis: When Bryden (1973) and Young (1973) published research undercutting the economic rationale for tourism development, tourism's social and cultural consequences came into question as well. Many saw tourism as a form of exploitative neocolonialism (Finney and Watson, 1975; Nash, 1977). Anthropologists became outspoken in their concern that tourism brought rapid degradation of culture and identity in societies on the "periphery" (Aerni, 1972; Greenwood, 1972, 1977; cf. Crick, 1989). A number of assessments of the positive and negative potentials of "North–South" tourism development followed, written by anthropologists (e.g., Wagner, 1977), sociologists (e.g., De Kadt, 1979), and subaltern scholars themselves, for example the Indonesian anthropologist I Gusti Bagus (1976).

Initial Interventions and Classic Concerns

With tourism allowed into the ethnographic picture, the first two decades of research focused primarily on its consequences in relation to social change, gender and sexuality, material culture ("tourist arts"), authenticity, ethnicity, and identity. Here we address each of these classic concerns in turn, showing how research has evolved up to the present. In the next section, we examine how recent changes to anthropological theory and practice have led to a reconfiguration of emphases in tourism-related research.

Tourism Development and Its 'Impacts'

As poorer nations came to achieve independence after World War II, they were often advised by experts from their former colonizers to develop tourism industries to earn foreign exchange and provide employment. In the Caribbean, Africa, and South and Southeast Asia, the relatively low capital and technical requirements of tourism and the ease of switching workers, especially women, from domestic to tourism work appeared attractive. Advisors asserted that tourism investments would produce a "multiplier effect," whereby every dollar spent by a tourist would circulate further as tourist institutions and their workers passed income on to other local workers and businesses. However, this model did not take into account the leakages of funds back to the metropolitan countries for loan interest, tax havens, payments for infrastructure and industrial necessities, training of locals, and the employment of expatriates as experts and business leaders, not to mention the consequences of inflation and displacement of locals.

These issues were of central concern in early ethnographic works on tourism, which explored "impacts" on social, cultural, and environmental aspects of so-called host communities (Finney and Watson, 1975; Smith, 1977), often implicitly using the acculturation model discussed above (e.g., Nuñez, 1963). Many of these studies assumed that tourist destinations in the "global South"—viewed as the powerless, the poor, the colonized—were reacting to overwhelming outside pressures from the rich, metropolitan North. While these early studies paved the way for a substantial body of scholarship on the social and cultural changes wrought by tourism development, more recent work has abandoned the "impact" model because it simplistically assumed that there were just two elements involved—"hosts" and "guests"—and that the tourist presence was the active vector of change, with the local population a passive recipient whose traditional lifeways were irreparably altered. As we discuss below, not only have more sophisticated studies shown that there is agency, i.e. purposeful action, exercised by all parties, but they have also demonstrated that the encounter is rarely two-sided. Both outside forces and destination populations are complex, manifold, and often involve competing sets of stakeholders (Abram et al., 1997; Daher, 2000). Nor is it a simple question of "outsiders" and "locals"; as Brennan (2004) argues in the case of Sosúa, a beach town in the Dominican Republic, tourist destinations often become "transnational spaces," attracting labor migrants from both within and outside the country, expatriates from various nations, and a range of other transient populations in addition to tourists.

More recent studies of the outcomes of tourism development offer a considerably more nuanced picture. "Impacts" can include cultural reinforcement as well as change: by providing an alternative source of employment, development in isolated regions can slow rural–urban labor migration, thus keeping intergenerational families intact and enabling the preservation of local ritual observance (Moon, 1989). Moreover, rather than being experienced as an external force impinging on otherwise pristine local lifeways, in heavily visited destinations such as Bali (Picard, 1996) tourists and the tourism industry at large can become an integral part of local culture. Contemporary research situates tourism development in relation to the local–global nexus, revealing that the repercussions of postcolonial relations and ongoing interactions with tourists are made still more complex by cross-sectoral networks and intermediaries, as well as global circuits of symbolic, cultural, and economic capital (Meethan, 2001; Ness, 2003).

Gender, Sexuality, and the Body

Early studies emphasized the "impacts" of tourism on local gender roles, especially in developing countries (Smith, 1977; cf. Kinnaird and Hall, 1994; Swain, 1995). Research showed that tourism employment opportunities often favored women over men, sometimes substantially shifting the balance of power. In some cases women's economic activities were welcome and benefited traditional family structures (Swain, 1977, 1993), but in others sharp restrictions were placed on women's involvement, in keeping with existing gender norms. For example, Scott (1995) found that women's employment in the tourism industry in Turkish Cyprus served to delineate boundaries between "insiders" and "outsiders": Cypriot women were able only to take tourism jobs deemed culturally appropriate, and female labor migrants from Romania and Russia were channeled toward tourism work considered sexually compromising, including prostitution. In addition to gender roles and differential access to employment, current research explores the interplay between local gender ideologies, tourists' gendered behavior and expectations, and local, national, and transnational cultural politics (e.g., Swain and Momsen, 2002).

Scholars have used sexuality, both literal and metaphorical, as a framework for articulating the exploitative aspects of tourism. In an early article reviewing literature on tourism and prostitution, Graburn (1983d) suggested that the prototypical rich North–poor South tourism dynamic can be thought of through the metaphor of the rich male purchasing or taking the services of the poor female, i.e., of countries that have "nothing to sell but their beauty" (their young people, landscapes, nature). Others have suggested more bluntly that "tourism is whorism" (Britton, 1982). Sex tourism itself has proven difficult to study, particularly through participant-observation. Research on male tourists seeking sexual contact with female sex workers or children of either gender (Kempadoo, 1999; Truong, 1990) typically assumes little more than predatory desires on the part of the prototypical white male. However, both Cohen's (1982) work on opened-ended prostitution in Bangkok and Askew's (1999) ethnographic research among Thai female sex workers provide rare insight into the varied motives, emotional entanglements, and outcomes of sex tourism as a social phenomenon. Together with an emerging body of increasingly nuanced literature on the subject (e.g., Babb, 2007; Brennan, 2004), their studies suggest that although the overall dynamic is indeed exploitative, the women involved have considerable agency and the men are not uniformly predatory on an interpersonal level.

While some scholars readily condemn sex between male tourists and their female "victims," ignoring the possibility of a romantic element or of female agency, sex between women tourists and local men has been analyzed almost entirely within the framework of "romance"—a fairly transparent application of deeply ingrained Western gender stereotypes. However, by assuming male agency this bias has enabled a more complete picture of the motivations involved. Early studies situated men's sexual involvement with tourists in terms of struggles for local status and for a viable economic future, possibly even abroad with a tourist-turned-lover (Bowman, 1989; Cohen, 1971; Wagner, 1977). Wright's (1992) insightful ethnographic film, *The Toured: The Other Side of Tourism in Barbados*, uses interviews and filmed conversations to show the unvarnished attitudes of both the tourist women and the local "beach boys," leaving the viewer sympathetic to both sides with few grounds for accusations or guilt.

A few early studies focused specifically on the gender of the tourist, such as Smith's (1979) "Women: The Taste Makers in Tourism," and a handful of ethnographers have since attended to tourists' gendered experiences of a given destination (e.g., Selänniemi, 2002). However, until relatively recently most theorists of tourist behavior and experience were silent on the issue, portraying "the tourist" as a theoretically gender-neutral sightseer whose dominant feature was "the gaze"

(MacCannell, 1976; Urry, 1990). Pritchard and Morgan (2000) have shown that the tourist gaze is in fact implicitly gendered as male, though it can be wielded by affluent females of a dominant nation, such as Japanese women tourists in the Pacific (Kelsky, 1999). An important breakthrough was Veilola and Jokinen's (1994) "The Body in Tourism," a playful but incisive essay that "tours" major theoretical paradigms through imagined conversations with a series of theorists on a beach holiday, showing that each fails to attend to the role of the body in tourism. Veilola and Jokinen's call for a multi-sensory, experiential approach paved the way for feminist considerations of the gendered body in tourism encounters, moving beyond the prevailing ocular-centric and implicitly male paradigm of "the gaze" (Ateljevic et al., 2007; Swain, 2004; see also Aitchison, Chapter 35, on gender and tourism discourses in this book). Since then, the role of the tourist's body has emerged as a subject of ethnographic study in its own right, not only in relation to gender but also with regard to such topics as outdoor adventure and "extreme" tourism (e.g., Abramson and Laviolette, 2007; Perkins and Thorns, 2001).

Tourist Arts

The "impact" framework was also informally applied to crafts produced by indigenous peoples for sale to tourists. Disparagingly referred to as "airport art," these products were considered a degeneration of "authentic" culture and ignored in ethnographic publications. With a single exception (Lips, 1937), until the late 1960s anthropological studies of arts and crafts focused solely on the structural, functional, and psychological aspects of expressive culture made for local or regional uses. The first collection of ethnographic studies on "ethnic arts" made expressly for sale (Graburn, 1976) revealed a considerable range of forms, from what appeared to be traditional, functional, and ritual paraphernalia to quickly made novelties that reflected the desires and expectations of the tourists more than the cultural norms of the makers. Some studies suggest that the purchase of these arts without direct contact between makers and buyers constitutes a form of "indirect tourism" (Aspelin, 1977; Graburn, 1967). Other tourist arts are hybrid products of the tourism "contact zone" (Clifford, 1997b), incorporating stylistic elements created *de novo* to bridge the cultural gap (Ben-Amos, 1977). In many circumstances, ethnic artists can command a number of styles, and continue making things for traditional use while simultaneously producing stereotypic souvenirs desired by tourists (Jules-Rosette, 1984). Having been exposed to the arts of the tourists' world, some aspire to acceptance as "Artists"—i.e., adepts of the fine arts—in the metropoles. This is happening in the very era when creations previously labeled crafts, artifacts, or "primitive art" are becoming accepted as "Art" in the global art market (Price, 1989).

More recent work shows that the field of tourist arts is dynamic and its categories labile; objects created for local use may end up being sold as "tourist art," and vice versa. For instance, Kuna women wear their appliquéd cloth *mola* blouses until they are worn out or out of fashion, then sell them to tourists (Salvador, 1997), whereas the Tlingit in Southeast Alaska may purchase their own tourist arts to decorate their homes and lives as part of asserting their contemporary Native identity (Bunten, 2005). Tourist arts are usually judged as less valuable than either the traditional "primitive" arts of earlier generations or those "high arts" that formally trained "ex-primitives" (MacCannell, 1990) manage to display in museums and galleries (Graburn, 1993). Yet when unmoored from the surveillance of traditional communities, producers of tourist arts may be immensely creative in producing new arrays of objects (Grunewald, 2006). These creations bear an ambiguous relationship to so-called "primitive art," which was reviled before it was collected and is now no longer made (in the traditional sense) even though it has become collectible and valuable in the global art-culture system (Clifford, 1988; Errington,

1998). Similarly, once early genres of tourist arts are no longer made, they in turn become valuable as collectibles (Thompson, 1979). As we discuss below, the shifting valuation, classification, and circulation of tourist arts continues to be a subject of substantial interest, particularly in light of contemporary anthropological concerns with globalization.

Authenticity

Authenticity has long been a key concept in anthropological studies of tourism, primarily because it is continuously invoked by tourists, tourism producers, and anthropologists critical of tourism "impacts," but also because it underpins a major theoretical debate. Following Goffman's dramaturgical approach (1959), MacCannell developed the concept of "staged authenticity" (1973) as a response to critics who assailed mass tourists for mindlessly enjoying the contrived and the fake. MacCannell claimed to the contrary that tourists, alienated from the shallowness of urban life, travel in search of authenticity elsewhere. In this radical modification of Marx's concept of alienation, tourists are said to seek wholeness and meaning in nature, in history, or in the supposedly simpler lives of other peoples (MacCannell, 1976). The tourism industry knows this and "stages"—i.e., creates, marks off, and advertises—tourist attractions, presenting tourists only with things created expressly for them. Knowing that everything "on stage" is put there as entertainment, tourists believe that the "real," authentic parts of the world are to be found backstage, hidden from view. The tourism industry responds by making the front stage look like a backstage, or by inviting tourists into what appears to be a backstage but is really only another front stage. According to this model, tourists are doomed to fail in their search for authenticity.

Three key challenges have been raised in response to MacCannell's argument: (1) Are all tourists really alienated and searching for authenticity? (2) Does involvement with the tourism industry necessarily render something

"inauthentic"? And (3) what precisely is meant by the term "authenticity"? In relation to the first of these, Cohen (1979) argues that tourists differ widely in their degree of alienation: some are satisfied with their home life, others search for something "different" away from home but happily return, and the most alienated experiment with or even emigrate to adopt more "authentic" lifestyles elsewhere. Cohen (1988) also argues that authenticity resides primarily in the minds of tourists (cf. Cary, 2004), and thus commodification for tourism does not automatically produce inauthenticity: objects, places, practices, and even peoples transformed for tourist consumption can themselves become accepted as "authentic" over time, in a process he calls *emergent authenticity*. In a penetrating analysis that makes liberal use of ethnographic examples, Wang (1999) summarizes the extensive debate prompted by MacCannell's model and suggests that we distinguish between three understandings of authenticity: (1) objectivist—where something can be examined by an expert to determine its true nature, also called "museum authenticity"; (2) constructivist—where authenticity is not an ontological condition, but a label or perceived status determined according to socially constructed criteria; and (3) existential—where tourists focus on the "truth" of their inner and interpersonal feelings during the journey.

Much ethnographic evidence has been marshaled to challenge and expand upon MacCannell's framework, for example in relation to tourist destinations and performances (Bruner, 1994; Daniel, 1996; Handler and Saxton, 1988), souvenirs (Phillips and Steiner, 1999; Shenhav-Keller, 1993), and displays of "heritage" (Kirshenblatt-Gimblett, 1998; Macdonald, 1997), among many others. Urry (1990) found that English white-collar workers were savvy enough to know that most things were created expressly for tourists, but enjoyed them precisely for the aesthetic and humorous qualities of their "inauthenticity." Labeled "post-tourists," these travelers are said to characterize postmodern tourism, which blurs the modernist distinction between real and fake (cf. Rojek and

Urry, 1997). Others argue that tourists are quite sincere in their quest for the "authentic," but locate it in a desire for unmediated interaction with local populations (Conran, 2006; Harrison, 2003). Overall, anthropological concern with the theoretical debate over "authenticity" has largely abated. Based on extensive fieldwork among tourists and tourism producers, Bruner provides a succinct articulation of the perspective now taken by many: "authenticity is a red herring, to be examined only when the tourists, the locals, or the producers themselves use the term" (2005: 5).[6]

Ethnicity, Identity, and Heritage

The commodification of ethnicity and institutionalization of tourist desire, which have wrought so many changes to arts and crafts, directly influence other aspects of identity. Ethnic tourism depends on conveying—through brochures, videos and descriptions off-site, tourist arts, and on-site settings and performances—the fascinating difference, even exoticism, of the host community. The same forces also shape regional and even national (self-) representations in those parts of the world that do not consider themselves "ethnic." Everywhere, "authentic culture" is put on display.

The tourism industry is one of the most productive in the modern world, re-creating historical and archaeological sites for the more serious and nostalgic tourists (Handler and Linnekin, 1984; Handler and Saxton, 1988; Graburn, 1995a; Peers, 2007), neatly packaging ethnic or national difference for easy consumption, and fashioning elaborate "postmodern" theme parks for those interested in imaginative fantasy (Rojek and Urry, 1997). Tourism producers play up appealing difference while promising some reassuring familiarities; this alterity becomes an expectation of the tourists and a burden (Greenwood, 1977) or opportunity for the communities visited. The greater the gap between expectations and reality, the more likely the need to "stage" culture for the tourists (MacCannell, 1973).

Ethnic communities in contemporary plural societies and newly formed postcolonial nations often collude with tourists by playing up their "ethnic difference." As Carpenter (1973: 101) puts it, "We have called primitive man from his retreat . . . taught him to carve the sort of art we like, and hired him to dance for us," implying that such peoples discover from their audience who they are "supposed to be" in this novel social predicament. MacCannell (1984) calls the outcome "reconstructed ethnicity." Numerous ethnographies show how small-scale societies attempt to adapt to these new demands without giving up their values or destroying their society. As formerly marginalized ethnic groups now receive formal education, travel the world, and realize their common predicament, they learn to play new roles while resisting the competition and intergenerational strains brought about by tourism and the demonstration effect of new lifestyles (Stanley, 1998). In some communities suffering from cultural erosion, subjugated peoples have learned to rebuild aspects of their overt culture (language, naming systems, religious rituals, material crafts) in response to tourist expectations (Grunewald, 2006; Stocker, 2007). Where such peoples are sufficiently re-empowered to run their own indigenous tourism operations, they consciously debate the fine line between "sharing culture" and "selling out" (Bunten, 2008).

Since the 1960s, ethnicity has surpassed "race" as a topic of great importance in sociocultural anthropology. Wood (1998) points out that tourism is a major form of ethnic relations, for instance in multiethnic Chiapas (van den Berghe, 1994), and is therefore central to broader anthropological concerns (cf. Keyes and van den Berghe, 1984). In examining ethnic tourism, Hitchcock (1999) reminds us of Barth's (1969) original proposition that ethnicity is about social boundaries, not biological essences, and is thus both flexible and situational. And just as national communities are "imagined" into existence through modernist representations and institutions (Anderson, 1983), the contemporary touristic portrayal of postcolonial nations as mosaics of iconically differentiated ethnic groups supplies a powerful integrative image for their citizens (Graburn, 1997: 205).

Heritage can play a similarly integrative or divisive role. The concept of heritage or patrimony (*patrimoine*) has been transformed in Western nations from its original meaning of inalienable family inheritance (ancestral farms, artisans' tools, etc.), to its current denotation of ethnic, regional, or national cultural phenomena considered the "inheritance" of a group at large. Heritage bears a relation to culture that is the inverse of Bourdieu's (1977) concept of habitus; the former is consciously chosen, explicitly valued, and public, whereas the latter is unconsciously learned, implicitly shared, and individually embodied. Heritage consists of material, natural, and intangible aspects of culture that are felt to be permanent and transmittable (Lowenthal, 1985, 1996), a concept closely allied to the equally loaded term *tradition*. Like tourist arts and ethnicity itself, "heritage" requires the selection of particular traits to be supported and exhibited, fomenting competition between ethno-national groups in plural societies and between status groups and classes in stratified societies. Heritage is thus those elements of culture that are chosen and commodified as "heritage products" for the very competitive tourism industry (Nadel-Klein, 2003; Tunbridge and Ashworth, 1996). The "politics of heritage" focuses on who gets to select and package, i.e., tell the story of, those features to be foregrounded out of the totality available (Meethan, 1996). Archaeological sites provide important foundations for heritage claims and can themselves become tourist sites. As such, control over archaeological research is key to buttressing and disseminating particular versions of history and can thus become a source of considerable political conflict (Habu et al., 2008).

Recently, anthropologists have begun to study the implementation of the universalist concept of "World Heritage" to sites around the world. Since 1972, UNESCO bureaucrats have negotiated with ambitious regional and national authorities to designate places as worthy of recognition as the cultural, historical, or natural heritage of all humankind (Di Giovine, 2009; Harrison and Hitchcock, 2005). This has put nations in competition with each other and has fostered intense internal struggles among ministries and regional authorities. At present, UNESCO World Heritage designation has been granted to over 400 sites internationally. Although it bestows little financial aid, it highlights cultural "value" that often attracts governmental, NGO, and commercial financial support for both the preservation of local heritage and the regulation of tourist development (see also Orbaşlı and Woodward, Chapter 18, on tourism and conservation in this book). This is an emerging critical direction for scholars looking at the nexus of ethnicity, heritage, and tourism (Adams, 2006: 209–215). For instance, through detailed ethnography in the World Heritage Site of Lijiang, China, Wang (2007) shows how homestay tourism enterprises provide a "customized authenticity" for visitors that runs counter to the objectivist model of heritage implicit in UNESCO recognition. In 2003, UNESCO began a similar program for the selection of world-class "intangible cultural heritage," referring to such expressive traditions as song, dance, music, folklore, crafts, and theater. This has set off another wave of presentation and competition, potentially ensuring the preservation and transmission of threatened traditions (Laske, 2005) and most certainly leading to further tourism development worldwide.

Current Trajectories

That the UNESCO World Heritage designation process has itself become an acceptable topic for anthropological study reflects fundamental theoretical and methodological changes in the discipline over the past two decades. As subaltern peoples began to speak for themselves in the global arena, anthropologists were confronted with the partiality and contingency of their knowledge and their questionable authority to represent the lives of others. This epistemological and ethical crisis, which coincided with a general trend in anthropology away from positivistic approaches and toward a more hermeneutic stance (Geertz, 1973), dominated theoretical debate throughout the 1980s and early 1990s (Clifford, 1988; Clifford and Marcus, 1986; Fox, 1991; Marcus and Fischer, 1986; cf. Wagner, 1975). One result was that anthropologists began to incorporate "their" people's own self-representations into their studies, treating them as an additional form of cultural activity to be analyzed. Interpretation of multiple layers of cultural representation soon followed: not only self-representations by the people studied, e.g. in art, film, local media, literature, and their own scholarship, but also outsiders" representations—in the international media, popular discourse, travel writing, academic scholarship—and even the anthropologist's own "authoritative" ethnographic account, all became fodder for analysis. This reflexive turn, and the attention to the construction of culture that it enabled, opened a space for the representational discourses and practices of tourism to be incorporated into the mainstream of anthropological research. Like the labeling of expressive culture as "intangible heritage" for UNESCO World Heritage status or the performance of ethnicity for tourist audiences, the representation, indexing, and marketing of places, people, things, and practices for others' consumption have become unignorable aspects of life around the globe.[7]

Anthropologists have also had to contend with the massive social and cultural changes wrought by globalization. As Appadurai (1996) and others have argued, in light of mass migration and international flows of media, capital, ideas, and imagery, we can no longer speak of culture as something that is rooted in place. On the contrary, anthropologists have had to rethink both their theoretical models and their methods in order to grasp the changing nature of human experience in a global era (Gupta and Ferguson, 1997; Kearney, 1995; Marcus, 1995). With the discipline turning increasingly to multi-sited studies that trace transnational connections among dispersed peoples, accompany mobile populations, follow the global flow of capital and development discourses, and track circuits of imagery and objects, the study of tourism offers a point of entry into cutting-edge debates in the field. Not only are scholars publishing articles on tourism-related topics in all of the major anthropological journals and even organizing special issues on the topic (e.g., Silverman, 2005), but recent years have seen a steady increase in the number of papers on tourism presented at anthropological meetings. Here we outline some of the key themes running through this rapidly expanding body of work: place, people, movement, things, and "the global."

Place

The production and marketing of places as tourist destinations is one of the most common topics in contemporary social scientific research on tourism. Having moved beyond straightforward "impact" studies, anthropologists approach the construction of tourist sites in terms of imagery, process, power, performance, and meaning. The most sophisticated of these link global politics with micropractices, political economy with semiotics (Babb, 2004; Selwyn, 2007).

Imagery representing tourist destinations circulates via brochures, postcards, travel photos, websites, films, novels, and other media, fomenting "myths" (Selwyn, 1996) or "narratives" (Bruner, 2005: 19–27) of place that shape tourists' expectations of what they will find long before they arrive. These myths/narratives in turn resonate with cultural metanarratives about discovery, adventure, global intercultural relations, and so forth, providing the "conceptual frame within which tourism operates" (Bruner, 2005: 21). Based on research at tourist sites on three continents, Bruner argues that "tourism is not that innovative in inventing new narratives but seeks new locations in which to tell old stories, possibly because those stories are the ones that the tourist consumer is willing to buy" (2005: 22). However, the processes through which destinations become so "enchanted" (Selwyn, 2007) unfold in the concrete world of infrastructure, politics, and economics, as well as that of narrative and imagery. Like the generic narratives underpinning tourist marketing and myth-making, resort development relies upon the creation of places that are simultaneously generic and exotic. Ness (2003) provides a detailed ethnographic account of the physical creation of "utopic" places in the Philippines, tracing the implementation of global development schemes through touristic landscaping, construction, and staff training programs. She also shows that the transformation of such destinations into consumable places for tourists may simultaneously render them "non-places" (Augé, 1995) for local populations, causing extreme disorientation, displacement, and disruption (Ness, 2005).

In order to be viable as a tourist destination, a locality must develop an identity that will attract visitors. This "branding" of place is often achieved through the selection of an emblematic ethnic or cultural trait—e.g., a festival, dance, craft, architecture, or food—or an entire ethnic group or historical event that can be packaged for tourist consumption (Abram et al., 1997; Coleman and Crang, 2002; Picard and Wood, 1997). Adams (2005a) provides a rare ethnographic account of the "branding" process as it transpires over a period of years on a remote Indonesian island. Although anthropologists (e.g., Greenwood, 1977) initially believed that commodification would drain local practices of their original value as they became increasingly adapted to suit the "tourist gaze" (Urry, 1990), subsequent research suggests that the marketing of place through ethnic or cultural features can serve local purposes, potentially increasing community interest in traditions that had been abandoned (Medina, 2003), promoting the interests of one locality over another (Chio, 2008), or shifting the balance of power among ethnic groups (Adams, 1997, 2006).

The packaging of place to highlight certain traits cannot guarantee that visitors will experience it as intended. A growing body of literature looks at how place is created anew in each tourist encounter, based on the imaginings, desires, and interests of the individual visitor and mediated by tour guides, guidebooks, and other "markers" (MacCannell, 1976). This is an intersubjective, phenomenological model of place, in which "tourists have agency, active selves that do not merely accept but interpret, and frequently question, the producers' messages" (Bruner, 2001: 899). Ethnographic studies show that the "place" tourists visit may vary widely depending upon their prior knowledge, values, and expectations (Bruner, 2005; Cheung, 1999; Chronis, 2005; Edensor, 1998). Smith (2003) offers a nuanced analysis of the "place" visited by elderly *pied-noir* tourists on a package tour from France to Malta. Because they cannot return to colonial Algeria, their remembered homeland, they visit Malta as a "place replaced," one that offers a particular combination of sights, sounds, and flavors they recall from childhood in colonial Algeria. Leite (2007) emphasizes the role of narrative and imagination, showing how package tours of "Jewish Portugal" rely upon tourists' imaginative and embodied engagement to materialize an historical "destination" of which few physical traces remain. In this extreme case, the tourist attraction is itself a narrative of absence, rendered visible and visitable only through the tourists' presence.

People

When viewed as a social field comprised of manifold interactions, "tourism" includes far more than the basic binary of "hosts" and "guests." Within the touristic contact zone, actors may include various groups of tourists, possibly from a variety of nations; their drivers and guides (who are not necessarily local nor of the same origin as the tourists); local guides; performers; employees at tourist sites; workers in restaurants, hotels, shops, and other service industries; street vendors; sex workers;

NGO representatives, researchers, and even other anthropologists (Picard, 2007); and people who live in the area but have no direct relationship to the tourism industry. Additional stakeholders might include local, regional, and national tourism officials; political leaders; owners of land and buildings; travel agencies; package tour companies; marketers; investors; and future tourists. Complicating the situation further, tourists may have friends, relatives, or ancestral ties in the destination, raising questions regarding the oft-made distinction between "domestic" and "foreign" tourism and that of "home" and "away" (Duval, 2003; cf. Graburn, 2008a).

Causey (2003) has proposed the term "tourate" for local people at a given tourist site who interact with tourists or tourism, as opposed to those who live in the destination but do not generally come into contact with them. His study of Toba Batak (Indonesia) carvers, who revived local carving traditions in the 1960s to meet tourists' demands for souvenirs, provides detailed portraits of carvers and their families based on extended participant-observation in their daily lives and in their marketplace negotiations with Western tourists. Brennan's (2004) ethnography of female sex workers in the Dominican Republic vividly recounts the stories of individual women's lives, the choices they face, and the hopes that motivate their involvement in the sex-tourist trade. Gmelch (2003) and Ness (2003) offer rich accounts of tourate perspectives in the Caribbean and the Philippines, respectively, drawing on in-depth interviews that reveal a wide range of roles, motivations, and concerns. In general, anthropologists have found it difficult to carry out fieldwork alongside tourism service workers, as employees may feel uncomfortable under the researcher's gaze and employers are often wary of outsiders' nosiness (Camacho, 1996). Those who are able to conduct participant-observation as an employee in the industry are ideally positioned to gain an understanding of tourate experiences. Drawing on her fieldwork as a tour guide for a Native Alaskan tour company, Bunten (2008)—herself an Alaskan Native, though from a different tribe—develops a general theory of "self-commodification" to capture the convergence of emotional labor, identity construction, and the politics of cultural representation in Native guides' encounters with tourists.

Interactions between tourists and members of the local population, however defined, reveal tensions, desires, animosities, affinities, and stereotypes that operate on interpersonal, intercultural, and international levels. As individual actors with agency, people living in tourist destinations respond in a variety of ways to the constant attention of outsiders, including ironic humor (Evans-Pritchard, 1989) and outright antagonism (Abbink, 2000), among other strategies (Adams, 1996; Boissevain, 1996). Some may actively seek intimate contact with tourists, as romantic partners or through the sex trade, in order to experience exotic difference, to transgress local gender dynamics, for immediate economic gain, or in hope of translating a relationship into a better life in a different country (e.g., Askew, 1999; Brennan, 2004; Dahles and Bras, 1999; Ebron, 2002; Meisch, 1995; Pruitt and LaFont, 1995). The mutual desire expressed in such intimate relations may thus be heavily inflected by cross-cultural stereotypes and local and geopolitical inequalities. Though there are notably fewer studies of sexual contact from the tourists' point of view (mostly Western women; e.g., Ebron, 2002; Meisch, 1995; Pruitt and LaFont, 1995), the existing literature suggests that these liaisons are sought as opportunities for self-expression, freedom, ease, and excitement that may be lacking in everyday life.

More broadly, ethnographers have documented that as long as it is perceived as "authentic," any kind of direct interaction with local people can be a highlight of tourists' journeys, particularly when the tourist perceives there to be significant cultural and linguistic difference involved (Conran, 2006; Harrison, 2003: 43–70; cf. Cary, 2004). "Roots" tourists, on the other hand, may find their expectations of easy affinity met with a more complicated reality. In his analysis of African American travel to the Elmina slave castle in Ghana, Bruner (1996) recounts how these tourists envision their journey as a "homecoming" and are thus disappointed to be treated no differently by locals than any other foreign visitors. Lehrer (2007) describes the discomfort some Jewish tourists feel upon learning that the Poles who serve as knowledgeable guides, caretakers, and performers of Krakow's Jewish heritage are not Jewish; rather, they are people who identify with Jewishness and, in the absence of a living local Jewish community, have stepped in to become the tourates.

It is notoriously difficult for anthropologists to capture the nuances of tourists' experiences during their travels. The various stages of the journey—preparation and anticipation (Liebman Parinello, 1992), travel to the destination, periods in the hotel and out touring, time spent during the trip discussing experiences with others, more periods in the hotel and out touring, travel home, readjustment, and subsequently narrating the experience to friends and family—each contribute to the overall whole (Bruner, 2005; Graburn, 2001; Harrison, 2003). In a study of pilgrim-tourists on Spain's Camino de Santiago, Frey (1998) offers a rare glimpse into the "inner journey" of dozens of travelers; her close and often long-term relations with participants both during and after their journeys allowed her to grasp both their day-to-day experience and its long-term effects. The practice-based knowledge Frey gleaned by walking the arduous Camino herself demonstrates that ethnographers can learn a great deal from their own embodied experiences as travelers alongside the tourists they study. In an analysis of an African American "roots" tour to West Africa, Ebron (2000) devotes significant attention to the impact of what Bruner (2005: 24) calls "the sheer materiality of being there," i.e. the physical sensations she felt while moving through the slave dungeons and other sites on the trip. Such attention to bodily sensation opens up richer understandings of tourist experience, as Selänniemi (2001) found in his study of Finnish sun-seeking tourists in the Canary

Islands (cf. Crouch, 2002; Crouch and Desforges, 2003; Leite, 2005; Feldman, 2008; Veilola and Jokinen, 1994).

Movement

If nothing else, it can be said of tourism that it involves movement from one place to another. But while tourism is fairly easily distinguished from the other major forces currently moving people around the globe, particularly migration and refugee flight, its relationship to other forms of travel is less clear. Business trips, "voluntourism," visiting friends and relatives, and other temporary journeys all share elements that are worthy of exploration. By far the most attention has been given to the overlap between tourism and pilgrimage. Graburn (1977, 1983a, 2001) argues that modern tourism bears both structural and experiential similarities to pilgrimage in earlier times (cf. MacCannell, 1976; Turner and Turner, 1978), given that it combines a liminal break from everyday routine with purposeful travel toward an often highly anticipated destination. Others have sought to distinguish the two, arguing that pilgrimage involves religiously motivated journeying toward the "spiritual center" of one's world, whereas tourism is primarily ludic and involves movement toward its periphery. But the feelings that motivate travelers or arise at their destination are often labile, revelatory, and very personal. Indeed, recent ethnographic considerations of the relationship between tourism and pilgrimage demonstrate that it is neither possible nor advisable to draw an abstract distinction between them; from an anthropological perspective, the difference can only be gauged in contextual and experiential terms (Badone and Roseman, 2004; Coleman and Eade, 2004; Frey, 1998; Smith, 1992).

More provocative are analyses of when the framework of pilgrimage is invoked in relation to tourism, and to what effects (Basu, 2004; Ebron, 2000; Graburn, 2004). In addition to explicitly religious-oriented travel, anthropologists have noted the use of the term pilgrimage by participants in various forms of identity tourism—"queer pilgrimage" to San Francisco as a gay homeland (Howe, 2001), Jewish "pilgrimages of memory" to Holocaust-related sites in Eastern Europe (Feldman, 2008; Kugelmass, 1992), and, perhaps most ubiquitously, "roots pilgrimages" to the homeland of one's ancestors (e.g., Basu, 2007; Bruner, 1996; Ebron, 2000). In invoking the concept of pilgrimage, tourists simultaneously indicate that the journey has great emotional resonance and stake a claim of ownership: it is *their* pilgrimage site, their "sacred center" (Cohen, 1979, 1992). As a diasporic identity practice, "roots pilgrimages" map a geography of elective affiliation and belonging that effectively bridges past and present, enacted through the traveler's own bodily experience of ancestral place (Leite, 2005). At the same time, these journeys reflect a "reconfiguration of the sacred," for "the 'mysterium tremendum' at [their] heart . . . is ultimately no more, and no less, than the self" (Basu, 2004: 170–171). Thus, ethnographic research suggests that tourists use "pilgrimage" as a label for what they consider a distinct category of experience, not in reference to religion, per se, but in opposition to the category "tourism." From the tourist's point of view, what is "sacred" here is the seriousness of purpose with which the journey is undertaken and the anticipated lasting impact of its completion.[8]

Things

The material trappings of tourism—museums and their collections, ethnic theme parks, and objects produced for and consumed by tourists as souvenirs—have attracted considerable attention from ethnographers, building on earlier research on tourist arts and the commodification of ethnicity and heritage. The resulting literature complements and often draws upon studies of touristic representation by scholars working in cultural studies,

performance studies, art history, and other allied fields.

Museums and Cultural Display

Kirshenblatt-Gimblett offers a cogent explanation of the relationship between museums and tourism: "[T]ourism stages the world as a museum of itself, even as museums try to emulate the experience of travel. Indeed, museums—and the larger heritage industry of which they are part—play a vital role in creating the sense of 'hereness' necessary to convert a location into a destination" (1998: 7). Local, regional, and national museums are thus quintessentially connected with tourism: they serve as authoritative guides, displaying objects that represent the important features of culture, history, art, and nature that tourists might want to visit. At the same time, metropolitan museums are attractions in their own right, gathering the world's treasures and presenting them to the public. As a powerful force shaping visitors' perceptions of people and destinations, museum exhibitions often become flashpoints for debate, especially when different groups wish to assert their own self-image or suppress those of others (Clifford, 1997a, 1997b; Karp and Lavine, 1991; Karp et al., 1992, 2006). When ethnic and minority peoples take charge of the display of their own culture and history, in contrast to their representation in official ethnographic museums, they may choose to avoid the colonial echoes of the term "museum" by referring to their own venues for curation and auto-ethnographic display as "cultural centers" (Clifford, 1997b). A parallel development in rural regions of Europe where agriculture and village life are threatened has been the creation of *ecomusées*, which attempt to preserve and demonstrate specifically local, artisanal ways of rural life by packaging them for tourists (Poulot, 1994).

Like museums, model culture villages and ethnic theme parks objectify emblematic features of an ethnic community or a nation. These tourist attractions, which may or may not include human "residents," raise a number of key issues around the commodification of culture and the possibility of virtual travel. While Smith (1977, 1989) suggests that they serve the positive function of drawing tourists away from a community's daily life, most such model villages, following the model of the Polynesian Cultural Center (PCC) in Hawaii (Stanton, 1989), are purpose-built condensations of regional and national entities. Jakarta's Taman Mini, a theme park representing Indonesia through its many ethnic regions, has been scrutinized by anthropologists as a politicized representation of national unity (Errington, 1998; Hitchcock, 1997). However, Bruner (2005) suggests that for the ethnic groups represented, Taman Mini's individual ethnic pavilions may simultaneously serve as a venue for reinforcement of minority identity in Jakarta's multiethnic metropolis. In China, regional "nationalities" theme parks (Gordon, 2005) offer the opportunity for tourists to "experience" the lifeways of China's far-flung rural minorities without traveling great distances. Japan, conversely, has themed villages, not only of its own people, but of foreign countries (Graburn, 2008b; Hendry, 2000). Here Japanese domestic tourists "experience foreignness" in the form of buildings, gardens, and historical sites, as well as food, drinks, shops, and the chance to dress in the ethnic and national costumes of other countries. For some, these places serve as training grounds in which to prepare for overseas tourism, whereas for others they offer a convenient, safe, and monolingual substitute for the daunting idea of going abroad.

Whether they portray national majorities or minorities, and whether run by commercial entrepreneurs, governments, or minority enterprises, model culture villages are typically presented in the "folkloric mode." Inhabitants and their clothes, crafts, songs, dances, architecture, and cuisines are portrayed as simple representatives of a time just past. In these mediated settings, Europeans may be princes or peasants, Native Americans and Chinese minorities are "traditional" and nonthreatening, Polynesians and Africans dance shoeless and bare-chested, and each group is charged to convey a single, sanitized narrative that often fits into the dominant schema of that minority's place in contemporary society. Indeed the whole atmosphere may resemble children's folktales, cartoons, or Disney characters more than strictly ethnohistorical realities.

Objects on the Loose

Things, like people, travel. The objects and photographs brought home from the journey—i.e., souvenirs—take on a wide range of significations for the tourist. Most tourists are satisfied with objects that suit their taste or remind them of the place, especially if personally acquired from a local person (Lee, 1991). Souvenirs may carry emblems of and ideological messages about the specific ethnicity or nationality of the tourist site (Shenhav-Keller, 1993), but they may also signify an occasion, a companion, a social group, or something altogether idiosyncratic (Hitchcock and Teague, 2000). Despite bearing quite specific meanings for their collectors, if they are deemed valuable and passed on to a museum or a gallery, such objects may be stripped of their personal "memory" function and assume an altogether different set of references for future owners or viewers. In this way, an object can be transformed from private possession into public culture (Graburn, 2000; Kirshenblatt-Gimblett, 1998). Souvenir practices also vary cross-culturally: in tourist systems such as those of Japan and Korea, souvenirs (omiyage) are bought to give to friends and family, often those who gave going-away gifts prior to the trip, so at the point of purchase the souvenir represents the homebound person for the tourist. To the eventual recipient, on the other hand, the souvenir signifies personal ties to the tourist as well as the place visited (Graburn, 1987).

While virtually anything can become a souvenir, "ethnic" or "primitive" tourist arts occupy a special category in anthropological analyses. Because a global system of meanings and markets is already in place for them, these objects can and do circulate on their own, entering regimes of value (Appadurai,

1986) entirely distinct from those in operation at their place of manufacture. Phillips and Steiner's (1999) comprehensive collection of essays examines the commodification and global circulation of tourist arts as souvenirs, artifacts, collectibles, and fine art. They explore the creativity and hybridity of tourist arts, the intense concern of elites with authenticity, related to a pervasive nostalgia for cultural communities that no longer exist (Rosaldo, 1989), and a gradual acceptance of such objects within art history and art institutions of the expanding (global) Western art world.

Other scholars focus on the practices surrounding production and sale of the objects themselves. Some arts and crafts are sold directly to tourists by their makers (Causey, 2003; Meisch, 2002); others travel via local traders and regional brokers to end up as souvenir objects sold in metropolitan centers, where they may also make their way to fine art dealers or craft distributors and enter the transnational ethnic art/craft market (Adams, 2006; Meisch, 2002; Myers, 2001; Steiner, 1994). Steiner (1994) examines the shifting meanings of African carvings as they are mediated by different actors on their way to being sold to tourists and regional brokers. Middleman-traders acquire the carvings from villages, then modify both the objects and the narratives that accompany them, based on their knowledge of the desires of tourists and dealers in both Africa and North America. Whatever their source, as these objects travel ever farther from their makers, they and the stories that accompany them contribute to the global spread of imagery and ideas about the tourist destinations where they began.

The Global

It is in relation to this last topic—the global circulation of imagery and ideas, as well as objects and people—that tourism is most fully integrated into contemporary anthropological research agendas. Mass media, international flows of products and capital, waves of migration, the Internet, development schemes and humanitarian missions, and the imagery and institutions of tourism itself, have together produced a world that is profoundly interconnected. Anthropologists view this global interconnectedness as both a meaningful context for study and a cultural phenomenon in its own right, one with important implications for identity, mobility, politics, the nature of place, and the possible futures that individuals and communities can envision for themselves (Appadurai, 1996; Inda and Rosaldo, 2002). Whether global interconnectedness is the setting or the subject of research, and whether the anthropologist stays in one location or undertakes multi-sited fieldwork (Marcus, 1995), it is increasingly common to find tourism included in ethnographies of global or transnational phenomena. In such studies, tourism is addressed as one among several ways in which far-flung people imagine and encounter one another (Adams, 1996; Ebron, 2002), build and maintain connections to distant places, and experience cultural and economic globalization in their daily lives.

Many anthropologists have explored the transnational connections and modes of diasporic identification forged among globally dispersed populations. Like heritage associations, ethnic festivals, Internet groups, and consumption of commercial "heritage products" (clothing, music, books, art), research shows that "homeland" tourism can be an important context for the construction and expression of diasporic and ancestral identities (cf. Clarke, 2006). While some roots-seeking travelers experience their journey as a profound and emotionally satisfying "homecoming" (Basu, 2007), for others the outcome is more equivocal. Some may even be alienated by their experience, finding to their surprise that they identify more strongly with the country of their birth, or with their fellow diasporic tourists, than with their ancestral homeland. By undertaking participant-observation on "homeland" tours within the context of long-term fieldwork among diasporic populations—thus accompanying people with whom they have ongoing contact both before and after the journey—ethnographers have been able to reveal the dynamic, often ambivalent nature of national, transnational, and diasporic identification in an era of hyphenated identities (Karam, 2007; Kim, 2003; Louie, 2001). It should be noted, however, that scholars working in this area rarely make tourism the primary focus of their research. Instead, tourism constitutes one of many "sites" through which they grapple with the broader topic of identity, identification, and belonging in a global context.

For their part, national governments may see political and economic benefit in attracting "homeland" tourists, whether through targeted marketing or officially sponsored package tours. In their respective analyses of Chinese-American youth tours to China and Arab-Brazilian tourism to Lebanon and Syria, Louie (2001) and Karam (2007) show how state officials attempt to produce a relation of "forged transnationality" (Schein, 1998) between visitors and their ancestral homeland, one that they hope will lead participants to consider future economic investment or serve as informal spokespeople on the nation's behalf. Governments may also promote foreign travel by their own citizens in order to strengthen national identity at home, as Feldman (2008) demonstrates in his nuanced ethnographic account of the emotional and social impact of commemorative package tours that guide Israeli youth through Holocaust sites in Poland.

In approaching transnational and global phenomena, anthropologists often argue for a reconceptualization of "the field" (i.e., the "location" of ethnographic research) as a translocal, even global social space (Gupta and Ferguson, 1997). This is the case even among ethnographers who limit their research to a single geographical location, for, in adopting "the native's point of view," they must take into account the local population's awareness of global forms and forces that permeate their daily lives and shape their understanding of their place in the world. In these studies, international tourism often

emerges as a primary means through which local lives become entangled with global processes. But it may not be the only one: in addition to being seasoned tourates, research shows that "the toured" may themselves travel internationally, embrace globally circulated aesthetic forms, sell their arts and music to audiences abroad, and utilize the Internet, international media, and contacts forged with foreign visitors to promote their interests in regional and national political struggles (Adams, 2006; Meisch, 2002). Here "the global" is not a separate force impinging upon "the local," but instead part and parcel of everyday life.

Indeed, ethnographers studying tourism in relation to globalization take pains to stress that the latter "does not supersede the local, and the two are not dichotomous. In fact, international tourism and global cultural circulation depend on the local, on culturally specific sites of production and on local differences" (Meisch, 2002: 266). In his study of a group of tour guides in Yogyakarta, Indonesia, Salazar (2005) explores how such "local differences" are packaged and highlighted for foreign tourists, drawing attention away from obvious signs of globalization and "glocalization" throughout the region. Fully engaged with global popular culture and themselves international travelers, these guides draw upon their knowledge of foreign tourists' desires to present the destination—and themselves—as pristinely and distinctively "local." Similarly, Brennan's (2004) sensitive ethnography of migration and the sex-tourist trade in the Dominican Republic shows how female sex workers, aware of their representation on the Internet and in other global venues as exotic and hyper-sexualized, play upon this imagery to meet sex tourists' fantasies. At the same time, many hope to transcend "the local" by forming a lasting relationship with a foreign client, as a means to financial security and potentially a visa to go abroad. Thus anthropological scholarship increasingly views tourism as a context in which the global not only affects, but *becomes* the local, and vice versa.

Future Directions

We began this chapter by questioning what might be meant by "the *anthropology* of tourism," given that anthropologists studying tourism draw upon theoretical models from a wide range of academic disciplines and given that scholars in other disciplines often utilize anthropological methods in their research. We conclude by questioning the other half of the phrase: "the anthropology of *tourism*." In the previous section, we showed how tourism is increasingly taken up by anthropologists as one strand in a densely interwoven system of representations, practices, and global interconnections. As Graburn (1983a, 2002) has suggested, we cannot understand the meaning of tourism as a social practice without situating it in the context of the traveler's life as a whole. The current trend in anthropological research presses still further in that holistic direction, seeing tourism as so deeply embedded in other social and cultural phenomena—from the personal to the global, from intimate ties to geopolitical relations—that it can hardly be considered a distinct category of human experience.

In this final section we briefly sketch some of the most interesting and perhaps unexpected ways in which this new perspective arises in connection with issues at the cutting edge of anthropological research. These emerging research directions, some of which could be considered postmodern or even postdisciplinary, reveal the blurring of boundaries between tourism and other phenomena linked with contemporary global mobilities, inequalities, and interconnections.[9]

Tourism/medicine: Gross international inequalities in the cost of and access to medical care have created a new niche tourism market. No longer simply a matter of seeking urgent medical procedures that are expensive or difficult to obtain in one's own country, people now travel internationally for optional cosmetic surgery, sex-change operations, infertility treatments (dubbed "reproductive tourism," Inhorn 2003), and even the black-market harvesting and receipt of organs in "transplant tourism" (Scheper-Hughes, 2000, 2006). Anthropologists explore these new developments in relation to the commodification of life and of body parts, cultural differences in attitudes toward various medical procedures, and the blurring of medicine and touristic consumption.

Tourism/media: New media research moves beyond analysis of representations of tourist destinations to examine how tourism and the media have become fully intertwined. Topics addressed include media consumption and/as world travel, international joint-ventures that link "product placement" of cities and sites in film and electronic media with emotional and physiological aspects of touristic consumption (Choe, 2008), and mass-media imagery of the practice of international travel, e.g. by celebrities or on reality television programs, that suggests how viewers should conceive of their country's roles and responsibilities in relation to other nations (Hubbard and Mathers, 2004).

Tourism/power: Emerging scholarship examines the articulation of tourism industry practices with power, resource management, and social (in)equality at the local, regional, national, and international levels. In addition to the consequences of neoliberal policies and labor migration and exploitation (Bianchi, 2002), this research explores ecotourism as a context for local community empowerment, through analysis of the nuances of NGO development and conservation initiatives and joint commercial/community-based ventures (Stronza, 2005).

Tourism/activism: With the commercialization of "voluntourism," work tourism, solidarity tourism, ecotourism, philanthropy tourism, and "reality tours" such as those offered by Global Exchange and other NGOs, tourists are invited to exercise their political and moral convictions while traveling, blurring the distinctions between tourism, activism, leisure, and humanitarian work. Walking tours of slums in the "global South," bus tours to sites of atrocities, and package tours offering opportunities to labor in fields or mines alongside impoverished local workers may connect tourists with "the real world," but raise disturbing questions about the commodification and sequestration of moral outrage.

Tourism/kinship: In light of the global dispersion of migrant populations and the popularity of genealogical research, international tourism now easily shades into a metaphorical version of "visiting friends and relatives" (VFR). At the same time, tourism can be a context in which *new* "familial" bonds are created, whether in fictive kinship that emerges in the makeup and interactions of tourist groups (Carroll, 2008), in the discovery of far-flung relatives during genealogical and roots tourism, or in the sense of experiential and ancestral "kinship" forged among participants in international homeland tours (Kim, 2003). As Leite (forthcoming) has found in her research on affective bonds created during solidarity and roots tourism, informal encounters among tourists and between foreign tourists and local people can generate lasting transnational ties, expanding participants' conception of community and reconfiguring their notions of self, ethnic and spiritual "kinship," and belonging on a global scale.

In 1991, Graburn and Jafari argued that "the maturity of tourism as a research topic was marked when researchers set out specifically to study tourism" (1991: 4). Today, we suggest that anthropological research on tourism has reached a still-higher stage of maturity: no longer segregated as a distinct topic of study, tourism is now seen by many scholars as an inextricable aspect of social, cultural, and economic life around the globe. Analyzed holistically, recognized as a crucial

medium for and reflection of globalization, and treated as just one component among many in overlapping spheres of meaning and action, tourism has found its place at the heart of anthropological scholarship.

Acknowledgements

We dedicate this chapter to Jafar Jafari, Founder and Editor-in-Chief Emeritus of the *Annals of Tourism Research*, without whose work and support the anthropological study of tourism would be immeasurably poorer. We are also grateful to Alexis Celeste Bunten, Jenny Chio, and the members of the Berkeley Tourism Studies Working Group for their critical engagement and feedback.

Notes

1 In recent years we have noticed a bifurcation among anthropologists conducting research on tourism. There are those who are engaged primarily in the interdisciplinary tourism studies community, focusing on journals and conferences specific to tourism research; these anthropologists may identify themselves with "the anthropology of tourism," but may not be in dialogue with anthropological research published and presented in other contexts (see, e.g., Nash, 2004). Others publish entirely in anthropological venues and seem unaware that an interdisciplinary tourism studies community exists. Only a handful of scholars effectively bridge the two (e.g., Adams, 2006; Bruner, 2005; Selwyn, 2007).

2 This does not include applied anthropologists, who are actively conducting research in the areas of tourism and political ecology, conservation and resource management, community-based tourism, and ecotourism, among other topics. Due to space limitations, we are unable to address the theoretical and methodological concerns specific to this important subfield; see Wallace (2005) for a representative sampling of contemporary research.

3 As a discipline, anthropology includes four subfields: social/cultural anthropology, linguistic anthropology, archaeology, and physical/biological anthropology. Some practitioners consider applied anthropology to be a fifth subfield. Although there is a growing body of tourism-related research

by archaeologists, particularly on the interplay of archaeological practice, tourism, and constructions of heritage, we limit our discussion here to sociocultural anthropology.

4 Studies of tourism development projects can be equally complex, given that there may not be an obvious local role for the anthropologist to step into as a participant-observer. See Ness (2003) for a thorough discussion of methodological adaptations in this situation.

5 This problem has been taken up by numerous anthropologists (see, e.g., Adams, 1996; Bruner, 2005; Graburn, 1977, 1983; Nash, 1981, 1996; Selwyn, 1994). Crick (1985) and Errington and Gewertz (1989) address the anthropologist–tourist relationship in great detail, and Ness (2003: 5–9) provides a helpful overview of the issues.

6 This is not to suggest that anthropologists are no longer interested in the topic. Like "race," another term that has profound social reality but whose application is labile and context-dependent, most sociocultural anthropologists do not accept "authenticity" as an ontological category and attend instead to the nature and consequences of its invocation in specific contexts. That is, "authenticity" is understood to be a folk category, not an analytic one.

7 Ironically, the essentializing, objectified concept of culture underpinning much contemporary tourism discourse was originally developed by anthropologists, who have since discarded it in favor of more nuanced, fluid understandings of identity and practice.

8 This distinction echoes the common differentiation tourists make between "tourist" and "traveler," here made even more emphatic by the invocation of a sacred element.

9 Although we know each these topics to be the subject of current research by anthropologists, to date few of them have reached the point of publishing this work.

References

Abbink, Jon (2000). "Tourism and its Discontents: Suri-Tourist Encounters in Southern Ethiopia." *Social Anthropology*, 8(1): 1–17.

Abram, Simone, Waldren, Jacqueline, and Macleod, Donald (Eds.) (1997). *Tourists and Tourism: Identifying With People and Places*. Oxford: Berg.

Abramson, Allan and Laviolette, Patrick (2007). "Cliff-Jumping, World-Shifting, and Value-Production." *Suomen Antropologi*, 32(2): 5–28.

Adams, Kathleen (1997). "Ethnic Tourism and the Renegotiation of Tradition in Tana Toraja (Sulawesi, Indonesia)." *Ethnology*, 36(4): 309–320.

Adams, Kathleen (2005a). "The Genesis of Touristic Imagery: Politics and Poetics in the Creation of a Remote Indonesian Island Destination." *Tourist Studies*, 4(2): 115–135.

Adams, Kathleen (2005b). "Generating Theory, Tourism, and 'World Heritage' in Indonesia: Ethical Quandaries for Anthropologists in an Era of Tourist Mania." *NAPA Bulletin*, 23: 45–59.

Adams, Kathleen (2006). *Art as Politics: Re-Crafting Identities, Tourism, and Power in Tana Toraja, Indonesia*. Honolulu: University of Hawaii Press.

Adams, Vincanne (1996). *Tigers of the Snow and Other Virtual Sherpas: An Ethnography of Himalayan Encounters*. Princeton, NJ: Princeton University Press.

Aerni, Mary Jane (1972). "Social Effects of Tourism." *Current Anthropology*, 13(2): 162.

Anderson, Benedict (1983). *Imagined Communities*. London: Verso.

Appadurai, Arjun (Ed.) (1986). *The Social Life of Things*. Cambridge: Cambridge University Press.

Appadurai, Arjun (1996). *Modernity at Large: Cultural Dimensions of Globalization*. Minneapolis: University of Minnesota Press.

Askew, Marc (1999). "Strangers and Lovers: Thai Women Sex Workers and Western Men in the 'Pleasure Space' of Bangkok." In Jill Forshee, et al. (Eds.), *Converging Interests* (pp. 109–148). Berkeley: IAS, University of California at Berkeley.

Aspelin, Paul (1977). "The Anthropological Analysis of Tourism: Indirect Tourism and Political Economy in the Case of the Mamainde of Mato Grosso, Brazil." *Annals of Tourism Research*, 4(3): 135–160.

Ateljevic, Irena, Pritchard, Annette, and Morgan, Nigel (Eds.) (2007). *The Critical Turn in Tourism Studies*. Oxford: Elsevier.

Augé, Marc (1995). *Non-Places: Introduction to an Anthropology of Supermodernity*. Trans. John Howe. London: Verso.

Babb, Florence (2004). "Recycled Sandalistas: From Revolution to Resorts in the New Nicaragua." *American Anthropologist*, 106(3): 541–555.

Babb, Florence (2007). "Love for Sale: Sex, Sentiment, and Tourism in Contemporary

Cuba." Paper presented at "States of Tourism," a symposium of the Tourism Studies Working Group, University of California, Berkeley.

Badone, Ellen and Roseman, Sharon (Eds.) (2004). *Intersecting Journeys: The Anthropology of Pilgrimage and Tourism*. Urbana: University of Illinois Press.

Bagus, I Gusti (1976). *The Impact of Tourism upon the Culture of the Balinese People*. Washington, DC: UNESCO/IBRD.

Barth, Fredrick (1969). "Introduction." In Fredrik Barth (Ed.), *Ethnic Groups and Boundaries* (pp. 9–38). London: George Allen and Unwin.

Basu, Paul (2004). "Route Metaphors of 'Roots Tourism'." In Simon Coleman and John Eade (Eds.), *Reframing Pilgrimage* (pp. 150–174). London: Routledge.

Basu, Paul (2007). *Highland Homecomings: Genealogy and Heritage-Tourism in the Scottish Diaspora*. London: Routledge.

Ben-Amos, Paula (1977). "Pidgin Languages and Tourist Arts." *Studies in the Anthropology of Visual Communication*, 4(2): 128–139.

Bianchi, Raoul (2002). "Towards a New Political Economy of Global Tourism." In Richard Sharpley and David Telfer (Eds.), *Tourism and Development: Concepts and Issues* (pp. 265–299). Clevedon: Channel View.

Boissevain, Jeremy (1977). "Tourism and Development in Malta." *Development and Change*, 8: 523–538.

Boissevain, Jeremy (Ed.) (1996). *Coping With Tourists: European Reactions to Mass Tourism*. Providence, RI: Berghahn Books.

Bourdieu, Pierre (1977). *Outline of a Theory of Practice*. Cambridge: Cambridge University Press.

Bowman, Glenn (1989). "Fucking Tourists: Sexual Relations and Tourism in Jerusalem's Old City." *Critique of Anthropology*, 9(2): 77–93.

Brennan, Denise (2004). *What's Love Got to Do With It? Transnational Desires and Sex Tourism in the Dominican Republic*. Durham, NC: Duke University Press.

Britton, S.G. (1982). "The Political Economy of Tourism in the Third World." *Annals of Tourism Research*, 9(3): 331–358.

Bryden, John (1973). *Tourism and Development: A Case Study of the Commonwealth Caribbean*. Cambridge: Cambridge University Press.

Bruner, Edward (1994). "Abraham Lincoln as Authentic Reproduction." *American Anthropologist*, 96: 397–415.

Bruner, Edward (1996). "Tourism in Ghana: The Representation of Slavery and the Return of the Black Diaspora." *American Anthropologist*, 98(2): 290–304.

Bruner, Edward (2001). "The Maasai and the Lion King: Authenticity, Nationalism, and Globalization in African Tourism." *American Ethnologist*, 28(4): 881–908.

Bruner, Edward (2005). *Culture on Tour: Ethnographies of Travel*. Chicago, IL: University of Chicago Press.

Bunten, Alexis (2005). "Commodities of Authenticity: When Natives Consume Their Own 'Tourist Art'." In Robert Welsch, Eric Venbrux, and Pamela Scheffield Rosi (Eds.), *Exploring World Art* (pp. 317–336). Long Grove, IL: Waveland Press.

Bunten, Alexis (2008). "Sharing Culture or Selling Out? Developing the Commodified Persona in the Heritage Industry." *American Ethnologist*, 35(3): 380–395.

Camacho, Michelle (1996). "Dissenting Workers and Social Control: A Case Study of the Hotel Industry in Huatulco, Oaxaca." *Human Organization*, 55(1): 33–40.

Carpenter, Edmund (1973). *Oh! What a Blow That Phantom Gave Me*. New York: Holt, Rinehart & Winston.

Carroll, Charles (2008). "My Mother's Best Friend's Sister-In-Law is Coming with Us: Exploring Domestic and International Travels with a Group of Lao Tourists." In Tim Winter, Peggy Teo and T.C. Chang (Eds.), *Asia on Tour: Exploring The Rise of Asian Tourism* (pp. 277–290). New York: Routledge.

Cary, Stephanie Hom (2004). "The Tourist Moment." *Annals of Tourism Research*, 31(1): 61–77.

Castaneda, Quetzil (1996). *In the Museum of Maya Culture: Touring Chichén Itzá*. Minneapolis: University of Minnesota Press.

Causey, Andrew (2003). *Hard Bargaining in Sumatra: Western Travelers and Toba Bataks in the Marketplace of Souvenirs*. Honolulu: University of Hawaii Press.

Cheung, Sidney (1999). "The Meanings of a Heritage Trail in Hong Kong." *Annals of Tourism Research*, 26(3): 570–588.

Chio, Jenny (2008). "The Internal Expansion of China: Tourism and the Production of Distance." In Tim Winter, Peggy Teo and T.C. Chang (Eds.), *Asia on Tour: Exploring the Rise of Asian Tourism* (pp. 207–220). New York: Routledge.

Choe, Youngmin (2008). "Affective Sites: Hur Jin-ho's Cinema and Film-Induced Tourism in Korea." In Tim Winter, Peggy Teo and T.C. Chang (Eds.), *Asia on Tour: Exploring the Rise of Asian Tourism* (pp. 109–126). New York: Routledge.

Chronis, Athinodoros (2005). "Co-Constructing Heritage at the Gettysburg Storyscape." *Annals of Tourism Research*, 32: 386–406.

Clarke, Kamari (2006). "Mapping Trans-nationality: Roots Tourism and the Institution-alization of Ethnic Heritage." In Kamari Clarke and Deborah Thomas (Eds.), *Global-ization and Race* (pp. 133–153). Durham: Duke University Press.

Clifford, James (1988). *The Predicament of Culture*. Cambridge, MA: Harvard University Press.

Clifford, James (1997a). "Four Northwest Coast Museums: Travel Reflections." In *Routes: Travel and Translation in the Late Twentieth Century* (pp. 107–145). Cambridge, MA: Harvard University Press.

Clifford, James (1997b). "Museums as contact zones." In *Routes: Travel and Translation in the Late Twentieth Century* (pp. 188–219). Cambridge, MA: Harvard University Press.

Clifford, James and Marcus, George (1986). *Writing Culture*. Berkeley: University of California Press.

Cohen, Erik (1971). "Arab Boys and Tourist Girls in a Mixed Jewish-Arab Community." *International Journal of Comparative Sociology*, 12: 217–233.

Cohen, Erik (1979). "A Phenomenology of Tourism Experiences." *Sociology*, 13: 179–201.

Cohen, Erik (1982). "Thai Girls and Farang Men: The Edge of Ambiguity." *Annals of Tourism Research*, 9(3): 403–428.

Cohen, Erik (1988). "Authenticity and Commoditization in Tourism." *Annals of Tourism Research*, 15(3): 371–386.

Cohen, Erik (1992). "Pilgrimage and Tourism: Convergence and Divergence." In Alan Morinis (Ed.), *Sacred Journeys: The Anthropology of Pilgrimage* (pp. 47–60). Westport, CT: Greenwood Press.

Coleman, Simon and Crang, Mike (Eds.) (2002). *Tourism: Between Place and Performance*. New York: Berghahn.

Coleman, Simon and Eade, John (Eds.) (2004). *Reframing Pilgrimage: Cultures in Motion*. London: Routledge.

Conran, Mary (2006). "Beyond Authenticity: Exploring Intimacy in the Touristic Encounter in Thailand." *Tourism Geographies*, 8(3): 274–285.

Crick, Malcolm (1985). "'Tracing' the Anthropological Self: Quizzical Reflections on Fieldwork, Tourism, and the Ludic." *Social Analysis*, 17: 71–92.

Crick, Malcolm (1989). "Representations of International Tourism in the Social Sciences." *Annual Review of Anthropology*, 18: 307–344.

Crouch, David (2002). "Surrounded by Place: Embodied Encounters." In Simon Coleman and Mike Crang (Eds.), *Tourism: Between Place and Performance* (pp. 207–218). New York: Berghahn Books.

Crouch, David and Desforges, Luke (Eds.) (2003). *The Sensuous in the Tourist Encounter*, special issue of *Tourist Studies*, 3(1): 5–22.

Daher, Rami (2000). "Dismantling a Com-munity's Heritage." In Mike Robinson et al. (Eds.), *Tourism and Heritage Relationships* (pp. 105–128). Newcastle: University of Northumbria.

Dahles, Heidi and Bras, Karin (1999). "Entrepreneurs in Romance: Tourism in Indonesia." *Annals of Tourism Research*, 26(2): 267–293.

Daniel, Yvonne (1996). "Tourism Dance Performances: Authenticity and Creativity." *Annals of Tourism Research*, 23(4): 780–797.

De Kadt, Emmanuel (1979). *Tourism: Passport to Development?* New York: Oxford University Press.

Di Giovine, Michael (2009). *The Heritage-scape: UNESCO, World Heritage, and Tourism*. Lanham: Lexington Books.

Durkheim, Emily (1965). *The Elementary Forms of the Religious Life*. (trans. by Joseph W. Swain) New York: Free Press.

Duval, David (2003). "When Hosts Become Guests: Return Visits and Diasporic Identities in a Commonwealth Eastern Caribbean Community." *Current Issues in Tourism*, 6(4): 267–308.

Ebron, Paulla (2000). "Tourists as Pilgrims: Commercial Fashioning of Transatlantic Politics." *American Ethnologist*, 26(4): 910–932.

Ebron, Paulla (2002). *Performing Africa*. Princeton, NJ: Princeton University Press.

Edensor, Tim (1998). *Tourists at the Taj*. London: Routledge.

Errington, Frederick and Gewertz, Deborah (1989). "Tourism and Anthropology in a Post-Modern World." *Oceania*, 60: 37–54.

Errington, Shelley (1998). *The Death of Authentic Primitive Art and Other Tales of Progress*. Berkeley: University of California Press.

Evans-Pritchard, Deirdre (1989). "How 'They' See 'Us': Native American Images of Tourists." *Annals of Tourism Research*, 16(1): 89–105.

Feldman, Jackie (2008). *Above the Death Pits, Beneath the Flag: Youth Voyages to Poland and the Performance of Israeli National Identity*. Oxford: Berghahn.

Finney, Ben and Watson, Karen Anne (Eds.) (1975). *A New Kind of Sugar: Tourism in the Pacific*. Honolulu: East-West Center.

Fox, Richard (Ed.) (1991). *Recapturing Anthropology*. Santa Fe: SAR Press.

Frey, Nancy (1998). *Pilgrim Stories: On and Off the Road to Santiago*. Berkeley: University of California Press.

Geertz, Clifford (1973). *The Interpretation of Culture*. New York: Basic Books.

Gmelch, George (2003). *Behind the Smile: The Working Lives of Caribbean Tourism*. Bloomington: University of Indiana Press.

Goffman, Erving (1959). *The Presentation of Self in Everyday Life*. New York: Anchor.

Gordon, Tamar (2005). *Global Villages*. Documentary film. New York: Tourist Gaze Productions.

Graburn, Nelson (1967). "The Eskimo and Airport Art." *Trans-action*, 4(10): 28–33.

Graburn, Nelson (Ed.) (1976). *Ethnic and Tourist Arts: Cultural Expressions from the Fourth World*. Berkeley: University of California Press.

Graburn, Nelson (1977). "Tourism: The Sacred Journey." In Valene Smith (Ed.), *Hosts and Guests* (pp. 17–32). Philadelphia: University of Pennsylvania Press.

Graburn, Nelson (1983a). "The Anthropology of Tourism." *Annals of Tourism Research*, 10(1): 9–33.

Graburn, Nelson (Ed.) (1983b). *The Anthropology of Tourism*, special issue of *Annals of Tourism Research*, 10(1).

Graburn, Nelson (1983c). *To Pray, Pay and Play: The Cultural Structure of Japanese Domestic Tourism*. Aix-en-Provence: Centre des Hautes Etudes Touristiques.

Graburn, Nelson (1983d). "Tourism and Prostitution." *Annals of Tourism Research*, 10(3): 437–456.

Graburn, Nelson (1987). "Material Symbols in Japanese Domestic Tourism." In Dan Ingersoll and Gordon Bronistky (Eds.), *Mirror and Metaphor: Material and Social Constructions of Reality* (pp. 15–27). Lanham, MD: University Press of America.

Graburn, Nelson (1993). "Ethnic Arts of the Fourth World." In Dorothea Whitten and Norman Whitten (Eds.), *Imagery and Creativity: Ethnoaesthetics and Art Worlds in the Americas* (pp. 171–204). Tucson: University of Arizona Press.

Graburn, Nelson (1995a). "Tourism, Modernity, and Nostalgia." In Akbar Ahmed and Cris Shore (Eds.), *The Future of Anthropology* (pp. 158–178). London: The Athlone Press.

Graburn, Nelson (1995b). "The Past in the Present in Japan: Nostalgia and Neo-Traditionalism in Contemporary Japanese Domestic Tourism." In Richard Butler and Douglas Pearce (Eds.), *Changes in Tourism: People, Places, Processes* (pp. 47–70). London: Routledge.

Graburn, Nelson (1997). "Tourism and Cultural Development in East Asia and Oceania." In Shinji Yamashita et al. (Eds.), *Tourism and Cultural Development in Asia and Oceania* (pp. 194–213). Bangi: Universiti Kebangsaan Malaysia Press.

Graburn, Nelson (2000). "Foreword." In Michael Hitchcock and Brian Teague (Eds.), *Souvenirs: The Material Culture of Tourism* (pp. xii–xvii). Aldershot: Ashgate.

Graburn, Nelson (2001). "Tourism as Ritual: A General Theory of Tourism." In Valene Smith and Maryann Brent (Eds.), *Hosts and Guests Revisited: Tourism Issues of the 21st Century* (pp. 42–52). London: Cognizant Communications.

Graburn, Nelson (2002). "The Ethnographic Tourist." In Graham M.S. Dann (Ed.), *The Tourist as Metaphor of the Social*

World (pp. 19–39). Wallingford: CABI Publishing.

Graburn, Nelson (2004). "The Kyoto Tax Strike: Buddhism, Shinto, and Tourism in Japan." In Ellen Badone and Sharon Roseman (Eds.), *Intersecting Journeys: The Anthropology of Pilgrimage and Tourism* (pp. 125–139). Urbana: University of Illinois Press.

Graburn, Nelson (2008a). "The Past and the Other in the Present: *Kokunai kokusaika kanko* (Domestic International Tourism)." In Sylvie Guichard-Anguis and Ok Pyo Moon (Eds). *Japanese Tourism and Travel Culture.* (pp. 21–36). London: Routledge.

Graburn, Nelson (2008b). "Multiculturalism, Museums, and Tourism in Japan." In Nelson Graburn, John Ertl, and R. Kenji Tierney (Eds.), *Multiculturalism in the New Japan* (pp. 218–235). New York: Berghahn Press.

Graburn, Nelson and Jafari, Jafar (1991). "Introduction." *Tourism Social Science*, special issue of *Annals of Tourism Research*, 18(1): 1–25.

Greenwood, Davydd (1972). "Tourism as an Agent of Change: A Spanish-Basque Case." *Ethnology*, 11(1): 80–91.

Greenwood, Davydd (1977). "Culture by the Pound: An Anthropological Perspective on Tourism as Cultural Commoditization." In Valene Smith (Ed.), *Hosts and Guests* (pp. 129–137). Philadelphia: University of Pennsylvania Press.

Grunewald, Rodrigo (2006). "Pataxó Tourism Art and Cultural Authenticity." In Melanie Smith and Mike Robinson (Eds.), *Cultural Tourism in a Changing World* (pp. 203–214). Clevedon: Channel View.

Gupta, Akhil and Ferguson, James (Eds.) (1997). *Anthropological Locations.* Berkeley: University of California Press.

Habu, Junko, Fawcett, Clare, and Matsunaga, John (Eds.) (2008). *Evaluating Multiple Narratives: Beyond Nationalist, Colonialist, Imperialist Archaeologies.* New York: Springer.

Handler, Richard and Linnekin, Jocelyn (1984). "Tradition, Genuine or Spurious." *Journal of American Folklore*, 97(2): 273–290.

Handler, Richard and Saxton, William (1998). "Dyssimulation, Reflexivity, Narrative, and the Quest for Authenticity in Living History." *Cultural Anthropology*, 3(3): 242–260.

Harrison, David and Hitchcock, Michael (2005). *The Politics of World Heritage.* Buffalo, NY: Channel View.

Harrison, Julia (2003). *Being a Tourist: Finding Meaning in Pleasure Travel.* Vancouver: University of British Columbia Press.

Hendry, Joy (2000). *The Orient Strikes Back: A Global View of Cultural Display.* Oxford: Berg.

Hitchcock, Michael (1997). "Indonesia in Miniature." In Michael Hitchcock and Victor T. King (Eds.), *Images of Malay-Indonesian Identity* (pp. 227–235). Kuala Lumpur: Oxford University Press.

Hitchcock, Michael (1999). "Tourism and Ethnicity: Situational Perspectives." *International Journal of Tourism Research* 1: 17–32.

Hitchcock, Michael and Teague, Ken (2000). *Souvenirs: The Material Culture of Tourism.* Aldershot: Ashgate.

Howe, Alyssa (2001). "Queer Pilgrimage: The San Francisco Homeland and Identity Tourism." *Cultural Anthropology*, 16(1): 35–61.

Hubbard, Laura and Mathers, Kathryn (2004). "Surviving American Empire in Africa: The Anthropology of Reality Television." *International Journal of Cultural Studies*, 7(4): 441–459.

Huizinga, Johan (1950). *Homo Ludens: A Study of the Play Element in Culture.* Boston, MA: Beacon Press.

Inda, Jonathan and Rosaldo, Renato (Eds.) (2002). *The Anthropology of Globalization.* Oxford: Blackwell.

Inhorn, Marcia (2003). *Local Babies, Global Science: Gender, Religion, and In Vitro Fertilization in Egypt.* New York: Routledge.

James, Wendy and Allen, N.J. (Eds.) (1998). *Marcel Mauss: A Centenary Tribute.* NY: Berghahn.

Jules-Rosette, Bennetta (1984). *The Messages of Tourist Art: An African Semiotic System in Comparative Perspective.* New York: Plenum.

Karam, John (2007). "Air Turbulence in Homeland Tourism." In *Another Arabesque: Syrian-Lebanese Ethnicity in Neoliberal Brazil* (pp. 144–165). Philadelphia, PA: Temple University Press.

Karp, Ivan and Lavine, Steven (Eds.) (1991). *Exhibiting Cultures: The Poetics and Politics* of Museum Display. Washington, DC: Smithsonian.

Karp, Ivan, Kreamer, Christine, and Lavine, Steven (Eds.) (1992). Museums and Communities: The Politics of Public Culture. Washington, DC: Smithsonian.

Karp, Ivan, Kratz, Corinne, Szwaja, Lynn, and Ybarra-Frausto, Tomás (Eds.) (2006). Museum Frictions: Public Cultures/Global Transformations. Durham, NC: Duke University Press.

Kearney, Michael (1995). "The Local and the Global: The Anthropology of Globalization and Transnationalism." Annual Review of Anthropology, 24: 547–565.

Kelsky, Karen (1999). Women on the Verge: Japanese Women, Western Dreams. Durham, NC: Duke University Press.

Kempadoo, Kamala (Ed.) (1999). Sun, Sex, and Gold: Tourism and Sex Work in the Caribbean. Lanham, MD: Rowman & Littlefield Publishers.

Keyes, Charles and van den Berghe, Pierre (Eds.) (1984). Tourism and Ethnicity, special issue of Annals of Tourism Research, 11(3).

Kim, Eleana (2003). "Wedding Citizenship and Culture: Korean Adoptees and the Global Family of Korea." Social Text, 21(1): 57–81.

Kinnaird, Vivian and Hall, Derek (Eds.) (1994). Tourism: A Gender Analysis. New York: John Wiley.

Kirshenblatt-Gimblett, Barbara (1998). Destination Culture: Tourism, Museums, and Heritage. Berkeley: University of California Press.

Kottak, Conrad (1983). Assault on Paradise: Social Change in a Brazilian Village. New York: Random House.

Kugelmass, Jack (1992). "The Rites of the Tribe: American Jewish Tourism in Poland." In Ivan Karp et al. (Eds.), Museums and Communities (pp. 382–427). Washington, DC: Smithsonian.

Laske, Tomke (Ed.) (2005). Diversidad Cultural y Turismo, special issue of Cultura y Desarrollo [Havana: UNESCO], 4.

Leach, Edmund (1961). "Time and False Noses." In Rethinking Anthropology (pp. 132–136). London: Athlone.

Lee, Molly (1991). "Appropriating the Primitive: Turn-of-the-Century Collection and Display of Native Alaskan Art." Arctic Anthropology, 23(1): 6–15.

Lehrer, Erica (2007). "Bearing False Witness? Vicarious Jewish Identity and the Politics of

Affinity." In Dorota Glowacka and Joanna Zylinska (Eds.), Imaginary Neighbors (pp. 84–109). Lincoln: University of Nebraska Press.

Leite, Naomi (2005). "Travels to an Ancestral Past: On Diasporic Tourism, Embodied Memory, and Identity." Antropologicas, 9: 273–302.

Leite, Naomi (2007). "Materializing Absence: Tourists, Surrogates, and the Making of 'Jewish Portugal.'" In Things That Move: The Material Worlds of Tourism and Travel. Conference Proceedings. Leeds, UK: Centre for Tourism and Cultural Change.

Leite, Naomi (forthcoming). "Global Affinities: Memory, Materiality, and Kinship in the Portuguese Marrano-Anusim Revival Movement." PhD dissertation, University of California, Berkeley.

Liebman Parinello, Giuli (1992). "Motivation and Anticipation in Post-Industrial Tourism." Annals of Tourism Research, 20: 233–249.

Lips, Julius (1937). The Savage Hits Back. New York: University Books.

Louie, Andrea (2001). "Crafting Places Through Mobility: Chinese American 'Roots-Searching' in China." Identities, 8(3): 343–379.

Lowenthal, David (1985). The Past is a Foreign Country. New York: Cambridge University Press.

Lowenthal, David (1996). Possessed by the Past: The Heritage Crusade. Cambridge: Cambridge University Press.

MacCannell, Dean (1973). "Staged Authenticity: Arrangements of Social Space in Tourist Settings." American Journal of Sociology, 79(3): 589–603.

MacCannell, Dean (1976). The Tourist. New York: Schocken Books.

MacCannell, Dean (1984). "Reconstructed Ethnicity: Tourism and Cultural Identity in Third World Communities." Annals of Tourism Research, 11(3): 375–391.

MacCannell, Dean (1990). "Cannibal Tours." Visual Anthropology Review, 6(2).

Macdonald, Sharon (1997). "A People's Story: Heritage, Identity, and Authenticity." In Chris Rojek and John Urry (Eds.), Touring Culture (pp. 155–175). London: Routledge.

Malinowski, Bronislaw (1922). Argonauts of the Western Pacific. New York: Dutton.

Marcus, George (1995). "Ethnography in/of the World System: The Emergence of

Multi-Sited Ethnography." *Annual Review of Anthropology*, 24: 95–117.

Marcus, George and Fischer, Michael (1986). *Anthropology as Cultural Critique*. Chicago: University of Chicago Press.

Marx, Karl (1999). *Capital* [abridged edition]. Oxford, NY: Oxford University Press.

Mauss, Marcel (1954). *The Gift* (trans. by Ian Cunnison) Glencoe, IL: Free Press.

Medina, Laurie Kroshus (2003). "Commoditizing Culture: Tourism and Maya Identity." *Annals of Tourism Research*, 30(2): 353–336.

Meethan, Kevin (1996). "Consuming (in) the Civilized City." *Annals of Tourism Research*, 23(2): 322–340.

Meethan, Kevin (2001). *Tourism in Global Society*. London: Palgrave.

Meisch, Lynn (1995). "Gringas and Otavaleños: Changing Tourist Relations." *Annals of Tourism Research*, 22(2): 441–462.

Meisch, Lynn (2002). *Andean Entrepreneurs: Otavalo Merchants and Musicians in the Global Arena*. Austin: University of Texas Press.

Michaud, Jean (2001). "Anthropologie, tourisme et sociétés locales au fil des textes." *Anthropologie et Sociétés,* 25(2): 15–33.

Moon, Ok Pyo (1989). *From Paddy Field to Ski Slope*. Manchester: Manchester University Press.

Myers, Fred (2001). "The Wizards of Oz: Nation, State, and the Production of Aboriginal Fine Art." In Fred Myers (Ed.), *The Empire of Things* (pp. 165–204). Santa Fe, NM: School of American Research Press.

Nadel-Klein, Jane (2003). *Fishing for Heritage: Modernity and Loss Along the Scottish Coast*. Oxford: Berg.

Nash, Dennison (1970). *A Community in Limbo: An Anthropological Study of an American Community Abroad*. Bloomington: Indiana University Press.

Nash, Dennison (1977). "Tourism as Imperialism." In Valene Smith (Ed.), *Hosts and Guests* (pp. 33–47). Philadelphia: University of Pennsylvania Press.

Nash, Dennison (1996). *Anthropology of Tourism*. Oxford: Pergamon.

Nash, Dennison (2004). "New Wine in Old Bottles: An Adjustment of Priorities in the Anthropological Study of Tourism." In Jenny Phillimore and Lisa Goodson (Eds.), *Qualitative Research in Tourism* (pp. 170–184). London: Routledge.

Ness, Sally (2003). *Where Asia Smiles: An Ethnography of Philippine Tourism*. Philadelphia: University of Pennsylvania Press.

Ness, Sally (2005). "Tourism-Terrorism: The Landscaping of Consumption and the Darker Side of Place." *American Ethnologist*, 32(1): 118–140.

Nuñez, Theron (1963). "Tourism, Tradition, and Acculturation: *El Weekendismo* in Mexico." *Ethnology*, 2: 328–336.

Peers, Laura (2007). *Playing Ourselves: Interpreting Native Histories at Historic Reconstructions*. Lanham, MD: Alta Mira Press.

Perkins, Harvey and Thorns, David (2001). "Gazing or Performing? Reflections on Urry's Tourist Gaze in the Context of Contemporary Experience in the Antipodes." *International Sociology*, 16(2): 185–204.

Phillips, Ruth and Steiner, Christopher (Eds.) (1999). *Unpacking Culture: Art and Commodity in Colonial and Postcolonial Worlds*. Berkeley: University of California Press.

Picard, David (2007). "Friction in a Tourism Contact Zone." *Suomen Antropologi*, 32(2): 96–109.

Picard, Michel (1996). *Bali: Cultural Tourism and Touristic Culture*. Singapore: Archipelago Press.

Picard, Michel and Wood, Robert (Eds.) (1997). *Tourism, Ethnicity, and the State in Asian and Pacific Societies*. Honolulu: University of Hawaii Press.

Poulot, Dominique (1994). "Identity as Self-Discovery." In Daniel Sherman and Irit Rogoff (Eds.), *Museum Culture* (pp. 66–84). Minneapolis: University of Minnesota Press.

Price, Sally (1989). *Primitive Art in Civilized Places*. Chicago: University of Chicago Press.

Pritchard, Annette and Morgan, Nigel (2000). "Privileging the Male Gaze: Gendered Tourism Landscapes." *Annals of Tourism Research*, 27(4): 884–905.

Pruitt, Deborah and LaFont, Suzanne (1995). "For Love And Money: Romance Tourism in Jamaica." *Annals of Tourism Research*, 22(2): 422–440.

Redfield, Robert, Linton, Ralph, and Herskovits, Melville (1936). "Memorandum for the Study of Acculturation." *American Anthropologist*, 38(1): 149–152.

Rojek, Chris and Urry, John (Eds.) (1997). *Touring Cultures*. New York: Routledge.

Rosaldo, Renato (1989). "Imperialist Nostalgia." *Representations*, 26: 107–122.

Salazar, Noel (2005). "Tourism and Glocalization: 'Local' Tour Guiding." *Annals of Tourism Research*, 32(3): 628–646.

Salvador, Mari Lyn (1997). *The Art of Being Kuna: Layers of Meaning Among the Kuna of Panama*. Los Angeles: Fowler Museum, UCLA.

Schein, Louisa (1998). "Forged Transnationality and Oppositional Cosmopolitanism." In Michael Smith and Luis Guarnizo (Eds.), *Transnationalism from Below* (pp. 291–313). New Brunswick, NJ: Transaction Publishers.

Scheper-Hughes, Nancy (2000). "The Global Traffic in Organs." *Current Anthropology*, 41(2):191–224.

Scheper-Hughes, Nancy (2006). "Mr. Tati's Holiday: Seeing the World via Transplant Tourism." Paper presented at the American Anthropological Association Annual Meeting, San José, California.

Scott, Julie (1995). "Sexual and National Boundaries in Tourism." *Annals of Tourism Research*, 22(2): 385–403.

Selänniemi, Tom (2001). "Pale Skin on the Playa del Anywhere: Finnish Tourists in the Liminoid South." In Valene Smith and Maryann Brent (Eds.), *Hosts and Guests Revisited* (pp. 80–92). New York: Cognizant Communication.

Selänniemi, Tom (2002). "Couples on Holiday: (En)gendered or Endangered Experiences?" In Margaret Byrne Swain and Janet Momsen (Eds.), *Gender/Tourism/Fun(?)* (pp. 15–23). New York: Cognizant Communications.

Selwyn, Tom (1994). "The Anthropology of Tourism: Reflections on the State of the Art." In A.V. Seaton et al. (Eds.), *Tourism: The State of the Art* (pp. 729–736). Chichester: John Wiley and Sons.

Selwyn, Tom (Ed.) (1996). *The Tourist Image: Myths and Myth-Making in Tourism*. Chichester: John Wiley & Sons Ltd.

Selwyn, Tom (2007). "The Political Economy of Enchantment: Formations in the Anthropology of Tourism." *Suomen Antropologi*, 32(2): 48–70.

Shenhav-Keller, Shelly (1993). "The Israeli Souvenir: Its Text and Context." *Annals of Tourism Research*, 20(1): 182–196.

Silverman, Helaine (Ed.) (2005). *Performance, Tourism, and Ethnographic Practice*, special issue of *Anthropology and Humanism*, 30(2).

Smith, Andrea (2003). "Place Replaced: Colonial Nostalgia and Pied-Noir Pilgrimages to Malta." *Cultural Anthropology*, 18(3): 329–364.

Smith, Valene (1953). "Travel Geography Courses for a New Field." *Journal of Geography*, 52: 68–72.

Smith, Valene (Ed.) (1977). *Hosts and Guests: The Anthropology of Tourism*. Philadelphia: University of Pennsylvania Press.

Smith, Valene (1979). "Women: The Tastemakers in Tourism." *Annals of Tourism Research*, 6: 49–60.

Smith, Valene (Ed.) (1989). *Hosts and Guests: The Anthropology of Tourism*, 2nd edition. Philadelphia: University of Pennsylvania Press.

Smith, Valene (Ed.) (1992). *Pilgrimage and Tourism*, special issue of *Annals of Tourism Research*, 19(1).

Stanley, Nick (1998). *Being Ourselves for You: The Global Display of Cultures*. London: Middlesex University Press.

Stanton, Max (1989). "The Polynesian Cultural Center: A Multi-Ethnic Model of Seven Pacific Cultures." In Valene Smith (Ed.), *Hosts and Guests* (2nd edition.) (pp. 247–262). Philadelphia: University of Pennsylvania Press.

Steiner, Christopher (1994). *African Art in Transit*. Cambridge: Cambridge University Press.

Stocker, Karen (2007). "Identity as Work: Changing Job Opportunities and Indigenous Identity in the Transition to a Tourist Economy." *Anthropology of Work Review*, 28(2): 18–22.

Stronza, Amanda (2001). "Anthropology of Tourism." *Annual Review of Anthropology*, 30: 261–283.

Stronza, Amanda (2005). "Hosts and Hosts: The Anthropology of Community-Based Ecotourism in the Peruvian Amazon." *NAPA Bulletin* 23: 170–190.

Swain, Margaret Byrne (1977). "Cuna Women and Ethnic Tourism." In Valene Smith (Ed.), *Hosts and Guests* (pp. 71–82). Philadelphia: University of Pennsylvania Press.

Swain, Margaret Byrne (1993). "Women Producers of Ethnic Arts." *Annals of Tourism Research*, 20(1): 32–51.

Swain, Margaret Byrne (Ed.) (1995). *Gender in Tourism*, special issue of *Annals of Tourism Research*, 22(2): 247–266.

Swain, Margaret Byrne (2004). "(Dis)embodied Experience and Power Dynamics in Tourism Research." In Jenny Phillimore and Lisa Goodson (Eds.), *Qualitative Research in Tourism* (pp. 102–118). London: Routledge.

Swain, Margaret Byrne and Momsen, Janet (Eds.) (2002). *Gender/Tourism/Fun(?)*. New York: Cognizant Communication.

Thompson, Michael (1979). *Rubbish Theory*. Oxford: Oxford University Press.

Truong, Thanh-Dam (1990). *Sex, Money, and Morality: Prostitution and Tourism in Southeast Asia*. London: Zed Books.

Tunbridge, J.E. and Ashworth, Gregory (1996). *Dissonant Heritage: The Management of the Past as a Resource in Conflict*. New York: Wiley.

Turner, Victor and Turner, Edith (1978). *Image and Pilgrimage in Christian Culture*. New York: Columbia University Press.

Urry, John (1990). *The Tourist Gaze*. London: Sage.

Van den Berghe, Pierre (1994). *The Quest for the Other: Ethnic Tourism in San Cristóbal, Mexico*. Seattle: University of Washington Press.

Van Gennep, Arnold (1960). *Rites of Passage*. (trans. by Monika B. Vizedom and Gabrielle L. Caffee) Chicago: University of Chicago Press.

Veblen, Thorstein (1934). *The Theory of the Leisure Class*. New York: Modern Library.

Veilola, Soile and Jokinen, Eeva (1994). "The Body in Tourism." *Theory, Culture, and Society*, 11: 125–151.

Wagner, Roy (1975). *The Invention of Culture*. Chicago: University of Chicago Press.

Wagner, Ulla (1977). "Out of Time and Place: Mass Tourism and Charter Trips." *Ethnos*, 42(1–2): 35–52.

Wallace, Tim (Ed.) (2005). *Tourism and Applied Anthropologists: Linking Theory and Practice*, special issue of *NAPA Bulletin*, 23.

Wang, Ning (1999). "Rethinking Authenticity in Tourism Experience." *Annals of Tourism Research*, 20(2): 349–370.

Wang, Yu (2007). "Customized Authenticity Begins at Home." *Annals of Tourism Research*, 34 (3): 789–804.

Wood, Robert (1998). "Touristic Ethnicity: A Brief Itinerary." *Ethnic and Racial Studies* 21(2): 218–241.

Wolff, Kurt H. (Ed.) (1950). *The Sociology of Georg Simmel*. Glencoe, IL: Free Press.

Wright, Julie (1992). *The Toured: The Other Side of Tourism in Barbados*. Documentary film. Berkeley: UC Extension Center for Media and Independent Learning.

Young, George (1973). *Tourism: Blessing or Blight?* Harmondsworth: Penguin.

The Sociology of Tourism

Adrian Franklin

Introduction

Sociology has arguably been the key discipline in the emergence of a scholarly interest in tourism. Certainly, many of its key and enduring theoretical perspectives have been developed by sociologists, from Simmel (1997a, 1997b) to Benjamin (1955) in the first half of the twentieth century, to Boorstin (1964) and MacCannell (1976) in the middle years of the twentieth century; to Urry (1991), MacCannell (1992), Rojek (1993, 1995), Veijola and Jokinen (1994), Lury (1997) Bauman (1998, 2000), Löfgren (1999) towards the end of the twentieth century, and Edensor (2001), Franklin (2001, 2002, 2003a, 2003b, 2004, 2008), Franklin and Crang (2001), Urbain (2003), Coleman and Eade (2004), Sheller and Urry (2004) in the early twenty-first century. While many other disciplines have become fully engaged in tourism research and studies, and many including social anthropology and human geography are fellow travelers (and are in many ways indistinguishable from sociology), few have such a track record of theoretical development over such a long period. This is because, from very early in the twentieth century,

sociologists began to understand how tourism and touristic behavior was implicated in the profound social and cultural transformations associated with urbanization and the transformation of city sensibilities, predispositions to the coast, water and health as well as travel, sporting and associational life, and the emergence of culture, consumption, consumerism and leisure as a new domain and organizing dimension of social life.

Curiously, sociology never spawned much in the way of a vigorous "sociology of tourism" subdiscipline in the same way that vibrant subdisciplines have emerged in geography and anthropology. This is perhaps explained by sociology's *core* historic interests in the domains of work, social reproduction (family, city, and housing) and social inequality with a strong sense of contributing practical policy research around urgent and compelling social issues and problems. As a perceived luxury, tourism posed nothing to be solved or, at any rate, nothing particularly pressing. In itself it was not a problem and thereof did not require fixing; if anything it was an activity that some were able to indulge in while others suffered basic needs (so therefore at their expense) and in that sense it was worse than merely of little interest. Worse still, it was seen as shallow and lacking in merit as a diversion or improving leisure and derived much of its negative reputation from the idle traveling classes of the aristocracy rentier classes. It did not appear to contribute anything to society and worse, was seen as wasting time and resources while at the same time indulging in dubious activities always associated with the social periphery (alcohol, theatre, brothels, pubs, dance halls, etc.). For this reason, the main interest in it has come from those developing social and cultural theories of change, particularly those interested in developing forms of class subcultures, those studying de-industrializing modernity (which often sought to replace production with consumption-based entertainment) and more recently consumption itself, the interest in the body, contemporary forms of social identity construction and global ordering.

Sociology was traditionally very "located" in, and focused on, cities and urbanized societies of the West and "ordinary working people" in Western nations and far less concerned with rural and peripheral spaces, still less on affluence and conspicuous consumption. Despite being Europeanized and Pan-American by the early twentieth century, tourism is also more historically associated with some modern national cultures (USA, UK) rather than others (Eastern Europe, France). As the French tourism sociologist Jean-Didier Urbain (Doquet and Evrard, 2008) noted, for example, in France tourism was for a very long time widely considered to be an English cultural phenomenon. According to Larrouse, the French Dictionary, "touriste" was an acceptable synonym for "English" around 1890. Not surprisingly perhaps, with tourism strongly associated with Englishness (read also as "English dissoluteness") and the survival of its idle leisure classes (aristocrats and their bourgeois emulators), the French academy was even more hostile to according any serious point to the study of tourism. According to Urbain, this is still more or less the case

for mainstream French sociology, (despite some interesting work being published more recently).

Beyond Formalism

One of the reasons why sociology has proved to be so valuable to the study of tourism is its interest in how and why tourism emerges in modern society and how its various iterations relate to and can be explained by key social changes in the nineteenth and twentieth centuries. In this way, sociology is able to problematize the conceptualization of tourism that has been generally given and taken-for-granted, or explained away through formalistic definitions, especially in the less theoretical tourism disciplines. I have specified the dangers and pitfalls of formalistic definitions of tourism elsewhere (see Franklin, 2007: 387–389), which tend to concentrate attention on notions of "temporary movements" (Bukart and Medlik, 1974: v; Mathieson and Wall, 1982: 1); those spaces beyond and marginal to the everyday (e.g., the cultural anthropologists Graburn, 1978; Smith, 1978; Voase, 1995; but see also Shields, 1991); periods of time spent in hotel or other temporary accommodation (Judd and Fainstein, 1999; Shaw and Williams, 1994), travel and movement itself (Bukart and Medlik, 1974: v); and the (somewhat tautological) "net effects" of the complex of tourism industries (see Weaver and Oppermann, 2000: 3) which "determine" demand as well as supply (Cooper et al., 1998).

This is all very well but for one thing. None of these attempts to define the object under study are in any way explanations (though they give the appearance of explaining what is at hand) and further, they tend to confuse more than they clarify. For example, an emphasis on travel itself simply confuses travel motives: a business person going off to work or to confer will thus be confused with others hoping to experience sex, nature, music, or whatever. To suppose that such behaviors are usefully lumped together in the same category is banal. Equally, an emphasis on non-everyday spaces on the social margin may obscure the cultural and social value placed on travel itself or, indeed, the styles and relative degrees of mobility itself (see Franklin, 2003a; see also Bauman's, 1998 essay "Vagabonds and Tourists" in his *Globalization* book). It may also obscure the fact that tourism is an established part of the everyday in most places (cities, for example) and for an increasing number of people wherever they live (almost every remote and peripheral area will be touched to varying degrees by the global network of tourism (Franklin, 2003a).

Sociology offers the potential to look beyond formal definitions and processes and asks why tourism emerged in the first place, how it relates to specific societies, contexts and cultures, and how social and cultural change has shifted and changed its expression, its impact and its experience. This chapter aims to explain first how sociology, particularly in the USA and UK, came to discover the significance of tourism, beginning with exploratory initial studies inspired by a growing interest in leisure, and later from the 1990s with studies of deindustrialization, consumerism and postmodernism. It will then set out the principal sociological theories of tourism that dominated tourist studies until quite recently when a critique was mounted based on a range of new issues relating to the body, sex, excitement and sensuality, the spatial dedifferentiation of tourism and its invasion of the everyday and new debates about tourism ontologies and orderings. A review of progress in these new debates will be offered by way of a conclusion.

Sociology Begins to Notice Leisure and Tourism

Sociology's early development predisposed it to ignore tourism. It was sociology's own juxtaposition in relation to an emerging modern world that influenced how it viewed the tourism phenomenon in the nineteenth century and why it was ultimately forced to take notice in the twentieth century. Sociology was fixated on production, work and social reproduction in the nineteenth century and while this continued to dominate the core of the discipline, consumption, culture and leisure grew so important in the twentieth century that new scion disciplines (cultural studies, leisure studies, tourism studies) began to form around it.

Sociology's disciplinary origins date back to a number of Enlightenment and counter-Enlightenment themes. To the extent that it has always considered itself scientific it was positively aligned with Enlightenment issues of human progress and development, democracy, scientifically based and rational approaches to planning and policy and most of all, producing an understanding of human behavior, society and culture that was based on scientific observation rather than religious or other forms of dogma. However, it was also influenced by certain more conservative counter-Enlightenment concerns, especially those that identified the potential harm that progress and change would wreak on fragile but important social bonds, social solidarity itself and long-established cultures and traditions. The concern that social anthropology has with tourism as a destroyer of culture and tradition, if not as a form of ethnocide, has its origins in the same counter-Enlightenment spirit. The modernity project *could* only deliver progress and change by destroying many aspects of tradition and so sociology as an emerging discipline found a compromise and a role for itself. It was going to monitor change and find ways to manage society through churning periods of social transition. It was primarily interested in uncovering and understanding the nature and social costs of change but it was equally *applied* to the solving of problems posed by it.

As it presented itself to the founding fathers of sociology in the nineteenth century, tourism did not seem like a problem needing a solution; or rather it appeared inversely related to the problem of immobilized poverty. It represented ostentatious consumption in its highest expression, a symbol of gross inequalities in the distribution of wealth and income that enabled some the luxury of idleness in pristine, sanitized resorts while most were consigned to a life of industrial toil in filthy and unhealthy cities. To be a tourist for most of the nineteenth century one had to be among the traveling class of the landed social elite or one of the new middle classes who were emulating their styles of consumption—largely centered on luxurious rural lifestyles and travel. Neither of these was of great concern to the emerging discipline of sociology.

For almost every sociologist in the early years and even until relatively recently, the heartland of their interest was in the industrial city, in the sphere of industry and work (production), the conditions of social reproduction and the nature of social relations and cultures among ordinary working people. Even though many workers had begun to receive paid holidays in the early twentieth century and were establishing their own patterns and places of vacationing, this form of leisure was most frequently seen as a solution to their earlier predicament of unrelenting work and poor health rather than something that required further investigation. Along with the puritanical capitalist class (that it was so critically monitoring), sociology also tended to view leisure and especially idle, non-improving leisure activities, with a great degree of suspicion and disapproval, even until relatively recently (see Rojek, 1993: 174–176). Thus it was that leisure first made its appearance in the sociological cannon as a social *problem* that owed its origins to more significant problems in the sphere of work and production.

One the earliest signs that sociologists were to take an interest in tourism came with the publication of Henry Durant's (1938) *The Problem of Leisure*, and it was unmistakably critical of the purely passive, spectatorial,

and consumerist forms of leisure. Although not specifically addressing tourism per se, he identified a theme about the rise of leisure in the 1930s that became more prominent later and specifically came to be associated with tourism.

Typical of sociological approaches, the problem with leisure was associated with, and located in, the problems associated with work and industrial communities. The core problem was an alienating English work place, where Fordist production techniques had robbed workers of those historic forms of "work satisfaction" associated with craft skills and mastery over entire production processes. Thus they were forced to find forms of satisfaction and self identity outside the work place, in forms of escapist leisure, epitomized by the newly dominant cinema.

Interestingly, Durant also alludes to the relative *immobility* of workers in 1930s Britain—*as a problem*. They were denied the opportunities to make work-based fortunes via easy access to cheap land and resources in the former colonies *and/or* the opportunity to emigrate to more favorable industrial labor markets elsewhere. "From this growing lack of mobility, with its consequent diminution of opportunity to seek a fortune, work has lost its thrill as the means of acquiring wealth and social position" (Durant, 1938: 14). Having lost the rationale for their existence, workers now looked to what Durant called the "Machinery of Amusement," a new and growing vortex of industries based on the spectacle, excitement and escape. These popular mass entertainment industries were perceived as a *problem* and therefore fit to be addressed by sociologists because, no matter how popular they were, they did not solve the problem they addressed. Rather than solve the problem of alienation in the workplace and in modern life generally, the new leisure industries, particularly cinema, offered workers unrealistic expectations in the form of dreams of individual salvation through romantic love (meeting the wealthy husband, for example), finding a fortune through unswerving self-advancement, making it to the top from nowhere as an entertainer or sports personality, plus other dreams of life in the newly constituted world of Hollywood lifestyle, luxurious idle living and celebrity.

For Durant these were trivial, inauthentic and unrealistic leisure life worlds for ordinary workers to inhabit and could only lead to further disappointment, alienation, and moral decay. Against the extension of further "machinery for amusement" (the highest expression of which was to be found in such holiday resorts as Blackpool and Margate—see Franklin [2003a]), Durant argued the case for local authorities to supplant commercial forms of leisure provision with those that would be healthy and improving, "an Institute providing free or very cheap facilities for indoor sports, lectures, committee and rehearsal rooms and a theatre; in short, all those premises and accessories which constitute the framework necessary for encouraging initiative and enterprise in organizing spontaneous leisure" (Durant, 1938: 254). In other words, if work itself lacked the possibility for creativity then it is preferable for leisure to be creative and healthy rather than passive and voyeuristic. A similar view was expressed in France in the early 1960s. According to Urbain (cited in Doquet and Evrard, 2008), the sociologist of leisure Joffre Dumazadier (1962) saw leisure "as something that was going to favor the loss of morality among citizens, leading to decadence and the breakdown of society" and further, in a manner identical to colleagues across the Channel, that "tourism was considered exclusively in relation to leisure, and leisure exclusively in terms of work."

In America, Boorstin's (1964) analysis of tourism maintained this essentially problematic essence of tourism but it was more sophisticated sociologically. Rather than relate the problem of leisure and tourism purely to workers' alienation in the work place and process, he considered the wider and emerging culture around them, particularly as it constituted a visual habitus. The ubiquitous semiotics and simulacra of advertising and other distortions and exaggerations of reality (such as film, television, urban design and planning, entertainment, and tourist resorts) rendered the "real" invisible or unreal. Indeed the modern world had so distorted everything, with new materials and new designs and styles creating annual changes in the look of the world that one might say that the real was no longer actually discernible or relevant (hence heralding the postmodern). But, back in the early 1960s, the pace of change, the intensity of advertising and the playful world of consumer luxury that it created disturbed a sense of reality (or what Giddens, 1990: 257, later called "ontological security") among cultural commentators and academics. Boorstin's pseudo world was organized around what he called "pseudo-events" and the archetype, the worst case scenario, was tourism.

According to Boorstin, modern American consumers were so habituated to contrived and clearly constructed environments that the real world, as might be encountered on the social periphery or pleasure periphery beyond America, was problematic and difficult to cope with for tourists. The solution was thus, clearly, to contrive specially touristic settings, stage familiar activities inside the protected and much managed spaces of tourism or "tourist bubbles" and prevent too much contact with reality on the outside. Then, over time the various manifestations of ideal tourism settings and action became the basis upon which tourism per se became selected and evaluated; an entirely new form of social space ("sights" especially) built around the "pseudo-event." But this very term carries a strong subjective evaluation of tourism and is unmistakably pejorative. It points to an assumed (rather than demonstrated) cultural idiocy of tourism and to a wider social pathology of modern consumer society. Interestingly, this seemed to find widespread agreement and threw up few other further pressing research questions to answer until

MacCannell (1976) questioned Boorstin's "idiocy" element in the tourist mentality.

Even as late as 1997, Crawshaw and Urry (1997: 178) could make the point that sightseeing "is commonly denigrated" as "irreducibly superficial" and they relate this to the commonly held view that the purely visual "is not seen as the noblest of the senses in travel, but one which would get in the way of what are deemed to be real experiences, which ideally should involve a variety of senses." This is certainly evident in the scathing attack on tourism by John Carroll (1980). However, it may not have been sight and the visual sense that was the problem so much as the passivity and voyeurism that it suggested. He repeats the content of Durant's objection to the "machinery of amusement" (particularly cinema) which he felt could be put right by providing the opportunity for workers to write and perform their own dramas. Dean MacCannell's (1976) *The Tourist* is a landmark study in the sociology of tourism because for the first time it was interested in what tourists *actually did* and their *motives* for it. It provided the platform for tourist studies because it linked forms of modern tourism with more universal forms of human culture, thus enrolling interest from ethnographers, anthropologists, and cultural sociologists ever since. It set in motion a series of books and articles that established a broadly agreed upon agenda of research that occupied much of the 1980s and 1990s, particularly after the publication of John Urry's *Tourist Gaze*. Together, MacCannell and Urry established a first wave of sociological theories of tourism which dominated debates and research until relatively recently.

The 'First Wave' Sociology of Tourism: Dean MacCannell and John Urry

Against Boorstin, MacCannell suggested that tourists were not passive or locked inside "pseudo events" but in fact the opposite: they were searching, in their own way, for universal truths, authentic expressions of the world and in this way their behavior was sociologically related to a range of other ritual and cultic practices involving carnival, pilgrimage and even homage. Nonetheless, while MacCannell argued for a more active and interested tourist, he retained the social alienation thesis that provides the motive for travel. MacCannell's (1976) *The Tourist* has to be judged in this context. Viewed from the position of American sociological theory at the time it was not surprising that it problematized and tried to explain tourism almost as a *deviant* activity, a somewhat disturbing behavior resulting from the alienation and cultural disturbance of modernization and modern social relations. Tourism was treated somewhat clinically as a necessary period of recovery from the intolerable conditions of modern life, not as Boorstin had it, a mirror image; a comfy extension. Some of the classical anxieties of 1960s sociology were wrapped up in this book: alienated workers, dysfunctional family life, and a world of synthetic unreality, a highly differentiated and fragmented world ruled by rationalized and bureaucratized procedures. In comparison with premodern cultures where the individual was locked into a stable and secure social framework, the modern individual was at sea, looking for meaningfulness and finding it the categorical, invariant opposites of modernity: the past, the exotic other, pristine nature. In short, MacCannell declared the modern world to be inauthentic and troubling and tourism was the somewhat pathetic and pointless search for the authentic and an antidote of some short-lived kind.

While plausible in itself, MacCannell's 1976 book left tourism characterized in very much the same manner it was found: a marginal, somewhat spurious escape attempt from some notional true reality, whether unsavory or not. It is all the more surprising then how this thesis and the authentic–inauthentic dualism continues to be drawn upon as a way of explaining tourism behavior or at least the taxonomy of tourist objects. Franklin and Crang (2001) argued that it was indicative of the stagnant or withering state of tourist studies at the turn of the twenty-first century. In the absence of many other general theories of tourism researchers are more or less obliged to refer to it. Of course the better studies refused to see tourists as cultural dupes, preferring to acknowledge a commonplace sense of ironic self-deception among tourists (see Cohen and Taylor, 1976; Feifer, 1986; Urry, 1990). Conceptualizing tourism and tourists as intellectually challenged and culturally vacuous is still extremely common but also revealing of something important, as will be discussed a bit later.

Accounts influenced by the philosopher Fredrick Nietzsche argue that capitalist societies of the West have trapped people inside the disciplines of work and education and buried them inside a bureaucratic and stifling culture of control. These accounts underline the manner by which a so-called true human nature has been constrained and needs to be released for more creative, physically demanding and less inhibited activities. Tourism in particular is identified as a principal escape valve of this sort. This is nowhere better demonstrated than in Cartmill's analysis of the dominant hunting and outdoor leisure activities in the USA, and the development of the national park areas and policy debates that even drew in presidents (Cartmill, 1993). After all, does not tourism take place outside normal everyday disciplines and beyond the gaze of everyday surveillance? Is not tourism characterized by a greater tolerance for sexual freedom, gambling, fooling around, adventure, drug taking, drinking, and looser controls over the purse strings? Other accounts, while not emphasizing this liberational rationale, nonetheless take as axiomatic that tourism provides a compelling series of pleasures derived through relief from the monotony of everyday life. So, in Urry's (1990) account, tourism is explained in terms of the pleasureabilty of the different and the unusual. How else are we to explain the somewhat

bizarre objects that tourists will pay money to see? For Urry, the ultimate goal of tourists is to feast their eyes on different and unusual objects, landscapes and townscapes. It is as if these visions are a reward in themselves, visions that can be captured by visual technologies and stored and kept rather like any other commodity.

Urry's (1990, 2002) *The Tourist Gaze* is the other landmark in sociological theory development in tourism of this period, although it is a very different sort of thesis.

Urry does not offer a particularly clear link between tourism and the *conditions* of modern life, and certainly tourism is not explained as a *response* to the conditions of modern life. Rather, tourism is located very clearly as an emerging cultural activity in modernity and a positive outcome of modernity; it is clearly linked to the extension of leisure and holidays to workers, the democratization of travel (and security in travel), the extension of the Victorian notion of improvement and approved leisure activities, and also globalization. Writing in the late 1980s, Urry linked tourism theoretically to patterns of social change in the last quarter of the twentieth century. Urry does not provide a particularly clear explanation for touristic behavior per se and this is a weakness. Vague references to the pleasurability of "the different" and "the unusual" or the non-everyday only *asserts* some form of pleasurability from these abstract things, it does not account for them. However the implication is that there is something about the everyday that drives people to seek respite or escape, as if the everyday is, as earlier analysts described it, somehow problematic. Missing is an account of the aesthetic sensibilities of tourism, especially in the new tourisms of recent decades.

At best, Urry's account draws upon historical momentum in which the educated middle classes acted as the initial travelers and tourists, establishing a pattern of touristic consumption that working class and mass markets simply emulated and copied through critical innovations such as Thomas Cook's package tours. Here, though, the emphasis is on notions of personal improvement through education, experience, exposure to different places and people, and the pursuit of health and fitness—all established values of Victorian modernism. However, the implicit aesthetic content of this diffusion model is based upon the older notion of high and low culture: tourism offered those born to low culture the opportunity of glimpsing and being improved by icons and displays of high culture. As I have argued more recently, however, this diffusion model is plausible but problematic. In particular, it fails to take into account the reality that the non-traveling classes of the nineteenth century were suspicious of travel and of unfamiliar places and had to be persuaded using a mixture of rhetoric and inducement to leave the everyday where they were apparently happy to stay, if not always happy (Franklin, 2004: 288–296). Evidence for this came from those who attempted to tour in England at the end of the eighteenth century, only to find that local people were universally poor at directing people to places beyond their everyday and still worse at identifying aspects of travel that might in any way be diverting or pleasurable. It also came from those like Thomas Cook, who tried in the mid-nineteenth century to expand the traveling public beyond the social elite. He met with so much resistance and refusal, consistently, that he set himself the task, within his own considerable organization, of extolling the virtues of tourism through his writing, particularly in his *Excursionist* magazine. It was not appealing to existing desires but *persuading* people to do something *unappealing* and new.

The concept of pleasurable travel, then, did not exist for anyone other than the traveling classes of the aristocracy and bourgeoisie; according to Jean-Didier Urbain, many of whom traveled through France and earned for the English a reputation for being *singular* in this regard. Historically, most French and most other European people shared the same incredulity for such a bizarre

practices (see Doquet and Evrard, 2008). This shortfall notwithstanding, Urry's main contribution has focused on explaining why tourism expanded and became more fragmented into lifestyle niches from the 1980s onwards, an account that drew on important processes of economic restructuring and post-Fordism (Urry, 1990, 2002). Post-Fordist forms of production, which grew rapidly from the late 1970s, favored smaller, leaner and more flexible forms of production that could respond better to fluctuations in the shaky aftermath of the postwar boom economy and the growing power of consumers in the credit-rich affluent markets of the Western world. Under conditions of greater choice, greater credit and the break down of mass popular culture, individuals tended to identify less with older repositories of identity such as social class, political alignment gender, region and workplace and more in terms of lifestyle groups, with their emphasis on consumption, leisure and style. Tourism industries responded to the emergence and proliferation of lifestyle groups by providing a range of specialist niche markets, greater flexibility, choice, and self-direction. The tourism market became segmented into a series of consumer groups catering quite specifically to different tastes and styles. Again, early examples were based on the desire of young people to spend their holidays together. Age, income, class and occupation continued to frame broad patterns of taste, but other dimensions such as generation, sexual orientation, subculture, style, family cycle stage, leisure and enthusiasms provided templates for quite specific forms of consumption. Even though such a general characterization as this is widely agreed upon, it sits awkwardly with Urry's emphasis on the necessary pleasurability of difference and the unusual at the heart of the tourism experience. To a major extent then, tourism is *increasingly not* offering an essentially different or unusual set of experiences for tourists but, rather, is tailoring their experiences in line with their chosen forms of *everyday* culture: their style, their preferences, their fellow travelers their fantasies, taste and so on.

This problem at the heart of attempts to understanding tourism during this period, particularly its basis on a set of dualisms such as everyday: extraordinary, home: away, profane: sacred; inauthentic: authentic; routine/usual: special/unusual; mundane: excitement; work: pleasure and so on, was the belief that there was a fundamental and structural opposition between the spaces, times and processes of tourism and the spaces, times and processes of the everyday, that there was in other words a fundamental difference between them. As I have written elsewhere (Franklin, 2003a, 2004, 2006b, 2007; Franklin and Crang, 2001), it was almost as if the theoretical logic of tourism had to be revealed through this abstract theorizing rather than through reconstructing precise historical and cultural accounts of its emergence and operation. From the late 1990s it seemed flawed to a growing number of people whose critiques and re-theorizations might be dubbed the "new wave" in sociological studies of tourism. Leadership in this venture was not dominated by sociological theorizing or reworking older structural logics but by the careful assembly and consideration of the huge stockpile of evidence that had been generated by first wave studies. As such the contributors to this critical turn came from disciplines interested in tourism as well as newly formed areas/ departments of tourism studies. Much of this new wave addressed and critiqued the sociological foundations of the first wave and still drew much inspiration from contemporary sociological theory.

Whereas sociology had historically seen tourism as a corrosive force, at work against the successful improvement of modern society, other disciplines had developed their own accounts of its essentially destructive nature or tendency. Social anthropology imagined it destroying fragile cultures just as geography and environmental studies imagined it to be wasting sensitive ecosystems, ecologies and environments. Then, a variety

of scholars addressing the difficult and contentious globalization thesis saw tourism as virus-like, spreading the disease of western domination, human dedifferentiation (one of sociology's identifiers of postmodern times), senseless commodification, cultural cleansing, and ethnocide. It is a character so central to the historic development of tourism that it occupied an unequivocal position on the bad side of a good: bad dualism. It is tempting to see this view cynically, as an artifact of the social class of academic writers rather than the result of much generalized solid evidence, since, despite their great propensity to travel, few scholars are ever self-identifying tourists themselves in the same way that other commentators include themselves as consumers. Rather they would always be the travelers whose preferred places and haunts, and whose roads and trails, homes and villages are spoiled by the canker of tourism. As someone who has always enjoyed the spectacle of the tourist crowd, the impossible cultural compression of the airport and has even enjoyed the confining company of the contemporary cruise ship I find this intolerance hard to understand, particularly since an entire world enrolled into regular national and international tourism would seem, on the face of it, to be one of the great triumphs of modernity. At best this attitude seems to be a willful expression of elitism or nimbyism and barely stops to consider the wider benefits of a touristic world order. A more generous and open-minded view of tourism was one of the characteristics of the new wave (Franklin and Crang, 2001; Hollinshead, 2007; Picken, 2006; Tribe, 2005) or the "critical turn" as it has been called (Ateljevic et al., 2007; Tribe, 2005).

The New Wave

By the late 1990s, there was sufficient disaffection with the entrenched dualisms and the repetition of agreed assumptions in so much tourism research that several new projects took off. In some cases these were in the form of strikingly new papers, often drawing on leading edges of sociological theory and enquiry. Veijola and Jokinen's (1994) *The Body in Tourism* in *Theory, Culture and Society* drew inspiration from the newly formed sociology of the body to strike killer blows to the essentially *visual* and cognitive character of tourism theory. Whereas the tourist gaze was portrayed as fleeting, passive and shallow, engaged mainly with the semiotics of sites, the tourist body might linger slowly on a beach, yet be more active, as a physical, flirting, sexualized, drinking, dancing body directed to and engaged with other tourists" or local people's bodies. This was both semiotic and sensual; moreover this new perspective insisted it could not be clear (in advance) to the tourist what their experience as a tourist was or should be because, in addition to being embodied, it was also open-ended, experimental and *performed*. Precisely because tourism had to be performed by the embodied subject it could never be the passive, absorbing, disconnected, blank slate subjectivity posed by earlier notions of tourism. Rather, it was always in performance, choreographed by designers of sites and operators to be sure, but never completely, and never in a manner that was entirely dominant. As Alain de Botton (2002) reminds us, tourists may be tempted by the pure imagery of the brochure and the promise of its prose, believing that somehow their experience will match their dream and transform them completely, but they always, inadvertently, bring themselves along too. This subjective "baggage" might be the body still saddled with that nagging worry from work, or a discernible headache from an oncoming cold; you might bring with you a characteristic shyness that will make the experience highly interiorized, a tired body that simply seeks rest, or an active body that will seek excitement and boundaries anywhere. Yours might be a black body, a brown body or a pigmentless body—whatever the color might be, it is likely to *matter*, both in terms of performances by and for you, as it has, for example, in relation to the cult of sunbathing in different cultures and places.

Later papers developed the theme of performance as an essential ingredient of tourism. It related well to other insights that attempted to show that the tourism experience was at least partly constituted by what tourists brought with them to the site, that the site was only part of a wider subjective and constructed landscape of tourism, where the everyday and the extraordinary, the home and away and the profane and the sacred were *in dialogue*, rather than *in contrast* (see Crouch [Chapter 5] as well as Edensor [Chapter 30] in this *Handbook*). Yet even this conception is deficient when it fails to take in the *experimental* character of tourism that results from the freedom to pursue *alternative* identities, personalities, and performances. As Löfgren (1999: 6–7) put it, we might ". . . view vacationing as a cultural laboratory where people have been able to experiment with new aspects of identities, their social relations or their interaction with nature . . . Here is an arena in which fantasy has become an important social practice."

Other projects under the new wave included the launch of new tourism journals dedicated not so much to the encouragement of tourism research, for there was plenty (a surplus?) of that, as to theoretical and conceptual *development*. *The Journal of Tourism and Cultural Change* and *Tourist Studies*, for example, both encouraged researchers and authors to view tourism less as a phenomenon that was understood and predictable and governed by a set of known parameters and processes, and more as a dynamic and complex multiplicity whose understanding had barely begun.

Launching *Tourist Studies*, the editors attempted to identify a set of problems characterizing tourism research and theory in the early 2000s. They began by identifying three general problems (Franklin and Crang, 2001). First, that tourism research had grown so rapidly that it had been unable to develop the concepts and theory necessary to make sense of its massive stockpiles of data. Worse it had developed an uncritical and descriptive style of writing that was becoming maddeningly repetitive. Second, that its theoretical base was relatively narrow and based on a very few, largely dated ideas and that the transmission of new ideas elsewhere was not getting through. Third, in the absence of finer theoretical appreciation of tourism, researchers had resorted to an endless and unproductive elaboration of typologies and ever-finer subdivisions of experience. While this is not bad in itself, it is not sufficient in itself: it was a mix of "flatfooted sociology and psychology" or the "unhappy marriage between marketing research and positivist ambitions of scientific labeling" (Löfgren, 1999: 267).

Gathering together ideas that had been brewing in the more creative edges of tourism and travel studies, Franklin and Crang identified several important departure points for a new wave they were trying to create. This sense of a plurality of departure points was important because they emphatically argued against the search for a singular account of, or explanation for, tourism and any singular solution that simply supplanted, say, the *resort cycle model* or the *tourist gaze*. This is because a great deal is happening in the social spaces of tourism and it needed unpacking and elaborating rather than being reduced differently or even further. It was also needed because tourism in a globalizing world is a dynamic and disturbing force in which new spaces and people are enrolled in new and changing circumstances, and a whole host of desires become subject to conflicting and contested patterns of promotion and control. Franklin and Crang's (2001) departure points included:

- the problem of locating tourism practices in a social field (specifically, avoiding the production

of a "rarefied language of commentary" that obscures "lay and popular knowledges produced through tourism");
- reconfiguring the everyday–extraordinary dualism (as the "extraordinary everyday") which recognizes that tourism or touristic experience is now everywhere; re-conceiving tourism as a routinized world of flows rather than activities on the social periphery or margin;
- recognizing that tourism operates in and through the body and not merely as a visual and mental register;
- realizing that the pleasurability of being a tourist is not confined to being away in a new and unusual place (i.e., through the experience of difference) but through the embodied expression of many potential desires, movements and excitements (many of which remain familiar and some of which arise through cultural hybridization);
- recognizing that tourism is not, predominantly a semiotic field of representations but also, crucially a theatre of enactment, performance and agency (Edensor, 1998, 2001a, 2001b)— and not merely in the humanist sense of humans among themselves, for clearly new research inspired by Deleuze and Guattari has become interested in the distribution and dispersal of action in which humans and nonhumans have affect and agency, and accounts not merely of being but of becoming (Fullagar, 2000). This research could be inspired by John Law's (1994) call for sociology of verbs rather than nouns, of doing and acting rather than being. This represented a call for a different form of anthropology or ethnography which searches less for meaning and more for new and painstaking descriptions of action. In many ways this was, as Latour has argued, a case for anti-theory (since there is nothing particularly hidden that we need theory to uncover).

The New Wave in tourism studies was an enormous undertaking and its results are reworking the terrain and landscape, as well as the discourse, of tourism. We can no longer cast the tourist as a cultural dupe or tourism itself as a singular and negative force unleashed on the world. Rather, as Franklin (2003a) argues, tourism has reconfigured our stance to a globalizing world, taught many people the repertoires of performance in a world which is generally fluid or liquid, in which most things and people are encountered as flows from elsewhere, which also become constituted in the everyday. Without tourism our ability to cope with the enormous flows of people and commodities would be less refined and arguably more fragile and tense. For clearly, as Bauman (2003—but see also Franklin, 2003b) argues, contemporary Western cities are characterized both by "mixophilia," where cultural aestheticization takes root when encountered and known forms of difference become valued and appreciated but also "mixophobia" where the opposite, cultures of fear, take root in the absence of appropriate opportunities for encounter or where flows outpace encounters. This is what Hollinshead (2007: 187) and his oft-cited source Meethan (2001) surely mean by tourism as *worldmaking*: "tourism is an immense agent in the worldmaking dynamics of change and transformation which are currently occurring to places and to cultures in the globalized world . . . tourism works in and alongside other processes to help transform places, all manner of new forms of creolization, hybridization, and of indigenization are being produced which have yet been scarcely identified . . ." It is very unlikely that without tourism such effects would have been created but tourism is curiously also something we take very much for granted and its origins and early worldmaking beginnings are also scarcely identified.

As I tried to show in my *Tourism* book (Franklin, 2003a) cities have become entirely touristic in the sense that they are spaces of flows, of objects, peoples and cultures. They market themselves in a touristic manner not only to visitors but to local people also. Tourism assists us in living in large complex modern cities because it provides repertoires of action and behavior to cope with such traffic but also to be *comfortable* amongst it and even stimulated by it. It is now so important in fact, as a globally desirable sensibility, that cities have to be made in the likeness of

tourist spaces, they encourage an open, tolerant manner and deliberately frame social and cultural difference as an attraction (see Franklin, forthcoming).

Nationalisms and Orderings

The perfect chapter on the sociology of tourism would somehow now, in the limited space left, work in as many examples and dimensions of research that exemplify the New Wave tourism sociology as possible, but in a way these lists are already available in the annals of *Tourist Studies* and other journals and in new books in this area, such as Ateljevic et al.'s (2007) *The Critical Turn in Tourism Studies*. Instead I want to conclude in a more specific way, by picking up and extending Hollinshead's points (above) about *worldmaking* and also our typical failure to identify it.

With this particular "new wave" we are in some danger of talking ourselves out of grand theory and grand narratives for tourism, as if they were essentially what were wrong with the first wave. That is true to a degree. However, providing we are not trying to reduce tourism to the structural logic of a few binary dualisms, and providing we do ask what tourism does, in addition to what it means, we ought to be on firm ground when we pose questions about tourism's wider social role and impacts. The new wave did temper the essentially negative character of tourism as a form of social action and suggested the true story is far messier and inconclusive. It also suggested that tourism was a more central and organizing social process than had been hitherto believed. Tourism was rescued from a position on the social margin and spatial periphery and shown to be more evenly distributed and perhaps more central to the heart of successful cities and creative industries than was formerly supposed (Florida, 2003; Landry, 2000; O'Connor and Wynne, 2000). The question this evokes is, how can we conceptualize tourism as a social process of *worldmaking*? While we can follow Hollinshead's notion of tourism disturbing local and regional social relations, warping, mixing, and hybridizing a series of largely unintended effects as it proceeds, how can we take into account the *intentional* qualities of tourism as well its *wider unintended effects* when, to all intents and purposes, agency is so widely distributed? I have argued in a different paper that the sociology of orderings offers a valuable means of understanding tourism as an expanding network of distributed agency that nonetheless fits all the criteria of an "ordering" (Franklin, 2004).

The sociology of orderings arose out of the widespread discomfort with structural understandings of social order. It is a mix of Foucauldian perspectives, and the relational materialism of Law, Latour, and Deleuzian philosophy. From Foucault comes the idea that the world is ordered even if there is not stable or achieved *order*. Rather there are discernible ordering attempts through history, many of which fail and many of which are unleashed against other orders but which nonetheless operate "out there" and have a social life of varying lengths of time. According to Kendall and Wickham (2001: 5) orderings are any attempts to control, organize, and manage, but they are never simple entities; they are materially heterogeneous, including machines and technologies, texts and administrative systems. Without these entities, human ordering attempts would have little impact on ordering the world. However, with them, and especially sophisticated networks of them, orderings are not only possible but can create new unintended effects due their combinations. Once unleashed on the world, any such ordering attempts are active rather than passive, and dynamic rather than stable. Following Deleuze and Guattari (1999), orderings are said to possess the quality of *becoming*, tracing lines of flight as their rhizomic assemblages interact with other orderings, enrolling new elements, cancelling others, expanding, contracting and changing over time.

Can tourism be thought of like this? It can perhaps be argued so in at least two senses. The first sense is in terms of how we investigate any one discrete tourist site, activity, place, or organization but also spaces of mobility, such as airports, cars, coaches, planes, boats, highways, routes, and itineraries. Here Law's (2001) essay on "machinic pleasure" serves as a place to start or the recent work on automobility published in *Theory, Culture and Society* (see, for instance, the 2004 Vol. 21, Issue 4/5 special issue on problematizing cultural knowledge). Second, world tourism itself can be thought of in these terms, historically and presently as an ordering of global space. It is a fundamentally *connected* rhizomic entity, even if it is extremely large, and it is an *organized* entity even if is comprised of many organizations. From the earliest days of modern tourism, perhaps a founding part of it was the establishment of timetables and schedules of timetables that allow the tourist or agent to plot an itinerary that connects many places, carriers, travel organizations, technologies, cultures, businesses, and nationalities. We take this for granted but I have attempted to show in my ordering paper just how important Thomas Cook was to this ordering and how many other orderings his had to tackle before it could create the effects it intended (Franklin, 2004). He was not merely the innovator of travel and tourism, innovating the world's first international system of credit; he was also credited with making the British Empire possible and was dubbed travel agent to the British Empire.

Once tourism was unleashed on the world, particularly in the form of capitalist organizations, its only logic or option was to expand and it was expanding into a world that had never experienced the sorts of connectivity it was to usher in. It connected a great many other orderings in the form of markets and governmental territories that had hitherto reached their outer limits but which could now consolidate, providing this travel ordering was maintained at all cost. International shipping, then airlines, and now Internet and computer networks have made this connectivity all the more powerful and simultaneous. The tourism ordering was in part a project establishing a *smoothness* of travel connections and conditions in a world whose mobilities were largely ungoverned or unordered (rough to say the least) up to then; it was now a world network of spaces in travel—places of travel and spaces of mobility in a world hitherto consisting only of the everyday, bounded universes of the (largely) sedentary.[1]

All this however was only secondary to, and perhaps the artifact or ordering effect of, a far more important ordering, namely the ordering of a traveling global public. How was it that, suddenly, ordinary, hitherto non-traveling cultures became traveling cultures; how did they acquire an inbuilt yearning and wish to see other places? Was it because their everyday was so much worse than before or was it that a widening, expanding world interpellated them? And if it was the latter, how did that happen?

The tourism ordering attempts of Thomas Cook and a few others around the same time were not simply providing something that was wanted, rather the opposite. When they first forwarded the idea of tourism it was scorned and rejected widely. As the early tourist-explorers such as John Bying found in the UK, a traveling and touristic mentality simply did not exist (Adamson, 1996). As Urbain argued recently in an interview:

In Europe, the specificity of the tourist was not recognized until the end of the eighteenth century. No earlier trace can be found anywhere. It is worth recalling Gustave Flaubert's anecdote about the tourist trip he took to Brittany with his friend Maxime Ducamp in 1847 (Flaubert, 1989: 234). On arriving in one village, they found it impossible to convince the inhabitants that they were traveling simply for pleasure. They were taken for spies, surveyors, cartographers, government road inspectors or controllers checking on the work of lighthouse keepers. In the end, they had to invent an official purpose for their visit, a function, a utility, to cease being incomprehensible, and therefore suspicious, in the eyes of the villagers. (cited in Doquet and Evrard, 2008: 37)

As with Hollinshead's notion of tourism as *worldmaking*, the process that was to hail ordinary Europeans beyond the safe confines of their localities and create the desire to visit other places was not the provision of transportation to do so, for that predated the idea of using it as such by a long time. Nor was it emulation of the traveling social elite, for ordinary people were quite resistant to the idea even when it was presented to them as a possibility. The ordering that created the possibility of a traveling public was nationalism or nation formation because it was only after the creation of nations, and its inhabitants as *citizens* of the wider social formation that nations encompassed and promoted, that a world beyond their everyday localities or where they made their living became relevant to them. As Gellner (1983) argued, national formation created nationalism and not the other way around; nation formation called into being forms of nationalism precisely because there was very little prior social solidarity among such far flung peoples. A wide variety of technologies beside travel made this sense of belonging to a wider social formation possible (the development of better printing presses the publication of national histories, folklore, natures geographies and national education schemes, for example) but it was also galvanized and consolidated by the building of spectacles and monuments of nation that were intended to be visited pilgrim-like, in much the same way that the Anglo Saxon kings used pilgrimage and the building of cathedrals and saints" shrines to produce webs and trails of belonging (Wood, 2000).

The incredible and unpredicted arrival of Thomas Cook's travel and tourism ordering appeared before the full force of European nation formation took place and this partly accounts for his early difficulties in growing the company, but the two orderings were more synchronized across Europe in the latter half of the nineteenth century and fully global by the first quarter of the twentieth century. At that point Thomas Cook operated around the world, and the world was more or less fully connected by a constantly expanding travel and tourism network. It may have been nationalism that prized many people from their more parochial village and city lifestyles and constructed national territories into spectacles to visit and appreciate. However it was tourism that extended that generalized curiosity for the world and indeed created a sense of the world that one also belonged to—a world, in other words, that *beckoned*.

Notes

1 Clifford's salutary correction of the myth of the essentially sedentary nature of premodern cultures is well taken here. Nonetheless, despite not being sedentary he was not saying they were touristic, which I take to be the desirability of travel for its own sake. See J. Clifford "Traveling Cultures." In L. Grossberg, C. Nelson and P.A. Treichler (Eds.), *Cultural Studies*. New York: Routledge.

References

Adamson, D. (Ed.) (1996). *Rides Round Britain by John Byng*. London: The Folio Society.

Ateljevic, I., Morgan, N. and Pritchard, A. (Eds.) (2007). *The Critical Turn in Tourism Studies: Innovative Research Methodologies*. London: Elsevier.

Bauman, Z. (1998). *Globalisation*. Cambridge: Polity.

Bauman, Z. (2000). *Liquid Modernity*. Cambridge: Polity.

Benjamin, W. (1955). *Illuminations*. London: Jonathon Cape

Boorstin, D. (1964). *The Image: A Guide to Pseudo Events in America*. New York: Harper.

Bukart, A.J. and Medlik, S. (1974). *Tourism: Past, Present and Future*. London: Heinemann.

Carroll, J. (1980). *Sceptical Sociology*. London: Routledge and Kegan Paul.

Cartmill, M. (1993). *View to a Death in the Morning*. Cambridge, MA: Harvard University Press.

Cohen, S. and Taylor, L. (1976). *Escape Attempts*. London: Routledge.

Coleman, S. and Eade, J. (2004). *Reframing Pilgrimage—Cultures in Motion*. London: Routledge.

Cooper, C., Fletcher, J., Gilbert, D. and Wanhill (1998). *Tourism: Principles and Practice*. Harlow, Essex: Pearson Education Ltd.

Crawshaw, C. and Urry, J. (1997). "Tourism and the Photographic Eye." In C. Rojek and J. Urry (Eds.), *Touring Cultures* (pp. 176–195). London: Routledge.

de Botton, A. (2002). *The Art of Travel*. London: Hamish Hamilton.

Deleuze, Giles and Guattari, Felix (1999). *A Thousand Plateaus*. London: Athlone Press.

Doquet, A. and Evrard, O. (2008). "An Interview with Jean-Didier Urbain." *Tourist Studies*, 8(2): 34–48.

Dumazedier, J. (1962). *Vers une société du loisir?* Paris: Le Seuil.

Durant, H. (1938). *The Problem of Leisure*. London: George Routledge and Son.

Edensor, T. (1998). *Tourists at the Taj: Performance and Meaning at a Symbolic Site*. London: Routledge.

Edensor, T. (2001a). "Performing Tourism, Staging Tourism: (Re)Producing Tourist Pace and Practice." *Tourist Studies*, 1(1): 59–81.

Edensor, T. (2001b). "Walking in the British Countryside: Reflexivity, Embodied Practices and Ways to Escape." In P. Macnaghten and J. Urry (Eds.), *Bodies of Nature*. (pp. 81–106). London: Sage.

Feifer, M. (1986). *Tourism in History*. New York: Stein and Day.

Flaubert, G. (1885/1989). *Voyage en Bretagne. Par les champs et par les grèves*, Brussels: Ed. Complexe.

Florida, R. (2003). *The Rise of the Creative Class*. London: Pluto.

Franklin, A.S. and Crang, M. (2001). "The Trouble with Tourism and Travel Theory?" *Tourist Studies*, 1(1): 5–22.

Franklin A.S. (2001). "The Tourist Gaze and Beyond: An Interview with John Urry." *Tourist Studies*, 1(2):115–131.

Franklin, A. S. (2002). *Nature and Social Theory*. London: Sage.

Franklin, A.S. (2003a). *Tourism*. London: Sage.

Franklin, A.S. (2003b). "The Tourism Syndrome: An Interview with Zygmunt Bauman." *Tourist Studies*, 3(2): 205–218.

Franklin, A.S. (2004). "Towards a New Ontology of Tourism: Tourism as an Ordering." *Tourist Studies*, 4(3): 277–301.

Franklin, A.S. (2006a). "The Humanity of the Wilderness Photo." *Australian Humanities Review*, 28(April): 1–16.

Franklin, A.S. (2006b). "Tourism." In C. Rojek, S. Shaw and A. Veal (Eds.), *Handbook of Leisure Studies* (pp. 386–403). London: Palgrave MacMillan.

Franklin, A.S. (2007). "The Problem with Tourism Theory." In I. Ateljevic, A. Pritchard, and N. Morgan (Eds.), *The Critical Turn in Tourism Studies* (pp. 131–148). Oxford: Elsevier.

Franklin, A.S. (forthcoming). *City Life*. London: Sage.

Fullagar, S. (2000). "Desiring Nature: Identity and Becoming in Narratives of Travel." *Cultural Values*, 4(1): 58–76.

Gellner, E. (1983). *Nations and Nationalism*. London: Basil Blackwell.

Graburn, N. (1978). "Tourism: The Sacred Journey." In V. Smith (Ed.), *Hosts and Guests*. Philadelphia: University of Pennsylvania Press.

Hollinshead, K. (2007). "Worldmaking and the Transformation of Place and Culture." In I. Ateljevic, A. Pritchard and N. Morgan (Eds.), *The Critical Turn in Tourism Studies* (pp. 165–196). Oxford: Elsevier.

Judd, D.R. and Fainstein, S.S. (Eds.) (1999). *The Tourist City*. New Haven, CT: Yale University Press.

Kendall, G. and. Wickham, G. (2001). *Understanding Culture: Cultural Studies, Order, Ordering*. London: Sage.

Landry, C. (2001). *The Creative City: A Toolkit for Urban Innovators*. London: Earthscan.

Law, J. (1994). *Organizing Modernity*. Oxford: Blackwell.

Law, J. (2001). "Machinic Pleasures and Interpellations." Centre for Science Studies and the Department of Sociology, Lancaster University.

Löfgren, O. (1999). *On Holiday: A History of Vacationing*. Berkeley: University of California Press.

Lury, C. (1997). "The Objects of Travel." In C. Rojek and J. Urry (Eds.), *Touring Cultures*. London: Routledge.

MacCannell, D. (1976). *The Tourist: A New Theory of the Leisure Class*. New York: Schocken.

MacCannell, D. (1992). *Empty Meeting Grounds: The Tourist Papers*. London: Routledge.

Mathieson, A. and Wall, G. (1982). *Tourism: Economic, Physical and Social Impacts*. London: Longman Cheshire.

Meethan, K. (2001). *Tourism in a Global Society*. Aldershot: Palgrave.

O'Connor, J. and Wynne, D. (Eds.) (2000). *From the Margins to the Centre: Cultural Production and Consumption in the Post-industrial City*. London: Arena.

Picken, F. (2006). "From Tourist Looking-glass to Analytical Carousels: Navigating Tourism through Relations and Context." *Current Issues in Tourism*, 9(2): 158–170.

Rojek, C. (1993). *Ways of Escape*. London: MacMillan.

Rojek, C. (1995). *Decentring Leisure: Rethinking Leisure Theory*. London: Sage.

Shaw, G. and Williams, A. (1994). *Critical Issues in Tourism*. Oxford: Blackwell.

Sheller, M. and Urry, J. (2004). *Places to Play, Places in Play*. London: Routledge.

Shields, R. (1991). *Places on the Margin*. London: Routledge.

Simmel, G. (1997a). "The Alpine Journey." In D. Frisby and M. Featherstone (Eds.), *Simmel on Culture* (pp. 219–220). London: Sage.

Simmel, G. (1997b). "The Adventure." In D. Frisby and M. Featherstone (Eds.), *Simmel on Culture* (pp. 221–232). London: Sage.

Smith, V. (Ed.) *Hosts and Guests*. Philadelphia, PA: University of Pennsylvania Press.

Tribe, J. (2005). "New Tourism Research." *Tourism Recreation Research*, 30(2): 5–8.

Urbain, J.-D. (2003). *At the Beach*. Minneapolis: Minnesota University Press.

Urry, J. (1990). *The Tourist Gaze*. London: Sage.

Urry, J. (1991). *The Tourist Gaze*. London: Sage.

Urry, J. (2002). *The Tourist Gaze* (2nd edition.). London: Sage.

Veijola, S. and Jokinen, E. (1994). "The Body in Tourism." *Theory, Culture and Society*, 11: 125–151.

Voase (1995). *Tourism: The Human Perspective*. London: Hodder and Stoughton.

Weaver, D. and Oppermann, M. (2000). *Tourism Management*. Brisbane: John Wiley.

Wood, M. (2000). *In Search of England*. Harmondsworth: Penguin.

The Diverse Dynamics of Cultural Studies and Tourism

David Crouch

Introduction

To the extent that tourism may be conceptualized as culture, the work of "cultural studies" is germane to an understanding of tourism, what happens *in* tourism, and the meanings it holds for both tourists and non-tourists. This chapter addresses the key threads of the dynamic relationships between the field of cultural studies and the conceptual work which is being undertaken to explain the dynamics of tourism. Conceptual developments in both arenas of intellectual activity have been rapid and complex. This chapter identifies dimensions of each arena where interactions and developments have taken place.

A core theme of the chapter is the convergence and multidisciplinarity of debates surrounding cultural studies amongst both the social sciences and humanities in recent decades. This theme is necessarily reflected in the influences and congruences relating to tourism studies that are conferred by this convergence and multidisciplinarity. Necessarily, this chapter does not attempt to be exclusive, but rather focuses on the dynamic character of the progressive debates that mutually relate cultural studies and tourism studies to one another.

In particular, this entails consideration of the debates regarding: the character, content and dynamic of the ways in which culture works; issues relating to representation, context, and subcultures and their emergence in examinations of heritage, identity and authenticity in tourism; conceptual discussions on practice and so-called "nonrepresentational" cultural theory and; critical thinking on consumption.

As this chapter unfolds, tourism will be described as the ongoing outcome of complex and dynamic cultural processes, in varying degrees attached and detached from their surrounding influences. Given that anthropology has consistently shaped the theoretical grasp of culture, cultural structure, and change, it is unsurprising that tourism has been a focus on attention within anthropology for decades (see, for instance: Bruner, 2005; Clifford, 1997; Cohen, 2004, Graburn, 1983; MacCannell, 1999; Nash, 1981; Selwyn, 1996; Smith, 1977), and arguably anthropologists have provided the most sustaining critical edge to the conceptualization of tourism (Selwyn, 1996). While this should be acknowledged, it is also necessary and legitimate to consider cultural studies as an important framework for examinations of tourism as a significant and popular "cultural" phenomena and a major marker of modernity (MacCannell, 1999).

At this juncture it is useful to note that cultural studies is usually taken to refer to a mode of inquiry which itself eclectically draws upon a number of different disciplines, methods and theoretical perspectives (sociology, communication and media studies, literary criticism, political economy, etc.) to analyze cultural forms in societies (Kraniauskas, 1998). It is widely taken to have its roots in the formation of the Centre for Contemporary Cultural Studies (CCCS) at the University of Birmingham in the UK in 1964, first under the leadership of Richard Hoggart and then Stuart Hall. The works of Richard Hoggart (b. 1918), Stuart Hall (b. 1932) and E.P. Thompson (1924–1993) are considered to among the foundational texts of cultural studies (all three theorists were associated with CCCS, which also came to be known as the Birmingham School of Cultural Studies or simply the Birmingham School). Cultural studies is both an outcome from, and a formative influence on, the so-called "cultural turn" (Hall, 2007), where culture and its meanings have been privileged as foci of academic study. While there is overlap between anthropology and cultural studies, the latter can be said to focus more (though not exclusively) upon the immediate "modern" world, the popular, and the processes and practices of meanings, drawing heavily upon literary analysis, postmodern, and poststructuralist criticism.

Core themes in the study of tourism and tourists—such as claims of "authenticity," notions of the "sacred," cultures of hosts and guests, together with issues of gender, nationalism, class, ethnicity, displacement and diaspora, mythologies, semiotics, and the power of representation of peoples and places—are all enriched, it is argued, by a dynamic engagement with cultural studies as a multidisciplinary conceptual lens. At the core of this engagement is the search for meanings within tourism and how meanings and identities are constructed amongst individuals and in society as a whole.

Unevenness and Shifts in Cultural Studies

The explanatory power of cultural studies across disciplines and fields such as tourism has frequently been acknowledged in the last decade (Franklin and Crang, 2001). Emerging from literary criticism in the mid-twentieth century, cultural studies has itself continued to experience profound "turns," and is on these which this section directs its attention, providing as they do positioning directions and reflections for the rest of the chapter. These thrusts of the discipline concern the character, content and dynamic of the ways in which culture works. From the 1950s, cultural studies evolved from the study of culture through languages to take in more recent significant interventions from a diverse intellectual portfolio, which would include the work of Noam Chomsky and Michel de Certeau, among others.

F.R. Leavis, an early figure of British cultural studies and a literary scholar bound to the moral superiority of "high" culture, emphasized the idea of institutionalized culture in the forms of museum and gallery collections, historic houses, and motifs of royalty (Leavis, 1930). Such forms, he argued, were by consensus the very essence of culture and should be encouraged by government. By way of contrast, Raymond Williams (1958), in his influential work *Culture and Society,* argued that culture is "ordinary" (see McGuigan, 1992). Williams suggested that, rather than being dominantly contextualized by the media and its powerful representations of meaning, value and significance, culture was also constituted profoundly through what individuals did in their own lives. He acknowledged the dynamic interactivity of culture and economy, not its linear determination, which was also a significant theme in the work of historian E.P. Thompson (1963) at the time, and later in the work of Hoggart and Bishop (1985) who, working from a non-Marxian position, documented working-class culture as worthy of acknowledgement. Political critique of culture, from a leftist perspective, as exemplified by Thompson and Williams, is an important and inherent theme, particularly in European cultural studies and continues to be an important dynamic.

Debates on the position and role of culture in societies emerged at the height of the Frankfurt School of sociology, which soon became enmeshed with cultural studies during the 1950s and 1960s. The Frankfurt School of critical theory emerged out of early Hegelian Marxism and was the name associated with the Institute of Social Research that was founded in 1923 in Frankfurt, Germany. Among the most famous thinkers associated with this school of critical theory were Max Horkheimer, Theodor Adorno, Erich Fromm, Herbert Marcuse and the more contemporary German sociologist and philosopher, Jurgen Haberman (cf. Ritzer, 1996). Adorno, who is widely credited with first using the term "culture industry" in his essay on popular music (1941), together with Max Horkheimer, were prominent amongst the Frankfurt School in emphasizing the power of mass consumption, contextualized through representations, as well as ongoing class structure, and through advertising and mass media (McGuigan, 1992). Advertising was a major thrust of their research, but they also focused on the press, popular magazines, and popular music. Their analysis chimed with Williams' reading of popular culture and each was influenced by Marxist notions of the power of superstructure and of capital in framing lives. Raymond Williams however, insisted on the acknowledgement of the active interface between this "superstructure" and that of individuals, and communities' everyday lives, actions, relationships, which were spread more widely than the structural frameworks of capitalism. Williams, emphasized a culturalist perspective through the notion of "structures of feeling" (McGuigan, 1992). He acknowledged the ways in which individuals, as routinely interpreted by social anthropologists, constitute their lives through rituals and their living and active authenticity in everyday life, as typically studied in pre, and non-western cultures. The debate turned upon how far, and to what intensity, such routines can survive and be sustained in contemporary western societies. Williams' insistence that culture is ordinary asserted power amongst individuals less in the face of, but more in relation to, apparent structures of capitalist, market, institutional and governmental power and their traditions.

The sociologist Bourdieu (1984) similarly engaged with this debate up to a point in his work on "cultural capital." In his work he produced extensive evidence of the production and reproduction of cultural capital, of lifestyles and their accompanying values, significance, and above all for cultural studies, *meaning* in relation to individuals' everyday activities, as well as their educational background, employment, and prospects. While essentially a class-dominated perspective, Bourdieu accounted for the sustainability of distinctions of what he called "cultural capital" between discrete identities of individuals accordingly, denoted as "habitus." He also acknowledged the potential fissures that could develop in these apparently encased, self-perpetuating positions. Progress, opportunity, social mobility proffered the opportunity for individuals to crack the traditional frame of cultural categories.

Stuart Hall (1980), a major figure in British cultural studies, along with Dick Hebdige (1979) offered further possibilities in their examination of cultural diversity and of subcultures. During the 1970s and 1980s the apparently obvious framing of British class, in relation to the working class as being somehow hermetically sealed, became evidently limited as numerous diverse cultural distinctions produced themselves, if partly through an emphasis upon a cultural-political resistance. Britain was not alone in this as revolutionary intensity for difference persisted in numerous hybrid ways across at least the western world, following the post-1968 period. Thus, for instance, Hebdige was able to interpret Rastafarian, punk and other cultures among a wider raft of potentialities. One of the most significant contributions on the power of the state to shape culture was made by Stuart Hall, who persistently argued the power of the media in asserting right-wing values in the Reagan–Thatcher years.

Williams' notion of culture as ordinary, and these more recent evident diversities of possibility have further questioned the straight jacket of structural contexts, such as class, in constructing and constituting culture. At the same time, feminist and blacks in cultural studies made similar innovative critical interventions (Gilroy, 1987). Ironically, as this work was being developed the power of structures persisted in other distinctive arenas of cultural studies, and became adopted in fields such as cultural geography, and tourism studies and, arguably, have persisted more strongly in the latter.

The Debate About Representation and Context

Social anthropology, in its habitual study of non-western cultures, mobilized in the nineteenth century in the assertion of imperialism and its cultures, as well as genuine intellectual curiosity, drew attention to the ritualistic character of "indigenous" cultures. The distinction and cohesion of the latter was sustained and marked via a system of signs that signified their identity, and often became reified in relation to myths of existence (MacCannell, 1999). In the western world of the mid-twentieth century, if not earlier, the understood "signs" or codes of identity, ritual practice, and social relationships through culture became increasingly complex, codified and themselves signified in semiotics. A common sense and linear singularity of relationship between sign and its meaning became increasingly contestable. The cultural philosopher Roland Barthes critiqued and deconstructed such codes of meaning, signified perhaps for tourism in his paper "The Writer on Holiday" (1993a: 29–31) and also,

importantly, in his conceptual essay, "Myth Today" (1993b: 109–159). Barthes argued that signs and their significance exert no simple, "natural," or obvious, transfer of meaning between those who make, or reproduce and communicate it; rather, they may be used in diverse ways to intentionally distort and or create agendas. Tensions, both cultural and (if distinguishable) political, are apparent in Barthes' thesis.

There is a lingering linearity in the ways in which much translation, often away from the core disciplines such as anthropology and psychology and through which such critical readings emerge, to other fields of study. Cultural studies pursued its rigorous critical, contexting edge. In fields such as tourism studies, this edge was lost in an effort to demonstrate, and often to assert, the "natural," linear value of, for instance, the promotion of tourism's commercial "products"; where the word "products" is used to denote, for example, places, buildings, and destinations (Ringer, 1998). Alongside such unquestioning application has emerged a more alert critical study which has sought to translate threads of the power of signs to confer meaning, value, significance, often with the exertion of particular, selected meanings. This is exemplified in the work within the frequently visual-spatial science of the geographies of landscape and place (Cosgrove and Daniels, 1988). In such core works, the play of signs was significantly taken to be an exercise of power (Duncan and Ley, 1991). Brought home to tourist/m studies in recent years, literature makes a direct link between cultural studies and new explorations in cultural material and its semiotic values for tourism (Robinson and Andersen, 2002).

Such work mobilizes neo-Marxian positions concerning the exercise of power through communication, that loops back to such as Adorno, the mass consumption thesis and the deployment of the so-called "mass media" in an effort to influence, and to persuade "the public" audiences and consumers. Until recently, positions regarding the understandings of the media in tourism studies have lacked critical rigor, assuming as they have tended fairly simple causal relationships and the absence of understanding power relations (Hughes, 1998). Yet, crucially, across the wide raft of debate broadly within, or informed by, cultural studies' attention to culture in the "west" has shared a perspective of the overriding power, however critically asserted, to affect. Writers such as Britton (1991) and Meethan (2001), from geography and sociology respectively, have, more critically scoped the potential misapplication of apparently anodyne messaging and communication through signs and symbols of significance in their reference to global effects that surround the sign-mobilization of tourism corporations. And across all of these intellectual interventions there is a presumption of the performative power of institutions and their "purposeful," or at least intentional message. Thus there has emerged a pervasive notion that signs and representations work in messages of direct communication to consumers providing the essential context for action by consumers in tourism. Often empowered by its use of the visual, pictures (and now film and the Internet), frame and contextualize expectations, desires and choice within the market. Such a process can be used in a formulaic manner, in tourism, exemplified by the sign-power, with strong visual content in its messaging, of both the landscapes of the Disney corporation that "delivers" ever-continuing childhood happiness and, the power of heritage, and at least, what heritage stands for in contemporary culture (Phillips, 1999; Zukin, 1990).

Within the complex debate of cultural studies' arguments concerning the framing (perhaps determination), of meaning and value by the play of signs in contemporary culture, through the media via visual material and also language (exemplified in the influential critical political and cultural thinker Noam Chomsky), there has emerged a remarkable shift in thinking. As growing critical awareness of diversity in contemporary culture has surfaced tensions have opened in cultural studies through the claim that, as diversity has increased, it has erased traditional distinctions of culture (even those such as Bourdieu had analyzed), by means of the multiple cultural adjustments of the mid-twentieth century. Baudrillard (1981), perhaps high priest of sign-flattening and its detachment from everyday meaning and life, argued that the overwhelming power of the media and its signs further erased both traditional and recent distinctions of culture. He argued the importance of "strategies of desire" (1981: 85) through which individuals', consumers' (read "tourists") needs are mobilized, or provoked and their nascent interests captured in a process of consumption before consumption. In this strange assertion, he argued that signs as such no longer referred individuals to what they may have experienced. Power thus shifts from things, events, and objects themselves to their circulation in representations, their fuller consumption dominated by their sign-value and the value invested in anticipation. These strategies, Baudrillard argued, consist of the signs on which the value of products are conveyed in the process of seduction.

For tourism, these signs may include brochures of destinations, their power lying in and systematized by their display and communication. This emerges as the world of the hyper-real where individuals become reliant upon floating signifiers that relate only to the life proffered in the experience of the advertisement, the image, and so on; a form of high postmodernism. Human activity becomes secondary to the images that circulate in culture. Meaning, or "meaninglessness" is composed of these free-floating signifiers from which the world according to Baudrillard is "made sense" as being somewhat detached from what people seem to do. Experience and its quality is therefore "flattened" and life becomes only vicarious. The experience of tourism is best interpreted as the experience of the sign; the anticipation delivered in reading the brochure, for example, and thus relates to nothing else. Of course, postmodernism in cultural studies (as in a host of related disciplines) also acknowledges the erosion of difference between art and everyday life. For Baudrillard, arguably, there was no everyday life, only the artifice of its representation. Furthermore, such a position erases the need to confront the contentious notion of authenticity, another cultural icon of tourism studies. If nothing (at least of value) is "real," authenticity ceases to exist, at least in terms of MacCannell's argument (MacCannell, 1999). Ironically, in effect, such postmodern positions erase what is understood to be "value" in tourism. The individual does not "need" to go anywhere, or "do" anything.

Yet it is of continuing concern to tourism studies that the aspects of this debate on "only signs matter" (although postmodern theory argued that nothing mattered anyway) percolate thinking. For example, most notably, Urry (2002) argued that tourism, in cultural/social terms and life, is encapsulated in the "gaze," looking detachedly at signs, whether of touristic directions, building style, themed imagery, or the content of the Internet. Through a privileging of the notion of the "gaze" Urry largely understates any other power of vision; haptic, touching, caring, loving in character, as well as its potential opposites. This issue is pursued later in this chapter; however, it is important to note at this stage that Urry's discourse was much less shaped in relation to postmodern emptiness than his reading of Foucault, another powerful influence on cultural studies in the 1980s. Foucault (1970) sustained his major critical position through his work on institutional dominance, exemplified in surveillance, in the organization of society, bringing order into culture. Yet in his use of Foucault, Urry drew upon the old Renaissance notion of sight as the "noblest of the senses," a position in continual and appropriate speculation and revision. Mediated visual material may be more prevalent in contemporary culture, but does the gaze—by tourists, at signs provided by "the industry" in the wider sense—completely enframe the meaning, value and significance of what tourism is to the tourist? It is around this question, and other conceptualizations of moments of

ordering in tourists' "doing" that the remaining sections of this chapter attend to.

Aspects of the importance of signs in tourism had of course been discussed by social anthropologist Dean MacCannell (1999) who argued powerfully for acknowledgement of the signification of tourist sites as locations of the authentic; i.e., where people could—and want to—"feel" their lives authenticated, anxiously seeking the reflection of something authentic into their own lives as the "man in the mirror." Building his argument on the interpretation of tourism as sightseeing, MacCannell argues that the baggage of visual material is constructed to deliver the tourist what is understood to be authentic, even though this may be a staged authenticity, achieved through the skilful manipulation of artifacts and signs. Indeed, artifacts, even constructed ones, become translated into commodities for tourism and privileged as "markers." MacCannell terms this "constructed recognition." In his words: "Sightseers have the capacity to recognize sights by transforming them into one of their markers ... not permitted to attach the marker to the sight according to his own method of recognition" (1999: 123–124). Tourists' photographs, too, are programmed by markers; the so-called "Kodakization" of tourism, which clearly marks sites from which to see, the direction of view, even the framing in a circuit of signification. This contributes to an interpretation of the alienated modern individual, anxious for identity.

Destination, site, landscape, heritage, and "other" often regarded "static" content remains powerful in the ways in which places are inured in tourist seduction by contemporary capitalism—the business sector and its marketing (Selwyn, 1996). There is a rich and varied body of work exploring how tourist spaces have historically been (as increasingly they are today), deeply implicated in the formation of identities. In the British case, few historical examinations of the shaping of the identities and dispositions of the upper and upper-middle classes would be complete without exploring the influences of the Grand Tour and travel more generally, including travel to classical Mediterranean sites (Inglis, 2000). Likewise, no examination of the shaping of more contemporary identities could be framed without extensive reference to, for example, sites in the Caribbean, the Indian subcontinent, and/or (once again, although in a rather different way) the crowded shores of the Mediterranean, or temples and mosques, exemplified in the Taj Mahal (Edensor, 1998).

In a series of contributions, Urry (1995, 2002) has developed the notion of the tourist gazing through an increasingly subjective vein, offering increasing options of tourist categories to exemplify its variation (Crawshaw and Urry, 1997). The tourist, or better, the human subject doing tourism, is less duped than aware, less desperately needing identity than using tourism in the negotiation of identity. While Urry (2002) stays with an emphasis on the visual and its evolution through increasing mobility, easily related to aspects of tourism, he is increasingly nonetheless attuned to the incompleteness of vision alone.

Critically for Lash and Urry (1994), this "making use of signs out there" became a focus for the mental reflexivity of the subject's own life in a practice of postmodern subjectivities. Following Baudrillard's desire, this might suggest that people come to respond to their life through the provided spectoral seduction. The sociologists of culture Cohen and Taylor (1993) argue for a subject-centered and less dependent seduction in terms of a reverie of self-seduction in an escape in an everyday sense of wanting change, adjustment, rediscovery, in emotion, identity, and relations.

Tensions between contexts and what tourists may arguably "do" and make of what they do themselves, may be exemplified in the context-driven analyses of the dynamics of cultural economies (Zukin, 1995). In their wide-ranging discussion of economies of signs and space Lash and Urry discuss possible ways in which "the aesthetic reflexivity of subjects in the consumption of travel and the objects of cultural industries create a vast

real economy" (1994: 59, my emphasis), through their engagement in the flows of diverse cultural producers and mediators. Yet this "real economy"—of art galleries, bars, taxi drivers, and brokers—conceals the complexity of the cultural economy and refers, again, only to the institutions and their animateurs. The burden of debate so far has concerned the shift to mental reflexivity, where the available contextual signification may be subjectively, perhaps ironically, made sense of by the individual. However, in contradistinction to a "floating signs" perspective, it may be claimed that human subjects live their lives, live space, encounter each other, and work through their own lives in a negotiation of the world around them/us.

Discussions on Practice and So-Called 'Nonrepresentational' Cultural Theory

Bourdieu's concept of cultural capital prioritized the sustaining, often entrapping, of habitual social positions and relations in an ongoing, perpetually reasserted set of actions. These, he argues, are dominated by traditions of interaction involving "upbringing," education, job opportunity, and class, and all would, for example, be brought to bear through one's choice of holidays (Bourdieu, 1984). However, there is evidence that Bourdieu grasped the potential of breaking from these apparent constraints to enable a more progressive possibility, and perspective on identity processes. His work focused significantly on practice; things that people do, enact, and ritualize. Of course generations of social and material anthropologists have long acknowledged the importance of practices in the sustaining of cultures and their shared identities, but again, in terms of *sustaining* rather than enabling difference and diversity. However, it is through a consideration of practice in the sphere of the multidisciplinary emergence of cultural studies debates that we can rediscover ways in which culture is ordinary, and also diverse, replete with subcultural distinctions that entail class, but also gender, age, ethnicity, and their multiple intersections. Yet these characteristics alone are insufficient for grasping the cultural diversity at work. Tim Edensor, who has taken cultural studies much closer to tourism studies, created a subtle and powerful critical discourse concerning the complex interrelations between practice and contexts, and their representations, in his work on tourists at the Edensor (1998). He tracked and identified the diverse ways in which different groups of visitors make their way around the site; engage and modulate their identities; amble and queue and make sense of their experience and the spaces they occupy. Edensor has also written informatively concerning contexts and practices in his discourse on national identity and everyday life, exemplified in festivals and fashion (Edensor, 2002). These critical observations open the way to enable cultural studies' deal with (often in preference) for context to be engaged with its more recent contributions to making sense of meaning, value, significance, and identity through greater attention to what individuals do, think, and feel.

As cultural studies has moved from its fascination with so-called postmodernism in its more detached phase (exemplified by Baudrillard), it has reengaged developing arenas of disciplines whose emergence it significantly informed. In a range of contributions, everyday life is not only propelled and given significance by context and representation, but by the "doing" of that life by individuals, inter-subjectively, perhaps in relation to particular subcultures, with its attendant cultural capital, that they may find themselves occupying. The following paragraphs briefly examine this apparently "non-contextual," so-called "nonrepresentational" approach across cultural studies. However, as will be acknowledged, the apparent rejection of context such titles imply need to be given attention, as it is in the complex interplay of these diverse dimensions that meaning is more likely to be constructed and constituted, as will be considered towards the close of this chapter.

Recent work over the last decade or so which has tried to unpack the dynamic character and power of everyday life, owes its origins to earlier cultural studies, not least the work of Raymond Williams and also the work of the sociologist of culture Michael de Certeau (1984). Both have engaged with the making of narrative and walking the city, as everyday practice and ways of writing culture (1984). Two discourses in particular focus on possible explanations. The first focuses on the discussions of embodied practice, in the wake of the reworking of the philosopher Merleau Ponty's (2002) work on the body, the senses and the perception of space by the likes of Crossley (1996), Radley (1990), and Crouch (2003). The second focuses on performance theory that surrounds cultural studies and emerges, in particular, from feminist theory (see, for instance, Butler, 1993). Both discourses may be related to the recent debates concerning the work of Deleuze and Guattari on the complexities, the nonlinear networks and flows of actions of life (see, for instance, Deleuze and Guattari, 2001, 2004).

The notion of embodied practice as expressive provides a useful orientation for thinking through relations between touch, gesture, haptic vision, and other sensualities and their mobilization in *feelings of doing* (Harre, 1993). The word "doing" distinguishes what people may do without particular practical outcome, from that oriented around "tasking." Expressively encountering, the individual engages in body-practice as an everyday activity of living (Radley, 1995). Burkitt (1999) has drawn together ideas of body-practice and social constructionist notions of identity (in particular Shotter's [1993] notion of ontological knowledge) to argue that embodied practice may be important in working identity. Similarly, Ingold (2000) identifies a process of *dwelling* whereby encounters with objects, individuals, space and the self, progresses life. So too has Grosz (1999) argued that performativity reconstitutes life and culture. There are resemblances between performativity and embodied practice that are briefly considered in the following summary of certain themes of performativity (see also Edensor [Chapter 30] in this *Handbook*).

The difficulties with performance and performativity, and between the performative and embodied practice, lies in the divergent perspectives between the former and the overlapping reasoning between the former and the latter, as has been discussed within cultural studies. These discourses disrupt the disembodied privileging of representations and the mediated world of *both* traditional representational discourses and postmodern claims of *hyperreality* and *simulacra* (Baudrillard, 1988). First, performativity and embodied practice are both profoundly bodily (Dewsbury, 2000). Second, each emphasizes the importance of the expressive body and its ability to change things, their meaning and significance (Radley, 1995; Tulloch, 2000).

The nature of performance is contested. The American philosopher Judith Butler (1993), drawing upon poststructuralism in her works on feminist theory, presented performance and performativity in terms of being ritualized practice, working to pre-given codes and habitually repeated (Carlsen, 1996). However, it seems Butler acknowledges the possibility whereby relations with contexts may be reconfigured, broken, adjusted, or negotiated (Thrift and Dewsbury, 2000), thus affecting, as well as being the *affect* of context. These debates that have brought the "culture" of cultural studies more into the arena of lived practice, "ordinary" [sic] lives and what cultural studies has termed "the everyday", has been advanced in relation to tourism in particular through work in cultural, and social geography in the last decade (Crouch, 1999; Franklin and Crang, 2001). This raft of work has produced new geographies of tourism (Crouch, 2005), with a welcome shift from debates concerning industry-framed tourism to a consideration of the individual, doing tourism, as the tourist, ironically recalling MacCannell's book, *The Tourist*, originally published in 1976. People matter.

While performance can emphasize the framework of everyday protocols, the performative errs to the potential of openness. The reconfiguring, or reconstitutive potential of performance, is increasingly cited in terms of performativity, as modulating life and discovering the new and the unexpected, in ways that may reconfigure the self, in a process of ". . . what life (duration, memory, consciousness) brings to the world: the new, the movement of actualization of the virtual, expansiveness, opening up" (Grosz, 1999: 25), enabling the unexpected. Cindy Patton seeks to distinguish performativity from what de Certeau (1984) called "tactics" in his discourse on practice *and* from performance, arguing that "only in the performative can new strategies be constituted" (Patton, 1995: 183). In contrast, Roach inflects that "practice" *and* performativity constitute a "cultural act, critical perspective, a political intervention," and argues that *performances* may be considered as *practices* that contain the transformative (Roach, 1995: 46).

Furthermore, both the performative and embodied practice are characterized in doing (again, see Edensor [Chapter 30] on tourism and performance in this book). Each is articulated for the individual in terms of doing as constituting and refiguring, their own significations, as material or embodied semiotics, and may respond to other representations of the world (Crouch, 2001; Game, 1991). Performance as performativity is taken further as the ongoing and multiple interrelations of things, space and time, in a process of *becoming*. Engaging the new, like Radley's (1990) consideration of embodied practice— unexpected and unconsidered—is suggestive of a similar performative shift beyond the mundane and the idea of routine habituality. The notion of "going further" may emerge from exactly those apparently momentary things (Dewsbury, 2000). Moreover the borders between "being" as a state reached and becoming, are indistinct and constantly in flow (Grosz, 1999), although may be focused in *the event* (Dewsbury, 2000). In the present discussion, *becoming* is distinguished from *being* in the sense of Grosz's becoming as "unexpected," where performance's performa- tivities may open up new, reconstitutive possibilities. It is in the notion of multiple routes of "becoming" that the discourse on performativity is particularly powerful to the study of culture in tourism.

Throughout this chapter lies the tension between the related threads of performance/ performativity/embodied practice and the "making sense" of the world and aspects of the world (Harrison, 2000). Through perfor- mativities, practice, and performance, indi- viduals are able to feel, think, and rethink. While Dewsbury suggests that we may eschew performativities as not being "moments of synthesis" (2000: 481), they may be consti- tuted as important informing elements; their fluidity merging in events, nodes or knots of complexity. The significance of performance, or what Roach (1995) terms "transformative practice," lies in the process of advancing the individual to the intimate worlds where indi- viduals are felt to be. The expressive charac- ter in performativity is especially significant in *becoming*. The significance of "becoming" tends to be considered in terms of a profound rearrangement of the self, and may consist of numerous momentary performativites that may themselves be significant (Dewsbury, 2000). The individual consumer, or tourist, engages the world through feeling; as a con- nector with the environment, destinations, activities, as well as referring to mediated images, brands and so on.

Critical Thinking on Consumption

The cultural context, practice and performance debate fascinatingly converges with recent cultural and social anthropological reconcep- tualizations of consumption. Too frequently, Miller (2000) argues, do examinations of the world of consumption produce a virtual world of production detached from actually how consumers work, think, "use" objects, events, and experiences in their lives. Consumption and its objects of production

material culture, considered securely within the frame of the market place, may not under- stand individuals who buy them. Consumption is much more than the moment of consump- tion and its ephemeral, and only apparent, stimuli (Miller, 1998). Miller takes consump- tion to be an active process whereby objects, products, places, and things can be made *to matter*; they are made to matter through the way individuals' consume them (Miller, 1998). Individuals, then, constitute their own meanings and significations in what they buy, do, consume. A decade earlier, Fiske (1989) explained the ways in which produc- ers' powerfully semiotic products can be resisted, adjusted, or profoundly changed in their consumption, or made alternatively symbolic. To get closer to understanding the way the individual may engage or encounter products, places, events, activities, it is neces- sary to go beyond a linear philosophy that interprets processes as "step by step."

Engaging culture, and especially cultural complexity and its processes, opens insight to the complexity of being a tourist. In this chapter the consumer is conceptualized as an active, reflexive individual whose power to constitute meaning and significance in what is done, also acts through embodied practice and lay knowledge. Thus the consumer- tourist is considered as an individual living her or his life, in relation to cultural frame- works. Products tend to be understood in terms of meaning and value-production pre- figured by a world of producers that under- stand their consumers' preferences and desires. There is some evidence that produc- ers and their marketing *do* influence the meanings these products are given by the consumer-individual. Yet this may be only partial. The consumer of culture emerges in this way as also its co-*producer*. The cultural and social power, and politics, of tourism is produced through the acts of individuals (pace consumers) as much as by any institu- tional forces (Crouch, 2005). Thus, human lives are an important and so often over- looked and misunderstood component of so-called "new economies" (Crouch, 2006).

The opportunity of this opening of ideas is not to deny commercial and institutional, and indeed "local"/indigenous cultural and social power, but to fill the dramatis personae (Clifford, 1997). Similarly, recent texts have animated a more critical reading of the flows of influence between and amongst cultural texts, literature, visual imagery, television, and film, to reveal their greater complexity than one dimensional linear influence working only from commercial and institutional "production" to the individual [consumer]. Indeed, the individual, previously held within a frame of "in receipt" of culture, as only consumer, becomes acknowledged as also producer, not least of the tourist experience of "tourism" (Crouch, 2005; Crouch and Lubbren, 2003).

In moving around, in watching, the body is expressive, the individual creative. With reference to the over-reductive interpretations of cultural significance in the prescribed, prefigured, *mediated* formalism of ritual, Michael Taussig argues that the features and gestures of performance are operated not of "sense so much as sensuousness, an embodied and somewhat automatic knowledge that functions like peripheral vision, not studied contemplation, a knowledge that is imageric and sensate rather than ideational" (1992: 141).

Of course this can happen in terms of the inscription of culture on the body surface—the wearing of adornments in tourism experiences—at a disco, surfing, or at a Balinese festival—but also as a means through which to express oneself, as "being," enjoying life, "making fun," or not. Thereby the "fun" of tourism may be a means of being in the world, of reaching and engaging the world, a medium through which it is enjoyed, and the subject declares the self within that world. Dance, whitewater rafting and other forms of "adventure tourism" (Cloke and Perkins, 1998), along with more mundane tourism such as camping and coach-touring and moments of emerging from the bus to stand and stare, provide exemplars that express not only systems of signs but expressions of feeling, subjectivity in the world, and our unique

personality. Thus, heritage, great views and intimate corners, adventure and theme parks are brought into our lives and may not remain detached from our own identities.

Culture is Ordinary-Extraordinary, Even in Doing Tourism

Each of the moments of doing, borne through the intimate complexity of the contemporary but also flickered with personal and wider memory, proffers the possibility of perpetual authenticity, and heritage. Tourism is familiarly associated with journeys to visit heritage and cultural authenticity, exemplified in terms of cultural time-distance from the contemporary culture (MacCannell, 1999). Artifacts, prefigured heritage features may be signified by cultural mediation, but also through personal and shared, collective memory, and performatively embodied, socially, through our relations with each other. In the doing, moments of memory are recalled, reactivated in what is done, and thus, while memory may be drawn upon to signify, it is made anew, drawn through performance, and thus flows in time with the other components of performance. It is less that memory is performed, than it is "in performance." Memory and immediate activities are experienced as complexities of time. Individuals do not simply remember by picking the memory up momentarily, they return to it through performance and reform it. Time, too, is performed again and again, differently, and embodied thereby, grasped from clock or other time and wound up in body-performance.

At the same time mediated representations of tourism events and sites do not act on a *tabla rasa*. Not least, most individuals have experienced a tourist site or event, or find it resonant in other parts of their own lives. Individual places and objects, too, are remembered as significant because of the ways in which they were encountered (Radley, 1990). The significance of places and artifacts is not merely constituted through significance that is pre-given and projected, but also gained in the practice and in combinations of the two, and through reflection. Memory is constantly refigured in practice and performance through what individuals do. As things are done, other "events" are remembered and replaced into the present. Memory is temporalized and can reinvigorate what one is doing "now," but also is reinvigorated and can be rerouted in the "now," but not in an exact rerun of the past (Crang, 2001). Performing time/spacing appears to be more than a linear "moving on" from ideas, and memory is operated as an active character of performativity. As Bachelard (1994: 57) argues, we have "only retained the memory of events that have created us at the decisive instants of our pasts." These are drawn into a focus through the character of performativity, in nodes and knots of significance.

Moreover, tourism can also be used to regulate the self, to sustain or achieve security in life, to "hold on" to life-references. Even in the apparently extreme tourism of white water rafting there is considerable effort to achieve security in the way things are done, and dance can be enacted with repetition in the maintenance of life identity rather than in "going further." The care that tourists may give to identifying the minutiae of their travel, of knowing what to expect, in advance, and the frequent repeated visits they may make, points to tourism as "holding on" as well as "going further." In pursuit of Crawshaw and Urry's (1997) notion of the imperative amongst tourists for ordering their experiences, these moments of "holding on," drawn through the lens of many other facets of the encounter and through performative encountering, arguably offer a fuller and more rounded interpretation of what tourists may want beyond merely (visual) ordering.

Tourism undoubtedly has components of seeking escape (Cohen and Taylor, 1993; MacCannell, 1999; Rojek, 1992), but may be better conceptualized as components of the performative "going further" with life *in relation* rather than as moments of experience

separated out, in the way that Cohen and Taylor (1993) imply. The arguments of performativity support this potential in what individuals may achieve, however momentarily, and possibly with longer significance. However it is in the complex tensions of going further that the individual tourist may make some resolution of what can be achieved. The awareness, or feeling, of being able to change one's life in the practices of being a tourist, however temporarily, may be significant in the tourist's oft desire to return and to experience this again. Yet, also what individuals do and feel when in tourist mode resonates with what they do and feel in other spheres of their lives.

Furthermore, as Ann Game (1991) argues, through her own reflections on being a visitor to Bondi Beach and to the English Pennines, the individual constructs their own "material semiotics" of places through the bodily encounters that are made. Acknowledging the significance of body-practices it is appropriate to argue that these become *embodied semiotics* rather thana prefigured, merely scripted semiotics or context-driven (Crouch, 2001). A reading of the signs of tourism needs to be reconfigured in terms of this practical ontology. The power of contexts in the tourist experience is thereby informed. The tourist may stand and stare at prepared sites/sights but engages them as a complex individual in the round and with an expressive character, extending character of her own to the site as well as using it as an available marker.

Recent work in material culture has argued that objects can be given new significance through the ways in which they are consumed. The programmed, mediated and, prefigured visual culture of tourism can be similarly refigured, as in the diverse versions of London Bridge in Arizona (Jewesbury, 2003). Sites, destinations, and particular locations are constantly being refigured. To practice and to perform are components of the flow of contemporary culture. Meanings change and are changed; they are also diversely approached and (re)figured in practice and performance, in the continuous production and reproduction of culture, out of "the ordinary."

The familiar argument of the making of the "real economy," of art galleries, bars, taxi drivers and brokers conceals the complexity of cultural economy. The incompleteness of this abstracted and reductive world view through which the world is understood to be mainly mediated for the consumer rather than by him or her, becomes explained through the work of Miller (2000) *and* in relation to performance debates in cultural studies, attending to the complexities of "real" economies. The relations, production, and circulation of meanings, the central concerns of cultural studies for over half a century, appear to be less driven by complex institutional processes than a differently constituted set of processes where individuals are actively involved, participate, in a more nuanced manner, engaging along the way the work of the institutional producer (Leyshon, Lee and Williams, 2003). Through their performances, individuals work to select significance amongst a complexity of things, feelings, relations and actions (a process of affect). The result may be a cacophony or patina, negotiated, different spaces, artifacts and experiences given embodied significance. The apparent "real economy" is worked through and mediated into their own relation with these other resources of economy.

Tourism is culture; embedded in the diverse complexities, rather than dualities, overtly reductive categories and oppositions that characterize so much tourism studies. Linking back into the work of Stuart Hall, this also engages a kind of politics, where individuals are more actively engaged, but in a less explicitly resistant way (Crouch, 2007). Perhaps the greatest challenge and intellectual, explanatory opportunity in tourism studies now is to deepen and articulate the multiple interrelations of different, often distinctive, cultural processes involved; not merely to break down but thereby to enhance explanation of how those "contexts" and

practices-performances work. Such a project acknowledges head-on the theories, issues, and serious challenges that surround tourism, the potentialities of engaging with the intellectual journeying of cultural studies, and also the progressive opportunities which are created.

Acknowledgements

Thanks go to numerous colleagues and conference and research seminar discussions amongst many colleagues in Cultural Geography, Cultural Studies, Anthropology and Sociology, including in 2007, Berkeley, Goteborg, Split Croatia, London Metropolitan University and the UK Royal Geographical Society.

References

Adorno, T. (1941). "On Popular Music." *Studies in Philosophy and Social Sciences*, 9(1): 17–18.

Bachelard, G. (1994). *The Poetics of Space*. Boston, MA: Beacon Press.

Barthes, R. (1993a). "The Writer on Holiday." In *Mythologies* (pp. 29–31). London: Vintage.

Barthes, R. (1993b). "Myth Today." In *Mythologies* (pp. 109–159). London: Vintage.

Baudrillard, J. (1981). *For a Critique of the Political Economy of the Sign*. St Louis, MN: Telos Press.

Baudrillard, J. (1988). "Simulacra and Simulations." In Mark Poster (Ed.), *Selected Writings* (pp. 166–184). Stanford, CA: Stanford University Press.

Bourdieu, P. (1984). *Distinction: A Social Critique of the Judgement of Taste*. London: Routledge.

Bruner, E. (2005). *Culture on Tour*. Chicago, IL: Chicago University Press.

Britton, S. (1991). "Tourism, Capital and Pace." *Environment and Planning D: Society and Space*, 9: 451–478.

Burkitt, J. (1999). *Bodies of Thought*. London: Sage.

Butler, J. (1993). *Bodies that Matter*. London: Routledge.

Carlsen, M. (1996). *Performance: A Critical Introduction*. London: Routledge.

Clifford, J. (1997). *Routes: Travel and Translation in the Late Twentieth Century*. Cambridge, MA: Harvard University Press.

Cloke, P. and Perkins, H. (1998). "Cracking the Canyon with the Awesome Foursome." *Environment and Planning: Society and Space*, 16: 185–218.

Cohen, E. (2004). *Contemporary Tourism: Diversity and Change*. London: Elsevier.

Cohen, S. and Taylor, L. (1993). *Escape Attempts*. London: Routledge.

Cosgrove, D. and Daniels, S. (1988). *The Iconography of Landscape*. Cambridge: Cambridge University Press.

Crang, M. (2001). "Rhythms of the City: Temporalised Space and Motion." In J. May and N. Thrift (Eds.), *Time/Space Geographies* (pp.187–207). London: Routledge.

Crawshaw, C. and Urry, J. (1997). "Tourism and the Photographic Eye." In C. Rojek and J. Urry (Eds.), *Touring Cultures: Transformations in Travel and Theory* (pp.176–195). London: Routledge.

Crossley, N. (1996). "Body-Subject/Body-Power: Agency, Inscription and Control in Foucault and Merleau-Ponty." *Body Society*, 2: 99–116.

Crouch, D. (Ed.) (1999). *Leisure/Tourism Geographies*. London: Routledge.

Crouch, D. (2001). "Spatialities and the Feeling of Doing." *Social and Cultural Geography*, 2(1): 61–75.

Crouch, D. (2003). "Spacing, Performance and Becoming: Tangles in the Mundane." *Environment and Planning A*, 35: 1948–1960.

Crouch, D. (2005). "Flirting with Space: Tourism Geographies as Sensuous/Expressive Practice." In C. Cartier and A. Lew (Eds.), *Seductions of Tourism*. London: Routledge.

Crouch, D. (2006). "Empowerment and Performance in the Making of Contemporary Cultural Economies." In T. Terkenli and A. Hauteserre (Eds.), *Landscapes of a New Cultural Economy of Space* (pp. 19–40). Amsterdam: Springer.

Crouch, D. (2007). "The Power of the Tourist Encounter." In A. Church and T. Coles (Eds.), *Tourism, Power and Space* (pp. 45–62). London: Routledge.

Crouch, D. and Lubbren, N. (Eds.) (2003). *Visual Culture and Tourism*. London: Berg.

De Certeau, M. (1984). *The Practice of Everyday Life*. Berkeley: University of California Press.

Deleuze, G. and Guattari, F. (2001). *A Thousand Plateaus*. London: Continuum.

Deleuze, G. and Guattari, F. (2004). *Anti-Oedipus*. London: Continuum.

Dewsbury, J.D. (2000). "Performativity and the Event: Enacting a Philosophy of Difference." *Environment and Planning D: Society and Space*, 18(4): 473–496.

Duncan, J. and Ley, D. (Eds.) (1991). *Representing Cultural Geography*. London: Routledge.

Edensor, T. (1998). *Tourists at the Taj*. London: Routledge.

Edensor, T. (2002). *National Identity, Popular Culture and Everyday Life*. London: Berg.

Fiske, J. (1989). *Understanding Popular Culture*. London: Routledge.

Foucault, M. (1970). *The Order of Things*. London: Tavistock.

Franklin, A. and Crang, M. (2001). "Introduction." *Tourist Studies*, 1(1): 5–22.

Game, A. (1991). *Deconstructing Sociology*. Buckingham: Open University Press.

Gilroy, P. (1987). *There Ain't No Black in the Union, Jack*. London: Hutchinson.

Graburn, N. (1983). "The Anthropology of Tourism." *Annals of Tourism Research*, 10(1): 9–33.

Grosz, E. (1999). "Thinking the New: Of Futures Yet Unthought." In E. Grosz (Ed.), *Becomings: Explorations in Time, Memory and Futures* (pp. 15–28). Ithaca, NY: Cornel University Press.

Hall, S. (1980). "Cultural Studies—Two Paradigms." *Media, Culture and Society* 2(2): 57–72.

Hall, S. (2007). "Richard Hoggart, The Uses of Literacy and the Cultural Turn." *International Journal of Cultural Studies,* 10(1): 39–49.

Harre, R. (1993). *The Discursive Mind*. Cambridge: Polity Books.

Harrison, P. (2000). "Making Sense: Embodiment and the Sensibilities of the Everyday." *Environment and Planning D: Society and Space*, 18: 497–517.

Hebdige, D. (1979). *Subculture: The Meaning of Style*. London: Methuen.

Hoggart, K. and Bishop, J. (1985). *Organising Around Enthusiasms*. London: Comedia.

Hughes, G. (1998). "Tourism and the Semiological Realisation of Space." In G. Ringer (Ed.), *Destinations* (pp. 17–32). London: Routledge.

Inglis, F. (2000). *The Delicious History of the Holiday*. London: Routledge.

Ingold, T. (2000). *The Perception of the Environment: Essays in Livelihood, Dwelling and Skill*. London: Routledge.

Jewesbury, D. (2003). "London Bridge in Arizona." In D. Crouch and N. Lubbren (Eds.), *Visual Culture and Tourism* (pp. 223–240). London: Berg.

Kraniauskas, J. (1998). "Globalization is Ordinary. The Transnationalization of Cultural Studies." *Radical Philosophy*, 90 (July/August): 9–19.

Lash, S. and Urry, J. (1994). *Economies of Sign and Space*. London: Sage.

Leavis, F. R. (1930). *Mass Civilisation and Minority Culture*. Cambridge: Cambridge University Press.

Leyshon, A., Lee, R. and Williams, C. (Eds.) (2003). *Alternative Economic Spaces*. London: Sage.

MacCannell, D. (1999). *The Tourist: A New Theory of the Leisure Class*. Berkeley: University of California Press.

McGuigan, J. (1992). *Cultural Populism*. London: Routledge.

Meethan K. (2001). *Tourism in Global Society*. London: Palgrave.

Miller, D. (Ed.) (1998). *Material Culture: Why Some Things Matter*. London: Routledge.

Miller, D. (2000). "Virtualism—The Culture of Political Economy." In I. Cook, D. Crouch, S. Naylor and J. Ryan (Eds.), *Cultural Turns/Geographical Turns: Perspectives on Cultural Geography* (pp.196–213). Harlow: Prentice Hall.

Nash, D. (1981). "Tourism as an Anthropological Subject." *Current Anthropology*, 22(5): 461–481.

Patton, C. (1995). "Performativity and Spatial Distinction: The End of AIDS Epidemiology." In A. Parker and E. Kosofsky Sedgwick (Eds.), *Performativity and Performance* (pp.173–196). London: Routledge.

Phillips, D. (1999). "Narrativised Space: The Function of Story in the Theme Park." In D. Crouch (Ed.), *Leisure/Tourism Geographies* (pp. 91–108). London: Routledge.

Ponty, M. (2002). *Phenomenology of Perception*. London: Routledge.

Radley, A. (1990). "Artefacts, Memory and a Sense of the Past." In D. Middleton and D. Edwards (Eds.), *Collective Remembering* (pp. 46–59). London: Sage.

Radley, A. (1995). "The Elusory Body and Social Constructionist." *Theory Body and Society*, 1(2): 3–23.

Ringer, G. (Ed.) (1998). *Destinations*. London: Routledge.

Ritzer, G. (1996). *Modern Sociological Theory*. New York: McGraw-Hill Companies, Inc.

Roach, J. (1995). "Culture and Performance in the Cirum-Atlantic World." In A. Parker and E. Sidgewick (Eds.), *Performativity and Performance* (pp. 45–63). New York: Routledge.

Robinson, M. and Andersen, H.C. (Eds.) (2002). *Literature and Tourism: Essays in the Reading and Writing of Tourism*. London: Continuum.

Rojek, C. (1992). *Ways of Escape*. London: Sage.

Smith, V. (Ed.) (1977). *Hosts and Guests: The Anthropology of Tourism*. Philadelphia, PA: Philadelphia University Press.

Selwyn, T. (Ed.) (1996). *The Tourist Image*. Chichester: Wiley.

Shotter, J. (1993). *Cultural Politics of Everyday Life: Social Constructionism, Rhetoric and Knowing of the Third Kind*. Cambridge: Taylor & Francis Group.

Taussig, M. (1992). *The Nervous System*. London: Routledge.

Thrift, N. and Dewsbury, J.D. (2000). "Dead Geographies—And How to Make Them Live." *Environment and Planning D: Society and Space*, 18(4): 411–432.

Thompson, E.P. (1963). *The Making of the English Working Class*. London: Victor Gollancz.

Tulloch, J. (2000). *Performing Culture*. London: Sage.

Urry, J. (1995). *Consuming Places*. London: Routledge.

Urry, J. (2002). *The Tourist Gaze*. London: Sage.

Williams, R. (1958). *Culture and Society*. London: Chatto and Windus, 1958. New edition with a new introduction. New York, Columbia University Press, 1963.

Zukin, S. (1990). *Landscapes of Power*. Berkeley: University of California Press.

Zukin, S. (1995). *The Culture of Cities*. London: Sage.

Tourism, Popular Culture and the Media

Philip Long and Mike Robinson

Introduction

An air of contestation hangs heavy around the words "culture" and "popular" and particularly so when the terms are combined. Despite relatively recent attempts to study what has been termed "popular culture," there is an absence of any generally accepted definition, a lack of consensus as to what it does and does not include, and a lack of agreement regarding methodologies for its study. Paradoxically, although it deals with issues of what is popular and the idea of "mass" phenomena, it remains largely on the periphery of both academic and political/policy discourse (unless concerned with popular cultural behaviors that are deemed to be socially undesirable) and frequently attracts a pejorative slant as a field of enquiry which oscillates between being over-theoretical and explicitly political, to lacking rigor (a frequent critique of its subjectivism) and a distinct lack of "seriousness" (Sontag, 2001). However, despite these accusations, the study of popular culture, within and without the more inclusive frame of (British) "cultural studies," continues to develop, not necessarily with the, usually leftist, political agenda that it once had or was perceived to have had, but as a valuable arena for understanding contemporary life and indeed contemporary tourism.

This chapter explores the relationships between tourism, popular culture, and the media. These are complex and multifarious relationships which see tourism as a form of popular culture and also with aspects of popular culture contributing to the shaping of contemporary tourism. These relationships are played out through both the production and consumption of tourism and also through the study of tourism. Central in these relationships, and central in this chapter, is the role of the media in a both a communicative sense and as a form of entertainment and enjoyment fuelling the development of tourism.

In this sense the media is used in a short hand way to refer to a grouping of products, institutions, distribution technologies and audiences: newspapers, magazines, television programs, films, and the emerging digital and web-based media, etc. The function of the media as a way of communicating or distributing messages and images of people, places, and events is central to the workings of international tourism. However, there is a further important dimension of the media which needs to be discussed; this is the role of the media beyond the notion of a mere distributive mechanism and as a form of entertainment in itself which feeds the production of popular cultural genres. This leisure function of the media and how our enjoyment and the extraction of pleasure from the media can feed and shape our discoveries about the world as tourists, is frequently overlooked but is worthy of more concerted research.

Despite the intimacies and importance of the relationships between tourism and the media in practice, there has been limited conceptual writing on this. Indeed, while there has been considerable research on issues of the conceptualization of destination image, its formation, representation and its linkages to tourist motivation (see for instance Baloglu and McCleary, 1999; Echtner and Ritchie, 2003; Font, 1997; Gartner, 1993), the role of the media has seldom moved from the realms of the implicit and within tourism studies in general is largely characterized as solely a mechanism of communication. Nielsen (2001) and Avraham (2007) offer useful perspectives on some of the more functional dimensions of the role of the media in international tourism, including its implications on tourist motivations and behavior and ways of dealing with negative media coverage. However, it is left to Crouch et al. (2005) to place the tourism and media relationship into a more theoretical frame but without a single theoretical perspective. Crouch et al. focus on the tourist imagination as an entry point into understanding the key point of interdependence between tourism and the media. So, not only does the media convey and distribute imaginary scapes which feed expectation, experience and reflection, the

ideas and experiences of tourism and tourists feed the imaginations of the media and are thus projected back into the world.

The Idea of the Popular

The concept of the popular and the idea of "mass culture" are inextricably linked. It is widely held that the notion of popular culture within the developed world was fed by the phenomena of "mass" production, "mass" consumption, and "mass" distribution associated with the industrial and technological developments of the late nineteenth century. However, in most historical periods, and in most societies, there have been versions of popular culture (Schroeder, 1980).

The persistent problems of trying to pin down the idea of culture are frequently dealt with by constructing a spectral approach where at one end lies the notion of "high culture" with its elite, critically acclaimed artistic and literary leanings, while at the other end, and drawing upon anthropological tradition is the notion of "folk culture" focusing upon the practices, institutions, and artifacts of communities or some ethnic grouping. Both ends of the spectrum share the idea of valued histories and traditions and also that of being somehow distant from the ordinary and the practices of the majority in some "special" way. Between these positions lies the discursive category widely referred to as "popular" culture which deals with the immediate, the imminent, and the contemporary, brought together and widely distributed by, and through, the mass media. Instinctively popular culture appears to refer to that which is "of the people"; an implicit acceptance of a kind of "folk" culture and this is an interesting area, because it also encompasses the idea of an "alternative" culture which includes minority groups, perhaps with subversive values (the "indie" music scene is an example of this). So "popular" (sub)cultures can and sometimes do, challenge the "dominant" cultural power groups (Jenks, 2005; Muggleton and Weinzierl, 2003).

Petracca and Sorapure (1998: 3) neatly summarize the location and essence of the popular: "If the Metropolitan Opera House represents high culture, then Madison Square Garden represents "pop." If the carefully crafted knives used in Asian cooking rely on a folk tradition, then the Veg-O-Matic is their pop counterpart." However, what appears as a somewhat two dimensional, bipolar and largely static approach to culture is of course multidimensional, dynamic, and laden with contradictions and ideology. So called "low-brow" culture, popular here and now, can shift along the spectrum to become the "high-brow" culture of the future. Focusing upon culture as representation, critics point to the ways in which the undoubted populism and popularity of authors such as, for instance, Mark Twain, Walter Scott, and Charles Dickens in the nineteenth century, have given way to their occupying more elite positions in contemporary literary culture. Thus is it argued that the works of J.K. Rowling or Stephen King may one day move to occupy positions of "high" culture.

Such shifts are in part related to the playing out of positions of power (with dominant power usually seen to reside in the maintenance of high cultural practices by the socially privileged) and associated trends in aesthetic value linked to the influence and perpetuation of a social elite. But the notion of movement along some cultural scale is also a function of normative demographic change as each generation connects with its own cultural values, not least through the media, and the values of former generations become contested ground. This generational dynamic has been occluded from many characterizations of tourism which still seem to be dominated by an almost romanticized view of tourism which positions the resources of tourism as somehow unchanging, untouchable icons and, unyielding, immutable traditions. That younger generations respond differently to edifices of culture constructed before they came along, and indeed generate

their own cultural landscapes from and through the media they are most familiar with, is a fact recognized by some cultural institutions more than others. For instance, in 2007, the Victoria and Albert Museum in London, itself a prominent tourist attraction, staged a hugely successful exhibition devoted to the costumes and photographs of singer and actress Kylie Minogue. The reactions to the exhibition highlighted the inherent tension in the term popular culture. The Director of the Museum Mark Jones came under attack from critics who took the exhibition to signal a "dumbing down" process and "pandering to pop culture." Jones responded by aligning the exhibition with the mission of the Museum; to showcase the best of British design and to broaden its visitor base. Jones was supported in his defense by attracting record numbers of visitors to the exhibition.

It is of course the case that, broadly speaking, contemporary tourism is inscribed with the patterns and neo-romantic discourses inherited from eighteenth- and nineteenth-century Eurocentric travel. Visits to the ruins of Rome or Athens are still as popular as ever and the images of Venice or Paris are still widely circulated. However, the ways in which such sites/sights are read/understood has shifted considerably. It is not that established understandings of "high" culture have evaporated, nor that aesthetic preferences have undergone wholesale revolution. However, they have been supplanted with additional, layered meanings more readily accessible to a younger audience. Hence, the Louvre is no longer merely a repository of fine art for the education and moral betterment of its visitors but, for some (and it is a significant number of visitors), it is also a site of the bestselling novel and film "The Da Vinci Code."

Such an overlay of meanings builds up somewhat organically, allowing for multiple readings of attractions and destinations. In this way culture is metaphorically and vicariously passed along the notional spectrum through the actions and interactions of its consumers/tourists. What is taken as reified "high culture" is made popular through consumption and what was popular is made more so through the same process. As Philips (2000: 98) suggests: "If Rider Haggard and Conan Doyle, Hans Christian Andersen, the Brothers Grimm, Bram Stoker, Mallory and Tennyson are not directly acknowledged, variations of their stories are to be found in Disneyland, and in almost all other theme parks." Arguably, this is not another cultural form but rather the same culture consumed by a different audience, or even just consumed "differently." Such shifts in consumer/tourist perceptions and interpretations of the sights and sites of "high" culture indicated here may, to a large extent, be explained through their representation in a range of "mass" media forms that reach large and increasingly global audiences.

The morphing of cultural interpretations, the intertextualities of cultural forms, coupled with global/cross-cultural exposure and readings and, the interrelations with the media, problematizes the very nature of what is widely presented as "cultural tourism." This category has emerged over recent years almost as a sign of resistance against the populist and relativist notions of culture. Certainly, among public authorities deemed to uphold inherited cultural capital, cultural tourism is widely taken to mean activities which would seem to support longstanding investments in heritage protection and conservation and support for "national" markers of culture such as opera, ballet, art galleries, and museums. However, if we insert the idea of "popular" into culture, then it becomes clear that state hegemonies played out through tourism—or at least the providing for certain types of tourists—are weakened as the popular lies more in the realms of the informal, the commercial and private sectors and is closely linked to the media and free form expressions. This also challenges the notion of the "cultural tourist"; usually taken to be one who is well educated, middle class, middle aged, and somewhat different from the hedonistic "mass" tourist (Richards, 1996, 2001, 2006). In line with the notion of the post-tourist (Rojek, 1997; Urry, 2002), the

very mediation of tourism, or rather the places, peoples, and pasts that constitute tourism through engaging with the imagination and human curiosity, cuts through such typologies and blurs boundaries so that tourists who visit museums at one moment may also visit sites associated with Hollywood movies.

The Mediation of Tourism

The interpretation of media as a "means" for mass communication, while widely accepted, has been criticized in the literature as failing to acknowledge the issues of differentiation and distinction amongst populations and audiences (Boyd-Barrett and Newbold, 1995; Fiske, 1990; Inglis, 1990; Louw, 2001; McQuail, 1983), and the fact that while the term communication implies a two way exchange, invariably it has been traditionally posited in communication and media studies as a one-way process *from* the media *to* receptive audiences (Gillespie, 2005; Hall, 1997; Lasswell, 1948). The media are pivotal for the distribution of popular culture and the cumulative construction of touristic mobilities. Important in this respect is the role of the media as a form of entertainment and how this dimension feeds into the very production of culture. In this sense, the media may be viewed as reflecting the cultural values which reciprocally shape texts and forms of representation.

Who audiences are, the ways in which they (we) use and interpret media texts and the possible "effects" of media texts on readers are central concerns of research on the media (Altheide, 1996; Berger, 2005; Devereux, 2003). Whether media outputs have discernible effects on audiences has been a contentious area within the media studies field. Early (post-World War II) media theorists tended to place emphasis on what the mass media *do* to their audiences; where power lies with the message and the audience is convinced into accepting meanings as intended by their producers (Branston and

Stafford, 1996; Fiske, 1990; Gillespie, 2005). In this conception, alternative viewpoints are filtered out and the critical capacity of the audience is reduced. The audience is a dependent, passive, mass public and the media confirms the established social order.

Media owners and controllers are seen to be creating and sustaining "mass culture," encouraging responses to advertising and reinforcing patterns of sociability, ways of thinking and, perhaps as a more or less intended byproduct, tourist choices and behavior. The origins of this propagandist model of media power can be traced to World War II and the importance attached to radio and newspapers at that time as agents of the state, presenters of (dis)information and upholders of public morale (Lasswell, 1948; Moores, 1993). This model of media power on audiences may also be illustrated in the part that may have been played by "Western" media, such as the Voice of America radio station, in undermining the former Communist regimes in Eastern Europe in the early 1990s. It may even be suggested that a contributory factor in the demise of these regimes was a desire among their populations, encouraged by Western media images, to be international tourists to western countries (Hall and O'Sullivan, 1996).

As far as media effects on audiences are concerned, research findings are often complex in pattern, difficult to interpret, inconclusive and rarely supportive of a picture of media impact as overriding, uniform or direct. Some audience research findings suggest that the effects of the media are usually hard to sustain; retention may not be long-term, reflecting the so-called "3 minute culture" attention span (Gurevitch et al., 1982: 237; Lull, 2001). Furthermore, media influences may undergo modification and reshaping at a personal or group level by "significant others," such as parents, teachers, friends and partners, either at the point of consumption or in later discussion about the content of a program or article. The degree of media influence is therefore open to question. As Gurevitch et al.

(1982: 12) suggest: "People tend to expose themselves to, understand and remember communications selectively, according to prior dispositions. They manipulate rather than are manipulated by the mass media."

An alternative perspective on media "effects" places emphasis on the uses and interpretations that audiences make of media outputs and the contexts within which "reading" of the media takes place; what audiences (we) *do with* the media rather than what the media *does* to them (us) (Bae and Lee, 2004; Creeber, 2001; Gillespie, 2005; Hall, 1997). In this perspective audiences are seen as being conscious consumers who make use of the media to gratify certain needs or desires. These may include: a diversion or escape from routines such as the "armchair traveler's" consumption of travel programs and features; the reinforcement of personal relationships and self-identity through shared use of the media, such as with reference to tourism media as part of the process of selecting family holiday options; personal identification with individual media commentators and celebrities who reinforce or challenge the reader's worldviews, including those broadcasters and journalists whose views on tourism attract respect; the need to gain information, resolve ambiguity or uncertainty and formulate attitudes, again, for example in relation to travel choices (Berger, 2005; Watson, 1998: 65). It may also be suggested that audiences make critical responses to particular media "texts," which can be classified as where: the "preferred reading" of the broadcaster/writer is approved, accepted and adopted by the reader; the presenter's interpretation of the subject is broadly accepted, but with parts of the message queried or doubted; the message is rejected altogether (Devereux, 2003; Hall, 1997; Watson, 1998: 54).

Any "effects" that the media may have on audiences are therefore not clear cut. "People are neither neutral nor passive audiences for either print or electronic media. Their consumption of media information is frequently interactive, taking place with other readers who may see different meanings" (Pearce et al., 1996: 85). Broadcast and print media may be particularly influential in some circumstances and less so on other occasions. It has been suggested that media effects on audiences may be most influential in situations where: information rather than attitude or opinion is sought; the media source is prestigious, trusted or liked; monopoly conditions exist, i.e., when alternative sources are limited or unavailable; the issue is remote and difficult to verify from personal experience; personal contacts support the message (Devereux, 2003; Gurevitch et al., 1982: 13). People therefore bring their worldviews and experiences (and those of other people) to their interpretation of media messages. However, the question remains of the extent to which those worldviews and experiences are, in turn, influenced and shaped by media representations. Furthermore, identifying the effects of individual television programs is far from straightforward. As Watson (1998: 78) suggests: "The use of the remote control has facilitated zipping, zapping and grazing, as digitalization makes channel scarcity a thing of the past, it has become increasingly difficult to define what 'watching television' actually means."

Media Tourism Categories

Media texts and images are ubiquitous, increasingly globalized and instantaneous in their circulation. It is hard to avoid or ignore news headlines and advertising imagery and for many people worldwide, "soap operas" and situation comedies, documentaries and sports broadcasts, and the latest film releases contribute significantly in shaping daily and weekly leisure patterns and provide subjects for diversion, reflection and discussion (Biltereyst and Meers, 2000; Couldry, 1998; Elasmar and Hunter, 1997; Hobson, 2003). The news and entertainment media, which overlap, present more or less objective and appealing textual, visual and aural information, images and representations of events, places and people situated in particular time and space. Some of these media texts and images are intended,

produced and presented as being concerned specifically with narratives on tourism; other media texts are indirectly and incidentally concerned with tourism or have more or less significant implications for the tourist, tourism industry, and destination image (Butler, 1990; Dann, 1996; Hanefors and Larsson, 1993). Media representations of the world and the extent to which they are interpreted by and influential on people in making decisions about where to travel as tourists (and where to avoid), how to get there and what to do when they arrive at the destination, are clearly important subjects in the study of the relationships between contemporary tourism, the media and popular culture. Tourism—media relationships are also significant strategic and operational matters for practitioners in both tourism and media sectors. However, this is a subject that has received relatively little research attention within a media theoretical framework.

The tourism industry makes extensive use of global distributive means; what Appadurai (1996) refers to as the "mediascape." Transportation operators advertise new routes, products and services; destination tourist boards, in partnership with tour operators, organize press "familiarization" visits in the hope or expectation of receiving favorable publicity; and visitor attractions issue press releases about their "biggest," "longest," "fastest" new ride hoping that the story will be picked up by editors as being "newsworthy." The media industries are also increasingly turning to travel and tourism as a source of "human interest" stories, advertising revenues, travel features, supplements, and program formats. The apparent indifference of tour operators to dangerous gas heating appliances or swimming pools in Mediterranean resorts complexes and allegations of price fixing or unsafe practices against airlines, for example, provides good material for investigative reporting. Visitor attractions, tour operator resort representatives, cruise ships, charter airlines, and hotels provide settings for "day-in-the-life," "fly-on-the-wall" documentaries, and "reality" television formats that make ephemeral celebrities of some of their participants. Destination tourism promotion agencies, politicians and law enforcement agencies respond swiftly through the media in response to any attack or threat against tourists (Crouch et al., 2005; Hall and O'Sullivan, 1996).

As we have indicated in the introduction to this chapter, it is important to recognize that the study of the media is not solely a matter of considering the content and circulation of messages and images. Media may usefully be categorized and applied to tourism in relation to types or modes of output; most obviously print and broadcast, tabloid and broadsheet; by audience and ownership—public and private sector; and in relation to the nature of its output, or genre, with our focus here on media as concerning both "serious" news and feature outputs and as leisure pursuit and entertainment. This is a useful starting point for the analysis of media "texts" (visual and aural as well as verbal) and their connections with popular culture and tourism. Thus we may consider mass media outputs reaching large audiences at international, national, regional, and local levels that are specifically and directly concerned with tourism. Examples include television holiday programs and newspaper travel supplements and feature stories. Here editorial and feature pieces typically convey the views of a commentator who may possess an authoritative, quasi-celebrity status who outlines their experiences, opinions and prejudices about particular destinations, peoples, accommodation, and modes of transportation (Morgan and Pritchard, 1999; Seaton, 1990). Investigative documentaries and extended features that report on tourism-related subjects extend this area where commentary and judgments relating to tourism are presented through the media. News reports that are directly concerned with the tourism industry and places represented as tourist destinations may also be included in this category. Mass media coverage in terms of news and features not directly or primarily concerned with tourism but which may have, at least potentially, a more or less positive or negative influence on readers" perceptions of, for example, destination

image, cost, security, and transportation safety are also pertinent.

Turning toward the media as leisure pursuits, we find extensive coverage of sport and other hallmark events which are effectively major tourist attractions. Critical reviews of arts exhibitions, major festivals and events and reporting on the football World Cup and Olympic Games, for example, and the reporting on the behavior of visitors to such events come into this category. Specialist media reaching narrower, more targeted, niche audiences, include those aimed directly at tourists. "Lifestyle" features and publications concerned with leisure, health, and personal fulfillment also often include a tourism angle. All of these "texts" can be analyzed in terms of their apparent assumptions about the audiences to which they are aimed. These assumptions are reflected in their "modes of address"; i.e., the ways in which the article or program "speaks" to its audience in terms of style, presentation, content and cultural references (Berger, 2005; Branston and Stafford, 1996: 313; Butler, 1990; Gillespie and Toynbee, 2006).

As part of the wider mediascape, tourism has developed its own media which have evolved to service its own needs. This includes pamphlets, guidebooks, maps, travelogues and, increasingly, websites and travel weblogs. It is a media which has developed its own linguistic familiarity where we are able to comprehend and structure, the spaces and practices of international tourism. We are able to "read" language, vocabulary, symbols, images, and codes used to animate space and place. We accept, use and play with the narratives and discourses of tourism. We formulate, tell, share, and memorize our own stories of touristic experience. We build up vocabularies of tourism and know terms such as "air miles," "charter flights," and "single supplements." To draw upon the metaphor of performance, we know how to perform tourism and we are usually well versed in reading our scripts (Gregory, 1999).

Given the notion of tourism as a time limited system of exchanges and mobilities (Jacobsen, 2003), some form of mediation is required.

With some necessity, tourism media has been developed to address the physical and psychic gap that exists between tourist purchase and experience; that is some form of representation of the complexities of a destination and its attributes is required prior to visitation. Over recent years, researchers have given attention to the wide variety of texts specifically developed for the tourist; what Dean MacCannell (1976) terms "transcultural materials." In the main, these texts are the "induced information sources" that Gunn (1972) referred to and which many people will be ultimately familiar with—tourism brochures and guidebooks. As Durkheim (1909: 238) put it; "the world exists only in so far as it is represented to us." In this sense, tourism brochures and guidebooks are part of a vast wave of knowledge forms and formats which, in line with the ever increasing pervasiveness of "print capitalism" (Anderson, 1983), represent the world to us. While clearly lacking the artistic creativity and social gravitas of the more "literary" works which so concerned critics such as Edward Said (1978) in his analysis of the construction of "the Orient," the tourism media compensate via their abilities to shape attitudes by virtue of their democratic "reach" into societies and a more complex and less superficial process of construction that has not been widely researched.

Within the category of "induced" media sources (Gunn, 1972), a vast range of leaflets are produced by the predominately commercial providers of tourism services. Independent hotels, hotel chains, transportation providers, visitor attractions, etc., all generate texts and images that not only locate themselves and the services they provide but also the places and the cultures in which they themselves are located. References and cross references are made to various aspects of the cultures in which they operate and collectively they circulate as ephemera, providing fleeting glimpses of larger narratives relating to destinations. Given that such texts are usually produced outside of the state/public structures of tourism they are often highly problematic to estimate in terms of their

number, are extremely difficult to regulate in any way, and moreover, it is complicated to assess their impact upon audiences.

In addition to tourism-oriented leaflets is a more substantive category of a wide range of magazines, again produced by various providers of tourist services. With higher production values and, usually, a far more focused distribution strategy, these include an expanding array of titles relating to particular "niche" forms of tourism (skiing, exploration, travel photography, etc.), overseas property investment and "in-flight" magazines. The latter have been the subject of research (Jaworski and Thurlow, 2003), but overall there is a major gap in our knowledge relating to the impact of these particular forms of tourism texts and the way in which they overlap with other categories of social activities. Further examples of media texts, which through their circulation have a fragmented yet arguably cumulative impact upon individual and collective constructions of the world, include: postcards (Pritchard and Morgan, 2005), newspaper travel supplements, television holiday programs (Dunn, 2005; Jaworski et al., 2003), travel exhibitions, and various promotional DVDs.

In the context of tourism specific media, the days of the tourism brochure or the guidebook existing only as physical objects are now gone. While the materiality of both is still very important it is clear that new communicative technologies and new networks of practice are shaping the messages and impact of the tourism brochure and the guidebook. The vast majority of tour operators and national tourism agencies have a web presence, but in the main this tends to be an edited version of texts and images already produced in hard copy. A number of tour operators, for instance, have destination narratives available on the web but site visitors are able to download copies of the brochures that are still produced. There are also many operators which "sell" directly via the internet without the aid of further hard copy brochures. Travel Republic (http://www.travelrepublic.co.uk), for instance, is an online travel agent based in the UK, which has been trading on the web for over 20 years. Effectively working as a standard tour agency with online brochures, Travel Republic has limited space to convey the cultural complexities of the destinations it features and thus majors upon a destination "highlights" model with an appeal to the younger, more technologically astute market. But, away from the travel agents and tour operators using the internet to sell holidays, is also a new form of guidebook which uses the interactivity of the web to generate contemporary representations of destinations and their cultures. Working on, but extending the principles already adopted by the likes of Lonely Planet, these virtual guidebooks act as points for information collection from the tourists themselves. One such example is a company called World66, founded originally by a Dutch couple in 1999 but now owned by the e-commerce company "Internet Brands," and run from California. World66 (http://www.world66.com) brings together information on 20,000 destinations and works on an open content system where anyone can add and edit the content via a company moderator who can accept or decline a modification. Each country featured is divided into sections, the majority of which contain practical information regarding transportation, eating, and accommodation, etc., though some sections have no information within them. The benefits of such a guidebook lie in its ability to reflect, almost immediately, the real experiences of tourists. The immediacy can be passed on to tourists via mobile phone downloads, which automatically start with the homepage of where you are.

A similar interactive virtual guidebook is operated by Wikitravel (http://www.wikitravel.org). In principle, this open system works very well for tourists in that it overcomes key problems of the standard guide in book format such as information dating quickly and not being able to reflect the vast spectrum of cultural opportunities of a destination. Commentaries tend to be submitted by the younger tourists and reflect a broader, more popular approach to local cultures. There are also frequent instances of practical advice which relate to dealing with local cultures. However, there are

disadvantages to these virtual guidebooks in respect of the validity of the information submitted and in terms of a general lack of depth with regard to many explanations of destination cultures. Also, as with standard guidebooks, the information put forward is generally provided by and for the tourists with little input from the local communities. A further problem relates to the funding of such guides and a number feature advertisements from companies to assist their operations.

What the tourism media has been very good at is prioritizing the visual and over the years researchers of tourism have given considerable attention to the importance of the image (Synott, 1993), or more precisely, to the visuality of tourism encompassing; the notion of "sightseeing" and the construction, deconstruction, and consumption of spectacle (MacCannell, 1976), the gaze (Urry, 2002), the production of "place-myths" (Shields, 1995), and a whole set of issues relating to the ways tourism and tourists play with, and practice visual culture in its widest sense (Crouch and Lübbren, 2003). Images, featured in the media generally as sources of knowledge that are encountered and used as a way to structure experience, are clearly a significant factor in what can be termed the "making" of tourists as well as having a role in the processes of destination decision making, and in shaping predispositions toward the tourist gaze (Strain, 2003). The role of the image in destination decision making has been widely researched (see, for instance, Baloglu and McCleary, 1999; Echtner and Ritchie, 1993; Gursory and McCleary, 2004; Therkelsen, 2003). However, the representational role of the tourism media is not all about the visual. As Barthes (1977) notes, images are not only received and perceived but are also "read." In this sense the cognitive context and the history/genealogy of the tourism image/tourist gaze becomes important. Seldom is the tourist merely exposed to media images without context, without caption, and without associated anchoring text.

In addition to the category of induced tourism media are "organic" media information sources which relate to all forms of texts which strictly lie outside of the influence of the tourism industry and its desire to shape our imaginings. This is, of course, a vast category and still poorly understood in terms of the inputs it may have in shaping the patterns of international tourism. It is clear, however, that the texts we encounter—both nonfiction and fiction—contribute subtly, often dramatically, and always cumulatively, to our understandings of cultures of the world (Robinson, 2005). Their influence and narrative power is impossible to separate from considerations of the role of a specific "tourism media." Indeed, the tourism media in total can be taken to be nothing more than composite derivations of a wide variety of existing texts.

As a reflection of the importance of tourism as a facet of modernity and echoing the feedback of images into media activity that Crouch et al. (2005) discuss, we can witness a serious increase in the ways in which tourism itself—as an industry and a social practice—is portrayed entertainingly, if at times stereotypically, through the media. For example, the popular British television comedy series *Benidorm* conveys scenes of British tourists' excessive consumption of alcohol and sexual exploits that refer back to very common portrayals in the UK tabloid press of the worst aspects of British tourist behavior abroad. Other examples include the best selling book and widely seen film adaptation of Alex Garland's *The Beach* that represented an arguably simplistic view of the negative consequences of backpacker tourism in Thailand (Cohen, 2005; Law, Bunnell and Ong, 2007) and; variations on the perils faced by the innocent abroad in the recent genre of "backpacker slasher" films such as *Hostel*. In such cases tourism is woven into the narratives of the media, but it is more than a setting or narrative device; rather, it is reflective of the ways tourism has *become* popular culture, cutting through social and economic barriers (Whetmore, 1989) and being absorbed as part of "everyday life," and a body of knowledge that through international exposure provides it with cross-cultural currency.

Transmission and Transformation

A cursory glance at tourist literature emanating from destinations across the globe, whether produced within the public or private sphere, reveals a series of formalized products and experiences highly, or critically, dependent upon the media. So, for instance, visitors to New York are able to undertake a three and a half hour *Sex in the City* tour based upon the long running and widely distributed television series. The tour, which features over 40 locations featured in the series, operates nearly all year around. Similarly, in Botswana, tours are being designed around the movie, *The Number 1 Ladies' Detective Agency*. The latter, based upon Alexander McCall Smith's novels, has already been dramatized for BBC radio and television. However, there is no inevitable causal relationship between media exposure and touristic behavior. Instead, such relationships are messy, drawn out over time, often cumulative, intimate, ephemeral, and, for the researcher, difficult to study and predict.

In the context of bringing a more rounded understanding as to how tourism is implicated in the flow and meanings of (popular) "texts," Appadurai's "mediascape" links well with Crouch et al.'s (2005) bridging concept of the imagination. For Appadurai (1996: 35): "Mediascapes, whether produced by private or state interests, tend to be image-centered, narrative-based accounts of strips of reality, and what they offer to those who experience and transform them is a series of elements (such as characters, plots, and textual forms) out of which scripts can be formed of imagined lives, their own as well as those living in other places." This moves beyond modalities of mere communication, representation and passive reception towards engagement and experience. Global tourism is littered with destinations which are now intimately linked with productions for the media or are popular because of national or international media coverage and are experienced on a daily basis. Important tourist sites such as Graceland, the once home of Elvis Presley (Boret and Attali,

2005; Wheeller, 2006) and Disneyworld/land (Ritzer and Liska, 1997), reflect both the dominance and the importance of popular culture and the dual role of the media in both its distributive and entertainment sense. Tourism, in many cases, has facilitated the three-dimensional existence of what were originally two-dimensional media forms so that novels, cartoons, and popular music can now be found represented as attractions and theme parks around the world.

Key in this explosion of both popular cultural tourism and popularized culture is the visual media producing, through film or television, not mass tourism but rather niche forms of tourism based around mass forms of entertainment. It is testimony to the importance of popular culture, particularly (but not exclusively) within a western, developed world context, that there exists increasingly close relationships between tourism and the consumption of film and fictional television programs (Beeton, 2001, 2005; Busby and Klug, 2001; Connell, 2005a, 2005b; Couldry, 1998; Eco, 1998; Fish, 2005; Kim and Richardson, 2003; Mordue, 2001; 1992; Riley et al., 1998; Schofield, 1996; Tooke and Baker, 1996; Urry, 2002). Such relationships vary between the commonly observed and measured, yet still largely opaque, process of visits to actual sites featured in film akin to a particular form of popular pilgrimage, to the very creation of tourist destinations through production and location processes and the creation of mythic places. The common denominator is the circulation, to a greater or lesser extent, of imagery; selectively framed, cropped, enhanced and in some cases wholly generated. Within a visual culture, prospective tourists are deemed to be drawn to destinations through the assimilation of images of places used as backgrounds and foregrounds in film and television productions (Crouch and Lübbren, 2006; Crouch et al., 2005; Urry, 2002). The concept of film induced "location" tourism is increasingly well explored throughout the tourism studies literature and focuses generally upon the interlinked issues of motivation (Macionis,

2004; Singh and Best, 2004), image (Kim and Richardson, 2003) and marketing with important subtexts relating to representation and identity-making.

But, despite the welcome growth in attention in considering film-induced tourism, there are some critical gaps in the way the phenomena has been approached to date. Among these, three are worth highlighting for future research. First, there are often naïve assumptions made about the seeming interchangeability of large screen, usually "big-budget" films and programs produced for the television (small screen). Both can have significant audience impact but in the case of the former this tends to be intense, sporadic and relatively short-lived (Beeton, 2005; Carroll, 1996; Creeber, 2001), while, in the latter, audiences are developed over a longer period of time, the programs generating a certain loyalty and more sophisticated relationship with the viewer (Hobson, 2003; Kincaid, 2002; Newcomb, 1974; Valaskivi, 2000). The body of theoretical literature in media and popular cultural studies also exists that offers insights on production values and audience responses to and engagement with popular dramatic film and television outputs (Bae and Lee, 2004; Sood, 2002; Sood and Rogers, 2000). However, this literature has been rarely explored in film tourism and destination image studies. Patterns of distribution differ, as do the environs, practice and social dynamics of viewing and there exist degrees of crossover between these elements so that we can view a blockbuster movie on the television, a DVD, or video at frequent intervals. The film tourism literature has also focused mainly on cinematic releases with a relative lack of attention to popular television series. There is also a lack of attention to non-Western popular television productions, audiences and tourism.

Second, little work has been carried out regarding the cross-cultural reception of film and television programs and the intercultural circulation of film and television programs as catalysts for tourism. One of the markers of globalization is the relative ease with which images now circulate around the globe (Appadurai, 1996). However, understanding the reception and processing of these entails some degree of contextualization. While we can recognize some pressures of globalization such as "westernization" and standardization, we should not assume that our understandings of the rudimentary mechanics of film tourism have universal value. Tourism as a social practice is culturally framed and there is a need to locate it, and the leisure activities of film-going and watching television, within the specifics of "local" values and behavior. Certainly the dominant flow of images from film and television is largely perceived to be from "west to east," developed to developing world (Beltran, 1978; Boyd-Barrett, 1977; Elasmar and Hunter, 1997; Golding and Harris, 1997; Lee, 1980; Nordenstreng and Varis, 1974; Schiller, 1976; Tunstall, 1977; Ware and Dupagne, 1994).

The longstanding pervasiveness and power of Hollywood as a source of global imagery is generally unchallenged in much of the work carried out on film tourism. However, there are other centers and sources of screen imagery and narrative—various traditions in European cinema, Indian "Bollywood" productions, Nigerian "Nollywood" and Latin American versions of daily television soap operas, especially *telenovelas* (Antola and Rogers, 1984; Bilteryst and Meers, 2000; Rogers and Antola, 1985; Tracey, 1988)—of which relatively little is known about the touristic spinoffs which may or may not be associated with their outputs.

Third, and related to the above, is the hegemony of the English language as the foremost mechanism of narrating what is on the screen and in the wider media. Most of the cases and examples which have been examined as focal points for tourism are drawn from English language and literary traditions. This implicit privileging is understandable to some extent, given the practical issues of researching screen productions in non-Anglophone linguistic and cultural settings. However, in being locked within the immediacy of the English language and our own recognizable histories of screen production, it is too easy to presuppose audience reactions and tourist behaviors.

The ways in which tourists encounter media-driven culture varies considerably, reflecting, as it does, the wide variety of media. Thus, for example, the imagined locations featured in A.A. Milne's children's book *Winnie the Pooh* and which are based on actual places experienced by the author at Ashdown Forest in Sussex, England, are promoted to, and experienced by, tourists in England within the context of "Winnie the Pooh Country." Following the Disney feature length cartoons, based on the books and produced and globally distributed over the past 30 years or so, and now constantly played as videos and DVDs, Winnie the Pooh and other characters derived from the books are also popular tourist draws at Disney attractions in the USA, France, and Japan. In addition, Winnie the Pooh is encountered in Canadian tourism media promoting White River, Ontario, the birthplace of the teddy bear which inspired the original stories. He is also a feature of the Burjuman shopping complex in Dubai where there are regular performances for visitors and where the latter can also buy a Pooh Bear comic book, a cuddly Pooh toy, a Piglet pencil case, an Eyore balloon, and a Pooh Bear brand of honey. In this highly complex multilayered and transnational example it would seem clear that various media are ever at work both in terms of communication and entertainment and, whatever the original "status" of Milne's book, it is now firmly part of popular culture.

Conclusion

Tourism is a key element of popular culture and is fed, and feeds from, the media which both circulates and produces culture. While the notion of a sliding spectrum of culture is useful in conceptual terms and, while there is still room for debate regarding the moralities of culture in societies, the very success of popular culture, embraced to a large extent by the tourism sector, cuts through the idea of a simplistic binary. It would seem clear that popular culture provides yet a further resource for the tourism sector to package through attractions and itineraries, in recognition of the connection that we develop and share with what Raymond Williams (1958) referred to as the "culture of the ordinary," constantly being made and remade. Two points are worth stressing here. First, is that in the functioning and imagingings of tourism, popular culture is not taken as a substitute for more "traditional" notions of culture. Visits to Bollywood locations in India are not about to displace the popularity of the Taj Mahal, rather, they can provide an additional experience. Second, as Williams hints at, it is important to recognize the dynamic within culture; a dynamic of invention/reinvention, disconnection and reconnection which also feeds the development and flows of tourism.

Despite only skimming the surface of the issues presented within this chapter it is apparent that the relationships between tourism, popular culture and the media are still under-researched in the academic literature. Approaches to so-called cultural tourism are still dogged by being site specific and often fail to take account of the role of the media in their production and consumption. Moreover, approaches to tourist behavior and performances sometimes neglect the role of media in shaping pre-visit expectations and imaginations. For those engaged in seeking deeper understandings of tourism, media studies and the work conducted in the frame of popular culture studies, provides a rich source of ideas, conceptual approaches, and methods. As tourism spills out into more popular cultural realms it is increasingly important to be able to draw upon ideas such as, for instance, translation, genre, intertextuality, and celebrity.

In relation to tourism the importance of the media as a communicative practice which is ideologically framed, as a leisure practice and form of entertainment and, as a source of imaginings, will continue to increase. Among the key issues that would warrant further attention from tourism scholars include: the extent to which images distributed by the media persist or alter over time (this is a crucial issue for destination tourism authorities in former and intermittent areas of conflict and in places where tourists have been subject to violent attacks); the ways in which the tourism industry and government agencies use the media to draw travelers" attention to security issues in destinations; the links between travel advertising, media editorial policies and demand for tourism products; and the effects that emerging media technologies have on tourism supply, intermediation, demand and inter-tourist communication.

References

Altheide, D.L. (1996). *Qualitative Media Analysis*. London: Sage.

Anderson, B. (1983). *Imagined Communities*. London: Verso.

Antola, A. and Rogers, E.M. (1984). "Television Flows in Latin America." *Communication Research*, 11(2): 183–202.

Appadurai, A. (1996). *Modernity at Large: Cultural Dimensions of Globalization*. Minneapolis: University of Minnesota Press.

Avraham, E. (2007). *Media Strategies for Marketing Places in Crisis: Improving the Image of Cities, Countries and Tourist Destinations*. London: Butterworth-Heinemann.

Bae, H. and Lee, B. (2004). "Audience Involvement and its Antecedents: An Analysis of the Electronic Bulletin Board Messages about an Entertainment-Education Drama on Divorces in Korea." *Asian Journal of Communication*, 14(1): 6–21.

Baloglu, S. and McCleary, K.W. (1999). "A Model of Destination Image Formation." *Annals of Tourism Research*, 26(4): 868–897.

Barthes, R. (1977). *Image, Music, Text*. New York: Noonday Press.

Beeton, S. (2005). *Film-Induced Tourism*. Clevedon: Channel View.

Beeton, S. (2001). "Smiling for the Camera: The Influence of Film Audiences on a Budget Tourism Destination." *Tourism, Culture and Communication*, 3(1): 15–25.

Beltran, L.R. (1978). "Communication and Cultural Domination: USA–Latin American Case." *Media Asia*, 5(4): 183–192.

Berger, A. A. (2005). *Media Analysis Techniques* (3rd edition). London: Sage.

Biltereyst, D. and Meers, P. (2000). "The International Telenovela Debate and the Contra-flow Argument: A Reappraisal." *Media, Culture & Society*, 22(4): 393–413.

Boret, A. and Attali, J. (2005). "Espaces, Tourisme & amp." *Loisirs*, 222: 21–49.

Boyd-Barrett, O. (1977). "Media Imperialism: Towards an International Framework for the Analysis of Media Systems." In J. Curran and M. Gurevitch (Eds.), *Mass Communication and Society* (pp. 116–135). London: Edward Arnold.

Boyd-Barrett, O. and Newbold, C. (Eds.) (1995). *Approaches to Media: A Reader*. New York: Edward Arnold.

Branston, G. and Stafford, G. (1996). *The Media Student's Book*. London: Routledge.

Busby, G. and Klug, J. (2001). "Movie-Induced Tourism: The Challenge of Measurement and Other Issues." *Journal of Vacation Marketing*, 7(4): 316–332.

Butler, R.W. (1990). "The Influence of the Media in Shaping International Tourist Patterns." *Tourism Recreation Research*, 15(2): 46–53.

Carroll, N. (1996). *Theorizing the Moving Image*. Cambridge: Cambridge University Press.

Cohen, E. (2005). "The Beach of 'The Beach'? The Politics of Environmental Damage in Thailand." *Tourism Recreation Research*, 30(1): 1–19.

Connell, J. (2005a). "Toddlers, Tourism and Tobermory: Destination Marketing Issues and Television-Induced Tourism." *Tourism Management*, 26(5): 763–776.

Connell, J. (2005b). "'What's the Story in Balamory?': The Impacts of a Children's TV Programme on Small Tourism Enterprises on the Isle of Mull, Scotland." *Journal Of Sustainable Tourism*, 13(3): 228–255.

Couldry, N. (1998). "The View from Inside the 'Simulacrum': Visitors' Tales from the Set of Coronation Street." *Leisure Studies*, 17(2): 94–107.

Creeber, G. (2001). "Taking Our Personal Lives Seriously: Intimacy, Continuity and Memory in the Television Drama Serial." *Media, Culture and Society*, 23(4): 439–455.

Crouch, D., Jackson, R. and Thompson, F. (Eds.) (2005). *The Media and the Tourist Imagination*. Chichester: Routledge.

Crouch, D. and Lübbren, N. (Eds.) (2006). *Visual Culture and Tourism*. Oxford: Berg.

Dann, G. (1996). "Tourists Images of a Destination—An Alternative Analysis." *Journal of Travel and Tourism Marketing*, 5(1/2): 41–55.

Devereux, E. (2003). *Understanding the Media*. London: Sage.

Dunn, D. (2005). "Venice Observed: The Traveller, The Tourist, The Post-Tourist and British Television." In A. Jaworski and A. Pritchard (Eds.), *Discourse, Communication and Tourism* (pp. 98–120). Clevedon: Channel View Publications.

Durkheim, E. (1909/1982). "The Contribution of Sociology to Psychology and Philosophy." In S. Lukes (Ed.), *The Rule of Sociological Method and Selected Texts on Sociology and its Method* (pp. 236–240). New York: The Free Press.

Echtner, C.M. and Ritchie, B. (1993). "The Measurement of Destination Image: An Empirical Assessment." *Journal of Travel Research*, 31(4): 3–13.

Echtner, C.M. and Ritchie J.R. (2003). "The Meaning and Measurement Of Destination Image." *The Journal of Tourism Studies*, 14(1): 37–48.

Eco, U. (1998). *Faith in Fakes: Travels in Hyperreality*. London: Vintage.

Elasmar, M.G. and Hunter, J.E. (1997). "The Impact of Foreign TV on Domestic Audiences: A Meta-Analysis." In B.R. Burleson (Ed.), *Communication Yearbook 20* (pp. 47–69). Thousand Oaks, CA: Sage.

Fish, R. (2005). "Media Producers and the Televisual Tourist." In D. Crouch, R. Jackson and F. Thompson (Eds.), *The Media And The Tourist Imagination: Converging Cultures* (pp. 119–134). London: Routledge.

Fiske, J. (1990). *Introduction to Media Studies* (2nd edition). London: Routledge.

Font, X. (1997). "Managing the Tourist Destination's Image." *Journal of Vacation Marketing*, 3(2): 123–131.

Gartner, W. (1993). "Image Formation Process." *Journal of Travel and Tourism Marketing*, 2(2/3): 191–215.

Gillespie, M. (Ed.) (2005). *Media Audiences*. Maidenhead: Open University Press.

Gillespie, M. and Toynbee, J. (Eds.) (2006). *Analysing Media Texts*. Maidenhead: Open University Press.

Golding, P. and Harris, P. (1997). *Beyond Cultural Imperialism: Globalisation, Communication and the New International Order*. London: Sage.

Gurevitch, M., Bennett, T., Curran, J. and Woollacott, J. (Eds.) (1982). *Culture, Society and the Media*. London: Routledge.

Gregory, D. (1999). "Scripting Egypt: Orientalism and the Cultures of Travel." In J. Duncan and D. Gregory (Eds.), *Writes of Passage: Travel Writing, Place and Ambiguity*. London: Routledge.

Gunn, C. (1972). *Vacationscape: Designing Tourist Regions*. Austin: Bureau of Business Research, University of Texas.

Gursoy, D. and McCleary, K.W. (2004). "An Integrative Model of Tourists' Information Search Behavior." *Annals of Tourism Research*, 31(2): 353–373.

Hall, C.M. and O'Sullivan, V. (1996). "Tourism, Political Stability and Violence." In A. Pizam and Y. Mansfeld (Eds.), *Tourism, Crime and International Security Issues*. Chichester: John Wiley.

Hall, S. (1997). "Encoding/Decoding." In D. Graddol and O. Boyd-Barrett (Eds.), *Media Texts, Authors and Readers: A Reader* (pp. 200–211). Milton Keynes: Open University Press.

Hanefors, M. and Larsson, L. (1993). "Video Strategies Used by Tour Operators." *Tourism Management*, 14(1):27–33.

Hobson, D. (2003). *Soap Opera*. Cambridge: Polity Press.

Inglis, F. (1990). *Media Theory: An Introduction*. Oxford: Blackwell.

Jacobsen, J.K.S. (2003). "The Tourist Bubble and the Europeanisation of Holiday Travel." *Journal of Tourism and Cultural Change*, 1(1): 71–87.

Jaworski, A. and Thurlow, C. (2003). "Communicating a Global Reach: Inflight Magazines as a Globalising Genre in Tourism." *Journal of Sociolinguistics*, 7(4): 581–608.

Jaworski, A., Thurlow, C., Lawson, S. and Ylanne-McEwen, V. (2003). "The Uses and Representations of Host Languages in Tourist Destinations: A View from British TV Holiday Programmes." *Language Awareness*, 12(1): 5–29.

Jenks, C. (2005). *Sub-Culture: The Fragmentation of the Social*. London: Sage.

Kim, H. and Richardson, S. (2003). "Motion Picture Impacts on Destination Image." *Annals of Tourism Research*, 30(1): 216–237.

Kincaid, D.L. (2002). "Drama, Emotion, and Cultural Convergence." *Communication Theory*, 12(2): 136–152.

Lasswell, H (1948). "The Structure and Function of Communication in Contemporary Society." In L. Bryson (Ed.), *The Communication of Ideas IRSS*. New York.

Law, L., Bunnell, T. and Ong, C.E. (2007). "The Beach, The Gaze and Film Tourism." *Tourist Studies*, 7(2): 141–164.

Lee, C.C. (1980). *Media Imperialism Reconsidered: The Homogenizing of Television Culture*. Beverly Hills, CA: Sage.

Louw, E. (2001). *The Media and Cultural Production*. London: Sage.

Lull, J. (Ed.) (2001). *Culture in the Communication Age*. London: Routledge.

MacCannell, D. (1976). *The Tourist: A New Theory of the Leisure Class*. New York. Schocken Books.

McQuail, D. (1983). *Mass Communication Theory*. London: Sage.

Macionis, N. (2004). "Understanding the Film-Induced Tourist." *Proceedings of International Tourism And Media Conference 2004* (pp. 86–97). Melbourne: Tourism Research Unit, Monash University.

Moores, S. (1993). *Interpreting Audiences: The Ethnography of Media Consumption*. London: Sage.

Mordue, T. (2001). "Performing and Directing Resident/Tourist Cultures in Heartbeat Country." *Tourist Studies*, 1(3): 233–252.

Morgan, N. and Pritchard, A. (1999). *Tourism Promotion and Power: Creating Images, Creating Identities*. Chichester: John Wiley.

Muggleton, D and Weinzierl, R. (Eds.) (2003). *The Post-Subcultures Reader*. Oxford: Berg.

Nielsen, C. (2001). *Tourism and the Media*. Melbourne: Pearson Education Australia.

Newcomb, H. (1974). *TV: The Most Popular Art*. New York: Anchor.

Nordenstreng, K. and Varis, T. (1974). Television Traffic: A One-Way Street? Paris: UNESCO.

Pearce, P.L., Moscardo, G. and Ross, G.F. (1996). *Tourism, Community Relationships*. Oxford: Elsevier.

Petracca, M. and Sorapure, M. (1998). *Common Culture: Reading and Writing about American Popular Culture.* New Jersey: Prentice Hall.

Philips, D. (2000). "Narrativised Spaces: The Function of Story in the Theme Park." In D. Crouch (Ed.), *Leisure/Tourism Geographies* (pp. 91–108). London: Routledge.

Pritchard, A. and Morgan, N. (2005). "Representations of "Ethnographic Knowledge": Early Comic Postcards of Wales." In A. Jaworski and A. Pritchard (Eds.), *Discourse, Communication and Tourism* (pp. 53–75). Clevedon: Channel View Publications.

Richards, G. Ed. (1996). *Cultural Tourism in Europe.* Wallingford: CAB International.

Richards, G. Ed. (2001). *Cultural Attractions and European Tourism.* Wallingford: CAB International.

Richards, G. (2006). *Cultural Tourism: Global and Local Perspectives.* New York: Haworth Press.

Riley, R., Baker, D. and Van Doren, C.S. (1998). "Movie Induced Tourism." *Annals of Tourism Research*, 25(4): 919–935.

Ritzer, G. and Liska, A. (1997). "McDisneyization and Post-Tourism." In C. Rojek and J. Urry (Eds.), *Touring Cultures: Transformations of Travel and Theory* (pp. 96–109). London: Routledge.

Robinson, M. (2002). "Between and Beyond the Pages: Literature-tourism Relationships." In M. Robinson and H.C. Andersen (Eds.), *Literature and Tourism: The Reading and Writing of Tourism* (pp. 39–79). London: Continuum Press.

Rogers, E.M. and Antola, A. (1985). "Telenovelas: A Latin American Success Story." *Journal of Communication*, 35(4): 24–35.

Rojek, C. (1997). "Indexing, Dragging and the Social Construction of Tourist Sights." In C. Rojek and J. Urry (Eds.), *Touring Cultures: Transformations of Travel and Theory* (pp. 52–74). London: Routledge.

Saïd, E. (1978). *Orientalism.* London: Routledge & Kegan Paul.

Schiller, H.I. (1976). *Communication and Cultural Domination.* New York: International Arts and Sciences Press.

Schofield, P. (1996). "Cinematographic Images of a City: Alternative Heritage Tourism in Manchester." *Tourism Management*, 17(5): 333–340.

Schroeder, F.E.H. (1980). "Introduction: The Discovery of Popular Culture Before Printing."

In F.E.H. Schroeder (Ed.), *5000 Years of Popular Culture: Popular Culture Before Printing* (pp. 1–9). Bowling Green, OH: Bowling Green University Popular Press.

Seaton, A.V. (1990). *The Occupational Influences and Ideologies of Travel Writers.* Sunderland: Business Education Publishers.

Shields, R. (1995). *Places on the Margin.* London: Routledge.

Singh, K. and Best, G. (2004). "Film-Induced Tourism: Motivations of Visitors to the Hobbiton Movie Set as Features in the Lord of the Rings." *Proceedings of International Tourism and Media Conference 2004* (pp. 98–111). Melbourne: Tourism Research Unit, Monash University.

Sontag, S. (2001). *Against Interpretation and Other Essays.* London: Picador.

Sood, S. (2002). "Audience Involvement and Entertainment-Education." *Communication Theory*, 12(2): 153–172.

Sood, S. and Rogers, E. (2000). "Dimensions of Parasocial Interaction by Letter-Writers to a Popular Entertainment-Education Soap Opera in India." *Journal of Broadcasting & Electronic Media*, 44(3): 386–414.

Synott, A. (1993). *The Body Social: Symbolism, Self and Society.* London: Routledge.

Therkelsen, A. (2003). "Imaging Places. Image Formation of Tourists and its Consequences for Destination Promotion." *Scandinavian Journal of Hospitality and Tourism*, 3(2): 134–150.

Tooke, N. and Baker, M. (1996). "Seeing is Believing: The Effect of Film on Visitor Numbers to Screened Locations." *Tourism Management*, 17(2): 87–94.

Tracey, M. (1988). "Popular Culture and the Economics of Global Television." *Intermedia*, 16(2): 9–25.

Tunstall, J. (1977). *The Media are American.* Beverly Hills, CA: Sage.

Urry, J. (2002). *The Tourist Gaze* (2nd edition.). London: Sage.

Valaskivi, K. (2000). "Being a Part of the Family? Genre, Gender and Production in a Japanese TV Drama." *Media, Culture & Society*, 22(3): 309–325.

Ware, W. and Dupagne, M. (1994). "Effects of U.S. Television Programs on Foreign Audiences: A Meta-Analysis." *Journalism Quarterly*, 71: 947–959.

Watson, J. (1998). *Media Communication: An Introduction to Theory and Process*. London: Macmillan.

Whetmore, E.J. (1989). *Mediamerica: Form, Content and Consequence of Mass Communication*. Belmont, CA: Wadsworth.

Wheeller, B. (2006). "The King is Dead. Long Live the Product: Elvis, Authenticity, Sustainability and the Product Life Cycle." In. R.W. Butler (Ed.), *The Tourism Area Life Cycle—Vol. 1: Applications and Modifications* (pp. 339–348). Clevedon: Channel View Publications.

Williams, R. (1958). *Culture and Society, 1780–1950*. London: Chatto and Windus.

Histories of Tourism

John K. Walton

Tourism History: A Developing Field

This chapter argues that a persisting failure to grasp the importance of tourism's past has impoverished the understanding of current developments and future prospects on an international stage, despite a recent explosion of new work on the history of tourism on several fronts. It examines key debates in tourism through a historical lens, while providing a contextualized commentary on developments in tourism on the world stage, mainly since the eighteenth century, and reflecting the Eurocentric and North American perspectives that dominate current outputs. Approaches, trends, and current foci of interest will be considered, along with problems of source material and interpretation. It also considers the contested relationships between history and the "heritage industry," which raise issues of authenticity, control and ownership in particularly challenging forms, not least when tourist destinations market versions of their own histories as distinguishing features and selling points.

As Paul Theroux has recently remarked, travel writers need to be aware that "every trip has a historical dimension": the social

and political landscape can change with remarkable speed, as can the transportation systems available to the traveler, pushing every current commentary into a shifting past with disconcerting rapidity (Theroux, 2008: 6). This is not a peculiarity of travel writing: it applies to every attempt to write about tourism, whether or not from a literary perspective, and it means that every practitioner of tourism studies, however immediately contemporary their ostensible concerns, needs to come to terms with the ever-moving frontier of the past. The present cannot be understood without reference to what has gone before; nor can we attempt to predict or preempt the future without achieving some understanding of where we, and others, have come from, or of how relevant interested parties understand and appreciate their versions of the past. Tourism studies, whether we view it as a field, a set of interests, or an emergent discipline, is no exception: it needs a sense of historical awareness, not least to inform the ways in which tourism itself tries to use history, through the marking, marketing and exploitation of traces, stories, heritage, authenticity, and, ultimately, distinctiveness.

Tourist businesses and destinations often pay lip service to the distinctiveness of their histories, even when cultural tourism based on architectural heritage, literary landscapes, or romantic stories of difference and otherness is not central to their marketing. Thus the tourism website of the English seaside resort of Bournemouth offers a timeline of development based almost entirely on "significant" personalities ("great men") and their contributions to the town, while the northern English county of Lancashire invites the visitor to "find out about Lancashire's history from the official tourist board," which proves not to be the reliable source that this implies, presenting an extraordinary farrago of inventions and misleading half-truths. In such cases history is seen to be useful, indeed a necessary part of the offering, but not important enough to take seriously in the sense of providing full, accurate, or stimulating supporting material.[1] A lack of discipline and attention to context, including existing historical writing, is sometimes also evident when practitioners of cultural studies present their versions of "tourism history" (Inglis, 2000). Buzard (2001) has pointed out that for many tourism promotion purposes "history" tends to be reduced to a scattering of attractive tales, traditions, and vignettes, which become problematic when set in opposition to the narratives celebrating modernity, comfort, and predictability which are also seen as essential to the competitive tourist offer. In much mainstream tourism marketing, modernity and history are set in perpetual (though often concealed) antagonism, the one seeking to sanitize and manipulate the other.

This should not be so. As Martín reminds us, following the cultural geographer David Harvey, although "the development of tourism on a grand scale . . . brings with it an ever-increasing homogenization of what was once unique and non-replicable," itself a set of historical processes too easily rendered down into universal notions of "globalization," there is always a countervailing celebration of the distinctive: ". . . if the goose of the golden eggs is not to be killed, if capital is to extract a surplus value from difference, it must sustain some level of specificity" (Martín, 2008: 222).

Moreover, many "cultural heritage" aspects of the tourist experience may have been constructed for the purpose, as part of systematic projects in the creation of national or regional identity and distinctiveness, through what Hobsbawm and Ranger long ago described as the "invention of tradition" in such forms as folk dancing and "peasant" dress (Hobsbawm and Ranger, 1983; Löfgren, 2001; Steward, in Baranowski and Furlough, 2001). But beyond all this, tourism studies itself also has its own history. Key concepts and approaches have evolved through the multiplication of case studies, the testing of theories and the challenging of assumptions over (at least) the past 30 or 40 years. Moreover, as Schwartz points out in her history of tourism in twentieth-century Cuba, tourism *as* history, as a way of understanding cultures through time, is just as important as histories *of* tourism as a phenomenon. This approach has the added merit of steering the historian's gaze towards the domestic as well as the international, and to "hosts" as well as "guests" (Schwartz, 1997).

The history of tourism is now a rapidly expanding field in its own right, complete with dedicated journal (*Journal of Tourism History*, Taylor and Francis, from 2009). It remains on the fringes of most professional historical activity, as a conservative academic area has been slow to recognize the global importance of this rapidly expanding, economically potent and culturally disruptive industry. It is just beginning to affect the wider agenda of tourism studies, in which the dominant paradigms have come from such present-focused (though often historically aware) disciplines as economics and business/management studies, geography, sociology, and anthropology (Berghoff et al., 2002; Walton, 2005a, 2005b). Significantly, a recent analysis of the relationship between tourism studies and the social sciences discusses every social science discipline except history (Holden, 2005).

Where introductions to tourism studies acknowledge that tourism has a history, they tend to encapsulate it briskly in three main themes: the aristocratic Grand Tour of France, Germany, Italy, and later Switzerland, from the sixteenth and especially the eighteenth to the early nineteenth centuries; the work of Thomas and John Mason Cook in democratizing access to British, then international tourism from the 1840s and especially the 1860s onwards, with acknowledgement of Cook as the presumed inventor of the "package tour"; and the rise of popular international tourism based on "sun, sea, sand, sex and *sangria*," sending large numbers of northern Europeans on cheap flights to Mediterranean shores, from the 1950s or 1960s onwards. The work of Alain Corbin on the eighteenth-century origins of positive perceptions of coastal environments in Western Europe has also made a widespread impact (Corbin, 1994). There is recurrent recourse to the concept of "mass tourism," which (like the bourgeoisie) seems always to be "rising" in historical terms. It has been used as a convenient label to apply to everything from the early Cook's tours, through the rail-borne working-class seaside holiday (which developed at different times, rates and intensities in different parts of the world), to the package tourism of the "jet age." This simplistic and unduly flexible coinage, which remains prevalent in historical writing and appears in the titles and subtitles of many excellent books, encourages over-simplification and distortion, not least because it promotes misleading assumptions about the uniformity of tourist experiences and the lack of agency and choice ascribed to the tourists themselves. The often-used distinction between the "traveler," trail-blazing and self-motivated, and the "tourist," reactive, following established channels and seeking prescribed experiences in predetermined ways, is also question-begging (Buzard, 1993; Edensor, 1998; Wright, 2002). It is also too easy to read off, retrospectively, Urry's much-cited concepts of the "romantic" and "collective" gaze as mapping neatly on to the dichotomy between the "traveler" and the "tourist" or the rise of "mass tourism," although Urry himself was aware of these dangers and called his readers' attention to variations on these themes (Urry, 1995).

Serious, critical historical research complicates such pictures while enriching them.

The Grand Tour was important in setting out and reinforcing enduring elements of the cultural capital expected of elite (and, later, of some middling and popular) tourists in Western (including North American) societies, and in defining where to go, what to see, and how to respond to prescribed experiences in parts of France, Germany, Italy (especially), and later Switzerland; but it was not the sole fountain-head of tourism in history. Moreover, the cultural meanings attached to the term have mutated over time, not least through the incursions of satire, snobbery, and self-mockery (Black, 2003; Chaney, 1998; Levenstein, 2004; Sketchley, 1870). A broad spectrum of tourist activity flourished in classical Greece and Rome, for example, and it is possible to write about tourism in "ancient India." Across the globe religious pilgrimage has motivated organized travel for millennia, entailing a mix of spiritual and secular activities that falls under many broader definitions of tourism than the basic, reductive one of being away from home for between 24 hours and a year (Feifer, 1985; Hunt, 1982; Lomine, 2005; Pearson, 1996; Singh, 2005; Swatos and Tomasi, 2002; Timothy and Olsen, 2006).

Spa and seaside tourism also have deep independent roots, with classical (or earlier) origins in the former case, while the latter's formal modern origins, whether at Scheveningen in the mid-seventeenth century or Scarborough in the early eighteenth, grew out of older popular traditions of therapeutic bathing and communal reveling at the late summer spring tides (Gibson, 2000: 105; Porter, 1990; Walton, 1997a). Nor are these purely Western traditions: Japanese religious pilgrimages to hot springs, described by a contemporary in 1832 as being 70% about pleasure and 30% faith, have equally deep roots, for example. Some of the 3000 or so "onsen" spa resorts trace their origins back for a millennium, although revived and transformed at various points from the seventeenth and eighteenth centuries (Miyazaki and Williams, 2001). Less obvious was Tunisian attachment to popular sea-bathing customs, which predated French colonial influences and the international literary and artistic community at Hammamet, and brought summer visitors from the desert interior to Sousse, long before these coastal settlements became centers of international tourism (Boukraa, 1993).[2]

Meanwhile, Thomas Cook's high visibility in potted histories of tourism is not only a reflection of the firm's important contribution to international tourism from a British perspective, especially in Europe and the eastern Mediterranean, from the 1860s onwards. It also reflects Cook's exemplary suitability as an entrepreneurial role model and individual illustration of "self-help" in action, with the survival of extensive archives and their deployment for publicity. There were other innovatory and enterprising travel agents in mid- to late nineteenth-century Britain alone, from Henry Gaze and Frames to Sir Henry Lunn, but we hear much less about them, although Gaze was offering 10-guinea tours to Switzerland by 1861 and 15-guinea tours of northern Italy and Venetia by 1864; but they did not keep archives (Gaze, 1861, 1864). Cook was not just a pioneer of popular tourism, but provided custom-built and luxurious tourist experiences for international and colonial high society, promoted his own distinctive form of pilgrimage to the Holy Land (also providing travel services to Mecca for the Hajj), and was in some contexts practically a commercial extension of the British Empire (Brendon, 1991; Hunter, 2004; Larson, 2000; Walton, 1974: 284–286). Discussion of the rise of package tourism has conflated diverse phenomena, from Cook's tours, through other kinds of rail- or motor coach-based collective tourism (common in Europe by the 1930s) based on shared itineraries and an all-in price for travel, accommodation, and, perhaps, entertainment and excursions, to the use of air travel (initially of a hair-raising kind using post-Second World War surplus military transport planes) alongside bus and train to reach new destinations from the 1950s. These were mainly Mediterranean in the early years, but such practices were spreading across the globe in proliferating variety by the later twentieth century, including distinctive socialist Eastern European variants by the 1960s. These were complex and variable developments, sometimes involving dedicated, segregated holiday camps or villages. The relationships between developers, hoteliers, and tour operators were by no means uniform, while visitors varied in their willingness to explore and mix with local people on their own account (Akhtar and Humphries, 2000; Bray and Raitz, 2001; Lyth, 2003; Turner and Ash, 1975; Wright, 2002). We need to create and take account of critical, textured, contextually aware contributions by historians to debates in these and many other areas, rather than recycling uncritically "truths universally acknowledged" about tourism's pasts.

What History Offers

A key role of history in tourism studies is to challenge or complicate disarmingly simple stories about the past through detailed and carefully documented research in archives as well as published texts. History as an academic discipline is protean in subject matter and methodology: it can be qualitative or quantitative in predominant approach, although historians often blur that imagined boundary. Its intrinsically interdisciplinary nature as the study of "the past" means that it engages with every thematic dimension that feeds into tourism studies, from demography (Hobbs's [2008] work on the illusory nature of the alleged problem of "illegitimacy" and its relationship with popular seaside tourism in twentieth-century Blackpool) to international politics (Endy's [2004] examination of the role of USA tourist traffic to Europe in the "Cold War" diplomacy of the 1950s and 1960s). It engages in dialogue between expectation (whether or not articulated formally as "theory") and evidence, with a requirement that statements should be validated or at least supported by reference to verifiable sources in print, archives, or other accessible media, wherever possible in the public domain. Historians do not always honor such commitments, and nor are they peculiar to historical practice; but widespread acknowledgement of their importance, and shared appreciation of a set of rules and conventions about the validation of statements, itself affects practice and the prevailing sense of what is and is not legitimate discourse (Evans, 1997). The "common sense" of the discipline tends to be suspicious of overarching theories and efforts to classify phenomena into rigidly defined boxes, and to resist formulaic approaches to the presentation of argument according to prescribed stages, often dominant and prescribed in the academic cultures of business and social science. Contrasting expectations about the construction of academic outputs, and editorial reluctance to recognize the validity of historical perspectives, have sometimes made it difficult for historians to publish in tourism studies outlets (Worthington, 2003).

Historians generally reject notions of history as "progress" to an ideal state (especially any suggestion that such a state has been achieved), or as the irresistible rise of "modernity" or "globalization"; and attempts to propose "stages of growth" models usually attract skeptical responses, although they sometimes emerge via econometric approaches to history or the adoption of modernization theory. For example, the Tourist Area Life Cycle can appear unduly schematic and mechanistic to historians, even in its more sophisticated recent forms: it is based on perceptions of and assumptions about change over time, but its credibility for historians has been undermined by a lack of grounded archival investigation into the historical processes at work, and a consequent tendency to "read off" the past in circular ways, especially when dealing with complex, extended histories. Prideaux's (2000) notion of a spectrum of resort experiences, and the "realist" approach advocated by Gale and Botterill (2005) in examining the decline and attempted regeneration of the Welsh seaside resort of Rhyl, show that tourism studies can address these issues, offering more scope for positive intervention by historians (Butler, 2005). Recent research in tourism studies has generated more convincing comparative understandings of the changing nature of resort destinations and processes at work in periods of transition, but the distinctive contributions of historians, as in Garner's elegant, evocative and nuanced study of the local and external influences on the French resort of Arcachon in the nineteenth and twentieth centuries, still shed indispensable additional light (Agarwal, 2002; Garner, 2005).

History offers depth of field, enhanced understanding of origins, trends and distinctiveness, awareness of the complex and provisional nature of our understandings of continuity and change over time and variations between societies and kinds of place, and critical awareness of context, the circumstances under which the materials we use as sources were created, and the ways in which our own assumptions affect the questions we ask and the answers we privilege. This is not to claim that all historians display all these attributes under all circumstances; nor is it to suggest that "history" as a category is separate and distinct from other fields of academic endeavor, or that other disciplines do not also display such distinguishing features. Quite the reverse, in fact; indeed this disclaimer is a necessary corollary of the argument that everything has a history. But it is to suggest that the contributions of historians are likely to be distinctive, enriching, and worthy of attention.

Histories of Tourism

The spectrum of histories of tourism extends from the economic to the cultural, engaging with contingent and overlapping disciplines in the process. Tourism's perceived legitimacy as a "proper" subject of economic history has suffered from problems of quantification and measurement. Its "product" is intangible, the sum of the satisfactions obtained by those who use its services and experience the associated attributes of journey and destination, and cannot be measured in material goods that can be counted and assigned a price. The technologies used to service tourism (accommodation, transportation, infrastructure, buildings, and machinery dedicated to the provision of pleasure) can be measured and accounted for, but they do not provide a surrogate for the sum, or collectivity, of the relevant tourist experiences as they change over time. The "aura" attached to more tangible kinds of consumer goods, in terms of how they are used and what they signify to (and about) the consumer, poses fewer problems because the statistics of manufacture and sale seem more firmly grounded, even though they tell us more about price than value, and about the number of outputs rather than what they mean to the consumer (Rapaport, 2000; Vickery, 1998). The more standardized and centralized the product, the more plausible the time-series and geographically comparative statistics of tourism may appear; but it remains difficult to get beyond the level of the individual firm, and the process is bedeviled by problems of definition and duration, especially in the many cases where tourism is seasonal or works to weekly or even daily rhythms.

Statistics of visitor and traveler numbers and per capita expenditure remain extremely dubious, although they have been gathered with increasing care and assiduity since the 1970s and 1980s. They become more doubtful still as we go further back in time (Gaviria, 1974: 14–15). If collected and classified at all, they have seldom been kept in standard or apparently reliable forms that enabled plausible comparisons between periods, places, and categories in ways that supported sophisticated statistical analysis. The use of destination population figures, data on individual attractions, or overall numbers traveling, provides unsatisfactory surrogates, although orders of magnitude and patterns of development are often discernable, especially for islands with a single dominant mode of access, where tourists could readily be counted in and out (Buades, 2004; Prentice, 1990: 248–253). Where, for example, individual tourist attractions have counted visitors in through turnstiles, and recorded the results, sturdy

basic comparative figures can be supplied; but most of the statistics deployed by tourist industries and organizations, and especially those in the public domain, are still based on projections and assumptions rather than hard evidence. Historians have tried to work with various quantitative sources, from official national and regional tourism statistics and census records to transportation statistics, the records of lodging or entertainment taxes, and commercially generated lists of visitors, but reliability and comparability (over time and between places) remain elusive (Chadefaud, 1987; Dye, 2005; Walton and O'Neill, 1993; Walton and Smith, 1996). The habit of skepticism this engenders is invaluable, but resource and archival problems ensure that the quantitative economic history of tourism will remain provisional and imprecise, while providing salutary reminders of the general vulnerability of time-series economic and social statistics. Such problems have not inhibited the construction of business histories of tourism in several settings, including Australia (Davidson and Spearritt, 2000).

The demographic history of tourism is equally problematic. Developed resort destinations often exhibit distinctive age, gender, and occupational profiles in census reports, and migration profiles can be configured for those who are captured by the census, as can tables showing the social and geographical distribution of ethnic and linguistic groups. But this kind of statistical evidence is usually only available for the larger centers. It often overlooks or downplays itinerant and seasonal migrant workforces and their characteristic occupations, even when triangulated with other materials such as taxation records or trade directories, especially as censuses tend to be taken outside peak holiday periods, and to understate female participation in the labor market. Household occupational classifications based on male economic activity are particularly distorting in tourist environments, especially those with many female-operated small outlets in accommodation, retail, and services (Higgs, 2005; Walton, 1994, 1997b). The demographic characteristics of guests, especially short-stay visitors, are even more elusive, especially if we seek to establish patterns of class, age, and gender. The professional visitor survey was mainly a postwar development, especially from the 1970s, while the visitors' lists provided by (mainly) nineteenth-century newspapers were always selective and unreliable. Statistics based on arrivals by public transportation are unable to disaggregate "tourists" from others, although in highly specialized tourist environments they can provide orders of magnitude; but they have difficulty in coping with the rise of the private motorist at different points in the twentieth century. Here, then, we depend particularly heavily on the critical assessment of commentary from contemporary observers, alongside the analysis of visual and cinematic representations of the tourist journey, its destinations and participants, which become available in some settings at the beginning of the twentieth century (Walton, 1983, 2004). Some of the literature privileges the analysis and ascribed significance of international tourism flows at the expense of national or local activity, as in the case of much work in English on tourism in twentieth-century Mexico, which shows much greater interest in Cancún than in Veracruz, and in new international destinations than traffic flows within Mexico (Clancy, 2001).

Tourist journeys also have more complex and problematic histories than might be assumed. It is tempting to "read off" successive transportation innovations as if they revolutionized the nature of the experience and the capacity of the system at a stroke, from road and carriage improvements that accelerated the speed and enhanced the comfort of travelers, through the application of steam power to transportation by sea and rail, to the internal combustion engine in its various incarnations and the jet engine. New transportation modes and infrastructures promoted new ways of experiencing and visualizing the tourist journey, and hastened the transition from one environment and culture to another; but we should consider the gradual and incomplete nature of such transitions, the time-lag before they were widely adopted, their variety (from mainline express to sleepy branch line, from paddle steamer to ocean liner, from lumbering war surplus vehicle to luxury express coach), and the way in which many tourist journeys have combined modes rather than confining themselves to the most modern and rapid (Armstrong, 2005; Featherstone et al., 2005; Lyth, 2003; Schivelbusch, 1980; Simonsen, 2005; Williams and Armstrong, 2006). Moreover, simple, archaic and rustic transportation modes have often been preferred by seekers after the authentic or nostalgic, and leisure travel on foot (hiking, rambling, trekking) has been a tourism mode and preferred experience in its own right (Taylor, 1997). The availability of new transportation systems does not simply create demand for tourism: it may have to be unlocked by other developments, such as improvements in real wages or family incomes, the availability of consecutive free time or even paid holidays, or the development of a preference for discretionary expenditure on travel and tourism above alternative modes of leisure or consumer spending on, for example, food, fashion, dancing, or the cinema (Walton, 1983: ch. 2; Walton, 2000a: ch. 3). It may have to be encouraged by government policies to promote tourism for nationalistic or other political reasons, the policies of transportation providers in offering and promoting cheap, flexible services on tourist routes, the advertising campaigns of travel agents and holiday destinations, or the spread of cheap travel-related literature (Furlough, 1998; Pagenstecher, 2004). Transportation innovation has usually been enabling or encouraging, responding to existing demand or visible opportunity, rather than making things happen in its own right.

Equally important to significant tourism growth, beyond tradition and "word of mouth" and developing at regional, national, and international levels, has been the development of literatures associated with tourism, from the iconic literary output to the travel book with literary pretensions, guidebook, and promotional leaflet. The role of the guide-book in prescribing, advising, and mediating between tourist, journey, destination, and experience, and the emergence of a distinctive genre of "travel journalism," are particularly important here (Koshar, 2002; Mackenzie, 2005; Steward, 2005). The emergence and expansion of tourism in particular places or regions has often been stimulated by celebra-tory "literary landscapes," as in responses to the work of the Lake Poets in England (where William Wordsworth himself boosted the process by writing an influential early guidebook and becoming a reluctant resident celebrity), or the novels of Sir Walter Scott in Scotland. Such influences now extend to film, television, and other media (Dekker, 2005; Durie, 2003; McCracken, 1984). Novels and other literary productions based in established resort settings have provided additional stimuli for their tourist economies, or for specific businesses within the larger destination. One example is the Hotel des Bains at Venice's Lido, where associations with Thomas Mann's *Death in Venice* (first published in 1912), were reinforced by Visconti's film of 1971, illustrating a recurrent alliance between written word and moving image. Depictions of desirable objects of the "tourist gaze" have also both responded to and contributed to tourist demand, from the Italian painters who were the fountainheads of the Picturesque, through Ruskin's didactic drawings, and the seaside and riverside scenes of the Impressionists, and the photographers and filmmakers (amateur and professional) who sought to capture "authenticity," "tradi-tion," and atmosphere in environments where engagement with an imagined romantic past was part of the allure, to the cheap reproduc-tion, the crude souvenir representation of iconic scene or building, and the picture post-card (Crouch and Lubbren, 2003; Herbert, 1994; Hitchcock and Teague, 2000; Kamm, 1984; Löfgren, 1999).

Broader perceived relationships between literature, the arts, architecture, landscape, and the ascribed atmosphere and aura of places, regions, and landscapes (whether within nations or transcending them: Tuscany, the Mediterranean, the American West or the Australian outback) are powerful cultural influences for tourism development, espe-cially for the snobbish. The British "stately home" as repository of art, architecture, and a romanticized imagined (and usually elite) past pulls many of these themes together; and increasingly, of course, the museum has become a tourist destination in its own right (Fussell, 1980; Horne, 2005; Mandler, 1997; Pemble, 1987; Lasansky and McLaren, 2004; Wrobel and Long, 2001). Such representations might domesticate the experience of new environments—or environments that became almost a "home from home" through repeat visiting—through the souvenir on the mantel-piece or picture rail, and the "armchair tourism" of reading guidebooks and travel literature as a substitute rather than a prelude or preparation for, or recapitulation of, a physical journey. Analyzing such material and its impact brings history, art history, literature, cultural, and film studies, and, increasingly, visual culture into creative contact. Such perceptions filter through into commercial guidebooks, publicity mate-rial, souvenirs, and artistic reproductions aimed at tourist markets, stimulating kinds of demand and encouraging ways of seeing that might subvert the values and intentions of the original writers, although they might equally provide protection for their cherished but besieged environments, as in the complex case of Robert Graves in his Mallorcan refuge (Waldren, 1996).

Particularly significant here have been interpretations of tourist development in imperial, colonial, and postcolonial settings, which can also be applied to the internal colonialism associated with the relationships between the "metropolitan" and the "periph-eral" within Western Europe and North America, as tourist mythologies are created around the inhabitants of "quaint" fishing villages, or "rustic" country folk, or "primitive" mountain settlements. Here, questions of "orientalism" remain central, as an anthropo-logical version of the "tourist gaze" is directed at unfamiliar sites and cultures, claiming the power to control and exploit them through classification and taxonomic appraisal, and appropriating what is placed on display through photography and the purchase of "local crafts" and other souvenirs (Furlough, 2003; Klein, 2003; Mackenzie, 1995, 2005; Pratt, 1992; Ryan, 2007; Sheller, 2003). Pre-existing settlements and ways of life have been swept aside to make room for tourist developments, based on generalized holiday preferences and uniform expectations regarding standards of provision, only for sanitized versions of local "cultures" to be staged and represented in folkloric style as part of the destination's competitive pursuit of distinctiveness and difference. Already in late nineteenth-century Brittany or Cornwall "traditional" festivals were being incorporated into tourist repertoires, changing their own nature (and the attitudes of the participants) in response. This has become a major theme in tourism history. But those at whom this orientalizing gaze is directed have agency of their own, and can return it with interest, as displayed in the mocking Mexican references to Cancún and other "circus-like spectacle(s) of the overbuilt resort" as "Gringolandia" (Deacon, 2001; Torres and Momsen, 2005). Further complications are added when empires return their inhabitants as tourists to the metropole, whether directing an adoring or ambivalent gaze at the sights of London or Paris as the center of an imperial universe, or commemorating their participation in imperial struggles through the "battlefield tourism" of, for example, Australians and Canadians in Belgium and northern France (Furlough, 2002; Gilbert and Henderson, 2002; Looker, 2002; Wharton, 1998; White, 2005).

Tourism thus has its political, diplomatic and military histories, as is clear from these references to relations between "center" and "periphery," to tourism and the delineation of empire, and to cultures of martial commemoration. It engages with the construction and elaboration of national identities by promoting domestic tourism in the sense of "see America first" (Shaffer, 2002), or encouraging

tourist mobility to achieve a sense of national belonging by direct appreciation of the best aspects of the nation, especially through early, self-consciously adventurous motor touring, as in Italy or Argentina in the 1920s and 1930s (Bosworth, 1997; Piglia, 2007), or stimulating national pride, political conformity and a sense of racial superiority, as in the case of Hitler's Germany and its Kraft durch Freude (Strength through Joy) organization (Baranowski, 2004; Semmens, 2005; Spode, 2004), or sustaining an ideal of shared democratic access to leisure and holidays through "social tourism," as in Argentina during the 1930s and 1940s (Pastoriza, 2003). Tourism might also be used to promote regional identities, politically as well as for the competitive advancement of ideas of distinctiveness, as in the case of the Basque Country in the early twentieth century, or the emergent nationalities within the Austro-Hungarian Empire before World War I (Steward, 1999, 2000, 2001; Walton, 2000b). But, just as Thomas Cook became entangled with late Victorian British imperialism, the expansion of Conrad Hilton's hotel chain in postwar Europe and the Middle East, in synchrony with US tourism policy, aimed at representing and projecting the lifestyle and ascribed virtues of international capitalism, offering distinctive high-rise architecture, and North American cuisine and comforts in ways that prefigured subsequent McDisneyfication (Endy, 2004; Klein, 2003; Ritzer, 2006; Wharton, 1999, 2001). Investment in tourism was also associated with national economic recovery and growth, in such contrasting settings as Britain, Spain, and Mexico, although governmental attempts to develop tourism from overseas in Britain were enduringly ineffectual, while the potentially destabilizing consequences of such a strategy were evident in Spain, as the relaxation of political and religious controls associated with the tourist boom of the 1960s and 1970s helped to undermine the Franco regime (Beckerson, 2002; Buzard, 2001; Clancy, 2001; Grant 2006; Pack, 2006).

Tourism history is also about class and class conflict, whether over access to and use of space for recreational purposes, as in

San Sebastián in the early twentieth century (Walton, 2001), or conflicts over the exploitation of labor forces, who usually suffer the disadvantages of being seasonal and under-unionized, lacking in formally defined skills, predominantly female and often operating as part-timers in the labor market, easily replaceable and either working in the informal economy of marginal family businesses, or for powerful national or multinational organizations. When questions of ethnicity or "race" are factored in alongside those of class and gender, the issues are exacerbated, as in the long history of contested exclusion of African Americans from public spaces in Atlantic City, and their consignment to menial and demeaning occupations (Clancy, 2001; Shorris, 2004; Simon, 2004; Smith and Walton, 1994). Popular tourism can also allow for hedonistic collective self-expression among a working class that finds release, relaxation, entertainment, and something resembling the safety-valve of carnival at certain kinds of destination, from working-class areas of British seaside resorts since the early railway age, to cheap package holiday destinations of the later twentieth century, from Spain to Florida and Thailand; but the balance between enjoyment and exploitation needs to be carefully weighed, and Aron's work reminds us of the enduring tension between holiday-making and the work ethic that cuts across the pursuit of pleasure through tourism in US society (Aron, 1999; Cross and Walton, 2005).

Gender will also become a central theme in tourism history, linking with ideas about the relationship between personal displacement and the suspension of cultural constraints, not least in terms of the performance of roles (whether as observer or observed, tourist or worker) and conventions of bodily display, as investigated in Desmond's (1999) work on Hawaii. Work in this field has focused mainly on women travelers, usually in adventurous circumstances, but there is extensive scope for further development of themes relating to gender and sexuality, including the provision of sexual services, which are deeply embedded in most aspects of tourism history.

The historical analysis of tourism's environmental impacts is also inescapable, as the rapid expansion of environmental history leads it into the history of tourism (Anderson and Tabb, 2002; Hassan, 2003). This in turn draws attention to the importance of the relationships between tourism, heritage and the built and "natural" environments, bringing us back to the tensions between authenticity (however "staged"), history, "heritage," and the drive to modernize that are inherent in the pursuit of profit through the expansion of tourism. British seaside "heritage" has broad parameters and emotive associations, as becomes apparent when threats are directed against favorite amusement park rides, or grounded nostalgia celebrates the family values of earlier incarnations of the popular seaside accommodation industry (Beckerson, 2007; Walton, 2007). But there are darker sides to heritage tourism, as providers, consumers, and campaigners negotiate the presentation of issues connected with slavery or holocaust memorials (Lennon and Foley, 2000). Here the uses of history in tourism studies turn out to be manifold, contested and problematic.

Conclusion: The Varieties of Tourism History

This necessarily brief survey makes no pretensions to comprehensiveness. It presents central themes in a rapidly expanding branch of the international historical enterprise, which needs to be connected more effectively with work in other disciplines, and especially with tourism studies itself. Tourism history can, and should, inform every aspect of tourism studies; and its relevance will often go back long before the immediate past, as phenomena regarded as new or recent have much deeper, and more revealing, roots than appear at first sight. History helps to shed light on the mixtures of motivations that guide and shape the demand for destinations and enjoyments. It challenges the "common sense" of assumed "human nature" by revealing the shifts in perception that can take place over comparatively short periods, as in the eighteenth-century sea change in Western culture when negative evaluations of seacoasts and mountain scenery gave way to positive appreciation and attraction. It covers the spectrum of intellectual activity in the arts, humanities and social sciences, and can help to redeem them from the silo mentalities that sometimes keep them in isolated, separate compartments. Much of the tourism history on offer is firmly anchored to the locality, not always as case study or in context; but even narrower academic contributions in these areas can contribute to more ambitious enterprises by providing reliable supporting evidence for general claim or counterclaim. The interdisciplinary area of tourism studies needs to embrace and make use of the work of historians, and this chapter has sought to make that case.

Notes

1 Bournemouth tourism pack (for students undertaking projects). Retrieved March 28, 2008 from http://www.bournemouth.co.uk. http://www.visit-lancashire.com accessed March 28, 2008, which supplies the misleading information that the world's first Industrial Revolution began precisely in the towns of Blackburn and Burnley.

2 Information about indigenous Tunisian seabathing traditions at Sousse comes from interviews undertaken there by the present author in April 1997 with the help of Nora Essafi.

References

Anderson, S. and Tabb, B. (Eds.) (2002). *Water, Leisure and Culture*. Oxford: Berg.

Agarwal, S. (2002). "Restructuring Seaside Tourism. The Resort Life-Cycle." *Annals of Tourism Research*, 29(1): 25–55.

Akhtar, M. and Humphries, S. (2000). *Some Liked it Hot*. London: Virgin.

Armstrong, J. (2005). "The Steamboat and Popular Tourism." *Journal of Transport History*, 26: 61–77.

Aron, C. (1999). *Working at Play*. New York: Oxford University Press.

Baranowski, S. and Furlough, E. (Eds.) (2001). *Being Elsewhere: Tourism, Consumer Culture and Identity in Modern Europe and North America*. Ann Arbor: University of Michigan Press.

Baranowski, S. (2004). *Strength through Joy: Consumerism and Mass Tourism in the Third Reich*. Cambridge: Cambridge University Press.

Beckerson, J. (2002). "Marketing British Tourism: Government Approaches to the Stimulation of a Service Industry, 1880–1950." In Berghoff et al. (Eds.), *The Making of Modern Tourism: The Cultural History of the British Experience, 1600–2000* (pp. 108–134). London: Palgrave.

Beckerson, J. (2007). *Holiday Isle: the Isle of Man*. Douglas: Manx Heritage Foundation.

Berghoff, H., Korte B., Schneider, R. and Harvie, C. (Eds.) (2002). *The Making of Modern Tourism: The Cultural History of the British Experience, 1600–2000*. London: Palgrave.

Black, J. (2003). *The British Abroad: The Grand Tour in the Eighteenth Century*. Stroud: Sutton.

Bosworth, R.J.B. (1997). "The Touring Club Italiano and the Nationalization of the Italian Bourgeoisie." *European History Quarterly*, 27: 371–410.

Boukraa, R. (1993). *Hammamet: Le Paradis Perdu*. Aix-en-Provence: CHET.

Bray, A. and Raitz, V. (2001). *Flight to the Sun: The Story of the Holiday Revolution*. London: Continuum.

Brendon, P. (1991). *Thomas Cook: 150 Years of Popular Tourism*. London: Secker and Warburg.

Buades, J. (2004). *On Brilla el Sol: Turisme a Baleares abans del Boom*. Eivissa, Spain: Res Publica Edicions SL.

Butler, R.W. (Ed.) (2005). *The Tourist Area Life Cycle, Vol. 1: Applications and Modifications*. Clevedon: Channel View.

Buzard, J. (1993). *The Beaten Track*. Oxford: Clarendon.

Buzard, J. (2001). "Culture for Export: Tourism and Autoethnography in Postwar Britain." In Baranowsky and Furlough (Eds.), *Being Elsewhere: Tourism, Consumer Culture and Identity in Modern Europe and North America* (pp. 299–319). Ann Arbor: University of Michigan Press.

Chadefaud, M. (1987). *Aux Origines du Tourisme dans les Pays de l'Adour*. Pau: Université de Pau.

Chaney, E. (1998). *The Evolution of the Grand Tour*. London: Frank Cass.

Clancy, M. (2001). *Exporting Paradise: Tourism and Development in Mexico*. London.

Corbin, A. (1994). *The Lure of the Sea*. Cambridge: Polity.

Cross, G. and Walton, J.K. (2005). *The Playful Crowd: Pleasure Places in the Twentieth Century*. New York: Columbia University Press.

Crouch, D. and Lubbren, N. (2003). *Visual Culture and Tourism*. Oxford: Berg.

Davidson, J. and Spearritt, P. (2000). *Holiday Business: Tourism in Australia since 1870*. Carlton: Miegunyal Press.

Deacon, B. (2001). "Imagining the Fishing: Artists and Fishermen in Late Nineteenth Century Cornwall." *Rural History*, 12: 159–178.

Dekker, G. (2005). *The Fictions of Romantic Tourism: Radcliffe, Scott and Mary Shelley*. Stanford, CA: Stanford University Press.

Desmond, J.C. (1999). *Staging Tourism: Bodies on Display from Waikiki to Sea World*. Chicago, IL: University of Chicago Press.

Durie, A.J. (2003). *Scotland for the Holidays: A History of Tourism in Scotland, 1780–1939*. East Linton: Tuckwell.

Dye, V. (2005). *All Aboard for Santa Fe: Railway Promotion of the South-West, 1890s–1930s*. Albuquerque: University of New Mexico Press.

Edensor, T. (1998). *Tourists at the Taj*. London: Routledge.

Endy, C. (2004). *Cold War Holidays: American Tourism in France*. Chapel Hill: University of North Carolina Press.

Evans, R. (1997). *In Defence of History*. London: Granta.

Featherstone, M., Thrift, N. and Urry, J. (Eds.) (2005). *Automobilities*. London: Sage.

Feifer, M. (1985). *Going Places: The Ways of the Tourist from Imperial Rome to the Present Day*. London: Macmillan.

Furlough, E. (1998). "Making Mass Vacations: Tourism and Consumer Culture in France, 1930s to 1970s." *Comparative Studies in Society and History*, 40: 247–286.

Furlough, E. (2002). "Une lecon dans les choses: Tourism, Empire and the Nation in Interwar France." *French Historical Studies*, 25: 441–473.

Fussell, P. (1980). *Abroad: British Literary Travelling between the Wars*. Oxford University Press.

Gale, T. and D. Botterill (2005). "A Realist Agenda for Tourism Studies." *Tourist Studies*, 5: 151–174.

Garner, A. (2005). *A Shifting Shore: Locals, Outsiders and the Transformation of a French Fishing Town*. Ithaca, NY: Cornell University Press.

Gaviria, M. (1974). *España a go-go*. Madrid: Turner.

Gaze, H. (1861). *Switzerland: How to See It for Ten Guineas*. London.

Gaze, H. (1864). *Northern Italy and Venetia: How to See Them for Fifteen Guineas*. London.

Gibson, W.S. (2000). *Pleasant Places*. Los Angeles: University of California Press.

Gilbert, D. and F. Henderson (2002). "London and the Tourist Imagination." In P.K. Gilbert (Ed.), *Imagined Londons* (pp. 121–136). Albany, NY: SUNY Press.

Grant, M. (2006). "'Working for the Yankee Dollar': Tourism and the Festival of Britain as Stimuli for Recovery." *Journal of British Studies*, 45: 581–601.

Hassan, J. (2003). *The Seaside, Health and Environment in England and Wales since 1800*. Aldershot: Ashgate.

Herbert, R.L. (1994). *Monet on the Normandy Coast*. New Haven, CT: Yale University Press.

Higgs, E. (2005). *Making Sense of the Census Revisited*. London: Institute of Historical Research.

Hitchcock, M. and Teague, K. (2000). *Souvenirs: The Material Culture of Tourism*. Aldershot: Ashgate.

Hobbs, A. (2008). "It Doesn't Add Up: Myths and Measurement Problems of Births to Single Women in Blackpool, 1931–1971." *Women's History Review*, 7: 435–454.

Hobsbawm, E.J. and Ranger, T. (1983). *The Invention of Tradition*. Cambridge: Cambridge University Press.

Holden, A. (2005). *Tourism Studies and the Social Sciences*. London: Routledge.

Horne, J. (2005). *The Pursuit of Wonder*. Carlton: Miegunyah Press.

Hunt, E.D. (1982). *Holy Land Pilgrimage in the Later Roman Empire*. Oxford: Clarendon.

Hunter, F.R. (2004). "Tourism and Empire: The Thomas Cook and Son Enterprise on the Nile, 1868–1914." *Middle Eastern Studies*, 140: 28–54.

Inglis, F. (2000). *The Delicious History of the Holiday*. London: Routledge.

Kamm, H. (1984). "Traces of Mann: A Dearth in Venice." *New York Times*, January 29.

Klein, C. (2003). *Cold War Orientalism: Asia in the Middlebrow Imagination 1945–1961*. Berkeley: University of California Press.

Koshar, R. (Ed.) (2002). *Histories of Leisure*. Oxford: Berg.

Larson, T. (2000). "Thomas Cook, Holy Land Pilgrims, and the Dawn of the Modern Tourist Industry." *Studies in Church History*, 36: 329–342.

Lasansky, M. and McLaren, B. (Eds.) (2004). *Architecture and Tourism: Perception, Performance and Place*. Oxford: Berg.

Lennon, J.J. and Foley, M. (Eds.) (2000). *Dark Tourism*. London: Continuum.

Levenstein, H. (2004). *We'll Always Have Paris: American Tourists in France Since 1930*. Chicago, IL: University of Chicago Press.

Löfgren, O. (1999). *On Holidays: A History of Vacationing*. Berkeley: University of California Press.

Löfgren, O. (2001). "Know Your Country: A Comparative Perspective on Tourism and Nation Building in Sweden." In Baranowski and Furlough (Eds.), *Being Elsewhere: Tourism, Consumer Culture and Identity in Modern Europe and North America* (pp. 137–154). Ann Arbor: University of Michigan Press.

Lomine, L. (2005). "Tourism in Augustan Society." In J.K. Walton (Ed.), *Histories of Tourism* (pp. 71–87). Clevedon: Channel View.

Looker, B. (2002). *Exhibiting Imperial London*. London: CURS.

Lyth, P. (2003). "'Gimme a Ticket on an Airplane': The Jet Engine and the Revolution in Leisure Air Travel, 1960–75." In L. Tissot (Ed.), *Construction of a Tourism Industry in the 19th and 20th Century: International Perspectives* (pp. 111–122). Neuchatel: Alphil.

McCracken, D. (1984). *Wordsworth and the Lake District: A Guide to the Poems and Their Places*. New York: Oxford University Press.

Mackenzie, J. (1995). *Orientalism: History, Theory and the Arts*. Manchester: Manchester University Press.

Mackenzie, J. (2005). "Empires of Travel: British Guide Books and Cultural Imperialism in the 19th and 20th Centuries." In J.K. Walton (Ed.), *Histories of Tourism* (pp. 19–38). Clevedon: Channel View.

Mandler, P. (1997). *The Fall and Rise of the Stately Home*. New Haven, CT: Yale University Press.

Martín, A. (2008). "Miniskirts, Polka Dots, and Real Estate: What Lies Under the Sun?" In E. Afinoguénova and J. Martí-Olivella (Eds.), *Spain is (Still) Different* (pp. 219–243). Lanham, MD: Lexington Books.

Miyazaki, F. and Williams, D. (2001). "The Intersection of the Local and the Translocal at a Sacred Site." *Japanese Journal of Religious Studies*, 28: 399–440.

Pack, S.D. (2006). *Tourism and Dictatorship: Europe's Peaceful Invasion of Franco's Spain*. Basingstoke: Palgrave Macmillan.

Pagenstecher, C. (2004). *Der bundesdeutsche Tourismus: Ansatze zu einer Visual History: Urlantsprospekte, Reisefuhrer, Fotoalban 1950–1990*, Hamburg: Kovac.

Pastoriza, E. (2003). "El ocio peronista: la conquista de las vacaciones. El turismo social en la Argentina" In various authors (Eds.), *Fiesta, Juego y Ocio* (pp. 383–420). Editorial Universidad Salamanca.

Pearson, M.N. (1996). *Pilgrimage to Mecca*. Princeton, NJ: Markus Wiener.

Pemble, J. (1987). *The Mediterranean Passion*. Oxford: Clarendon Press.

Piglia, M. (2007). "Los Orígenes del Turismo Como Política Pública." Retrieved April 6, 2008 from www.economia.unam.mx.amhe/cladhe/simposios8/html.

Porter, R. (Ed.) (1990). *The Medical History of Spas and Waters*. Medical History, Supplement 5.

Pratt, M.L. (1992). *Imperial Eyes: Travel Writing and Transculturation*. London: Routledge.

Prentice, R. (1990). "Tourism." In V. Robinson and D. McCarroll (Eds.), *The Isle of Man: Celebrating a Sense of Place* (pp. 248–267). Liverpool: Liverpool University Press.

Prideaux, B. (2000). "The Resort Development Spectrum—A New Approach to Modeling Resort Development." *Tourism Management*, 21(3): 225–240.

Rapaport, E. (2000). *Shopping for Pleasure.* Princeton, NJ: Princeton University Press.

Ritzer, G. (2006). *McDonaldization: The Reader.* Thousand Oaks, CA: Pine Forge Press.

Ryan, C. (Ed.) (2007). *Battlefield Tourism.* London: Elsevier.

Schivelbusch, W. (1980). *Railway Journey: Trains and Travel in the Nineteenth Century.* Oxford: Blackwell.

Schwartz, R. (1997). *Pleasure Island.* Lincoln: University of Nebraska Press.

Semmens, K. (2005). *Seeing Hitler's Germany: Tourism in the Third Reich.* Basingstoke: Palgrave Macmillan.

Shaffer, M.S. (2002). *See America First: Tourism and National Identity 1880–1940.* Washington, DC: Smithsonian Institute.

Sheller, M. (2003). *Consuming the Caribbean.* London: Routledge.

Shorris, E. (2004). *The Life and Times of Mexico.* New York: W.W. Norton.

Simon, B. (2004). *Boardwalk of Dreams: Atlantic City and the Fate of Urban America.* New York: Oxford University Press.

Simonsen, D.G. (2005). "Accelerating Modernity: Time-Space Compression in the Wake of the Aeroplane." *Journal of Transport History,* 26: 98–117.

Singh, A. (2005). *Tourism in Ancient India.* New Delhi: Serials Publications.

Sketchley, Arthur (pseudonym of George Rose) (1870). *Mrs Brown on the Grand Tour.* London.

Smith, J. and Walton, J.K. (1994). "The Rhetoric of Community and the Business of Pleasure: The San Sebastián Waiters' Strike of 1920." *International Review of Social History,* 39: 1–31.

Spode, H. (2004). "Fordism, Mass Tourism and the Third Reich." *Journal of Social History,* 38: 127–155.

Steward, J. (1999). "'Gruss aus Wien': The Tourist Culture of Fin-De-Siecle Vienna." In M. Gee, T. Kirk and J. Steward (Eds.), *The City in Central Europe* (pp. 125–143). Aldershot: Ashgate.

Steward, J. (2000). "The Spa Towns of the Austrian-Hungarian Empire and the Growth of Tourist Culture: 1860–1914." In P Borsay, G. Hirschfelder and R. Mohrmann (Eds.), *New Directions in Urban History* (pp. 87–126). Munster: Waxmann Verlag.

Steward, J. (2001). "Tourism in Late Imperial Austria." In S. Baranowski and E. Furlough

(Eds.), *Being Elsewhere: Tourism, Consumer Culture and Identity in Modern Europe and North America* (pp. 108–134). Ann Arbor: University of Michigan Press.

Steward, J. (2005). "'How and Where to Go': The Role of Travel Journalism in Britain and the Evolution of Foreign Tourism, 1840–1914." In J.K. Walton (Ed.), *Histories of Tourism* (pp. 39–54). Clevedon: Channel View.

Swatos, W.H. Jr. and Tomasi, L. (Eds.) (2002). *From Medieval Pilgrimage to Religious Tourism.* London: Praeger.

Taylor, H. (1997). *A Claim on the Countryside.* Edinburgh: Keele University Press.

Theroux, P. (2008). "To the End of the Line." *Guardian Review,* March 22: 6.

Timothy, D.J. and Olsen, D.H. (Eds.) (2006). *Tourism, Religion and Spiritual Journeys.* London: Routledge.

Torres, R.M. and Momsen, J.D. (2005). "Gringolandia: The Construction of a New Tourist Space in Mexico." *Annals of the Association of American Geographers,* 95: 314–335.

Turner, L. and Ash, J. (1975). *The Golden Hordes: International Tourism and the Pleasure Periphery.* London: Constable.

Urry, J. (1995). *Consuming Places.* London: Sage.

Vickery, A. (1998). *The Gentleman's Daughter.* New Haven, CT: Yale University Press.

Waldren, J. (1996). *Insiders and Outsiders: Paradise and Reality in Mallorca.* Oxford: Berghahn.

Walton, J.K. (1974). "The Social Development of Blackpool, 1788–1914." PhD thesis, Lancaster University.

Walton, J.K. (1983). *The English Seaside Resort: A Social History, 1750–1914.* Leicester: Leicester University Press.

Walton, J.K. and O'Neill, C. (1993). "Numbering the Holidaymakers: The Problems and Possibilities of the June Census of 1921 for Historians of Resorts." *Local Historian,* 23: 205–216.

Walton, J.K. (1994). "The Blackpool Landlady Revisited." *Manchester Region History Review,* 8: 23–31.

Walton, J.K. and Smith, J. (1996). "The First Century of Beach Tourism in Spain: San Sebastián and the "Playas del Norte"from the 1830s to the 1930s." In J. Towner, M. Barke and M.T. Newton (Eds.), *Tourism in Spain: Critical Issues* (pp. 35–61). Wallingford: CAB Publications.

Walton, J.K. (1997a). "The Seaside Resorts of Western Europe, 1750–1939." In S. Fisher (Ed.), *Recreation and the Sea* (pp. 36–56). Exeter: University of Exeter Press.

Walton, J.K. (1997b). "The Seaside Resorts of England and Wales, 1900–1950: Growth, Diffusion and the Emergence of New Forms of Coastal Tourism." In A. Williams and G. Shaw (Eds.), *The Rise and Fall of British Coastal Resorts* (pp. 21–48). London: Cassell.

Walton, J.K. (2000a). *The British Seaside: Holidays and Resorts in the Twentieth Century*. Manchester: Manchester University Press.

Walton, J.K. (2000b). "Tradition and Tourism: Representing Basque Identities in Guipúzcoa and San Sebastián, 1848–1936." In N. Kirk (Ed.), *Northern Identities* (pp. 87–108). Aldershot: Scolar Press.

Walton, J.K. (2001). "Policing the Alameda: Shared and Contested Recreational Space in San Sebastián, 1863–1920." In S. Gunn and R.J. Morris (Eds.), *Identities in Space: Contested Terrains in the Western City since 1850* (pp. 228–241). Aldershot: Ashgate.

Walton, J.K. (2004). "The Seaside and the Holiday Crowd." In V. Toulmin, P. Russell and S. Popple (Eds.), *The Lost World of Mitchell and Kenyon: Edwardian Britain on Film* (pp.158–168). London: *bfi* Publishing.

Walton, J.K. (Ed.) (2005a). *Histories of Tourism*. Clevedon: Channel View.

Walton, J.K. (2005b). "Introduction." In Walton (Ed.), *Histories of Tourism* (pp. 1–18). Clevedon: Channel View.

Walton, J.K. (2007). *Riding on Rainbows: Blackpool Pleasure Beach and its Place in British Popular Culture*. St Albans: Skelter Publishing.

Wharton, A. (1999). "Economy, Architecture and Politics: Colonial and Cold War Hotels." *History of Political Economy*, 31: 285–299.

Wharton, A. (2001). *Building the Cold War: Hilton International Hotels and Modern Architecture*. Chicago, IL: University of Chicago Press.

Wharton, L.D. (1998). *Battlefield Tourism*. Oxford: Berg.

White, R. (2005). *On Holidays: A History of Getting Away in Australia*. North Melbourne: Pluto Press.

Williams, D. and Armstrong, J. (2006). "Steam Shipping and the Beginning of Overseas Tourism." *Journal of European Economic History*, 35: 125–148.

Worthington, B. (2003). "Change in an Estonian Resort: Contrasting Development Contexts." *Annals of Tourism Research*, 30: 369–385.

Wright, S. (2002). "Sun, Sea, Sand and Self-Expression." In Berghoff et al. (Eds.), *The Making of Modern Tourism—The Cultural History of the British Experience, 1600–2000* (pp. 181–202). Houndmills, UK: Palgrave.

Wrobel, D. and Long, P. (Eds.) (2001). *Seeing and Being Seen: Tourism in the American West*. Lawrence: University of Kansas Press.

8

Tourism Geographies: A Review of Trends, Challenges, and Opportunities

Sanjay K. Nepal

Introduction

Geography, as a subject matter of enquiry, is rooted in antiquity; however, it was formally organized as a separate discipline only around the last quarter of the 19th century (Mitchell and Murphy, 1991). Although various dichotomies of geographic research have existed in the past, from an academic perspective, almost all geographers identify themselves with the broader distinction of either physical or human geography. Irrespective of the division, geographers usually associate themselves with the analysis of spatial and temporal patterns of development and change in the environment, economy, culture, social norms and values, and politics. Today, geography is a highly pluralistic discipline, and geographic research represents a hybrid of various contemporary issues conducted from the positivist, humanistic, and interpretive perspectives, and utilizing a combination of different research methods and analytical techniques.

Mitchell and Murphy (1991) trace tourism geography's genealogy to the 1920s in the USA. They note that the first refereed article on a tourism topic in a major US geographic journal was published in 1933. In Germany, Hans Poser's work on the Riesengebirge Mountains in the 1930s is considered the main awakening of interest in the geography of tourism in the German-speaking world (Kreisel, 2004). Before discussing what tourism geographers have been interested in and what research approaches they have considered, a definition of tourism is necessary, followed by a brief discussion of what commonalities exist between tourism and geographers and how geographers may have helped define the field of tourism studies.

The definition of tourism, as mentioned in a widely adopted undergraduate textbook, places emphasis on ". . . processes, activities, and outcomes . . . from the interactions among tourists, tourism suppliers, host governments, host communities, and surrounding environments that are involved in the attracting and hosting of visitors" (Goeldner and Ritchie, 2003: 5–6). Four components stand out in this definition and include processes (mechanisms and structures necessary for the development of tourism), activities (tourist interests, and motivation and behavior associated with interests), outcomes (positive and negative impacts), and interactions between different stakeholders (power, participation, and representation). Geographers are interested in the central notions of place, space and the environment, and scale is of fundamental importance to them (Hall and Page, 2002; Mitchell, 1984). Therefore, some commonalities that can be used to describe the study of both tourism and geography include their multifaceted characteristics, interdisciplinary perspectives, and spatial and temporal dimensions. Geography is concerned with the spatial arrangements of tourist attractions and travel patterns, and their temporal variations. Geographers' interests in key attributes of a location, or a feature, and at different scales (e.g., points, lines, and polygons) are relevant to the distribution and arrangement of tourist attractions, travel flows, and core–periphery relationship. Both geography and tourism can be characterized as complex, diverse, and dynamic. Geographers are keenly interested in temporal changes. Changes to the economy, society, and the environment as a result of tourism are very rapid and dramatic. All these factors make the study of tourism an exciting one for many geographers.

To geographers, then, tourism is a study about change, and particularly the processes and the variability of change. Some key questions that a tourism geographer may ask include:

1 How do destinations evolve over time?
2 Where do tourists come from, where and how do they travel?
3 What attractions are they interested in and why?
4 What motivates them to travel?
5 What forms of travel behavior do they exhibit?
6 How do they interact with the environment and people at the destination?
7 How do they understand and interpret the images they acquire from their travel experience?

8 What is the outcome of the interactions between various players at the tourism destination?
9 How is tourism organized at the destination and who are involved in its organization?
10 What is the dynamics of power relations between various stakeholders of the tourism industry?

This chapter provides an overview of tourism geography studies. It is organized into three main parts. The first part discusses the era, language, and themes of tourism research, the second part deals with contemporary trends in geographic research on tourism, looking particularly at papers presented at three annual meetings of the Association of American Geographers (AAG) and several recent volumes of the journal *Tourism Geographies*. The final (third) part outlines emerging trends in tourism geography and the challenges of continuing a strong tradition of research in tourism geographies. At the outset, it should be stated that this chapter focuses on research in tourism geographies. With the exception of *Tourism Geographies* (TG), given the lack of distinct tourism geography journals, and the increasing tendency among geographers to accept appointments in non-geography departments, it is practically challenging to identify who is or is not a tourism geographer. Butler (2004) addresses this challenge in more detail. This chapter takes a generalized approach to tourism research conducted by people who have received their academic training in geography and includes work identified by others as contribution by a geographer. Further, the review presented here is selective, as it is a daunting task to provide a complete review within the necessary constraints of a *Handbook* chapter. Readers are suggested to consult Pearce (1979), Mitchell and Murphy (1991), Crouch (1999), Meyer-Arendt and Lew (1999), Hall and Page (2002), Lazzarotti (2002), Butler (2004) and Kreisel (2004) for further perspectives. Apart from these sources, a whole issue of *Geojournal* in 1984 had been devoted to the geography of tourism and leisure (Barbier, 1984). Papers in this volume discussed the status of tourism research in the USA, Canada, the UK, Germany, France, several East European countries, Japan, Australia and New Zealand; interestingly, papers on Third World countries were not covered.

Tourism Geographies by Era, Language and Theme

By Era

Butler (2004) has identified three eras in the development of tourism. Although his review is limited to the English-speaking world, and includes leisure and recreation, it nevertheless provides a good overview of trends over the last several decades. The three eras include: (1) the descriptive era between 1930s–1950s; (2) the era between 1950s–1980s, when different themes started to emerge; and (3) the contemporary era, which indicates to a rapidly changing landscape of tourism research.

During the descriptive era, research on tourism geography was conducted mainly from two perspectives. First, tourism was conceptualized as a significant form of land use (Brown, 1935; McMurray, 1930), which reflects the geographic tradition of research on human–land interactions. Second, following the empiricist-positivist tradition, many geographers analyzed the economic aspects of tourism (Carlson, 1938; Deasy, 1949). The emphasis during this era was on describing the tourism phenomenon, for example, analyzing the influence of geographic characteristics on development patterns of tourism destinations (Poser, 1939; Selke, 1936), morphology of tourist attractions (Gilbert, 1939), and patterns of tourist flows (Miége, 1933). Butler (2004) comments that most of the pioneering studies conducted during this period did not gain momentum, as interest in tourism geography as an academic subject was marginal and viewed as being of lesser importance.

The second era, between 1950s–1980s, was characterized by both the emergence of

the first wave of geographers specializing in tourism, and the development of tourism themes (Butler, 2004). The geography of tourism and leisure was accepted as a commission within the International Geographic Union at its Montreal conference in 1972, with a formal start at the Tokyo conference (Barbier, 1984). Geographers such as Coppock (1977), Wolfe (1952), Murphy (1963, 1985), Butler (1980), Pearce (1989), Marsh (1975), and Wall (1988) firmly established their expertise in tourism. They have contributed to creating a second generation of tourism geographers, many of whom are today well respected academics themselves. Butler (2004), citing Smith's (1982) review of recreation geography, notes three major themes of tourism research emerging during this era: area studies, human–land tradition, and spatial analysis. Area studies dealt with regional development and the effect of tourism, the human–land tradition focused on resource conservation and land management, and spatial analysis centered on patterns and movements of resources, people, and tourist perceptions. Of particular note is that all three traditions are deeply rooted in the broader discipline of geography, and many tourism specialists have remained loyal to the geographic knowledge base informing these traditions.

Pearce (1979) states that since the early 1960s geographers have become increasingly concerned with the nature and place of tourist geography, both in prefacing their own writings and in general reviews of the subject. The European geographers were mainly concerned with the spatial differentiation of tourism (Jacob, 1966; Juls, 1965; Merlini, 1968; Ritter, 1966, all cited in Pearce, 1979), conditioned by geographical characteristics (Poser, 1939, cited in Kreisel, 2004), and increased urbanization and regional development (Lazzarotti, 2002). The early American geographers tended to focus on economic geography, but this quickly gave way to a diverse range of research topics (Matley, 1976; Robinson, 1976, cited in Pearce, 1979).

Tourism research branched into impacts on the environment, demographics, transportation, settlement and urban planning, and social impacts. Pearce (1979) takes a critical view that tourism geographers during this era failed to sustain a systematic line of enquiry, resulting in ". . . the lack of cohesiveness and the fragmented nature . . ." of tourism research. He then suggests particular components of the geography of tourism and appropriate lines of research, which include (1) spatial patterns of supply and demand, (2) forms and functions of resorts, (3) tourist movement and flows, (4) economic, environmental, and social/cultural impacts of tourism, and (5) models of tourist space.

The contemporary era, since the 1990s, has experienced a dramatic growth in tourism research, contributed due to a second wave of tourism specialists and diversity of topics examined (Butler, 2004). The fragmentation of tourism research is much more clearly evident. While tourism geographers have continued to research the five themes identified by Pearce (1979), the diversity of tourism research has been incredible in recent years (see Part III for details). Of particular note is the increasing interest in (1) culture and heritage, (2) race, ethnicity, and gender, (3) globalization, mobility, and migration, (4) climate and energy, and (5) technological applications, including geographic information systems. Kreisel (2004: 177) observed that "geographical research has attempted to keep pace with the recent rapid transformations in the production and consumption of tourism and leisure, in particular those that reflect the fundamental restructurings of culture, society, economy and governance." The diversity of tourism research in geography reflects the increasing diversity of specialties and subdisciplines in geography itself. For example, the AAG lists 47 specialty groups under which geography membership is distributed. It is no wonder then that tourism geography has increasingly become hybrid. While new research frontiers are opening up, providing opportunities to "discover" something new, concerns about fragmented research

remain as valid today as they did 70 years ago. At the same time, the emergence of the journal *Tourism Geographies*, which is now in its ninth year of publication, could also suggest a more coherent approach to tourism research that is focused on three critical components of geography, i.e., space, place, and the environment. There are also concerns about tourism disappearing from many geography departments' curricula, forcing tourism researchers to accept positions in other departments where tourism is taught. These issues are discussed further below.

Language

This section relies mainly on three papers that have reviewed the state of tourism research in English (Butler, 2004), German (Kreisel, 2004), and French (Lazzarotti, 2002). Additional references were consulted to provide a brief synopsis below of the state of tourism geography in China, which is a growing area of research interest.[1]

Butler (2004) states that in the English-speaking world, tourism and leisure research trends can be identified by comparing the papers written by the North American and non-North American (particularly UK, Australian and New Zealand) geographers. As noted earlier, the focus of the North American geographers is mostly on economics of leisure and recreation, and less so on tourism. The non-Americans, in contrast, focus more on tourism and less on recreation and leisure. The American researchers are trained in the positivist-empiricist traditions, while the non-Americans approach tourism research from critical and humanist perspectives. While early attempts to tourism research were very fragmented and appeared occasionally, research after the 1970s increased substantially. Butler, originally from the UK, was the first to establish the first undergraduate courses in tourism geography in Canada, and possibly in North America (Butler, 2004). Significant contributions were made early on by geographers such as Richard Butler, Leslie Mitchell, Peter Murphy, and Geoffrey Wall, and later by Alan Lew, Dallen Timothy, David Weaver, and David Fennell, to name but a few. Outside North America, pioneer tourism geographers included Coppock (1977), Gilbert (1939), Mercer (1970), and Patmore (1968); all cited in Butler (2004), and later, scholars such as Douglas Pearce and Michael Hall have made significant contributions to tourism geography. Some of the most significant scholarly contributions, in the author's opinion, include Butler's evolutionary perspective of tourist development (Butler, 1980), tourism impacts (Mathieson and Wall, 1982), political economy (Britton, 1982, 1991), ecotourism (Fennell, 1999), resort morphology (Pearce, 1979), community-based tourism (Murphy, 1985), "Third World" tourism (Weaver, 1998), and what is arguably one of the best undergraduate textbooks on the geography of tourism (Hall and Page, 2002).

Through a literature review of the geography of leisure and tourism in the German-speaking world (mainly Germany, Austria and Switzerland), Kreisel (2004) identified three pillars of progress in tourism research. Giving much credit to the pioneering work of Hans Poser (1939), Kreisel suggests that the first pillar of tourism "as established by Poser" considered holistic approaches to understanding tourism, and its consequences not only on the immediate environments but more broadly and in all spheres of development and planning. Poser's work was significant in that ". . . he shifted the focus of interest in tourism and leisure to where tourism actually takes place; that is, to space, the region and the landscape" (Kreisel, 2004: 166). To Poser, tourist regions were unique, "special entities with a definite character that sets them apart from other regions" in terms of "their settlement, economy, traffic and lifestyle, all of which are subject to change in space and time" (Kreisel, 2004: 166). Regions and space were central elements in later studies, for example Christaller's (1955, 1964) application of central place theory to tourism, based on

which Butler (1980) later advanced his ideas of the life cycle of tourist destinations. Christaller asserted that touristic developments are based on the interactions between the center and its periphery, and that the periphery offered more favorable conditions for tourism development (Kreisel, 2004; Pearce, 1979). Early research on tourism space followed the positivist tradition and models like Christaller's were criticized for their failure to incorporate normative and humanist perspectives into their models. The second pillar of tourism geographies, largely driven by what Kreisel considers the "Munich School" of thought, attempts to fill this gap. The emphasis on human behavior, through the "action-space approach," attempted to provide explanations to human interactions and their effects on space (Heinritz and Popp, 1978, cited in Kreisel, 2004). The third pillar relates to current tourism studies, with a strong focus on applied tourism geography. Sustainable development and management of tourism, carrying capacity considerations, natural and protected areas, and interpretation of heritage landscapes, have been the major subjects of interest. Krippendorf's (1976, 1984) seminal work on mass tourism and its environmental and social impacts of tourism, can perhaps be considered as a precursor to the establishment of the third pillar of tourism.

Lazzarotti (2002) notes that research on tourism started much earlier in French geography, but failed to keep up with research conducted in the German- and English-speaking worlds. The early work of Le Lannou, conducted in the 1930s, which was a description of tourist attractions and the geography of Brittany, had a distinctive regional geography flavor. Lazzarotti (2002) states that prior to the 1950s, geography departments were preoccupied with more established research traditions in geomorphology and regional geography and that tourism was considered outside the purview of geography. This changed after the post-World War II economic boom, as Hall and Page (2002) suggest in their assertion that the French geography in the 1960s and 1970s was much advanced in both theoretical development and extent of publication than in the English-speaking world. Indeed, tourism students get some exposure to French tourism geography in Pearce's (1995) book *Tourism Today – A Geographical Perspective*, which references several seminal studies. Pearce (1979, 1995) identifies Miège (1933) and Defert (1967) as the pioneer French geographers who laid the foundations for the geographical study of tourism. According to Miège, geographers were interested in tourism in two directions: as the movement of people, and as a regional resource (cited in Pearce, 1979). Both Defert (1967), and later Miossec (1976), analyze *espace* (space) as the focal point of tourism studies. Miossec "speaks of *l'espace parcouru* [travel space] and as an *espace occupé* [business space] involving a *lieu de déplacement* [place of movement] and a *lieu de séjour* [place of visit]" (Pearce, 1995: 1). Much of this era's work in tourism focused on urban areas; for example, the seminal text *Traité de Géographie urbaine*, had a chapter on recreational relationships, which were treated with the same form of analysis as rural–urban relationships (Beaujeu-Garnier and Chabot, 1967, cited in Lazzarotti, 2002). Lazzarotti points out that the "book marked the beginning of a discourse that was characterized by condescension, whereby tourism was seen as an outcome of the dehumanized lifestyles produced by modern society" (2002: 138). He further states that this point of view has been constantly reiterated to this day through the works of George (1974), Michaud (1983) and Bavoux (1997).

The 1970s and the early 1980s were reported as being a highly productive period, with many studies conducted from a regional geography perspective (Lazzarotti, 2002). Throughout the 1990s, the scope of tourism geography was broadened considerably, as studies were conducted on a variety of topics, including tourist flows, tourism production, and the relationship between tourism and the environment. Lazzarotti (2002) references

the works of Lozato-Giotard (1993), Cazes (1992), Dewailly and Flamment (1993), and Debarbieux (1995), among others, and notes that discourses in other disciplines such as history, anthropology, and sociologists were beginning to imprint the works of geographers. This period also saw tremendous growth in tourism studies related to the Third World, environment, climate, globalization, transportation, and town and country planning.

Contrary to the Anglo-American, German, and French traditions, Chinese tourism geography has a relatively short history, starting mainly in the 1970s, but it has quickly become a well established subdiscipline. However, the study of geography combining traveling can be traced back to the Ming Dynasty, around 1640, when Xiake Xu wrote his traveling diary named *The Traveling Diary of Xiake Xu* (Zhang and Wang, 1992). Xiake Xu traveled more than 30 years in his life and had been to a majority of Chinese territory. Xu's diary offered a vivid description of the natural resources, and geographic and geologic landscapes of China (Zhang and Wang, 1992). Modern tourism research in China can be traced back to 1930s with Junru Zhang's paper *Comparison of Scenery Areas in Zhejiang* in 1934 and Meie Ren's *Natural Scenery and Geologic Structure* in 1940 (Guo and Bao, 1990). However, the systematic study of tourism geography and tourism study began in the late 1970s, with the establishment in 1979 of the first Tourism Geography Research Center in China, founded under the Institute of Geographic Sciences and Natural Resources Research, within the Chinese Academy of Sciences (Wang, 1996).

The first PhD dissertation with a focus on geographical aspects of tourism in China was written by Yifang Chu (1989), although he received his PhD from the economics department (Bao, 2002). Bao (2002) provides an overview of doctoral dissertations completed in tourism geography since 1989. His list indicates that spatial organization of tourism, tourism systems, tourism development and planning, sustainable tourism, and tourism behavior were the main topics of interest. Currently, tourism geography research in China has concentrated on tourism resource evaluation (Chen, 1985; Guo and Wu, 2000), tourism destination life cycle (Bao and Peng, 1995; Lu, 1997), spatial structure of regional tourism destinations (Wang and Wang, 2003; Wu, 1994 and 2001), destination image (Li, 1995). Lu (1997) has stated that two-thirds of this China-focused research in tourism geography is related to tourism resource and tourism development and planning. A more recent trend, since the early 1990s, indicates increased interests in tourist behavior and marketing studies (Bao, 2002; Wang and Zhou, 2001). Similarly, environmental dimensions of tourism including carrying capacity (Feng and Bao, 1999; Zhao, 1983), and ecotourism development (Liu and Wang, 2001; Niu, 1999; Wang and Yang, 1998) have generated a lot of interest, while tourism impact studies (Chen and Yang, 2004) and GIS applications (Deng and Wang, 2003) are topics of current interest.

Thematic Developments

Pearce observed in 1979 that ". . . it is difficult to speak of the geography of tourism as a subject with any coherence within the wider discipline of geography or in the general field of tourism studies" (1979: 246). Looking back at nearly three decades of tourism research, it is tempting to agree with Pearce's observation. However, if tourism geography, as a sub-discipline, is viewed in light of the advances in geographic research and changes that the discipline has gone through (Wolman, 2004), it would seem that tourism geography research has reflected broader trends in geography and academic discourse. The majority of tourism geographers have remained faithful to advancing geographic knowledge about place, space, and environment. As an academic discipline, geography has continued to push its boundaries, and has kept abreast of emergent societal and global issues. Many issues that were peripheral to a geographer's horizon two decades ago are now mainstream topics.

For example, there is an increased level of interest in issues of transnationalism, neo- and post-colonialism, post-Fordist, and post-modern economic and social structures, new urbanism and urban revitalization, feminism, GISciences, health and crime, globalization, and global change. Indeed, geography as a discipline remains very healthy and vibrant (Marston, 2006) and geographers are constantly pushing the frontiers of knowledge (Hanson, 2004; Lawson, 2005). This fertilization is evident in tourism geographies too. It is worth reconsidering Mitchell:

> The geographer's point of view is a trilogy of biases pertaining to place, environment, and relationships . . . the geographer has traditionally claimed the spatial and chorographic aspects as his realm . . . is concerned about earth space in general and about place and places in particular. The description, appreciation, and understanding of places is paramount to his thinking although two other perspectives (i.e., environment and relationships) modify and extend the primary bias of place. (1979: 237)

Mitchell considers place, environment, and relationships central elements of exploration for a geographer studying tourism. Interestingly, two decades after Mitchell's statement, the first journal in tourism geography, *Tourism Geographies*, was established, which separated papers into three categories: space, place, and environment. The editor of this journal has acknowledged that while certain papers have attempted to focus on one of the themes identified above, most papers transcend these boundaries (Lew, 2001). More recently, this division has been abandoned in favor of an "open" approach. Reflecting on papers published in a recent issue (Volume 8, Issue 1), the editor states that ". . . place, space, movement, global, local are all combined in different ways from one article to the next" and expects future papers submitted to the journal to be more reflective of this integration than separation (Lew, 2006: 95).

The 'Geographic Advantage'

Similar to what Mitchell has noted above, geography scholars argue that they have what one might refer to as "the geographic advantage" (Hanson, 2004: 720). This advantage confers an understanding of the relationships between people and the environment; the importance of spatial variability (the place dependence of processes); processes operating at multiple and interlocking geographic scales; and the integration of spatial and temporal analysis (Hanson, 2004). Expanding this argument to tourism, this author argues geographers engaged in tourism scholarship have "the tourism geographic advantage." Geographers are able to bring unique insights to tourism studies with their focus on the interactions between people and the environment at multiple scales, across different spatial units and at different time scales. These characteristics set tourism geographers apart from other scholars of tourism, and provide coherence to their research.

Exploration of the relationships between society and the environment has been, and continues to be, of interest to tourism geographers. Wolman argues that "[T]he professional geographer is the primary custodian of the concern for the interrelationship of human beings and the environment" (2004: 723). Since Marsh's (1864) classic treatise on human–land interactions, geographers have had strong interests in studying the consequences of human actions on the environment. Tourism scholars have been engaged in this discourse in touristic environments, particularly as they relate to changes in land use: from rural to urban; from natural to built; and from traditional (extractive-oriented) to modern (service-oriented) environments. Current concerns about sustainability and global change will continue to fuel geographers' interests in addressing the complex and intertwined aspects of tourism development and its consequences on the society and the environment. The scale of human impact has grown exponentially and all over the world, extending from land to water and air, as well as to more distant regions. Tourism geographers have kept pace with this as they have studied, more recently, human impacts on natural environments (Butler and Boyd, 2000), marine environments (Stewart and Draper, 2006), remote (Nepal, 2000, 2005), and polar regions (Hall and Johnston, 1995). Pearce (1979) provides an early overview of tourism impact studies conducted by geographers. Tourism impact studies, since the 1980s, have focused mostly in the developing countries (Weaver, 1998).

From Spatial to Critical Reflexive Themes

Geographers' traditional interests in gravity model, morphological characteristics, and spatial and temporal concentrations, have influenced earlier research on tourist flows (Guthrie, 1961; Ullman, 1956; Wolfe, 1966), spatial patterns of supply and demand (Defert 1967; Wolfe 1951), evolution of tourist space (Butler, 1980; Miossec, 1977), and resort morphologies (Pearce, 1978; Robinson, 1976). Tourism research between the 1950s and 1980s was influenced by the contemporary positivist-empiricist paradigm. Contributions from English, German, and French geographers during this period were numerous (Barbier, 1984; see the discussion above too), and it was arguably the golden era of tourism geography, both in volume and quality, of contributions to tourism scholarship in general. Hall and Page (2002) note that two very influential tourism textbooks by Pearce (1995) and Shaw and Williams (1994) have treated tourism geography in contrasting ways. The former has treated the subject matter mostly from a spatial perspective while the latter take a more critical approach, applying perspectives from political economy, production, consumption, globalization, and commodification. In addition to these two dominant approaches, a third perspective of a reflexive form of analysis focused on identities, encounters, and people as socialized and embodied subjects is getting greater recognition (Crouch, 1999, cited in Hall and Page, 2002). Based on these observations, we can conclude that contemporary tourism geography research may be considered as consisting of three broad approaches: spatial, behavioral, and reflexive.

Quantitative Continuity

Geography's quantitative tradition—some consider it the "unifying force" of the discipline ". . . in bringing different interests within the field into common conversation" (Wolman, 2004: 726)—has continued today in computer modeling, geographic information systems (GIS) and remote sensing applications. Indeed, it may be argued that the modern (post-1980) quantitative era has made geography immensely popular as an academic field of study, fueled largely by interests in GIS and remote sensing (Goodchild, 2004). Advances in GIS and remote sensing have transformed the field and made possible more comprehensive studies of both landscape processes and human activities and their interaction. Tourism scholars have taken advantage of these spatial technologies and have attempted to apply them in tourism settings; however, their full potential in examining form and processes of touristic development, travel flows and tourist movement, and tourism impacts, has not been realized yet. Early examples of GIS applications to tourism studies can be found in Li (1987), and later in Boyd and Butler (1993), and more recently in Nepal and Nepal (2004), who analyzed the effect of trekking tourism on a mountain trail.

Contemporary Perspectives

This section provides a brief overview of current trends in tourism geographies. In particular, it looks at the contributions at three annual meetings of the Association of American Geographers (AAG), and papers published in *Tourism Geographies*.

Table 8.1 shows the frequency of papers presented at the AAG meetings held during 2005 and 2007. Four major themes and 17 sub-themes have been identified; this division is based on abstracts and keywords posted on AAG's website. A total number of 260 papers were presented during the three annual meetings of the AAG. Tourism planning, regional development, heritage tourism, tourism impacts, and protected areas/landscapes were the major concentration of research. Papers on these themes (Group I) constituted roughly 41.9% of all articles presented. Representation and identity, tourism image and aesthetics, gender, race and class, and romance, sex and

Table 8.1 Foci of Tourism-Related AAG Papers*

Focus Areas	2005 (n = 97)	2006 (n = 121)	2007 (n = 142)
Group I Planning & Development			
Tourism planning	12	11	15
Regional development	8	11	15
Heritage tourism	11	18	9
Tourism impacts	5	12	5
Protected areas/ landscapes	5	4	10
Group II Representation & Image			
Representation and identity	0	15	14
Tourism image and aesthetics	7	1	6
Gender/race/class	3	6	4
Romance/sex/sexuality	5	0	0
Group III Sustainable Development			
Ecotourism	7	7	7
Sustainability	3	5	8
Mountain tourism	2	2	5
Urban revitalization/ land use	1	3	3
Climate/energy	0	1	1
Group IV Economics & Education			
Globalization/ post colonialism	2	2	5
Tourism education	2	2	0
Technology	2	4	6

*includes all papers with tourism as a keyword.
Source: www.aag.org. Accessed February 28, 2007.

sexuality (Group II) represented approximately 17% of all papers. Around 15.3% papers had sustainable development as their main theme (Group III) and covered topics such as ecotourism, sustainability, mountain tourism, urban revitalization, and climate. Tourism economics, education and technology (Group IV) were covered by 7% of the papers. Other topics included health (5), ethics (5), cruise (5), religious/pilgrimage tourism (3), wine (3), second homes (3), and indigenous tourism. There were several other eclectic papers such as Peter Adey's (2005) "Airport affection: bodies, motion, feeling," Robert Kruse's (2006) "Contemporary geographies of John Lennon," Keiron Bailey's (2006) "Mileage runners, weedeaters, and the 'R' bucket: an actor network investigation of the geographies of elite frequent flyers," and

Table 8.2 Focus of Papers Published in Tourism Geographies (2003–2006)

Research Area	Topics (Number of Papers)
Geography (n = 26)	Spatial patterns, analysis, models of tourist space (6)
	Trans-nationalism, borders, migration and mobility (8)
	General (3)
	Location (1)
	Life cycle (2)
	Settlements (1)
	Land use planning (1)
	Tourist space (2)
	Travel model (1)
	Peripheral regions (1)
Sociology (n = 12)	Cultural understanding, cross-cultural relationships, resident perceptions (7)
	Sports tourism (1)
	Creative tourism (1)
	Globalization and economics (2)
	Leisure (1)
Psychology (n = 3)	Tourist motivation, tourist behavior (3)
Anthropology (n = 13)	Authenticity, ethnic identity, heritage (6)
	Cultural tourism (7)
Political Science (n = 1)	Occupied zones (1)
Planning and community development (n = 19)	Planning, development and policy (12)
	Resort development (1)
	Sustainable development, ecotourism (5)
	Tourism impacts (1)
Marketing (n = 4)	Destination image (3)
	Travel writing (1)

Source: Compiled from *Tourism Geographies* journal, 2003–2006.

Mary Conran's (2007) "Returning the gaze: Exploring the possibility for a dialogical tourism."

Similarly, preliminary examination of four years of refereed papers published in the *Tourism Geographies* indicates that the majority of the papers were distinctly geographic (Table 8.2). Although contributors to tourism geographies come from many different backgrounds and are not necessarily always from geographers, papers published in *Tourism Geographies* may be considered as one of the indicators of research direction in tourism geography. Papers are confined not only to geographic approaches, but are based also on sociology, psychology, anthropology, planning, political science, and marketing approaches. This could also be an indication that many geographers apply interdisciplinary perspectives to tourism geography research.

The above analysis indicates that tourism geography has never before been this diverse. Topics such as heritage tourism, wine tourism, and mountain tourism today are as common as more traditional topics like tourism impacts, tourism planning, regional development. It is no surprise that the editor of a new journal *Journal of Heritage Tourism* is a geographer, two of the three authors of a new book on mountain tourism are geographers too (Clark et al., 2006), and so is the lead author of the book on wine tourism (Hall et al., 2002).

Future Trends and Challenges

The recognition of human–environment relationships as a product of very complex processes, at different spatial scales, has meant that geographers are now exploring these issues not only with the aid of sophisticated technologies such as GIS, but also through cooperation with scholars from other specialties and disciplines. Indeed, federal agencies like National Institute of Health (NIH), National Science Foundations and National Research Council (1999) have recognized that solving complex problems requires multidisciplinary, interdisciplinary, and inter-institutional collaborations,[2] as well as applications of both linear and nonlinear scientific approaches. Tourism geographers are aware of this, as indicated by their contributions to addressing issues about tourism vis-a-vis sustainable development and recognition of the research challenges that lie ahead (Farrell and Twining-Ward, 2004). Innovative research techniques, systems modeling, combination of linear, and nonlinear approaches, are increasingly being applied to address sustainability issues in an interrelated, local-global (tourism) system. As Wolman states:

> [O]nce one recognizes the scale and myriad of interactions of humans and the environment, it becomes

increasingly difficult to make sharp distinctions between the influence of environment on society and humans as geographic agents . . . this reciprocal relationship includes recognition that the way the land is used at a place is driven not simply by indigenous features of the landscape, but often by social forces remote from the site. (2004: 726)

This is quite fitting for tourism scholars, who have traditionally grappled with issues of indivisibililty of tourism impacts, problems in discerning human caused impacts from natural impacts, and issues of comparisons at multiple and interlocking scales. The integration of the three broad approaches—spatial, behavioral, reflexive—remains a challenge, despite the recent improvements noted above.

Barriers to collaboration for tourism research are another important issue, and two important challenges can be identified here. The first relates to Butler (2004) and Hall and Page (2002) have commented that communication between English- and non-English-speaking (particularly, German-, French-, and Chinese-speaking) scholars has been very limited (Butler, 2004; Hall and Page, 2002). Pioneering works conducted by German and French geographers have been translated into English, and vice versa, but much greater attention is needed to encourage both collaboration and translation of tourism research being conducted in different academic and research institutions worldwide.

The second challenge relates to the position of tourism geographers within the overall discipline of geography. Mitchell (1979), Hall and Page (2002), and Butler (2004) all have discussed the legitimation issues related to the study of tourism and tourism geographers' low standing within geography. A related issue that has not been well addressed but deserves urgent attention is the declining number of tourism scholars within geography departments. For example, Canadian geography departments were once the powerhouse of noted tourism scholars like Richard Butler, John Marsh, Peter Murphy, Simon Milne, Geoffrey Wall, among others. With the exception of Wall, the others have

either retired or moved overseas and their positions are now replaced by non-tourism scholars. With the emergence of medical geography, GIS, and the recent resurgence of urban development, tourism, at least in North America, has been pushed aside to make way for these new specialties. While this may be justified, as tourism geographers increasingly seek academic positions outside geography and in tourism management or business schools, it is likely that the type and quality of tourism scholarship they produce may be very different from what geographers have traditionally contributed. For instance, critical theory and philosophical discourses have been the hallmarks of geographic research. With more tourism geographers moving to business and management type schools, these approaches might take more of a back seat in future.

Conclusion

Just as geography is prospering today, tourism geography is thriving too. Tourism's complex, diverse, dynamic nature has allowed it to continuously evolve in interesting ways. Specialties are narrowing down to subspecialties; subspecialties are unifying, integrating, and morphing into new specialties. Advances in tourism geography may be analogous to Darwin's evolutionary perspective: species evolve, adapt, mutate and become extinct only to reemerge as a new species. Tourism geography will continue to evolve; it will adapt to the scientific community's and society's thirst for discovery and new knowledge, some topics will be less popular, others will grow in importance; some traditional concepts will become obsolete, fresh perspectives and techniques will emerge; and the cycle will continue. Tourism geographers are actively engaging in current discourses, including but not limited to, climate change, energy management, immigration and border relations, globalization and rural change.

Carl Sauer has noted: "The interest [in geography] is immemorial and universal; should we disappear, the field will remain, and it will not become vacant" (1956: 287). Tourism matters, it is all-pervasive in today's world. We see changes in people's attitudes and behavior as a result of travel, and because of it many of us have seen changes in our neighborhood, community, and society at large. Scholars of tourism geography may no longer exist as such within major departments of geography, but the field will continue. Wolman (2004) states that despite the inevitability of change, it is likely that the four themes of geography—place, spatial location, mapping, and the interaction of society and the environment—will remain and so will tourism geographers.

Acknowledgement

The author wishes to thank Ms Juejue Xing, a PhD student in the Department of Recreation, Park and Tourism Sciences at Texas A&M University, for help in writing the section on tourism geography in China.

Notes

1 Rapid economic growth in India is also beginning to garner attention as new tourism offerings come on line to make this a growing contender in the global tourism economy.

2 See, for example, NSF's Integrative Graduate Education and Research Traineeship funding program. Retrieved May 10, 2008 from www.nsf.gov/funding/pgm_summ.jsp?pims_id=12759&from=fund.

References

Adey, P. (2005). "Airport Affection: Bodies, Motion, Feeling." Paper presented at *The Annual Meeting of the Association of American Geographers*. Denver, April 5–9.

Bailey, K. (2006). "Mileage Runners, Weed Eaters, and the 'R' Bucket: An Actor Network Investigation of the Geographies of Elite Frequent Flyers." Paper presented at *The Annual Meeting of the Association of American Geographers*. Chicago, March 7–11.

Bao, J. (2002). "Tourism Geography as the Subject of Doctoral Dissertations in China, 1989–2000." *Tourism Geographies*, 4(2): 148–152.

Bao, J. and Peng, H. (1995). "A Study on the Expansion Development of Tourist Resorts: Taking Yangyuan Section, Danxia Scenic Spot as an Example." *Scientia Geographica Sinica*, 15(1): 63–69 (in Chinese).

Barbier, B. (1984). "Geography of Tourism and Leisure." *GeoJournal*, 9(1): 4–95.

Bavoux, J. (1997). *Les Littoraux Français*. Paris: A. Colin.

Beaujeu-Garnier, J. and Chabot, G. (1967). *Traité de Géogrpahie Urbaine*. Paris: A. Colin.

Boyd, S. and Butler, R. (1993). "Identifying Areas for Ecotourism in Northern Ontario: Application of a Geographical Information System Methodology." *Journal of Applied Recreation Research*, 19(1): 41–66.

Britton, S. (1982). "The Political Economy of Tourism in the Third World." *Annals of Tourism Research*, 9(2): 331–358.

Britton, S. (1991). "Tourism, Capital and Place: Towards a Critical Geography of Tourism." *Environment and Planning D: Society and Place*, 9: 451–478.

Brown, R. (1935). "The Business of Recreation." *Geographical Review*, 25: 467–475.

Butler, R. (1980). "The Concept of a Tourist Area Cycle of Evolution, Implications for Management of Resources." *Canadian Geographer*, 24(1): 5–12.

Butler, R. (2004). "Geographic Research on Tourism, Recreation, and Leisure: Origins, Eras, and Directions." *Tourism Geographies*, 6(2): 143–162.

Butler, R. and Boyd, S. (2000). *Tourism and National Parks. Issues and Implications*. Chichester: John Wiley.

Carlson, A. (1938). "Recreation Industry of New Hampshire." *Economic Geography*, 14: 255–270.

Cazes, G. (1992). *Fondements pour une géographie du tourisme et des loisirs*. Paris: Bréal, coll. Amphi-géographie.

Chen, C. (1985). "Research on Tourism Evaluation of Physiognomy." *Journal of Henan University (Natural Science)*, (1): 65–74.

Chen, B. and Yang, G. (2004). "Quantitative Study of the Impact of Tourist Trampling on Ecotourism Scenic Region: A Case Research of the Shangri-la Bita Lake Ecotourism Scenic Region." *Scientia Geographica Sinica*, 24(3): 371–375 (in Chinese).

Christaller, W. (1955). Beitrage Zu Einer Geographie des Fremdenverkehrs. *Erdkunde* 9(1): 1–19.

Christaller, W. (1964). "Some Considerations of Tourism Location in Europe: The Peripheral Regions—Under Developed Countries—Recreation Areas." *Regional Science Association Papers*, 12: 95–105.

Chu, Y. (1989). *The Spatial Organization of Tourism*. PhD Dissertation. Nankai University (in Chinese).

Clark, T., Gill, A. and Hartmann, R. (2006). *Mountain Resort Planning and Development in an Era of Globalization*. New York: Cognizant.

Conran, M. (2007). "Returning the Gaze: Exploring the Possibility for a Dialogical Tourism." Paper presented at *The Annual Meeting of the Association of American Geographers*. San Francisco, April 17–21.

Coppock, J. (1977). *Second Homes: Curse or Blessing?* Oxford: Pergamon Press.

Crouch, D. (Ed.) (1999). *Leisure/Tourism Geographies: Practices and Geographical Knowledge*. London: Routledge.

Deasy, G. (1949). "The Tourist Industry in a North Woods County." *Economic Geography*, 25(2): 240–259.

Debarbieux, B. (1995). *Tourisme et montagne*. Paris: Économica, coll. Géopoche.

Defert, P. (1967). Le Taux de Fonction Touristique: Mise au Point et Critique. Aix-en-Provence: Centre des Hautes Etudes Touristiques. *Les Cahiers du Tourisme*, C–13.

Deng, Y. and Wang, Z. (2003). "Several Geocomputation Problems on Tourism Distribution Center Planning." *Acta Geographica Sinica*, 58(5): 781–788 (in Chinese).

Dewailly, J.-M. and Flamment, É. (1993). *Géogrpahie du tourisme et des loisirs*. Paris: DIEM, SEDES.

Farrell, B. and Twining-Ward, L. (2004). "Reconceptualizing Tourism." *Annals of Tourism Research*, 31(2): 274–295.

Feng, X. and Bao, H. (1999). "Preliminary Research on Tourist Activity Influence Upon the Soil and Cover Plant of Scenic Spot." *Journal of Natural Resources*, 14(1): 75–78 (in Chinese).

Fennell, D. (1999). *Ecotourism: An Introduction*. London: Routledge.

George, P. (1974). *Précis de géographie urbain*. Paris: PUF.

Gilbert, E. (1939). "The Growth of Inland and Seaside Health Resorts in England." *Scottish Geographical Magazine*, 55: 16–35.

Goeldner, C. and Ritchie, B. (2003). *Tourism: Principles, Practices, Philosophies* (9th edition.). New Jersey: John Wiley.

Goodchild, M. (2004). "GIScience, Geography, Form and Process." *Annals of the Association of American Geographers*, 94(4): 709–714.

Guo, L. and Bao, J. (1990). "Review on Chinese Tourist Geography and its Prospect." *Geographical Research*, 9(1): 78–87 (in Chinese).

Guo, L. and Wu, B. (2000). "Study on the Tourist Resources Classification System and Types Evaluation in China." *Acta Geographica Sinica*, 55(3): 294–301 (in Chinese).

Guthrie, H. (1961). "Demand for Tourists' Goods and Services in a World Market." *Papers, Regional Science Association*, 7: 159–175.

Hall, M. and Johnston, M. (Eds.) (1995). *Polar Tourism: Tourism in the Arctic and Antartic Regions*. Chichester: Wiley.

Hall, M. and Page, S. (2002). "Chapter 1. Introduction: Tourism Matters!" In M. Hall and S. Page (Eds.), *The Geography of Tourism and Recreation—Environment, Place and Space* (2nd edition.) (pp. 1–29). London: Routledge.

Hall, M., Sharples, L., Cambourne, B. and Macionis, N. (2002). *Wine Tourism Around the World*. Oxford: Butterworth-Heinemann.

Hanson, S. (2004). "Who are 'We'? An Important Question for Geography's Future." *Annals of the Association of American Geographers*, 94(4): 715–722.

Heinritz, G. and Popp, H. (1978). "Reichweiten von Freizeiteinrichtungen und aktionsräumliche Aspekte des Besucherverhaltens." *Mitteilungen der Geographischen Gesellschaft München*, 63: 79–115.

Jacob, G. (1966). "Der Gegenwartige Stand und die Aufgaben der Geographie des Fremdenverkehrs." *Wiss. Z. Hocsh Verkehrs wes Dresden*, 13(1): 185–190.

Juls, F. (1965). "Praktische Hinwesie für wissenschaftliche Arbeiten in de Fremdenverkehrsgeographie." In *Festschrift Leopold G. Scheidl zum 60 Geburstag* 1 Teil: 56–67.

Kreisel, W. (2004). "Geography of Leisure and Tourism Research in the German-speaking World: Three Pillars to Progress." *Tourism Geographies*, 6(2): 163–185.

Krippendorf, J. (1976). *Die Landschaftsfresser. Tourismus und Erholungslandschaft— Verdeben oder Segen?* Bern: Hallwag.

Krippendorf, J. (1984). *Die Ferienmenschen. Für ein neues Verständnis von Freizeit und Reisen.* Zürich and Schwäbisch. Hall: Orell Füssli.

Kruse, R. (2006). "Contemporary Geographies of John Lennon." Paper presented at *The Annual Meeting of the Association of American Geographers.* Chicago, March 7–11.

Lawson, V. (2005). "President's Column: We are all the AAG." *The Association of American Geographers (AAG) Newsletter*, 40(1): 38.

Lazzarotti, O. (2002). "French Tourism Geographies: A Review." *Tourism Geographies*, 4(2): 135–147.

Lew, A. (2001). "Editorial: Tourism and Geography Space." *Tourism Geographies*, 3(1): 1.

Lew, A. (2006). "Editor's Note: Tourism Geographies' Space, Place and Environment." *Tourism Geographies*, 8(1): 95.

Li, L. (1987). "GIS for the Tourism Professional." Proceedings of the American Society for Photogrammetry and Remote Sensing.

Li, L. (1995). "A Discussion on the Positioning of Tourism Resort Image." *Tourism Tribune*, (3): 29–31 (in Chinese).

Liu, Z. and Wang, Y. (2001). "Landscape Ecology and Ecotourism Planning/ Management." *Geographical Research*, 20(2): 206–212 (in Chinese).

Lozato-Giotard, J-P. (1993). *Géographie du tourisme* (4th edition.). Paris: Masson, coll. géographie.

Lu, L. (1997). "A Study on the Life Cycle of Mountain Resorts: A Case Study of Huangshan Mountain and Jiuhuashan Mountain." *Scientia Geographica Sinica*, 17(1): 63–69 (in Chinese).

Marsh, G. (1864). *Man and Nature or Physical Geography as Modified by Human Action.* London: Sampson Low, Son, and Marston.

Marsh, J. (1975). *Tourism as a Factor in National and Regional Development.* Occasional Paper 4. Peterborough: Department of Geography, Trent University.

Marston, R. (2006). "President's Column: The AAG—Expanding who we are." *The Association of American Geographers (AAG) Newsletter*, 41(1): 3 and 6.

Mathieson, A. and Wall, G. (1982). *Tourism: Economic, Physical and Social Impacts.* London: Longman.

Matley, I. (1976). *The Geography of International Tourism.* Resource Paper No. 76–1. Washington, DC: Association of American Geographers.

McMurray, K. (1930). "The Use of Land for Recreation." *Annals of the Association of American Geographers*, 20: 7–20.

Merlini, G. (1968). "Problemi Geografici del Tourismo in Italia." *Bollettino della Societa Geografica Italiana*, 9(1–3): 1–30.

Mercer, D. (1970). "The Geography of Leisure: A Contemporary Growth Point." *Geography*, 55(3): 261–273.

Meyer-Arendt, K. and Lew, A. (1999). "Commentary: A Decade of American RTS Geography." *Tourism Geographies*, 1(4): 477–487.

Michaud, J-L. (1983). *Le tourisme face à l'environnement.* Paris: PUF, coll. Le géographe.

Miège, J. (1933). La Vie Touristique en Savoie. *Revue de Géographie Alpine*, 23: 749–817.

Miossec, J. (1976). Eléments pour une Théorie de l'Espace Touristique. Aix-en-Provence: Centre des Hautes Etudes Touristiques. *Les Cahiers du Tourisme* C–36.

Mitchell, L. (1979). "The Geography of Tourism. An Introduction." *Annals of Tourism Research*, 6(3): 235–244.

Mitchell, L. (1984). "Tourism Research in the United States: A Geographical Perspective." *GeoJournal*, 9: 5–15.

Mitchell, L. and Murphy, P. (1991). "Geography and Tourism." *Annals of Tourism Research*, 18(1): 57–70.

Murphy, P. (1963). "Geography and Outdoor Recreation: An Opportunity and an Obligation." *Professional Geographer*, 15(5). 33–34.

Murphy, P. (1985). *Tourism: A Community Approach.* New York: Methuen.

National Research Council. (1999). *Our Common Journey: A Transition to Sustainability.* Washington, DC: National Academy Press.

Nepal, S. (2000). "Tourism and Environment in the Nepalese Himalaya: Opportunities and Constraints." *Annals of Tourism Research*, 27(3): 661–681.

Nepal S. and Nepal, S. (2004). "Visitor Impacts on Trails in the Sagarmatha (Mt. Everest) National Park, Nepal." *Ambio*, 33(6): 334–340.

Nepal, S. (2005). "Tourism and Remote Mountain Settlements: Spatial and Temporal Developments of Tourist Infrastructure in the Mt. Everest Region, Nepal." *Tourism Geographies*, 7(2): 205–227.

Niu, Y. (1999). "Sustainable Tourism, Ecotourism and Implementation." *Geographical Research*, 18(2): 179–184 (in Chinese).

Patmore, J. (1968). "The Spa Town of England and Wales." In G. Beckinsale (Ed.) *Problems of Urbanization* (pp. 168–194). London: Methuen.

Pearce, D. (1978). "Form and Function in French Resorts." *Annals of Tourism Research*, 5(1): 142–156.

Pearce, D. (1979). "Towards a Geography of Tourism." *Annals of Tourism Research*, 6(3): 245–272.

Pearce, D. (1989). *Tourist Development*. Harlow: Longman.

Pearce, D. (1995). *Tourism Today: A Geographical Perspective*. Harlow: Longman.

Poser, H. (1939). Geographische Studien uber den Fremdenverkehr in Riesengebirge: Ein Beitrag zur Geographischen Betrachung des Fremdenverkehrs. *Abhandlungen der Gesellschaft der Wissenschaften zu Gottingen*. Dritte Folge. Heft 20: 1–173.

Ritter, W. (1966). *Fremdenverkehr in Europa*. Leiden: Sijthoff.

Robinson, H. (1976). *A Geography of Tourism*. London: MacDonald & Evans.

Sauer, C. (1956). "The Education of a Geographer." *Annals of The Association of American Geographers*, 46: 287–299.

Selke, A. (1936). "Geographic Aspects of the German Tourist Trade." *Economic Geography*, 12: 206–216.

Shaw, G. and Williams, A. (1994). *Critical Issues in Tourism: A Geographical Perspective*. Oxford: Blackwell.

Smith, S. (1982). "Reflections on the Development of Geographic Research in Recreation: Hey, Buddy, Can You's Paradigm?" *Ontario Geography*, 19: 5–29.

Stewart, E. and Draper, D. (2006). "Sustainable Cruise Tourism in Arctic Canada: An Integrated Coastal Management Approach." *Tourism in Marine Environments*, 3(2): 77–88.

Ullman, E. (1956). "The Role of Transportation and the Bases for Interaction." In W. Thoman (Ed.), *Man's Role in Changing the Face of the Earth* (pp. 862–880). Chicago, IL: Chicago University Press.

Wall, G. (1988). "Implications of Climatic Change for Tourism and Recreation in Ontario." *Climate Change Digest*, 88–05. Ottawa: Ministry of Supply and Services Canada.

Wang, X. (1996). "The Development and Prospect of China's Modern Tourism Geography Research." *Human Geography*, 11: 72–79 (in Chinese).

Wang, Z. and Wang, Y. (2003). "Research of Reconstitution of Tourism Location of Guizhou Province in China." *Geographical Research*, 22(3): 313–323 (in Chinese).

Wang, Z. and Zhou, W. (2001). "An Analysis for Market Area of Chinese National Park Based on Railway Corridor." *Acta Geographica Sinica*, 56(2): 206–213 (in Chinese).

Wang, Y. and Yang, X. (1998). "A Study on Landscape Ecology of Regional Tourism Development Taking Anning City as an Example." *Geographical Research*, 17(4): 383–388 (in Chinese).

Weaver, D. (1998). *Ecotourism in the Less Developed World*. Wallingford: CAB International.

Wolfe, R. (1951). "Summer Cottages in Ontario." *Economic Geography*, 27(1): 10–32.

Wolfe, R. (1952). "Wasaga Beach—The Divorce from the Geographic Environment." *The Canadian Geographer*, 2(1): 57–66.

Wolfe, R. (1966). "Recreation travel: The New Migration." *The Canadian Geographer*, 10(1): 1–14.

Wolman, M. (2004). "The More Things Change." *Annals of the Association of American Geographers*, 94(4): 723–728.

Wu, B. (1994). "A Research on Urban Recreationist's Travelling Behavior in Shanghai." *Acta Geographica Sinica*, 49(2): 117–126 (in Chinese).

Wu, B. (2001). "A Study on Recreational Belt Around Metropolis (ReBAM): Shanghai Case." *Scientia Geographica Sinica*, 21(4): 354–359 (in Chinese).

Zhang, X. and Wang, X. (1992). *100 Books Which Influenced China.* Nanning: Guangxi People Press (in Chinese).

Zhao, H. (1983). "A Study on Tourism Environmental Capacity of Suzhou City." *City Planning Review*, 5: 46–53 (in Chinese).

9

Development Studies and Tourism

David J. Telfer

Introduction

With its promise of foreign exchange and employment, tourism is seen as an attractive development strategy; thereby placing it within the realm of development studies, a highly contested field of enquiry with roots in the late 1940s being institutionalized in the 1950s and 1960s (Hettne, 2002). Proponents of tourism argue that the industry in its various forms has a role to play, not only in economic development but also in development more broadly defined. With tourism being used as a strategy for development, there are opportunities to further explore the relationship between tourism and various competing development ideologies, theories and strategies that have evolved over time within the overriding discipline of development studies. For example, tourism development can be examined in the context of globalization where neoliberal policies facilitate foreign multinationals investing and controlling large-scale resorts. This can be juxtaposed with indigenous NGOs providing grassroots assistance to community-based organizations

in pro-poor tourism producing handmade craft souvenirs for tourists. The first option illustrates a macro-level policy aimed at broader level goals of attaining foreign exchange and employment at a national level, while the latter option can be observed at a more micro level in terms of a direct attack on poverty in a specific location. The challenge is not only to investigate to what degree these two very different tourism development strategies can contribute to development, but also how the strategies relate to the concepts within the discipline of development studies.

Development studies as a multi- and interdisciplinary field of investigation (Potter, 2002) "has changed in everything except its normative concern with emancipation from inequality and poverty" (Hettne, 2002: 11). While initially focused on economic growth, the meaning and measurement of development has expanded to include broader concepts such as human development and the environment. How development is purportedly achieved can be traced through a set of competing development paradigms that have evolved since the end of World War II, including modernization, dependency, economic neoliberalism, and alternative development. However, development studies reached an impasse in the 1980s, with the failure of development in developing countries along with the postmodern critique and trends in globalization (Desai and Potter, 2002) all giving rise to post-development. The global political economy shifted markedly towards the Washington consensus (see Williamson, 2003) in the 1990s, following the neoliberal policy approach of the Bretton Woods Institutions (e.g., International Monetary Fund and World Bank) (Burnell and Randall, 2005). Nevertheless, cracks are appearing in the globalized economy (Saul, 2005) with the recognition that a completely free market may not be the best answer for development. Development studies has crossed the millennium threshold though, admittedly, not with a gracious jump (Schuurman, 2000). It is at a crossroads and the search for a new paradigm has begun, yet the shape that development thought will take in the coming years is open to debate (Rapley, 2002). As a way forward, there are interesting emerging approaches that may help build towards the future, including elements of international political economy, links between peace and development, cultural studies, and a continuing concern for the excluded (Hettne, 2002).

In tourism too there has been an evolution, beginning with the drive for economic growth and modernization through tourism in the 1950s, to a shift towards sustainable tourism and, most recently, a focus on poverty reduction, mirroring shifts in development studies. However, there has been limited investigation of the role of tourism in development studies and likewise in the development literature, tourism has yet to receive significant attention (Telfer, 2002). The purpose of this chapter is to address this gap and explore the relationship between development studies and tourism. It will begin by exploring the linkages between these two areas of study and then outline the changes in the meaning and

measurement of development. The chapter will then trace the evolution of development thought along with related strategies of tourism development. The chapter will conclude by reevaluating the relationship between tourism and development.

Tourism and Development Studies

Development is very much a normative concept and though the various theories and strategies have changed, it is focused on freeing people from inequality and poverty (Hettne, 2002). What role then can tourism play in a narrower conceptualization of development tied to economic growth and distribution or to part of a broader notion of development that includes elements such as empowerment, self-sufficiency, and environmental sustainability? The challenges of development are many and are extremely complex. There are over one billion people living in extreme poverty, representing about one-sixth of the world's population (Addison, 2005). Using the analogy of economic growth as being a ladder where the rungs are steps to economic well-being, Sachs (2005) points out that only one billion (approximately one-sixth of the world population) live in the high-income world. Addison (2005) goes on to note the challenges that developing countries have include very mixed economic performance, with success in much of Asia but also poor performance in sub-Sahara Africa and economic instability in Latin America. Fields (2001) reminds us that economic growth alone does not ensure that the distribution of development benefits all. Can tourism offset developmental challenges even in a small way? Advocates for tourism present the positive impacts that tourism can have for development. Table 9.1 contains selected examples of ways that tourism can contribute positively to development. As one moves beyond the basic economic indicators (e.g., GDP, employment), the complexity of the development goals and indicators increases

Table 9.1 Potential Positive Examples of Tourism Contributing to Development

Area of Development	Potential Positive Contribution
Economic	• GDP • Foreign exchange • Employment • Income • Poverty reduction • Infrastructure development
Social/Cultural	• Strengthening local culture • Self-reliance • Revitalization of crafts
Environmental	• Sustainable development • Environmental management • Protected areas
Political	• Empowerment • Self-reliance • Freedom • Image of stability and security

for areas such as the environment, the social/ cultural realm and the political realm.

Development studies as a subject emerged after World War II and was initially focused on macroeconomic problems, especially those concerning global inequalities between rich and poor nations (Brohman, 1996). Economists played a lead role in postwar development theory and over time it has become interdisciplinary in focus, with contributions from fields such as anthropology, sociology, political science, social psychology, and geography (Brohman, 1996; Potter, 2002). It should be stressed that there are significant barriers (both endogenous and exogenous to the destination) related to all of the items listed in Table 9.1 that prevent the maximum developmental benefit from occurring. Moreover, just as there are disputes as to the effectiveness of development, there are some who argue that tourism reinforces inequalities and generates exploitation.

There is little doubt that tourism has economic potential and most countries around the world participate to some degree in the industry. In 2008, tourism is expected to generate US$ 5,890 billion of economic activity, 9.9% of total GDP and 238.3 million jobs or 8.4% of total employment (WTTC, 2008). Table 9.2 illustrates international tourist arrivals and receipts for 2005 and 2006.

It is clear, however, from the table that the distribution of tourists and hence wealth is far from equal, as Europe received 54.4% of the tourists and 51.1% of the receipts. These marked differences are also apparent when one looks at the sub regions in the table, and also when one considers the role that tourism plays in individual countries. Table 9.3 illustrates that the USA, Japan, and France had the highest travel and tourism industry GDP in 2006, while Macau, Antigua and Barbuda, and Aruba had the highest travel and tourism economy GDP as a percentage of total GDP. Clearly tourism plays a greater role in the economy of some developing island destinations than in some of the large developed countries. Statistics, however, can be deceiving, as they often do not indicate to what extent local communities or even individuals benefit from tourism. Cawthorne (2007), for example, notes the controversy that has emerged over "slum tourism" to Kibera, a community of 800,000 in Nairobi, Kenya where tourists come to see poverty yet few benefits come to the community.

In answering the question what kind of discipline is development studies and what should it be, Hettne responds that development studies is interdisciplinary, "problem oriented, concerned with global disparities in material resources, the social consequences of this situation in different societies, and political strategies to change it" (1995: 11–12). The field has undergone drastic changes since the early focus on economic growth. It has been at the center of many debates, with criticism coming from those that suggest it is a concept that "stands like a ruin in the intellectual landscape" (Sachs, 1996: 1) while others have examined the evolution of the development project into the globalization project (McMichael, 2004). There has been a search for new theoretical conceptualizations of development and this has been mirrored in changes in how development is practiced (Potter, 2002). These changes have been evident in how tourism has been used as a development tool, influenced by shifts in the larger theoretical conceptualizations of development (Telfer, 2002).

Table 9.2 International Tourist Arrivals and Receipts

	International Tourist Arrivals (millions)		Market Share (%)	International Tourist Receipts (US $ billions)		Market Share
	2005	2006	2006	2005	2006	2006
World	803	846	100	676	733	100
Europe	438.7	460.8	54.4	348.8	374.5	54.1
Northern Europe	51.0	54.9	6.5	53.9	59.9	8.2
Western Europe	142.6	149.8	17.7	122.5	130.8	17.9
Central/Eastern Europe	87.8	91.2	10.8	32.4	37.3	5.1
Southern/Mediterranean Europe	157.3	164.9	19.5	140.0	146.5	20.0
Asia & Pacific	155.3	167.2	19.8	134.5	152.6	20.8
North-East Asia	87.5	94.0	11.1	65.4	74.3	10.1
South East Asia	49.3	53.9	6.4	33.8	40.6	5.5
Oceania	10.5	10.5	1.2	25.6	26.3	3.6
South Asia	8.0	8.8	1.0	9.6	11.5	1.6
Americas	133.2	135.9	16.1	145.2	154.0	21.0
North America	89.9	90.7	10.7	107.4	112.5	15.4
Caribbean	18.8	19.4	2.3	20.8	22.1	3.0
Central America	6.3	7.0	0.8	4.6	5.4	0.7
South America	18.2	18.8	2.2	12.4	14.0	1.9
Africa	37.3	40.7	4.8	21.7	24.3	3.3
North Africa	13.9	14.9	1.8	7.0	8.5	1.2
Sub Saharan Africa	23.3	25.8	3.0	14.7	15.8	2.2
Middle East	38.3	41.8	4.9	26.3	27.3	3.7

Source: UNWTO, 2007a.
Note: 2006 data provisional.

Meaning and Measuring of Development

There has been a great deal of debate and controversy surrounding development, with many changing views as to its definition and the strategies by which development, however defined, may be pursued (Potter, 2002).

The term has had several meanings including "economic growth, structural change, autonomous industrialization, capitalism or socialism, self-actualization and individual, national, regional and cultural self-reliance" (Harrison, 1988: 154). Reflecting on the changes over time, Marks and Andreassen state that "in the last decades of the twentieth century,

Table 9.3 Selected Top 10 Tourism Statistics

Travel & Tourism Industry GDP 2006 (US$ MN)		Travel and Tourism Economy 2006 (% of Total GDP)	
United States	518,336.0	Macau	93.6
Japan	168,500.8	Antigua and Barbuda	85.4
France	97,794.2	Aruba	78.0
Spain	81,638.8	Anguilla	74.7
Italy	81,617.8	Maldives	66.6
United Kingdom	79,874.4	British Virgin Islands	54.7
Germany	77,952.4	Seychelles	54.1
China	63,424.0	Saint Lucia	51.0
Mexico	41,975.3	Bahamas	50.1
Canada	41,457.7	Vanuatu	47.0

Source: WTTC, 2007.
Note: The Travel and Tourism Industry captures the explicitly defined production-side "industry" contribution (i.e., direct impact only) while the Travel and Tourism Economy captures the broader economy-wide impact direct and indirect of Travel and Tourism.

development thinking has shifted from a growth oriented model to a human development model" (2006: vii). In looking for areas of consensus around development, Desai and Potter (2002) state that economic growth is necessary but not sufficient condition for development. They go on to argue that "development must be regarded as synonymous with enhancing human rights and welfare, so that self-esteem, self respect and improving entitlements become central concerns" (2002: 2). With the shift away from an economic focus, other areas come into focus, including political, social, ecological, cultural, and other wider aspects of development. On the environmental front, sustainable development came to the forefront to address growing concerns about resource exploitation and degradation, and the need for corporate social responsibility in this regard. Most notably, sustainable development as defined by the World Commission on Environment and Development (WCED) is "development that meets the needs of the present without compromising the ability of future generations to meet their own needs" (1987: 43). The 1992 Earth Summit in Rio produced *Agenda 21*, an action plan for achieving sustainable development, and subsequent Earth Summit conferences have revisited the progress made towards *Agenda 21*. In an analysis of the discourses of sustainable development, Redclift (2002) highlights the complexity and broadening of the term, indicating that sustainable development can be increasingly connected to notions of human rights and democracy.

A useful way of examining development has been outlined by Hettne (1995). He suggests that development can be examined in terms of development theory, development strategies and development ideology. Building on Hettne's work, Potter (2002) suggests that theories can be regarded as sets of ostensibly logical propositions that aim to explain how development has occurred in the past. The theories can be either normative (what should happen in an ideal world) or positive (what has generally been the case in the past). Development strategies, then,

are the practical paths to development pursued by international agencies, states, NGOs, community-based organizations, or individuals to stimulate change within nations, regions, and continents (Potter, 2002). Development ideologies reflect that different development agendas will reflect different goals and objectives. These goals in turn reflect social, economic, political cultural, ethical, moral, and religious influences (Potter, 2002). Goldsworthy (1988) argues that more attention is needed on the political ideological underpinnings of development thinking whether it is conservative, liberal, or radicall, for example. When one considers various ideologies, it is important to keep in mind the concepts of power and control with respect to development. Who has power and what ideology do they subscribe to will often dictate the selected development strategy. In the context of tourism, who has control of the industry and who is allowed to participate and benefit are central to the tourism development debate.

The complexity and sometimes contradictory concerns of the term "development" are also reflected in how development is practiced (Goulet, 1995). Goulet (1995: 1–2) illustrates this through a short list of "bewildering, and at times contradictory, assortment of policy prescriptions:

- a "'big push' into self sustained economic growth or rapid shock treatment reform of the economic system;
- the Westernization of social institutions and practices;
- the repudiation of Westernization in favor of an 'endogenous' model of change;
- the mobilization of national resources and energies around 'giant projects'; or conversely
- the glorification of the 'small is beautiful' strategy based on small, locally controlled projects."

Examples of these "prescriptions" can be found in tourism developments around the world, whether through community based ecotourism projects in places like Costa Rica or Kenya, or large scale resort complexes with national government involvement, such as in Cancun, Mexico.

The shift away from the primary income based development indicators is apparent in published indices. Elliot (2002) outlines the changes in measuring development by the United Nations Development Program (UNDP). In 1990, the UNDP introduced the Human Development Index (HDI), which is a composite index designed to reflect achievements in the most basic human capabilities defined as having a long life (measured by life expectancy at birth), being knowledgeable (measured by adult literacy rate and the combined primary, secondary, and tertiary gross enrollment ratio), and enjoying a decent standard of living (measured by GDP per capita) (see UNDP 2008). In 1995, the Gender Related Human Development Index (GDI) and the Gender Empowerment Measure (GEM) were both introduced; these recognized that gender equality is also a measure and means for both human and national development. In 1997, the Human Poverty Index (HPI) was introduced, measuring the percentage of the population not expected to live to age 40, illiteracy rates, the percentage lacking access to health services and safe water, and the percentage of children less than five years old who are moderately or severely underweight. These changes reflect that development is increasingly conceived in terms of human rights, freedom and the recognition that the various aspects of development are interconnected and multidimensional in nature (Elliot, 2002). As evidence of this, the UN General Assembly adopted the Declaration on the Right to Development in 1986 and at the 1993 Vienna Conference on Human Rights called the right to develop "fundamental" (Marks and Andreassen, 2006). At the 1998 General Assembly celebrating the 50th anniversary of the Universal Declaration of Human Rights (UDHR), a proposal was put forward that the Declaration on the Right to Development be put on par with the UDHR (Marks and Andreassen, 2006).

The most recent focus of development is on poverty reduction, as evident in the UN Millennium Development Goals outlined in Table 9.4. These goals have a target date of 2015 and each has further specific indicators (not included in the Table). If the focus has shifted towards poverty reduction, consideration needs to be given as to how tourism can contribute to the UN Millennium Goals. At a macro level, if there is additional revenue and taxes generated through tourism there is potential that the additional revenue can contribute towards the developmental goals of a nation. How this additional income is used to specifically combat poverty is an area for further investigation in individual countries. In September 2005, the UN World Tourism Organization released a declaration on how tourism can be harnessed to help contribute to the Millennium Goals (UNWTO, 2005). The declaration has 17 key recommendations for tourism to effectively contribute to the Millennium Goals. The UNWTO has also established the ST-EP program (Sustainable Tourism—Eliminating Poverty).[1]

A Brief History of Development Thought

Charting the evolution of development thought since the ending of World War II is a path through competing and at times contradictory theories, ideologies, and strategies. "When the idea of 'development' took hold in the middle of the last century, it seemed possible that all that countries had to do was to emulate the rich—following roughly the same development path towards a similar destination" (Fukuda-Parr et al., 2002: 2). This simple linear progression has proven not to work for a multitude of reasons and has given rise to a variety of approaches and critiques. There are many ways to categorize development thinking through time (Potter, 2002). Hettne (1995) argues that in the social sciences, "paradigms" tend to accumulate rather than replace each other, one reason for this being that they may fulfill ideological purposes, even after their explanatory power (if there ever was any) has been lost. Not only have the overriding theories changed,

Table 9.4   United Nations Millennium Development Goals

1. Eradicate extreme poverty and hunger
   - reduce by half the people living on less than a dollar a day and the proportion who suffer from hunger
2. Achieve universal primary education
   - ensure all boys and girls receive a full course of primary schooling
3. Promote gender equality and empower women
   - eliminate gender disparity in primary and secondary education, preferably by 2005 and all levels by 2015
4. Reduce child mortality
   - reduce by two-thirds the mortality rate for children under five years of age
5. Improve maternal health
   - reduce by three quarters the maternal mortality ratio
6. Combat HIV/AIDS, malaria and other diseases
   - halt and begin to reverse the spread of HIV/AIDS, malaria and other major diseases
7. Ensure environmental sustainability
   - integrate principles of sustainable development into countries' policies and programs; reverse the loss of environmental resources; reduce by half the proportion of those without sustainable access to safe drinking water; and achieve significant improvements in the lives of 100 million slum dwellers by 2020
8. Develop a global partnership for development
   - develop open trading financial system with commitment to good governance, poverty reduction and development; address least developed countries' special needs (debt relief and assistance for countries focusing on poverty reduction); address needs of landlocked and small island developing states; deal comprehensibly with debt problems; provide access to affordable medications; make the benefits of new technologies available

Source: United Nations, 2005.

but so too have the strategies to secure development. Preston (1996) identifies three main paradigms in terms of characterizing and securing development. The first paradigm focuses on state intervention to secure development. The second focuses on the role of the free market. The third relates to the power of the political community to secure the goals of development. In this third option, a central role is allocated to the public sphere, with the approach oriented to securing formal and substantive democracy. The institutional vehicle for this approach lies in the realm of NGOs, charities, and dissenting social movements. Two of the major social movements include the environmental movement and the women's movement.

In linking the evolution of tourism and development theory, Telfer (2002) examined four main development paradigms since the ending to World War II: modernization, dependency, economic neoliberalism, and alternative development. Under these four main paradigms, the author examined selected corresponding theoretical approaches or models and their respective key concepts and strategies. These are explored below, along with corresponding developments in tourism, as illustrated in Table 9.5. However, as mentioned above, development theory is at a crossroads and a search is underway for a new paradigm (Rapley, 2002). As Schuurman points out, until the mid-1980s, post-World War II development thinking shared three basic paradigms, which included "essentializing the Third World and its inhabitants as homogeneous entities, an unconditional belief in progress and the makeability of society and the importance of the (nation) state in realizing progress" (2000: 7). From the 1980s onward, these three have lost their hegemonic status in the impasse of development, giving way to "a loose set of partly descriptive, partly heuristic notions like civil society, social capital, diversity and risk" (Schuurman, 2000: 7). Table 9.5 also illustrates some examples of the range of concepts that are emerging in development studies.

It must be noted that, given the volume of work in development studies, it is not possible to comprehensively explore the main paradigms or the various subfields within each major theory or approach (see Telfer [2002] for more detailed explanation of development theory). It also must be stressed that this is only one perspective of looking at development theory and there are a variety of different classification systems (for example, see Potter, 2002). The time guide is only a guide and meant to illustrate when the paradigm gained prominence after World War II (many of the key components are still applicable today). In a sense, there is an ongoing conversation and debate between these paradigms and their processes, which can be seen in part as a reaction to those that precede it. It is interesting to see that in the most recent period there are

Table 9.5   Linkages Between Development Theory and Tourism

Time Guide	Development Paradigm or Process	Selected Theoretical Approaches, Strategies & Critiques	Illustrations in Tourism
1950s 1960s	*Modernization*	Stages of economic growth Diffusion of growth impulses and trickle down	use of tourism to generate foreign exchange, employment, growth poles and promote modern or Western way of life; demonstration effect; evolution of destination resorts
1950s 1960s	*Dependency*	Neocolonialism: underdevelopment caused by developed countries Dualism: poverty functional to global economic growth Structuralism: domestic markets, import substitution, state involvement	critique of power structures in tourism; multinational tourism industry exploits developing country; loss of local culture to tourism culture; state led tourism development projects as a response to dependency
mid 1970s and 1980s	*Economic neoliberalism*	Free competitive markets; privatization Structural Adjustment: market forces, competitive exports One World: new world financial system, deregulation, globalization	states open doors to foreign investment in tourism to compete in global market; rise of multinational tourism operators looking globally for lowest costs of production; international loans for tourism projects on the condition of opening the economy to world trade
1970s early 1980s	*Alternative development*	Basic needs: food, housing, water, health, education Grassroots: people centered development, empowerment Gender: women in development, gender relations Sustainable Development: meeting present & future needs	sustainable tourism development; community based tourism; pro-poor tourism; fair trade; ecotourism; alternative tourism; empowerment of women through tourism; local involvement in planning; tourism codes of conduct and ethics; corporate social responsibility in tourism
1990s, 2000 and beyond	*Beyond the impasse: the search for a new paradigm?*	Post-Development: rejection of "development" Developmental State Theory: state-led development Civil Society and Social Capital: connect citizens and state Transnational Social Movements: movements of, e.g., environmentalists, indigenous peoples, feminist, peace, etc. Culture Studies: different worldviews are accommodated Development and Security: conflict and chaos with state disintegration	critique of tourism as a "development" tool; state-led tourism development; focus on local communities and the importance of indigenous knowledge; increasing role for tourism NGOs in both service provision and campaigns (local to international) against exploitation; concerns over safety and security

Source: After Telfer, 2002; Hettne, 2002.

ideas which have similarities to development thinking from the past.

Modernization and Tourism

Modernization is a process of socioeconomic development that follows an evolutionary path from a traditional society to a modern society, such as those in Western Europe or America (Schmidt, 1989). Modernization theory was constructed around three interrelated components: an uncritical vision of the West; a view of non-West or traditional societies in a way that ignored their own histories and measured their innate values in terms of their level of Westernization; and an interpretation of the West–non-West encounter based on the governing assumption that the non-West could only develop and throw off its backwardness and traditions by embracing relations with the West (Slater, 2002: 92). Modernization is multidisciplinary and encompasses questions of economic growth, social institutions, political change, and psychological factors (Slater, 2002). With the ending of World War II, the reconstruction of war-torn Europe provided the model of state-directed modernization of "new nations" (Hettne, 2002). Modernization theory represented a deepening and extension of growth theory grounded in Keynesian economics that took a strongly interventionist stance toward Third World development, stressing comprehensive development planning by reformist states in cooperation with foreign donors (Brohman, 1996). Rostow's (1960) unilinear model, which was primarily based on the Euro-American experience and suggested that a country's economy and society must pass through a series of stages, is undoubtedly the most influential modernization theory in the early 1960s (Binns, 2002). According to the model, societies must pass through the following five stages: traditional society; preconditions for takeoff; takeoff; drive to maturity; and age of high mass consumption. Developing countries were still in the early states of the model, while developed countries had already passed through the early stages and were past the takeoff stage. Modern society (as contrasted with a traditional society) is composed of "typical economic patterns (e.g., capitalist work rhythms, mass consumerism, high savings, and investment rates), typical social patterns (e.g., high literacy and urbanization rates), and typical psychological attributes (e.g., rationalism, achievement motivation)" (Brohman, 1996: 15).

The patterns and concepts of modernization can be seen in tourism development. As illustrated in Table 9.5, tourism has been used to generate foreign exchange, employment, and growth as well as promoting a modern way of life. Early tourism developments after World War II were focused on the

positive economic benefits associated with tourism and the "tourism industry" has been used as a growth pole to generate trickle down of resources thereby increasing the tourism multiplier (Telfer, 2002). Just as modern society focuses on mass consumerism, large-scale mass tourism is also about mass consumption.

Dependency and Tourism

Criticism to modernization arose in the 1960s out of the Latin American *dependencia school* and together with the more global *world systems theory* which articulated the weak structural position of the Third World countries in the world system (Hettne, 2002). The work of neo-Marxists in this area has been referred to variously as dependency theory, world systems theory and underdevelopment theory (Harrison, 1988). The analysis of dependency includes a variety of related theories and focuses on the unequal economic and political exchange that takes place between the advanced capitalist countries, known as the "core," and developing countries of the South, referred to as the "periphery" (Routledge, 2002). The periphery economies are conditioned and dependent upon the expanding economies of the core and wealth is accumulated in the core (Routledge, 2002). The *"dependentistas"* or "neo-Marxists" demanded a radical political transformation within the developing countries, the delinking of their economies from the world market and a focus on state-driven industrialization (Hettne, 2002). Arguments within the neocolonial dependency model suggest that developing countries are in a state of underdevelopment due to the historic evolution of a highly unequal international capitalist system with unequal rich to poor country relationships (Todaro, 1994). Routledge (2002) identifies three main ways in which development projects can foster economic dependency of developing countries: (1) through technology that is required for development is produced in developed countries; (2) reliance on foreign investment to accelerate development, thus creating strong debt obligations; and (3) exacerbated dependency and underdevelopment due to leakage of foreign aid revenues; while such aid is important to developing countries, factors such as interest payments on foreign loans results in money being transferred back to developed countries.

Elements of the dependency paradigm emerged in tourism research after the negative impacts of tourism started to appear, particularly the high rates of leakages associated with international tourism in developing countries. Britton (1982) examined the power structures in the tourism industry that reinforced the dependent and vulnerable positions of developing countries. He developed a three-tiered structural model of Third World tourism, which included the headquarters, branch offices and small-scale tourism enterprises. The control of the tourism industry, he argued, is in the hands of foreign corporations and dominant capitalist firms (Britton, 1982). Dependency relationships have also been addressed with respect to government–industry structures. Under the structural school in dependency, a number of newly independent states pursued stateled tourism development programs with domestic hotel chains (Curry, 1990).

Economic Neoliberalism and Tourism

One of the reactions to state intervention in the previous two paradigms is neoliberalism, which is based on the doctrine of "economic liberty" for the powerful and its global reach can be seen to be popularly named "globalization" (Routledge, 2002). In the 1980s the private sector and the power of the market were championed while the state was seen as a brake on development (Slater, 2002). As the neoliberal doctrine goes, an economy must be free from the restrictions placed upon it by states, such as national economic regulations, social programs, and class compromises (i.e., bargaining agreements between employers and trade unions), as they are barriers to free flow of

trade, capital, and the freedom of transnational corporations to exploit labor and the environment in their own best interest (Routledge, 2002). Neoliberalism has been framed in terms of structural adjustment, privatization, deregulation, free trade and market-based development and is seen as the new emerging model from the West prescribed for the rest of the world (Harvey, 2005; Slater, 2002). International organizations such as the International Monetary Fund, the World Bank, and the World Trade Organization have been seen to enforce the doctrine of neoliberalism on developing nations who have traditionally relied on them for financing; this has led to a reduction in government spending on health, education, welfare, and environmental protection across the globe (Routledge, 2002). One example of such funding was the Structural Adjustment Lending Programs (SALPs), which have been heavily criticized for the changes they brought about in developing countries. Governments had to restructure their economies to accommodate the neoliberal agenda and cut back on some of the public programs mentioned above. In the more recent shift to poverty reduction, SALPs have largely been replaced by Poverty Reduction Strategy Papers. However, these too have been met with similar criticism for the changes they bring to developing countries.

As trade barriers continue to be dismantled, concerns continue to be voiced that the world economy is increasingly being controlled by multinational corporations and the power of the state continues to be eroded. Routledge argues that as "transnational corporations strive to become 'leaner and meaner' in this highly competitive global environment, they engage in massive cost-cutting and 'downsizing,' reducing the costs of wages, healthcare provisions, and environmental protection in order to make production more competitive" (2002: 316). The neoliberal policies of the West have certainly facilitated the international expansion of tourism corporations, especially as states remove trade barriers in order to participate in the world economy.

There is intense competition between developing countries to attract tourism developers by offering investment incentives (Reid, 2003). Neighboring governments can end up competing with each other by trying to offer the best incentives (e.g., allow foreign investment, tax benefits, import allowances, the permission to repatriate profits, etc.) in order to attract much needed foreign capital and expertise for tourism development. The power of multinational tourism operators has grown and consolidation is occurring globally in the industry as multinational hotel chains acquire other hotel chains, and airlines form alliances across the globe in an era of deregulation and privatization (Sinclair and Stabler, 1997). Another industry that has been able to successfully take advantage of neoliberal policies is the rapidly growing cruise ship industry. Flying under "flags of convenience" (often registering the ship in a developing country) the cruise ships are able to operate under labor and environmental policies governed by where the ship is registered, which can be less strict than developed countries (Wood, 2004; also see Wood [Chapter 33] in this *Handbook*). As multinationals continue to spread their operations globally it raises the question as to whether the power of the state is subsiding. Economic neoliberalism is also evident in the lending policies of international financial organizations who have lent money to developing countries for tourism developments.

Alternative Development and Tourism

The alternative development approach can be seen in contrast to the top-down development strategies that focused on economic growth. In the early 1970s, many international and bilateral aid agencies began searching for more people-oriented approaches (Brohman, 1996). The change in development focused on bottom-up strategies and more focused on people and basic needs such as infant mortality, malnutrition, disease, literacy, and sanitation (Streeten, 1977). Increased recognition was given to indigenous theories of development along with recognizing the role of women in the development process. The decade from 1975 to 1985 was designated as the Decade for Women by the United Nations. Development also began to focus on community-based initiatives stressing local participation and self reliance. NGOs began to take on larger roles, primarily in the areas of service delivery and policy advocacy, and many began to work with grassroots organizations and marginalized groups. In this respect they have both widened (socially and geographically) and deepened (in both personal and organizational capacity) the possibilities of citizen participation (Desai, 2002). According to Desai (2002) NGOs also have a role to play in the mitigation of adverse costs of structural adjustment.

Another major element of the alternative development paradigm is concern over the environment. Sustainable development came to the front with the release of *Our Common Future* in 1987 (WCED, 1987) and *Agenda 21* in 1992 (see Holden [Chapter 12] in this *Handbook*). Meanwhile, recent concerns over climate change are reviving debates and stimulating new conversations around the 1997 Kyoto Accord. Critiques of alternative development range from the difficulties of empowering local communities who may not be homogeneous to the difficulties in defining and implementing sustainable development.

As highlighted in Table 9.5, tourism development has followed many of the concepts associated with the alternative development paradigm with respect to empowerment and sustainability. One of the pillars of the alternative development paradigm is local empowerment and this has been the focus of research on indigenous tourism, community based tourism, ecotourism, and the empowerment of women through tourism (Telfer, 2002). Pro-poor tourism is a more recent development and coincides with the global poverty reduction efforts, as illustrated though the UN Millennium Development

Goals (Table 9.4). In the 2005 UNWTO declaration to support the use of tourism to help achieve the Millennium Goals, there is a call to mobilize domestic resources in cooperation with financial institutions, micro credit entities, and business service providers; the aim here is to encourage the local private sector to facilitate community driven tourism programs and small to medium tourism enterprises (UNWTO, 2005). Work in the area of NGOs and tourism has ranged from investigations of service delivery and specific projects in developing countries to more policy advocacy such as demonstrated by the work of the UK-based NGO Tourism Concern.

There has been a great deal of research and debate over the notion of "sustainable tourism." Initial debates concerned the differences between foreign controlled, large-scale mass tourism development at one extreme and small scale, locally controlled and environmentally friendly tourism at the other end. The debate has now moved on to making all forms of the industry and its impacts more "sustainable." Work has also been done on codes of conduct/ethics, guides and indicators for sustainable tourism for destinations, tourism corporations and tourists (see Mbaiwa and Stronza [Chapter 19] in this *Handbook*). Two common criticisms that can be heard are: (1) that some of the efforts to make the industry more sustainable are more of a marketing ploy; and (2) empowerment through tourism is not as easy as it might appear on paper (Stabler, 1997).

The Impasse in Development Studies

Development studies in the 1980s underwent what has become known as an impasse where the current theories of development were no longer able to successfully explain the difficulties that developing nations were facing. The 1980s have been referred to as "the lost decade" for many developing countries and perhaps for development theory as well (Schuurman, 1996). The standard development theories such as modernization or

dependency theory no longer seemed able to fully explain the experiences of development and underdevelopment (Schuurman, 2002). Schuurman (1996) outlined seven main reasons for the rise of the impasse in development studies. First, there was a realization that the gap between rich and poor nations was continuing to widen. Second, there was a recognition that developing countries were more concerned with short-term policies to keep their own heads above water in terms of debt and were not able to implement policies on an intermediate- or long-term basis. Third, there was growing understanding that economic growth was having major impacts on the environment, but advocates of sustainable development were calling for reduced growth that did not correlate with existing development theories. Fourth, socialism was no longer seen as a legitimate viable political means of solving the problems of development. Fifth, with the rise of world markets and globalization, there was a realization that traditional development theories that are focused on the nation within did not coincide with a reduction in the power of the state. Sixth, there was a growing recognition that a homogeneous "Third World" did not exist and global theories of development based on universalist discourses of "First World" and "Third World" could not accommodate these differences. Seventh, there was the rise of postmodernism in the social sciences, which further undermined grand master narratives (such as capitalism, socialism, communism, etc.) and argued for more individual and particular attention. Therefore, development theories based on metadiscourses ended up being severely challenged. Despite the presence of the "impasse," the spread of tourism as a development strategy continued in all forms worldwide, from large-scale resort developments to small-scale, locally controlled developments (Torres, 2002). The variety of strategies is also reflected in the diversity of voices now speaking in development thought, as outlined in the next section as scholars look "beyond the impasse" (Schuurman, 1996).

Beyond the Impasse: The Search for a New Paradigm?

The questions arises what then is the state of development thought at the beginning of the 21st century? The title of Saul's (2005) book on globalization is *The Collapse of Globalism and the Reinvention of the World*. As he charts out the reasons for the collapse of globalism, he also acknowledges other forces causing social change, all very much linked to development studies.

> To shape society we need to think about the origins of what is now passing—the origins of Globalization, its promise, its rise, and gradual collapse from the mid-1990s on. If we don't focus on that magisterial appearance, rise, hesitation and fall, we cannot understand what has happened to us, good and bad and where we now are. And we need to look carefully at the other forces that increasingly set the pace today, from irregular warfare to NGOs to reinvigorated nation-states, from the reappearance of genocides and oligopolies and hidden forms of inflation to a new practical interest in ethics and positive forms of nationalism and a new interest in citizenship. Much of this is exciting. Some of it is dangerous. All of it is real. (Saul, 2005: 14)

The diversity of forces highlighted by Saul is a window into the diversity of theories and approaches being put forward in development studies, a few of which are highlighted in Table 9.5.

With the apparent impasse in development studies a radical critique to the concept of "development" itself came forward in the 1990s from post-development scholars. In an often quoted passage from *The Development Dictionary*, Sachs stated, "The idea of development stands like a ruin in the intellectual landscape. Delusion and disappointment, failures and crimes have been the steady companions of development and they all tell a common story: it did not work" (1996: 1). While not a homogeneous paradigm or group with a singular message, those in the post-development school focus on the problematization of poverty, the portrayal of development as Westernization and the critique of modernism and science (Nederveen Pieterse, 2000). Escobar is frequently quoted with respect

to the power relations that are endemic to development, for "development can be best described as an apparatus that links forms of knowledge about the Third World with the deployment of forms of power and interventions, resulting in the mapping and production of Third World societies" (1996: 213). Slater identifies some of the shared assumptions and concerns presented in the critique of the discourse on development which include "an interest in local knowledge and cultures as bases for redefining representation and societal values; a critical stance with respect to the established discourse of development knowledge, as produced and disseminated by international organizations; and the defense and promotion of indigenous grassroots movements" (2002: 97). Many concerns of post-development are not really new as they have been shared by other critical approaches, but the rejection of development as previously conceived stands out clearly (Nederveen Pieterse, 2000; see also Sidaway, 2002).

Post-development has some parallels to dependency theory and alternative development. In seeking autonomy from dependence, post-development is similar to dependency theory and the emphasis on self-reliance is similar to both dependency and alternative development (Nederveen Pieterse, 2000). But by rejecting the concept of "development" itself, post-development is based on a paradox and has been heavily criticized for having little to offer as an alternative in terms of policies, except the self-organizing capacity of the poor (Nederveen Pieterse, 2000). In the context of studying ecotourism in Celestun, Mexico, Azcárate (2006) criticizes post-development, stating that the reliance of post-development approaches has severely restricted the understanding of how tourism works in practice. Nonetheless, even while not providing answers and not originating within the traditional boundaries of development theory, it has been acknowledged for the questions it raises (Rapley, 2002). Vandergeest et al. state that the critiques of development remain influential for "people seeking to draft into practice values for alternative forms of development and they continue to inform many of the normative dispositions of these practical and activist networks that critique development in action" (2007: 5). These authors go on to argue that even organizations such as World Bank have had to be cognizant of the critical post-development assessments and attempt to incorporate or pay lip service to the emphasis on the values of participation and the importance of culture in development.

In another trend, Batley (2002) argues that in the 1990s and the first decade of the 21st century there has been a shift away from the simple commitment to market liberalization to a renewed concern with the capacity of states and their support of the institutional conditions where markets and citizens can flourish. Neo-institutionalist economics, for example, stresses the regulatory role that the state must play in a capitalist economy. The developmental state model focuses on selecting industries and intervening extensively to build them up, not in order to supply the local market but to export. Clancy (1999) notes this state-led development in the context of tourism development in Mexico. However, Rapley (2002) argues that many of the least developed countries lack the essential features required to lead a state-led development policy and they still must operate in an unbalanced world market. Others suggest the concepts of civil society and social capital have an important role to play in development as states downsize. A civil society links citizens to the state and thus highlights democracy; social capital builds on trust to reduce transaction costs in the economy, thereby facilitating growth. Both civil society and social capital concepts have been put forward to build up society and to make up for the deficiencies that have emerged as states have downsized; some of this work has been linked to the efforts of NGOs (Rapley, 2002). The importance of partnerships and collaborations has been examined in tourism as has NGOs contributions to tourism-related

development projects (Archabald and Naughton-Treves, 2001; Burns, 1999).

Transnational social movements are also listed in Table 9.5. They began to emerge in the early to mid-1990s in opposition to neoliberal policies. A significant event was the large protests in Seattle in November of 1999 at the World Trade Organization ministerial meeting. Since the "battle in Seattle," the presence of large groups of protesters linked to transnational social movements have become a prominent feature at most major international economic summits (Helleiner, 2006). The Internet has facilitated the growth of many of these movements. It is important to note that there are many different voices in the transnational social movements, ranging from environmentalists and feminists to those interested in peace. There are strong links here to the alternative development paradigm as highlighted in Table 9.5, clearly illustrating the continued evolution of the environmental movement and women's movement (among others). NGOs have launched a variety of campaigns against exploitation by the tourism industry. Tourism Concern, for instance, has campaigned for improved labor conditions in holiday destinations and Fair Trade Tourism to name a few. Global warming, the debates over the Kyoto Accord and activist groups have put the environment on many political agendas. Partly in response in the tourism industry, carbon credits are being sold to offset emissions during jet flights and hotels are signing on to Green Globe 21 (Brown, 2007).

The fifth element in this section in Table 9.5 is cultural studies. Hettne (2002) argues that feminism, postmodernism, and cultural studies can be credited with deconstructing the myth or Grand Narrative of development thought. Citing the work of Munck and O'Hearn (1999), Hettne states that the "the significance of culture and identity in development has to do not so much with the cultural factor in the process in development as with abandoning Eurocentric development thinking, i.e. development as catching up and imitation, and instead conceiving and conceptualizing development as an inclusive, liberating process, in which different world views are accommodated and constitute a dialogical process" (2002: 9). This raises the question of how tourism should be developed within different country contexts. What may well work in one destination may not work in another destination. It raises the question of the role of cultural tourism in the development process. Does selling living cultures as a tourism attraction to promote development further create dependency on an industry thriving under neoliberal trade policies? Some cultures adapt and become part of the tourism industry while others may want little to do with tourism yet are incorporated into the tourism industry.

The last element in Table 9.5 is development and security and reflects comments made by Saul (2005) in terms of the rise in irregular warfare and reappearance of genocides. Unwin (2002) states that despite the tendencies towards an increasingly global economy, violence, death and the horrors of war continue to dominate the lives of tens of millions. Hettne (2002) questions the meaning of development in a context where the nation-state is abdicating, people act in a vacuum, global inequalities are rising, new wars are multiplying and the poverty problem is reduced to a civil form of intervention through complex humanitarian emergencies. A fundamental premise for tourism development is safety and security and any threat, real or perceived, can keep tourists away and impact development plans (Hall et al., 2003).[2]

The preceding section has illustrated some of the various theories and approaches that have emerged out of the impasse in development studies, along with their relationship to tourism. It has been suggested that the selected ideas presented here may help contribute toward the search for a new paradigm in development studies. Some of the ideas are new, while others seem, in some respect, a newer version of an old idea. As we look to the future and towards a possible new paradigm in development theory, what is the way forward? Hettne suggests that the "emerging approach

can be described as transcendence: development studies as a precursor of a comprehensive and universally valid historical social science, devoted to the contextual study of different types of societies in different phases of development, struggling to improve their structural positions within the constraints of one world economy and one, albeit multilayered, world order. Furthermore, development theory needs to be reconstructed in terms of content as well" (2002: 11). Hettne goes on to suggest that some of the building blocks or emerging approaches that can assist in building towards the future and a global social theory include certain strands of international political economy theory (IPE), a theory of new development-related conflicts along with the links between peace and development, a new cultural study with an emphasis reflecting the relevance of alternative thinking, a concern for the excluded, and an examination of the nature of the world order since the framework for development will no longer be solely the nation state. Exploring alternatives to neoliberalism within the context of IPE, Helleiner argues that the neoliberal policy revolution "now seems to be running out of steam. Public officials at international conferences declare that the neoliberal 'Washington Consensus is passé,' while activists across the world mobilize confidently behind the slogan 'Another World is Possible'" (2006: 77). He explores the ideologies that are prominent in the opposition movement to neoliberalism including green, feminist, and "civilizational" thought. He also points out that there is little consensus whether the alternatives should be at the global, regional, national, or local level.

While there is no consensus as to the future direction of development studies, Rapley (2002) suggests that a number of questions have to be considered in putting together a new paradigm, a new approach to development:

- Can development models be universalized?
- What role will environmental issues play in development theory?

- Is there a population time bomb and how will it affect the Third World?
- What will be the new balance between state and society be?

The answers to these questions and the various ideologies outlined above are part of the chorus of voices taking development studies into the future. These questions also have relevance for tourism as a development strategy. It is important to keep in mind, however, that previous development paradigms do not fade away entirely (see Inglehart and Welzel, 2005).

Reevaluating Development and Tourism

While development can be regarded as a normative concept it is also very much about power and control. Who has power, what are their values and beliefs, how do they exercise their power, will they share power and who benefits as a result of their actions? In a critique of neoliberalism, Harvey asks the basic question, "in whose particular interests is it that the state take a neoliberal stance, and in what ways have those interests used neoliberalism to benefit themselves rather than as is claimed, everyone, everywhere?" (2007: 24). In a similar context, Hall (1989) noted that tourism will have positive or negative effects depending on the scale of analysis, along with the perceptions, interests and values of those who are impacted, and those that conduct the impact studies. Questions of who benefits and who loses reflect the very nature of the relationship between tourism and development studies.

This chapter has illustrated examples of the range of competing ideas surrounding the nature of development and the strategies, which accompany them. It is important not only to consider the various strategies of development but also the theories and ideologies behind them. Those in the post-development camp take this level of analysis one step

further and question the value of the very concept of "development" itself. While the theoretical debates over the way forward continue, tourism is increasingly being utilized as a strategy to promote development. Preston's (1996) three main paradigms in terms of characterizing and securing development crystallize the debate between the various camps. The first focuses on state intervention, the second on the role of the free market and the third relates to the power of the political community. Should tourism be developed with strong state intervention or should the free market reign allowing multinational tourism corporations to freely operate across borders? What risks and benefits do states take in opening up to the global tourism market? Can they risk not to? Alternatively, should tourism be more community based as a better way to contribute to a nation's developmental goals? These questions raise the issue of whether development is highly relative: does success depend upon the conditions in the destination or are there modes and models of tourism development that are transferable from place to place? Can one mode of development be followed to success or is a combination of strategies the best option?

Addison (2005) argues that in terms of development policy, there are areas where there is considerable consensus and others where there is deep controversy. One area of consensus in today's development policy community is that there must be an explicit focus on poverty reduction (Addison, 2005). This is in contrast to the 1970s when it was assumed that economic growth would automatically lead to poverty reduction. Addison (2005) argues that while economic growth can lead to some poverty reduction, pro-poor policies are necessary to maximize the benefits of growth for the poor. There has been a recent shift through the UN Millennium Development Goals to focus on poverty and this is also evident in the rise in pro-poor tourism (Zhao and Ritchie, 2007). The 2006 Noble Peace Prize went to Muhammad Yunus and Grameen Bank in Bangladesh for the work on microcredits as an instrument against poverty. This highlights the link between poverty reduction and peace. Providing microcredits for pro-poor tourism initiatives may be one strategy in facilitating development. Kiva, for example, operates as a person-to-person online microlending website providing funds to various entrepreneurs in developing countries, including tourism entrepreneurs (Kiva, 2008). Mowforth and Munt (1998) state it is not a tool for eliminating poverty, nor even necessarily alleviating it, rather it can be viewed as a measure for making some sections of poorer communities "better-off," thereby reducing vulnerability of poorer groups to shocks (such as hunger). Development of tourism on a larger scale may also generate significant economic benefits that, *if fairly distributed*, may also help alleviate poverty.

Another area of agreement noted by Addison (2005) is that poverty reduction is not just linked to income, it is also linked to improving human development indicators. The focus here involves improving pro-poor services such as basic health care, safe water and sanitation, along with primary education and an emphasis on rural areas where there is a great deal of poverty. The question for tourism then is: How can tourism or the associated benefits of tourism best promote these broader human development indicators? There is no doubt that within tourism the process of globalization has opened borders to multinational companies, including tour operators, hotels and airlines that have generated new tourism growth in developing countries. However, these multinationals have been criticized for limited economic linkages to host communities, and it has become clear that more is not necessarily better: growth in terms of tourism numbers or tourism income does not necessarily lead to development. Globalization has not lived up to all its promises and poverty remains a major issue (Saul, 2005). Criticism of neoliberal policies has come from a wide audience and has been championed by the environmental movement and other transnational social movements. Despite the roll back of the state in many countries, it still has many roles to play, including the provision of public goods

and regulation of markets in the public interest (Addison, 2005).

As Addison (2005) suggests, getting development policy right has the potential to lift millions out of poverty; however, getting it right is not just a technical matter but requires careful political judgment on how to promote economic and social change that stand the best chance of succeeding. Tourism is only one strategy for development, yet in many developing countries it is the leading industry. If tourism is to contribute towards development goals, it is important to understand tourism within the field of development studies and its various theories, ideologies and strategies. As Hettne (1995) indicates, theorizing about development is a never-ending task.

Notes

1 See also (UNWTO 2007b) "Increase Tourism to Fight Poverty." New Year Message from UNWTO. Retrieved January 21, 2009 from http://www.unwto.org/newsroom/Releases/2007/january/newyearmessage.htm.

2 Sharpley et al. (1996) explored the relationships between travel advice to tourists and whether they are also used as trade embargos. Note that tourists are sometimes attracted to sites of war and conflict; i.e., dark tourism.

References

Addison, Tony (2005). "Development." In Peter Burnell and Vicky Randall (Eds.), *Politics in the Developing World* (pp. 205–230). Oxford: Oxford University Press.

Archabald, K. and Naughton-Treves, L. (2001). "Tourism Revenue-Sharing Around National Parks in Western Uganda: Early Efforts to Identify and Reward Communities." *Environmental Conservation*, 28(2): 135–140.

Azcárate, Matilde C. (2006). "Between Local and Global, Discourses and Practices: Rethinking Ecotourism Development in Celestun (Yucatán, Mexico)." *Journal of Ecotourism*, 5(1&2): 97–111.

Batley, Richard (2002). "The Changing Role of the State in Development." In Vandana Desai and Robert B. Potter (Eds.), *The Companion to Development Studies* (pp. 135–139). New York: Oxford University Press.

Binns, Tony (2002). "Dualistic and Unilinear Concepts of Development." In Vandana Desai and Robert B. Potter (Eds.), *The Companion to Development Studies* (pp. 75–80). New York: Oxford University Press.

Britton, S. (1982). "The Political Economy of Tourism in the Third World." *Annals of Tourism Research*, 9(3): 331–358.

Brohman, John (1996). *Popular Development Rethinking the Theory and Practice of Development.* Oxford: Blackwell Publishers.

Brown, Dana (2007). "Green's Going Places Environmentally–Minded Tourism Taking Off." *The Hamilton Spectator*, February 16.

Burnell, Peter and Randall, Vicky (Eds.). (2005). *Politics in the Developing World.* Oxford: Oxford University Press.

Burns, P. (1999). "Editorial—Tourism NGOs." *Tourism Recreation Research*, 24(2): 3–6.

Cawthorne, Andrew (2007). "Slum Tourism Stirs Controversy in Kenya." *Reuters*, February 9. Retrieved June 18, 2008 from www.reuters.com/article/inDepthNews/idUSL0681899920070209.

Clancy, M. (1999). "Tourism and Development: Evidence from Mexico." *Annals of Tourism Research*, 26(1): 1–20.

Curry, S. (1990). "Tourism Development in Tanzania." *Annals of Tourism Research*, 17(1): 133–149.

Desai, Vanda (2002). "Role of Non-Governmental Organizations (NGOs)." In Vandana Desai and Robert B. Potter (Eds.), *The Companion to Development Studies* (pp. 495–499). New York: Oxford University Press.

Desai, Vandana and Potter, Rob (2002). "The Nature of Development and Development Studies." In Vandana Desai and Robert B. Potter (Eds.), *The Companion to Development Studies* (pp. 1–2). New York: Oxford University Press.

Elliot, Jennifer, A. (2002). "Development as Improving Human Welfare and Human Rights." In Vandana Desai and Robert B. Potter (Eds.), *The Companion to Development Studies* (pp. 45–49). New York: Oxford University Press.

Escobar, A. (1996). "Imaging a Post-Development Era." In J. Crush (Ed.), *The Power of Development* (pp. 211–227). London: Routledge.

Fields, Gary S. (2001). *Distribution and Development, a New Look at the Developing World.* Cambridge, MA: MIT Press.

Fukuda-Parr, Sakiko, Lopes, Carlos and Malik, Kahalid (2002). "Institutional Innovations for Capacity Development." In Sakiko Fukuda-Parr, Carlos Lopes and Kahalid Malik (Eds.), *Capacity for Development New Solutions to Old Problems* (pp. 1–22). New York: UNDP.

Goldsworthy, D. (1988). "Thinking Politically About Development." *Development and Change*, 19(3): 9–33.

Goulet, Dennis (1995). *Development Ethics: A Guide to Theory and Practice.* London: Zed Books.

Hall, C.M. (1989). "The Politics of Hallmark Events." In G.J. Syme, B.J. Shaw, D.M. Fenton, and W.S. Mueller (Eds.), *The Planning and Evaluation of Hallmark Events* (pp. 20–39). Aldershot: Avebury.

Hall, C.M., Timothy, D.J. and Duval, D.T. (Eds.), (2003). *Safety and Security in Tourism: Relationships, Management and Marketing.* New York: Haworth.

Harrison, David (1988). *The Sociology of Modernisation and Development.* London: Routledge.

Harvey, David (2005). *A Brief History of Neoliberalism.* Oxford: Oxford University Press.

Harvey, David (2007). "Neoliberalism as Creative Destruction." *Annals AAPSS 610*, (March 2007): 22–44.

Helleiner, Eric (2006). "Alternatives to Neo-liberalism? Towards a More Heterogeneous Global Political Economy." In Richard Stubbs and Geoffrey R.D. Underhill (Eds.), *Political Economy and the Changing Global Order* (3rd edition.) (pp. 77–87). Don Mills, ON: Oxford University Press.

Hettne, Björn (2002). "Current Trends and Future Options in Development Studies." In Vandana Desai and Robert B. Potter (Eds.), *The Companion to Development Studies* (pp. 7–12). New York: Oxford University Press.

Hettne, Björn (1995). *Development Theory and the Three Worlds Second Edition.* Harlow: Addison Wesley Longman Limited.

Inglehart, Ronald and Welzel, Christian (2005). *Modernization, Cultural Change and*

Democracy: The Human Development Sequence. Cambridge: Cambridge University Press.

Kiva (2008). "Kiva Loans that Change Lives." Retrieved May 21, 2008 from www.kiva.org.

Marks, Stephen P. and Andreassen, Bård A. (2006). "Introduction." In Bård A. Andreassen, and P. Marks Stephen (Eds.), *Development as a Human Right* (pp. vi–xxii). Cambridge, MA: Harvard University Press.

McMichael, Philip (2004). *Development and Social Change A Global Perspective* (3rd edition). London: Pine Forge Press.

Mowforth, M. and Munt, I. (1998). *Tourism and Sustainability Development and New Tourism in the Third World*. London: Routledge.

Munck, Ronaldo and O'Hearn, Denis (Eds.) (1999). *Critical Development Theory: Contributions to a New Paradigm*. London: Zed Books.

Nederveen Pieterse (2000). "After Post-Development." *Third World Quarterly*, 21(2): 175–191.

Potter, Robert B. (2002). "Theories, Strategies and Ideologies of Development." In Vandana Desai and Robert B. Potter (Eds.), *The Companion to Development Studies* (pp. 61–65). New York: Oxford University Press.

Preston, P.W. (1996). *Development Theory: An Introduction*. Oxford: Blackwell.

Rapley, John (2002). *Understanding Development Theory and Practice in the Third World*. London: Lynne Reinner Publishers.

Redclift, Micheal (2002). "Sustainable Development." In Vandana Desai and Robert B. Potter (Eds.), *The Companion to Development Studies* (pp. 275–278). New York: Oxford University Press.

Reid, D. (2003). *Tourism, Globalisation and Development*. London: Pluto Press.

Rostow, Walt (1960). *The Stages of Economic Growth: A Non-Communist Manifesto*. Cambridge: Cambridge University Press.

Routledge, Paul (2002). "Resisting and Reshaping Destructive Development: Social Movements and Globalizing Networks." In R.J. Johnston, Peter J. Taylor and Michael J. Watts (Eds.), *Geographies of Global Change Remapping the World* (2nd edition.) (pp. 310–327). Oxford: Blackwell.

Sachs, Jeffrey D. (2005). *The End of Poverty: Economic Possibilities of Our Time*. New York: Penguin Books.

Sachs, Wolfgang (Ed.) (1996). "Introduction." In Wolfgang Sachs (Ed.), *The Development Dictionary A Guide to Knowledge as Power* (pp. 1–6). London: Zed Books.

Saul, John Ralston (2005). *The Collapse of Globalism and the Reinvention of the World*. Toronto: Penguin Group.

Schmidt, H. (1989). "What Makes Development?" *Development and Cooperation*, 6: 19–26.

Schuurman, Frans (2002). "The Impasse in Development Studies." In Vandana Desai and Robert B. Potter (Eds.), *The Companion to Development Studies* (pp.12–15). New York: Oxford University Press.

Schuurman, Frans (2000). "Paradigms Lost, Paradigm Regained? Development Studies in the Twenty-First Century." *Third World Quarterly*, 21(1): 7–20.

Schuurman, Frans (1996). "Introduction: Development theory in the 1990s." In F. Schuurman (Ed.), *Beyond the Impasse: New Direction in Development Theory* (pp. 1–48). London: Zed Books.

Sharpley, R., Sharpley, J. and Adams, J. (1996). "Travel Advice or Trade Embargo? The Impacts and Implications of Travel Advice." *Tourism Management*, 17(1): 1–7.

Sidaway, James D. (2002). "Post-Development." In Vandana Desai and Robert B. Potter (Eds.), *The Companion to Development Studies* (pp. 16–19). New York: Oxford University Press.

Sinclair, M. and Stabler, M. (1997). *The Economics of Tourism*. London: Routledge.

Slater, David (2002). "Trajectories of Development Theory: Capitalism, Socialism and Beyond." In R.J. Johnston, Peter J. Taylor and Michael J. Watts (Eds.), *Geographies of Global Change Remapping the World* (2nd edition.) (pp.88–99). Oxford: Blackwell.

Stabler M.J. (Ed.) (1997). *Tourism and Sustainability: Principles to Practice*. Wallingford, Oxon: CAB International.

Streeten, P. (1977). "The Basic Features of a Basic Needs Approach to Development." *International Development Review*, 3: 8–16.

Telfer, David J. (2002). "The Evolution of Tourism and Development Theory." In Richard Sharpely and David J. Telfer (Eds.), *Tourism and Development: Concepts and Issues* (pp. 35–78). Clevedon: Channel View Publications.

Todaro, M. (1994). *Economic Development* (5th edition.). New York: Longman New York University Press.

Torres, R. (2002). Cancun's Tourism Development from a Fordist Spectrum of Analysis. *Tourist Studies*, 2(1): 87–116.

United Nations (2005). *UN Millennium Development Goals*. Retrieved August 22, 2006 from www.un.org/millenniumgoals.

UNDP (2008). "What is the Human Development Index (HDI)?" Retrieved January 14, 2009 from http://hdr.undp.org/en/statistics/indices/hdi/question,68,en.html

Unwin, Tim (2002). "War and Development." In Vandana Desai and Robert B. Potter (Eds.), *The Companion to Development Studies* (pp. 440–444). New York: Oxford University Press.

UNWTO (2005). *Declaration: "Harnessing Tourism for the Millennium Development Goals'."* Madrid: World Tourism Organization.

UNWTO (2007a). *Tourism Highlights 2007 Edition*. Retrieved May 22, 2008 from www.worldtourism.org/facts/eng/pdf/highlights/highlights_07_englr.pdf.

UNWTO (2007b). "Increase Tourism to Fight Poverty." New Year Message from UNWTO. Retrieved January 21, 2009 from http://www.unwto.org/newsroom/Releases/2007/january/newyearmessage.htm.

Vandergeest, Peter, Idahosa, Pablo, and Bose, Pablo, S. (2007). "Introduction." In Peter Vandergeest, Pablo Idahosa and Pablo S. Bose (Eds.), *Developments, Displacements, Ecologies, Economies and Cultures at Risk* (pp. 3–29). Vancouver: UBC Press.

Williamson, John (2003). "From Reform Agenda to Damaged Brand Name." *Finance and Development*, 40(3): 10–13.

Wood, R. (2004). "Global Currents: Cruise Ships in the Caribbean." In David Duval (Ed.), *Tourism in the Caribbean Trends, Development, Prospects* (pp. 152–171). London: Routledge.

WCED. World Commission on Environment and Development (1987). *Our Common Future*. New York: Oxford University Press.

WTTC (2007). "League Tables: Travel and Tourism Climbing to New Heights: The 2006 Travel and Tourism Economic Research." Retrieved from www.wttc.org/2006TSA/pdf/League%20Tables202006.pdf.

WTTC (2008). "Progress and Priorities 2008/09 World Travel & Tourism Council." Retrieved May 21, 2008 from www.wttc.travel/bin/pdf/original_pdf_file/progress_and_priorities_2008.pdf.

Zhao, W. and Ritchie, J.R.B. (2007). "Tourism and Poverty Alleviation: An Integrative Research Framework." *Current Issues in Tourism*, 10(2–3): 119–114.

10

Economics of International Tourism

John Fletcher

Introduction

Tourism is an activity that takes place in all continents and its economic significance and impacts are far reaching. The economic significance of international tourism is concerned with both the size of international tourism activity and an economy's level of dependency and can be examined at global, regional, national, and sub-national levels. Because tourism is not an industry in the sense of being a single productive sector in national accounts, it tends to be measured according to the consumer spending that takes place (tourism receipts). This is fraught with difficulties, not only in the way in which tourism receipts are estimated but also in terms of drawing distinctions between tourism and non-tourism spending. Tourism satellite accounts (TSA) have been devised as an attempt to provide a consistent framework within which the economic impact of tourism activity can be measured at the national, regional, or state level within the country (see Jones et al., 2003). The economic impacts of international tourism are quite different in that they are concerned with the effects of the

spending of international tourists on net foreign exchange flows, income, employment, and government revenue within a specific economy. The models used to estimate these impacts are quite different from TSAs because they are attempting to measure the effects of changes in specific variables as a result of a marginal change in tourist spending. However, tourism affects economies in many ways, including, for example, the effects on labor supply and capital (where there are opportunity costs to the hosting economy), the often high development costs that take away from other needed areas of operational spending, and the levels of economic dependence that different destinations may experience.

The main purpose of this chapter is to examine the economic significance of international tourism, so that the discussions can take into account not only the scale of tourism activity but also the speed of its development over the past half century. The speed of development is an important aspect because the faster that economies change, the more pronounced the effects on the economic structure, other industries and the local community, as there is less time for adaptation. This latter point can influence the long-term benefits that destinations may derive from international tourism by exacerbating the level of economic leakages. The chapter also looks at some of the main driving forces behind the current influences on tourism development and the role of tourism within the sphere of international trade. Finally, aspects such as internationalization and globalization, including advances in technology and multilateral agreements such as GATS, are briefly examined to consider the influences they may have on the liberalization of tourism and the sustainability of tourism in destinations, particularly with respect to developing countries.

Global and Regional Economic Significance

Global Significance

World travel and tourism in 1950 was an emerging industry but few could have predicted the speed and strength of its development over the rest of the twentieth century. In 1950, the number of international tourist arrivals was 25 million. Impressive as these figures may have seemed at the time, it was the late 1960s and 1970s that saw international tourism transformed and placed on to the strong growth path that has become part of twenty-first century life. World tourist arrivals in 2007 were just under 900 million, which represents a 36-fold increase over the 1950 level, and the recent growth trend demonstrates that this growth continues unabated, with an increase of 200 million over the two years from 2005 to 2007. There are many drivers of this strong development performance, including the economic growth of industrialized countries and the accompanying increase in paid leisure time, together with the technological developments in transportation and information systems. Figure 10.1 shows the strong growth in tourist arrivals from 1950 to 2000.

Although globally the last decade of the twentieth century may have been considered economically benign, the twenty-first century

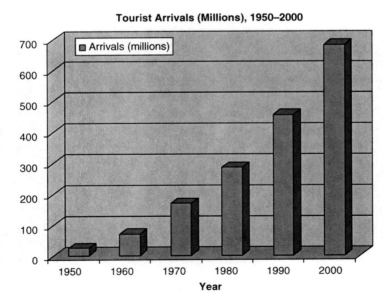

Tourist Arrivals (Millions), 1950–2000

Figure 10.1 World Tourist Arrivals, 1950–2000.
Source: Derived from World Tourism Organization Vision 2020.

has witnessed greater economic volatility as it has progressed and the tourism industry has been beset by problems that have, to some extent, hindered its development. The 9/11 attacks in 2001 caused shock waves around the world that still reverberate today. The bombings in Bali, London, Madrid, and Kenya all amplified the risks to the travel industry caused by acts of terrorism and the December 2004 tsunami reminded us all that natural disasters can leave a path of devastation; one that is still being cleared up four years later. These events have left their mark on tourism development, changing not only the way that transportation systems (particularly airlines) operate, but also the patterns of international tourism flows.

In spite of these major forces that have worked to slow down the increasing rate of growth of tourism development, the industry has proven its resilience and continued to consolidate its position as one of the largest international trading activities in the world. Figure 10.2 shows world tourist arrivals during the period from 1995 to 2007 to demonstrate that, although figures flattened off in

the immediate aftermath of 9/11 they have since continued to grow at their relentless pace. Indeed, the growth from 2005 to 2007 has been stronger than that experienced during the period from 1995 to 1997.

However, the adoption of international tourism from the destination's viewpoint has not been driven by the number of tourist arrivals, but by its economic impacts and the significance of the industry to national and local economies in terms of the acquisition of foreign exchange and the creation of income and employment opportunities. International tourism receipts in 1950 were US$2.1 billion; by the year 2006 the volume of receipts had increased to US$733 billion (WTO, 2008).[1] In nominal terms receipts seem to have grown 10 times faster than arrivals. The long term growth of tourism receipts from 1950 to 2000 and the rapid growth experienced during the last three decades of the twentieth century are evident in Figure 10.3.

The economic significance of international tourism in the twenty-first century is outstanding. In 2006 there were 75 countries that earned more than US$1 billion and the year

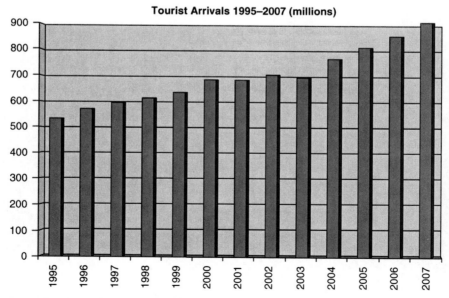

Figure 10.2 World Tourist Arrivals, 1995–2007.
Source: World Tourism Organization (UNWTO) (2008).

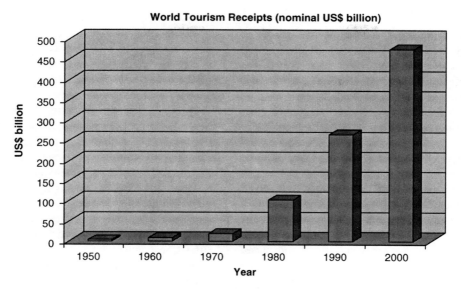

Figure 10.3   World Tourism Receipts, 1950–2000.
Source: Derived from World Tourism Organization Vision 2020.

saw a growth in the volume of tourism receipts of US\$ 57 billion, almost half of which (46%) was for European destinations, a region which in total accounted for 51% of world total receipts (US\$374 billion). Figure 10.4 shows the strength of the growth of international tourist arrivals and receipts over the 16 years from 1990 to 2006.

Global international tourism receipts in 2004 were estimated to be approximately 10% of world gross domestic product (GDP) and 2.7% of world employment (WTTC, 2003: 6). These global proportions disguise an enormous range of values and changes at the individual country level. The increasing significance of tourism to specific countries

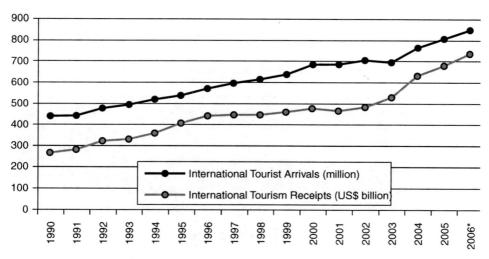

Figure 10.4   International Tourist Arrivals and Receipts, 1990 to 2006.
Source: World Tourism Organization (UNWTO) (2008).

can be remarkable, for instance in Cambodia tourism receipts accounted for 13.4% of GDP in 2005, whereas only 10 years earlier the corresponding figure was just 1.6%. Their significance to individual countries can vary, however, according to the level of diversification within their economies; they may also be the only source of foreign exchange earnings for some countries For some small islands destinations, for example, international tourism receipts can be the largest proportion of GDP attributable to a single activity. Such is the case in the Republic of Palau and Macao, China, where they account for almost 70% of GDP. Even in islands where there are other significant industries, such as Jamaica, tourism still accounts for almost 35% of GDP. However, the majority of tourism activity takes place between the industrialized countries of the world, where tourism receipts represent only a small percentage of GDP. Figure 10.5 shows international tourism receipts as a percentage of GDP for the top 10 countries with respect to tourism receipts.

Figure 10.5 shows that tourism receipts are most significant for Austria and Turkey, accounting for 5.2% and 4.2%, respectively. These figures contrast with those of the USA which receives the largest volume of tourism receipts, yet this only accounted for 0.65% of GDP in 2006. In fact, as Figure 10.5 shows, tourism accounts for only a small proportion of GDP in all of the major receiving countries.

The significance of international tourism receipts may be more accurately reflected not as a percentage of GDP but as a percentage of exports of goods and services. This approach shows the strength of tourism from a country's international trading perspective. Therefore, Figure 10.6 shows the top 10 countries in terms of tourism receipts and explores the proportion of their exports that can be attributed to international tourism. In this case it can be seen that some countries, such as Spain and Turkey, are highly dependent upon international tourism as part of their export portfolio, where international tourism receipts account for 16% and 16.6% of total exports, respectively.

There are a variety of reasons why some countries are more dependent upon tourism than others and why many countries, such as those in Europe, are both "importers" and "exporters" of tourism services. The level of dependency may be because the economy has few other forms of production, as may be the case in some small island developing states (SIDS), as noted earlier. Or it may be because the country, although relatively well-developed with a wide array of productive sectors, chooses to specialize in the production of tourism services. The issues surrounding why some economies specialize in tourism more than others are discussed in greater detail below when the theories of competitive and comparative advantage are examined.

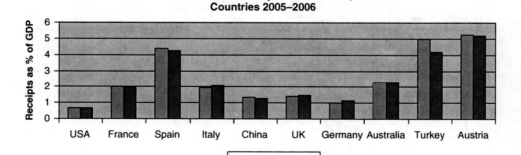

International Tourism Receipts as % of GDP, Selected Countries 2005–2006

Figure 10.5   International Tourism Receipts as a Percentage of GDP for Selected Countries 2005–2006.
Source: WTO and World Bank (2008).

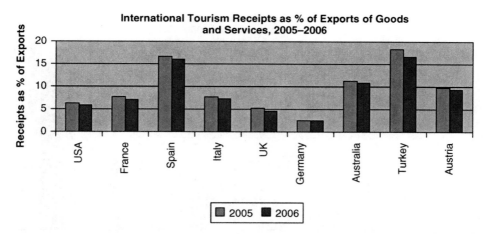

Figure 10.6   International Tourism Receipts as a Percentage of Exports of Goods and Services, Selected Countries 2005–2006.
Source: UNWTO (2008) and United Nations Common Database (2008).

Although there has been much emphasis on the importance of industrialized countries in accounting for the majority of tourism flows, it should also be noted that international tourism accounts for 7% of developing countries' exports in goods and services and more than 45% of their exports in commercial services. The corresponding figures for the least developed countries are even higher and stand at 9% and 65%, respectively. This demonstrates the importance of tourism to such countries, even if the absolute volumes are relatively small.[2]

Simple trend pictures do not reflect the real value of international tourism receipts over this period, nor do the arrival and expenditure figures reflect the enormous amount of domestic tourism activity that takes place, which often exceeds the volume of international tourism by many times. One of the difficulties in examining international tourism receipts over a long time period is that the purchasing power of currencies can change quite significantly over time; although in US dollar terms it appears that the growth in tourism receipts has exceeded the growth in the number of international tourist arrivals by a wide margin, the reality is that travel is relatively much cheaper now than it was in the 1950s and the real value of tourism receipts (when examined in constant price terms) is far less than the increase that appears

to be present when looked at in current prices. It should be noted, too, that the devaluation of currencies over time, combined with the fact that products tend to change both in terms of improved quality and falling relative prices, makes it difficult to make "real price" comparisons, especially with tourism, which is a composite product. To demonstrate the magnitude of this problem Figure 10.7 shows the numbers of international tourism arrivals to North America from 1950 through to 2000 along with international tourism receipts in both current prices and in 1950 constant prices.

In current or nominal prices, Figure 10.7 shows that tourism receipts have grown at a much faster rate than the growth in tourist arrivals, with receipts increasing by a factor of almost 148 compared with the corresponding factor of 15 for arrivals. However, using the US Government's CPI index to express tourism receipts in 1950 prices it can be seen that the growth of international tourism receipts at constant prices is only a fraction of the growth expressed in current prices, with the receipts of US$101 billion in 2000 only being equivalent to US$14.2 billion at 1950 prices. Even so, tourism receipts in North America have grown faster than arrivals, growing by a factor of more than 20 over the 50 year period. This is, of course, a simplistic approach to

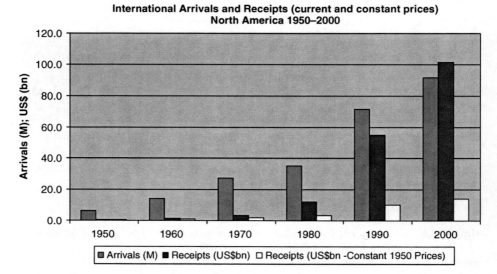

**International Arrivals and Receipts (current and constant prices)
North America 1950–2000**

Legend: ■ Arrivals (M) ■ Receipts (US$bn) □ Receipts (US$bn -Constant 1950 Prices)

**Figure 10.7   International Tourist Arrivals and Receipts, North America 1950–2000,
in Current and Constant Prices.
Source: 1950 to 1980, Archer (1989); 1990 and 2000, WTO (2008).**

a complex problem. The cost of air fares in real terms has fallen dramatically over the period from 1950 to 2000 and so too has the costs of accommodation services. Therefore, although the purchasing power of the US dollar may have declined, the prices of tourism services have also declined in real terms. The quality of both transportation and accommodation has also improved over this period, making it difficult to be precise about the relative value for money in 2000 compared with 1950.

Furthermore, the fact that international tourism receipts are recorded in US dollars means that changes in exchange rates disguise the real trends for specific countries and a declining value of the US dollar, as experienced over the past few years, will give the impression that tourism receipts are growing faster than they are in countries where the national currency has strengthened against the US dollar.

Regional Significance

At the regional level Europe has dominated with respect to tourist arrivals in absolute terms, even though year on year growth rates show that other regions, such as Asia and the Pacific, are growing at a much faster rate. Figure 10.8 shows the growth in arrivals by region from 1950–2000.

The growth in tourism receipts by region is no less impressive and Figure 10.9 gives a clear indication of the strength of growth of international tourism receipts over the last half of the twentieth century.

It should be noted here that the value of tourism receipts is estimated at national levels and there are wide variations in the way these estimates are made. One of the most reliable methods for estimating international tourism receipts is by undertaking exit surveys at the main ports of entry and exit. Tourists are surveyed and asked to recall the amount of money they have spent on goods and services as a result of their visit. Although most tourists may have precise knowledge about their overall expenditure it is often difficult for them to be able to break these down by expenditure category. The introduction of alternative means of payment, such as credit and debit cards, compound the problem of travelers recalling their expenditures and,

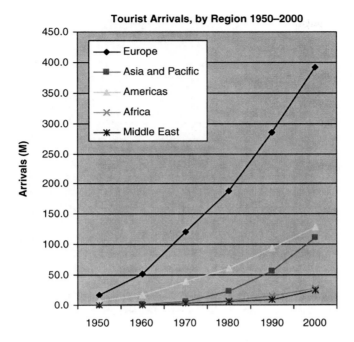

Figure 10.8 Tourist Arrivals by Region 1950–2000.
Source: Derived from World Tourism Organization Vision 2020.

within Europe, the introduction of the euro also hinders the task of identifying exactly what visitors spend when traveling. If tourists travel on a package tour it may be impossible for them to know how much of their expenditure took place at a particular destination locale (as opposed to the cost of services outside of that local economy). The development of all-inclusive hotels adds to the difficulty of identifying just how much of the package cost paid by the visitor actually ends up in the destination's economy. The value of tourism receipts estimated will also be influenced by the proportion of exit points sampled and the proportion of visitors completing the survey. These words of caution aside, it is only possible to work with the data that are available to build a picture of the national, regional, and global significance of tourism.

In order to gain a more complete picture of the economic significance of tourism to any economy it is necessary to construct a set of accounts that reflect the wide range of economic activities that fall under the umbrella of tourism. This includes not simply the transportation and accommodation sectors but all sectors that produce goods and services that are consumed directly and indirectly by tourists. The favored method of estimating this comprehensive picture of tourism is the TSA system. Although TSAs were given the official seal of approval by the UN and WTO in 1993, and organizations such as the OECD published guidelines for constructing such accounts, they are still in their infancy and the majority of countries do not have the data necessary to construct an accurate set of tables. However, there is a global trend to construct TSAs to accurately reflect the true significance of tourism to national economies (see Suich, 2002). It should be noted that TSAs only provide an insight to the economic significance of tourism activity and do not, on their own, provide a tool for studying the economic impact of tourism, the models used to determine the economic impact of tourism are discussed later in this chapter.

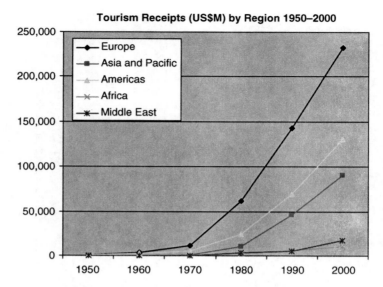

Figure 10.9   Tourism Receipts (US$M) by Region 1950–2000.
Source: Derived from World Tourism Organization Vision 2020.

Economic Development: Impact Considerations

There have been many attempts to provide theoretical underpinning to the process of economic development. An early start was the English Classical Theory, supported by economists such as Malthus, Ricardo, and Mill, which painted a fairly depressing picture of economic growth and development—they projected that population growth would always exceed any progress being made to the means of subsistence. The more dynamic world perceived by Marx later suggested economies would be in some constant state of revolution. The "vicious circle" theory of poverty in economic development suggests that poor economies are poor because they always have been so and have neither the capital available to invest and increase productivity nor the level of demand (because of low wages) to warrant investment in capital to increase productivity (see Perry et al., 2006). During the 1950s, when international tourism was beginning to make a global impression, Rostow (1960) formulated a model that suggested that there were five stages that

all economies must pass through as they move from a traditional based economy to one of mass consumerism. Rostow's model came to be known as "Rostow's Stages of Growth" and his theory owes much to the Harrod-Domar inspired work developed by Solow and Swan that broke the fixed relationship of capital to output and capital to labor to provide a framework which facilitated productivity growth.[3] His theory contributed strongly to theories of modernization which have also been incorporated into studies of tourism and development. Telfer's chapter in this Handbook addresses this as well as other development paradigms in tourism.

Irrespective of which theory achieves the most empirical support, development requires dynamics and increases in capital as well as increasing demand. International tourism can provide a significant stimulus to development for a number of reasons. It requires investment in infrastructure, because without such investment tourism will be very small scale and unlikely to develop. Tourism induces investment, either from within the economy or from outside (foreign direct investment) and tourism expenditure increases an economy's level of aggregate demand. Furthermore, since it involves a variety of productive sectors, tourism activity is an excellent lead sector to act as a catalyst for development—it can enhance the development of agricultural production, transportation, communications, financial services, and construction, as well as the many other services that either directly or indirectly support tourism.

Tourism therefore exhibits inherent characteristics that make it an attractive option for economic development. These characteristics include the fact that it appears to be an "easy" product to develop, is dominated by small- and medium-sized enterprises (SMEs) that often require little in the way of capital to set up, is not technically daunting, and can be a rapid earner of foreign exchange. Many of tourism's sectors are labor-intensive and therefore attractive to destinations which have an abundance of labor. But there are also disadvantages associated with using tourism development as means to achieving general economic development. Paradoxically, the poorer countries that have the greater need for increases in net foreign exchange flows and the income generation associated with tourism, are often less able to profit from it because of the heavy demands it places on infrastructure and the significant amounts of economic leakages that are incurred, particularly if tourism is developed at a pace more rapidly than can be accommodated by local businesses and capital resources. Moreover, in spite of the fact that many tourism enterprises are low capital businesses, the infrastructure that is necessary for tourism to develop successfully is considerable and much of its related impacts do not enter into the pricing system for tourism. Training and educational programs are necessary but may be difficult to implement due to funding constraints and lack of local expertise to conduct them. Lack of experience and knowledge in operating SMEs can result in higher than average business failure rates. The labor demands are often limited to a small segment of the population (women and young men), may be subject to seasonality, and are often

entry level positions with little room for professional or career development. The issues of gender, work, and tourism are especially important concerns with respect to international tourism (see Kinnaird and Hall, 1994; Sinclair, 1997; Swain, 1995).

Other potential negative impacts should also be factored into the development picture. Tourism can be a precursor to urbanization and takeover by second home owners and amenity migrants as associated infrastructural needs are developed. It requires reliable transportation and communication networks, energy production, and public health and security systems, all of which lend themselves to attracting not only visitors but also new businesses, employees, and residents—growth management could quickly become a problem as destinations become "discovered," particularly ones located in scenic areas with high recreational and amenity value. As these grow in tourism popularity, economic flows shift to accommodate rising demand for both goods and services.[4] Values shift as well; for instance, land values may shift from agriculture to tourism and social repercussions can be extensive, not only in terms of cultural relationships to the land, but also with respect to basic sustenance and social well-being. Where tourism is developed rapidly in resorts, for instance, the price of land can increase significantly, putting the property prices out of reach of local residents and non-tourism businesses. This can displace whole communities, with the consequential environmental and social costs associated with that displacement (see Harrison, 1992).

Whenever there is a limit to supply there will be opportunity costs, therefore if tourism employs labor it will do so at the expense of labor availability for other activities. The introduction of tourism, like the introduction of any economic activity, can displace workers from existing industries into tourism with a consequential loss of output in the former. In developing countries this means that workers may be displaced from traditional industries such as agriculture, forestry, and fishing into the service sectors. The loss of output resulting from this switch in labor should be taken into account when considering the economic impact of tourism but often this is not the case because most economic impact studies focus only on the positive aspects. These less tangible economic impacts tend to be ignored unless a larger systems approach is adopted in calculating economic impacts (Bergh, 1991). A related example here is that rapidly developing tourism can consume capital available for investment, leaving other sectors short of capital and thereby damaging their productivity and long term survival.

Dependency issues are a serious concern with respect to international tourism (Britton, 1981). Although tourism is dominated by SMEs there are also some very large corporations that are either fundamental to international tourism or significant in their influence over the way that tourism develops. For instance, airlines are major players, require significant capital, and are often not owned by the destination to which they transport the passengers. This is particularly true for small developing countries. Tour operators, like airlines, are focused on volume and these two aspects of tourism can drive the speed and magnitude of tourism development beyond that which would be optimal from the destination's point of view. The past half century is littered with examples where the expansion of tourism development has been way in excess of what was optimal from the destination's perspective (see Sinclair and Stabler, 1991). In such circumstances tourism development can have severe negative economic impacts as well as the more obvious social and environmental impacts that accompany rapid development.

Impacts on the Economy Itself

The first part of this chapter discussed the economic significance of tourism and is largely concerned with the volume of tourism receipts and the value of tourism in relation to the rest of the economy. As identified in that section, an appropriate tool for measuring the economic significance of tourism are TSAs, which provide an excellent picture of tourism's relative size in the economy. In this section, the *significance* of the economic impact of tourism is considered. Here, the economic impact of tourism is concerned with the effects of tourism expenditure on the economy rather than its size. It is primarily concerned with the economic impact with regard to marginal value, i.e., what happens to the economy for each additional tourism dollar that is spent. Multiplier analyses are a common method of measurement when discussing this type of tourism economic impact.

Multiplier Analysis

Multiplier analysis is concerned with estimating the direct, indirect, and sometimes induced economic effects associated with a given change in the volume and/or pattern of tourist expenditure. Each of these different levels of effect can be defined as follows (see Archer, 1976; Archer and Fletcher, 1988, 1996; Archer and Owen, 1971):

Direct Effects

The direct effects refer to the changes in income, output, employment, and government revenue experienced by those businesses that directly receive the increased tourist spending, such as the accommodation, catering, and transportation sectors. It does not include any of the consequential effects, nor does it include the import value of the goods and services that the tourists directly purchase.

Indirect Effects

The indirect effects refer to the consequential or secondary effects associated with the *direct effects* of tourist spending. For instance, where a restaurant that receives money from the additional tourist spending re-spends that money on food and beverages from wholesalers or manufacturers, accountants, telecommunications, rent for the premises, etc., these are all secondary or consequential expenditures because of the increased spending by tourists. In turn, the businesses that receive money from the restaurant will also make expenditures to buy their inputs of goods and services and so the secondary effects percolate throughout the economy. These are all indirect effects.

Induced Effects

As noted above, the direct and indirect effects will result in increases in income in the form of wages, salaries, rent interest and dividends, not just in the tourism-related businesses, but in all businesses that are directly and indirectly affected by the initial change in tourist spending. A proportion (generally a large proportion) of this additional income will be re-spent by the recipients of that income, for instance, on goods and services, some of which will be bought within the local economy. This means that an additional layer of economic activity is generated from which there will be increases in income, employment, output, and government revenue. The effects associated with the re-spending of income earned as a result of the initial change in tourist spending is known as the induced effect.

There are a number of approaches to the formulation of multipliers, including those that are based on the ratio of the direct plus indirect effects to the direct effects (Type I multipliers) as opposed to those that show the ratio of the direct plus indirect plus induced to the direct effect (Type II multipliers). Induced effects are sometimes left out of the analysis (Type I) on the basis that such effects would be the same regardless of the industry that created the additional income. However, such an assumption means that all recipients of income would have the same marginal propensity to consume and this need not be the case, particularly given the fact that tourism and agriculture both have a preponderance of low paid job opportunities associated with them, yet is likely to result in fairly high propensities to consume. The Type I and Type II multipliers are not as

useful to planners and policymakers as the unorthodox multipliers which show the changes in income, employment, output, and government revenue brought about by a unit change in tourism expenditure. This latter approach provides a value that is much easier to understand by the planners and policymakers.

The unorthodox "multiplier" is the ratio between the initial change in tourist spending and the effect it has on one of the economic variables. For instance, there is a tourist income multiplier which demonstrates the amount of additional income generated as a result of a unit change in tourist spending. There is also an output multiplier which refers to the change in total output created by the initial change in tourist spending by one unit. There is an employment multiplier which refers to the number of employment opportunities supported by additional tourist spending. Because employment multipliers tend to be quite small they are usually expressed in relation to a larger change in tourist spending, say, per US$20,000 of additional expenditure. Finally, there can also be a government revenue multiplier which shows the relationship between a unit change in tourist spending and its effect on either local or national government revenue.

Although the value of multipliers can be estimated using different methodologies, there are some commonalities about all multiplier values. First, the bigger the economy, the larger the multiplier value tends to be. This is obviously not a spatial issue but is determined by the ability of an economy to produce the goods and services required by tourist businesses and those that support them from within the economy rather than importing them. For instance, multiplier values for cities such as Edinburgh, London, Paris, Rome, or New York will all be significantly smaller than the corresponding figures for Scotland, England, France, Italy, and the USA. Similarly, one would expect the various multipliers of, say, Cyprus, to be much smaller than the corresponding ones for Spain (see Table 10.1 for examples of tourism income multipliers). Greater levels of economic

Table 10.1   Income Multipliers (input-output) for a Selection of Destinations

Income Multiplier Values for a Selection of Destinations	
Turkey	1.96
UK	1.73
Egypt	1.23
Dominica	1.20
Bermuda	1.10
Antigua	0.88
The Bahamas	0.78

Source: Archer and Fletcher (1988).

Table 10.2   Tourism Multipliers for Sub-National Economies (input-output): Urban, Rural and Remote Rural Areas (Scotland)

Tourism Multiplier Values for Urban, Rural and Remote Rural Areas	
Output Multipliers	
Urban	1.481
Rural	1.292
Remote Rural	1.254
Income Multipliers	
Urban	0.314
Rural	0.307
Remote Rural	0.291
Employment Multipliers (per £18,000 expenditure[a])	
Urban	0.363
Rural	0.342
Remote Rural	0.363

[a] In the original table the employment data were based per £10,000 expenditure but this figure has been adjusted to take into account inflation over the period from 1991 to 2007.

Source: Derived from the Scottish Tourism Multiplier Study, Fletcher et al. (1993).

diversification can help increase the ability of a specific economy to produce goods and services within its own boundaries. This means that leakages (imports) can be reduced and hence the multiplier values will be higher.

Table 10.1 shows the income multiplier vales for selected destinations and demonstrates quite clearly how the multiplier values are lower for smaller economies. The less diversified the economy, the greater the leakages, and hence, the smaller the multiplier values. The same is true when examining multiplier values for sub-national economies. Table 10.2 shows the income, output, and employment multipliers for sub-national economies in Scotland. In general, the urban areas (cities) are associated with larger multiplier values than rural areas and rural areas isolated from nearby urban areas are again subject to even greater leakages and hence have smaller multiplier values than their rural counterparts that are closer to urban areas. There will always be some exceptions to this, such as in an area that may be so isolated that it is economically attractive to be more self-sufficient or provide tourism products and services that can be produced locally (hence the level of leakages would diminish and the size of the multiplier would increase).

As can be seen from Table 10.2, the output multiplier values are always larger than the income multiplier values. This is because only a part of increases in output accrues as income and hence it is necessary for output to increase greater than income. The direct effect of tourism expenditure on output using these unorthodox multipliers will always be "1" which is the unit of tourist spending. Note

also that the employment multipliers are significantly smaller than either income or output multipliers because of the amount of tourist expenditure required to support one full-time equivalent (FTE) job opportunity. Therefore, in Table 10.2 the values shown are per £18,000 of tourist spending. In an urban area it shows that tourist spending would need to increase by almost £50,000 in order to support one FTE job opportunity in 2007. Many governments use employment multipliers for their planning and policy purposes because of the importance set on using tourism to create employment opportunities. However, because of the nature of employment multipliers this needs to be done with caution. Unlike the income and output effects, there is likely to be a time lag or buffer between a change in tourist spending and its impact on employment. This is because businesses may not be fully utilizing their current employment levels and can increase their output without increasing their staffing levels. In this case, an increase in tourism spending may simply increase labor utilization. Second, because labor in many countries is an input that is difficult to vary in the short-term, particularly downwards, businesses may wish to see if an increase in tourist spending is "permanent" before taking on additional units of labor. In the latter case one might expect a lag of at least two years between an increase in tourism spending and a corresponding increase in employment levels.

Estimating Multiplier Values

The various multiplier values can be estimated using either partial or general equilibrium analysis.

Partial Equilibrium Analysis

The term partial equilibrium analysis refers to the fact that only selected economic sectors are included in the model that is used to estimate economic impact. Such a partial approach reduces the costs of undertaking the economic impact study by reducing the number of sectors that have to be targeted when collecting the primary data. This approach was devised by Brian Archer in the 1970s and is known as the *Ad Hoc Multiplier Model*, and it is an excellent way of approximating the economic impact of tourism at a relatively low cost (Archer, 1976). The *Ad Hoc Multiplier Model* takes its pedigree from Keynesian multiplier theory and can produce estimates for marginal changes in tourist expenditure on the levels of income, employment, government revenue and output for a national or sub-national economy. The fact that it is a partial equilibrium approach makes it particularly attractive as an efficient method for undertaking sub-national impact assessments because it does not rely upon the gross output and employment totals that are the framing variables for general equilibrium analysis. The structure of the *Ad Hoc Model* is as follows:

$$k = A * \frac{1}{1 - BC} \qquad (1)$$

where k = the multiplier; A = the proportion of tourist expenditure that is left in the economy after the first round leakages; B = the proportion that local residents consume of each unit of additional income within the local economy; and C = the proportion of expenditure made by local residents which accrues as income throughout the local economy.

But this model is a little simplistic and needs to be expanded further to reflect the different expenditure patterns of different type of tourists, the different production functions of different businesses, and those who receive the additional income from the increased tourist spending.

$$\sum_{j=1}^{N} \sum_{i=1}^{n} Q_j K_{ij} V_i \frac{1}{1 - c \sum_{i=1}^{n} X_i Z_i V_i} \qquad (2)$$

where j = the type of tourist ($j = 1$ to N); i = each type of business establishment ($i = 1$ to n); Q_j = the proportion of total tourist expenditure that is spent by the jth type of tourist; K_{ij} = the proportion of total expenditure by the ith type of tourist in the jth category of business; V_i = the direct and indirect income generated by unit of expenditure by the ith type of business; X_i = the pattern of consumption, i.e., the proportion of total consumer expenditure by the residents of the area in the ith type of business; Z_i = the proportion of X_i which takes place within the study area; and c = the marginal propensity to consume.

In order to trace the flows of expenditure through successive rounds, separate equations are estimated for a range of V_i values. Examples of these are provided in the literature (see, for example, Archer and Owen, 1971).

Such an approach has distinct advantages over the original Keynesian multiplier approach, which is too blunt an instrument. The Keynesian model implies that all sectors have the same propensity to employ, import, generate income, etc. and this is clearly not the case. The *Ad Hoc Multiplier Model* allows the researcher to impose a different marginal propensity to consume, pay taxes, and employ workers for each sector of the economy disaggregated in the model. This facilitates the exploration of the effects of tourism on each of the sectors chosen as part of the model's structure. It is this choice of sectors that is the Achilles' heel of the model. Because the inclusion of economic sectors into the model's framework is left to the discretion of the researcher it becomes subjective. This means that there may be some sectors that are influenced by tourism activity but because the linkages are not obvious, may be overlooked during the model's construction. This would result in multiplier values that underestimate the economic impact of any given tourist expenditure. The second category of models is designed to overcome this subjective limitation.

General Equilibrium Analysis

Alternative approaches to the *Ad Hoc Multiplier Model* are the General Equilibrium Models. As their name suggests, these latter models are based on a framework that encompasses all sectors of the economy rather than the selective approach used by the partial equilibrium model. This type of model has the advantage of not being subjective because it includes all sectors of the economy, no matter how far it seems removed from the impacts of tourism activity. Some authors have suggested that because they pick up some of the more obscure economic linkages, general equilibrium models yield multiplier values that can be up to 30% higher than their partial equilibrium counterparts (see Wanhill, 1994). One such general equilibrium approach is that used in *input–output analysis*. A model that was initially derived by Leontief (1965) to examine the sectoral linkages within the US economy has subsequently been developed to determine the economic impact of tourism (see Fletcher and Archer, 1991; Fletcher and Snee, 1985). The model includes all economic sectors and is therefore more suited to the estimation of economic impacts at national rather than sub-national levels; however, it has been utilized at

sub-national levels to great effect (Fletcher and Archer, 1991).

If we let X be a column vector for each sector of the economy; Y be a column vector of sales to the final user; A be a matrix showing the proportion of total inputs purchased by each sector from each other sector of the economy (inter-industry matrix); I be the identity matrix (a matrix with the same dimensions as A where all of the cells are zero except for the diagonal cells that are equal to 1); and Δ be a change in value of a variable.

Then the basics of the model can be described as:

$$X = AX + Y \qquad (3)$$
$$X - AX = Y$$
$$(I-A)X = Y$$
$$X = (I-A)^{-1}Y$$
$$\Delta X = (I-A)^{-1}\Delta Y \qquad (4)$$

The model shown as Equation (4) states that a change in final demand, ΔY, which in this case would be a change in tourist expenditure, will bring about a change in output ΔX through the changes in inter-sectoral purchases that are needed to support that change in final demand. Having established the changes in output for each sector the input–output model can be extended to determine changes in primary inputs (wages, salaries, and profits), government revenue (taxes, licenses, duties, and fees) and imports. Imports can be disaggregated to distinguish between competitive and noncompetitive imports in order to improve the model's predictive power. The input–output approach is based on the assumption that there is homogenous output from uniform production functions for each economic sector. The linkages between sectors are assumed to be stable and proportionate to production. In this way it is possible to examine the effects of a change in demand for one sector's output and how it affects each other sector's output as a consequence.

Input–output models have been constructed for the largest industrialized economies to the smallest developing island. They are extremely effective in demonstrating economic linkages, impacts, potential supply restrictions, and identifying the most beneficial nature of tourist spending. More recently input-output models have been developed that include environmental matrices to allow economic and environmental impacts to be assessed within a common framework. This combination of economic and environmental impacts within a common framework is absolutely vital if the two aspects of impacts are to be considered equitably and fairly.

Even with these extensions, input–output models have their limitations. They do not sit comfortably with relative price changes that can bring about substitutions in terms of methods of production and their assumptions of linear production functions denies the existence of economies of large scale production. Such shortcomings can be overcome my modifying the model further using linear programming techniques. Computable general equilibrium (CGE) models have gained much popularity in recent times and although their pedigree stems from input–output analysis they tend to give prices a much greater role in determining the outcome. CGE models are particularly strong in cases where there is greater volatility in the economy, such as in developing countries where structural and political changes can cause severe disturbances to the economy. The CGE models allow researchers to get away from the Leontief input-output rigidities, such as having fixed amounts of labor to produce a given level of output for specific sectors and allow, say, increases in wages to affect the demand for labor (see Dwyer et al., 2004). However, such models do require a precise understanding of the price sensitivities of factors of production and in a world where the data required for input–output models is often seen as expensive, for CGE models the issue is even more acute. Researchers then have to weigh up the relative costs and advantages of constructing more detailed and flexible models for policy makers who often work with rather "blunt" strategies.

As a final note in this section, it is useful to recall that the methodology that is used to estimate the economic impact of tourism can influence the size of the multiplier. For instance, Wanhill (1994) has estimated that the *ad hoc* multiplier models produce multiplier values that are around 30% less than those values that would have been derived if input–output analysis had been used. However, the adoption of some of the assumptions that are implied within input–output analysis, particularly those relating to substitution between factors of production and the ability to meet the intermediate needs of the economy, mean that the input–output models can also overestimate the true economic impacts.

International Tourism and International Trade

The strong growth of international tourism outlined at the start of this chapter is impressive, not only due to the absolute growth in the global number of tourists traveling and spending but also with regard to the number of countries that are involved in tourism. In the 1950s (which mark the start of the above analysis of visitor numbers), just 15 countries were responsible for almost the total movement of visitors; by the end of the twentieth century, international tourism receipts are a part of most countries' balance of trade and the top 15 destinations only account for 60% of all international flows. In addition to the number of countries involved in tourism, the competition for those that account for the largest share of tourism receipts is also evident, with countries such as China entering into the top 10 category for the first time.

Table 10.3 shows the value of tourism receipts, gross domestic product, and exports for the top 10 countries in terms of tourism receipts. The table also shows how open the economies are (exports as a percentage of GDP) and how dependent upon tourism they are (tourism receipts as a percentage of GDP and as a percentage of exports). The most

Table 10.3   Tourism Receipts, GDP and Exports for the Top 10 Countries (2006)

International Tourism Receipts, GDP and Exports, Top 10 Tourism Countries (2006)

	Tourism Receipts US$ (b's)	GDP US$ (b's)	Exports US$ (b's)	Exports as % of GDP	Tourism Receipts as % of GDP	Tourism Receipts as % of Exports
USA	85.70	13,200	1,466	11.11	0.65	5.85
France	42.90	2,200	614	27.91	1.95	6.99
Spain	51.10	1,200	320	26.67	4.26	15.97
Italy	38.10	1,800	517	28.72	2.12	7.37
China	33.90	2,700	1,056	39.11	1.26	3.21
UK	33.70	2,300	719	31.26	1.47	4.69
Germany	32.80	2,900	1,297	44.72	1.13	2.53
Australia	17.80	768	164	21.35	2.32	10.85
Turkey	16.90	403	102	25.33	4.20	16.57
Austria	16.70	322	177	54.90	5.18	9.44

Source: Derived from UNWTO (2008) and UN Statistics (2008).

open economy is Austria, where exports are equal to almost 55% of GDP, followed by Germany with a corresponding figure of almost 45%. Tourism receipts account for some 16% of total export earnings for Spain and yet only 4.26% of GDP is attributable to tourism. Whereas in Austria tourism receipts are equivalent to 9.44% of total exports, and tourism is responsible for 5.18% of GDP. In the USA, which tops the table in terms of tourism receipts and can be regarded as being the least open economy, exports are equivalent to just over 11% of GDP, and international tourism receipts are accountable for 5.85% of export earnings (0.65% of GDP).

Why some countries specialize in tourism as opposed to others has been the subject of debate in the literature and much of the reasoning has focused on competitive advantage. There have been a number of attempts to examine international tourism flows using theories of competitive advantage (see Gooroochurn and Sugiyarto, 2005). Taking data from more than 200 countries these authors derived an index based on eight distinct characteristics:

1 the environment;
2 human resources;
3 human tourism;
4 infrastructure;
5 openness;
6 price;
7 social development; and
8 technology.

Their analysis concluded that the social and technological indicators were the most important in explaining the competitiveness of tourism destinations, and the human tourism and environmental factors performed worst in terms of providing explanatory power (Gooroochurn and Sugiyarto, 2005). It should be noted that variables such as social development and technology are composite indicators and there are a number of factors at work that might generate the correlations observed.

By focusing on competitive advantage, researchers have also created demand functions and used these to forecast future tourist arrivals.[5] But such analysis is based on past arrival trends and does little to explain the international ranking of destinations. Tourism has some unique characteristics that hinder the application of general international trade theory. Such factors include the multi-sector structure of tourism as an activity, the way in which the activity utilizes the priced factors of production (land, labor, and capital), and its utilization of non-priced elements that include infrastructure as well as environment and culture. Finally, the simultaneity of production and consumption (the fact that tourists have to travel to the place of production for any output to take place) means that tourism allows countries to trade in what are normally non-tradable products and services.

Another challenge worth noting here is that international tourism for leisure purposes is not isolated from international tourism for business purposes, which itself is related to international trade flows. Therefore, one might expect to find correlations between international trade and international tourism. Khan and Lin (2002) explored such aspects of causality in international tourism in their study of co-integration in Singapore. Given the significance of international business travel as a part of total visitor arrivals (around 20% of total traffic) it is not surprising that they found a relationship between this aspect of travel and international trade. Furthermore, the authors found that the direction of causality ran both ways and that greater international trade led to greater international visits for business purposes, which in turn led to greater international trade. However, their work did not find any conclusive evidence that there was a statistically significant relationship between international trade and visitor arrivals for leisure purposes.[6]

An alternative approach to examine why some destinations are more successful than others and to explain their global ranking is to analyze the comparative advantage of destinations. Originally based on the work of Robert Torren, and subsequently David Ricardo, comparative advantage theory suggests that, under competition, a country's domestic price ratio without trade taking place is determined by the relative efficiency in the production of the goods and services it produces (see Hunt and Morgan, 1995). If international trade then takes place, the price ratio would change to reflect not only the supply-side efficiency of production but also the relative demand for traded products by consumers. The Heckscher–Ohlin theorem (Ohlin, 1933), which is commonly used as an explanation of international trade, goes further than this by suggesting that it is not the efficiency of production that is important in determining the domestic price ratio but the relative abundance or scarcity of factors of production (factor endowments of land, labor, and capital) (see Deardorff, 1982). Tourism is generally regarded to be a labor-intensive form of economic activity; therefore,

from an international tourism perspective, one would expect countries that have an abundance of land and labor together with a favorable climate and attractive environment to have a comparative advantage in tourism. However, tourism production is not the outcome of a homogenous industry and there are elements of tourism production that are capital intensive, such as air transportation. Furthermore, the tourism "product" itself is not homogenous and their tourism activities that are relatively labor intensive or capital intensive, such as theme parks. A variety of authors have attempted to calculate capital–output ratios for various tourism destinations and it has been found that there are indeed wide variations in the incremental capital–output ratios, with Kenya yielding one of the lowest ratios at 2.4 and Turkey yielding one of the highest at 4.0.

Moreover, the theory of comparative advantage was conceived on the basis of trade in tangible goods rather than services and there is far less ambiguity when attempting to measure the quantities involved. Tourism as a service employs many factors (some priced and many non-priced) that are extremely difficult to quantify. Furthermore, the theory of comparative advantage was put forward and then developed at a time when factors of production were far less mobile than they are in the twenty-first century. If all factors of production were perfectly mobile then relative differences between the supply-side conditions in trading countries would soon be equalized. However, land is fixed and labor, although far more mobile than in Ricardian times, is still well short of being described as mobile. Capital, however, is highly mobile and this is likely to influence the outcome of relative abundance of the factors of production.

The complexity of applying comparative advantage theory to international tourism is compounded by the fact that tourism requires simultaneous production and consumption; i.e., tourists have to travel to the destination to enjoy the tourism product. This means that while at the destination tourists can consume goods and services that may otherwise have been deemed to be non-traded goods and services. This adds a new dimension to the theory of comparative advantage and results in the fact that international tourism demand can influence the price of non-traded commodities. Hazari and Sgro (2004) explored the issue of international tourism consuming non-traded goods and found that tourists consume non-traded commodities such as the infrastructure, the superstructure, the environment, and the culture of the destination. Tourism is also an activity that involves real estate development, and the competition between residents and tourists for these non-traded commodities can result in land and building price inflation, which can in turn have significant effects on the local economic structure.[7]

International Tourism, Globalization and GATS

Globalization is a term that reflects the effects of increased technology on the movement of capital, labor and information. Advances in technology and the concentration of capital have the same effect as making the world a smaller place. Markets that were once considered to be confined to relatively small geographical areas are now able to extend over greater areas and across national boundaries. The process of globalization began with mankind's first steps of travel and has progressed throughout history. But technological advances, particularly with respect to transportation and communication, have accelerated this process so rapidly that, by the closing stages of last century, globalization became a recognized phenomenon and the term itself became a buzzword. The movement away from fixed exchange rates and the ease with which capital can be moved around the planet have also played their part in liberalizing trade and extending markets across national and continental boundaries. This liberalization of trade has become more uniformly present across the planet with the demise of planned economies and the spread of market economies in their place.

The process of globalization helps deliver the wealth that feeds tourism demand and, in turn, increased demand for tourism and the thirst for new and different destinations helps drive forward the globalization process. The relatively fast growth of tourism in the Asia Pacific Region, as noted earlier in this chapter, is to a large extent a manifestation of the influence of globalization on tourism activities. New destinations appear on the destination portfolios and the success of these destinations is enhanced by improving living standards within them that are driven forward by competitive markets. While operating within a global system, tourism can be seen as an activity that has local "anchors" that help develop the economies in which it takes place. In other words, it is a local–global system: the production process is still largely locally based, although the ownership of the enterprises may not be local and the drivers are primarily global policies and institutions such as the World Trade Organization (WTO), among others.

The WTO sets its primary goal to be the liberalization of trade in goods.[8] The significant growth in trade of services prompted the WTO to implement the General Agreement on Trade in Services (GATS) to capture the dynamics of international trade and the ever increasing importance of services. A variety of international policies and strategies have added to the globalization of tourism services, including the International Monetary Fund's inclusion of tourism in its Structural Adjustment Programs (SAPs) and the implementation of the GATS. Both of these bring requirements to liberalize and open up economies and make it easier to move capital and labor across national boundaries as well as set up overseas offices and brands and repatriate returns on foreign direct investments (FDI). Clearly, the liberalization of international markets and the ease with which companies can move labor and capital from one country to another will influence the significance of the competitive and comparative advantages that destinations possess.

Globalization affects the markets for tourism by making them more competitive and providing greater awareness and information while standardizing the levels of comfort and facilities that tourists seek. Global instant reservation and booking systems are improving the transparency of relative prices, enabling tourists to play a much greater role in their decision-making (see Gretzel and Fesenmeier [Chapter 31] in this *Handbook*). While globalization provides greater opportunities for transnational corporations to extend their market reach, it also places locally owned SMEs at a significant disadvantage as they attempt to develop and establish a foothold within this globalized corporate marketplace. Tourism has not been comfortably accommodated within the World Trade Association and GATS because of the way that the sectors related to tourism sit across more than one industrial classification; it results in some sectors being included and some not, and allows participating countries to agree to conditions relating to some activities but not to others. In its present form, GATS does not provide a sound platform for sustainability with respect to tourism (see Wood [Chapter 33] in this *Handbook*). Efforts made to protect emerging tourism-related businesses, the environment, and the culture can be seen as the imposition of barriers to trade and thereby result in penalties. Globalization as a process is much wider than simply large transnational businesses setting up their store in other countries or regions—it brings with it changes in production processes, employment, and finance that will materially alter the economies subjected to it.

Conclusion

International tourism represents a large and increasing part of the global economy. As an economic activity within and between countries it creates opportunities and problems that extend beyond the scope of this chapter. However, it is clear that international tourism is an economically significant activity at the global, regional, and national level. It is also a resilient activity and has continued to grow

in spite of major events that have acted as deterrents to its future development. Tourism is difficult to measure because it does not fit comfortably in the UN SIC framework and spans a wide variety of productive sectors, few of which are exclusively involved in tourism. Attempts have been made to make the measurement of tourism's economic significance more consistent through the adoption of TSAs. The economic impact of tourism can be measured using a variety of models, all of which have their advantages and disadvantages, and the choice of approach is likely to be the result of a balancing act between resources and data availability.

International tourism can be used as a catalyst for economic development but it is not without its problems, especially those relating to pressures on land and building prices, as well as the opportunity costs experienced as tourism attracts labor and capital away from other forms of economic activity. The relationship between international tourism and international trade is complex and although theories of competitive and comparative advantage go some way to explaining why some countries specialize in tourism, they do not provide a complete answer. The development of international policies such as GATS, although helping to liberalize world trade in services, including tourism, does bring areas of concern for developing countries that are attempting to protect not only their emerging tourism businesses but also their environment and culture. Increasing concerns about climate change and global warming are also worth factoring into future sustainability considerations in international tourism, e.g., with respect to long-haul flights and destinations at various altitude levels (see Becken, 2002).

Notes

1 Also see WTO publication report called Tourism Market Trends 2006—World Overview & Tourism Topics. Available online from March 13, 2008. Retrieved May 25, 2008 from http://www.wtoelibrary.org/content/u8pk83/.

2 Ibid. note 1). Also see Luzzi and Fluckiger (2003).

3 A good introduction to development theories can be found in Chapter 7 of Nafziger (1984).

4 Webster et al. (2007) undertook an empirical investigation of 45 countries constructing Balassa and Grubel-Lloyd Indices as well as the construction of dynamic indices. The authors found that many countries specialize as both "importers" and "exporters" of international tourism and that this was not dependent upon the level of development of the economy.

5 For studies measuring impact of international tourism on demand for tourist services at the country level, see, for instance, Divisekera (2003), Garin-Munoz and Amaral (2000), Turner and Witt (2001), Witt and Song (2001). Also see Archer (1984).

6 Such a finding runs counter to other research that has in the past linked visits to trade fairs and conferences to subsequent leisure visits (see Rogers [2003] for a discussion on the size and economic value of global conferences and conventions). This may be explained in part by the adoption of mis-specified time lags in the analysis.

7 International tourism is not only a part of international trade it can also influence international trade flows in a more discrete manner. Tourism literature abounds with examples of where tourist behavior and dress codes may influence the destination community's behavior and purchasing habits (Harrison, 1992).

8 www.wto.org/English/thewto_e/whatis_e/tif_e/fact1_e.htm. Accessed May 25, 2008.

References

Archer, B. and Owen, C. (1971). "Towards a Tourist Regional Multiplier." *Regional Studies*, 5: 289–294.

Archer, B.H. (1976). "The Anatomy of Multiplier." *Regional Studies*, 10: 71–77.

Archer, B.H. (1984). "Trends in International Tourism." In S.F. Witt and L. Moutinho (Eds.), *Tourism Marketing and Management Handbook* (2nd edition.). Hemel Hempstead: Prentice Hall.

Archer, B.H. and Fletcher, J. (1988). "The Tourist Multiplier." *Teoros*, 7: 6–10.

Archer, B.H. and Fletcher, J. (1996). "The Economic Impact of Tourism in the Seychelles." *Annals of Tourism Research*, 23(1): 32–47.

Becken, S. (2002). "Analysing International Tourist Flows to Estimate Energy Use Associated with Air Travel." *Journal of Sustainable Tourism*, 10(2): 114–131.

Britton, S. (1981). "Tourism, Capital and Place: Towards a Critical Geography of Tourism." *Environment and Planning D: Society and Space*, 9(4): 451–478.

Deardorff, A.V. (1982). "The General Validity of the Heckscher-Ohlin Theorem." *The American Economic Review*, 72(4): 683–694.

Divisekera, S. (2003). "A Model of Demand for International Tourism." *Annals of Tourism Research*, 30(1): 31–49.

Dwyer, L., Forsyth, P. and Spurr, R. (2004). "Evaluating Tourism's Economic Effects: New and Old Approaches." *Tourism Management*, 25(3): 307–317.

Fletcher, J. and Snee, H. (1985). "The Need for Output Measurement in the Service Industries: A Comment." *Service Industries Journal*, 5(1): 73–78.

Fletcher, J. and Archer, B.H. (1991). "The Development and Application of Multiplier Analysis." In C.P. Cooper and A. Lockwood (Eds.), *Progress in Tourism, Recreation and Hospitality Management* (Vol. 3) (pp. 28–47). Chichester: Wiley.

Fletcher, J., Wanhill, S. and Cooper, C. (1993). *The Scottish Tourism Multiplier Study* (Vols. 1–3). ESU Research Paper, The Scottish Office, UK.

Garin-Munoz, T. and Amara, T.P. (2000). "An Econometric Model for Internacional Tourism Flows to Spain." *Applied Economics Letters*, 7(8): 525–529.

Gooroochurn, N. and Sugiyarto, G. (2005). "Competitiveness Indicators in the Travel and Tourism Industry." *Tourism Economics*, 11(1): 25–43.

Hazari, B.R. and Sgro, P.M. (2004). *Tourism, Trade and National Welfare*. Amsterdam: Elsevier.

Harrison, D. (Ed.) (1992). *Tourism and the Less Developed Countries*. London: Belhaven Press.

Hunt, S.D. and Morgan, R.M. (1995). "The Comparative Advantage Theory of Competition." *Journal of Marketing*, 59(2): 1–15.

Jones, C., Munday, M. and Roberts, A. (2003). "Regional Tourism Satellite Accounts: A Useful Policy Tool?" *Urban Studies*, 40(13): 2777–2794.

Kinnaird, V. and Hall, D. (1994). *Tourism: A Gender Analysis*. Chichester: Wiley.

Khan, H. and Lin, C. (2002). "International Trade and Tourism: Evidence from Cointegration and Causality Tests by Using Singapore Data." *The 33rd Annual Conference of Travel and Tourism Association (TTRA)*. Arlington, VA, June 23–26.

Leontief, W. (1965). "The Structure of the US Economy." *Scientific American*, 212(4): 25–35.

Luzzi, G.F. and Fluckiger, Y. (2003). "Tourism and International Trade." *Pacific Economic Review*, 8(3): 239–243.

Nafziger, W.E. (1984). *The Economics of Developing Countries*. Belmont, CA: Wadsworth Inc.

Ohlin, B. (1933/1968). *Inter-Regional and International Trade*. Cambridge, MA: Harvard University Press.

Perry, G.J. Arias, O.S., López, H. Maloney, W.F. and Servén, L. (2006). "Poverty Reduction and Growth: Virtuous and Vicious Circles." Washington: The World Bank. Retrieved May 26, 2008 from siteresources.worldbank. org/EXTLACOFFICEOFCE/Resources/870892-1139877599088/virtuous_circles1_complete.pdf.

Rogers, T. (2003). *Conferences and Conventions: A Global Industry*. Oxford: Butterworth-Heinemann.

Rostow, W.W. (1960). The Stages of Economic Growth: A Non-Communist Manifesto, Cambridge: Cambridge University Press.

Sinclair, T. (1997). *Gender, Work and Tourism*. London: Routledge.

Sinclair, T. and Stabler, M.J. (1991). *The Economics of Tourism*. Wallingford, Oxon: CAB International.

Song, H. and Witt, S.F. (2001). "Forecasting International Tourist Flows to Macau." *Tourism Management*, 27(2): 214–224.

Suich, H. (2002). "Development of Preliminary Tourism Satellite Accounts for Namibia." *Development Southern Africa*, 19(1): 105–121.

Swain, M.B. (1995). "Gender in Tourism." *Annals of Tourism Research*, 22(2): 247–266.

Turner, L.W. and Witt, S.F. (2001). "Factors Influencing Demand for International Tourism: Tourism Demand Analysis Using Structural Equation Modelling, Revisited." *Tourism Economics*, 7(1): 21–38.

United Nations Common Database (UNCDB). Retrieved June 14, 2008 from unstats.un. org/unsd/cdb/cdb_help/cdb_quick_start.asp.

van den Bergh, J. (1991). Dynamic Models for Sustainable Development. Amsterdam: Tinbergen Institute.

Wanhill, S. (1994). "The Measurement of Tourist Income Multipliers." *Tourism Management*, 15(4): 281–283.

Webster, A., Fletcher, J., Hardwick, P. and Morakabati, Y. (2007). "Tourism and Empirical Applications of International Trade Theory." *Tourism Economics*, 13(4): 657–674.

Witt, S.F. and Song, H. (2001). "Forecasting Future Tourism Flows." In A. Lockwood and S. Medlik (Eds.), *Tourism and Hospitality in the 21st Century* (pp. 106–118). Oxford: Butterworth-Heinemann.

World Bank Development Data and Statistics (2008). Retrieved June 14, 2008 from web. worldbank.org/WBSITE/EXTERNAL/DATASTATISTICS/0,,menuPK:232599~pagePK:64133170~piPK:64133498~theSitePK:239419,00.html.

WTO (2008). *UNWTO World Tourism Barometer* (Volume 6, Issue 1). Retrieved May 26, 2008 from www.unwto.org/facts/menu.html.

World Travel and Tourism Council (2003). Blueprint for New Tourism. London.

11

Power, Politics, and Political Science: The Politicization of Tourism

Linda K. Richter

Introduction

The politicization of tourism has two dimensions: its growth as a research subject for political scientists and its increased importance in politics at all levels. This chapter considers both facets.

The study of political science has always had much to offer the study of tourism, but few political scientists have investigated such linkages. Whether they consider them to be too frivolous, too multifaceted, or too unlikely to advance individual careers, political scientists have largely ignored tourism.

As one indicator, my research assistant Teola Dorsey examined 10 leading American political science journals from 1980–2006 and found only one referred to the subject of travel or tourism in its article titles. That was my 1985 *Public Administration Review* article on public-sector employment in tourism development. There were also two articles and a reprinted act in *American Journal of International Law (*Baskmeijer and Roura,

2004; Enactment of PROTECT Act Against Sex Tourism, 2004; Nelson, 1987). Two caveats are important. It is possible some articles referred peripherally to tourism. Also, political scientists outside the USA may have been more active in the non-English journals (Richter, 1985a, 1985b).

Some tourism issues are subsumed under topics such as planning, confidence-building initiatives, capacity building, patronage, integration, or emergency management. Tourism—the world's largest industry—never quite makes it into the political science curriculum.

Twice before, once in 1983 and again in 1991 with Harry Matthews, I sought to look at tourism and political science. In 1983, my focus was the subfields of political science and the myriad of tourism issues of relevance to the discipline and vice versa (Richter, 1983). In 1991, we looked at political science concepts and their appropriateness for research on tourism including tourism development, planning international and comparative analysis (Matthews and Richter, 1991).

Neither article ignited a flurry of political science research on tourism, but some political scientists and other social scientists have applied political questions, concepts, and analytical tools. Concepts such as legitimacy, power, stakeholder analysis, sovereignty, ideology, democracy, equity, political development, colonialism, risk analysis, heritage preservation, sustainability, and gender roles are but some of those applied to tourism issues (Butler and Mao, 1995; DeKadt, 1979; Elliott, 1983 and 1997; Finney and Watson, 1976; Francisco, 1983; Hall, 1994; Hoivik and Heiberg, 1980; Jeffries, 2001; Richter, 1991b, 2004a).

In this chapter tourism will be discussed in three parts tracing the growing politicization of tourism. Part I tracks some of the early efforts of political scientists and others to explore basic political topics involving tourism. Part II looks at the emergence of new issues of tourism politics. These parallel the emergence of mass tourism, rising demands for equality and development by minorities, labor and women and raise issues of heritage representation and environmental concerns.

Part III focuses on the role tourism plays and can play in the relations among countries. In some cases the emphasis is on the facilitation of global travel, its economic, political, and environmental impacts. More recently, travel and tourism law has been studied as a factor in immigration control, the spread of disease, and tourism policy's role in the challenges of eradicating terrorism and trafficking in persons and drugs.

In that context new tools have been developed for both ideological and technological reasons that have influenced these issues. Deregulation, privatization, and democratization have changed whatever governance nations and the international community have had. The computer, the Internet, and the cell phone have altered the make up of the haves and have nots (Friedman, 2005). Finally, the chapter sketches a future where politics and policy will be increasingly global of necessity even as

the role of the nation state may be increasingly problematic. Tourism, like other forms of migration, will be politically challenged by the twin impulses to facilitate cross-border travel and build walls against it (Bookman, 2006).

Part I: Exploring the Politics of Tourism

For more than 30 years this writer has been fascinated with the politics surrounding tourism policy and the impact it exerts. The few political scientists who have studied tourism have not been trained to do so in political science courses but have rather stumbled upon it. In my case I was researching a supposed priority of the Marcos dictatorship in the Philippines: agrarian reform. Yet, while land reform was receiving scant resources, Manila was being transformed by the simultaneous building of 12, 5-star hotels in the space of 18 months—all for the 1976 IMF-World Bank conference. Slowly, it became apparent to me that tourism could transform perceptions of a nation's desirability, attractiveness, and commitment to modernization. Tourist comments and receipts could serve to convey a veneer of legitimacy that masked the unequal distribution of wealth. It could be a source of power and patronage; financed in this case by raiding the country's social security system (Richter, 1980, 1982, 1989). Agrarian reform had no such political promise.

President Marcos was not the first to recognize the political usefulness of tourists. Franco's Spain, Taiwan under Chiang Kai-shek, and many other leaders have used tourism, especially international tourism, as a vehicle for promoting their political regime (Henderson, 2003; Pi-Sunyer, 1979; Richter, 1989, 1999c).

Other political scientists had on occasion noticed tourism in the course of their work on other topics. Arend Liphjart (1964) observed its impact on national integration and communication in the 1960s. Harry Matthews (1978) noted the decidedly mixed effects of tourism's impact in the Caribbean in promoting dependency and a monoculture in the region. Other social scientists were coming to similar concerns in the edited volume, *Tourism: A New Kind of Sugar*, which traced in the South Pacific the cultural impacts of moving from a dependency on sugar to a similar dependency on international tourism (Finney and Watson, 1976).

Meanwhile, political scientist Cynthia Enloe (1975), studying comparative responses to pollution in several nations, was one of the first to call some forms of tourism "pollution." She would develop a more sophisticated and compelling critique of tourism and its relationship to militarism and gender roles in developing nations in her classic, *Bananas, Beaches, and Bases* (1990).

The emerging impetus to recognize tourism's political and social impacts focused first in developing nations. Nations that were newly independent and eager to exploit their "exotic" cultures in order to earn scarce foreign exchange and prestige while easing unemployment and encouraging foreign investment. Scholars studying these nations noted that the distribution of power, the relative influence of the tourists versus the local citizens or even their governments, was decidedly lopsided. The international tourist industry held most of the bargaining power.

Early critiques echoed Harold Lasswell's admonition to look at "who gets, what, when, and how?" (Dekadt, 1979; Farrell, 1984; Franda, 1979; Kent, 1984; Lasswell, 1936; Rosenau, 1979). Their research, in contrast to the boosterism of the tourist industry, was highly critical of the promise of tourism as a development strategy for poor nations. Too often, most citizens were ignored by unrepresentative governments and powerful elites. Interest in minorities was frequently limited to their usefulness as quaint and colorful ethnic attractions. Ownership and management of the industry was often in the hands of foreigners or domestic elites even in areas that were part of developed countries—such as Hawaii or Alaska (Kent, 1984; Richter, 2006).

Scholars saw the pernicious "demonstration effect" of tourist wealth and the bastardization and commoditization of culture. Political scientists and especially public administration specialists might be involved in the implementation and promotion of government tourism policies, but too rarely were they on the frontlines confronting opposing factions or cautioning planners to see stakeholders as other than powerful developers (Richter, 1985b). Nor did they see the potential for tourist disruption of local lives by the type and pace of tourism development favored. An exception was David Edgell (1999, 2002, 2006), a political scientist who saw the increasing political ramifications of developing tourism and would write about them extensively both as a policymaker and as an academic.

Critics often lacked access to government and planners seldom asked tough questions about net benefits and costs (Wanhill, 2005). Skeptics were considered obstacles to development even as their opposition to tourism development went unheard. Rather than attempt to understand or include critics in planning, more emphasis was placed on enclave tourism development, removing both tourists and their economic receipts from the general population (Richter and Richter, 1985).

Tourism schools and curricula blossomed but generally were founded on the premise of tourism being an economic bonanza to be harnessed and promoted. Training of employees but not their treatment; the development of the local environment but not worker housing or displacement of other laborers were the subjects of study. No discussion of the encouragement of development that supported local craftspeople, indigenous materials, and foods took place; nor was attention given beyond issues of transportation. Coordination with other sectors of the economy was lacking even in developed countries (Wheatcraft, 1994).

A wake-up call for the USA was the OPEC oil crisis of the mid-1970s. Sunday gas station closings or every-other-day access to gas pumps significantly reduced car travel even as other forms of travel grew more costly. The US federal policy only narrowly considered the gas shortage not the effects on the wider domestic travel industry. Calls for closer coordination among economic sectors highlighted the interconnectedness of tourism and government policy. But it was the industry not political scientists that noticed what had happened to the USA's second largest industry.

American tourism was at that time 97% domestic and had more than 43 federal agencies with some tourist-related jurisdiction. Still, neither the federal government nor the industry itself had fully realized how much the growth of mass tourism and its associated employees needed to be factored into energy policy. The government's obliviousness may have arisen because, unlike most nations, it had no national airline or train service (Richter, 1985a). The energy crisis awakened major tourist-generating nations to the linkages that were required between the industry and government. Tourism development, however, was a self-chosen policy not one forced upon developed countries (Hirschman, 1975).

For newly independent and other poor countries the only entities capable of developing tourism were foreign investors or the government. Moreover, alternative development streams, such as oil, mining, and diamond extraction, required export of finite resources; export that often increases dependence on the very colonial powers from which they had achieved independence. Tourism looked increasingly like a better option. As Milica Bookman put it: "Perhaps they chose tourism because tourism chose them . . . It is often the cheapest alternative since resources are already in place and exploiting them usually does not require much capital" (2006: 81).

Some may have underestimated the costs of developing the required infrastructure and the foreign exchange leakage that surrounds tourism. For countries with a tradition of religious pilgrimage, like India, some tourism accommodations are already in place. Also, countries with lengthy colonial histories have

tourism infrastructure in place such as hill stations where the colonists used to retreat in the hot season. (Crossette, 1999; DeKadt, 1979; Richter, 1989).

In any event, the tourism industry, both at home and abroad, would increasingly seek government support, especially for promotion and to ease travel. Sectors dependent on international tourism particularly relied on national government policies for border control (Airey, 1983; Butler and Mao, 1995; Edgell, 1999; Jeffries, 2001; Timothy, 2001).

Liberal border control policies were in violation of the Helsinki Accords of August, 1975 (Act III). They called for freedom of travel. The USA particularly sought to emphasize its slogan, "Travel—the Perfect Freedom," to contrast its policies with those of the former Soviet Union, which sought to restrict travel of its citizens beyond the USSR and the other Warsaw-Pact Nations. However, even the USA at that time did not permitted travel to mainland China (since 1949), or to North Korea, Libya, Cuba, and Yemen among others. Still other nations like South Korea and the Republic of China (Taiwan) controlled travel abroad to reduce foreign exchange leakage and to assure that draft age men could not escape military duty (Richter, 1989).

Part II: Emerging Issues in Tourism Politics

The 1970s onward saw the global rise in government activity to encourage tourism. All governments recognized the economic benefits; others also viewed the arrival of international tourists as an indication of political legitimacy and even territorial claims. A country such as Bhutan, that feared tourism, nonetheless saw tourists as a way to accentuate its fragile nationhood at a time when India had already absorbed other small princely kingdoms on its border (Richter, 1989).

Another example is Israel. Unlike Bhutan, it had no wish to keep the tourist from despoiling its culture but rather saw in tourism a way to share and promote Israeli values. Travel to Israel became a rite of passage for many high school children from Jewish homes around the globe. Adult Christians and Jews alike started traveling to Israel, less for the kibbutz experience of their offspring and more to "touch the stones" of the Old and New Testament stories. Tourist expenditures not only enhanced Israel's claim to land contested by Palestinians, but tourism also softened Israel's image as a militarized state. Tourism subsidized theater, arts, museums, excavation of antiquities, and other forms of entertainment that might otherwise have been unavailable.

Other nations in the region, especially Egypt, Lebanon, Jordan, and Syria would also see tourism in politico-economic terms. Moreover, their own citizens would benefit from these attractions at least as much as the tourists (Stock, 1977). Political accords between Israel and Egypt were prompted in part by the conviction that travel between the nations could benefit both their respective economies and serve as a confidence-building step that could further the peace process.

However, tourists acquired considerable leverage. The threat or actual boycott of a country because of its political repression or relations with the tourist-generating countries became a way for tourists to protest against political behavior. Such protests depressed the affected country's tourist revenues and assaulted the political legitimacy of its policies. China immediately after the Tiananmen Square Massacre, Burma since its military coup in 1990, and the USA and Soviet boycotts of each other's Olympic Games illustrate this pattern (Gartner, 1992; Richter, 1999a).

Governments increasingly recognize that ethnic minority or marginal cultures within their borders may be more valuable as tourist attractions than the homogenization of society and the suppression of minority customs. Governments also are well aware that if tourism becomes controversial to a particular sector of society, it is a very easy industry to sabotage. The Light-a-Fire Movement in the Philippines that burned lavish hotels during the Marcos dictatorship and the cancellations that followed China's crackdown on dissidents in the late 1980s illustrate tourism's fragility (Gartner, 1992; Richter, 1989).Two coups in Fiji during 1987 also protested the perceived loss of Fijian control over the tourist economy to Indian citizens (Kent, 1984; Richter, 2006).

The tourist, in contrast to the business traveler, has many choices of destination and rarely seeks out places in turmoil, thus even minor disturbances in the region can deter tourism. The example of Croatia is a good one, following its disastrous war with Serbia and its attempts to rebuild its once thriving tourist industry. Its postwar slogan tells it all: "Come to Croatia, the Coast is Clear" (Richter and Richter, 2000). For a few travelers, however, the danger visiting an unstable nation provides is a prerequisite. Regrettably, they will never want for places to go (Pelton et al., 1998; Prideaux and Seongseop-Kim, 2004).

Dependency on tourism can leave a nation or community very vulnerable. Diversification is certainly desirable where possible. While tourism may provide an incentive for friendly relations among regions, external events such as tsunamis, war, hurricanes, recession, and disease can always play havoc with the tourism planning. However, there is growing recognition that governments can and should plan carefully to assure that those elements within their control—labor, ethnic, and geographical conflict—be minimized.

The importance of a stable political situation provides leverage for underrepresented groups (Richter, 2006, 2007a.) New claimants to political power have expanded. This is particularly evident in heritage tourism as sites are no longer the monopoly of the strongest, most numerous, or those that most glorify the political elites (Horne, 1984; Richter, 1999a; Timothy and Boyd, 2006). Tourism industries seek out new destinations, packaging disparate sites into theme journeys (Seaton, 1999). A whole tourism niche has developed known as "dark tourism" or "thanatourism" (see Seaton [Chapter 29] in this *Handbook*) around infamous sites of barbarism. Examples include battlegrounds and concentration camps. Museums have also flourished such as the Holocaust Museum, and the Museum of Tolerance (Richter, 1999b; Seaton, 1999; Smith, 1996).

In the USA, sites on the Underground Railroad that helped Southern slaves escape to freedom in the North are featured. Specific museums dedicated to black history, sports, and culture have been founded not because people suddenly noticed the absence of monuments of the black experience in America but because of the growing economic and political clout of African-Americans (Hayes, 1990, 1991; Richter, 1995, 1999b, 2006). Something similar has happened with women, Japanese Americans, and Native American tourist sites (Richter, 1995, 1999b, 2006).

Blacks, women, and gays have also on occasion used their interest groups to attempt to influence tourism decisions based on the presentation of their group at tourism locales. For example, pro-Equal Rights Amendment (ERA) supporters in the early 1980s attempted to use their choice of convention venue as political leverage; boycotting states that had not ratified the ERA. Millions of convention dollars were lost by such states but the attempt did not lead to further ratified states. The boycott was too blunt a tool. Cities in such states generally favored the amendment, but the often rural control—unaffected by urban convention revenues—of state legislatures prevented pro-ERA action (Richter, 1995: 86).

More successful was the black travel boycott supported by many other groups that persuaded recalcitrant state legislatures to change their minds and support a Martin Luther King holiday to remember America's foremost civil right leader. Black associations have tended to select convention venues based on attractions of relevance to their heritage. Decision-makers are also attentive to the power structure of the cities they select, including the percentage of blacks in positions of political and economic power (Hayes, 1981, 1990). Native Americans have had a two-pronged strategy: protection of sacred sites from inappropriate development and aggressive marketing of tourist ventures, such as gambling, seen as critical to tribal economic development (Richter, 2006).

More recently there has been increased recognition of the political clout and disposable income of gay and lesbian travelers. An estimated US$65 billion is spent annually by gays and lesbians in the USA. This has led to more explicit marketing to this demographic group. Atlanta, Georgia's targeted campaign, illustrates this point. Its slogan: "Get Your History Straight and Your Nightlife Gay" (Clark, 2006). Entire cruise ships have been marketed to gays, their families, and friends. Such moves have been popular and profitable, but there have been some political issues when such ships have docked in conservative ports of call such as the Bahamas. The local tourism industry has so far been able to defuse the political issue by emphasizing the economic rewards of tolerance.

Not all minorities succeed in leveraging ascendant tourism into political and economic clout. Occupational minorities, such as those in the fishing industry, may find their way of life shut out by tourist development. Hunters or subsistence farmers may discover too late the land they had called their own is now restricted for parks and other sanctuaries. Others find their neighborhoods seized by the power of eminent domain for world fairs, expositions, or other public uses.

Recent US court decisions have gone beyond the compensated seizure and nationalization of private ventures and have now extended seizures to private ventures that may enhance public tax rolls through the gentrification of communities developed for private purposes (*Kelo v. City of New London*, 545 US 469, 2005). This decision has huge implications for tourism, pitting modest neighborhoods against developers whose projects could greatly enhance tax rolls even as affordable housing disappears. Yet, to some communities, no action also has consequences if it perpetuates an unfair status quo (Bachrach and Baratz, 1963).

Recently, tourism has grown and increased its ability to create more participants and stakeholders, doing so in spite of growing recognition of its fragility and dependence on local peace. Court decisions, political insensitivity, and international events continually threaten tourism. If tourism developers ever labored under the illusion that their fate was dependent only on economics, they have been increasingly made aware of their vulnerability to politics.

Part III: Tourism's International Impact

International and even domestic tourism has moved well beyond decision-makers in individual nations. Neither localities nor national governments, nor even segments of the tourist industry, "call all the shots" on tourism. Of course, the degree of independence decision-makers have had has always depended on local options and opportunity costs in other sectors, the power structure, and the overall economy of tourist-receiving and tourist-generating countries. The assumption that a minimal level of scenic beauty or a requisite number of exotic attractions is required has been dispelled. Tiny island states or territories such as Hong Kong, Macau, and Singapore regularly trounce large beautiful island chains such as the Philippines or Indonesia in tourism receipts and arrival numbers. The former were first and foremost catering to business travelers who could not be as fickle as those traveling for recreation. But ordinary tourists also flocked to these places based on their clean, safe surroundings with shopping or gambling opportunities (Butler and Mao, 1995; Chang, 2004).

Successful tourism must have political stability. Economists rather than political scientists have typically measured the costs of political instability. Tourism developers too often make lucrative deals with the elites in power and are frequently left vulnerable to the changing fortunes of those in power (Putra and Hitchcock, 2006; Richter, 1982, 1989, 1992, 1999c; Richter and Waugh, 1991; Sönmez and Graefe, 1998). Tourists will readily choose another destination if their safety, schedules, and comfort cannot be assured. Publicity of even isolated riots, bloodless coups, and even large electoral demonstrations and labor strikes, are usually sufficient to see tourism arrival numbers plummet (Henderson, 2003; Teye, 1988).

Democratic government is not a necessary requirement for tourism success. However, brutal or unstable political destinations regardless of beauty, attractions, and favorable exchange rates, cannot sustain tourism (Richter, 1992). Even the most repressive government cannot hide such events in the age of 24-hour news and the Internet. Pakistan, for example, has been plagued with both persistent political problems and sporadic violence crippling its tourism efforts in its 60 years of independence despite having abundant scenic attractions and heritage treasures (Richter, W., 1978). It has also had the misfortune even in periods of relative calm to be sandwiched between turbulent Afghanistan and Iran and its bitter enemy, India, with which it has fought several wars. India has been affected by the tension in terms of overland tourists but it enjoys a massive core of domestic tourists and extensive pilgrimage tourism (Richter, 1989).

Tourism development in an age of globalization and rising concerns with terrorism is not simply uncontrollable for countries such as Pakistan and an increasing number of other nations. The USA, even five years after the 9/11 attacks, has still not fully recovered its international tourism rates. That may be in part because international goodwill expressed following 9/11 has largely evaporated. The preemptive strike of the USA against Iraq has engendered rising anti-Americanism throughout the world, especially in Western Europe and other favorite destinations of traveling Americans. Moreover, much as nations need the economic impact of tourists, countries such as the USA are increasingly ambivalent towards foreigners despite the fact that international visitors spend twice as much as domestic tourists. "Right now, we live in an environment where members of Congress are not convinced they want more travelers in this country" (De Lollis, 2006: 3B).

Also, the spread of terrorist attacks to the allies of the USA and the growing number and complexity of such events have spooked leisure travelers disproportionately to the actual risks (Richter and Waugh, 1991). A single tsunami in South and Southeast Asia in 2004 killed many more tourists, let alone nationals, than a decade of terrorist actions. However, it is not just the collateral damage affecting tourists, but the deliberate targeting of visitors that has occasioned fear. The motives for which range from trying to hurt the regime in power, to protest the modernity travelers represent, or to draw attention to the skewing of priorities they are perceived to create (Henderson, 2003; Putra and Hitchcock, 2006; Richter, 1992). Such violence has not been confined to Islamic jihadists but has occurred as a result of all kinds of terrorist groups (Adams, 2001).

The globalization of information and commerce has also meant virtual travel through new forms of media to almost everywhere. This has led to an increasing inability for repressive regimes to spin their own image of the nation both abroad and for domestic consumption. China's recent attempt to censor the Internet is real but is unlikely to succeed. Author Thomas Friedman (2005) has said that the globalization revolution augers well for the world's societies as brands of fast food and hotels spread. He reminds us that no nations with McDonalds have ever fought each other. However, such globalization does pose the threat of a "race to the bottom" among nations eager to be competitive, even at the risk of their environment, health, labor safety, and tax base.

For example, the amenities competition both within and among hotel chains has led to ever more elaborate bedding and mattresses. As a consequence, there has been a sharp rise in injuries sustained by hotel workers as they attempt to clean and replenish heavier and more luxurious beds. These workers are the least likely to be paid a living wage or to enjoy health coverage and other employee benefits. Yet, most social scientists are unlikely to follow trends in bedding in their criticisms of the tourist industry (Rasell, 2006).

The mantra of free trade may conjure up a borderless world but it is certain that the emerging world order has not come free of costs. The new reality has increased attention to international law, illegal immigration, and terrorists posing as tourists. Thus countries have been pulled both toward the relaxation of some regulations even as they develop more protective postures for international tourism (Richter, 2001a, 2001b). It is hard to believe that in the early 20th century there were actually few constraints on travel. As late as the mid-1990s the US government emphasis on tourist facilitation had led to the US exempting a number of friendly nations' citizens from visas requirements. The "visa waiver" program was extremely popular with inbound tourists as was the process by which tourists and returning nationals could go through US customs before boarding or embarking for the USA (Richter, personal observation while on United States Travel and Tourism Advisory Board, 1990–1994).

The US tourist industry succeeded in protecting its interests within the Department of Commerce and had one of the largest caucuses in the Congress (Hayes, 1981). Despite many divergent, contradictory, and competitive interests, for a time in the 1990s, the industry seemed to be getting its political act together. President H.W. Bush did television ads welcoming international tourists. The industry fended off a departure tax which is the norm in most countries, forestalled indexing the minimum wage to inflation, and discouraged greater scrutiny of seasonal and low-paid workers, many of whom were illegal aliens.

Even earlier, by the mid-1980s as government employment declined at all levels, state tourism initiatives were growing and with it public-sector employment in tourism planning, marketing, and destination development. Unfortunately, monitoring and evaluation and other cautionary measures were not put in place (Richter, 1985a, 1985b).

Nor was there any reporting of some of the increased costs associated with increased tourism–traffic, noise, litter, prostitution, parks and recreation staff, police. Everything was reported in terms of gross rather than net receipts. Private facilities typically reaped the benefits; the public sector absorbed the costs (Richter, 1985a). Similar criticism has been voiced by Stephen Wanhill (2005) with respect to British tourism development (Wanhill, 2005).

While US state tourism budgets continue to grow and national promotion remains significant in most tourist-receiving countries, international tourism growth has slowed. A series of terrorist attacks in such tourist havens as the USA, the UK, Spain, and Indonesia have left travelers more wary of traveling. Moreover, the international environment has led to a tightening of the recently loosened borders, long delays for security checks, and new requirements for hard-to-forge passports and visas. The cost of travel in time and money has taken a lot of the spontaneity from tourism. Many nations have raised both visa requirements and their costs. It is almost as if, in a world increasingly beyond national control, those demands that can be made will more likely be made.

Still, global threats have elicited a new degree of international cooperation in several important areas. Governments have taken heed of these niches for sharing information and increasing security. Transparency, accountability, law and protocols for international cooperation are emerging in areas of weather, health, trafficking, transportation, and terrorism. There is also a growing concern about areas where international law relies on an eroding consensus. Tourism to outer space and Antarctica may well be future issues where national interests and international controls collide (Basmeijer and Roura, 2004).

The United Nations' World Tourism Organization (WTO) has since its formation become a valuable clearinghouse for information on tourism problems and initiatives around the world. Its publications have also tallied basic statistics on the industry. Though organized to promote tourism globally, the WTO has featured issues on particular regions and on such demographic groups as the traveling disabled, elderly tourists, and student tourism (Jafari, 1975).

It has also adopted a Code of Ethics for the international tourism industry after more than a decade of urging by such interest groups as the Ecumenical Coalition on Third World Tourism, Ecumenical Coalition on Child Prostitution in Asian Tourism, Just Tourism (New Zealand), Tourism Ecumenical Network (TEN) in Europe, Tourism Concern in the UK, and the Center for Responsible Tourism in the USA. WTO has taken up such issues as prostitution and international trafficking, though its effectiveness has been hampered by the failure of major powers to pay more than lip service to its recommendations (Anon, 2003; Bales, 1994; Richter, 1991b, 2004b, 2005, 2007b; Richter and Richter, 2003; *WTO News*, 2002a, 2002b, 2003).

The WTO has also responded to scores of conservation and heritage preservation groups by providing forums and publicity for ecotourism efforts, labeling for green projects, and supported the work of heritage groups including UNESCO World Heritage Sites. UNESCO has helped to identify important sites and focus a political spotlight on the behavior of nations and their adversaries (Singh et al., 2001, 2003; Turco, 1997).

Two examples illustrate this point. First, the importance of Dubrovnik in Croatia, which had been a protected city since medieval times, made the Serbian attack on this non-military but priceless city all the more horrific. Some would argue Dubrovnik's historic and touristic importance helped garner opposition to Serbia and encourage NATO's entry into the war against Serbia in Bosnia. Without dispute, publicity surrounding the shelling of Dubrovnik marshaled massive resources globally for the recovery of Dubrovnik's cultural treasures (Richter and Richter, 2000).

Second, the destruction of the enormous Buddhist sculptures at Bamian by the Taliban government in Afghanistan in March, 2001, further isolated the Taliban even before the attack on the US World Trade Center. Only Pakistan maintained diplomatic relations with the government (Maycuth, 2006: A12).

Today, within nearly any geographical or ideological alliance, there are committees and groups dealing with tourism. The Association of Southeast Asian Nations (ASEAN) is such an example. There is also explicitly tourism organizations formed on a regional basis like the Pacific Area Tourism Association (PATA) (Timothy, 2003).

Recently, tourism has been politicized at the international level by its association with prostitution at international sporting events. Tourism also highlights the inadequacy of international law to deal with the kidnapping of children by noncustodial parents or strangers posing as tourists, crimes in international waters, and the threat to world health posed by travelers (Clift and Grabowski, 1997; Exploited Child Unit 2001; Fidler, 2004; Garrett, 1996, 2000; Klein, 2005; Langewiesche, 2003; Lowe, 1999; Rave, 2006; Richter, 2003, 2004b, 2005).

So porous are the regulations both within and among nations regarding travel-related health risks, the very impotence of the World Health Organization (WHO) has been a matter of international concern for more than a decade (Nelson, 1987; "Fortress WHO," 1995). The WHO is underfunded and without the necessary authority to police global health. Nations with chronic disease or sporadic health threats such as malaria, tuberculosis, Severe Acute Respiratory Syndrome (SARS), or avian flu or widespread AIDS are loathe to advertise any problems that would discourage tourism (Richter, 2003; "TB Bug Gaining Ground in US," 2006).

Moreover, nationals of countries with endemic disease are rarely required to be vaccinated or tested before entering other countries, unless they are coming to study or work for an indefinite time. The global community actually relaxed its already inadequate scrutiny. Requirements for health safety are today less than before mass air

travel and cruising began in the 1960s. Despite the emergence of nearly two dozen new infectious diseases in the last 20 years, monitoring and evaluation of disease is lacking and requirements for informing travelers have actually lessened. This writer can only conclude that the success in largely eliminating smallpox and polio, coupled with the economic hunger for tourists, has led to the crippling of the one international body charged with global public health (Klein, 2005; Richter, 2003).

WHO cannot even go into a nation unless invited by that nation and as the SARs scare illustrated, nations may well hide cases rather than seek help and risk the loss of trade and tourism (Fidler, 2004). Similarly, the Centers for Disease Control in the USA have had to wait for a specific state's request for help in cases of outbreaks before it could act. The threat of biological terrorism and the possibility of an avian flu pandemic may trigger global and regional action (Specter, 2005). Certainly, the ease with which deliberately or accidentally infected individuals can move around the world has made tourism a legitimate concern for government scrutiny.

Currently, there is a new and growing form of health-related travel. It, too, deserves government scrutiny because the consumer protections for the traveling tourist may be slight indeed. Thousands are now traveling to other countries for medical care (Kamps, 2006: 108–111). Typically, the travelers are from the most industrialized countries, especially the USA, where health costs are the highest in the world. They travel to the finest facilities, both more labor-intensive and luxurious hospitals and clinics in developing nations. The countries most active in providing such services are Thailand, the Philippines, and India. In most cases the doctors have been trained in the West but can afford to offer the best care at a fraction of the cost charged in the West. In the process, however, "it has to invest a disproportionate share of finite resources in services for the affluent, thus distorting any redistributive effect of better care" (Wolfe, 2006: 3).

Medical tourism, historically was to "take the waters" in some reputedly curative spring or to make pilgrimages to shrines to pray for cures. Now, it has moved from largely cosmetic surgery to very sophisticated and complicated procedures. Nor has all the health-related travel been to developing countries. Many US citizens travel to Canada for their prescriptions, which are often 75% lower for the same drugs as in the USA. Members of Congress, dependent on pharmaceutical companies for campaign funds, have so far been unwilling to prevent, particularly American seniors, from combining travel and medicine purchases.

Of course, for many decades the wealthy elites of other countries have come to the USA for specialized treatments at leading hospitals and clinics. Today, however, there is a new clientele: those who travel to US fertility clinics for the purpose of being able to select the sex of their baby. Such non-medically necessary sex selection is illegal in most countries (Johnson, 2006: A6).

Conclusion

The politicization of tourism only has been sketched in this essay. Still, tourism's importance and multifaceted nature has elicited an incredible amount of research in the last 30 years. The twenty-first century may be the era when political scientists belatedly recognize that the core issues of political science inquiry are germane and compelling for the world's largest industry. Phenomena such as globalization, terrorism, deregulation, privatization, and the Internet have challenged nations in new ways to protect citizens and freedom of movement. They have also required a level of cooperation and integration of approaches that countries were heretofore unwilling to consider.

By 2015, over 1.6 billion travelers are predicted to cross international borders annually (Edgell, 1999). This is the largest migration on earth and will not occur smoothly without incredible political skill and cooperation. The political issues these travelers raise and which must be confronted will require greater not less regulation, strict standards not laissez-faire trade, and levels of political commitment from nations to international protocols that will guarantee heightened levels of scrutiny within, among, and above nations. With or without the insights of political scientists, the politics of tourism will only grow in importance and will be played for the highest economic and political stakes.

References

Adams, K. (2001). "Danger Zone Tourism: Prospects and Problems for Tourism in Tumultuous Times." In Peggy Teo, T. Chang and K.C. Ho (Eds.), *Interconnected Worlds: Tourism in Southeast Asia* (pp. 265–281). London: Pergamon.

Airey, D. (1983). "European Government Approaches to Tourism." *Tourism Management*, 4(4): 324–244.

Bachrach, P. and Baratz, M.S. (1963). "Decisions and Non-Decisions: An Analytical Framework." *American Political Science Review*, September: 632–642.

Bales, K. (1999). *Disposable People: The New Slavery in the Global Economy*. Berkeley: University of California Press.

Bastmeijer, Kees and Rora, R. (2004). "Regulating Antarctic Tourism and the Precautionary Principle." The *American Journal of International Law*, 98(4): 763–781.

Bookman, M.Z. (2006). *Tourists, Migrants and Refugees: Population Movements in Third World Development*. Boulder, CO: Lynne Reinner.

Butler, R.W. and Mao, B. (1995). "Tourism Between Quasi-States: International, Domestic or What?" In Richard W. Butler and Douglas Pearce (Eds.), *Change in Tourism: People, Places, Processes* (pp. 92–113). London: Routledge.

Chang, T.C. (2004). *Tourism in a "Borderless" World: The Singapore Experience*. Monograph No. 73, May. Honolulu: East-West Center.

Clark, J. (2006). "Cities in the Red States Play Ball with Gay Travelers." *USA Today*, February 10.

Clift, S. and Grabowski, P. (1997). *Tourism and Health*. London: Pinter.

Crossette, B. (1999). The Great Hill Stations of Asia. New York: Basic Books.

DeKadt, E. (Ed.) (1979). *Tourism: Passport to Development?* New York: Oxford University Press.

DeLollis, B. (2006). "State of Foreign Travel Lamented." *USA Today*, Oct. 4, 2006: 3B.

Dorsey, T. (2006). Unpublished review of major political science journals: 1980–2006. Manhattan, KS. The journals examined were *The American Political Science Review*, the *Journal of Politics*.

Edgell, D.L., Sr. (1999). *Tourism Policy: The Next Millennium*. Champaign, Illinois: Sagamore.

Edgell, D.L., Sr. (2002). *Best Practices Guide Book for International Tourism Development for Rural Communities*. Provo, UT: Brigham Young University.

Edgell, D.L., Sr. (2006). *Managing Sustainable Tourism: A Legacy for the Future*. New York: Hawthorn Press.

Elliott, J. (1997). *Tourism Politics and Public Sector Management*. London: Routledge.

Elliott, J. (1983). "Politics, Power and Tourism in Thailand." *Annals of Tourism Research*, 10(3): 377–393.

"Enactment of Protect Act Against Sex Tourism" (2004). *American Journal of International Law*, 98(1): 182.

Enloe, C. (1975). *The Politics of Pollution in a Comparative Perspective*. New York: David McKay Co.

Enloe, C. (1990). *Bananas, Beaches, and Bases: Making Feminist Sense of International Politics*. London: Pandora.

Exploited Child Unit (2001). *Annual Report*. Washington, DC: National Center for Missing and Exploited Children.

Farrell, B. (1979). "Tourism's Human Conflicts: Cases from the Pacific." *Annals of Tourism Research*, 6(2): 122–136.

Fidler, D.R. (2004). *SARS and the Globalization of Disease*. New York: Palgrave.

Finney, B. and Watson, K.A. (1976). *A New Kind of Sugar: Tourism in the South Pacific*. Honolulu: East-West Center.

"Fortress WHO: Breaking the Ramparts for Health's Sake" (1995). *Lancet*, January 28, 345: 203–204.

Francisco, R. (1983). "The Political Impact of Economic Development on Tourism in Latin America." *Annals of Tourism Research*, 10(3): 363–376.

Franda, M. (1979). *Quiet Turbulence in the Seychelles, Part 1: Tourism and Development*. American University Field Staff Reports, 10.

Friedman, T.L. (2005). *The World is Flat*. New York: Farrar, Straus and Giroux.

Garrett, L. (2000). *Betrayal of Trust: The Collapse of Global Public Health*. New York: Hyperion.

Garrett, L. (1996). "The Return of Infectious Diseases." *Foreign Affairs*, 75(1): 66–79.

Gartner, W.C. (1992). "Impact of Tiananmen Square on China's Tourism." *Journal of Travel Research*, Spring: 47–52.

Hall, C.M. (1994). *Tourism and Politics: Power, Policy and Place*. London: John Wiley and Sons.

Hayes, B.J. (1990). "What's So Special About Atlanta?" *Dollars and Sense*, October/November: 22–24.

Hayes, B.J. (1991). "The Economics of Travel: Do African-Americans Get Their Share of the Travel Dollar?" *Dollars and Sense*, December/January: 52–56.

Hayes, B.J. (1981). "The Congressional Travel and Tourism Caucus and U.S. National Tourism Policy." *Tourism Management*, 2(2): 126–137.

Henderson, J. (2003). "The Politics of Tourism in Myanmar." *Current Issues in Tourism*, 16(2): 97–118.

Hirschman, A. (1975). "Policy-Making and Policy Analysis in Latin America: A Return Journey." *Policy Sciences*, 6: 385–402.

Hoivik, T. and Heiberg, T. (1980). "Centre-Periphery Tourism and Self Reliance." *International Social Science Journal*, 32(1): 69–98.

Horne, D. (1984). *The Great Museum*. London: Pluto.

"Human Trafficking Sanctions Mulled" (2003). *Kansas City Star*, June 12: A12.

Jafari, J. (1975). "Creation of the Inter-governmental World Tourism Organization." *Annals of Tourism Research*, 2(5): 237–245.

Jeffries, D. (2001). *Governments and Tourism*. Oxford: Butterworth-Heinemann.

Johnson, C.K. (2006). "It's Your Choice, Boy or Girl, at U.S. Clinics." *Kansas City Star*, June 15: A16.

Kamps, L. (2006). "The Medical Vacation." *Travel and Leisure*, July: 108–111.

Klein, R.A. (2005). *Cruise Ship Squeeze*. Gabriola Island, BC: New Society Publishers.

Kent, N. (1984). *Hawaii: Islands Under the Influence*, Monthly Review.

Langewiesche, William, (2003). "Anarchy at Sea." *The Atlantic Monthly*, September: 50–80.

Lasswell, Harold (1936). *Politics: Who Gets What, When and How*. New York: P. Smith.

Lijphart, A. (1964). "Tourism Traffic and Integration Potential." *Journal of Common Market Studies*, 2(3): 251–262.

Lowe, N. (1999). *Report. International Forum on Parental Child Abduction*, Washington, September 15–16, 1998.

Matthews, H.G. (1978). *International Tourism: A Political and Social Analysis*. Cambridge, MA: Schenkman Publishing Company.

Matthews, H.G. and Richter, L.K. (1991). "Political Science and Tourism." *Annals of Tourism Research*, 18(1): 120–135.

Maycuth, A. (2006). "Rubble in History Too." *Kansas City Star*, Oct. 7: A12.

Nelson, L.J. III (1987). "International Travel Restrictions and the AIDS Epidemic." *The American Journal of International Law*, 81(1): 230–236.

Pelton, R.Y., Aral, C. and Dulles, W. (1998). *Fielding the World's Most Dangerous Places*. Redondo Beach, CA: Fielding World Wide, Inc.

Pi-Sunyer, O (1979). "The Politics of Tourism in Catalonia." *Mediterranean Studies*, 1(2): 46–69.

Putra, N.D. and Hitchcock, M. (2006). "The Bali Bombs and the Tourism Development Cycle." *Progress in Development Studies*, 6(2): 1–10.

Rasell, E. (2006). Excerpt from Witness Ministries. *UCC Bulletin*, September 3, 12.

Rave, J. (2006). "Crime Rocks the Boat." *Time*, March 13: 23–24.

Richter, L.K. (1980). "The Political Uses of Tourism: A Philippine Case Study." *Journal of Developing Areas*, 14 (January): 237–257.

Richter, L.K. (1982). *Land Reform and Tourism Development: Policy-Making in the Philippines*. Cambridge, MA: Schenkman.

Richter, L.K. (1983). "Political Science and Tourism: A Case of Not So Benign Neglect." *Annals of Tourism Research*, 10(3): 313–335.

Richter, L.K. (1985a). "The Fragmented Politics of U.S. Tourism." *Tourism Management*, 6(3) September: 62–73.

Richter, L.K. (1985b). "State-Sponsored Tourism Development: A Growth Area for Public Administration." *Public Administration Review*, 45(6): 832–839.

Richter, L.K. (1989). *The Politics of Tourism in Asia*. Honolulu: University of Hawaii Press.

Richter, L.K. (1991a). "The Search for Appropriate Tourism." In Tej Vir Singh, Valene L. Smith, Mary Fish and Linda K. Richter (Eds.), *Tourism Environment: Nature, Culture, Economy*. New Delhi: Inter-India Publications.

Richter, L.K. (1991b). "The Impact of American Tourism Policy on Women." In M.L. Kendrigan (Ed.), *Gender Differences and Public Policy* (pp. 201–222). CO: Greenwood Press.

Richter, L.K. (1992). "Political Instability and Tourism in the Third World." In David Harrison (Ed.), *Tourism and the Less Developed Countries* (pp. 35–46). London: Belhaven.

Richter, L.K. (1995). "Gender and Race: Neglected Variables in Tourism Research." In Richard W. Butler and Douglas Pearce (Eds.), *Change in Tourism, People, Places, Processes*. London: Routledge.

Richter, L.K. (1999a). "Myanmar," *Encyclopedia Americana Yearbook* (p. 375). Danbury, CT: Grolier Press.

Richter, L.K. (1999b). "The Politics of Heritage Tourism Development." In Douglas Pearce and Richard Butler (Eds.), *Emerging Issues for the New Millennium* (pp. 108–126). London: Routledge.

Richter, L.K. (1999c). "After Political Turmoil: The Lessons of Rebuilding Tourism in Three Asian Countries." *Journal of Travel Research*, 38(1): 41–45.

Richter, L.K. (2001a). "Where Asia Wears a Smile: Lessons of Philippine Tourism Development." In Valene L. Smith and Maryann Brent (Eds.), *Hosts and Guests Revisited: Tourism Issues of the 21st Century* (pp. 283–297). New York: Cognizant Publications.

Richter, L.K. (2001b). "Continuity and Change: Tourism Challenges in Developing Nations at the Millennium." In David Harrison (Ed.), *Tourism and the Less Developed Countries: Issues and Cases.* London: CABI, Wallingford.

Richter, L.K. (2003). "International Tourism and Its Global Health Consequences." *Journal of Travel Research*, 41(4): 340–347.

Richter, L.K. (2004a). "Exploring the Political Role of Gender in Tourism Research." In William Theobald (Ed.), *Global Tourism* (3rd edition.) (pp. 426–439). Maryland Heights, MO: Butterworth-Heinemann.

Richter, L.K. (2004b). "Not Home Alone: International Issues Surrounding the Traveling Child." *Tourism Recreation Research*, 29(1): 27–35.

Richter, L.K. (2005). "Not a Minor Problem: Developing International Travel Policy for the Welfare of Children." *Tourism Analysis*, 1: 27–36.

Richter, L.K. (2006). "The Politics of Negotiating Culture in Tourism Development." In Peter M. Burns and Marina Novelli (Eds.), *Tourism and Social Identities*. London, Elsevier: 27–38.

Richter, L.K. (2007a). "Democracy and Tourism: Exploring the Nature of an Inconsistent Relationship." In Peter Burns and Marina Novelli (Eds.), *Advances in Tourism Research: Tourism and Politics, Global Frameworks and Local Realities*. London: Macmillan.

Richter, L.K. (2007b). "Tourism Policy-Making in Southeast Asia: A 21st Century Perspective." In Michael Hitchcock (Ed.), *Tourism in South-East Asia Revisited*. Copenhagen: NAIS.

Richter, L.K and Richter, W.L. (2003). "Human Trafficking, Globalization and Ethics." *PA Times*, 26(2): 4.

Richter, L.K. and Richter, W.L. (2000). "Back from the Edge: Recovering a Public Tradition in Dubrovnik." In Stuart Nagel (Ed.), *Handbook of Global Social Policy*. New York: Marcel Dekker.

Richter, L.K. and Richter, W.L. (1985). "Policy Choices in South Asian Tourism Development." *Annals of Tourism Research*, 12(2): 201–217.

Richter, L.K. and Waugh, W. (1991). "Tourism and Terrorist as Logical Companions." In S. Medlik (Ed.), *Managing Tourism* (pp. 318–327). Oxford: Butterworth-Heinemann.

Richter, W.L. (1978). "Persistent Praetorianism: Pakistan's Third Military Regime." *Pacific Affairs*, 51(Fall): 406–426.

Rosenau, J.N. (1979). "Le Tourists et le Terrorist ou les Deux Extremes du Continuum Transnational." *Etudes Internationales*, 10(June): 231–252.

Seaton, A.V. (1999). "War and Thanatourism: Waterloo 1815–1914." *Annals of Tourism Research*, 26(1) 130–158.

Singh, S., Timothy, D.J. and Dowling, Ross K. (2003). *Tourism and Destination Communities*. London: CABI, Wallingford.

Singh, T.V., Smith, V.L., Fish, M. and Richter, L.K. (Eds.) (1991). *Tourism Environment: Nature, Culture, Economy*. New Delhi: Inter-India Publications.

Smith, V.L. (1996). "War and Tourism: An American Ethnography." *Annals of Tourism Research*, 23(1): 202–227.

Sönmez, S.F. and Graefe, A.R. (1998). "Influence of Terrorism Risk on Foreign Tourism Decisions." *Annals of Tourism Research*, 25(1): 112–114.

Specter, M. (2005). "Nature's Bioterrorist: Is There Any Way to Prevent a Deadly Avian-Flu Pandemic?" *The New Yorker*, February 28: 50–61.

Stock, R. (1977). "Political and Social Contributions of International Tourism to the Development of Israel." *Annals of Tourism Research*, 4(4): 30–42.

"TB Bug Gaining Ground in U.S." (2006). *Manhattan Mercury*, September 22, p. B9.

Teye, V. (1988). "Coup d'etat and African Tourism: A Study of Ghana." *Annals of Tourism Research*, 15(3): 329–356.

Timothy, D.J. and Boyd, S.W. (2006). "Heritage Tourism in the 21st Century: Valued Traditions and New Perspectives." *Journal of Heritage Tourism*, 1(1): 1–16.

Timothy, D.J., Prideaux, B. and Seongseop Kim, S. (2004). "Tourism at Borders of Conflict and Demilitarized Zone." In Tej Vir Singh (Ed.), *New Horizons in Tourism*. Cambridge, MA: CABI.

Timothy, D.J. (2003). "Supranationalist Alliances and Tourism: Insights from ASEAN and SAARC." *Current Issues in Tourism*, 6(3): 250–266.

Timothy, D.J. (2001). *Tourism and Political Boundaries*. London: Routledge.

Turco, M. (1997). "The Greed Behind the Green in Tourism." *Contours*, 7: 6–7.

WTO News (2002a). "Bali to Host Future Meeting of Child Protection Task Force."4th Quarter: 8.

WTO News (2002b). "Child Protection Code of Conduct Endorsed by Tour Operators' Initiative." 4th Quarter: 8.

WTO News (2003). "Costa Rica to Lead National Effort Against Sexual Exploitation in Children." 4th Quarter: 8.

Wanhill, S. (2005). "Role of Government Incentives." In William Theobald (Ed.), *Global Tourism* (3rd edition.) (p. 370). Amsterdam: Elsevier.

Wheatcraft, S. (1994). *Aviation and Tourism Policies*. London: Routledge.

Wolfe, S.M. (Ed.) (2006). "Patients without Borders: The Emergence of Medical Tourism." *Public Citizen Health Letter*, July 22 (7): 1–3.

12

Tourism and Natural Resources

Andrew Holden

Introduction

The use of nature and natural settings for recreational tourism is something that is axiomatic in holiday advertising and is reflected in the major spatial flows of tourism. However, the temporal movement of hundreds of millions of international tourists each year,[1] combined with the movement of similar numbers of domestic tourists, inevitably has implications for how tourism interacts with natural resources. The essential elements of a typical vacation; i.e., transportation, accommodation, and the facilitation of amusement, all involve the use of natural resources in various ways. For example, air travel is reliant upon the use of oil as fuel and also the atmosphere as a sink for pollutants. However, it is only comparatively recently that the manner of how tourism interacts with natural resources has become a topic of study and debate; a consequence of its relatively recent growth and now prominent global significance.

The type of relationships that tourism can have with its natural resources has been categorized as being positive, neutral, or negative (Wall and Mathieson, 2007). The extent to which tourism can be viewed as having an overall positive or negative effect on natural resources is highly debatable and contentious. While originally having been advocated as a smokeless industry in the 1960s, it is observable that tourism can place considerable pressure on natural resources, in certain situations leading to negative environmental consequences. In trying to understand tourism's relationship with natural resources, one field of academic knowledge that is especially relevant is environmental studies. A historical context is provided below, followed by a discussion of tourism in relation to natural resources (including challenges related to environmental ethics) and future considerations.

Environmental Studies

The emergence of environmental studies as a subject for academic study can be identified in the 1960s. Its development was a consequence of a realization that human activity was impacting upon and creating a state of disequilibrium in the environment. Instrumental to this understanding was scientific enquiry that has made us aware of many of the environmental concerns with which we are familiar today: e.g., global warming, ozone depletion, biodiversity loss, and pollution. However, although science has highlighted these problems it does not necessarily have the solutions to them. There also exists a high level of scientific uncertainty over the magnitude and timescale of many of the environmental effects of human induced change.

Given that many environmental problems are seemingly a consequence of human behavior, the social sciences have an essential role to understanding and helping find solutions to them. Hence, a suitable definition of environmental studies would be the one given by Nelissen et al. as: "We define environmental studies as the interdisciplinary field of studies concerned with problems in the relationship between man, society, and environment" (1997: 13). Although not specified by the authors, it is assumed that in this definition the term "man" is used in a neutral sense, referring to both men and women.

Besides the support of scientific measurement it is perhaps our own observations and experiences of environmental change that draw our attention to the human impact on nature. According to Hodgson (1996), the first incident that created public concern about the state of the environment was the poisoning of water and fish from chemical discharges released by the Chisso Corporation factory in Minamata Bay, Japan, in the mid-1950s. The discharges damaged people's nervous systems and lead to a high incidence of birth defects and brain damage. Yet, as Hodgson (1996) points out, during the 1950s, many people in the world also regarded smoke and dirt as signs of industrial progress, especially in a post-World War II world that was attempting to reconstruct national economies. However, a decisive moment in the questioning of scientific progress came in 1962 with the publication of biologist Rachel Carson's book *Silent Spring*, which heavily criticized the ecological damage caused by the use of agrochemicals on farmland in the USA. The book emphasized the dangers to human health of chemicals being passed through the food chain. The book became a bestseller and had a major

influence on public consciousness and subsequently on regulatory policy, with the banning or restriction of use being placed on 12 of the pesticides and herbicides that Carson identified as being most dangerous, including the notorious DDT. *Silent Spring* marks the rise of a strong environmental movement in the USA that took up a number of major issues over the next couple of decades.

As Western societies became progressively dependent upon oil during the 1960s to power factories, heat homes, and to fuel the increasing number of vehicles, in 1967 the first major "environmental disaster" in the West occurred. In March of that year, the Torrey Canyon oil tanker, carrying a full load of 120,000 tons of crude oil, hit rocks off the coast of England, leading to the release of oil onto its southwest coast. This was the first time anything like this had ever happened, as the oil polluted the water and washed onto the beaches. Media images of birds with black oil and tar stuck were poignant, as was the knowledge that the oil had killed fish and shrimps and other forms of life. Besides causing a high level of public concern, the disaster highlighted that a higher material standard of living did not come without environmental risk and cost. In the same year, the first major oil spill in the USA occurred from an offshore rig near Santa Barbara, releasing millions of tons of crude oil onto the coasts of California. In 1969, toxins leaked into the River Rhine, poisoning millions of fish and threatening the quality of drinking water for millions of Europeans (Dalton, 1993).

Subsequently, there arose a growing body of evidence that industrial growth and progress was not free of environmental cost. In 1968, perceptions of the world as having unlimited and abundant resources were also challenged by the first widely broadcast television images of the Earth shot from the American spacecraft Apollo 8, showing the earth as a sphere floating in space. The concept of a "spaceship earth" was the subject of a famous essay in environmental studies by Boulding (1973), questioning the "cowboy economy" associated with the reckless and exploitative use of nature, which he believed typified the Western approach to development.

In place of the cowboy he argued we should begin to conceptualize the earth as having a "spaceman economy," in which the Earth, like a spaceship, does not have unlimited reserves of anything, and in which humans must find their place without threatening its cyclical ecological system.

Newly arisen public concern over the environment manifested itself in "Earth Day," which took place in the USA on April 22, 1970. Organized by Senator Gaylord Nelson, an estimated 20 million Americans participated, with 100,000 converging on New York's Fifth Avenue. As Spowers (2002) observes, this large demonstration pressured American politicians into being seen to do something on the environment. In 1972, the first international conference on the environment, organized by the United Nations, was held in Stockholm, one outcome being the formation of the United Nations Environment Programme (UNEP), which remains influential in directing global environmental policy today. Evidence of an increasing public environmental concern was also illustrated by the founding of major environmental nongovernmental organizations (NGOs) including Greenpeace and Friends of the Earth in the early 1970s. One particular focus of Greenpeace was its campaign against whaling, as many species of whale faced extinction from over hunting (Hodgson, 1996). The role of NGOs was important in attracting and maintaining media attention on the environment and lobbying government about environmental issues.

In 1972, the "Limits to Growth: A Report for the Club of Rome project on the Predicament of Mankind" (Meadows, 1972) was also published. This report was the result of collaborative research between a group of scientists and business leaders into population growth, resource use, and other environmental trends. Predictions of pollution, resource depletion, and heightened death rates resulting from a lack of food and health services, drew attention to environmental issues, even if they have been proven incorrect with the passage of time. In 1979, the near melt down of the nuclear reactor at Three Mile Island in Pennsylvania in the USA and the subsequent threat of a major environmental and civil catastrophe, alerted the public to the dangers of the nuclear power program being pursued in many counties. Opposition to nuclear power became a central focus of the environmental movement in the 1970s, based upon both the environmental consequences of the program, and its strong link to the production of plutonium for nuclear weapons.

By the 1980s, environmental problems caused by human action had become regular media items. The explosion, in 1984, at the Union Carbide factory at Bhopal in India, killing 2000 people and maiming 20,000 more, raised the issue of corporate responsibility for the environment, Union Carbide being forced to pay US$470 million compensation (Hodgson, 1996). Even though the plant is no longer used, water supply pollution, high cancer rates, and ongoing claims for compensation are still issues more than 20 years later.

Global warming associated with the burning of the Earth's carbon stocks to supply the energy for an increasing consumer society and the associated release of "greenhouse gases" (GHG) gained increased media coverage in the 1980s, as did the depletion of the ozone layer. The predicted climatic changes associated with global warming, and the increased risk of melanoma or skin cancer resulting from ozone depletion, became issues of human welfare. Disquiet was also being voiced by NGOs over the rate of depletion of the most biodiverse ecosystem in the world, tropical rain forests, for the purposes of agriculture and logging. Nuclear power remained an ongoing concern. In 1986, the world experienced its worst nuclear disaster to date with the meltdown of the nuclear reactor at Chernobyl in the Ukraine, the effects of the nuclear fall out being felt across Europe. One year later, the "European Year of the Environment" was held in the European Union. In 1987, the World Commission on Environment and Development (WCED) report "Our Common Future" was published. Also known as the Brundtland Report (after Mrs. Gro Harlem Brundtland, the chairperson of the commission), it emphasized a reevaluation of global resources, and advocated development based upon sustainable principles to arrest degradation of the environment. This seminal document mobilized global public and private sector attention towards the concept of "sustainable development."

During the 1990s, campaigns for the rights of animals and against animal experimentation became more vocal and violent. Protests against road building became a focus for environmental campaigners in the UK and other European countries as concerns grew over the pace of the loss of countryside and nature grew. Green politics in Europe gained increasing recognition through formal political routes, notably the formation of a governing red–green coalition in Germany, and by the end of the decade green politicians were in charge of the environment ministries of Germany, France, Italy, and Finland (Bowcott et al., 1999). Concerns over the practices employed by farmers were also heightened with the outbreak of bovine spongiform encephalopathy (BSE) in the UK, which not only threatened animal life, but could also be transmitted to humans in the form of Creudtzfeld–Jakob Disease (CJD). The economic impacts of this were strongly felt by farmers as British beef exports were boycotted around the world. Worries over genetically modified crops were also raised in Europe and there has been a subsequent increased demand for organically produced vegetables, fruits, and meats. The emergence of a new "green" consumer culture represented another channeling of environmental action (Burchell and Lightfoot, 2001).

The 1990s also marked a time of collective international policy making on the environment. In 1992. in Rio de Janeiro, more than 140 countries were represented at the United Nations Conference on Environment and Development (UNCED), more commonly termed the "Earth Summit." Alongside this official event, 20,000 members of NGOs from around the world met at a separate event, the "Global Forum" (Spowers, 2002). Two successive Earth Summits followed in New York in 1997 and in Johannesburg in

2002. Although the Earth Summits have been criticized for being nothing other than sophistry to satisfy public opinion, an outcome of the summits has been two biodiversity conventions, a commission on sustainable development, and Agenda 21, which sets out guidelines for governments to follow. In 1997, the "Kyoto Protocol," the world treaty attempting to control global warming, was agreed with the aim of reducing green house emissions.

How we interact with our natural surroundings is now a major concern of global society at the beginning of the twenty-first century. The Fourth Assessment Report "Climate Change 2007" of the International Panel on Climate Change in the autumn 2007 raised wide public awareness and has gained public and private sector acknowledgement worldwide of the need to address global warming and related challenges.[2] Tourism as a phenomenon of society does not operate in a void of policy and environmental concern. In attempting to comprehend how environmental issues have relevance to tourism's interaction with natural resources it is necessary to understand the historical background of environmental change, and also to consider the meaning and value ascribed by humans to natural resources.

Natural Resources and the Tragedy of the Commons

Natural resources from an anthropocentric perspective are those that are a derivative of processes of nature and are utilized for our survival and development. There are natural resources upon which we depend for our physical survival, e.g., air and water; and others upon which we may create a false-dependency, e.g., oil. A commonly used scientific categorization is to divide natural resources into two main types: renewable and nonrenewable. Renewable resources include those that naturally regenerate and possess an infinite quality such as the wind, the seas, and forests.

According to Collins a natural resource is one: "That is replaced by natural processes in a reasonable amount of time. Soil, water, forests, plants, and animals are all renewable resources as long as they are properly conserved. Solar, wind, wave and geothermal energies are based on renewable resources" (2004: 334). Nonrenewable resources include those that do not naturally regenerate, are consequently finite in quality, and subsequently can be over extracted, e.g., oil and gas.

Hardin's (1968) "Tragedy of the Commons" parable is useful when considering how tourism can result in an overuse of natural resources. This is one of the most cited writings in environmental studies, questioning the assumption of classical economics that behavior driven by self-interest automatically acts for the greater social good. Using the analogy of an area of common land termed "the commons" on which farmers in a village are at liberty to freely graze their cattle, Hardin suggests that an existing state of equilibrium between the numbers of cows grazing on it and its ability to regenerate itself, can be threatened by the self-interest of the farmers. Specifically, one farmer may decide he wants to increase his herd's milk production, and therefore his profit, by the addition of an extra cow to his herd. While this one extra cow may not directly threaten the commons' long-term stability, the other farmers witness this action and decide that they too would like to increase the size of their herds and their subsequent profit. Ultimately the pressures placed upon the commons from the extra cattle lead to a situation of over-grazing; the commons becomes unsustainable, as the grass is not permitted to regenerate in sufficient quantities, threatening the long-term existence of the resources and the livelihoods of the farmers that are dependent upon it.

This scenario illustrates that the use of openly available natural resources based upon human behavior driven by self-interest may result in the exhaustion of the resource. Similar to the analogy of the commons, many types of natural resources that tourism typically relies upon often display characteristics of what in environmental studies are referred to as "common pool resources" (CPRs). These may be categorized by criteria of exclusion and exploitation, where exclusion is impractical on the basis of cost, and the exploitation of the resource by one person reduces the benefit for another (Ostrom et al., 1999). A major threat to the well-being of CPRs exists from the mentality of "finders keepers," viewed by Hardin (1968) as a rush to harvest and secure the benefits of the resource before someone else does so; a manifestation of behavior based upon competitiveness and self-interest. Typical CPRs used by tourism include the oceans and seas, the atmosphere, beaches, coral reefs, and mountains and it is upon these natural resources and ecosystems that the impact of tourism is often felt.

The Impact of Tourism

Healy (1994: 597) states that tourism landscapes are subject to both the "overuse problem" and the "investment incentive problem" that characterize CPRs. These problems occur on spatial scales, varying from the global to the local and are well charted in the literature on the environmental impacts of tourism (Holden, 2000; Hunter and Green, 1995; Mathieson and Wall, 1982; Mieczkowski, 1995). The threats tourism poses to CPRs originate from both overuse and inappropriate use. Sometimes tourism may be a contributor, alongside other activities to environmental problems, while on other occasions it may be the main causal factor.

On a global scale, the contribution of air transportation to energy consumption and pollution is an issue of growing concern to private- and public-sector interests, and especially for some governments and NGOs. Atmospheric pollution by air travel accounts for 3% of the total global emissions of carbon dioxide (Malone, 1998), alternatively expressed as being equivalent to 60% more than the CO_2 emissions of the 1.1 billion population of India.

Although a contested figure as a consequence of the difficulties in its measurement and scientific determination, independent scientific assessments calculate aviation's contribution to GHG emissions to be between 3.4 to 6.8% (Gössling and Peeters, 2007). The exhaust fumes of jet aircraft also contain sulfur trioxide, which is thought to contribute to the destruction of the ozone layer. Air transportation represents one of the fastest growing sources of greenhouse gas emissions and is a major threat to the natural functioning of the atmosphere. It is predicted by the OECD (2000, cited in Dubois and Ceron, 2000), that the contribution of air transportation to global warming is likely to exceed that of car transportation between 2010 and 2040. The potential threat of global warming to tourism includes the modification of climatic amenities, lack of snow for winter sports, excess heat, beach erosion, coral bleaching, and an increased incidence of malaria (Dubois and Ceron, 2000).

Tourism also affects CPRs at a local level. Tourism development can directly threaten and destroy ecological habitats, although the global scale of transformation is difficult to estimate in the absence of detailed empirical research. However, at a local level there are observed effects that tourism can have on the functioning of ecosystems. For, example tourism adversely affects coral reefs, the world's second most biodiverse ecosystem after tropical rain forests. Coral reefs are threatened by the use of coral in the construction of tourism facilities; inadequate sewage disposal systems; and the behavior of local tour enterprises, local people, and tourists. Reefs have been mined for building materials in Sri Lanka, India, Maldives, East Africa, Tonga, and Samoa (Mieczkowski, 1995). In the Red Sea, sediment runoff as a byproduct of construction from tourism; nourishment to enhance tourist beaches; and sewage and rubbish disposal associated with tourism, threaten the well-being of over an estimated 70% of the reefs off the coast of Egypt (Goudie and Viles, 1997). The irony being that the lucrative diving industry in the area is dependent upon the well-being of the reefs and their continuing biodiversity. Other problems associated with the use of coral reefs for tourism include: tourists walking upon it, divers breaking it off for souvenirs, tour operators dragging their boat anchors though it and local people breaking it off to sell or make handicrafts with. This is in accord with Hardin's (1968) analogy of the overgrazing of the commons by farmers seeking to maximize their individual gain is apparent, the major difference being the variety of stakeholders involved, a characteristic of tourism's interactions with CPRs.

Other examples of the pressures tourism can place on ecosystems include the deforestation of mountainsides, the draining of coastal wetlands, the over-extraction of water sources causing the lowering of water table levels, and disruption to the eating and breeding patterns of wildlife. Problems also arise from what is put into CPRs as a byproduct of tourism in the form of water, noise, aesthetic, and air pollution. The disposing of untreated human waste into the seas in coastal areas is a problem associated with tourism, while noise pollution can adversely affect residents in resort areas and around airports. Noise pollution associated with tourism can also affect wildlife in districts not used to a high level of human intrusion.

Localized air pollution as a consequence of the movement of extra vehicular traffic in generating, transit, and destination zones is also a problem. The aesthetic pollution of coastlines and mountain environments from overbuilding and uniform development is a further criticism that has been made of tourism. For example, nearly 40 years ago Mishan wrote: "Once serene and lovely towns such as Andorra and Biarritz are smothered with new hotels and the dust and roar of motorized traffic" (1969: 141). More recently, commenting on tourism development in the islands of Guadeloupe and Martinique, Burac states: "The most worrying problem now prevalent in the islands relates to the anarchic urbanization of the coast" (1996: 67). In summary, tourism can negatively affect CPRs through overuse, both in terms of extraction and pollution.

However, it is misleading to portray tourism purely as having a negative effect upon natural resources. Within a global economic system, which in the vast majority of cases continues to emphasize the instrumental value of natural resources, the demand for tourism can play a key role in giving an economic value to a natural resource. Such a value in turn provides resources with a conserved state for the enjoyment of tourists. Tourism may also play a significant role in raising awareness to support the management of protected areas.

The Case for Tourism as an Agent of Conservation

While nature has been a key component of recreational tourism since the periods of Romanticism and the Industrial Revolution, recent trends towards ecotourism, nature tourism, sustainable, and responsible tourism, emphasize the importance of natural resources as part of the tourism system. However, despite a range of other values carried by natural resources, including those of the recreational, scientific, aesthetic, genetic-diversity, historical, cultural-symbolization, character building, and religious (Holmes Rolston, 1988: 111), these have often been held as secondary to their market value.

Dissimilar to other kinds of economic land use, e.g., agriculture, forestry and mining, which usually require the modification or destruction of natural resources, tourism may realize the instrumental value of a natural resource in a conserved state from tourists' willingness-to-pay to view natural ecosystems and species. The fact that tourists are willing to pay to travel, use accommodation, and other services, brings varying degrees of economic benefit at a national and local level. The extent of the benefits is largely determined by the political economy of tourism development. Consequently, an economic value is given to natural resources in their conserved state. The link to sustainable tourism development is axiomatic, as summed up in a more general context by Pearce who comments: "If, on the other hand, conservation and the sustainable use of resources can be shown to be of economic

value, then the dialogue of developer and conservationist may be viewed differently, not as one of necessary opposites, but of potential complements" (1995: 15; also see Mbaiwa and Stronza's [Chapter 19] discussion on sustainable tourism, plus Telfer [Chapter 9] on development studies and tourism in this *Handbook*).

While estimates of the economic value of natural resources in a conserved state given by tourism are rare, research in the Amboseli National Park in Kenya found that the economic value of a lion was US$27,000 per annum, measured against the tourists' willingness to pay to see it in its natural habitat (Boo, 1990). In terms of relative economic use, the park's net earnings from tourism were found to be 50 times higher than the most optimistic projection for agricultural use.

Although the revenues that can be obtained through tourism can help protect the environment from other more environmentally destructive development alternatives, an important *caveat* of this line of argument is that if natural habitats or wildlife are judged not to have sufficient economic value in comparison to other development options, then a pretext is set for their removal. Shackley (1996) also highlights another danger of the economic valuation process with particular regard to wildlife. There are many species of wildlife that are not attractive to tourists in the dramatic sense that elephants and lions are but which have a role to play in the ecological system of the area. By their lack of inclusion or the lack of ability to be able to value them because they are not on the tourists' itinerary of animals to view, their value will be undermined in economic terms, placing their continued survival under threat.

Environmental Ethics

While the economic case for the conservation of tourism through natural resources may in some cases be a relatively strong one, at the beginning of the twenty-first century we are being forced to reevaluate our place and obligations to nature, on the premise of our own and future generations' well-being. The growing awareness of the human ability to alter and harm nature has led to the advent of a growth in environmental ethics as a course of philosophical enquiry. Key questions include the extent of human moral obligation to the environment and the degree that the environment has "rights." As Holmes Rolston III comments: "Environmental ethics in the primary, naturalistic sense is reached only when humans ask questions not merely of prudential use but of appropriate respect and duty" (1988: 1). It is suggested that this realization that we are helped or hurt by the condition of our environment is now widely accepted in most societies. Cooper (1992) suggests that without a new environmental ethic for society, we shall plunge into catastrophe. He also advocates that a new ethic needs to pass beyond pragmatism to give a new appreciation of the place of human beings in the world.

This appreciation of our place would, as Westra (1998) observes, require that we pass beyond an anthropocentric viewpoint of the world to establish who or what may possess moral standing and have rights. Clearly associated with this principle is the type of value we attach to nature. That is do we view nature as purely a "resource" in the sense of its instrumental value or do we recognize its "intrinsic value" independent of human usage? This latter position is the one adopted by "deep" or "radical" ecologists, who argue that all forms of life have an equal right to existence and that nature has its own worth independent of humankind (Benson, 2000). Consequently, this means that living things and systems containing living things have a moral status independent of that granted to them by humans.

This acceptance of the intrinsic values of nature held by deep ecologists means that nature should be protected for its own sake and not because of its usefulness to us. It entails the giving of absolute rights to the environment. However as Walker (2000) suggests, such a position raises some interesting dilemmas. For instance, if it is the absolute right for all

living things to be free from harm, then how should the human species feed itself? Also, if the right to life is absolute, how should humans respond to the instances in nature when one animal takes the life of another? It would make little sense to prosecute a lion for killing prey that is essential for its survival. As Walker (2000) suggests, the solution to this particular issue may lie in the acceptance of rights as being "relative" rather than absolute.

The development of an environmental ethic would in the words of Singer: "[R]egard every action that is harmful to the environment as ethically dubious and those that are unnecessarily harmful as wrong" (1993: 285). Applied to tourism, this would mean our selection of recreational activities would no longer remain ethically neutral. What has previously been a matter of choice or preference now becomes an ethical decision. For example, in the knowledge that aircraft emissions are a major source of carbon dioxide emissions and contribute to the global warming that threatens the long-term survival of species and ecosystems, is it ethically correct to take holidays which are dependent upon air travel?

The Future Relationship of Tourism with Natural Resources

The tourism system does not exist in a vacuum devoid of political and economic influence. At the beginning of the twenty-first century, the consideration of our relationship with nature has gained a prominence on the global political agenda, which many environmentalists would have viewed as being inconceivable 20 years ago. The political debate is being followed by shifts in economics to incorporate the environmental costs of natural usage into economic models and the market system. Pollution charging, carbon trading, congestion charging, and calls for tax on aviation fuel are now a feature of the economic and political landscape. These political and economic changes are representative of a shifting ground in ethical consciousness, arriving at a point where many people realize that a conservation ethic is necessary for "our own and future generations" survival, even if not recognizing a wider intrinsic right of nature "to be."

In the context of tourism an ethical debate has already emerged from sections of the industry. The development of environmental codes of conduct for self-regulation, and the sponsorship of environmental prizes such as the British Airways "Tourism for Tomorrow Awards" and the Association of Independent Tour Operators (AITO) "Award for Responsible Tourism" are indicative of a higher profile for the environment, although the reasons why these initiatives have been taken are debatable. Conceivably, these initiatives are representative of the emergence of a new corporate climate that more readily incorporates environmental and social ethics as a part of organizational planning that was the case in the past. However, a reluctance to take actions that would damage the market competitiveness of businesses, as exemplified by the opposition of the International Air Transport Authority (IATA) to the proposition from the European Union and some national governments to place a tax on aviation fuel, points to inconsistencies in the approach of the industry.

The development of codes of conduct by various coordinating organizations was particularly prolific in the 1990s and they continue to represent the guiding principles of ethical operations. Typically, the codes are centered upon a conspicuous conservation ethic, the basic premise being that a clean and healthy environment is essential for the development and continuance of tourism. For example, the Canadian Tourism Industry's code of ethics adopted in 1992 states: "The Canadian Tourism Industry recognizes that the long-term sustainability of tourism in Canada depends on delivering a high quality product . . . It depends as well on the wise use and conservation of our natural resources; the protection and enhancement of our environment; and the preservation of our cultural,

historic and aesthetic resources" (Tourism Industry Association of Canada, 1992: 2; also see Smith [Chapter 34] on ethical perspectives in tourism in this *Handbook*).

In direct reference to an ethic for the environment, the Travel Industry Association of America cited in UNEP suggests that: "Green travel companies should adopt or reaffirm an ethic of environmental stewardship and a commitment to achieving greater harmony between human activities and nature," adding that they "Pay attention to the 'double bottom line' by placing equal value on ecological and fiscal considerations" (1995: 17). The Pacific Asia Travel Association's (PATA) "Code for Environmentally Responsible Tourism" also emphasizes "the need for an environmental ethic amongst all those involved in tourism" (UNEP, 1995: 18).

That this ethic should be one of conservation for human benefit is exemplified by their definition of conservation as: "Conservation: means the management of human use of the environment to yield the greatest sustainable benefit to present generations while maintaining the potential to meet the needs and aspirations of future generations." Similarly, PATA's "Code for Sustainable Tourism," adopted in 2001, urges PATA members to: "Contribute to the conservation of any habitat of flora and fauna affected by tourism" (PATA, 2004). Hotel groups have utilized environmental auditing, notably through The Charter for Environmental Action in the International Hotel and Catering Industry, as part of the International Hotel Environment Initiative (IHEI) launched in 1993. The opening sentence of this charter cited by the UNEP states: "Recognizing the urgent need to support moral and ethical conviction with practical action, we the hotel industry have established the International Hotel Environment Initiative to foster the continual upgrading of environmental performance in the industry worldwide" (1995: 13). This charter prioritizes the development of environmental auditing and management systems to address issues including energy conservation and pollution reduction.

The influence of the conservation ethic in the framework of reasoning of tourism's interaction with the environment is also emphasized by the World Tourism Organization (WTO). In their "Global Code of Ethics," Article 3, point 1 states: "All the stakeholders in tourism development should safeguard the natural environment with a view to achieving sound, continuous and sustainable economic growth geared to satisfying equitably the needs and aspirations of future generations" (WTO, 1999). However, given that the business decisions of the private sector are likely to remain to be primarily driven by market forces, the environmental ethics of consumer demand will therefore be highly influential in determining the level of action taken to ensure conservation. Consequently, the market may act as a regulatory mechanism towards conservation if it is influenced by an environmental ethic. While it can be argued that the increase in demand for "eco" and "nature" tourism is reflective of a growth in "green consumerism," we understand little about the extent to which consumers who purchase nature based tourism holidays do so because they feel they are making a genuine contribution towards conservation, or because they simply want to enjoy nature and visit "new" or "unspoilt" places.

Tourism as a facet of consumerism does not operate in a vacuum of the wider trends in society. An emerging tendency for purchasing behavior to be influenced by ethics, consequently suggests that the buying of tourism is likely to have a greater ethical component in the future. However, although customers may expect companies to demonstrate a higher ethical awareness, the degree to which an environmental ethic will influence their own behavior remains uncertain. For example, the extent to which people will be willing to forego the lure of exotic locations because of the effects of flying upon the atmosphere will be a thorough test of the depth of a society's environmental ethic. Or their willingness to wait for limited number of permits to access fragile natural areas or highly impacted protected areas, or their willingness to pay for

biodiversity conservation and technologies to manage climate change (Eagles, 2007; Paloniemi and Tikka, 2008).

Ultimately, a continued use of nature in an instrumental way will be unsustainable. At present there is little evidence to point to a valuing of nature by either the industry or the consumer that moves beyond the extrinsic. The emphasis remains upon the value of nature to our selves, whether this is expressed in economic, aesthetic, or recreational terms, rather than recognition of the intrinsic value of nature to the "right to be." Yet, at some point in the future, the benefits of consumerism pursued within an unsustainable framework will involve costs that make them no longer worth pursuing. This may manifest itself through a perception that tourism can no longer fulfill a role of contributing to an individual's well-being. For instance it may be that too many destinations are viewed as being overdeveloped, environmental quality has been lost, and participation in tourism cannot bring the rewards it once did. Environmental impacts often have direct social consequences at the local level, such as: changes in lifestyle and livelihood due to resource depletion (e.g., loss of traditional fishing practices, fish populations decline) and habitat loss (e.g., due to development), lack of access to hunting/gathering areas due to protection measures, as well as tourism-related stress on resident access to environmental goods, such as water (Fennell, 2006; Floyd and Johnson, 2002; Stonich, 1998).

As tourism researchers progress through the challenging environmental climate of the twenty-first century, much is to be gained by drawing from different disciplinary areas to develop a knowledge base on scientific and social issues related to the environmental resources that tourism depends on, as well as theoretical, ethical, practical, and policy directions. The issues go beyond conflicts over resource use, growth management, or biodiversity conservation. At the level of planning and decision making, sustainability involves making tradeoffs to address current and future needs. Much greater attention has to be focused on understanding societal values (e.g., how wilderness is valued), the diverse human–environmental relationships of various cultural groups, plus drawing upon scientific, indigenous, and local knowledge to address environmental issues (Agrawal, 1995; Berkes, 1999; Christ et al., 2003). Among others, environmental justice, political ecology, political theory, philosophy, environmental management, ecosystem management, conservation anthropology, cultural anthropology, and critical and human geography, as well as a wide range of sociological theories, are available to inform the study of tourism and natural resources.

Notes

1 A figure that is predicted to reach 1.6 billion by 2020 (WTO, 2003). Also see UNWTO (2007) *World Tourism Barometer,* 5(3) for regional trends and outlooks (2007/2008). Retrieved April 26, 2008 from unwto.org/facts/eng/pdf/barometer/UNWTO_Barom07_3_en.pdf. See *UNWTO Tourism Highlights, 2007 Edition* for online facts and overview of international tourism in 2006. Retrieved April 26, 2008 from www.unwto.org/facts/menu.html.

2 See http://www.ipcc.ch/ (accessed April 28, 2008). Also see the "Acceptance Speech for the Nobel Peace Prize Awarded to the Intergovernmental Panel on Climate Change (IPCC)," delivered by R.K. Pachauri, Chairman, IPCC, Oslo, December 10, 2007. Retrieved April 28, 2008 from www.ipcc.ch/graphics/speeches/nobel-peace-prize-oslo-10-december-2007.pdf.

References

Agrawal, A. (1995). "Bridging Research and Policy Dismantling the Divide between Indigenous and Scientific Knowledge." *Development and Change,* 26(3): 413–439.

Benson, J. (2000). *Environmental Ethics: An Introduction with Readings.* London: Routledge.

Berkes, F. (1999). *Sacred Ecology: Traditional Ecological Knowledge and Resource Management.* London: Taylor & Francis.

Boo, E. (1990). *Ecotourism: The Potentials and Pitfalls* (Vol. 1). Washington, DC: World Wide Fund for Nature.

Boulding, K.E. (1973). "The Economics of the Coming Spaceship Earth." In H.E. Daly (Ed.), *Toward a Steady-State Economy.* San Francisco, CA: W.H. Freeman and Company.

Bowcott, O., Traynor, I., Webster, P. and Walker, D. (1999). "Analysis: Green Politics." *The Guardian* (London), March 11.

Burac, M. (1996). "Tourism and Environment in Guadeloupe and Martinique." In L. Briguglio, R. Butler, D. Harrison, and W.L. Filho (Eds.), *Sustainable Tourism in Islands & Small States: Case Studies* (pp. 63–74). London: Pinter.

Burchell, J. and Lightfoot, S. (2001). *The Greening of the European Union?: Examining the EU's Environmental Credentials.* London: Continuum.

Carson, R. (1962). *Silent Spring.* Boston, MA: Houghton Mifflin.

Christ, C., Hillel, O., Matus, S. and Sweeting, J. (2003). *Tourism and Biodiversity: Mapping Tourism's Global Footprint.* Washington, DC: United Nations Environment Program and Conservation International.

Collins (2004). *Dictionary of Geography.* Glasgow: HarperCollins.

Cooper, D.E. (1992). "The Idea of Environment." In D.E. Cooper and J.A. Palmer (Eds.), *The Environment in Question: Ethics and Global Issues* (pp. 165–180). London: Routledge.

Dalton, R.J. (1993). Cited in Burdell, J. and Lightfoot, S. (2001). *The Greening of the European Union?: Examining the EU's Environmental Credentials.* London: Continuum.

Dubois, G. and Ceron, J.P. (2000). "A la recherche d'une éthique du tourisme." *Cahiers Espaces,* 67: 10–29.

Eagles, P. (2007). "Global Trends Affecting Tourism in Protected Areas." In R. Bushell and P. Eagles (Eds.), *Tourism in Protected Areas: Benefits Beyond Boundaries* (pp. 27–43). Wallingford: CAB International.

Fennell, D. (2006). *Tourism Ethics.* Clevedon: Channel View.

Floyd, M. and Johnson, C. (2002). "Coming to Terms with Environmental Justice in Outdoor Recreation: A Conceptual Discussion with Research Implications." *Leisure Sciences,* 24: 59–77.

Gössling, S. and Peeters, P. (2007). "It Does Not Harm the Environment! An Analysis of Industry Discourses on Tourism, Air Travel and the Environment." *Journal of Sustainable Tourism*, 15(4): 402–417.

Goudie, A. and Viles, H. (1997). *The Earth Transformed: An Introduction to Human Impacts on the Environment*. Oxford: Blackwell.

Hardin, G. (1968). "The Tragedy of the Commons." *Science*, 162: 1243–1248.

Healy, R. (1994). "The 'Common Pool' Problem in Tourism Landscapes." *Annals of Tourism Research*, 21: 596–611.

Hodgson, G. (1996). *People's Century*. London: BBC Books.

Holden, A. (2000). *Environment and Tourism*. London: Routledge.

Holmes Rolston III (1988). *Environmental Ethics: Duties to and Values in the Natural World*. Philadelphia: Temple Press.

Hunter, C. and Green, H. (1995). *Tourism and the Environment: A Sustainable Relationship?* London: Routledge.

Malone, P. (1998). "Pollution Battle Takes to the Skies." *The Observer* (London), November 8.

Mathieson, A. and Wall, G. (1982). *Tourism: Economic, Physical and Social Impacts*. Harlow: Longman.

Meadows, D.H. (1972). *Limits to Growth: A Report for the Club of Rome Project on the Predicament of Mankind*. New York: Universe Books.

Mieczkowski, Z. (1995). *Environmental Issues of Tourism and Recreation*. Lanham, MD: University Press of America.

Mishan, E.J. (1969). *The Costs of Economic Growth*. Harmondsworth: Penguin.

Nelissen, N., Van der Straaten, J. and Klinlers, L. (1997). *Classics in Environmental Studies: An Overview of Classic Texts in Environmental Studies*. The Hague: International Book.

OECD (2000). *Sustainable Tourism: Sector Case Stuffy Series*. Draft final report on Household Tourism Travel Patterns. Report No. ENV/EPOC/GEE1(2000)5/REVI, November 15. Paris: OECD.

Ostrom, E., Burger, J., Field, C., Norgaard, R. and Policansky, D. (1999). "Revisiting the Commons: Local Lessons, Global Challenges." *Science*, 284: 278–282.

Paloniemi, R. and Tikka, P.M. (2008). "Ecological and Social Aspects of Biodiversity Conservation on Private Lands." *Environmental Science and Policy*, 11(4): 336–346.

PATA (2004). "APEC/PATA Code for Sustainable Tourism." Retrieved May 30, 2008 from www.pata.org/patasite/index.php?id=72.

Pearce, P. (1995). *Blueprint 4: Capturing Global Environmental Value*. London: Earthscan.

Shackley, M. (1996). *Wildlife Tourism*. London: International Thomson Press.

Singer, P (1993). *Practical Ethics* (2nd edition.). Cambridge: Cambridge University Press.

Spowers, R. (2002). *Rising Tides: A History and Future of the Environmental Movement*. Edinburgh: Canongate.

Stonich, S.C. (1998). "Political Ecology of Tourism." *Annals of Tourism Research*, 25(1): 25–54.

Tourism Industry Association of Canada (1992). *Code of Ethics*. Ottawa: Tourism Industry Association of Canada.

UNEP (1995). *Environmental Codes of Conduct for Tourism. Technical Report: 29*. Paris: United Nations Environmental Program.

Wall, G. and Mathieson, A. (2007). *Tourism: Change, Impacts and Opportunities*. New York: Prentice Hall.

Walker, J. (2000). *Environmental Ethics*. London: Hodder and Stoughton.

Westra, L. (1998). Environment and Environmental Ethics. In P.H. Werhane and E.R. Freeman (Eds.), *Encyclopedic Dictionary of Business Ethics* (pp. 205–208). Oxford: Blackwell.

World Commission on Environment and Development (1987). *Our Common Future*. Report of the Brundtland Commission. Oxford: Oxford University Press.

WTO (1999). *Global Code of Ethics for Tourism*. Madrid: WTO.

WTO (2003). *Tourism Highlights (Edition 2003)*. Madrid: World Tourism Organization.

13

Tourism: A Strategic Business Perspective

Nigel Evans

Introduction

Although the antecedents of modern tourism can be traced back to Thomas Cook in 1850s Britain (Hamilton, 2006; Withey, 1998), as a highly structured sector of many economies it can be viewed as a creation of more recent times. Its rise has been traced by a number of authors, including Gee et al. (1997) and Holloway and Taylor (2006). Since the early 1950s the growth of tourism, both domestically in the developed countries and internationally, has been phenomenal in its scale, and remarkably resilient to periodic economic and political adversity. In product life cycle terms (Evans et al., 2003: 138–141) and taking a global perspective, international tourism might be categorized as having passed through the "introductory" phase into the "growth" phase. The number of international arrivals, for example, has risen from a mere 25 million international arrivals in 1950 to an estimated 806 million in 2005, corresponding to an average annual growth rate of 6.5% (WTO, 2008). As many more countries and new consumers are being drawn into the international tourism net, further growth is to be expected before "maturity" is reached.

Such growth will be uneven, spatially and temporally, and is likely to take place against the backdrop of a post-9/11 world combined with dramatic changes in the business environment. This creates both managerial and marketing opportunities and dilemmas for private-sector leaders and public-sector policymakers. Given the dominance and drive of the private sector in the development of tourism and the growth in the services that support this, a business management approach to tourism studies has evolved over the past 25 years or so. It has arguably become a dominant frame for teaching tourism in higher education institutes. Tourism is frequently referred to as an "industry" within this context and is framed by the practical needs of organizations seeking commercial success to understand not only the actual business changes taking place, but also to have an understanding of the underlying characteristics of the industry. Such characteristics raise a number of managerial issues, which, if not unique, are certainly highly distinctive.

Managers working within the industry, policymakers, regulators, and others concerned with the industry's continuing development need not only to be knowledgeable about these characteristics and issues, but also to recognize the potential managerial responses that are possible and the impact they might have. These managerial actions and responses often fall within one of the recognized functional areas of business: marketing, human resources, accounting, finance, operations management, or the emerging academic field of strategic management.

This chapter concentrates primarily on the applied business dimensions of human resources, marketing, and strategic management in tourism. This is not to underplay accounting, financial, and operational concerns but it is argued that the accounting and financial issues are normally of a more generic type which may be common to many industries (Evans et al., 2003). The operational management issues can be viewed as being highly context specific, varying greatly according to the type, location, and scope of the business, and are thus beyond the scope of this chapter. They are, however, discussed in Sharpley (2002), Cooper et al. (2004), and Holloway and Taylor (2006). Neither is it to ignore the "alternative" critical and cultural narratives within business schools that attempts to temper the mainstream business education curricula and research programs; consider, for instance the area of critical accounting (Broadbent, 2002; Oguri, 2002). Tourism studies within business schools is predominantly an applied mainstream discourse, and will be addressed as such in this chapter.

A Business Approach to Tourism—A Disciplinary Dilemma?

Since its entry into mainstream higher education the study of tourism has attracted debate regarding its disciplinary status and the advantages and disadvantages of various approaches to its understanding. The debate has primarily focused upon the conceptualization of tourism (Faulkner and Ryan, 1999) and specifically on whether or not tourism should be treated as a distinct discipline. The articulation of this debate continues to reveal division of opinion (Evans, 2001). On the one hand, authors such as Leiper (1981), Jovicic (1988), Comic (1989), and Rogozinski (1985) have advocated that tourism should be treated as a distinct discipline. Others, on the other hand, maintain that tourism as an area of study fails to meet the necessary criteria in order to be treated as a distinct discipline (Dann et al., 1988; Echtner and Jamal, 1997; Gunn, 1987; Jafari, 1990; Morley, 1990; Pearce, 1993; Pearce and Butler, 1993; Ritchie and Goeldner, 1994; Tribe, 1997).

Jafari (1990), for instance, argues that four platforms of tourism studies have emerged chronologically but also that they are not mutually exclusive. The "knowledge based" platform, the last of the four identified, aims to study tourism holistically, in so doing, it strives for the formation of a scientific body of knowledge in tourism while maintaining bridges with other platforms (Jafari, 1990). Echtner and Jamal (1997), in a wide-ranging review of the "disciplinary dilemma," argue that the knowledge-based platform is consistent with the move toward the treatment of tourism as a distinctive discipline. However, in order to reach such a position, these authors argue that tourism needs to overcome its theoretical fragmentation and research has to move towards an interdisciplinary (as opposed to a multidisciplinary) approach.

Tribe (1997) goes further when he maintains that not only is tourism not currently a discipline, but also that the search for tourism as a discipline should be abandoned. To continue to advocate that tourism should be viewed as a discipline would involve "casting adrift of important parts of tourism studies in the quest for conceptual coherence and logical consistency" (Tribe, 1997: 656). Instead, Tribe (1997), Gunn (1987), and Jafari and Ritchie (1981) argue that tourism should be treated as a "field" of study. In this way it becomes similar to housing or engineering studies (Tribe, 1997), which concentrate on particular phenomena or practices and call upon a number of disciplines to investigate and explain their areas of interest. Contrasting fields and disciplines, Henkel noted that disciplines "are held together by distinctive constellations of theories, concepts and methods" whereas fields "draw upon all sorts of knowledge that may illuminate them" (1988: 188).

Many of the concepts utilized in tourism, such as life cycle analysis, impact studies, multiplier analysis and yield management, are those that have been adapted for use in tourism but are not unique to tourism studies. They have been borrowed from other well-established theoretical paradigms, for instance, classical or neoclassical economics informs some of the views commonly presented in tourism text books (Goeldner and Ritchie, 2004). While economics, sociology, and psychology are generally perceived to be disciplines, since they represent a *way* of studying, it can be argued that tourism (as with education or leisure) is not, since it represents something *to* be studied (Tribe, 1997).

If it is accepted that tourism is a field of study rather than a discipline it has a significant consequence. It follows that many different approaches can be applied to examine the multi-faceted topic of "tourism." Mill and Morrison's (1985) first edition of *The Tourism System* presented four interconnected parts of the system (market, travel, destination, and marketing) and showed how one might study the various functions within the system. The study of tourism and the associated international travel industry in these types of texts fitted well with the business and management subject areas. The techniques and applied knowledge in the "functional" business areas of tourism, such as marketing, human resource management, accounting, finance, operations management, and the holistic study of organizations through the study of strategic management,

are, "derivative partly from the disciplines that contribute to them and partly from the world of business practice" (Henkel, 1988: 188).

Business and business schools within universities have exerted a powerful gravitational pull upon the field of tourism studies. In Tribe's words: "The tourism studies that is developing in higher education tends to be crystallizing around the business interdisciplinary approach" (1997: 653). This is because there is some coherence and structure to be observed in the field of tourism business studies and it is consistent with many employers' views as to the necessary attributes required of tourism graduates (note here that the close link between business and tourism programs manifests itself in various aspects, including internship programs, scholarship, research funding, etc.). This is not to say that other approaches to the field are not possible and indeed desirable—the complex nature of tourism impacts, local–global interdependencies, and the numerous stakeholders involved with diverse often divergent interests in tourism makes for a complex domain requiring an understanding of related social, cultural, political, and environmental issues, plus the skills to manage them. Tourism studied within disciplines such as sociology forms a small component of the overall discipline and does not appear to have formed in a unified manner. In the UK, most tourism courses situated in business schools have adopted structures that have incorporated a large business-based component (Evans, 2001).

Travel and Tourism Characteristics and Managerial Challenges

Tourism and the international travel industry that has grown up to support it are characterized by: fragmentation of ownership and control; a diversity of products and destinations; development that is often divided by public and private sectors and therefore largely uncoordinated from a planning perspective. Travel and tourism products have a number of characteristics that are of relevance to the way in which they are managed and are thus relevant to any business-oriented study of tourism. Some of these characteristics are shared with other service products, while others are, if not unique, certainly of particular relevance to travel and tourism products in particular (Evans et al., 2003). These defining features lead to particular challenges for managers and result in distinctive managerial responses that can be briefly reflected on here. In addition to the four characteristics of services that the services marketing literature discusses (intangibility, inseparability, perishability, and heterogeneity), three others that are pertinent to tourism are summarized below (interdependence, seasonality, and ownership) (Ehrlich and Fanelli, 2004).

Intangibility

The tourism product is not a physical object but an amalgam of products and "invisible" (i.e., intangible) services that results in, among other things, a tourist *experience*. This creates some unique challenges and problems for organizations operating in the sector. To overcome the purchasing uncertainties that may arise due to intangibility, managers sometimes attempt to create some form of tangible offering that potential customers can relate to, such as a DVD demonstrating the attributes of a destination, pictures of a hotel and its rooms plus amenities in brochures, advertisements, and on the Internet (e.g., a virtual tour of the hotel on a website). Following the trend commencing in the business field toward serving a new "experience economy" (Pine and Gilmore, 1999), tourism organizations are increasingly recognizing the importance of ensuring a satisfactory visitor *experience* and adopting new strategies and practices for enhancing it, such as technology-based tools for interactive learning, storytelling, etc.

Inseparability

The production and consumption of services are inseparable. To take advantage of an air flight, for example, both the traveler and the means of transportation must make the journey at the same time. The implication of this inseparability is that the consumers have direct experience of the production of the service that has profound implications for staffing, training, and the successful delivery of the service encounter.

When a physical product is purchased, the circumstances under which the product is produced and how it is delivered are usually of little relevance to the customer. In the case of a service product, however, customers are likely to be very concerned about the way in which the product is delivered; i.e., the level of customer service. At a hotel reception desk, for example, the customer is likely to notice if the receptionist is rude and mistakes can prove very costly in terms of lost future custom.

Interdependence

The business of tourism (i.e., the travel and tourism industry) can be viewed as comprising five component sectors: accommodation; attractions; transportation; travel organizers; and destination organizations (Middleton and Clarke, 2001). Each of these sectors can be further subdivided (as shown in Figure 13.1) into a range of organizational types and stakeholders within these sectors. Some organizations, such as tour operations, are operated for profit while others such as museums and national parks are often operated on a noncommercial basis.

The important point to note in this context is that the sectors are closely linked and often depend upon one another; i.e., there is an interdependence between them. The accommodation sector, for example, relies upon the transportation sector to transport guests to and from the accommodation. Similarly, the transportation and accommodation sectors

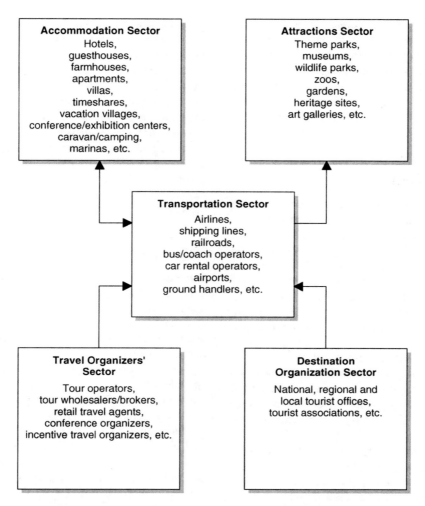

Figure 13.1   Sectors and Organizational Stakeholders/Types.
Source: Adapted from Middleton and Clarke (2001).

both rely upon the travel organizers' sector to provide them with customers. The fragmentation of tourism planning, ownership and control in the tourism "supply chain" means that if one sector fails to deliver a service it can have an adverse effect on other sectors.

Figure 13.1 shows how the various sectors in the industry "fit" together. In reality, the world is not as simple as the diagram suggests. Individual companies will often straddle two or more sectors. Some hotel companies, for example, organize inclusive tour packages and thereby also operate in the travel

organizers sector. In the late 1990s, travel companies in the UK and elsewhere undertook strategies of "vertical integration" whereby a single company may sell travel arrangements to customers (retail), provide travel arrangements (tour operations), transportation customers (airline operations), and in some cases also own accommodation in a so-called vertically integrated structure. Similarly, consolidation into larger operating units has seen the process of "horizontal integration" occurring. In this case companies, such as Air France and KLM airlines, have joined together to derive benefits such as economies of scale (see Debbage and Gallaway [Chapter 32] in this *Handbook*).

The challenge for managers is to coordinate different aspects of the tourist supply chain so that the tourist can derive benefits from each of the constituent parts even though they may be under different ownership.

Perishability

Since production and consumption are simultaneous, services are instantly perishable if they have not been sold at the time of production. The empty train seat, the empty hotel bed, or the unsold holidays all represent lost opportunities, which can never be recovered. Companies cannot just keep on producing services and store them for future sales; striking the correct balance between capacity and sales (supply and demand) is extremely difficult (Bull, 1995).

The problems of perishability can be made even more acute by fluctuating demand but relatively fixed supply. Demand can vary during the day, during the week, or from season to season. Many resort hotels, for instance, are full for only a few months of the year. Capacity (supply) may be insufficient to meet demand at peak times, but in excess of what is required at slack times.

Supply is also much more difficult to alter, at least in the short term. For example, a hotel has a fixed bed-stock that it has to try and fill. The management challenge is to make sure that the company is operating at full capacity for as much of the time as possible. To be successful, the company will need carefully designed strategies to stimulate demand and "smooth out" occupancy levels and seasonal variations (e.g., by implementing appropriate pricing strategies).

Seasonality

Bull (1995: 44) argued that, "Tourism has one of the most highly seasonal patterns of demand for any product, having less variation than the demand for Christmas cards or air conditioners, but more than nearly all high value individual purchases." This seasonality has implications for the price and quantity of tourism products supplied between seasons, as well as for hiring of staff (full-time, part-time, temporary, or permanent), and for profitability. One way in which management can respond to these problems of seasonality is to develop or acquire counter-seasonal businesses, for instance, to develop or to purchase businesses that operate primarily at other times of the year.

Heterogeneity

Services, unlike manufactured goods, are never identical. One hotel in a chain of hotels or one person's holiday will never be identical to another. The human element and other factors in delivering services ensures that services will be heterogeneous.

Tourism products in particular are usually "people oriented," and the human factor plays a key role. The enjoyment gained from a holiday cannot be separated from the personalities that go to make up that holiday, such as the service provided by cabin staff on a long-haul flight. Human behavior, however, is highly variable and it is difficult for a company to ensure that its employees display good customer relation skills all of the time.

To take account of this variability, managerial responses include providing potential customers with sufficient advanced information so as to mange their expectations, and an emphasis on the recruitment and training of frontline personnel to enable them to deal effectively with customers. In many cases in travel and tourism it is the heterogeneity that the customer finds attractive and can provide for competitive advantage. For example, hotel chains try hard to maintain a consistent brand image while at the same time trying to differentiate each hotel through varying design features. Managing this variability is a challenge for industry managers attempting to simultaneously deliver differentiated products and consistent service quality levels.

Ownership

When a customer buys a manufactured product ownership is transferred from seller to buyer. When a consumer buys a service he or she does not usually receive ownership of anything tangible. A car is hired, but ownership is not transferred, a hotel room is reserved for a period of time but nothing in it is ever owned by the customer (as noted above, an important part of the transaction is the intangible tourist experience). The fact that service buyers are buying only access to or use of something has important management implications. The task of building a relationship with customers and building brand loyalty often becomes more difficult. Managerial responses to this issue are, for example, reflected in the many loyalty schemes prevalent in the industry, such as the popular frequent flyer schemes operated by the world's airlines.

The Impacts of Tourism— A Business Based Perspective

Tourism is, it can be argued, different from other services in at least one important respect. Tourism is highly visible as well as invisible in its impact and is capable of making profound societal and cultural changes, not only to host destinations, but also to tourist "exporting" areas. The impacts that tourism has are wide-ranging, controversial and subject to widespread debate in the tourism academic literature. The focus of attention is usually upon the impact tourism has upon host destinations, but tourism can also have an impact on tourist generating areas and on the territories affected by the travel between destinations and tourist generating areas (Mason, 2008).

Krippendorf (1987), for instance, in his highly influential work "The Holiday Makers," discussed aspects of the impact tourists have on their destination. He quotes a leading Swiss researcher writing in the early 1960s who argued that since its focal point is people and not the economy, tourism can be one of the most important means, especially in developing countries, of bringing nations closer together and of maintaining good international relations. Krippendorf takes a contrary view when he argues that no communication can develop where the main reason for traveling is to get away from things, where the tourist ignores the existence of other people, where assembly line techniques are the only way of dealing with huge numbers, where profit making rules supreme, and where there are feelings of superiority and inferiority.

Any discussion on the impacts of tourism from a business perspective tends to center on mitigating the effects of so-called "mass tourism," but more is being addressed in recent years on smaller scale alternatives to such as ecotourism and other forms of low-impact and responsible travel (Getz and Page, 1997). Mass tourism has been defined as, "a phenomenon of large-scale packaging of standardized leisure services at fixed prices for sale to a mass clientele" (Poon, 1993: 32). Indeed, Poon (1993: 17–21) argues that a "new tourism" is emerging whose characteristics tend towards being more differentiated and less "mass" oriented. The signs of the emerging new tourism that Poon describes include:

- The growing demand for "independent" non packaged holidays.
- The growing demand for choice and flexibility.
- Information technologies, such as computer reservations systems (CRS) and the Internet are rapidly diffusing and allowing customers to deal directly with companies and organizations as a means to flexibly make travel arrangements as an alternative to "packaged" holidays.
- The rate of growth of the traditional sun package tour business is slowing.
- There is increasing environmental planning and control of tourism in host countries such as Belize and Bermuda.
- There is an increasing "segmentation" of travel markets to cater for differing lifestyle characteristics.
- The travel behavior and motivation of tourists are changing with increasing short breaks and activity oriented travel.

The relevance of the preceding discussion on the impacts of tourism to managers is two-fold. First, consumers are becoming sensitive to the impacts of what they consume, whether it is the effect that the detergents they use might have on the environment or the impacts that tourism has, particularly on the host community (Getz and Page, 1997). In successfully managing their tourism products, managers, and marketers must be sensitive to this issue in a way in which they often failed to be in the past. Second, while mass tourism would appear to be here to stay, nevertheless changes are taking place in the marketplace. Consumers are becoming more knowledgeable, experienced, and sophisticated in their tastes and rather more complicated to understand. Many new forms of tourism have emerged to suit the needs of this vastly more discriminating travel market, including wine tourism, culinary/food tourism, dark tourism, extreme adventures, and various specialized forms of learning-based travel for a growing segment of active older population as the baby boomers continue to age with increased longevity. Health and wellness travel continues to evolve from spa resorts to providing medical services, and medical travel is another new trend that is expected to grow (Connell, 2006).

Technology, while creating some barriers to learning and adoption, has also democratized decision making and control over product development (see Gretzel and Fesenmeier [Chapter 31] on IT and Tourism in this *Handbook*). Managers have to research and attempt to understand these changes that are undoubtedly taking place. Furthermore, in the highly competitive travel and tourism industry, they have to design their products to appeal to these changing tastes and then to promote, distribute and price the products appropriately.

'Adding Value'—A Key Consideration for Tourism Managers

Acknowledging that tourism businesses are different in a number of ways from businesses that produce physical products they are also different in emphasis from other service industries. These differences lead to important considerations which managers of tourism businesses have to consider and result in various distinctive managerial responses to the issues faced.

In all industries, including the component sectors of travel and tourism, some organizations are more successful than others. The superior performers conceivably possess something special that competitors do not have access to that allow them to outperform their rivals. The sources of "competitive advantage" lie in combining the superior application of competences (skills) and the deployment of superior resources (assets) in creating value for consumers. Sustainability (the terminology is used here in a business context) is achieved when the advantage resists erosion by competitive behavior (Porter, 1985). Thus, in order to achieve the goal of competitive advantage, managers must have an understanding of how value is added in an organization and a number of approaches have been used in the emergence of a new managerial paradigm—"strategic management."

Strategic Management in a Tourism Context

The overall aim of strategy and strategic management is to develop an effective framework for thinking ahead—for thinking strategically (Evans et al., 2003). Since the 1960s, the subject area has been widely considered as a topic of academic interest and a vast literature in the field has been assembled, including influential early works from writers such as Chandler (1962) and Ansoff (1965) through to widely quoted texts such as Porter (1980, 1985), Kay (1993), and Hamel and Prahalad (1994), Grant (2002), Mintzberg (1994) and Mintzberg et al. (2002), and Johnson et al. (2008).

As the subject has matured differing schools of thought have emerged. McKiernan (1997) usefully characterizes four such schools, which are not, however viewed as being mutually exclusive or as encompassing all contributions.

- The "planning and practice" school (See for example, Ackoff, 1970; Argenti, 1974) deals primarily with the "fit" between the external and the internal environments, as well as between strategy formulation and strategy implementation (See for example, Mintzberg, 1994; Mintzberg et al., 2002).
- The "learning" school (see, for example, Johnson, 1988; Wildavsky, 1973) assumes that the environment is so unpredictable and complex that models do not present any protection from the constant buffeting organizations have to face. In this school organizational adaptability is stressed in recognition of the unpredictable environmental circumstances faced by organizations.
- In the "positioning" school, often associated with the work of Michael Porter (1980, 1985), it is differences in market structure that govern any differences in strategy. In deciding on price organizations could decide to either to "differentiate" their products or adopt a "cost leadership" approach—to do neither is to be "stuck in the middle and risk failure."
- The "resource based" view of the firm' (See for example, Grant, 1991; Prahalad and Hamel, 1990; Rumelt, 1984; Wernerfelt, 1984) sees understanding the acquisition and interaction of scarce resources, along with human intervention to create competencies which are difficult to replicate, as being the key to corporate success.

The subject is also widely taught as part of hospitality and tourism related courses but has received relatively little attention in the specialist literature. Some papers and a limited range of texts have, however, been developed, including: Athiyaman (1995), Athiyaman and Robertson (1995), Evans et al. (2003), Go and Pine (1995), Holloway with Taylor (2006), Moutinho (2000), Olsen et al. (1998), Phillips and Moutinho (1998), Schwaninger (1986), Teare and Boer (1991), and Tribe (1997). In view of this limited, but developing literature, it is difficult to disagree with the assertion of two leading researchers (Olsen and Roper, 1998: 119), when they state that ". . . whilst it is clear that there is scope

for significant development of strategy research as applied to the hospitality industry, . . . the area is hardly 'embryonic' (an accusation made by Taylor and Edgar, 1996)."

Recent years have seen the strategy process and related frameworks applied in a more focused way to certain aspects of tourism. For example, Buhalis (2002) connects the strategic management analysis with the emergence of electronic commerce in tourism while Murphy and Murphy (2004) consider the management of tourist communities in the context of a strategic conceptualization.

Strategic Management Frameworks for Tourism

Measuring organizational success and implementing effective strategies for future success represent continuous challenges for managers, researchers, and consultants. Frameworks have increasingly been developed which purport to represent not merely a way of measuring the success of an organization but go further in that they offer managers a "road map" by which they can manage. In particular they focus on the way in which a strategic vision can be realized, and strategic planning and implementation can occur (Johnson et al., 2008; Lynch, 2003; Mintzberg et al., 2002).

One of the most widely used approaches—the "value chain analysis" (Porter, 1985)—seeks to provide an understanding of how much value an organization's activities add to its products and services compared to the costs of the resources used in their production. Although, it has been applied widely in the manufacturing sector, several writers have applied the model successfully to a services setting. Poon (1993), for example, adapts the model to the travel and tourism industry. Value chain analysis seeks to help managers understand how effectively and efficiently the activities of their organization are configured and coordinated.

In relation to the service industries in particular, during the 1990s a team of researchers at Harvard University introduced an alternative framework. The Service Profit Chain (Heskett et al., 1997) assesses the sources of profitability and growth in labor dominated service firms. Such companies are those where labor is both an important component of total cost and capable of differentiating the firm's service from that of its competitors.

The Service Profit Chain's purpose is to provide managers with a framework to help them manage by enabling them to focus on (predominantly) quantifiable measures that lead to financial performance measures. In this respect the model is similar to the "Balanced Scorecard" approach to strategy developed by Kaplan and Norton (2001). Focusing as it does on the service delivery aspects of performance, the model is useful but does not represent a holistic approach to managing service-based organizations.

The Service Profit Chain (shown in Figure 13.2) emphasizes the roles of employees internally to the organization, the way in which services are delivered and the targeting of marketing to customers' needs as key drivers of profitability. Thus the ways in which the organization effectively utilizes its human resources and the ways in which it positions its products so that they appeal to particular target markets are two of the most important aspects of an organization's competitive strategy. The remainder of this chapter will thus focus on these crucial aspects in the management of successful tourism businesses.

Human Resources as a Key Differentiator in Tourism Businesses

People are an important resource to most organizations, but in service-based organizations in particular, it is often the human resources; i.e., people that represent the key factor in delivering successful performance. As Richard Lynch puts it "There are some industries where people are not just important but they are, arguably *the key factor* for successful performance, as for example: in leisure and tourism, where a company has a

direct, intangible interface that relies on individual employees to give interest and enjoyment to customers" (2003: 254).

Tourism is a labor-intensive service sector in which the human factor is often the key differentiator between different competing organizations. Pursuing this theme, Tom Baum (1995) considers the experience of the guest or consumer within the tourism industry to be both highly intense and intimate in a way rarely replicated in other service industries. Furthermore, their interactive experience is commonly within the industry's frontline staff who often are those who have the lowest status, are the least highly trained and are the poorest paid employees and several authors, including Baum (1995), Choy (1995), and Nickson (2000), have investigated these characteristics.

In labor-intensive industries (such as tourism) employees or groups of employees are critical to strategic success. These are the people that the organization's success may have been built upon in the past and it is likely that the existing structures continue to be centered on them. In some organizations, the human resources (employees) thus represent what is often referred to in the literature as a "critical success factor" (CSF) (See for example, Johnson et al., 2008: ch. 3). In some cases the CSFs may be found on the board of directors giving strategic direction to the company as a whole. In others, they might be found in research, developing the new products upon which the future success will be built. The CSFs might also include a unique location, a brand image, an enviable reputation, a legally protected patent or license, a unique production process or technology, but in tourism it is often the people employed by the organization that can make a real difference to overall success. Certain marketing personnel or operations managers might also be critical in some businesses. For example, in some tour operators the management of the operational aspects of tours may involve local knowledge and experience of destination areas and individual suppliers. This knowledge and experience may be held by key

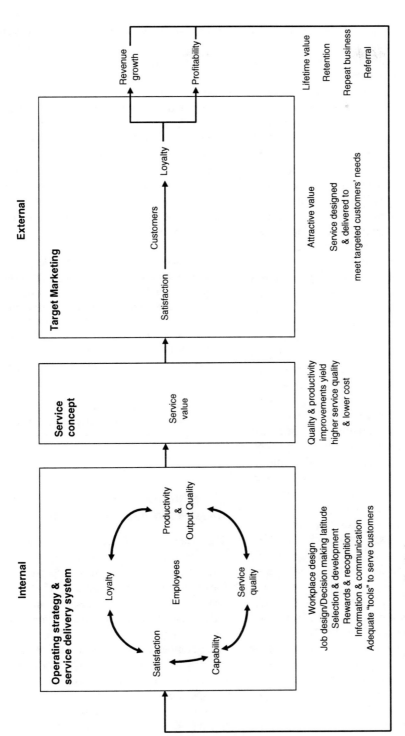

Figure 13.2 The Service Profit Chain.
Source: Adapted from Heskett et al. (1997).

individuals whose sudden loss to a company could cause operational problems.

Well-managed companies try to reduce the inherent risk involved in losing key employees or losing optimal functioning of such strategically important personnel. To minimize the risk one approach taken to a CSF is to defend it. This usually takes the form of "locking it in" to ensure that the advantage is maintained or that competitors are prevented from gaining the same advantage. If the CSF is in the form of a human resource, this might involve contractual arrangements providing financial incentives, long periods of notice to leave the company, providing the right working environment for employees or, as Lashley (1995) and Jones and Davies (1991) describe, through the "empowerment" of employees.

Worldwide employment in tourism is forecast to grow to 251.6 million jobs (one in every 11 jobs) according to the World Travel and Tourism Council (WTTC, 2000). The industry presents managers with specific challenges insofar as it employs a large proportion of young and female employees and has a large number of part-time and seasonal workers and is often characterized by: high staff turnover rates; recruitment difficulties; and poor levels of training and low pay. In such circumstances the challenge to managers is to recruit and retain well-motivated employees. In order to do this, employers may offer more training opportunities, provide higher levels of pay and bonuses, and pay attention to the design of jobs and roles, as well as changes to employee profiles (e.g., diversity in the workplace, outsourcing or increasing home-based employees) (Evans et al., 2003: ch. 4; Hoque, 1999; Kelliher and Johnson, 1997).

In relation to the high staff turnover often evident in tourism organizations, one study in the USA (Woods et al., 1998) for example, found that annual staff turnover in the hotel sector was running at 51.7% for "front-line" employees (although the figures were somewhat lower for supervisory and managerial staff). As a counter-balance to some of the negative aspects of the industry, it must be said that the industry is often seen as an attractive industry in which to work. Staff often have access to concessionary travel and accommodation rates, opportunities are presented for meeting people and seeing something of the world, and many employees are situated in attractive surroundings. In such circumstances the challenge to managers is to recruit, motivate, and retain well-motivated employees (Lucas, 1997: 99–113). In order to do this employers may offer more training opportunities, provide higher levels of pay and bonuses and pay attention to the design of jobs and roles through:

- Job enlargement—employees' jobs are made more worthwhile and interesting in that they are given a wider variety of tasks to carry out.
- Job rotation—employees rotate jobs between them so that teamwork is encouraged, knowledge and skills are gained and everyone has to take a share of less popular tasks.
- Job enrichment—employees are given a greater deal of discretion or *empowerment* to make decisions.
- Job sharing—employees' jobs are shared between two or more employees thereby sharing burdens and responsibilities.

The Management of the Guest–Employee Encounter

The management of the guest (or customer)–employee encounter remains one of the most difficult but ultimately most important tasks for tourism managers (Baum, 1997). Thus, in fast moving markets, especially in service industries which are relatively "labor intensive," it may be that the key drivers in delivering commercial success are: the ability and knowledge of people; the ability of people to learn; and the ability of people to adapt to change (Pettigrew and Whipp, 1991).

Writers on service quality have suggested that the proof of service (quality) is in its flawless performance (Berry and Parasuraman, 1991); this is a concept similar to the notion of "zero defects" which is often discussed in a manufacturing context. From the customer's point of view, the most immediate evidence of service quality occurs in the service encounter or "the moment of truth" when the customer interacts with the organization (Augustyn and Ho, 1998; Bitner et al., 1994). The derivation of the term "moment of truth" is often attributed to Jan Carlzon (1987), a past President of Scandinavian Airline Systems (SAS) who used the terminology to describe every point of contact that a customer, or potential customer, has with the organization in question.

As both Baum (1995) and Ryan (1996) have argued, the tourism industry presents particular challenges in the management of "moments of truth" because of the "fragmentation" of the travel experience through different points in the journey from home to elsewhere and back. The mix of physical "product" (e.g., a souvenir, or ticket to a theme park) and it's intangible and social-psychological aspects (e.g., visiting a theme park with one's children, or giving of souvenirs as a gift) has led to the recognition that the tourism "product" is a complex amalgam that spans various moments between home and the destination. The concept of the "moment of truth" as a manifestation of the guest (or customer)–employee encounter clearly has applicability throughout the three parts (traveler generator region, transit route region and tourist destination region) of what Leiper (1981) has called "the tourism system."

Baum, building on Leiper's representation has produced a model of "moments of truth" in relation to the wide range of organizations that go to make up the tourism system. The model (Figure 13.3) recognizes that "moments of truth" need not carry equal weighting; i.e., that some will be more important to customers than others "so that as far as the guest is concerned . . . a positive or negative experience in one area may elicit a very different response to a similar experience elsewhere in the guest cycle" (1997: 101).

The model provides through its vertical axis a measure (albeit rather crude and subjective) of the intensity and therefore the importance of the interaction to customers. In so doing the model allows tourism managers who are responsible for the tourists' experience to attempt to predict those areas of greatest potential impact and consequently to recognize those areas on which resources might be focused.

The temporal and spatial scales involved for tourism businesses are local–global in range and highly interrelated. Added to a post-9/11 world in which safety and security concerns influence travel, are addition risk concerns such as physical/nature-based hazards, and disease. Sustainability issues will also affect service provision and the tourist experience. Following the turn from product to services, and then to relationship marketing and societal marketing, marketing has been shifting its focus towards sustainable marketing and "green" product development. More recently, study areas such as social entrepreneurship have begun to gain attention as climate change and conservation concerns, as well as new social movements, intrude on mainstream objectives of profitability and growth. Stakeholder management (and stakeholder theory), inter-organizational collaboration, conflict management, integrated planning processes, environmental auditing and environmental management systems, corporate social responsibility, monitoring strategies, and certification schemes will be essential considerations for tourism managers (Font and Harris, 2004; Honey, 2002).

Strategic Marketing for Competitive Advantage

The way in which an organization's products relate to its markets is one of the most important aspects of competitive strategy, the aim of which is to gain a competitive advantage over competitors. The idea of a market as a place where buyers and sellers come together can apply to both inputs of resources and outputs of services. Output (or product) markets are those in which an organization competes for sales, while resource markets

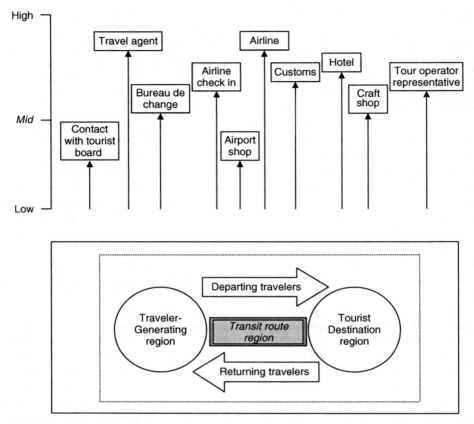

Figure 13.3   A Model of the Tourist Experience and Moments of Truth.
Source: Adapted from Baum (1997).

are those in which an organization competes for its resource inputs. In both cases, a tourism organization attempts to put itself into a position where it achieves an advantage over competitors through the strategy it adopts.

A company may have great technical and operational capabilities but these capabilities only become a source of competitive advantage when such "distinctive capabilities" are applied in the marketplace (Kay, 1993). Hence it is of critical importance that managers are able to define and understand the markets in which they are operating (see also Fletcher [Chapter 10] in this *Handbook*). Building on this theme, Horner and Swarbrooke (1996) consider markets in a tourism context and assert that success in the development of tourism, leisure, and hospitality products lies in the ability to match product offerings with the range of specific benefits sought by tourists. The authors concede however, that the matching of the two is a challenging process for managers.

Modern management writers view marketing less as one of the main constituent departments of an organization and more as a holistic, competitive orientation for a business (generally described as the firm's "marketing orientation"). In such a way marketing takes on a strategic role for an organization and indeed the "strategic" dimension to marketing reflects its growing impingement on traditional "strategic management" territory (Fyall and Garrod, 2005). Authors such as Faulkner (1998), Lumsdon (1997), and Papadopoulos (1989) discuss strategic approaches to marketing in a tourism context. However, to the most widely quoted author on the subject, Kotler (1997), the heart of modern strategic marketing can be described as "STP Marketing" namely: Segmenting, Targeting and Positioning. In STP or "Target Marketing" the seller distinguishes the major *segments* (identifiable parts) of the market, *targets* one or more of these segments and *positions* products and marketing programs so that they will appeal to the needs and wants of these chosen target segments.

Market Segmentation

Markets are rarely completely homogenous. Within markets there are groups of customers with requirements that are similar, and it is this similarity of needs and wants that distinguishes one market segment from another. By considering the extent to which the segments should be treated differently from others, and which ones will be chosen to serve, organizations can develop *target markets* and gain a focus for their commercial activity. As Moutinho states "the concept of market segmentation arises from the recognition that consumers are different. Market segmentation is a strategy of allocation of marketing resources given a heterogeneous tourist population" (2000: 12).

There is no single way of segmenting a market. Each organization has to choose *bases*, or variables, that are appropriate in respect of its consumers. Furthermore, the literature provides various ways of differentiating between bases. Middleton and Clarke (2001) for example, refer to seven "bases": the purpose of travel; buyer needs, motivations and benefits sought; buyer behavior/characteristics of product usage; demographic, economic and geographic characteristics; psychographic characteristics; geodemographic profile; and price. When the possible range of segments have been identified and the characteristics of each of the segments has been analyzed, the tourism organization then has to decide which market segments to target using criteria such as; market size; market growth; and how easy it is to access each identified segment.

Product Positioning

All organizations need to differentiate themselves and their products, from competing organizations and products. "Product positioning" is the way in which a product or a brand is perceived in relation to preferences of segments of the market, and in relation to competitive products. The perceptual image that a consumer holds about an organization or product is important because a positive and favorable image can lead to the consumer purchasing products from the organization in question, whereas a negative image inevitably results in consumers looking elsewhere for their product purchases. Image management and impression management continue to be important tasks.

Thus tourism strategists and (marketers) must seek to match the attributes of their product, and buyers' perceptions of those attributers, with the needs and priorities of customers in that segment. A number of authors have considered positioning in a travel and tourism context (see, for example, Connell, 1994; Dev et al., 1999; Harris, 1988; Lovelock et al., 1999).

The development of the mid-market Courtyard hotel brand by the US-based Marriott Corporation provides an example of product positioning (Crawford-Welch, 1994). Research allowed Marriott to identify a niche in the mid-level market, which was not being filled by any hotel concept at that time. Marriott developed a product positioning statement for the hotel concept, which stated that the Courtyard product was to serve business travelers who wanted moderately priced hotels of consistent high quality and pleasure travelers who wanted an affordable room that was a safe base of operations. A basic conceptual framework for the product was then developed. The product would be positioned to have a number of features in that it would: be tightly focused for the transient mid-priced market segment; be relatively small; serve a limited menu, be a standardized product managed in clusters (i.e., five to eight hotels in one area); with the Marriott name attached for recognition and a "halo effect."

From Firm Level to Destination Level

The principles of positioning and repositioning can also be applied to tourist destinations and a large literature has developed around the subject area (see, for instance, Ahmed, 1994; Alford, 1998; Ashworth and Voogd, 1994; Bramwell and Rawding, 1996; McKercher, 1995; Morgan and Pritchard, 1998; Scott et al., 2000; Walmesley and Young, 1998). For instance, Tourism Queensland—a state government owned enterprise charged with the promotion of Queensland as a tourist destination—has over recent years promoted five key destination areas to visitors as distinctive destinations (Scott et al., 2000). This positioning strategy was initiated as a response to the emergence of a number of sub-regions, each having distinctive attributes, target markets, and a sufficiently developed tourist industry to warrant a portfolio approach to their management as destinations (see also Harrill [Chapter 25] and Ford and Peeper [Chapter 24] in this *Handbook*).

However, as Scott et al. (2000) go on to point out, destinations differ from organizations in that the assumptions of strong leadership and clear goal-driven decisions to which all participants adhere may be lacking since destinations may be viewed as conglomerates of attractions, operators and agencies which each have individual objectives. Destination branding and place marketing thus take on different levels of complexity and challenges (Ashworth and Voogd, 1994; Dev et al., 1999; Kotler, et al., 1993; Morgan and Pritchard, 1998). The highly diverse range of touristic offerings, the local to global scale and scope of tourism and the unique characteristics of the tourism "product" makes product development and marketing extremely challenging.

Conclusion

Tourism is many faceted and multidisciplinary. Its definition and conceptualization are fraught with difficulty since the industry boundaries (unlike say the automotive industry) are far from clear. These conceptual issues mean that tourism as a field of academic enquiry lends itself to study from a number of disciplinary angles, but can also be studied from a business perspective. In doing so it can be argued that tourism as a business is something to be studied; a field that draws heavily on various disciplines and a large literature has developed over the last 20 years or so which focuses on tourism as a business.

This literature has pointed to the defining characteristics of tourism which managers and researchers need to be aware of since these characteristics lead to managerial responses that need to take into account the particular and specific characteristics which tourism exhibits. In this chapter particular emphasis has been given to the human resources, marketing and strategy as key drivers of corporate success in a tourism setting. Such an emphasis reflects the distinctiveness of tourism as an industry in respect of these issues but it also reflects the growth of the literature that is far better developed in these fields than in say the operational and financial aspects of tourism businesses.

Tourism is dynamic, growing and its future course difficult to predict. Tourism as a business phenomenon is a product of economic development and so it is no accident that tourism is growing fastest where economic growth is also at its fastest, such as in South East Asia and India. Both the scale and the complexity of tourism are set to increase as more countries develop both their domestic and international tourism industries. It is necessary for managers and researchers to understand both conceptually and practically the changes that are taking place and to design policies and managerial strategies that respond to them. Moreover, the tourism "product" continues to evolve. New offerings are being developed, older ones are enhanced and repositioned (cruise travel and casino/gambling destinations like Las Vegas, for instance, have undergone makeovers). New skills will be needed to service niche products and growing market segments.

It is difficult to be precise as to the exact nature of these changes but they will include changes to tourism's products, markets and impacts and increasing levels of complexity and interaction with other sectors. Likely changes (Robinson et al., 2000) will include:

- Mass tourism being replaced by mass customization in an industry that has to cater for ever more discerning and experienced consumers.
- Increasing polarization as companies have to make the strategic choice to become complex vertically, horizontally, or, in some cases, diagonally integrated organizations or to specialize as niche players targeted at discrete market segments.
- Emerging policy and regulatory frameworks such as the move towards deregulated market structures, the privatization of state owned companies, and the removal of foreign ownership restrictions, all of which serve to lower entry and exit barriers in the industry and to increase competitive pressures.
- Competitive and resource pressures necessitating newer ways of working such as the increasing emphasis on collaborative strategy through the formation of strategic alliances, franchising and the separation of ownership of tourist assets from their management in the commercial sector and through the formation of innovative public–private partnerships to facilitate development and regeneration opportunities.
- The threat to the role of "traditional" travel agency intermediaries as new technology empowers consumers to deal through Internet-based intermediaries or directly with principals.

References

Ackoff, R.L. (1970). *A Concept of Corporate Planning*. New York: John Wiley.

Ahmed, I.S.Z. (1994). "Determinants of the Components of a State's Tourist Image and Their Marketing Implications." *Journal of Leisure and Hospitality Marketing*, 2(1): 55–69.

Alford, P. (1998). "Positioning the Destination Product—Can Regional Tourist Boards Learn from Private Sector Practice?" *Journal of Travel and Tourism Marketing*, 7(2): 53–68.

Ansoff, I. (1965). *Corporate Strategy*. New York: McGraw Hill.

Argenti, J. (1974). *Systematic Corporate Planning*. Sunbury-on-Thames: Thomas Nelson.

Ashworth, G.J. and Voogd, H. (1994). "Marketing of Tourism Places: What are we doing?" In M. Uysal (Ed.), *Global Tourist Behavior* (pp. 5–20). New York: Haworth Press.

Athiyaman, A. (1995). "The Interface of Tourism and Strategy Research: An Analysis." *Tourism Management*, 16(6): 447–453.

Athiyaman, A. and Robertson, R.W. (1995). "Strategic Planning in Large Tourism Firms: An Empirical Analysis." *Tourism Management*, 16(3): 199–205.

Augustyn, M. and Ho, S.K. (1998). "Service Quality and Tourism." *Journal of Travel Research*, 37(1): 71–75.

Baum, T. (1995). *Managing Human Resources in the European Hospitality and Tourism Industry—A Strategic Approach*. London: Chapman Hall.

Baum, T. (1997). "Making or Breaking the Tourist Experience: The Role of Human Resource Management." In C. Ryan (Ed.), *The Tourist Experience—A New Introduction* (pp. 92–111). London: Cassell.

Berry, L.L. and Parasuraman, A. (1991). *Marketing Services*. New York: The Free Press.

Bitner, M.J., Booms, B.H. and Mohr, L.A. (1994). "Critical Service Encounters: The Employee's Viewpoint." *Journal of Marketing*, 58 (October): 95–106. Reprinted in M. Gabbott and G. Hogg (Eds.) (1997), *Contemporary Services Marketing Management—A Reader* (pp. 149–170). London: The Dryden Press.

Bramwell, B. and Rawding, L. (1996). "Tourism Marketing Images of Industrial Cities." *Annals of Tourism Research*, 23(1): 201–221.

Broadbent, J. (2002). "Critical Accounting Research: A View from England." *Critical Perspectives on Accounting*, 13(4): 433–449.

Buhalis, D. (2002). *Etourism: Information Technology for Strategic Tourism Management*. London: Financial Times/Prentice Hall.

Bull, A. (1995). *The Economics of Travel and Tourism* (2nd edition.). Melbourne: Longman.

Carlzon, J. (1987). *Moments of Truth*. Cambridge, MA: Ballinger.

Connell, J. (1994). "Repositioning Forte Hotels Portfolio." *English Tourist Board Insights*, March: C43–51. London: English Tourist Board.

Connell, J. (2006). "Medical Tourism: Sun, Sea, Sand and Surgery." *Tourism Management*, 27(6): 1093–1100.

Crawford-Welch, S. (1994). "The Development of Courtyard by Marriott." In R. Teare, J.A. Mazanec, S. Crawford-Welch and S. Calver (1995), *Marketing in Hospitality and Tourism: A Consumer Focus* (pp. 166–193). London: Cassell.

Chandler, A. (1962). *Strategy and Structure.* Cambridge, MA: MIT Press.

Choy, D. (1995). "The Quality of Tourism Employment." *Tourism Management*, 16(2): 129–137.

Comic, D. (1989). "Tourism as a Subject of Philosophical Reflection." *Revue de Tourisme*, 44(2): 6–13.

Cooper, C., Fletcher, J., Gilbert, R., Wanhill, S. and Fyall, A. (2004). *Tourism Principles and Practice* (4th edition.). Harlow, UK: Longman.

Dann, G., Nash, D. and Pearce, P. (1988). "Methodology in Tourism Research." *Annals of Tourism Research*, 15: 1–28.

Dev, C.S., Morgan, M.S. and Shoemaker, S. (1998). In T. Baum and R. Mudambi (Eds.), *Economic and Management Methods for Tourism and Hospitality Research* (pp. 124–137). Chichester, UK: John Wiley.

Ehrlich, E. and Fanelli, L.A. (2004). *The Financial Services Marketing Handbook: Tactics and Techniques that Produce Results.* Princeton, NJ: Bloomberg Press.

Echtner, C.M. and Jamal, T. (1997). "The Disciplinary Dilemma of Tourism Studies." *Annals of Tourism Research*, 24(4): 868–883.

Evans, N. (2001). "The Development and Positioning of Business Related University Tourism Education: A UK Perspective." *Journal of Teaching in Travel & Tourism*, 1(1):17–36.

Evans, N., Campbell, D. and Stonehouse, G. (2003). *Strategic Management for Travel and Tourism* (pp. 28–32). Oxford: Butterworth-Heinemann.

Faulkner, B. (1998). "Developing Strategic Approaches to Tourism Destination Marketing: The Australian Experience." In W.F. Theobald (Ed.), *Global Tourism* (2nd edition.). Oxford: Butterworth-Heinemann.

Faulkner, B. and Ryan, C. (1999). "Innovations in Tourism Management Research and Conceptualization." *Tourism Management*, 20(1):3–6.

Font, X. and Harris, C. (2004). "Rethinking Standards from Green to Sustainable." *Annals of Tourism Research*, 31(4): 986–1007.

Fyall, A. and Garrod, B. (2005). *Tourism Marketing: A Collaborative Approach.* Clevedon, UK: Channel View Publications.

Gee, C.Y., Makens, J.C. and Choy, D.J.L, (1997). *The Travel Industry* (3rd edition.). New York: John Wiley.

Getz, D. and Page, S.J. (Eds.) (1997). *The Business of Rural Tourism: International Perspectives.* London: International Thomson Business Press.

Go, F. and Pine, R. (1995). *Globalization Strategy in the Hotel Industry.* London: Routledge.

Goeldner, C.R. and Ritchie, J.R.B. (2004). *Tourism: Principles, Practices, Philosophies* (10th edition.). New York: John Wiley.

Grant, R.M. (1991). "The Resource Based Theory of Competitive Advantage: Implications for Strategy Formulation." *California Management Review*, 33(Spring): 114–135.

Grant, R.M. (2002). *Contemporary Strategy Analysis: Concepts, Techniques, Applications* (4th edition.). Oxford: Blackwell.

Gunn, C.A. (1987). "A Perspective on the Purpose and Nature of Tourism Research Methods." In J.R.B. Ritchie and C. Goeldner (Eds.), *Travel, Tourism and Hospitality Research:—A Handbook for Managers and Researchers* (pp. 3–11). New York: John Wiley.

Honey, M. (2002). *Ecotourism and Certification: Setting Standards in Practice.* Washington, DC: Island Press.

Hamel, G. and Prahalad, C.K. (1994). *Competing for the Future.* Cambridge, MA: Harvard Business School Press.

Hamilton, J. (2006). *Thomas Cook: The Holiday Maker.* Stroud, UK: Sutton Publishing Ltd.

Harris, M. (1988). "Economical Positioning." *Cornell Hotel and Restaurant Administration Quarterly*, 31(2): 97–115.

Henkel, M. (1988). "Responsiveness of the Subjects in Our Study: A Theoretical Perspective." In C. Boys, J. Brennan, M. Henkel, J. Kirkland, M. Kogan, and P. Youll (Eds.), *Higher Education and Preparation for Work* (pp. 134–195). London: Jessica Kingsley.

Heskett, J.L., Sasser, W.E. and Schlesinger, L.A. (1997). *The Service Profit Chain.* New York: Simon and Schuster.

Holloway, J.C., with Taylor, N. (2006). *The Business of Tourism* (7th edition.). London: FT/Prentice Hall.

Hoque, K. (1999). "New Approaches to HRM in the UK Hotel Industry." *Human Resource Management Journal*, 9(2): 64–76.

Horner, S. and Swarbrooke, J. (1996). *Marketing Tourism, Hospitality and Leisure in Europe*. London: International Thomson Business Press.

Jafari, J. (1990). "Research and Scholarship: The Basis of Tourism Education." *Journal of Tourism Studies*, 1(1): 407–429.

Jafari, J. and Ritchie, J.R.B. (1981). "Towards a Framework for Tourism Education." *Annals of Tourism Research*, 8(1): 13–34.

Johnson, G. (1988). "Rethinking Incrementalism." *Strategic Management Journal*, 9: 75–81.

Johnson, G., Scholes, K. and Whittington, R. (2008). *Exploring Corporate Strategy* (8th edition.). London: Financial Times/ Prentice Hall.

Jones, P. and Davies, A. (1991). "Empowerment: A Study of General Mangers at Four Star Hotel Properties in the UK." *International Journal of Hospitality Management*, 10(3): 211–217.

Jovicic, Z. (1988). "A Plea for Tourismological Theory and Methodology." *Revue de Tourisme*, 43(3): 2–5.

Kaplan R.S. and Norton, D.P. (2001). *The Strategy Focused Organization*. Boston, MA: Harvard Business School Press.

Kay, J. (1993). *Foundations of Corporate Success*. Oxford: Oxford University Press.

Kelliher, C. and Johnson, K. (1997). "Personnel Management in Hotels—An Update: A Move to Human Resource Management?" *Progress in Tourism and Hospitality Research*, 3(4): 321–331.

Kotler, P., Haider, D.H. and Rein, I. (1993). *Marketing Places*. New York: Free Press.

Kotler, P. (1997). *Marketing Management Analysis, Planning, Implementation, and Control* (Ninth edition.). Englewood Cliffs, NJ: Prentice Hall International.

Krippendorf, J. (1987). *The Holiday Makers— Understanding the Impacts of Leisure and Travel*. London: Heinemann.

Lashley, C. (1995). "Towards an Understanding of Employee Empowerment in Hospitality Service." *International Journal of Contemporary Hospitality Management*, 7(1): 27–32.

Leiper, N. (1981). "Towards a Cohesive Curriculum in Tourism: The Case for a Distinct Discipline." *Annals of Tourism Research*, 8(1): 69–84.

Lovelock, C., Vandermerwe, S. and Lewis, B. (1999). *Services Marketing: A European Perspective*. London: Prentice Hall Europe.

Lumsdon, L (1997). *Tourism Marketing*. London: International Thomson Business Press.

Lucas, R. (1997). "Maximizing Labour Flexibility." In M. Foley, J. Lennon and G. Maxwell (Eds.), *Hospitality, Tourism and Leisure Management*. London: Cassell.

Lynch, R. (2003). *Corporate Strategy* (3rd edition.). London: Financial Times/Prentice Hall.

Mason, P. (2008). *Tourism Impacts, Planning and Management* (2nd edition.). Oxford: Butterworth-Heinemann.

McKercher, B. (1995). "The Destination-Market Mix: A Tourism Market Portfolio Analysis Model." *Journal of Travel and Tourism Marketing*, 4(2): 23–40.

McKiernan, P. (1997). Strategy Past, Strategy Futures. *Long Range Planning*, 30(5): 790–798.

Mill, R.C. and Morrison, A.M. (1985). *The Tourism System*. Englewood Cliffs, NJ: Prentice-Hall.

Middleton, V.T.C. and Clarke, J. (2001). *Marketing in Travel and Tourism* (3rd edition.). Oxford: Butterworth-Heinemann.

Mintzberg, H. (1994). *The Rise and Fall of Strategic Planning*. New York: The Free Press.

Mintzberg, H., Lampel, J.B, Quinn, J.B. and Ghoshal, S. (2002). *The Strategy Process: Concepts, Contexts and Cases* (4th edition.). Englewood Cliffs, NJ: Prentice Hall.

Morgan, N. and Pritchard, A. (1998). *Tourism Promotion and Power: Creating Images, Creating Identities*. Chichester: John Wiley.

Morley, C. (1990). "What is Tourism? Definitions, Concepts and Characteristics." *Journal of Tourism Studies*, 1(1): 3–8.

Moutinho, L. (2000). *Strategic Management in Tourism*. Wallingford: CABI Publishing.

Murphy P. and Murphy, A.E. (2004). *Strategic Management for Tourism Communities: Bridging the Gaps*. Clevedon: Channel View.

Nickson, D. (2000). "Human Resource Issues in Travel and Tourism." In L. Moutinho (Ed.), *Strategic Management in Tourism* (pp. 169–185). Wallingford: CABI Publishing.

Olsen, M.D. and Roper, A. (1998). "Research in Strategic Management in the Hospitality Industry." *International Journal of Hospitality Management*, 17(2): 111–124.

Olsen, M.D., West, J. and Tse, E.C. (1998). *Strategic Management in the Hospitality Industry* (2nd edition.). New York: John Wiley.

Papadopoulos, S. (1989). "Strategy Development and Implementation of Tourism Marketing Plans: Part 2" *European Journal of Marketing*, 23(3): 37–47.

Pearce, P.L. (1993). "Defining Tourism Study as a Specialism: A Justification and Implications." *TEOROS International*, 1: 25–32.

Pearce, P.L. and Butler, R. (1993). *Tourism Research: Critiques and Challenges*. London: Routledge.

Pettigrew, A. and Whipp, R. (1991). *Managing Change for Competitive Success*. Oxford: Basil Blackwell.

Phillips, P.A. and Moutinho, L. (1998). *Strategic Planning Systems in Hospitality and Tourism*. Wallingford, UK: CABI.

Pine, J.P. and Gilmore, J.H. (1999). *The Experience Economy*. Boston, MA: Harvard Business School Press.

Poon, A. (1993). *Tourism Technology and Competitive Strategies*. Wallingford: CABI Publishing.

Porter, M.E. (1980). *Competitive Strategy: Techniques for Analyzing Industries and Competitors*. New York: Free Press.

Porter, M.E. (1985). *Competitive Advantage*. New York: Free Press.

Prahalad, C.K. and Hamel, G. (1990). "The Core Competence of the Corporation." *Harvard Business Review*, 68 (May–June): 79–91.

Ritchie, J.R.B. and Goeldner, C.R. (1994). *Travel, Tourism and Hospitality Research*. New York: John Wiley.

Robinson, M., Evans, N., Long, P., Swarbrooke, J and Sharpley, R. (2000). "Introduction." In M. Robinson, N. Evans, P. Long, J. Swarbrooke and R. Sharpley (Eds.), *Reflections on International Tourism—Management, Marketing and the Political Economy of Travel and Tourism* (pp. v–vii). Sunderland: Business Education Publishers.

Rogozinski, K. (1985). "Tourism as a Subject of Research and Integration of Sciences." *Problemy Turystyki*, 4: 7–19.

Rumelt, R.P. (1984). "Towards a Strategic Theory of the Firm." In R. Lamb (Ed.), *Competitive Strategic Management* (pp. 556–570). Englewood Cliffs, NJ: Prentice Hall.

Ryan, C. (1996). "Market Research in Tourism: Shifting Paradigms for New Concerns." In L. Moutinho (Ed.), *Marketing Research in Tourism*. London: Prentice Hall.

Schwaninger, M. (1986). "Strategic Business Management in Tourism." *Tourism Management*, 7(2): 74–85.

Scott, N., Parfitt, N. and Laws, L. (2000). "Destination Management: Co-operative Marketing, A Case Study of the Port Douglas Brand." In B. Faulkner, G. Moscardo and E. Laws (Eds.), *Tourism in the 21st Century: Lessons from Experience* (pp. 198–221). London: Continuum.

Sharpley, R. (Ed.) (2002). *The Tourism Business: An Introduction*. Sunderland: Business Education Publishers.

Taylor, S. and Edgar, D. (1996). "Hospitality Research, The Emperor's New Clothes." *International Journal of Hospitality Management*, 15(3): 211–227.

Teare, R. and Boer, R. (1991). *Strategic Hospitality Management*. London: Cassell.

Tribe, J. (1997). "The Indiscipline of Tourism." *Annals of Tourism Research*, 24(3): 638–657.

Oguri, T. (2002). "A Theoretical Survey of Critical Accounting Studies in Japan." *Critical Perspectives in Accounting*, 13(4): 477–495.

Walmesley, D. and Young, M. (1998). "Evaluative Images and Tourism: The Use of Personal Constructs to Describe the Structure of Destination Images." *Journal of Travel Research*, 36(3): 65–69.

Wernerfelt, B. (1984). "A Resource-Based View of the Firm." *Strategic Management Journal*, 5: 171–180.

Wildavsky, A. (1973). "If Planning is Everything, Maybe It's Nothing." *Policy Sciences*, 4: 127–153.

Withey, L. (1998). *Grand Tours and Cook's Tours: A History of Leisure Travel, 1750 to 1915*. London: Aurum Press.

Woods, R.H., Heck, W. and Sciarini, M. (1998). *Turnover and Diversity in the Lodging Industry*. American Hotel Foundation. Washington, DC.

WTO (2008). World Travel Organization. Retrieved April 27, 2008 from www.wto.com.

WTTC (2000). *Tourism Satellite Accounting Research, Estimates and Forecasts for Governments and Industry*. London: World Travel and Tourism Council.

PART II

Key Topics in Tourism

Ha Ling Peak and the mountain resort town of Canmore nestled in the Bow Valley, Alberta, Canada.

Tourism, Religion, and Spirituality

Richard Sharpley

Introduction

The institutions of religion and tourism have long been associated. Human migration has been linked to religion from the earliest times (Sigaux, 1966; Vukonić, 1996). Furthermore, religious tourism—or tourism "whose participants are motivated either in part or exclusively for religious reasons" (Rinschede, 1992: 52)—is widely considered to be one of the oldest forms of travel (Kaelber, 2006). In particular, institutionalized religious tourism in the form of pilgrimage was, during the medieval period, a widespread "social movement" (Digance, 2006) that was evident in the world's main religious traditions of Hinduism, Buddhism, Christianity and Islam. To a great extent, that social movement remains to this day, with many traditional pilgrimage centers, such as Mecca, Rome, Jerusalem, Lourdes, Santiago de Compostella, Guadeloupe, and Varanasi (Benares) having remained or reestablished themselves as popular contemporary tourism-pilgrimage destinations. Consequently, as Collins-Kreiner and Gatrell (2006: 33) note, "it is impossible to understand the development of . . . tourism without studying religion and understanding the pilgrimage phenomenon" of bygone eras.

In more recent times, religious tourism or, more generally, tourism that is religiously or spiritually motivated, has increased both in scale and scope and now represents a significant sector of the international tourism market. Traditional pilgrimage has remained a widespread form of travel. It is estimated, for example, that some 240 million people go on pilgrimages annually (Olsen and Timothy, 2006). As tourism has evolved into a major global social and economic phenomenon, the number of people traveling wholly or partly for religious or spiritual purposes in particular (including attendance at religious festivals/ events and visiting religious sites/attractions) has increased both proportionally and in absolute terms. To an extent, this can be explained by both the increased accessibility of sacred places and sites to international tourist markets and also, in recognition of their economic potential, by the greater propensity of governments and other agencies to market such places to tourists (Vukonić, 2002).

India, for example, is actively promoting the Mahabodhi Temple in Bodhgaya and other Buddhist sites as attractions to potential spiritual tourists (Contours, 2004). At the same time, however, a broadening and, perhaps, secularization of notions of religion and spirituality has resulted in a wider interpretation of what constitutes sacred tourism places and experiences (Olsen and Timothy, 2006) and, hence, increased participation in such forms of travel. So-called "New Age" tourism, for example, embraces both travel or pilgrimage to particular "sacred" (often pagan) sites, such as Glastonbury in the UK (Bowman, 1994), and also the consumption of specific experiences, such as "holistic holidays" (Smith, 2003). The issue of secular religion/ spirituality and its relevance to tourism is a central theme in this chapter and is returned to below. In short, there is no doubt that what may be collectively referred to as "religious tourism" has, over time, evolved into a significant, increasingly diverse, and continually growing sector of the overall tourism market (McKelvie, 2005; Russell, 1999).

Given this long and increasingly complex association between tourism and religion, it is perhaps surprising that, until recently, relatively little attention has been paid to the subject in the tourism (or, indeed, religious studies) literature. This is not to say, of course, that it has been completely overlooked. Reflecting the origins of contemporary religious tourism, a number of early studies addressed the relationship between tourism and pilgrimage, albeit principally from a sociological structural-functional perspective (Cohen, 1998). In other words, attention was focused on the extent to which modern tourism practices can be compared with, or are distinct from, traditional pilgrimage in terms of both social form and meaning. MacCannell (1973, 1976), for example, was the first to suggest that the modern tourist is a secular pilgrim, that tourism is a "secular substitute for organized religion" (Allcock, 1988: 37), providing tourists with the opportunity to seek meaning or authenticity through the rituals of sightseeing.

Similarly, Graburn (1983, 1989) compared the practice of tourism with that of pilgrimage. Drawing heavily on the work of Turner and Turner (1978), he explored the distinctions between sacred and profane time and space, as well as the concepts of liminality and communitas, and their relevance to modern tourism, concluding that "tourism . . . is functionally and symbolically equivalent to other institutions that humans use to embellish and add meaning to their lives" (Graburn, 1989: 22).

Subsequently, Smith (1992) proposed that the relationship between tourism and pilgrimage may be conceptualized as a continuum based upon the degree of intensity of religious motivation in what she refers to as the "quest in guest." At one extreme lies sacred pilgrimage, a journey driven by faith, religion and spiritual fulfillment; at the other extreme lies the secular tourist who may seek to satisfy some personal or spiritual need through tourism. Between these two points may be found innumerable religious/secular combinations of religious tourism defined by an individual's religious or cultural/ knowledge needs. Thus, Smith (1992) suggests that although tourists and pilgrims share the same fundamental requirements for travel (time, financial resources, and social sanction), a distinction between tourism and pilgrimage may be identified within the meaning or personal belief attached to each activity.

Expanding on these earlier analyses, the tourism–religion relationship has been explored more recently by commentators from a number of disciplinary perspectives. Collectively, their work embraces a number of identifiable themes, the most popular of which remains the pilgrim-tourist debate and the links between tourism and pilgrimage within (post)modern societies more generally. For example, in Timothy and Olsen's (2006) edited text *Tourism, Religion and Spiritual Journeys*, the majority of chapters focus on pilgrimage and tourism from either a conceptual or religion-specific perspective. In addition, however, the contemporary literature explores four other broad yet interrelated themes:

- The historical development of religious tourism (e.g., Swatos and Tomasi, 2002).
- The flows, characteristics and activities of religious tourists, including the contrasting behavior of religious and nonreligious tourists (or pilgrims and other tourists) at sacred sites (Collins-Kreiner and Gatrell, 2006; Collins-Kreiner and Kliot, 2000; McKelvie, 2005; Poira et al., 2003; Rinschede, 1992).
- The negative consequences and management implications of religious/spiritual tourism, including both cultural impacts (the commoditization of religious culture, and the violation of the sanctity of sacred places) and physical impacts on the natural and built environment (Olsen, 2006; Shackley, 1999, 2001).
- The economic potential of religious tourism, in terms of both the economic development of the local area around sacred sites (Gupta, 1999; Jackowski and Smith, 1992; Vukonić 2002) and the preservation of sacred sites themselves (Shackley, 2002).

A full review of what may be collectively referred to as the "religious tourism" literature is beyond the scope of this chapter (see Olsen and Timothy, 2006, for a useful summary). However, not only is it evident that this literature is both eclectic and lacking theoretical cohesion, but also the following observations can be made.

First, much of the literature adopts a tourism-centric perspective. That is, with a few notable exceptions (including the aforementioned edited text by Timothy and Olsen), few attempts have been made to locate the analysis of religious/spiritual tourism within a theological context. Consequently, little account is taken of the changing attitudes towards, or the role of, religion and spirituality in modern societies and the consequential implications for the consumption of tourism.

Second, a significant proportion of the more recent literature is concerned with exploring pragmatic issues such as the volume, value, and scope of the religious tourism market, the development of religious tourism for economic purposes, the necessity of effective site or visitor management, associated challenges relating to commoditization, authenticity and so on.

While of undoubted importance to the management of religious tourism as a particular sector of the overall tourism market, these issues are, in essence, relevant to all forms of heritage or cultural tourism rather than peculiar to religious or spiritual tourism. As Shackley (2006) notes, religious or spiritual tourism is often seen as a subset of cultural tourism and, consequently, many of these issues are generic and applicable to many other forms of tourism.

Third, arguably little progress has been made in advancing research into the conceptual links between tourism and religion and/or spirituality within modern societies. In other words, the well-rehearsed arguments relating to the nature of modern tourism as a form of secular pilgrimage or secular spiritual experience continue to draw on the early conceptual foundations developed by MacCannell, Graburn and others, yet, in general, a fuller understanding of the spiritual meaning or role of tourism remains elusive. More particularly, as Sharpley and Sundaram (2005) observe, there also exists relatively little empirical research into the religious or spiritual motives or experiences of tourists.

In short, religious tourism is, subject to definition, an identifiable and significant sector of global tourism (McKelvie, 2005). For the purposes of this book, however, there is little to be gained in describing its nature, extent, impacts, and relevant management challenges. These are generic practical issues applicable to many forms of tourism. Conversely, the most fruitful area of research remains the experiential aspects of religious or spiritual tourism, a greater understanding of which would undoubtedly inform the management, development and promotion of religious/sacred tourism sites and experiences. This chapter, therefore, explores what can be described as the "spiritual dimension of tourism." That is, drawing on recent work in the area, it reviews and adds to the understanding of the role of tourism as a modern-secular religious or spiritual experience. The first task, however, is to review briefly the transforming role of religion in contemporary society to provide a broad conceptual framework for the rest of the chapter.

From Religion to Spirituality . . . To Religion?

To compare the modern socioeconomic institution of tourism with religion, it is necessary to consider the place of religion in modern societies. In other words, it is not possible to explore critically the relationship between tourism and religion without some understanding of the latter phenomenon. However, although a number of studies consider religious tourism within the context of particular religions or religious/sacred sites, rarely is the debate about tourism as a modern sacred experience more generally located in the wider framework of religion in society. That is, religion is often, but erroneously, viewed as a "given" within the tourism–religion relationship.

Two points must immediately be emphasized. First, "religion" itself is difficult, if not impossible, to define. Not only are there, of course, many competing sociological and theological perspectives on religion but also, given the numerous religions that may be identified globally, the concept of religion cannot, as Vukonić observes, "be described in a simple definition" (2000: 497). Nevertheless, it is generally accepted that religion is, within the context of specific societies, an institutionalized or organized system of beliefs and practices that some or all members of that society follow; moreover those beliefs and practices are, as Durkheim suggested, "relative to sacred things" (cited in Jary and Jary, 1991: 527) or focused upon one or more supreme gods or deities. Indeed, "almost all people who follow some form of religion believe that a divine power created the world and influences their lives" (Vukonić, 2000: 497).

Thus, in many if not all societies, religion is an integral part of the social system (Vukonić, 1996: 26), a fundamental element

of culture that is manifested in people's attitudes, beliefs and behavior (Lupfer et al., 1992). Such behavior, in turn, emanates from two principal sources (Poira et al., 2003). On the one hand, certain religions impose particular obligations and restrictions upon believers, such as with clothing or eating and drinking (Levin, 1979), or demand adherence to particular rituals (Turner and Turner, 1978). Religions also contribute more generally to a society's attitudes and values amongst both believers and nonbelievers. Together, these suggest that any society's values, attitudes and behavior (including touristic activity) will vary and, in part, be determined by the nature, extent, and strength of religious following within that society. In some countries or societies, the contribution or influence of religion remains dominant, whereas in modern and, by definition, secular societies (the USA, perhaps being a notable exception) religion plays a more limited cultural role.

This leads directly to the second point underpinning the argument that tourism is a modern, secular pilgrimage. Modern societies are generally characterized by increasing secularization or, to put it another way, by a decline in the perceived relevance or significance of religious institutions and practices. Such a decline, evidenced by the decreasing participation in organized religion or, specifically, attendance at church services (Stark et al., 2005), is usually explained by industrialization, globalization, consumerism, and scientific rationality (Maguire and Weatherby, 1998), although it is suggested that a postmodern search for individual freedom and expression has also reduced dependence on or respect for religious traditions (Tomasi, 2002). Conversely and somewhat paradoxically, however, immigration and cultural pluralism in many modern societies has resulted in the resurgence in participation in organized religion, while some commentators suggest that a genuine religious revival is in evidence around the world (Tilson, 2001).

Importantly, the alleged secularization of modern societies has not resulted in a religious vacuum. That is, religion, in the traditional sense of the word, is not in decline but, rather, is taking on a different form. Modern societies remain religious (Tomasi, 2002) but religion has become increasingly deinstitutionalized (Harvey, 2003). To put it another way, a more traditional social adherence to religious beliefs and practices has been replaced in modern societies by a more private, individualized "religiosity without belonging, especially among young people" (Lambert, 2004). As Wilson puts it, "people have made new choices about what to believe, and what to do about what they believe" (1976: 2). Thus, the practice of religion has evolved beyond adherence to religious dogma and unquestioning acceptance of religious institutions and rituals; religious freedom has, in a sense, become freedom from religion. This is, perhaps, most effectively revealed in the ongoing religion-spirituality debate evident in the religious studies literature over the last two decades (Zinnbauer et al., 1997) and, in particular, the distinctions that have emerged between the terms "religiousness" and "spirituality."

Religiousness

Prior to the rise of secularization, the concept of religiousness embraced both traditional institutional/individual beliefs and activities and the more general notion of spirituality. However, according to Zinnbauer et al. (1997), disillusionment with religious institutions and religious leadership has given rise to distinctive meanings of religiousness and spirituality. Thus, religion, or religiousness, has come to be viewed from two perspectives (Pargament, 1999): the substantive approach explores the beliefs and practices of people with respect to a higher power, central to which is the notion of the sacred, while the functional approach focuses upon the role that religion plays in people's lives with respect to issues such as death, and suffering. From both perspectives, however, religiousness is now considered narrowly as "religious

institutions and prescribed theology and rituals" (Zinnbauer et al., 1997: 551). Moreover, the term has also come to attract negative connotations, being perceived by many as a barrier to personal experiences of the sacred or spiritual. A number of studies have demonstrated that increasing numbers of people prefer to define themselves as spiritual rather than religious (Lambert, 2004; Zinnbauer et al., 1997), perhaps reflecting the argument that, throughout history, "the power and force of religion . . . have been beyond question, analysis, or inspection (Wellman and Tokuno, 2004: 294).

Spirituality

According to Brown, spirituality "has become a kind of buzzword of the age . . . an all purpose word, but one that describes what is felt to be missing rather than specifying what is hoped to be found ... The spiritual search has become a dominant feature of late twentieth-century life; a symptom of collective uncertainty" (1998: 1). However, from a theological perspective, spirituality is viewed more positively. Rather than a desired antidote to the perceived anomic condition of (post)modern life, spirituality is a "personal and subjective," as opposed to an impersonal and institutionalized, perspective on religion (Zinnbauer et al., 1997). Spirituality has always been an element of human existence (Vukonić, 1996), but has become a more powerful force in popular religions. It is a label applied to an enormous variety of beliefs and practices "concerned with things of the spirit as opposed to the material" (Stark et al., 2005: 7). Spirituality assumes the existence of the supernatural, though not necessarily a god or gods, and therefore represents a wider connotation of the sacred. As a broad concept, spirituality embraces a number of beliefs and practices that do not conform with traditional religions—people may have what they believe to be spiritual experiences even though they may not hold religious beliefs (Heelas, 1998)—yet, interestingly, research has also demonstrated that, for many people, the concepts of spirituality and religiousness retain a degree of congruence (Zinnbauer et al., 1997). In other words, it has been found that many of those who consider themselves to be religious also consider themselves to be spiritual, while spirituality remains defined in traditionally religious perceptions of the sacred (i.e., belief in God) and of ritual (e.g., prayer, attendance at church). What may be changing is the way that such spirituality is manifested in practice. Shackley (2002), for example, notes that, although church congregations in the UK are declining, tourist visits to churches and cathedrals are on the increase. This, she suggests, may be a consequence of a pressurized modern world that drives some people to seek a "quick-fix spiritual experience by being a temporary tourist entering a place of worship for a transient, but none the less significant, encounter with the numinous" (Shackley, 2002: 350).

Nevertheless, there is little doubt that the search for the "spiritual" has, for many, become distinct from the search for the "religious." Moreover, the concept of the spiritual, released from the constraints of the prescribed beliefs and rituals of traditional religions, embraces a significantly broader range of practices, beliefs, and sacred places. Consequently, and as noted above, not only have new forms of spiritual tourism, such as "New Age" or "wellness" tourism, emerged (Timothy and Conover, 2006), but also the variety of places considered "sacred" (and, hence, the journeys, or pilgrimages, to such places) has increased enormously. Thus, contemporary spiritual tourism may include visits to so-called dark tourism sites (Lennon and Foley, 2000; Sharpley, 2005), to battlefields and war cemeteries (Seaton, 2002), to the homes/graves of famous artists or authors (MR/HCA ref), to places associated with the lives and/or death of music or movie stars (Alderman, 2002), or even to sporting events (Gammon, 2004). At the same time, of course, tourism in general (cities, the countryside, wilderness areas, the seaside) may, as MacCannell (1973, 1976) and others originally proposed, be considered contemporary spiritual experiences.

This latter point, with specific reference to visiting a traditional tourism destination—the seaside—is considered in more detail later in this chapter. The important point is, however, that the concept of religion is both dynamic and difficult to define. Moreover, although many consider that, in modern, secular societies, religion has been replaced by, or has evolved into, a broader-based, secular spirituality, the distinction between traditional religiousness and contemporary interpretations of spirituality may be less clear than is immediately apparent. Consequently, the distinctions between the pilgrim, the religious/spiritual tourist, and the secular tourist are also fuzzier than suggested by earlier writings on the tourism–religion relationship. The implications of this are explored shortly in the context of three particular spiritual dimensions of tourism. Before doing so, however, it is useful to add an extra dimension to the study of tourism, religion, and spirituality by reviewing briefly the extent to which theological interpretations of tourism exist.

Tourism: Theological Interpretations

Few attempts have been made to consider the relationship between tourism and religion from a theological perspective. This may, in part, be due to the fact that, as Cohen (1998) suggests, most religions consider tourism to be a secular activity and, hence, "of little relevance to religion." Indeed, theological considerations of the relationship between religion and tourism are generally reduced to the view that tourism is but one of numerous phenomena that define modern life, while the concepts closest in traditional religions to tourism are traveling, learning, peace, and hospitality for strangers (WCC, 2005). One notable exception is Grimshaw (2001) who, inverting the "tourism as religion" thesis, raises the possibility that religion is analogous to the tourist experience. Drawing on David Lodge's (1991) *Paradise News*, he asks: "what if popular religion is a form of spiritual tourism, a weekly package deal that takes the participants on a journey to encounter the expected exotic other that is experienced in a nonconfrontational way and then transports them back to their embarkation point?" (Grimshaw, 2001: 255).

Typically, theological perspectives on tourism begin with the notion of tourism as free time and, hence, an opportunity for people to learn about the natural world (God's creation) and for their own spiritual enrichment (Vukonić, 2000). However, religious interpretations of "free time" and its appropriate use vary significantly, as do the concepts of travel, hospitality and religious tourism. For example, Cohen (1998) suggests that the attitude of traditional religions to strangers and the provision of hospitality is one of ambivalence, where innate suspicion of strangers is balanced by "religiously sanctioned rules of hospitality." Nevertheless, different religions are more or less ambivalent to strangers; some Islamic countries have little interest in welcoming non-Islamic visitors, with consequential implications for the scope of tourism in those countries (Poirier, 1995), while Christianity and Buddhism are more tolerant in their provision of hospitality to strangers (Cohen, 1998). Similarly, different religions are more or less open to the concept of religious tourism. While Roman Catholicism does not deny the phenomenon of religious tourism, other religions, such as Buddhism and Islam, do not accept the intermingling of profane and religious motives in traveling (Vukonić, 1996) and, hence, implicitly reject the concept of religious tourism.

Generally, then, "the world's religions find it . . . hard to formulate a principled theological position to the phenomenon [of tourism]" (Cohen, 1998: 8), suggesting that the relationship between tourism, religion and spirituality is conceptually one-sided; that is, its basis lies within the profane phenomenon of tourism. Nevertheless, and somewhat paradoxically, theological ambivalence or antagonism towards tourism is often contradicted by pragmatic support for the promotion of religious sites and festivals as vital sources of income, while the development of church tourism in some countries is motivated by both economic necessity and the opportunity of exposing visitors to religious/spiritual experiences. Therefore, a greater understanding of the spiritual dimensions of tourism, albeit from a profane-tourism perspective, may provide insights into the effective promotion and management of religious sites, while also contributing to potential theological interpretations of tourism.

Tourism: Spiritual Dimensions

The principal focus of the academic study of the relationship between tourism and religion has been on the links between the tourist and the pilgrim. Structurally, the activities of tourism and pilgrimage are considered to share similar characteristics with respect to the use of transportation, accommodation facilities and other services, while pilgrims also participate in "touristic" behavior, such as sightseeing or purchasing souvenirs (Eade, 1992). Thus, pilgrimage may be seen as one form of tourism. From a motivational perspective, however, significant distinctions are evident; Cohen (1992) notes, for example, that pilgrims travel towards the center of their world whereas tourists travel away from their center to a pleasurable "Other." Similarly, de Sousa (1993) suggests that, while pilgrims follow religious convictions and behave respectfully and piously in the destination, tourists seek fun, pleasure and relaxation and are driven by egocentric, hedonistic needs. Nevertheless, it is also argued that, in modern societies, pilgrimage and tourism are functionally similar, providing pilgrims/tourists with spiritual experiences in liminal time and space (Graburn, 1989, 2001; MacCannell, 1976).

Smith's (1992) widely cited pilgrim–tourist continuum proposes that there are numerous combinations of tourist–pilgrim lying between the "true" pilgrim and the secular tourist. At the midpoint are located religious tourists (or religious heritage tourists). However, while this continuum provides a useful means of classifying forms of pilgrimage or religious tourism, it is unable to embrace the diverse and complex interpretations of religion, spirituality and pilgrimage in contemporary society. There is a need to progress beyond both relatively simplistic structural-functional comparisons of tourism-pilgrimage and polarized definitions of the spiritual pilgrim and secular tourist (and identifiable combinations of the two), taking account of the nature of religion/spirituality within modern societies and how this may influence tourist experiences. Drawing on recent work in this field, three specific issues are now considered: the spirituality of the journey; the spirituality of religious sites; and, the spirituality of tourist places.

The Spirituality of the Journey

Typically, pilgrimage and tourism have been considered structurally similar with respect to the stages of the journey—the separation stage (journey out to the destination), the liminal stage (the stay in the destination) and the reintegration stage (the return home). Functionally, the two phenomena are similar in that they both represent sacred, as opposed to ordinary, obligated, profane time, or the transference of the individual from an ordinary into another, non-ordinary state of existence. This is often referred to a liminal existence in a state of anti-structure, where pilgrims/tourists experience so-called "communitas" (Turner and Turner, 1978). This liminal stage of communitas is seen by some as fundamental to the contemporary spiritual experience offered by tourism (Graburn 2001; Passariello, 1983).

Less attention, however, has been paid to the ways in which the journey itself (irrespective of motive or destination), the act of traveling away and home again, may represent for the participant a spiritual experience. Graburn relates rites of passage to the journey where "kinds of tourism may be purposely self-imposed physical and mental tests" (2001: 44), such as arduous trips (e.g., cycling across a continent) or backpacking on a minimal budget (Riley, 1988), yet this tends to be specific to particular journeys at specific periods in peoples' lives. In other words, it remains unclear to what extent tourist journeys in general are spiritually meaningful or significant.

Addressing this issue, Laing and Crouch (2006) explore the spiritual dimension of what they refer to as "frontier tourism," or journeys to the Earth's more remote places involving physical danger and hardship. Relating such journeys to pilgrimage in terms of the nature of the journey, as opposed to its stages, they identify five particular characteristics of pilgrimage that may equally enhance the spiritual significance of frontier travel:

Sacrifice, Danger, and Hardship
Journeys to remote, inhospitable places, such as deserts or the polar regions, frequently require frontier travelers to face up to dangerous situations, to endure hardships and make personal sacrifices in terms of personal comfort, safety, and well-being. Enduring (and surviving) such dangers and hardships may contribute to a deeper understanding of the self and the learning of personal spiritual truths.

Transformation
In addition to the endurance of hardship and danger, frontier travel may provide a transforming experience. That is, it enables people to discover a new or real self through a desocializing process; the standards, conventions and concerns of their home society are shed, enabling the "real," inner self to emerge. In other words, frontier travel becomes

a "means of spiritual purification" (Laing and Crouch, 2006), a cleansing process resulting in enhanced self-knowledge.

Enrichment

Related to the endurance of hardship, the overcoming of danger and the potentially transforming power of the experience, frontier travel may also provide individuals with spiritual enrichment. Such enrichment may emanate from the successful completion of the journey or adventure, or from particular "moment in time" experiences when everything "falls into place," representing inner spiritual peace or knowledge. In either case, the experience is enriching inasmuch as it becomes an abiding memory, a never to be forgotten experience that frames the individual's future life and, perhaps, a form of addiction as similar experiences are continuously sought out.

Communitas

Not surprisingly, perhaps, Laing and Crouch identify communitas as a defining spiritual characteristic of frontier travel. While personal transformation and enrichment may be the outcome of solo journeys, it is the common sharing of the journey, its dangers, hardships, successes, and enriching moments amongst the members of the group or team that may provide the most significant or spiritual reward. Such communitas develops from the shared experience, from mutual respect and dependence and, perhaps, from the unwritten lore or code of ethics that surrounds particular activities, such as mountaineering.

Return

All journeys inevitably involve a return to the traveler's home society from whence the journey commenced. Such return or reintegration may be difficult—the spiritually enriching character of frontier travel may render "normal" life unattractive. Conversely, the frontier traveler may seek to add meaning to others' lives by sharing his or her experiences, whether through educating them about other places or by motivating them to face up

to challenges, to grow spiritually or to seek out similar experiences. In this sense, the frontier traveler becomes a secular "preacher," conveying the message of the spiritual experiences of travel to frontier places.

While Laing and Crouch's (2006) research focuses specifically on those who have participated in, or written about, frontier travel, the outcomes may nevertheless be applied to all forms of tourism. In other words, for frontier travelers, the "frontier" represents the border between the safe, predictable, ordered and, perhaps, tamed world, and the dangerous, unpredictable, unexplored, untamed, and challenging places on or beyond that border. In a sense, however, all people, all tourists, perceive that there are frontiers to their safe, predictable world and existence. Such frontiers may be social, represented by networks of family or friends or by the security of routine and ritual; the routines of work, obligatory activities and leisure often provide the boundaries or meaning of "normal" life. Conversely, such frontiers may be geographical; the familiarity of place (or the unfamiliarity of other places) may also represent a boundary to peoples' lives. They may also be defined by an individual's travel experience. Thus, all people have frontiers beyond which, through tourism, they may travel. Consequently, it may be argued that all tourists may potentially experience the spiritual characteristics of frontier travel (or pilgrimage) identified by Laing and Crouch. An obvious example is the backpacker or independent traveler, the role, attitudes and motivation of whom has long been addressed in the literature (Cohen, 1973; Loker-Murphy and Pearce, 1995; Riley, 1988; Vogt, 1978). Backpacking, whether or not a rite of passage, may indeed provide meaningful spiritual experiences, whether through hardship, transformation, enrichment, or communitas (Binder, 2004). Similarly, secular tourists following traditional pilgrimage routes, such as that to Santiago de Compostella in northern Spain, may experience some or all of the spiritual elements of pilgrimage although, as Gatfield (2006) notes, this claim requires validation on the basis of individual experiences. However, for a tourist inexperienced in international travel, the first holiday overseas, or a holiday in a more distant, exotic location, may provide similar spiritual experiences. In short, exploring the spirituality of the journey from this perspective provides credence to the argument that contemporary tourism is a modern spiritual experience.

The Spirituality of Religious Sites

The boundaries between tourism and pilgrimage are, arguably, least distinct within the context of religious sites, such as churches, cathedrals, temples, and other religiously significant places and structures including, for example, the Wailing Wall in Israel or the Swayambhunath Buddhist Stupa near Kathmandu, Nepal. On the one hand, religious sites act as foci for religious practice, ritual or observance; they attract people who are primarily motivated by the desire for religious experiences of one form or another, from peaceful spiritual contemplation, through an "encounter with the numinous" (Shackley, 2002), to salvation and healing (Eade, 1992). On the other hand, they also fulfill a number of other functions. They may be architecturally significant structures in their own right, they may house important works of art, they may play host to a variety of events, such as concerts or exhibitions, or they may simply be iconic tourist sites, visited simply because they are, as Urry puts it, "famous for being famous . . . entail[ing] a kind of pilgrimage to a sacred center which is often a capital or major city" (1990: 12). It is unlikely, for example, that a tourist in Paris would feel that his or her stay in the city is complete without a visit to either Notre Dame on the Ile de la Cité or the Basilica of the Sacré Coeur on Montmartre; similarly, a tourist stay in Istanbul would almost

certainly include a visit to the Sultan Ahmet Camii, or Blue Mosque. In short, there are at least four possible motives for visiting religious sites:

- Spiritual/religious purposes, including individual contemplation/prayer or participation in formal services or ceremonies.
- Heritage or cultural purposes, such as an interest in architecture or religious culture.
- Special interests, for example, musical concerts, brass rubbing, or photography.
- Planned or impulse visit "because it's there"; that is visiting religious sites as iconic tourist markers.

Implicitly, therefore, the management of religious sites is potentially problematic given the diversity of motives amongst visitors, the fact that, frequently, religious visitors are outnumbered by those with other motives (Shackley, 2002), and the need to meet and balance the needs of all visitors while recognizing that tourism may represent a vital source of income to maintain the fabric of the site.

At the same time, however, greater knowledge and understanding of the behavior, expectations and experiences of visitors (both religious and "nonreligious") to religious sites, particularly with respect to the extent to which to seek out or benefit from spiritual experiences, serendipitously or otherwise, may go some way towards informing the management and promotion of such sites. In other words, while it may be safe to assume that certain groups of visitors are religiously motivated, it may be less safe to assume that other, secular visitors do not have some form of spiritual motivation or experience.

A small number of previous studies address this issue, albeit to a limited extent. Jackson and Hudman (1995), for example, explored the motivations of visitors to five English cathedrals, finding that less than 4% cited religion as the basis for their visit. Overall, the primary reason for visiting cathedrals was an interest in the history or architecture of the building although, significantly, those in the older age group (60 or over) cited religion as their main reason for visiting. Conversely, over half of all respondents indicated that their visit "prompted some type of religious feeling" (Jackson and Hudman, 1995), although the study did not enquire into respondents' self-perceptions of religiousness or spirituality.

Adopting a different perspective, Collins-Kreiner and Gatrell (2006) compare the differing behaviors of secular and religious tourists to the Bahái Shrine and Garden in Haifa, Israel, concluding that secular tourists and religious tourists differ greatly in terms of their experience of the site (although this is, to a great extent, determined by the differing structures of tours provided to secular or religious tourists, the former group being permitted only to observe from tourist space, the latter enjoying a more performative role in pilgrim space). More usefully, perhaps, Poira et al.'s (2003) study of two groups of tourists at the Wailing Wall in Jerusalem investigates the relationship between tourists' religious affiliation, the strength of their religious beliefs, and their subsequent visitation patterns. They identify a strong correlation between religious affiliation of tourists (i.e., their religious heritage) and both their visitation patterns and personal involvement with the site; conversely, strength of religious belief is a less dominant factor. Thus, nonreligious Jews feel more involved with the site (the Wailing Wall is considered the holiest religious site for Jewish people) than religious Christians, who do not attach the same religious significance to the site.

While these latter studies perhaps reinforce the perceived distinction between religious and secular tourists in terms of motivations and experiences, recent work by Williams et al. (2006) not only adds a new dimension to the understanding of tourists' relationship with, or response to, spiritual places, but also, importantly, begins to challenge the assumption that religious and nonreligious tourists inevitably experience such places in different ways. Based on a survey

of visitors to a Welsh cathedral, Williams et al. (2006) assess visitors' experience of visiting the cathedral under four broad headings, namely: overall impressions; spiritual and religious; aesthetic and historic; and, commercialization. Significantly, however, they also segment respondents according to their degree of "religiosity" (measured, perhaps somewhat simplistically, by frequency of church attendance) in order to identify the extent to which expectations and experiences vary among different groups of visitors.

Some results of the research are unsurprising. For example, for frequent churchgoers' (the most religious group), the overall impression of their visit tends to be most positive; similarly, a majority of this group also claim to "sense God's presence" during their visit to the cathedral and, overall, feel satisfied and refreshed by their visit. Conversely, only a small proportion of those who never attend church (the least religious group) sense God's presence and are less positive in terms of their overall impressions. Interestingly, however, among this latter group there is evidence of a spiritual dimension to the cathedral visit. For example, over one-third of nonchurchgoers, secular visitors who "stand outside the Christian tradition," find the cathedral to be spiritually alive, half feel a sense of peace from their visit and a significant majority find the cathedral awe-inspiring and uplifting. In other words, as Williams et al. (2006) suggest, "many aspects of the visit were able to stir the soul" of these secular tourists.

This particular outcome of this study might support Shackley's (2002) assertion, noted earlier, that the pressures of modern society lead people to seek a "quick fix" spiritual experience. In a sense, just as physical hunger may be satisfied by fast food, so too may spiritual hunger be satisfied by fast religion. Conversely, the research may suggest that secular visitors are susceptible to spiritual experiences while visiting religious sites. A lack of apparent religiosity does not necessarily preclude some sense or experience of the spiritual. As Williams et al. (2006) observe, this suggests that there exists the opportunity for religious sites, such as cathedrals, to "build bridges between contemporary spiritualities, implicit religious quests, and explicit religious traditions," thereby enabling them to extend the ministry to this group. It also suggests that the distinction between "pilgrims" and "tourists" at religious sites may not be as great as previous research suggests (see also Sharpley and Sundaram, 2005). Nevertheless, there is quite evidently a need for wider, more in-depth research in this area focusing upon different sites and different religious contexts.

The Spirituality of Tourist Places

It has long been recognized that certain tourism places (or spaces) may provide tourists with spiritual experiences. For example, it has been observed that, in general, the link between sublimity and religion has long been explicit: "it is no coincidence that the Western attraction to sublime landscapes developed at precisely the moment when traditional beliefs in God began to wane" (de Botton, 2003: 171). Thus, gazing upon sublime views or landscapes may provide some form of spiritual refreshment or meaning.

More specifically, particular categories of tourism places or destinations have been associated in one way or another with spirituality or spiritual refreshment. MacCannell (1976), by asserting that tourism is a modern form of pilgrimage, implies that reality, meaning, and authenticity can be found in other times and places which remain traditional or untainted by modernity. In other words, tourism places in the "Other" may be the setting for spiritually meaningful tourism experiences. Similarly, the countryside (or, more specifically, the social construct of rurality that may be associated with rural places) has long been seen as possessing a

symbolic significance in modern societies. Contrasting with the physical and sociocultural characteristics of urban areas, the countryside has come to be seen as a rural utopia, a green and pleasant land (Newby, 1985) offering tourists the opportunity to immerse themselves in a nostalgic past. In other words, as MacCannell (1976) more generally suggests, the countryside is a "refuge from modernity" (Short, 1991: 34), a place that may provide visitors with spiritually refreshing experiences.

Although little or no research has been undertaken into this topic, it may be safe to assume that other types of tourist destination, such as historic cities, industrial heritage urban areas, or "dark tourism" sites, may similarly provide visitors with spiritual experiences. Collectively, however, the potential spirituality of such places lies in their history, heritage or links with a more "authentic" past. In other words, the spirituality of such places lies in the historic meaning or reality they provide in an anomic, (post)modern world—they provide a focal point, a kind of historical spiritual rock in the uncertain and dissatisfying contemporary world of modernity (Hewison, 1987).

In contrast, recent work by Bull (2006) explores the extent to which the continuing popularity of a traditional tourist space—the seaside—may be linked either wholly or in part to its spiritual "pull"; that is, he considers the aspects of coastal-based tourism that might be more spiritual than temporal. There are, according to Bull (2006), three different uses of the sea/coast by tourists:

- Activities occurring on, in or under the water (e.g., paddling, swimming, water sports).
- Activities that make use of the coastal margin, such as walking or seabird watching.
- Activities that do not depend on the coastal resources but nevertheless occur at the seaside (e.g., socializing, visiting amusement arcades, parks, cafés, and so on).

In the first two cases, it is important to explore why such activities may have a deeper spiritual meaning for visitors; in the third case, the question is: what pulls tourists to the seaside to participate in activities that could take place anywhere?

In addressing these issues, Bull (2006) identifies eight influences that pull tourists to the seaside, each of them possessing "in some measure a degree of natural spirituality." At the same time, there are significant symbolic characteristics of the sea that transcend many religions and belief systems and that, collectively, elicit a "set of human spiritual responses." These eight influences may be summarized as follows:

1   *Spiritual and physical well-being.* The sea has long been considered beneficial to both physical health (seawater as a natural healer) and spiritual well-being.
2   *Correspondence of the sea's rhythms* to life's rhythms. An unconscious sense of the connectivity between the sea's rhythms (the tides, the waves breaking on the shore) with life rhythms (heartbeat, breathing, human biorhythms) provides spiritual peace and relaxation.
3   *Freedom of the limitless.* The sea's edge provides the spectacle of infinity, limitlessness, and the wonder of the Earth's dimensions; it provides the sense of escape, freedom and unconstrained movement in an environment uncontrolled by humankind.
4   *The beach as liminality.* The coastal margin is a safe liminal space between the danger and unpredictability of the sea and the ordered serenity and stability of the land, from which people may contemplate the "latent anger and chaos of the ocean, its punishment of sins."
5   *Adventure and daring.* As with other adventure places, the sea provides opportunities for, and the spiritual refreshment from, participating in adventurous or daring activities and pastimes.
6   *Regression to childhood.* As a liminal space, the beach/sea allows people to return to a childlike existence of fun and play, of innocence and spiritual freedom from adult codes, norms and cynicism.
7   *Return to the womb/pre-terrestriality.* Swimming in the sea may be equated with a return to the womb, a prenatal comfort, or even perhaps a spiritual link with pre-terrestrial existence.
8   *Surrender to a greater spiritual power.* The sea may draw people back spiritually to their creator and the contemplation of their final resting place.

To "toy" with this greater power (surfing, diving, and so on) is to confront the final journey.

As Bull (2006) accepts, it would be difficult to claim that there is a spiritual dimension to every seaside visit (just as it would be difficult to claim that there is a spiritual dimension to every tourist journey or experience). Nevertheless, the seaside does appeal to people's spiritual consciousness and unconsciousness in a number of ways, and provides a setting where a variety of spiritual experiences may be possible. The question, therefore, is: can other tourist places, either in the natural or built environment, provide similar spiritual opportunities?

Conclusion

The relationship between tourism and religion can be considered from two perspectives. On the one hand, religious tourism, defined as tourism that is motivated either partly or entirely by religious or spiritual purposes, is not only one of the oldest forms of touristic activity but has also evolved into a significant and growing sector of the global tourism market. Consequently, as a consequence of both its economic potential and the need for appropriate environmental and cultural management policies, increasing attention is being paid to the management and promotion of religious tourism and tourists. On the other hand, tourism may be considered *as* religion—a contemporary spiritual journey. It is seen to be either structurally and functionally the modern equivalent of traditional pilgrimage, the experience of liminality and communitas being common to both phenomena, or more generally a modern spiritual experience that contrasts with the anomic condition of (post)modern societies.

As this chapter has suggested, many of the issues surrounding the former (religious tourism) perspective are common to many, if not all, forms of tourism; religious tourism may, in a sense, be utilized as a case study for exploring the challenges of managing and promoting tourism. Conversely, the latter (tourism as religion) perspective is a unique phenomenon, yet one that remains relatively under-researched. That is, although the tourism-as-religion discourse has explored the conceptual links among tourism, pilgrimage, and spirituality, few attempts have been made either to locate the debate within the context of contemporary theological perspectives on religion and spirituality or, more specifically, to undertake empirical research into this issue. Consequently, little account has, to date, been taken of the shifting role of religion/ spirituality in contemporary societies and the subsequent ways in which tourist journeys, sites and places may be experienced by apparently secular or nonreligious tourists.

Drawing on recent research in this area, this chapter has demonstrated that the distinction between pilgrims, religious/religious heritage tourists and secular/nonreligious tourists is less clear than is suggested in the extant literature. That is, the dynamic, multilayered nature of religion and spirituality in modern societies may be reflected in a multitude of spiritual tourist experiences that have yet to be revealed or understood. Therefore, in conclusion, there is evidently a need for more extensive empirical research into the spiritual characteristics of contemporary tourism in order to better inform the management and promotion of religious sites and places. Not only would this enable such places to meet the needs of all tourists but also, perhaps, enhance the religious or spiritual message that they convey.

Acknowledgements

The latter section of this chapter draws upon research presented in a number of papers at the *Tourism: The Spiritual Dimension* Conference held at the University of Lincoln, UK, in April 2006. I am grateful to the authors of those papers for permission to cite their work.

References

Alderman, D. (2002). "Writing on the Graceland Wall: On the Importance of Authorship in Pilgrimage Landscapes." *Tourism Recreation Research,* 27(2): 27–35.

Allcock, B. (1988). "Tourism as a Sacred Journey." *Loisir et Société,* 11(1): 33–48.

Binder, J. (2004). "The Whole Point of Backpacking: Anthropological Perspectives on the Characteristics of Backpacking." In G. Richards and J. Wilson (Eds.), *The Global Nomad: Backpacker Travel in Theory and Practice* (pp. 92–108). Clevedon: Channel View Publications.

Bowman, M. (1994). "New Age Pilgrimage: The Glastonbury Experience." *Tourism in Focus* (Tourism Concern), 11 (Spring): 6–7.

Brown, M. (1998). *The Spiritual Tourist.* London: Bloomsbury.

Bull, A. (2006). "Is a Trip to the Seaside a Spiritual Journey?" Paper presented at *The Tourism: The Spiritual Dimension* Conference, University of Lincoln, UK (unpublished).

Cohen, E. (1973). "Nomads from Affluence: Notes on the Phenomenon of Drifter Tourism." *International Journal of Comparative Sociology,* 14(1–2): 89–103.

Cohen, E. (1992). "Pilgrimage and Tourism; Convergence and Divergence." In A. Morinis (Ed.), *Sacred Journeys* (pp. 47–61). Westport, CT: Greenwood Press.

Cohen, E. (1998). "Tourism and Religion: A Comparative Perspective." *Pacific Tourism Review,* 2(1): 1–10.

Collins-Kreiner, N. and Gatrell, J. (2006). "Tourism, Heritage and Pilgrimage: The Case of Haifa's Bahá'í Gardens." *Journal of Heritage Tourism,* 1(1): 32–50.

Collins-Kreiner, N. and Kliot, N. (2000). "Pilgrimage Tourism in the Holy Land: The Behavioural Characteristics of Christian Pilgrims." *Geojournal,* 50: 55–67.

Contours (2004). "India Promotes Spiritual Tourism." *Contours,* 14(1): 21.

de Botton, A. (2003). *The Art of Travel.* London: Penguin Books.

De Sousa, D. (1993). "Tourism and Pilgrimage: Tourists as Pilgrims?" *Contours,* 6(2): 4–8.

Digance, J. (2006). "Religious and Secular Pilgrimage: Journeys Redolent with Meaning." In D. Timothy and D. Olsen (Eds.),

Tourism, Religion and Spiritual Journeys (pp. 36–48). Abingdon: Routledge.

Eade, J. (1992). "Pilgrimage and Tourism at Lourdes, France." *Annals of Tourism Research* 19(1): 18–32.

Gammon, S. (2004). "Secular Pilgrimage and Sport Tourism." In B. Ritchie and D. Adair (Eds.), *Sport Tourism: Interrelationships, Impacts and Issues* (pp. 30–45). Clevedon: Channel View Publications.

Gatfield, T. (2006). "Pilgrimage and Tourism— Two Different Paradigms. Personal Reflections on the Santiago de Compostella Experience." Paper presented at the *Tourism: The Spiritual Dimension Conference*. University of Lincoln, UK (unpublished).

Graburn, N. (1983). "The Anthropology of Tourism." *Annals of Tourism Research,* 10(1): 9–33.

Graburn, N. (1989). "Tourism: the Sacred Journey." In V. Smith (Ed.), *Hosts and Guests: The Anthropology of Tourism* (2nd edition.) (pp. 21–36). Philadelphia: University of Pennsylvania Press.

Graburn, N. (2001). "Secular Ritual: A General Theory of Tourism." In V. Smith and M. Brent (Eds.), *Hosts and Guests Revisited: Tourism Issues of the 21st Century* (pp. 42–50). New York: Cognizant Communications.

Grimshaw, M. (2001). "Tourist, Traveler, or Exile: Redefining the Theological Endeavour." *The Journal of Religion,* 81(2): 249–270.

Gupta, V. (1999). "Sustainable Tourism: Learning from Indian Religious Traditions." *International Journal of Contemporary Hospitality Management,* 11(2 and 3): 91–95.

Harvey, D. (2003). "Cell Church: Its Situation in British Evangelical Culture." *Journal of Contemporary Religion,* 18(1): 95–109.

Heelas, P. (1998). "Introduction: On Differentiation and Dedifferentiation." In P. Heelas (Ed.), *Religion, Modernity and Postmodernity* (pp. 1–18). Oxford: Blackwell.

Hewison, R. (1987). *The Heritage Industry: Britain in a Climate of Decline.* London: Methuen.

Jackowski, A. and Smith, V. (1992). "Polish Pilgrim-Tourists." *Annals of Tourism Research,* 19(1): 92–106.

Jackson, R. and Hudman, L. (1995). "Pilgrimage Tourism and English Cathedrals: The Role of Religion in Travel." *The Tourist Review,* 50(4): 40–48.

Jary, D. and Jary, J. (1991). *Collins Dictionary of Sociology.* London: Harper Collins.

Kaelber, L. (2006). "Paradigms of Travel: From Medieval Pilgrimage to the Postmodern Virtual Tour." In D. Timothy and D. Olsen (Eds.), *Tourism, Religion and Spiritual Journeys* (pp. 49–63). Abingdon: Routledge.

Laing, J. and Crouch, G. (2006). "From the Frontier: Sacred Journeys in Far Away Places." Paper presented at the *Tourism: The Spiritual Dimension Conference*. University of Lincoln, UK (unpublished).

Lambert, Y. (2004). "A Turning Point in Religious Evolution in Europe." *Journal of Contemporary Religion,* 19(1): 29–45.

Lennon, J. and Foley, M. (2000). *Dark Tourism: The Attraction of Death and Disaster.* London: Continuum.

Levin, S. (1979). "Understanding Religious Behavior." *Journal of Religion and Health,* 18(1): 8–20.

Lodge, D. (1991). *Paradise News.* London: Viking.

Loker-Murphy, L. and Pearce, P. (1995). "Young Budget Travelers: Backpackers in Australia." *Annals of Tourism Research,* 22(4): 819–843.

Lupfer, M., Brock, K. and DePaola, S. (1992). "The Use of Secular and Religious Attributions to Explain Everyday Behavior." *Journal of the Scientific Study of Religion* 31(4): 486–503.

MacCannell, D. (1973). "Staged Authenticity: Arrangements of Social Space in Tourist Settings." *American Journal of Sociology,* 79(3): 589–603.

MacCannell, D. (1976). *The Tourist: A New Theory of the Leisure Class.* New York: Schocken Books.

Maguire, B. and Weatherby, G. (1998). "The Secularization of Religion and Television Commercials." *Sociology of Religion,* 59(2): 171–178.

McKelvie, J. (2005). "Religious Tourism." *Travel and Tourism Analyst,* (4): 1–47.

Newby, H. (1985). *Green and Pleasant Land? Social Change in Rural England.* London: Wildwood House.

Olsen, D. (2006). "Management Issues for Religious Heritage Attractions." In D. Timothy and D. Olsen (Eds.), *Tourism, Religion and*

Spiritual Journeys (pp. 104–120). Abingdon: Routledge.

Olsen, D. and Timothy, D. (2006). "Tourism and Religious Journeys." In D. Timothy and D. Olsen (Eds.), *Tourism, Religion and Spiritual Journeys* (pp. 1–22). Abingdon: Routledge.

Pargament, K. (1999). "The Psychology of Religion and Spirituality? Yes and No." *International Journal for the Psychology of Religion*, 9(1): 3–16.

Passariello, P. (1983). "Never on a Sunday? Mexican Tourists at the Beach." *Annals of Tourism Research*, 10(1): 233–249.

Poira, Y., Butler, R. and Airey, D. (2003). "Tourism, Religion and Religiosity: A Holy Mess." *Current Issues in Tourism*, 6(4): 340–363.

Poirier, R. (1995). "Tourism and Development in Tunisia." *Annals of Tourism Research*, 22(1): 157–171.

Riley, P. (1988). "Road Culture of International Long-Term Budget Travelers." *Annals of Tourism Research*, 15(3): 313–328.

Rinschede, G. (1992). "Forms of Religious Tourism." *Annals of Tourism Research*, 19(1): 51–67.

Russell, P. (1999). "Religious Travel in the New Millennium." *Travel and Tourism Analyst*, (5): 39–68.

Seaton, A. (2002). "Thanatourism's Final Frontiers? Visits to Cemeteries, Churchyards and Funerary Sites as Sacred and Secular Pilgrimage." *Tourism Recreation Research*, 27(2): 73–82.

Shackley, M. (1999). "Managing the Cultural Impacts of Religious Tourism in the Himalayas, Tibet and Nepal." In M. Robinson and P. Boniface (Eds.), *Tourism and Cultural Conflicts* (pp. 95–111). Wallingford: CABI.

Shackley, M. (2001). *Managing Sacred Sites: Service Provision and Visitor Experience*. London: Continuum.

Shackley, M. (2002). "Space, Sanctity and Service: The English Cathedral as Heterotopia." *International Journal of Tourism Research*, 4(5): 345–352.

Shackley, M. (2006). "Keynote Address: Tourism—The Spiritual Dimension." Paper presented at the *Tourism: The Spiritual Dimension Conference*. University of Lincoln, UK (unpublished).

Sharpley, R. (2005). "Travels to the Edge of Darkness: Towards a Typology of Dark Tourism." In C. Ryan et al. (Eds.), *Taking Tourism to the Limits: Issues, Concepts and Managerial Perspectives* (pp. 217–218). Oxford: Elsevier.

Sharpley, R. and Sundaram, P. (2005). "Tourism: a Sacred Journey? The Case of Ashram Tourism, India." *International Journal of Tourism Research*, 7(3): 161–171.

Short, J. (1991). *Imagined Country: Society, Culture and Environment*. London: Routledge.

Sigaux, J. (1966). *History of Tourism*. London: Leisure Arts.

Smith, M. (2003). "Holistic Holidays: Tourism and the Reconciliation of Body, Mind and Spirit." *Tourism Recreation Research*, 28(1): 103–108.

Smith, V. (1992). "Introduction: The Quest in Guest." *Annals of Tourism Research*, 19(1): 1–17.

Stark, R., Hamberg, E. and Miller, A. (2005). "Exploring Spirituality and Unchurched Religions in America, Sweden and Japan." *Journal of Contemporary Religion*, 20(1): 3–23.

Swatos, W. and Tomasi, L. (Eds.) (2002). *From Medieval Pilgrimage to Religious Tourism*. Westport, CT: Praeger.

Tilson, D. (2001). "Religious Tourism, Public Relations and Church-State Partnerships." *Public Relations Quarterly*, 46(3): 35–40.

Timothy, D. and Conover, P. (2006). "Nature Religion, Self-Spirituality and New Age Tourism." In D. Timothy and D. Olsen (Eds.), *Tourism, Religion and Spiritual Journeys* (pp. 139–155). Abingdon: Routledge.

Timothy, D. and Olsen, D. (Eds.) (2006). *Tourism, Religion and Spiritual Journeys*. Abingdon: Routledge.

Tomasi, L. (2002). "Homo Viator: From Pilgrimage to Religious Tourism." In W. Swatos and L. Tomasi (Eds.), *From Medieval Pilgrimage to Religious Tourism* (pp. 1–25). Praeger: London.

Turner, V. and Turner, E. (1978). *Image and Pilgrimage in Christian Culture*. New York: Columbia University Press.

Urry, J. (1990). *The Tourist Gaze*. London: Sage Publications.

Vogt, J. (1978). "Wandering: Youth and Travel Behavior." *Studies in Third World Societies*, 5: 19–40.

Vukonić, B. (1996). *Tourism and Religion*. Pergamon: Oxford.

Vukonić, B. (2000). "Religion." In J. Jafari (Ed.), *Encyclopedia of Tourism* (pp. 497–500). London: Routledge.

Vukonić, B. (2002). "Religion, Tourism and Economics: A Convenient Symbiosis." *Tourism Recreation Research*, 27(2): 59–64.

Wellman, J. and Tokuno, K. (2004). "Is Religious Violence Inevitable?" *Journal for the Scientific Study of Religion*, 43(3): 291–296.

WCC (2005). "Respect for People and Nature." World Council of Churches News Release. Retrieved May 28, 2008 from www2.wcc-coe.org/pressreleasesen.nsf/index/pr-05-56.html.

Williams, E., Francis, L., Robbins, M. and Annis, J. (2006). "Visitor Experiences of St. David's Cathedral: The Two Worlds of Pilgrims and Secular Tourists." Paper presented at *The Tourism: The Spiritual Dimension Conference*. University of Lincoln, UK (unpublished).

Wilson, B. (1976). *Contemporary Transformations of Religion*. Oxford: OUP.

Zinnbauer, B., Pargament, K., Cole, B., Rye, M., Butter, E., Belavich, T., Hipp, K., Scott, A. and Kadar, J. (1997). "Religion and Spirituality: Unfuzzying the Fuzzy." *Journal for the Scientific Study of Religion*, 36(4): 549–564.

15

Breaking Down the System: How Volunteer Tourism Contributes to New Ways of Viewing Commodified Tourism

Stephen Wearing and Jess Ponting

Introduction

This chapter argues that models of tourism based on commodified agendas continue to hold dominance in both the theory and practice of tourism. Tourism in the free market economy represents the commercialization of the human need to travel and exploits natural and cultural resources as means to profit accumulation. Despite impressive foreign exchange earnings, transnational tourism corporations operating in developing countries incur high rates of economic leakage. Through high rates of imports, profit repatriation, high levels of expatriate management staffing, and investment incentive schemes, neoliberalist models of tourism generally result in tourist experiences which not only prevent tourists and destination communities from interacting on an equal footing, but which also provide only limited contributions to local communities in developing countries (Meyer, 2007; Schilcher, 2007). This reflects a broader neoliberalization agenda which sees rich country governments use access to their markets and foreign aid as leverage to induce developing countries to adopt neoliberal policies; international economic organizations giving loans conditional upon the adoption of neoliberal policies; and, vigorously pursue free trade agreements skewed in favor of the rich countries. The position taken here is that rather than helping poorer countries to develop, the dogmatic pursuit of economic neoliberalism actually prevents alternative models of tourism being investigated and pursued, and "kicks away the ladder" of careful government regulation and control which the rich countries ascended to prosperity in the first instance (Chang, 2008). This chapter presents volunteer tourism as a shift away from commodified, neoliberalist approaches to tourism and tourism research and, based upon benefits to the subjectivities of both the tourist and host, advocates a severing of exclusive ties to this paradigm of practice and analysis.

Volunteer tourism challenges established models of practice and highlights a need for more theoretically inclusive ways of understanding tourism. Broadening research philosophies allows access to approaches that pursue decommodification in tourism and which place social, cultural, and ecological value on local communities, their environments and economics. In a global society that increasingly uses dogma and marketing to instill values and exploit social relations (Chang, 2008), volunteer tourism represents both an opportunity and a means of value adding in an industry that can represent consumer capitalism at its worst.

Volunteer tourism has been described as when people "volunteer in an organized way to undertake holidays that might involve the aiding or alleviating the material poverty of some groups in society, the restoration of certain environments, or research into aspects of society or environment while furthering knowledge and awareness of these" (Wearing and Neil, 2001: 241). People who have discovered the pleasures, challenges, and adventures of volunteer tourism often return to it year after year because they build new friendships and develop deeper understandings of others, and while helping others, they strengthen their own self-identity and worth and those of the communities they interact with (Wearing, 2001). These are facets of tourism not encompassed by dominant neoliberal paradigms of tourism research and practice.

This chapter draws on examples of both commodified and decommodified/volunteer forms of surfing tourism in Indonesia to demonstrate and explore the polarization between commodified tourism and decommodified tourism. The argument is then progressed beyond the simplistic polarized analysis to examine the power relationships inherent in guest–host interactions and socially constructed tourist spaces. It is argued that volunteer tourism provides a vehicle for exploring the "Third Space"[1]

of tourism interaction that becomes possible when the dominant paradigms of tourism research and practice are challenged and transcended.

Volunteer Tourism

Volunteer tourism experiences have in recent years become of some interest as a significant and growing form of alternative tourism (Britton and Clarke, 1987; Cohen, 1987; Dernoi, 1981, 1988; Ellis, 2003; Halpenny and Caissie, 2003; Holden, 1984; Pearce, 1980; Sorensen, 1997; Uriely et al., 2003; Wearing, 2001, 2003, 2004; Wearing and Neil, 2000, 2001). Volunteer tourism represents an expanding tourism niche, its growth reflected in the mounting body of research on volunteers and volunteer tourism within tourism literature and, most recently, the addition of a dedicated academic journal. Indeed, a Google search of the words "volunteer tourism" on April 17, 2008 returned 230,000 hits, including large numbers of volunteer tourism operators and support NGOs such as San Diego based VolunTourism (voluntourism.org. accessed April 30, 2008), as well as a great deal of published literature. Callanan and Thomas (2005) demonstrated the scope of the volunteer tourism industry by identifying 698 individual volunteer tourism products—largely community welfare, teaching, business, environmental, cultural development, medical, and journalism related activities—on a single volunteer database (GoAbroad.com). Some individual volunteer tourism organizations have reached an impressive scale. Earthwatch, for example, between 1971 and 2008 has involved upwards of 90,000 volunteers in 1350 projects across 120 countries and contributed US$67 million and 11 million hours to scientific fieldwork (Earthwatch Institute, 2008).

Existing volunteer tourism research has tended to focused on reconciliation, development, impacts on host communities and volunteer tourists, personal development, participation in social movements, and what volunteering represents as a tourism product (Broad, 2003; Brown and Morrison, 2003; Callanan and Thomas, 2005; Campbell and Smith, 2006; Ellis, 2003; Galley and Clifton, 2004; Grey and Campbell, 2007; Halpenny and Caissie, 2003; Higgins-Desbiolles, 2003; Lyons, 2003; McGehee, 2002; McIntosh and Zahra, 2007; Ryan et al., 2001; Simpson, 2004; Sin, 2005; Stoddart and Rogerson, 2004; Uriely and Reichel, 2000; Uriely et al., 2003; Wearing, 2001, 2002; Wearing, 2004; Wearing and Dean, 2003; Wearing and Neil, 2000). Recent research has also developed typologies of volunteer tourism providers (Coghlan, 2007) and products (Callanan and Thomas, 2005) and explored the role of volunteer tourism expedition leaders (Coghlan, 2008).

For many researchers volunteer tourism has provided a means to step away from the commodified centrality that has driven tourism research and allowed a focus on a more decommodified agenda. Some, however, have challenged both the value of a decommodified research agenda (Butcher, 2006) and the decommodified nature of volunteer tourism (Grey and Campbell, 2007). However, under close scrutiny Butcher's (2006) arguments against a decommodified research agenda over simplify the term and mistakenly assume it to be antidevelopment (Wearing and Ponting, 2006). Grey and Campbell's (2007) study of volunteer tourism that failed to deliver decommodified experiences in Costa Rica is an example of what Callanan and Thomas (2005) describe as "shallow volunteer tourism." That is short term, flexible itineraries decided upon by the tourists in a setting where the destination and promise of specific wildlife sightings dominate motivation and thus satisfaction (Grey and Campbell, 2007). We suggest that while shallow volunteer tourism experiences may be in danger of becoming another example of commodified tourism, deeper volunteer tourism products can represent a glimmer of resistance to neoliberal models of tourism and research.

Volunteer Tourism as Resistance to the Dominant Research Paradigm

Neoliberal ideologies regard people as consumers rather than producers (Comaroff and Comaroff, 2001). This shift in the mode of contemporary citizenship from production to consumption has become the axis upon which identity and experience is constructed in free market societies (Beder, 2001; Birch and Paul, 2003; Cohen, 2003; Hamilton, 2002; Kasser, 2003; Lury, 1996; Slater, 1997) causing the tourism industry to contrive, and the tourist to seek out, neoliberal utopias located in, but disembedded from, host cultures and environments (Ponting et al., 2005). Difference is perceived as inferiority and reinforces the capital accumulation logic of the tourists' original culture. The discourses of tourist literature and marketing have in many ways implicitly adopted this top down hegemonic view. Its deconstruction and contestation with alternate perspectives from the margins is overdue (Ponting, 2006, 2009). The polarization of tourist encounters with hosts provides a little more theoretical space and is useful in providing perspective, however, it is moving beyond conceptualizations of essentialized culture and reductionist views of "mass tourism bad, alternative tourism good" that opens up a plethora of other meanings and allows a better understanding of the exchanges that occur in destination spaces.

Bhabha's (1994) imperialized cultural space suggests a discursive and primordial struggle over and against hegemonic constructions. Volunteer tourism, particularly where NGOs are involved, provides a framework from which to reconceptualize this imperialized cultural space. When destination communities' views are given credence, possibilities emerge for alternate programs of tourism and counter-discourse to hegemonic modes of interaction. Spaces within destination areas that provide experiences to destabilize and transform the constructed self then become possible. Otherness within this framework can include difference without inferiorization and identity fixity. A concept that can include, as illustration, modes of tourist experience that allow for a fluid two-way process of co-presence and co-construction between tourist and host with possible benefits for both.

Deep volunteer tourism enables social value and identities to be developed within the host's cultural presentation by allowing a higher degree of experiential interaction (cf. Wearing, 2001). Social value is developed where cultural Third Spaces of hosts are included through community consultation, policy decision-making, and other participation opportunities. This enables a breakdown of the self-other in the dominant-subordinate dichotomy, and provides sufficient freedom in the re-presentation of host identity to explore a Third Space of the hybrid selves created for both parties. How these cultural worlds are accessed and experienced is influenced by the socially constructed nature of otherness in tourist experience, the resistance and subversion of host cultures to this programmatic coding, and the counter-discourses to the gaze/surveillance of touristic power.

Often, in deep volunteer tourism, tourists are placed in new and unfamiliar settings, forced to rely only on themselves, pushed to their limits, and tested beyond their normal skill and comfort levels (Wearing, 2001). In such cases volunteers nearly always come away from the experience with a deeper understanding of themselves and a high level of satisfaction with their efforts to help in social or ecological contexts.

> The social interaction between the volunteer tourist, the host community and natural environment forms an exchange of influence that creates a social value of the site for the volunteer tourist that effects a change in self and identity. As such, the behavior and values of the volunteer tourist have been impacted upon, and they come away from the experience with a changed value for the social and physical environments visited. (Wearing and Neil, 2000: 409)

This interaction can move us beyond the more accepted views of the interaction between host and guest in tourism research.

Finally, volunteer tourism allows arguments to be drawn together into a model of tourism which challenges cultural hegemony and offers alternatives to hegemonic cultural logic. This re-presentation of touristic identities can allow for a cultural and experiential process of interaction and exchange between tourist and host communities. In this way, the domination of the tourist experience by Western countries can be challenged and, following de Certeau's (1988) arguments on experiential resistance, the balance of knowledge–power destabilized and resisted to favor the cultural uniqueness of host communities.

As we have argued elsewhere (Ponting et al., 2005; Wearing and Ponting, 2006; Wearing et al., 2005) there is an important sense of public ethic and a role for local governance, local economies, and indigenous self-management by host communities in counter-imperialistic strategies. In effect, these and other strategies provide a revitalized social ethic of association amongst minority and marginal groups in the developed and developing nations of global civil society to overcome the highly commodified, normalizing and marketized nature of globalized Western tourism (Wearing and Wearing, 1999). Such strategies can constitute a new politics of Third Space tourist cultures. Volunteer tourism can represent an alternative way of constructing self/other in tourist space in resistance to objectified destinations representing cultural exoticism for the voyeuristic gaze, fleeting pleasure, and individualized escape of visiting tourists.

Breaking Down the System

By empathizing with and valuing the host community for whom the tourist destination is "home" and the cultural product a "way of life" volunteer tourism can find specificity and uniqueness in the host culture. These tourist destinations are places in which many people from the host culture have interacted over a long period of time. Through this inter-action and associated activities and rituals the place acquires cultural meanings which are deeply and uniquely tied to identities of the community and the individual selves of its members—place becomes *space*, taking on a social value.

Space and place are now widely accepted as complex sociocultural constructions, rather than simply physical locations (Gustafson, 2001; Meethan, 2001). Social scientists have traditionally referred to space in terms of a physical location, and the meanings that people bring to it as place. Place has come to be considered as the product of social, cultural, and political processes with differ-ent discourses constructing and reappraising individual notions of place (Eade, 1997; Gustafson, 2001; Massey, 1994, 1995; Pries, 1999). Michel de Certeau (1988) and Michel Foucault (1986) parallel these ideas though invert the traditionally held relationship between space and place. De Certeau (1988) conceptualizes "space" as being a geographi-cal "place" that resonates with experience and stories which act to provide spatial organiza-tion, open a "legitimate theatre for practical actions," and authorize the "establishment, displacement and transcendence of limits" (De Certeau, 1988: 125). In this view a vari-ety of discourses, or spaces, may interact in one geographic location, or place, without one of these spaces necessarily assuming absolute authority or legitimacy. Foucault refers to these contested places as heteroto-pias: "the juxtaposing in a single real place (of) several spaces, several sites that are in themselves incompatible" (1986: 25). Tourist spaces, then, can act as heterotopias for resistance to domination, allowing room for discourse other than that of the powerful.

In the context of volunteer tourism, places are not simply gazed upon but are interacted with, thus ascribing them with the hybridity of a new space and a social value that is different for all (Australian Heritage Commission, 1992: 10). If experiential worth derived from the history of the place and its representation sets the scene for its social

worth, then its maintenance and the continual interaction of people with it ensure the persistence of its social and, hence, cultural value. If the creation of social value of a space is dependent on dynamic relation-ships with those who use it, the meaning may change and develop over time. The transfor-mation to Third Space occurs precisely because the interactions involved in volun-teer tourism create a hybrid space that has meaning ascribed across a wider set of values. The people who give social value to the space are those who "practice" the place. If they are given a voice this value may be passed on through empathy and listening skills of the volunteer tourist. Unfortunately, as the term "Third Space" implies, the repre-sentational order of host places hinders direct access to such experience and meaning for tourists. From the commodified research perspective these tourist spaces are seen as purely profitable. Volunteer tourism allows us to explore other ways of "doing" tourism.

Re-Presenting the Space of Commodified Tourism

One recent example of the re-presentation of commodified tourist space is the juxtaposition between commodified and decommodified/ volunteer forms of surfing tourism amongst the islands off the west coast of Sumatra, Indonesia. In surfing tourism's most com-modified incarnation to date, tourists, primar-ily from the USA, Australia, Europe, Brazil, and Japan fly into Padang international airport on Sumatra's west coast where they are met by company representatives and are transported directly either to a local five star hotel or their chartered live-aboard boat (Buckley, 2002; Ponting, 2001, 2002, 2006; Ponting et al., 2005; Ponting and Wearing, 2003). Paying up to US$500 per day, surfing tourists are taken around the Mentawai Islands, which are con-sidered to be one of the world's richest surf fields, in the relative luxury of custom outfit-ted live-aboard yachts complete with high-tech entertainment systems, on board chef, and surf guide. The popularity of this product and what it represents in terms of a commodified space disembedded from its local "place" is evident in the words of *Tracks* surf magazine editor Sean Doherty:

> The Mentawais has created the ideal of "The Boat Trip" . . . It created that fantasy. Now you can be in the most isolated corner of the world, i.e. the Mentawais, and you can have DVD. You can have sat phones! You've got all your mod cons there. I think the whole creation of the luxury boat trip ideal is a reflection that we live in a mod con society. People chase convenience. If you can have convenience and at the same time have the dream of isolated uncrowded waves and marry the two together, you can begin to understand why there are fifty boats up there working. (Sean Doherty, pers. comm., October 20, 2005)

A range of publications have demonstrated that this model of tourism, viewed from within the Western dominated cultural hegemonic ideal, is based upon a socially constructed reductionist "Wonderland," or "Nirvana," symbolized by perfect surf, uncrowded conditions, a pristine tropical environment and "cushioned adventure" (meaning limited interactions with local communities and the logistics of travel) (Ponting, 2006, 2009; Ponting et al., 2005). Historically, within this construction it has been normal in the surf media and in the discourse of marketing to simply ignore the presence of local communities as the use of yachts removes the necessity of interacting with them. This component, coupled with the presence of the cultural buffer of the tour company, has played a large role in the current popularity of this type of trip among those surfing tourists who may not have otherwise felt comfortable traveling to such a remote and poverty stricken region. For these people the idea of visiting a widely acknowledged surfing Nirvana has been a long held dream of surf media construction made real by the availability of the commodified Mentawai surf charter (Ponting, 2006, 2009; Ponting et al., 2005). (See Photo 15.1).

If we add the benefit of alternative philosophies of tourism analysis and acknowledge that this surfers' Nirvana is a commercially driven sociocultural construction—the success of which is dependent upon the facade of adventure, uncrowded perfect surf

Photo 15.1   Surfing tourists in a socially constructed surfing nirvana off the village of Katiet in the Mentawai Islands.
Photo: Jess Ponting.

and compliant friendly locals—cracks appear in the discourse that holds this mythical space together. The disconnection of the Nirvanic myth from its true place (the Mentawai) and the communities that live in this place reveal the broader impacts of a neoliberal tourism model. This is a form of package tourism which attempts to prevent the tourist from entering into a Third Space with local communities, establishing and protecting experiences of a mythical tourist space created in the surf media (Ponting, 2006). The following excerpt is from an interview with a surfing tourist volunteering in a village and reflecting upon yacht charter tourism.

> With charter boats, people fly in they're picked up at the airport and taken to the boat. They go out there surfing, they might get off the boat onto an island a couple of times, then back to Padang, one night here and then home. Basically a boat trip isn't really an Indonesian experience. It's not meeting Indonesians. They might spend two or three weeks here and not speak to an Indonesian person apart from the Indonesian crew working on the

boat. I guess if they just want to go surfing and go on a boat ride its good but its hardly what you'd call going to Indo. (Will, surf tourist/volunteer, pers. comm., October 28, 2003)

By contrast, Will was using his personal skills and equipment to provide first aid for the community in which he was staying; traveling to the mainland to retrieve medicines for the village; providing materials for a local guesthouse; teaching English for tourism purposes; and teaching local children to surf. The differences between those tourists experiencing only the mythical space of Nirvana onboard surf charter yachts and those offering their services in the villages was noted by Mentawaian villagers who encounter both types of tourists. (See Photo 15.2).

> The surfers on the yachts are quite arrogant. They have no desire to build a good relationship with the local community. Surfers on the land want to make friends with the locals even teach them how to surf. I think that is a good thing. (Andi, Mentawaian villager, pers. comm., August 5, 2003)

There are many stories arising of surfing tourists in Indonesia becoming volunteer tourists.

Photo 15.2   The only regular interaction between yacht charter surfing tourists and Mentawai villagers is the sale of handicrafts direct to tourists on boats mediated by surf guides. Offshore from Katiet village, Mentawai Islands.
Photo: Jess Ponting.

These range from individuals who organize, supply materials for, and teach English classes to local communities, to those that raise funds in their home communities to build and staff schools in surfing tourism destinations. One tourist who arrived as crew on a charter boat started a joint-venture tourism business with a local community, providing training and employment as well as a proportion of income to a community fund (Ponting, 2005). Perhaps the most marked example of self-motivated volunteering among surfing tourists comes from a yacht charter tourist who went ashore with a view to pursuing an element of volunteer tourism in his commodified tour. Dr. Dave Jenkins advised the Katiet community that he would return later that day to give free medical treatment. He was shocked when over one hundred people arrived for his impromptu clinic. This experience of coming to know and value local people and to understand the challenges they face led Dr. Jenkins to establish a medical aid/humanitarian NGO, Surf Aid International (SAI). In five years SAI had grown from one volunteer tourist to 60 full-time staff in four countries and thousands of members, supporters, and donors around the world (Dave Jenkins, pers. comm, 2005). At the peak of SAI's tsunami response in Indonesia it managed 140 staff, 13 supply boats and a helicopter (SAI, 2005).

Volunteer surfing tourists have led the way in the Mentawais and surrounding areas in terms of developing ways of doing surfing tourism which are beginning to break down the established system of what it means to be a tourist. While volunteer surfing tourism began in the region through the actions of individual tourists forming relationships with local communities, volunteer surf tourism products are beginning to be offered through mainstream surfing tourism wholesaler/retailers (World Surfaris, 2008). The different views established by volunteer tourists and volunteer tourism organizations enable a decommodifying of analysis and offer a basis to say "it can be done differently" and that some hope for meaningful change and development in these

areas is possible. In this sense, the ideas stemming from volunteer tourism and, represented by academics and NGOs can challenge the more oppressive nature of larger tourism operators. Unlike the anti-universalist stance towards ethics of postmodernist thought, we suggest a principled approach to the global economic agendas and enterprise culture of surfing tourism in developing countries that acknowledges the Third Space of community members and tourists. In this ethical agenda tourist policy is not fixed but performed and re-performed in the everyday identities and governance of self (Chabbott, 1999; Yudice, 1995).

If communities can be encouraged to represent the local symbolic order-identity, clarify and advocate their own positions and values with regard to the images that are presented to the tourist, destinations become spaces of experience strongly tied to place and culture. The idea of space when associated with social value provides a spiritual or traditional connection between past and present. Within tourism this may help give a disempowered group back a version of its history. Often images constructed to market destinations have been constructed without the adequate and meaningful participation of the communities who confer social value. Importantly, the images then often do not match the tourist experience. Social value recognizes that the community holds extensive knowledge about areas and that this knowledge is a key part of the tourist experience. The tourism experience can thus transcend the defined "otherness" to become a process that allows the existing marginalized images of the host community to become more central. The images are then related to the social value these communities hold for the space that the tourist enters.

Operationalizing Change

We have used commodified surfing tourism and volunteer tourism to demonstrate different ways of analyzing tourist space. We now ask, how can this be operationalized? Historically, and particularly during the modernization period of development theory in the 1960s and 1970s, tourism development in less developed countries proceeded in rather ad hoc fashion. This has been addressed with varying degrees of success by the involvement of all levels of government and nongovernment organizations in local planning processes. In developing countries the involvement of government planners in tourism development is seen as crucial for building local social capital (Wilson, 1997). Haywood (1988) argues that if tourism is not planned and organized in such a way that is sensitive to the host community, the tolerance thresholds of that community are liable to be exceeded. The result will be antagonism between hosts and their guests. When a breakdown in host–guest relations occurs, the tourism industry is liable to "peak, fade and self destruct" (Haywood, 1988: 105).

If the idea of social value is used in the construction of the meaning of the tourist destination and its relevant image, revisioning the past and consultation with those whose history has contributed to this social value becomes essential. Members of the host community can then play a valuable part in determining the "identity" of the destination through the value that they have for particular places, events and traditions. Alternate forms of tourism produced by more mission driven (principled) and less commercialized operators have sought to consider input from host communities. They base their operations on a two-way interactive process between host and guest whereby the local community and the visitor have opportunities to access different space-place dimensions to those available in conventional profit-driven modes of tourism.

Holidays With Purpose is a volunteer surfing tourism business initiated by an Australian couple who initially worked as independent small business owners and community volunteers in the Hinako islands off central west Sumatra for five years before beginning to formalize their desire to provide volunteer tourism experiences for others and bring benefits to

the communities they lived in. Income from Holidays With Purpose is now used to fund a Local Empowerment Assistance Project (LEAP), a project established by the owners to address poverty in the islands off North West Sumatra through small industry implementation. Community projects which involve Holidays With Purpose volunteers working on LEAP activities include the establishment of a cold pressed coconut oil industry, the rebuilding of infrastructure in the wake of the 2004 Indian Ocean tsunami and March 2005 earthquake, construction of fishing canoes to replace those lost in the twin disasters, the planting of community gardens to generate income and improve nutrition, and the delivery of health education (Ruby Senaratne, pers. comm., 2006). The following copy from the Holidays With Purpose website explains the philosophy of the operation and the emphasis upon tourists establishing genuine relationships with the local community.

> Holidays with Purpose is not just your regular surfing or holiday charters. The trip is designed to give you a unique experience to become part of a village community, not simply as a tourist observing, but as a member. You will have the opportunity to build relationships as you work and play alongside the local people. By being part of a project that is benefiting the community, the hearts of the people are open to you and you will experience their lives in ways that you never would simply as a tourist . . . Each day you will spend a few hours taking part in the LEAP community development project. You may be helping in a building project or making a water tank, helping to plant a garden, hosting children's activities or presenting educational plays on health issues. (Holidays With Purpose, 2008)

Holidays With Purpose guiding principles relate to understanding the culture visited and to respect and be sensitive to the people who are hosting the visit, while treading softly on the environment of the host community. Local food is consumed, local transportation is utilized, and cultural and survival issues are presented realistically. By working on community projects alongside community members all the volunteer tourists gain an understanding of the factors and difficulties facing the host community. Contrasting with the provision of experiences of mythical Nirvanic space by the commodified products offered by the Mentawai surf charter fleet, this approach encapsulates our concept of "re-presenting" tourist spaces and allowing for greater possibilities and access to new identities of host and tourist to develop reflexively.

Where To From Here?

The view we have brought to this discussion through alternative analysis enabled by volunteer tourism demonstrates that the concept of "otherness" in Westernized models of tourism, exemplified by commodified Mentawai Island surf charter tourism, is underpinned by a power relationship in which Western developed countries use economic resources and representations to construct tourist destinations as places for exotic voyeurism of a different and "inferior" culture (MacCannell, 1992: 125), or indeed to utilize the natural resources of destination communities for leisure purposes while ignoring the very existence of these communities (Ponting, 2006; Ponting et al., 2005). Through the commodification of these places and the use of their indigenous inhabitants as servants in the commercialized process, the tourist endeavor eventually becomes cannibalistic as the essentialized view of tourist culture assumes the form of a powerful hegemony, which submerges, ingests, and, eventually eclipses the "other" culture of the host nation. What began as an attraction due to its difference and "otherness" becomes merely incorporated as more of the same dominant culture with its identities and values intact. The self that goes home from the tourist destination has a reinforced sense of superiorityconstructed around the hegemony of the home culture. The selves of the hosts through interaction with the tourists have also been reinforced, but theirs is a reinforcement of inferiority as identities of self-destruction in the white man's logos, his mimics, and mythology.

We indicate that volunteer tourism is able to bring a different understanding and framework for tourist-host interaction and exchange of cultural identity and symbols in local places. The alternate model that is suggested here is dependent on understanding that a more equitable distribution of power between Western and host cultures where interaction occurs in the third tourist space, decision making responsibility involves the hosts and they receive economic returns. In this model tourism is not exploitative of local populations and the benefits flow to local residents. The culture of the host community is respected and the tourist is open to experiencing aspects of the "other" culture with a view to learning and expanding the self and to some degree a spiritual element. This shift in the relationships of power between tourist and host culture enables both to interact and to learn from each other with an eventual hybridization of cultures. The tourist destination becomes a space for interaction and learning and tourism does not damage or destroy the culture of the host community. The tourist becomes a "chorister" (Wearing and Wearing, 1996) who is actively involved in the re-presentation of the host culture with aspects of his/her own culture. Hosts become reflexive educators and interpreters. The selves of both tourist and host move beyond the constraints of a dominant hegemonic culture into Third Spaces. Hybridization of the self enables a communication in which "they" or the "other" is transposed into "you" and "I." Instead of hegemony, where one culture dominates and inferiorizes the other, there are possibilities for cultural interaction, respect and growth of the selves involved.

In some senses this alternative model of tourism is idealized, as it depends on considerable shifts in power between Western and host societies. However, not to engage in the ideas that volunteer tourism brings to this discourse and to remain within the assumptions of "cannibalistic tourism" means a reinforcement of the self-destruction of unique cultures and artifacts. To create a shift in thinking suggests meaningful re-presentations of cultures and alternative progressive procedures and practices are possible. One element that is essential here is the idea of hybridized and unfixed cultural identity formation. MacCannell (1992), drawing on both his legacy to Goffman and postcolonial approaches (Bhabha, 1994), sees tourism to and from the Western world as an opportunity to form hybrid cultures. As we suggest this will be a precondition for inventive re-presentation in creating subjectivities which resist cultural constraints and cultural determinism. The result being that the tourist and host in hybridized cultures can have possibilities to cross over their own cultural boundaries, the tourist not as invader, but as imaginative traveler, and the host not as existing within an essentialized static culture but as engaged in an evolving culture (MacCannell, 1992: 7; Wearing, 1998: 58). We find that the face-to-face interactions of tourist and hosts in the postcolonial contact zones are then constructed as a Third Space. The individual tourist or community member is able to challenge the way culturally specific discourses construct the "I" and "you" of their cultures in opposition to the "other" inferiorized ethnic, indigenous or national culture (MacCannell, 1992: 25; Wearing, 1998: 59).

Volunteer tourism then allows both tourist and host community member to move beyond oppressive interactions to self-enhancing ones (for an explicit application of these ideas see Wearing and Wearing, 1996). This involved a focus on the experiential micropolitics of interactionist theory (Mead, 1934/1972; Simmel, 1911/1971) in conjunction with the Third Space reconceptualizing in postcolonial theory (Bhabha, 1994) and concept of social re-presentations (Latour, 1986). The face-to-face interactions of host-tourist exchange provides plural spaces for individuals to challenge the way culturally specific discourses construct social, personal and cultural identity. As we suggest in the alternate model for cultural re-presenting and understanding, the "I" and "you" of selves and identities in culture are then placed in opposition to the "he" and his "White man mimics"

that inferiorize difference as otherness in cross-cultural exchange and encounters. We have shown that interactions in the tourist spaces of host cultures have the potential to break down, destabilize and reconstruct as hybrid the othering created by the cultural prescriptiveness.

Conclusion

In this chapter we have presented a way of theorizing volunteer tourism which enables us to reconceptualize views of tourism. The hegemonic constructions of powerful Western industrialized countries in a period of neoliberal ascendency require views that provide different ways of interacting. Such constructions can be imposed on developing countries with the risk of destroying culture and values. Modes of "cultural cannibalism" are also means of reinforcing and homogenizing the cultural constraints of the dominant Western culture. In this model there is a fixity of both host and tourist identity and little room for self-reflexivity through tourism. The economic and, hence, representational power of tourist marketers has enabled them to commodify and package their own interpretations of otherness in Third World domains. Surfing tourists engaged with commodified forms of tourism, such as the Mentawai surf charter, are encouraged to be voyeurs who glimpse aspects of the other culture, often dressed up to conform to the image which has been presented in the surf media's selling of the perfect wave. Surfing tourist destinations are presented as places for satisfying self or escaping to Nirvana rather than as spaces for interaction with local communities.

Volunteer tourism, such as that provided by Holidays With Purpose in the islands off North West Sumatra, allows us to shift this view, requiring Third Space interaction that negotiates and reinvigorates identities to sharing cultures in the resisted and contested performance by hybrid selves. In this way the tourist experience can then include the other's embodied self and partial culture as the tourist or Simmel's (1971) "adventurer" that opens up the possibilities of self-reflexive Third Spaces. Where local communities have been involved in the planning, preparation, management and implementation of tourism, rather than absent or present only as exoticized and objectified others, the people become part of the "you," instead of the White "he" and his mimics. Exclusion and inferiorization of otherness can then give way to dialogue in which there is a semblance of sharing and exchange of cultures. In the co-presence of tourist and host the dominant system can be broken down, the power balance between tourist and host can be destabilized, cultural hegemony can be challenged and tourist spaces constructed for Third Space exchange, which will benefit all the selves involved.

Notes

1 In terms of Bhabha's thesis the concept of a hybrid or Third Space is used to convey the possibilities of a different ordering of lived experience by rereading these spaces to that given by hegemonic constructions of tourism with host and indigenous cultures in developing countries in particular. Both hosts and tourists, amongst other social actors, can participate in reconstructing tourist spaces as Third Space (see also for example the collection of essays in Hall and Tucker (2004) for an analysis of how the postcolonial has been applied to tourism). Following Bhabha's (1994: 37) conceptualization of imperialized cultural space, discursive and primordial struggles over and against hegemonic constructions are occurring within what we call the "Third Space" of tourist-host interactions and in tourist destinations.

References

Australian Heritage Commission (1992). *What is Social Value?* Canberra: Australian Government Printing Service.

Beder, S. (2001). *Selling the Work Ethic: From Puritan Pulpit to Corporate PR*. London: Zed Books.

Bhabha, H.K. (1994). *The Location of Culture*. London: Routledge.

Birch, C. and Paul, D. (2003). *Life and Work*. Sydney: University of New South Wales Press.

Britton, S. and Clarke, W.C. (Eds.) (1987). *Tourism in Small Developing Countries*. Suva: University of the South Pacific.

Broad, S. (2003). "Living the Thai Life: A Case Study of Volunteer Tourism at the Gibbon Rehabilitation Project, Thailand." *Tourism Recreation Research,* 28(3): 63–72.

Brown, S. and Morrison, A.M. (2003). "Expanding Volunteer Vacation Participation: An Exploratory Study on the Mini-Mission Concept." *Tourism Recreation Research,* 28(3): 73–82.

Buckley, R. (2002). "Surf Tourism and Sustainable Development in Indo-Pacific Islands. II. Recreational Capacity Management and Case Study." *Journal of Sustainable Tourism,* 10(5): 425–442.

Butcher, J. (2006). "A Response to Building a Decommodified Research Paradigm in Tourism: The Contribution of NGOs by Stephen Wearing, Matthew G. McDonald and Jess Ponting. Journal of Sustainable Tourism, Vol. 13, No. 5, 2005: 424–455." *Journal of Sustainable Tourism,* 14(3): 307–310.

Callanan, M. and Thomas, S. (2005). "Volunteer Tourism: Deconstructing Volunteer Activities within a Dynamic Environment." In M. Novelli (Ed.), *Niche Tourism: Contemporary Issues, Trends and Cases* (pp. 183–200). Oxford: Butterworth-Heinemann.

Campbell, L.M. and Smith, C. (2006). "What Makes Them Pay? Values of Volunteer Tourists Working for Sea Turtle Conservation." *Environmental Management,* 38: 84–98.

Chabbott, C. (1999). "Development INGOs." In J. Boli and G.M. Thomas (Eds.), *Constructing World Culture: International Nongovernmental Organizations Since 1875* (pp. 222–248). Stanford: Stanford University Press.

Chang, H.J. (2008). *Bad Samaritans: The Myth of Free Trade and the Secret History of Capitalism*. New York: Bloomsbury Press.

Coghlan, A. (2007). "Towards and Integrated Image-Based Typology of Volunteer Tourism Organizations." *Journal of Sustainable Tourism,* 15(3): 267–287.

Coghlan, A. (2008). "Exploring the Role of Expedition Staff in Volunteer Tourism." *International Journal of Tourism Research,* 10(2): 183–191.

Cohen, E. (1987). "Alternative Tourism—A Critique." *Tourism Recreation Research,* 12(2): 13–18.

Cohen, L. (2003). *A Consumers' Republic: The Politics of Mass Consumption in Postwar America.* New York: Knopf Publishers.

Comaroff, J. and Comaroff, J.L. (Eds.) (2001). *Millenial Capitalism and the Culture of Neoliberalism.* Durham, NC: Duke University Press.

de Certeau, M. (1988). *The Practice of Everyday Life.* Berkley, CA: University of California.

Dernoi, L.A. (1981). "Alternative Tourism: Towards a New Style in North-South Relations." *International Journal of Tourism Management,* 2(4): 253–264.

Dernoi, L.A. (1988). "Alternative or Community Based Tourism." In D.A.L. and J. Jafari (Eds.), *Tourism—A Vital Force for Peace.* Montreal: D'Amore. L.

Eade, J. (Ed.) (1997). *Living in the Global City: Globalization as a Local Process.* London: Routledge.

Earthwatch_Institute. (2008). "Earthwatch Institute Fact Sheet." Retrieved April 17, 2008 from earthwatch.org/earthwatch_fact_sheet.

Ellis, C. (2003). "Participatory Environmental Research in Tourism: A Global View." *Tourism Recreation Research,* 28(3): 45–55.

Foucault, M. (1986). "Of Other Spaces." *Diacritics,* 16(1): 22–27.

Galley, G. and Clifton, J. (2004). "The Motivational and Demographic Characteristics of Research Ecotourists: Operation Wallacea Volunteers in South-East Sulawesi, Indonesia." *Journal of Ecotourism,* 3: 69–82.

Grey, N. and Campbell, L.M. (2007). "A Decommodified Experience? Exploring Aesthetic, Economic and Ethical Values for Volunteer Tourism in Costa Rica." *Journal of Sustainable Tourism,* 15(5): 463–482.

Gustafson, P. (2001). "Meanings of Place: Everyday Experience and Theoretical Conceptualizations." *Journal of Environmental Psychology,* 21: 5–16.

Halpenny, E.A. and Caissie, L.T. (2003). "Volunteering on Nature Conservation Projects: Volunteer Experience, Attitudes and Values." *Tourism Recreation Research,* 28(3): 25–33.

Hamilton, C. (2002). *Overconsumption in Australia: The Rise of the Middle-Class Battler.* Canberra: The Australia Institute.

Haywood, K.M. (1988). "Responsible and Responsive Tourism Planning in the Community." *Tourism Management,* 9(2): 105–118.

Higgins-Desbiolles, F. (2003). "Reconciliation Tourism: Tourism Healing, Divided Societies!" *Tourism Recreation Research,* 28(3): 35–44.

Holden, P. (1984). *Alternative Tourism: Report on the Workshop on Alternative Tourism with a Focus on Asia.* Bangkok: Ecumenical Coalition on Third World Tourism.

Holidays With Purpose. (2008). "The Purpose." Retrieved April 17, 2008 from holidayswithpurpose.com/go2/Purpose.

Kasser, T. (2003). *The High Price of Materialism.* Cambridge, MA: MIT Press.

Latour, B. (1986). "The Powers of Association." In P. Kegan (Ed.), *Power, Action and Belief* (pp. 264–280). London: Routledge.

Lury, C. (1996). *Consumer Culture.* Oxford: Polity.

Lyons, K. (2003). "Ambiguities in Volunteer Tourism: A Case Study of Australians Participating in a J-1 Visitor Exchange Programme." *Tourism Recreation Research,* 28(3): 5–13.

MacCannell, D. (1992). *Empty Meeting Grounds: The Tourist Papers.* London: Routledge.

Massey, D. (1994). *Space, Place and Gender.* Cambridge: Polity.

Massey, D. (1995). "The Conceptualization of Place." In D. Massey and P. Jess (Eds.), *A Place in the World? Places, Cultures and Globalization* (pp. 44–77). Oxford: Open University/Oxford University Press.

McGehee, N. (2002). "Alternative Tourism and Social Movements." *Annals of Tourism Research,* 29(1): 124–143.

McIntosh, A.J. and Zahra, A. (2007). "A Cultural Encounter Through Volunteer Tourism: Towards the Ideals of Sustainable Tourism." *Journal of Sustainable Tourism,* 15(5): 541–556.

Mead, G.H. (1934/1972). *Mind, Self, Society.* Chicago, IL: University of Chicago Press.

Meethan, K. (2001). *Tourism in Global Society: Place, Culture, Consumption.* Basingstoke: Pelgrave.

Meyer, D. (2007). "Pro-Poor Tourism: From Leakages to Linkages. A Conceptual Framework for Creating Linkages Between the Accommodation Sector and 'Poor' Neighbouring Communities." *Current Issues in Tourism,* 10(6): 558–583.

Pearce, D. (1980). *Tourist in the South Pacific: The Contribution of Research to Development and Planning.* Christchurch: National Commission for UNESCO.

Ponting, J. (2001). *Managing the Mentawais: An Examination of Sustainable Tourism and the Surfing Tourism Industry in the Mentawai Archipelago, Indonesia*: Sydney: University of Technology. Unpublished Report.

Ponting, J. (2002). *Locating Surfing Tourism in Tourism Literature.* Paper presented at the *School of Leisure, Sport and Tourism Research Conference.* University of Technology, Sydney.

Ponting, J. (2005). "A Worthy Secret." *Pacific Longboarder,* 8(5): 62–66.

Ponting, J. (2006). *Castles Made of Sand: The Nirvanification of the Mentawai Islands.* Paper presented at the *International Tourism and Media Conference.*

Ponting, J. (2009). "Projecting Paradise: The Surf Media and the Hermeneutic Circle in Surfing Tourism." *Tourism Analysis,* 14(2).

Ponting, J., McDonald, M. and Wearing, S. (2005). "De-constructing Wonderland: Surfing Tourism in the Mentawai Islands, Indonesia." *Society and Leisure,* 28(1): 141–162.

Ponting, J. and Wearing, S.L. (2003). "Beyond Wonderland: How 'Tourist Space' and Ecotourism Principles can Facilitate Moves towards Sustainable Surfing Tourism in the Mentawai Archipelago, Indonesia." Paper presented at the *International Ecotourism Conference.* Selangor, Malaysia, April 15–17.

Pries, L. (1999). *Migration and Transnational Social Spaces.* Aldershot: Ashgate.

Ryan, R., Kaplan, R. and Grese, R. (2001). "Predicting Volunteer Commitment in Environmental Stewardship Programs." *Journal of Environmental Planning and Management,* 44: 629–648.

SAI (2005). *Annual Report 2004.*

Schilcher, D. (2007). "Growth Versus Equity: The Continuum of Pro-Poor Tourism and Neoliberal Governance." *Current Issues in Tourism,* 10(2 and 3): 166–192.

Simmel, G. (1911/1971). "The Adventurer." In D.N. Levine (Ed.), *George Simmel: Individuality and Social Forms* (pp. 187–198). Chicago, IL: Chicago University Press.

Simpson, K. (2004). "Doing Development: The Gap Year. Volunteer Tourists and a Popular Practice of Development." *Journal of International Development* (16): 681–692.

Sin, H.L. (2005). *Involve Me and I Will Learn: A Study of Volunteer Tourism Originating from Singapore.* Paper presented at the *Third Global Summit on Peace Through Tourism—Education Forum.* October 2–5.

Slater, D. (1997). *Consumer Culture and Modernity.* Cambridge: Polity Press.

Sorensen, H. (1997). *International Travel and Tourism.* New York: Delmar.

Stoddart, H. and Rogerson, C. (2004). "Volunteer Tourism: The Case of Habitat for Humanity South Africa." *GeoJournal,* 60: 311–318.

Uriely, N. and Reichel, A. (2000). Working Tourists and Their Attitudes to Hosts. *Annals of Tourism Research,* 27(2): 267–283.

Uriely, N., Reichel, A. and Ron, A. (2003). "Volunteering in Tourism: Additional Thinking." *Tourism Recreation Research,* 28(3): 57–62.

VolunTourism.org. (2008). "Voluntourism." Retrieved April 17, 2008, from voluntourism.org/.

Wearing, B.M. (1998). *Leisure and Feminist Theory.* London: SAGE.

Wearing, B.M. and Wearing, S.L. (1996). "Refocusing the Tourist Experience: The Flaneur and the Chorister." *Leisure Studies,* 15(4): 229–243.

Wearing, S. (2001). *Volunteer Tourism: Experiences that make a Difference.* Wallingford: CABI.

Wearing, S. (2002). "Re-centring the Self in Volunteer Tourism." In G.M.S. Dann (Ed.), *The Tourist as a Metaphor of the Social World* (pp. 237–262). Wallingford: CABI.

Wearing, S. (2003). "Volunteer Tourism." *Tourism Recreation Research,* 28(3): 3–4.

Wearing, S. (2004). "Examining Best Practice in Volunteer Tourism." In R.A. Stebbins and M. Graham (Eds.), *Volunteering as Leisure/Leisure as Volunteering: An International Assessment* (pp. 209–224). Wallingford: CABI.

Wearing, S. and Dean, B. (2003). "Seeking Self: Leisure and Tourism on Common Ground." *World Leisure,* 1: 6–13.

Wearing, S., McDonald, M. and Ponting, J. (2005). "Building a Decommodified Research Paradigm in Tourism: The Contribution of NGOs." *Journal of Sustainable Tourism,* 13(5): 424–439.

Wearing, S. and Neil, J. (2000). "Finding Self and Identity Through Volunteer Tourism." *Society and Leisure,* 23(2): 389–419.

Wearing, S. and Neil, J. (2001). "Expanding Sustainable Tourism's Conceptualization: Ecotourism, Volunteerism and Serious Leisure." In S.F. McCool and R.N. Moisey (Eds.), *Tourism, Recreation and Sustainability: Linking Culture and the Environment* (pp. 233–254). Wallingford: CABI.

Wearing, S. and Ponting, J. (2006). "A Reply to Butcher's Response to Decommodifying Tourism." *Journal of Sustainable Tourism,* 14(5): 512–515.

Wearing, S.L. and Wearing, M. (1999). "Decommodifying Ecotourism: Rethinking Global–Local Interactions with Host Communities." *Society and Leisure,* 22(1): 39–70.

Wilson, P. (1997). "Building Social Capital: A Learning Agenda for the Twenty First Century." *Urban Studies,* 34: 5–6.

World_Surfaris (2008). *Holidays with Purpose, North Sumatra.* Retrieved April 20, 2008 from worldsurfaris.com/package_1.asp?pkgid=88.

Yudice, G. (1995). "Civil Society, Consumption, and Government in an Age of Global Restructuring: An Introduction." *Social Text,* 14(4): 209–230.

16

Theme Parks and the Representation of Culture and Nature: The Consumer Aesthetics of Presentation and Performance

Keith Hollinshead

Introduction

According to *The Routledge Encyclopedia of Tourism* (Pearce, in Jafari, 2000: 578), theme parks are highly developed, capital intensive, self-centralized recreational spaces, which contain a pre-designated mix of entertainment facilities, specialty food outlets, and attractions-of-specific interest which are somehow arranged and organized around a "theme" or "unifying idea" which has been deliberately taken from the history, the heritage, or the nature which (normally, but not always!) pertains to the immediate region within which that park is located. While all of these theme parks tend to be very large in scale, some of them are highly commercial undertakings where entertainment rules and others have a more pointed *preservation* or

public education role in terms of the public/ exhibited "culture" of that area or the public/ exhibited "nature" of that area. In Pearce's view, theme parks have evolved from the carnivals, fairs, and ubiquitous amusement parks of yesteryear to become a sizeable and imaginative (but highly variegated) classification of leisure-cum-tourism attractions in their own right. To Davidson (1992: 74), theme parks are those sites of immense and ever-evolving leisure attractions which have particularly followed the mid-twentieth century model developed by the Walt Disney Company/ Corporation model at *Disneyland* in California: the most famous of them have grown to become prominent and permanent international destinations in their own right, providing a clustered mix of activity-experiences and shopping/catering amenities cohesively packaged and presented towards family leisure and tourism markets.

This chapter will loosely take a cultural studies approach to analyzing the phenomenon of theme parks in tourism today, whereby it will inspect what is going on within theme park development from a transdisciplinary—and here and there from a postdisciplinary—viewpoint. In this sense, the chapter critiques theme parks as a discursive formation: that is, as a notional, institutional site (or a mix of physical sites) which present and perform (and thereby create or help create particular forms of *culture, heritage, nature,* or *whatever*). To this end, this chapter conceives of theme parks as an important setting of cultural selection and cultural production in leisure and tourism where received and established forms of *being, identity,* and *difference* are not only projected but are unmade and remade through the exhibition of that phenomenon as a leisure and/or tourism drawcard. In this sense, this cultural studies approach draws eclectically—as do most cultural studies inspections (see Grossberg's edited comments on *Postmodernism and Articulation: An Interview With Stuart Hall* in Morley and Chen [1996])—from Marxist, structuralist and postmodernist perspectives. In particular, it will seek to reveal the play of power at work in the ways in which contemporary theme parks socially construct visions of being, identity, and difference, and will highlight some of the fashions through which theme parks serve as highly important settings of signification in the current era as they borrow, invent, and articulate certain meanings and representations while they deny, silence, or de or rearticulate other such interpretations of knowing and seeing. In this light, this chapter is (like most cultural studies approaches [Barker, 2004: 43]) something of *an intellectual magpie* as it examines the relations of culture and power in which theme parks are highly influential "agents." By this it is meant that the chapter will therefore be of value not only to *critically minded* cultural studies enthusiasts here and there in social science today, but also to *creatively minded* management and development

specialists who work on planning and programming matters in leisure and tourism, and who might want to reflect upon the power and political consequences of theme parks as either agents of the received local/national/international symbolic order or as agents of preferred cultural change.

The History and Development of Theme Parks

The origins of the theme parks of the current age go back to medieval Europe where *pleasure gardens* were established in many countries. These "gardens" tended to offer dance and entertainment activity, and provided the kinds of games, ride, and firework amusements which were popular of the particular time (Goeldner et al., 2000: 216). During the mid-to-late twentieth century, theme parks gradually changed in form and concept from being these sorts of "thrill ride," "show," or "food and foolishness" amusement-attractions to become popular mass-market, multi-activity themed destinations in their own right (Lundberg, 1985: 37). They also proliferated to such an extent (notably in North America) that, by the mid-1980s, there were some 700 amusement parks that could be styled *theme parks* in this fashion in the USA alone (Lundberg, 1985: 37), though not all researchers in the tourism industry and the globe might agree whether *open zoos* (like Longleat and Woburn Abbey in England) or *museum towns/townscapes* (like Obidos in Portugal and Colonial Williamsburg in Virginia, USA) are indeed theme parks, and others might maintain that "ride-and-thrill" sites like the Children's Park in Santa Barbara, California (which are perhaps only tokenistically thematic?) ought *not* be classified as theme parks, per se.

An inspection of the development of theme parks in the USA reveals that the sorts of high profile theme parks which exist today have largely been catalyzed in form by the multimillion dollar corporate investments which have been made at world famous sites

THEME PARKS AND THE REPRESENTATION OF CULTURE AND NATURE

such as Disney, Universal Studios, and Busch Gardens. The first boost in the theme park concept in the USA occurred in 1955 with the opening of Disneyland at Anaheim in California: "it expanded the concept of amusement parks from simply rides and car-nival barkers to include shows, shops, and restaurants in theme settings with immaculate cleanliness, promising adventure, history, science fiction, and fantasy" (Goeldner et al., 2000: 218). Despite the subsequent opening of Walt Disney World, on 27 thousand acres in central Florida in 1971 (Fjellman, 1992), the late 1970s and early 1980s then witnessed something of a slump in theme park building programs, until Sea World of Texas opened its doors in San Antonio in 1988. That devel-opment can be seen to have reinvigorated the theme park industry in the USA and the fol-lowing other sizeable operations appeared on the scene shortly after:

- Fiesta Texas: San Antonio, TX (1992);
- Knott's Camp Snoopy: Bloomington, MN (1992);
- MGM Grand Adventures: Las Vegas, NV (1993);
- Hecker Pass: Gilroy, CA (1998);
- Disney's Wild Kingdom (at Walt Disney World): Orlando, FL (1998);
- Lego World: Carlsbad, CA (1999);
- Heartland America: Indianapolis, IN (1999);
- Universal's Island of Adventure: Orlando, FL (1999);
- Jazzland: New Orleans, LA (2000). (Goeldner et al., 2000: 245).

If one scrutinizes the map of the USA, the nation's principal theme parks have been established in the sunbelt of California and Florida (a state where the city/region of Orlando has the most concentrated mix of theme parks and aggregated-attractions any-where in the world). At the time of writing, a new "Hogwarts" theme park is being added to the existing theme park "heaven" of Orlando, to keep alive the life and times of Hogwarts Castle and The Forbidden Forest of Harry Potter fame. It is ironic to note that while Hogsmeade village (there) will be permanently snow-covered, it is being built for visitation in sun-drenched Florida: the implication—and clear Warner Brothers

corporative logic—is that few of the most ardent of Potter-zealots would want to take a Hogwarts Express train to see the castle, the village, and the snow in the (author) J.K. Rowling's own damp, chilly, but only sometimes-snowy UK (see Reynolds, 2007: 15). Even the wintery world of wizards has to be consumed in the florid warmth of Florida, it seems. And just as ironic is the fact that at the very same time that the magic of Harry Potter is being hailed as a precious "British" cultural icon—with the release of seven first-class postage stamps by the Royal Mail (Govan and Reynolds, 2007: 8)—it appears that in *The Land of True Tourist Themery*, Harry Potter, Phoenix Orders, Deathly Hallows, Hogwarts-And-All are best experienced in and from *American* vantage points. To reapply a Bill Clintonism: "It is the economics, stupid!!"

So much for the sunny themery of the southern USA. In contrast, in Europe the growth of theme parks has largely had a non-sunzone profile, for such sites remain largely Northern European entities (notably in the Netherlands and Germany) situated in prox-imity to large urban-industrial centers. Indeed, Derek Oliver (Head of Sales and Marketing at the Thorpe Park theme park in the UK) maintain that "in order to succeed a theme park [in Europe] must be placed on a site with a population of 15 million people within 12 hours driving time" (cited in Davidson, 1992: 75). While the development of theme parks in Europe has generally been at a rather more gradual pace than that of the USA, recent years in Europe have also seen the trend across "the old continent" for the pro-duction of new instant construction large-scale theme parks similar in concept to the so called American model. Taken in toto, these major recent European theme parks are inclined:

- to be constructed on greenfield sites;
- to offer a critical mix of amenities—that is everything required for a day visit (viz., entertainment, plus catering, plus shopping facilities, plus, plus, plus);
- to include a large-scale white-knuckle side of some kind;
- to service a range of performance activity in live theatre and/or cinema, and/or music;

- to project the site via a familiar character (such as Astérix) or group of symbolic characters (such as the Smurfs) which constitute the overriding *theme* for the development—or otherwise via the linked provision of "thematic areas" or "lands" (such as with the programmed journeys through "Chinatown," "the Wild West," "Old Berlin," and "Space Center" *lands* at Phantasialand near Cologne in Germany);
- to be operated with a meticulously clean, safe, and orderly environment free of long queuing and free of litter; and,
- to function via one "single-payment" admission policy, thereby entitling visitors to use rides and amenities without having to meet other entry costs. (Davidson, 1992: 75–77)

In recent decades the theme park concept has spread across to other continents, and family targeted entertainment centers oriented to a particular subject or historical area have particularly begun to appear in Asia. These Asian theme parks like Disney Tokyo (which opened in 1984) rely upon the integration of topic-based costuming with topic-based architecture and then with (as much as can be achieved) topic-based entertainment and topic-based merchandising to generate overall a fantasy-loaded atmosphere. As in North America and Europe, there has been a tendency for these Asian theme parks to become even-more *artificial* in their location and design whereby "all their indoor and outdoor exhibits and amusements [are inclined to] rely little on the physical and cultural features of the areas where they have been developed . . . [Thus] they can create a major tourist attraction in an area which has virtually no physical or cultural features of note" (Mill and Morrison, 1985: 197). As theme parks have spread around the world in this fashion, the aim has been to create in situ a separate world or a controlled "reality" around the selected theme, which the rides, the created characters, and the live entertainment all interfusively augment. In such clustered controlled-reality theme parks, "culture," "history," and "nature" are mined in ways that harness or which appeal to all of the senses (Mill and Morrison, 1985: 211).

Increasingly, these theme parks utilize highly sophisticated technology such as lasers, holographs, interactive games, and robots to complement the resort theme. And as these parks have grown to become huge business and technological "townships," closely calibrated computer control systems have been introduced not only to regulate the rides and the animated entertainment, but almost every operational detail in the running of the park (Nickerson, 1996: 195). These turnkey packages of preprogrammed computer systems are supplied by vendors who provide all the essential system development features (i.e., the hardware/the software/the manual procedures) and all of the installation services (i.e., the training and the follow up assessments) (Gee, 1988: 519).

To a certain extent, notwithstanding the continued concrete pouring and magic-making in and around key nodes like Orlando in central Florida, it appears that the development of large-scale theme parks in North America has come to something of a standstill during the last decade (to 2007). Simply put, the volume of land required for such operations and the depth and range of public sector planning and infrastructure support renders them easy targets for local resident groups to attack. If they are not pitchforked right into the surety of an endless play-zone roost like sunny and ever-reliable Orlando, significant new theme parks (of scale and scope) in North America appear to pass muster only if they are attached to already-established lead tourism and leisure attractions—such as is occurring with the new construction of The Space Race theme park being designed for the NASA headquarters at Cape Canaveral (also conveniently in Florida) (Arnold, 2007). Consonantly, the theme park type has clearly begun to declassify in North America. Smaller theme parks and specialized "resorts" like Sesame Place in Langhorne, Pennsylvania (Anderson, 1991) and dedicated but contained "water parks" are now much more commonplace. And many of the later theme parks in North America have followed the long-expected trend towards creative leisure, where bodies such as The Disney Institute in Florida have experimented with the provision of vacations combined with intellectually challenging and/or physically stimulating self-improvement pursuits (Gee, 1988: 500). Many of these other/emergent theme parks in North America have readapted the social science idea of the lyceum of previous centuries—known as *the Chautauqua* in the USA—where a program of public lectures, musical activities, and specific-subject theater creatively brings vacationers to the theme park "to be stimulated, amused and revitalized" (Gee, 1988: 500), notably during periods of low visitation to or at such places.

Theme parks also offer other competitive realities in the market place today:

- Through the use of clever and composite technology, rival businesses can provide equivalent experiences to theme park exhilarations or small sites at a fraction of the operating costs of theme parks, per se (The Economist, 1994).
- Virtual reality parks have emerged during the last decade which can provide a whole range of variably stimulated experiences—and again these largely "experience-zone" parks do not need the space of traditional theme parks, nor do they need to meet the same level of extremely high insurance costs (Lundberg et al., 1995: 127).
- Major theme parks are also being outshone by immense shopping malls of our era such as West Edmonton Mall (Edmonton, AB, Canada) and Mall of America in Minneapolis, MN where a mix of thrill rides and water play zones can be provided alongside fancy shopping opportunities, and alongside associated/co-managed restaurants and theaters. Often provided under one composite roofing structure, these "localized" malls tend to be immune to external weather conditions, and tend to be much more accessible to large concentrated populations, thereby reducing the clamor of youngsters to travel to "the real thing" at a major (and usually distant, land-consuming) aggregate theme park (Gee, 1988: 200, 238, 241, 245).
- Elsewhere large hotel complexes such as MGM's Grand Hotel in Las Vegas have blurred the distinction between what is a theme park and what is seemingly a hotel by providing an array of cinematic and gaming amenities on its hotel site. All in all, these huge casino hotels, water parks, and mall areas destroy the unique appeal of theme parks as they encroach upon each other's characteristics-of-old (Lundberg et al., 1995: 127).

The Design and Management of Theme Parks

The design and management of theme parks necessarily involve many interrelated facets of development and operation in terms of the choice of the site's "theme" and the subsequent arrangement and appearance of the resultant "park." Indeed, to many commentators on the sphere(s) of tourism, leisure, and hospitality, theme parks are one of the key areas of what could be described as the overall resort development industry. As such, theme park managements are decidedly charged with the responsibility of preserving and enhancing the more "rare" or "desirable" elements of the inherited historic and/or natural environment in which they are located, not just in running a profitable business operation. Hence, master plans for the given theme park tend to have to consider all manner of componential activities that give rise to a litany of ownership, governmental, local community, and sanctioning body/special interest group concerns.

Principally, master plans for theme parks tend to seek to ensure that:

- the identifying theme of the park will be *consistently symbolized* in terms of the actual image potential visitors "read" from everything encountered about the theme parks from its name, its logo, its design, its staff, etc.;
- the visitor, on entering the particular park, has indeed moved into a different/rare/special/better fantasy world with its own atmosphere, rules, and logic;
- the density of attractions is consistent with the historic (fantasy) appeal or the natural visual and activity (fantasy) capacity of the utilized/captured site; and,
- the architecture and technology deployed is sympathetic to the local cultural-heritage and the local environment qualities, and *also to the fantasy illusions being developed in parallel with these hinterland qualities of culture and/or nature.*

The targets are not always consistently upheld at many theme parks around the globe where the lure of the immediate "easy-dollar" has been found overtime to sap the initial fast-paced development drive of management bodies. Such organizations have to learn to take time and effort to neatly fit their attraction sensitively into the surrounding public cultural/public heritage/public natural "atmosphere." Much too frequently, however, easy-to-construct "notice-me" theme park buildings often eventually appear and proliferate at new theme park locations as the original expressed community-oriented rhetoric of the or an early participation plan exercise is all-too-readily forgotten or ignored.

Table 16.1 illustrates the sorts of design and management considerations that lead industry consultants recommend to theme park developers when producing their master plans. It is based upon the common assumption that a thorough market segmentation study is being conducted in parallel (or preferably has already been conducted) to ascertain which:

1 segments have the best growth potential for the site;
2 segments can realistically be attracted to and/or be accommodated at the site; and,
3 of these segments can best be adopted to best meet the park's overall special development objectives (given what generally is each park's own idiosyncratic "distinct advantages").

Table 16.1 thereby lists the componential strategies which industry consultants tend to suggest that theme park designers (and subsequent operators) ought to consider in order to confirm or establish the given park's identity, image, and (unique) character. The table is adapted from the work of Helber in Hollinshead (Helber, 1986a), and constitutes a list of many of the key elements of design and management which help package the theme park "creation"—i.e., its available "products" and its offered "services." As in all resort or park developments, product recognition is deemed to be cardinal in the positioning of the site in what is always (?) an increasingly competitive marketplace. Thereby theme park and tourist resort consultants are inclined to work to the principle that elements and features must collectively and consistently generate a strong positive identity and must exude the right sort of "appeal" to the specific target markets selected. That said, Table 16.1 first lists a number of paramount strategies that routinely facilitate such sorts of "product recognition." Park and resort consultants tend to stress the fact that these elements should be considered in tandem with each other, for the park logo "should have design components which can be incorporated in logos for [current or subsequent] sub-developments within the resort" (Helber, 1986a: 30), and "the theme and character [of the site] should also be incorporated in the resorts logo and promotional graphics" (Helber, 1986a: 30). All told, the product recognition strategies listed in Table 16.1 provide a unifying thread that "knits the resort together" (Helber, 1986a: 30).

Thereafter, the second part of Table 16.1 lists a number of other follow-up strategies, which theme park consultants are inclined to recommend that operating management bodies should take advantage of in appropriately selling the given concept. This second part of Table 16.1 consists of activities pertaining to the running of a large *integrated* theme park. In contrast, a more "low key" or "remote" park complex might be more closely networked with special interest bodies, adventure clubs, or pertinent publications for cost effective promotional exposure, and would require the theme park managing organization to engage in a raft of *good citizenship* local commitments in (perhaps) heritage preservation, wildlife conservation, indigenous sacred-spiritual storytelling, or similar, to yield clear evidence that it is bona fide and trustworthy where it counts in terms of local/hinterland nuances (Helber, 1986a: 31–32).

The Financial Management of Theme Parks

A single chapter of this short length precludes the author from making anything more than

Table 16.1 Marketing Development Strategies for Theme Parks: Components of the Park Master Plan

- **Strategies Based Upon Product Recognition**

The resort master plan should focus upon the finely judged integrated placement and functional interrelationships of the following unique identity-giving/image-bestowing/character-building elements:

Image Building Name
which must be an honest representation of what the park offers, and must appeal to the target markets sought;

Logo or Symbol
which must be simple and tasteful and of a unique style to stimulate instant recognition and product identification;

The Theme, Per Se
which must encapsulate the site's total development image, and which must be incorporated in the project's architecture, the landscape architecture, the signage, and the other main park fixtures;

Continuity In Design
which constitutes an extension of the project's overall theme involving building forms, colors, architecture style, building materials, graphics, common landscape elements, et cetera. These elements must help give the theme park/the theme resort distinct boundaries and limits;

Unifying Signature
which must be conveyed via the park's graphic style and street furniture, viz., via its adopted information signs, its street and night lighting, and its other site amenities;

Identifiable Place "Atmosphere"
which must be considered where the theme park is within or in close proximity to a well known place or identifiable natural/historic feature: the theme park should reflect the character of that location, and incorporate it into the name, the logo, and the unifying signature being created.

- **Strategies Related to the Promotion and Sales of the Park/Resort Product**

Once the theme park has been master-planned (with its design and packaging, as above) the following promotion strategies should be evaluated for implementation:

The Incorporation of Quality (Four Star/Five Star) Hotels
which should have extensive amenities and target-market "relevant" recreational activities and be managed by a well known international chain;

Provision of Onsite Information/Sales and Display Center (Part of Phase 1 of the Development)
which should have models of the perspectives and renderings selected for the total theme park / theme resort and for specific subprojects (which might have their own particular but related "treatments");

Use of Hotel Guest Lists for Subsequent Mail-outs
which should be used for the personal mail-outs, notifying (i) major park events; (ii) off-season bargain packages there; (iii) new theme-appropriate developments, in situ; (iv) etc.;

Hosting of Apposite TV Programs/Apposite Outdoor Activity Events/Apposite Sports Tournaments
which should be designed to attract target-market-relevant "lead guests" and potential buyers, thereby cultivating high national/international recognition to the theme park/theme resort;

Subsidy of Internationally-Known Celebrities and Movie Stars
which should ensure that such celebrities do not only endorse the park, but also become a high-profile part of it through their well-publicized home or condominium ownership there;

Implementation of a Direct "Personal Contact" Real Estate Program
which should create the illusion that the theme park has a scarcity of product in relationship to expressed demand;

Joint Packaging With Major Airline/Airlines
which should help broaden the marketing/promotional coverage of the theme park/theme resort;

Joint Packaging With Rental Car Agency/Agencies
which should help broaden the packaging/programming possibilities for the park/resort.

Source: Adapted from Helber (1986a).

generalized comments on the financial management of theme park developments. Thus, this section will be limited to the provision of some fundamental observations on the complexities involved in investing in and financing such park development.

In terms of investment analysis, it ought to be noted at the outset that the level of risk and uncertainty involved with theme park operation (indeed, with the running of any large any large "resort" or "composite attraction") is far more demanding than the risks commonly involved with or at an ordinary attraction in the tourism industry, especially where the proposed park (or resort) is destined to be built in a remote location. This is principally because the market for the theme parks (resort) is "frequently *far removed* from the location of the development, and is not [generally] committed to visiting the area of [the theme park (resort)] as is the case with [ordinary] business travel or with [regular] travel to visit friends or relatives" (emphasis added) (Lamb, 1986: 47). The market for theme park (resorts) also commonly results from the external catalytic or multiplicative drawing power of many such theme park sites, where they are often "strangled by the greed of its own [and other aroused] developers in over-developing the [target] area" (Lamb, 1986: 47).

Investors interested in supporting a particular theme park operation must be aware of motivations of the numerous parties involved in the project. The objectives of the principal participants are likely to be diverse and conflicting, for instance:

- The (regional/provincial/state/national) government's objectives are generally to develop the tourism industry, generate foreign exchange earnings, provide employment, and stimulate economic growth via the multiplier effect.
- The owner's objectives may cover a wide range of interests. Profit (and return on investment) is certainly a prime motivating factor, but many investors have other pressures to respond to. For instance, development companies frequently participate in projects in order merely to secure profits from construction, while other "international investors" may be looking for a safe haven in which to deposit their wealth.
- The theme park operator's objectives are perhaps simplest to define, routinely being to maximize the profit of the enterprise (and thereby its management fees) and minimize the investment (if any) of that business or that chain in the given park. Operators also seek to avoid or limit their own financial obligations under the park's particular operating agreement. Accordingly, very few operators are willing to enter into a fixed lease agreement with owners, and most are reluctant to provide working capital for the site and thereby expose themselves to operating losses. At the same time, the operator may wish to maintain high standards of site management in order to continue to impress other parties and thereby expand "the chain" (or the new theme park "stylization") in new geographical and conceptual areas where it is not yet active.
- The lender's objectives are (apart from making loans at rates that represent a fair return in relation to the risks involved) largely dependent on the nature of the financial institution itself. Commercial financiers rarely have collateral interests in park or resort projects and the projects tend to be judged entirely on their own merits. In contrast, government fringe financiers frequently are influenced by a mix of local and other political pressures (Lamb, 1986: 50).

In recent years, tourism industry consultants have concluded that it is crucial, therefore, that the developer of a theme park takes time to understand the disperate requirements of those involved. Table 16.2 clarifies at greater length the particular interest of the last named "party" above—viz., *the lender*. It constitutes an attempt to detail the information required by lenders. It is adapted from Mackay's (1986) account, in Australia, of the preferred sorts of information, research, and procedural frameworks that bankers commonly demand. In the original source, Mackay adds the following caveat—that the lending banker will commonly look at five basic risks, which would relate to the

Table 16.2 Financing a Resort/Park Development:
Bank Perspectives and Information Requirements

1. Information On The Developers' Development Objectives
- What are the developer's short-term objectives? [e.g., to sell the developed site?]
- What are the developer's long-term objectives? [e.g., to invest in tourism, or to harness the selected theme, over the long run?]
- Is the development part of an integrated approach to tourism?
- Is the development part of an integrated approach to the thematic subject?
- How does the proposed theme park fit in with the local "cultural"/"heritage"/"natural" environment?
- Which segments of the leisure/tourism/special-interest market is the theme park project intended to serve?

2. Information On The Developers' Financing Objectives
- [Obviously the lowest cost of money is required, but...] ...where should it be raised from?
- Should the finance raised be fixed rate or floating rate?
- What gearing is appropriate for the project?
- What interest servicing is available for the project?
- What is the repayment source?
- What security is being offered to the bank?

3. Information On The Theme Park Project, Itself
- Brief Summary of the Project
  - The Location
  - Site Information [Current Status/Contract Price/Physical Description/Title Description]
- Zoning and Approval Status
  - Permitted Uses
  - Planning Feasibilities [Floor Space Ratios/Heights/Setbacks]
  - Government Authorities involved (with known or potential interest) in general matters of "Conservation"/"Buildings"/"Roads"/"Whatever"
  - Other Sanctioning Bodies (with known or potential interest) in specific thematic matters of "culture," "heritage," "nature," etc.

Nota Bene: alternative courses of action may needed to be provided for critical areas of attention, in the above zoning matters

- The Development Proposal
  - Brief Description
  - Schedule of Income Generating Areas
  - Outline Specifications
  - Plans
- The Construction
  - Costing Summaries [for land and acquisition/adopted gross building area/construction costs/design costs/legal costs/contingencies/escalations/finance]
  - Total Project Costs
  - The Proposed Building Program [a chart showing approvals/design aspects/construction criticalities/documentation records]
  - The Theme Park Project Team [detailing the experience and performance of the builder/the use of major subcontractors/the role of consultants]
  - The Industrial Relations Policy [detailing the team's record and specifying any anticipated problems]
- The Market
  - Current and Anticipated Supply in the Identified Price Brackets
  - Current and Projected Demand
  - Outgoings
  - Projected Growth
  - Adopted Vacancy Levels
  - Anticipated Yields
  - Current Gross Retail Values
  - Net Rental

Continued

Table 16.2 Financing a Resort/Park Development:
Bank Perspectives and Information Requirements *(Continued)*

- Rate of Lease-Up
- Anticipated End Values
- Projected Profit

Risk Identification

Involved bankers will generally assess the theme park project proposal in relation to the following main risks:
- Planning Risks
- Construction Risks
- Market Risk
- Funding Risk
- Security Risk.

Source: Adapted from Mackay (1986). Based on requirements for a hypothetical theme park development in Australia.

development of a sizeable theme park or resort. They are:

1 Planning risks—i.e., have the required consents and licenses been obtained?
2 Construction risks—i.e., is the builder technically capable of completing (and initially stable enough to complete) the proposed development?
3 Market risks—i.e., is the proposed price structure (distribution structure, and such like) appropriate for the intended market? And, is the associated complementary mix of roads, railways, airports, and other infrastructure elements, adequate to deliver the expected flow of visitors to the site?
4 Funding risk—i.e., are the projected cash flow projections reasonable to ensure that loan and interest charges will be met?
5 Security risk—i.e., is there adequate security offered to cover the entire construction phase, to minimize the likelihood that the bank will itself have to sell or even run the development (as mortgagee in possession) in order to get lent monies back?[1]

A number of other useful observations are available in the theme park literature of Tourism Management/Tourism Studies on matter of finance and investment. The following mul-tum-in-parvo statements are taken from, for instance, Lundberg et al. (1995: 124–127):

- **Infrastructure costs.** The critical initial consideration concerns the degree to which the theme park owners and developers have to pay for capital projects to render the site viable. For instance, the Disney Corporation has been rather successful in convincing Florida government authorities to undertake transport and access projects that

benefited Walt Disney World immensely— as with the construction of proximate high-way interchanges by the Florida State Road Development (Fjellman, 1992).

- **Employment costs.** Theme parks have to employ high numbers of workers, and full- and part-time labor costs constitute lead operating expenditures. Large theme parks tend to employ thousands of people.
- **Other lead costs.** Other principal expenditures are food and beverage supplies, service provision, marketing, maintenance, and utilities.
- **Quality level costs.** The Walt Disney Corporation has set the standard for the provision of clean, safe, and tidy family-oriented park environments. Accordingly, in the light of the high standards they have set, sanitation, police, fire protection, and related "quality control" costs are nowadays inclined to be high at theme parks.
- **Vulnerable character of theme park atten dance.** Visitor numbers fluctuate owing to weather conditions, petrol prices, and general economic conditions.
- **Training costs.** Many of the jobs at theme parks are "specialist" despite their extreme seasonality. Accordingly, theme park operators have to carefully select their employees (i.e., their *cast* team at Walt Disney World [Fjellman, 1992]) and much time, effort, and expenditure has to be spent on training them, and continually endeavoring to ensure that they are performing in a fit-for-purpose fashion.
- **The park hinterland and associated profit-ability.** Where theme park operators lack the money to purchase the land surrounding their development, they can end up generating much "lost income" for other (outside) parties that move

in to set up external, but still readily accessible, hotels, restaurants, and leisure operations close to the park.

- **The pressure to spend and respond on technology.** Large and popular theme parks are under pressure to add "rides" or "kinetic and technological features" which are newer or bigger and more challenging than those of competitors. These new attractions not only generally demand land but can be extremely costly to first provide. Lundberg et al. (1995: citing Roy Aron, CEO of Showcase, a corporate maker of simulator rides) point out that—in mid-1990s figures—a roller coaster fixture costs US$4–6 million to build, and there are a myriad of operating costs to subsequently carry on top of that.

- **High profitability potential militated by crowding costs.** Overall, theme parks can be highly profitable once the fixed costs have been met, and subsequently, each additional visitor received (after breaking point has been reached) can yield a high "profit" percentage. This scenario is diminished by the fact that highly popular theme parks can generate high crowd-management costs immediately, and can affect the quality of visitor satisfaction (leading to diminished attendances thereafter). It is not at all easy to get the balance right in terms of high income-yielding attendance versus perceived quality of visitor experience.

- **Overall costs of provision.** Taking the above multum-in-parvo points into consideration, the cost of building a theme park in the USA that had critical mass and a modicum of state-of-the-art technological features was—during the height of the 1990s explosion in provision—estimated at US$300–500 million (*Wall Street Journal*, February 2, 1993—cited in Lundberg et al., 1995: 127). Given the previously mentioned competition from smaller virtual reality "parks" and from "expansive-hotels," etc., and given the intensity of local opposition to theme park provision in North America, nowadays, few corporations or public authorities *there* are believed to even be contemplating the provision of these sorts of cutting-edge, multi-amenity theme parks from yesteryear. It seems that North American knowhow-muscle and knowhow-magic in the theme park business will now be focused upon other contained and totalized regions of the world where consolidated oppositional voices are far less common—such as has occurred with the planned Hollywood Studio DreamWorks theme park of "Dubailand" in the thriving Persian Gulf emirate of Dubai (Elsworth,

2008: 9), for which Jeffrey Katzenberg (a onetime senior figure in Disney theme park operations) is a prominent player.

Theme Parks and Tourism: The Power of Worldmaking

Clearly, theme parks have been highly popular "stars" in the tourism industry's constellation of drawcard attractions, and many of them have been in the van of experience-generating, knowledge-creating, and affiliation-confirming tourist endeavors. It is important, therefore—given the commonplace identity of crises of recent decades (when matters of projected difference have been key issues in national identity debates, in gender identity campaigns, and in diasporic identity articulations of the identity politics "wars" of the late twentieth century and early twenty-first century)—that those who work in senior management or research positions in or on tourism explore the challenge of these contests of being and aspiration (Bauman, 2003). Tourism is not an isolated industry removed from such questions of difference and becoming. It is a highly involved realm of human expression and cultural/societal projectivity: representatively, it is not only axially connected to the en groupe fond hopes of each sort of local, regional, national, or transnational interest group, it is dependent upon them for its source of usable narratives and promotion-worthy inheritances (Robins, 2002: 14–19). It is these sorts of storylines and felt-communal-resources that spawn the very themes the industry seeks to articulate and exploit. Theming is not only big business, it is cultural business (after Appadurai, 1986).

In this expansive light, it is vital that increasing numbers of individuals who work in tourism management and tourism studies understand (and are schooled in) the relations between things economic and things cultural. Through the narratives and the storylines of themed tourism, particular versions of culture, heritage, and nature are circulated, and other versions of en groupe interpretations are otherwise frustrated or foreclosed. It is crucial, then, that those who work in the culture-selection industry that is tourism— and in the culture-production play-space that is tourism—learn to appreciate how the profession of "tourism management" in general (and the business of theme park operation in particular) helps re-elevate certain old identities and received aspirations (yet coterminously fouls up others), and helps to fertilize certain new identities and raw-and-recent aspirations (yet coterminously fails to recognize others). Such is the stuff of the concept of *worldmaking*—an old concept on the mediated meanings of things in and of individual, group, and institutional life (Goodman, 1978), which Hollinshead (2002, 2004) has revivified for tourism studies.

Table 16.3 explains the projective reach and authority of the worldmaking effectivity of tourism. In the table, "worldmaking" is defined as that mix of large and small representations and significatory pursuits which all sorts of people and organizations engage in via their special and elevated programs and their ordinary and mundane actions as they consciously or unconsciously advance accepted versions of the world while simultaneously denying others. The table thereby attests to the commonplace authority of tourism as a worldmaking force, and to the dynamic character of the sorts of worldmaking accounts, which begin in (or which rather more frequently percolate through tourism). To these ends, Table 16.3 also seeks to orientate those who work in tourism management and tourism studies to the generally collaborative and reinforcive thrust of all of this banal but constant worldmaking activity, and to the often under-examined political footprint that such quiet (and even loud) worldmaking culture-production, heritage-production, and nature-production generates. All told, Table 16.3 advances the view that tourism does not just mirror the world about it—tourism manifestly mediates and helps make that very world.

Since space in this chapter is limited and militates against any fulsome explication of

what worldmaking is, those who are eager to read further about the power of the discourse and praxis of tourism in the psychic and material production of peoples, places, and pasts are advised to inspect Hollinshead's (2007) portrayal of tourism as a worldmaking cultural intermediary (a worldmaking heritage intermediary, and a nature making intermediary). Otherwise, one can explore the commentaries—on related worldmaking outlooks in and through tourism—of Fjellman (1992), Horne (1992), Buck (1993), Hall (1994), McKay (1994), Thomas (1994), Kirshenblatt-Gimblett (1998), and Rothman (1998). While none of the above explicitly uses the singular term worldmaking, per se, they each differentially speak with insight and force on the under-appreciated role and function of tourism in the mediation of our understandings of narratives about people, places, and pasts, and on the objectifying governance of particular visions of the locality and/or celebrated reality through tourism.

Prospect: New Sense, New Significations—Old Issues, Old Identities

It may well be that the traditional concept of the massive and singular theme park has had its day in Europe and North America, at least, as had been mentioned earlier in this chapter. It does appear in the developed nations of the West, nowadays, that it is becoming increasingly hard to distinguish what is a theme park from what is a mammoth-sized hotel or resort complex, from what is a massive regional retail complex, from what is a crossroads leisure and educational play park. To Henry James (as discussed in Zukin, 1993: 218), such confluences and confusions comprise a postmodern synergy where the landscape and the vernacular are admixed within a novel realm of an apparent *hotel-civilization* falsity. In such emergent false and faux locations, whole new landscapes are created which blur the liminality between

**Table 16.3 The Representational Power of "Worldmaking" Defined:
The Concept Applied to the Inventive Agency of Theme Parks**

- **Working Definition**

"Worldmaking," as used in this chapter, is the creative and often or faux imaginative processes and projective promotional activities which management agencies, other mediating bodies, and individuals strategically and ordinarily engage in to purposely (or otherwise unconsciously) privilege particular dominant/favored representations of people/places/pasts within a given or assumed region, area, world, over and above other actual or potential representations of those subjects.

- **Some Caveats On the Agency or Effectivity of "Worldmaking"**

Caveat 1: Authority Through Worldmaking

The worldmaking imaginary tends to consist of a representational repertoire of sites, subjects, and storylines, which view the world from standpoints which are important to that authorizing management or mediating agency or engaged individual.

Illustration: *The Application of the Concept to Theme Park Management/Development*

After Fjellman (1992) on Walt Disney World—what does the given theme park authorize through the stories and symbolizations it captures/appropriates/projects?

Caveat 2: The Dynamic Life of Worldmaking Projections

The worldmaking imaginary tends to be platformed upon received narratives revered by the interest group/subpopulation/society with which that management, mediative agency, or individual associates (or seeks to affiliate), but those foundational narratives may be given subtle or substantive (and not always recognized or admitted) reinterpretations over time.

Illustration: *The Application of the Concept to Theme Park Management/Development*

After (Thomas, 1994) on the changing life of discourses about peoples and places—how have the significations of place and space projected at the given theme park (i) deliberately, and (ii) accidentally/adventitiously altered the views that are commonly held of particular cultural or natural entities?

Caveat 3: The Collaborative and Cumulative Force of Worldmaking

The worldmaking imaginary sometimes tends to purposely or unwittingly take on board interpretations of other hues (about history/nature/the cosmos) which have either originated or been consolidated elsewhere either within distant/removed/foreign invasive populations, or within collaborative industrializing corporate settings which are powerful in the prevailing regional/national/international marketplace.

Illustration: *The Application of the Concept to Theme Park Management/Development*

After Kirshenblatt-Gimblett (1998) on the collaborative "madeness" and "hereness" of performed projections of place and space—how do the stories and significations emanating from the given theme park support (or otherwise conflict with) previously hegemonic interpretations of locality ABC?

Caveat 4: The Often Undersuspected Political Reach of Worldmaking

The worldmaking imaginary is always inherently (and sometimes pungently) political, inevitably advantaging some populations over others in particular ways, while coterminously suppressing those other peoples in large or small ways—though those who give voice to such normalizing or mainstreaming acts of articulation may not always be alert to the culuro-political effects of that symbolic/significatory dominance.

Illustration: *The Application of the Concept to Theme Park Management/Development*

After Hall (1994) on the industrial production of culture and place through tourism—in what senses are the corporate symbolizations found at the given theme park indeed "political," and which local/regional/national special interest groups do these mobilized (political) significations thereby tend to silence/subdue/suppress?

Source: the above definition predominantly constitutes a condensation of the broad ideas on the *frequently fabricative* nature of the held cultural heritage and the received sociopolitical inheritances of populations, as given in Hollinshead (2002, 2004, 2007). The definition does however also draw from Goodman's (1978: 6) old explanation of symbolic worldmaking, where the found ways of worldmaking alluded to in any context (particularly those in art, craft, and music) always start from worlds already on hand; i.e., are always constructed within familiar regimes of ordering the world as already known and supported by the given worldmaker/worldmaking group.

what is ostensibly "market" and what is ostensibly "place" (Zukin, 1993: 219). Such fantasy environments and such spectral landscapes are built in both grandness of scale and scope, becoming a noted magnet for external *footloose capital*. In these ways, the old form of entertainment—the amusement park—is elevated and translated into a new landscape, hotelscape, or cityscape of power in which the fantasy realms created constitute a seemingly false orb or a faux theatre where "the visual consumption [that is constantly generated] is inseparable from the centralized structures of economic power" (Zukin, 1993: 221) which spawn and control it. Hence, hotel-civilization becomes a mixed-up zone of imaginary landscapes that form various prototype designs for a new sorts of collective life—that is, of an aspirant way of living pointedly reinforced through the regular display of appropriated and authorized celluloid visualization. In such fantasy landscapes, preferred or designated collective life is one based upon domestic consumption itself, where corporate symbols determine the boundaries of the consumers' held and lived realities. In such onstage and mixed-up landscapes (or rather, storyscapes), it is hard to determine where nature or culture actually stop and start and where artifice indeed takes over. Under hotel civilization, "culture" becomes anything that can be captured for presentation within this dominant and aggrandizing realm of consumption.

So, all sorts of private-for-profit, private-not-for-profit, and government bodies nowadays seem to be wedded to the concept of "theming" as each seeks to give their particular tourist site, their historical, heritage, or natural "park" cum "center" cum "complex" an easily understandable tag, title, or tailoring in pursuit of this endless consumerism. Such is the constant merchandising of "all things" in all sorts of hotel civilization settings. For this reason, it may be more sensible to concentrate now (in this chapter) upon the broader subject of "theming" (rather than upon the specific subject of "theme parking") to account for such hybrid operational circumstances in

the various tourism-plus, leisure-plus, and heritage-plus *national, ethnic, local*, and *psychic-aspirational* (and, of course, *business*) visions of the communal or the new-tribal present. Thus it is important that those who work in research and advocacy positions in tourism management and tourism studies become rather well versed in the new plural (and often open-ended) consumption-oriented conceptualities which these prospective mixed-theme settings generate—as evidenced, for example, in the island-creating or "Universe"—making work of Australian developer Chris O'Donnell in what he regards as "the real estate heaven" of Dubai (Hewitson, 2008: 3), or in the work of Heron International in wanting to build no less than 20 brand new *Heron City* developments ("blending leisure, retail, and entertainment" [Thomas, 1999: 22]) across Europe in Lille, Madrid, Stockholm, etc. In tourism studies, it is nowadays essential that researchers evaluate not merely the role and function of *theme parks* as the privatization of public space, but the role and function of *theme cities* and *theme landscapes* in the private conquest of cultural and natural narratives, and in the private appropriation of community inheritances (Davis, 1999).

It would therefore be highly relevant for those who plan tourism management and tourism studies programs of study to include tuition and/or training that more directly addresses these ideoscapes of social control—that is, of the dynamic *consumer aesthetics* of place. These matters of globalized and glocalized contemporary tourism are very much part and parcel of the resymbolization and the reproduction of seemingly local and seemingly indigenous local life. They constitute the play of power in the de-aesthetization and re-aesthetization of places and spaces: that is, of the sorts of contests of value, and sorts of predominantly urban form "profusions and confusions" in which cultural studies and media studies scholars are perhaps rather more assiduous (Griffin, 1998) than those who have been schooled in tourism management/tourism studies. Such fresh/innovative schooling in tourism studies would conceivably cover some of the following terms to describe who is doing what to whom and which in and through the themed complexes of the moment—where these five defined constructs are taken from a glossary of 53 concepts on "representation" and "signification," as recorded in Hollinshead (1998b):

1 **Commodity aesthetics.** The rhetorical activity or process through which corporations create commodity niches for their products and services, where the power of such marketplace discourse distinguishes their offerings in a pervasive language of image (based on cleverly harnessed design, packaging, and advertising "treatments") rather than upon product/service content.

2 **Creeping surrealism.** The decided, creative, and repeated intermixture of the real with the fantastic to such an extent that a state of euphoric disorientation commonly results where it becomes difficult for many to distinguish one from the other, where some may fear that there *is nothing "real" anymore, and where some may not even care about that possible loss of "reality."*

3 **Culture redux.** The condition where powerful organizations invent new cultural symbols and appropriate others in order to neutralize the "real" differences between things thereby to project certain preferred narratives about the world, where culture and commodity become dialectically intertwined to serve as a medium of legitimacy for that narrower/prescribed realm of living in nature and geography and being in heritage and culture.

4 **Emplotment.** The creative doctoring of text where the basic facts are cleverly packaged (notably through technological brilliance and technological exhilaration) and deconstructed and/or juxtaposed in order to gain particular added or replacement significances, and extra reach.

5 **Pasteurized history.** That sort of orchestrated historical amnesia where an organization purposely and carelessly recontextualizes or decontextualizes the past in order to fit particular favored emplotments of events and particular projections of value: the resultant treatment of history thus tends to have its unpalatable "truths" removed, just as pasteurized culture and pasteurized nature might consist of like sterilizations of received local inheritances or environment, respectively.

The other terms offered in that *Current Issues in Tourism* glossary—a list originally inspired by the commentaries of Fjellman (1992) on World Disney World in Florida—are:

- ambiguity;
- ambivalence;
- bricolage/bricoleur;
- commodification;
- commodity form;
- commodity zen;
- cross-corporate power;
- cross-referential;
- marketing;
- dature;
- decontextualization;
- deography;
- disneyification;
- disneylaw;
- discourse;
- distory;
- duture;
- entrepreneurial;
- violence;
- euphoric disorientation;
- exteriority;
- fantasmatics;
- hegemonic values;
- historicide;
- hyperreality;
- Huxleyan control;
- imagineering;
- intended shrine;
- interpretive autonomy;
- intertextuality;
- legerdemain;
- metastasis;
- metastory;
- microveracity;
- Orwellian control;
- Other, the;
- performativity;
- postmodernity;
- postmonauts;
- public culture;
- referential reason;
- self-referential;
- marketing;
- signification;
- simulacrum;
- soma;
- symbolic legitimacy;
- tao;
- techne;
- universe maintenance;
- utopia.

It may well be that the future decades in theme park design and development—or, rather, in themed center, themed complex design and development—will very much be one of bricolage and of highly imagineered narrative-making as various private sector bodies and public institutions contend amongst each other to maintain their favored "universes" (i.e., to privilege their received or refined worldviews on particular public culture, public heritage, and public nature subjects) via their own controlled technologies and/or channels of symbolic legitimacy. We already have, at the Rover's Return television studios in Lancashire, for instance "a representation of a representation of a representation" (Goodwin, 1989): we already visit such themed sites "traveling in hyperreality" (Eco, 1986). Our already-developed "society of the spectacle" (Debord, 1983) is likely to be even more *spectacular*, as powerful new techno-kinetic production-houses like the highly ideative Pixar Studio join forces with (or contend against) established theme park players like the Disney Corporation (Rushe, 2005). Such are the creative, but often volatile, co-productive synergies of the consumer aesthetics, which typify the financial and operational dealings of the moment.

What is important, in the theming of places and spaces, is not so much that the so called contemporary demise of received history and the supposed decay of orthodox heritage metanarratives (Lyotard, 1984) which have seemingly brought about *the death of tradition*. What considerably matters is how "our conception of what tradition is [is changing]" (AlSayyad, 2004). It is increasingly wise and necessary for those who work in tourism development to expect contestation as to what it is appropriate to celebrate or show of in our contesting public cultures, public heritages, and public natures. Globalization has unsettled the conventional connections between place and culture, place and heritage, and place and nature, and our new more democratic, more pluralized, more admixed politics of difference are conceivably giving rise to all sorts of new acceptable visions of peoples, places, and pasts (Appadurai, 1990). Just as Roy (2004) has encountered an end to the traditional ways in which we think about tradition, so we may now have encountered *an end to the traditional ways of thinking about theming*. While recent decades in tourism studies may have required scholars—after Hobsbawm and Ranger (1983)—to chronicle how traditions have in fact been *invented* and thereby manufactured, packaged, and deployed through tourism, notably by dominant modes of capitalistic social consumerism, the future of theming (and the future of projection through tourism?) is likely to be much more "open" (Venn, 2006). Invented traditions and invented cultures, heritages, and natures will continue to appear, but the twin fields of tourism management and tourism studies will need more flexible ways of characterizing and differentiating them.

Indeed, if it is the job of a theming imagineer like California's Joe Rohde (for the Walt Disney family of companies) "to create the illusion of reality in the minds of [site visitors]" (Higgins, 2006: 90), it is the job of tourism studies and tourism sciences scholars to analyze and interpret what is happening through the production of, and customer adoption of, these new imaginary worlds (Davis, 1996; Ellwood, 1998; Tuan, 1997).

Today, it appears that the future of theming through tourism (and its new, evolving, and dynamic gazes) are likely to be much more about the more inaugurate possibilities of thematic projection. Many more of the invented traditions of the future of tourism are not so much expected to be globalized as highly glocalized (Irazábal, 2004: 18), that is, they will be projected differentially from hybrid and fluxional positions in different particular places and in different particular contexts. In Bhabha's (1994) view, the postcolonial world will give to all sorts of new restless or unsettled spaces—new *third space* positions (see Hollinshead, 1998c, 1998d, both translating Bhabha's thoughts on interstitial culture to tourism)—that is, to half-light locations of considerable ambivalence and ambiguity (Platenkamp, 2007). Yet it is from these emergent but difficult restless and halfway positions that much of the will to articulate "self" and "identity" is expected (by Bhabha) to arise. If Bhabha is indeed correct, "traditions" will persist and grow, but in unanticipated and unexpected ways. Just as many unfolding traditions will be articulated via all sorts of new and flickering *new sense* positions of difference, of being, and of becoming, so one might expect these to be all sorts of new and flickering *new sense* thematized expressions. And amongst them is bound to be not only "the new," "the latest," and "the previously suppressed," but "the-old-creatively-resurrected-as-the-third-space" or as "the-new-creatively-resurrected-as-the-old." If the words of Lu (2004: 228) may be adopted here, "the debris [of old themes and subjects] that has been smashed by the previous storm [of recent postmodern and postcolonial global and local truthmaking] is more than just a residue: it holds the potential to bring about another [representational/symbolic] storm."

The future of *theming* is likely therefore to be shaped not just by the authoritarian state and the aggrandizing market, but also by emergent enunciating "affinity groups" (Platenkamp, 2007)—that is, by the hybrid ethnic community, by the unfolding special interest group, and/or by the cross-national ideo-mongers of culture, of heritage, and of cultural versions of "nature" at each particular place of exploitable difference or celebration (Whatmore, 2002). The future of theming is unlikely to be static: it will have new transitional, consumptive, and aesthetic contours of possibility. One can turn to a miscellany of authors who can help fill in for us where the art and craft of theme park provision has been over the past three decades, for instance:

- on matters of design and development—via Helber (1986b and 1986c);
- on the so called "impacts" of theme park placement—via Stynes and Stewart (1996); McCrone et al. (1995); Hendry (2000); Brodie (2006);
- on community or special interest group critiques of theme park operation—via Powers (1987); Keelan (1996); Walsh (1996); Macdonald (1997); Hannam and Halewood (2006); and,
- on the commodity aesthetics of theme park placemaking—via Urry (1990); Hollinshead (1998a, 1998b); Byrne and McQuillan (1999); Philips (1999); Warren (1999); Rojek (2002); and Stewart (2005).

But the future of theming is likely to in volve new narrative possibilities and new technological hegemonies not necessarily or fully depicted by the above 20 authors. All sorts of new possible group-to-industry relationships (Venn, 2006) are likely to emerge across the world through tourism, where reformed authorities and/or newly enunciating bodies join forces with emergent techno-capitalistic enterprises to have their say, to project their view, and have you and I celebrate their long-esteemed or their recently captured sacred or profane themes. Such are

the possible, the alternative, and the not fully anticipatable standpoints and dynamic spaces from which future themes will be issued.

Yet, much of the old, received worldmaking agency of theme park design and development will continue in specific parts of the world where corporative bodies can rule the roost both over grand storylines and large blocks of matching territory. Some old-sense businesses in the theme park industry will continue to give the tourist or leisure seeker under-examined representations and unreconstructed interpretations of peoples and places. Some fast-buck merchants will continue to crop up in the industry, rather insensitive to the contested political and symbolic contours of culture, of heritage, and of nature. There will always be hackneyed and trivialized interpretations of people, places, and pasts in tourism. In an industry so tentacular and impossible to regulate as tourism, there will always be representers, symbolizers, and themers who will conjure up for us visitable versions of our culture, our history, and our nature that never were quite like that (Hollinshead, 1988; Urry, 1990). Certainly, the cognoscenti in history, in literature, and such, will axiomatically and long bemoan such looseness of interpretation which are being generated day-by-day through the new consumer aesthetic power plays of tourism and themed "cityscape civilization." A pungent example of this contempt for the trivialities of unbridled theming has indeed arisen as the last lines of this chapter are being written in the UK—that is, with the opening of a new "Tribute to Dickens" theme park in Kent. But (as Davidson [2007] ponders for that perhaps loose treatment of Dickensian life there in the southeast corner of England, and—by extension—for all tourism *themevilles* and all hotel civilization *themezones*), will the Playstation® generation really care? Do googlers and bloggers of today's buzzing immediacy indeed value knowing which century Dickens lived in, or what he had to say about the poor? Who is ever going to vet each example of good or bad theming: and who is ever going to vet the selection of those good or bad inspectors of the industrialized scripting of peoples, places, and pasts? Who has the mandate to examine the faithful interpretation of serious and not-so-serious things?

Note

1 Adapted from Mackay in (Hollinshead, 1986: 58–59); for a related list of developer perspectives (involving an account of theme motivations of (1) professional development companies; (2) track record developers; and (3) "new" developers, see Harston in (Hollinshead, 1986: 64–67). Again—as for Mackay—the illustrated context is Australian).

References

AlSayyad, N. (Ed.) (2004). *Consuming Traditions, Manufacturing Heritage: Global Norms and Urban Forms in The Age of Tourism*. London: Routledge.

Anderson, J. (1991). "Sesame Place through Children's Eyes." *Fun World*, August: 38–41.

Appadurai, A. (Ed.) (1990). "Disjunctive and Difference in the Global Cultural Economy." In M. Featherstone (Ed.), *Global Culture: Nationalism, Globalization and Modernity* (pp. 295–310). London: Sage.

Appadurai, A. (1986). *The Social Life of Things: Commodities in Cultural Perspective*. Cambridge: Cambridge University Press.

Arnold, K. (2007). "Fifty Years On: The Space Race is Still a Blast." *The Daily Telegraph* (London), May 26.

Barker, C. (2004). *The Sage Dictionary of Cultural Studies*. London: Sage.

Bauman, Z. (2003). "From Pilgrim to Tourist—or a Short-History of Identity." In S. Hall and P. du Gay (Eds.), *Questions of Cultural Identity* (pp.18–36). London: Sage.

Bhabha, H. (1994). *The Location of Culture*. London: Routledge.

Brodie, S. (2006). "Sex 'Theme Park' Without Any Rides—But Lots of Interactivity." *The Daily Telegraph* (London), April 14.

Buck, E. (1993). *Paradise Remade: The Politics of Culture and History in Hawaii*. Philadelphia, PA: Temple University Press.

Byrne, E. and McQuillan, M. (1999). *Deconstructing Disney*. London: Pluto Press.

Davidson, M. (2007). "Dickens Theme Park Hopes—To Live Up To Expectations." *The Daily Telegraph* (London), May 26: 11.

Davidson, R. (1992). *Tourism in Europe*. London: Pitman.

Davis, S.G. (1996). "The Theme Park: Global Industry and Cultural Form." *Media, Culture and Society*, 18: 399–422.

Davis, S.G. (1999). "Space Jam: Media Conglomerates Build the Entertainment City." *European Journal of Communication*, 14(4): 435–459.

Debord, G. (1983). *Society of the Spectacle*. Detroit, MI: Black and Red.

Eco, U. (1986). *Travels in Hyper-Reality*. London: Picador.

Economist (1994). "Theme Parks: Feeling the Future." February 19–25: 74–79.

Ellwood, W. (1998). "Inside the Disney Dream Machine." *New Internationalist*, 308 (December).

Elsworth, C. (2008). "DreamWorks Magic Comes to Dubai." *The Daily Telegraph* (London): 9.

Fjellman, S.M. (1992). *Vinyl Leaves: Walt Disney World and America*. Boulder, CO: Westview Press.

Gee, C.Y. (1988). *Resort Development and Management*. East Lansing, MI: The Educational Institute of the American Hotel and Motel Association.

Goeldner, C.R., Ritchie, J.R.B. and McIntosh, R.W. (2000). *Tourism: Principles, Practices, Philosophies*. New York: John Wiley.

Goodman, N. (1978). *Ways of Worldmaking*. Hassocks: Harvester.

Goodwin, A. (1989). "Nothing Like The Real Thing." *New Statesman and Society*, August 12.

Govan, F. and Reynolds, N. (2007). "Wizard's Army Hunt for Madelaine." *The Daily Telegraph* (London), July 17: 8.

Griffin, G. (1998). "The Good, the Bad, and the Peculiar: Cultures and Policies of Urban Planning and Development on the Gold Coast." *Urban Policy and Research*, 16(4): 285–291.

Hall, C.M. (1994). *Tourism and Politics: Policy, Power, and Place*. Chichester: John Wiley & Sons.

Hannam, K. and Halewood, C. (2006). "European Viking Themed Festivals: An Expression of Identity." *Journal of Heritage Tourism*, 1(1): 17–31.

Harston, J. (1986). "Financing a Tourist Development: Developer Perspectives." In K. Hollinshead (Ed.), *Tourist Resort Development: Markets, Places and Inpacts* (pp. 64–67). Proceedings of National Conference. Artarmon, NSW, Australia, November 1985. Lindfield, NSW, Australia: Centre for Leisure and Tourism Studies, Kuring-gai College of Advanced Education.

Helber, L. (1986a). Market Development Strategies for Tourist Resorts. In K. Hollinshead (Ed.), *Tourist Resort Development: Markets, Places and Inpacts* (pp. 27–32). Proceedings of National Conference. Artarmon, NSW, Australia, November 1985. Lindfield, NSW, Australia: Centre for Leisure and Tourism Studies, Kuring-gai College of Advanced Education.

Helber, L. (1986b). "Integrated Approaches to Resort Development." In K. Hollinshead (Ed.), *Tourist Resort Development: Markets, Places and Inpacts* (pp. 75–81). Proceedings of National Conference. Artarmon, NSW, Australia, November 1985. Lindfield, NSW, Australia: Centre for Leisure and Tourism Studies, Kuring-gai College of Advanced Education.

Helber, L. (1986c). Site Development and Project Implementation. In K. Hollinshead (Ed.), *Tourist Resort Development: Markets, Places and Inpacts* (pp. 126–132). Proceedings of National Conference. Artarmon, NSW, Australia, November 1985. Lindfield, NSW, Australia: Centre for Leisure and Tourism Studies, Kuring-gai College of Advanced Education.

Hendry, J. (2000). *The Orient Strikes Back: A Global View of Cultural Display*. Oxford: Berg.

Hewitson, J. (2008). "Master of the Universe." *The Daily Telegraph* (Special Supplement on "Overseas Property") (London), March 29: 3.

Higgins, R. (2006). "A Life in the Day: Joe Rohde." *Sunday Times,* December 3 (Magazine) (London), 90.

Hobsbawm, E. and Ranger, T. (1983). *The Invention of Tradition*. New York: Cambridge University Press.

Hollinshead, K. (1988). "Publications in Review: 'A Sunny Place for Shady Peoples: The Real Gold Coast Story.'" *Annals of Tourism Research*, 15(3): 449–557.

Hollinshead, K. (1998a). "Cross-Referential Marketing Across Walt Disney's 'World': Corporate Power and Imagineering of Nation and Culture." *Tourism Analysis*, 2(2): 217–228.

Hollinshead, K. (1998b). "Disney and Commodity Aesthetics: A Critique of Fjellman's Analysis of 'Distory' and the 'Historicide' of the Past." *Current Issues in Tourism*, 1(1): 58–119.

Hollinshead, K. (1998c). "Tourism, Hybridity and Ambiguity: The Relevance of Bhabha's Third Space Cultures." *Journal of Leisure Research*, 30(1): 121–156.

Hollinshead, K. (1998d). "Tourism and the Restless Peoples: A Dialectical Inspection of Bhabha's Halfway Populations." *Tourism, Culture and Communication*, 1(1): 49–77.

Hollinshead, K. (2002). "Tourism and the Making of the World: Tourism and the Dynamics of Our Contemporary Tribal Lives." *The Year 2002—Honors Excellence Lecture*. The Honors College. Miami: Florida International University.

Hollinshead, K. (2004). "Tourism and New Sense: Worldmaking and the Enunciative Value of Tourism." In C.M. Hall and H. Tucker (Eds.), *Tourism and Postcolonialism: Contested Discourse, Identities and Representations* (pp. 25–42). London: Routledge.

Hollinshead, K. (2007). "'Worldmaking' and the Transformation of Place and Culture." In I. Ateljevic, A. Pritchard and N. Morgan (Eds.), *The Critical Turn in Tourism Studies: Innovative Research Methodologies* (pp. 165–193). Amsterdam: Elsevier.

Horne, D. (1992). *The Intelligent Tourist*. McMahon's Point, NSW, Australia: Margaret Gee Holdings.

Irazábal, C. (1994). "Architecture and the Production of Postcolonial Images: Invocations of Tradition Versus Critical Transnationalism in Curitiba." In N. AlSayyad, (Ed.), *The End of Tradition?* (pp. 144–170). London: Routledge.

Jafari, Jafa, (Ed.) (2000). *Encyclopedia of Tourism*. London: Routledge.

Keelan, N. (1996). "Maori Heritage: Visitor Management and Interpretation." In C.M. Hall and S. McArthur (Eds.), *Heritage*

Management in Australia and New Zealand (pp. 195–201). Melbourne: Oxford University Press.

Kirshenblatt-Gimblett, B. (1998). *Destination, Culture: Tourism, Museums, and Heritage*. Berkeley: University of California Press.

Lamb, A.N. (1986). "Investment Analysis for Resort Development." In K. Hollinshead (Ed.), *Tourist Resort Development: Markets, Places and Inpacts* (pp. 46–54). Proceedings of National Conference. Artarmon, NSW, Australia, November 1985. Lindfield, NSW, Australia: Centre for Leisure and Tourism Studies, Kuring-gai College of Advanced Education.

Lu, D. (2004). "The Latency of Tradition: On the Vicissitudes of Walls in Contemporary China." In N. AlSayyad (Ed.), *The End of Tradition?* London: Routledge.

Lundberg, D.E. (1985). *The Tourist Business*. New York: C.B.I. [Van Nostrand Reinhold].

Lundberg, D.E., Krishnamoorthy M. and Staverga, M.Hcn. (1995). *Tourism Economics*. New York: John Wiley.

Lyotard, J-F. (1984). *The Postmodern Condition: A Report on Knowledge*. Manchester: Manchester University Press.

Macdonald, S. (1997). *Reimagining Culture: Histories, Identities and the Gaelic Renaissance*. Oxford: Berg.

Mackay, K.I. (1986). "Financing a Resort Development: Bank Perspectives." In K. Hollinshead (Ed.), *Tourist Resort Development: Markets, Places and Inpacts* (pp. 55–58). Proceedings of National Conference. Artarmon, NSW, Australia, November 1985. Lindfield, NSW, Australia: Centre for Leisure and Tourism Studies, Kuring-gai College of Advanced Education.

McCrone, D., Morris, A. and Kiely, R. (Eds.) (1995). *Scotland—The Brand: The Making of Scottish Heritage*. Edinburgh: Edinburgh University Press.

McKay, I. (1994). *Quest for the Folk*. Montreal: McGill and Queens University Press.

Mill, R.C. and Morrison, A.M. (1985). *The Tourism System. An Introductory Text*. Englewood Cliffs, NJ: Prentice Hall.

Morley, D. and Chen, D.K. (Eds.) (1996). *Stuart Hall*. London: Routledge.

Nickerson, N.P. (1996). *Foundations for Tourism*. Upper Saddle River, NJ: Prentice Hall.

Philips, D. (1999). "Narrativised Space: The Functions of Story in the Theme Park." In D. Crouch (Ed.), *Leisure/Tourism Geographies* (pp. 91–108). London: Routledge.

Platenkamp, V. (2007). *Contexts in Tourism and Leisure Studies: A Cross-Cultural Contribution to the Production of Knowledge*. Wageningen: Wageningen University.

Powers, R. (1987). *White Town Drowsing*. New York: Penguin.

Reynolds, N. (2007). "Harry Falls for The Charm of a Florida Retirement." *The Daily Telegraph* (London), June 1: 15.

Robins, K. (2002). "What in the World's Going On." In P. du Gay (Ed.), *Production of Culture/Cultures of Production* (pp. 11–66). London: Sage.

Rojek, C. (2002). "Fatal Attractions." In D. Boswell and J. Evans (Eds.), *Representing the Nation: A Reader—Histories, Heritage and Museums*. London: Routledge. [First published in collaboration with The Open University in 1999].

Rothman, H.K. (1998). *Devil's Bargains: Tourism in the Twentieth-Century American West*. Lawrence: University Press of Kansas.

Roy, A. (2004). "Nostalgias of the Modern." In N. AlSayyad, (Ed.) *The End of Tradition?* (pp.63–86). London: Routledge.

Rushe, D. (2005). "Disney and Pixar Head for Divorce." *Sunday Times* (London), November 13.

Stewart, J. (2005). *The Disney Wars*. New York: Simon and Schuster.

Stynes, D.J. and Stewart, S.I. (1996). "Impacts of the Grand Traverse Resort, Michigan, U.S.A.: Are Perceptions Consistent with Reality?" In L.C. Harrison and W. Husbands (Eds.), *Practicing Responsible Tourism* (pp. 239–260). New York: John Wiley.

Thomas, M. (1999). "Heron Cities." *Leisure Management*, 19(6): 22–23.

Thomas, N. (1994). *Colonialism's Culture: Anthropology, Travel and Government*. Princeton, NJ: Princeton University Press.

Tuan, Y. (1997). "Disneyland: Its Place in World Culture." In K.A. Marling (Ed.), *Designing Disney's Theme Parks: The Architecture of Reassurance*. New York: Flammerion.

Urry, J. (1990). *The Tourist Gaze: Leisure and Travel in Contemporary Society*. London: Sage.

Venn, C. (2006). *The Postcolonial World: Towards Alternative Worlds*. London: Sage.

Walsh, B. (1996). "Authenticity and Cultural Representation: A Case Study of Maori Tourism Operators." In C.M. Hall and S. McArthur (Eds.), *Heritage Management in Australia and New Zealand* (pp. 202–207). Melbourne: Oxford University Press.

Warren, S. (1999). "Cultural Contestation at Disneyland Paris." In D. Crouch (Ed.), *Leisure/Tourism Geographies: Practices and Geographical Knowledge* (pp. 109–125). London: Routledge.

Whatmore, S. (2002). *Hybrid Geographies: Natures, Cultures, Spaces*. London: Sage.

Zukin, S. (1993). *Landscapes of Power: From Detroit to Disney World*. Berkeley, CA: University of California Press.

17

Architecture and Urban Planning: Practical and Theoretical Contributions

Robert Mugerauer Jr.

Introduction

Architecture, planning, and tourism have been partners in shaping urban and rural places for commerce, consumption, and inhabitation, but this collaboration is deeply interwoven with political as well as economical and social needs.

The first section below presents the main analytic categories and approaches to urban destination development in a historical framework. Though laid out in a temporal sequence in order to be followed more easily, this is not a historical narrative covering tourism in relation to architecture and urban planning. Rather, it is the "effective history"—what is alive now, bearing on the present and future—and thus opens up to the later sections covering problems, debates, and future directions. The goal is to assess the progress and remaining tasks if collectively we are to deal with what Ashworth, perhaps shockingly, called the double neglect of urban tourism, where tourism studies "have tended to neglect the urban context," while "urban studies . . . have been equally neglectful of the importance of the tourism function" and though the area is growing, it "still remains comparatively unresearched" (Ashworth 1989: 33, cited in Hall and Page, 2002: 185–186).

A Rich Heritage

As political, religious, economic, and cultural centers, cities have long been the destinations of travelers and have impressed visitors with their monumental buildings and clearly ordered urban planning. In ancient Rome we already find almost all the facilities and great public spaces associated with modern tourism: the Appian Way, allowing visitors easy access to the forums (shopping mall, city hall, and civic center all in one), the Pantheon, Coliseum, Circo Massimo, Trajan's Column, the Baths of Agrippa, as well as summer retreats away from the heat and noise of the city such as Hadrian's Villa near Tivoli—all of which remained tourist attractions through the Renaissance "Grand Tour" (Clelland, 2000; MacDonald, 2000a). Similar stories can be told about Beijing, Kyoto, Angkor-Jayavarman, Varanasi, Mekka, Istanbul, London, Teotihuacán-Mexico City, Lima and other major cities and pilgrimage sites around the world. Thus, tourism and urban architecture and planning are scarcely new phenomena.

In the modern era, the great expositions and World Fairs drew thousands to wonder at the latest technological inventions and cultural displays from around the globe. Following the London Exhibition of 1851, housed in the Crystal Palace (considered the first true World's Fair), the great cities of the world vied to assert their leadership in the industrial era by hosting these events: Philadelphia in 1876 featured the telephone and typewriter; Paris in 1878, motorcars, refrigeration, electricity; New York in 1939, television, air conditioning and plastics; Brussels in 1958, the nuclear reactor and the atomic clock (Badger, 1979: 9). The modern resuscitation of the Olympics also was urban focused and prestige oriented.

It is not an exaggeration to claim that through these events cities learned to coordinate teams of diverse professionals and workers to transform existing, dense environments to host millions of visitors. For example, the World Exposition of 1893 in Chicago required financial planning, extensive landfill on the site, a transportation system to allow access by 35 different railroad lines, parks, and the buildings and activities themselves (Badger: 1979). Cities came to understand that beyond facilities and planned land uses, hosting large numbers of visitors involves complex political, economic, management, and marketing processes, all operative within historical, social, and economic contexts. Whether such events can be counted on to be financial successes remains an unresolved issue: many lost substantial money and continue to do so—the Paris World's Fair of 1855 returned barely over 10% of the money expended, while the same city's 1889 Fair (featuring the Eiffel Tower) was a financial success with 25–30,000,000 visitors attending (Badger, 1979). Chicago declined hosting the 1992 commemoration of Columbus' landing because of concerns with the cost and likely losses, while civic promoters and developers continually push for substantial public expenditures to become hosts for such mega-events. Research in event tourism has brought attention to the economic impacts and to a lesser extent to the social and political impacts of hosting various types of events in the urban destination (Getz, 2005, 2008; Roche, 1992; also see Quinn [Chapter 27] on festivals and events in this *Handbook*).

Lessons of the 1960s and 1970s

Contemporary tourism is seen to be a feature of the modern era, and particularly as an outcome of the industrial age, at a time when there is an unprecedented amount of disposable income for leisure and recreational pursuits, intensified international business activity and transportation systems that were developed in order to accommodate huge numbers of travelers. Many scholars point to Thomas Cook as the progenitor of mass tourism. The emergence and rapid growth of rail travel (as well as declining cost) and passenger steamship services made travel much easier. Thomas Cook organized the first group excursion tour from Leicester to Loughborough (England) in 1841 and went on to become an international tour operator by the 1860s (Cormack, 1998; Gladstone, 2005). However, it was not obvious after World War II that tourism would have an urban focus. There were new resorts aiming to capitalize on the traditions of sea bathing and spas as well as on the increasing popularity of golf, gambling, and the newly affordable tropical destinations promising "sun, sand and sex" (Schwartz, 1997). Major urban centers did attract people to their historical landmarks, cultural treasures, landscaped parks, and a variety of stimulating nightlife; but, especially in Europe and the USA, cities were experiencing hard times as the industrial era waned (King, 1990; Schöllmann et al., 2000: 66–67). While domestic tourism continued, two world wars and the 1930s' economic recession between them curtailed the growth of international tourism and slowed the postwar modernization processes that would soon arrive.

The urban renewal process driving much of the urban planning and architecture discussed below was neither in effect everywhere nor unfolded at the same pace across even the USA and the UK. Though different in cities around the world, the processes have many features similar to those in the USA. There, with white residential and business flight to the suburbs, the multiple-lane interstate highway system inserted into urban fabric, and the correlate severage and collapse of inner city services, employment, and building stock, big cities were perceived to be not only unattractive, but dangerous. Begun in the mid-1950s, but more fully implemented in the 1960s and 1970s, urban renewal was a hoped-for cure for urban ailments, though success could not be assumed. The fundamental dynamic was not tourist-oriented, but rather was meant to resuscitate city centers for residents and businesses. The basic question was how to attract reinvestment and repopulation, using government and local

dollars to replace "blighted" areas with modern buildings and art-filled plazas. The process led to new relationships in which city officials and staff learned to "make deals" with the private sector in order to fully plan and construct infrastructure and buildings, and then fill them with more affluent occupants than before. As cities promoted early successes with festivals and sporting events, local and regional inhabitants began to perceive the downtown as attractive (Gratton and Taylor, 1995; McBee, 1992). At the same time, urban renewal displaced many former residents, especially the poor and minority populations, arguably a substantial cause of urban homelessness that still exerts pressure to develop "tourist enclaves" to separate visitors from remaining urban problems (Anderson, 1964; Fotsch, 2004) (see Photo 17.1).

The conventional wisdom became that an economically successful downtown required "a shopping mall, new office towers, a convention center, an atrium hotel, a historic neighborhood, domed stadium, aquarium or cleaned-up waterfront, [plus] sports stadiums" (Frieden and Sagalyn, 1989: 259, 277). Obviously, along the way in planning such

**Photo 17.1   Pittsburgh's urban renewal highway and stadium: problem
and solution?**
Photo: Robert Mugerauer Jr.

facilities, a new appreciation developed for the role of tourists in economic recovery. Insofar as cities had a redevelopment plan at this point, it was what has been called the "corporate center strategy . . . to make downtown efficient for business firms and attractive to visitors and middle-class residents" (Friedan and Sagalyn, 1989: 260; also see Judd, 2003; Urtasun and Gutiérrez, 2006). Because the traditional business traveler was seen to be central to the demand for hotels, restaurants, and other retail activity, in addition to reestablishing offices and many service businesses in the central business district, urban renewal regularly centered around construction and promotion of convention centers, pavilions and exhibition halls, as was the case with Chicago's major investment in McCormick Place (Logan and Molotch, 1987; Williams and Shaw, 1988).

Since it was assumed that retail sales were one of, if not the most important, component of urban success, (re)establishing shopping for residents as well as business visitors was critical. It was recognized that few cities could sustain retail prosperity from tourists alone, so the goal became a well-balanced downtown catering to different market segments (each with specific implications for retailing), including business visitors, convention and meeting attendees, tourists and other transient visitors (McBee, 1992). To the mix, then, were added pedestrian malls and festival marketplaces (urban specialty centers) as part of the development of shopping as a recreational experience. Shopping continues to be a major theme in urban revitalization. Urban centers have used this strategy to attract international as well as regional tourists (consider Orchard Row in Singapore with it's high-end designer shops, and the multilevel shopping, accommodation and recreational facilities in West Edmonton Mall in Edmonton, Alberta, Canada) (see Photo 17.2).

Historic cities such as York in England have also targeted the provision of attractive shopping facilities and experiences in order to revitalize declining historic cores and facilitate heritage conservation (see Orbasli and Woodward [Chapter 18] on heritage

conservation in this *Handbook*). With hotels, excellent architectural design often was a critical ingredient because beyond merely providing more rooms, the buildings were expected to draw visitors—successfully accomplished, for example, by Portman's Hyatt Regency atrium buildings in Atlanta (1967) and San Francisco (1974), by Wimberly Allison Tong and Goo's Four Seasons in Mexico City or their Chinzan-So in Tokyo (Gaardboe, 2000; MacDonald, 2000b: 142–151).

A common controversy in urban renewal projects was whether to sweep away old buildings or to preserve some of the most historic ones. With public support (in which designation of heritage or historical status is critical, as with England's National Trust), many significant buildings were handsomely restored (Goodall, 1993). Generally, financing comes from private donations and corporate sponsorships and, in the public realm, often indirectly from tax incentives (most recently via environmental credits) (Jókövi, 1992: 141). Because a major part of the urban heritage is industrial, industrial archeology and tourism have combined to adaptively reuse factories, power plants, warehouses, and their transportation infrastructure (such as railroads and canals) for commercial, retail, and residential use (Goodall, 1993; Hospers, 2002).

The problems of the great cities should not be exaggerated. Economic and cultural activity continued, essentially enhanced by new developments, but also amid the already famous buildings. In New York business and recreational visitors came to the Empire State Building (1930), the Chrysler Building (1930), Rockefeller Center (1932), Times Square, Frank Lloyd Wright's Guggenheim Museum (1959), the Pan Am Building by Gropius (1963), and the World Trade Center (1966–1973) (Ellis, 2000; Wurman, 1983). The same was true in smaller cities: Washington, DC kept pace with I.M. Pei's East Wing of the National Gallery (1969–1979), Fort Worth with Louis Kahn's Kimbell Art Museum (1967–1972).

This also was an era of progress in understanding the importance of, and means to,

**Photo 17.2   York's historic core: shopping experience and
heritage conservation.
Photo: Robert Mugerauer Jr.**

achieve active public spaces. Led by sharp observation and research in behavior, perception, and environment, the dynamics that foster urban social interactions were studied and physical and regulatory changes implemented. Key lessons included: more people make places attractive and safer, the key to which is active streets, driven by mixed-use, 24 hours a day; and the flow of pedestrians along streets, then into and across plazas can be promoted by proper street furniture and landscaping, outdoor cafes and vendors, and traffic dampening. Breakthroughs with several exemplary mixed-use waterfront projects in Baltimore (Inner Harbor) and Boston (Feneuil Hall) showed what public–private partnerships could accomplish in once vital, but now abandoned and problematic, areas. Well-planned, executed, and managed projects changed parts of the city for a worldwide audience.

In addition to the regional draw of sports, arts, entertainment, and shopping, cities created

a larger field of attraction by hosting genuinely major events, such as the Olympics and World Fairs. The 1968 World's Fair in San Antonio involved the creation of the HemisFair complex (an arena, theater of performing arts, the Tower of the Americas), a convention center, and more than 2000 hotel and motel rooms. The Alamo Dome was added, the River Walk system expanded, a museum of cultures installed, and to continue from the initial base, the Rivercenter Mall developed more recently. In 1968, the year of the Fair, there were 6.4 million visitors, and in 1993 there were 10.1 million; in 1995 tourism accounted for US$ 2 billion and 35,000 jobs (Minter, 1995). Similar stories can be told for sites of the Olympic Games (Montreal, Mexico City, Sydney, and Atlanta) or other such events such as the Commonwealth Games (Manchester) (Hiernaux-Nicolas, 2003; Macdonald, 2000c; Van den Berg, van der Borg and Russo, 2003). Yet, not all these events are successful economic catalysts, and even the successful ones do not necessarily benefit residents and the public–private sector equitably (Srinivasan, 1990).

All of these urban planning and architectural elements and processes from this era remain with us today, many as viable as ever, with lessons regarding the types of facilities and offerings, behavior and perception, and especially the careful planning and management of urban spaces that have proven effective in attracting and satisfying tourists, as well as residents. Though there are lapses, generally these insights have generally been incorporated into professional practice. In fact, following the conservative principle of staying with what works, the physical elements required of cities for economic success have become codified:

- Cultural-entertainment facilities: concert halls, museums, art galleries, theatres, media-techs, film centers.
- Business facilities: exhibition halls/convention centers, trade pavilions.
- Sports facilities: indoor and outdoor.
- Secondary elements: hotels and accommodation, catering, bars, and restaurants, shopping and retail.
- Leisure settings: ancient monuments, ecclesiastical buildings, harbors/docklands.
- Historically interesting buildings, parks and green areas, waterfronts, canals, and riverfronts.
- Amusement facilities: casinos, festival halls-markets, night clubs, event spaces/arenas
- Additional elements: car parking, public transportation and accessibility, tourism information offices/red boxes, street signage, guide books/urban trails/travelogues/video, guides, maps/leaflets, websites and the Internet. (Adapted from Jansen-Verbeke, 1988; Law, 1993; MacDonald, 2000c)

New Politics and Post-Industrial Economics to the Fore: 1980s and 1990s

Urban tourism in the 1980s and 1990s continued previous accomplishments with the same types of facilities, yet changed to function within a markedly different political and economic situation. With the shift in politics to the right and to strongly pro-free market policies and neoliberalism, government funding for urban projects dried up in the USA and the UK, resulting in ever more entrepreneurial public–private partnerships, intense marketing, and new or more pronounced patterns of spatial differentiation (Jókövi, 1992: 187; McBee, 1992: 49). In addition, the arrival of the post-industrial, post-colonial, and global era brought new attention to well-established urban centers in Asia and to new policies, resources, and built environments there that were soon to contribute significantly to international tourism, adding to the growing number and diversity of new tourism offerings worldwide (Tham, 2001).

Mixed Successes

Around the world some central cities continued to slide into worse positions while others managed to work out one or another tactic for economic and social recovery. Included here were differing stages of incorporating tourism as part of a fully planned overall strategy. Whereas, earlier, tourism had been ignored by some cities, reluctantly and ambivalently engaged by others, and sophisticatedly developed by cities that assumed leadership, in the 1980s enthusiasm and energy spread quickly and widely to cities of many different sorts and sizes (MacDonald, 2000a; Page, 1995a). In Europe, Spain, Italy, Greece, Portugal, Switzerland, Austria, France, the UK, Germany, and the Netherlands, all saw an increased awareness of the economic importance of tourism, as did Australia, Indonesia, Malaysia, Singapore, and Thailand (Smith, 1992; Williams and Shaw, 1988).

Despite 20 years of urban renewal, in the UK and the USA some city centers were abandoned by the 1970s and had to continue to struggle mightily to rescue themselves (Law, 1993, 1996; O'Conner and Wynne, 1996). For example, in Manchester, whereas in the 1970s urban policies were based on retail and office expansion, in the 1990s the focus shifted to leisure, tourism, and residence facilities (Law, 2000: 117, 122–128). Nor were the 1980s a good time for Singapore, where a world recession, combined with the decade's oversupply of hotel rooms, dampened the contribution of tourism, even as it was considered an important part of overall economic diversification (Yeoh et al., 2001: 5). Yet despite failures, setbacks, and many non-participants, there was enough success that broad appreciation could be voiced about "the remarkable transformation of cities from places of necessity (work, shopping), through a phase when 'urban life seemed doomed' (in the 1960s and 1970s), to being positively valued as popular sites and places of freedom in the 1980s and 1990s" (Frieden and Sagalyn, 1989: xi; see also Burgers, 1995).

Political Changes

The political atmosphere changed dramatically in the USA and the UK as a result of the urban turmoil of the 1960s and 1970s, the criticism of government, and the simultaneous rise in expectations for personal freedom and satisfaction, coupled with the economic recession of the 1970s and 1980s. Public planning and management increasingly were perceived as hindrances to prosperity, while the answer appeared to lie in openness to market forces (McBee, 1992: xx). Thus, with the administrations of Reagan and Thatcher the role of government was reduced as the private sector was entrusted more and more with the critical task of managing the economy (Benington, 1986). The change in urban economies with the "changes in thinking about public planning . . . encouraged planning authorities to react to urban change by intervention in markets" (Ashworth and Voogd, 1990: 2–16). This may sound contradictory, but is not insofar as the new planning intends to intervene—in entrepreneurial partnership with the private sector—in order to manage markets successfully. Similarly, in Shanghai, national macroeconomic policy developed new flexibility to adjust to market and consumer demands (Yeoh et al., 2001).

Post-Industrial Economy

The shift from production to consumption in previously industrialized sectors meant a continuing collapse of some manufacturing and supportive economies, the transfer of those capacities elsewhere, the development of a new telecommunications and electronic economy that continued to privilege certain "world cities," and a shift in, but not elimination of, face-to-face business and political meetings (Castells, 1989, 1996; Harvey, 1989). These demographics and spatial networks of business connections and mass expendable income naturally had a major impact on travel In those areas that shifted into a post-productivism, many manufacturing and service jobs disappeared; but, new freedom of movement, choice of living place, and flexibility of leisure–work times provided perhaps even greater resources for travel, and certainly different expectations and activities, which were reconceptualized and pragmatically redirected in terms of "global flows" (Ateljevic, 2000; Shaw and Williams, 2004; Urry, 2000).

Competition

In the new global market-oriented capitalism, "Cities all over the world have entered into a vigorous international competition for tourists, and the terms of this competition require cities not only to market themselves, but also to provide a constantly improving level of facilities, amenities, and services" (Judd, 2003: 3). In regard to both holiday and business travelers coming into and out of Asia, for example, Singapore sees itself competing with Hong Kong, Tokyo, Seoul, Bangkok, Denpasar, Beijing, San Francisco, Sydney, Taipei, and Los Angeles (Hui, Wan and Ho, 2007; Low, 2001) (see Photo 17.3).

The globalization of technology, culture, finance, labor, and capital has enabled a new "creative class" seeking local and global amenities, aesthetic environments and experiences—arts, culture, culinary, fashion, film, festivals, museums, etc. (Florida, 2002). These are situated in larger urban centers (metropolitan cores) as well as increasingly

Photo 17.3   Bangkok as holiday and business gateway: global market orientation.
Photo: Robert Mugerauer Jr.

in the urban-rural interface (periphery), in touristic communities set amid "spectacular nature." Competition for business and leisure travelers requires attending to the local-global stage of a complex urban tourism system—the tourist, the tourism industry and cities—along with new modes of interdependencies, dependences, and stakeholder relations (Judd and Fainstein, 1999).

New Modes of Public–Private Partnerships

There now have been a considerable number of case studies of the new modes of public–private partnerships that attempted to deal with the global competition of cities. London's redevelopment of the Docklands allowed a documentation and analysis of the struggle of policies between free market and interventionist forces and the shifting roles of the London Tourist Board and Planning Advisory Committee. At the heart of the venture, the new forms of top-down planning implemented by the central government's London Dock Development Corporation coordinated the complex transfers of land control and changes in use, the massive investments in infrastructure (in 1987 the transportation

system involved investments of £57,000,000 for the Docklands Light Railway and £3,000,000 for links with the London City Airport, as well as work with the Jubilee underground line, in progress at the time; serious attention was given to the "misdistribution" of accommodations, considered to be "overly concentrated in the West End in the 1970s and 1980s"), and the negotiations with the surrounding community that resulted in provision of services for "the outside" rather than for locals (Page and Sinclair, 1989: 131–133, 126–127, 134; see also Page, 1995b; Villamarin, 1990). In the USA, mayors and other city officials further developed as deal-makers, working with the private sector on various "creative financing mechanisms—tax increment financing, ground leasing, and tax abatements," and a wide range of visitor and pooled taxes (McBee, 1992: 45, 54–55, 224–232; see also Fromm, 2005).

Consumer Preference, Perception, Image, and Marketing

At the same time that there were new public–private entrepreneurial relationships to develop and market cities to tourists, the context of late capitalism meant that vying for consumer and investor resources operated in the realm of images. In postmodern media's consumption-oriented representations, consumer behavior is substantially based on the way people perceive themselves, commodities and services, and the places that might satisfy needs (consider Las Vegas as an extreme example of this—Braun-LaTour et al., 2006; Douglass and Raento, 2004). "Urban residential, social, recreational, and cultural services" that provide amenities are "now active determinants in attracting or repelling the location of [preferred] activities; . . . the perception of cities, and the mental image of them, have become active components of economic success or failure" (Ashworth and Voogd, 1990: 1–3).

In addition, new tourist preferences and expectations were emerging: the highly educated and culturally sophisticated travelers who benefited from the new information economies sought enhanced experiences— opportunities to learn about local history, culture, traditions, and the natural environment (Falbey, 2002; Smith, 2001). The expanding study of tourist motivation and social psychology helps us appreciate the complexity of motivations: enjoying nature, escaping routine and responsibility, physical exercise, creativity, relaxation, social contact, meeting new people, heterosexual [sic] contact, family contact, recognition status, social power, altruism, stimulus seeking, self-actualization, achievement via challenge or competition, avoiding boredom, and intellectual aestheticism (Crandall, 1980; Iso-Ahola, 1999; Kabanoff, 1982). Overall, as Law (2000: 119) and others explain, with greater prosperity and focus on satisfaction in the near term, people had come to expect more out of life, wanting excitement, fun, and entertainment: "the spatial correlate of this kind of society is something like a leisure city, or 'fun city'." It is the city which provides the facilities and audiences to display a great variety of "lifestyles," especially "the avant-garde and well-off" (Burgers, 1995: 154; O'Conner and Wynne, 1996).

Global and Local Identity and Place

The new image production required not only the assemblage of facilities and services, but negotiating the global–local dynamics of the post-industrial, post-colonial age. Both dimensions remain simultaneously affective: on the one hand, the excitement and accessibility of the global means that the local is displaced and may even be seen as negatively provincial; on the other hand, dissatisfaction with the homogeneity of the global systems and products and the damage it does to a sense of local place and identity stimulates appreciation of and interest in the latter (Paskaleva-Shapira, 2007). Clearly, place promotion is a necessary and increasingly dominant feature of global competition among cities (Ashworth and Goodall, 1990; Ashworth and Voogd, 1990; Gold and Ward, 1994; Philo and Kearns, 1993; Ward, 1998). Since what can be marketed ranges from mere image (innocuous at best, deceptive at worst) to significant characteristics of local bio-cultural environments, "the information that cities themselves provide about the local situation" needs to be critically assessed as we engage the "uneasy mix of image building, boosterism, and economic purpose" (Burgers, 1995: 155–156; Frieden and Sagalyn, 1989: 260).

While the huge literature on sense of place and identity cannot be covered here, two points are noteworthy: first, the conjunction among tourism, heritage, and (local, regional, national and postcolonial) identity (Ashworth and Larkham, 1994: xii, 19; Bissell, 2005). Usually, the branding of cities is related to distinctive features. Tourism manuals offer whole lists of successes and possibilities: Stratford, Ontario with its Shakespeare festival, Monterrey, California with its music events, or Philadelphia and Williamsburg via history, and Orlando in terms of family fun (Fromm, 2005; Rubin and Bragitikos, 2001). This marketing of cities attempting to take advantage of their differences is as wide-ranging as any of the interesting typologies of tourism cities suggests: (world showcase) capital cities, metropolitan centers, walled historic and small fortress cities, large historic cities, inner city areas, revitalized waterfront areas, industrial cities, pilgrimage destinations, cultural art cities, sustainable tourist locations, etc. (Mullins, 1992; Richards, 2001).

Second, the intersection of the global and the local is both opportunistic and conflictual; the almost aspatial urban systems of globalism are tensed against older forms of local ways of life (Castells, 1997; Schöllmann et al., 2000). Though the polarity clearly is operating, for the most part the globalized elements are "grafted onto what may be termed existing tourist landscapes" (Shaw and Williams, 2004: 7). Many urban plans manifest the features of the most advanced, "world-class" city: smoothly integrated transportation, accommodation, business, and entertainment facilities and services in the latest architectural mode in order to differentiate themselves from their earlier forms and rural surroundings; other cities with a strong sense of local identity might either have a record of already caring for their traditional built forms, natural environments, and customs or seek to reconnect with their authentic past, as Singapore did to its traditional places of worship and as it intended to do when it shifted from "fast Asia" to redeveloping "ethnic 'enclaves' such as Chinatown, Little India, and Kampong Glam" (Chin, 2001; Yeoh et al., 2001: 6;). Increasingly, the universalisms and metanarratives of modernity are giving way to postmodern, situated perspectives, incorporating local and subjective perspectives. Multiculturalism, local narratives, storytelling, and various interpretive tools are employed to provide for personalized, interactive tourist experiences in various spaces ranging from museums to theme parks and architectural tours. In Chicago, for instance, involving local residents in urban neighborhood tours is a key strength of cultural promoters and marketers; the tourist experience is further personalized by means of web-based and other technological innovations (e.g., geocaching, iPods, GPS) (http://www.chicagoneighborhoodtours.com accessed April 23, 2008) (see Photo 17.4).

Facilities, Services, Amenities for both Visitors and Residents

Cities increasingly are alert to the interdependence among the diverse populations using its services and the need to balance costs and benefits among the different groups. The most inclusive cases attempt to achieve multiple goals at the same time—among types of users, between short- and long-term benefits, or at neighborhood and regional (or even national) scales. Now cities are expected to provide amenities that will simultaneously attract visitors and new residents as well as satisfy current inhabitants (Fromm, 2005: 24). Culture, for example, not only is seen as a significant economic factor and attraction in destination promotion, but also as a possible condition for innovation, creating an environment where the rich diversity of cultural events fosters innovation and creative advertising, marketing, design, fashion, and media feel at home (Florida, 2002 YES IT IS). The reach of such planning may be substantial, as in Singapore's macroeconomic diversification plan "which encourages local tourist enterprises to go regional" while bringing in "lifestyle concepts from abroad," extending government-government partnerships with other regional countries (China, Vietnam, Myanmar, Indonesia, Thailand, the Philippines, and China) for linked tourist products and regional flows (Chang, 2001; Ser et al., 2001: 8).

Old and New Features

Many well established urban dimensions continued to successfully serve visitors: in New York, I.M. Pei's Javitz Convention Center (1982–1986) contributed to urban renewal's focus on business, as did the IBM Tower (1982) and Philip Johnson's postmodern AT&T corporate headquarters (1983). Overall, the skyscraper remained the supreme index of status: towering buildings demonstrated Hong Kong's status in the 1980s and 1990s: Foster's Hong Kong and Shanghai Bank Building (1986), the Bank of China Tower by I.M. Pei (1990), the Central Plaza (1992), and the Hong Kong Convention and Exhibition Center extension (1997); since 1997 title to the world's tallest building has passed around Asia with Taipei 101 the titleholder as of 2009. Though already taller than Taipei 101, the Burj Dubai will not be declared the world's tallest building until it is completed and inhabited.

At the same time, given the changes in perceptions, preferences, and the large number of short stays (the average stay is 2.2 days for Paris, 2.5 for Berlin, 6.5 for London, and 2.5 for Mexico City), the 1980s and 1990s also saw the development of several new forms (Ashworth, 1995; Hiernaux-Nicolas, 2003: 204; Law, 2002). While attention continued to focus on both business and leisure travelers, there was a decided move "upscale," to more luxurious hotels, more elaborate mixed-used complexes, more spectacular "signature" buildings (Falbey, 2002: 50–51). Boutique hotels and the conversion of historic homes and buildings to upscale accommodation provide

unique packaging of heritage and hospitality to visitors seeking unique, cultural experiences or keen to avoid mass customized accommodation but still wanting modern comforts wrapped in the "authenticity" of the past (see Orbasli and Woodward [Chapter 18] in this *Handbook*) (see Photo 17.5).

Museums as Civic Catalysts

The importance of historical urban features remained strong, especially where major cities asserted their preeminence as multifaceted attractions, marketing their unparalleled array of historically important buildings and qualitatively superior open spaces, accumulations of art works, and well developed musical and theatrical traditions (Hamnett and Shoval, 2003). Both to affirm status and attract tourists there was a great surge of new museums, theaters, and performing arts centers during the 1980s and 1990s (Crosbie, 2003;

Photo 17.4   Hong Kong's urban center: skyscrapers as measure of status.
Photo: Robert Mugerauer Jr.

**Photo 17.5   Helsinki's Chiasma Museum: star architecture by Stephen Holl.
Photo: Robert Mugerauer Jr.**

Forster, 2004: 60–63; Lampugnani and Sachs, 1999). More than any other major capital, following the success of the earlier Centre Pompidou, Paris "undertook a definite policy at the end of the seventies to relaunch its cultural infrastructure . . . carrying out major projects . . . [including] the thorough transformation of the Louvre" (Buzas et al., 2004; Montaner, 1995: 63). More recently, a substantial area of derelict London was renewed by means of the Tate Gallery of Modern Art at Bankside (from 1994 onwards), for which Herzog and de Meuron adapted the disused South Bank power station across the river from St. Paul's Cathedral, and that was linked with the North Bank by Norman Foster's new footbridge (Forster, 2004). The same was true with Piano's new Metropolis Museum of Science in the Amsterdam harbor (1997), Daniel Libeskind's additions to the Berlin Museum 1989–1999), Mexico City's development by means of cultural activities (including the Children's Museum by Legoretta (1991) combined with shopping and residence), and dozens more (Hiernaux-Nicolas, 2003; Lampugnani and Sachs, 1999). The serious management of heritage resources spread beyond the capitals, as is seen in

England, in the thrust of the World Heritage designations, and in Dresden, where the restoration of Green Vault displaying Augustus the Strong's amazing treasure cabinet of art works has been so successful that at the opening (the end of August 2006), all tour tickets had already been sold out for the next several months.

The trend to anoint some buildings as instantly famous and their architects as international stars sometimes is referred to as the "Bilbao effect" because the Guggenheim Museum building in Bilbao, Spain, designed by Frank Gehry, and completed in 1997 at a cost of US$100,000,000, is credited with having had a spectacular impact on recognition of the city's importance, as is seen in the statistics for average tourist visits to Bilbao per month before and after the Guggenheim opened (comparing January 1994–September 1997 to October 1997–July 1999): total arrivals increased from 83,898 to 112,887 (+34.6%), including overseas guests, who increased from 22,175 to 32,058 (+44.5%) (Shaw and Williams, 2004).

Though not at all the origin of the phenomena, and though the fact that the city invested simultaneously in a new underground system, an airport, the Law Courts, and the Congress Centre is totally overlooked in the hype. The sensational success that the city had in transforming an abandoned industrial site and warehouses and gaining global recognition by virtue of the museum (rather than the art collection it housed) was not lost on anyone (Forster, 2004). Such signature projects continue apace: Calatrava's lakeshore Art Museum (1994–2000) put Milwaukee on the international map; "with his winning entry in the competition for the Walt Disney Concert Hall in Los Angeles (1998), Frank Gehry ushered in a decisive stage in the evolution of cultural buildings"; James Stirling's Tate Gallery of Art was part of rejuvenating Liverpool (Couch and Farr, 2000; Forster, 2004; Lampugnani and Sachs, 1999).

Themeing and Megamalls— Destination Developments

Other types of buildings and spaces were further developed in the 1980s and 1990s through the material and symbolic production of space: fantasy spaces from Disneyland and Las Vegas (globalizing of the theme park), to shopping malls, restaurants, heritage centers, museums, art galleries, music venues, festival market places, parks, landscapes, virtual environments, and cruise ships. These spaces are created anew on the viewpoint that "the most inventive solution is to shed history and the natural environment altogether and create destinations from scratch"; they offer what might be called "amazing" sensory experiences, such as the 17 theme parks in Singapore, restaurants from Hard Rock cafes to Planet Hollywood, virtual environments and cruise ships (Clelland, 2000: 111; Teo and Yeoh, 2001; also see Hollinshead [Chapter 16] on theme parks in this *Handbook*).

A dramatically expanding form in the new millennium is the themed megamall. As places of leisure, downtowns maximize the development of shopping as a recreational experience, to be combined with eating, drinking, and watching people. Thus, Water

Tower Place was developed on North Michigan Avenue in Chicago in 1976. The currently most advanced version of the megamall extends the idea to complexes that combine more forms of entertainment and retail than ever. Elaborate multi-block entertainment-retail complexes have developed into the most popular successes today—touted not as megamalls, but as "destination developments." The Urban Land Institute's major article on destination development identifies six basic forms: mixed use development, destination-levered urban revitalization, sports and cultural links, suburban centered development, regional leisure, and second wave destination development, all of which offer a wide variety of attractions. The "critical mix and massing" of elements includes upscale retail merchandizing, restaurants, bars, and music venues (an upscale megaplex theater typically would include 12–20 screens, stadium seating, the latest sound systems, a great choice of what to view) closely connected to facilities such as museums, galleries, concert halls, sports stadiums, gardens, and convention centers (Rubin and Bragitikos, 2001).

The intention is to "unfold or orchestrate" the experience of visitors; products are presented in a manner explicitly intended to be read as "personalized and customized" (Rubin and Bragitikos, 2001: 47). A menu of experiences is offered so that consumers can choose what they want and when, encouraging them to move from one item to another, lingering and personally "composing" multiple ways to satisfy their wants. Providers offer branded identity (theme, image, sense of place) for the entire destination (perhaps incorporating distinctive local features) as well as for the products within. Retailers, it goes without saying, are brand stores (the adjective used to describe these is not "chain" but "signature"; similarly, P.D. Chang and Rainforest are described as "concept" restaurants (Rubin and Bragitikos, 2001: 45–46). Some of the most notable projects include: the Sony Metrocon Entertainment Center, Times Square in New York, Ybor City in Tampa, Hollywood and Highland in Los Angeles,

Plaza San Marino in Guayaquil, Ecuador, Pottsdamer Platz in Berlin, and megaprojects in Rotterdam, Birmingham, and Lisbon (van den Berg et al., 2003).

Indeed, entire cities can take on branding from such destination centers, as may be happening in Dubai, where the airport as well as "over–the–top" array of 47 themed megamalls attract people from the entire Middle East, Russia, India, and indeed from around the world, to the extent that it is touted to be a safe meeting place for the most diverse people (Fichtner, 2006).

Problems and Debates

Distributive Justice

Segregated Spaces

Insofar as urban destination development (though not unique) exemplifies the leading edge of global tourism, it embodies some of the more troubling aspects of urban tourism. The first concern is that it accelerates a problem of tourism in general in that the attractive spaces created anew remove us from our ordinary experiences. Since this seems true of much traditional tourism (pilgrimages to reach the sacred, holidays from the work routine), what is the concern? Clelland argues that current designs reinforce the notion of the holiday as "an experience filtered from everyday life," and that newly minted themed environments are unable to provide "substantial engagements with the world" (2000: 109). Beyond individual experience, the substantial concern is that "tourist bubbles" (that as an integral part of urban renewal, appear not only in resorts but as urban enclaves) are exclusionary, prejudicial, and destructive of urban public life. While economically successful and appreciated by many of their users, others find them troubling: "By building demarcated and defended tourist spaces, cities could hide the sordid and unsightly aspects of local urban life" (Judd, 2003: 7). Here we find (perhaps insurmountable)

differences in interpretation and a social split in values. Some case studies of cities focus on constructing a well-defined tourist space as a means to reclaiming downtown (e.g., Indianapolis, Baltimore, Denver, Mexico City, and New Orleans); these are distinct from those that "emphasize quality of life and culture" (e.g., San Diego, Santiago, Tijuana, Montreal, Vancouver, Amsterdam, Rotterdam, Birmingham, and Lisbon). These seem to provide mixed evidence as to what succeeds and what might be desired as a goal: tourism is concentrated in a few cultural spaces in Mexico City; Mardi Gras spaces of consumption in pre-Katrina New Orleans were also perceived to be sites of "inequality and struggle" (Gotham, 2002; Hiernaux-Nicolas, 2003; Judd, 2003: xii, 4–5).

Benefits and Burdens

Because the spatial polarizations involve disadvantaging some for the gain of others the larger issue is distributive justice. Whether touristic development is unfair is an issue in the not unusual situations where the local population is concentrated and subject to congestion, pollution, generally stressed infrastructure and services (water, waste disposal, transportation systems), increased flooding, increased crime (including that wrought by visitors), and dramatically changed characteristics of the place, while simultaneously profitable for a range of stakeholders including city government, mortgage lenders, developers, merchants, equity investors, and various residents (Beke and Elands, 1995; De Albuquerque and McElroy, 1999; Ryan, 1993). As Fagence (2004) notes, the opportunities and ramifications of a range of policy alternatives (e.g., entrepreneurialism, development partnerships, leveraging private sector investment, using flagship projects) in Christopher Law's (2002) 2nd edition of *Urban Tourism* focuses on issues related to demand, leveraging and development strategies, but pays passing attention to questioning issues such as the sources of the money or the sustainability of the development. As Fagence (2004) notes, urban tourism is the outcome of

Photo 17.6   Pottsdamer Platz, Berlin. Destination development as urban renewal.
Photo: Robert Mugerauer Jr.

complex interlocking decisions by a range of interests (for instance, investment, development, and subcontracting industries), agencies, governments of various kinds and at different levels, local communities, and tourists. Yet, the organizations, psychological and political consequences of urban tourism development are still not rigorously assessed (Fagence, 2004) (see Photo 17.6).

The question of who benefits and who loses from tourism and, for the purpose of this chapter, urban tourism, is not easy to answer theoretically or empirically because the phenomena are difficult to disaggregate. Data gathering and analysis involve prior, often implicit assumptions and interpretations, and surprisingly, relatively little investigation has been undertaken concerning project financing and the eventual flows of earnings and profits. Even where quantitative shortcomings might be remedied through further detailed studies using a variety of empirical methodologies (such as space paths or Markov chain analysis); conceptual issues remain (Dietvorst, 1994).

Economic factors are not clearly understood and are hard to disaggregate because they include so many interrelated factors and ripple effects (Gratton and Taylor, 1995;

Page and Sinclair, 1989). Some costs are paid by developers and eventually customers, others (such as infrastructure, historical, and cultural environments) by governments, corporate sponsors, or nongovernmental organizations; nested social and environmental costs resulting from local actions that impact other regions would require a "full cost accounting" to become more intelligible and a better understanding of leakage and multiplier effects would be needed (Jókövi, 1992: 138). The vast literature on multipliers and economic impact calculations has yet to effectively address related socioeconomic, social and environmental costs and benefits.

The problem of how to assess the costs and benefits of the facilities and services is not only empirical, but epistemological and axiological. In addition to questions about who and where, there are substantial issues about what matters: money, politics-culture, identity-autonomy, amenity, health, and environmental well-being (the perhaps obvious measure—money—in fact is widely contested in social debates about value systems and worldviews, especially by those advocating that the "new tourism" must be inclusive) (Hiernaux-Nicolas, 2003; Poon, 1990).

Planning and decision making become even more problematic when sites and structures involve issues of history, heritage, identity and ideology—places like Old Havana (Cuba), Cuzco (Peru), and Trogir (Croatia) are urban world heritage sites; war memorial sites like the Vietnam Memorial in Washington, DC, and projects like the redevelopment of the World Trade Center at Ground Zero, New York, are places of collective memory as well as national ideology. History, and what a nation wants to remember and display of its past and present, can be reconstructed through development, planning and interpretation to make some sites and their stories more or less visible, as is occurring in a number of post-colonial, post-apartheid, post-socialist, and post-communist settings (Castillo, 1992; Vale, 1992). Neocolonialism through tourism can exact similar effects on diverse cultural heritage and urban spaces as the planned development of Cancun (Torres, 2002), and the various transformations of Cuba (Sanchez and Adams, 2008) illustrate.

Among the most vexed issues are the allocation of resources for tourism-oriented development instead of for other uses and the distribution of benefits that accrue. "The cost of . . . the infrastructure and amenities of tourism . . . often . . . absorb[s] most of a city's public development resources"; yet "little scholarly attention has been devoted to [that] infrastructure" so that "the overall benefits to the city are often ambiguous or impossible to measure" (Judd, 2003: 4, 8). Again, inadequate concepts and disaggregation are key problems. That costs and benefits are difficult to discern is clear even in the simplest cases of publicly supported facilities. For example, through the 1990s convention centers showed no sign of abating, even amid "financial distress" and consistent rejection by voters (Logan and Molotch, 1987; Peterson, 1998; Sanders, 1992: 135–137). Similarly, exhibition halls, sports stadiums, and arenas do not produce profits, but are perceived by downtown business and developers to generate prestige and spinoff revenues—a point contested by those who feel that investment decisions tend to be effectively removed from public review and control (Noll and Zimbalist, 1997; Perry, 2003; Peterson, 1998; Sanders, 1992).

Theorization and Methodology

Inadequate and Fractured Theorization and Methodology

Even what might seem straightforward issues, perhaps to be resolved by the "neutral categories" of positive science, need further conceptualization; for example, the "roles of size, spatial clustering, and design" (form), or those of "recreation resource typology: design, organization, function, space/use characteristics, scale, catchment, source of provision" (Ashworth, 1995). Or, researchers argue that it is still necessary to try to explain the location and distribution of visitor-oriented functions, plus find adequate and acceptable categories for multifunctional land use in central areas of cities: the naming of touristic zones include the RBD (recreational business district), the CBD (central business district), and the CTD (central tourist district) (Hall and Page, 2002).

Tourism scholars find theoretical and methodological shortcomings in regard to the complex contexts that shape tourism, and reciprocally, the ways that tourism acts as a catalyst to those contexts. Utilizing Habermas' analysis, Ashworth and Dietvorst argue that "the most central challenge . . . is still to deepen our understanding of recreation and tourism as features of social change . . . [in order to establish] any legitimation for intervention or nonintervention" (1995: 3). Burgers contends that since urban transformation "is rooted in more encompassing social changes, historical-sociological analysis" is needed to understand the "different qualities of urban public space" (1995: 148). Even global capitalism and the political economy of urban destinations needs to be more consistently and fully conceptualized, whether using Urry's (2000) "scapes and flows" or other concepts, in order to deal with the most obvious and pressing questions (Britton, 1991; Held, 2000).

The above argument documents that—setting aside the exemplary exceptions—urban tourism studies are notably under theorized, with key phenomena, contexts, categories and issues not yet adequately conceptualized, which means that empirical methodology is limited, as are identifying and implementing best practices. The causes of this deeper problem are complex, but two aspects merit a brief look in order to facilitate future courses of corrective action and change.

1   Separation of the academic, professional, and business realms. An important cause lies in the fact that the diverse areas are too separate from each other. Academic research, professional practices, and the tourism business itself all have very different, uncoordinated, or even mutually exclusive approaches, as do their sub-specializations. While sensitive to political, economic, and historical dimensions, urban studies" literature rarely treats the actual physical environment in any detail, much less conveys the vivid experiences of buildings or open spaces. The design and other professional areas do compellingly present the character of the built environment, but seldom attend to the historical-social context, much less engage in critical analysis (though the best architectural publications present both the visual phenomena and analysis, for example: Buzas et al., 2004; Crosbie, 2003; Lampugnani and Sachs, 1999). The tourism business trade publications, guidebooks and brochures also present the attractions in an interesting manner, but again rarely are concerned with substantial historical, social, or critical analysis.

2   The academic disciplines, theories, and methodologies. As to the sub-specializations within the academic disciplines related to tourism and urban planning or architecture, the usual theories and methods are represented: positivism, structuralism, semiotics, phenomenology, hermeneutics, critical theory, communicative action, varieties of post-structuralism, and complexity theory (though, because of the different categorizations in each discipline, working out a complete matrix of which methods are used by each discipline contributing to urban tourism studies would be no small task) (on classifications of tourism planning approaches, see Hall and Page, 2002; see Pearce, 2001, for a proposed integrative framework for urban tourism research). The real problem, however lies not in which approaches are "used," but in the failure to adequately engage primary theories and sophisticated methodologies or to develop them. Despite all the good work that has been done, tourism research in general, and certainly in regard to architecture and urban design, is strikingly behind most other areas of research (literary, cultural, architectural, planning, geographical, anthropological, cinema, or art history studies all are much richer in this regard): "tourism research is still too often descriptive, atheoretical, and chaotically conceptualized in being abstracted from broader social relationships. . . . Remedying these deficiencies . . . requires a collective endeavor by tourism researchers," but is an enormous task (Shaw and Williams, 2004: 1). Since this chapter cites a disproportionate number of the exceptional figures, it does not provide many examples of the shortcomings, common as they are—from among the many major theorists directly treating topics relevant to tourism, beyond Barthes, the following are more notable by absence than significant use: Wallerstein, Eco, Baudrillard, Derrida, Foucault, Virilio, Benjamin, Lefebvre, Heidegger, or Althusser (Meethan, 2001; Shaw and Williams, 2004).

Future Directions

Developments will continue to spring from the problems and debates just identified concerning conceptualization of key concepts and categories and detailed empirical research. Additionally, several new areas are emerging of focal interest: the experience of visitors and residents with respect to urban tourism, the impact of the World Wide Web, sustainability and social justice issues in the local–global spaces in which tourism is enacted. A few of these topical issues are summarized below.

Experiences

We think we understand the factors that matter in evaluating urban tourism experiences, or how tourists and residents use the mixed used destination complexes connected with cities' existing attractions, "However, when the actual behavior of visitors is investigated, it has become clear from what detailed research exists that the role of such spatial clusters is much more complex," and requires detailed information that address both temporality and spatiality; e.g., the local-global relationships between places, sites, those who inhabit them, as well as those who visit them (Ashworth, 1995: 278–279).

Given the importance of providing environments and services that draw and satisfy people, the lack of focus on the sensory dimensions is striking: very little academic literature focuses on the sensory in the sites that interest tourists. Urban studies will become more robust by developing well-established perception and behavior approaches as well as using new techniques to explore multisensory experiences and engage diverse populations, such as in Berlin, where a "series of city tours [to otherwise inaccessible construction sites]. . . helped to promote an envisioned future to local residents" (Till, 2003: 52). Future work will also reflect on the core phenomena of experience and satisfaction, investigating the differences between touristic and everyday experiences by combining tourism studies knowledge with research on cognition, perception, and feelings from other areas (Trauer and Ryan, 2005). Ashworth and Dietvorst (1995) encourage proceeding by way of Husserl, Schutz, and Bergson; Heidegger offers theoretical direction for the study of space, place and experience (Mugerauer, 1995; Seamon and Mugerauer, 1989). Certainly, phenomenology could help analyze the "negative" dimensions of tourism usually ignored such as criminality, the spread of disease, or more ordinarily, the processes of going through customs and immigration.

Impact of the World Wide Web and E-Commerce

With all the recent attention to the World Wide Web, the study of its impact specifically on urban tourism has begun. More studies are being done concerning how the e-commerce

informs and attracts; consumers interacting with various technologies play an increasingly active role in influencing travel and accommodation, as well as activities and experiences (see Gretzel and Fesenmeier [Chapter 31] on IT and tourism in this *Handbook*). Future economic development strategies will also continue to draw upon architecture, urban design, and planning for competitive advantages in this technological age. Singapore, self-identified as a "'wired-up' nation," has shifted strategy due to substantial analysis of what will be required for corporations to be competitive in the new commerce, aiming not only to be a "tourism hub," but "a business hub" providing the latest info-communication technology, including the "architecture of an Internet airport" (a "highly secure and reliable data center that connects and attracts companies"), and then ultimately becoming a premier location providing infrastructure and services to the tourism business itself (Chang, 2001: 183–184; Low, 2001: 16–17, 38).

Sustainability

Climate change, global warming and conservation issues have impacted urban planning and development in wide-ranging areas; e.g., designing high density, mixed-use, pedestrian-friendly neighborhoods, developing sustainable transportation and "green" buildings using sustainable materials and incorporating conservation measures and technologies (ranging from long-life light bulbs and wind and solar power technologies to low-flush toilets, rainwater and grey water reuse). Certification schemes for buildings (e.g., the Gold LEED rating of the landmark David L. Lawrence Convention Center by the US Green Building Council) and for accommodations (e.g., various ecolodge and green hotel certification programs) are important areas for future research.

Whether urban tourism can also be "sustainable tourism" is increasingly important, with environment, economics and social equity issues coming under greater scrutiny

(Sanchez and Adams, 2008). Serious attention will be given to the costs of transportation, the rapid spread of diseases, the degradation of sought-after destinations, and terrorism that targets touristic sites (such as Bali in 2002). In addition, ethical considerations, social justice issues and the political economy of (urban) tourism deserve much greater scrutiny. The competition for luxury travelers and the aesthetically attuned new leisure class has enabled numerous trends focused on the body: resorts offering spa, as well as other health and wellness programs, medical travel, romantic getaways to all-inclusive hotels or luxury ecolodges set in spectacular landscapes and seascapes. But at what cost? Who benefits, who loses? (see Photo 17.7).

With the collapse at the beginning of the new millennium of the dot.com craze and the stock markets that fed on it, along with increased worldwide resistance to neoliberal economic policies, a resurgence of the local, new post-global and post-postcolonial analyses are developing (AlSayyad, 2001, 2004). This is not to say that globalism will cease to provide the major post-industrial context for urban tourism, architecture, and planning, but that globalism itself and its emerging alternatives require deeper reflection than hitherto. Parallel, a new "integral" political philosophy that aims to wend between particularism and universalism, might help mitigate the factionalism in which the radical reassertion of differences often results in deadly conflicts (Agamben, 1998; Bardiou, 2003; Tsing, 2005)—the latter approach has not yet impacted tourism studies, though it soon will (it already is appearing in planning, anthropology, and cultural studies).

Photo 17.7   Dubai as the future? Competition for luxury travel.
Photo: Robert Mugerauer Jr.

References

Agamben, G. (1998). *Homo Sacer: Sovereign Power and Bare Life*. Stanford, CA: Stanford University Press.

AlSayyad, N. (2001). *Consuming Tradition, Manufacturing Heritage*. New York: Routledge.

AlSayyad, N. (2004). *The End of Tradition?* New York: Routledge.

Anderson, M. (1964). *The Federal Bulldozer: A Critique of Urban Renewal*. Cambridge, MA: MIT Press.

Ashworth, G.J. (1989). "Urban Tourism: An Imbalance in Attention." In C.P. Cooper (Ed.), *Progress in Tourism: Recreation and Hospitality Management* (Volume 1). (pp. 33–54). London: Belhaven Press.

Ashworth, G.J. (1995). "Managing the Cultural Tourist." In G.J. Ashworth and A.G.J. Dietvorst (Eds.), *Tourism and Spatial Transformations: Implications for Policy and Planning* (pp. 265–283). Wallingford: CAB International.

Ashworth, G.J. and Dietvorst, A.G.J. (Eds.) (1995). *Tourism and Spatial Transformations: Implications for Policy and Planning*. Wallingford: CAB International.

Ashworth, G.J. and Goodall, B. (Eds.) (1990). *Marketing Tourism Places*. New York: Routledge.

Ashworth, G.J. and Larkham, P.J. (Eds.) (1994). *Building a New Heritage: Tourism, Culture, and Identity in the New Europe*. London: Routledge.

Ashworth, G.J. and Voogd, H. (1990). "Can Places Be Sold For Tourism?" In G.J. Ashworth, G.J. and H. Voogd (Eds.), *Selling the City: Marketing Approaches in Public Sector Urban Planning* (pp. 1–16). London: Belhaven Press.

Ateljevic, I. (2000). "Circuits of Tourism: Stepping Beyond the 'Production/Consumption Dichotomy.'" *Tourism Geographies*, 2(4): 369–388.

Badger, R. (1979). *The Great American Fair: The World's Columbian Exposition and American Culture*. Chicago, IL: Nelson Hall.

Bardiou, A. (2003). *Saint Paul: The Foundation of Universalism*. Stanford, CA: Stanford University Press.

Beke, B. and Elands, B. (1995). "Managing Deviant Tourist Behavior." In G.J. Ashworth and A.G.J. Dietvorst (Eds.), *Tourism and Spatial Transformations: Implications for Policy and Planning* (pp. 285–301). Wallingford: CAB International.

Benington, J. (1986). "Local Economic Strategies: Paradigms for a Planned Economy." *Local Economy*, 1(1): 7–24.

Bissell, W.C. (2005). "Engaging Colonial Nostalgia." *Cultural Anthropology*, 20(2): 215–248.

Braun-LaTour, K.A., Hendler, F. and Hendler, R. (2006). "Digging Deeper: Art Museums in Las Vegas?" *Annals of Tourism Research*, 33(1): 265–268.

Britton, S. (1991). "Tourism, Capital and Place: Towards a Critical Geography of Tourism." *Environment and Planning D: Society and Space*, 9(4): 451–478.

Burgers, J. (1995). "Public Space in the Post-Industrial City." In G.J. Ashworth and A.G.J. Dietvorst, A.G.J. (Eds.), *Tourism and Spatial Transformations: Implications for Policy and Planning* (pp. 147–161). Wallingford: CAB International.

Buzas, S., Carmel-Arthur, J., Forster, K., Knapp, G. and Thorne, M. (2004). *Four Museums*. London: Edition Axel Manges.

Castells, M. (1989). *The Informational City*. Oxford: Blackwell.

Castells, M. (1996). *The Rise of the Network Society: The Information Age: Economy, Society, and Culture* (Volume I). Oxford: Blackwell.

Castells, M. (1997). *The Power of Identity: The Information Age: Economy, Society, and Culture* (Volume II). Oxford: Blackwell.

Castillo, G. (1992). "Cities of the Stalinist Empire." In AlSayyad, N. (Ed.), *Forms of Dominance* (pp. 261–285). Aldershot: Avebury.

Chang, T.C. (2001). "The Business of Pleasure: Singapore as a Tourism Business Center." In Tan Ern Ser, Brenda Yeoh and Jennifer Wang (Eds.), *Tourism Management and Policy: Perspectives from Singapore* (pp. 183–206). Singapore: World Scientific Publishing.

Chin, K. (2001). "Marketing Authenticity in Tourism: Success and Limitations." In T.E. Ser, B. Yeoh, and J. Wang (Eds.), *Tourism*

Management and Policy: Perspectives from Singapore (pp. 289–308). Singapore: World Scientific Publishing.

Clelland, D. (2000). "Tourism and Future Heritage." *Built Environment*, 26(2): 99–116.

Cormack, B. (1998). *A History of Holidays, 1812–1990*. London: Routledge/Thoemmes Press and the Thomas Cooke Archives.

Couch, C. and Farr, S.J. (2000). "Museums, Galleries, Tourism and Regeneration: Some Experiences from Liverpool." *Built Environment*, 26(2): 152–163.

Crandall, R. (1980). "Motivations for Leisure." *Journal of Leisure Research*, 12: 45–54.

Crosbie, M. (2003). *Designing the World's Best Museums and Art Galleries*. Victoria: Images Publishing.

De Albuquerque, K. and McElroy, J. (1999). "Tourism and Crime in the Caribbean." *Annals of Tourism Research*, 26(4): 968–984.

Dietvorst, A.G.J. (1994). "Cultural Tourism and Time-Space Behavior." In G.J. Ashworth and P.J. Larkin (Eds.), *Building a New Heritage: Tourism, Culture, and Identity in the New Europe* (pp. 69–89). London: Routledge.

Douglass, W.A. and Raento, P. (2004). "The Tradition of Invention: Conceiving Las Vegas." *Annals of Tourism Research*, 31(1): 7–23.

Ellis, D. (2000). *New York City*. Oakland, CA: Lonely Planet Publications.

Fagence, M. (2004). Book review of C. Law's *Urban Tourism* (2nd edition. 2001, London: Continuum). *Tourism Management*, 25(5): 638–640.

Falbey, W. (2002). "Market Views: Industry Leaders Share Their Views on Major Trends in the Resort and Recreational Development Market." *Urban Land*, 61(8): 48–53.

Fichtner, U. (2006). "Leben und Shoppen Lassen." *Der Spiegel*, No. 30/24.7.06: 109.

Florida, R. (2002). *The Rise of the Creative Class*. New York: Basic Books.

Forster, K. (2004). "The Museum as Civic Catalyst." In Stefan Buzas et al. (Eds.), *Four Museums* (pp. 60–63). London: Edition Axel Manges.

Fotsch, P.M. (2004). Tourism's Uneven Impact: History on Cannery Row. *Annals of Tourism Research*, 31(4): 779–800.

Frieden, B. and Sagalyn, L. (1989). *Downtown, Inc.: How America Rebuilds Cities*. Cambridge, MA: MIT Press.

Fromm, D. (2005). "Cultural Planning: Harnessing Cultural Facilities to Further Economic Development Has Been the Dream of Hundreds of Cities, Including Second-Tier Cities." *Urban Land*, 64(3): 24, 26–27.

Gaardboe, M. (2000). "Urban Tourism: Global Projects of Architectural Excellence." *Built Environment*, 26(2): 130–141.

Getz, D. (2005). *Event Management and Event Tourism* (2nd edition). Elmsford, NY: Cognizant Communication.

Getz, D. (2008). "Event Tourism: Definition, Evolution, and Research." *Tourism Management*, 29(3): 403–428.

Gladstone, D.L. (2005). *From Pilgrimage to Package Tour: Travel and Tourism in the Third World*. New York: Routledge.

Gold, J.R. and Ward S.V. (1994). *Place Promotion—The Use of Publicity and Marketing to Sell Towns and Regions*. Chichester: John Wiley.

Goodall, Brian (1993). "Industrial Heritage and Tourism." *Built Environment*, 19(2): 92–104.

Gotham, K. (2002). "Marketing Mardi Gras: Comodification, Spectacle and the Political Economy of Tourism in New Orleans." *Urban Studies*, 39(10):1735–1756.

Gratton, C. and Taylor, P.D. (1995). "Impacts of Festival Events: A Case-Study of Edinburgh." In G.J. Ashworth and A.G.J. Dietvorst (Eds.), *Tourism and Spatial Transformations: Implications for Policy and Planning* (pp. 225–238). Wallingford: CAB International.

Hall, C.M. and Page, S. (2002). *The Geography of Tourism and Recreation: Environment, Place, and Space* (2nd edition.). London: Routledge.

Hamnett, C. and Shoval, N. (2003). "Museums as Flagships of Urban Development." In L. Hoffman, S. Fainstein, and D. Judd (Eds.), *Cities and Visitors: Regulating People, Markets, and City Space* (pp. 219–236). Oxford: Blackwell.

Harvey, D. (1989). *The Condition of Postmodernity*. Oxford: Blackwell.

Held, D. (Ed.) (2000). *A Globalizing World? Culture, Economics, Politics*. London: Routledge.

Hiernaux-Nicolas, D. (2003). "Tourism and Strategic Competitiveness: Infrastructure Development in Mexico City." In D.R. Judd (Ed.), *The Infrastructure of Play: Building the Tourist City* (pp. 202–214). Armonk, NY: M.E. Sharpe.

Hospers, Gert-Jan (2002). "Industrial Heritage Tourism and Regional Restructuring in the European Union." *Europe Planning Studies*, 10(3): 397–403.

Hui, T.K., Wan, D. and Ho, A. (2007). "Tourists Satisfaction, Recommendation and Revisiting Singapore." *Tourism Management*, 28(4): 965–975.

Iso-Ahola, S. (1999). "Motivational Foundations of Leisure." In E.L. Jackson and T.L. Burton (Eds.), *Leisure Studies: Prospects for the Twenty-First Century* (pp. 35–51). State College, PA: Venture Publishing.

Jansen-Verbeke, M. (1988). *Leisure, Recreation and Tourism in Inner Cities*. Amsterdam: Geographical Studies, No. 58.

Jókövi, E.M. (1992). "The Production of Leisure an Economic Developments in Cities." *Built Environment*, 18(2): 138–144.

Judd, D.R (Ed.) (2003). *The Infrastructure of Play: Building the Tourist City*. London: M.E. Sharpe.

Judd, D.R. and Fainstein, S.S. (Eds.) (1999). *The Tourist City*. New Haven, CT: Yale University Press.

Kabanoff, B. (1982). "Occupational and Sex Differences in Leisure Needs and Leisure Satisfaction." *Journal of Occupational Behavior*, 3(3): 233–245.

King, A.D. (1990). *Urbanism, Colonialism, and the World-Economy—Cultural and Spatial Foundations of the World Urban System*. London: Routledge.

Lampugnani, V, and Sachs, A. (Eds.) (1999). *Museums for a New Millennium*. New York: Prestel.

Law, C. (1993). *Urban Tourism: Attracting Visitors to Large Cities*. London: Mansell.

Law, C. (Ed.) (1996). *Tourism in Major Cities*. London: International Thompson Business Publishing.

Law, C. (2000). "Regenerating the City Centre Through Leisure and Tourism." *Built Environment*, 26(2): 117–129.

Law, C. (2002). *Urban Tourism: The Visitor Economy and the Growth of Large Cities* (2nd edition.). London: Continuum.

Logan, J.R. and Molotch, H.M. (1987). *Urban Fortunes: The Political Economy of Place*. Berkeley: University of California Press.

Low, L. (2001). "Singapore's New Economic Initiatives and Implications for Tourism." In Tan Ern Ser, Brenda Yeoh, and Jennifer Wang (Eds.), *Tourism Management and Policy: Perspectives from Singapore* (pp. 16–42). Singapore: World Scientific Publishing.

MacDonald, R. (2000a). "Urban Tourism: An Inventory of Ideas and Issues." *Built Environment*, 26(2): 90–98.

MacDonald, R. (2000b). "Urban Hotel: Evolution of a Hybrid Typology." *Built Environment*, 26(2): 142–151.

MacDonald, R. (2000c). "Urban Tourism: An Introduction." *Built Environment*, 26(2): 88–89.

McBee, S. (1992). *Downtown Development Handbook* (2nd edition). Washington: Urban Land Institute.

Meethan, K. (2001). *Tourism in Global Society: Place, Culture, Consumption*. Basingstoke: Palgrave.

Minter, J. (1995). "Keeping Up With the Convention Boom." *Urban Land*, 54(4): 47–50.

Montaner, J. (1995). *Museums for the New Century*. Barcelona: GG Publishers.

Mullins, P. (1992). "Cities for Pleasure: The Emergence of Tourism Urbanization in Australia." *Built Environment*, 18(3): 187–198.

Mugerauer, R. (1995). *Interpreting Environments*. Austin: University of Texas Press.

Noll, R.G. and Zimbalist, A. (1997). "Build the Stadium—Create the Jobs." In R.G Noll and A. Zimbalist (Eds.), *Sports, Jobs, and Taxes: The Economic Impact of Sports Teams and Stadiums* (pp. 55–91). Washington, DC: Brookings Institution Press.

O'Conner, J. and Wynne, D. (Eds.) (1996). *From the Margins to the Center: Cultural Production and Consumption in the Post-Industrial City*. Aldershot: Arena.

Page, S. (1995a). *Urban Tourism*. London: Routledge.

Page, S. (1995b). "Waterfront Revitalization in London: Market-Led Planning and Tourism in London Docklands." In S. Craig-Smith and M. Fagence (Eds.), *Recreation and Tourism as a Catalyst for Urban Waterfront Development* (pp. 53–70). Westport, CT: Greenwood Publishing.

Page, S. and Sinclair, M.T. (1989). "Tourism and Accommodation in London: Alternative Policies and the Docklands Experience." *Built Environment*, 15(2): 125–137.

Paskaleva-Shapira, K.A. (2007). "New Paradigms in City Tourism Management: Redefining

Destination Promotion." *Journal of Travel Research*, 46(1): 108–114.

Pearce, D. (2001). "An Integrative Framework for Urban Tourism Research." *Annals of Tourism Research*, 28(4): 926–946.

Perry, D. (2003). "Urban Tourism and the Privatizing Discourses of Public Infrastructure." In Dennis Judd (Ed.), *The Infrastructure of Play: Building the Tourist City* (pp. 19–49). London: M.E. Sharpe.

Peterson, D.C. (1998). *Sports, Convention, and Entertainment Facilities*. Washington, DC: Urban Land Institute.

Philo, C. and Kearns G. (Eds.) (1993). *Selling Places—The City as Cultural Capital, Past and Present*. Oxford: Pergamon.

Poon, A. (1990). "Competitive Strategies for a 'New Tourism.'" In C.P. Cooper (Ed.), *Progress in Tourism, Recreation and Hospitality Management* (pp. 1, 91–102). London: Belhaven Press.

Richards, G. (Ed.) (2001). *Cultural attractions and European Tourism*. Wallingford: CABI Publishing.

Roche, M. (1992). "Mega-Events and Micro-Modernization: On the Sociology of the New Urban Tourism." *British Journal of Sociology*, 43(4): 563–600.

Rubin, M. and Bragitikos, C. (2001). "Destination Development Arrives." *Urban Land*, 60(2): 40–49, 111.

Ryan, C. (1993). "Crime, Violence, Terrorism and Tourism: An Accidental or Intrinsic Relationship." *Tourism Management* 14(3): 173–183.

Sanchez, P.M. and Adams, K.M. (2008). "The Janus-Faced Character of Tourism in Cuba." *Annals of Tourism Research*, 35(1): 27–46.

Sanders, H. (1992). "Building the Convention City: Politics, Finance, and Public Investment in Urban America." *Journal of Urban Affairs*, 14(1): 135–159.

Schöllmann, A. Perkins, H. and Moore, K. (2000). "Intersecting Global and Local Influences in Urban Place Promotion: The Case of Christchurch, New Zealand." *Environment and Planning A*, 32(1): 55–76.

Schwartz, R. (1997). *Pleasure Island: Tourism and Temptation in Cuba*. Lincoln: University of Nebraska Press.

Seamon, D. and Mugerauer, R. (Eds.) (1989). *Dwelling, Place and Environment: Towards a Phenomenology of Person and World*. New York: Columbia University Press.

Ser, T.E., Yeoh, B. and Wang, J. (Eds.) (2001). *Tourism Management and Policy: Perspectives from Singapore*. Singapore: World Scientific Publishing.

Shaw, G. and Williams, A. (2004). *Tourism and Tourism Spaces*. London: Sage.

Siong, V. (2001). "Convention Tourism Development in Singapore: A Study of the Delegates' Family Members." In T.E. Ser, B. Yeoh, and J. Wang (Eds.), *Tourism Management and Policy: Perspectives from Singapore* (pp. 309–348). Singapore: World Scientific Publishing.

Smith, R. (1992). "Coastal Urbanization: Tourism Development in the Asia Pacific." *Built Environment*, 18(1): 27–40.

Smith, M. (2001). *Issues in Cultural Tourism*. London: Routledge.

Srinivasan, Sumatra (1990). "New Life For Old Fairs." Masters' Thesis, University of Texas, Austin.

Teo, P. and Yeoh, B. (2001). "Theme Parks in Singapore." In T.E. Ser, B. Yeoh, and J. Wang (Eds.), *Tourism Management and Policy: Perspectives from Singapore* (pp. 23–255). Singapore: World Scientific Publishing.

Tham, E. (2001). "Regionalism as a Strategy for Singapore's Tourism Development." In T.E. Ser, B. Yeoh, and J. Wang (Eds.), *Tourism Management and Policy: Perspectives from Singapore* (pp. 50–54). Singapore: World Scientific Publishing.

Till, K. (2003). "Construction Sites and Showcases: Mapping 'The New Berlin' Through Tourism Practices." In S. Hanna and V. Del Casino (Eds.), *Mapping Tourism* (pp. 51–78). Minneapolis: University of Minnesota Press.

Torres, R. (2002). "Cancun's Development from a Fordist Spectrum of Analysis." *Tourist Studies*, 2(1): 87–116.

Trauer, B. and Ryan, C. (2005). "Destination Image, Romance and Place Experience—An Application of Intimacy Theory in Tourism." *Tourism Management*, 26(4): 481–491.

Tsing, A. (2005). *Friction: An Ethnography of Global Connection*. Princeton, NJ: Princeton University Press.

Urry, J. (2000). *Sociology beyond Societies: Mobilities for the Twenty-First Century.* London: Routledge.

Urtasun, A. and Gutiérrez, I. (2006). "Hotel Location in Tourism Cities: Madrid 1936–1998." *Annals of Tourism Research,* 33(2): 382–402.

Vale, L.J. (1992). *Architecture, Power, and National Identity.* New Haven, CT: Yale University Press.

Van den Berg, L. van der Borg, J. and Russo, A.P. (2003). "The Infrastructure of Urban Tourism: A European Model? A Comparative Analysis of Mega-Projects in Four Eurocities." In D.R. Judd (Ed.), *The Infrastructure of Play: Building the Tourist City* (pp. 296–320). Armonk, NY: M.E. Sharpe.

Villamarin, M. (1990). "London Docklands: Development and Learning Experience." Masters Thesis, University of Texas, Austin.

Ward, S. (1998). *Selling Places: The Marketing and Promotion of Towns and Cities 1850–2000.* New York: Routledge.

Williams, A. and Shaw, G. (Eds.) (1988). *Tourism and Economic Development: Western European Experiences.* London: Belhaven Press.

Wurman, R. (1983). *NYC.* New York: Access Press.

Yeoh, B., Ser, T.E., Wang, J. and Wong, T. (2001). "Tourism in Singapore: An Overview of Policies and Issues." In T.E. Ser, B. Yeoh, and J. Wang (Eds.), *Tourism Management and Policy: Perspectives from Singapore* (pp. 1–15). Singapore: World Scientific Publishing.

18

Tourism and Heritage Conservation

Aylin Orbaşlı and Simon Woodward

Introduction

A broad description of cultural heritage today encompasses archaeological sites, places of historic and/or architectural significance, monuments, castles and forts, historic towns and settlements, cultural landscapes, and the linked heritage of pilgrim and trade routes to historic railways. These tangible assets (both built and natural) also have intangible qualities of meaning and association that past and present communities have linked to places, and that enrich our understanding and appreciation of the physical remains. The built heritage is an important physical manifestation of history, some of the rare evidence that comes to our time from the past. At the same time, historic buildings embody the craft skills that enabled their production, and will ultimately be required for their maintenance and conservation.

Some historic places are of local or regional interest, while others are viewed or promoted as symbols of national identity. Today there is greater acceptance that the cultural heritage is the inheritance of humankind rather than the exclusive property of a single interest group.

This is exemplified in the UNESCO (1972) list of World Heritage Sites, which lists sites of global natural and cultural significance across the world. The Word Heritage Committee meets annually to consider new nominations made by State Parties of sites of "universal" natural or cultural significance. While the judgment of cultural significance may include intangible elements, intangible heritage is listed through the more recent UNESCO (2003) Convention for the Safeguarding of Intangible Cultural Heritage. Each year countries compete for the inclusion of their sites on the World Heritage Sites list. Competition is not only for the prestige of being included on the list, but quite often an anticipation of increased tourist numbers as a result.

The definition of heritage tourism is broad ranging (Jamal and Kim, 2005), though it is increasingly considered as a subgroup of cultural tourism (Timothy and Boyd, 2003). Others, however, argue that all tourism is cultural in some way as it involves encounters outside of the visitors' own cultural environment (McKercher and du Cros, 2002; Robinson and Smith, 2006). Although these classifications continue to be debated, it is incontrovertible that cultural heritage is not only the focus of special interest groups but is often part of the holiday experience for a broader range of tourists (Timothy and Boyd, 2003). Heritage is experienced by a wide range or tourist types: from special interest groups that may be visiting archaeological sites in the Middle East; to those on beach or adventure holidays taking a day out of their schedule to visit a major monument; or those visiting a historic town for a romantic weekend. For many, cultural heritage may not be the ultimate purpose of a journey, but will add value to their holiday experience.

The purpose of this chapter is to examine the relationship and dependency between tourism and conservation. Tourism is often seen as a vehicle for conservation, both as a reason and in financial terms, but inevitably it also influences what is conserved and how it is conserved. The chapter considers all forms of the built heritage, from archaeological sites to monuments and historic settlements and urban areas. Although in the context of conservation much of the focus is on the physical qualities of the heritage, this is not to diminish the intangible heritage. The chapter is in two sections. The first is an introduction to the fields of conservation and cultural (heritage) tourism. The second section analyses the often conflicting relationship between tourism and conservation, starting with the impacts of tourism on cultural heritage, then identifying the ways in which tourism both benefits and influences conservation, and finally discussing the issue of authenticity as seen by conservation professionals, the tourism industry, and tourists.

The Two Spheres of Cultural Heritage and Tourism

Definitions and understandings of heritage can vary significantly according to the social-political context it is interpreted in (Jokilehto, 1999). Graham et al. define heritage as "what contemporary society chooses to inherit and to pass on" (2000: 6). Others argue that heritage is a creation of the present, with history being interpreted and packaged mainly to serve the purposes of the tourism industry (Hewison, 1987; Timothy and Boyd, 2003). Cultural heritage will represent different meanings for different people and different groups in society. These will often be based on their own cultural values and those they attribute to the physical relics of the past. Values most commonly associated with the cultural heritage are historic, architectural, aesthetic, rarity, or archaeological values. Other values are less tangible and relate to the emotional, symbolic, and spiritual meanings of a place. Some buildings are built as monuments and continue to be valued as such; others lose their intended value and significance in the passing of time, while some gain value for other reasons as society attributes new values to them and as they come to symbolize something else. The buildings and places valued, protected, and conserved as cultural heritage today are a reflection of current societal values, and may not be those that will be held by future generations (Orbaşlı, 2008).

The Protection and Conservation of Cultural Heritage

Cultural heritage assets are generally safeguarded in a formal sense through legislation and the management mechanisms established by policy. While international conventions and charters provide guidance on best-practice conservation principles on a global scale, decisions regarding the level and nature of protection for a nation's cultural heritage tend to be made by departments of antiquity and/or planning at the national level. Responsibility for the protection of historic towns tends to be the remit of local municipalities, working to directions from national agencies that may also have responsibility themselves for protecting and managing some of the most important

archaeological or built heritage sites. The
various departments and their divisions concerned with the protection of the cultural
heritage often have an established working
relationship, at times including arrangements
with nongovernmental and voluntary sector
heritage bodies as well. What they are less
likely to have, however, is an established
working relationship with the departments,
organizations, and agencies that are directly
responsible for the development and planning of tourism.

The definition of the word conservation
varies in different languages and cultures
and in some cases both preservation and restoration may be used interchangeably with
conservation. Here we will use conservation
to mean the process of understanding, safeguarding and, where necessary, maintaining,
repairing, restoring, and adapting historic
property to preserve its cultural significance.
Conservation is the sustainable management
of change, not simply an architectural delibera-
tion but also an economic and social concern.
Conservation involves making balanced
judgments in respect of historic evidence,
present day needs and resources available,
and future sustainability (Orbaşlı, 2008).
Historic buildings are part of a larger network
of areas, places, towns, and landscapes. In
making decisions regarding the conservation,
setting and context of a historic building is as
important as the building and its material
components.

Conservation philosophies also vary for
each culture, but it is worth noting some
internationally accepted principles that are
also emphasized in the *Operational Guidelines of the World Heritage Convention*
(UNESCO, 2005):

- Historic buildings and places should be considered in the context of their setting.
- Most historic buildings, structures, and places
  have changed and evolved over time. In conservation each of these layers should be recognized
  as a valuable contribution to the building and our
  understanding of it.
- Rebuilding or reconstructing historic buildings
  should only be undertaken where this is necessary

for the protection of historic fabric and where
there is firm material evidence of the original.
- The authenticity of the material, place, and
  meaning should be respected.
- The integrity of the building, place, city, and setting
  should not be jeopardized and conservation judgments should be carried out with professional
  integrity.

The approach taken to the conservation of
any building, place, site, or structure will be
a specific response to the building type, particular situation and use. Architectural conservation can involve everything from
carrying out preventative maintenance
through minimal repairs, restoring decorative
features with skilled craftsmen, undertaking
significant modifications to allow a new
function to thrive in an existing building or
maintaining the character of a historic quarter
while still allowing it to evolve as a place to
live in (Orbaşlı, 2008). While some buildings
continue to be used for the original function
for which they were designed, many others
have had to be changed and adapted for new
uses or changing user needs over time. When
new uses are being proposed for historic
buildings these will need to be in keeping
with the spatial and architectural character of
the building and not damaging to its cultural
significance.

There are many reasons why cultural heritage is preserved, much of it linked to the
values attributed to it as discussed above.
However, cultural heritage is not universally
valued and indeed some may see it as a hin-
drance to development. In some cases political will may favor one period or type of
heritage over another. In many places around
the world the cultural and architectural heritage of a colonial power is suppressed or even
discarded in favor of the cultural legacy of
a precolonial period that is appropriated for
the creation of "new" national identities
(Harrison, 2005). In many Eastern European
countries the transition has been a case of reestablishing a "European" as well as an individual
national identity in the post-socialist era (Young
and Light, 2001). Tourism, on the other hand,
can also influence political preconceptions

when a new tourism value is recognized in the relics of the previously unwanted colonial, socialist or occupier period (Ashworth and Larkham, 1994).

Often though, finance becomes the determining factor in choices of what is conserved and the degree to which it is conserved. Ownership therefore plays a significant role in conservation. National (public) authorities may own major sites. Such national ownership can bring with it political implications for how something is conserved (political and ideological dimension) and the choice of what is conserved (such as precolonial heritage or simply those with high tourism attraction). At the urban level most buildings are privately owned and these owners may not always be able to afford conservation to the standards expected of them.

Conservation is very dependent on the availability of financial resources to fund the necessary capital works and the willingness of the society in question to conserve the building(s) in question. It is impossible for any government to shoulder the burden of maintaining and conserving a nation's entire stock of historic buildings. Cultural heritage also needs to prove its worth and the principal way in which this is demonstrated is through the level of activity that it can stimulate in the local, regional, or national economy. Tourism therefore is often seen as a savior for the protection of historic buildings. Binney and Hanna (1978), in their seminal book *Preservation Pays*, were among the first to identify tourism as a significant contributor to the economics of building conservation to the extent that now "at most historic sites it is nostalgia that pays the bills" (Lowenthal, 1985: 345).

Cultural Heritage as a Visitor Attraction

Buildings of historic significance and often monumental quality have been visitor attractions for centuries. A Grand Tour of Italian and Greek classical sites was seen as a part of a young gentleman's education in the eighteenth century. In the nineteenth century some adventurers almost saw it as a challenge to visit, in disguise, the holy cities of Makkah and Madinah in order to understand more fully the cultural heritage of Islam (see, for example, Burton, 1964; Keane, 2006). Many archaeological expeditions in Egypt, Palestine and Transjordan in the nineteenth century also involved the restoration of the finds to meet western visitors' expectations (Johnson, 1993).

Tastes in what constitutes "real heritage" are still changing, and visitors are now as eager to visit servant's quarters in English country houses or the slave quarters attached to antebellum plantation houses in the Southern USA as preceding generations of tourists were keen to view the sumptuous interiors of the main property (Lowenthal, 1985).

The wide-ranging remit of cultural heritage also has implications for how a local community is using cultural heritage and how it is being presented to the tourist. In many places of the world, what the tourist perceives to be cultural heritage is part of everyday life and may not even be recognized as being of any cultural significance locally. In some developing countries historic urban quarters that appeal to outsiders as "quaint" are perceived as being old and backward by residents who aspire to new and modern ways of living. Urry (1990) refers to the concept of the "tourist gaze" and its consumption of places, suggesting that tourists view their environment in a different way to local residents and that their values do not always reflect those of their hosts. There is all too often a differentiation between the built heritage as it is used and viewed by a community and the way in which it is packaged and marketed to tourists as a heritage attraction. Marketing strategies also influence the way in which tourists will view a place, or the culture they will assign to a community. Robinson and Smith (2006) argue that must-see tourist sites such as Petra and other classical sites for Jordan are not representative of the local "living" culture, which is not being actively promoted.

In order to better understand cultural tourism practices and the implications for tourism, cultural heritage attractions can be divided into several broad categories, depending on how they are being managed.

Site-Specific Heritage Attractions

First are the recognized heritage attractions, archaeological sites, monuments, castles, stately homes, or manor houses, where the site has a defined boundary or "pay perimeter" and an entrance fee, which is an indication that both the visitors and the attraction/asset is managed in some way. Such heritage attractions have often been places of wonder and bewilderment, testimony of architectural, and artistic achievements of their time. These are often the sites and monuments that are afforded the highest level of protection nationally and therefore already singled out for high quality conservation. There will nonetheless be competition between the attractions, with some "must-see" attractions receiving too many visitors while others are ignored for either not being as good as the top end attractions or simply not located conveniently for the tourist trail. For example, the Pyramids of Giza receive in excess of 1.7 million overseas visitors each year and a further 800,000 domestic (Egyptian) visitors, while the Pyramids at Dashour, located around 30 km to the south and which are equally interesting in archaeological and architectural terms, receive around 100,000 international visitors per annum and fewer than 1000 from domestic visitors (Egyptian Council for Antiquities—pers. comm., 2007).

The built heritage is a way and means of engaging with history, a past time, or specific events in history and it therefore incorporates not only the "wondrous" and the beautiful but also less illustrious episodes of human history. Today the concentration camp at Auschwitz is a grim reminder to visitors of events that took place during World War II. Indeed, there is now a discipline of tourism devoted to the study of dark tourism or "thanotourism" (see Chapter 29) and its appeal to certain markets (Lennon and Foley, 2000).

Many former industrial sites and mines are now being restored and opened to the public as visitor attractions. For instance, the Big Pit Mining Museum in South Wales attracts more than 100,000 visitors a year and acts as an introduction both to the mining heritage of Wales but also to the Blaenavon Industrial Landscape World Heritage Site.

This broadening understanding of heritage and its presentations to visitors also brings with it new challenges to its conservation. A dormant industrial heritage site is no longer a dirty, noisy, and smoke spewing environment and tends to be presented to visitors as a sanitized object, relying on interpretation to illustrate conditions at the time. The remit of conservation is also extended in such cases as it is not only a case of repairing the building fabric, but also of the working elements of the machinery, which was often an integral part of the architecture (see Photo 18.1). In other instances major attractions can be places that continue to be actively used, most notably religious buildings. This can give rise to conflicts between visitor and user needs and expectations (Woodward, 2004).

Historic Cities and Settlements

Historic towns, city quarters, or rural settlements on the other hand are very different from managed heritage attractions. They are living environments that have evolved over time and continue to do so, an attribute that is one of their most important characteristics. While such settlements retain a physical character of past times, they have also had to adapt to remain relevant to contemporary society. In historic towns it is almost always the value of the group or collection of buildings that is more important than the architectural value of each individual building. This also necessitates the different approaches taken in urban conservation. The way in which historic towns are presented to tourists and the ways in which tourists experience them are also very different from other types of "designated" heritage attractions (Ashworth and Tunbridge, 1990). The paradox of a living environment and an experience sought by visitors can lead to a number of conflicts that are less likely to arise in other types of attractions.

Photo 18.1   Helmshore Mill in East Lancashire in England is now managed as an industrial heritage attraction and museum by the Lancashire County Museums Service. Industrial heritage is often presented to visitors in sanitized and "safe" surroundings.
Photo: Helen Wilkinson.

The size of a historic place can also influence how it is affected by tourism. Where the impacts of even a small number of visitors will be immediately felt in a small rural location, a historic quarter in a major city can readily absorb much greater numbers before impacts are felt (Orbaşlı, 2000a). Ashworth and Tunbridge (2000) revisit their concept of the "tourist-historic" city, expanding on the concepts of cohabitation and coexistence of tourist services with those used by locals. Tourist-historic cities vary in their physical character and in the make up of their resident population the world over. Cities such as Venice are well known as must-see destinations (MacCannell, 1976) where tourist flow cannot be diverted and is only marginally managed. The outcome is a city that is more a tourist destination than a living environment. A similar situation is evident in Quebec City in Canada, a rare historic city destination in North America, where much of the walled city has been taken over by tourist functions

(Viau, 2005). The walled city of Jaipur in India on the other hand may be in need of serious infrastructure regeneration and conservation but continues to be a living city alongside its attraction as a major tourist destination (see Photo 18.2).

Open Air Museums

The third category is heritage attractions that are specifically created for tourism purposes. Open air museums are managed attractions in which vernacular buildings are presented to visitors and are explicitly about a "past" time. The intentions of each open air museum will be different, whether it has a building type (architectural) focus, a regional focus or brings together a national collection of vernacular buildings. These objectives consequently influence the way in which the buildings are conserved and how they are being presented to visitors (Oliver, 2001). Conservation in such instances is determined by the objective of the museum and buildings are inevitably

**Photo 18.2   Visitors to Jaipur, India are encouraged to walk through the old town, where their experience is of life as it is rather than a contrived "tourist" place.
Photo: Aylin Orbaşlı.**

displayed out of context. Conservation will generally be focused on the authenticity of the physical fabric although this may not always be the case. In one example from Japan house plans were altered from "as found" to the curatorial desire for depicting what they should have been like and to assist visitor flow and interpretation.

Theme parks on the other hand do not constitute cultural heritage (yet), nor should they be seen as a substitute for cultural heritage. Theme parks according to Ghirardo (1996) redefine public spaces as exclusively middle class "safe" environments constructed of idealized urban screen sets, all in all a "commercialized reality." There is concern that over-management and commodification

of cultural heritage will start turning historic places into theme parks (Boniface and Fowler, 1993). Colonial Williamsburg in Virginia, USA is a peculiar hybrid, where the eighteenth century settlement has been "restored" and recreated to become a visitor attraction with the operational management of a theme park, including costumed interpretation.

The Volume and Value of Cultural Heritage Tourism

In 2007, worldwide tourist arrivals numbered almost 900 million, a 6% increase on the previous year and evidence that the tourism sector continues to experience relatively rapid growth (UNWTO, 2008). The World Tourism Organization claims that cultural tourism represents between 35 and 40% of all tourism worldwide, and that it is growing at around 15% per annum—three times the rate of growth of general tourism (Failte Ireland, 2006).

As a motivation for travel, the desire to engage with different cultures has long been a significant factor for many people. However, not all tourists share the same motivations for travel—while many people travel just for pleasure, large numbers also travel on business or to visit family and friends. Often, the distinction between business and leisure tourists is at best ambiguous. For example, the medical profession regularly holds seminars in locations where the working element of the trip is subsumed by the opportunity to experience cultural heritage or engage in cultural activities such as visiting the opera, theatre, or museums. Moreover, business travelers often combine a business trip with one or more days of pleasure travel, particularly when in cities with a high destination appeal. Finally, there are the scores of pilgrims and other religious travelers whose trips have very little in common with the traditional "western" holidaymaker (Gladstone, 2005).

What all of the above tourists have in common is that their trip will almost always include an element of engagement with the cultural heritage of the destination in question. However, the many and varied definitions of culture and cultural tourism (Poria et al., 2003) make it difficult to provide detailed statistics on levels of cultural heritage tourism in different destinations. Some benchmarking information from different countries does however give an indication of the scale of the sector:

- 90% of package tours to Sri Lanka include a visit to the Sri Dalada Maligawa (Temple of the Tooth) in Kandy (Woodward, 2004);
- 60% of international travelers responding to a survey on cultural tourism carried out for Tourism New Zealand said that visiting sites associated with the destination's history was very important to them, and 59% indicated that they would visit historic buildings (Brunton, n.d.);

- 30% of international tourists to Morocco visit Marrakesh where cultural tourism is the principal activity (Ambrose, 2002);
- around 30% of European tourist destinations are chosen by virtue of the cultural heritage sites that can be visited (Bellini et al., 2007);
- in a 1999 survey of international tourists traveling to Australia, some 5% of visitors stated that a factor influencing their decision to visit Australia was to experience Australian culture and 3% stated that the opportunity to experience Aboriginal culture was a factor (Bureau of Tourism Research, 2000).

The economic, employment, and social benefits associated with cultural tourism are of course very significant. Economists at the Fondazione Eni Enrico Mattei in Milan report that cultural tourism has a stronger impact on local economies than other forms of tourism (Bellini et al., 2007). In post-apartheid South Africa, cultural tours to townships are reported to have not only increased local employment chances, but also increased local civic pride and community confidence (Briedenhann and Ramchander, 2006).

It is obvious from these findings that however much the cultural heritage and tourism sectors may wish to operate independently they are in fact intimately connected. This relationship may be one of conflict, cautious coexistence, or interaction. The following section evaluates the often complex and tense relationship between the tourism and cultural heritage sectors in their struggle to dominate the management of the heritage asset.

Conflict, Coexistence and Interaction

Visitor Impacts on the Cultural Heritage

Alongside the economic development opportunities of heritage tourism are the impacts of tourists on the cultural heritage. Tourism and tourists can cause damage to cultural heritage assets, thus negatively impacting on their significance and cultural values. The level of impact depends on both the fragility of the monument or place and the volume of tourists (McKercher and du Cros, 2002).

Some of the most commonly noted and measured impacts of tourists on historic buildings and places of historic interest are:

- Historic fabric becomes worn with heavy foot traffic, especially steps and thresholds, but also exposed ruins at archaeological sites or walls and doorways. The older the fabric, the more valuable it is due to its rarity and is equally likely to be more fragile. Increased car traffic in historic towns can also damage building fabric, especially corners or overhangs.
- Changes in internal conditions, humidity, even the transfer of microorganisms have impacts on material conservation. This can particularly affect wall paintings, such as the damage to wall paintings inside many of the tombs in the Valley of the Kings, Egypt.
- Wear and tear, where large numbers of visitors magnify the levels of disturbance to the building fabric above levels that would have been experienced prior to the development of tourism. Large numbers of visitors in historic interiors not only knock against surfaces but also impact on the microclimate and increase the level of dust that could impact on the care of collection items. Dirt and grit brought in on shoes is known to damage historic floors.
- The congestion and pollution associated with tourist buses and cars, especially in historic town centers. Indeed, tourist coaches generally are a major polluter in many environments. In Durham City in northern England, a charging scheme had to be introduced when large numbers of cars and coaches taking visitors to the Cathedral and Castle were creating considerable problems in the narrow medieval streets leading to the core of the World Heritage Site (Woodward, 2004).
- Vandalism, graffiti, and even theft of the historic fabric can be common outcomes of visitor activity (although graffiti on the Pyramids at Giza left by Napoleonic soldiers is now part of the historic asset and thus of the tourism product).
- A change in circumstances, such as inscription onto the World Heritage List, or a major event can result in an unexpected and sudden increase in visitors, causing damage, especially if sufficient management precautions are not in place.

- Loss of character may be experienced as high numbers impact on the appreciation of the place. There is a threshold limit where visitors to a museum gallery stop appreciating the work on display due to overcrowding. The same is true for major sites and even historic towns where overly crowded streets detract from the enjoyment of experiencing a city.
- The desire to locate tourism services close to major attractions can directly impact on the cultural heritage attraction itself and especially its setting. In Istanbul, the Four Seasons hotel chain has been granted permission to extend over the ruins of a medieval (Byzantine) Palace in the much visited historic peninsula, a World Heritage Site.

Lowenthal raises the interesting paradox that in many cases, pressures from tourists threaten "the very fabric and feeling of history" (1985: 276), arguing that often the process of preventing or mitigating such damage further affects the surviving fabric and relics, with the result that the preservation process actually sets in train the extensive remodeling of the very past that it aims to protect.

In most cases the response to reducing or mitigating impacts is through appropriate management practices. In the most extreme cases, places of high historic value and high vulnerability have to be closed to visitors, such as caves with paintings that are deemed to be too fragile or the backfilling of archaeological excavation where exposed material cannot be safeguarded. Other management techniques range from dispersion and spreading of visitors over place and time, traffic management, or improved information and interpretation provision. Nonetheless, one of the major conflicts between cultural heritage and tourism lies in the way in which the two disciplines approach management through different structures and objectives. Although tourism management and cultural heritage management are both concerned with the same assets or resource base, cultural heritage promoters have broader social goals, while the tourism sector is predominantly concerned with profit making and improving economic benefits, primarily to its investors (McKercher and du Cros, 2002).

Tourism: An Opportunity for Conservation?

Despite the impacts, in many places tourism is seen as an opportunity for economic development and for the conservation of the built heritage. Even places with heritage assets of modest or local interest are seeking ways in which they can be marketed and made attractive to a wider audience. In many cases cultural tourism is seen as a desirable and "clean" economic activity. With the continuous emergence of new cultural tourism destinations, the market has also become competitive and even well established destinations are having to continuously better their offer and ensure they are maintaining quality standards (Ashworth and Tunbridge, 2000; Lowenthal, 1996).

In the first instance tourists showing an interest in the cultural heritage may help raise local awareness of its value. Tourism creates a demand for conservation and often is the key motivator for investment funding that enables a greater degree of conservation than would otherwise be possible. The conservation of a historic building enables it to be displayed and attract more tourists (Timothy and Boyd, 2003). However, tourism revenue very rarely directly pays for conservation, with the exception of some nationally important (and thus heavily visited) sites where the significant revenues generated from admission fees, retailing, and catering may well pay for the upkeep of a site. At larger managed sites, secondary spending may also help in generating additional revenues that can be diverted to maintenance, upkeep, and even conservation. In other instances the income generated elsewhere in the economy by cultural tourists will be seen as a benefit and reason for investing in historic building conservation.

Tourism also provides an opportunity to reuse otherwise redundant historic buildings for tourism purposes (Orbaşlı, 2000a). Staying in a historic building provides added value and enhances the visitor experience. In India providing tourist accommodation in historic houses and palaces has become a popular enterprise and a means through which many of these exquisite buildings can continue to be used and maintained. In Oxford, England, the old prison located in the city center has been converted into a luxury hotel and is proving very popular with visitors who stay in the converted prison cell bedrooms. A restaurant or café in a historic building will make it stand out to the extent that even chain eateries or cafes are seeking out historic buildings as venues (see Photo 18.3).

In historic towns there are no entrance fees and tourism revenues are very rarely directly channeled into conservation. Conservation is either speculative by owners of individual buildings hoping to directly benefit from tourism or funded through grants made available through the local council to promote tourism and/or local economic regeneration. Conversely, in places where tourism profit is perceived to benefit a minority group or outsiders, local communities can feel resentment towards tourists, especially if they are being displaced though tourism activity (Aas et al., 2005).

Regeneration initiatives that are directly tourism-led can sometimes prove too weak or can even be too overwhelming. Unlike culture-led regeneration that can work with and for the benefit of local communities (Evans, 2005), an overly tourism based approach to regeneration will not only fail to recognize community values and connections to a place, it will leave the place vulnerable to a single economic activity. Prague, the capital of the Czech Republic, is a well preserved historic town; mostly central European in character, it has a mixture of architectural styles from the medieval through to the present day. Although much of the older quarters of Prague have been protected since 1950, problems faced during the communist period, when most buildings were in state ownership, included high levels of pollution as well a lack of regular maintenance practices. This did, however, mean that many original features were preserved rather than replaced over time. After the Velvet Revolution property reverted to private ownership and tourist

**Photo 18.3   The former Power Plant in Baltimore's Inner Harbor
has been regenerated and adapted for tourism use.
Photo: Simon Woodward.**

numbers grew 70-fold between 1989 and 1995 to reach an annual figure of 60 million visitors. Although tourism has created the financial incentive to restore and care for the historic buildings, this has not necessarily resulted in conversions and conservation that are in the best interest of the historic buildings. Fueled by "aggressive investors" acting very fast and often uncontrollably there has been a loss of residential use to more profitable commercial use and an abundance of advertising signs obliterating the delicate details of historic frontages and shops. Notably, high tourist numbers are causing damage to monuments and crime levels have also increased (Stulc, 1995; see also Photo 18.4)

Tourism Influences on Conservation

By financing conservation, or being influential in its realization, tourism plays a role in what is conserved and how it is conserved. It is often the case that limited government budgets for conservation favor sites that are known tourist attractions or have a potential to be so. A major consideration in nominating sites for the World Heritage Site list is to increase their tourism potential and therefore revenue generation. Although there have not as yet been any full-scale and longitudinal studies undertaken, anecdotal evidence indicates that although World Heritage Site status will increase the likelihood of a site being visited, the site still needs to be recognizable to visitors and easily accessible to sustain numbers in the long term. However, in many cases, increased visitors also mean increased pressure on resources to maintain and manage a site. Visitors with substantial travel and cultural heritage experience will have high expectations on how a site is managed and interpreted, especially if it is a World Heritage Site. Visitors may also demand more conservation, at an archaeological site for example, which could be controversial if there are strong reasons against this course of action.

Visitors to historic towns generally experience the public domain of a city, in which building frontages are a major component

Photo 18.4   The character of the historic center of Prague in the Czech Republic has largely been eroded as tourist services and signage has taken over.
Photo: Aylin Orbaşlı.

of the appreciated streetscape and urban char-acter. The common use of "heritage" style designs in the urban settings, much of it unre-lated to the local historic character, is leading to formulaic approaches to the design of open spaces in historic towns. Nelle (2007) recorded, in a recent in-depth study of tourism trends in three historic towns in Mexico, Cuba, and the Philippines, an increase in heritage style street furniture in parts of historic towns that were specifically "tourist" areas (Photo 18.5).

The desire to create an attractive tourism destination frequently results in an emphasis on tackling the outward appearance of build-ings during the conservation process as it is the façade, rather than the interior, that tends to be seen by tourists. Even grant programs support-ing conservation tend to favor façade ren-ovation. These pressures can also result in a historicist approach towards the design of new buildings in historic towns and, in the extreme, the creation of "heritage zones" within set boundaries that become isolated from the wider urban development context (Orbas‚lı, 2000b). Once buildings start being purchased speculatively for tourism purposes, it can also influence the conservation process whereby historic features may be repositioned to comply

with the new functional needs or even added to emphasize a desired "historic" image. When income generation becomes more important than the heritage and cultural values of the historic environment, then their very signifi-cance is in danger of being devalued.

The way a building or place of historic interest is conserved can directly lead to how it is interpreted and quite often in ways that may not have been anticipated. Conservation might place emphasis on a certain element or part of a site, thus reducing the apparent value of another part for which there may be insuf-ficient evidence or simply for which funds are not available. Furthermore, while international conservation philosophy may be understood and respected by conservation professionals, the outcome may be perceived very differ-ently by the visiting public. A common method in conservation practice since the nineteenth century has been to differentiate new interventions by using a different mate-rial to the original. For example, the repairs to a stone wall carried out using brick may simply be interpreted as a traditional building technique, especially once the repair work starts to weather over time. At some key sites there are now over two centuries of repairs

Photo 18.5　"Heritage" style street furniture from benches and bollards to lampposts is commonly used all over the world to adorn historic towns and signal them as "heritage places" to visitors. Often the chosen items have no historic relevance to the place, as in this example in Eskişehir, Turkey.
Photo: Aylin Orbaşlı.

and conservation, each undertaken according to the accepted conservation philosophy of their time. The increasing complexity of heritage presentations and the difficulty of interpreting heritage for different cultural audiences (Boniface and Fowler, 1993) often add to the confusion. New buildings in historic style along a high street advocated by the local planners to "fit in" may some years later be incorrectly interpreted as being part of the historic fabric (see Photo 18.6).

At the same time, planned interpretation can assist with conservation, making visitors aware of the fragility of the fabric or parts of a heritage site (Chitty and Baker, 1999; Hall and McArthur, 1996). Similarly, visitors having access to or seeing conservation in progress will increase awareness and possibly even assist in generating funds for conservation. For instance, tours are now being offered to the mason's yard at Durham Cathedral in northern England to raise public understanding of the skills required to conserve the fabric of this World Heritage Site.

The direct engagement of local communities in the conservation, interpretation and presentation of the heritage will not only strengthen local links with their heritage but the research and preservation process will also benefit from local knowledge and understanding (Doughty and Orbaşlı, 2007). In addition, local involvement can positively enhance visitors' experience as they engage with the local culture.

Once heritage becomes a visitor attraction, then preservation of the physical fabric is not the only goal. Other intentions include accessibility, education, recreation, financial, community engagement, and the delivery of high quality service (Timothy and Boyd, 2003). Improving disabled access to historic buildings is also a conservation issue, as is making heritage more accessible to a wider audience. Invariably a delicate balance will need to be reached where access is not at the cost of the historic fabric, or does not interfere with it in such a way that its significance is seriously diminished. In this respect innovative solutions

Photo 18.6 **Visitors to the Forum Romanum in Rome, Italy are confronted with a broad historical spectrum of ancient buildings, many of which have been varyingly altered over time for different uses and restored in different ways. For many visitors this provides a very rich experience, but one that is likely to be interpreted in many different ways.**
Photo: Aylin Orbaşlı.

rather than add-on additions are always more successful.

Authentic Places and "Authentic" Experiences

In the European (western) conservation tradition, with its beginnings in the nineteenth century (Jokilehto, 1999), authenticity generally implies the original material of a building and therefore its preservation wherever possible. This is partly in recognition of the evidence base such material provides of historic building practices that cannot be replicated or captured in replacements. For other cultures, in contrast, authenticity can be more closely associated with place or location rather than the material values of a building, which may be regularly renewed or replaced.

In the remit of tourism, authenticity has come to mean different things to different people. The tourist desire for an "authentic experience" may well be in conflict with the academic or conservation professionals understanding of "authentic," especially as the visitor may not always wish to be confronted by reality (McKercher and du Cros, 2002). The industry's desire to cater to the tourist experience to ensure "satisfactory" experiences can lead to various degrees of mediation and staging of the heritage attraction (Timothy and Boyd, 2003). The results of this commodification vary from omitting information about architectural or planning-related changes over time to the production of replica buildings and places, themed environments set up specifically to deliver specific types of managed experiences.

Heritage conservation in the context of tourism can also be used to generate new identities. One such example is Singapore where new and often invented heritage buildings were rebuilt to compensate for the loss of genuine heritage buildings to development some years previously (Teo and Yeoh, 1997). Interestingly, creating urban spaces that were attractive to tourism was one of the objectives of the project.

In a museum situation, conversely, the objective may indeed be to re-create a historically accurate environment of a certain period in history. This may allow for some historic installations to be retained and reused in ways that would not be practical if the building in which they were housed needed to be reused. Similarly, a country house open to the public as a heritage display can retain much of the original furniture and finishes, and even be lit by candlelight if so desired. A similar building converted for use as a hotel on the other hand may need to accommodate new bathrooms, and services that provide the expected quality and comfort levels to the intended target market (which may include tourists seeking a luxury experience). Despite the changes, such a place will most likely be packaged and promoted to the visitor as an "authentic" country house experience.

It should be noted, however, that even museum/display approaches can create conflicts with good conservation practice. The removal, for example, of later layers of building fabric simply to illustrate a certain chosen period of history may well be at the expense of valuable historic material and evidence. There are clearly multiple issues revolving around "authenticity," ranging from the authenticity of the site or object itself to the authenticity of the tourist experience (Wang, 1999). The extant material retained and consolidated in an archaeological site may be historically authentic, but the visitor may not experience the size or scale of the original structure if the project did not involve restoration or rebuilding to its historic/scientific known origins. Visitors to many of the standing remains of the Roman Hadrian's Wall in northern England and the Antonine Wall in Central Scotland (both part of the Frontiers of the Roman Empire World Heritage Site) suffer from this problem. However, tourists to Hadrian's Wall do have an opportunity to see reconstructions offering an insight into

the original scale and appearance of the Wall at two locations—Vindolanda in Tynedale and Segedunum on Tyneside. Whether these recreations are more or less appealing to tourists is a topic meriting further research.

Interpretation plays an important role in increasing public understanding of ruined heritage sites in particular, although it is of course equally valuable in helping visitors appreciate the special qualities of built heritage, whether a medieval town square, a historic walled town or a planned industrial community such as New Lanark (Scotland) or New Harmony (Indiana, USA). The role of interpretation in enhancing the visitor experience is also important in established destinations seeking to recover lost market share and increase penetration into new markets (Stuart-Hoyle and Lovell, 2006).

Paradoxically, while most western historic towns have now reached outwardly well preserved appearances, the western sense of the romantic continues to be attracted to the slightly dilapidated. This is also an element of the search for a place being more authentic, real, and lived-in. At the same time there is a growing trend in using pastiche "heritage" styles in the architecture of tourist destinations, from theme parks to shopping malls and entire resorts. While so much of the urban heritage in the Middle East and particularly the Gulf region is being wantonly destroyed by development pressures, new holiday resorts and hotels are being designed in quasi-historical styles, which is then promoted as their unique selling point (see Photo 18.7).

Although cultural heritage represents the physical evidence of the past, providing a link to the past or strengthening our association with it, it can be argued that visiting a historic place cannot re-create a past experience that is not mediated, either by those in the heritage industry who "produce" the heritage experience, or by other mediators such as the culture industry. Destination image and heritage destinations are (re-)presented and reproduced through multiple media such as films, novels, magazines, travel writings, and websites (including personal sites where

**Photo 18.7   Completed in 2004, the Madinat Jumeirah shopping mall, hotel
and leisure complex in Dubai, UAE, is adorned with historic
architectural features and ornamentation of the region to
create a tourist destination with a unique selling point.
Photo: Aylin Orbaşlı.**

photos and travel accounts or narratives are posted). Hence, the past (heritage) is (re)constructed and viewed in the context of the present through our current day values and indeed through contemporary media formats. While definitions of heritage vary (ICOMOS, 1999; Jokilehto, 1999), it is clear that heritage, historic conservation (or heritage preservation as some prefer to call it) and heritage tourism are highly political and highly contested areas, where issues of multiculturalism, national ideology, collective (group, ethnic), and personal identity, as well as cultural survival are some of the stakes involved.

Multiple stakeholders are involved in heritage management, so collaboration, partnerships, and resident involvement has been advocated as essential for the sustainable development and protection of natural and cultural heritage. A stakeholder is defined as "anyone who is impacted on by tourism development" (Aas et al., 2005: 30), negative or positive. The complexity of tourism supply and demand chains can often mean that local communities will have little influence in the way tourism is generated, marketed, or managed. There is often a misconception that investment and development for the benefit of tourism will also benefit the locals, whereas this can equally lead to their marginalization. Stakeholder involvement is fundamental to sustainable tourism development, but can only be successful if all major industry players and decision makers are involved in the process and the objective is local empowerment and direct benefits from tourism development.

Conclusion

Heritage tourism and historic building conservation are inherently linked. The economic benefits of cultural heritage tourism are undisputed and are the reason why so many destinations seek to conserve, manage, and promote their built heritage. The historic environment adds considerable value to the overall visitor experience, whether it is a single historic building converted into a boutique hotel or a centuries old town recently opened up to tourism as a result of a budget airline taking on a new route. Cultural tourists do not just look at historic buildings and visit museums and art galleries; they also browse bookshops, drink coffee, watch the locals go about their daily business, and generally enjoy the sense of place provided at the destination (Robinson and Smith, 2006). It is this integrated experience and the desire to see "real life" that town planners, tourism planners and cultural heritage managers need to consider as they strategize and plan.

While tourism is a stimulus for investment in conservation, it can also seriously influence which places are conserved and more importantly how they are conserved. Conservation involves choices and tourism will play a significant role in determining or influencing those choices. In the absence of clear decision-making structures and integrated management practices, approaches to the conservation of the built heritage will be significantly influenced by tourism developers and perceived tourist expectations. McKercher and du Cros refer to past practices where management at heritage tourism sites has been seen as a trade-off between tourism and conservation to reach a balance, but argue that "conservation values should drive the process" (2002: 62). It is therefore essential that, from the outset, destination managers are clear about the type of experience they wish to market to tourists and that they work with conservation professionals to ensure that the historic building, site or settlement in question can accommodate such activity and volume without detriment to its cultural significance. Sustainability of tourism development in historic locations can only be achieved through close, regular and well-informed negotiations between all key stakeholders, including local communities who can become the best guardians of cultural heritage.

References

Aas, C., Ladkin, A. and Fletcher, J. (2005). "Stakeholder Collaboration and Heritage Management." *Annals of Tourism Research*, 32(1): 28–48.

Ambrose, T. (2002). Eastern Promise: Cultural Tourism Opportunities in Morocco. *Locum Destination Review*, Winter: 26–28.

Ashworth, G.J. and Larkham, P.J. (1994). *Building a New Heritage: Tourism, Culture and Identity in the New Europe*. London: Routledge.

Ashworth, G.J. and Tunbridge, J.E. (1990). *The Tourist-Historic City*. London: Belhaven Press.

Ashworth, G.J. and Tunbridge, J.E. (2000). *The Tourist-Historic City: Retrospect and Prospect of Managing the Heritage City*. Amsterdam: Pergamon.

Bellini, E., Gasparino, U., Del Corpo, B. and Malizia, W. (2007). *Impact of Cultural Tourism on Urban Economies: An Econometric Exercise*. Working Paper 85.2007. Milan: Fondazione Eni Enrico Mattei.

Binney, M. and Hanna, M. (1978). *Preservation Pays*. London: SAVE Britain's Heritage.

Boniface, P. and Fowler, P.J. (1993). *Heritage and Tourism in the "Global Village."* London: Routledge.

Briedenhann, J. and Ramchander, P. (2006). "Township Tourism: Blessing or Blight? The Case of Soweto in South Africa." In M. Smith and M. Robinson (Eds.), *Cultural Tourism in a Changing World* (pp. 124–142). Clevedon: Channel View.

Brunton, C. (n.d.) *Demand for Cultural Tourism: Research Findings*. Retrieved March 2008 from www.mch.govt.nz/publications/summreport.pdf.

Bureau of Tourism Research (2000). *International Visitors in Australia: Annual Results of the International Visitor Survey*. Bureau of Tourism Research, Canberra, BTR.

Burton, R.F. (1893/1964). *Personal Narrative of a Pilgrimage to Al-Madinah and Meccah*. New York: Dover Publications Inc.

Chitty, G. and Baker, D. (Eds.) (1999). *Managing Historic Sites and Buildings*. London: Routledge.

Doughty, L. and Orbaşlı, A. (2007). "Visitor Management and Interpretation at Prehistoric Sites" In I. Hodder and L. Doughty (Eds.),

Mediterranean Prehistoric Heritage: Training, Education and Management (pp. 43–56). Cambridge: McDonald Institute Monograph.

Evans, G. (2005). "Measure for Measure: Evaluating the Evidence of Culture's Contribution to Regeneration." *Urban Studies*, 42: 959–983.

Failte Ireland (2006). *Cultural Tourism. Making it Work for You. A New Strategy for Cultural Tourism*. Dublin: Failte Ireland.

Ghirardo, D. (1996). *Architecture after Modernism*. London: Thames & Hudson.

Gladstone, D.L. (2005). *From Pilgrimage to Package Tour: Travel and Tourism in the Third World*. New York: Routledge.

Graham, B., Ashworth, G.J. and Tunbridge, J.E. (2000). *A Geography of Heritage: Power, Culture and Economy*. London: Arnold, and co-published in NY: Oxford University Press.

Hall, CM. and McArthur, S. (Eds.) (1996). *Heritage Management in Australia and New Zealand*. Melbourne: Oxford University Press.

Harrison, D. (2005). "Contested Narratives in the Domain of World Heritage." In D. Harrison and M. Hitchcock (Eds.), *The Politics of World Heritage. Negotiating Tourism and Conservation* (pp. 1–10). Clevedon: Channel View Publications.

Hewison, R. (1987). *The Heritage Industry: Britain in a Climate of Decline*. London: Methuen.

ICOMOS (1999). *International Cultural Tourism Charter*. ICOMOS.

Jamal, T. and Kim, H. (2005). "Bridging the Interdisciplinary Divide: Towards an Integrated Framework for Heritage Tourism Research." *Tourist Studies*, 5(1): 55–83.

Johnson, J. (1993). "Conservation and Archaeology in Great Britain and the United States: A Comparison." *Journal of the American Institute of Conservation*, 32: 249–69.

Jokilehto, J. (1999). *History of Architectural Conservation*. Oxford: Butterworth-Heinemann.

Keane, J.F.T. (1881/2006). *Six Months in the Hijaz, Journeys to Makkah and Madinah 1877–1878*. Barzan Publishing Ltd, Manchester.

Lennon, J. and Foley, M. (2000). *Dark Tourism: The Attraction of Death and Disaster*. London: Continuum.

Lowenthal. D. (1985). *The Past is a Foreign Country*. Cambridge: Cambridge University Press.

Lowenthal, D. (1996). *Possessed by the Past: The Heritage Crusade and the Spoils of History*. London: Free Press.

MacCannell, D. (1976). *The Tourist: A New Theory of the Leisure Class*. London: Macmillan.

McKercher, B. and du Cros, H. (2002). *Cultural Tourism: The Partnership Between Tourism and Cultural Heritage Management*. New York: The Howarth Hospitality Press.

Nelle, A. (2007). "Museälitat im städischen Kontext." PhD Thesis. Brandenburg Technical University, Germany.

Oliver, P. (2001). "Re-Presenting and Representing the Vernacular: The Open Air Museum." In N. AlSayyad (Ed.), *Consuming Tradition, Manufacturing Heritage* (pp. 191–211). London: Routledge.

Orbaşlı, A. (2000a). *Tourists in Historic Towns: Urban Conservation and Heritage Management*. London: Spon Press.

Orbaşlı, A. (2000b). "Is Tourism Governing Conservation in Historic Towns?" *Journal of Architectural Conservation*, 6(3): 7–19.

Orbaşlı, A. (2008). *Architectural Conservation*. Oxford: Blackwell Publishing.

Poria, Y., Butler, R. and Airey, D. (2003). "The Core of Heritage Tourism." *Annals of Tourism Research*, 30(1): 238–254.

Robinson, M. and Smith, M.K. (2006). "Shifting Contexts of Cultural Tourism." In M.K. Smith and M. Robinson (Eds.), *Cultural Tourism in a Changing World* (pp. 1–17). Clevedon: Channel View.

Stuart-Hoyle, M. and Lovell, J. (2006). "Liberating the Heritage City: Towards Cultural Engagement." In M.K. Smith and M. Robinson (Eds.), *Cultural Tourism in a Changing World* (pp. 290–303). Clevedon: Channel View.

Stulc, J. (1995). "Prague—A City Poised at the Cross-Roads." In P. Burman, R. Pickard and S. Taylor (Eds.), *The Economics of Architectural Conservation*. York: Institute of Advanced Architectural Studies.

Teo, P. and Yeoh, B.S.A. (1997). "Remaking Local Heritage for Tourism." *Annals of Tourism Research*, 24(1): 192–213.

Timothy, D.J. and Boyd, S.W. (2003). *Heritage Tourism*. Harlow, UK: Prentice Hall.

UNESCO (1972). The World Heritage Convention.

UNESCO (2003). The Convention for the Safeguarding of Intangible Cultural Heritage.

UNESCO (2005). *Operational Guidelines for the Implementation of the World Heritage Convention*. Paris: World Heritage Centre.

UNWTO (2008). *UNWTO World Tourism Barometer*, 6(1).

Urry, J. (1990). *The Tourist Gaze*. London: Sage.

Viau, S. (2005). "The Difficult and Perpetual Conciliation Between the Residents, the Business and the Tourist: The Case of City of Québec." *8th OWHC World Symposium*, Cusco, Peru. Retrieved January 2008 from urbo.ovpm.org/index.php.

Wang, N. (1999). "Rethinking Authenticity in Tourism Experience." *Annals of Tourism Research*, 26(2): 349–370.

Woodward, S.C. (2004). "Faith and Tourism. Planning Tourism in Relation to Places of Worship." *Tourism and Hospitality Planning & Development*, 1(2): 173–186.

Young, C. and Light, D. (2001). "Place, National Identity and Post-Socialist Transformations: An Introduction." *Political Geography*, 20: 941–955.

19

The Challenges and Prospects for Sustainable Tourism and Ecotourism in Developing Countries

Joseph E. Mbaiwa and Amanda L. Stronza

Introduction

The tourism industry has been described as one of the global economic success stories of the last 40 years (Coccossis and Parpairis, 1995). Governments in developing countries often invest in tourism with the assumption that it will contribute to economic development (Hall, 1995). Tourism is viewed as a means for national and regional development to increase employment, foreign exchange earnings, balance of payments advantages, and infrastructure (Edwards, 2004; Glasson et al., 1995). In developing countries, sustainable tourism is especially important because it has the potential to bring social, economic, and environmental benefits. The objective of this chapter is to assess the practices and prospects of sustainable tourism and ecotourism

in developing countries. We begin by examining definitions and concepts, and then we move to a discussion of socioeconomic and environmental impacts, and strategies for managing impacts. Examples of sustainable tourism projects in Botswana in Southern Africa are provided, followed by implications for planning and policy, particularly in developing countries.

Origins and Significance of Sustainable Tourism

Sustainable tourism seeks to meet three overarching goals: to improve the quality of life for host communities; to achieve visitor satisfaction; and to protect natural resources in destination countries (Ahn et al., 2002;

Hunter and Green, 1995). Inskeep defines sustainable tourism as that which:

> . . . meets the needs of present tourists and host regions while protecting and enhancing opportunities for the future. It is envisaged as leading to management of all resources in such a way that economic, social and aesthetic needs can be fulfilled while maintaining cultural integrity, essential ecological processes, biological diversity and life support systems. (1991: 461)

This definition shows the influence of the Brundtland Commission's Report to the United Nations in 1987. The Brundtland Report *Our Common Future* (World Commission on Environment and Development [WCED], 1987) focused business and government attention on the need to address global environmental issues and related economic-social factors, using a long-term perspective (Briassoulis and van der Straaten, 2000). Sustainable development is "development that meets the needs of the present without compromising the ability of future generations to meet their own needs" (WCED, 1987: 43).

Prosser (1994) and Liu (2003) argue that four forces of social change influenced sustainable tourism: (1) dissatisfaction with existing products; (2) increasing environmental awareness and cultural sensitivity;

(3) the realization by destination regions of the resources they possess and their vulnerability; and (4) the changing attitudes of developers and tour operators. Some argue that sustainability hinges on the three broad concerns of social equity, economic efficiency, and ecological sustainability (Angelsen et al., 1994; Munasinghe and McNeely, 1995; Swarbrooke, 1999). According to Coccossis (1996), sustainable tourism has adapted these same three principles (see Figure 19.1).

The principle of *economic efficiency* requires the production of maximum output within the constraints of existing capital, in order to achieve a high standard of living (Markandya, 1993; Paehlke, 1999). The principle of *social equity*, among other things, advocates fairness and equal access to resources by all user groups (Thompson, 1997). This includes equity in the distribution of costs, benefits, decision-making, and management (United Nations Conference on Environment and Development, 1992). Jamal et al. (2006: 22) argue that social equity revolves around societal concerns such as healthcare, social support services, education, housing, livelihoods, access to resources and recreation, and gender and ethnic relations. They further note that social equity

Figure 19.1 Interpretation of Sustainable Tourism.
Source: Adapted from Coccossis (1996).

includes equity in host–guest relationships, such as respectful encounters. The principle of *ecological sustainability* states that the rate that renewable natural resources are used should not be faster than the rate at which the natural process renews those resources (Munasinghe and McNeely, 1995; Serageldine, 1993; Thompson, 1997).

Tosun (2001) argues from these principles that sustainable tourism is an adaptive paradigm that is capable of addressing widely different situations and articulating different goals. It requires a multidisciplinary approach, touching upon a wide range of issues such as economic development policy, environmental concerns, social factors, and structure of the international tourism system. These assumptions are in line with Wall's (1997) argument that sustainable tourism should be economically viable, socio-culturally sensitive, and environmentally friendly. However, these three pillars of sustainable tourism are interrelated and effects on one are likely to affect the others. For example, Oliveira (2003) explains that an environment that is adversely impacted by tourism risks losing future investment and faces disruption to local livelihood.

Other scholars have offered similar principles for sustainable tourism. For example, Cater (1993) identified three objectives: (1) meeting the needs of the host population both in the short and long terms; (2) satisfying the demands of tourists; and (3) safeguarding the natural environment. Hardy et al. (2002) suggested that sustainable tourism is defined primarily by the social context and that stakeholders analyses must be conducted to ensure conflicting needs are met (Bramwell and Lane, 1993).

The notion of sustainable tourism has received numerous criticisms as well. A number of authors note it is disjointed and flawed, lacking in theoretical rigor (Harrison, 1996; Liu, 2003; Sharpley, 2000). While sustainable tourism attempts to redress the negative impacts of mass tourism and establish environmentally, economically, and culturally sustainable alternatives, this effort can devolve into a purely rhetorical

strategy, as commodification, dependency, subservience, and a range of other problems persist (see also Britton, 1982; Cater, 1993; Dixon et al., 2001; Sindiga, 1996; Sofield, 2003).

Of particular interest here is Redcliff (1987), who feels that the debate on sustainable development fails to view sustainability in developing countries as a function of the internationalization of capital, labor, and markets. Often, the costs of environmental degradation and exploitation are passed to those who are less powerful (such as the poor) and future generations. Indeed, a lack of well-established principles and indicators has allowed a number of international tour operators and managers to promote their products under the banner of sustainability, while in reality only legitimizing their power to control destination areas as usual (Cohen, 2002; Mowforth and Munt, 2003).

Despite the numerous criticisms, proponents of sustainable tourism argue that it holds considerable promise to manage the complex interactions between the tourism industry, tourists, the environment and the host communities, and strive for long-term sustainability of natural and cultural resources. It is a goal that is applicable to all tourism ventures regardless of scale. Its principles can be used to address mass tourism as well as other forms of tourism (Hardy et al., 2002). However, sustainability is a norm that should be applied to tourism development in a responsible manner. The tourism industry is complex, fragmented, and multisectoral; furthermore, it still tends to be product-centered rather than people-centered. Much of the tourism industry focuses on bottom-line profit rather than striving for societal goods expressed as intragenerational and intergenerational equity (Hunter, 1995; Sharpley, 2000). Integrated planning and policymaking between the local, regional, national, and international levels is crucial if more of the projected benefits of tourism are to be realized than has occurred to date in the developing world (Gladstone, 2005).

New Directions for Sustainable Tourism?

Research in sustainable tourism continues to grow, with new contributions to theory development, principles, and practice being made in a range of journals, including tourism journals such as the *Journal of Sustainable Tourism*. Some of the concerns and critiques of "sustainable tourism" have also (re)stimulated interest in "responsible tourism." See, for instance, the Cape Town declaration formed at the Cape Town Conference on Responsible Tourism in Destinations, held in Johannesburg in 2002, which defines responsible tourism[1] as having the following characteristics:

- minimizes negative economic, environmental, and social impacts;
- generates greater economic benefits for local people and enhances the well-being of host communities, improves working conditions, and access to the industry;
- involves local people in decisions that affect their lives and life chances;
- makes positive contributions to the conservation of natural and cultural heritage, to the maintenance of the world's diversity;
- provides more enjoyable experiences for tourists through more meaningful connections with local people, and a greater understanding of local cultural, social, and environmental issues;
- provides access for physically challenged people; and
- is culturally sensitive, engenders respect between tourists and hosts, and builds local pride and confidence.

Another area of strong research interest that is closely related to sustainable tourism and responsible tourism is ecotourism, a practice that is argued to be oriented towards the achievement of sustainability. A short overview of this area is provided below, followed by a discussion of environmental impacts in developing countries. The final part of the chapter summarizes a number of tools and processes for sustainable resource use and tourism development.

Ecotourism

Origins and Significance

Ecotourism is defined as nature-based tourism with three additional goals: (1) to minimize the negative environmental, economic, and social impacts often associated with mass tourism; (2) to deliver a net positive contribution to environmental conservation; and (3) to improve the livelihoods of local people (Barkin, 1996; Cater and Lowman, 1994; Lindberg and Hawkins, 1993; Wallace and Pierce, 1996; Wearing and Neil, 1999). In summary, ecotourism is tourism that attempts to minimize the negative impacts of conventional tourism and instead make instead positive contributions to environmental and social challenges.

Though most market-based approaches to conservation have been challenged in recent years (e.g., Oates, 1999; Terborgh, 1999), ecotourism is an exception. Many conservationists endorse ecotourism as a way to provide economic incentives for local people to protect biodiversity (Daily and Ellison, 2003; Terborgh, van Schaik, Davenport and Rao, 2002: 6–7). Especially since the Brundtland report, considerable capital and technical expertise has been channeled to local communities near protected areas around the world (Weaver and Lawton, 2007). In 2003, 170 nations attending the World Parks Congress in South Africa called for increased measures to make ecotourism a more effective "vehicle" for conserving biodiversity and reducing poverty (International Union for the Conservation of Nature [IUCN], 2003). In just a couple of decades, the United States Agency for International Development (USAID) spent more than US$2 billion on ecotourism projects (Kiss, 2004).

There are conflicting views among scholars about the origins of ecotourism. However, Hector Ceballos-Lascurain, a Mexican architect, is regarded as one of the people who coined the term ecotourism in 1983 (Ceballos-Lascurain, 1996). As a result, the IUCN adopted Ceballos-Lascruain's definition of ecotourism:

> Environmentally responsible travel and visitation to relatively undisturbed natural areas, in order to enjoy, study and appreciate nature (and any accompanying cultural features–both past and present). It is a type of tourism that promotes conservation, has low visitor impact and provides for beneficially active socioeconomic involvement of local populations. (1996: 20)

Honey adapted the International Ecotourism Society's shortened version of ecotourism and defines it as: ". . . responsible travel to natural areas that conserves the environment and sustains the well-being of local people" (1999: 6).

An important aim of ecotourism is to raise public environmental awareness and thus support for conservation. Many tours include interpretative activities that help visitors learn about conservation and ecology as they see new landscapes and communities (Orams, 1997; Thaites et al., 2002). Some tours also present information on cultural history and human–environment interactions, encouraging visitors to consider not only the beauty of the destination, but also the environmental challenges it is facing.

The terms "ecotourist" and "ecotourism" continue to be subjects of controversy and contrasting definitions in academia. Despite this, they are being accepted by planners in developing countries as possible strategies for conservation and improved livelihoods. For example, the Department of Tourism in Botswana adopted the National Eco-Tourism Strategy in 2002. This strategy adopted the IUCN definition of ecotourism and this was viewed by the Government of Botswana as one way to promote sustainable tourism development in country.

Understanding Ecotourism's 'Benefits'

Though conservationists generally agree that conservation may result if ecotourism delivers benefits to local communities, they tend to disagree on what benefits are, or how and why such benefits might lead to long-term and locally sustained conservation. Broadly speaking, one divide occurs between economists and biologists, on the one hand, and

anthropologists and other social scientists, on the other. Among many economic studies, ecotourism "benefits" have been defined primarily as new employment and cash income (Campbell, 1999; Gossling, 1999; Wunder, 2000). Langholz (1999), for example, argued that ecotourism income can minimize or eliminate economic dependence on other activities that exploit natural resources, such as commercial agriculture, hunting, logging, cattle ranching, and gold mining (see also Lindberg, 1994; Taylor et al., 2003). Bookbinder et al. (1998) also measured benefits in economic terms and concluded that ecotourism generally does not generate enough of such benefits to provide sufficient interest or incentive for local communities to conserve wildlife or biodiversity. In general, these kinds of ecotourism analyses support the idea that resource use and conservation are primarily the result of economic decisions people make, divorced from larger political, cultural, and historical values and relations.

Anthropologists, particularly those using a political ecology approach, have paid more attention to social relations and politics in their analyses of ecotourism impacts. This view has led to more holistic understandings of ecotourism "benefits," and includes noneconomic factors, such as empowerment and local participation in ownership and management (Scheyvens, 1999; Stonich, 1998; Stronza, 2007; Young, 1999). Stonich (2000), for example, found that at least some devolution of control from private tour operators and the government to local residents made a positive difference for conservation and community development in the Bay Islands off the coast of Honduras. Borman (1999) also described the benefits of local control over ecotourism for protecting Cofan indigenous territories and achieving community development goals. The catalyzing effect of participation may be that it can help build skills in leadership and strengthen local institutions while also ensuring that residents are able to translate economic benefits from ecotourism into broader goals (Stem et al., 2003; Stronza and Gordillo, 2008).

Ecotourism thus promises a wide range of outcomes, from environmental conservation to social justice, economic development, and environmental education (Honey 1999; Stronza, 2001). Kutay (1989) described ecotourism as a potential model for development in which natural areas are planned as part of the tourism economic base, and biological resources and ecological processes are clearly linked with social and economic factors. Conservation, however, has been a primary driver of ecotourism, and the generation of economic and social benefits to local inhabitants is often described as the primary means to this end (Jamal et al., 2006).

Environmental Costs

Despite its popularity, theorists and practitioners have yet to understand the conditions under which ecotourism works effectively as a tool for conservation (Doan, 2000; Kruger, 2005). In some cases, ecotourism has been able to generate economic incentives for conservation (Alexander, 2000; Wunder, 1999, 2000). In other cases, ecotourism has failed to deliver benefits either for people and/or the environment (Belsky, 1999; West and Carrier, 2004). Success and failure in ecotourism have varied over time as well. Short-term economic gains in some places have led to environmental degradation over time (Barrett et al., 2001). Hillery et al. summarize the paradox that nature-based tourism can lead to: "The more attractive a site, the more popular it may become, and the more likely it is that it will be degraded due to heavy visitation, which in turn may diminish the quality of the experience" (2001: 853–854).

Though many tourism destinations in developing countries now bask in the status of popularity, some are beginning to wonder: How many are too many tourists? Will tourism here begin to kill the goose that laid the golden egg? Will nature based tourism destinations in developing countries suffer the same negative impacts as early ecotourism

destinations such as Kenya, Belize, and the Galapagos Islands? Potential "tourism horror stories" in such places as the Mediterranean coastlands, Greek Islands, Himalayan valleys, and the coast of Kenya (Cooke, 1991: 15) have been told. The Okavango Delta in Botswana is at the moment threatened with environmental problems created by tourism development (Mbaiwa, 2003). As a result, a tourist visiting the Okavango Delta recently made the following remark: "Too many tourists will destroy the very product that is marketed."

International tourism development in developing countries has also been found to take little consideration of its environmental impacts (Cater, 1991; Honey, 1999). As a result, issues of carrying capacity or limits of acceptable change in tourism destinations are not given the attention they deserve. Environmental damage can arise if the number of tourists visiting a particular place is large or the environmental resources are overused (Cohen, 1978; Dixon et al., 2001; Glasson et al., 1995; Plog, 1974). An example of environmental problems caused by tourism in destination areas is poor waste (e.g., sewage) disposal in the sea by international tourism companies in the Caribbean, particularly in Negril and Jamaica (Dixon et al., 2001). In the Okavango Delta in Botswana, Mbaiwa (2003) argues that tourism development causes environmental problems such as the creation of illegal tracks, poor waste disposal, noise pollution; wildlife displacement, wildlife feeding, the spread of invasive species like *Salvinia molesta*, and the development of squatter settlements. The increase in human settlements creates a population sprawl, which causes resource degradation in the Okavango Delta (Van der Post, 2004). Some of the indicators that have been suggested to monitor and manage tourism impacts in this area include:

- The rate of growth of tourism in the destination area.
- The extent to which government tourism agencies implement and monitor environmental management strategies, policies, and development.

- Direct environmental impacts, such as the disturbance of flora, fauna, and topography in the destination area/site.
- Seasonal effects of tourism activities on natural resources.

Additional Impact Considerations in Developing Countries

While tourism development in destination areas has several positive socioeconomic impacts (such as employment opportunities, income generation for host communities, and infrastructure development), tourism studies from the late 1970s indicate that tourism development, particularly in developing countries, does not necessarily act as a positive agent of development (Britton, 1982; Matthew, 1977; Oppermann and Chon, 1997). The multiplier effects of tourism in developing countries were considerably less than expected, the international orientation and organization of mass tourism required high investment costs and led to a high dependency on foreign capital, skills, and management personnel (Bryden, 1973; Oppermann and Chon, 1997; Pavaskar, 1982). Tourism has not lived up to its promises in many developing countries, though some positive benefits do result (Oppermann and Chon, 1997).

Foreign Domination
Foreign domination of the tourism sector is an especially significant problem in developing countries. Seckelmann (2002) notes that with the expansion of tourism in Turkey from the 1990s, small, local investors, who formed the bases of the first developments, were displaced by superregional, often foreign-based companies. The foreign ownership of tourism facilities and control of the industry in developing countries has led to revenue leakage out of the host nation's economy; this is generally typical of enclave tourism throughout the world (Britton, 1982; Cater, 1991; Ceballos-Lascurain, 1996; Oppermann and Chon, 1997). Britton (1982) claims that where tour packages are

offered by foreign airlines, and foreigners run hotels, the destination countries in developing countries receive on average 22–25% of the inclusive tour retail prices paid by the tourists. In Botswana, the foreign dominated tourism industry in the Okavango Delta results in only 29% of the tourist revenue being retained in the country, while the remainder (71%) is being repatriated to industrialized countries (Mbaiwa, 2005). International tourism companies also enjoy tax holidays, hence little revenue is retained in destination areas, as is the case in the Caribbean (Dixon et al., 2001).

The dominance of the tourism industry by foreign investors and nonlocal investment can result in loss of local control over the destination's resources and loss of local autonomy. A local resident may also suffer a loss of sense of place, as his/her surroundings are transformed to accommodate the requirements of a foreign-dominated tourism industry. In this regard, foreign domination of the tourism industry in developing countries violates the principles of social equity that advocates for fairness in the distribution of benefits, costs and decision making process in resource use.

Losses in the Employment Sector
The violation of the norms of social equity in the tourism industry in developing countries is especially noticeable in the employment sector. Local participation in tourism in developing countries is primarily in employment rather than the tourism business where the high capital costs of entry, language, education, and skills are constraints (Healy, 1994). However, citizens and local people usually hold poor and unskilled jobs while management and better paying positions are held by expatriates (Britton, 1982; Oppermann and Chon, 1997). This problem was found to be true by Mbaiwa (2005) in the Okavango Delta, Pantin (1998) and Dixon et al. (2001) in the Caribbean and Seckelman (2002) in Turkey. As a result, approaches such as ecotourism, and community-based tourism management programs are some of the efforts that are being used to promote more sustainable

tourism in nature-based destinations of developing countries.

Sustainable Management of Tourism-Related Resources

There are several approaches and tools that have been developed to address and manage environmental impacts from tourism in destinations' areas. These include techniques for environmental impact management, visitor impact management, and a range of planning processes. A few key topics and approaches are described below.

The Concept of Carrying Capacity

The concept of carrying capacity has a long history among scholars of various disciplines (Goldsmith, 1974; Inskeep, 1991; McIntyre, 1993; O'Reilly, 1986; Odum, 1959; Shelby and Herberlein, 1986; Stankey and McCool, 1984; Williams and Gill, 1994; World Tourism Organization/United Nations Environmental Program, 1992) that it appears in some form in almost all tourism planning and management textbooks. Carrying capacity modeling is still a slice of the current research pie, especially in explorations of the meaning of sustainable tourism (Brown et al., 1997; Hawkins and Roberts, 1997; Saveriades, 2000; Wahab and Pigram, 1997). Borrowed from range science and ecology, the notion of carrying capacity seems simple: there is a threshold or set of thresholds, usually measured in tourism numbers, densities, or uses, beyond which economic, social, psychological, and environmental systems are threatened and sustainability unlikely. Tourism, like any other economic activity, can lead to undesirable impacts.

More specifically, the environmental component of carrying capacity recognizes that no environmental system can withstand unlimited utilization. As such, a threshold of tourist activity must be defined beyond which

irreversible and detrimental change in the physical environment will occur, such as loss of habitats and elimination of species or populations of species (Stankey and McCool, 1984). The sociocultural component of carrying capacity recognizes that detrimental impacts on local populations will occur if tourism exceeds a certain level. The psychological component of carrying capacity refers to the maximum number of visitors for whom an area is able to provide a quality experience at any one time. Management implies setting limits, such as the number of lodges and beds per lodge or the amount of use allowed in a given site. Unfortunately, the intuitive allure and apparent simplicity of carrying capacity have led to more obfuscation than clarification and, judging from the literature of the past few years, there is much disenchantment with the concept.

The Problem of Carrying Capacity

Criticism of carrying capacity research in tourism and recreation, which began in the mid-1980s, is now strong (e.g., Brown et al., 1998). Lindberg et al. (1996) and Boyd and Butler (1996) identify some of the problems with carrying capacity: (1) definitions often provide insufficient guidance for effective implementation; (2) despite perceptions to the contrary, carrying capacity is imprecise and relative; it is anything but a scientific concept; (3) there is an almost infinite number of measures of economic, social, psychological, and even ecological impact and all to some degree are subjective and vary by region, user, end use, and ecological situation; and (4) carrying capacity often confuses inputs and outputs, typically collecting data on use levels or number of visitors instead of what management really requires—bottom-line site conditions. In other words, limiting numbers or uses is ineffective without a context of management objectives. Lindberg et al. conclude that carrying capacity is "simply not adequate to address the complexity found in tourism situations" (1996: 461). Yet managers still need to know how and when to control use and users, for without this information the ecological integrity of a site may be jeopardized.

An array of promising strategies and frameworks, most of which derive from "management by objectives" thinking, has tried to resolve this management predicament. Instead of asking "How many is too many?" the focus is on "What conditions do we desire?" (Boyd and Butler, 1996; Stankey et al., 1985). This shift is not simply a matter of emphasis. It is a wholly new approach to exploring limits and managing tourism as a sustainable economic activity. Basing planning and management on desired outcomes builds a foundation for an iterative process in which present conditions are continuously monitored according to predetermined standards. A cocktail of acronyms symbolize these tools: VAMP—the Visitor Activity Management Process of Canadian National Parks (Graham et al., 1988); VERP—Visitor Experience Resource Protection; and VIM—Visitor Impact Management process of the US National Park System (Graefe et al., 1990; National Park Service, 1993;); ROS and TOS—Recreational Opportunity and Tourism Opportunity Spectrums, respectively (Butler and Waldbrook, 1991; Clark and Stankey, 1979); ECOS—Ecotourism Opportunity Spectrum (Boyd and Butler, 1996); and LAC—Limits of Acceptable Change (McCool 1994, 1995; Stankey et al., 1985). Two popular approaches are described below (LAC and VIM).

Limits of Acceptable Change (LAC)

The LAC framework was developed by Stankey et al. (1985) to help manage increasing demands and impacts by hikers and backpackers in the US wilderness system. It assesses the probable impact of an activity, decides in advance how much change will be tolerated, monitors what is happening systematically and regularly, and determines what actions are appropriate if agreed-upon quality standards are surpassed. It was therefore an attempt to provide reasonable answers to questions such as: Has tourism already surpassed some critical environmental and social thresholds? Is tourism endangering the ecological well-being of physical environments in destination areas? It seems to have the broadest applicability to the complex tourism setting, and attempts to take into consideration the multiple stakeholders involved (Ahn et al., 2002; Boyd and Butler, 1996; Oliver 1995; Roggenbuck et al., 1993).

Ceballos-Lascurain (1996) notes that the LAC approach concentrates on establishing measurable limits to human-induced changes in the natural and social setting of parks and protected areas, and on identifying appropriate management strategies to maintain and/or restore desired conditions. In this way, knowledge of the physical-biological environment is combined with knowledge of the sociopolitical context in order to define appropriate and unacceptable future conditions. Although the original LAC framework involved nine planning steps, Glasson et al. (1995) reduce it to six. These are: (1) identifying *issues* and (2) *goals*; (3) developing *standards*; (4) conducting *inventory*; (5) implementing *actions*; and (6) *monitoring*. Tentative standards (e.g., polluted channels and lagoons) are unacceptable outcomes of tourism development.

The LAC system proved to be a valuable management tool in several wilderness areas in the USA (Cebbalos-Lascurain, 1996). In the USA, the LAC system has been mostly used by the Forest Service. The system has not been tested and used in developing countries, hence much of its applicability in promoting sustainable tourism remains largely unknown. As environmental impacts from tourism continue to mount, LAC may become an effective tool to employ.

Visitor Impact Management (VIM)

The VIM approach was developed by the National Parks and Conservation Association of the USA to manage visitor impacts in the

US national parks system. VIM is not a single sector approach to examining use–impact relationships as is carrying capacity. It integrates the various approaches used in other disciplines and attempts to move beyond the carrying capacity limits identified in ecological and social studies. Recognizing that simply establishing limits may do little to reduce the impacts they were intended to resolve, it tries to address human impacts and interactions (Glasson et al., 1995; Graefe et al., 1990).

Like LAC, VIM is a set of procedures that first reviews management objectives of tourism, then identifies indicators related to these management objectives. Standards for these indicators are then selected and compared with existing conditions to look for specific problems, probable causes for the various impacts, and possible breaches of quality standards (Glasson et al., 1995). Potential management strategies are devised, which should lead to the mitigation of the impacts. Finally, a continual monitoring process is devised to ensure effective management actions, so that the process becomes dynamic and able to respond to changing conditions of use and impact (Williams and Gill, 1994).

As Glasson et al. (1995) indicate, the relationships between use and impacts are neither linear nor uniform. They identify five key principles to explain the relationship between visitor use and impacts that are important in order to have any affect on impact mitigation. These include:

- Impact interrelationships. There is no single predictable response between the use of a setting and the visitor/host experience. As a result, an interrelated set of impact indicators can be identified of which some can be more direct or evident than others. As such, a combination of indicators could become the basis of a management strategy.
- Use-impact relationships. Most impacts do not exhibit a direct linear relationship with user density. This suggests that various impact indicators are related to the amount of recreation use of a given area, even though the strength and nature of the relationships vary widely for different types of impact and in accordance with different measures of visitor use and the particular situational factors.
- Varying tolerance of impacts. There is an inherent variation in the levels of tolerance between different user groups in different settings. Different destination areas respond differently to visitor impacts. This suggests that some species may benefit at the expense of others that are negatively impacted or displaced. Various recreational user groups may also have different responses in that some may enjoy higher densities, yet others find these levels unacceptable.
- Activity-specific influences. Some types of activity cause different impacts due to varying intensities of use and visitor characteristics. This means that the extent of an impact resulting from a given activity can vary according to factors such as type of transportation or equipment used, and visitor characteristics, particularly size and behavior.
- Site-specific influences. Tourism impacts are influenced by any number of site specific and seasonal variables. That is, the outcome for using a specific area may depend on the time and place of the human activity given the basic tolerance level for a particular tourist activity.

Although the VIM framework has not received wide use in nature-based tourism destinations, it may be useful in helping planners and managers to identify tourism-related impacts, ascertain related drivers and factors, plus select potential strategies to deal with them.

Community-Based Natural Resource Management

Community-based natural resource management (CBNRM) and ecotourism projects are carried out in most developing countries as an attempt to achieve sustainable tourism development. CBNRM is a collective term used for a number of similar but unconnected programs in different countries of Eastern and Southern Africa. CBNRM aims at addressing problems of land use conflicts, the lack of direct wildlife economic benefits to people living in wildlife areas, and local community participation in wildlife resource management (Mbaiwa, 2005). The basic principle behind the CBNRM program is that of reforming the conventional "protectionist conservation philosophy" and "top-down" approaches to development; it is based on common property theory, which discourages open access resource management and promotes resource use rights of the local communities (Kgathi et al., 2002). The CBNRM program assumes that once rural communities derive economic benefits from nature resource use, they will feel greater stewardship over their environments and support conservation (Tsing et al., 1999; Twyman, 2000). The CBNRM program has been carried out in Botswana, Namibia, Zimbabwe, Kenya, Tanzania, Malawi, Mozambique, and Zambia so far.

Case Study: The CBNRM Program in Botswana

In Botswana, CBNRM projects are carried out in areas around national parks and game reserves known as wildlife management areas (WMAs). The concept of WMAs arose from a need for conservation and controlled utilization of wildlife outside national parks and game reserves, along with the desirability of creating buffer zones between parks and reserves and areas of more intensive land use. WMAs are further subdivided into smaller land units known as controlled hunting areas (CHAs). Botswana is divided into 163 CHAs, which are zoned for various types of wildlife utilization (both consumptive and nonconsumptive uses). The government leases CHAs to rural communities for CBNRM projects and to safari companies for safari hunting purposes. The CHAs that are directly leased to safari companies are also known as concession areas. The Department of Wildlife and National Parks (DWNP) uses CHAs as administrative blocks to determine wildlife quotas for safari hunting by rural communities involved in CBNRM and safari hunting companies in concession areas.

The number of CBNRM projects in Botswana has grown rapidly since 1996.

Arntzen et al. (2003) provide the following figures. In 2002, there were 42 registered CBNRM projects and 12 of them were involved in joint venture agreements (JVA) with at least seven private safari companies. Revenues from JVAs have also grown to P8.5 million[2] by 2002 with an average cash for communities of over P700,000 per annum; this is a lot of money considering the small size of villages involved in CBNRM in Botswana. Arntzen et al. (2003) also indicate that employment generated by CBNRM projects is estimated to be around 1000–1500 jobs with an average employment of 21 employees per project in 2001. CBNRM projects thus serve as an alternative form of employment in wildlife regions. People employed by the CBNRM project at Sankoyo Village in the Okavango (Photo 19.1) and by the joint venture safari hunting company have improved their shelter (homes), support siblings to meet the costs associated with school and provide support for their families (Arntzen et al., 2003). CBNRM has clearly had a fairly substantial socioeconomic impact on the livelihoods of Sankoyo residents and other communities in Botswana.

Sankoyo residents have gone further to reinvest tourism profits from wildlife hunting into ecotourism lodges and campsites. The Sankoyo community established a 16-bed photographic lodge known as Santawani Lodge (Photo 19.2), a cultural tourism center (Shandrika) where tourists can view the cultural activities and way of life of the people of Sankoyo (Photo 19.3), and a campsite known as Kazikini (Photos 19.4 and 19.5) where tourists who do not want to stay in a lodge can camp. Santawnai Lodge, Kazikini, and Shadrika generate income and employment for the people of Sankoyo. Santawani Lodge and Kazikini Campsite respectively employed 16 and 15 people in June 2004.

The Sankoyo CBNRM project is heavily dependent on wildlife resources, particularly the community's wildlife quota: over 70% of its income is from sale of its wildlife quota to safari hunters (Arntzen et al., 2003). This income subsequently ends up in local

Photo 19.1   Waters in the Okavango Delta flow from Angola.
Photo: Amanda Stronza.

households in the form of dividends. Data from annual reports of the Sankoyo CBNRM project show that between 1996 and 2001, each household was paid P200. This sum increased to P250 in 2002, P300 in 2003, and P500 between 2004 and 2007 (in 1996, all 34 households at Sankoyo received the dividends; households increased to 49 households in 2004). Because of the economic benefits that rural communities derive from safari hunting, illegal wildlife exploitation is reported to have gone down in the last decade (Arntzen et al., 2003). Botswana's CBNRM program reflects a tourism development approach that promotes the well-being of local people, and environmental conservation. Furthermore, it enables local participation in the decision making process.

Certification and Self-Regulation in Tourism

The pressure to promote sustainable tourism development in destination areas has resulted in practitioners developing certification

programs to protect their businesses. According to McLaren (2006) tourism certification attempts to ensure the quality of products and services beyond simple labeling. As a result, current efforts to certify tourism include sustainable tourism certification, responsible tourism certification, and fair trade tourism certification. In this regards, certification labels serve as useful marketing tools and can motivate the industry to develop more environmentally friendly products. Certification programs and ecolabeling schemes therefore reflect the tourism industry and the operator's efforts to gain credibility and visibility in an increasingly competitive marketplace (Honey, 1999; Jamal et al., 2006). Certification can provide consumers with valuable information on sustainable tourism products, helping them to make more informed travel choices (McLaren, 2006).

Certification is one avenue by which tourism operators attempt to meet the requirements of Agenda 21 for Travel and Tourism. As Mowforth and Munt (2003) summarize, Agenda 21 impinges on tourism in two ways: first, tourism is considered to be having a sustainable development potential to certain communities,

Photo 19.2   A two bed chalet at Santawani Lodge.
Photo: Joseph Mbaiwa.

Photo 19.3   Basarwa Peoples of the Okavango participate in tourism through
the community-based Natural Resource Management Program.
Photo: Amanda Stronza.

Photo 19.4   A restaurant facility at Kazikini.
Photo: Joseph Mbaiwa.

particularly fragile environments. Second, tourism has many impacts that may need to be altered by the legal framework, policies and management practices under which it operates. The Agenda 21 directive urges governments and the tourism industry to respectively adopt policies and code of conducts to promote sustainability in tourism development. For example, the tourism business and industry sector is required to adopt codes of conduct promoting best environmental practice, to ensure responsible and ethical management of products and processes and to increase self-regulation (Mowforth and Munt, 2003).

Synergy (2000) and World Tourism Organization (2002) indicate that over 100 international, national, and regional sustainable tourism certification schemes were being promoted around the start of the twenty-first century. The Australian Nature and Ecotourism Certification Program (NEAP), the Costa Rican Sustainable Tourism Certification (STC), and the Canadian Saskatchewan Ecotourism Accreditation System (SEAS) are tourism certification programs; they generally provide tourism companies with a logo that allows businesses to demonstrate their environmental credentials to consumers. These credentials are earned by engaging in recognized industry practices such as ecolabeling, earning a specific trademark through a certification process involving a membership fee, self-assessed accreditation programs and third party audits. Certification programs have guidelines and criteria, which particular schemes should adopt for self-regulation purposes. For example, the Costa Rican Sustainable Tourism Certification is noted for having 152 sustainable tourism criteria that include environmental, social, economic, and quality indicators (Jamal et al., 2006).

While tourism certification is a tool for enabling sustainable tourism, it is difficult to monitor as it depends to a greater extent on voluntary certification and services than does the certification of many products. Certification is easier to verify for businesses like camping sites, guesthouses, restaurants and farm houses

Photo 19.5   A signboard of Kazikini Campsite. Behind it is the campground.
Photo: Joseph Mbaiwa.

than for community development projects like local tours, cultural preservation and integrated development strategies (McLaren, 2006). Font and Harris (2004) state, furthermore, that certification of corporate social responsibility in developing countries is problematic. This is because the programs used by tourism companies have ambiguous social standards and assessment methods and are inconsistent and open to interpretation. Greater research and effective legal and policy frameworks are needed to address these challenges, and facilitate the use of certification programs and other mechanisms to enable sustainability in tourism development.

Future Issues and Challenges

Since the adoption of the Brundtland Report by the United Nations in 1987 (WCED, 1987), the concepts of sustainable development and sustainable tourism have become important

tools that inform tourism research and practice. Despite the rich body of literature that has emerged, the meaning of sustainable development (and subsequently sustainable tourism) remains problematic. Williams and Millington state that "sustainable development is a notoriously difficult, slippery and elusive concept to pin down" (2004: 99). Peterson (1997) says the concept of sustainable development has become celebrated as a public policy goal to be supported and furthered on the basis of scientific research and management—she argues persuasively that the concept is based on modernist principles of economic growth and progress.

The concept of sustainable tourism as it has evolved in the 1990s follows the definition and principles of sustainable development (WCED, 1987). It calls for both intra- and intergenerational equity; that is, fair and equitable opportunities for people, both in the present and in the future. Yet, the flows and the structures of international tourism indicate that equitable development through tourism is difficult to achieve.

Europe and North America remain major beneficiaries of tourism investment in developing countries. Tourism in most developing countries has so far resulted in uneven distribution of resources and few opportunities for equitable development (Britton, 1982; Oppermann, 1993).

Sustainable tourism and responsible tourism principles and practices can be applied to a wide array of tourism services and facilities, including large hotels, and cruise ships as well as small lodges and tour guiding services. If implemented appropriately, sustainable tourism has the potential to link the conservation of nature with the well being of local communities through a number of benefits including revenue generation, renewed cultural pride, and capacity building. Complexity and interdependence among environmental, social and economic issues and policies is important to recognize and address if sustainability goals are to be achieved (Myburgh and Saayman, 1999). Shifting towards responsible forms of tourism may require major change in the sociopolitical, legal, administrative, and economic structures, as well as education. Tourism planning should be designed such that policies that are adopted contribute to needs of local communities and biodiversity conservation in host regions and countries. Greater attention to the issues raised in this chapter is needed if present generations of tourists, host communities, tourism operators, and government agencies are to derive satisfactory benefits from environmental resources that also happen to be tourism products.

Notes

1 The website of the International Center for Responsible Tourism provides information on the Cape Town declaration and the 2008 Kerala Declaration on Responsible Tourism, see www.icrtourism.org/capetown.shtml. Accessed May 2, 2008.

2 US$1 equals 5 Botswana Pula as of the writing of this chapter.

References

Alexander, S.E. (2000). "Resident Attitudes Towards Conservation and Black Howler Monkeys in Belize: The Community Baboon Sanctuary." *Environmental Conservation*, 27(4): 341–350.

Angelsen A., Fjeldstad, O. and Rashid-Sumaila, U. (1994). *Project Appraisal and Sustainability in Less Developed Countries*. Fantoft-Bergen, Norway. Bergen Print Services.

Ahn, B., Lee, B. and Shafer, C.S. (2002). "Operationalizing Sustainability in Regional Tourism Planning: An Application of the Limits of Acceptable Change Framework." *Tourism Management*, 23(1): 1–15.

Arntzen, J., Molokomme, K., Tshosa, O., Moleele, N., Mazambani, D. and Terry, B. (2003). *Review of CBNRM in Botswana*. Gaborone: Centre for Applied Research.

Barkin, D. (1996). "Ecotourism: A Tool for Sustainable Development in an Era of International Integration?" In J.A. Miller and E. Malek-Zadeh (Eds.), *The Ecotourism Equation: Measuring the Impacts* (pp. 263–272). New Haven, CT: Yale University.

Barrett, C, Brandon, K, Gibson, C. and Gjertsen, H. (2001). "Conserving Tropical Biodiversity Amid Weak Institutions." *BioScience*, 51(3): 497–502.

Belsky, J.M. (1999). "Misrepresenting Communities: The Politics of Community-Based Rural Ecotourism in Gales Point Manatee, Belize." *Rural Sociology*, 64(4): 641–666.

Bookbinder, M.P., Dinerstein, E., Rijal, A., Cauley, H. and Rajouria, A. (1998). "Ecotourism's Support of Biodiversity Conservation." *Conservation Biology*, 12(6): 1399–1404.

Borman, R. (1999). "Cofan: Story of the Forest People and the Outsiders." *Cultural Survival Quarterly*, 23: 48–50.

Boyd, S. and Butler, R.W. (1996). "Managing Ecotourism: An Opportunity Spectrum Approach." *Tourism Management*, 17(8): 557–566.

Bramwell, B. and Lane, B. (1993). "Interpretation and Sustainable Tourism: The Potentials and Pitfalls." *Journal of Sustainable Tourism*, 1(2): 71–80.

Briassoulis, H. and ver der Straaten, J. (Eds.) (2000). *Tourism and the Environment: Regional, Economic, Cultural and Policy Issues*. London: Kluwer Academic Publishers.

Britton, S.G. (1982). "The Political Economy of Tourism in the Third World." *Annals of Tourism Research*, 9(3): 331–358.

Brown, K., Turner, R.K., Hameed, H. and Bateman, I. (1997). "Environmental Carrying Capacity and Tourism Development in the Madives and Nepal." *Environmental Conservation*, 24: 316–325.

Brown, K., Turner, R.K., Hameed, H. and Bateman I. (1998). "Reply to Lindberg and McCool: A Critique of Environmental Carrying Capacity as a Means of Managing the Effects of Tourism Development." *Environmental Conservation*, 25: 293–394.

Bryden, J.M. (1973). *Tourism and Development: A Case Study of the Commonwealth Caribbean*. Cambridge: Cambridge University Press.

Butler, R.W. and Waldbrook, L.A. (1991). "A New Planning Tool: The Tourism Opportunity Spectrum." *Journal of Tourism Studies*, 2(1): 1–14.

Campbell, L. (1999). "Ecotourism in Rural Developing Communities." *Annals of Tourism Research*, 26(3): 534–553.

Cater, E. (1991). *Sustainable Tourism in the Third World: Problems and Prospects*. Discussion Paper No. 3. London: University of Readings.

Cater, E. (1993). "Ecotourism in the Third World: Problems for Sustainable Tourism Development." *Tourism Management,* 14(2): 85–90.

Cater, E. and Lowman, G. (Eds.) (1994). *Ecotourism: A Sustainable Option?* Chichester: John Wiley & Sons.

Ceballos-Lascurain, H. (1996). *Tourism, Eco-tourism and Protected Areas*. Glad, Switzerland: International Union for Conservation of Nature and Nature Resources.

Clark, R.N. and Stankey, G.H. (1979). *The Recreation Opportunity Spectrum: A Framework for Planning, Management, and Research*. USDA Forest Service, Pacific Northwest Forest and Range Experiment Station, General Technical Report PNW-98.

Coccossis, H. (1996). "Tourism and Sustainability: Perspectives and Implications." In G.K. Priestley, J.A. Edwards and H. Coccossis (Eds.), *Sustainable Tourism? European Experiences* (pp. 1–21). Wallingford: CAB International.

Coccossis, H. and Parpairis, A. (1995). "Assessing the Interaction between Heritage, Environment and Tourism: Mykonos." In H. Coccossis and P. Nijkamp (Eds.), *Sustainable Tourism Development* (pp. 107–126). Hong Kong: Avebury.

Cohen, E. (2002). "Authenticity, Equity and Sustainability in Tourism." *Journal of Sustainable Tourism*, 10(4): 267–276.

Cohen, E. (1978). "The Impact of Tourism on the Physical Environment." *Annals of Tourism Research*, 5(2): 215–237.

Cooke, J. (1991). "Tourism and its Impact on a Developing Country." In L. Pfotenhauer (Ed.), *Tourism in Botswana*. Gaborone: The Botswana Society.

Daily, G.C. and Ellison, K. (2003). *The New Economy of Nature: The Quest to Make Nature Profitable*. Washington, DC: Island Press.

Doan, T. (2000). "The Effects of Ecotourism in Developing Nations: An Analysis of Case Studies." *Journal of Sustainable Tourism*, 8(4): 288–304.

Dixon, J., Hamilton, K., Pagiola, S. and Segnestan, L. (2001). *Tourism and the Environment in the Caribbean: An Economic Framework*. New York: Environment Department, World Bank.

Edwards, V.M. (2004). "The Commons in an Age of Global Transition: Challenges, Risks and Opportunities." *The 10th Biennial Meeting of the IASCP*. Oaxaca, Mexico, August 9–13.

Font, X. and Harris, C. (2004). "Rethinking Standards from Green to Sustainable." *Annals of Tourism Research,* 31(4): 986–1007.

Gladstone, D.L. (2005). *From Pilgrimage to Package Tour: Travel and Tourism in the Third World*. New York: Routledge.

Glasson, J., Godfrey, K. and Goodey, B. (1995). *Towards Visitor Impact Management: Visitor Impacts, Carrying Capacity and Management Responses in Europe's Historic Towns and Cities*. Aldershot: Avebury.

Goldsmith, F.B. (1974). "Ecological Effects of Visitors in the Countryside." In A. Warren and F.B. Goldsmith (Eds.), *Conservation in Practice* (pp. 217–231). London: Wiley.

Gossling, S. (1999). "Ecotourism: A Means to Safeguard Biodiversity and Ecosystem Functions?" *Ecological Economics*, 29(2): 303–320.

Graefe, A.R., Vaske, J.J. and Kuss, F.R. (1990). *Visitor Impact Management: The Planning*

Framework. Washington: National Parks and Conservation Association.

Graham, R., Nilsen, P. and Payne, R.J. (1988). "Visitor Management in Canadian National Parks." *Tourism Management*, 9(1): 44–61.

Hall, C.M. (1995). *Introduction to Tourism in Australia: Impacts, Planning and Development*. London: Longman.

Hardy, H., Beeton, R.J.S. and Pearson, L. (2002). "Sustainable Tourism: An Overview of the Concept and its Position in Relation to Conceptualization of Tourism." *Journal of Sustainable Tourism*, 10(6): 475–496.

Harrison, D. (1996). "Sustainability and Tourism: Reflections from a Muddy Pool." In L. Briguglio, B. Archer, J. Jafari and G. Wall (Eds.), *Sustainable Tourism in Islands and Small States* (pp. 69–89). London: Pinter.

Hawkins, J. and Roberts, C. (1997). "Estimating the Carrying Capacity of Coral Reefs for Scuba Diving." *Proceedings of the Eighth International Coral Reef Symposium*. Balboa, Panama: Smithsonian Tropical Research Institute: 1923–1926.

Healy, R. (1994). "Tourist Merchandise as a Means of Generating Local Benefits from Ecotourism." *Journal of Sustainable Tourism*, 2(3): 137–151.

Hillery, M., Blair, N., Graham, G. and Syme, G. (2001). "Tourism Perception of Environmental Impact." *Annals of Tourism Research*, 28(4): 853–867.

Honey, H. (1999). *Ecotourism and Sustainable Development: Who Owns Paradise?* Washington, DC: Island Press.

Hunter, C. (1995). "Sustainable Tourism as an Adaptive Paradigm." *Annals of Tourism Research*, 24(4): 850–867.

Hunter, C. and Green, H. (1995). *Tourism and Environment*. London: Routledge.

Inskeep, E. (1991). *Tourism Planning: An Integrated and Sustainable Development*. New York: Van Nostrand Reinhold.

International Union for the Conservation of Nature (IUCN) (2003). "World Commission on Protected Areas." Retrieved February 14, 2008 from www.iucn.org/themes/wcpa/wpc2003/.

Jamal, T., Borges, M. and Stronza, A. (2006). "The Institionalisation of Ecotourism: Certi-fication, Cultural Equity and Praxis." *Journal of Ecotourism*, 5(3):145–175.

Kiss, A. (2004). "Is Community-Based Ecotourism a Good Use of Biodiversity Conservation Funds?" *Trends in Ecology and Evolution*, 19(5): 231–237.

Kgathi, D.L., Mbaiwa, J.E. and Motsholapheko, M.R. (2002). *Local Institutions and Natural Resource Management in Ngamiland*. Maun: Harry Oppenheimer Okavango Research Centre, University of Botswana.

Kutay, K. (1989). "The New Ethic in Adventure Travel." *Ecotourism*, 20: 27–32.

Kruger, O. (2005). "The Role of Ecotourism in Conservation: Panacea or Pandora's Box?" *Biodiversity and Conservation*, 14(3): 579–600.

Langholz, J. (1999). "Exploring the Effects of Alternative Income Opportunities on Rainforest Use: Insights from Guatemala's Maya Biosphere Reserve." *Society and Natural Resources*, 12(2): 139–150.

Lindberg, K. (1994). *An Analysis of Ecotourism's Economic Contribution to Conservation and Development in Belize: A Report*. Washington: World Wildlife Fund.

Lindberg, K. and Hawkins, D.E. (Eds.) (1993). *Ecotourism: A Guide for Planners and Managers*. North Bennington, VT: Ecotourism Society.

Lindberg, K., Enriquez, J. and Sproule, K. (1996). "Ecotourism Questioned: Case Studies from Belize." *Annals of Tourism Research*, 23(3): 543–562.

Liu, Z. (2003). "Sustainable Tourism Development: A Critique." *Journal of Sustainable Tourism*, 11(6): 459–475.

Matthew, H.G. (1977). "Radicals and Third World Tourism: A Caribbean Focus." *Annals of Tourism Research*, 5(5): 20–29.

Markandya, A. (1993). "Criteria for Sustainable Agricultural Development." In A. Markandya and J. Richardson (Eds.), *Environmental Economics: A Reader* (pp. 289–293). New York: St Martins Press.

Mbaiwa, J.E. (2003). "The Socio-Economic and Environmental Impacts of Tourism in the Okavango Delta, Northwestern Botswana." *Journal of Arid Environments*, 54(2): 447–468.

Mbaiwa, J.E. (2005). "Enclave Tourism and its Socio-Economic Impacts in the Okavango Delta, Botswana." *Tourism Management*, 26(2): 157–172.

McCool, S.F. (1994). "Planning for Sustainable Nature Dependent Tourism Development: The Limits of Acceptable Change System." *Tourism Recreation Research*, 19: 51–55.

McCool, S.F. (1995). "Linking Tourism, the Environment, and Concepts of Sustainability: Setting the Stage." In *Linking Tourism, the Environment and Sustainability*. USDA Forest Service Technical Report INT-GTR-323: 3–6.

McIntyre, G. (1993). *Sustainable Tourism Guide for Local Planners*. Madrid: World Tourism Organization.

McLaren, D. (2006). "The Responsible Travel Movement." In D. Beardsley, D. Clemmons and M. DelliPriscoli (Eds.), *Responsible Travel Handbook 2006* (pp. 10–13). Bennington: Transition Abroad Magazine.

Mowforth, M. and Munt, I. (2003). *Tourism and Sustainability: New Tourism in the Third World*. London: Routledge.

Munasinghe, M. and McNeely, J. (1995). "Key Concepts and Terminology of Sustainable Development." In M. Munasinghe and W. Shearer (Eds.), *Defining and Measuring Sustainability: The Biological Foundations* (pp. 19–46). Washington, DC: The World Bank.

Myburgh, E. and Saayman, M. (1999). *Ecotourism in Action: Practical Guidelines and Principles*. Potchefstroom: Institute for Tourism and Leisure Studies.

National Park Service (US National Park Service) (1993). *Visitor Experience and Resource Protection Process*. Denver: National Park Service.

O'Reilly, A.M. (1986). "Carrying Capacity: Concept and Issues." *Tourism Management*, 7(4): 254–258.

Oates, J.F. (1999). *Myth and Reality in the Rainforest: How Conservation Strategies are Failing in West Africa*. Berkeley: University of California Press.

Odum, E.P. (1959). *Fundamental of Ecology*. Philadelphia: W.B. Saunders.

Oliver, J. (1995). "Is the 'Limits of Acceptable Change' Concept Use for Environmental Managers? A Case Study from the Great Barrier Reef Marine Park." In G.C. Grigg, P.T. Hale and D. Lunney (Eds.), *Conservation through Sustainable Use of Wildlife* (pp. 131–139). Brisbane: Centre for Conservation Biology, University of Queensland.

Oliveira, J.A.P. (2003). "Governmental Responses to Tourism Development: Three Brazilian Case Studies." *Tourism Management*, 24(1): 97–110.

Oppermann, M. (1993). "Tourism Space in Developing Countries." *Annals of Tourism Research*, 20(3): 535–556.

Oppermann, M. and Chon, K.S. (1997). *Tourism in Developing Countries*. London: International Thomson Business Press.

Orams, M.B. (1997). "The Effectiveness of Environmental Education: Can We Turn Tourists into 'Greenies'?" *Progress in Tourism and Hospitality Research*, 3: 295–306.

Paehlke, R. (1999). "Towards Defining, Measuring and Achieving Sustainability: Tools and Strategies for Environmental Valuation." In E. Becker and T. Jahn (Eds.), *Sustainability and the Social Sciences*. London: Zed Books.

Pantin, D.A. (1998). *Tourism in St. Lucia*. St Augustine: Sustainable Economic Development Unit for Small and Island Development States, University of the West Indies.

Pavaskar, M. (1982). "Employment Effects of Tourism and the Indian Experience." *Journal of Tourism Research*, 21(2): 32–38.

Peterson, T.R. (1997). *Sharing the Earth: The Rhetoric of Sustainable Development*. Columbia: University of South Carolina Press.

Plog, S.C. (1974). "Why Destination Areas Rise and Fall in Popularity." *Cornell Hotel and Restaurant Quarterly*, 14(4): 55–58.

Prosser, R. (1994). "Societal Change and the Growth in Alternative Tourism." In E. Cater and G. Lowman (Eds.), *Ecotourism: A Sustainable Option* (pp. 19–37). New York: John Wiley & Sons.

Redcliff, M.R. (1987). *Sustainable Development: Exploring the Contradictions*. London: Methuen.

Roggenbuck, J.W., Williams, D.R. and Watson, A.E. (1993). "Defining Acceptable Conditions in Wilderness." *Environmental Management*, 17: 187–197.

Saveriades, A. (2000). "Establishing the Social Tourism Carrying Capacity for the Tourist Resorts of the East Coast of the Republic of Cyprus." *Tourism Management*, 21(2): 147–156.

Scheyvens, R. (1999). "Ecotourism and the Empowerment of Local Communities." *Tourism Management*, 20(2): 245–249.

Seckelmann, A. (2002). "Domestic Tourism—A Chance for Regional Development in Turkey?" *Tourism Management*, 23(1): 85–92.

Scheyvens, R. (1999). "Ecotourism and the Empowerment of Local Communities." *Tourism Management*, 20(2): 245–249.

Serageldine, I. (1993). "Making Development Sustainable." *Finance and Development*, (December): 6–13.

Sharpley, R. (2000). "Tourism and Sustainable Development: Exploring the Theoretical Divide." *Journal of Sustainable Tourism*, 8(1): 1–19.

Shelby, B. and Herberlein, T.A. (1986). *Carrying Capacity in Recreational Settings*. Corvallis: Oregon State University Press.

Sindiga, I. (1996). "International Tourism in Kenya and the Marginalization of the Waswahili." *Tourism Management*, 17(6): 425–432.

Sofield, T.H.B. (2003). *Empowerment for Sustainable Tourism Development*. Oxford: Pergamon.

Stankey, G.H. and McCool, S.F. (1984). "Carrying Capacity in Recreational Settings: Evolution, Appraisal, and Application." *Leisure Sciences*, 6: 453–473.

Stankey, G.H., Cole, D., Lucas, R.C., Patterson, M.E. and Frissell, S.S. (1985). *The Limits to Acceptable Change System for Wilderness Planning*. USDA Forest Service, Intermountain Forest and Range Experiment Station, General Technical Report INT-176.

Stem, C., Lassoie, J., Lee, D. and Deshler, D. (2003). "How 'Eco' is Ecotourism? A Comparative Case Study of Ecotourism in Costa Rica." *Journal of Sustainable Tourism*, 11(4): 322–347.

Stonich, S. (1998). "The Political Ecology of Tourism." *Annals of Tourism Research*, 25(1): 25–54.

Stonich, S. (2000). *The Other Side of Paradise: Tourism, Conservation and Development in the Bay Islands*. Cognizant Communications.

Stronza, A. (2001). "The Anthropology of Tourism: Forging New Ground for Ecotourism and Other Alternatives." *Annual Review of Anthropology*, 30: 261–283.

Stronza, A. (2007). "The Economic Promise of Ecotourism for Conservation." *Journal of Ecotourism*, 6(3): 170–190.

Stronza, A. and Gordillo, J. (2008). "Community Views of Ecotourism." *Annals of Tourism Research*, 35(2): 448–468.

Synergy, (2000). *Tourism Certification (Report)*. London: WWF.

Swarbrooke, J. (1999). *Sustainable Tourism Management*. Wallingford: CAB International.

Taylor, J.E., Yunez-Naude, A. and Ardila, S. (2003). "The Economics of Ecotourism: A Galápagos Islands Economy-Wide Perspective." *Economic Development and Cultural Change*, 13(3): 978–997.

Terborgh J. (1999). *Requiem for Nature*. Washington, DC: Island Press.

Terborgh, J., van Schaik, C., Davenport, L. and Rao, M. (Eds.) (2002). *Making Parks Work: Strategies for Preserving Tropical Nature*. Washington: Island Press.

Thaites, R., Lipscombe, N. and Smith, E. (2002). "Providing Education in a Growth Industry: Issues in Ecotourism Education and Employment in Australia." *Journal of Teaching in Travel and Tourism*, 2(1): 81–97.

Thompson, P.B. (1997). "Sustainability as a Norm." *Philosophy and Technology*, 2(2). Texas A&M University, Unpublished Paper.

Tosun, C. (2001). "Challenges of Sustainable Tourism Development in the Developing World: The Case of Turkey." *Tourism Management*, 22(3): 289–303.

Tosun, C. (2000). "Limits to Community Participation in Tourism Development Process in Developing Countries." *Tourism Management*, 21(6): 613–633.

Tsing, A.L., Brosius, J.P. and Zerner, C. (1999). "Assessing Community-Based Natural Resource Management." *Ambio*, 28: 197–198.

Twyman, C. (2000). "Participatory Conservation? Community-Based Natural Resource Management in Botswana." *The Geographical Journal*, 166(4): 323–335.

United Nations Conference on Environment and Development (UNCED) (1992). *Report of the United Nations Conference on Environment and Development, Volume I–III*. New York: United Nations.

Van der Post, C. (2004). "Human Sprawl and the African Wilderness of the Okavango." *South African Geographical Journal*, 86(2): 65–73.

Wahab, S. and Pigram, J.J. (Eds.) (1997). *Tourism, Development and Growth: The Challenge of Sustainability*. London: Routledge.

Wall, G. (1997). "Is Ecotourism Sustainable?" *Environmental Management*, 21(4): 483–491.

Wallace, G. and Pierce, S. (1996). "An Evaluation of Ecotourism in Amazonas, Brazil." *Annals of Tourism Research*, 23(4): 843–873.

Wearing, S. and Neil, J. (1999). *Ecotourism: Impacts, Potentials, and Possibilities*. Oxford: Butterworth-Heinemann.

Weaver, D.B. and Lawton, L.J. (2007). "Twenty Years On: The State of Contemporary Ecotourism Research." *Tourism Management*, 28(5): 1168–1179.

Wearing, S. and Neil, J. (1999). *Ecotourism: Impacts, Potentials, and Possibilities*. Oxford: Butterworth-Heinemann.

West, P. and Carrier, J. (2004). "Ecotourism and Authenticity: Getting Away from it All?" *Current Anthropology*, 45(4): 483–491.

Williams, C.C. and Millington, A. (2004). "The Diverse and Contested Meanings of Sustainable Development." *The Geographical Journal*, 170(2): 99–104.

Williams, P.W. and Gill, A. (1994). "Tourism Carrying Capacity Management Issues." In W.F. Theobald (Ed.), *Global Tourism: The Next Decade* (pp. 231–246). Boston, MA: Butterworth-Heinemann .

World Tourism Organization/United Nations Environmental Program (1992). *Guidelines: Development of National Parks and Protected Areas for Tourism*. Madrid: World Tourism Organization.

World Commission on Environment and Development (WCED) (1987). *Our Common Future*. London: Oxford University Press.

World Tourism Organization (WTO) (1996). *What Tourism Managers Need to Know: A Practical Guide to the Development and Use of Indicators of Sustainable Tourism*. Madrid: WTO.

World Tourism Organization (WTO) (2002a). *Tourism Market Trends, Africa: 1999, 2002*. Madrid: WTO.

World Tourism Organization (WTO) (2002b). *Voluntary Initiatives for Sustainable Tourism*. Madrid: WTO.

Wunder, S. (1999). *Promoting Forest Conservation Through Ecotourism Income? A Case Study from the Ecuadorian Amazon Region*. Bogor, Indonesia: CIFOR.

Wunder, S. (2000). "Ecotourism and Economic Incentives—An Empirical Approach." *Ecological Economics*, 32: 465–479.

Young, E. (1999). "Balancing Conservation with Development in Small-Scale Fisheries: Is Ecotourism an Empty Promise?" *Human Ecology*, 27(4): 581–620.

20

Rural Tourism: An Overview

Bernard Lane

The Background

Introduction

During the 1970s, 1980s, and 1990s a wave of change, redemption, and regeneration swept the rural world. The wave began in Western Europe, swept on to North America, over Australia and New Zealand, across to Japan and into Eastern Europe. Its broader impacts can be felt worldwide. The wave was called rural tourism. It signaled a new era for the rural world, but it also reflected a new phase in the changing and growing world of tourism development.

Rural tourism was, however, not new in the 1970s. Its origins lie deep in the Romantic Movement that began to develop in the late eighteenth century and flourished in the nineteenth century. Romanticism was an intellectual concept that raised the natural world to prominence: romanticism is typified by William Wordsworth's nature poems, by Beethoven's music, by Caspar David Friedrich's landscape paintings, and by the literature of Henry David Thoreau and Ralph Waldo Emerson. It sees values in natural landscapes, in folk memories, and folklore, and above all in contact with nature. It grew as an antidote to industrial cities and the industrial revolution (see Fiero, 2006: 3–27, for a global summary of romanticism; see also Roe, 2005; Thompson, 2005). Tourism developed around those romantic images in the nineteenth century through rail links to rural resorts. In Europe, the Alpine regions came within 24-hour train journeys of the major continental cities. In North America, journeys were twice as long, but transcontinental rail lines opened the way for many to see the Rocky Mountains: by 1930 no less than five railroads served Yellowstone National Park, bringing 40,000 people there in that year (Runte, 1990)

The nineteenth century helped create the powerful imagery of the rural scene, and began the concept of the rurally based holiday, but it did not create rural tourism as we know it today. Rail-based rural tourism was essentially resort/hotel based and was in many respects urban in its style. Modern rural tourism began in the post-World War II era, breaking free of the resort, changing in scale and character, and became a much more widespread phenomena, spreading from the much publicized scenery of famous protected areas to many more "ordinary" landscapes. There was a remarkable coming together of a range of technical, demand and supply factors that occurred by lucky chance. From about 1970 to the end of the century, growth was easy. Rural tourism now faces more hostile market conditions.

But What is Rural Tourism?

This author was asked to define rural tourism by the Organization for Economic Cooperation and Development (OECD) in 1991.[1] It was considered an essential task because of the powerful impact that rural tourism was then seen to be having. The once largely agricultural rural world was being diversified— economically and socially—by growing numbers of tourists and tourist enterprises. The once resort based world of tourism was also being diversified—economically and spatially—by several new forms of tourism, of which rural tourism was one. It was felt essential to seek a definition so that the size, geographical spread, and value of rural tourism could be quantified.

After intensive and lengthy debates across the agricultural and tourism committees of that institution, and through the OECD's Council on Rural Development, an answer was published in 1994 (Lane, 1994a). It is paraphrased and discussed below. It was an answer that did not allow for easy quantification, for reasons that will become apparent.

The OECD definition noted the many problems in defining rural tourism. Rural tourism is tourism that takes place in the countryside. But rural areas are themselves difficult to define, and the criteria used by different nations vary considerably (Robinson, 1990). The OECD's Council on Rural Development (OECD, 1993) agreed that at a very simple level, rural areas should be classified as:

- Economically Integrated Areas—close to cities and towns, rural in appearance but economically and culturally close to cities. These areas tend to have high levels of day visit tourism, and tend

to have farm economies increasingly related to visitation. Pressures to both use and conserve land and landscapes can be considerable.

- Intermediate Areas—the rural heartland, comprising the majority of rural land, relatively distant from urban areas with largely agricultural/ forestry land uses. Here tourism tends to be largely in terms of overnight stays, with growth concentrated in scenic areas, often in protected areas, in areas with heritage/cultural strengths, and in areas with special qualities and niche market attractions such as bird breeding/feeding grounds, or good cycling routes. Intermediate areas with good road, rail, or even air connections can be especially attractive in tourism terms.

- Remote Areas—often sparsely populated, far from major urban areas, often with low quality land, form the third part of the typology. Tourism in remote rural areas functions largely as a result of outstanding natural heritage and scenery, but also as a niche market for those who wish to escape into a quiet zone, away from the pressures of modern life.

It was noted in the discussions of the early 1990s that rural areas themselves were in a complex process of change. Traditional self-sufficient communities were changing as a result of global markets, communications, and telecommunication. Those changes are now far more advanced. Power structures have changed markedly. The rise of environmentalism has led to increasing control by "outsiders" over land use and resource development; protected areas have increased in numbers and area covered. That trend, and the trend for protected areas themselves to change their focus to become more market and therefore tourism orientated, have been reflected in a number of studies, including those by Butler and Boyd (2000), Eagles (2002, 2004), and Sharpley and Pearce (2007).

Although some rural areas still suffer depopulation, others are experiencing an inflow of people to retire, to commute or to develop new "nontraditional" businesses. Retirees often follow tourism visits (OECD, 1995; Perry et al., 1986). But perhaps most striking in its impact has been the rise of the life style entrepreneur, keen to set up small tourism (and other) businesses, bringing with them financial capital, contact networks, market knowledge, and entrepreneurial ideas from the cities (Ateljevic and Doorne, 2000; Lane, 1995; OECD, 1995). Some of the new entrepreneurs come as spouses or partners, some as families, some as couples. However, not all of the new entrepreneurial skills that have powered rural economies have come recently from the cities. Persson et al. (1997) noted the transition of traditional rural people from being members of the "Short Distance Society" to members of the "Open Society," part of the wider concept of rural society changing its control systems, conflicts and empowerment levels as part of an evolving and complex "Arena Society."

Within the background scenario outlined above rural tourism itself is a complex, multi-faceted activity. It may have had its roots in farm based or agritourism, but it is now much more diverse, and continues to diversify. It is a series of niche activities within a larger niche activity (Clemenson and Lane, 1997). It is an umbrella concept, accepting rather than one that is tightly defined. It includes:

Ecotourism

Probably the best known subset of rural tourism, its generally accepted definition comes from Hector Ceballos Lascurain (1996: 14):

> environmentally responsible travel and visitation to relatively undisturbed natural areas, in order to enjoy and appreciate nature (and any accompanying cultural features—both past and present), that promotes conservation, has low visitor impact, and provides for beneficially active socioeconomic involvement of local populations.

That definition has been used by TIES, the International Ecotourism Society.[2] Ceballos Lascurain has issued two riders, words of caution, and explanation. Ecotourism is a rural subset of the wider concept of sustainable tourism. And he has cautioned that ecotourism is shifting from small-scale, nature-based responsible tourism to a set of general principles rather than just small-scale tourism. Ecotourism should be *in* scale, not necessarily small scale.

Overall, then, ecotourism may be seen as a specialized form of rural tourism, restricted to relatively natural areas (rather than intensively farmed or forested areas), and largely avoiding small towns as destinations in themselves. It promotes the concept of sustainable rural tourism: not all types of rural tourism expressly do that. Ecotourism is often associated with protected areas or with rural parts of the developing world, but it need not be so restricted. Norway, with one of the world's highest per capita GDPs, has an ecotourism certification strategy (Lamark, 2007). Shepherd and Royston-Airey (2000) describe ecotourism in Central Southern England. Compare the definition of ecotourism above with that of rural tourism below as adopted by OECD.

Nature Tourism

Nature tourism is differentiated from ecotourism for a variety of reasons. For instance, it lacks explicit commitment to environmental conservation and to local communities.

Farm Holidays/Agritourism

Farm holidays/agritourism is normally rural tourism that involves staying on a working farm, or, for day visitors, making farm visits. In many countries, farm tourism has its own organizations. An example of best practice in this field is generally accepted to be Austrian Farm Holidays.[3] For a fuller discussion of the agritourism sector see Jennings et al. (2007) and Weaver and Fennell (1997).

Activity Tourism

Activity tourism is a general term that indicates physical activity while on holiday, and usually this type of holiday takes place in rural areas. Examples of activities include walking, climbing, cross country skiing, and various kinds of cycling. Downhill skiing is a grey area: some major skiing complexes are now urban, some almost industrial (see Clifford, 2002).

Adventure Tourism

Adventure tourism also usually takes place in rural areas. Difficult to define, Hall suggests that "adventure tourism is categorized by the deliberate seeking of risk and danger by participants in outdoor activities" (1992: 143). The degree of risk is difficult to quantify, but the term reflects the recent market growth for holidays that are different, challenging and individual—a phenomenon discussed later in this chapter. Buckley (2007) provides a detailed review of this sector.

Sports Tourism

Sports tourism is related to adventure and to activity tourism and as Hall (1992) points out, can be divided into two parts—participants and observers. In rural settings sports include cycle sports, climbing of all types, and specialties such as fell running. Golf falls into the sports category, as does angling and some cross-country skiing. Ritchie and Adair (2004) provide a useful overview.

Equestrian/Equine Tourism

Equestrian/equine tourism is a strong niche market in many rural areas, covering a range of activities from trekking through to horseback safaris and working ranch holidays. Ollenburg (2005) suggests that there could be 20 million active recreational horse riders in the developed world. Horse tourism is usually, but not necessarily, linked to farm tourism.

Cultural and Heritage Tourism

Cultural and heritage tourism is a vast field within which rural heritage and culture plays a strong role. Richards (1996), quoted in McKercher and du Cros (2002), suggests that between 35% and 70% of all international travelers can be considered cultural tourists. As those figures suggest, definitions are difficult; many tourists seek multiple experiences even on short holidays.

Food and Wine Tourism

Food and wine tourism is a growing and important relative newcomer to the rural tourism scene. It is clearly linked to agricultural diversification, but also to cultural and heritage tourism. Du Rand and Heath make the important point that food and wine help build imagery for rural tourism, and that "food is seldom the key reason for visiting a destination" (2006: 209). Hall et al. (2003) provide a full discussion on food and wine tourism.

There is also a large general interest market for less specialized forms of rural tourism. This aspect has long been shown to be important by studies of the important German tourism market, where a major requirement of the main holiday is the ability to provide peace, quiet and relaxation in rural surroundings (Studienkreis fuer Tourismus, 1987). Contributors to Butler et al. (1998) confirm that fact. But generalizations based on just one country can be misleading. Japanese main holiday rural tourists, for example, demand a much more intensive, non-relaxing, though still non-specialized, rural holiday (New Zealand Tourist Board, 1995, 1996).

The OECD (1993) finally published the following, stating that rural tourism should be:

1 Located in rural areas.
2 Functionally rural—based upon the rural world's special features of small-scale enterprise, open space, contact with nature and the natural world, heritage, "traditional" societies and "traditional" practices.
3 Rural in scale—both in terms of buildings and settlements and, therefore, usually—but not always—small-scale.
4 Traditional in character, growing slowly and organically, and connected with local families. It will often be very largely controlled locally.
5 Based on farms, and in villages and small towns.
6 Of many different kinds, representing the complex pattern of rural environment, economy, history, and location.

The question of the element of sustainable development was not included in the OECD definition; sustainable tourism was in its infancy as an accepted global concept in 1994. But Lane pointed out that if rural tourism is to be sustainable, it should "seek to avoid an unbalanced approach to economic growth by using tourism as a tool for broader economic progress" (1994b: 19).

He also restated Frederick's (1992) views that sustainable development in rural tourism must involve local business and communities in ownership decision-making and benefits. Sharpley (2003) takes the discussion of sustainable rural tourism further.

These definitional questions are more than just academic debates. Page and Getz (1997) in *The Business of Rural Tourism* note that a definition of rural tourism is valuable for public sector policy makers and planners. They need to define the subject to determine eligibility for grants and other incentives, and equally, to have definitions which ensure that permission for development goes to rural initiatives which can help conserve the countryside, rather than urbanize it. But these two authors are less sure of the value of defining rural tourism for others: "the question of what is rural is irrelevant to rural tourism business operators . . . (and) not really of importance to visitors either" (Getz and Page, 1997: 192). This view is worth reexamining. Businesses need to consider very carefully how they pitch their enterprises, to take maximum advantage of the marketing opportunities afforded by rural images. They also need to understand the notion of "perceived rurality" so that their activities do not damage either the reality or the perceived image of the countryside to visitors. And rurality is an essential requirement for many visitors: tourism is ultimately a form of escapism from everyday urban and suburban life: understanding how the market defines rural is, therefore, vital. There is also a broad environmental and ethical goal in seeking a definition. The search for a definition of rural tourism brings with it a search for the value judgments that should underlie the rural tourism planning, development, and management process. Only when the subject is defined or at least well described can its future be charted.

How Large is Rural Tourism?

Even given the loose definition above, it might just be possible to make an informed guess at the size of rural tourism; few areas, let alone nations, have attempted a detailed survey. In the UK, however, the major outbreak of foot and mouth disease in 2001 led to the cessation of visits to most parts of the countryside through much of that year. The need to compensate rural tourism businesses then arose. Government research showed that UK rural tourism produced revenues in 2000 of c.£12 billion, compared to £15 billion from the agricultural sector. That £12 billion figure was part of the total UK tourism revenue of £64 billions in 2000. British rural tourism was found to employ over 380,000 people in 25,000 businesses (Sharpley and Craven, 2001). In many UK rural regions, tourism is more important financially than farming.

What Impacts has Tourism had on the Rural World?

This chapter opened with the claim that rural tourism has been a wave of change, redemption, and regeneration. Change came by opening a new economic opportunity to rural areas that, since the industrial revolution, had lost the manufacturing sector, and not gained jobs in the service sector. That change boosted incomes. It also boosted the job and business opportunities for rural women—an impact commented on later in this chapter. It boosted rural property values. It was especially valuable in creating new uses for heritage properties, small and large, vernacular and polite. Redemption came from tourism's part in turning around "failing" areas. Since the mid-nineteenth century increasing numbers of rural regions worldwide had begun to lose population through out migration. Rural France became known as *Le Désert Français* (Gravier, 1947). So great was its population loss that the phrase haunted French and other European rural planners for decades. While rural tourism cannot claim to have been alone in turning around the position of many rural areas, it has been a key part of a wider series of societal, managerial, and technological trends that have seen increasing numbers of rural areas see strong inward migration over the last 20 years.

Regeneration was part of the redemption package, and the classic example of regeneration techniques using tourism has become the European Union's rural regeneration LEADER Programs.[4] Of the 217 Leader I Projects (1991–1994) 71 had a major rural tourism component (Jenkins et al., 1998). Of the 887 Leader II Local Action Groups (1995–1999) the majority had a rural tourism component of some kind.[5] The last completed Leader program (2000–2006), Leader Plus, has followed a similar pattern to Leader II, but has yet to publish final figures.

However, not all the impacts of rural tourism have been seen as beneficial. Many commentators have noticed the environmental, cultural, and social impacts that change through rural tourism have brought. Bouquet and Winter (1987) were early critics on a range of issues: their book opens with the famous words from Victorian diarist Francis Kilvert— "of all noxious animals, the most noxious is the tourist." Detailed papers have since reported on specific problems with increasing pressure on for example hiking and horse trekking trails (see Cole and Spildie, 1998; Newsome et al., 2008). Discussions on broader ecological impacts can be found in Buckley (2004). Stronza and Gordillo (2008) assess a range of wider community and cultural impacts. Most commentators now conclude that tourism management is essential to mitigate the negative effects of tourism in rural areas, and to maximize its positive effects; these issues are discussed below.

What Impacts has Rural Tourism had on the World of Tourism?

When, in 1991, the OECD began its enquiries into rural tourism, OECD staff members knew that the rise of rural tourism, a "new" type of non-resort tourism, was of concern to many established and traditional tourism regions. In practice the rise of rural tourism

was part of a much wider series of trends in the tourism market that had been foreshadowed by Stanley Plog (1991) in his seminal book *Leisure Travel: Making it a Growth Market Again*, predicting the rise of the Allocentric traveler, intellectually curious, marginally risk taking, confident explorers, seeking new and often different experiences. The same people were to drive the growth of heritage and cultural tourism, and city tourism. They were also able to help the development of a range of small, independent tour operators, pushing the boundaries of the industry, characterized by the Association of Independent Tour Operators (AITO).[6] The scene was set for a range of "tourism alternatives," amply discussed in Smith and Eadington (1994).

Academic Responses

As the last 30 years of the twentieth century unfolded, the risk takers in the real rural world readily grasped the potential value of tourism for rural areas. The planners and political policy makers also—though a little more slowly—grasped the possible development implications. Many felt that rural tourism was the first effective rural regeneration policy available since the widespread use of guaranteed farm gate prices in the 1940s. Protected area managers and some NGOs were, however, much more wary of the new ideas involved. Academics took a middle course: analysis and criticism of change is an academic tradition. The response was fragmented—a whole range of subject specializations have been and are involved in rural tourism research: it has been studied as a tourism issue, as a rural development issue, as an agricultural issue, as a sociological issue, as a conservation issue, and as a business studies issue. Recent rural tourism literature searches reveal that three big themes seem to run through rural tourism research: ecotourism development, gender roles and gender issues, and the business issues of rural tourism.

Operational and Motivational Questions

An understanding of the day to day working of contemporary rural tourism requires information on the supply and demand issues that drive the activity, along with knowledge of the technology which rural tourism uses, and perhaps the most fascinating issue of all—the organizational frameworks on which it depends. This section discusses the factors that have allowed rural tourism to grow.

Supply Side Issues

Put simply, why did rural tourism emerge? Visitors to most rural areas in the 1960s would have found few signs of visitation, and notably, few places to stay. A series of key factors transformed the supply of rural tourism:

Farm Diversification

As farm gate prices fell over the last 30 years, more and more farmers have diversified into tourism. The UK's experience is typical of the situation across the developed world. The UK is a land of large farms: 70% of all agricultural units are over 100 hectares in size. But despite those large farm sizes, net farm incomes have fallen steadily: 2005/2006 figures showed that most farms earned less than the national average wage for men.[7] Farmers have had to turn to a whole range of ideas to diversify their activities and raise their incomes.[8] New enterprise has become the feature of the modern British countryside. 46% of UK farms have now diversified their enterprise mix to include one of 224 recognized on-farm but nonagricultural enterprises. Tourism related activities have been the most popular choice.

Post-Fordism

Post-Fordism is a name applied to many forms of late twentieth-century production. It implies the use by business of new information technologies, an emphasis on service

and service delivery according to individual needs, flexibility of producer response and the feminization of the workforce (Amin, 1994). The rural world has taken all those factors into account, especially in farm enterprises.

Rural Entrepreneurs

Rural entrepreneurs have increased in number, skills, and market knowledge (Getz and Carlsen, 2000). The change has come through necessity—as farm incomes declined—through education and advisory services (see below), and through rapid dissemination of the success of rural tourism possible in a world of mass media and, at a later stage, the Internet. And the basic concept of rural land holding has changed from that of farming to produce food as a way of life, to that of using rural land as a way of life. In 1961, a best selling book, called *Farming for Profits* was published in Britain (Dexter and Barber, 1961). Like similar publications in other countries, it marked a management change across the rural world. The new aim was to use rural land profitably and not necessarily for food production. If tourism could make profits, then tourism could and should be farmed.

Entrepreneurial Rural Women

The rise of the entrepreneurial rural woman has been especially central to many rural tourism enterprises of all kinds, from farm shops, to cycle hire, open gardens, and of course accommodation provision, serviced and unserviced. That rise has produced many changes within rural society and a wide range of research enquiries: early works include Bouquet and Winter's writing in 1987; a recent work is that by Jennings et al. (2007).

Life Style Entrepreneurs

Life style entrepreneurs have joined rural people generally and rural women in particular in creating a supply of new rural tourism products (Ateljevic and Doorne, 2000; OECD, 1995). Life style entrepreneurs draw on their market knowledge, skills, and capital, usually gained in the cities, and also draw inspiration from the romantic, healthy, community rich, crime free images of the countryside, which remain powerful for many. William Wordsworth's well-known lines have a resonance for many people even after 200 years:

One impulse from a vernal wood
May teach you more of man,
Of moral evil and of good
Than all the sages can . . . Sweet is the lore which
Nature brings . . .

(from "The Tables Turned," composed and published in 1798).[9]

Rural Tourism Infrastructure

In most rural tourism destinations, infrastructure has been improved via the public sector, aware of the need for quality infrastructure to allow rural regions to compete in the rural tourism market. That infrastructure includes organizational and marketing help—see below—as well as physical developments such as better signing of regions, roads, paths and attractions, visitor information and heritage centers, and improvements to the communication network.

Demand Side Opportunities

Despite the growth of powerful motivations and opportunities from the supply side, rural tourism could not have grown without growth in the demand for the many products that rural tourism could offer. Why did that demand emerge?

In large part, demand has been driven by increasing wealth among travelers, allowing more frequent holidays, and in part by the elevation of many aspects of rural tourism to high fashion status. The majority of Britons, for example, now take more than one holiday per year, and those second and third trips are typically short breaks, many to rural destinations in the UK or continental Europe.[10] The rise in obesity and the increase in diabetes

have made a powerful case for more physical activity, supported by the health agendas pursued by governments and the media world wide. Rural holidays are seen as enjoyable and fashionable ways to take physical exercise. Walking as a recreational activity—mainly in the countryside—now ranks top of all the physical and sports activities undertaken in the UK, with 35% of the population reporting regular participation (Office for National Statistics, 2005). Walking is a growth area in most developed countries, illustrated by the large number of walking and hiking magazines, and walking websites, such as US-based walking.about.com and www.nordicwalkingusa.com. Cycling has also experienced a boom as a rural leisure pursuit in recent years and has also become both a fashionable activity and a healthy living pursuit (see BMA, 1992; Lumsdon, 1994, 2001). Off-road, quiet road, and dedicated cycle trails have become special growth areas. Successful NGOs drive rural cycle trail development: in the USA that movement is led by the Rails to Trails Conservancy;[11] in the UK, Sustrans has a similar role.[12] Both have over 10,000 miles of route way, largely rural, both are membership organizations—Sustrans has over 35,000 members, Rails to Trails Conservancy over 100,000.

It is also important to mention the growing interest in fashionable, "authentic," healthy, and specialty foods. Hall et al. (2003) discuss the key drivers behind those interests and their impacts on tourism. A special role is played by the slow food movement, founded in Italy by Carlo Petrini in 1986 and now active in over 100 countries. It is best illustrated by the web site www.slowfoodusa.com (accessed May 25, 2008).

Overall, rural tourists emerge from surveys as being of all ages, better educated and better off than most. It is a powerful demand group; it is also one that is mobile, fickle, and demands quality. It reflects the continuing numerical growth of the free and independent traveler, seeking different, slightly challenging, and individual holiday experiences—the Plog allocentrics.

Transportation and Technological Improvements

Tourism to rural areas began by using rail communications. Low in capacity, and offering few points of access, rural rail was no match for the car based transportation systems that have in many places now replaced local rural rail services. Mass car ownership has allowed rural tourism to flourish; over 90% of rural tourists travel by car to most destinations. Car travel is not only convenient and flexible, it also appeals to the freedom of movement that runs strongly through the motivations of rural visitors, the much vaunted "thrill of the open road." Long distance road improvements along quality divided highways have also helped. Along with widespread car use has been the ready availability of maps and information via the Internet.

Telecommunications generally have allowed the supply side of the equation to flourish: low cost, direct dial telephone systems, the World Wide Web, and the use of credit and debit cards via telephone lines have all destroyed the tyranny of distance which once rendered many rural areas too remote for visitation. Finally, the growth of regional air services, often until recently at low cost, have added a further supply side advantage to rural tourism. In the UK, German ice climbers fly into the Scottish Highlands for a weekend's climbing; in rural France and Italy, UK second home-owners fly into regional airports to reach their properties.

One often forgotten part of the new technology, which allows rural tourism to flourish, must also be mentioned: equipment. Better waterproof footwear, breathable rain proofed garments, lightweight walking poles, lightweight canoes, hang gliders, mountaineering equipment such as carabiners, cams, quickdraws, nuts, hexes, crampons, and countless other items have revolutionized the tourism supply possibilities of rural areas. Cycles, too, have benefited from high tech and fashionable developments, with lightweight frames, multi gears, disc brakes, and full suspension, as well as the introduction of the mountain bike as an off road adventure tool.

Organization and Support

Rural tourism is a difficult activity to organize and regulate. It consists of innumerable numbers of small suppliers, many different types of business, and large numbers of often conflicting stakeholders. But, as has already been mentioned, its ability to regenerate rural areas, and to help fund and support conservation efforts of many kinds, has helped convince the public sector—international, national, regional, and local—to supply organization and support. The public sector can rightly take credit for much of the rise in rural tourism.

At the international level, the major role has been taken by the support measures offered by the European Union. These have included:

- Supporting numerous rural tourism development projects via Leader Plus programs, see ec.europa.eu/agriculture/rur/leaderplus/index_en.htm.
- Supporting a pan-European rural tourism marketing partnership, Eurogites,[13] with a membership of 28 professional organizations from 24 countries. Eurogites organizes regular international conferences on rural tourism, and is running a major web based survey of market preferences in the field.
- Publications of various kinds detailing the outcome of demonstration sites and partnership projects. At one end of the scale come the regular issues of the Internet bulletin *Flash News*. The regular print media publication on rural development is the thrice-yearly *Leader Plus Magazine*. Available on the Internet and in print form comes the annual Leader Plus Best Practices publication, typically 80 pages in length.

Full details of these materials can be found on the European Union's website: ec.europa.eu/agriculture/rur/leaderplus/publications/bp_en.htm (accessed May 25, 2008).

At the national level, many countries have produced guidelines and best practice advice notes. Many have organized—via a variety of providers—training courses for new participants. One of the most interesting early developments nationally took place in the USA in the late 1980s with the work of the US National Rural Tourism Development Project, hosted by the Extension Service at the University of Minnesota. The project worked with 197 communities to produce a major training manual (Koth et al., 1991) and accompanying video. The project culminated in a national teleconference on rural tourism development entitled *Turn it around with Tourism*. From that teleconference came audience questions, which were then answered by a panel of 60 experts, and published (Koth et al., 1993).

Regional level support is illustrated by the work of a number of US states and Canadian provinces, also working in the late 1980s and early 1990s. The most striking work done at this level was the implementation of training programs for several hundred rural communities across the huge province of Alberta, backed by training and marketing manuals (Alberta Tourism, 1988, 1991). Many of these programs were well thought out and well delivered, were perhaps slightly too early in their distribution, but above all suffered from lack of ongoing back up to keep the momentum of ongoing development, learning, and change moving forward. Rural tourism is often slow growing and needs some years of support.

Two forms of local level organizational work illustrate a more gradual, long-term support system, a perhaps more sustainable approach.

Via Local Government

Local government level support for rural tourism is common in many countries. In England, over the period c.1987–2002, it became the major support system for rural tourism, using the resources of many of the 34 rural counties, and within those counties, many of the over 220 district councils which have substantial rural areas. The great majority of the 254 authorities employed and trained tourism officers, with backup staff and resources, to assist the growth of tourism, to assist change in the countryside and to restructure the rural economy. This allowed the development of strategies suited to local needs, local geographies, and local opportunities. While national guidelines were laid

down, especially for quality standards and for items like signage, experimentation was encouraged locally; there were problems, but rarely major and usually quickly put right by local action. In addition, local level organization:

- Encouraged the development not just of tourism accommodation facilities but also encouraged the vital creation of tourism *product*, things for visitors to do and enjoy.
- Helped create a *range of places to stay* in the countryside, from farms to villages to market towns, and from bed and breakfasts through self catering to a range of high class specialist accommodation, broadening market appeal.
- Began the process of developing rural areas as *destinations*, not just places for farm holidays.
- Worked with wider rural groups to bring farm enterprises into fruitful partnership with other local businesses.
- Produced and coordinated market research and marketing materials professionally but with close links to tourism providers.
- Set up local Tourism Information Centers, using a variety of formats, and staffed by both trained volunteers and professionals.
- Prioritized use of the Internet and developed websites: 49% of English tourists now choose their accommodation by using the Internet (Enjoy England, 2006).
- Helped district wide sustainable tourism strategies to be developed in consultation and partnership with farmers, other business stakeholders, communities and conservation and heritage interests.
- Facilitated creation of a huge range of infrastructure, including signage, local, regional and long distance footpaths, cycle routes, historic sites and buildings, nature reserves, local partnerships, and a range of heritage interpretation materials, all of which transformed countryside into valuable product.
- Made training available in relevant subjects, including starting up tourism businesses, quality care and marketing. Business support services were offered, updates on market conditions, and advice offered on obtaining planning permission for developments (see Dewhurst and Thomas, 2003)
- Enabled central government agency funds to be applied for and obtained for specific local projects.
- Networked with neighboring tourism officers and across the UK, which allowed the rapid development of successful ideas and early warning of problems.

Via Local Self-Help Groups

Often parallel to, and working closely with local government, were self-help groups. Austrian Farm Holidays encouraged (and still encourages) accommodation providers to create "Guest Circles" to discuss, train, and coordinate (Embacher, 1994). Clarke (1999) provides a valuable and detailed discussion of the workings of local farm holiday providers groups in the UK, developing a telling typology ranking those groups in a continuum. Low activity groups are categorized as survivors. The continuum continues through drifters, laid back, and organized groups until it reaches the top achievers, the dynamic groups, innovative and with high levels of business success.

The Partnership Concept

Partnerships are now recognized as a key to rural business and service survival across many fields (Cavazzani and Moseley, 2001). They are also recognized as central to the development of sustainable tourism (Bramwell and Lane, 2000). Within rural tourism, there are many forms of tourism partnerships now operational. They allow small businesses to work together; they offer a framework for the public and private sector to work together. Bramwell and Lane (2000) describe the pros and cons of partnership working in detail; Knowd (2006) describes and analyzes a successful partnership in Australia—Hawkesbury Harvest. The early world of rural tourism partnerships is likely to become more important in the future—see section below—as rural tourism enters a period of crisis and reassessment.

The Future: Uncertainty and the Need for Future Proofing

The golden days of rural tourism expansion may now be coming to an end, necessitating new ideas to deal with new problems. Long and

Lane (2000) foreshadowed the onset of more difficult market conditions, noting the rapid growth of rural tourism supply, notably in the former "closed" lands of eastern Europe, a supply that could easily outrun demand. They also noted the need for more coordination and quality in rural tourism product.

Since 2000, uncertainties and problems have multiplied. While intra-rural competition has grown as predicted, so has competition from new forms of tourism, including cruise tourism, cultural and heritage tourism, shopping tourism, but above all city tourism. The last three of those growth areas have been boosted by the rapid growth of air travel using low cost airlines, and low cost hotel provision in urban centers keen to exploit tourism as a form of urban renewal. On the supply side, the recent rises in farm gate prices may reduce the need to diversify into tourism. In organizational terms, the public sector is beginning to reduce its financial assistance, cutting back on the support for marketing and training. Oil prices are rising, reaching US$135 per barrel at the time of writing. This trend puts a large question mark over car use and, in particular, over the short-break holiday that has been such a useful growth market for rural tourism. Within rural areas, there are conflicts about the scale of tourism intrusion, and its long-term impacts on rural character and that slippery question—authenticity.

Rural tourism therefore is at a crossroads. It needs to examine a number of ways to adjust and future proof its status and viability.

Business Strategy Reassessment

Business strategy reassessment will be essential for many enterprises. Mitchell and Hall noted the problems that many rural tourism businesses have weak business strategies: "there has been a tendency for businesses to develop in an ad hoc manner, with little or no meaningful strategy" (2005: 3). Single enterprises have been slow to recognize the changing conditions, but cooperative ventures and partnerships have realized the problems. Austrian Farm

Holidays—marketing and advising 3,400 farms in Austria—began the process of creating its new vision for 2010 back in 2002. Its methodology and new strategy is described in Embacher (2003). One of the pioneers of rural tourism, the 50-year-old cooperative Gîtes de France, with 44,000 business members, presented its Horizon 2015 concept at the 3rd European Congress on Rural Tourism, held at Eger in Hungary in 2007. Its President, Phillipe Hellio, illustrated the need for new products, new marketing concepts, better quality control and above all a new vision.[14] He felt that Gîtes de France faced a crisis. And, in an earlier conference in 2007 held in Scotland, Ian Henderson outlined the new business strategies being introduced by Ireland's innovative Green Box program for rural tourism in the North West of Ireland.[15]

Integrated Management

Integrated management has long been a dream of rural planners, discussed at length in Europe since the 1960s. Interestingly, integration is a key aim of the new Austrian Farm Holiday Strategy discussed above. Integration is a holy grail for rural tourism because of the number and variety of stakeholders, public and private, involved, and the wide range of resources required. The lack of integrative frameworks has long been known and discussed (Bramwell and Sharman, 1999). Integration should be able to add value to tourism product and performance and bring stakeholders together to ward off competition and boost sustainability across the triple bottom line. The latest research into integrated management practice in rural tourism comes from Cawley and Gilmour (2008) working in the west of Ireland. Their paper sets out the requirements for producing an integration model to reduce deficiencies in planning and provision, identify areas of agreement and disagreement and produce viable ways of collaborative working.

The need for integrated management as a way of overcoming uncertainty is also set out in Vernon et al. (2005), describing and analyzing a successful collaborative partnership in Cornwall, UK. It emphasizes the role of the public sector in promoting integrated bottom-up forms of governance, the temporal dynamics of the process and the realities of innovation in policy making.

Destination Management Organizations

Destination management organizations (DMOs) are becoming increasingly common in rural areas. They save public sector money by bringing councils together to fund fewer but theoretically more effective organizational and marketing units. They are a further type of partnership organization. They can—like Hadrian's Wall Heritage Ltd[16]—be private companies working to fixed fees against targets. DMOs can use the Visitor Experience Planning concept pioneered by the US National Park Service, and now being used in Europe. DMOs allow for the idea of branding rural destinations, first floated by Clarke (2000). They should also be able to address the difficult question of developing on line booking of rural accommodation, 24/7, to compete against low cost city hotels. And they could develop synergy marketing of local products *and* tourism outside their regions.

Product Development

Product development will be especially important. Until recently short breaks have been a central plank in the rural tourism offer. Peeters et al. (2009) describe the powerful forces that will depress the short break market in the future as travel costs rise. Better product development will be needed to provide confidence in taking longer rural holidays. The case for integrated quality management (IQM) in rural tourism is strongly made by Youell (2003), outlining experiences in professionalizing product through IQM in rural Wales.

Visitor Experience Planning can be a useful tool here. Character retention in product development is also a key area that needs to be addressed. If rural tourism is to be different, and attractively different, it needs to remain special. The concept of authenticity is important. It has been tackled successfully by a number of commentators, including Midtgard (2003) and Xie and Lane (2006). The latter introduce a multilayered management concept to authenticity management according to market focus.

Carbon Neutral Destination

Carbon neutral destination status will become a new "must have" for many destinations in the future (Gössling, 2009). Given the inherent perception among the public that rural holidays are—however vaguely—"green," it would seem logical to pursue this status as part of a move to attain an ecolabel, or some form of green accreditation. Transportation will be a key issue here. Air travel will be a major problem. Some areas may be able to go back to the future by reviving rail-based, rural holidays. In the USA, Amtrak have long worked with the National Park Service to encourage and enhance rural tourism by rail. In the UK, the Devon and Cornwall Rail Partnership and others have worked hard to gain marketing and product integration between rail and rural tourism on branch lines.[17] New marketing techniques borrowing ideas from both demarketing and social marketing will be needed. And car use, using car sharing and hybrid and other low consumption cars may allow use of cars for many rural journeys (Peeters et al., 2009).

Conclusion

Rural tourism has come far since the Romantic Movement first developed the rural idyll image 200 years ago. The flowering of modern rural tourism over the last 30 years is now over. We are moving into a new era of uncertainty and challenge, where a new professional approach to rural tourism will become essential. Paradoxically, a key challenge will be to retain the individual post-Fordism approach inherent in rural tourism, retaining personal discovery and an artisan approach, while being keenly professional. Skilled approaches to heritage and product will be necessary too. Tourism is a fashion business—holidays are dream times, times for energizing the body and uplifting the soul. The far north of Scotland might perhaps be showing the way for some aspects of the rural tourism of the future. That once fashionless and harsh land of emigration, wind and rain has changed utterly in the last 30 years. It has achieved a vibrant blend of tradition and innovation. It produces traditional haggis *and* modern edible flowers, it has Harris Tweed and uses that tweed not just for those tweed jackets once worn by old administrators in the public service, but for high fashion craft textiles aimed at the under 30 and the under 50 cool generations. It turns nature into spell binding products through interpretation and guiding. It exploits foul weather through ice climbing. It uses the Gaelic language with panache to develop poetry, dance, and song that evoke a special sense of place. It has brought Highland cooking back from the past to offer a new cuisine using low food mile, often organic, raw materials. Young, skilled, educated and innovative people are at the helm. With product models like this rural tourism can beat the city tourism challenge. And amazingly, rural Scotland has retained much of its network of long-distance, rural rail lines, giving it a chance to beat the carbon challenge too.

Notes

1 http://www.oecd.org. Accessed May 25, 2008.
2 http://www.ecotourism.org. Accessed May 25, 2008.
3 http://www.farmholidays.com. Accessed May 25, 2008.
4 Leader is a French acronym, standing for "Liaison Entre Actions de Développement de l'Économie Rurale," meaning "Links between the rural economy and development actions."

5 http://ec.europa.eu/agriculture/rur/leader2. Accessed May 25, 2008.

6 http://www.aito.co.uk. Accessed May 25, 2008.

7 http://www.statistics.defra.gov.uk/esg/; www. statistics.gov.uk. Accessed May 25, 2008.

8 http://www.defra.gov.uk/erdp/schemes/default. htm. Accessed May 25, 2008.

9 http://rpo.library.utoronto.ca/poem/2373.html. Accessed May 27, 2008.

10 http://www.visitbritain.com/research. Accessed May 25, 2008.

11 http://www.railtrail.org. Accessed May 25, 2008.

12 http://www.sustrans.org. Accessed May 25, 2008.

13 http://www.eurogites.org. Accessed May 25, 2008.

14 http://www.europeanrtcongress.org/new/ hellio.ppt. Accessed June 4, 2008.

15 http://www.visitscotland.org/print/research_ and_statistics/scenarios/scenarioplanning_policies/ green_futures.htm, and also www.greenbox.ie. Accessed June 4, 2008.

16 http://www.hadrians-wall.org. Accessed May 25, 2008.

17 See Dallen (2007); also see http://www.carfree daysout.com, http://www.heartofwessex.org.uk. Accessed May 25, 2008.

References

Alberta Tourism (1988). *Community Tourism Action Plan*. Edmonton: Alberta Tourism.

Alberta Tourism (1991). *Market Planning Skills Program*. Edmonton: Alberta Tourism.

Amin, A. (1994). *Post-Fordism: A Reader*. Oxford: Blackwell.

Ateljevic, I. and Doorne, S. (2000). "Staying within the Fence: Lifestyle Entrepreneurship in Tourism." *Journal of Sustainable Tourism*, 8(5): 378–392.

BMA (British Medical Association) (1992). *Cycling towards Health and Safety*. Oxford: Oxford University Press.

Bouquet, M. and Winter, M. (Eds.) (1987). *Who from Their Labours Rest: Conflict and Practice in Rural Tourism*. Aldershot: Avebury.

Bramwell, B. and Sharman, A. (1999). "Collaboration in Local Tourism Policymaking." *Annals of Tourism Research*, 26(2): 392–415.

Bramwell, B. and Lane, B. (Eds.) (2000/2004). *Tourism Partnerships and Collaboration: Politics, Practice and Sustainability*. Clevedon: Channel View Press.

Buckley, R.C. (Ed.) (2004). *Environmental Impacts of Ecotourism*. Wallingford: CAB International.

Buckley, R.C. (Ed.) (2007). *Adventure Tourism*. Wallingford: CAB International.

Butler, R.W., Hall, C.M. and Jenkins, J. (Eds.) (1998). *Tourism and Recreation in Rural Areas*. Chichester: Wiley.

Butler, R.W. and Boyd, S.W. (Eds.) (2000). *Tourism and National Parks: Issues and Implications*. Chichester: Wiley.

Cavazzani, A. and Moseley, M. (2001). *The Practice of Rural Development Partnerships in Europe*. Soveria Mannelli, Rubbettino Editore.

Cawley, M. and Gilmour, D.A. (2008). "Integrated Rural Tourism: Concepts and Practice." *Annals of Tourism Research*, 35(2): 316–337.

Ceballos-Lascurain, H. (1996). *Tourism, Ecotourism, and Protected Areas*. Cambridge: IUCN.

Clarke, J. (1999). "Marketing Structures for Farm Tourism: Beyond the Individual Provider of Rural Tourism." *Journal of Sustainable Tourism*, 7(1): 6–25.

Clarke, J. (2000). "Tourism Brands: An Exploratory Study of the Brands Box Model." *Journal of Vacation Marketing*, 6(4): 329–345.

Clemenson, H.A. and Lane, B. (1997). "Niche Markets, Niche Marketing and Rural Employment." In R.D. Bollman and J.M. Bryden (Eds.), *Rural Employment: An International Perspective* (pp. 410–426). Wallingford: CAB International.

Clifford, H. (2002). *Downhill Slide: Why the Corporate Ski Industry is Bad for Skiing, Ski Towns and the Environment*. San Francisco: Sierra Club Books.

Cole, D.N. and Spildie, D.R. (1998). "Hiker, Horse and Llama Trampling Effects on Native Vegetation in Montana USA." *Journal of Environmental Management*, 53(1): 61–71.

Dallen, J. (2007). "Sustainable Transport, Market Segmentation and Tourism: The Looe Valley Branch Line Railway, Cornwall, UK." *Journal of Sustainable Tourism*, 15(2): 180–199.

Dewhurst, H. and Thomas, R. (2003). "Encouraging Sustainable Business Practices in a Non-Regulatory Environment: A Case Study of Small Tourism Firms in a UK National Park." *Journal of Sustainable Tourism*, 11(5): 383–403.

Dexter, K. and Barber, D. (1961/1967). *Farming for Profits*. Harmondsworth: Penguin Books.

Eagles (2002). "Trends in Park Tourism: Economics, Finance and Management." *Journal of Sustainable Tourism*, 10(2): 132–153.

Eagles (2004). "Tourism at the 5th World Parks Congress, Durban, South Africa." *Journal of Sustainable Tourism*, 12(2): 169–173.

Embacher, H. (1994). "Marketing for Agri-Tourism in Austria: Strategy and Realisation in a Highly Developed Tourist Destination." *Journal of Sustainable Tourism*, 2(1&2): 61–76.

Embacher, H. (2003). "Strategy Formulation in Rural Tourism—An Integrated Approach." In D. Hall, L. Roberts and M. Mitchell (Eds.), *New Directions in Rural Tourism* (pp. 137–151). Aldershot: Ashgate.

Enjoy England (2006). *UK Market Profile*. Retrieved from www.tourismtrade.org.uk.

Fiero, G.K. (2006). *The Humanistic Tradition. Book 5, Romanticism, Realism and the Nineteenth Century World*. Boston, MA: McGraw-Hill.

Frederick, M. (1992). *Tourism as a Rural Economic Development Tool: An Exploration of the Literature*. Washington, DC: USDA.

Getz, D. and Carlsen, J. (2000). "Characteristics and Goals of Family and Owner Operated Businesses in the Rural Tourism Industry and Hospitality Sectors." *Tourism Management*, 21(6): 547–560.

Getz, D. and Page, S.J. (Eds.) (1997). "Conclusions and Implications for Rural Business Development." In D. Getz and S.J. Page (Eds.), *The Business of Rural Tourism: International Perspectives* (pp.191–205). London: International Thomson Business Press.

Gössling, S. (2009). "Carbon Neutral Destinations: A Conceptual Analysis." *Journal of Sustainable Tourism*, 17(1): 17–37.

Gravier, J.F. (1947). Paris et le Désert Français. Paris: Portalon.

Hall, C.M. (1992). "Adventure, Sports and Health Tourism." In B. Weiler and C.M. Hall (Eds.), *Special Interest Tourism*. London: Belhaven.

Hall, C.M., Sharples, L., Mitchell, R., Macionis, N. and Camborne, B. (Eds.) (2003). *Food Tourism around the World*. Oxford: Butterworth-Heinemann.

Jenkins, J., Hall, C.M. and Troughton, M. (1998). "The Restructuring of Rural Economies: Rural Tourism and Recreation as a Government Response." In R.W. Butler, C.M. Hall and J. Jenkins (Eds.), *Tourism and Recreation in Rural Areas* (pp. 43–69). Chichester: John Wiley.

Jennings, G., Kim, K. and McGehee, N.G. (2007). "Gender and Motivation for Agri-Tourism Entrepreneurship." *Tourism Management*, 28(1): 280–289.

Knowd, I. (2006). "Tourism as a Mechanism for Farm Survival." *Journal of Sustainable Tourism*, 14(1): 24–42.

Koth, B., Kreag, G. and Robinson, M. (1993). *Q and A about Rural Tourism Development*. St. Paul: University of Minnesota Extension Service.

Koth, B., Kreag, G., Sem, J. and Kjolhaug, K. (1991). *A Training Guide for Rural Tourism Development*. St. Paul: University of Minnesota Extension Service.

Lamark, L. (2007). *Norwegian Ecotourism Certification Criteria*. Oslo: GRIP (Green In Practice).

Lane, B. (1994a). "Tourism Strategies and Rural Development." In *Tourism Policy and International Tourism in OECD Countries 1991–2* (pp. 13–76). Paris: OECD.

Lane, B. (1994b). "What is Rural Tourism?" *Journal of Sustainable Tourism*, 2(1&2): 7–21.

Lane, B. (1995). "Creating Niche Markets in a Growing Sector: Rural Tourism." In *Niche Markets and Rural Development* (pp. 81–110). Paris: OECD.

Long, P. and Lane, B. (2000). "Rural Tourism Development." In W.C. Gartner and D.W. Lime (Eds.), *Trends in Outdoor Recreation, Leisure and Tourism* (pp. 299–308). Wallingford: CAB International.

Lumsdon, L. (1994). *Cycle UK*. Wilmslow: Sigma Leisure.

Lumsdon, L. (2001). "Cycling Tourism." In L. Roberts and D. Hall (Eds.), *Rural Tourism and Recreation—Principles to Practice* (pp. 173–174). Wallingford: CAB International.

McKercher, B. and du Cros, H. (2002). *Cultural Tourism: The Partnership Between Tourism and Cultural Heritage Management*. New York: Howarth Hospitality Press.

Midtgard, M.R. (2003). "Authenticity—Tourist Experiences in the Norwegian Periphery."

In D. Hall, L. Roberts and M. Mitchell (Eds.), *New Directions in Rural Tourism* (pp. 102–114). Aldershot: Ashgate.

Mitchell, M. and Hall, D. (2005). "Rural Tourism as Sustainable Business: Key Themes and Issues." In D. Hall, I. Kirkpatrick and M. Mitchell (Eds.), *Rural Tourism and Sustainable Business* (pp. 3–16). Clevedon: Channel View Publications .

New Zealand Tourist Board (1995). *Product Development Opportunities for Asian Markets*. Wellington: NZTB.

New Zealand Tourist Board (1996). *Japan Market Brief*. Wellington: NZTB.

Newsome, D., Smith, A. and Moore, S.A. (2008). "Horse Riding in Protected Areas: A Critical Review and Implications for Research and Management." *Current Issues in Tourism*, 11(2): 144–166.

OECD (1993). *What Future for our Countryside? A Rural Development Policy*. Paris: OECD.

OECD (1995). *Niche Markets and Rural Development*. OECD: Paris.

Ollenburg (2005). "Worldwide Structure of the Equestrian Tourism Sector." *Journal of Ecotourism*, 4(1): 47–55.

Office for National Statistics (2005). *Social Trends 35*. London: ONS.

Page, S.J. and Getz, D. (1997). "The Business of Rural Tourism: International Perspectives." In D. Getz, and S.J. Page (Eds.), *The Business of Rural Tourism: International Perspectives* (pp. 3–37). London: International Thomson Business Press.

Peeters, P., Gössling, S. and Lane, B. (2009). "Moving Towards Low Carbon Tourism: New Opportunities for Destinations and Tour Operators." In S. Gössling, C.M. Hall and D. Weaver (Eds.), *Sustainable Tourism Futures: Perspectives on Systems, Restructuring and Innovations* (pp. 240–257). London: Routledge.

Persson, L.O., Westholm, E. and Fuller, T (1997). "Two Contexts, One Outcome: The Importance of Lifestyle Choice in Creating Rural Jobs in Canada and Sweden." In R.D. Bollman and J.M. Bryden (Eds.), *Rural Employment: An International Perspective* (pp. 136–163). Wallingford: CAB International.

Perry, R., Dean, K. and Brown, B. (1986). *Counterurbanization: Case Studies of Urban to Rural Movement*. Norwich: Geo Books.

Plog, S.C. (1991). *Leisure Travel: Making it a Growth Market Again*. New York: Wiley.

du Rand, G.E. and Heath, E. (2006). "Towards a Framework for Food Tourism as an Element of Destination Marketing." *Current Issues in Tourism*, 9(3): 206–234.

Richards, G. (1996). "The Scope and Significance of Cultural Tourism." In G. Richards (Ed.), *Cultural Tourism in Europe* (pp. 19–46). Wallingford: CAB International.

Ritchie, B. and Adair, B. (Eds.) (2004). *Sport Tourism: Interrelationships, Impacts and Issues*. Clevedon: Channel View Books.

Robinson, G.M. (1990). *Conflict and Change in the Countryside*. London: Belhaven.

Roe, N. (ed.) (2005). *Romanticism: An Oxford Guide*. Oxford: Oxford University Press.

Runte, A. (1990). *Trains of Discovery*. Niwot, CO: Roberts Rinehart.

Sharpley, R. and Craven, B. (2001). "The 2001 Foot and Mouth Crisis—Rural Economy and Tourism Policy Implications." *Current Issues in Tourism*, 4(6): 527–538.

Sharpley, R. (2003). "Rural Tourism and Sustainability—A Critique." In D. Hall, L. Roberts and M. Mitchell (Eds.), *New Directions in Rural Tourism* (pp. 38–53). Aldershot: Ashgate.

Sharpley, R. and Pearce, T. (2007). "Tourism, Marketing and Sustainable Development in the English National Parks: The Role of National Park Authorities." *Journal of Sustainable Tourism*, 15(5): 557–573.

Shepherd, K.L. and Royston-Airey, P.C.M. (2000). "Exploring the Role of Part-Time Ecotourism Guides in Central Southern England." *Journal of Sustainable Tourism*, 8(4): 324–332.

Smith, V.L. and Eadington, W.R. (Eds.) (1994). *Tourism Alternatives: Potentials and Problems in the Development of Tourism*. New York: Wiley.

Stronza, A. and Gordillo, J. (2008). "Community Views of Ecotourism." *Annals of Tourism Research*, 35(2): 448–468.

Studienkreis fuer Tourismus (1987). *Urlaubsreisen 1986*. Starnberg, Studienkreis fuer Tourismus.

Thompson, C. (2005). "Travel Writing." In N. Roe (Ed.), *Romanticism: An Oxford Guide* (pp. 555–573). Oxford: Oxford University Press.

Vernon, J., Essex, S., Pinder, D. and Curry, K. (2005). "Collaborative Policymaking: Local Sustainable Projects." *Annals of Tourism Research*, 32(2): 325–345.

Weaver, D.B. and Fennell, D.A. (1997). "The Vacation Farm Sector in Saskatchewan: A Profile of Operations." *Tourism Management*, 18(6): 357–365.

Xie, P. and Lane, B. (2006). "A Life Cycle Model for Aboriginal Arts Performance in Tourism: Perspectives on Authenticity." *Journal of Sustainable Tourism*, 14(6): 545–561.

Youell, R. (2003). "Integrated Quality Management in Rural Tourism." In D. Hall, L. Roberts and M. Mitchell (Eds.), *New Directions in Rural Tourism* (pp. 169–182). Aldershot: Ashgate.

21

Transportation and Tourism: A Symbiotic Relationship?

Stephen Page and Yue (Gurt) Ge

Introduction

Transportation is a fundamental driver of the tourism industry: it is a precondition for travel, since it facilitates mobility and the movement of tourists from their place of origin (i.e., their home area) to their destination and back. In this respect it has a symbiotic relationship with tourism: one cannot occur without the other and the two are codependent. This has many similarities with the tourism–environment relationship also discussed in this volume, although it has certainly not attracted the same level of research activity that the environment–sustainability debate has raised, even though transportation is a key element of that debate.

Despite many influential books being published on tourism since the 1970s, few ever address in any level of depth, this symbiotic relationship or the dependencies which exist between tourism and transportation. For example, many of the early texts on tourism (e.g., Burkart and Medlik, 1974) describe how tourism developed as transportation technology changed and mass tourism became possible in domestic and international contexts.

In conceptual terms, these key changes or tipping points have led to major growth in domestic and international travel and are depicted as contributing to tourism time-space compression. That is, how the world has become a more accessible place in terms of tourist travel, where no part of the world is more than a 24–30-hour flight between the origin and destination.

It would be fair to characterize the study of transportation and tourism as something which is relegated to a passive element of the tourist experience, where it is conceptualized as a major driver of tourism activity, but invariably glossed over despite its crucial role in both time spent and in the distance traveled. In this context, transportation is an essential service element of tourism, and in some cases it can form the focus of the tourism experience per se (e.g., cruising and scenic train journeys). Various forms of transportation have been associated with the development of tourism and technological developments in transportation, combined with the rise in personal disposable incomes, have led to the expansion of both domestic and international tourism.

One of the main explanations of the lack of integration in research is the failure to develop a common language, a joint knowledge base that helps to create greater understanding of the relevance, meaning, and value of transportation to tourism. It has contributed to impeding coherence and collaboration among different social science disciplines which study transportation (e.g., geography, economics, and psychology), Where transportation and tourism are, for example, included as a subtheme at a conference, the papers are invariably disciplinary based (e.g., the Institute of British Geographers conference) and are not holistic in approach or in what they seek to report. Instead, they are invariably lacking in new conceptualizations that would otherwise advance knowledge beyond empirically biased approaches which only communicate with their own discipline.

A similar disciplinary divergence is also evident within the planning spheres too. Lack of collaboration is noticeable between experts or planners of urban and regional planning, transportation planning and tourism destination marketing. Even in the subfield of spatial planning, it is rare to see these actors embark on associations between tourism and transportation policy. Commenting on the relationship between tourism development and transportation, Palhares observed that "most of the existing research has been conducted from a single discipline perspective (economics, geography, management, psychology or sociology), without a multidisciplinary approach" (2003: 403). A perusal of research in tourism studies, where one might expect synergies with transportation, shows a focus on supply–demand, the tourism industry (hospitality) and tourists, preservation and development, even in inner city revitalization where one might expect greater mention of transportation (Formica and Uysal, 1996; Lee and Han, 2002; Lim, 1997; Sinclair, 1998; Weisbrod and Lawson, 2003). An exploration of the limited literature on tourism and transportation shows a tendency for tourism scholars to focus more on economic, social, and environmental impacts rather than spatial/physical interrelationships and impacts (Pearce, 2001).

Without seeking to promote one's own research activity, it is apparent from any detailed review of the transportation–tourism literature, that the transportation–tourism nexus did not receive any real synthesis until the publication of Page's (1994) *Transport for Tourism*. This short review of the subject sets out the conceptualization needed to undertake more substantive research on this area, reflected in its citation in journal articles and book chapters, along with its more detailed successors (Page, 1999, 2005), the collection by Lumsdon and Page (2004a), and the monograph by Duval (2007). Duval (2007) made a constructive attempt to analyze the synergy of transportation and tourism within a network of flows and nodes. Moreover, transportation was positioned at the center of the discussion that included the physical description of transportation in a variety of spatial levels (global, regional, and local) as well as the highlight of three main modes of transportation (ground, marine, and air). Generally, the subject still remains a niche area despite the overwhelming significance of the subject, and has not attracted a major quantum of output as this review of the field suggests. Rising commodity prices (oil especially more recently) and increasing attention to climate change and global warming has started to bring greater attention to various transportation sectors and issues, as will be discussed further below.

The above notwithstanding, the 35-page list of references in Page (2005) demonstrates that transportation research per se is healthy, and that where the tourism dimension is mentioned or covered in any detail, it tends to be published in nontourism journals (e.g., *Journal of Transport Geography*, *Transportation Research A–F*, *Transport Policy* and *Journal of Air Transport Management*) although one notable exception to this is the special issue of the *Journal of Sustainable Tourism* on tourism and transportation. Research has also started to emerge on new topics like tourism transportation for the disabled (Cavinato and Cuckovich, 1992), the relationship between urban leisure and public transportation (Evans and Shaw, 2001), transportation policy in historic inner cities (Israeli and Mansfeld, 2003), suburban and regional transportation spatial models for urban tourism (Wu and Cai, 2006), etc.

It is not the intention of this chapter to reiterate the existing and emerging literature; Page (2005) offers a starting point for anyone embarking on the subject. Instead, this chapter sets out to provide a road map of the field, with signposts to key concepts, debates, and some of the contemporary issues that are associated with the prevailing paradigm of transportation and tourism research. For this reason, it is useful to commence with an initial conceptualization of the fundamental relationships that exist between transportation, recreation, and tourism.

The Transportation, Recreation and Tourism Nexus: Fundamental Relationships

Within the growing literature on recreation and tourism as a social science subject, the much debated positioning of recreational and tourism activities as a subset of leisure is important to any understanding of the transportation–tourism–recreation nexus (Hall and Page, 2006). The assumption here is that leisure activities are discretionary because they occur in juxtaposition to work and other household functions and occur in three contexts: "time not required for work or basic functions such as eating and sleeping, of activities or recreation within leisure time, and an attitude of mind based upon a perception of pleasure and enjoyment, recognizing that there may be blurring within and between these areas" (Patmore, 1983: 5–6). Complications arise in seeking to understand the relationship between leisure, recreation, tourism, and the role of transportation. For instance, in the postwar period in developed countries, the amount of "leisure" time has generally increased as the hours of work

have decreased. Often described as non-work time, the growth in daily, weekly, and annual leisure time has not been distributed evenly in social and spatial terms. There is an issue of equity of access and distribution of such leisure time and its use when one looks at the increasing urbanization of the world's population and how the most affluent neighborhoods have relative easy access to recreational and leisure resources, reflected not only in the spatial distribution of such resources but also through increased levels of car ownership and other means of transportation in such neighborhoods, compared to residents in poorer districts (Curry, 2001a, 2001b; Litman, 2002). Therefore, if transportation is a prerequisite for tourism and recreation to occur, then there are substantial social issues over access to transportation to facilitate even domestic tourism and recreation, let alone international travel. It is not a universal right enshrined in legislation, despite some attempts to promote social tourism in some countries. Instead, it is dependent upon wealth, disposable income and the time to engage in this activity (i.e., an absence of barriers to participation). This may seem a straightforward issue, and while some recreations and leisure research have addressed issues of access and equity (e.g., Floyd and Johnson, 2002; Tarrant and Cordell, 1999), few analyses within tourism studies seek to recognize the issues of inequality and access to tourism as a public good, with the cost of transportation a key obstacle or inhibitor to participation (e.g., Lee and Jamal, 2008). When one attempts to distinguish between the use of transportation for leisure purposes such as tourism and day-use recreationalists it becomes increasingly difficult. As Page observed:

> on a rail journey through a National Park, the train may be carrying local passengers who are enjoying a passive use of their leisure time by sightseeing and it may also be carrying fell walkers who are using the train as a mode of transport into the National Park to reach the starting point for their walk and thereby participate in outdoor recreation. The train may also be carrying non-residents journeying from point A to B. These may be domestic

tourists who are staying away from home for more than 24 hours or international tourists who are on holiday. Herein lies the complexity of disentangling the complex relationship between leisure, recreation and tourism and the fact that tourists also undertake recreational activities at their destination area. (1998: 219)

For this reason, we need to begin any analysis of transportation and tourism with a clear attempt to conceptualize the relationships and basic propositions that define the subject and to delineate what we are trying to analyze.

Conceptualizing Transportation and Tourism

There have been surprisingly few attempts to conceptualize the transportation–tourism relationship, with some notable exceptions (e.g., Duval, 2007; Hall, 1999; Lumsdon and Page, 2004a, 2004b; Page, 1994, 1999, 2005). It is generally accepted that two fundamental modes of analysis exist.

Transportation for Tourism

Where transportation is construed as a utilitarian or functional act that comprises travel on a mode or modes of transportation to achieve the goal of moving from origin to destination. It also serves a valuable facilitation role for tourist travel within the destination. Consequently, as a means of facilitating international tourist travel, as Lumsdon and Page (2004a: 5) show using UN World Tourism Organization (UNWTO) data, the various modes of transportation impact upon tourism in the following way:

- international air travel accounts for 43% of international tourist trips;
- road transportation accounts for 42% of trips;
- rail travel comprises 8% of trips;
- sea transportation account for 7% of trips.

These global estimates of the importance of transportation in tourist travel will, of course,

vary by region of the world. Land-based travel is extremely important in Europe due to the large geographic areas served by road and rail there. Air travel is growing rapidly in Asia due to the vast land mass, difficult terrain to be traversed, and large distances involved. As the above noted statistics show, in an international context, air is not necessarily as dominant as many commentators would lead us to believe, with road-based travel accounting for almost as many trips.

Transportation as Tourism

Transportation as tourism occurs where the form of transportation is integral to the overall experience of tourism such as cruising or taking a scenic railway journey. This is reflected in T.S. Eliot's famous quotation "the journey, not the arrival, matters," epitomized in the nostalgic marketing being used by Cunard Line, a major cruise ship line in 2006 in the UK market for journeys on the Queen Mary II ship: "in an age when travel is measured in hours, we are still proud to measure it in luxury." Some of the luxurious tourist products available, such as the Orient Express in Europe, the Rocky Mountaineer train tour through the Canadian Rockies, and a multitude of exclusive cruises utilize the elegance, opulence and quality service attributes of the mode of travel. Page (2007) outlines the growing significance of luxury travel in the evolving tourist markets for travel, as transportation providers have recognized this niche and seek to meet the demand.

These two fundamental approaches to tourism have led Lumsdon and Page (2004b) to identify a tourist transportation continuum in which transportation for tourism offers a low intrinsic value in relation to the overall tourist experience (i.e., typified by using a mode of transportation to simply get from origin a to destination b) through to the position where transportation is developed, designed, and harnessed as the containing context and the central element—as tourism (see Figure 21.1). Research by Moscardo and Pearce (2004) has begun to present motivational arguments for this type of continuum, only a starting point for further research to delineate the dimensions and niches of tourist interaction along this continuum.

In reality, a tourist will have several service encounters along this continuum (Figure 21.1), making it a complex process to model or produce a blueprint of the tourist service experience of the transportation used in a typical trip. It is not surprising, therefore, that researchers have avoided the detailed modeling of these encounters, preferring to resort to more conventional analysis such as a modal approach. A modal approach typically follows the descriptive classification of such activity by transportation researchers into land-based, air-based, and water-based travel within which different classifications and modal forms of transportation are explored and discussed. This approach has been widely used by transportation geographers and economists, particularly where they seek to model and analyze the competition between modes and how different consumers use different modes of transportation. Therefore, attention now turns to a modal approach in the absence of more conceptual

modes of analyzing tourist transportation. The section below commences with a brief discussion of recent trends, followed by an overview of various transportation models.

A Modal Approach to Tourist Travel

At an international scale, there are no studies which begin to show the interactions and scale of tourist use of different modes of transportation. Where studies exist, these are usually focused on air travel. In a European context, bodies such as the European Union (EU) document the usage of different modes of transportation showing that two modes of transportation dominate: the car and air travel. In terms of air travel to Europe, much of the demand is largely fueled by intraregional travel (that is travel originating from and destined for locations within the EU). Much of this travel originates in Western Europe and Scandinavia and is destined for Southern Europe, especially tourist destinations in the Mediterranean. Such growth can be traced to the initial rise of charter travel in the late 1960s to the Mediterranean coastline.

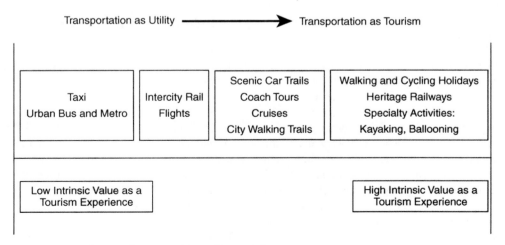

Figure 21.1 The Tourism Transportation Continuum.
Source: Adapted from Lumsdon and Page (2004: 7).

In the period since the late 1990s, this pattern has also been modified by the rapid expansion of low cost airlines (Calder, 2002; Gittell, 2003). Similar geographical migrations in the summer season can also be observed by air in the USA and Canada with mass travel to southern sunshine states (e.g., Florida and California) and the Caribbean, using charter and lower priced air travel, though not on the same scale as the European migrations in the summer. In the USA, one of the largest tourist flows exists cross border (USA–Canada; USA–Mexico) by road and similar land-based tourist migrations exist in other parts of the world (e.g., trans-European border crossings in Eastern and Western Europe by car) although in Europe the absence of any statistical cross border counts due to the absence of border checks for Europeans make it difficult to precisely enumerate such flows. Low cost air travel has also led to a growth in Western European travel to Eastern Europe after the collapse of the Berlin Wall and liberalization of trans-European travel. For example, destinations such as Prague have witnessed a major transformation of their local economies as low cost airlines have provided services to the city. Another phenomenon aiding this growth is the rise of urban short breaks over the past decade, fueled initially by package holidays and more recently by the revolution in low cost air travel (Dobruszkes, 2006; Warnock-Smith and Potter, 2005).

In contrast, the trends in rail and bus/coach travel in Europe (and many other countries) by tourists mirror many international trends that show relative declines in their use. These modes of transportation do not perform the same function in moving high volumes of mass tourists that they did historically in the nineteenth and up to the mid-twentieth century as air-based and car-based transportation dominate. The rapid growth in leisure travel in Asia-Pacific and in countries such as China illustrates this point: while the overall volume of travel has increased, the proportions using air travel have grown rapidly (Page, 2004). Rail and bus/coach transportation for tourists

may best be described as secondary or *complementary modes of transportation* (except where they perform a dedicated tourist function; e.g., coach touring and long-distance scenic rail travel or airport rail links), given the tourist preference for car and air-based travel, with its perceived speed, ease of access, and cost. This reflects a shift from tourist-use of transportation in the public domain unless it is faster, more accessible and time efficient to more private modes of travel. Although exceptions exist such as the use of the fast rail TGV in France, AVE in Spain, the Channel Tunnel rail link between the UK and France, and the bullet train in Japan, high-speed rail services which are time competitive with air and road transportation remain the exception rather than the rule. One explanation is that that safety, security and convenience are key factors shaping travel behavior, as Table 21.1 shows (QUATTRO, 1998). Table 21.1 suggests that eight principal variables and sub-variables shape the desire to use public transportation as well the perception of quality. Attempting to convince tourists to switch transportation modes (i.e., from the car to public transportation) depends upon operator and government action around these key variables to influence passenger behavior.

Land-Based Transportation

The Car

The car is still widely neglected in tourism studies because it is now such an accepted part of everyday life that the impact and use in tourism is taken for granted and overlooked. Both the early study by Wall (1971) and Patmore (1983) identify the fundamental changes in mobility in the postwar period in Western industrialized society and the rise in car ownership. These studies also depict the behavioral attributes of recreational travel and tourist travel to nonurban areas, the impact on National Parks (Eckton, 2003) and coastal areas as the car posed management challenges for planners in accommodating

Table 21.1 The Public Transportation Quality Matrix

QUALITY		
	1. Availability	1.1 Network
		1.2 Timetable
	2. Accessibility	2.1 External interface
		2.2 Internal interface
		2.3 Ticketing
	3. Information	3.1 General information
		3.2 Travel information—normal conditions
		3.3 Travel information—abnormal conditions
	4. Time	4.1 Journey time
		4.2 Punctuality and reliability
	5. Customer care	5.1 Commitment
		5.2 Customer interface
		5.3 Staff
		5.4 Physical assistance
		5.5 Ticketing options
	6. Comfort	6.1 Ambient conditions
		6.2 Facilities
		6.3 Ergonomics
		6.4 Ride comfort
	7. Security	7.1 Safety from crime
		7.2 Safety from accident
		7.3 Perception of security
	8. Environment	8.1 Pollution
		8.2 Natural resources
		8.3 Infrastructure

Source: Common work Quattro/CEN TC320 WG5 as cited in "Final Report: Synthesis and Recommendations," QUATTRO, Contract No. UR-96-SC-1140, p. 9, June 1998. www2.eur.nl/quattro/final_report/QuattroFinalReport.pdf. Accessed May 24, 2008.

the volume of usage. These studies typify the major effect of the car on patterns of travel. Despite this, bodies such as the EU have introduced policies (e.g., the September 2001 White Paper, European Transport Policy to 2010) with 60 measures designed to make policy more user-orientated. Specific research projects and policies as a result of this action seek to reverse the decline in rail travel in Europe, to increase rail use to 40% over the period 1998–2010, from the low base of 6–10% a share of the market for all travel. In the bus and coach sector, similar measures are also a fact in Europe and in specific countries, although research by Lumsdon et al. (2006) does point to the key role which public transportation can play in visiting National Parks and in shaping tourist itineraries. For this reason, it is useful to examine what is meant by tourist itineraries, their role in transportation and tourism and how they help us to understand tourist travel behavior (Shailes et al., 2001).

The Tourist Itinerary: A Neglected Concept in Transportation and Tourism

What the car has done is transform the tourists' ability to organize and develop their own itineraries and activity patterns without being dependent upon existing transportation provision. An itinerary is a method of analyzing how a tourist travels from an origin to a destination, including the routes they travel along, the stopping points, and activity patterns. By modeling such travel behavior, the use of transportation modes, such as the car, can be more fully understood in relation to the destinations visited, tourist resources consumed en route and likely impact of such activity in time and space. Yet as McKercher and Lew observe:

little empirical or conceptual work has been conducted examining and modeling tourism itineraries, in spite of the long understood need to study this phenomenon . . . one of the reasons for this lack of research is that the study of itineraries presents significant practical problems in gathering data. (2004: 36)

McKercher and Lew (2004) review the main studies since the 1960s, which evolved around itineraries and tourist travel (e.g. Campbell, 1966), as well as recreational travel (e.g. Coppock and Duffield, 1975; Forer and Pearce, 1984). In addition, Becken (2005) and Becken et al. (2003) modeled coach itineraries in New Zealand and reconstructed the itinerary of international tourists visiting New Zealand to measure the energy use associated with their travel. Schiefelbusch et al. (2007) introduced the concept of "travel chain" by analyzing such a travel chain in Germany.

For National Parks, the impact of the car on key sites (e.g., honeypots, which are high use sites) and popular locations which tourists visit, has proved a continuous problem since the 1960s and understanding tourist itineraries is invaluable when trying to manage such impacts. In some cases (e.g., The Goyt Valley in the Peak District National Park) have managed the use of cars by providing alternative forms of transportation to key tourism and recreational sites where overuse is a potential threat. Many National Parks in the UK are concerned about their ability to accommodate the forecast growth in car use of 267% between 1992–2025, which illustrates the scale of the problem. Similar problems also affect tourist destinations like small cities and Dickinson et al. (2004: 105) highlight the range of initiatives developed to try and manage the tourist use of the car because in Western developed countries such as the UK, 40% of mileage traveled is for leisure use. Dickinson et al. also point to leisure travel initiatives which have sought to: (1) encourage closer travel to home; (2) to introduce containment/restriction strategies such as the Goyt Valley in the Peak District; (3) generate tourist traffic to support uneconomic public transportation, such as the seasonal use of rail routes to peripheral areas; and (4) make improvements to cycling and walking opportunities.

Yet the major obstacle to getting visitors to switch to alternatives is inertia, a lack of understanding of alternatives and the perception of public transportation as undesirable as Table 21.1 illustrated. In historic cities, Orbaşli and Shaw (2004) identified the need to reconfigure the road network to reroute tourist cars away from city centers to catchment areas with park and ride schemes. It also requires the separation of the car from tourists on foot by provision of pedestrian only and cycle tracks to reduce pollution, noise and conflicts. But such action poses a poison chalice for many local authorities charged with car-management measures, as epitomized by congestion charging in London: the car brings the volume of visitors many towns "and cities" local economies depend upon. Therefore, any measures to limit, deter or make city center access inconvenient (i.e., by pricing mechanisms) or the perceived inconvenience of park and ride, is opposed by business groups who do not wish to see the visitor deterred. In stark contrast, where the car is a major polluter of the built environment, environmental, and resident groups want to a solution that reduces such impacts. Whatever stance a local authority adopts, it is going to be a no win situation, as one group will feel aggrieved.

Coach and Bus Transportation

In contrast to the car, the evolution of bus and coach transportation since the 1930s was a technological advance on rail travel, making destinations not on rail routes more accessible. These modes of travel also played a major role up until the 1960s in access to areas within countries for domestic travel, by offering a low cost and competing mass transportation mode. In the USA for example, the famous Greyhound coach network for long-distance travel has reexamined a major feature of land-based travel and not challenged as a low cost mode of transportation until the 1980s and the low cost airline model was introduced. In the EU, the bus/coach mode of travel for tourism and leisure purposes is used by around 12% of the population (TPR Associates, 1999) and the countries with the greatest use were Greece, Denmark, Germany, and Spain, with the lowest levels of use of under 5% were in the UK, Ireland, Italy, and France. Recent policy changes in the EU such as the White Paper, *European Transport Policy for 2010* outlined the potential of this sector to substitute road-based car travel for bus/coach travel. Changes in policy approaches have led to different market structures for the management of bus and coach travel, from a public ownership model to market-led approaches and major competition. One outcome in the UK is the development of large integrated bus–coach–rail operators such as First, Stagecoach, and National Express. Some of these operators have European and global operations, such as Stagecoach's acquisition of Coach USA in July 1999 and its operation of services in New Zealand. Yet the most profound change in the fortunes of the bus and coach can be charted by the decision by Stagecoach in the UK to embark on a low cost coach operation to challenge both the low cost airline and the existing express coach operator—National Express.

In August 2003, the UK's Stagecoach bus company launched a low cost Internet booking coach service based on trips between the UK's main cities. Its dark blue vehicles proudly boasted singe fares for £1.00 plus a booking fee. By 2005, the Megabus network had developed a network of services covering 40 UK cities since 2004, with around 1.5 million passengers a year, and two-hourly services on major trunk routes such as London–Birmingham and lower frequencies on longer distance routes (e.g., London–Aberdeen). This was the first major competition of any significance for the UK's National Express intercity coach service that operates to 1200 possible pick up/drop off locations in the UK. The service is modeled on the low cost airline model of ticketless travel, seats are yield managed and cheaper fares offered the further in advance you book.

Cycling

The bicycle is arguably the most sustainable form of tourist transportation (Lumsdon and Tolley, 2004; Lumsdon et al., 2004): it is non-motorized and it does not require fuel while having a minimal impact on the built and physical environment, with the exception of mountain biking, where it constitutes a recreational activity with resource impacts. As Lumsdon and Tolley (2004) argue, after walking, cycling is the most important form of transportation globally, given its significance for leisure use in developing countries such as China where it comprises 65% of all trips made. In a European context, cycling remains a popular form of transportation in Denmark, Germany, and the Netherlands, even though motorized transportation has dominated transportation policy in the interwar and postwar period in most Westernized countries.

Up until the 1990s, cycling symbolized many of the key principles of sustainable tourism, with minimal environmental impacts and limited infrastructure requirements. Since the late 1990s, cycling has become part of a wider renaissance of interest in walking and cycling in North America, Australasia, and in Eastern Europe where the issue of quality of life is moving higher up the political agenda (Lumsdon and Tolley, 2004: 147) in contrast to developing countries seeking to emulate symbols of modernization and affluence such as car ownership. Yet the major change, in recreational terms, in the late 1990s has been the demand for purpose-built infrastructure such as dedicated bike lanes, marked cycling routes, multiuse pathways to accommodate local commuters and urban visitors, as well as cycle tourism in scenic rural, coastal, and mountain landscapes.

Rail Travel

Train transportation for tourism takes two forms: combined leisure and business travel, which is scheduled, and predominantly leisure-based services "where train travel becomes the focus of the tourist experience" (Prideaux, 1999: 73). As discussed earlier, rail transportation was one of the prime movers of the leisure revolution in Victorian and Edwardian times, linked with the rise of seaside resorts since it offered an efficient mode of moving volumes of urban passengers from a city to a coastal destination. Yet, for rail transportation to operate effectively, a vastly expensive capital investment is needed in fixed infrastructure, and many current day rail networks were built by private investment in Victorian times, and further developed under state ownership.

In the case of tourist journeys by rail, the traditional postwar market for rail holidays has seen competition emerge with other forms of transportation, most notably the car in the 1960s and more recently, the low cost airlines. Yet leisure day trips remain a key element of rail travel, for leisure and business use, while high-speed routes have seen significant growth. In Europe, rail has been subject to deregulation and it remains a sector with ongoing investment requirements, although it does perform well in carbon emissions as a relatively sustainable mode of tourist travel. Yet some of the most profound changes in rail travel have occurred with the "transportation and tourism" luxury market, such as the Orient Express train journey, an innovative tourism product based on luxury, nostalgia, class, and opulent consumption. Similar examples have been developed in many countries, such as Queensland Rail, which have packaged scenery and sightseeing as key elements as discussed by Prideaux (1999).

In terms of the future development of rail for tourism uses, Page (2005) observes that in Europe, further investment by the EU to create a pan-European, high-speed network is a key component of its transportation policy, to create a Trans-European Network (TEN) with infrastructure projects designed to provide links across country borders.

Water-Based Transportation

Waterborne transportation is frequently overlooked in many studies of tourism since air travel dominates the world patterns of travel, although prior to air travel, it was the principal form of long-distance travel, epitomized in the 1930s by the transatlantic cruiselines. Within the water-based transportation sector, three main forms of transportation can be identified: cruising, ferries, and pleasure craft.

Cruising

Cruising is among the most high profile sectors of the sea-based travel market, having seen a market renaissance in the 1990s (Wood, 2000, 2004). The cruise product can take many forms; small-scale, specialist ships exist to take niche market clients to locations such as the Galapagos Islands; and, at the other end of the spectrum, there are massive mass entertainment ships, which are themselves the destination. As tour operators have expanded the market for these products to a mass market, a budget product has emerged where new luxury ships have a higher capacity. The product base for cruising comprises both transportation and accommodation—and a number of cruises out of Asia go "nowhere" since they are provided for the gambling market.

As an activity, cruising has increased rapidly as Peisley (2004) acknowledges, with large cruising companies dominating the market (e.g., Carnival Cruises, www.carnival.com and Princes Cruises www.princess.com). This level of concentration of capacity into two large groups had been accompanied by the growing size of cruise ships (i.e., over 100,000 ton plus ships) to provide significant economies of scale. For example, in July 2006, Europe's largest cruise ship, the 3780 passenger and 112,000 ton Costa Concordia entered service with 1430 cabins to illustrate the scale of the new cruise ships. In the USA, the Cruise Lines International Association saw the volume of passengers grow from 8.6 million in 2002 to 9.5 million in 2003 and the USA dominates the world cruising market, followed by the UK and Europe. In the new millennium, cruising has been relaunched as a luxury activity which is now more accessible to greater numbers of people, and a much wider range of people from different age groups (including families) now choose this as a holiday option. Increased competition and the growth in new larger ships have led many cruise operators to discount prices to fill capacity. A good example of increased competition alongside this segmentation is the introduction of the low cost brand in 2005 with the rise of the Easy.com band—Easycruise, representing another product to enter a crowded market.

Ferries

Ferries are used to cross water where it constitutes a barrier to travel. One of the busiest waterways in the world is the English Channel and a ferry service has been recorded in history between Dover and Calais since Roman times, meeting the need for tourist travel. Ferries tend to operate on strategic trade routes with a mix of passenger and freight. Up until the 1970s, ferries remained almost entirely functional and spartan in terms of their provision of services for tourists. The recognition that a ferry could be a "product" is combined with the increasing size of ships in order to provide more of an "experience" for travelers and a major business activity onboard the vessels for the ferry operators. Such a trend intensified with the opening of one of the largest ever European tourist transportation infrastructure projects, in the form of the Channel Tunnel. This altered services on this route by the end of the 1990s and provided a new form of competition with the sea-based services, which were subsequently rationalized, reorganized, and repositioned to compete with the new operator.

In some peripheral locations, which have a highly seasonal tourist market, such as the Highlands and Islands of Scotland and many Scandinavian islands, the ferry services not only operate under a government grant to subsidize the operation, but provide a vital lifeline to a scattered series of communities and similar situations can be seen in other countries. In Scotland, the volume of traffic on these services is around 6 million passenger journeys a year, including nearly 2 million car crossings. The tourist market remains a key element of their business, supporting the highly seasonal tourism trade on remote and dispersed islands and similar patterns also exist in the case of the Greek Islands. More recent innovations, with new technology to support time-speed improvements in sea crossings, have come in the form of catamaran services to offer a high-speed alternative to ferries, in much the same way the hovercraft did with its revolutionary impact in the 1970s. Again, innovations in technology have changed the nature and impact of tourist travel.

Pleasure Craft on Inland Waterways

Within countries which have an industrial heritage based on canals and inland waterways (e.g., Northern European countries, especially the UK, Eire, and the Netherlands) a significant vacation market has developed based on pleasure boats designed to use the former canal and waterways that were previously developed to serve the transportation needs of a former era. For example, in Scotland the development of pleasure steamers on the river Clyde in Glasgow and the development of Loch Lomond as a day trip destination saw the rise of a large urban demand for these services in the nineteenth and twentieth centuries, only losing ground in the 1970s and 1980s with the rise of the car and decline of this mass form of leisure. In contrast to large inland bodies of water, such as lochs, inland waterways in cities such as Birmingham and Gloucester, in the UK, the network of canals is so extensive that they have become the focus of tourism-related urban regeneration projects. In areas where tourist use of pleasure craft exists, this market has become an integral part of the strategy by bodies such as British Waterways Board to relaunch the area's appeal to the tourist seeking a heritage product. The extent of the canal network in the UK still offers considerable potential for expansion as a tourism and leisure resource using the historic canal boats, converted for holidays by companies such as Hoseasons.

One indication of the scale of this growing market for pleasure craft as part of a holiday experience is the Norfolk Broads in the UK. To many observers this form of tourist transportation is a seemingly sustainable mode but the canal or pleasure boat is not without its environmental impacts. The Norfolk Broads is a wetland region in East Anglia created through the flooding of peat diggings in the medieval period. The region comprises a number of rivers and their tributaries that offer opportunities for recreational and tourism-related boating activities. The hire-boat industry, pioneered by John Loyne in the 1880s and popularized in 1908 by H. Blake and Company, created purpose-built vessels for hire aimed at the rail-based visitors. In 1995, the boat companies in the region comprised 1481 motor cruises and launches hired to approximately 200,000 visitors a year but there are over 13,000 licensed boats using the Broads each year. Yet these forms of transportation and tourism pale into significance when one examines the area that has seen the greatest exponential growth in demand since the 1970s—air travel.

Air Transportation and Tourism

Travel by air, compared to other modes of tourist transportation is the most recent innovation that has provided access to international locations, previously only possible by long-distance sea travel. Although air travel dates to the 1930s, its use was confined to the affluent traveler until the 1950s and 1960s, until the rise of the charter aircraft (Hanlon, 2004). The air charter provided low cost travel, initially to short haul destinations for leisure purposes and is widely credited with the rapid development of destinations in the Mediterranean in the 1960s and 1970s. Subsequent innovations in long-distance air travel reduced the unit cost of travel progressively, with the DC10 aircraft in the 1960s and the Boeing 747 jumbo jet in the 1970s. Further improvements in operating costs of jet aircraft reduced the relative cost of air

travel, especially on short-haul routes with the Boeing 737 and 1980s variants from Airbus Industries.

Scheduled airlines are those operating to a clearly defined, published timetable, irrespective of whether a flight is full or not. Until the 1980s, many schedule airlines were state owned and run for reasons of national prestige; a classic example of privatization occurred in 1987 with British Airways. In contrast, chartered aircrafts are hired out to a third party such as a tour operator who may use the aircraft for a summer or winter season's flying. In many cases, large European tour operators such as Airtours, Thomson and First Choice possess their own airline. The evolution of air travel is a complex area that is historically determined by international bodies such as the International Civil Aviation Organization (ICAO) and the International Air Transport Association (IATA). The regulations they established have, combined with bilateral agreements, established the framework for international air travel up until the deregulation era in the late 1970s. One of the most complex areas is the political regulation of air travel that dates to the 1930s, and the 1944 Chicago Convention. Current day aviation is regulated by international aviation law and this provides the context in which national and global carriers operate. At the national level, different countries have varying approaches to aviation competition and regulation. In the USA, the existence of antitrust laws seeks to encourage competition and reduce price fixing. This was extended under the Airline Deregulation Act 1978 (Debbage, 2004). In the USA, deregulation led to larger carriers taking over many of the smaller operators and the introduction of a hub and spoke operation (Gillen, 2005; Morrell, 2005). An interesting trend running contrary to this is the growth of low-cost carriers like South West airlines in the USA, using smaller secondary airports and offering point to point services, rather than a national and international network (Alderhighi et al., 2005).

TRANSPORTATION AND TOURISM

383

At an international scale, the right of airlines to fly are governed by the five freedoms of the air (Page, 2005) where airlines gain technical and traffic rights to operate between countries, based on the 1944 Chicago Convention. The rights have also been developed in subsequent years with sixth and seventh freedoms being added. With the major changes posed by deregulation and the complexities of freedoms of the air, airline management has emerged as a key feature of tourism and civil aviation since the 1980s (Weber and Dinwoodie, 2000).

Globalization and Airline Alliances

Aviation is one of the clear examples of globalization in the tourism sector as national carriers have sought to collaborate to reduce investment costs in operating international networks while seeking to enter protected markets (some useful reviews of this expanding area of research include: Albers et al. (2005); Gudmundsson and Lechar (2005); Iatrou and Alandari (2005); Ito and Lee (2005); Kleymann and Seristö (2005); Oum et al. (2000); also see Chapter 32 by Debbage and Gallaway in this *Handbook*). In Asia and South America, many airlines are still state owned and enjoy a degree of protectionism (Findlay et al., 1997). In Asia, as Page (2005) shows, airlines in the other parts of the world have forged strategic alliances to enter these "protected" markets, thereby gaining competitive advantages. The protectionism had meant than many of the state owned airlines are less competitive, leading to high fares for Asian travelers except where they operate low staffing cost structures (Findlay et al., 1997). Evans (2001) addresses the different collaboration and alliance options available to airlines in the competitive marketplace, for example, as an alliance may offer passengers a global network without one airline having to provide all the services. Alliance membership as an equity or non-equity member also offsets some of the risks of merger or acquisition by competing airlines and provides new focus for inter-alliance competition (Zhang and Zhang, 2006).

Managing the Tourist Experience and Tourist Volumes: The Airport

The scale of air travel at individual airports is apparent from the data recorded by the Airport Council International (ACI). At a global scale, in 2003, of 3.5 billion passenger movements, 1.3 billion were in North America and 1 billion were in Europe followed by 720 million in Asia-Pacific. ACI airports accommodated 66.7 million total aircraft movements (including cargo flights), dominated by North America, Europe and Asia-Pacific, although US airports dominate the top 20. Current and future airport projects illustrate the greater focus now being placed on the environment for consumption and retailing to generate revenue (Graham, 2003). As these environments generate large volumes of traffic with many revenue opportunities, the scale of travel raises the wider research agenda for the tourist transportation sector, especially the challenge for sustainability and the effects on the environment (Peace et al., 2006; Price and Probert, 1995; Schipper, 2004).

Sustainability Issues in Transportation and Tourism

A range of contemporary issues impinges upon the area of tourist and transportation as strong growth is being experienced in many domestic and international travel and tourism destinations. Predominant among these is concern about environmental impacts and sustainable development.

Several key issues related to this important global agenda are summarized briefly below and offer some insight and implications for future tourism and transportation research. Case studies illustrating various themes are provided further below. While the focus below is on impacts related to the biophysical environment, social issues of equity and access should not be forgotten (touched on briefly earlier in the chapter), as well as issues related to human health in relation to transportation.

Environmental Impacts

The single most important environmental impact of the hire boat and recreation and boat industry described in the water transportation section above has been the damage to the river banks caused by the wash from vessels as they travel along the river. This impact has combined with a number of other effects induced by potential conflict between wildlife, other activities such as angling, and visitors. Managing these impacts is problematic given the economic impact of boating in the region, estimated to contribute £25 million to the local economy. Similar examples exist in Ireland, where the large Lough Erne and Shannon-Erne waterways have provided opportunities for pleasure cruising (Guyer and Pollard, 1997). Likewise, in the USA personal watercraft have had major ecological impacts on inland waterways (Burger and Leonard, 2000). Cruise ships and water-based craft also generate significant environmental impacts on marine and coastal environments, including endangered coral reefs (Davenport and Davenport, 2006).

In other forms of transportation, the greenhouse gas emissions of the airline industry (especially long-haul travel) and land transportation forms are increasingly coming into popular consciousness, aided by "corporate social responsibility practices" offering carbon offset schemes and other efforts to manage the significant pollution from jet engines and other transportation forms (De Lollis, 2007). Gössling (2002) assessed and quantified the impacts of tourism on the environment, and provided a series of useful estimates on car use, air travel, and train use, and travel distances for leisure and tourism for different countries. Transportation was identified as the most important factor contributing to leisure-related energy use and emission of greenhouse gases, contributing to 94% of the overall contribution of tourism to global warming (Gössling, 2002). Similarly, Becken et al. (2003) measured energy use associated with different travel choice in New Zealand.

They determined usage of different modes of transportation (the car accounted for 91% of all domestic tourist trips). Transportation was found to be "the dominant subsector in terms of energy use with a contribution of 73% to the domestic tourist's energy bill and 65% to the international tourist's one" (Becken et al., 2003: 274).

Impact Management Responses

While tourism and transportation are likely to be one of the largest contributors to the forecasted growth in green house emissions in the next 20 years, there has been little debate from tourism researchers. One is more likely to see a tacit acceptance of the necessity of air travel to facilitate tourism and a naivety and failure of critical debate and engagement by tourism researchers. However, change is occurring, albeit slowly. Researchers and practitioners in the sustainability arena are beginning to develop impact management and assessment tools. In a study of inbound tourism and transportation to Amsterdam, Peeters and Schouten (2006), using the Ecological Footprint Analysis, established that 70% of the environmental pressure of inbound tourism originated from transportation to Amsterdam. They suggest two strategies for sustainable tourism in Amsterdam: selective marketing and managing flows of tourists and day visitors. Carbon calculation and carbon-offset sites are provided by nongovernmental or research-oriented organizations through the Internet (see www.climatefriendly.com, www.carbonfootprint.com, www.oneplanetliving.com, www.footprintnetwork.org. All accessed May 21, 2008). These websites offer programs to manage impacts of transportation on the environment and arouse the public awareness of environmental protection.

The rise of biofuels as alternatives to depleting nonrenewable, highly polluting carbon based fuels is being widely addressed in transportation policymaking. In the UK, the *Renewable Transport Fuel Obligation (RTFO)* (Department for Transportation, UK, 2005) was announced in 2005 with the requirement that by 2010 5% of all road vehicle fuel should consist of renewable resources. In the USA, the *Energy Independence and Security Act of 2007* requires American "fuel producers to use at least 36 billion gallons of biofuel in 2022" (US 110th Congress, 2007). In some developing countries such as Brazil (a leader in this initiative), India, and China, new types of biofuels like bioethanol and biodiesel are being increasingly developed as substitutes of gas and diesel. Despite the controversial reception that the biofuel movement is receiving, such global efforts can be viewed as a promising sign for reducing adverse environmental effects of tourist transportation if more and more countries will be participating in the biofuel research and development.

Policy Responses

An important research area is policy issues in transportation studies, as reflected in the contributions to the journal *Transport Policy*, plus other academic and professional literature on this subject. Transportation policy informs practice and more importantly shapes the actions that governments take to manage the impacts and effects of transportation as an economic activity (Williams et al., 2002, on aviation). The most high profile and significant area of policy debate on tourist transportation is associated with the environmental consequences of air travel, closely followed by the impact of the car. Much rhetoric has also emanated from the tourism sector in response to these issues, especially associated with the way in which greener transportation options (e.g., cleaner fuel and engine technology such as the new Airbus A380) will help solve these problems. The rapid growth in low cost air travel is among the worse culprits for it has converted travelers from rail and more sustainable energy

options to air travel. Low cost air travel generates new discretionary travel due to its low price and failure to pay a tax on aviation fuel, a subsidy also enjoyed by the global aviation sector. Greater policy scrutiny of the externalizing of environmental costs is needed, but the aviation sector and transportation sector in general has a powerful political lobby, which has ensured its profit-oriented interests are met. This is well demonstrated by environmental debates and arguments over airport expansion. Attempts to restrict airport development are usually futile when the economic development role is used to justify growth and expansion, as the UK White Paper on Airports Policy in 2003 exemplified.

Planning Issues

Tourism impact studies illustrate a wide variety of economic, sociocultural, and environmental impacts that result through travel and visitation, for example, overcrowded attractions and services (like restaurants on a big event day), inadequate transportation alternatives and infrastructure (e.g., narrow roads causing traffic congestion), noise and air pollution, competition for access to scarce resources between locals and tourists, habitat fragmentation and soil erosion as vegetation is cut for development of touristic facilities, etc. Highly popular tourist destinations experience large numbers of visitors and environmentally sensitive areas are particularly vulnerable, as are fragile heritage sites and tourist-historic cities (Ashworth and Tunbridge, 2000). Israeli and Mansfeld conducted a pioneer research on the transportation accessibility of the Old City of Jerusalem, pointing out a number of problematic issues, noting that "such syndromes are predominantly a reflection of poor planning and bad management of the transportation systems, which is supposed to support the influx and movement of tourists in and around these historic districts" (2003: 462).

Both urban planners and transportation planners tend to neglect the relatively strong effects from external factors like tourism on the overall urban or regional planning. Variability in travel flows, lack of information on tourist itineraries and lack of detailed visitation statistics at the local level contribute to the data collection problem in transportation–tourism research. Managing tourism mobility in urban destinations such as cities and metropolitan areas is a critical planning issue, but is also crucial for community, rural, and environmental destinations seeking to develop a viable tourism trade. Likewise, the symbiotic relationship between transportation and tourism at a regional or an international level at a necessary condition for moving visitors from one locale to another. A number of examples are provided below to further illustrate the issues outlined above.

Example 1: Integrated Planning for Urban Tourism—Wuxi City, Jiangsu Province, China

Wuxi is one of the most famous tourist cities in China. It is located in the heart of the Yangtze River Delta in the southeast of Jiangsu Province, encompassing a total area of 4650 square kilometers, and a downtown of 1931 square kilometers. This area houses a population of 5.18 million, some 1.1 million of who reside downtown. It is located strategically about 128 kilometers west of Shanghai and 183 kilometers east of Nanjing; it abuts Zhejiang Province across Taihu Lake on the south. The tourism boom began in the 1980s when several movie/television induced theme parks were launched. In addition, the excellent waterfront amenities, as well as the historic water-downtown, helped to promote this as an urban tourism destination nationally. Wuxi tourism statistics in 2007 revealed the following classification: 760,000 inbound tourist trips and 33.51 million domestic tourist trips (Wuxi City Department of Statistics, 2008).

An important planning component is the Great Yangtze River Delta Tourism Ring, a convenient and multimodal set of transportation facilities (including aviation, highway system, high-speed intercity rail, tourist waterways, etc.) that has contributed instrumentally to the rapid improvement of Wuxi tourism development.

In 2003, the *Tourism Development Master Plan of Wuxi City, Jiangsu Province (2003–2020)* (China Academy of Urban Planning and Design, 2003) adopted the urban transportation plan from the newly updated *Urban Master Plan of Wuxi City, Jiangsu Province (2002–2020)* (Jiangsu Province Academy of Urban Planning and Design, 2002), in order to enable better integration of tourist routes with the urbanization and motorization process. In 2005, a downtown-focused *Integrated Transportation Network Plan in the 11th Five-year Urban-rural Construction Plan of Wuxi City (2006–2010)* (Wuxi City Academy of Urban Planning and Design, 2005) also helped to address urban tourism transportation demands. Construction of the planned high-speed intercity railway has commenced as outlined in the *11th Five-year Urban-rural Construction Plan*. Similar coordination between the tourism plan and the urban plan can also be found in the construction of thoroughfares between the downtown and major suburban tourist areas. These planning initiatives can be considered innovative in bring synergies between tourism and transportations systems that traditionally tend to be treated separately or in a fragmented manner (see Photos 21.1 to 21.4).

Example 2: Sugar Cane-Based Ethanol Biofuels in Brazil

Cleaner burning agricultural based fuels, such as biofuels or mixed ethanol-based fuels, are a promising alternative to reduce air pollution and exhaust pipe emissions in both developed and developing countries. Brazil, which is considered to have the world's first sustainable biofuels economy and the biofuel industry leader (Budny and

Photo 21.1   The ancient canal through downtown Wuxi.
Photo: Yue Ge (2002).

Photo 21.2   A historic mansion on the canal.
Photo: Yue Ge (2002).

Photo 21.3   The Classic Garden—Jichang Yuan.
Photo: Yue Ge (2002).

Photo 21.4   An ancient battle show in the Three-Kingdom Studio
**   Theme Park.**
Photo: Yue Ge (2002).

**Photo 21.5   A Petrobras gas station at São Paulo with dual fuel service
marked "A" for Alcohol (ethanol) and "G" for gasoline (2008).
Source: Retrieved on May 21, 2008 from http://en.wikipedia.org/wiki/
Biofuel_in_Brazil.
Photo: Mariordo Mario Roberto Duran Ortiz.**

Sotero, 2007), has successfully developed sugar cane-based ethanol biofuels. In 2006, Brazil produced 16.3 billion liters (4.3 billion US liquid gallons) (Renewable Fuels Association, 2008) representing 33.3% of the world's total ethanol production and 42% of the world's ethanol used as fuel (The World Bank, 2008). It has been a nationwide technology innovation since 1977, producing blended fuels such as 20% ethanol with gasoline or 25% ethanol with gasoline, which have become a realistic choice for regular gasoline vehicles in this popular touristic destination and important conservation region (see Photo 21.5).

Example 3: Heritage Streetcars in the USA
Heritage streetcars, also called tramcars, trolleys, or trams, are among the many rail modes popular in European, Oceanic, and American cities, especially those with historic downtowns. In addition to being an effective public transit mode, these vintage vehicles or replicas of historic vehicles are also part of the historic and cultural landscape for

tourism. Another advantage of heritage streetcars is their convenience to set up and the relatively low operational costs than other types of rail transportation. Commemorating early industrialization years, heritage streetcar systems are being operated in a couple of old cities in the USA: Little Rock, Arkansas, Memphis, Tennessee, Dallas, Texas, New Orleans, Louisiana, Philadelphia, PA, Tampa, Florida, Charlotte, North Carolina, San Francisco, California, Boston, Massachusetts, etc. These old-fashioned rail vehicles bring people to the past and connect the tourist hotspots in downtowns; often driven by electricity, they offer an important alternative to mass capacity vehicles using gasoline or diesel. Millikin (2005) reported that 14 propane-fueled American Heritage Streetcars were introduced and operated by VIA Metropolitan Transit San Antonio, Texas, which may be a promising avenue for combining heritage streetcars with tourist transportation in the USA to provide for a "sustainable heritage tourism" experience (see Photo 21.6).

Photo 21.6   Vintage trolley—formerly of Poroto, Portugal—on the Memphis Main Street Trolley Line (2003).
Source: Retrieved on May 22, 2008 from http://en.wikipedia.org/wiki/ Heritage_streetcar.
Photo: Jeremy Atherton.

Photo 21.7   Bikes in a European city (2006).
Source: Retrieved on May 22, 2008 from http://www. bike-eu.com/news/article.asp?id=1973.

Example 4: Cycling in Europe

Though highly motorized, many European countries, such as the Netherlands, France, Germany, the UK, Spain, and Ireland, are bicycle friendly, offering touring routes that provide a great chance to travel along canals, past windmills, through hills, and villages (see Photo 21.7). Ireland, for instance, has emerged as a popular destination for bike touring through beautiful rural landscapes and visiting small local eateries and accommodation establishments (e.g., Iron Donkey Bicycle Touring, www.irondonkey. com; and The Great Irish Pub Ride 2008, www.bikithikit.com/ireland-cycling.htm. Accessed on May 24, 2008). Being on two wheels can facilitate rich experiences for cross-cultural encounters, enjoying area-based culinary fare, and local hospitality. The smaller-scale distances between places in Europe make it possible for bicycling tourists to ride between villages within a short time while enjoying the scenery and cultural–historic attractions. Well-designed routes on lesser used, secondary roads help avoid high traffic and facilitate road safety. Nowadays, more and more European cities advocate policies to encourage tourists as well as local residents to use bicycles, as an environmentally preferable product (Mygatt, 2005). For instance, Copenhagen provides 3000 free bicycles for public use through its City Bike program and allows them on most trains, plus is currently working to increase and upgrade bicycle parking facilities at rail stations (Mygatt, 2005).

Conclusion

Tourist transportation remains a significant area for research but it still remains a niche subject despite its mainstream role in tourist movement and tourism researchers tend to follow the lead from the mainstream transportation areas. One result has been the lack of engagement by tourism researchers in the wider significance of transportation as a research subject underpinning the very basis of tourism as an activity. Tourism and transportation clearly have a crucial, symbiotic relationship. Tourism affects local, regional and international transportation in terms of travel flows and passenger volume, transit modes, travel behaviors, transportation economy, access to new developments, etc. Wider conceptual debate and interconnected dialogue with other disciplines will be essential for the investigation of transportation and tourism to progress in any meaningful manner.

Interdisciplinary research remains a crucial priority in order to address the implications for travel and tourism of these sustainability issues. As climate change and global warming continue to occupy the global agenda, sustainable forms of transportation, and alternative fuels will demand greater attention in research and practice. An urgent precursor to effectively addressing these major challenges is joint research and collaboration to fully appreciate the implications, meaning, and values attached to tourist transportation, and begin to bridge the knowledge gap that still exists between the tourist as traveler and their consumption of tourist transportation.

References

Albers, S., Koch, B. and Ruff, C. (2005). "Strategic Alliances Between Airlines and Airports—Theoretical Assessment and Practical Evidence." *Journal of Air Transport Management*, 11(2): 49–58.

Alderhighi, M., Cento, A., Nijkamp, P. and Rietveld, P. (2005). "Network Competition—The Coexistence of Hub-and-Spoke and Point-to-Point Systems." *Journal of Air Transport Management*, 11(5): 328–334.

Ashworth, G.J. and Tunbridge, J.E. (2000). *The Tourist-Historic City* (2nd edition.). Amsterdam: Pergamon.

Becken, S., Simmons, D.G. and Frampton, C. (2003). "Energy Use Associated With Different Travel Choices." *Tourism Management*, 24: 267–277.

Becken, S. (2005). "Towards Sustainable Tourist Transport: An Analysis of Coach Tourism in New Zealand." *Tourism Geographies*, 7(1): 23–42.

Budny, D. and Sotero, P. (2007). "The Global Dynamics of Biofuels." *Brazil Institute Special Report*, 3: 1–7. Brazil Institute of the Woodrow Wilson Center. Retrieved May 21, 2008 from www.wilsoncenter.org/topics/pubs/Brazil_SR_e3.pdf.

Burger, J. and Leonard, J. (2000). "Conflict Resolution in Coastal Waters: The Case of Personal Watercraft." *Marine Policy*, 24: 61–69.

Burkart, A. and Medlik, R. (1974). *Tourism: Past, Present and Future*. London: Heinemann.

Calder, S. (2002). *No Frills: The Truth Behind the Low-Cost Revolution in the Skies*. London: Virgin.

Campbell, C.K. (1966). *An Approach to Recreational Geography*. B.C. Occasional Papers No. 7.

Cavinato, J.L. and Cuckovich, M.L. (1992). "Transportation and Tourism for the Disabled: An Assessment." *Transportation Journal*, 31(3): 46–53.

China Academy of Urban Planning and Design (2003). *Tourism Development Master Plan of Wuxi City, Jiangsu Province*. Beijing: China Architectural Press.

Coppock, J.T. and Duffield, B. (1975). *Outdoor Recreation in the Countryside: A Spatial Analysis*. London: Macmillan.

Curry, N. (2001a). "Access for Outdoor Recreation in England and Wales: Production, Consumption and Markets." *Journal of Sustainable Tourism*, 9(5): 400–416.

Curry, N. (2001b). "Rights of Access to Land for Outdoor Recreation in New Zealand: Dilemmas Concerning Justice and Equity." *Journal of Rural Studies*, 17(4): 409–419.

Davenport, J. and Davenport, J.L. (2006). "The Impact of Tourism and Personal Leisure Transport on Coastal Environments: A Review." *Estuarine, Coastal and Shelf Science*, 67(1–2): 280–292.

De Lollis, B. (2007). "Can you be Traveling Green by Buying Offsets?" *USA TODAY*, March 2. Retrieved May 22, 2008 from www.usatoday.com/travel/news/2007-03-02-offsetsusat_x.htm.

Debbage, K. (2004). "Airlines, Airports and International Aviation." In L. Pender and R. Sharpley (Eds.), *The Management of Tourism*. London: Sage.

Department for Transportation, UK (2005). *Renewable Transport Fuel Obligation (RTFO) Feasibility Report*. Retrieved May 18, 2008 from www.dft.gov.uk/pgr/roads/environment/rtfo/secrtfoprogdocs/renewabletransportfuelobliga3849.

Dickinson, J., Calver, S., Watters, K. and Wilks, K. (2004). "Journeys to Heritage Attractions in the UK: A Case Study of National Trust Visitors in the South West." *Journal of Transport Geography*, 12: 103–13.

Dobruszkes, F. (2006). "An Analysis of European Low-Cost Airlines and Their Networks." *Journal of Transport Geography*, 14(4): 249–264.

Duval, D.T. (2007). *Tourism and Transport: Modes, Networks and Flows*. Clevedon, Buffalo and Toronto: Channel View Publications.

Eckton, G. (2003). "Road-User Charging and the Lake District National Park." *Journal of Transport Geography*, 11: 307–317.

Evans, G. and Shaw, S. (2001). "Urban Leisure and Transport: Regeneration Effects." *Journal of Leisure Property*, 1(4): 350–372.

Evans, N. (2001). "Collaborative Strategy: An Analysis of the Changing World of International Airline Alliances." *Tourism Management*, 22(3): 229–243.

Findlay, C, Sien, C and Singh, K. (1997). *Air Transport in Asia-Pacific: Challenges and Policy Reforms*. Singapore: Institute for South East Asian Studies.

Floyd, M. and Johnson, C. (2002). "Coming to Terms with Environmental Justice in Outdoor Recreation: A Conceptual Discussion with Research Implications." *Leisure Sciences*, 24: 59–77.

Forer, P. and Pearce, D.G. (1984). "Spatial Patterns of Package Tourism in New Zealand." *New Zealand Geographer*, 40: 34–42.

Formica, and Uysal (1996). "The Revitalization of Italy as a Tourist Destination." *Tourism Management*, 17(5): 323–331.

Gillen, D. (2005). "The Evolution of Networks with Changes in Industry Structure and Strategy: Connectivity, Hub-and-Spoke and Alliances." *Research in Transportation Economics*, 13: 49–73.

Gittell, J. (2003). *The Southwest Airlines Way*. New York: McGraw Hill.

Gössling, S. (2002). "Global Environmental Consequences of Tourism." *Global Environmental Change*, 12: 283–301.

Graham, A. (2003). *Managing Airports* (2nd edition.). Oxford: Butterworth Heinemann.

Gudmundsson, S.V. and Lechar, C. (2005). "Multilateral Airline Alliances: Balancing Strategic Constraints and Opportunities." *Journal of Air Transport Management*, 12(3): 153–158.

Guyer, C. and Pollard, J. (1997). "Cruise Visitor Impressions of the Environment of the Shannon-Erne Waterways System." *Journal of Environmental Management*, 51: 199–215.

Hall, C.M. and Page, S.J. (2006). *The Geography of Tourism and Recreation: Environment, Place and Space* (3rd edition.). London: Routledge.

Hall, D.R. (1999). "Conceptualising Tourism Transport: Inequality and Externality Issues." *Journal of Transport Geography*, 7(3): 181–188.

Hanlon, P. (2004). *Global Airlines*, Oxford: Butterworth Heinemann.

Iatrou, K. and Alandari, F. (2005). "The Empirical Analysis of the Impact of Alliances on Airline Operations." *Journal of Air Transport Management*, 11(3): 127–134.

Israeli, Y. and Mansfeld, Y. (2003). "Transportation Accessibility to and within Tourist Attractions in the Old City of Jerusalem." *Tourism Geographies*, 5(4): 461–481.

Ito, H. and Lee, D. (2005). "Domestic Code-sharing Practices in the US Airline Industry." *Journal of Air Transport Management*, 11(2): 89–97.

Jiangsu Province Academy of Urban Planning and Design (2002). *Urban Master Plan of Wuxi City. Jiangsu Province*.

Kleymann, B. and Seristö, H. (2005). *Managing Strategic Airline Alliances*. Aldershot: Ashgate.

Lee, C. and Han, S. (2002). "Estimating the Use and Preservation Values of National Parks' Tourism Resources Using a Contingent Valuation Method." *Tourism Management*, 23(5): 531–540.

Lee, S. and Jamal, T. (2008). "Environmental Justice and Environmental Equity in Tourism: Missing Links to Sustainability." *Journal of Ecotourism*, 7(1): 44–67.

Lim, C. (1997). "Review of International Tourism Demand Models." *Annals of Tourism Research*, 24(4): 835–849.

Litman, T. (2002). "Evaluating Transportation Equity." *World Transport Policy & Practice*, 8(2): 50–65.

Lumsdon, L. and Page, S.J. (Eds.) (2004a). *Tourism and Transport: Issues and Agenda for the New Millennium*. Oxford: Elsevier.

Lumsdon, L. and Page, S.J. (2004b). "Progress in Transport and Tourism Research: Reformulating the Transport-Tourism Interface and Future Research Agendas." In L. Lumsdon and S.J. Page (Eds.), *Tourism and Transport Issues and Agenda for the New Millennium* (pp. 1–28). Oxford: Elsevier.

Lumsdon, L. and Tolley, R. (2004). "Non-Motorised Transport: A Case Study of Cycling." In L. Lumsdon and S.J. Page (Eds.), *Tourism and Transport: Issues and Agenda for the New Millennium* (pp. 157–170). Oxford: Elsevier.

Lumsdon, L., Downward, P. and Cope, A. (2004). "Monitoring of Cycle Tourism on Long Distance Trails: The North Sea Cycle Route." *Journal of Transport Geography*, 12(1): 13–22.

Lumsdon, L., Downward, P. and Rhoden, S. (2006). "Transport for Tourism: Can Public Transport Encourage a Modal Shift in the Day Visitor Market?" *Journal of Sustainable Tourism* 14(2): 139–156.

McKercher, B. and Lew, A. (2004). "Tourist Flows and the Spatial Distribution of Tourists." In A. Lew, C.M. Hall and A. Williams (Eds.), *A Companion of Tourism* (pp. 36–48). Oxford: Blackwell.

Millikin, M. (2005). "The Week in Sustainable Transportation." Retrieved May 23, 2008 from www.worldchanging.com/archives/003790.html.

Morrell, P. (2005). "Airlines within Airlines: An Analysis of US Network Airline Responses to Low Cost Carriers." *Journal of Air Transport Management*, 11(5): 303–312.

Moscardo, G. and Pearce, P. (2004). "Life Cycle, Tourist Motivation and Transport: Some Consequences for the Tourist Experience." In L. Lumsdon and S.J. Page (Eds.), *Tourism and Transport: Issues and Agenda for the New Millennium* (pp. 29–44). Oxford: Elsevier.

Mygatt, E. (2005). "Bicycle Production Remains Strong Worldwide." Retrieved May 23, 2008 from www.earth-policy.org/Indicators/Bike/2005.htm.

Orbasli, A and Shaw, S. (2004). "Transport and Visitors in Historic Cities." In L. Lumsdon and S.J. Page (Eds.), *Tourism and Transport Issues and Agenda for the New Millennium* (pp. 93–104). Oxford: Elsevier.

Oum, T.H., Park, J-H. and Zhang, A (Eds.) (2000). *Globalisation and Strategic Alliances: The Case of the Airline Industry.* Oxford: Pergamon.

Page, S.J. (1994). *Transport for Tourism.* London: Routledge.

Page, S.J. (1998). "Transport for Recreation and Tourism." In B. Hoyle and R. Knowles (Eds.), *Modern Transport Geography* (2nd edition.) (pp. 217–240). Chichester: Wiley.

Page, S.J. (1999). *Transport and Tourism* (1st edition.). Harlow: Addison Wesley Longman.

Page, S.J. (2004). "Air Travel—Asia." *Travel and Tourism Analyst,* 12:1–66.

Page, S.J. (2005). *Transport and Tourism: Global Perspectives* (2nd edition.). Harlow: Prentice Hall.

Page, S.J. (2007). *Tourism Management: Managing for Change* (2nd edition.). Oxford: Butterworth Heinemann.

Palhares, G.L. (2003). "The Role of Transport in Tourism Development: Nodal Functions and Management Practices." *The International Journal of Tourism Research,* 5(5): 403–407.

Patmore, J.A. (1983). *Recreation and Resources.* Oxford: Blackwell.

Peace, H., Maughan, J., Owen, B. and Raper, D. (2006). "Identifying the Contribution of Different Airport Related Sources to Local Urban Air Quality." *Environmental Modelling & Software,* 21(4): 532–538.

Pearce, D.G. (2001). "Tourism and Urban Land Use Change: Assessing the Impact of Christchurch's Tourist Tramway." *Tourism and Hospitality Research,* 3(2): 132–148.

Peeters, P. and Schouten, F. (2006). "Reducing the Ecological Footprint of Inbound Tourism and Transport to Amsterdam." *Journal of Sustainable Tourism,* 14(2): 157–171.

Peisley, T. (2004). "Cruising in Europe." *Travel & Tourism Analyst,* 2: 1–39.

Price, T. and Probert, D. (1995). "Environmental Impacts of Air Traffic." *Applied Energy,* 50(2): 133–162.

Prideaux, B. (1999). "Tracks to Tourism: Queensland Rail Joins the Tourist Industry." *International Journal of Travel Research,* 1(2): 73–86.

QUATTRO (1998). *Quality Approach in Tendering Urban Public Transport.* Brussels: European Union.

Renewable Fuels Association (2008). *Industry Statistics: Annual World Ethanol Production by Country.* Retrieved May 21, 2008 from www.ethanolrfa.org/industry/statistics/#E.

Schiefelbusch, M., Jain, A., Schafer, T. and Muller, D. (2007). "Transport and Tourism: Roadmap to Integrated Planning Developing and Assessing Integrated Travel Chains." *Journal of Transport Geography,* 15(2): 94–103.

Schipper, Y. (2004). "Environmental Costs in European Aviation." *Transport Policy,* 11(2): 141–154.

Shailes, A., Senior, M.L. and Andrew, B.P. (2001). "Tourists' Travel Behaviour in Response to Congestion: The Case of Car Trips to Cornwall, United Kingdom." *Journal of Transport Geography,* 9(1): 49–60.

Sinclair, M.T. (1998). "Tourism and Economic Development: A Survey." *Journal of Development Studies,* 34(5): 1–51.

Tarrant, M. and Cordell, H.K. (1999). "Environmental Justice and the Spatial Distribution of Outdoor Recreation Sites: An Application of Geographic Information Systems." *Journal of Leisure Research,* 31(1): 18–34.

The World Bank (2008). *Biofuels: The Promise and the Risks, in World Development Report 2008* (pp. 70–71). Retrieved May 21, 2008 from siteresources.worldbank.org/INTWDR2008/Resources/2795087–1192112387976/WDR08_05_Focus_B.pdf.

TPR Associates (1999). *The European Tourist: A Market Profile.* London: TPR Associates.

US 110th Congress (2007). *Energy Independence and Security Act of 2007* (Pub. L. 110–140).

Wall, G. (1971). "Car Owners and Holiday Activities." In P. Lavery (Ed.), *Recreational Geography.* Newton Abbot: David and Charles.

Warnock-Smith, D. and Potter, A. (2005). "An Exploratory Study into Airport Choice Factors for European Low-Cost Airlines." *Journal of Air Transport Management,* 11(6): 388–392.

Weber, M. and Dinwoodie, J. (2000). "Fifth Freedoms and Airline Alliances: The Role of Fifth Freedom Traffic in an Understanding of Airline Alliances." *Journal of Air Transport Management*, 6(1): 51–60.

Weisbrod, R.E. and Lawson, C.T. (2003). "Ferry Systems: Planning for the Revitalization of U.S. Cities." *Journal of Urban Technology*, 10(2): 47–68.

Williams, V., Noland, R. and Toumi, R. (2002). "Reducing the Climate Change Impacts of Aviation by Restricting Cruise Altitudes." *Transportation Research D*, 7: 451–464.

Wood, R. (2000). "Caribbean Cruise Tourism: Globalization at Sea." *Annals of Tourism Research*, 27(2): 345–370.

Wood, R. (2004). "Cruise ships: Deterritorialised Zones." In L. Lumsdon and S. J. Page. (Eds.), *Tourism and Transport: Issues and Agenda for the New Millennium* (pp. 133–146). Oxford: Elsevier.

Wu, B. and Cai, L.A. (2006). "Suburban Leisure in Shanghai." *Annals of Tourism Research*, 33(1): 179–198.

Wuxi City Academy of Urban Planning and Design (2005). *The 11th Five-year Urban-Rural Construction Plan of Wuxi City, Jiangsu Province*.

Wuxi City Department of Statistics (2008). *2007 Statistics Gazette on Economic and Social Development, Wuxi City*. Retrieved May 21, 2008 from 203.207.226.100/image/infopic08/wxtjgb2007.htm.

Zhang, A. and Zhang, Y. (2006). "Rivalry between Strategic Alliances." *International Journal of Industrial Organization*, 24(2): 287–301.

Innovative Approaches for Managing Conservation and Use Challenges in the National Parks: Insights from Canada

Kathy Rettie, A.P. Clevenger and Adam Ford

Introduction

Global visitation to national parks and protected areas continues to experience robust growth, and while this is positive in terms of revenues for park management, managing growth and visitor numbers can add additional burdens to the conservation of protected areas, as Eagles (2007) pointed out, these trends, along with decreasing tax-based budgets are requiring new shifts in protected areas management. Conflict with respect to conservation, visitation and habitation (local residents) is expected to rise, and new forms of governance are emerging to cope with these changes. Healey (2003) noted that traditional organizational structures and functions tend to isolate destination marketing, land-use planning, resource use and conservation from each other *and* from societal values and learning. An informed public is a valuable ally for protected area administrators

with respect to gathering support for policy and conservation initiatives, appreciating the purpose and mandate of the protected area as visitors, and assuming stewardship roles. As Leopold stated, obligations "have no meaning without conscience, and the problem we face is the extension of the social conscience from the people to the land" (1949: 209).

Biodiversity is a people's resource, a local common resource, as much as it might claim to be a global heritage. In many parks and protected areas, as well as the communities within and around them, there is increasing contestation over the use of space and resources for human and other natural species. In the pluralism of perspective and views on the rights and values of wilderness and ecosystems are also questions related to who represents future generations and the voice of the natural environment, which cannot speak for itself in conservation and development decision-making in natural areas. Over the years, public participation in decision-making has become part of the "cultural anchors" of Canadian society, particularly evident in environmental decision-making. Operating within the federal Department of Environment, the Parks Canada Agency (Parks Canada) is responsible for the management of Canada's national parks, with a relatively recently mandated emphasis on ensuring ecological integrity (environmental sustainability). As with the majority of the world's national parks, management decisions are directed by a dual mandate: protection versus use. Creative approaches to addressing both traditional human-use values and ecological integrity-based management policies have become necessary, especially where human use levels are high. Seeking to achieve the balance demanded in its mandate, Parks Canada has expanded its focus to include ecological integrity (resource protection), visitor experience, and public awareness and understanding; each having equal importance. Ultimately, through positive one-on-one experience in nature and better understanding of ecological integrity, it is hoped that a sense of ownership and stewardship for parks' natural resources will emerge. This body of informed and involved citizenry can then provide stronger support for national park conservation-based policy and subsequent management actions.

This chapter presents an innovative and unique initiative to bring conservation and the public together to address an important issue in Canada's oldest national park, Banff National Park (also a UNESCO World Heritage Site). Tourism and conservation are the mainstays of Banff National Park's economy. Successful marketing of the park's natural wonders has resulted in over three million visitors per year, most of whom arrive via the Trans-Canada Highway that runs through the park. To mitigate the significant negative impacts of this traffic on wildlife, beginning in the early 1980s, crossing structures were created to allow animal movement across the highway. The mitigation process is charted below, along with the involvement of the visiting

and resident public through the various phases of this process. By learning more about the success of the crossing structures, Banff National Park's visitors join a community of informed citizens; they are connecting with nature through increased understanding. The hope is that, ultimately, this understanding will lead them to support decisions derived from ecological integrity values.

The chapter commences with a brief literature review, followed by a detailed description of the innovative greening of transportation initiative undertaken in Banff National Park Canada. The final section discusses some implications for conservation and citizen involvement in parks and protected areas.

Conservation Challenges in the National Parks

Public support for resource protection-based management actions is key to meeting conservation challenges in national parks. Clearly, one method of attaining this support is through increased public involvement and understanding. The critical balance between ownership and stewardship rests partly with the role that the public plays in decision-making. Shared knowledge increases the public's awareness of which management actions need to be taken and the consequences associated with those actions. The impacts of tourism (and other) traffic on ecological integrity in national parks and protected areas are one example of a contemporary challenge for conservation managers.

Public/Citizen Involvement in National Parks (or Protected Areas) Decision-Making

Public participation has been a legislated requirement for national parks in Canada since 1968.[1] Typically, public participation has taken the form of consultation, often staged as town hall meetings, and published materials available at public venues (i.e., local libraries). Using the comprehensive study guidelines under the Canadian Environmental Assessment Act as a guide, public consultation is often limited to 14 days.[2] While this form of public participation meets legal requirements, it has proven to be rather unsuccessful at truly engaging the public and is often viewed by the public as "tokenism." Recognizing the need for more positive engagement with Canadians, the Parks Canada Agency has in recent years adopted a more responsive approach to public involvement. One example, discussed later in this chapter, is the stakeholder advisory group formed to review plans for expansion and mitigation of the Trans-Canada Highway through Banff National Park. This more elaborate method is not unlike efforts made in other protected areas. Globally, levels of participation range from exclusion to full empowerment; see, for instance, Borrini-Feyerabend's (1996) compilation of case studies entitled *Collaborative Management of Protected Areas: Tailoring the Approach to the Context* and also in (1997) *Beyond Fences: Seeking Social Sustainability in Conservation.*

Rettie (2001, 2006) describes a model for park management in Cairngorms National Park (Scotland's newest national park) that is built on community involvement. There, the National Park Authority (NPA) board of directors has 25 members: five are directly elected by local people, 10 are appointed by local authorities, and 10 are appointed by the Scottish Ministers. Candidates for the first NPA were rated on their knowledge of the Cairngorms and Cairngorms issues, of sustainable growth, of current initiatives (i.e., partnerships), and of the environment, and also for their communications skills. Members of the NPA are collectively responsible for everything done in the name of the NPA: strategic direction, policies, and proper and effective management of the national park. As the park lands are primarily privately owned, this model was essential to garner local support for the creation of the national park in 2003.

In *Community Involvement in Marine Protected Areas: the Case of Puerto Morelos Reef, Mexico* Rodriquez-Martinez (2007) presents another example where a community-based approach was taken in the creation of a protected area. In this case, the local community works in an advisory capacity, while the federal government holds jurisdiction over the marine protected area and controls the finances and decision-making. The author sees much need and room for stronger community involvement, and suggests, among other things, environmental education and supportive legal mechanisms (Rodriquez-Martinez, 2007). Also with respect to inclusionary processes, Bramwell and Sharman (1999) examine the effectiveness of a working group formed to develop a visitor management plan in Peak District National Park in England. Members of the The Hope Valley collaborative working group, representing relevant stakeholders, achieved consensus on some key issues and agreed on a possible course of action for visitor management. However, the authors suggest that consultation was limited due to a lack of resources. As well as key areas of concern, such as tourism carrying capacity, local costs and benefits were not sufficiently examined due to divisive views and an uneven distribution of power that favored the authorities rather than the national park residents.

Transfer of authority to local communities is, perhaps, the ultimate in public participation. Collins and Fabricius (2007) assess the governance systems under such a regime. Using four case studies in South Africa, they site numerous community-based resource conservation strategies that promote the development of a governance system for local involvement. Much of this revolves around building community capacity and enforceable rules for management. They also recognize numerous shortcomings and propose, amongst other things, that to be successful, community-based management must draw upon broad knowledge and experience and develop formal structures for decision-making. Hiwasaki's (2006) article on sustainability for Japan's protected areas, gives an account of how institutional arrangements and partnerships provide a basis upon which community-based tourism may be facilitated in that context. As described later in this chapter, partnerships can successfully support research and monitoring in national parks and protected areas.

Authors who have focused on unsuccessful efforts towards citizen and community involvement in resource management include Hibbard (2000), who explores why participatory planning failed in Jackson/Teton County, Wyoming. Lane and Corbett (2005) reveal the systematic marginalization of indigenous peoples as a key barrier to community-based environmental management in Australia. In the results of their study at Sherburne National Wildlife Refuge, Payton, Fulton and Anderson (2005) consider collaborative efforts in the context of declining citizen involvement in community affairs and declining level of trust in individual and institutions.

In Canada, the move towards greater public participation in environmental and land-use decision-making in Canada has been perceived as both positive and problematic. Study of local involvement in protected area management by Rettie (2000) outlines some of the challenges faced by residents seeking to incorporate local knowledge into the decision-making process in Canada's oldest national park, Banff National Park. Richardson et al.'s study of environmental public hearings on the Alberta-Pacific bleached Kraft pulp mill in northern Alberta, demonstrated the difficulty of addressing representation issues in public processes and asked "who should be identified as speaking with authority for a community?—for science?—for nature?—for native people?—for the silent majority?—for future generations?" (1993: 18). In this vein, identifying sectors for representation on the Trans-Canada Highway stakeholder advisory board in the innovative conservation and transportation related project shown further below was purposefully comprehensive.

Resident (and Visitor) Education About Conservation, Transportation Greening (Highways, etc.)

Public awareness and understanding of the motives and consequence of ecological integrity-based actions are key to building support for natural resource management decisions. In the BNP project described below, this relates to the installation of costly highway mitigation. In their study of a reef volunteer monitoring program Pattengill-Seemens and Seemens (2003) describe the education and stewardship benefits gained through a partnership of government agencies, scientists, conservation organizations, and private institutions. In their case, citizen science resulted in a successful resources monitoring program. Johnson and Mappin (2005) take a very different view of the efforts made to advance knowledge and understanding of the natural environment, suggesting that environmental education often alludes more to advocacy and the promotion of particular belief and values. This would contradict with the more altruistic outcomes sought by the Parks Canada Agency that were mentioned earlier.

Greening of Transportation in National Parks

Banff National Park is unique in that a transcontinental highway runs through the most important habitat for humans and wildlife; the montane ecosystem. However, other national parks are also exploring ways of reducing the impacts of traffic on nature and on visitor experience. In *the Evaluation of Public Transport Alternatives to the Car in British National Parks*, Eaton and Holding (1996) examine actions taken to encourage the use of public transportation as a solution to the expected growth in car use in England and Wales. Cullinane (1997) also reviewed traffic management measures proposed for British National Parks. He concluded that "without a change in the public's attitude towards the use of cars and a stronger lead taken by government, the success of traffic management . . . remains in doubt" (1997: 267). In their publication for the National Cooperative Highway Research Program, Petraglia and Weisbrod review the relationship between tourism and transportation US national parks. Their focus is on tourism transportation and planning; case studies show that planning activities focus on building solutions to infrastructure, access, and environmental issues that impact on the success of tourism in the region" (2004: 2). Their literature review cites numerous studies completed on transportation needs in national parks linked to visitor demand exceeding infrastructure capacity.

Greening of the Trans-Canada Highway, Banff National Park

In Canada, federally designated protected areas are created through national parks. The mandate of the National Parks Act 1930, guides the dual purpose of these areas, stating that national parks are "dedicated to the people of Canada for their benefit, education and enjoyment . . . and National Parks shall be maintained and made use of so as to leave them unimpaired for the enjoyment of future generations."[3] Designated in 1885, Banff is Canada's first national park. It provides abundant evidence of how the culture of park management has changed over the years. Since the 1970s, the human desire to connect with the wilderness in the national parks has been tempered with strict regulations on economic development, based on the equally strong need to preserve the wilderness for future generations. Banff is also a good example of the current challenges faced by Parks Canada management as they begin to implement the most recent ecological integrity policies.

Located in the Rocky Mountains on the western border of Alberta, Banff National Park is one of seven contiguous sites that make up the Canadian Rocky Mountain

Parks World Heritage Site (Figure 22.1).[4] Banff National Park encompasses 6,641 square kilometers of glaciers, mountains, forest, lakes, and rivers. The park management plan, approved by the Canadian Parliament, provides direction on how the park will meet objectives outlined in national policies and Parks Canada Agency corporate plans.

For management purposes, the park is divided into five zones, defined by varying degrees of conservation and development. Zones I, II and III—which encompass 95% of the park—are designated as "natural environment" and contain very limited infrastructure and no motorized traffic. Zone IV contains areas developed for recreation and accessible by motorized vehicles, including three ski areas and several roadside picnic and lakeside day-use areas. Zone V is for high visitor use and contains necessary infrastructure and services. It covers less than 1% of the park. Within these zones, three ecoregions are identified: alpine (above tree line), subalpine (steep slopes just below tree line), and montane (lower slopes and large valley bottoms).

The montane ecoregion, which covers less than 4% of the park, provides the most effective habitat for wildlife in this mountainous landscape. However, it's also the most hospitable area for people, so humans and wildlife share this environment on a daily basis. Two communities, the Town of Banff (population 6,700) and the Village of Lake Louise (population 938),[5] are located in this montane ecoregion, as is a 73-kilometer section of the Trans-Canada Highway (TCH). Situated between the major population centers of Vancouver and Calgary, the TCH in Banff National Park experiences significant through-traffic in addition to an estimated three million annual visitors destined for Banff itself. Traffic volumes average over 16,000 vehicles per day, peaking at over 35,000 vehicles per day during the summer months. The concentration of facilities and people in the valley has raised concerns that this area's ecological integrity is at risk (Banff Bow Valley Task Force, 1996: 9), resulting in numerous studies, much publicity,

Figure 22.1   Location Map of Banff National Park in Canada.
Source: Courtesy of Parks Canada.

Figure 22.2   Trans-Canada Highway Through Banff National Park.
Source: Courtesy of Parks Canada.

and sporadic political intervention in how the area is managed. There has been much interest in "greening" the national park experience to provide a better environment for all who share it, and to promote biodiversity conservation.

History and Policy

During the 1960s, entrepreneurs proposed a grand development scheme for Lake Louise that included a bid to host a Winter Olympics (Touche, 1990: 100–119), construction of an airstrip, and high-rise hotels. Plans were brought before a public hearing, where national conservation organizations objected vociferously. The well-publicized battle between "tree huggers" and "money-grubbing developers" was a reflection of opposing values in 1960s Canadian society. In the end, it became clear that most Canadians did not approve of this type of development in their national parks, and the proposal was rejected. The federal government recognized the danger of unilaterally entertaining future development proposals, and ski areas were henceforth required to prepare long-range development plans to be approved following public review. Further, in 1968, the National Parks Act was amended to require national park management plans to be reviewed every five years and rewritten every 15 years, with a provision for public consultation.

In the mid-1990s, the entire Canadian national parks system shifted its priority to focus on ecological integrity. This was spurred, in part, by the ministerial appointment of a five-member panel to assess the state of Canada's national parks. The panel concluded that all but one of Canada's national parks was subject to external and human-caused stressors that threatened the long-term health of the ecosystem. Stressors identified included habitat loss, habitat fragmentation, loss of large carnivores, air pollution, and pesticides (Parks Canada Agency, 2000).

Scientists in Banff National Park selected an indicator species, the grizzly bear, to measure changes in ecological integrity. The current management plan is divided into carnivore management units identified by grizzly bear habitat and use. Policy related to visitor activity and experience is built upon a framework for the conservation of grizzly bears. For example, trail and area closures have been put into effect to protect wildlife from human-caused mortality and habituation to humans. These closures have increased dramatically throughout the park over the past ten years. Since one's nature experience in Banff National Park depends heavily upon access to a network of hardened trails, these restrictions have had a direct negative impact on visitor experience. Critics of this biocentric approach to management ask whether the park is for bears or humans (Cooper et al., 2002).

In 2001, the Canada National Parks Act was amended to state that "maintenance or restoration of ecological integrity . . . shall be the first priority . . ." in park management.[6]

The act fixes boundaries of all urban communities within the national parks and strictly limits commercial development within those communities. Parks Canada further solidified its stance through subsequent park management plans prioritizing ecological integrity (EI) initiatives. Funding of over CAN$210 million for such initiatives was announced publicly between the years of 2003 and 2005.[7]

With management culture steeped in ecological integrity, economic and social sustainability were not given equal weight. Developers, residents, park users, academics, and lobbyists challenged the narrow focus on environmental sustainability (Cooper et al., 2002; Green and LeRoy, 2005).

Elements internal and external to the Parks Canada Agency are affecting its recent approach to decision making. In 1998, Canada's national parks became the responsibility of the Parks Canada Agency, a Canadian crown corporation with a more businesslike administrative and financial structure than existed previously. Under Section 20 of the Parks Canada Agency Act 1998, the agency exercises the right to retain a certain percentage of revenues gathered from visitors in the national parks and historic sites. Revenue is generated via park entrance fees, camping fees, and backcountry overnight permits. Large parks, like Banff National Park, are expected to generate sufficient revenue to fully finance reinvestments in infrastructure and long-term capital projects.

The agency is moving to increase support for national parks and historic sites by emphasizing a memorable visitor experience and increasing the relevance of parks and historic sites to all Canadians. This creates interesting challenges, given the rapidly changing Canadian demographic: more than 200 ethnic origins were reported in the 2001 Canadian census, creating within the population widely varying perceptions of cultural heritage. The underlying premise is that having a better understanding of—and a personal connection to—national parks garners public support for environmental priorities.

Parks Canada's latest corporate orientation documents prepare for an important shift, one that recognizes that ecological integrity cannot be achieved without people. There is a new emphasis on human relations and interactions with nature and the involvement of Canadians as partners and advocates for national park policy. Focusing on the visitors' needs and expectations requires a move away from emphasizing the provision of services, facilities and programs in a way that meets only Parks Canada's EI goals and objectives (Parks Canada, 2005). This new approach to national parks has its complications: there are obvious contradictions inherent in trying to reduce human use while at the same time encouraging more visitors to experience the parks firsthand.

The Parks Canada Agency faces another challenge that calls for a shift in approach and policy. The agency is mandated to finish a national system of parks that represents each of Canada's distinct natural regions. The system is 60% complete; hence, numerous new parks must be established. Support from communities in or near proposed new parks is not forthcoming; rather, the opposite is happening, with communities banding together to protest the creation of new and/or expanded national parks. Parks Canada's single-minded focus on ecological integrity at the expense of social and economic sustainability is one of the obvious key reasons. Communities believe a new park nearby will mean more restrictions and fewer opportunities for local empowerment and economic development.

New national parks in northern Canada have broken from tradition: local communities are fully engaged in the management of the parks' natural resources. Traditional land uses are permitted, and tourism is seen as a means to enhance the local economy. Parks Canada may have to look to other countries, Scotland, for example,[8] for advice on how to include all three pillars of sustainability in all new park proposals, not just those in the north. It is unlikely that Banff National Park, however, can expect to see a dramatic shift in governance, in part because the resident social and economic realities have been shaped by Banff's own unique historical circumstances.

Tourism

Banff National Park was established for profit (Bella, 1987), and tourism has been the mainstay of the park's economy since its creation in 1885. As William Van Horne, general manager of the Canadian Pacific Railway, famously put it: "If we can't export the scenery, we'll import the tourists." Conservation was adopted more recently as a crucial tool to protect the wilderness that would keep the tourists coming. Though mining and hunting were common in the park until as recently as the 1930s, today Banff National Park does not support land-use industries in the typical sense of the term. There is no agriculture, forestry, or field sports; the only industry one could consider being directly related to the land is the ski industry, which in this paper is included as an element of the tourism industry.

The significance of Banff to the provincial and national tourism industry is undisputed. In 2004, Banff National Park contributed over CAN$800 million to Alberta's economy (Alberta Economic Development, 2007). On a busy summer's day, Banff's population increases by up to 40,000 people with overnight and day-use visitors. The upper Lake Louise area receives 20,000 visitors a day in summer, thanks to its renowned beauty and status as a Canadian icon.

Nearly 50% of Banff's residents and 60% of Lake Louise's residents are directly employed in sales and services tied to the tourism industry.[9] Banff National Park's well-established system of visitor services includes 50 hotels and 40 bed and breakfasts. There are 150 restaurants, 250 retail shops, and 1,180 businesses. (All businesses are subject to various levels of government approval, based on appropriate use of the limited space within the town boundaries.) In the greater park area, there are 13 campgrounds with 2,500 campsites; three of the campgrounds are open year-round. There are six hostels and nine lodges in outlying areas. While most services are geared toward visitors, the Banff townsite also provides a number of basic services, including service stations, a hospital, a community health unit, medical clinics, grocery stores, a public library, and public schools. Services in the village of Lake Louise, located in the upper and lower reaches of the valley at the base of famous Lake Louise, are limited to one central shopping mall and adjacent service stations. Residents and frequent park visitors will drive the 57 kilometers to Banff to avoid paying the high prices for groceries at the single food market found in Lake Louise.

In 2007, Banff Lake Louise Tourism members voted to increase their budget from CAN$1.5 million to CAN$4.3 million to boost marketing efforts (*Banff Crag and Canyon*, March 27, 2007). Overseas marketing by this group—particularly in the UK and Germany, where the public is known to be environmentally conscious—focuses on environmentally friendly tourist activities and services. Simultaneously, Banff businesses have launched national park awareness programs that extol the virtues of the national park, inform visitors of the local history, and promote the importance of ecological integrity.

Clearly, Parks Canada managers face considerable challenges linked to Banff's long history as a tourism destination, high levels of human use, and nationally important natural features, which must be protected. Managers must address these challenges in a manner that follows directions set out in national policy.

A shining example of a successful intervention to increase ecological integrity in the face of high human use and involve the public in the process comes from an unlikely spot: the 73 kilometers of the TCH running through Banff National Park. Managers, engineers, biologists and researchers have worked together for a dozen or more years to implement measures along the highway to lessen its deadly impact on wildlife. In this case, successfully addressing and communicating the ecological integrity goals for the park and beyond requires a multifaceted approach. Key goals focus on two broad categories: (1) monitoring and research; and (2) installation of new wildlife crossing structures in future phases of highway twinning. Both require sufficient funding and support from strategic sources. An international public–private partnership continues to play an integral role in meeting the key goals.

Mitigation Measures Along the Trans-Canada Highway

The TCH is part of a national transportation system that responds to civil engineering demands that are not always compatible with national park objectives (McGuire and Morrall, 2000). Less than 100 years ago, the first car to reach Banff National Park traveled a dusty, narrow road from Calgary. By the early 1970s, four paved lanes of TCH linked Calgary to the park's east gate. Once inside the park, vehicles were funneled onto an untwinned (two-lane highway) section. As traffic increased, so did collisions.

In the late 1970s, work began on creating a four-lane highway within the park, beginning at the east gate and heading west; this so-called "twinning" project continues today. However, between 2000 and 2002, total collisions per kilometer on the remaining two-lane section were twice as high as along similar highways in other parts of Canada; and fatalities were five times higher (Morrall, 2004).

Roads are known to affect wildlife populations by increasing mortality; creating a barrier to movement; removing habitat from the landscape; and facilitating the spread of invasive species (Forman et al., 2003). With between 16,000 and 35,000 vehicles per day passing through Banff National Park, a vehicle passes a given point on the TCH every three seconds—a formidable barrier indeed for human or animal seeking to cross the road.

The most obvious effect of roads on wildlife is mortality due to wildlife–vehicle collisions (WVCs). WVCs are a concern to human safety, property damage, and insurance costs (Morrall, 2004), as well as to wildlife population conservation. Parks Canada has been able to track the spatial distribution of WVCs for a variety of species over several decades along more than 70 kilometers of highway. Thanks to a large pool of trained staff (e.g., wardens and highway service personnel) regularly traveling the highway within Banff National Park, WVC data are gathered on a daily basis. This information is stored in a central database, and each record may include location, timing of event, physiological information from necropsies, and demographic information of the animal. During the 1980s, the focus of this effort was directed at ungulate—specifically elk—mortality, as well as large carnivores (Woods, 1990). During the 1990s, this effort was expanded to track WVCs for small mammals, birds, and herpitiles, as well as sections of the highway in other jurisdictions adjacent to Banff National Park. Furthermore, Parks Canada staff has a fence-intrusion reporting system, which records observations of large animals on the highway side of the fence. This central database contains information on the location, species, and timing of the event.

In some cases, rates of WVCs may be high enough to cause wildlife populations to decline. For example, the 1990 elk population in the Bow Valley was estimated at 800 individuals and was predicted to fall to fewer than 175 individuals by 2010, largely due to a constant mortality rate from WVCs along the highway (Woods, 1990). Within Banff National Park, estimates from population surveys and WVC reporting from 1981–1996 along the highway blamed roads for 48% of all ungulate mortality and 65% for carnivores (Shury, 1996). If mortality due to WVCs is high enough, genetic mixing of populations bisected by roads can be compromised (Jaeger et al., 2005), negatively affecting the long-term genetic fitness of wildlife populations.

In addition to mortality, roads are also known to create a barrier to animal movement through avoidance behavior. Road avoidance has been documented in songbirds

(Reijnen et al., 1995), small mammals (Ford and Fahrig, 2008), ungulates (Rost and Bailey, 1979), and large carnivores (Mace et al., 1996). Many species need to move daily to forage. They may move intra-annually to find mates or to seek seasonally available resources, and move inter-annually as part of a juvenile dispersal process. Disruption of these movements can have negative consequences for individual survival (e.g., inability to reach needed resources) and population persistence (e.g., loss of genetic connectivity) (Gerlach and Musolf, 2000). Seasonal and once-in-a-lifetime movement patterns may involve several hundred kilometers for the large mammal species within Banff National Park. Yet several studies have shown that animal movement in the Bow Valley is disrupted by the presence of the TCH (Clevenger et al., 2002).

Mitigating the effects of the highway must therefore focus on reducing WVCs to ensure wildlife have enough access to food, shelter, and mates across the landscape and throughout the year to enable populations to persist. Parks Canada responded with both structural and management initiatives to help minimize the effect of the TCH on driver safety and wildlife populations. Through engineering and monitoring, a greening of the highway began to occur (Figure 22.2).

In 1978, Public Works Canada proposed to twin the highway;[10] the first phase was the section from the east gate entrance of the park to the Banff townsite, followed by a series of phases that will eventually stretch to the Alberta/British Columbia border. Before any work was undertaken, the Federal Environmental Assessment and Review Office studied the proposals, convened a panel, and conducted public participation meetings (Federal Environmental Assessment Review Office 1979, 1982). Engagement during this stage of public review consisted, primarily, of public meetings, handouts and open house-style events. After a lively public debate—would a bigger highway be safer for people at the expense of wildlife?—the first twinning project was approved with the goals of improving travel safety for people and

reducing roadkill of deer and elk. Highway fencing and the use of wildlife underpasses were recommended. Public review for the most recent stage of twinning, phase IIIB from Castle junction to the Alberta British Columbia, adopted a more comprehensive and interactive form of consultation. Based somewhat on the Banff Bow Valley Round table model (Bow Valley Task Force, 1996), representatives from thirteen relevant sectors, I including commercial transportation associations, environmental organizations and tourism boards, were invited to join a stakeholder advisory broad (SAB), the board meet regularly to review each stage of development of the draft plan for the continued expansion and mitigation of the highway. Each representative was given equal opportunity to voice the views of his/her constituents. A record of each meeting was distributed for ratification by all members. Scientific data collected through previous years of monitoring informed the board's decisions on the number, locations, and types of crossing structures that would be incorporated into the design. The SAB was instrumental in reviewing the environmental assessment and in recommending avenues for connecting with the broader public audience.

The Science

Banff National Park represents one of the best testing sites in the world for innovative techniques for reducing road impacts on wildlife populations. The 47-kilometer stretch of highway from the park's east gate to Castle Junction now has the most concentrated system of wildlife crossing mitigation measures on the planet. In 1996, Parks Canada contracted Dr. Tony Clevenger to begin long-term research monitoring of the Banff highway mitigation measures. Under his direction, researchers use a variety of methods to monitor animal use of the wildlife crossings; these include raked track-beds and infrared-operated cameras, checking the structures every three days year-round.

Since 1996, when consistent monitoring protocols of the WCS were implemented,

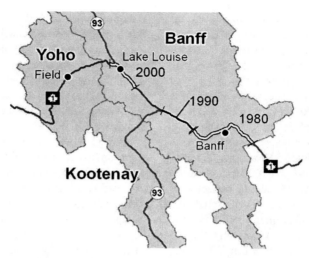

**Figure 22.3   Highway Mitigation Phases and
Locations.
Source: Courtesy of Parks Canada.**

over 120,000 crossing events have been recorded by moose, sheep, deer species, lynx, cougar, fox, coyote, wolf, black bear, and grizzly bear. Of these, over 65,000 have been ungulates (mostly deer and elk), although 88 have been moose and 4,600 bighorn sheep. Carnivore crossing totals to 2006 include 3,914 wolf passes, 1,043 cougar, 1,039 black bear, and 342 grizzly bear.

As each phase of twinning and mitigation was completed, researchers discovered replicable patterns in wildlife-vehicle collision reduction and fence intrusions. Clevenger et al. (2001) showed that fencing reduced WVC by 90% for ungulates and 16% for carnivores over two years. Furthermore, Clevenger et al. (2002) showed that the fence intrusions were 83% lower on highway sections with buried fence aprons compared to those with unburied fence sections. Concurrent measures of population abundance for a variety of species clearly indicate that the reduction in WVC is related to fencing, rather than to decreases in population size. These results indicate that structural improvements to highway fencing were effective at reducing WVC within Banff National Park.

Moreover, use of wildlife crossing structures by some species has increased during

that time at a rate exceeding even the most conservative estimates for changes in population size. For example, grizzly bear use of the WCS has increased exponentially, from six passages in 1997 to 115 passages in 2007 (Figure 22.3). Meanwhile, the population of grizzly bears was relatively consistent over that time (unpublished field data). The following demonstrates the importance of long-term monitoring: had the results of the first three years been considered finite, the structures would have been considered a failure. However, having had sufficient time to adapt, the bears now use the crossings on a regular basis.

With respect to the DNA research, during the 2005 field season, there were a total of 56 approaches to the two wired pilot underpasses by carnivores. Of these, 43 were made by bears (24 by black bears and 19 by grizzly bears). Bears turned around or avoided the underpasses less than 10% of the time (two black bears and only one grizzly bear). The hair-capture success rate was high for both bear species; more than 90% of the time a bear passed through the underpasses, it left hair, and 81% of the hair samples yielded sufficient DNA to allow genetic profiling. The results? A total of nine different

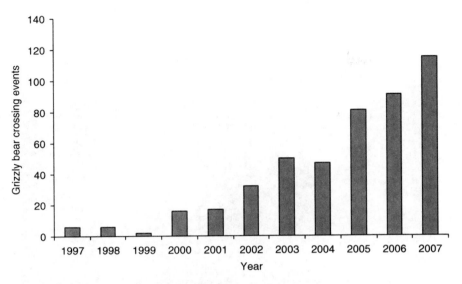

Figure 22.4   Grizzly Bear Use of Wildlife Crossing Systems: 1997–2007.
Source: Courtesy of Parks Canada.

bears used the two underpasses during the three-and-half-month study period in 2005. There were five different grizzly bears (three females, two males) and four black bears (two females, two males).

In 2006, the DNA study was expanded: two overpasses and 19 underpasses were wired for hair collection. That year, 109 individuals were recorded—66 grizzlies and 43 black bears (Figure 22.4). Banff National Park now has the most complete data set on wildlife crossing structures in the world. The next challenge is informing park residents, the public and visitors about the success of the crossing structures—to create a community of informed citizens with a connection to nature through increased understanding and, ultimately, to build support for ecological integrity-based actions (see Photo 22.1).

Public and Financial Support

Consistent evidence of both the performance and effects of these crossings is needed to support their continued and growing implementation by transportation and resource management agencies. There is still skepticism

among some organizations regarding the conservation benefits of wildlife crossings.

Funding for the new structures draws upon taxpayer dollars allotted for the twinning of the highway. This means that for every new WCS erected, fewer kilometers can be twinned. The budget for the Phase I and II construction of 27 kilometers of twinned highway, which took place between 1982 and 1986, allocated 13% for wildlife mitigation. By contrast, the construction of 19.8 kilometers in the 1990s allocated 25% of the budget toward mitigation, and for the remaining 33 kilometers of construction, the mitigation cost has increased to 36% of the budget (see Figure 22.2). Many taxpayers perceive it to be more valuable to have extra miles of four-lane highway without wildlife mitigation measures than to have fewer lanes with wildlife mitigation. Therefore it is essential to educate Canadians about the purpose and effectiveness of the crossing structures and how they help to protect people driving the highway as well as wildlife living adjacent to it.

Public support will come from increased understanding. By elevating the visibility and profile of ecological integrity and highway mitigation, Parks managers are working on

Photo 22.1 Grizzly bear on wildlife overpass.
Source: Parks Canada/WTI.

the cultivation of an expert community. Ideally this community of "citizen experts" will emerge who can readily support and defend decisions to adopt necessary but often expensive mitigation measures to maintain ecological integrity.

Key to garnering support is first to dispel suspicions that the structures did not work and were a waste of taxpayers' dollars. Without focused public education and outreach programs, these types of rumors circulated in the early days among the public and Parks staff. As the most visible structures, the overpasses came in for the most aggressive criticism. Many drivers who frequently used the highway thought the overpasses were constructed for hikers who needed to cross the highway; they clearly had no idea how many and what species of wildlife were crossing overhead as they drove through the structures.

Reaching the public has become a full-time occupation for one member of the research and monitoring team. Key tools for informing the public are the scientific data recorded from the track pads, the undeniable evidence

collected via the still and video cameras, and the results of the DNA analysis.

The ambitious schedule of outreach activities includes museum exhibits, school programs, presentations, newspaper articles, and television coverage. In the summer of 2006, the Wildlife Crossings exhibit at Banff's Whyte Museum of the Canadian Rockies creatively transmitted information to 19,000 visitors and residents. The theme for the exhibit was "art and science." With the assistance of museum photographers, black and white images of animals using the wildlife crossing structures (generated by the motion-sensor cameras) were tastefully presented. A touch screen with video footage of large mammal species was installed for interactive display, and the past, present and future story of the TCH through Banff National Park was told through a series of panels, maps, and photographs. The exhibit won the Banff Heritage Tourism Award for its innovative approach to educating residents and tourists. It was clear from the comments in the guest book that, prior to experiencing the exhibit, most visitors were unaware of the purpose or success of the wildlife crossing structures. They were appreciative of the opportunity to learn more about wildlife species, stressors, and manmade solutions in the Bow Valley.

Starting in April 2007, anyone who purchased an annual park pass at the east gate of Banff National Park received a DVD entitled "Survival on the Move: Why Did the Bear Cross the Road?" The 30-minute video tells the story of the crossing structures: why they are necessary, how many are in place, and how they work. Footage also focuses on the ongoing research and monitoring work: "How do we know animals are using the structures? Why, and how, are we collecting DNA samples?" and so on. The DVD was created for a broad audience. It is informative and entertaining, appealing to children and adults. Many vehicles now have built-in in DVD players, so ideally the DVD is "live" as the visitors travel along the highway through Banff. The goal is to connect visitors with nature, so they can better understand what we are protecting and how.

In 2006 and 2007, information on the crossings project was presented to over 2,300 students in and near the Bow Valley. Classes from kindergarten to Grade 12 were engaged in various learning processes using games, props, and presentations aimed at communicating the role that humans and roads play in their environment and the importance of maintaining habitat connectivity in transportation corridors (Gill, 2007).

Opening in early summer of 2008, the Crossings Exhibit at the Calgary Zoo incorporates scientific data, photographic evidence and interactive displays that tell the story of the success of the crossing structures. Visitation to the Calgary Zoo was 1.2 million people in 2007 (Calgary Zoological Society, 2008), and zoo visitors are an attractive key audience for the project, since they are interested, inquisitive and diverse sections of the local population. The theme for the zoo exhibit is "conservation and science." Once again, the goal is to inform the public of the success of science by illustrating how the wildlife crossing structures are helping to achieve conservation goals. This exhibit should strengthen public support for maintaining ecological integrity, at least on the highway.

Numerous articles on the success of the wildlife crossings have appeared in local and national media, with stories appearing in the *New York Times*, on CBC radio and television, and in many other media outlets across North America. Local media, in particular, serves as a convenient venue for distributing news on the latest developments: for example, the early season arrival of a grizzly bear approaching a snowy wildlife overpass in March 2008. Momentum builds as printed media from various locations continue to cover the "action" on wildlife crossings, for example: *Animal Overpasses, Tunnels Offering Roadkill Remedy* (Walker, 2004), *A Highway runs Through It* (Savage, 2000) and *Rights of Passage* (Crane, 2008). Over 10,000 posters illustrating the wildlife crossings and the species that use them were distributed at information centers, campgrounds and entrance gates in Banff, Yoho and Kootenay National Parks.

Importantly, electronic media are also engaged in the story. For example, the CBC has done several spotlights on the crossings, and in the summer of 2007 CTV featured a television interview with researcher Michael Sawaya discussing the success of the DNA research project. These powerful images, linked to popular discourse, shape the culture of how we use/view national parks and their role in maintaining ecological integrity.

Sustained funding is crucial to the success of any monitoring project. Between 1996 and 2003, the Parks Canada Highways Service Centre provided CAN$2 million for research and monitoring of the wildlife crossings structures on the 54 kilometers of twinned highway through Banff National Park (Phases I, II and IIIA, reaching as far as Castle Junction). This enabled scientists to collect multiyear data that clearly showed that, while it took three years for wildlife to adapt to the crossings, use was increasing exponentially and reaching a magnitude that demonstrated unequivocal success. In 2003, the Highways Service Centre was prepared to proceed with the next phase of highway twinning, but faced with skyrocketing construction costs and a restricted budget, they could contribute limited money to monitoring only.

At this point, in order to determine whether its ecological integrity goals were being met by the wildlife crossing structures, Parks Canada sought funding to advance research on connectivity and species viability which used the noninvasive DNA technology. An international public–private partnership agreement was created that included the Parks Canada Agency, the Western Transportation Institute (WTI) at Montana State University in Bozeman, Montana, and three American foundations: the Woodcock Foundation, the Wilburforce Foundation and the Henry P. Kendall Foundation. WTI is the academic home of Dr. Tony Clevenger, whose work has informed so much of this project. The international partnership contributed initially to the 2004 pilot project, and the Parks Canada Agency secured matching funds through the Ecological Integrity Innovation and Leadership Fund (CAN$80,000 per year for three years) and through the Mountain Park field units and National Office (CAN$60,000 per year for three years).

Since its inception, this public–private international partnership has contributed more than CAN$1 million to support the research and monitoring of wildlife populations and movements affected by the TCH and other highway transportation systems in the mountain national parks. It now operates with an annual combined budget from Parks Canada and the partners of over CAN$500,000. This arrangement benefits all parties: the foundations achieve one of their goals of supporting road ecology research in North America; the WTI's scientists have access to an exceptional field laboratory; and Parks Canada can continue to gather data needed to address a key ecological integrity issue in one of Canada's most complex national park landscapes.

The public–private partnership funding has afforded the research team the luxury of branching out its work to include public education and outreach. The Banff Wildlife Crossings Project is sharing its scientific findings through a diverse mix of venues to inform the general public, students, and transportation professionals. The research has led to seventeen peer-reviewed scientific journal articles. Numerous articles have been published in academic journals with the intent of expanding interest in practical solutions to road ecology issues. Four graduate students completing their theses are studying the effects of the TCH on natural resources in Banff National Park. The cover of *Essentials of Conservation Biology*, a popular college textbook by Richard B. Primack (2006), features the wildlife crossing structures.

In the fall of 2006, with the support of the public–private partnership and the Canadian Institute for Transportation Engineers, a technicians' workshop was held at the Banff Centre. The course was designed for decision-makers and transportation professionals interested in gaining field-based knowledge of—and learning the guiding principles for—planning, designing, evaluating, and maintaining highway mitigation measures aimed at reducing WVCs and increasing habitat connectivity for wildlife and fisheries. The workshop was designed to bring science and solutions together. Workshop topics included: (1) basic concepts of road ecology; (2) impact assessment and planning of environmental mitigation; (3) motorist safety and wildlife mortality reduction; (4) mitigation of barrier effects and landscape fragmentation; (5) engineering considerations for fish passage at culverts and bridges; and (6) engineering considerations of wildlife crossings and fencing.

Importantly, the success of the crossing structures in Banff National Park has directly influenced highway design in other nature-based tourism areas. Three examples in the USA are: Highway 93 in Montana; Interstate 70 in Vail Pass, Colorado; and Interstate 90 in Washington State. These highways all include wildlife mitigation measures modeled on the Banff wildlife crossings.

Insights for Conservation and Stewardship in Park Management

> Natural areas are not made less natural by human presence . . . the world of nature and culture overlap. (Chase, 1986: 317)

National parks evoke important, unique and utilitarian imagery—not least by providing a globally visible display of a nation's environmental ethics and commitment to biodiversity conservation. Aldo Leopold describes an ethic, ecologically, as "a limitation on freedom of action in the struggle of existence," as "possibly a kind of community instinct in-the-making" (1949: 202–203). A land ethic changes our role from "conqueror of the land-community to plain member and citizen of it. It implies respect for his fellow-members and also respect for the community as such" (1949: 204).

Major conservation issues and concerns worldwide are leading to greater focus on ecological integrity but also recognize Leopold's wisdom with respect to stewardship of the land and the biophysical systems that inhabit it. Put into the context of today's discourse, environmental sustainability has to work alongside social and economic sustainability in national parks and other protected areas. A few planning/policy considerations for valuable conservation initiatives, like the greening of highways and visitor/resident roles in parks and protected areas, are summarized in closing.

Managing for Environmental and Social Sustainability

Conservation measures such as greening of transportation have to address human dimensions, with respect to both visitors

(e.g., education and experience) and residents (e.g., education and involvement). As discussed above, successful mechanisms for doing so include partnerships, institutional arrangements, citizen science, knowledge transfer among specialists and outreach programming that connect to visitors and residents in key public areas and through popular media. In Canada the long-standing paradigm for use and protection of national park resources is spelled out in Section 4 of the National Parks Act 2000. This necessarily puts managers in the difficult position of finding the balance between public education, enjoyment and use, and the protection of the natural resources for future generations. Over the more than 100 years since its creation, Banff National Park and its managers have experienced shifts in policies and priorities. Tourism remains the cornerstone of the local economy, while ecological integrity is now legislated as the priority for management decisions. Successfully mitigating negative environmental impacts of human activity (tourism-based and otherwise) is the primary goal. Thanks to the wildlife crossing structures in Banff National Park and informed public education and involvement, human and wildlife safety has been improved.

Evaluating Effectiveness and Monitoring Performance

Evaluating the success of highway mitigation measures from a WVC reduction and landscape connectivity view must address several levels of biological organization. Namely, mitigation effectiveness needs to be weighed against the preservation of genetic, species-population and community-ecosystem diversity. From the top down, mitigation measures have ensured that wide-ranging species are able to interact at scales that invariably overlap with the TCH. Monitoring has shown that all species common to the Bow Valley ecosystem are using the crossing structures, and more recently, we are beginning to get a clearer picture of genetic flow across the highway.

In simple terms, highway mitigation is an engineering effort capable of improving traffic flow and motorist safety by excluding animals from the road surface. When combined with a mandate to allow wildlife movement across the road, as it is in Banff National Park, mitigation can be seen as a management initiative that effectively addresses several scales of biodiversity conservation. Performance monitoring continues at all 24 wildlife crossing structures in the park. These results will provide measurable data on the value of these different crossing structures in maintaining or restoring wildlife populations. The Banff research results guided the design and location of 17 new crossings to be built as part of the latest phase of TCH twinning near Lake Louise; the project described above is a prime example of evolving science being used to inform transportation management planning decisions.

Implications for Parks Policy and Public Participation: The "Citizen Experts"

As a growing literature on protected areas and co-management indicates, projects that attempt to garner wider public support for conservation initiatives and provide arenas that accommodate citizen science and local knowledge will be critical for environmental and social sustainability (Borrini-Feyerabend, 1996, 1997). The importance of greening the national park experience cannot be overestimated. Informed stakeholder involvement and ongoing public consultation will be necessary for future conservation measures in relation to any proposed twinning and highway expansion in the national parks and elsewhere. Visitor and resident awareness of the necessity of pursuing ecological integrity can be increased by communicating the science and the actions taken on success stories like the wildlife crossing structures on the TCH. As the public gains a better understanding of ecological integrity—what it is, how it can be achieved, what role we play—the human

connection to nature takes on new meaning. One has an increased understanding of the natural dynamic that is playing out over, under and beside the highway. There is a growing appreciation for the human interventions made to maintain a balance between education, enjoyment, and protection. It is hoped that this *Handbook* chapter and the experience and expertise of residents and scientists in the Banff National Park transportation example will help to raise international awareness and be valuable to other regions worldwide.

Notes

1 Section 5. (1) Subject to section 8.2, the administration, management and control of the parks shall be under the direction of the Minister. (1.3) The Minister shall review the management plan of a park every five years and shall cause any amendments to the plan to be laid with the plan before each House of Parliament. (1.4) The Minister shall, as appropriate, provide opportunities for public participation at the national, regional and local levels in the development of park's policy, management plans and such other matters as the Minister deems relevant (Government of Canada, 2000).

2 Canadian Environmental Assessment Act (1992 c.37): Section 4 (d) and Section 16 (1) (Canadian Environmental Assessment Agency).

3 Section 4, Canada National Parks Act 2000 c.32.

4 The seven contiguous sites are: Banff, Jasper, Kootenay and Yoho National Parks and Mount Assiniboine, Hamber, and Mount Robson Provincial Parks.

5 Statistics Canada (2007) reports for 2006.

6 Section 8.2, Canada National Parks Act (2000).

7 2005 Report of the Commissioner of Environment and Sustainable Development. www.oagbvg.gc.ca/internet/English/aud_parl_cesd_200509_e_1122.html.

8 The National Parks Act (Scotland) 2000 includes an important fourth aim that is not usually included in national park mandates. While the first three aims mimic those of most other national parks throughout the world—conservation of cultural and natural heritage, sustainable use of natural resources and promoting public understanding and enjoyment of the area—the Scottish fourth aim focuses on maintaining or enhancing the social and economic well-being of the residents within the national park.

9 Percentages are based on Statistics Canada (2007) information for 2006.

10 "Twinning" refers to the expansion of a highway to include two lanes for traffic traveling in opposite directions—aka a four lane highway.

References

Alberta Economic Development (2007). "Frequently Requested Alberta Tourism Statistics." Retrieved from www.albertacanada.com. Accessed on May 2008.

Bella, L. (1987). *Parks for Profit*. Montreal: Harvest House Ltd.

Borrini-Feyerabend, G. (1996). "Collaborative Management in Protected Areas: Tailoring the Approach to the Context." *Issues in Social Policy*. Gland: IUCN.

Borrini-Feyerabend, G. (1997). *Beyond Fences: Seeking Social Sustainability in Conservation*. Gland, Switzerland: IUCN.

Bow Valley Task Force (1996). *Banff Bow Valley: At the Crossroads: Technical Report of the Banff Bow Valley*. Task Force (Robert Page, Suzanne Bailey, J. Douglas Cook, Jeffrey E. Green and J.R. Brent Ritchie) prepared for the Honorable Sheila Copps, Minister of Canadian Heritage, Ottawa, ON.

Bramwell, B. and Sharman, A. (1999). "Collaboration in Local Tourism Policy-making." *Annals of Tourism Research*, 26(2): 392–415.

Calgary Zoological Society (2008). *Annual Report (2007)*. Retrieved from www.calgaryzoo.org. Accessed on May 2008.

Chase, Alston (1986). *Playing God in Yellowstone: The Destruction of America's First National Park*. Boston, MA: The Atlantic Monthly Press.

Clevenger, A.P., Chruszcz, B. and Gunson, K.E. (2001). "Highway Mitigation Fencing Reduces Wildlife-Vehicle Collisions." *Wildlife Society Bulletin*, 29: 646–653.

Clevenger, A.P., Chruszcz, B., Gunson, K. and Wierzchowski, J. (2002). *Roads and Wildlife in the Canadian Rocky Mountain Parks—Movements, Mortality and Mitigation*. Final Report (October 2002). Report prepared for Parks Canada, Banff, AB.

Collins, S. and Fabricius, C. (2007). "Community-Based Natural Resource Management: Governing the Commons." *Water Policy*, 9(2): 83–97.

Cooper, B., Hayes, J. and LeRoy, S. (2002). *Science Fiction or Science Fact? The Grizzly Biology Behind Parks Canada Management Models*. Fraser, BC: The Fraser Institute.

Crane, M. (2008). "Right of Passage." *Whistler Weekly Newsmagazine*, February 7, 2008

Cullinane, S. (1997). "Traffic Management in Britain's National Parks." *Transport Reviews*, 17(3): 267–279.

Eagles, P. (2007). "Global Trends Affecting Tourism in Protected Areas." In R. Bushell and P. Eagles (Eds.), *Tourism in Protected Areas: Benefits Beyond Boundaries* (pp. 27–43). Wallingford: CAB International.

Eaton, B. and Holding, D. (1996). "The Evaluation of Public Transport Alternatives to the Car in British National Parks." *Journal of Transport Geography*, 4(1): 55–65.

Federal Environmental Assessment Review Office (1979). *Banff Highway Project: East Gate to km 13*. Report of the Environmental Assessment Panel. October.

Federal Environmental Assessment Review Office (1982). *Banff Highway Project: km 13 to km 27*. Report of the Environmental Assessment Panel. April.

Flygare, H. (1979). "Mitigated Measures for Reducing Trans-Canada Highway Ungulate Mortality in Banff National Park, East Gate to Sunshine Turn-Off." A Report for Banff National Park.

Ford, A. and Fahrig, L. (2008). "Movement Patterns of Eastern Chipmunks (Tamias striatus) Near Roads." *Journal of Mammalogy*, 89(4): 895–903.

Forman, R.T.T., Sperling, D., Bissonette, J.A., Clevenger, A.P., Cutshall, C.D., Dale, V.H., Fahrig, L., France, R., Goldman, C.R., Heanue, K., Jones, J.A., Swanson, F.J., Turrentine, T. and Winter, T.C. (2003). *Road Ecology: Science and Solutions*. Washington, DC: Island Press.

Gerlach, G. and Musolf, K. (2000). "Fragmentation of Landscape as a Cause for Genetic Subdivision in Bank Voles." *Conservation Biology*, 14(4): 1066–1074.

Gill, C. (2007). *Banff Wildlife Crossings Project—Classroom Presentations: How Effective Are They?* A report prepared for the Parks Canada Agency.

Government of Canada (2000). *The Canada National Parks Act* (R.S., c, N-13, s.1) Ottawa: Queens Printer.

Green, K. and LeRoy, S. (2005). *Can Markets Save Canada's National Parks?* Fraser, BC: The Fraser Institute.

Harrison, G., Hooper, R. and Jacobson, P. (1980). *Trans-Canada Highway, Wildlife Mitigation Measures, Banff National Park (East Gate to Banff Traffic Circle).* A Report Prepared for Banff National Park.

Healey, P. (2003). "Collaborative Planning in Perspective." *Planning Theory,* 2(2): 101–123.

Hibbard, M. (2000). "Saving Land but Losing Ground." *Journal of Planning Education and Research,* 20(2): 187–195.

Hiwasaki, L. (2006). "Community-Based Tourism: A Pathway to Sustainability for Japan's Protected Areas." *Society and Natural Resources,* 19(8): 675–692.

Johnson, E.A. and Mappin, M. (2005). *Environmental Education and Advocacy: Changing Perspectives of Ecology and Education.* Cambridge, MA: Cambridge University Press.

Jaeger, J.A., Bowman, G.J., Brennan, J., Fahrig, L., Bert, D., Bouchard, J., Charbonneau, N., Frank, K., Gruber, B. and von Toschanowitz, K.T. (2005). "Predicting When Animal Populations Are At Risk From Roads: An Interactive Model Of Road Avoidance Behavior." *Ecological Modeling,* 185: 329–348.

Lane, K. and Corbett, T. (2005). "The Tyranny of Localism: Indigenous Participation in Community-Based Environmental Management." *Journal of Environmental Policy and Planning,* 7(2): 141–159.

Leopold, A. (1949). *A Sand County Almanac and Sketches Here and There.* New York: Oxford University Press.

Mace, R. Waller, J. Manley, T., Lyon, J. and Zuuring, H. (1996). "Relationships Among Grizzly Bears, Roads and Habitat in the Swan Mountains Montana." *The Journal of Applied Ecology,* 33(6): 1395–1404.

McGuire, T. and Morrall, J. (2000). "Strategic Highway Improvements to Minimize Environmental Impacts Within the Canadian Rocky Mountain National Parks." *Canadian Journal of Civil Engineering,* 27: 523–532.

Morrall, J. (2004). *Project Needs/Options Analysis Castle Junction to the Alberta/British Columbia Border Trans Canada Highway, Banff National Park.* A report prepared for Parks Canada.

Parks Canada Agency (2000). "Unimpaired for future generations? Protecting Ecological Integrity with Canada's National Parks Vol. 1." *Report of the Panel on the Ecological Integrity of Canada's National Parks.* Ottawa: Minister of Public Works and Government Services.

Parks Canada Agency (2005). *National Performance and Evaluation Framework for Engaging Canadians: External Communications at Parks Canada.* Unpublished. Produced by the Performance, Audit and Review Group, February. Government of Canada.

Pattengill-Seemens, C. and Seemens, B. (2003). "Conservation and Management Applications of The Reef Volunteer Fish Monitoring Program." *Environmental Monitoring and Assessment,* 81(1–3): 43–50.

Payton, M., Fulton, D. and Anderson, D. (2005). "Influence of Place Attachment and Trust on Civic Action: A Study at Sherburne National Wildlife Refuge." *Society and Natural Resources,* 18(6): 511–528.

Petraglia, L. and Weisbrod, G. (2004). *Integrating Tourism and Recreation Travel with Transportation Planning and Project Delivery.* National Cooperative Highway Research Program, American Association of State Highway and Transportation Officials, National Research Council (US). Transportation Research Board.

Primack, R. (2006). *Essentials of Conservation Biology* (4th edition). Sunderland, MA: Sinauer Associates.

Reijnen, R., Foppen, R., Ter Braak, C. and Thissen, J. (1995). "The Effects of Car Traffic on Breeding Bird Populations in Woodland III. Reduction of Density in Relation to the Proximity of Main Roads." *The Journal of Applied Ecology,* 32(1): 187–202.

Rettie, K. (2000). "Involvement of Resident Peoples in Protected Area Management: A Case Study of Banff National Park." University of Calgary, thesis.

Rettie, K. (2001). *The Report on the Proposal for a National Park in the Cairngorms.* Report 4, an independent assessment of the consultation on the proposed National Park for the Cairngorms. Aberdeen: Scottish Natural Heritage.

Rettie, K. (2006). "At Home in National Parks: A Study of Power, Knowledge and Discourse in Banff National Park and Cairngorms National Park." St. Andrews University, thesis.

Richardson, M., Sherman, J. and Gismondi, M. (1993). *Winning Back the Words: Confronting Experts in an Environmental Public Hearing.* Toronto: Garamond Press.

Rodriquez-Martinez, R.E. (2007). "Community Involvement in Marine Protected Areas: The Case of Puerto Morelos Reef, Mexico." *Journal of Environmental Management.* In press.

Rost, G. and Bailey, J. (1979). "Distribution of Mule Deer and Elk in Relation to Roads." *The Journal of Wildlife Management,* 43(3): 634–641.

Savage, C. (2000). "A Highway Runs Through It." *Canadian Geographic,* 120(5): 34–43.

Shury, T.K. (1996). *A Summary of Wildlife Mortality in Banff National Park, 1981–1995:* *Final Report.* Submitted to the Warden Service of Banff National Park, March 1.

Statistics Canada (2007). Government of Canada www.statcan.gc.ca

Touche, R. (1990). *Brown Cows, Sacred Cows: A True Story of Lake Louise.* Calgary: Gorman Publishers.

Walker, C. (2004). "Animal Overpasses, Tunnels Offering Roadkill Remedy." Retrieved from news.nationalgeographic.com. Accessed on May 2008.

Woods, J. (1990). *Effectiveness of Fences and Underpasses on the Trans-Canada Highway and Their Impact on Ungulate Populations Project.* A report prepared for Parks Canada.

23

Planning for Tourism at Local and Regional Levels: Principles, Practices, and Possibilities

Brian King and Michael Pearlman

Introduction

As has been frequently observed, tourism has grown dramatically during the past 60 years (Theobald, 2004). Over the period from 1945 to 1980 growth was concentrated in the developed world, though the developing countries have attracted increasing visitor numbers since the early 1980s, albeit still receiving a small proportion of overall international arrivals. The rapid increase in tourism arrivals has had major implications for planning with an expansion of tourism related business activity and the pursuit by governments of the employment and other economic benefits of tourism, increasingly at local and regional levels.

This chapter examines tourism planning provision as it has evolved in response to the rapid growth of visitation. It considers how distinct approaches have been developed for the planning of tourism leading to a more integrated approach, influenced by the principles of sustainable development. The emerging planning structures and frameworks are explained. It is noted that newer planning models have espoused a more active approach to the management of tourism, though achieving the flexibility that this implies is particularly difficult to implement at the local and regional levels, where resource limitations are most evident. Local and regional level tourism planning has stronger roots in the developed world, but globalization and the rapid economic growth of Asia and of China and India, in particular, has demanded the application of stronger institutional frameworks to deal with the associated issues and challenges. Many of the various development issues impact disproportionately on the developing countries since they involve the empowerment and engagement of disadvantaged sections of society. These are discussed in more detail later in the chapter.

Tourism planning is complex and many of the ongoing challenges are not new. According to Hall (1995), tourism planning is varied in terms of form (e.g., infrastructure and marketing), structures (government and industry), scale (national, regional and local) and timing (cycles and implementation). While there is no universally accepted definition of tourism planning, some common elements have been identified (Getz, 1987; Murphy, 1985). The literature suggests that tourism planning is a strategic decision-making process about the allocation of resources, which aims to derive optimum economic, environmental and sociocultural outcomes for destinations and their stakeholders. It is conceived as being dependent on the conduct of research, the monitoring of changing environments, the evaluation of alternative strategies and the achievement of commitment amongst stakeholders. Planning structures and processes are responses to a range of very fundamental questions about development, including: What type of tourism is appropriate? What scale of development should occur? How fast should tourism be allowed to grow? Where should development take place?

Traditionally, tourism planning in both the developed and developing countries focused on marketing and infrastructure development through interventions by government and international agencies. These interventions sought to exercise a considerable degree of control over tourism development. The results were mixed. Gradually, involvement by national governments has diminished, particularly in the developed countries where the planning framework is well established. Within this planning hierarchy, national governments increasingly set the broad policy agenda for tourism development, often through a long-term vision or strategy document rather than through a detailed "master plan." Such strategic documents provide guidance for more detailed regional and local plans, which reflect specific locational issues and typically have shorter time horizons (one to five years). They involve the identification of target markets and associated marketing strategies, development opportunities and constraints, visitor management issues and strategies, and propose organizational frameworks to undertake the implementation phase. Gunn (1988) has emphasized the need

for continuity of approach towards planning over time with integration at all levels and ongoing revisions being made in response to changing conditions.

A further complication of the planning hierarchy is that definitions of "local" and "regional" are not universally consistent. For example, Tosun and Jenkins (1998) suggest that regions are sub-national areas that possess a degree of jurisdictional status (i.e., administrative, economic, political) and have a common sense of purpose (e.g. significant tourism activity). Whereas Smith (1989) believes that a region or locality is a simple identification mechanism which allows comparison with equivalent entities elsewhere. Murphy and Dore (2000) have pointed out that this ambiguity extends to existing practice whereby many government agencies allocate funding for "regional tourism" without clearly defining regional boundaries for eligibility purposes. To complicate matters further, international tourism organizations such as the Pacific Asia Travel Association (PATA) attempt to serve the needs of the tourism industry in a regional area (in this case the Asia-Pacific region) but are in effect engaged in tourism planning at the supranational level (i.e., between two or more countries). Similarly, in the case of the Greater Mekong Sub-Region, several adjacent sovereign states are actively engaged in tourism planning. These examples indicate that there is no consensus about an established framework of regional tourism planning for comparative purposes. Murphy and Dore's (2000) regional tourism research framework incorporates multiple dimensions, including demand and supply factors. It is a useful framework as it is not too prescriptive and acknowledges that the various dimensions may change over time as different priorities evolve (e.g. risk management).

The Evolution of Tourism Planning

The early expansion of mass international tourism during the 1960s was based on standardized package tours and occurred in a laissez-faire manner, exemplified by the ribbon development and sprawl along Spain's Mediterranean coastline. This expansion was planned to the extent that it was a deliberate move on the part of the Franco government to attract overseas investment and transform the tourism and services sector. However the ensuing development was not controlled in a systematic manner and has been widely viewed as exemplifying the ugly face of unplanned tourism. It also highlights the negative consequences of the type of rapid tourism expansion which often occurs when weak local government authorities are unable to exercise adequate controls over development.

The evolution of tourism planning is closely associated with attempts to minimize the adverse effects of tourism development while maximizing the potential benefits. This has been accompanied by the creation of various planning models. In his seminal paper, Getz conducted an extensive review of tourism planning models, classifying them into theoretical, planning and management process, and forecasting models. He identified over 150 models in the literature "pertaining explicitly to tourism" (1986: 24). This profusion of models was illustrative of the complex and interdisciplinary nature of tourism. In a subsequent paper he noted that tourism models can be applied in a variety of settings and scales – site, locality, region, national, or international and proposed some alternative approaches for tourism planning (Getz, 1987). These were subsequently extended and integrated by Hall (1995). Some of these approaches are summarized below.

Economic Development and Planning

During the 1960s and 1970s, tourism in the developed countries was regarded as primarily a private sector domain. Though governments were often interested in the balance of payments advantages of attracting high spending overseas visitors, there was little government support for the specific regulation of tourism activity at the destination. Many of the fundamentals of tourism planning were however already in place, e.g. controlling and regulating recreational access to rural areas. Such controls were often exercised by local planning authorities (Heeley, 1981).

Tourism is well established as a contributor to national and regional economic development. Economic development models have been embedded within many of the most established approaches to tourism master planning (Lawson and Baud-Bovy, 1977). Market-oriented planning models (e.g., Heath and Wall, 1992; Mill and Morrison, 1985) provide an alternative approach, which attempts to match existing and potential tourism resources and products to existing and potential target markets, with the aim of increasing the economic benefits of tourism. In general, these models tend to focus on macro-destination planning issues, though consideration of resources, products, and markets can be related to micro (local and regional) destinations within a broader strategic macro framework.

The economic and market oriented models have been the dominant influence on government tourism planning in many countries at national, regional, and local levels. Governments have increasingly pursued the income, employment, foreign exchange earnings, and regional development benefits of tourism. However, it is clear that the prevailing regional and local planning infrastructures have been stronger in the developed countries than in the developing countries. This is closely related to resourcing. During the 1980s, for example, the European Union (then EEC) funded numerous studies to develop tourism strategies for the economic rejuvenation of regional areas suffering hardships due to the decline of traditional industries. Relative to the developed countries of Europe and elsewhere, the developing countries have been more reliant on receiving ongoing assistance from international agencies such as the United Nations World Tourism Organization (UNWTO).

Such assistance has involved the development of national tourism master plans and, in more recent times, regional tourism plans.

Physical/Spatial Planning

During the 1980s, environmental issues were increasingly prominent within the language and rhetoric of tourism planning. The initial impetus for this focus was Butler's (1980) classic work on the Tourist Area Life Cycle (TALC) or "resort cycle," which described the growth of destinations confronting capacity constraints. While TALC incorporates more than environmental issues, most interpretations focus on the environmental problems and associated management implications of visitor growth. There have been many critics of the model, notably Prideaux (2000) who has provided a useful review. However despite its weaknesses, TALC remains very influential.

A major issue for tourism planning during the 1980s was the emerging debate on sustainability. The tourism literature quickly responded to the various deliberations into sustainability by the Brundtland Commission. The Commission had far-reaching consequences for many industry sectors but had particular impact in the case of tourism because of the symbiotic relationship between tourism and the physical environment. Importantly the Commission proposed a conceptualization that drew upon the experiences of both the developed and the developing world (World Commission on Environment and Development, 1987). While references to the natural environment had been evident in Gunn's (1979) early work and were not new, there was growing environmental consciousness in the global and transnational contexts during the 1980s, including in the political realm.

Physical/spatial models of tourism planning have evolved from Butler's TALC Model and are based on an assumption that tourism has an ecological base. In recognition of this relationship, it has been widely accepted that

planning and development should incorporate spatial patterns, capacity constraints, and thresholds (Getz, 1983; Gunn, 1988; Inskeep, 1991). This philosophy is also apparent in visitor management models such as Clarke and Stankey's Recreation Opportunity Spectrum (ROS) (1979) and Stankey et al.'s (1985) Limits of Acceptable Change (LAC). These models adopt a micro-level approach to destination planning and management issues.

Some of these models have been applied by a range of National Park agencies, as the basis for zoning and visitor management strategies aimed at protecting the natural environment from overuse and degradation (Fagence, 1990). These models are also implicit in various decisions about land use planning undertaken in the coastal and urban planning contexts (Dredge, 1999). In practice political interests can, however, usurp the power to make such decisions and the original intentions of these models (Craik, 1991). This has occurred in the case of various corrupt regimes in the developing world. The former Marcos regime in the Philippines is a notable example.

Community Planning

Within the various planning approaches which emerged during the 1980s, tourism concepts were still largely confined to the experience of the developed world. An example is Murphy's (1985) *Tourism: A Community Approach*. This was an important breakthrough in the tourism literature, but overwhelmingly described applications in the developed world context. Murphy's community model of tourism planning placed a stronger emphasis on the social acceptability of tourism development on the basis that tourism takes place within community settings and impacts upon residents. Various authors in this field have subsequently highlighted the need to incorporate community participation in the planning process (Garrod, 2003; Haywood, 1988; Simmons, 1994).

Haywood's (1988) community planning paradigm identifies various constituencies as being involved in the process. Reid et al.'s (2004) community tourism development planning model gives particular emphasis to the role of effective leadership. The growing acceptance of the crucial importance of communities in tourism planning is consistent with the trend within the developed countries towards destination planning at the micro level. However it should be acknowledged that the circumstances encountered in developing countries are markedly different, notably in the case of the income and cultural disparities between wealthy tourists and poorer residents.

The earlier models of community-based tourism planning were developed in North America, as is exemplified by Murphy's work in British Columbia, Canada and Ritchie's (1993) community-based visioning process in Calgary (also in Canada). These models have subsequently been extended to other (mainly developed country) settings, and in some cases have embraced the role of indigenous communities. One example is Horn and Simmons's (2002) work with the Maori in New Zealand. In view of the very different parameters encountered in developing countries, the various attempts to integrate communities into the tourism planning process have met with mixed success. King et al. (2000) drew upon the examples from the Pacific islands of Vanuatu and Niue to demonstrate how host communities can participate actively in the tourism planning process, though the compact dimensions of these microstates provide a more manageable scale and better prospects for engagement to take place. In these examples and others, achieving continuity is often dependent on government commitment and on the receipt of ongoing guidance from external professional advisors.

The community approach to tourism planning has emphasized the human dimension. Over time the advocates of this approach could not ignore the experience of the developing countries. Key elements of this experience were the critical role of indigenous communities, and interactions between the cultures of the major tourist generating countries and the recipients of mass tourism. In the case of Murphy's approach, it is only quite recently that other authors have tested the underlying principles in the context of developing countries. The increasing consideration of so-called "Pro-Poor Tourism" during the past decade is a notable example of this. The "Pro-Poor Tourism" concept seeks to promote the benefits of tourism amongst the most financially disadvantaged groups in the community and has forced writers to contemplate the changing nature of tourism communities and the relationship between visitors and hosts (Ashley et al., 2000).

Integrated Tourism Planning

US planner and researcher Clare Gunn (1979) was one of the first authors to advocate a comprehensive and integrated approach to tourism planning, incorporating the geographic, land use and systems perspectives. Though placing particular emphasis on these issues, Gunn also attempted to consider the full range of tourism industry components, including both the supply and demand aspects. Gunn's work was paralleled in Europe by the contributions of Lawson and Baud-Bovy (1977). These contributions to the literature introduced some important conceptual advances, but did not give full consideration to the tourism development dilemmas encountered in developing countries. These concerns were considered in the wider tourism development literature, notably by Smith (1977), De Kadt (1979), and others. Tosun and Jenkins (1998) have provided a useful summary of the various contributions. The pursuit of globally applicable solutions only gathered momentum during the 1980s.

A large proportion of tourism activity occurs either in urban areas or else in regional areas located away from major population centers.

Urban and regional planners have been confronting tourism related issues over many years, though often their own professional training has been in the generic field of planning as opposed to tourism specific applications. In city settings urban planners have increasingly been confronted by tourism related issues, such as the development of conference and convention facilities, accommodation and visitor attractions. Tourism is playing a major part in the development of dynamic cities such as Dubai, Shanghai, and Hong Kong. Tourism is also integral to urban planning in the regeneration of deindustrialized cities often through the mechanism of integrated waterfront development.

While some of the advocates of the earlier planning models did acknowledge the merit of alternative theoretical approaches, few models prior to the 1990s could be considered to be either truly integrated, or as inclusive of the many variables associated with tourism activities and tourism planning. Lawson and Baud-Bovy (1977) alluded to this complexity 30 years ago when they formulated their Products Analysis Sequence for Outdoor Leisure Planning model (PASOLP), one of the earliest models to recognize the need for an integrated approach. PASOLP considered the full range of economic, social, and environmental impacts of tourism as well as the challenges of matching market demands with the provision of tourism resources. The tourism systems model proposed by Mathieson and Wall (1982) also recognized the need for an integrated approach to tourism planning and management (see also the more recent work by Wall and Mathieson, 2006). The model incorporated three integrated components—a dynamic (demand/tourist) element, a static (supply/destination) element and a consequential (impacts) element. Hall (2000) has however noted that such models tend to be prescriptive and to assert how planning should occur, rather than explaining what occurs over the course of the planning and decision-making process. Pearlman (1999) highlighted the need for research to be undertaken on destination case studies where integrated tourism planning

has been attempted, including the evaluation of planning processes and outcomes.

The principles of integrated tourism planning have been given impetus by the work of the UNWTO (Inskeep, 1991). As the resourcing of UNWTO has improved and the organization has gained greater political clout, it has been in a better position to advocate for improved tourism planning, particularly in the developing countries. Such advocacy has involved the application of universal planning principles to particular settings and an acknowledgment that the practices undertaken in diverse tourism settings may be instructive for the planning dilemmas being confronted in other parts of the world. Applying the principles of "community-based tourism" principles to Pro-Poor Tourism and the alleviation of poverty is an interesting example of an attempt to connect the experiences of the developed and developing worlds (Meyer, 2003).

Convergence of Tourism Planning

Debate about whether certain forms of tourism may be accurately described as "sustainable" or whether tourism is fundamentally antipathetic to sustainability, have gradually entered the tourism planning literature and have progressively manifested themselves as the focus of emerging tourism planning models (Mowforth and Munt, 1998). Hall (1995) has argued that integrated tourism planning, which incorporates the economic, environmental/physical, and community components, is a necessary though not sufficient condition for sustainable tourism development. The latter is described as providing host communities with "lasting and secure livelihoods with minimum depletion of resources, degradation of the environment, cultural disruption and social instability" (Hall et al., 1997: 19).

In the early to mid-1990s, a paradigm shift became evident in the various approaches to tourism planning, with increasing attention being given to what has become known as the "triple-bottom line." Models continue to draw upon the established market and economic approaches, but are integrating elements from other traditions outside the tourism field, indicative of a move towards convergence. Examples of this trend include the economic/market tradition of Ritchie and Crouch's (2000) Model of Destination Competitiveness and Sustainability, the physical/spatial tradition of Dowling's (1993) Environmentally-Based Model for Regional Tourism Development, and the community tradition of Reid et al's. (2004) Community Tourism Product Development Planning Process. The trend towards triple-bottom line considerations has also had practical implications. The terms of reference drawn up by funding agencies in support of major tourism projects, strategies and plans have increasingly demanded that attention is given to such concerns.

Convergence of tourism planning has also occurred between practices occurring in different political and economic systems. During the final two decades of the 20th century, governments placed an increasing emphasis on the principles and practice of eliminating barriers to tourism flows, though some of the momentum was lost in the aftermath of the 9/11 terrorist attacks and the safety threats which followed. The lowering of barriers exemplified the prevailing fashion for "liberating" market forces, with fewer, though more targeted controls in place. During the 1970s and early 1980s the experience of tourism in the communist, centrally planned countries appeared to be fundamentally different from what was occurring in the capitalist world. Though a small number of communist bastions remain at the time of writing (North Korea and Cuba, for example, and China and Vietnam more nominally), the culture of tourism has infiltrated all corners of the globe. Following the Velvet Revolution in Eastern Europe, the experience of tourism planning in the formerly communist countries has proven to be remarkably similar to the practice of tourism planning in

capitalist countries. This has facilitated the development of universal principles applicable at both local and regional levels.

Convergence has also affected the experience of tourism in the developed and developing countries. Prior to the 1980s, it was possible to make a clear distinction between the tourism experience of the developed and the developing countries. Tourists were overwhelmingly from developed countries and were traveling to or within other developed countries, with smaller numbers traveling to the developing world. The travel propensities of residents in the developing countries were low with minimal domestic tourism occurring in these settings. Striking contrasts do remain between the rich OECD countries and the world's least developed nations. While there are still many examples of extreme poverty throughout the world, particularly in Africa, economic growth has permeated many countries (including the developing countries) and this has enabled greater participation in international tourism across the globe. As a result, similar issues in tourism planning arise across many countries.

The growing incomes of the Asian nations generally and the most populous countries of China and India, in particular have created an audience of tens of millions exhibiting the type of consumption patterns more commonly found in the developed world. In these contexts, tourism planning concepts will need to incorporate lessons learnt from past experience to accommodate the implications of mass domestic tourist movements in China and India. For example, planners in China have struggled to deal with the huge number of visitors notably when the government granted worker entitlements to several extended holidays (King et al., 2005). More significantly, the prospect of China emerging as the world's number one tourist destination by 2020 and as the fourth largest international tourism generating country, will require a consistent planning approach across many countries to manage the massive tourism flows which are likely to occur.

Planning Structures and Frameworks

Running parallel to the evolution of approaches to tourism planning, are a range of formal planning structures and frameworks. As tourism has evolved, national governments have increasingly incorporated tourism considerations into the statutory planning process. Based on established legislation, most governments do exercise responsibilities for a range of tourism-related issues. Some examples include visa and other entry formalities, transport regulations, legislation governing national parks, the licensing of tourism-related businesses, workforce laws and foreign investment and ownership regulations. Most of these laws are generic but others are specific to tourism. In both developed and developing countries, most of these laws and regulations are the responsibility of national governments, though in the developed countries some powers are commonly devolved to the local or regional level. In a number of countries, powers have been increasingly vested in local government as a means of empowering local communities about decisions which affect them. An example is the granting of planning and building permits for new tourism developments, though such powers are periodically overridden by authorities higher up in the hierarchy (Craik, 1991). In developing countries there is comparatively less opportunity for local government to exercise control, though there has been a gradual devolution of power where economic development has spread to regional areas.

In addition to statutory planning, many developing countries have embraced indicative planning as prescribed by the WTO (now UNWTO) (Inskeep, 1994) in their terms of reference for tourism master plans. Indicative planning involves an "indication" of a preferred direction, rather than prescription via statute, as is the case with statutory planning. Both aspects are critical accompaniments to tourism development. According to King et al. (2000), the established approach to master planning has been typified by an older style rigid top-down approach to planning with excessive reliance on overseas consultants, emphasis on land use planning, over-optimistic market forecasts, lack of consultation with local communities and an inadequate commitment to implementation. As a result of considering these and similar weaknesses, the UNWTO progressively revised its approach. This resulted in a new model incorporating stronger community inputs and making greater use of local counterparts to work with overseas consultants. The scrutinizing of final outputs by academics can make a contribution to greater accountability over the process. Reflective of the evolution of tourism planning, tourism plans have also placed increasing emphasis on environmental and sociocultural concerns, with local counterparts playing a direct role in the implementation of the final plans. King et al. (2000) have cited the Niue and Vanuatu examples as representative of this new approach to planning. Similar models have been adopted by United Nations ESCAP in planning tourism for small island states more generally (ESCAP, 1996).

Emerging Models

The traditional tourism planning models have tended to be prescriptive and technical in their focus. More recently, descriptive tourism planning models, attaching greater importance to planning process issues, have gained wider acceptance. These models have emerged as a result of engagement with a wide range of stakeholders. A number of authors have applied stakeholder theory as a tourism planning and management tool. Jamal and Getz (1995) were early exponents of collaboration in community-based tourism planning and identified six propositions as a prospective guide for tourism destination managers and planners. Applying this work to Britain's Peak District National Park, Bramwell and Sharman (1999) proposed a framework to assess whether local collaboration is inclusive, involves collective learning, and builds consensus. On the basis of their experience with past planning failures, governments in many developed countries have recognized the importance of collaboration and partnerships between stakeholders. This philosophy has influenced more recent tourism planning within Spain as the authorities have attempted to combat the problems encountered in the most overdeveloped destination regions, such as Mallorca. This is addressing the repercussions of the unplanned approach which characterized 1960s and 1970s Spain and was referred to previously.

A number of authors have documented instances of conflict between tourism stakeholders, particularly where entrenched local power relations are threatened by the arrival of a new order (Bramwell and Lane, 2000; Hall, 2000; Hall and Jenkins, 1995; Murphy and Murphy 2004; Reed, 1999). The nature of power relations often plays a part in determining whether the views of particular stakeholder groups will be incorporated into the tourism planning and management process or whether the political process will be monopolized by a dominant group or individual. Unfortunately, there are many examples in the literature of failed tourism planning processes in both developed and developing countries arising from conflicts between stakeholder groups (Boyd and Singh, 2003; Ioannides, 1995).

The emerging focus on stakeholder engagement and process issues has prompted a shift of emphasis in the literature away from "tourism planning" models to "tourism management" models. This transformation has arisen in part because the term "planning" can have negative connotations and has sometimes been associated with excessive bureaucracy and inaction. As was alluded to by Gunn over 25 years ago, the term "management" has the advantage of being associated with positive terms such as "action" and "problem solving." Murphy and Murphy (2004) have emphasized that strategic planning still has a role to play, though recent tourism planning models attribute greater prominence to decentralized decision-making and to the role of stakeholders.

Such approaches are preferred because they consider multiple scenarios, can build a more widely shared vision and can bring about tangible commitments to collaborative effort. "Soft" management techniques have become more prominent, drawing upon the applications of Peter Senge and others within the wider business context to "systems thinking" and "learning organizations" (Senge et al., 1994). These concepts and philosophies have recently been applied to problem solving for tourism and to managing change at the micro destination level.

Australia has recently produced some interesting examples of emerging models and processes and their application, stimulated in part by the establishment of the Sustainable Tourism Co-operative Research Centre (STCRC), a collaboration between universities, government and industry. Most of the preliminary development has been undertaken by academics with subsequent applications in regional destination settings. Examples include the Tourism Futures Simulator (Walker et al., 1999), which has been applied in Far North Queensland and in Western Australia, the Tourism Optimization Management Model (McArthur, 2000) which has been applied on Kangaroo Island, South Australia, and the Destination Strategic Management and Planning Model, which has been applied as a component of the Gold Coast Visioning Project (Faulkner, 2002). The practical application of such integrated planning and management models remains in its infancy, partly because the financial and human resources needed for effective implementation are often lacking. Attempts to implement similar processes in developing countries have encountered even more obstacles, primarily due to traditional hierarchies and to the lower level of industry development prevalent in regional areas (Timothy, 1999).

Implementation Factors

While various planning models and processes have been described comprehensively in the tourism literature, evidence of their implementation and outcomes has been limited. Researchers have suggested that the prevailing institutional structures and the incidence of conflict and/or collaboration between stakeholders are key determinants of whether a destination has the capacity to implement plans and policies effectively. Goodrick (1996) has identified some implementation issues and challenges within the statewide tourism planning undertaken in Queensland, Australia. Blackman et al. (2004) have proposed some key factors influencing the effectiveness of tourism development in peripheral regions, drawing upon eleven international case studies. Based on the literature and in particular drawing upon the Australian experiences examined by Pearlman (2003), the following key issues for implementing tourism plans arise:

- Since the funding required to support planning processes is beyond the scope of most regions, it is critical to address the capacity for long-term funding and implementation of tourism plans at the outset.
- The support of key stakeholders and agencies (notably the local tourism operators, local community, government and international agencies, international tour wholesalers) is critical. These are the key drivers, providing financial and administrative support. From a political perspective the planning process often needs to be "sold" to a wide range of agencies, though government will often need to assume the role of lead agency.
- The role of local champions and visionary leaders with a long-term commitment to the process is crucial. Those with credibility and who command respect within the community will have the greatest capacity to tap into local networks.
- Stakeholder collaboration can facilitate the sharing of knowledge and collective learning and can enhance the prospects for innovation. A collaborative approach entails continuous reflection about what is being learnt through the planning process and about any outcomes that are achieved.
- The development of capacity and resources at the local level is particularly important in the case of smaller destinations. Since continuity is needed to provide impetus for the process, this should include mentoring and succession planning.

- The scale of the destination will influence which type of planning process is most appropriate. Larger regions are generally more complex but have the benefit of access to greater funding, whereas smaller regions benefit from greater coherence but are confronted by a lack of financial resources.
- A combination of technical and communication/ facilitation skills are required through the planning process. Industry operators often demand tangible outcomes from the research component, but this will not be achievable without professional data analysis. Despite the complexity of the various issues surrounding tourism planning, the various models and outcomes will need to be communicated to operators and the broader community in a nonthreatening manner, using readily understandable language. This approach enhances the prospects of achieving a sense of commitment and ownership.
- Tourism planning must fit into a broader planning framework for all sectors of the local/regional economy, environment and community. Tourism is only one of several interrelated elements and Getz (1986) has noted that tourism planning should not be undertaken in isolation from other social, economic and environmental planning.

Emerging Issues at Local and Regional Level

The issues confronting those involved in the tourism planning process at local and regional level are a curious combination of convergence and divergence. Convergence is occurring as a component of the accelerating process of globalization, manifested through the proliferation of transnational brands and through mediated global culture. Greater human mobility has increased the number of tourists exploring the remotest corners of the globe and in many countries has increased the diversity of the tourism workforce. Local and regional destinations are increasingly encountering visitors from diverse source markets, with major implications for human resources development planning. Training programs will increasingly be required to ensure that tourism employees possess knowledge and understanding about different cultures as well as the skills to communicate with and service the needs of visitors from different cultural backgrounds.

While indicators of global uniformity and convergence are evident in the tourism sector, regional and local pressures are pulling in the opposite direction. Tourists are increasingly attracted to destinations which offer experiences conveying local cultural peculiarities and/or distinctions. Such distinctiveness may manifest itself through performance, cuisine, language or artifacts and often incorporates insights into the way in which local people have engaged with their immediate surroundings over time. In confronting the challenges of convergence and divergence, tourism planners will need to establish a clearly defined destination positioning (i.e. distinctiveness) but also be conscious of global competition and evidence of best practice service delivery. In this brief summary chapter it is not possible to document the full range of approaches that are used to reconcile these conflicting pressures, but it is clear that tourism planners need to strike an appropriate balance.

Development pressures are evident at both the local and regional destination levels and planners are confronted by a number of fundamental questions. To what extent, for example, should indigenous people and their representatives be actively involved in the planning process? Should they be represented on all relevant public tourism bodies? Who should determine the extent to which indigenous culture is packaged and available for tourist consumption? In countries where incoming settlers have acquired land, there are often unresolved issues about land tenure with prospective impacts for developers who are seeking security over any land earmarked for tourism purposes.

Indigenous representatives are one of a number of potential stakeholder groups in the tourism development process. Though it is increasingly common to acknowledge the potential contribution of such groups, tourism plans are often silent about the requirement to engage with multiple stakeholders through the

planning and development process. After being largely ignored and marginalized during much of the early tourism development in Hawaii, the voice of the indigenous Hawaiians is increasingly being incorporated within the development process (Liu, 2005). The role of such groups as stakeholders and as agents is magnified by the genuine interest of visitors in the contributions of indigenous cultures to the destination experience.

The challenge of engagement with indigenous communities is not shared by all destinations, but the indigenous example is symbolic of the increasing recognition that social justice and social inclusion are relevant for tourism. This is an argument that has been championed by Burns (2004). Marginal groups within the community are often excluded from decisions which have the potential to affect them subsequently. Excluded groups may include women (in male dominated societies or communities), the poor and those discriminated against (e.g. gays, ethnic minorities, or the sick). The practice of tourism planning may be viewed as a manifestation of the authority of those who exercise power. Though the exercise of inclusive decision-making often falls short of the ideal, there is an increasing recognition in the literature that an inclusive approach to planning is good for social justice and is also good for the business of tourism. Destination communities will be more receptive to visitor expectations where genuine community consultation has occurred during the tourism planning process.

As a business activity, tourism is not immune from trends occurring more widely in the business sector. The "Fair Trade" concept has been regarded as a means of strengthening social justice within distribution and production systems and has been widely applied to key agricultural commodities such as coffee. Tourism businesses in South Africa in the post-apartheid era have been active in the application of the principles of fair trade (Rogerson, 2003). Currently the implementation of such principles is concentrated at the project level and, as such, generally cannot be described as being incorporated into the tourism planning process. Over time it can be expected to become more commonplace.

Another symptom of globalization has been the identification of entrenched poverty in Africa as a barrier to tourism and the application of pressure on planning authorities to demonstrate a commitment to poverty alleviation. Planners are sometimes required to choose between locating tourist developments adjacent to areas of poverty and malnutrition or deliberately avoiding such settings. The growing influence of the Pro-Poor Tourism movement is emblematic of international recognition that tourism can no longer be considered to be immune from other global concerns and must play its part in the elimination of injustices. The principle is sound but the challenge for planners is to make adequate provision for economic redistribution. If the established planning structures make no provision for involvement of the most marginal groups within tourism, then appropriate processes will need to be put in place. The application of pro-poor tourism is most widespread in Africa where a disproportion of the world's poorest citizens live, but is also evident in parts of Asia and parts of Latin America.

Regional dispersal of incomes and economic impacts is a further aspect of social justice for tourism planning at regional level. Tourism has often been advocated as a sector offering the potential to stimulate economic redistribution, typically from cities to country areas and also to pristine regional destinations offering residents few alternative employment opportunities. However, rapid economic development in some of the developing countries can lead to heightened income disparities. In the world's most populous nation of China, the population living along the eastern coastal fringe generally and in the eastern seaboard cities in particular is much wealthier than its inland and rural counterparts, particularly in the western region. Tourism planning becomes particularly important as one of the few means of

redirecting economic activity towards the least developed areas. Ensuring that adequate resources are available for the poorer areas is often outside local hands and requires discretionary activity on the part of the central authorities.

As previously mentioned, there is a strong tradition of undertaking tourism "master plans" in the developing world. Is there a future for such comprehensive documents, which often appear to advocate the regulation of tourism, reminiscent of the now discredited Soviet era? While there is a fashion for management rather than for planning, the business community itself recognizes that in an increasingly uncertain global environment (with terrorism, environmental threats, and increasingly fickle consumers), there is a continuing need to anticipate future scenarios and to plan for them. While commentators will differ in their enthusiasm for regulation, the need for professional tourism planning at local and regional levels is likely to increase. The widespread accessibility of tourism planning documents on the web and the associated accountability to electors and pressure groups, signals an end to the tendency for planning documents to gather dust in the drawers of planning officers.

The Future

Much of what is known and has been written about tourism planning is based upon the experience of the developed world generally and of Europe and North America in particular. This is unsurprising, given that the bulk of tourist arrivals and the planning resources have been concentrated in these settings. Looking forward though, many of the key global issues are as likely to be confronted by tourism planners in China or India, as by their counterparts in the UK or the USA. The rapid expansion of domestic tourism in China as a result of extending the weekend holidays into four week long holidays across the calendar, for example, has prompted Chinese authors to contemplate Chinese solutions to problems of overcrowding. The growing prominence of the most populous nations was recognized some years ago, when the World Tourism Organization (now UNWTO) embarked upon the preparation of provincial masterplans for both China and India in conjunction with the provincial and the national authorities (King, 2006; King and McVey, 2003).

Prompted by recent disruptions such as 9/11, the London, Madrid, and Mumbai bombings and the tsunami in the Indian Ocean, future tourism planning is likely to place greater emphasis on the need for risk management. At the local and regional levels, planning will also need to account for the risks of global warming (in island microstates such as the Maldives or Tuvalu), cyclones (in tropical settings) and political uncertainty (in anywhere that the political structure is volatile and violent outbreaks are possible). The increasing interest in risk management is manifested in the emerging tourism literature (Mansfield and Pizam, 2006).

The increasing autonomy exercised by consumers is a further challenge for local and regional tourism planners. Internet technology permits consumers anywhere in the world to make direct contact with small-scale suppliers such as homestays and bed and breakfast establishments. This opportunity for direct business-to-consumer (B2C) transactions challenges the established tourism planning hierarchies and some consumers may cease to make any use of intermediaries. Small- and medium-sized tourism enterprises often require training to improve their IT and marketing skills in responding to increasing customer expectations. Their need to share their experiences with other businesses will not diminish. If one conceptualizes a local or regional destination as a network of tourism related businesses, planning may well need to embrace network theory rather than rely on traditional tourism planning hierarchies. Such networks may enhance the capacity for mobilization in crisis situations.

As tourism continues to expand its intrusion into human activity throughout the world, it is likely that those who are responsible for tourism planning will be increasingly scrutinized by consumers, by the general public and by pressure groups. To handle such scrutiny, planners at the local and regional level will need to demonstrate a higher level of professionalism. They will need laws and regulations which integrate tourism with generic planning concepts. They will need to be sensitive to the particular needs of the locality, as well as have an appreciation of global trends and convergence. We can be confident that the burgeoning theoretical literature on tourism planning will continue to flourish. It should also be hoped that there is an increasing emphasis on implementation and evaluation of the various theoretical contributions.

References

Ashley, C., Boyd, C. and Goodwin, H. (2000). "Pro-Poor Tourism: Putting Poverty at the Heart of the Tourism Agenda." *Natural Resource Perspectives*, 51: 1–12.

Blackman, A., Foster, F., Hyvonen, T, Kuilboer, A. and Moscardo, G. (2004). "Factors Contributing to Successful Tourism Development in Peripheral Regions." *Journal of Tourism Studies*, 15(1): 59–70.

Boyd, S.W. and Singh, S. (2003). "Destination Communities: Structures, Resources and Types." In S Singh, T.J. Timothy and R.J. Dowling (Eds.), *Tourism in Destination Communities*. Wallingford: CABI.

Bramwell, B. and Lane, B. (2000). "Collaboration and Partnerships in Tourism Planning." In B. Bramwell and B. Lane (Eds.), *Tourism Collaboration and Partnerships: Politics, Practice and Sustainability* (pp. 1–19). Clevedon: Channel View Publications.

Bramwell, B. and Sharman, A. (1999). "Collaboration in Local Tourism Policymaking." *Annals of Tourism Research*, 26(2): 392–415.

Burns, P. (2004). "The 1990 Solomon Islands Tourism Plan: A Critical Discourse Analysis." *Tourism and Hospitality: Planning and Development*, 1(1): 57–78.

Butler, R.W. (1980). "The Concept of a Tourist Area Cycle of Evolution: Implications for Management of Resources." *Canadian Geographer*, 24(1): 5–12.

Clark, R.N. and Stankey, G.H. (1979). *The Recreation Opportunity Spectrum: A Framework for Planning, Management and Research*. Portland, OR: USDA Forest Service.

Craik, J. (1991). *Resorting to Tourism*. North Sydney, Australia: Allen & Unwin.

de Kadt, E. (1979). *Tourism: Passport to Development? Perspectives on the Social and Cultural Effects of Tourism in Developing Countries*. New York: Oxford University Press.

Dowling, R.K. (1993). "An Environmentally-Based Planning Model for Regional Tourism Development." *Journal of Sustainable Tourism*, 1(1): 7–37.

Dredge, D. (1999). "Destination Place Planning and Design." *Annals of Tourism Research*, 26(4): 772–791.

ESCAP (1996). "Integrated Tourism Planning in Pacific Island Countries." *ESCAP Tourism Review*, No. 17. New York: United Nations.

Fagence, M. (1990). "Geographically Referenced Planning Strategies to Resolve Potential Conflict between Environmental Values and Commercial Interests in Tourism Development in Environmentally Sensitive Areas." *Journal of Environmental Management*, 31(1): 1–18.

Faulkner, B. (2002). "Rejuvenating a Maturing Tourist Destination: The Case of the Gold Coast." *Current Issues in Tourism*, 5(5): 472–519.

Garrod, B. (2003). "Local Participation in the Planning and Management of Ecotourism: A Revised Model Approach." *Journal of Ecotourism*, 2(1): 33–53.

Getz, D. (1983). "Capacity to Absorb Tourism: Concepts and Implications for Strategic Planning." *Annals of Tourism Research*, 10(2): 239–263.

Getz, D. (1986). "Models in Tourism Planning: Towards Integration of Theory and Practice." *Tourism Management*, 7(1): 21–32.

Getz, D. (1987). "Tourism Planning and Research: Traditions, Models and Futures." Paper presented to *The Australian Travel Research Workshop*. Bunbury, Australia.

Goodrick, Y. (1996). *Integrated Tourism Frameworks-Avoiding the Implementation Slump*. Lismore, NSW: Centre for Tourism, Southern Cross University.

Gunn, C.A. (1979). *Tourism Planning*. New York: Crane Russak.

Gunn, C.A. (1988). *Tourism Planning: Basics, Concepts and Cases*. Washington, DC: Taylor and Francis.

Hall, C.M. (1995). *Introduction to Tourism in Australia: Impacts, Planning and Development* (2nd edition.). Melbourne: Longman.

Hall, C.M. (2000). *Tourism Planning, Policies, Processes and Relationships*. Harlow: Pearson Education.

Hall, C.M., Jenkins, J. and Kearsley, G. (1997). "Introduction: Issues in Tourism Planning and Policy in Australia and New Zealand." In C.M. Hall, J. Jenkins and G. Kearsley (Eds.), *Tourism Planning and Policy in Australia and New Zealand: Cases, Issues and Practice* (pp. 16–36). Roseville, Australia: McGraw-Hill.

Hall, C.M. and Jenkins, J.M. (1995). *Tourism and Public Policy*. Routledge, London.

Haywood, K.M. (1988). "Responsible and Responsive Tourism Planning in the Community." *Tourism Management*, 9(2): 105–118.

Heath, E. and Wall, G. (1992). *Marketing Tourism Destinations: A Strategic Planning Approach*. New York: John Wiley & Sons.

Heeley, J. (1981). "Planning for Tourism in Britain." *Tourism Planning Review*, 52: 61–79.

Horn, C. and Simmons, D. (2002). "Community Adaptation to Tourism: Comparisons between Rotorua and Kaikoura, New Zealand." *Tourism Management*, 23(2): 133–143.

Inskeep, E. (1991). *Tourism Planning: An Integrated and Sustainable Development Approach*. New York: Van Nostrand Reinhold.

Inskeep, E. (1994). *National and Regional Tourism Planning: Methodologies and Case Studies*. London: Routledge.

Ioannides, D. (1995). "A Flawed Implementation of Sustainable Tourism: The Experience of Akamas, Cyprus." *Tourism Management*, 16(8): 583–592.

Jamal, T.B. and Getz, D. (1995). "Collaboration Theory and Community Tourism Planning." *Annals of Tourism Research*, 22(1): 186–204.

King, B. (2006). "India." *Mintel Country Reports – Asia Pacific 1* (pp. 1–30).

King, B. and McVey, M. (2003). "China Outbound." *Travel and Tourism Analyst*, 1: 1–32.

King, B., McVey, M. and Simmons, D. (2000). "A Societal Marketing Approach to National Tourism Planning: Evidence from the South Pacific." *Tourism Management*, 21(4): 407–416.

King, B., Yu, S. and Tang, C. (2005). "The Implementation of China's 'Golden Weeks Holiday' Policy. A Preliminary Assessment." *Journal of Hospitality and Tourism*, 3(1): 33–54.

Lawson, F. and Baud-Bovy, M. (1977). *Tourism and Recreation Development*. Boston: CBI.

Liu, J.C. (2005). "Tourism and the Value of Culture to Regions." *The Annals of Regional Science*, 39(1): 1–9.

Mansfield, Y. and Pizam, A. (Eds.) (2006). *Tourism, Security and Safety: From Theory to Practice*. Oxford: Butterworth–Heinemann.

Mathieson, A. and Wall, G. (1982). *Tourism: Economic, Physical and Social Impacts*. Harlow: Longman Scientific & Technical.

McArthur, S. (2000). "Visitor Management in Action: An Analysis of the Development and Implementation of Visitor Management Models at Jenolan Caves and Kangaroo Island." Doctor of Philosophy Thesis. University of Canberra.

Meyer, D. (2003). "Review of the Impacts of Previous Pro-Poor Tourism Research: Results of a Survey to Follow-Up Pro-Poor Tourism Research Carried Out in 2000–2001." *PPT Working Paper No 9*. Retrieved April 10, 2006 from www.propoortourism.org.uk/9_impacts.pdf.

Mill, R.C. and Morrison, A.M. (1985). *The Tourism System: An Introductory Text*. Engelwood Cliffs, NJ: Prentice-Hall.

Mowforth, M. and Munt, I. (1998). *Tourism and Sustainability: New Tourism in the Third World*. London: Routledge.

Murphy, P.E. (1985). *Tourism: A Community Approach*. New York: Methuen.

Murphy, P.E. and Dore, L.R. (2000). "A Conceptual Framework for Regional Tourism Research and Training." Paper presented to *Council of Australian Universities Tourism and Hospitality Education Conference*. Mt. Bulla, Australia.

Murphy, P.E. and Murphy, A.E. (2004). *Strategic Management for Tourism Communities: Bridging the Gaps*. Clevedon: Channel View.

Pearlman, M. (1999). "A New Model for Integrated Tourism Destination Planning." Paper presented to *International Geographic Union Sustainable Tourism Study Group Conference on Tourism Policy and Planning*. Dunedin.

Pearlman, M. (2003). "A Comparison of Tourism Management Models in Australia." Paper presented to *CAUTHE 13th Australian Tourism and Hospitality Research Conference*. Lismore.

Prideaux, B. (2000). "The Resort Development Spectrum – A New Approach to Modeling Resort Development." *Tourism Management*, 21(3): 225–240.

Reed, M.G. (1999). "Collaborative Tourism Planning as Adaptive Experiments in Emergent Tourism Settings." *Journal of Sustainable Tourism*, 7(3&4): 331–355.

Reid, D., Mair, H. and George, W. (2004). "Community Tourism Planning: A Self-Assessment Instrument." *Annals of Tourism Research*, 31(3): 623–639.

Ritchie, J.R.B. (1993). "Crafting a Destination Vision: Putting the Concept of Resident Responsive Tourism into Practice." *Tourism Management*, 14(15): 29–38.

Ritchie, J.R.B. and Crouch, G.I. (2000). "The Competitive Destination: A Sustainability Perspective." *Tourism Management*, 21(1): 1–7.

Rogerson, C.M. (2003). "Towards Pro-Poor Local Economic Development: The Case for Sectoral Targeting in South Africa." *Urban Forum*, 14(1): 53–79.

Senge, P.M., Kleiner, A., Roberts, C., Ross, R.B. and Smith, B.J. (1994). *The Fifth Discipline Fieldbook: Strategies and Tools for Building a Learning Organisation*. London: Nicholas Brealey.

Simmons, D.G. (1994). "Community Participation in Tourism Planning." *Tourism Management*, 15(2): 98–108.

Smith, S.J. (1989). *Tourism Analysis: A Handbook*. Harlow: Longman Scientific and Technical.

Smith, V.L. (1977). *Hosts and Guests: The Anthropology of Tourism* (1st edition.). Philadelphia: University of Pennsylvania Press.

Stankey, G.H., Cole, D.N., Lucas, R.C., Petersen, M.E. and Frissell, S.S. (1985). *The Limits of *Acceptable Change (LAC) System for Wilderness Planning*. Intermountain Forest and Range Experiment Station, USDA Forest Service Ogden, UT.

Theobald, W.F. (Ed.) (2004). *Global Tourism*. Oxford: Butterworth-Heinemann.

Timothy, D.J. (1999). "Participatory Planning: A View of Tourism in Indonesia." *Annals of Tourism Research*, 26(2): 371–391.

Tosun, C. and Jenkins, C.L. (1998). "The Evolution of Tourism Planning in Third World Countries: A Critique." *Progress in Tourism and Hospitality Research*, 4(2): 101–114.

Walker, P.A., Greiner, R., McDonald, D. and Lyne, V. (1999). "The Tourism Futures Simulator: A Systems Thinking Approach." *Environmental Modelling & Software*, 14: 59–67.

Wall, G. and Mathieson, A. (2006). *Tourism: Change, Impacts and Opportunities*. Harlow: Pearson Education Limited.

World Commission on Environment and Development (1987). *Our Common Future*. London: Oxford University Press.

24

Destination Marketing Organizations: Convention and Visitors Bureaus

Robert C. Ford and William C. Peeper

Introduction

Although destination marketing organizations (DMOs) include various organizational entities, perhaps there are none more dominant than convention and visitors bureaus (CVBs) in North America. This type of DMO has a long history, a competitive present and a challenging future. This chapter will briefly review the history to show why they came to exist in the form they now have, what their present situation is, and how the dynamics of the market, technological change, and competitive forces are challenging the relevance of their business model and strategy.

These are challenging times for CVBs and this chapter should interest those that teach and research on this topic. A significant portion of this review is drawn from an extensive DMAI endorsed research project in which the authors personally conducted structured interviews with 22 CVB executives to ask them what they saw as the tasks, roles, and responsibilities of the CVB executive. The results of

this research are reported in a book, *Managing Destination Marketing Organizations: The Tasks, Roles and Responsibilities of the Convention and Visitors Bureau Executive* (Ford and Peeper, 2008). Readers are referred to this work, as well as Ford and Peeper (2007), for further detail on the topics discussed below and the document sources and research method that undergirds our assessments about CVBs.

We organize this review into three parts; first we present a brief history of the CVB industry and its major professional organization (Destination Marketing Association International or DMAI) to set the stage for why these organizations exist and the roles they are expected to perform. Next we discuss the current situation, including the structure and roles of these organizations, and include here a brief comparison between US and non-US CVBs. Finally, we close by addressing key challenges and some considerations for the future to help assist CVBs and researchers in this area.

The Past

Although many consider conventions a uniquely American invention, there have been conventions of some kind taking place around the globe for centuries. But it was in the USA that the idea came into its own (Turner, 1958). Besides the early political conventions held every four years to nominate presidential candidates, other organizations were bringing people together to discuss issues of common interest. For example, the Writing Paper Manufacturers Association and the National Education Association were reportedly meeting prior to the American Civil War. The American Medical Association was formed in 1847, and the American Bar Association's first meeting was in 1878 (Denton, 1950). Up until the late 1890s, the people who met were for the most part either religious, abolitionist, military (veterans), or members of political, social, and educational groups (Denton, 1950). There was also meeting activity in the pre-rail and preindustrial era by buyers and sellers of agricultural products who followed the agricultural cycle. Compared with today's events, these conventions tended to be quite small and limited in duration.

In early February 1896 a *Detroit Journal* newspaper writer, Milton J. Carmichael, wrote an article pointing out the obvious value of conventions to Detroit and suggested that local businesses should band together to promote Detroit as a desirable convention destination. The argument was effective. On February 19, 1896, members of the Chamber of Commerce joined with the Manufacturers Club to form an organization that was called The Detroit Convention and Businessmen's League. The founding committee of hoteliers, railroad agents, and other interested parties defined the mission of the new organization as "hustling for all these conventions" (Metropolitan Detroit Convention and Visitors Bureau, 1996: 2).

While Detroit may be recognized as the place of origination of the CVB industry and profession, convention and meetings activity had been going on for some time, with an increasing number of cities sending salesmen on the road to promote their destinations. What Detroit contributed was a model of how to turn the casual and typically uncoordinated efforts by cities and local businesses to attract convention visitors into a focused and organized profession. In a pamphlet published by Turner, the International Association of Convention Bureaus (IACB) stated that "the convention as we know it in this county is a unique institution, representing a complete reversal of the European tradition of secrecy in the business and industrial world" (1958: 24). Three factors appear to be key contributors to the development of the convention business and the CVB profession.

Key Factors in CVB Development

Growth in Large Scale Production
The industrial revolution was a major contributor to CVB development. The growth in large-scale manufacturing organizations across the country created the need for a way to communicate to a market spread out across a broad geographical area about products made in quantity at some central location. Manufacturers recognized that they had to get their sales people together to learn about their new products and also get their customers together to see these products. As manufacturers grew in size and complexity and geographical dispersion, new manufacturing techniques and ways to manage their increasingly specialized workforce also had to be learned. These forces created a need for meetings and conventions.

Railroads
A second major contributing factor was the rapid growth of the railroads (Zelinsky, 1994). At the time of the Chicago fire, in 1871, fewer than 75 trains left the city each day. By 1885, daily departures had grown to 178, and more than 500 miles of new intracity railroad tracks had been built (Harper, 1971). Railroads not only moved

goods and products quickly across the vast space of the North American continent, they also moved people. Now, instead of riding days on horseback or in carriages on dusty roads to get to a meeting, people could take the train and arrive the same day. It is no accident that the earliest conventions of the Association of Convention Secretaries (later to be renamed the International Association of Convention Bureaus, or IACB, and now called Destination Marketing Association International, or DMAI) tended to be held in urban railroad hubs of the industrial Midwest than in larger but less centralized cities such as New York and Boston.

Panic of 1893

A third contributing factor to the growth of the CVB industry was the panic of 1893 and the resulting depression that engulfed cities throughout the USA. The depression led civic leaders to think of selling their cities as convention centers as a way to promote economic recovery and development. They reasoned that if only company owners and managers would come and see their cities, the benefits of relocating their companies would be apparent (Hughes, 1987a). Joining the civic leaders in their efforts to attract businesses to the city through conventions were the hoteliers, city retailers, and railroad agents who would stand to make money from the influx of convention attendees. "Conventions have a two fold value," Fred Butler, executive secretary of the Jamestown (NY) Board of Commerce, said in a published speech in 1916. "First, there is the money they leave in a city to enter the channels of trade. The second is the advertising value to the city." (Butler, 1916: 230).

Founding of the Association of Convention Secretaries

By the turn of the last century city salesmen were bumping into each other at various national conventions as they vied to sell their respective destinations. Eventually, when

they realized that they were all chasing the same groups at the same time, several of them decided to get together and organize. The Association of Convention Secretaries was formed the next year—1915—in St. Louis. The *St. Louis Republic* reported that the original organization included 28 members (Love, 1915).

The first non-US member joined the Association of Convention Secretaries in 1919, an event that likely caused the name to be changed to the International Association of Convention Bureaus (IACB) in 1920 (Hughes, 1987b). Other sources confirm that the IACB became a regularly meeting organization in 1920 and that it then created a Constitution and By Laws (Gartrell, 1994). In 1974, after what some report as a contentious debate, the IACB changed its name to the International Association of Convention and Visitors Bureau and its initials to IACVB to include organizations that focus on tourists and other non-convention visitors. This change also recognized the changing nature of conventions as convention goers increasingly brought spouses and stayed extra days as tourists. In 2005, the IACVB again changed its name to the Destination Marketing Association International (DMAI) to better recognize the common purpose of its membership.

Reasons for Forming the Association of Convention Secretaries

Three reasons motivated the 28 city salesmen to form the landmark Association of Convention Secretaries in 1915:

1 To share information with their colleagues in other cities and find out what organizations that met in conventions really did—how many conventioneers did they actually attract, for example as opposed to what they said they attracted.
2 To adopt standards that excluded unscrupulous acts in selling cities as convention destinations and the salesmen who performed them.
3 To develop scientific management principles for their profession, as other professions were already doing.

Share Information

In regard to their need to talk to each other about what they did, this association did what most trade organizations do—shared information, particularly information about pricing and convention attendee behavior. The people who joined the association made a commitment to share information about any conventions held in their respective cities (Turner, 1965). Sharing information allowed an accurate database to be created so that members did not have to worry about whether convention organizers were telling them the truth. In 1920, the IACB members agreed to create a formal systematic reporting system that became the early version of what today's DMAI calls MINT (Meeting Information Network). This system allowed IACB to collect data on each convention hosted in their city and distribute the information to its members. These reports were and are vital to the IACB and now the DMAI and their member organizations.

Adopt Standards

The second reason they formed the Association of Convention Secretaries in 1915 was to promote sound and ethical sales practices and to exclude those who did not. The adoption of a Code of Ethics in 1925 indicates that early members considered some ethical principles important enough to be recorded in an official written document. It also suggests that convention selling was at that time a fairly rogue business with *caveat emptor* as its guiding rule. Markarian (1989) reported that convention salesmen of the time created a sort of Dun & Bradstreet rating system and tipped each other off about the "bloomers"— conventions that offered no value to the community. Sharing information only with fellow members and subscribing to a Code of Ethics was the IACB's member's way to distinguish themselves and the conventions they deemed of value from their unethical colleagues and the bloomers they supported.

Develop Scientific Management Principles

The third reason behind the formation of the Association of Convention Secretaries was to develop a science of their profession and the industry they served. In that founding year, 1915, Charles Hatfield of St. Louis wrote a pamphlet arguing that convention organizers should charge registration fees to help defray the costs of conventions so that they would not have to rely entirely on the host city and business community for financing (Flynn et al., 1987). In the 1930s the IACB published a pamphlet on site selection to help convention organizers (Trafton, 1987). The IACB recommended that the cities select professional salespersons and that the convening organization create a site selection committee to evaluate potential sites. At the same time the IACB published another pamphlet entitled "Convention Planning" directed at the many amateurs struggling to organize a convention without any background or training (Turner, 1958).

By helping convention organizers carry out their responsibilities in a more scientific way, these publications also served to reduce the burden of IACB members. If convention organizers financed their conventions with registration fees and relied less on financial support from the host city; if they made their site selection processes after listening to factual sales presentations and avoided direct emotional appeals to their organization's memberships; and if they learned how to run their conventions in a professional manner without help from the CVBs—then CVBs could concentrate on their real job, selling their cities. Furthermore, the conventioneers would have a better convention, a happier visit, and a higher opinion of the host city.

In the mid-1980s the IACVB turned its attention to its member CVBs and developed professional programs to help improve its own members' professionalism. This initiative became formalized as a key part of its strategic mission (IACVB, 1989). Today the association (now DMAI) is heavily involved in member education and professional development and has expanded its focus on the overall CVB by developing performance standards and an accreditation process.

The Present: Drivers of CVB Growth in the Modern ERA

A key factor in the growth of CVBs and the convention center industry was the recognition in the 1980s of the need to rebuild inner cities that had deteriorated after decades of flight by the middle class to the suburbs (Fenich, 1992). Since a new convention center tends to spur the development of hotels and restaurants and entertainment and retail facilities, it is well suited to anchor an urban renewal project. Building a convention center complex with hotels, restaurants, stores, theaters, arenas, and the like provides employment in the form of high-paying construction jobs. When construction is over people have to be employed on an ongoing basis to operate, support, and maintain these facilities. This approach to urban renewal was driven by the belief that meeting attendees were an untapped and available source of funding. Estimates of the multiplier effect of conventions are that every dollar spent by a conventioneer generates two dollars of business in the community with the associated employment (Fenich, 1992, 1995) (see Photo 24.1).

Another, and perhaps more important, driver of growth in CVBs and convention centers was the initiation of the bed or tourism tax (Migdal, 1991; Morrison et al., 1998). The first reported use of this tax was in 1946 when New York City passed a 5% tax to be added to the rate of each hotel room. The tax was vigorously opposed by the New York Hotel Association who feared it would make New York City uncompetitive: "Smaller cities looking for convention business are quick to point out that New York may be the largest city in the country but that it costs visitors more because of the 5 per cent hotel tax" (Hotel Association of New York, 1954: 2). The hoteliers felt abused, especially since the tax generated only US$5 million annually,

Photo 24.1   North–South Building of the Orange County Convention Center, Orlando, FL. It contains 1 million sq. ft. of exhibit space and is part of the total 2.1 million sq. ft. of exhibit space that makes up the convention center campus.
Source: Orange County Convention Center.

or 0.5% of the city's US$1 billion budget (Hotel Association of New York, 1954). The tax's advantage, however, was clear. It transferred the costs (to the extent of the tax) of constructing meeting facilities and marketing the destination from city taxpayers who voted to visitors who did not (Hiemstra and Ismali, 1993). In 1955, Las Vegas picked up on this and enacted a 3% tax on motel rooms and a 4% tax on hotel rooms, and applied the receipts to marketing its newly built Convention Center (Flynn et al., 2002).

Structure of the Modern CVB

Most US CVBs today are tax-exempt "business leagues" under §501(c)(6) of the Internal Revenue Code. They are required to engage primarily in the not-for-profit business that justifies the tax exemption, such as marketing their destination, and to limit any for-profit type of activities (Fenich, 2007; Gartrell, 1994; Lathrop, 2005). They also tend to be membership-based organizations with the membership categories, qualifications, governance structure, director responsibilities and authority, and voting processes spelled out in their constitution and bylaws. CVB members are expected to elect the organization's Board of Directors, pay some dues, and generally to become engaged in the oversight of the CVB and its executive. This governance structure also gives the CVB executive a new board chair every one or two years.

The nonprofit, tax-exempt, membership form of organization contributes greatly to the challenges of leading a CVB. In most communities, the hoteliers have the most at stake in the CVB's activities since they collect the governmentally imposed bed tax and are the primary beneficiaries of CVB activities. Hotelier members are required by their own corporate evaluation structure to focus on short-term results such as quarterly profits, EBITA (earnings before interest, taxes, and amortization), REVPAR (revenue per available room), and bottom line measures. Simply put, they want to get heads in their hotel's

beds *tonight*. Since the bed tax is collected from their guests, hoteliers strongly believe that they actually pay the tax themselves, not simply collect it. They often take exception when politicians, other community interests, and the CVBs try to tell them otherwise. The CVB executive thus mediates between two opposing and largely opposite interests—the destination's political structure that oversees the bed tax and the CVB's own membership structure, which is generally dominated by hotels with a proprietary interest in the bed tax.

The advent and widespread adoption of the bed tax changed CVBs in subtle but important ways. First, the stream of funds coming from this tax took away the imperative to seek general community support, in that the bed tax encouraged the CVB to refocus energies on selling outside the community and away from selling people in the community on the value of its CVB. Second, hotels became more interested and involved in the decision processes of CVBs and their executives to make sure that the CVBs were spending "their" money in ways that would benefit the hotels. Third, CVB executives, in turn, came to see hotels as their major constituency, and some CVB executives started spending more of their local community involvement time with hoteliers and less on other stakeholders. The bed taxes' influence in concentrating the focus of the CVB and its executive on the hotel stakeholders is exacerbated when the CVB is a nonprofit membership organization, as the larger and better funded CVBs tend to be.

Regardless of conflicting interests and points of view, industry and community stakeholders of CVBs, as well as those who study them, generally agree that CVBs add value to destinations and to the people who live there. Although some argue that the CVB industry should be charged with the costs to the community of lower wage jobs that attract younger employees who will require more community support services (e.g., food stamps, education of the employees' children, higher crime rates) and increased usage of roadways, others argue that it provides badly needed jobs for those with fewer skills, education, or other employment options and offers a starting point on the economic ladder.

Differences Between US and Non-US CVBs

While the basic function of any CVB is the promotion of its community as a destination for visitors, different CVBs fulfill it in different ways according to the needs of their local community and industry, and their resources and capabilities. Some devote themselves to selling and supporting conventions and meetings, others focus on tourists; still others assume a larger role in the community's economic development and marketing, perhaps even taking the lead role in managing the destination's brand image. There are important differences between US CVBs and their non-US counterparts, but besides discussions from Kim et al. (2003), Koutoulas (2005), Rogers (2003), and Weber and Chon (2002) surprisingly little has been written about this. Based on the information we gathered from the DMAI survey of its members, our interviews with CVB directors (mentioned at the beginning of this chapter), correspondence with several of the sources named above, and sparse literature sources, at least three key differences between US and non-US convention bureaus that affect what their CVB executives do can be identified: size (of both the CVB and its destination), funding patterns, and specific operational activities.

Size

The first of the major differences between US and other CVBs is their size. Data collected by DMAI (2005) and Koutoulas (2005) and a study by Mutschlechner (2003) of the International Congress and Convention Association (ICCA) show that US CVBs tend to be larger. The size difference is largely caused by the difference in the role and structure of the CVB. US CVBs typically have a responsibility for the visitor part

of destination marketing (the "V" in "CVB"). Although Canada and Mexico also have CVBs, our discussion is driven by the data reported by DMAI, and this is primarily derived from US CVBs. Many outside of North America tend to be CBs (Convention Bureaus) or tourist offices because they are often subsidiaries or junior partners of larger and well-established tourism bureaus, and are not responsible for tourism or leisure travel to the degree found in the USA. Local meetings and convention marketing organizations in Europe, for instance, consist primarily of CBs. The primary responsibility of these CBs is to sell their destination to the Meeting, Incentive, Convention, and Exhibition (MICE) meeting planners and the Professional Congress Organizers (PCOs). Furthermore, those structured as subordinate units of tourism bureaus generally have their overhead costs carried by the larger tourism bureaus and require fewer employees to operate. Also, these non-US CBs tend to focus on selling and not on delivery and servicing of a convention, which, after the sale is closed, are turned over to a PCO. Thus their role is more limited than in the USA and their size reflects that more limited role.

Size is also related to the types of meetings that the non-US CBs concentrate on attracting. Convention Bureaus outside the US generally focus on international association meetings. They are easier for them to identify, more cost-efficient to sell, and have a higher yield for their respective communities. While US CVBs do concentrate on selling to associations, their focus also extends to the corporate market and the Social, Military, Educational, Religious, and Fraternal (SMERF) market, on which they spend considerable marketing and sales effort. The meeting's market, moreover, is structured differently in many markets outside of the USA—the meetings are smaller than in the USA, as is the destination hotel room capacity (both guestrooms and meeting space) is smaller, and meeting types differ as well. Although there are several large trade shows and trade fairs outside of the USA (for example, in Germany) that are noteworthy exceptions, they tend to represent a small proportion of the total conference and convention market in that CVB's home market.

Meetings outside of the USA in meetings markets like Europe are even defined differently for record-keeping purposes. A major organization representing meetings and conventions outside the US market, the International Conference and Conventions Association (ICCA), defines a meeting as one that has more than 50 attendees and that rotates across a minimum of four countries on a regular basis (International Congress and Convention Association, 2008). The Union of International Associations (UIA), which publishes the *Yearbook of International Organizations* and *International Congress Calendar*, defines an international meeting as one lasting at least three days and having at least 300 attendees representing more than five nationalities, with at least 40% of the attendees being foreign to the host nation (Union of International Associations, 2007). Both definitions attest to the importance attached by non-US organizations to the international meeting market.

Because there are so many conferences and meetings held in the US market, US CVBs spend less time and effort recruiting international meetings, preferring to concentrate on the more easily solicited domestic business. This tendency to market close to home is true for non-US CBs as well as US CVBs. In non-US meetings markets, the generally smaller domestic meetings have planners that are completely familiar with the domestic destinations but not with foreign destinations, leaving the CBs to spend most of their effort marketing internationally. One other difference worth noting in marketing between US and non-US organizations is the marketing data. For non-US CBs, the DMAI's MINT database is largely irrelevant whereas the ICCA data are valued. In the US market the reverse is true.

Funding Patterns

The second key difference between US CVBs and non-US CBs is in funding. US CVBs are heavily funded with the bed tax and other public funds. In 2005, the average public funding reported by CVBs represented nearly 82% of their total budget. The largest contributor to this amount however is the bed tax collected and remitted by hotels and amounts on average to about 73% of a CVB's funding (DMAI, 2005). Outside of the North American CVB based countries (the USA, Mexico, and Canada), the contribution of bed taxes tend to vary. The majority of funding for many CBs comes from a direct grant or allocation from a governmental body and is often supplemented by local members. While the CB is typically funded by the national government through its tourism office or board, it may also be funded by a regional or even local government eager to increase the number of visitors to its destination.

One consequence of this difference is that the non-US CBs tend to have smaller budgets than their US counterparts. A second is that CB funding is unrelated to marketing effectiveness and grants are the same regardless of the number of visitors. In the US markets, with their tourism/bed tax, generally, more visitors mean greater revenues. A third consequence lies in stakeholder management strategies. While the US hotel industry takes a strong interest in how CVBs spend bed tax money the non-US hotel industry is less aggressive in helping the CBs get funding. Instead, the non-US CBs tend to listen closely to the convention centers, which are government entities that would be unhappy if event business is not forthcoming.

The funding for non-US CBs is dependent upon the success of the CB executive to convince either the government or the tourism board (or both) of the value of the CB activity in order to get the allocations of the funding necessary to operate and to fill the convention center. While on its surface this appears similar to the stakeholder management challenge faced by US CVB executives, the US executive is arguing for a slice of tax funds that increase with the CVB's success, whereas the non-US CB counterpart is arguing for a slice of a relatively fixed and stable tax pie.

Specific Operational Activities

A key difference between US CVBs and non-US CVBs concerns operations. In the US market, CVB activities generally fall into three major functional areas: (1) marketing to the tourist and leisure traveler; (2) sales to the convention and meeting market; and (3) services for the convention and meeting market. While other functions may be performed by member services, publications, etc., people and resources are mostly dedicated to supporting its tourist marketing, selling the convention and meeting planner on the destination, and supporting meeting logistics after it begins. In the USA, once the meeting begins, CVBs tend to offer their services to the meeting planners and attendees to help them solve their problems and fulfill their needs at the destination. Outside the North American market these services are by and large not provided by the CBs, but rather by the PCO.

The types of convention or meeting services are also different in the two markets. An early breakfast meeting for hundreds is routine in the US market, but not common elsewhere. Help with visa problems, currency conversions, or language translation services are offered in international conferences in markets outside the US, but are rare in the US market because international conferences are rare. Another difference is national tax laws. The US puts strict guidelines on the ability of US taxpayers to deduct travel expenses for attending meetings outside of the country. Other nations are beginning to enact legislation that will tighten up the deductibility by businesses of meetings and conventions that do not serve a real business purpose (e.g., pharmaceutical companies paying doctors to attend a meeting with little educational content at a resort destination).

The long US history of volunteerism translates into additional differences between US CVBs and foreign CBs. Many organizers of meetings of volunteer type groups are themselves volunteers. Groups typically are categorized under the general heading of SMERF and constitute a large segment of the convention and meetings business. While many of the larger SMERF groups can afford to hire professional meeting planners, a large number of the smaller ones are run by volunteers who are not full-time meeting planners. US CVBs need support personnel on their staff to help these volunteers run a successful meeting. CBs outside US do not have this unique SMERF market segment to attend to.

A final difference is in the role that non-US CBs play in marketing the overall destination. The non-US CB tends to play a largely tactical role in marketing meetings and conventions to the MICE market, while a national tourism office or board is responsible for the destination brand strategy. The tourist office or board is typically responsible for coming up with the brand identity, developing a marketing plan for the destination, and executing that plan to attract the leisure traveler. The US CVB executive has increasingly come to see his or her role as the person responsible for crafting and disseminating the destination's brand.

Changes and Challenges to CVB Futures

CVB strengths have traditionally been filling beds by selling destinations as sites for conventions and meetings, assisting with on site operations of conventions and meetings, and providing information to convention and meeting planners and tourists. CVBs usually know why a location is chosen by meeting planners and tourists, what made them happy or unhappy, and the approximate value the visitor industry adds to a destination. CVB leaders provide a vital communication link between the local tourism industry and the various community stakeholders in the destination. They have taken on the responsibility for explaining the needs, wants, and expectations of each group to the other. They are effective at articulating the balance between the interests of the overall destination and the interests of the tourism industry's individual members.

Today, many CVB executives have also accepted major responsibility for marketing the destination to the travel trade and directly to tourists and other potential visitors, and for destination branding, which can be used to sell the community not only to visitors but to new industry and others involved in economic development (Braley, 2006). The added challenges for the CVB executive as they assume these new roles are to:

- identify assets of the destination that yield competitive advantage;
- identify market segments whose interests and expectations match destination assets;
- identify current and future interests and expectations of current visitors;
- identify current and future interests and expectations of potential visitors;
- translate those visitor interests and expectations into the required individual components of the whole experience;
- motivate the destination stakeholders to fund, create, change, fix, update, or otherwise adjust the individual assets to ensure that the asset owners meet the interests and expectations of the targeted market segment; and
- communicate the destination assets to potential leisure and convention visitors through the development of a brand that should drive all marketing and sales activities.

If the past history of this business and its leaders is prologue to its future, we should be able to make some reasonable extrapolations into the future by further examining some key challenges facing CVB executives (see also Gretzel et al. [2006] as well as Harrill [Chapter 25] in this *Handbook*). We have organized this examination into the five categories where the executives we interviewed saw important changes happening:

1 funding and governance,
2 job responsibilities,
3 technological change,
4 information's changing role, and
5 competition.

Funding and Governance

Almost everyone we talked to regarded the growing political pressure to use more of the bed tax revenues to fund things besides CVB related activities as a major future challenge. One successful middle sized CVB executive told us, "I think economics are troubling in that there is so much demand for public money now in our state and I guess other states. There's just a real need for public dollars in areas other than visitor marketing. That's a challenge." There is growing recognition by CVB executives that they have to have a solid objective and defensible answer to give when the local politicians ask what is the value they get in return for the money the CVBs spend (Gartrell, 1992, 1994; Sheehan and Ritchie, 2005). The importance of accountability in sustaining the CVB funding is already a major issue and will continue in the future.

Attempts to find supplemental or alternative funding sources will be challenging in light of limited tax revenues, limited revenue enhancements, increased marketing costs driven by increased competition among destinations, and greater stakeholder expectations notwithstanding the decrease in funding availability. The CVB leaders interviewed recognized that the increased competition for funding requires them to more aggressively and effectively market their value to their own communities and local stakeholders. They felt a strong need to do a better job of telling their community about their contributions to its economic health. But most of those interviewed believed that their stakeholders did not understand either what they did or the value of their work to their community. As a smaller CVB executive told us, "everybody knows what the Chamber of Commerce does, but not many people know what a CVB does. That goes for my own relatives."

Job Responsibilities

The second current challenge is the change in individual job responsibilities of the CVB executive. Recalling what Carmichael did for Detroit in 1896 gives us some insight into the future of this issue (Carmichael, 1896). He sold the city to potential conventioneers.

As such he represented the city and not the industry, although the industry benefited. Boosterism was an early driver of this profession, and civic pride made it important to get the word out to anyone that met in conventions so that perhaps they would come to live, work, or play in that city after the meeting was over. It is hard to see that boosterism today in the CVB leader's tasks, roles, and responsibilities, for a couple of reasons. First, the automatic funding from the bed tax means that revenues are driven by people who come and go and not people who come and fall in love with the community and stay and bring their jobs with them.

Second, the professional growth and development of the CVB executive role means that the person running the CVB is more often a newcomer to the community than a native. Given the small size of most CVBs, it is hard to make career progress by staying in a single CVB, and career professionals move around a lot in pursuit of growth opportunities. This movement makes it harder to develop the deep roots of local involvement and community acquaintances that were characteristic of many early CVB leaders. Lack of deep roots in the community has led necessarily and appropriately to an increasing emphasis by the community on objective accountability measures, formal performance appraisals, and measurable goals. Successful CVB executives seek more objective measures to balance the short-term goals of one segment of the travel and tourism industry with longer-term community goals. Since what gets measured is usually what gets managed, the precision and adequacy of the measures adopted to evaluate the CVB's success become an increasingly critical issue for the future of the CVB (Ryan and Zahra, 2004).

Recently DMAI undertook an ambitious and, the authors believe, overdue initiative and established an accreditation process (Destination Management Accreditation Program) to define and assess some important industry-wide criteria associated with successfully managed CVBs. This DMAI accreditation program allows, for the first time, a CVB to assess itself against best practices established by the profession itself and helps their boards of directors and CEOs to find a common starting point for discussing and understanding the CEO's total job tasks, roles, and responsibilities. Accreditation should become a fundamental key to mutual understanding on all issues of accountability and can add to the CEO's credibility as accreditation requirements are met.

Technological Change

Technology is the third historical trend that continues to be an important influence on the business today (see Gretzel and Fesenmaier [Chapter 31] on information technology and tourism in this *Handbook*). CVBs and the travel industry have to keep up with changing technologies in order to serve an increasingly globalized marketplace. With the advent of virtual meetings, instant conferencing, and even virtual communities, the opportunities to bring people together virtually will become greater, especially with rising costs of bringing people together. Similar challenges exist in serving the evolving visitor market. Diminishing rapidly are the postcards, letters, and phone calls to CVBs requesting their "tourist information kit" as visitors become technologically sophisticated. Commercial travel information websites like Expedia and Travelocity already compete with one of the CVB's traditional roles, the distributor of destination information.

Competitive independent-minded CVB executives will have to explore new ways of doing business, such as cooperating with their rival cities or TIA, or perhaps even calling on DMAI to help members form and market an official destination web portal that can be jointly marketed to a global marketplace. If the future providers of travel information in general and destination specific information in particular are those that can establish a strong web presence, this collaboration among CVBs will need to happen if they intend to stay relevant in providing destination information.

CVB executives will thus have to spend more time and resources learning to use the web as a proactive marketing tool and apply it to reach previous and new customers alike. The website can also serve as a coordinating mechanism to help ensure that all destination sales and marketing efforts are aligned to consistently promoting the destination brand and make it easy for customers to access and assess the assets of a destination (Ha and Love, 2005; Hughes, 1985; Pan and Fesenmaier, 2006; Wang and Fesenmaier, 2006; Woolford, 2005; Yuan et al., 2005).

In our interviews with CVB executives, the general discussion of technology became quickly focused on information technology (IT). IT was the most often mentioned change that the CVB leaders felt would impact their business. They see IT making their job both easier and harder in a variety of ways. Their job becomes easier as the web allows them to make available a wider variety of destination specific information to both meeting planners and visitors that used to require expensive FAM tours or large volumes of costly printed material. But these respondents were also concerned about how some CVB functions might be replaced by web based services in ways that they could see coming but could not clearly define. This is discussed further below.

Information's Changing Roles

One of the original reasons that the DMAI was created was to share information about conventions with each other. Somebody had to collect it, store it, and make it available to other CVBs, and DMAI has performed these tasks well. Although the need for information has not changed, technology has changed the way in which it can be gathered, stored, and distributed. DMAI collects its information from its member CVBs and stores it in its MINT database, to which other member CVBs have access. Today the data in MINT are available from sources other than DMAI. The increasing sophistication of the databases of national hotel sales offices and the

meeting planners means that they often have better information than CVBs, and are not under any obligation to share it. This loss of exclusive control on the part of DMAI over convention and meeting information is bound to change the traditional role of DMAI as the collector, organizer, and disseminator of this information.

How they put the information to use is also changing. Early CVBs provided information to their city's visitors by printing pamphlets or brochures and, later, building and staffing visitor centers. They also sponsored FAM tours for meeting and convention planners, sent representatives to a variety of travel and trade association conventions, and actively pursued other ways to market their destination. While these roles will continue to be performed, they will increasingly be supplemented or even replaced by technology and new business models. Leisure tourists will be more inclined to find information on MapQuest and Google, and convention and meeting buyers will take virtual tours of destinations to save the time and expense of multiple site visits. And if third party intermediaries begin locating their representatives in destinations, they could even take over the traditional CVB role of familiarizing the meeting planners with the destination.

The changing roles of the CVBs and DMAI being described above is not only driven by changing information technology and growing sophistication on the part of modern travelers but also by diminished funding on the part of local governments, as noted earlier. Since travelers do not care whether the destination information they seek is produced in India or Indiana, the outsourcing trend seen in manufacturing industry may just be starting in the CVB industry.

Competition

Historically the early CVB leaders or Convention Secretaries used every tactic they could invent to get a convention to come to their destination. A story is told of a woman telling the delegates of an entire convention, who were about to vote on the site of their next convention, that her boss's dying request was for the convention to be held in the boss's city. She got their votes. While marketing techniques have grown more sophisticated than these dying pleas, the intensity of the competition between destinations has not. In fact, most CVB executives believe the competition is greater than ever and likely to continue in the future.

Competition in conventions and trade shows is increased by the growing pace of construction of new or expanded convention centers and "big box" hotels with large amounts of meeting and exhibit space. If the bed tax revenues have had a down side, it has been the creation of too much convention center capacity across the country. As a recent analysis of the industry has shown, this overcapacity has become a weak spot that meeting planners and convention organizers have found and effectively exploited (Sanders, 2005). Some destinations have rented their convention space at highly reduced rates, while other destinations have filled the center with whatever paying customers they could find, including local groups and gate shows that bring no new visitors to the destination. Given the governance split in many destinations between convention centers and CVBs, the potential for conflict can only increase in the future. Communicating to the governmental owners of the center the need to consider the total revenues generated for the city and not just the center's revenue stream will continue to be a major challenge.

There is clearly a need for new thinking about competition and the future role of the CVB that blends competition and cooperation into "coopetition." As a middle sized CVB executive said, "I think with increased competition coming on, you'll see more of a need for coopetition, working closely with your competitors, more of a regional approach to many things. You'll need to collaborate with people that you might have looked on as competition before."

Future Trends

While technology and competition are often mentioned in predictions of any industry's future, there are two or three other trends that seem to stand out. The first is related to *financing*. There is an inevitable decline of the CVB's (and industry's) access to the bed tax revenues as governments become increasingly inclined to siphon off this source of revenue for other purposes. This decline is likely to change the CVB business model so that it looks more like it did originally when it relied on local beneficiaries to fund it or even to eliminate the present model altogether in favor of some new business form. The new form could even be a for-profit model that eliminates the challenges and frustrations of competing for tax revenues and membership support and allow CVBs to aggressively compete for commission dollars and promote new ways of doing business across the industry.

The second trend is the growing role for CVB executives as *spokesperson* of the meeting, visitor, and tourist industry in their destination. Although it does reflect somewhat the early role of the convention chasers who presented the advantages of the entire destination as they courted convention and meeting planners, serving as a spokesperson of the industry to the community is a new role for most CVBs. But it has become clear to the people we talked to that this is a role they must perform because there is no one else to do it. While their motives are partly to preserve their revenues from further government intrusions, a stronger motive, coming from their passion for the business, is their belief that their industry produces substantial benefits for their community. Thus our interviewees are increasingly convinced that they must take the responsibility for both marketing their destination to potential visitors and managing the destination's resources to ensure that the benefits they claim their destination offers to visitors are realized.

A third trend is the realization that CVBs may need to find new paths of *cooperation* with other CVB executives due to the increasing competition for financial resources, pressure to accomplish more with the resources they get, and competition from destinations all over the world and, at home, from private sector intermediaries. There are several illustrations of individual CVBs forming sales partnerships but the Best Cities' alliance of destinations offers one of the better illustrations of a group alliance of competitors. Although other alliances can be found in New England and on the Gulf Coast, Best Cities (2008) claims on its website that it is the world's first. It consists of eight city partners on five continents—Cape Town, Copenhagen, Dubai, Edinburgh, Melbourne, San Juan, Singapore, and Vancouver—and it claims to be recognized internationally for its innovative approach to setting and delivering the world's best convention bureau practices for the meetings industry. These practices are embodied in 35 service standards it established for each partner city to meet to claim membership in the Best Cities group. The standards are spelled out on its website where it can advertise this valued consistency in meeting standards to its meeting planner customers.

Whether in funding, a new role as spokesman and keeper of the destination brand, *coopetition* with other CVBs, or some other some way or ways, or a combination of all of these ways, we predict that the future of the CVB will be different. Tomorrow's CVB will be different than today's CVB in possibly major ways. Pressures for funding and accountability by local stakeholders will require that CVBs collaborate more closely with the wide variety of local stakeholders, rather than focusing on satisfying it's traditionally largest interest group, the hotel industry. The chapter by Rich Harrill (Chapter 25) in this *Handbook* addresses some of the strategic challenges related to "destination management" and should be read as a complement to this chapter.

We conclude by noting that the web will be more widely used and may be a source of revenue to the CVBs sponsoring them.

The world expects sophisticated web-based technological solutions to its information needs, but individual CVBs cannot afford to provide them without collaboration and joint marketing campaigns. The most serious future threat for CVBs and DMAI may well be failing to meet the needs of potential visitors to their destinations because they lacked the willingness to collaborate and pool their resources.

References

Best Cities (2008). *Best Cities*. Retrieved May 29, 2008 from www.bestcities.net/.

Braley, S. (2006). "2006 Meetings Market Report." *Meetings & Conventions*, 41(8): 13.

Butler, F.C. (1916). "Financing and Entertaining of Conventions." *American City* (City edition), 15(3): 230.

Carmichael, M.J. (1896). "Open Arms." *The Detroit Journal*, February 6: 1, 5.

Denton, L.H. (1950). "The Convention Business—Past and Present." Unpublished manuscript.

DMAI. (2005). *CVB Organizational & Financial Profile*. Washington, DC: Destination Marketing Association International.

Fenich, G.G. (1992). "Convention Centre Development: Pros, Cons and Unanswered Questions." *International Journal of Hospitality Management*, 11(3): 183–196.

Fenich, G.G. (1995). "Convention Centre Development: Some Questions Answered." *International Journal of Hospitality Management*, 14(3): 311–324.

Fenich, G.G. (2007). *Meetings, Expositions, Events & Conventions* (2nd edition.). Englewood Cliffs, NJ: Pearson/Prentice Hall.

Ford, R.C. and Peeper, W.C. (2007). "The Past as Prologue: Predicting the Future of the Convention and Visitor Bureau Industry on the Basis of its History." *Tourism Management*, 28(4): 1104–1114.

Ford, R.C. and Peeper, W.C. (2008). *Managing Destination Marketing Organizations: The Tasks, Roles and Responsibilities of the Convention and Visitors Bureau Executive*. Orlando, FL: ForPer Publishing.

Gartrell, R.B. (1992). "Convention and Visitor Bureaux: Current Issues in Management and Marketing." *Journal of Travel and Tourism Marketing*, 1(2): 71–78.

Gartrell, R.B. (1994). *Destination Marketing* (2nd edition.). Dubuque, IA: Kendall/Hunt.

Gretzel, U., Fesenmaier, D.R., Formica, S. and O'Leary, J.T. (2006). "Searching for the Future: Challenges Faced by Destination Marketing Organizations." *Journal of Travel Research*, 45(4): 116–126.

Ha, M. and Love, C. (2005). "Exploring Content and Design Factors Associated with Convention and Visitors Bureau Web Site Development: An Analysis of Recognition by Meeting Managers." *Journal of Convention & Event Tourism*, 7(1): 43–59.

Harper, G.E. (1971). "Chicago: City on Fire." *Commerce*. Commemorative Supplement: 1F–160F.

Hiemstra, S.J. and Ismali, J.A. (1993). "Incidence of the Impacts of Room Taxes on the Lodging Industry." *Journal of Travel Research*, 31(4): 22–26.

Hotel Association of New York. (1954). *New York City 5% Tax on Hotel Room Rentals* (p. 2). New York: Hotel Association of New York.

Hughes, A. (1985). "The Computer Age Dawns for Convention and Visitors Bureau." *Successful Meetings*, 34(3): 49–56.

Hughes, A. (1987a). "How IACVB Got Started." *Successful Meetings*, 36(1): 114.

Hughes, A. (1987b). "The Evolution of the C&VB." *Successful Meetings*, 36(1): 100.

IACVB (1989). "1988–89 Strategic Plan Executive Summary." Champaign, IL: unpublished manuscript.

Kim, S.S., Chon, K.S. and Chung, K.Y. (2003). "Convention Industry in South Korea: An Economic Impact Analysis." *Tourism Management*, 24(5): 553–562.

Koutoulas, D. (2005). "Operational and Financial Characteristics of Convention and Visitors Bureaux." *Journal of Convention & Event Tourism*, 7(3/4): 139–156.

Lathrop, J. (2005). "Board Governance." In R. Harrill (Ed.), *Fundamentals of Destination Management and Marketing* (pp. 191–218). Lansing, MI: Educational Institute of the American Hotel & Lodging Association.

Love, R. (1915). "Angling for Conventions— A New Sport Highly Developed." *The St. Louis Republic*, July 31: 1.

Markarian, M. (1989). "Turning Back the Clock: The History of C&VBs." *Meeting News* (Supplement), 13(11): 8.

Metropolitan Detroit Convention and Visitors Bureau (1996). *A Century of Economic Development*. Detroit, MI: Metropolitan Detroit Convention and Visitors Bureau.

Migdal, D. (1991). "25th Anniversary CVBs: Making Cities Slicker." *Meetings and Conventions*, 26(9): 64–67.

Morrison, A.M., Bruen, S.M. and Anderson, D.J. (1998). "Convention and Visitor Bureaus in the USA: A Profile of Bureaus, Bureau Executives, and Budgets." *Journal of Travel & Tourism Marketing*, 7(1): 1–19.

Mutschlechner, C. (2003). "The Annual Assembly of the International Meetings Association ICCA in Copenhagen and Malmo." *TW -FRANKFURT AM MAIN*, 27(1): 26-33.

Pan, B. and Fesenmaier, D.R. (2006). "Online Information in Search Vacation Planning Process." *Annals of Tourism Research*, 33(3): 809–832.

Rogers, T. (2003). *Conferences and Conventions: A Global Industry*. Boston, MA: Butterworth-Heinemann.

Ryan, C. and Zahra, A. (2004). "The Political Challenge: The Case of New Zealand's Tourism Organizations." In N. Morgan, A. Pritchard and R. Pride (Eds.), *Destination Branding* (pp. 79–110). Amsterdam: Elsevier.

Sanders, H. (2005). *Space Available: The Realities of Convention Centers as Economic Development Strategy*. Washington, DC: The Brookings Institution.

Sheehan, L.R. and Ritchie, J.R.B. (2005). "Destination Stakeholders: Exploring Identity and Salience." *Annals of Tourism Research*, 32(3): 711–734.

Trafton, W.L. (1987). "The International Association of Convention and Visitor Bureaus: Then and Now." Unpublished manuscript.

Turner, J.S. (1958). *Conventions: An American Institution*. Cincinnati, OH: International Association of Convention Bureaus.

Turner, J.S. (1965). *The History and Heritage of I.A.C.B.* Presentation to IACB members in Convention. Syracuse, NY.

Union of International Associations (2006/2007). *Yearbook of International Organizations*. Retrieved from www.uia.be/yearbook.

Wang, Y. and Fesenmaier, D.R. (2006). "Identifying the Success Factors of Web-Based Marketing Strategy: An Investigation of Convention and Visitor Bureaus in the United States." *Journal of Travel Research,* 44 (3): 239–249.

Weber, K. and Chon, K.S. (2002). Convention Tourism: International Research and Industry Perspectives. New York: Haworth Hospitality Press.

Wood, J.T. (2002). "How the Distribution of the Hotel Bed Tax Impacts the Destination Marketing Organization." Providence, RI. Unpublished manuscript.

Woolford, L. (2005). "Technology." In R. Harrill (Ed.), *Fundamentals of Destination Management and Marketing* (pp. 125–145). Lansing, MI: Educational Institute of the American Hotel & Lodging Association.

Yuan, Y., Gretzel, U. and Fesenmaier, D.R. (2006). "The Role of Information Technology Use in American Convention and Visitors Bureaus." *Tourism Management,* 27(2): 326–341.

Zelinsky, W. (1994). "Conventionland USA: The Geography of a Latterday Phenomenon." *Annals of the Association of American Geographers,* 84(1): 68–86.

25

Destination Management: New Challenges, New Needs

Rich Harrill

Introduction

Changing consumer demographics and preferences, rapid technological advances, globalization of trade and increasing pressure on the physical environment, are some of the key drivers of the changes in tourism destinations and among the industry sectors that facilitate travel and tourism. Various authors have identified and discussed issues and strategies related to destination management, such as growth management (Gill and Williams, 1994), planning within environmental and sociocultural capacity limits of (Inskeep, 1991), and organizations for marketing destinations (Pearce, 1992). But progress is slow in showing how the various and highly varied characteristics and issues facing tourism destinations can be integrated for effective destination management, rather than the piecemeal approach that appears to be the status quo.

The tourism literature also emphasizes the importance of involving the local community in tourism planning and development (Gunn, 2004; Murphy, 1985). For the local residents within a tourism destination, tourism development impacts on their economic, social, and cultural lifestyle, hence directly affecting their quality of life. Adverse effects of tourism development on the integrity of the natural habitat surrounding a destination can affect both the ecological integrity and the lifestyle which residents may wish to experience in that locality. But, again, the processes by which the local community members can work most effectively together with other actors and stakeholders, in order to achieve the strategic tourism planning goals of a community, are not well understood and neither are the organizational structures that might be optimal for managing such a challenging setting.

Promising approaches have been forwarded within various areas that are relevant to planning and managing tourism in destinations (Farrell and Twining-Ward, 2004; Healey, 1997; Schianetza et al., 2007), but the issue of strategic destination management per se has not been clearly addressed and a coherent paradigm around destination management continues to be lacking.

The chapter commences with a brief review of some key characteristics of tourism destinations and the need for integrated management strategies, followed by a review of destination management organizations (DMOs). Challenges and critiques of DMOs are introduced, followed by two case examples illustrating how two DMOs (a local and a county level DMO) are engaging in collaboration with residents and other stakeholders to manage sustainability and development challenges. A short discussion and conclusion draws the chapter to a close.

Characteristics of Tourism Destinations

The Destination System

A tourist destination is "a place that a traveler chooses to visit for a stay of at least a night in order to experience some feature or characteristic of the place perceived as a satisfying leisure time experience" (Leiper, 1990: 95). Blank (1989: 22) defines a tourist destination area (TDA) as having the following characteristics: (1) a recognized, definable appeal to travelers; (2) a tourist industry of sufficient scale to deserve treatment as a factor in the local economy; (3) coherence in its geography and among its tourist-related features; and (4) political integrity, so that effective communications can take place and viable decisions can be made. The TDA is therefore well defined geopolitically and could contain an urban or rural community within its boundary. A "tourist destination," as used in the literature, can refer to a country, a region, an area, or a local habitation; e.g., a city, town, village. Without each of the elements outlined above, the tourism system would not be a functioning system; i.e., there is no tourist attraction (subsystem) without a tourist there to enjoy the leisure experience or without the ability to conserve the attraction (Laws, 1995). Similarly, without transportation and access, the tourist would not reach the destination, which makes infrastructure development an essential requirement in order to enable visitor access. Leiper (1990) thus advocates a systems approach to studying tourism.

Interrelationships Within and Outside the Destination

The elements of the tourism system are therefore closely interlinked. Strong interrelationships exist among the private sector, the government authorities, the residents and other public members; actions by one party with respect to planning or management can impact on the rest of the stakeholders. Furthermore, these stakeholders and the natural environment coexist in an almost symbiotic fashion, where the natural environment often performs the dual function of being a source of tourism attraction and a habitat for local residents (Blank, 1989). A major resort project in one community can have far reaching impacts that might extend well beyond the immediate region, to the natural environment in addition to its sociocultural and economic effects. Similarly, destination marketing organizations try to accrue benefits to their immediate constituencies, but can inadvertently create not merely positive but also negative social-cultural impacts if the destination is not marketed responsibly (e.g., with respect to it image and the expectations generated by their advertising and promotional strategies). Moreover, with the interconnection and access enabled by transportation and other technological innovations (include information technology), few destinations can claim to be "remote" and visitors, along with the infrastructure and services needed to ensure a "satisfactory" tourism experience, enable a range of positive and negative impacts, and changes on the destination area (Smith, 2002; Tosun, 1998).

The Public 'Good' Issue

One of the issues to be considered in managing the destination's resources is that of a "public good." A public good, by its very nature, is a candidate for government activity. Tourism, it can be argued, is a public good for several reasons beyond the leisure benefits it provides for societal well-being (much of which is provided by the private and public sector). Tourism may be of strategic importance to a country, both as an export commodity to generate foreign currency earnings and a potential generator of taxes for local authorities. Government investment and development of tourism infrastructure benefits all sectors of the tourism industry, foreign and domestic tourists, as well as the local inhabitants in a tourism destination area. Well conceived development of a critical mass of attractions by the combined efforts of private and public interests then provides a direct benefit to all the industry sectors involved in the tourism system, by improving the attractiveness and competitiveness of the destination. Residents and tourists also benefit if development is adequately tailored to their needs. To this extent, tourism development takes on the characteristics of a public and social good whose benefit is shared by numerous stakeholders; this characteristic also lends support for public involvement and public–private partnerships in tourism development and management. The flow-through of such benefits to various stakeholders and the local to global interconnections and interdependencies that destinations are embedded in are better discernible by adopting a systems view of tourism, as noted earlier (Leiper, 1990).

Multiple Stakeholders

The tourism destination is also challenging due to the presence of numerous stakeholders who may hold diverse views about development. These stakeholders range from those providing diverse tourism-related services to those who service primarily local residents (but stand to be impacted by tourism development/growth) and those who reside in the local area. They may be long-term inhabitants whose history, identity and belonging are closely related to the land, or they may be incomers—relatively new arrivals. Stakeholders at the local destination level can include the local destination management organizations, local real estate and development organizations,

local resident organizations and the local residents, environmental groups, planning, healthcare, housing and transportation authorities, as well as hospitality related (accommodations, restaurants, etc.) and other commercial businesses. There may be a range of attractions like theme parks, shopping, zoos, botanical gardens, whose owners and operators have a stake in destination development. In addition, there are the cultural institutions and associations, like those related to the arts, museums, theatre, as well as historic and cultural heritage stakeholders (e.g., festival associations, historic district commissions, individual festival groups, etc. A state or nationally endorsed heritage site or a World Heritage Site adds further complexity, as stakeholders extend quickly to the "global" domain on environmental and cultural heritage issues (see Orbaşlı and Woodward [Chapter 18] in this *Handbook*). Banks, hospitals, local law enforcement are other important stakeholders.

Strategies for Destination Development and Management

Numerous strategies and processes have been advocated to manage the fragmented and challenging characteristics of tourism destinations, in particular, collaborative planning and partnerships (Araujo and Bramwell, 2002; Bushell and Eagles, 2007; Bramwell and Lane, 2000). In the Caribbean destinations, Poon (1993) noted that the multifaceted nature of the tourism industry has led tourism ministries and authorities at the national level to look after marketing and promotion rather than overall product development. She argued that this approach is no longer optimal and "new and innovative ways have to be devised to take the entire tourism product in hand" (Poon, 1993: 239). Poon (1993) describes the industry subsystem as comprised of producers (e.g., airlines, on-site service suppliers), distributors (e.g., tour operators), facilitators (e.g., financial service suppliers), and consumers (passengers/tourists). At the producer level, she also felt that due to the level of sophistication and development of marketing companies, these will have the ability to shift value creation to the product development side and integrate the two functions. Though integration of marketing and planning at the regional and local level is not discussed in detail, Poon notes that public-private sector collaboration and cooperation is key to the success of building a dynamic private sector in Caribbean tourism. Fostering this new dimension would require regional cooperation and developing new institutions (Poon, 1993).

This problem is evident when one examines the role and functions of tourist organizations which are primarily involved in the marketing and promotion of tourist destinations (Gartrell, 1994). An examination of tourist organizations in several developed nations, as provided by Pearce (1992) in "Tourist Organizations," shows that most tourist organizations typically did not get involved in the planning aspect of destinations, with some exceptions. For example, the New Zealand Tourism Department, one of the earliest National Tourist Organizations (NTOs), traces its roots back to 1901. Its activities up to 1984 included directly managing and developing resort areas, running an extensive tour operating division and overseas sales and promotions; however, since 1984, the department has been divested of its business operations and now focuses on assisting the private sector in developing and marketing New Zealand as a tourism destination, within government objectives (Pearce, 1992). DMOs, due to their important role in tourism destinations, are discussed in further detail below.

Destination Management Organizations

There are many different types of DMOs deserving study. These include convention and visitors bureaus, regional marketing organizations, and state and local tourism offices (Pearce, 1992). In North America, the most common type of destination management organization is the Convention and Visitors Bureau (CVB), but there are several other types of tourist offices; e.g., small rural communities may have a tourist office that is administered under the local Chambers of Commerce. According to Gehrisch (2005: xxv), these organizations are defined as "serving as a coordinating entity, bringing together diverse community stakeholders to attract visitors to their area." Internationally, DMOs have different structures and names. All of these organizations are assuming new importance as globalization and demographics make the service sectors, specifically tourism, the primary industry in many areas of the world.

Pike (2004: 14–15) provides the following definitions for various types of DMOs: (1) a *destination marketing organization* is any organization at any level responsible for the marketing of an identifiable destination. This definition excludes government departments that are responsible for planning and policy; (2) a *national tourism office* (NTO) is an entity with overall responsibility for marketing a country as a tourism destination. Examples of national tourism offices include the China National Tourism Administration (CNTA) and the Mexico Government Tourism Office; (3) a *state tourism organization* (STO) is an organization with the overall responsibility for marketing a state, province, or territory as a tourism destination, in a country that has a federal political system. Examples of state tourism organizations include the California Division of Tourism and the Hawaii Visitors and Convention Bureau; (4) a *regional tourism organization* (RTO) is an organization responsible for marketing a concentrated tourism area as a tourism destination. Examples of regional tourism organizations are the European Travel Commission, and the South Pacific Tourism Organization.

The Meaning and Purpose of DMOs

However, despite these definitions, there remains some confusion about the acronym "DMO." Because these tourism development organizations arose initially to focus on marketing, the "m" in DMO is typically thought to mean marketing. However, today's DMOs have evolved to take an active management role in their own environs as well, both built and natural. This evolution has occurred from simple recognition that the very tourism product that DMOs market must be sustained and maintained, not only out of moral and ethical concerns, but to continue a healthy tourism revenue stream. For simplicity, the acronym remains DMO rather than DMMO—although many modern destination management organizations embrace these dual missions. The major professional association for DMOs— Destination Marketing Association International (DMAI)—retains the marketing designation out of the practical recognition that it represents a wide variety of DMOs, many of which still function primarily as local marketing organizations (e.g., CVBs). While DMAI's textbook, *Fundamentals of Destination Marketing and Management* (Harrill, 2005), amply acknowledges a broader conceptual framework, most veteran DMO directors will admit that marketing is still at the heart of the industry and the "selling" characteristic is one that all DMOs share.

As noted by Pike (2004), the purpose of destination marketing organizations is to foster sustained destination competitiveness. According to the author, specific goals of DMOs can be summarized as relating to four main themes: (1) enhancing destination image; (2) increasing industry profitability; (3) reducing seasonality; and (4) ensuring long-term funding. Related topics that have emerged of interest to researchers include brand promise and identity, research (including return-on-investment and visitor conversion), and employment and leadership (see Ritchie and Crouch, 2003 for more on these and others). Leadership includes many facets here, ranging from leadership in operations and management decision making, as well as well as leadership in place marketing. Leadership in destination image and branding has been examined, for instance, by Blain et al. (2005) and Pike (2004), among others. Exploring the branding process for DMOs, Blain et al. (2005) found that many such organizations narrowly define branding as the creation of logos and taglines.

Through a survey of DMOs, the researchers constructed a more comprehensive definition of branding, including identification, differentiation, experience, expectations, image, consolidation, reinforcement, recognition, consistency, brand messages, and emotional response.

Partnerships and Collaboration

The most successful DMOs excel in establishing partnerships and collaborative networks. Sheehan et al. (2007) explore the relationship between DMOs and its two most powerful stakeholders, the city and hotel. The researchers assert that DMOs operate as a powerful "triad" with hotels and city government. They conclude that while such an arrangement can be productive and functional, it may also be problematic and highly political. Sheehan et al. recommend four key strategies for DMO survival: (1) employ a strategy of collaboration with strategic stakeholders; (2) institutionalize the collaboration with strategic stakeholders by ensuring they are represented on the board of directors; (3) ensure regular, frequent, and clear communication with triad members using personal relationships; and (4) receive, interpret, and disseminate market information to stakeholders. Wang and Fesenmaier's (2007) study on collaborative destination marketing in Elkhart, Indiana, is also instructive. They found that collaboration destination marketing evolves through stages and results in three important types of outcomes: strategy-oriented, organizational-learning-oriented, and social capital oriented. The authors found that collaboration and cooperation may improve a DMO's marketing skills and operations, but may also result in particular learning problems, such as uncontrolled information disclosure.

Marketing-Planning Gap

Noting various social and cultural disparities and global destination competition, Jamal and Jamrozy (2006) contend that there is a serious gap between destination marketing and planning (including urban planning) that results in unsustainable destination development. They argue that overcoming this disconnect calls for a new, integrated model of destination sustainability emphasizing diversity and equity in addition to environmental and economic balance. This new model's objectives "are not to design a product, price, place and promotion of a tourism destination or attraction, but to ensure quality of life and environments through tourism development" (Jamal and Jamrozy, 2006: 168). To this end, they have proposed an integrated destination management (IDM) framework based on: (1) a collaborative and systems-based approach; (2) sustainable tourism and community-based principles; and (3) the destination's sense of place, as well as its economic and cultural diversity.

Yet to use this framework, according to the authors, existing destination management practices must change. First, sustainable destination development requires closing the traditional marketing-planning gap using planning innovations and cross-sectoral collaboration. Second, they call for governance structures and processes that enable informed participation in destination development from those who stand to be most impacted by tourism, including residents, NGOs, etc. Third, the authors noted that enabling social equity in tourism development will be an increasingly important principle for socioeconomic sustainability as new values and ethnic voices arise through globalization.

Most contemporary DMO directors understand that advocacy and politics are central to their roles. As advocates for the tourism industry, they educate residents and community leaders that tourism is economic development. This advocacy effort may be supported by research that explains the tourism industry's ROI (return-on-investment) to the community. With new responsibilities that may outstretch hotel tax dollars, entry into the political arena is seen as necessary to find funding alternatives. However, advocacy and political efforts are not without costs—accountability is the new watchword for the DMO industry as members and sponsors ask for accountability and performance in return for their support.

It is clear that the role of DMOs will need to expand towards assuming greater leadership and participating in issues beyond traditional marketing and promotional goals. One area where this changing role may be increasingly needed is in planning and managing responses to external disasters or crises (Hanbury, 2005; Pike, 2004). Their emerging role as emergency coordinator has already commenced in response to recent disasters and crises that occurred in major destinations: terrorist attacks in New York and Washington and Hurricane Katrina in New Orleans. Once only concerned with visitation immediately after crises, the new DMO role emphasizes the dissemination of information about the safety and security in the weeks following crises. Where hospitality and tourism is an economic mainstay, the local DMO is able to monitor and report steps taken toward economic recovery. In addition, these organizations may play an important role in rebuilding, making recommendations to city planners and public administrations about where new facilities may be built or requirements for rebuilding historic districts and economic zones.

Two examples are provided below of organizations that embody the dual mission, those adept at both destination marketing and management. While *Fundamentals of Destination Marketing and Management* describes the things DMOs do—service, sales, marketing, research, communications, product development, technology, human resources, member care, financial management, board governance, and alliances—the two examples will explore the diversity of collaborative practices among these DMOs, and the multiple stakeholders and interests managed by these DMOs. These organizations are the Juneau, Alaska, CVB, and Queen Anne's County Office of Tourism, Maryland. The following two cases have been adapted from case studies found in *Best Practices in Tourism and Destination Management, Vol. 2* (Harrill, 2005), a practitioner-oriented publication for sharing best practices among DMOs.

Case Example: Juneau Convention and Visitors Bureau

Background on Convention and Visitors Bureaus

The history of CVBs in North America dates back to 1896 when a prominent Detroit journalist, Milton Carmichael, suggested that local businessmen band together to promote the city as a convention destination and represent the city's many hotels to bid for business (Gehrisch, 2005; see also Ford and Peeper [Chapter 24] in this *Handbook*). From these beginnings, bureaus evolved and broadened in scope to include leisure travelers, spurred by improvement transportation infrastructure after World War II. From the mid-1960s into the 1970s, DMOs gained new stability and legitimacy though hotel tax funding. Reagan-era economic policy from 1980 dictated that cities find funding alternatives, leading to new recognition of tourism as a legitimate economic development strategy. To lure more visitors (and dollars), DMOs became increasingly sophisticated about destination marketing and branding through the 1980s and 1990s. This new emphasis on strategic thinking met with the emergence of sustainability as a mainstream development concept. Furthermore, globalization has made these organizations the primary drivers of economic development in many locales, yet with this new credibility came new responsibilities for performance accountability and accreditation standards. Cooperating and involving key stakeholders in managing issues and resolving conflicts was an important changing role assumed by DMOs like the Juneau Convention and Visitors Bureau.

Juneau, Alaska's capital city, is a small coastal community (population 30,000) located on the Inside Passage. Over the last two decades, the city has felt the effects of the significant growth of the cruise ship industry. The number of cruise passengers rose from 87,000 in 1982 to more than 760,000 in 2003 (Lorene Palmer, CEO Juneau Convention and Visitors Bureau, pers. comm.). As the number of cruise passengers grew, so did the effects associated with air traffic and bus transportation grow, as well. This rapid growth has had both positive and negative impacts on the community. Detriments have included increases in traffic and noise. As the industry grew, residents became more concerned about these impacts, but city officials and cruise operators did not proactively manage them. Increased tension in the community led to a management program that attempted to mitigate negative impacts retaining tourism's positive benefits. Far from perfect, the management program is nonetheless a model for sustainable destination management in that it represents an attempt to deal with issues among all stakeholders, including residents, local officials, and tour operators.

The year 2005 marked the 20th year of the Juneau Convention and Visitors Bureau (JCVB) serving as a vehicle for local business and city government working together to promote Juneau as a destination for leisure and business visitors (Photos 25.1 and 25.2). According to the bureau JCVB is a private, nonprofit organization dedicated to economic development in Juneau, Alaska through promoting and marketing Juneau as a year-round visitor destination. The bureau claims that its primary goal is to increase the overnight stays of business and pleasure travelers who support local businesses through consumer spending, and the city through payment of bed tax. In addition to its marketing goals, the bureau asserts that "overall, the JCVB seeks to ensure Juneau enjoys a more stable, sustainable year-round economy." Currently, the JCVB is funded solely from bed tax collections. Additional revenues for the CVB come from membership dues and marketing-program receipts. The bureau also receives cruise ship passenger fees to offset the cost of providing hospitality services to such visitors (Lorene Palmer, pers. comm.).

The profile of Juneau's tourism industry has changed over the last 20 years. The cruise

Photo 25.1 View of Gastineau Channel, Juneau, Alaska.
Source: Courtesy of the Juneau Convention and Visitors Bureau.

industry has become the city's primary visitor market. With the increasing strength of the cruise market, the JCVB's resources have been directed toward bolstering the overnight visitor market. In addition to marketing the destination to potential travelers, the bureau also provides hospitality and information services to both cruise and non-cruise visitors. It also supports the management of the TBMP program by providing administrative

Photo 25.2 Flightseeing by Floatplane, Juneau, Alaska.
Source: Courtesy of the Juneau Convention and Visitors Bureau.

services to assist with the program's promotion and managing the tourism hotline. Concerns about the impacts of Juneau's growing tourism industry first surfaced in 1993 when local residents expressed opposition to the increasing presence of fixed-wing aircraft or "flightseers" in the Gastineau Channel. In 1994, conflicts between residents and commercial hiking operations on local trails prompted the local city council to institute a tourism working group (TWG) to address tourism growth issues. The working group is a loose knit, informal coalition of community grassroots activists and concerned corporations.

In January 1995, the TWG became an active entity. Composed of industry and public-sector members, the TWG was urged by some in the community to enact regulations to curb the growth of visitor activities in Juneau's neighborhoods. The tourism industry resisted the implementation of arbitrary regulations and urged the city to gather statistically valid data on tourism attitudes in Juneau to determine exactly what and where the key problems were. The city subsequently undertook research to determine the influence of these problems on resident attitudes toward tourism development. By 1997, it because obvious that, while Juneau's tourism operators did not want additional municipal regulation, they were very interested in working with the community to resolve the conflicts identified in the search.

The Tourism Best Management Practices (TBMP) Program

Begun in 1997, the Tourism Best Management Practices (TBMP) program is an outcome of resident and tourism industry dialogue concerning the impacts associated with visitor increases. Currently, 60 tour operators and more than 1100 employees voluntarily implement practices designed to reduce congestion, noise, and conflicts with residents' use of recreational areas. Also, residents can contact a tourism hotline to report violations, ask questions, or raise concerns. Emerging from TWG, the TBMP program grew from the recognition that the cumulative effect of

numerous and diverse annoyances experienced by the local residents during the tourist season can culminate in major problems form the industry and the community. The Juneau Convention & Visitors Bureau (2007) developed guidelines are divided into categories: (1) transportation and vehicles; (2) helicopter and fixed-wing "flightseeing"; (3) walking, biking, and hiking tours; (4) cruise ships; (5) docks, harbors, and the airport; (6) marine tour and sightseeing operations; and (7) general agreements for all operators and/or agents. Within each category, specific areas of concern identified by local residents are enumerated. Through a series of public meetings each spring during which community input is gathered, tourism industry businesses develop an ongoing operation to ensure that each item is responsibly addressed. For example, in agreements regarding transportation and vehicles, 16 specific items are included, from engine idling to impeding pedestrian traffic. By listing each actual and potential irritant and offering the best possible way for motor coaches, vans, shuttles, and taxis to operate, each root issue is addressed before it can develop into a full-blown conflict within the community. Because residents are urged to read the guidelines and feel empowered to call the tourism hotline to report operators who ignore those guidelines, accountability for operator behavior is ensured. The TBMP is not designed to address long-range tourism planning; rather, it serves as a viable method to adjust specific tourism operational procedures and address short-term issues.

Indicators of success of the TBMP program include both objective data and anecdotal information. Research shows consistent stabilization of resident attitudes regardless of increase in number of visitors. Complaint-oriented letters to the editor and opinion pieces critical of visitor industry activity—once staples in the local press—have virtually disappeared. Since the TBMP's implementation, the program has seen gradually increasing participation, including rising numbers of operators and companies (and their employees) taking part.

The number of hotline calls has also increased, showing increased awareness and participation on the part of residents. The program has been successful, according to a recent community survey showing that the number of residents who believe that tourism has an overall positive impact grew from 29% in 1998 to 40% in 2006 (McDowell Group, 2006) According to survey information compiled by the McDowell Group, nearly half of all residents the tourism industry paid its fair share—or more—for services used by visitors. However, the survey also found that foot traffic and vehicle congestion were the leading tourism-related impacts, followed by helicopter noise. In addition, nearly half of Juneau resident believed that the city and borough of Juneau was still not doing enough to manage the impacts of tourism. The percentage of residents who felt that the city was not doing enough fell from 52% in 2002 to 47% in 2006.

The program is both an organized effort to reduce impacts and an example of an industry trying its best to be a good neighbor. However, the TBMP has had challenges. For example, awareness of the TBMP must be continually promoted to ensure that residents know operators are being good corporate neighbors. It is also sometimes difficult to get all corporate operators on board; many companies are hesitant to lose control over their tourism activities and operations by participating in the program. Finally, because participation in the program is voluntary, there is no mechanism for punishing repeat offenders. At this time, companies use an internal audit form to track complaints, and they meet two or three times during the summer to "self-police" travel-related firms.

The most important point for instituting such a program is that it should be implemented sooner rather than later. Communities should anticipate tourism growth and attempt to neutralize negative impacts before they become too prominent. At that point, it is often difficult to change negative perceptions about the tourism industry and its corporate members. Emerging destinations are especially vulnerable to cumulative impacts in a short period of time. However, community officials are often caught by surprise concerning the growth of tourism because the industry still does not receive the respect it deserves as an economic development engine. Overall, the key to Juneau's TBMP is to create opportunities for operators to become involved and to shoulder accountability. They realize that participation in the program will only increase their own product lifecycle. Finally, most realize that voluntary participation is much more desirable in the long run than laws and regulations instituted by the local government responding to citizen complaints.

Case Example: Queen Anne's County Office of Tourism

Queen Anne's County is located in Maryland on the eastern side of the Chesapeake Bay. It resides only 34 miles from Baltimore, 48 miles from Washington, DC, and 66 miles from Philadelphia. Kent Island, the county's westernmost section and the largest of the several islands in the Chesapeake Bay, was the earliest site of English settlement in Maryland, established in 1631. Today, the famed Chesapeake Bay Bridge touches down on the island's shoreline, providing the major gateway to Maryland's Eastern Shore. Queen Anne's County occupies 373 square miles. Its topography is largely rolling farmland, all of it close to sea level and mostly by water, including the Chesapeake and Eastern Bays and the Chester, Corsica, and Wye rivers. Residents and visitors enjoy many outdoor-recreation opportunities, such as boating, fishing, golf, birdwatching, hiking, and hunting. The advantageous geographic location and the diverse natural resources provide residents with a remarkable quality of life and travelers with an incentive to visit a unique destination.

Some of the finest bird watching opportunities in this region occur in the fall, winter, and spring. Among other natural advantages, the county lies on the Atlantic Flyway, a high significant ecological pathway followed by waterfowl, neotropical warblers, and other birds.

One of the largest bird counts in the Eastern Shore—248 species—is found just north of Kent Island at the Eastern Neck National Wildlife Refuge (Queen Anne's County Department of Business and Tourism, 2002).[1] Many of the region's sites are recognized by the Chesapeake Bay Gateways Network, a new program associated with the Chesapeake Bay Program and the National Park Service. In addition, over the years Queen Anne's County has made a significant investment in outdoor recreation activities and associated facilities. Together, these sites compose a critical mass that can support an ecotourism initiative designed to expand the region's tourism on a year-round basis. In this way, Queen Anne's Office of Tourism is an example of a local DMO that has created a brand identity that supports and maintains the natural environment.

The Growth of Nature-Based Tourism Activities

Trends in ecotourism, adventure recreation, heritage tourism, and general visitor interest in the Chesapeake Bay region led to the county recognizing an opportunity to attract a growing number of visitors. Officials also saw that additional initiatives to attract travelers could result in significant private and public revenues. The Queen Anne's County Office of Tourism became a government department in 1994, and in 1998 it merged with the Office of Economic Development. In 2001, the county created the Natural Advantage program. A year later, the Queen Anne's County Department of Business and Tourism created a plan to enable the county to compete effectively in the new market for ecotourism and adventure tourism related to the Chesapeake Bay.

The purpose of the Queen Anne's County ecotourism initiative is to encourage visitors to tour the region. The primary economic benefit to the county lies in encouraging tourists to purchase meals, lodging, and other services within its boundaries. The county has a well-developed tourism service infrastructure and lies close to large metropolitan markets. With improvements suggested in its plan called

Natural Advantage: An Initiative to Development Ecotourism in Queen Anne's County (Queen Anne's Office of Business and Tourism, 2002), the county has made greater use of this infrastructure and gained a larger share of visitation from primary markets.

The county believes tourism as an economic development strategy holds many benefits. Officials believe that a well-designed tourism program can benefit not only visitors but also residents, for the visitors targeted by the tourism initiative are seeking many of the same things that residents enjoy—from restaurants to wildlife—and are predisposed to support the protection of the assets they appreciate. From an economic development perspective, tourism offers additional value to the county. Tourism in Queen Anne's County is "locally grown"—that is, to provide a return on an owner's investment, a tourism business must grow in place. Thus, every dollar Queen Anne's County invests to support the tourism industry is a dollar that will stay in the community. The county also believes that tourism contributes to a desirable level of diversity in the local economy, as it behaves differently from agriculture, manufacturing, service, government, and other jobs that make up the bulk of the county's employment.

Tourism also contributes to socioeconomic diversity in another way, less evident in tourism statistics. In Queen Anne's County, and the Chesapeake region as a whole, tourism supports small business, largely independent or independently owned franchises. The resilience of these entrepreneurs is an important feature of the county's economy. Finally, the county realizes that without tourism some of its businesses would not be available for residents. In other words, the county recognizes the link between tourism and quality of life. This quality of life makes Queen Anne's County a more desirable place to live and invest, which means it helps the county attract business investment other than tourism.

The Queen Anne's County ecotourism initiative was designed to help meet the goal set by the county's Economic Development Commission to develop tourism as a way to sustain the county's economy, in keeping with an ethic to maintain a healthy natural environment. The county's ecotourism development plan provides a systematic look at ecotourism attractions in the region. It identifies steps that the county and its partners can take to create additional ways of attracting visitors and further enhancing the enjoyment of the region's natural sites and environmental education opportunities by visitors and residents alike. These steps include enhanced programming: more links between sites; capital investments such as site improvements; directional signage; and trails; collaboration among sites and the hospitality industry; and the development of associated business enterprises. Ecotourism is defined broadly in the plan to mean both recreational and educational offering—often together—that are related to the region's environment and natural resources. As used in the plan, ecotourism is relatively interchangeable with another term often used in the industry— "nature-based tourism," which in Maryland signifies active recreation in natural settings. The county chose to use the term "ecotourism" to reflect an approach that includes environmental education, but also supports the nature-based tourism initiative of the Maryland Department of Natural Resources (supported by the Maryland Office of Tourism Development). The aim of the department's Nature Tourism Program is to increase the number of visitors to the state's parks and wildlife management areas and encourage the licensing of more vendors who serve these new users. That program has increasingly included environmental education as well such activities as coastal kayaking.

By pursuing ecotourism, the county seeks to expand beyond the area's more traditional and extensive outdoor recreation—boating, fishing, hunting, golfing, and shooting clays. These are very valuable components of the county's current tourism, and all will continue to receive a high level of service from the county's tourism staff. The county believes it is possible to enlist these businesses and outfitters in the forms of outdoor recreation and environmental education discussed in the plan,

such as expanding offerings to tours and outings for visitors interested in birding, nature photography, hiking, boating, and sightseeing.

Funding for the ecotourism initiative was provided by the University of Maryland's Rural Development Center at the University of Maryland-Eastern Shore; the Maryland Tourism Development Board and the state's Office of Tourism Development (OTD); and the Queen Anne's County Commission. In addition, the Nature Tourism Program of the Maryland Department of Natural Resources (DNR) provided staff support. The initiative was designed to investigate potential partnerships among compatible businesses; county, state, and federal agencies; and private, nonprofit organizations managing sites and programs relating to environmental education and outdoor recreation. Although work naturally includes Queen Anne's sites and businesses, the Department of Business and Tourism also considered opportunities for collaboration with compatible sites and businesses elsewhere on the Eastern Shore.

Other Tourism Related Initiatives
Also, with Caroline, Kent, and Talbot counties, Queen Anne's County participated in the development of a heritage area program under the Maryland Heritage Preservation and Tourism Areas Program.[2] It is hoped that this plan will provide the background for creating regional collaboration on ecotourism, as well as heritage tourism in general.

In addition to the state-level partnerships and its effort with the University of Maryland—Eastsern Shore, Queen Anne's County worked with its neighboring counties on tourism-related initiatives. The county collaborated with Kent and Cecil counties in the corridor management plan for the proposed Chesapeake County National Scenic Byway. This route follows state routes 213 and 18, and has been nominated for the US Department of Transportation's National Scenic Byways program. Like the heritage area program, this initiative is expected to create additional visitation to the county, with many travelers seeking ecotourism experiences related to the byway. Growth in the number of visitors interested in ecotourism in all its forms is expected to continue in Maryland for the foreseeable future. Many of these represent the baby boomer generation, a large segment of the population whose travel and expenditures are rapidly expanding.

Finally, the county's Chesapeake Exploration Center is named a regional information center within the Chesapeake Bay Gateways Network.[3] The center thus has accepted responsibility for providing regional orientation and information for Chesapeake Bay visitors, promoting not only the county's attractions, but others that may interest travelers stopping for advice about their visit to the Eastern Shore. According to Barbara Siegert, Director of the Office of Tourism, many of the recommendations of the Natural Advantage program have been implemented, demonstrating that the initiative was not an empty exercise. To date, major recommendations completed include: creating a "desk book" for visitors, centers and county businesses that receive visitors; creating a programming plan and programs for the exhibit and grounds at the Chesapeake Exploration Center; reprinting and improving distribution of the *Nature Explorer's Guide;* and promoting Chesapeake Bay Environmental Center as the "first stop" for anyone interested in birding; organizing annual familiarization tours for nature and travel writers.

The Queen Anne's County case study provides an example of a local government investing in sustainable tourism as an economic development tool. Based on this commitment, the county then identified a tourism strategy most appropriate for the community— ecotourism. Then the Natural Advantage program was developed. To implement the plan, the county pursued funding and partners to help it carry out specific recommendations. However, the route to sustainable tourism development is not always easy, especially when attempting to integrate tourism into more traditional economic development strategies. These steps are often gradual, and the Office of Tourism tries to complete

one major recommendation program a year. It also councils that perseverance is necessary, as funding for tourism can be difficult to obtain and public support can be tough to gain. As with any tourism initiative, Natural Advantage has been a success because it was supported by local government officials and implemented by dedicated persons working on behalf of the environment and quality of life in Queen Anne's County.

Discussion

The destinations described above represent two very different environments: one, northern, subarctic; and the second, temperate, coastal. But both contain fragile ecosystems and it seems more than coincidental that these destinations would be among the first to expand the meaning of DMO to include management. But it should be noted that both cases attempted to integrate marketing and management through the adoption of guidelines intended to mitigate conflict. In other words, both the JVCB and Queen Anne's County Office of Tourism moved toward a management role due to external pressures and conditions. In the case of the JCVB, the sustainable tourism guides were a preemptive effort on the part of the cruise industry and the bureau to stem growing community resentment arising from increasing effects on the locality. The program then found a functional home in the bureau—a DMO that was seen as a natural mediator and facilitator between the community and the industry. However, it is worth noting that the bureau would perhaps not have embraced a management role had it not been confronted with the possible rejection of the cruise tourism industry in Juneau. Because it happened to be the organization positioned between the tourism industry and community, it assumed the mantle of management somewhat reluctantly and to this day is careful not to assume all responsibility. Implementation of the TBMP guidelines is spread evenly among all community stakeholders. While limited as a sustainable tourism model, the process and resulting document do attempt to strike a balance between environment, economy, and society.

Destination lifecycle stage matters as well (Butler, 1980). In the Juneau case, management was induced to protect an industry nearing saturation with the local community. Conversely, the Queen Anne's case study shows a community in the early stages of the industry lifecycle, but already performing a crucial economic role in the community. As globalization accelerates and traditional industries continue to move abroad, the Queen Anne's case study might become a more prevalent model. In this model, an organization was created out of the realization that tourism is a major revenue generator for the county. For all intents and purposes, tourism *is* the business of Queen Anne's County. This realization is often followed by a call to develop a formal management plan in order to protect those natural resources that form the basis of the local tourism industry. These management plans should have an organizational home, likely within or attached to offices of business or economic development. For example, many chambers of commerce are now seeking to hire a tourism manager or director. Depending on the local social, political, and economic context, the tourism and economic development functions remain separate or work together under the same roof.

Certainly, organizations with marketing and management objectives face many challenges. The credit crisis of the late 2000s may drain the flow of discretionary dollars that destinations count upon to survive. As if the globalization of tourism does not already make for stiff competition, only those destinations with the strongest brands can remain competitive through economic recession. Socially, many destinations are becoming more highly fragmented by age, race, and income, leaving some DMOs to tackle issues far removed from the narrow metrics of tourist dollars. Serious, interrelated problems of local pollution and global warming may drastically threaten a destination's environment and one

of the strongest elements of destination branding. Essentially, many destinations are ill-suited to tackle what urban planners once termed "wicked problems." According to Gretzel et al. (2006) research areas identified by DMO executives required to address these problems include: (1) building organizational capacity to change; (2) understanding tourism experiences; and (3) establishing appropriate performance measures and benchmarking methodologies. First, however, the authors assert that DMOs must become reflective and reflexive organizations able to look critically within as they attempt to move into the future.

In the future, many traditional DMOs will be compelled to address management issues such as the ones addressed in this chapter and subsequently be subject to rough-and-tumble municipal politics far outside the usual service sector politics. Most DMO directors might claim that this political context of their work has always been present. Increasingly, however, urban politics will be part of the director's job as well as providing a new lens for evaluating the role and function of DMOs within communities. Needless to say, the expansion of destination marketing to encompass an integrated management approach will be greatly needed, and it is anticipated that destination management will become an important companion field to tourism studies, thus belonging in this *Handbook of Tourism Studies*.

While research interest is beginning to grow in this area, there is still a need to better recognize destination management as a specialized subcategory of travel and tourism. University programs have tended to focus on the facts and figures of tourism, in addition to quantitative research borrowed from psychology, sociology, and the anthropological and historical foundations of tourism. While graduates receive good training to research why people travel and how tourism is perceived by prospective travelers and residents, the broader strategic picture (e.g., the interorganizational contexts of tourism marketing and development, and managing the diversity of stakeholders and interests) appears to receive less attention. Those graduating from the fields of planning, public policy, and management studies, should be better equipped to understand the complex tourism domain and the organizational culture of tourism businesses, including the various evolving forms and functions of DMOs.

Conclusion

Destination planning and management are challenging problems. Engaging tourism planning, development and marketing in a way that contributes to effective destination management is complicated due to a number of factors. This chapter and the two case examples above reveal a number of these. First of all, the complex nature of tourism destinations was discussed. Tourism destination has multiple stakeholders, with no individual stakeholder able to fully control development and planning. Fragmentation of control is further exacerbated by the element of public and social good contained in tourism development and marketing, which enhances public sector involvement in tourism, but provides for different goals, policies, and desired outcomes. This section illustrates the importance of approaching destination management from an integrated holistic approach and a systems-based perspective.

Second, the chapter discussed the role and characteristics of destination marketing organizations. Destination marketing is of common public interest, both to the government (taxes and revenues), the private sector which benefits from tourism, and the local residents whose livelihoods may depend on tourism. But, more importantly, the changes being brought by globalization, sustainability, and conservation issues both locally and globally are requiring DMOs to take on much more responsibility and accountability. collaboration and partnerships for integrated management of human community and biophysical world will continue to be a critical issue. The changes, as the two cases above demonstrate, cannot be handled by one organization

alone and the leadership of the DMO at the destination level in facilitating sustainable development and integrated management will be crucial. However, new organizational structures may also be needed to manage the needs and interests of multiple stakeholders, ecological conservation and social-cultural sustainability in the globalized tourism system in which local destinations are now situated.

Notes

1 For more on the Eastern Neck National Wildlife Refuge, see gorp.away.com/gorp/resource/us_nwr/md_eastn.htm. Accessed May 31, 2008.
2 The Maryland Heritage Areas Program is a statewide initiative to protect heritage and promote heritage tourism. The Maryland Heritage Areas Authority (MHAA) oversees implementation of this initiative. For more information see www.marylandhistoricaltrust.net/hb-1.html. Accessed May 31, 2008.
3 For more information on this center and photos of the area's attractions, see www.baygateways.net/general.cfm?id=74f. Accessed May 31, 2008.

References

Araujo, L.M. and Bramwell, B. (2002). "Partnership and Regional Tourism in Brazil." *Annals of Tourism Research*, 29(4): 138–1164.
Blank, U. (1989). *The Community Tourism Imperative: The Necessity, The Opportunities, Its Potential*. State College, PA: Venture Publishing Inc.
Blain, C., Levy, S.E. and Brent, J.R. (2005). "Destination Branding: Insights and Practices from Destination Management Organizations." *Journal of Travel Research*, 43: 328–338.
Bushell, R. and Eagles, P. (Eds.) (2007). *Tourism in Protected Areas: Benefits Beyond Boundaries*. Wallingford: CAB International.
Butler, R.W. (1980). "The Concept of a Tourist Area Cycle of Evolution: Implications for Management of Resources." *Canadian Geographer*, 24(1): 5–12.
Farrell, B. and Twining-Ward, L. (2004). "Reconceptualizing Tourism." *Annals of Tourism Research*, 31(2): 274–295.

Gartrell, R.B. (1994). *Destination Marketing* (2nd edition.). Dubuque, IA: Kendall/Hunt.

Gehrisch, M. (2005). "Introduction." In Rich Harrill (Ed.), *Fundamentals of Destination Management and Marketing* (pp. xxv–xxix) Lansing, MI: Educational Institute of the American Hotel & Lodging Association.

Gill, A. and Williams, P. (1994). "Managing Growth in Mountain Tourism Communities." *Tourism Management*, 15(3): 212–220.

Gretzel, U., Fesenmaier, D.R., Formica, S. and O'Leary, J.T. (2006). "Searching for the Future: Challenges Faced by Destination Marketing Organization." *Journal of Travel Research*, 45(2): 116–126.

Gunn, C.A. with Var, T. (2002). *Tourism Planning*. New York, NY: Taylor and Francis.

Gunn, Claire A. with Var, T. (2004). Tourism Planning: Basics, Concepts, Cases (4th edition.). New York: Routledge.

Hanbury, W.A. (2005). "Case Study in Crisis Management—Management Lessons Learned from 9/11 and Its Aftermath." In Rich Harrill (Ed.), *Fundamentals of Destination Management and Marketing* (pp. 99–108). Lansing, MI: Educational Institute of the American Hotel & Lodging Association.

Harrill, R. (2005). *Guide to Best Practices in Tourism and Destination Management, Vol. 2*. Lansing, MI: Educational Institute of the American Hotel & Lodging Institute.

Healey, P. (1997). *Collaborative Planning: Shaping Places in Fragmented Societies*. London: Macmillan Press.

Inskeep, E. (1991). *Tourism Planning: An Integrated and Sustainable Development Approach*. New York: Van Nostrand Reinhold.

Jamal, T. and Jamrozy, U. (2006). "Collaborative Networks and Partnerships for Integrated Destination Management." In D. Buhalis and C. Costa (Eds.), *Tourism Management Dynamics* (pp. 164–172). Amsterdam: Elsevier.

Juneau Convention & Visitors Bureau (2007). Tourism Best Management Practices Guidelines. Juneau, AK: Juneau Convention & Visitors Bureau.

Lane, B. and Bramwell, B. (Eds.) (2000). *Tourism Collaboration and Partnerships: Politics, Practice and Sustainability*. Clevedon: Channel View.

Laws, E. (1995). *Tourist Destination Management: Issues, Analysis, and Policies*. NY: Routledge.

Leiper, N. (1990). *Tourism Systems: An Interdisciplinary Perspective*. Massey University, Department of Management Systems. Palmerston North, New Zealand.

Murphy, P.E. (1985). *Tourism: A Community Approach*. New York: Methuen.

McDowell Group (2006). Summary of Recent Juneau Tourism Research. Juneau, AK: McDowell Group.

Pearce, D. (1992). *Tourism Organizations*. London: Longman.

Pike, S. (2004). *Destination Marketing Organizations*. Amsterdam: Elsevier.

Poon, A. (1993). *Tourism, Technology and Competitive Strategies*. Wallingford: CAB International.

Queen Anne's County Department of Business and Tourism (2002). *Natural Advantage: An Initiative to Develop Ecotourism in Queen Anne's County*. Chester, MD: Queen Anne's County Department of Business and Tourism.

Queen Anne's Office of Business and Tourism (2002). Natural Advantage: An Initiative to Develop Ecotourism in Queen Anne's County. Chester, MD: Queen Anne's Office of Business and Tourism.

Ritchie, J.R. and Crouch, G.I. (2003). *The Competitive Destination: A Sustainable Tourism Perspective*. Cambridge, MA: CABI Publishing.

Schianetza, K., Kavanaghb, L. and Lockington, D. (2007). "The Learning Tourism Destination: The Potential of a Learning Organisation Approach for Improving the Sustainability of Tourism Destinations." *Tourism Management*, 28(6): 1485–1496.

Sheehan, L., Brent Ritchie, J.R. and Hudson, S. (2007). "The Destination Promotion Triad: Understanding Asymmetric Stakeholder Interdependencies Among the City, Hotels, and DMO." *Journal of Travel Research*, 46(1): 64–74.

Smith, M. (2002). *Issues in Cultural Tourism Studies*. London: Routledge.

Tosun, C. (1998). "Roots of Unsustainable Tourism Development at the Local Level: The Case of Urgup in Turkey." *Tourism Management*, 19(6): 595–610.

Wang, Y. and Fesenmaier, D.R. (2007). Collaborative Destination Marketing: A Case Study of Elkhart County, Indiana. *Tourism Management*, 28(3): 863–875.

26

Tourism Safety and Security

Peter E. Tarlow

Introduction

On June 2, 2007, the TSA (Transportation Security Administration) announced that a planned attack on New York's John F. Kennedy Airport had been averted.[1] This incident serves as a reminder that ever since September 11, 2001 tourism security has become a "hot" topic within the tourism industry. The tourism world is now so sensitive to security matters that the 2007 shootings at Virginia Tech University not only impacted education, but also the local and broader tourism community (Davies, 2008).

Although security issues have always played a role in tourism, for most of the industry's life it was often placed on the back burner, or was a subject few people examined. While Israeli scholars, such as Raphael Raymond Bar-On,[2] Abe Pizam and Yoel Mansfeld (1996) have examined several security issues from the perspective of both crime and terrorism, in the past few universities had offered courses in this field. Police departments did not train their people in TOPs (tourism oriented policing/protection services),[3] and tourism marketers tended to take the position that the more visible security the higher the risk that the public would

be frightened and go somewhere else. This chapter offers a brief glimpse into this now rapidly changing field. The chapter is divided into the following subsections: an overview of some of the literature within the field, a short theory section, some of the multiple aspects of tourism security, plus managing for surety. A note on perception and risk is contained in the final section.

A Review of the Literature

Over the last 10 years tourism scholars have begun to seek to understand the concepts of tourism as it relates to security. The earliest works, in reality, were less concerned about protecting tourists and visitors than they were about finding relationships between tourism and issues of crime. The basic research question was: does tourism produce higher levels of criminal activities? The work of Meda Chesney-Lind and Ian Lind (1986) looked at precisely this side of the equation. The same theme can be seen in the research by Klaus de Albuquerque and Jerome McElroy of crimes against tourists in the Caribbean. They found that while residents suffered from higher rates of violent crime, tourists suffered higher rates of property crimes. The prevailing literature in the late 1980s and 1990s centered around three major questions. First, what were the patterns of tourism victimization? Second, did tourism incite crime or higher rates of crime? Last, were crimes against tourists different from crimes against local residents in form and in frequency of occurrence (Ellis, 1999)? As the literature developed, however, it began to become clear that not all scholars found the same answers to the above-mentioned questions. Thus, J.M. Knox and Associates (2004: ii) prepared a study entitled "Effects of Tourism on Rates of Serious Crime in Hawaii." This study looked at the interrelationship between tourism and crime, and noted that:

> . . . past statistics based studies almost always turned up some relationship between crime and tourism, but that the exact nature of the relationship varied from time to time or place to place. For example, one study would find a link between tourism and say, robbery, but no link with larceny. Another study—in a different time or place—would find a link between tourism and larceny, but no link with robbery. This was also generally true for the limited number of past Hawaii studies, though there was some tendency in previous Hawaii research to find links with burglary and (to a lesser extent) rape.[4]

In the 1990s some scholars began to wonder what methods might be used to protest tourists and for the first time they began to consider such questions as the differences between tourism safety and security. If tourists were victims of crime, were there methodologies that might be used to protect tourists? Pizam et al. (1997) attempted to move the discussion to the issue of caring for tourists. Based on previous research, they assumed that tourists needed to be protected and thus asked not only to whom this responsibility belonged, but also what some of the best practices that police and security professionals used to ensure visitor safety and security were.[5]

The book *Tourism, Crime, and International Security Issues* (Pizam and Mansfeld, 1996) was ground breaking in that it provided for the first time a theoretical perspective on tourism security and moved past data collection and analysis to present a more global vision of the problem. This book served as a motivational instrument for academic conferences held in Dubrovnik, Croatia (1997) and in Kalmar, Sweden (1999), resulting. in a special issue of the *Journal of Travel Research* on "War Terrorism and Tourism" (August, 1999) edited by Pizam and Tarlow.

The relationship between tourism, terrorism, and political instability started to gain attention in the late 1990s (Sonmez, 1998). Since September 11, 2001, the world of tourism has become less innocent and scholars have begun to explore the relationship between not only tourism and acts of crime but also tourism and terrorism. In 2006 two major works were published. *Tourism in Turbulent Times*, edited by Jeff Wilks, Donna Pendergast and Peter Leggat (2006), seeks to create a total understanding of tourism surety, from issues of health safety and food illnesses to acts of terrorism. The book divides its theoretical focus between the theories of tourism crime and those of terrorism. A second major work, *Tourism Security & Safety* (Yoel Mansfeld and Abraham Pizam, Eds., 2006) takes a broader view of the issue of tourism surety and seeks to unite the theories behind both terrorism activities against tourism and crime issues.

Some Theoretical Underpinnings

Yoel Mansfeld and Abe Pizam (2006: 1) have written that a tourism theory dealing with crimes and terrorism should be able to explain the following:

- Why do incidents of security, such as crime, terrorism, wars, riots, and civil unrest exist at tourism destinations?
- What are the motivators of the perpetrators/offenders?

Mansfeld and Pizam take the position that both crime and terrorism can be subsumed under the broad heading of "incidents of security." This author has taken a different approach, pointing out that there are key differences between acts of crime and terrorism in tourism (Table 26.1). Terrorism is often confused with criminal behavior. In a world of tourism, however, terrorism and crime can be very different social ailments (Tarlow, 2006). However, it should be noted that, at times, the results of a crime or terrorism incident to the industry may overlap or be similar.

Classical neo-Marxist theorists assumed that tourism crimes (that is crimes committed against tourists) were a manifestation of the economic disparity between the wealthier tourist and the poorer members of the economy. These assumptions are/were based on the following principles:

- Visitors are wealthier than the people who rob them.
- The robberies come out of economic frustration, that is to say poor locales observe wealthy visitors flaunting wealth and therefore rob out of resentments.
- Tourists are therefore guilty or at least almost guilty of their own victimization.

Such a Marxist outlook may be called "Robin Hood Tourism" (Tarlow, 2007b: 36).

Huddy (2008) offers a useful example of Robin Hood criminal terrorism, where the culprit believes that what s/he is doing is for social gain. Huddy's book is a detailed examination of Cuban-born José Manuel Vigoa, and his two-year Las Vegas crime rampage, a series of major criminal raids on the Las Vegas Strip during the first part of this decade:

> Vigoa would tell the guards to their face how foolish they are: 'I'm not trying to take the money away from you or steal anything from your families. I want to take the money from the fat pig casino owners who have millions and millions and exploit their employees with peanut wages.' (2008: 16)

Note that in the Robin Hood stories there are only two classes of people, the poor and the rich. It is assumed that the rich are evil and the poor are by nature good, and that the sheriff functions as the bully of the rich. In the Marxist approach there is no possibility that the thief may be richer than the victim or that the thief (criminal) may enjoy his or her work. Marxists also assume that the natures of those in the upper classes (*la bourgeoisie*) are by nature evil. Thus, managers and tourism executives (*les petits bourgeoisies*) exist to serve the needs of the leisure class.

Table 26.1   Key Differences Between Acts of Tourism Crime and Terrorism

	Crime	*Terrorism*
Goal	Usually economic or social gain	To gain publicity and sometimes sympathy for a cause.
Usual type of victim	Person may be known to the perpetrator or selected because he/she may yield economic gain	Killing is a random act and appears to be more in line with a stochastic model. Numbers may or may not be important
Defenses in use	Often reactive, reports taken	Some proactive devices such as radar detectors
Political ideology	Usually none	Robin Hood model
Publicity	Usually local and rarely makes the international news	Almost always is broadcast around the world
Most common forms in tourism industry	Crimes of distraction Robbery Sexual Assault	Domestic terrorism International terrorism Bombings Potential for biochemical warfare
Statistical accuracy	Often very low, in many cases the travel and tourism industry does everything possible to hide the information	Almost impossible to hide. Numbers are reported with great accuracy and repeated often
Length of negative effects on the local tourism industry	In most cases, it is short term	In most cases, it is long term unless replaced by new positive image

Source: Tarlow (2002: 134–135).

Perhaps the pinnacle of this can be seen in the work Thorstein Veblen's (1899) *The Theory of the Leisure Class*. Veblen defines leisure as "the non-productive consumption of time (1) from a sense of the unworthiness of productive work, and (2) as an evidence of the pecuniary ability to afford a life of idleness" (Veblen, 1899: 46). In such a scheme, Veblen never saw working in the leisure world as possible nor did he imagine that the proletariat would also be the beneficiaries of leisure time. Further insights into Veblen's thoughts can be seen in his analysis of male domination over women (paralleling the leisure class' domination of the proletariat) when he writes:

Unproductive consumption of goods is honorable, primarily as a mark of prowess and a perquisite of human dignity; secondarily it becomes substantially honorable in itself, especially the consumption of the more desirable things. The consumption of choice articles of food, and frequently also of rare articles of adornment, becomes taboo {sic} to the women and children; and if there is a base (servile) class of men, the taboo holds for them. (1899: 61)

A counter-theoretical perspective to the Marxist approach would be a Durkheimian way of viewing tourism crime. The theories of David Emile Durkheim form the basis for Functionalism. Functionalist theory forwards that society is a stable living system and that a change in any one aspect of the system produces unexpected consequences in other parts of the system. From a Functionalist perspective, crime is not a result of a wealth-disparity but rather the result of the introduction of new social groupings into society, thus taking it from a stable system to an unstable system. In such a paradigm, crimes exist when instability enters into the system. Durkheim theorists might assume a state of anomie when one travels, that is a state of normlessness. Because tourists operate outside of their normal patterns of behavior, they are open to those who would take advantage of them. A good example of anomic crimes is "crimes-of-dispersion." These are "minor" crimes that are never reported. For example, a taxi cab driver who continually makes one wrong turn per trip causing a slight increase in the fare. No tourist will suspect or report a small overcharge and yet when compounded over multiple passengers much greater amounts of money will have been stolen then first expected.[6]

From Crime to Terrorism

Despite the often mistaken notion that terrorism is just another form of crime, at least from the tourism perspective, nothing could be farther from the truth. As shown in Table 26.1, terrorists and criminals can act in a very different manner vis-à-vis tourism. The world famous sociologist Francis Fukuyama, reflecting on his work, *The End of History* (1989), wrote:

Fifteen years ago in my book *The End of History and the Last Man*, I argued that if a society wanted to be modern, there was no alternative to a market economy and democratic political system. Not everyone wanted to be modern, of course, and not everyone could put in place the institutions and policies necessary to make democracy and capitalism work, but no alternative system would yield better results.

While the 'End of History' thus was essentially an argument about modernization, some people have linked my thesis about the end of history to the foreign policy of President George W. Bush and American strategic hegemony. But anyone who thinks that my ideas constitute the intellectual foundation for the Bush administration's policies has not been paying attention to what I have been saying since 1992 about democracy and development. (Fukuyama, 2007)

What Fukuyama did not consider was that the early twenty-first century might become an age of active nostalgia for the "past." This active nostalgia has impacted many as is seen in the groundbreaking research of the Russian social thinker Svetlana Boym. Terrorism is a form of what she calls restorative nostalgia in which there is an attempt by force to move from the modern to the restorative past (Boym, 2001). The targets of terrorism then can very easily include tourism destinations and major cities where tourism is a visible part of capitalism and development. Tourism, in this instance, is perceived as a symbol of modernization and change. While there is no one formula to predict a terrorism attack and there is no set geographic pattern, the following points are helpful in determining a tourism site's terrorism vulnerabilities. Areas that have proven to be most vulnerable are:

- Iconic centers. Those centers that have a great deal of symbolic meaning to the host society or to a particular religion or ethnic grouping.
- Places that if attacked would produce mass casualties.
- Places that would impact a national, regional, or world economy.
- Places that will draw a great amount of media attention. (Tarlow, 2003).

Tourism Safety, Security, and Surety

Many disciplines make a clear distinction between security and safety, but some tourism scientists and professionals do not. Tourism security and safety are not like other forms of security and safety. Rather than divide safety from security, some tourism experts merge these two notions into one overall term, "tourism surety" (Tarlow, 2007b). While there is no one universally accepted definition among practitioners the term "security" often is used to mean the protection of a person, place, or reputation from an intended harm. Safety, as opposed to security, is often defined as protecting people against unintended consequences of an involuntary nature. In the case of the travel and tourism industry, both a safety and a security mishap can destroy not only a vacation but also the industry.

Although tourism security and safety are different, in the applied world the terms are often used almost interchangeably. For purposes of this chapter all three terms will be used. Safety will refer to security in the reflexive mode, that is to say, things that people do to themselves. For example, a person may not see the sign indicating a slippery floor and fall. The wet floor is a safety issue. If on the other hand, another person removes the sign so that the first person falls, that is no longer a safety issue, but a security issue. Safety is defined here as protecting a visitor from damaging him/herself. It should be noted that intentional damage done by a visitor to his/her property however is non-reflexive and therefore a security rather than a safety issue. For example, in some gaming communities, police departments have noted that locals visiting the casino will break the windows of their car to recuperate losses by charging a theft. In this case, although the perpetrator of the crime appears to be its "victim" in reality the victim may be either the casino or an insurance company.

Security can be defined as protecting a visitor from the negative actions produced by another person. It would be very difficult (if not impossible) to guarantee 100% safety or security; the best that can be hoped for is to lower the level of the probability that something will happen. "Tourism surety" is the resulting concept when safety and security are combined (Tarlow, 2007b: 473). It is the word that is used to indicate that professionals will keep the level of risk (be that risk self inflicted or inflicted by another) to the lowest levels possible. *Tourism surety* works under the assumption that any negative act, be it one of safety or security, can ruin a vacation and destroy a location's reputation. For example, if people suffer from poor food their vacation may well become a nightmare. In the same manner, having one's wallet stolen can easily become the negative focus of a vacation. It should be noted that often these three terms are confused and used interchangeably throughout the industry. Lastly, because personal surety often impacts the industry's surety, tourism surety seeks not only to protect the visitor but also the locale's reputation and economy.

A good example of personal surety is loss of life at sea through drowning. A study commissioned by the Hawaii Visitor Authority (HVA) in 2007 shows a close relationship between drowning and tourism security. The HVA considers drownings in the sea to be of equal importance to acts of violence committed against tourists.[7] Australia considers the issue of beach safety to be so important that on November 8–9, 2007 a special conference was dedicated to the issue (Gold Coast Beach Safety and Law National Summit, November 2007). The Queensland law society published the results of that conference in the book *Beach Safety and the Law: Australian Evidence* (Wilks, 2008). To further complicate the issue, so called "victimless crimes" such as prostitution may constitute both a safety and security element. It is for this reason that the two are combined into the term *tourism surety*. The May 2005 case of a missing woman in Aruba demonstrates that tourism security is about more than merely caring for tourists. Its other components are the protection of a place's reputation and tourism industry. These latter issues are so important that the state of Hawaii has an entire organization, VASH (Visitors Aloha Society of Hawaii), dedicated to caring for victims of tourism crimes.[8]

Tourism surety then is the point where safety, security, reputation, and economic viability meet.[9] Terrorists are also very much aware of this combination of factors. The reasons for this mélange are numerous and include the realization that both a lack of security and safety can destroy vacation experience, that visitors choose to come to a place rather than being forced to come to a spot, and that perceptions, while not always true, tend to be true in their consequences (Sonmez and Graefe, 1998).

Another example of this interfacing between safety and security is in the issue of health related matters. Visitors are capable of carrying diseases from one part of the world to another. The 2007 incident of an international airplane passenger carrying tuberculosis from the USA to Europe and then from Europe to Canada and the USA serves as an example of new forms of risks, both to other travelers and to local populations. The US Media reported that, "A man, with a form of

tuberculosis so dangerous he is under the first government-ordered quarantine since 1963, told a newspaper he took one trans-Atlantic flight for his wedding and honeymoon and another because he feared for his life."[10] The Black Hills Travel Medicine home page reports that the top travel diseases currently are: acute mountain sickness, bedbugs, dengue fever, hepatitis A and B, Japanese encephalitis, malaria, meningococcal meningitis, polio, rabies, tick-borne encephalitis, travelers' diarrhea, typhoid fever, whooping cough (pertussis) and yellow fever.[11]

If anyone doubts how vulnerable tourism is to negative publicity coming from illnesses one only has to review what happened to Toronto, Canada in 2003 after its reported SARS epidemic (Chon and McKercher, 2004). At the time, Neil Seeman of *National Review* wrote:

> As a consequence, economic tremors are rippling through the city. Major League Baseball has even advised players to refrain from signing autographs. An analysis by J. P. Securities Canada, Inc. on Tuesday estimated that the epidemic will cost Canada $30 million a day; the firm then reversed its forecast to 1% from the 2–2.5% national economic growth rate in the current economic quarter, which, pre-SARS, had been reason for economists here to herald Canada's impending emergence as an economic powerhouse.[12]

Visitors are also subjects of poor health standards in food preparation and the transferal of health problems from local tourism employees to visitors (MacLaurin, 2001, 2002). This issue will be discussed briefly further below.

As noted above, tourism surety is then defined for the purposes of this chapter as the point where tourism safety and security issues intersect with a place's reputation and economic well-being (Figure 26.1).

Tourism safety and security issues clearly play an important role in tourism's viability and credibility. Tourism needs a safe and secure environment in order to survive. Crimes against tourists come in many forms. Table 26.2, taken from *Tourism in Turbulent Times* (Tarlow, 2006: 96), gives a brief outline of many of the crimes from which

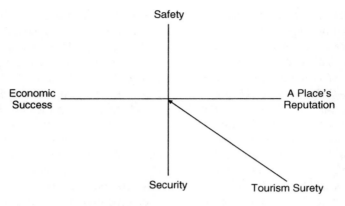

Figure 26.1   Tourism Surety.

tourists suffer. Table 26.3 provides a taxonomy for the types of crime committed.

The Center for Problem-Oriented Policing publishes an online booklet called "Crimes against Tourists" (Guide 26, 2004).[13] The authors Ronald W. Glensor and Kenneth J. Peak (2004) list crimes such as

- prostitution;
- pick pocketing (now called crimes of distraction);
- confidence schemes (fraud);
- fencing of stolen property;
- organized crime and gang activities;
- offenses relating to casino gambling;
- crimes involving the elderly;
- burglary of holiday homes;
- robberies at bars and other businesses;
- terrorism against tourists; and
- mass transit crimes (e.g., at bus or airport terminals; on subways or trains) as major tourism crimes.

Table 26.2   Types of Tourism Surety Issues

Types of Problems	Classification
Act of Terrorism	Security Issue
Crimes Against Personal Property	Security Issue
Crimes of Distraction	Security Issues
Drugs	Security Issue
Sexual Assaults	Security Issue
Crimes Against Sites	Security Issues
Food Poisoning	Safety Issue
Airborne Illnesses	Safety Issues
Pandemics	Safety Issues
Drowning	Safety Issues
Sun Illness	Safety Issues
Tsunami	Safety/Security Issues
Ecological Damage	Safety/Security Issues

We may also add to this list crimes such as other crimes of distraction (for example, the stealing of luggage at airports and in hotel/motel lobbies) and site stealing or defacement. Tourists often "take" things as souvenirs. In some areas of the world, this "souvenir taking" is big business and causes not only a great deal of damage to the historical ecology of the place but also to the site itself. To begin to understand tourism surety we can divide the field into six major components. These are listed in Table 26.4 and explained more fully further below.

Drawing from Table 26.4, tourism surety can be divided into a number of subfields. The article on tourism security in the *Encyclopedia of Security Management* (Tarlow, 2007a) notes that the field of Tourism surety has six major components:

1 Visitor protection. Tourism surety works under the assumption that it is protecting "righteous visitors." The term "righteous visitors" refers to people who come to a place either for business reasons or pleasure and seek to do no intended harm. Even righteous visitors however are capable of harming themselves. Visitors are tired; they suffer from location confusion, called anomie, and often do things that demonstrate a lack of common sense. It is then the job of the tourism surety professional (STP) to develop plans to protect visitors against themselves. In a like manner, both types of unscrupulous people, who may be locals or other visitors, often prey on the "righteous visitor." This preying on righteous visitors may come in the form

Table 26.3   Tourism/Visitor Crime Taxonomy

Crimes Committed by	Against Whom	Some Examples of	Goal of Crime
Tourists	Other visitors or local, population or tourism personnel	Robbery, pickpockets,	Usually economic or social gain
Locals	Visitors	Assaults, petty theft, con artists, crimes of distraction	Usually economic gain
Tourism Industry	Visitors	Fraud, Business Misrepresentation	Economic

of assaults, room entries, or even scams in which the visitor participates in his/her own victimization. Additionally, despite the best efforts of the tourism and lodging industries, not all staff members are always honest. Staff members may rob both their guests and their employers, and/or may be "spies" or implants for local criminals to whom they pass information.

2   Protection of staff. To travel is to know frustration and this frustration often turns into tourism rage or abuse by people who would otherwise never consider such behavior appropriate. Often tourism employees are subjected to abuse or even forms of sexual and physical assault. A second aspect

of a tourism surety is the realization that in open and at times sexually free societies, staff members may be exposed to numerous health risks. Blood left on a towel may be simply blood or may infect another person with a disease. Staff members must work in environments, such as hotels or aircraft, where infectious diseases are prevalent. Thus a tourism security program must find ways to assure honest staff members that they can work in an environment that is crime free, not hostile and from the perspective of health, safe. Issues of a hostile or abusive workplace are not unknown in the world of tourism, which often produces high levels of anxiety coupled with high expectations.

Table 26.4   Tourism Surety Groups

Surety Group	Victimizers	Some Victimization Venues
Visitors	• Visitors themselves • Visitors against other visitors • Locals • Industry employees • Secondary tourism industry personnel • Nature/animals	• Places of lodging • Streets/open spaces • Attractions • Meetings and convention centers • Transportation modules
Staff	• Visitors/guests • Staff on staff	• Visitors' rooms • Staff locales • Ingresses and egresses to tourism centers
Tourism Site	• Visitors to the site • Staff at the site • Ecological issues • Nature/weather	• The physical plant
Ecology	• Staff • Visitors • Nature	• Urban and Rural settings
Economy	• Staff • Visitors • Local government officials	• Salaries • Employment • Tax revenues
Reputation	• Staff • Visitors • Local government officials • Media	• The media • Word-of-mouth • Other tourism centers

3   Site protection. A third component of tourism security is site protection. The term "site" can mean anything from a place of lodging to an attraction site. While in an age of terrorism there are those who might intend to destroy or harm a specific site, site protection must also take into account the careless or selfish traveler. Travelers may also seek to "take" a part of a site home as a souvenir. For example, so many visitors wanted a "piece" of Plymouth Rock that a special protected area had to be constructed to preserve the rock from souvenir seekers. Another aspect of site protection is assuring that the industry's property is not mishandled. For example, hotel guests may damage the room in which they are staying or may chose to take home a towel as a souvenir of their stay. Tourism surety also takes into account the needs of cleaning staffs and hotel engineers and seeks to assure that the site's environment is both attractive and as secure/safe as possible.

4   Ecological and health management. Closely related to and yet distinct from site security is the protection of the area's ecology. No tourism entity lives in a vacuum. The care of a locale's streets, lawns, and internal environment has a major impact on tourism surety. In fact, one of the easiest and most efficient ways to lower crime is through beautification plans. Ecology also involves the cultural ecology. When cultures tend to die; crime levels tend to rise. Protecting the cultural ecology along with the physical ecology of a locale is a major preventative step that tourism surety professionals can do to lower crime rates and to assure a safer and more secure environment.

5   Reputation protection. Tourism crimes and acts of terrorism against tourism entities receive a great deal of media attention. As such tourism surety professionals must develop clear risk management strategies in order to avoid the need for a major marketing effort to counteract negative perceptions and bolster reputation. Often tourism professionals, seeking to cut corners, forget that it is much less expensive to prevent an economic loss than it is to repair a reputation once the incident has occurred and produced negative publicity.

6   Economic protection. Around the world tourism is a major generator of income. The recent thwarted airplane attacks from the UK to the USA serve as another example of the interrelationship between tourism and economic stability. Tourism centers are based around the concept of hospitality and as such are easy prey. To make economic protection even more difficult, tourist professionals and tourism surety professionals do not control people living and working in the community. As such, almost anyone in the community can harm the industry's reputation and through it the industry's economic base. (Tarlow, 2007b: 474)

Managing for Surety: Some Examples[14]

Lodging Surety

While the media often focus on transportation security, one of the tourism components that has been hard-hit by issues of tourism surety is the lodging industry. Be the problem one of safety or security, crimes or acts of terrorism, few hotels exist in a vacuum. While most people go to a place rather than a hotel, any negative security impact within the hotel can have disastrous consequences. Hotel and motel guests have long been victims of robberies and even room invasions. In 1999, a nationally televised program, Dateline NBC broadcast a program dealing with crimes against tourism at places of lodging. The impact of this program was felt by certain brand named motels almost immediately.

To add to the security difficulties of many places of lodging, terrorism acts against the tourism industry have occurred in hotels around the world. Hotels in such places as Bali, Cuba, Israel, Jordan, and Kenya have been targeted, resulting in multiple deaths and causing economic havoc for the host country. These attacks at what should be safe centers for both leisure and business travelers have left guests with both a sense of ennui and of fear. These attacks mean that the lodging industry must now find ways to combine tourism surety with hospitality, and create a sense of safety and surety along with an open and hospitable environment.

In an age of terrorism, the traditional needs of protecting guests and staff (Table 26.6) have now acquired new meaning. No longer do lodging surety professionals worry about crimes of distraction, kidnappings, and robbery, but they must also now be concerned with a vast array of new surety issues such as food safety, biochemical poisoning, and bombings. Furthermore, meeting and convention planners are now asking questions of hotels seeking to gain their business. This new awareness signifies a major change in attitudes. No longer do meeting planners simply assume that all is "secure and safe." Now they ask specific questions and thus shift issues of liability to the hotel's management. Lodging surety professionals need to create overall security plans. These plans include knowing the major threats against their establishment. Do they need to fear terrorism, acts of crime or both? Do their guests need protection from other visitor/guests, from locals who might seek to do the visitor harm, or even from less than honest staff members? How often do hotel guests place themselves in dangerous situations and as such need protection? To add to the difficulties in providing safe and secure lodging, as noted above, many people when away from home change their moral standards in a way that results in exposing themselves to additional risks.

Lodging security is often subdivided into hotel, motel, bed & breakfast (B&B), and other forms of lodging security. The other category subsumes such groupings as campsites, trailer parks, and campers. Table 26.5 presents an overview of many of the security issues found within three of these categories: hotels, motels, and B&B.

Because each place of lodging is different there is no single surety solution. Instead this chapter provides basic questions that hotel security people should ask in developing a lodging surety plan. The following list provides several of the key areas of surety concerns. They are given in alphabetical order and do not indicate a ranking of importance. Such a ranking can be done on site and by the hotel/motel's staff. Concerns to be considered by hotel surety staffs include:

- baggage storage areas;
- check-in areas (reception areas);
- delivery areas;
- door and key access and control;
- equipment security;
- evacuation plans;
- food safety;
- hotel clientele's demographics;
- kitchen safety and security;
- parking lots;
- room security;
- site's location;
- staff loyalty;

Table 26.5 Common and Unique Problems in Places of Lodging

	Lodging Type		
Problem	Hotels	Motels	Bed and Breakfasts
Primary types of keys used	Standard or electronic	Standard or electronic	Standard or electronic
Security of room	Ranges from good to poor	Ranges from good to poor	Tends to be poor
Conventions at the place of lodging	High probability	Low probability	No
Staff knows guests	Usually not	Usually not	Yes
Location well-known	Yes	Yes	Often no
Security staff on premises	Yes in the larger hotels	Rarely	Never
Staff trained in matters of security	Often	Rarely	Almost never
Secure parking	Often	Often	Almost never
Large numbers of people staying at place of lodging	Yes	Yes	No
Secure access to room	Often	At times	Rarely
Lobby	Yes	Often	Parlor may serve as lobby during awake hours

Source: Taken from Tarlow (2007: 456).

- staff training;
- telecommunications security.

Attraction Security

Much of the material presented concerning hotels is also true of attractions. In fact, in some cases a hotel and attraction may be one and the same (such as an all-inclusive resort) or a hotel and attraction may have a symbiotic relationship, such as the hotels found on an amusement park's grounds. Therefore there is a great amount of overlap between tourism surety procedures as they impact a hotel and an attraction. There are however several differences. For example, rarely do hotels hold iconic status. Thus, an attraction such as a national monument may have international fame. Places such as the Coliseum in Rome, Paris' Eiffel Tower, London's Houses of Parliament, and the Statue of Liberty all hold international iconic status. There are several other differences between hotels and attractions; Table 26.6 illustrates some of these.

Attractions are both crime and terrorism sensitive; therefore tourism surety professionals must develop a dual approach to the problem. For example, in the area of terrorism, attractions may have long lines waiting to purchase entrance tickets. These lines are similar to those at airport security lines where the public is exposed prior to entering into the

Table 26.6   Tourism Surety by Location

Issue	Attraction	Hotel/Place of Lodging
Iconic value	Often	Rarely
Set times	Yes	24 hours
Crowd control issues	Yes	Rarely
Owned by Government	Often	Rarely toward never
Major economic impact	Often	Lower probability
Opportunity for mass murder	Yes	Yes
Attack will be well publicized	Yes	Yes
Police in charge of security	Often	Rarely

"sanitized" zone. The need to develop passive restraints against terrorism attacks means that tourism security officials working at attractions must consider such challenges as:

1 What is the possibility of an explosion in tourist gathering points?
2 How easily can emergency vehicles access the property and is this access a danger?
3 If vehicles cannot access the property does this create an additional evacuation problem or a problem for medical personnel?
4 What explosive products are available in the locale?
5 Can perimeter streets be closed?
6 Do you measure the weight of a vehicle coming into your garage?
7 Can you reduce ceiling heights?
8 What unloading dock security do you have?
9 Do employees have numbered parking spaces?
10 How much visible law enforcement presence is there?
11 How well do first responders know the property?
12 How well is the area lighted?

Food Security

Starting around 2002 the media reported that the cruise industry suffered from what some people at the time believed to be an issue of food terrorism (MacLaurin, 2001, 2002). In reality no such thing happened, rather it was a case of the Norwalk virus (NV) that attacked cruise passengers due to some employees not properly washing their hands. According to the website of the Dietary Mangers, the NV is linked but not totally to food safety issues.[15] To the question of the NV is really a food service problem, the answer is two-fold: The NV can travel through food but not all NV cases are transmitted through food. Results from a five-year analysis of NV show: 39% passed through food, 12% from person-to-person, 3% through water, and 18% unknown.[16] Like institutions, cruise ships are subject to routine sanitation inspections, and officials have reported good scores in recent inspections.[17]

Although the situation was quickly handled, the incident serves as a case in point as to the importance of food safety and its potential impact on the tourism industry. The literature makes a clear distinction between food safety (the hygiene of food) and food security, a term that is often used in a technical sense to mean "freedom from hunger." To a great extent, vacations are about eating. Business travelers on short trips cannot afford to become ill from food. Food then plays not only a vital physical role in keeping us healthy, but also a vital economic role in how people often judge a vacation. Tourists and business travelers usually eat either at local restaurants or at their hotels. Hotel surety departments should meet with their kitchen staffs on a regular basis to insure the highest food safety possible. In the case of individual restaurants, the public is often at the mercy of local health departments and the restaurant's reputation.

The Center for Disease Control (CDC) maintains a website in regards to food safety and provides up-to-date information on a multitude of topics dealing with food safety issues.[18] According to the CDC website some 76 million people become sick from contaminated food in the USA, resulting in approximately 300,000 people per year being hospitalized. Even greater details can be found at the website of the "Center for Food Safety and Applied Nutrition" at the US Food and Drug Administration.[19] It provides up to the minute information on what food is being recalled, dangerous ingredients, and regulations for meats, poultry, fish, vegetables, and fruit. A list of critical questions that the researcher will want to ask in this regard is:

- Who knows the kitchen staff's personal medical history? Does everyone in the kitchen staff, cooks, cleaners, waiters, and waitresses, know all food safety regulations and follow them?
- Are background checks done on all people who handle foods (ancient kings and European royalty understood this principle when they insisted on food tasters prior to eating)?
- Are random inspections of the food locale held on a periodic basis?
- How are salad bars protected, and in an age of terrorism special observation, must be given to foods that are open to the public?

- Do the waiters/waitresses know the ingredients found in all meals?
- Are label menus correct?
- Do you know which foods can be contaminated at the tourism establishment and which can be contaminated at the production source? For example, shellfish may come to the preparation kitchen already contaminated. The same is also true of berries and some vegetables that have been grown in contaminated water or places with unsatisfactory sanitation.

Urban and Rural Tourism Security

Although many of the principles of tourism surety are the same for both urban and rural settings, there are some important differences that need to be considered. Table 26.7 indicates some of the differences between rural and urban tourism in this regard. It should be noted that suburban tourism is often at a midway point. Some suburbs manifest higher degrees of urban problems, others are sociologically closer to rural tourism. Many combine the best and worst features of the rural–urban continuum.

Because rural tourism tends to be spread out over a larger geographic area than urban tourism it is often more difficult to develop an overall tourism plan. Local police departments may not work well together and often these departments are not willing to develop common task forces that will deprive them of scarce manpower and resources. To further complicate the issue, there may be several layers of law enforcement present. These may include local police departments, sheriffs' offices, and state troopers. In such situations it is essential that the travel and tourism industry personnel work with police on local, regional and state levels. When working with police, tourism researchers may want to ask such questions as:

1 How do tourism professionals and the police work together from an organizational perspective?
2 What information do you, the members of the police department, need from tourism professionals?
3 How can tourism professionals be supportive of your department throughout the year?

Table 26.7   Differences Between Tourism Surety Issues for Rural and Urban Tourism

	Rural Tourism	Urban Tourism
Police	• Often under trained and lack resources • Know the local population and may feel close to local population	• Police have more access to training and experiences. • May not know the local population or feel alienated from it
Place	• Perceived as safe and friendly, tourists expect more and often left their guard down	• Perceived to be more dangerous and tourists tend to be more on guard against street crimes
Populations	• May be xenophobic toward outsiders	• Tend to be more tolerant of diverse societies
Ease of crime reporting	• Visitors may find it difficult to return to report crimes or to testify in court	• More convenient to return to, travelers may be more willing to report crimes
Accuracy of security and safety perceptions	• Under reporting of sexual assaults and drug usage	• Sensational journalism often produces fear in visitors.
Terrorism threats	• Low probability of terrorism attack	• High probabilities of terrorism attacks
Tourism preparedness	• Poor signage and poor foreign language skills	• Better (not always good) signage and access to foreign language speakers.
Weather issues	• Most activities are outdoors with few indoor bad weather alternatives	• May have numerous indoor alternatives
Nightlife	• Often little to none	• May have active nightlife which needs tourism surety protection
Gang violence	• Present	• Present
Tourism geography	• Dispersed over a large area	• Often concentrated in tourism districts

4   Are tourism professionals willing to have a police officer sit on our planning sessions?
5   What types of uniforms do you use? Can we use uniforms to create a positive image?
6   When working out events/parades etc., how much lead time do you need?
7   Would you share some of the police department's problems with us? How can we aid you?

Cruise Travel

To a great extent, a cruise ship is an all-inclusive hotel on the seas. As such, much of the information given in the section on lodging security also applies to cruise ships. The profile of many of the cruise industry's passengers, however, may be different. For example, cruises can attract specific niche markets, such as the gay traveler or single travelers. The following general sociological profile often applies to standard (non-niche oriented) cruise passengers (Sirakaya et al., 2004):

• Cruise goers tend to be more pyschocentric than allocentric, that is to say that they expect to be pampered and on the whole tend to be less adventure seeking.

• Cruise goers tend to bring large amounts of luggage that makes luggage control difficult.
• Lowering of inhibitions may be manifested by demands and rudeness to staff.
• Many cruise goers are in a state of denial, believing that nothing can happen to them.
• Reality loss, especially on shore leave, may become dangerous.
• Many communities have mixed feelings toward cruises and often do not have adequate police forces.
• Cruise goers often transfer any form of discomfort into anger.
• As on airplanes, anger can easily be displaced onto staff.

Concerns about cruise ship surety include the fact that cruise ships spend a great deal of their time in international waters and therefore are often sitting ducks without local protection. They are also similar to iconic security in that were one sunk there is the potential for a large number of casualties, a great deal of publicity, and severe economic impact to those nations and ports of call that are dependent on cruise passenger income. Lastly, due to their confined quarters, cruise ships, just alike airliners, are open to a great many health risks. They tend to face five types of problems (Tarlow, 2006):

1   Criminal activity committed by passengers against other passengers or staff.
2   Criminal activity committed by staff against passengers or other staff.
3   Issues of health safety.
4   The possibility of a port security breach.
5   The possibility of a terrorism attack while at sea.

A Note on Risk and Perceptions

It has been said that to live is to experience risk. Despite the public's desire for total security and safety there is simply no such thing. Instead, the best that can be hoped for is a stochastic model in which the risk of a negative incident, be it a crime or a terrorism attack, is lessened. Because risk is ubiquitous, it is essential that the tourism surety professional be aware of where there is potential for conflict. No tourism security plan can be developed without first considering the political, economic, and social problems that exist both within and surrounding the tourism entity or locale. Furthermore, a tourism safety and security specialist must have some idea as to how his locale is perceived. Many of our opinions of a place's security are formed as much on perception as it is on hard data. Often these perceptions are based on data from other locales. Thus, how dangerous a place may be considered has as much to do with what the person is accustomed to in his/her own community as the crime rate in the host community. Furthermore, perceptions of a destination and the way that the media portray the destination may both be essential factors in how a visitor decides if a destination is secure (Chen and Noriega, 2003).

Perceptions impact our sense of risk in many other ways. For example, the perception that a specific crime may be replicable will have a major impact on the local tourism industry (Araña and León, 2008). The now world famous case of the American teenager Natalee Holloway is a good example of such a perception.[20,21] In May of 2005 Natalee Holloway disappeared, leading to a media frenzy that cost the island of Aruba millions of dollars.[22] Despite the fact that Aruba is one of the Caribbean's safest locales,[23] the fact that the media created the idea that her disappearance is symbolic of the island's lack of surety has produced a great deal of economic damage. From that perspective it is fair to state that the perception of a crime may be as important as the actual victimization from that crime. Additionally, from a tourism risk perspective, tourism clusters (zones) tend to increase the risk of a criminal or terrorism incident occurring. Risk managers must then measure not only actual risks against visitors' and staff's property, persons, and potential for assault, but also must measure the risk perception if they are to protect the industry's economy and reputation. This risk perception increases for foreign visitors, who may not speak the local language or may be traveling alone.

A number of factors impact a visitor's perceptions of his/her surety in a host locale:

• Is the home nation of the visitor perceived to be safe?
• Are crimes in the tourism host country/city well publicized?
• Is the visitor a male or female?
• How far is the visitor from his/her home?
• Has the visitor experienced crime in the visitor's home country?
• Is the visitor coming to the host locale for business, pleasure or a special event?
• How old is the visitor?
• Does the visitor speak the local language?
• Is the visitor the same race as that of the majority of locals?
• Is there a chance that the visitor may enter into a self-victimizing situation such as the purchase of drugs or prostitution services?

Different locales will have to place their emphasis on different risks. For example, Caribbean islands must face the fact that during half the year, hurricanes are a major threat not only to life and property but also to the region's

Table 26.8   Sample Risk Table

	State the Risk	What Motivates the Risk?	Rank the Risk: High Medium or Low?	How Will You Identify the Risk?	What Are the Consequences Should the Risk Occur?
Weather					
Gangs					
Terror					
Food Poisoning					
Fire					
Theft					

Table 26.9   Classifying Risks Accordingly

Risk	Type 1 High Probability, Low Consequences	Type 2 Low Probability, High Consequences	Type 3 Low Probability, Low Consequences	Type 4 High Probability, High Consequences
Fire				
Natural Disaster				
Bad Publicity due to Illness				
Crime Wave				
Terrorism				

reputation and ability to market itself against other warm weather sun and sea destinations. Conversely, hurricanes pose no threat to a desert destination such as Nevada. Tourism officials must face a myriad of risks that range from weather to crime, from acts of terrorism to natural disasters such as earthquakes, tsunamis, or forest fires. Table 26.8 is not meant to be a comprehensive compilation of risks. Rather, it is meant to give the reader some idea of how to develop a risk chart. Variables should be selected that best match the needs of the local situation.

Table 26.9 demonstrates how to classify tourism risks according to both the probability of their occurrence and their impact.

Today, tourism impacts a world that is much less innocent than it was almost 60 years ago. Modern tourists must confront a world filled with gangs, criminals, drug lords, and terrorists. Tourism specialists must think about the safety and security of his/her guests. They cannot depend on mere marketing efforts to make things better. Those communities and businesses that offer tourism surety in addition to fair pricing, well maintained attractions, and good customer service stand a better chance of success. It is this author's hope that this chapter will help facilitate this success.

Notes

1 www.tsa.gov/press/happenings/jfk_terror_plot. shtm. Accessed April 25, 2008.

2 Bar-On, Raphael Raymond Bar-On. Pers. Comm., November 5, 2001.

3 The term TOPs did not exist prior to January 1999 when the term was coined by Dr. Peter Tarlow and Officer Chris Peña at the First California Tourism Security Conference in Anaheim, California.

4 hawaii.gov/ag/cpja/main/rs/sp_reports_0306/ crime_and_tourism.pdf. Accessed April 26, 2008.

5 In 2004, the COPS program of the US Department of Justice asked Ronald W. Glensor and Kenneth J. Peak to publish a pamphlet in its series *Problem Oriented Guides for Police*, #26 entitled "Crimes Against Tourists." www.tsa.gov/press/happenings/ jfk_terror_plot.shtm. Accessed April 26, 2008.

6 Note that police departments tend to focus on behavior when it comes to crimes against tourists. See, for example, the handbook of the Center for Problem Oriented Policing called *Crimes Against Tourists*, Guide No. 26 (Glensor and Peak, 2004). The police guide sees these crimes often as crimes of opportunity (see also Michalko, 2003).

7 This 2007 study was conducted by the author and will come online in late 2008 and will be found on the Hawaii Tourism Authority official website www.hawaiitourismauthority.org/.

8 See the VASH website for further details. visitoralohasocietyofhawaii.org.

9 www.khqa.com/news/news_story.aspx? id=36816. Accessed April 12, 2007.

10 www.khqa.com/news/news_story.aspx? id=36816. Accessed June, 6, 2007.

11 www.bhtm.org/travel_diseases_brief.htm. Accessed May 12, 2008.

12. www.nationalreview.com/comment/comment seeman042503.asp. Accessed June 6, 2007.

13 www.popcenter.org/Problems/problem-crimes_tourists.htm. Accessed April 12, 2008.

14 Air travel security is a large topic and has not been covered here due to the constraints of chapter length; readers are referred to the various sources cited in the reference section, including Barnett et al. (2001) and Seidenstat (2004). It should be noted that the various stressors of air travel can make for difficult conditions for service providers in this sector. Airport security people, for instance, may have to work with a relatively nervous public. Great care must be taken to maintain calm situations as often small events can become large events. Airport security is an easy target for media attention.

15 www.dmaonline.org/fppublic/connect35. html. Accessed July 19, 2007.

16 Center for Disease Control, wwwn.cdc.gov/. Accessed April 26, 2008.

17 www.dmaonline.org/fppublic/connect35. html. Accessed August 13, 2006.

18 www.cdc.gov/foodsafety. Accessed April 14, 2008.

19 www.cfsan.fda.gov/~news/whatsnew.html. Accessed April 26, 2008. Note also HospitaliltyLawyer. com (Accessed May 13, 2008) which is a website for tourism law that offers some academic information about safety and security from a law perspective, but much further research is needed to address the paucity of research in the area of food safety and tourism.

20 www.msnbc.msn.com/id/8417771/. Accessed April 26, 2008.

21 The website news.yahoo.com/fc/World/ Natalee_Holloway (April 26, 2008) provides continual updates on this case with an index of the multiple news stories and articles.

22 *The Eagle*, Bryan, Texas, July 29, page 1

23 travel.state.gov/travel/cis_pa_tw/cis/cis_1153. html. Accessed April 26, 2008.

References

Barnett, A., Shumsky, R., Hansen, and Odoni, A.M. (2001). "Safe at Home? An Experiment in Domestic Airline Security." *Operations Research*, 49(2): 181–195.

Boym, S. (2001). *Nostalgia*. New York: Basic Books.

Chen, R. and Noriega, P. (2003). "The Impacts of Terrorism: Perceptions of Faculty and Students on Safety and Security in Tourism." *Journal of Travel and Tourism Marketing*, 15(2): 81–97.

Chesney-Lind, M. and Lind, I. (1986).[1] "Visitors as Victims: Crimes Against Tourists in Hawaii." *Annals of Tourism Research*, 13(2): 167–191.

Chon, K. and McKercher, B. (2004). "The Over-Reaction to SARS and the Collapse of the Asian Tourism Industry." *Annals of Tourism Research*, 31(3): 716–719.

Davies, G. (2008). "Lessons from the Virginia Tech Shootings." *Magazine of Higher Learning*, 40(1): 8–15.

Ellis, R. (1999). *Security and Loss Prevention Management*. Lansing, MI: Educational Institute of the American Hotel and Motel Association.

Fukuyama, F. (1989). "The End of History." *The National Interest*, 16 (Summer): 3–18.

Fukuyama, F. (2007). *"The History at the End of History."* Retrieved May 15, 2008 from commentisfree.guardian.co.uk/francis_fukuyama/2007/04/the_history_at_the_end_of_hist.html.

Glensor, R.W. and Peak, K.J. (2004). "Crimes Against Tourists." *Problem Oriented Guides for Police*, 26 (August). Washington, DC: US Department of Justice.

Huddy, J. (2008). *Storming Las Vegas*. New York: Ballantine Books.

J.M. Knox and Associates (2004). "Effects of Tourism on Rates of Serious Crime in Hawaii." Prepared for use of the Hawaii State Department of the Attorney General, Crime Prevention and Justice Assistance Division.

MacLaurin, T.L. (2001). "Singaporeans' Attitudes, Perceptions, and Knowledge of Safe Food Preparation Practices." *Journal of the Society of Environmental Health*, 15: 25–36.

MacLaurin, T.L. (2002). "Singapore Public Health Officers' Opinions of the Relationship Between Food Safety and Food Quality." *Journal of the Society of Environmental Health*, 16: 23–27.

Mansfeld, Y. and Pizam, A. (2007). *Tourism Security & Safety*. Elsevier: Amsterdam.

Michalko, G. (2003). "Tourism Eclipsed by Crime: The Vulnerability of Foreign Tourists in Hungary." In M. Hall, D. Timothy and D. Timothy Duval (Eds.), *Safety and Security in Tourism: Relationships, Management, and Marketing* (pp. 159–172). New York: Routledge.

Pizam, A. and Mansfeld, Y. (Eds.) (1996). *Tourism Crime and International Security Issues*. London: John Wiley & Sons.

Pizam, A., Tarlow, P. and Bloom, J. (1997). "Making Tourists Feel Safe." *Journal of Travel Research*, 36(1): 23–28.

Paul Seidenstat (2004). "Terrorism, Airport Security, and the Private Sector." *Review of Policy Research*, 21(3): 275–291.

Sirakaya, E., Petrick, J. and Choi, H. (2004). "The Role of Mood on Tourism Product Evaluations." *Annals of Tourism Research*, 31(3): 517–539.

Sonmez, S. (1998). "Tourism, Terrorism, and Political Instability." *Annals of Tourism Research,* 25(2): 416–456.

Sonmez, S. and Graefe, A. (1998). "Influence of Terrorism Risk on Foreign Tourism Decisions." *Annals of Tourism Research*, 25(1): 112–144.

Tarlow, P. (2002). *Event Risk Management and Safety*. New York: John Wiley & Sons.

Tarlow, P. (2003). "The Changing Face of Tourism Security in Emergency Management."

Paper delivered at the *FEMA (Federal Emergency Management Agency) Conference*. Emmitsburg, MD, February, 2003.

Tarlow, P. (2006). "Crime and Tourism." In J. Wilks, D. Pendergast, and P. Legeat (Eds.), *Tourism in Turbulent Times* (pp. 93–106). Amsterdam: Elsevier.

Tarlow, P. (2007a). "Lodging Security." In John J. Fay (Ed.), *Encyclopedia of Security Management* (2nd edition.) (p. 455). Newton, MA: Butterworth-Heinemann.

Tarlow, P. (2007b). "A Social Theory of Terrorism and Tourism." In Y. Mansfeld and A. Pizam (Eds.), *Tourism Security & Safety*. Amsterdam: Elsevier.

Veblen, T. (1899). *The Theory of the Leisure Class*. New York: Mentor Books.

Wilks, J. (Ed.) (2008). *Beach Safety and the Law: Australian Evidence*. Brisbane: Queensland Law Society.

Wilks, J., Pendergast, D. and Leggat, P. (2006). *Tourism in Turbulent Times*. Amsterdam: Elsevier.

PART III

Critical Issues and Emerging Perspectives

Cruise ships at Cozumel, Mexico.

27

Festivals, Events, and Tourism

Bernadette Quinn

Introduction

The study of festivals and events is now an important and prolific area of tourism research enquiry. Festivals and events have flourished in recent decades and interest in understanding their significance in the tourism academy has risen accordingly. Even the most cursory scan of leading tourism journals demonstrates that literature on festivals and events is now one of the most prolific of any area of tourism research and there is now a burgeoning collection of monographs, academic textbooks, and practical handbooks available. Perhaps most obviously associated with this research activity is the body of literature dealing with the strategic and operational management of events. This is now a very significant literature, dating back to the 1970s, and several sub-streams with corresponding research specializations can now be identified. This literature is largely concerned with production and supply-side issues and tends to be applied in nature. There is also a smaller yet significant social sciences/humanities inspired tourism literature on festivals and events. This dates to at least the early 1970s and questions here often involve cultural and social change, the reproduction of place and of tradition, and the role of communities as producers/consumers. Thus, overall, there is a multiplicity of perspectives being brought to the study of festival and event-tourism relationships and this is a defining feature of the literature. To a large degree, the complexity that this introduces mirrors the breadth of tourism research more broadly, involving as it does a variety of theoretical and methodological approaches, with diverse applied and conceptual orientations.

Great strides have been made in recent times to define the nature and extent of tourism related festival and event research. In its entirety, and in components, it is an area that has been extensively reviewed in recent times and several "state of the art" type articles are available (e.g., Formica, 1998; Getz, 2004; Hede et al., 2003). A notable development has been the emergence of the term "events tourism" and more recently "event tourism." Getz (1989) began to discuss planning for "events tourism" in 1989 and with his 2008 review article defines the parameters of "event tourism." As Stokes (2005) notes, the perspective here is that of strategic management, and event tourism is construed as a sector primarily driven by the goal of economic benefits. Conceptualized as encompassing festivals and events, event tourism is understood to be at the nexus of tourism and event studies. Specifically, this nexus is posited as being the set of interrelationships that underpin "the marketing of events to tourists, and the development and marketing of events for tourism and economic development purposes" (Getz, 2008: 406). "Event tourism" has been the subject of a comprehensive review article published in a recent volume of *Tourism Management*, where the author (Getz, 2008), outlines a framework for knowledge creation and theory development.

This chapter takes the opportunity to review and reflect on the existing body of knowledge and to pose a number of questions about developments in the area. In the past, the literature on tourism and events has been accused of lacking in advanced theory and sophisticated and multiple research methods (Formica, 1998). Certainly, the literature is characterized by a diversity of disciplinary approaches and priorities. However, as Getz (2008) points out, this is typical of any relatively new field of enquiry. As will be argued, much of the management/economics inspired literature demonstrates a marked tendency to dislocate events and festivals from broader processes, other than to investigate their apparently unidirectional "impacts" on contextual environments. Meanwhile, sociological and cultural orientations within the social sciences (and humanities) tend to be concerned with processes and not to any great extent with the tangible dimensions related to planning, implementing, and measuring outcomes. Those with sociocultural investigative foci tend to concern themselves with tourism contexts where festivals and events are socially constructed, are mutually reproductive of place and place identity, and are bound up with the appropriation and evolution of cultural practices and traditions (i.e., social and cultural change). Here we see a clear dichotomy between an approach that arguably has historically treated events and festivals as discrete entities, and privileges them because they have strategically useful tourism potential, and another that problematizes the instrumental development of festivals and events in the interests of tourism.

A key question is whether potential exists for different disciplinary approaches to align more closely in the interest of creating a holistic understanding of the nature, meanings, and management of festival and event tourism relationships. As Getz (2008) clearly acknowledges in the opening paragraphs of his review, events have many partners and proponents and many important societal and economic roles to play. What is critical to appreciate in this context is that the mutual engagement of tourism and events informs the subsequent reproduction of both in particular ways. Understanding and explaining the kind of engagements that occur is an important research endeavor for a variety of reasons. One pragmatic reason is to effectively promote event tourism as a sustainable form of development. As Waitt (2003) discusses, a planning/management regime sensitive to quality of life and equity outcomes is essential for sustainable tourism. Sustainability in tourism requires hosts to be positively disposed towards developments, so as to enhance the tourists' experience and contribute to the destination's attractiveness.

This chapter briefly, but critically, considers some recent developments in the management literature. It then turns its attention to the research contributions emanating from social science and humanities disciplines, and identifies a number of core research areas. In essence, a core concern of this chapter is to begin to seek ways of strengthening dialogue and exchange between the management literature on event tourism and those other literatures whose engagement with the study of tourism has stemmed from a more central interest elsewhere, be it with place, society, or culture. If, for instance, the event tourism literature asks "how can planned events effectively contribute to the development of sustainable tourism?" a suggestion from this chapter is that it is also worthy to ask "how does the interaction of tourism and events influence their mutual reproduction as well as the reproduction of places, cultures and communities?" The chapter begins with definitions and a brief chronological overview of literature developments.

A Brief Historical Overview

Janiskee explained that festivals and events can be understood as "formal periods or programs of pleasurable activities, entertainment, or events having a festive character and publicly celebrating some concept, happening or fact" (1980: 97). The festive and public celebratory characteristics noted in this definition are important because festivals and events have long existed as significant cultural practices devised as forms of public display, collective celebration and civic ritual. In fact, according to Turner (1982: 11) people in all cultures recognize the need to set aside certain times and spaces for communal creativity and celebration. These practices date back centuries. Often they were allied to the rhythms of agrarian society (Rolfe, 1992). Very often there were religious underpinnings, as in many of the festivals that Fox Gotham (2005a) reminds us existed in the Middle Ages. Public displays and civic ritual were significant in Renaissance times (Muir, 1997), while Geppert (2004) explains how imperial and international exhibitions came to be part of both public life and the collective imagination in Europe from the middle of the nineteenth century onwards. Researchers consistently point to the fact that throughout these earlier periods, festivals and events "encapsulate identity, in terms of the nation state, a sense of place, and the personal and heterogeneous identities of a people" (Matheson, 2005: 224). Historical research demonstrates how festivals and events have a long history of acting as tourist attractions and of effecting the reproduction of places as tourism destinations. Gold and Gold (2005: 268) describe how the recognition of Greenwich as the fulcrum of the Earth's time zones in 1884 inspired the hosting of a year long festival intended to boost international tourism to the city. Adams (1986) discusses how, as long ago as 1859, the Handel Centenary Festival held in London's Crystal Palace was marketed as a tourist attraction with the organizers distributing 50,000 prospectuses in the European offices of the railway companies serving the Crystal Palace.

Simultaneously, these transient, albeit often recurring, phenomena acted as an important means of collective identification for the communities hosting the events. Then, as now, they engendered local continuity and constituted opportunities for asserting, reinforcing, reproducing, and sometimes contesting prevailing social norms, cultural values, and beliefs. Falassi argued that festivals "renew periodically the life stream of a community and give sanctions to its institutions" (1987: 3). In a similar vein, Bonnemaison (1990) argued that what the literature terms the "hallmark event" (see below for definition) functions like a monument, supporting and reinforcing the image of established power, whether religious or secular.

Festivals and events thus have a long historical trajectory, and embody the traditions of various pasts. They have flourished again in contemporary society, following a decline from the mid-20th century onwards (Boissevain, 1992). Their recent proliferation is noted by many researchers (e.g., Gursoy et al., 2004; Manning, 1983; Prentice and Andersen, 2003; Quinn, 2005a; Rolfe, 1992) and is allied to their tourism potential. A set of demand-driven factors underpin their growth, including socialization needs, the growth of serious leisure (Prentice and Andersen, 2003) and the move towards the consumption of experiences (Getz, 2008). On the production side, as discussed consistently in contributions to urban studies and urban geography literatures, the contemporary explosion of festivals and events is explained in terms of urban restructuring processes. A key driver for the growth and reinvention of festivals and events internationally has been their potential to deliver a series of development outcomes in terms of economic restructuring and revitalization, destination repositioning, inward investment, and tourism revenue generation (good items for evaluating the "success" of festivals and events). For example, Schuster (2001) has argued that festivals and events staged as urban ephemera or urban spectacle yield economic benefits by raising the profile of places, their products and institutions and attracting flows of tourists, capital, and inward investment. For many western cities, a key motivation in developing festival and event strategies has been to recover from long-term economic decline. Festivals and events have been part of a wider range of new "cultural strategies" (Fox Gotham, 2005a) used to regenerate and orient postproduction economies towards consumption (Zukin, 1995) where leisure, entertainment and tourism underpin an "experience economy" (Pine and Gilmore, 1999). Meanwhile, for these cities, as well as for those trying to get onto the global stage for the first time, festivals and events form part of place-marketing strategies, fueled by an ideology of globalization, localization and competition among cities. Shin (2004), for instance, presents the case of the Gwangju Biennale Festival as being representative of recent cultural festivals in South Korea, where the image of a "city of art" was one of the standardized images developed by local governments to reshape the images of several South Korean cities. As in the past, festivals and events entail public display and festive celebration, thus creating interest and attracting attention as they invigorate and enliven places.

Definitions

While Hede (2007) explains that special event research emerged as an area of tourism management in the mid-1970s, it was during the 1980s that the study of events began to grow dramatically in academia (Getz, 2008). The marked rise of academic interest in events in that decade was closely linked to their role in place-marketing, a type of civic boosterism that views culture instrumentally (Loftman and Nevil, 1996). Undoubtedly, this was an important context shaping research enquiry into festivals and events from then onwards. While the use of hallmark events as a civic boosterism instrument has been critiqued (Boyle, 1997), it was widely viewed as a positive development among tourism researchers. Events are seen as an important motivator in tourism (Getz, 2008), and as an effective enhancer of destination image

(Hall, 1992; Ritchie, 1984). Hallmark events, for example, usually held in city locations, have been labeled "our new image-builders" (Burns and Mules, 1986) and a whole new discourse, including a new set of definitions and terminology, has been developed to examine the phenomenon. "Special events" was an early and encompassing term used in the literature. This was understood to encompass different types of events, including mega events (e.g., Olympic Games and World Cup), hallmark events (those closely linked with a destination), festivals and other more modest events. Over time, definitions were refined. Mega events, for example, were defined by Ritchie as "major one-time or recurring events of limited duration, developed primarily to enhance the awareness, appeal, and profitability of a tourism destination in the short and/ or long term" (1984: 2). Within a place-marketing ethos, and from a supply perspective, festivals came to be increasingly defined simply as just one more type of event. Their festive, playful, celebrative qualities were recognized and prized because festivals offer tourists glimpses of local uniqueness (Litvin and Fetter, 2006), diverse cultural experiences (Hall, 1992) and opportunities to participate in distinctive, collective experiences (Getz, 1989). However, there was little attempt to draw on established understandings of festivals as socially and culturally important phenomena involved in the construction of place and community identity (as distinct from image identity). While their reproduction as tourist attractions was sometimes problematized (e.g., Greenwood, 1972), critical perspectives such as this did not noticeably influence the emerging event literature.

Dominant Themes: Management Perspectives

Previous literature reviews have identified the core areas of research and publication. Formica (1998) determined that economic impacts, then marketing, event profiles, sponsorship, management and forecasting/trend description were the main topics. Getz's (2000) conclusions were very similar. More recently, Moscardo (2007) asserted that the existing tourism literature on festivals and events is dominated by four main topics including economic impacts, audience analysis with a view to improving marketing and service quality, the management of events with a particular concern to enhance marketing and service quality, and broader event impacts as perceived by residents. Clearly, there remains scope for extending these emphases. As Getz (2008: 421) concludes, event tourism studies and related research are still in the early stage of development.

Economic Impact

The emphases evident in the literature to date must be understood in context. Not surprisingly, as festivals and events became increasingly incorporated into urban and regional development agendas, the obvious growth in early academic interest was in management and economics, and research agendas were closely attuned to practitioners' needs. There was a pronounced orientation towards understanding the impact of events, and from early on, events came overwhelmingly to be conceived as discrete entities with an ability to unidirectionally create a series on impacts, both positive and negative, on contextual environments. Ritchie's (1984) identification of a range of impacts associated with what he called hallmark events was an important and influential publication. Although he identified a wide range of impact types, most subsequent research attention focused on measuring and evaluating the economic impacts of events on host economies, a development at least partially inspired by the realities of city and regional government needs for justifying investment in festival and event development strategies (e.g., Burgan and Mules, 2001; Burns et al., 1986; Crompton and McKay, 1994; Dwyer et al., 2000; Getz, 2000; Mules and McDonald, 1994). As early as 1989,

voices were cautioning the need for a broader set of research concerns, including "the anticipation and regulation of the impact of the event on the host community, and the promotion of associated development in a manner which maximizes short- and long-term economic, environmental and social benefits" (Hall, 1989: 21).

Gursoy et al. (2004) note that researchers have been very slow in directing research beyond economic impacts and motivations. The overtly "economic impact" orientation of the literature has been well acknowledged by others (Getz, 2008; Hede, 2007; Moscardo, 2007). Furthermore, there has been much debate concerning both the robustness of the methodologies and approaches used to determine economic outcomes and the accuracy of gains attributed to events. The measurement of economic outputs has employed a variety of mechanisms. Lee and Taylor (2005) critically reviewed the problems that beset economic impact studies, citing critical observations from *inter alia* Burgan and Mules (1992), Crompton (1999), Lee and Kim (1998), and Tyrrell and Johnston (2001). They concluded that on the basis of past research only direct expenditure attributable to an event should be considered in estimating the economic impact of an event. However, elsewhere, Wood et al. (2006) argued that a focus on direct expenditure benefits will produce an incomplete picture. Thus the debate continues.

Other Impacts

The concern with demonstrating significant, predominantly economic impact automatically led to a strong emphasis on large scale events (Gibson et al., 2003). Much of the focus has been on sports events. As Getz states: "Sports as 'big business' is an enduring theme in the literature" (2008: 411) and mega events, including most notably the Olympic Games but also the FIFA World Cup, the Commonwealth Games, and various motor racing events, have received considerable attention. While there is a vast literature on the economic impact of major events, research enquiry in this area has also asked questions about destination image-enhancement, national identity, and pride enhancement, and longer-term regeneration outcomes in the form of sporting and commercial infrastructure as well as community-building and social legacies. The research evidence suggests that large scale events create both positive and negative impacts in both the short and the long term. Many studies have documented positive outcomes (e.g., Decco and Baloglu, 2002; Ritchie and Smith, 1991). A strong theme here is the enhancement of the international image of the host community, and the generation of short and long term visitor flows. With respect to the former, considerable attention has been paid to how events can reshape a city's image (Jeong and Faulkner, 1996; Lee et al., 2005) although Boo and Busser (2006) claim that few studies have empirically examined the role of festivals in destination image improvement and call for longitudinal research on this question. Meanwhile, the literature on the European City of Culture (ECOC) event is often preoccupied with the tourism outcomes of this annual cultural event (Bailey et al., 2004; García, 2005). One of the ECOCs most frequently discussed in the literature, Glasgow 1990, is widely attributed with having transformed the city's image from a rarely visited, depressed post industrial city into a lively and attractive city that, subsequent to the event, increased its inbound tourist flows dramatically. The generation of environmental outcomes in the form of infrastructural legacies is another notable theme in the literature. Large events have come to be seen as catalysts for urban regeneration (García, 2004) although mixed outcomes have been reported in respect of the latter with several acknowledging negative outcomes (Hall and Hodges, 1996; Hiller, 1998; Ritchie, 1999; Roche, 1994). Examples of such negativities include the accumulation of large debts for host communities and the displacement of local residents to make way for infrastructural improvements.

Some studies have pointed to positive, yet somewhat intangible and often surprising outcomes. Lee and Taylor in an economic impact study, concluded in respect of the 2002 FIFA World Cup held in South Korea that "the success of the South Korean football team provided the country with a sense of national pride and cohesiveness that no economic impact assessment could ever put a dollar value on" (2005: 602). Lee et al. (2005) make the point that mega sports events such as the Olympic Games draw a great deal of international attention to sport and in the process contribute to increased interest in sports tourism. Meanwhile Kim et al. (2006) argue that several researchers (e.g., Mihalik and Simonette, 1998; Ritchie and Aitken, 1984) have suggested that residents in places that have held sports mega events can believe the positive social outcomes to be as important as economic outcomes or even more so. Elsewhere, Thomas and Wood (2004) and Wood (2005) indicated that in a UK context, the social benefits of local authority funded events are likely to outweigh the economic benefits.

Planning and Evaluating Events

As might be expected, there is a long-standing literature on event planning and what seems like dozens of text books are now available on the topic. Of late, a number of important themes in this area can be identified. One has been the move towards a more collaborative decision making approach to mega event planning. Gursoy and Kendall (2006) argue that hallmark decision-making/political planning is gradually being abandoned as key decision-makers realize the value of local involvement and support. An underpinning argument for involving residents in event planning relates to the fact that if residents' quality of life is adversely affected by the staging of events, then visiting tourist populations may be adversely affected in consequence because of the ensuing animosity or ill feeling. Another recent theme is the need to adopt a more strategic approach to events so as to leverage as many benefits as possible for the host economy/community (Pugh and Wood, 2004).

In terms of the post-event outcomes, there has been a growing awareness of the need for evaluation to be increasingly broadly defined. The literature is peppered with calls for researchers to move beyond the economic domain into other equally fruitful terrains where social, cultural and political issues can be addressed (Bowdin et al., 2006; Gnoth and Anwar, 2000; Moscardo 2007; Wood et al., 2006). Recent work on evaluating and assessing the impacts associated with events has reflected this awareness. It has also been influenced by developments in the literature on the social impact of tourism more generally (e.g., Lankford and Howard, 1994) and an upsurge of publications on the topic is now evident. Early research came from Fredline and Faulkner (2000), with Delemare (2001) developing a Festival Social Impact Attitude Scale (FSIAS) and Fredline et al. (2003) and Fredline (2006) progressing the literature in this area. As Hede notes, "research on event evaluation is currently focused on amalgamating the economic, social and environmental forms of evaluation into one framework" (2007: 14). In this context, she emphasizes the emergence of the triple bottom line (TBL) approach. "The rationale behind Triple Bottom Line reporting is to illuminate the externalities associated with business activities and therefore to promote sustainability through planning and management practices that ameliorate negative outcomes and promote positive ones" (Fredline et al., 2005: 3, cited in Hede, 2007: 24).

Marketing and Motivation

From a tourism perspective, events clearly require audiences. As Faulkner et al. (2000) argue, the destination development engendered by an event is largely driven by the attendance it is expected to generate. Meanwhile, as Whitelegg (2000) notes, the impact of mega events on international tourism is related to their capacity to attract international audiences. Thus, the promotion and marketing of events is a key area of interest, and the question as to what motivates people to attend events has been an important social psychological question dating back to the early 1990s. There is now a substantial literature on the topic, including a recent review by Li and Petrick (2006). The complexity of motives at issue has been debated in general (e.g., Backman et al., 1995; Crompton and McKay, 1997, Formica and Murrmann, 1998; Getz and Cheyne, 2002; Robinson and Gammon, 2004) as well as in specific areas like sports events (Gibson, 1998, 2006), and business and convention events (Rittichainuwat et al., 2001). The importance of understanding constraints has been discussed (Kim and Chalip, 2004) as has the importance of market segmentation, with Formica and Uysal (1998) demonstrating that successful promotion depends on effective segmentation.

Local Residents and Stakeholder Relationships

A supply-side perspective is very evident in most of the above literature, but in the move towards a wider interpretation of event impacts (e.g., Hede, 2007) we see a growing interest in other stakeholders, including residents. One well established line of enquiry in the literature has concerned residents, and research into the perceived impacts of events on host communities is well established (Delamere, 2001; Fredline and Faulkner, 2002; Fredline et al., 2003; Gursoy and Kendall, 2006). Social exchange theory underpins a great deal of this research, and studies have tried to assess the extent and manner in which individuals are likely to participate in an exchange if they believe they are likely to gain benefits without incurring unacceptable costs (Homans, 1974, cited in Gursoy and Kendall, 2006: 607). Residents have also been central in the research that has explored how festivals and events are associated with enhanced community well-being, improved social cohesion, enhanced pride in place, building of community cohesion and identity, all of which have been investigated in festival and event settings (e.g., Derrett, 2003).

With respect to stakeholders more generally, there has been a growing interest in theorizing stakeholder relationships in festival and event settings from a number of management perspectives. Larson and Wikstrom (2001) and Larson (2002), for example, introduced the political market square concept into the event stakeholder literature. In the context of relationship marketing, Larson (2002) used the political market square concept to analyze the power dynamics evident in a project network of actors marketing a festival. Her analysis identified a series of political processes including gatekeeping, negotiation, coalition building, trust, and identity building. More recently, Getz et al. (2007) have argued that festivals are produced not by stand-alone organizations but by voluntary networks of stakeholders that must be managed effectively by the festival organization. Elsewhere, MacKellar (2007) used a network analysis methodology to study the relationships between organizations staging an event.

Most of the above literature orients itself around the idea that events are first and foremost tourist attractions. Its main priority is to understand how the tourism industry can produce events that attract and satisfy tourists, plus generate a series of beneficial outcomes (tourist expenditure, image enhancement, related investment, etc.). However, it is clear that there is now an increasing interest in moving away from a preoccupation with the event as a discrete entity towards a much broader conceptualization of festivals and events as phenomena embedded in a multiplicity of spatial, sociocultural, political, and environmental contexts. There is further an increasing inclination to problematize the relationships between festivals, events, and tourism and to adopt a more critical and reflexive approach. This is very apparent in recent developments emerging in the literature on collaborative planning and social outcomes, for instance, in the work examining how events link into their contextual environments and host communities through stakeholder relationships and networks of various kinds (Getz et al., 2007; Larson and Wikstrom, 2001;

Moscardo, 2007). It is in these literature areas that the distinction between management and other disciplinary approaches becomes blurred, and interchange between researchers working in diverse domains on closely related problems is most apparent.

Dominant Themes: Social Sciences and Humanities Perspectives

If the management literature has been profoundly conscious of development, planning, and marketing-related outcomes, the more sociological and cultural orientations within the social sciences/humanities literature has tended to be concerned with processes. Undoubtedly, this reflects the differential weight attached to applied and conceptual enquiry in the different areas, although the conceptual preoccupation of the latter does not necessarily imply a more advanced theoretical underpinning or even a more clearly defined research agenda. To date, few, if any, critical reviews or syntheses of what Getz (2008) has termed the "studies" literature have been published, unlike in the management domain, and there has been little attempt to identify dominant research strands. This section makes an attempt to do this by identifying some of the key ways in which festival and event settings have been analyzed to further mainstream tourism debates. Much of the following literature, when empirical, uses qualitative case study methodology, in contrast to the management-related literature, which much more frequently uses large-scale survey tools and quantitative techniques in its empirical investigations. Discussions generally point to the complexity and multidimensionality of festivals and events and conceive of them as being dynamic and continuously evolving, reproduced through a multiplicity of local and extra-local relationships, and implicated in the construction of identity (of culture groups, communities, places, and nations). Relationships that might be usefully explored in future research are considered towards the end of the discussion.

Tradition and Modernity—Processes of Cultural Change

The role that tourism plays in affecting cultural change has been of enormous interest to tourism researchers for decades. Very often, enquiries have been located in festival and event sites. Indeed, this is an example of an area where festivals and events were originally at the fore in initiating a mainstream tourism debate, with Greenwood's (1972) analysis of a Basque festival being highly influential. Following Marx, Greenwood argued that the Spanish Ministry of Tourism's involvement in the *Fuenterrabia* transformed the festival from an authentic, locally embedded, and meaningful cultural practice into a public spectacle for outsiders. The intervention, he argued, led to a decline of local interest and a loss of meaning such that "the ritual has become a performance for money. The meaning is gone" (Greenwood, 1972: 78). Greenwood's paper initiated a still ongoing debate about tourism and commoditization. As Sofield and Li note, his commoditization thesis was a very attractive one, and it became "one of the most powerful indictments of the corrosive effects of tourism" (1998: 270). It also quickly became one of the most frequently cited, strengthened by its inclusion in Cohen's (1988) paper on authenticity and commoditization in tourism. Greenwood's interpretation, however, has been subsequently critiqued (Wilson, 1993), and the usefulness of his commoditization thesis hotly debated ever since. Originally, the core question was whether the commoditization of festivals and events through tourism renders these cultural practices and the social relations inherent therein, inauthentic (Matheson, 2005). Recently, however, Shepherd (2002: 195) has argued that commodification within the sphere of culture is a social fact, and suggests that discussion should now focus less on what has been commodified and more on how authenticity becomes constructed and decided.

As implied here, the commodification discussion is closely linked to the equally intense and lengthy debate on authenticity and tourism. It was MacCannell (1976) who first argued that the search for authentic experience is crucial to the tourist endeavor. In this context, the festival or event is particularly appealing because it is understood to offer "outsiders" genuine insights into particular "insider" cultural practices, traditions and heritages. Furthermore, the very nature of festivals entails an overt outward orientation which sees communities of people generate cultural meanings expressly to be read by the outside world (Quinn, 2005b). The problem, however, as expressed early on in the literature, is that tourists are condemned to experiencing only a semblance of authenticity. Drawing on Goffman's (1959) models of front and back regions of social space, MacCannell (1976) argued that tourist settings are constructed to comprise six staged settings, all of which tourists strive, and ultimately fail, to "get behind" in their quest to access the authentic back stages of the host community. MacCannell's theorization, however, was later criticized because it equates the authentic with some sort of pristine, "original" state which becomes automatically destroyed upon contact with tourism (Bruner, 1994). Researchers like Bruner (1994), Olsen (2002), and Shepherd (2002) have argued instead that authenticity is a socially constructed process and that the critical question is "how do people themselves think about objects as authentic?" In this line of thinking, authenticity is no longer seen as a quality of the object but as a cultural value constantly created and reinvented in social processes (Olsen, 2002). Cohen (1988) further elaborates this thinking by arguing the negotiability of authenticity. Being socially constructed, it has many potential forms and so "a cultural product, or a trait thereof, which is at one point generally judged as contrived or inauthentic may, in the course of time, become generally recognized as authentic, even by experts" (Cohen, 1988: 379).

Thus, within mainstream tourism debates, it is becoming increasingly accepted that there are many reasonable answers to the question of what is authentic (Olsen, 2002); that questions about the meanings of authenticity are always open to negotiation (Timothy and Boyd, 2003); and that it is now necessary to speak of "competing authenticities, all products of particular social forces engaged in a process of cultural (re)invention and consumption within the context of existing social relations" (Shepherd, 2002: 196). Recent empirical investigations in festival and events settings are moving to reflect this theoretical position, although the idea that authenticity pertains to the quality of the object is still being explored. McCartney and Osti, examining the cultural authenticity of the Dragon Boat races in Macau, discuss the risk of commercialization diminishing the meaning of an event, transforming it into a spectacle or entertainment and "thereby destroying its cultural authenticity" (2007: 26). Richards (2007), however, following on from the work of researchers such as Cohen (1988) and Shepherd (2002), explores the value that different event audiences attach to authenticity. He explored how residents and visitors view commercialization processes and authenticity in traditional events and found that while residents and visitors generally agree that the Catalan festival studied, La Mercè, is authentic, their perceptions of authenticity vary. Drawing on Wang (1999), Richards (2007) argues that residents were more likely to emphasize a "constructive authenticity" based on familiar cultural norms (particularly those related to the role of tradition and language in Catalan society), while visitors tended to appreciate an "existential authenticity," one reliant on enjoying the festivity and the attendant socialization. Elsewhere, Müller and Pettersson's (2005) analysis of a Swedish festival celebrating Sami heritage shows how different sets of meanings can be produced simultaneously and apparently satisfactorily

for both producers and consumers. They describe how the experiences available to tourists, local residents and indigenous peoples range from being variously "staged" to being "non-staged." Furthermore, they conclude that it is probably the coexistence of more or less staged, authorized and unauthorized representations of Sami heritage that makes the festival attractive to a range of audiences, all of whom can relate to, and engage in, the festival in different ways. Thus, an important theoretical argument becoming established in the literature is that local residents, as producers and as established audiences, can engage meaningfully in festivals in ways that address both their own needs and those of visitors at the same time. However, more empirical research is needed to further elaborate this position.

Local and Global: Reproducing Place

Festivals and events have long been of interest to researchers because they constitute a vehicle for expressing the close relationship between identity and place (Aldskogius, 1993; Ekman, 1999; Lavenda, 1997; Lewis and Pile 1996; Smith, 1996). Festivals in particular have been a focus for empirically investigating how people connect with their place and with other people through their festival practices. The type of identity in question can be linked to different spatial spheres, ranging from the local to the international. The literature on place-marketing is most often interested in mega events and in country or major city destinations, but equally, a breadth of spatial spheres have been studied. Hall (1992), for example, has written about the role of events in developing or maintaining community or regional identity. De Bres and Davis (2001) discuss how a Kansas River Festival helped to promote a sense of pride, kinship, and community among the river communities involved. Derrett (2003) focused on how events contribute to an enhanced sense of place. More recently,

Moscardo (2007) examined 36 case studies of regional festivals and events, seeking to broaden understanding of how events contribute to regional development.

Throughout this literature, there has been an understanding that the meanings produced in festival sites display the influence of forces prevailing both locally and in other geographic spheres. Important questions have been: how do particular constellations of internal/external linkages emerge over time? Can events remain embedded in specific locales and retain meanings for place-based communities while meeting the needs of visiting audiences? In this, the reproduction of events is conceptualized as being akin to the reproduction of tourism places: it illuminates at once the twin processes of global homogeneity and local heterogeneity that characterize modern capitalism (Fox Gotham, 2005a). Thus, Green (2002), writing about carnival practices in Trinidad, argues that outside influences have always been a part of carnival, with much borrowing, adaptation and reinvention of traditions implicit over time. Quinn (2003) writing about an arts festival in Ireland, argues that the practice of producing a festival is an evolving one, partially informed by the introduction of externally sourced traditions, and by their subsequent reinvention through local lenses.

The link between globalization and cultural homogenization has been problematized in event settings. Some researchers have argued that large scale events erode place distinctiveness, leading to a process of homogenization and ultimately ending up being counterproductive to the original place marketing objectives (Richards and Wilson, 2006). McCartney and Osti, for example, raise the issue of "event homogenization," as "destinations jostle to reproduce successful themed festivals of their own" (2007: 26). Yardimci, writing about festivals in Istanbul, describes how festivals' failure to create difference in their content "pushes them to emphasize instead the difference of the city—in a monumental image of oriental Istanbul—that merges its socio-historical heritage with a western

techno-economic level of material development, familiarity with culture and adherence to secularism" (2007: 5). As McCarthy (2005) explains, the fact that events may not be culturally embedded in the locality and have but few linkages to local ideas of identity and local lifestyles is problematic. Isar's (1976: 126) argument that genuine festivals must be "rooted in society, in real life," and Degreef's (1994: 18) belief that "artistically responsible" arts festivals must respond and evolve in tandem with the changing artistic needs felt by diverse resident and visitor groups, may be lost in the bid to achieve place marketing or other goals. Thus, the result may be a privileging of the global and all that that entails, at the expense of the local. Yardimci's (2007) analysis of recent festival development in Istanbul, for example, posits the positioning of the West as a reference point against which Turkey's success in cultural development can be assessed. Fox Gotham (2005a) argues that as part of tourism, festivals and events can be promoted by powerful economic forces in ways that may undermine local traditions and decision making. For example, the literature has been conscious of the possibility that in the preoccupation with meeting visitor needs, events may disregard local residents. Eisinger (2000) suggested that events may have little to do with local citizens, being designed for a "visitor class," attracted into the event location from elsewhere. The implicit notion of displacement here is taken up by Misener and Mason (2006) who, writing about sports events, examine how events transiently reproduce space in ways that disrupt or at least alter, local ways of living in place. They suggest that local citizens "often struggle to find meaning, a sense of identity and a sense of connectedness in their own neighborhoods" as one-off strategies like sporting events transport the space around them (Misener and Mason, 2006: 385).

Conversely, there is an increasingly well supported argument that "local actors can use urban spectacles for positive and progressive ends" (Fox Gotham, 2005a: 235). Writing about New Orleans, he cites the example of the Essence Festival which functions as a vehicle for encouraging critical dialogue and debate over the causes and consequences of social inequality and continuing black marginalization in US society. Elsewhere, Nurse's (1999) analysis of Caribbean carnivals found that the substantial tourism and economic dimensions do not overshadow the profound social meanings of these festivities. While Alleyne-Dettmers (1997) analysis of London's Notting Hill Carnival conceives of local celebrations, such as carnival, as settings where the local becomes reworked in a dynamic and constantly changing global environment. In a discussion on Mardi Gras, Fox Gotham urges researchers to "develop our understanding of how places and extra-local flows constitute each other, rather than seeing them as opposing principles" (2005b: 323).

The Politics of Identity and Representation

A further key theme in the literature is that the reproduction of festivals and events as tourist attractions is strongly shaped by power dynamics. Boyle (1997) pointed to the power dynamics involved in their production and argued that events are socially constructed in specific ways by certain groups to promote particular ideas and beliefs. Events are never "impromptu or improvised ... and arts festivals in particular, are never spontaneous" (Waterman, 1998: 59). Shin's case of the Gwangju Biennale, for example, shows that "a festival is cultural, but its aim is economic—in advertising the city to tourists and investors— and that its process is immersed in political dynamics that influence potential transformations in the image of a city and urban space" (Shin, 2004: 630). Meanwhile, Hitters' (2000) analysis of Rotterdam as European Cultural Capital 2001 showed the event to be socially and politically contested. As Matheson (2005) notes, festivities offer an opportunity to decode the inner structures and workings of a society. Hence, a strong line of enquiry has been to explore both the reproduction of

dominant meanings by powerful stakeholders and the resistance that this has evoked in response. Clearly, the urban literature explains how and why powerful stakeholders like city governments and the tourism industry favor the development of events. Elsewhere, researchers have been at pains to demonstrate how the construction of festivals and events involves the elevation of selective cultural details/social positions and community voices to symbolic status and the simultaneous downgrading or silencing of others (De Bres and Davis, 2001; Quinn, 2005b). This process unfolds not simply in the interest of constructing a desirable image of place to be represented in the international tourism market-place, but also more profoundly for the sake of promoting vested interests, maintaining social order and the cultural status quo. Power divisions have many, often multiple, bases including social class, race, gender, and sexuality. Waterman (1998), for example, argues that highbrow arts festivals still explicitly prefer to present themselves as elitist, citing the case of the Israel Festival as one that is unashamedly so. Jamieson's (2004) analysis of the Edinburgh Festival, for example, reveals a festival city that is spatially constructed in ways that privilege visiting audiences, containing them within parts of the city considered "appropriate" for cultural consumption, while leaving the socially deprived outskirts of the city relatively free of festival activity. Lewis and Pile (1996) focuses on gender and analyzes how the performance of "woman" in the Rio de Janeiro Carnival unfolds through power, knowledge, and social equivocation about what "woman is or might be." While Waitt (2005) asks questions about the reconstitution of sexuality in Australian national space through an analysis of the Sydney 2002 Gay Games.

The idea that the particular sets of meanings reproduced through events are open to challenge, contestation and disruption from those who disagree or think differently is well accepted in the literature. Boyle and Hughes wrote about local opposition to Glasgow's 1990 City of Culture event, describing the "discomfort locals have experienced with the willingness of city leaders to forego cultural traditions" (1994: 468). Spooner (1996) conceived of an annual African-Caribbean carnival in Bristol as a potential site of resistance and analyzed black women's experiences in this light. Shin examined how the Gwangju Bienniale in South Korea "initiated power struggles among promoters who had different goals and images of the city in mind" (2004: 625). Waitt's (2005) analysis of the Sydney 2002 Gay Games discussed the contentiousness, exclusions, and resistance fostered by the Games. He found them to be associated with, for example, the fixing of sexual identities in the dualism of homosexual/ heterosexual, the privileging of the culture of masculinity and its imposition onto gay bodies, and the imposition of meanings of togetherness onto people who are materially and socially differentiated.

While considerable attention has been paid to the power dynamics that underpin the reproduction of events, Crespi-Vallbona and Richards (2007) make the point that insufficient attention has been paid to the manner in which particular constituencies of actors may actually share meanings and consensus. They argue, for example, that in the case of cultural events it may be quite common for a range of actors to agree on the importance of the event being staged but to diverge on the aims or content of the event itself, and call for a closer investigation of the politics of consensus as well as of conflict. This call for a more nuanced interpretation of event processes could be usefully applied more broadly within the social sciences literature on festival and event tourism. It seems accurate to suggest that the literature under review in the latter part of this chapter has tended to emphasize the tensions and dichotomies that characterize the reproductive dynamics evident in festival and event tourism relationships. What is and is not authentic? What is and is not rooted in place? Who is included and excluded? Are the audience tourists or residents? All these have been key questions. Now that many of these tensions have been aired, increasing attention

is currently being paid to the many complexities that blur and diminish these dichotomies. This sort of development is evident in all of the social sciences literature areas under review and might be advanced still further by examining two sets of relationships that have not yet received much attention in the literature: namely those between leisure and tourism, and between production and consumption.

Relationship between Leisure and Tourism in Festival and Event Settings

Urry (1995), among others, has pointed to the dedifferentiation of tourism and leisure in recent times, while the merits of conceptualizing leisure and tourism as two very closely related phenomena have been persuasively argued by Crouch (1999, 2000). Yet to date, the tendency to conceptualize festivals and events as tourism affairs has overwhelmed any inclination to understand them as leisure phenomena. Tourism researchers coming from strategic/management perspectives have been preoccupied with large scale events because they constitute tourist attractions. Smaller scale events have been of lesser interest precisely because they are thought to attract fewer tourists. Consequently, festival and event audiences have tended to be understood quite distinctly as either visitors or local residents by researchers adopting both management and social science perspectives. This constitutes a limitation in the literature. There has been much passing acknowledgement of how events largely depend on locally sourced audiences and indeed on how their tourism appeal is linked to how engaging they are for local communities. Yet, it is only recently that there has been a move to collapse these distinctions somewhat and to appreciate that the significance of events lies in the meanings they hold for both local and visiting populations, and in both their leisure and tourism functions. There is also increasing acknowledgement that individuals can seamlessly move between leisure and tourism worlds. This can be seen particularly in the literatures on small events and on sporting events. Shipley and Jones (2007), for example, show how individuals' leisure and tourism practices can merge in event settings. They employ the concept of serious leisure to examine the behavior of long-distance runners participating in an international running event. From another perspective, Gibson et al. (2003) found that college sports events, historically outside the domain of event tourism research, actually attract a significant proportion of fans from outside of the local community. They use this finding to call for a stronger emphasis on small scale sports events, arguing that they merit more attention from tourism researchers. Daniels (2007) draws attention to the fact that research on regular events (leisure) is sparse relative to that on mega events (tourism). She suggests that an economic argument exists for paying greater attention to smaller events and draws on central place theory to develop an understanding of how location influences economic outcomes. In shifting focus onto smaller, regular events that primarily draw on resident demand, researchers simultaneously begin to move tourism enquiries closer to those of leisure. These ways of thinking encourage a move away from a dichotomous line of enquiry that separates tourists and tourism from residents and leisure to a more complex yet holistic approach that understands people capable of playing different roles at different times.

Production—Consumption

Conceiving of events as both leisure and tourism settings also raises questions about the consumption of events. To date, there has been relatively little interest in analyzing the intricacies of how festivals and events are consumed (Boyle, 1997). While there is a well established literature on what motivates people to travel to events, there has been less interest in enquiring about how people engage with events, both in leisure and tourism domains. Motivational research, for example, has

established that socialization is an important factor motivating people to attend events, yet little attention has been paid to understanding how individuals come together to collectively engage in events. In this context, the concept of "practicing" festival and event settings might be usefully employed to analyze what Larsen (2008:28) has called the "emotional geography of sociability, of being together with close friends and family members from home." Clearly, also, the consumption of events is shaped by power dynamics. In the festival literature there has been a suggestion that festivals can reproduce place so as to privilege consumption by visitors, with space being transformed such that it is tourists who feel at home and locals who feel dislocated (Jamieson, 2004; Quinn, 2003). However, further implied here is the idea that tourists' engagement in an event informs that event's reproduction. This draws attention to the fact that the production and consumption of events are closely linked rather than being two distinct arenas of activity, and that the consumption of events, like tourist products and experiences more generally, is an important part of the ongoing reproduction of both the event and the host place.

Towards a More Holistic Research Approach

The literature on festivals, events, and tourism is an important and growing area of tourism research. It is characterized by quite different sets of disciplinary approaches, all of which conceive of the study topic in fundamentally different ways. The resulting breadth of enquiry is impressive, but it is not holistic in the sense that different disciplinary approaches do not yet seamlessly fit together in ways that are always mutually beneficial. This is to be expected of an area of study that is still relatively young, yet it would be undoubtedly beneficial for greater dialogue to occur across disciplinary boundaries.

Two central and interconnected points are made in this chapter. First, closer links could be usefully drawn between the research focused on understanding the dynamics of process and that which seeks to plan, implement and market festivals, plus identify and measure sets of outcomes for "success." Second, conceiving of festivals and events as phenomena that are embedded in diverse spatial, cultural, social and political environments is fundamental to fully understanding the relationships between festivals, events, and tourism.

A closer convergence of disciplinary approaches would yield greater understanding of the links between processes and outcomes in respect of a multiplicity of issues. Events are socially and politically constructed phenomena that require deconstruction to fully understand how and why they function as they do. Outcomes are rarely inevitable or natural, but rather are reproduced in particular ways in order to achieve particular sets of meanings. Thus, for example, in the impact literature, while there has been some discussion of the generation of social capital in the guise of, e.g., community pride, sense of place, and community well-being, an obvious area for further research is not only the measurement of these impacts but also a more thorough understanding of how and why such outcomes materialize.

As already discussed, recent developments in the literature demonstrate a growing agreement of the need to conceive of events more broadly, and to investigate the manifold ways in which they link into contextual environments. Moscardo (2007), for example, seeks to broaden the preoccupation with the role that festivals and events play in tourism or destination development to incorporate questions about their role in the development of regions more generally. Gursoy and Kendall (2006) signal a need to understand more about stakeholders and speak of the need to consult with local residents and in effect, to embed events in locality. Getz et al. (2007) have stressed how events cannot be produced on their own, without external resources and willing coproducers. Schuster (2001) has written about how successful events are those that are embedded in particular locales, of interest to local populations and driven by local agendas. The embedding of events in contextual environments automatically increases the complexity of research enquiries in that it raises questions about a multiplicity of concerns that include, but extend beyond, tourism-related economic outcomes into social, cultural and political issues. As numerous researchers have noted, the potential for further research enquiry into these issues is extensive as is the potential for further enquiry to advance mainstream tourism debates. This potential will be realized most effectively through dialogue and a cross fertilization of ideas from researchers examining the relationships between festivals, events, and tourism from a multitude of disciplinary perspectives.

References

Adams, R. (1986). *A Book of British Music Festivals*. London: Robert Royce Ltd.

Alleyne-Dettmers, P. (1997). "Tribal Arts: A Case Study of Global Compression in the Notting Hill Carnival." In J. Eade (Ed.), *Living the Global City: Globalization as a Local Process*. London: Routledge.

Aldskogius, H. (1993). "Festivals and Meets: The Place of Music in 'Summer Sweden'." *Geografiska Annaler Series B*, 75: 55–72.

Backman, K., Backman, S., Uysal, M. and Sunshine, K. (1995). "Event Tourism: An Examination of Motivations and Activities." *Festival Management & Event Tourism*, 3(1): 15–24.

Bailey, C., Miles, S. and Stark, P. (2004). "Culture-led Urban Regeneration and the Revitalization of Identities in Newcastle, Gateshead and the North East of England." *International Journal of Cultural Policy*, 10(1): 47–65.

Boissevain, J. (1992). *Revitalizing European Rituals*. London: Routledge.

Bonnemaison, S. (1990). "City Politics and Cyclical Events." *Design Quarterly*, 147: 24–32.

Boo, S. and Busser, J.A. (2006). "Impact Analysis of a Tourism Festival on Tourist Destination Image." *Event Management*, 9(4): 223–237.

Bowdin, G., Allen, J., O'Toole, W., Harris, R. and McDonnell, I. (2006). *Events Management* (2nd edition.). Oxford: Elsevier.

Boyle, M. (1997). "Civic Boosterism in the Politics of Local Economic Development— 'Institutional Positions' and 'Strategic Orientations' in the Consumption of Hallmark Events." *Environment and Planning A*, 29: 1975–1997.

Boyle, M. and Hughes, C.G. (1994). "The Politics of Urban Entrepreneurialism in Glasgow." *Geoforum*, 25(4): 453–470.

Bruner, E.M. (1994). "Abraham Lincoln as Authentic Reproduction." *American Anthropologist*, 96(2): 397–415.

Burgan, B. and Mules, T. (1992). "Economic Impacts of Sporting Events." *Annals of Tourism Research*, 19(4): 700–710.

Burgan, B. and Mules, T. (2001). "Reconciling Cost-Benefit and Economic Impact Assessment for Event Tourism." *Tourism Economics*, 7(4): 321–330.

Burns, J.A. and Mules, T.J. (1986). "A Framework for the Analysis of Major Special Events." In J. Burns, J. Hatch and T. Mules (Eds.), *The Adelaide Grand Prix: The Impact of a Special Event*. Adelaide: The Centre for South Australian Economic Studies.

Cohen, E. (1988). "Authenticity and Commodification in Tourism." *Annals of Tourism Research*, 15(3): 371–386.

Crespi-Vallbona, M. and Richards, G. (2007). "The Meaning of Cultural Festivals: Stakeholder Perspectives in Catalunya." *Journal of Cultural Policy*, 13(1): 103–122.

Crompton, J. (1999). *Measuring the Economic Impact of Visitors to Sports Tournaments and Special Events*. Ashburn, VA: National Recreation and Park Association.

Crompton, J. and McKay, S.L. (1994). "Measuring the Economic Impact of Festivals and Events: Some Myths, Misapplications and Ethical Dilemmas." *Festival Management and Event Tourism*, 2(1): 33–43.

Crompton, J. and McKay, S.L. (1997). "Motivations of Visitors Attending Festival Events." *Annals of Tourism Research*, 24 (2): 426–439.

Crouch, D. (1999). "Introduction: Encounters in Leisure/Tourism." In D. Crouch (Ed.), *Leisure/Tourism Geographies: Practices and Geographical Knowledge* (pp. 1–16). London: Routledge.

Crouch, D. (2000). "Places Around Us: Embodied Lay Geographies in Leisure and Tourism." *Leisure Studies*, 19(2): 63–76.

Daniels, M.J. (2007). "Central Place Theory and Sport Tourism Impacts." *Annals of Tourism Research*, 34(2): 332–347.

De Bres, K. and Davis, J. (2001). "Celebrating Group Identity and Place Identity: A Case Study of a New Regional Festival." *Tourism Geographies*, 3(3): 326–337.

Decco, C. and Baloglu, S. (2002). "Nonhost Community Resident Reactions to the 2002 Winter Olympics: The Spillover Impacts." *Journal of Travel Research*, 41(1): 46–56.

Degreef, H. (1994). "European Festivals: Confrontations of Cultural Establishments and Popular Feast." *Carnet*, 2: 16–22.

Delamere, T.A. (2001). "Development of a Scale to Measure Resident Attitudes Towards the Social Impacts of Community Festivals, Part II: Verification of the Scale." *Event Management*, 7(1): 25–38.

Delamere, T., Hinch, T. and Wankel, L. (2001). "Development of a Scale to Measure Resident Attitudes Toward the Social Impacts of Community Festivals, Part I: Item Generation and Purification of the Measure." *Event Management*, 7(1): 11–24.

Derrett, R. (2003). "Making Sense of how Festivals Demonstrate a Community's Sense of Place." *Event Management*, 8(1): 49–58.

Dwyer, L., Mellor, R., Mistillis, N. and Mules, T. (2000). "Forecasting the Economic Impacts of Events and Conventions." *Event Management*, 6(3): 191–204.

Eisinger, P. (2000). "The Politics of Bread and Circuses: Building the City for the Visitor Class." *Urban Affairs Review*, 35(3): 316–333.

Ekman, A.K. (1999). "The Revival of Cultural Celebrations in Regional Sweden: Aspects of Tradition and Transition." *Sociologia Ruralis*, 39(3): 280–293.

Falassi, A. (1987). *Time Out of Time: Essays on the Festival.* Albuquerque: University of New Mexico.

Faulkner, B., Chalip, L., Brown, G., Jago, L., March, R. and Woodside, A. (2000). "Monitoring the Tourism Impacts of the Sydney 2000 Olympics." *Event Management*, 6(4): 231–246.

Formica, S. (1998). "The Development of Festivals and Special Events Studies." *Festival Management and Event Tourism*, 5(3): 131–137.

Formica, S. and Murrmann, S. (1998). "The Effect of Group Membership and Motivation on Attendance: An International Festival Case." *Tourism Analysis*, 3(3/4): 197–208.

Formica, S. and Uysal, M. (1998). "Market Segmentation of an International Cultural-Historical Event in Italy." *Journal of Travel Research*, 36(4): 16–24.

Fox Gotham, K. (2005a). "Theorizing Urban Spectacles. Festivals, Tourism and the Transformation of Urban Space." *City*, 9(2): 225–245.

Fox Gotham, K. (2005b). "Tourism from Above and Below: Globalization, Localization and New Orleans' Mardi Gras." *International Journal of Urban and Regional Research*, 29(2): 309–326.

Fredline, E. (2006). "Host and Guest Relations and Sport Tourism." In H. Gibson (Ed.), *Sport Tourism: Concepts and Theories* (pp. 131–147). London: Routledge.

Fredline, L. and Faulkner, B. (2000). "Host Community Reactions: A Cluster Analysis." *Annals of Tourism Research*, 27(3): 763–784.

Fredline, L. and Faulkner, B. (2002). "Residents Reactions to the Staging of Major Motorsport Events within Their Communities: A Cluster Analysis." *Event Management*, 7(2): 103–114.

Fredline, L., Jago, L. and Deery, M. (2003). "The Development of a Generic Scale to Measure the Social Impacts of Events." *Event Management*, 8(1): 23–37.

Fredline, E., Raybould, R.; Jago, L. and Deery, M. (2005). "Triple Bottom Line Event Evaluation: A Proposed Framework for Holistic Event Evaluation." Paper presented at the *International Event Research Conference*. Sydney.

García, B. (2004). "Urban Regeneration, Arts Programming and Major Events: Glasgow 1990, Sydney 2000, Barcelona 2004." *International Journal of Cultural Policy*, 10(1): 103–118.

García, B. (2005). "Deconstructing the City of Culture: The Long-Term Cultural Legacies of Glasgow 1990." *Urban Studies*, 42(5/6): 841–868.

Geppert, A.C.T. (2004). "Città breva: storia, storiografia e teoria della pratiche espositiva Europee, 1851–2000." In A.C.T. Geppert and M. Baioni (Eds.), *Esposizioni in Europa tra Otto e Novecento* (pp. 7–18) Milan: FrancoAngeli.

Getz, D. (1989). "Special Events: Defining the Product." *Tourism Management*, 10(2): 135–137.

Getz, D. (2000). "Festivals and Special Events: Life Cycle and Saturation Issues." In W. Gartner and D. Lime (Eds.), *Trends in Outdoor Recreation, Leisure and Tourism* (pp. 175–185). Wallingford: CABI.

Getz, D. (2004). "Geographic Perspectives on Event Tourism." In A. Lew, M. Hall and A. Williams (Eds.), *A Companion to Tourism* (pp. 410–422). Oxford: Blackwell Publishing.

Getz, D. (2008). "Event Tourism: Definition, Evolution, and Research." *Tourism Management*, 29(3): 403–428.

Getz, D. and Cheyne, J. (2002). "Special Event Motives and Behaviour." In C. Ryan (Ed.), *The Tourist Experience* (2nd edition) (pp. 137–155). London: Continuum.

Getz, D., Andersson, T. and Larson, M. (2007). "Festival Stakeholder Roles: Concepts and Case Studies." *Event Management*, 10(2/3): 103–122.

Gibson, H. (1998). "Sport Tourism: A Critical Analysis of Research." *Sport Management Review*, 1: 45–76.

Gibson, H. (2006). *Sport Tourism: Concepts and Theories.* London: Routledge.

Gibson, H., Willming, C. and Holdnak, B. (2003). "Small-Scale Event Sport Tourism: Fans as Tourists." *Tourism Management*, 24(2): 181–190.

Gnoth, J. and Anwar, S.A. (2000). "New Zealand Bets on Event Tourism." *Cornell Hotel and Restaurant Administration Quarterly*, August: 72–83.

Goffman, E. (1959). *The Presentation of Self in Everyday Life.* Mayflower: Doubleday.

Gold, J.R. and Gold, M.M. (2005). *Cities of Culture: Staging International Festivals and the Urban Agenda, 1851–2000.* Aldershot: Ashgate.

Green, G.L. (2002). "Marketing the Nation: Carnival and Tourism in Trinidad and Tobago." *Critique of Anthropology*, 22(3): 283–304.

Greenwood, D. (1972). "Tourism as an Agent of Change: A Spanish Basque Case Study." *Ethnology*, 11: 80–91.

Gursoy, D. and Kendall, K.W. (2006). "Hosting Mega-Events: Modeling Locals' Support." *Annals of Tourism Research*, 33(3): 603–623.

Gursoy, D., Kim, K. and Uysal, M. (2004). "Perceived Impacts of Festivals and Special Events by Organizers: An Extension and Validation." *Tourism Management*, 25(2): 171–181.

Hall, C.M. (1989). "Hallmark Events and the Planning Process." In G.J. Syme, B.J. Shaw, D.M. Fenton and W.S. Mueller (Eds.), *The Planning and Evaluation of Hallmark Events*. Aldershot: Ashgate.

Hall, C.M. (1992). *Hallmark Tourist Events: Impacts, Management, and Planning.* London: Belhaven Press.

Hall, C.M. and Hodges, J. (1996). "The Party's Great, But What About the Hangover? The Housing and Social Impacts of Mega-Events with Reference to the 2000 Sydney Olympics." *Festival Management & Event Tourism*, 4(1/2): 13–20.

Hede, A. (2007). "Managing Special Events in the New Era of the TBL." *Event Management*, 11(1–2): 13–22.

Hede, A., Jago, L., Deery, M. (2003). "An Agenda for Special Events Research: Lessons from the Past and Directions from the Future." *Journal of Hospitality and Tourism Management*, 10 (supplement): 1–14.

Hiller, H. (1998). "Assessing the Impact of Mega Events: A Linkage Model." *Current Issues in Tourism*, 1(1): 47–57.

Hitters, E. (2000). "The Social and Political Construction of a European Cultural Capital: Rotterdam 2001." *Cultural Policy*, 6(2): 183–199.

Isar, R.F. (1976). "Culture and the Arts Festival of the Twentieth Century." *Cultures*, 3: 125–145.

Jamieson, K. (2004). "Edinburgh: The Festival Gaze and its Boundaries." *Space and Culture*, 7(1): 64–75.

Janiskee, R. (1980). "South Carolina's Harvest Festivals: Rural Delights for Day Tripping Urbanites." *Journal of Cultural Geography*, 1 (Fall/Winter): 96–104.

Jeong, G.H. and Faulkner, B. (1996). "Resident Perceptions of Mega-Event Impacts: The Taejon International Exposition Case." *Festival Management & Event Tourism*, 4(1): 3–11.

Kim, H.J., Gursoy, D. and Lee, S.B. (2006). "The Impact of the 2002 World Cup on South Korea: Comparison of Pre-and Post-Games." *Tourism Management*, 27(1): 86–96.

Kim, N.S. and Chalip, L. (2004). "Why Travel to the FIFA World Cup? Effect of Motives, Background, Interest and Constraints." *Tourism Management*, 25(6): 695–707.

Lankford, S.V. and Howard, D. (1994). "Development of a Tourism Impact Attitude Scale." *Annals of Tourism Research*, 21(1): 121–139.

Larson, M. (2002). "A Political Approach to Relationship Marketing: Case Study of the Storsjöyran Festival." *International Journal of Tourism Research*, 4(2): 119–143.

Larsen, J. (2008). "De-Exoticizing Tourist Travel: Everyday Life and Sociality on the Move." *Leisure Studies*, 27(1): 21–34.

Larson, M. and Wikstrom, E. (2001). "Organizing Events: Managing Conflict and Consensus in a Political Market Square." *Event Management*, 7(1): 51–65.

Lavenda, R.H. (1997). *Corn Fests and Water Carnivals: Celebrating Community in Minnesota.* Washington: Smithsonian Institution Press.

Lee, C.K. and Kim, J.H. (1998). "International Tourism Demand for the 2002 World Cup Korea: A Combined Forecasting Technique." *Pacific Tourism Review*, 2(2): 1–10.

Lee, C.K. and Taylor, T. (2005). "Critical Reflections on the Economic Impact Assessment of a Mega-Event: The Case of 2002 FIFA World Cup." *Tourism Management*, 26(4): 595–603.

Lee, C.K., Lee, Y.K., Lee, B. (2005). "Korea's Destination Image Formed by the 2002 World Cup." *Annals of Tourism Research*, 32(4): 839–858.

Lewis, C. and Pile, S. (1996). "Woman, Body, Space: Rio Carnival and the Politics of

Performance." *Gender, Place and Culture*, 3(1): 23–41.

Li, R. and Petrick, J. (2006). "A Review of Festival and Event Motivation Studies." *Event Management*, 9(4): 239–245.

Litvin, S.W. and Fetter, E. (2006). "Can a Festival be Too Successful? A Review of Spoleto, USA." *International Journal of Contemporary Hospitality Management*, 18(1): 41–49.

Loftman, P. and Nevil, B. (1996). "Going for Growth: Prestige Projects in Three British Cities." *Urban Studies*, 33: 991–1020.

MacCannell, D. (1976). *The Tourist: A New Theory of the Leisure Class*. New York: Schoken Books.

Mackellar, J. (2007). "Conventions, Festivals and Tourism: Exploring the Network that Binds." *Journal of Convention & Event Tourism*, 8(2): 45–56.

Manning, F.E. (Ed.) (1983). *The Celebration of Society: Perspectives on Contemporary Cultural Performance*. Bowling Green: Bowling Green University Press.

Matheson, C.M. (2005). "Festivity and Sociability: A Study of a Celtic Music Festival." *Tourism Culture & Communication*, 5: 149–163.

McCarthy, J. (2005). "Promoting Image and Identity in 'Cultural Quarters': The Case of Dundee." *Local Economy*, 20(3): 280–293.

McCartney, G. and Osti, L. (2007). "From Cultural Events to Sports Events: A Case Study of Cultural Authenticity in the Dragon Boat Races." *Journal of Sport & Tourism*, 12(1): 25–40.

Mihalik, B.J. and Simonette, L. (1998). "Resident Perceptions of the 1990 Summer Olympic Games—Year 11." *Festival Management & Event Tourism*, 5(1): 9–19.

Misener, L. and Mason, D.S. (2006). "Developing Local Citizenship Through Sporting Events: Balancing Community Involvement and Tourism Development." *Current Issues in Tourism*, 9(4/5): 384–398.

Moscardo, G. (2007). "Analyzing the Role of Festivals and Events in Regional Development." *Event Management*, 11(1–2): 23–32.

Müller, D. K. and Pettersson, R. (2005). "What and Where is the Indigenous at an Indigenous Festival?—Observations from the Winter Festival in Jokkmokk, Sweden." In *Indigenous Tourism: The Commodification and Management of Culture*. Elsevier.

Muir, E. (1997). *Ritual in Early Modern Europe*. Cambridge: Cambridge University Press.

Mules, T. and McDonald, S. (1994). "The Economic Impact of Special Events: The Use of Forecasts." *Festival Management and Event Tourism*, 2(1): 45–53.

Nurse, K (1999). "Globalization and Trinidad Carnival: Diaspora, Hybridity and Identity in Global Culture." *Cultural Studies*, 13(4): 661–690.

Olsen, K. (2002). "Authenticity as a Concept in Tourism Research." *Tourist Studies*, 2(2): 159–182.

Pine, B.J. and Gilmore, J.H. (1999). *The Experience Economy*. Boston, MA: Harvard University Press.

Prentice, R. and Andersen, V. (2003). "Festival as Creative Destination." *Annals of Tourism Research*, 30(1): 7–30.

Pugh, C. and Wood, E.H. (2004). "The Strategic Use of Events within Local Government: A Study of London Borough Councils." *Event Management*, 9(1–2): 61–71.

Quinn, B. (2003). "Symbols, Practices and Myth-Making: Cultural Perspectives on the Wexford Festival Opera." *Tourism Geographies*, 5: 329–349.

Quinn, B. (2005a). "Arts Festivals and the City." *Urban Studies*, 42(5/6): 927–943.

Quinn, B. (2005b). "Changing Festival Places: Insights from Galway." *Social and Cultural Geography*, 6(2): 237–252.

Richards, G. (2007). "Culture and Authenticity in a Traditional Event: The Views of Producers, Residents and Visitors in Barcelona." *Event Management*, 11(1–2): 33–44.

Richards, G. and Wilson, J. (2006). "Developing Creativity in Tourist Experiences: A Solution to the Serial Reproduction of Culture." *Tourism Management*, 27(6): 1209–1223.

Ritchie, J.R.B. (1984). "Assessing the Impacts of Hallmark Events: Conceptual and Research Issues." *Journal of Travel Research*, 23(1): 2–11.

Ritchie, J.R.B. (1999). "Lessons Learned, Lessons Learning: Insights from the Calgary and Salt Lake City Olympic Winter Games." *Visions in Leisure and Business*, 18(1): 4–13.

Ritchie, J.R.B. and Aitken, C.E. (1984). "Assessing the Impacts of the 1988 Olympic Winter Games: The Research Program and Initial Results." *Journal of Travel Research*, 22(3): 17–25.

Ritchie, J.R.B. and Smith, B. (1991). The Impact of a Mega-Event on Host Region Awareness: A Longitudinal Study." *Journal of Travel Research*, 29(1): 3–10.

Rittichainuwat, B., Beck, J. and LaLopa, J. (2001). "Understanding Motivations, Inhibitors and Facilitators of Association Members in Attending International Conferences." *Journal of Convention and Exhibition Management*, 3(3): 45–62.

Robinson, T. and Gammon, S. (2004). A Question of Primary and Secondary Motives: Revisiting and Applying the Sport Tourism Framework." *Journal of Sport Tourism*, 9(3): 221–223.

Roche, M. (1994). "Mega-Events and Urban Policy." *Annals of Tourism Research*, 21(1): 1–19.

Rolfe, H. (1992). *Arts Festivals in the UK*. London: Policy Studies Institute.

Schuster, J.M. (2001). "Ephemera, Temporary Urbanism and Imaging." In L.J. Vale and S.B. Warner (Eds.), *Imaging the City— Continuing Struggles and New Directions* (pp. 361–396). New Brunswick: CUPR Books.

Shepherd, R. (2002). "Commodification, Culture and Tourism." *Tourist Studies*, 2(2): 183–201.

Shin, H. (2004). "Cultural Festivals and Regional Identities in South Korea." *Environment and Planning D: Society and Space*, 22: 619–632.

Shipley, R. and Jones, I. (2007). "Running Away from Home: Understanding Visitor Experiences and Behaviour at Sport Tourism Events." *International Journal of Tourism Research*, 9(5): 373–383.

Smith, S.J. *(1996)*. *"Bounding the Borders: Claiming Space and Making Place in Rural Scotland." Transactions, Institute of British Geographers,* 18: 291–308.

Sofield, T.H.B. and Li, F.M.S. (1998). "Historical Methodology and Sustainability: An 800 Year Old Festival from China." *Journal of Sustainable Tourism*, 6(4): 267–292

Spooner, R. (1996). "Contested Representations: Black women and the St Paul's Carnival." *Gender, Place and Culture*, 3(2): 187–204.

Stokes, R. (2005). "Network-Based Strategy Making for Events Tourism." *European Journal of Marketing*, 40(5/6): 682–695.

Thomas, R. and Wood, E. (2004). "Event-Based Tourism: A Survey of Local Authority Strategies in the UK." *Local Governance*, 29(2): 127–136.

Timothy, D.J. and Boyd, S.W. (2003). *Heritage Tourism*. London and New York: Prentice Hall.

Turner, V. (1982). "Introduction." In V. Turner (Ed.), *Celebration: Studies in Festivity and Ritual* (pp. 11–29). Washington, DC: Smithsonian Institution Press.

Tyrrell. T. and Johnston, R. (2001). "A Framework for Assessing Direct Economic Impacts of Tourist Events: Distinguishing Origins, Destinations and Causes of Expenditures." *Journal of Travel Research*, 40(1): 94–100.

Urry, J. (1995). *Consuming Places*. London: Routledge.

Waitt, G. (2001). "The Olympic Spirit and Civic Boosterism: The Sydney Olympics." *Tourism Geographies*, 3(3): 249–278.

Waitt, G. (2003). "Social Impact of the Sydney Olympics." *Annals of Tourism Research*, 30(1): 194–215.

Waitt, G. (2005). "The Sydney 2002 Gay Games and Querying Australian National Space." *Environment and Planning D: Society and Space*, 23: 435–452.

Wang, N. (1999). "Re-Thinking Authenticity in Tourism Experiences." *Annals of Tourism Research*, 26(2): 349–370.

Waterman, S. (1998). "Carnival for Elites? The Cultural Politics of Arts Festivals." *Progress in Human Geography*, 22(1): 54–74.

Whitelegg, D. (2000). "Going for Gold: Atlanta's Bid for Fame." *International Journal of Urban and Regional Research*, 24: 801–817.

Wilson, D. (1993). "Time and Tides in the Anthropology of Tourism." In M. Hitchcock, V.T. King and M.J.G. Parnwell (Eds.), *Tourism in South-East Asia* (pp. 32–47). London: Routledge.

Wood, E. (2005). "Measuring the Economic and Social Impacts of Local Authority Events."

International Journal of Public Sector Management, 18(1): 37–53.

Wood, E.H., Robinson, L.S. and Thomas, R. (2006). "Evaluating the Social Impacts of Community and Local Government Events: A Practical Overview of Research Methods and Measurement Tools." In S. Fleming and F. Jordan (Eds.), *Events and Festivals, Education, Impacts and Experiences*. LSA Publication No 93. Eastbourne: LSA.

Yardimci, S. (2007). *Festivalising Difference: Privatisation of Culture and Symbolic Exclusion in Istanbul* (pp. 1–26) EUI Working Papers, Mediterranean Programme Series, RSCAS 2007/35.

Zukin, S. (1995). *The Cultures of Cities*. Cambridge, MA: Blackwell Publishers.

28

Tourism as Postcolonialism

Hazel Tucker and John Akama

Introduction

While the concept and study of postcolonialism has informed cultural theorizing for over two decades, it has only more recently begun to garner interest in the intellectual terrain of tourism studies (Hall and Tucker, 2004a). Studies of tourism in the less developed countries, concerns over identity and representation, and theorizing over the cultural, political, and economic nature and implications of tourism encounters, have increasingly been referring to postcolonial discourse. However, the title of this chapter is infused with ambiguity and tension. They arise due to different usages of the concept, for instance, between the use of the term postcolonialism to simply mean neocolonialism and a concept that could better be called *critical* postcolonialism. Furthermore, postcolonialism represents both the state of being "post" or "after" the condition of being (or perhaps even becoming) a colony and, importantly, a reflexive body of Western thought that seeks to reconsider and interrogate the terms by which the duality of colonizer and colonized, along with its accompanying structures of knowledge and power, has been established and is perpetuated. This chapter thus attempts to clarify the relationship

between tourism and postcolonialism by drawing upon postcolonial theory to discuss both the ways in which tourism relationships are embedded in and reinforcing of colonial relationships—neocolonialsm, and also the ways in which tourism might act as a medium for offering postcolonial counter-narratives of resistance to those colonial relationships—critical postcolonialism.

Indeed, a debate exists within postcolonial theory itself about the appropriateness of its name in that the term "post" could imply that the inequities of colonial rule are ended (Loomba 1998; Williams and Chrisman, 1993). Ashcroft et al. (1989), in *The Empire Writes Back*, posed the question why, since nearly all postcolonial societies have achieved political independence, should these societies continue to engage with the imperial experience? Why is the issue of coloniality still relevant at all? One answer is in the *ongoing* political, economic, and cultural influence of the former imperial powers in postcolonial states. Indeed, examination of neocolonial relationships, a situation in which an independent country continues to suffer intervention and control from a foreign state, is also often incorporated into the postcolonial corpus. Much of postcolonial theory's focus, then, is on the core–periphery relationship that exists in economic and political terms between the developed and the less-developed countries, as well as some focus on internal peripheries. More generically, though, postcolonial refers to a position *against* imperialism, colonialism, and Eurocentrism, including Western thought and philosophy.

Postcolonial theory itself has developed out of the belief that colonialism has been, and still is, one of the main sources of influence on the West's interpretations of and relationships with people from other (mainly non-Western) places and cultures. Said's *Orientalism* (first published in 1978) is widely considered to represent the first phase of postcolonial theory in that it directed attention to the discursive and textual production of colonial meanings and thus to the consolidation of colonial hegemony (Gandhi, 1998). Rather than being an account of "the Orient" itself, Said's book is an analysis of European scholarship and construction of the Orient and the Oriental Other. Said argued that this construction showed the Orient as exotic, mysterious, and sensual, but also cruel, despotic, and sly. Following Said, Ashcroft et al. (1989) contend that one of the main features of imperial oppression was control over language and text. They noted that language has become the medium through which a hierarchical structure of power is perpetuated, as well as being the medium through which conceptions of "truth," "order," and "reality" have become established. As we shall see in this chapter, in the tourism context, the hegemonic structures of language and representation have created particular conceptions of "truth" and "reality" for both tourism practice and tourism destinations. Postcolonial theory maintains that colonial discourse continues to dominate any form of representation of the "Third World" by the First World (Mishra and Hodge, 1991).

Postcolonial theory is not a unified set of ideas, however, and while much of the postcolonial work within literary/cultural studies relies on psychoanalytic theory, it is the emphasis on being *critical* of the colonial condition that is of particular relevance to

tourism studies. As well as emphasizing the pervasiveness of the legacies of colonialism in tourism, postcolonial theory highlights the *oppositionality* to colonizing discourses and practices. As Young explains, postcolonial theory "disturbs the order of the world. It threatens privilege and power. It refuses to acknowledge the superiority of the western cultures" (2003: 7). Particularly apt in the tourism context is Moore-Gilbert's (1997) summary of postcolonial criticism as being "preoccupied principally with analysis of cultural forms which mediate, challenge or reflect upon … relations of domination and subordination" (Moore-Gilbert, 1997: 12). Moore-Gilbert continues that these relations "have their roots in the history of modern European colonialism and imperialism," but they also "continue to be apparent in the present era of neocolonialism" (1997: 12).

There have been important intersections of work between postcolonial theory and poststructuralism, Marxism, postmodernism, and feminism (Williams and Chrisman, 1993). One of the main reasons for the intersection between postcolonial studies and feminist and gender studies, for example, is that concepts such as gender, class, ethnicity, and race become a ground for "internal colonialism" in which identities are constrained and oppressed, and selectively represented. Authors such as Gayatri Spivak (1987) and Ashcroft et al. (1989) used this trope to describe how women in many societies have been relegated to the position of "Other," marginalized and, in a metaphorical sense, "colonized" (Spivak, 1987). There are also important linkages to feminism with respect to the representation of other places and people (Aitchison et al., 2002; Ang, 1995; Blunt and Rose, 1994; Kappeler, 1986; McClintock, 1995; Spivak, 1986; Ware, 1992). The sexual imagery used in the tourism marketing of certain postcolonial destinations such as the Caribbean or the Pacific (Opperman and McKinley, 1997) tends to be a continuation of the Western representations of a sensual, sexually available, and subservient female oriental other that began in the seventeenth century (Hall, 1998). A poignant intersection between these issues and tourism lies thus in the colonial and neocolonial dimensions of sex tourism. Here, the institutionalized exploitation of women within patriarchal societies has been extended and systematized by the unequal power relationships that exist not only between genders and members of ethnic groups but also between "host" and advanced capitalist societies (Ong, 1985).

Postcolonial theory is thus useful in analyses of tourism in that, in the first instance, it directs our attention to the continuation of colonial power relations in tourism on both a structural and ideological level. Although formal territorial control of the colonized world ended with the rise of independent nationhood in the 20th century, the West continues to maintain a dominant and central ideological position, marginalizing the non-West to the peripheries (Mishra and Hodge, 1991). Second, there appears to be little doubt that most readings and uses of postcolonial theory imply both a continuous colonialism *and* a continuous postcolonialism, in the sense that the term "post" indicates contestation and resistance.

The intention in this chapter is to draw together the key issues at the intersection of postcolonial studies and tourism studies in order to consider the ways in which tourism practices and relationships are based on past and present-day colonial structural relationships, and also to look at the various ways in which tourism practices in postcolonial settings are, or could potentially be, sites of postcolonial resistance and contestation. The chapter begins with a short discussion of the colonial basis of tourism, or of tourism as neocolonialism, and the colonial core–periphery relationships that persist in the economy of tourism. This discussion of the colonial narrative that underpins much of the tourist activity throughout the world then moves on to look more specifically at the colonial legacy of particular attitudes, behavior, and promotional images that continue to be reified through tourism, as highlighted by

postcolonial theory. The chapter finally turns to look more precisely at both tourism studies and tourism practice as what will be referred to as critical postcolonialism. That section examines the ways in which tourism studies has begun to engage with postcolonial theory, and also the ways in which tourism practice can be a medium for postcolonial forms of resistance.

Tourism as Neocolonialism

Colonial Structural Relationships in Tourism

Postcolonial issues have had considerable influence on the tourism literature, beginning in the 1970s and 1980s. For example, Matthews described tourism as potentially being a new colonial plantation economy in which "[m]etropolitan capitalistic countries try to dominate the foreign tourism market, especially in those areas where their own citizens travel most frequently" (1978: 79). More recently, the connection between tourism and neocolonialism has been drawn by Craik (1994), Edensor (1998), Echtner and Prasad (2003), and various authors who contributed to the volume edited by Hall and Tucker (2004b), arguing that many of the economic structures, cultural representations and exploitative relationships that were previously based in colonialism, are far from over.

The development of tourism in most so-called "Third World" or "developing" countries is closely linked to the era of colonial rule in those countries. Furthermore, the current forms of tourism development initiatives in most of these countries are still, to a large extent, influenced by Western philosophical values and ideological orientation, and mainly respond to external political and economic interests. Moreover, the global structure of international tourism as a "luxury and pleasure seeking industry" usually entails, predominantly, rich tourists from the metropolis (mainly from developed Northern countries) visiting and coming to enjoy tourist attractions in the periphery (mainly poor and resource scarce countries in the South) (Britton, 1982). These forms of tourism development accentuate the economic structure of dependency on external market demand. These lead to "alien" forms of tourism development (i.e., the establishment of enclave resorts in these countries) to which local people cannot relate or respond to either socially or economically (Akama, 1997; Sindiga, 2000; Williams, 1993). In consequence, the management and long-term sustenance of the tourism and hospitality establishment, in most instances, depends on external control and support. This accentuates existing neocolonial tendencies and reinforcement of structures of economic dependency in developing countries.

Moreover, initial investment costs for mostly large-scale, capital intense tourism projects are usually too high for "Third World" governments and indigenous investors and, therefore, must depend on external capital investment mainly from multinational conglomerates. These structures of economic dependency usually lead to high leakages of tourism revenues to external sources (Akama, 1997; Britton, 1980, 1982; Oglethorpe, 1984; Opperman, 1992). In this regard, not much of the tourism revenue remains within these countries to be utilized in various initiatives of socioeconomic development. Recent shifts towards more responsible form of tourism and ecotourism (see Mbaiwa and Stronza [Chapter 19] in this *Handbook*) are attempting to ensure more equitable distribution of costs and benefits.

Furthermore, global economic trends also indicate that such developing economies are highly vulnerable and are increasingly being affected by processes of economic globalization and increasing dominance and control by the multinational corporations of global markets. As Debbage postulates, "the increasing oligopolistic structure of the international tourism industry indicates the intrinsic value of the profit cycle in explaining how oligopoly

can shape the product-cycle of a resort" (1990: 515). Consequently, the development of tourism in most developing countries is increasingly being influenced by unpredictable exogenous processes of global oligopoly and external market demands (i.e., the increasing control of the international tourism market by a small number of multinational companies). The multinational tourism and travel companies can, for instance, shift international tourism demand among various undifferentiated destinations, thus causing unforeseeable disruption to tourism development in developing countries.

The Kenyan case study provides a good example of a "Third World" country that has embraced tourism as an export tool for development and consequently illustrates the neocolonial structure of the tourism industry in such countries. At the attainment of independence in 1963 Kenya, as is the case with most other Third World countries that underwent colonial rule, inherited a colonial economy that was characterized by inequitable distribution of resources, high levels of poverty, and poor living conditions among the indigenous population. Furthermore, the country's economic structure was controlled by expatriates who had relatively high standards of living vis-à-vis that of the indigenous population. Specifically, as concerns tourism, its initial development in the country was initiated by resident European developers and the colonial government. For instance, the first conventional hotels and lodge facilities to be developed in Kenya were built by resident European developers.

These initial facilities include Hotel Stanley (the present New Stanley) in 1890, the Nairobi Club in 1891, the Norfolk Hotel in 1904, and the Commercial and Express Hotel in 1906. Most of these accommodation and hospitality facilities were built in Nairobi, which became the hub for commerce, business and administration in the East Africa region (Bosire, 1995). As a consequence, the initial development of tourism in Kenya was colonialist in orientation and served mainly the social and economic interests of the expatriate community and international tourists. At this initial stage there was minimal social interaction between pioneer Western travelers and indigenous Kenyans. Perhaps the only form of interaction that existed between the class in power and the governed was a "master–servant" relationship. Africans were hired mainly to work in servile positions as gardeners, cleaners, waiters, cooks, and guards.

At independence the Kenya government depended almost exclusively on export crops, tea and coffee, for the foreign exchange earnings needed to import manufactured goods and other items for urban consumption (Akama, 1996; Chege, 1987; Migot-Adholla, 1984). Over the years, however, prices of agricultural products in the world market fell relative (and in many cases absolutely) to manufactured goods. Thus, starting from the late 1970s, the government experienced persistent shortfalls in foreign exchange earnings due to decreased receipts from export crops. It was within this national and international socioeconomic context that the Kenya government realized that the country had an already existing "commodity" that could be readily marketed to generate much sought after foreign exchange and to create jobs. The alternative commodity was the country's unique tourism attractions, particularly the wildlife heritage and the pristine beaches.

With the realization of the importance of tourism development in generating much sought after foreign exchange, the Kenyan government turned to foreign and multinational tourism investors to provide initial capital for the establishment and development of large-scale, capital intense tourism and hospitality facilities. The government adopted an "open door" laissez-faire policy towards multinational tourism investors and developers. It also introduced specific financial incentives such as tax concessions, favorable fiscal policies for external capital investment, and profit repatriation. These financial incentives were aimed at attracting increased and accelerated foreign capital investment in tourism and hospitality.

Owing to increased foreign investment in Kenya's tourism industry over the years, there is increased ownership and management of the industry by foreign and multinational companies. Some of the international tourism companies that have invested in Kenya's tourism industry include Hayes & Jarvis, Lonrho Corporation, United Tour Company, Kuoni, Africa Club, Universal Safari Tours, Pollmans, France Russo, and Grand Viaggi. These multinational tourism companies have established first-class hotel and lodge facilities in the country's major tourist centers, particularly in Mombasa, Nairobi, Malindi, and in the country's popular wildlife parks and reserves.

As a consequence it has been estimated that over 60% of Kenya's tourism and hospitality establishment in major tourist centers is under foreign ownership and management (Sinclair, 1990; Sindiga, 2000). Furthermore, the state tourism policy has over the years mainly promoted the development of large-scale tourism projects such as beach resorts, high-rise hotels, lodges, and restaurants. These forms of capital intense programs tend to preclude local participation in tourism project design and management and local use of tourism resources. The following quotation highlights the nature of the Kenyan tourism industry:

> The ground operation of the country's tourism industry reflects (this) outwards-orientation. Typically a tour operator sends a micro-bus to the airport to collect tourists. Such visitors may be in an inclusive package tour already paid for overseas. The tour firms, for example, Abercrombie and Kent, United Tour Company, Kuoni Worldwide, Thomas Cook, and Hayes and Jarvis, would likely be foreign owned, or a subsidiary of a foreign company. The firms take the tourists to an assigned hotel in Nairobi or Mombasa for overnight stay. On the following day, the tour operators take the tourists for a wildlife safari in one of the national parks. This safari lasts several days. The average length of stay for departing tourists in (the 1990s) was 13.4 days . . . At the end of the tour, the process is re-enacted in preparation for departure from the country. (Sindiga, 1996: 29)

It has previously been noted that over 60% of the international tourists who visit Kenya travel using inclusive tour packages (Akama, 1997; Sinclair, 1990). In these forms of travel arrangements, prospective visitors pay tour operators for a complete travel package. The payment arrangements include almost all travel components such as air ticket, food, accommodation, and recreational activities. Tour operators contract non-Kenyan air carriers to bring visitors to the country. Even within Kenya, foreign-owned tourism and hospitality facilities, internal flights, and car rentals are contracted. It has been estimated that due to these forms of tour packages, leakages of tourism receipts to overseas contractors may range between 40 and 80% (Akama, 1997; Dieke, 1991; Sinclair, 1990).

A good example of the increasing overseas retention of Kenya's total tourism receipts can be demonstrated by the case of Malindi (one of the leading tourist centers in the Kenyan coast). Over the last 30 years Malindi has been a popular tourist destination for Italian visitors seeking tropical exoticism and adventure (Sindiga, 2000). In order to cater for the increased demand, Italian investors established tourism facilities such as hotels, villas, guesthouses, and car and helicopter rentals at Malindi (Sindiga, 2000). By the late 1990s a high percentage of tourist facilities in Malindi were under Italian ownership. As a consequence, in recent years Italian visitors to Malindi have ended up using exclusively Italian-owned or contracted air carriers. When the visitors arrive in Kenya, they are ferried by Italian-owned domestic flights to Malindi. While in Malindi the visitors stay in Italian-owned hotels. Also, whenever the visitors make inland visits to view the Kenyan wildlife in the national parks and reserves they use Italian owned car rentals and aircraft companies. Thus, the end result is a tourism product that is almost exclusively owned and managed by Italians. It has been estimated that these forms of travel arrangements account for leakage of as much as 80% of total tourism receipts (Sinclair, 1990; Sindiga, 2000).

Furthermore, the promotion and marketing of Kenya's attractions in tourist generating countries is mainly conducted by overseas tour operators and travel agents. In this regard, and as will be discussed in the next section, these overseas tour companies play an important role in influencing tourist attitudes and behaviors, and in determining the types and volume of tourists who visit a given tourist destination (Morgan and Pritchard, 1998; Shaw and Williams, 1994). Driven by the profit motive most tour operators focus on marketing those tourist attractions that can yield immediate and maximum profit returns. For instance, most tourist advertisements for Kenyan attractions in Western media focus on the "Big Five" (elephant, lion, rhino, cheetah, and giraffe), and the glittering white coastal beaches. Little effort is expended in giving a more complete picture of Kenya's diverse cultural and environmental attractions (Akama, 1997; Kibara, 1994; Sinclair, 1990).

A further example of this is in the tourism presentation of the Maasai as the only African community that exists in Kenya (this notwithstanding the fact that Kenya is made up of more than 40 ethnic communities with diverse cultures and historical experiences). Thus, when tourists visit Kenya for a wildlife safari they are also supposed to catch a glimpse of the exotic African culture as represented by the Maasai tribesmen. Consequently, in tourism circles, wildlife and the Maasai are usually wrapped together as one and the same thing. The African culture that the international tourists are presented with is that of the Maasai tribesmen and their physical adornments, dance, and other Maasai cultural artifacts. The Kenyan tourism image is constructed and reconstructed to revolve around wildlife and the Maasai image and thus the tourist image of the Maasai does not appear to have changed since early European explorers and adventure seekers first encountered the Maasai over 200 years ago.

The Maasai are thus prominently featured in brochures, advertisements, electronic media, and other forms of tourism commercials that promote Kenya as a leading tourism destination in Africa. Scenes of the Maasai dressed in red ochre shuka and/or traditional regalia are juxtaposed with the "Big Five" and are promoted as ideal African tourist attractions. The Maasai Moran (youthful warriors), carrying traditional long spears and clubs, are projected in the media as people who "walk tall" amid the deadly Africa wildlife. Scenes of Maasai livestock are also projected in commercials, grazing in harmony with other savanna herbivores such as antelopes, zebra, wildebeest, buffalo, and elephants. Overseas tour operators can thus be said to reinforce existing stereotypes and images of Kenya in particular, and Africa in general. Images of wild and darkest Africa, complete with roaring lions, trumpeting elephants, semi-naked and bare-breasted natives, are frequently used as catch phrases to lure Westerners keen for exoticism and adventure. Bruner and Kirshenblatt-Gimblet have also provided a critical analysis of the necessity of local inhabitants to appear in a primitive state in an African postcolonial setting, noting that the tourism performance of the Maasai people "enacts a colonial drama of the savage/pastoral Maasai and the genteel British, playing upon the explicit contrast between the wild and the civilized so prevalent in colonial discourse and sustained in East African tourism" (1994: 435). As the next section will discuss, the design and development of promotional messages and images that are used in sales promotion and the marketing of tour packages in tourist generating countries derive from, and are frequently based on, existing dominant Western cultural values and economic systems.

The Colonial Narrative Underpinning Tourism

Place promotion and representation in tourism is a prominent arena in which a colonial relationship is continuously played out (Echtner and Prasad, 2003; Huggan, 2001; Morgan and Pritchard, 1998). Spurr (1993) has argued that travel narratives are discourses of colonialism through which one culture works to interpret, to represent, and finally to dominate another.

Simmons (2004), too, has shown how colonial discourse is all-pervading in contemporary travel discourse in travel articles in Australian popular magazines. Her study highlights how it is that "the remains of imperialism not only linger in Western imaginations about cultural, racial and gender superiority, but are in fact central to a contemporary travel discourse that is reproduced in the written travelogue text" (Simmons, 2004: 54). A good example is the way in which the term "paradise" is often used in the promotion of postcolonial island states in a manner that reinforces western colonial ideas of a Romantic "tropical" Other. Almost all "tropical paradise" destinations, such as the Caribbean, Indian Ocean, and South Pacific islands, are former colonies. Importantly, however, and as is the case for Kenya as discussed above, it is Western multinational tour operators and travel agencies who primarily promote these destinations for tourism (Adams, 1984; Reimer, 1990). Most representations of "tropical paradise" islands are therefore aimed at and controlled by tourism interests entrenched in the West. As such, promotional images are clearly embedded in, and perpetuating of, colonial discourse. They define and fix both the tourist and the toured "other" in a relationship with each other which stems from colonialism and is always inherently colonial in nature.

The images used to market tourism destinations are highly influential not only in tourists' understanding and perception of those places, but also regarding their own identity and position as tourists in relation to those places. Although tourism promotional literature becomes the framework through which the tourist filters perception and experience, the creator of that literature "remains firmly lodged in the cultural values and orientations of his own society. He deals in the ethnicity of others, packaging and marketing it to members of his own culture" (Adams, 1984: 472). As Richter puts it, the images portrayed in the travel media tend to "always assume a particular kind of tourist—white, western, male and heterosexual" (1995: 81). While such a description is clearly problematic, "gay tourism" is even more so given the homophobia adopted from the colonizers and entrenched in the colonized's "new culture" only to see homosexuality turn into a late twentieth century niche market; a turn that is an anathema to many "postcolonial" societies in the Pacific Islands.

Bhattacharya (1997) highlights the colonial narrative underpinning tourism practice in India in her semiotic analysis of the Lonely Planet guidebook to India. Bhattacharyya's examination of the narrative voice used in the guidebook shows how it claims to represent India in a legitimate and authoritative way and also with a judgmental, ethical posture. The "voice" of the guidebook's authors(s) invites collusion with the tourist in a tone which implies that any reasonable person would view this in this way and "we" are reasonable people. The ethical posture also stipulates that the behavior of local Indian inhabitants is subject to moral judgment while the behavior of the traveler is not. The implication is that tourists are above any obligation to attend to the potential ethical consequences of their behavior. Moreover, the guidebook provides guidelines for tourists' interactions with local inhabitants. Setting Indians up as being there either to serve tourists or to act as interesting Others, the guidebook inadvertently highlights significant power differentials between local inhabitants and the traveler.

The construction of the Other, which stems from colonialism, is particularly essential in tourism since the "tourist gaze" (Urry, 1990) is altogether based on *difference*. As Selwyn has argued, "Encounters with the 'other' have always provided fuel for myths and mythical language. Contemporary tourism has developed its own promotional lexicon and repertoire of myths" (1993: 136). Echtner and Prasad (2003), through the prism of postcolonial theory, discuss three different myths that are upheld in tourism marketing of developing countries in the "Third World," each of which replicate colonial forms of discourse. The myth of the unchanged is used to represent destinations as timeless places that are firmly fixed in the past. Relating to countries embedded in the discourse of Orientalism such

as Egypt, India, Thailand, and Turkey, the tourist is invited to journey "backward in time to a world of ancient civilizations" (Echtner and Prasad, 2003: 669). This myth thus portrays the destinations as set in a time ripe for discovery and, as such, encourages modern day tourists to relive the experiences of colonial explorers, treasure hunters and archaeologists. The myth of the unrestrained, in contrast, represents a present-day paradise. This myth is related more to "tropical paradise" islands such as Fiji, Jamaica, and Cuba, and presents natural surroundings that entice the tourist to be self-indulgent and sensuous. Importantly, also, the people in these destinations must be smiling, servile, and submissive, thus resurrecting "the asymmetrical relationships between the former colonizers and colonized, relationships often characterized by the power divisions between master and servant" (Echtner and Prasad, 2003: 674). The last myth discussed by Echtner and Prasad (2003) is the myth of the uncivilized. This myth represents destinations as untouched and untamed, inviting tourists to encounter primitive, untamed nature, and natives. The myth of the uncivilized portrays nature and people in almost the opposite way from the myth of the unrestrained, creating instead destinations which are perfect for journeys of discovery and adventure. This myth pertains to the areas of Africa, South America, and Oceania, and follows the trope of the primitive, but also noble, savage.

By outlining these three main myths present in tourism marketing of developing countries, Echtner and Prasad (2003) are drawing attention to a colonial legacy of particular attitudes, images and stereotypes that continue to be reflected and reified through tourism. Morgan and Pritchard (1998: 15) also argue that tourist promotion of the Orient is always "now constructed around notions of Western superiority and dominance over Oriental inferiority and subservience." They continue:

A tourism image reveals as much about the power relations underpinning its construction, as it does about the specific tourism product or country it promotes. The images projected on brochures, billboards and television reveal the relationships between countries, between the genders and between races and cultures. (1998: 6)

Seen at this level, tourism marketing can serve to maintain and reinforce colonial discourse and power relations. As Gandhi points out, there is a "persisting Western interest in the . . . production of what we might call exotic culture[s]" (1998: 59–60). Marketing representations in tourism reinforce ideologies that "are grounded in the relations of power, dominance and subordination which characterize the global system" (Morgan and Pritchard, 1998: 3).

Moreover, following Dann, tourism is a tautology where tourists "merely confirm the discourse which persuaded them to take the trip" (1996: 65); tourism marketing representations form a highly influential framework for tourists' actual expectations, attitudes, and behaviors in those destinations. Indeed, the presence of colonial discourse in travel fantasy and behavior is prominent throughout the postcolonial world. For example, a favorite tourist activity in Singapore is to visit the famous Raffles Hotel for a cocktail (Henderson, 2004). In Hong Kong, many tourists have their photograph taken sitting in a rickshaw pretending to be pulled around by a Chinese "pigeon-chested pensioner" (du Cros, 2004). These tourist enactments of colonial performance are among the more obvious examples of tourism's heavy reliance on a colonial narrative base.

Another obvious and prominent example of tourist expectation and activity based on the colonial myth of the uncivilized is in the practice and promotion of so-called "ethnic" tourism. For example, Maori have been used in New Zealand's tourism imagery since the 1870s, a process which has clearly been dominated by a colonial discourse of the noble savage. Destinations such as Rotorua in New Zealand's North Island have long used quintessential aspects of Maori culture as a mechanism to attract overseas tourists (Carr, 1999), and these are the same essentialized features that were attributed to Maori culture during the colonial period.

Wels (2004) has also argued that the colonial myths and fantasies that shaped the European social constructions of African landscapes and peoples continue to play a powerful role in shaping the current gaze of Europeans in "ethnic" tourism today. Wels traces violence in the way that the continued colonial representation of the "Bushmen"[1] of southern Africa (who are perhaps the most victimized and brutalized people in the colonial history of southern Africa) has led to them being presented for tourism today as a beautiful people living in primeval paradise. As Wels argues:

That is the Otherness (i.e., "them") Europeans (i.e., "us") want to experience in Africa and for which they are prepared to pay money. This is the imagery or staged authenticity to which the tour-operators have to relate in their brochures in order to persuade clients/tourists to book a holiday with them. This is the imagery of African culture which cultural tourism must reflect in its programs. (2004: 90)

Such tourism "products" are not only clearly based on a colonial narrative, but for them to be maintained it is essential that the "Other" remains unchanged, unrestrained and uncivilized. As a consequence, in the postcolonial setting, indigenous people often find themselves trapped in "a sort of tourized confinement in the suffocating straightjacket of enslaving external conceptions. They are caught in the objectifying slant of 'Whites,' 'Westerners' and 'Wanderers-from-afar' in an anonymous but continuing process of subjugation" (Hollinshead, 1992: 44). Nevertheless, the very nature of the tourism industry may well create processes of acculturation and value change which are peculiar to tourism. This so-called "impact of tourism" has incited many studies of tourism themselves to echo colonial discourse. As Bruner commented, "Tourism scholarship thus aligns itself with tourism marketing, in that scholars tend to work within the frame of the commercial versions of their sites" (2001: 881). This frame is that of the binaries inherent in colonial discourse, such as advanced/primitive, civilized/uncivilized and controlled/unrestrained (Echtner and Prasad, 2003).

In their discussions of authenticity, tradition and cultural commodification in relation to tourism the same imperialist imagery that is employed in tourism promotions has unfortunately been maintained by many commentators on tourism, thus showing a desire by them also to fix the "ethnic" identities of peoples in tourism destinations into perpetual "Otherness." Moreover, the actual *process* of much tourism research in postcolonial settings could be considered to echo and perpetuate colonial processes, particularly where researchers conduct their activities in a non-reflexive and uncritical manner. Not only has much of tourism promotion and activity been underpinned by the colonial ideological narrative, therefore, but so too has much of the work within tourism studies. The realization of this in itself is a move towards tourism and tourism studies as a form of *critical* postcolonialism.

Tourism as Critical Postcolonialism

Definitions of the postcolonial, of course, vary widely, but the concept proves most useful not when it is used synonymously with a post-independence historical period in once-colonized nations, but rather when it locates a specifically anti- or *postcolonial discursive* purchase in culture, one which begins in the moment that the colonizing power inscribes itself onto the body and space of its Others and which continues as an often occluded tradition into the modern theatre of neocolonialist international relations (Slemon, 1991: 3).

If postcolonial studies is the analysis or unpicking of, as well as the contestation of, the legacies of colonialism and colonial domination, then to engage with postcolonial theory, tourism studies must take a critical perspective that draws attention to the discursive aspects of power and control present in "First World" (Western/European) representations of, and interest in, the developing countries, also referred to as the "Third World." Issues of representation and

identity have not only recently become a major concern in tourism studies, but work on these issues has begun to mature in its relation to postcolonial thought (Hollinshead, 2004).

Hollinshead has identified a number of other scholars (including himself) who have come in their research to uncover "the partly conscious and partly subconscious ways in which tourism is used politically to articulate the so called 'real' nature of populations" (2004: 25). By pointing out the "declarative" value of tourism, these researchers have highlighted the potential of tourism to be used by postcolonial states to readdress the social, cultural and political problems of domination which have arisen through their experiences of colonialism. Just as much of the discussion on postcolonial writing in literary and cultural studies is focused on how language and writing, with its power and signification of authority, can be wrested from the dominant European culture in order to provide an effectively subversive voice (Ashcroft et al., 1989; Bhabha, 1984), so too is tourism surely inseparable from such cultural politics, which can be defined as "the struggles over the official symbolic representations of reality that shall prevail in a given social order at a given time. One could argue that they are the most important kind of politics, for they seek to control the terms in which all other politics, and all other aspects of life in that society, will take place" (Ortner, 1989: 200). Rather than seeing postcolonial representations of identity as passively accepted by the colonized, a truly postcolonial stance views cultural identity as "an ongoing process, politically contested and historically unfinished" (Clifford, 1988: 9). This is also in line with McClintock's (1992) call for recognition of "multiplicity" in discussions of postcolonialism; recognition of the uneven development and experience of postcolonialism.

The trouble is that tourism might always be an activity and indeed an industry that feeds off the essentialisms and myths as outlined above. Perhaps tourism activities will continue to be based upon and to reenact colonial narratives and the industry will continue to perpetuate colonial core-periphery relationships. As Hollinshead (1993a, 1993b, 2004) puts it, perhaps tourism will always be the violence-rendering rhetorical instrument of imperialism, perpetually dealing in Eurocentric accounts which assert the Western/North Atlantic view as the proper one. Indeed, when tourism scholarship so frequently aligns itself with the predominant tourism image-making and joins in on the imperial essentializing desires of the Western forms of consciousness driving the industry (Meethan, 2001), it is no easy task to form counter-narratives within such a context.

However, following Bhabha's (1994) claim that the "hybrid subject" offers the possibility of resistance to the totalizing repression of colonialism, Hollinshead (1998a, 1998b, 2004) argues that tourism can and should begin to act as a medium for offering those counter-narratives, to act as "a vital medium of being and becoming" (2004: 38). The role that tourism can play in transforming collective and individual values is inherent in ideas of "commoditization" (Cohen, 1977). This term implies that what were once personal "cultural displays" of living traditions or a "cultural text" of lived authenticity becomes a "cultural product," which meets the needs of commercial tourism. Such a situation may, on the one hand, lead to the invention of traditions and heritage for external consumption; those that meet visitor conceptions of the other as described above (Ashworth and Tunbridge, 1996; Buck, 1993; Cronin et al., 2002; Errington and Gewertz, 1989; Fisher, 2004; Helu-Thaman, 1993; Picard and Wood, 1997; Webb, 1994). However, on the other hand, it may be difficult to distinguish between the creation of tradition for tourist consumption and its creation for other political and cultural ends of either the colonizers or the colonized (Hanson, 1989; Otto and Verloop, 1996; Trask, 1991).

For example, in destinations such as Singapore and Penang, Malaysia (Henderson, 2004) and Levuka in Fiji (Fisher, 2004),

colonial buildings and other monuments are preserved and used as tourist attractions. However, in some of these destinations a situation of ambivalence and even downright confusion seems to exist for governments that are driven on the one hand to preserve and promote colonial heritage for the purposes of generating revenue from tourism, while on the other hand being careful not to dwell upon and over glorify the colonial past in their post-independence national mythmaking. Many tourism commentators have now discussed the contestation and negotiation surrounding the use of colonial legacies in heritage tourism (e.g., du Cros, 2004; Fisher, 2004; Henderson, 2004; Marschall, 2004). Du Cros (2004), for example, describes the debate that took place in the Hong Kong media regarding a proposal to establish a working rickshaw stand on the southern side of Hong Kong Island in order to revive this colonial practice with "more authenticity" for a tourist population of the previous colonial power. Such promotion and use of the colonial past for tourism clearly does not go uncontested in the post-independence setting. Henderson's (2004) discussion of Singapore and Malaysia also provides a good example of the tensions that exist between the economic motives of tourism promotion and development and the ideological, political and social currents that inevitably underpin any heritage conservation movement. Henderson (2004) acknowledges that colonialism's bringing together of people from a diverse range of racial and cultural backgrounds can result in the decolonized state presenting itself for heritage and cultural tourism as multiethnic and multicultural, thus transcending a straightforward colonizer/ colonized dichotomy. Marschall (2004), similarly but in an entirely different context, describes the process whereby "postcolonial agents" (those previously marginalized who have become empowered to "speak") have used heritage to counter the biased accounts of the colonizer and to tell *their* side of the story. Heritage can thus be a highly proficient means for these "postcolonial agents," including governments, to assert a new decolonized identity.

Ambivalence can still arise when it is the postcolonial agent's precolonial heritage being used to mark the end of colonization. The cause of the ambivalence is that the precolonial heritage might tend to draw upon images and representations of the colon*ized* that were generated and used by the colon*izers*. Marschall takes a postcolonial stance on this practice by arguing that the use of heritage "that mimics or imitates western models can thus be interpreted as a strategy of the postcolonial agent to appropriate the (visual) language of the colonizer in order to 'write back' (Ashcroft et al., 1989), to respond to and 'de-scribe' the discourses of the colonizer" (2004: 102). This reflects the postcolonial ideas of Bhabha as described by Hollinshead: "At times, such in-between peoples will appear to mimic or imitate the cultural institutions of their erstwhile colonizers, and at times they may even appear to parody the supposed voices of their own precolonial 'Other'" (2004: 35). It is often quite difficult, therefore, for tourism commentators to know when cultural identities which appear to mimic and play according to colonial representations should be read as empowering forms of "cultural hybridity" and when they should be read as passive submission to the tourist colonial narrative. This issue might be particularly complex in what McClintock (1992) refers to as "break-away settler colonies," which have not undergone decolonization.

Besides the tensions and negotiations surrounding the role that heritage and cultural tourisms play in national and individual identity construction, ambivalence is also often felt by post-independence governments, and indeed individual actors such as tourism entrepreneurs, when, as described above, direct economic ties are retained with the ex-colonizing nation. Since the initial investment costs for large-scale, capital intensive tourism projects are often too high for postcolonial governments and indigenous investors, they depend on external capital investment, usually from multinational conglomerates. Indeed, Jaakson (2004) has

pointed out that, whereas classical colonization was state globalization, postcolonialism is characterized by a more minor role of the state and a greater role of multinational corporations. In this context, postcolonial governments often welcome this form of intervention and investment.

While state organizations in developing countries are unlikely to have the political power or wherewithal to challenge this form of neo-imperialism (Jaakson, 2004), there might be opportunities for the marketplace itself to enact a challenge through boycotts and protest against selected tourism corporations and activities. Simmons (2004) raises this point when she asks how present-day tourists, whether Westerners or not, might negotiate, dismantle, resist, or sustain the colonial elements of contemporary travel discourse and industry in their travel practices. This, along with the same question regarding all people engaged with the tourism industry, is clearly a crucial topic of future research in tourism studies (Tucker and Hall, 2004: 187). The same question should also be directed at those researching tourism: How, and to what extent, do they/we negotiate, dismantle, resist, or sustain the colonial elements of contemporary travel discourse, the tourism industry, *and* tourism research? These are important questions to ask if tourism practice and tourism research is to more fully engage with postcolonial theory and thereby become tourism as critical postcolonialism. In particular, discussants of tourism (especially in postcolonial settings) must at least attempt to locate and evaluate the ideological, political and aesthetic bases of their research and analysis.

Conclusion

Postcolonial analysis in tourism reflects the essential contested nature of postcolonial studies elsewhere in the social sciences and humanities, providing a critical perspective that draws attention to the hegemonic discourse as well as the material operations of tourism as both neocolonialism and genuine postcolonialism. A key perspective forwarded in this chapter is that an analysis of colonialism is crucial to a critique of past and present power relations within tourism, precisely because tourism relationships are an echo of, and perpetuate, colonial relationships. First, with direct economic ties often being retained between postcolonial governments and the ex-colonizing nations, neocolonial relationships persist through tourism when air services, resort and recreational developments are owned by foreign, often former colonizing, interests. Rather than just being used to refer to external state intervention, therefore, the term neocolonialism can be used to refer to the core powers continuing to exercise economic and cultural influence over the periphery. Moreover, colonial discourse is all-pervading in travel promotional text so that the language and representation within tourism perpetuates particular conceptualizations of place and identity. The colonial myths and fantasies that shaped the European social constructions of the colonized landscapes and peoples continue to play a powerful role in shaping the current gaze of Europeans in postcolonial tourism today.

As the "industry of difference" par excellence, the tourism industry (as well as tourism research) all too frequently helps to misinterpret and misrepresent the hybridity, ambiguity and multidimensionality of postcolonial landscapes and life (Hollinshead, 1998b). So while issues of image and representation of identity have become a major concern in tourism studies in recent years, particularly with respect to so-called "ethnic," indigenous and heritage tourism, there continues to be a need for more nuanced ethnographic (Bruner, 2001) and ethnohistorical (Duval, 2004) analyses of the range of heritage and culture displays and the range of tourism relationships within any one cultural area. There is a need to recognize the emergent nature of culture and identity, and to acknowledge and celebrate cultural hybridity rather than to lament the loss of some *a priori* notion of cultural tradition (Tucker, 2003).

It will never be possible "to return to or to rediscover an absolute precolonial cultural purity, nor to create national or regional functions entirely independent of the historical implication in the European colonial enterprise" (Ashcroft et al., 1989: 195–196), and so tourism practice and scholarship needs to more fully engage the postcolonial way of thinking that "identity is a matter of 'becoming' as well as of 'being'" (Loomba, 1998: 181).

Postcolonial theory and criticism clearly have a very important role to play in current and future tourism studies, especially if research and theorizing in tourism studies is to keep up with current thinking in related disciplines. Many of the areas of tourism research that are now becoming more central to the field, such as culture and identity, migration, sex and gender, and disabilities can all benefit from the contributions that postcolonial theory and criticism can bring. Fortunately, as outlined in this chapter, many scholars engaging in tourism studies have begun to highlight the ability of tourism to be used by post-independence states and other postcolonial agents to address and contest situations of social, cultural and political domination that had arisen through colonialism. This work is important, especially if it is conducted in a reflexive and critical manner, thereby accentuating the ways in which contemporary tourism research can engage in postcolonial critique.

Notes

1 These are the indigenous hunter-gatherer people of southern Africa, also referred to by other names such as the San and the Basarwa. The term Bushman [or Bushmen] is viewed as pejorative by some.

References

Adams, K. (1984). "Come to Tana Toraja, 'Land of the Heavenly Kings': Travel Agents as

Brokers in Ethnicity." *Annals of Tourism Research*, 11(3): 469–485.

Aitchison, C., Macleod, N.E. and Shaw, S.J. (2002). *Leisure and Tourism Landscapes: Social and Cultural.* Geographies. London and New York: Routledge.

Akama, J.S. (1996). *Wildlife Conservation in Kenya: A Political-Ecological Analysis of Nairobi and Tsavo Regions.* Washington, DC: African Development Foundation.

Akama, J.S. (1997). "Tourism Development in Kenya: Problems and Policy Alternatives." *Progress in Tourism and Hospitality Research*, 3(2): 95–105.

Ang, I. (1995). "I'm a Feminist but ...'Other' Women and Postnational Feminism." In B. Caine and R Pringle (Eds.), *Transitions: New Australian Feminisms* (pp. 57–73). New York: St Martin's.

Ashcroft, B., Griffiths, G. and Tiffin, H. (Eds.), (1989). *The Empire Writes Back: Theory and Practice in Post-Colonial Literatures.* London: Routledge.

Ashworth, G.J. and Tunbridge, J.E. (1996). *Dissonant Heritage.* Chichester: Wiley.

Bhabha, H. (1984). "Representation and the Colonial Text: A Critical Exploration of Some Forms of Mimeticism." In F. Gloversmith (Ed.), *The Theory of Reading* (pp. 93–122). Brighton: Harvester.

Bhabha, H. (1994). *The Location of Culture.* London: Routledge.

Bhattacharyya, D.P. (1997). "Mediating India: An Analysis of a Guidebook." *Annals of Tourism Research*, 24(2): 371–389.

Bosire, S. M. (1995). "Training Hospitality Manager in Kenya: A Re-Appraisal." Staff Seminar, Department of Tourism. Eldoret, Kenya: Moi University. (unpublished).

Blunt, A. and Rose, G. (Eds.) (1994). *Writing Women and Space: Colonial and Postcolonial Geographies.* New York: The Guildford Press.

Britton, S. (1980). "The Spatial Organisation of Tourism in a Neo-Colonial Economy: A Fiji Case Study." *Pacific Viewpoint*, 21: 144–165.

Britton, S. (1982). "The Political Economy of Tourism in the Third World." *Annals of Tourism Research*, 9(3): 331–358.

Bruner, E. (2001). "The Maasai and the Lion King: Authenticity, Nationalism, and Globalization in African Tourism." *American Ethnologist*, 28(4): 881–908.

Bruner, E. and Kirshenblatt-Gimblet, B. (1994). "Maasai on the Lawn: Tourist Realism in East Africa." *Cultural Anthropology*, 9: 435–470.

Buck, E. (1993). *Paradise Remade: The Politics of Culture and History in Hawaii.* Philadelphia, PA: Temple University Press.

Carr, A. (1999). "Interpreting Maori Cultural and Environmental Values: A Means of Managing Tourists and Recreationists with Diverse Cultural Values." In Te Waipounamu (Ed.). Unpublished seminar paper. Dunedin: Centre for Tourism, University of Otago.

Chege, M. (1987). "The Political Economy of Agrarian Change in Central Kenya." In M. Schatzberg (Ed.), *The Political Economy of Kenya.* New York: Praeger.

Clifford, J. (1988). *The Predicament of Culture: Twentieth-Century Ethnography, Literature and Art.* Cambridge, MA: Harvard University Press.

Cohen, E. (1977). "Toward a Sociology of International Tourism." *Social Research*, 39(1): 164–82.

Craik, J. (1994). "Peripheral Pleasures: The Peculiarities of Post-Colonial Tourism." *Culture and Policy*, 6(1): 153–182.

Cronin, M., Gibbons, L. and Kirby, P. (Eds.). (2002). *Reinventing Ireland: Culture, Society and the Global Economy.* London: Pluto Press.

Dann, G. (1996). *The Language of Tourism.* Wallingford, UK: CAB International.

Debbage, K. (1990). "Oligopoly and the Resort Cycle in Bahamas." *Annals of Tourism Research*, 17(4): 513–527.

Dieke, P.U. (1991). "Policies for Tourism Management in Kenya." *Annals of Tourism Research*, 9(1): 69–90.

Du Cros, H. (2004). "Postcolonial Conflict Inherent in the Involvement of Cultural Tourism in Creating New National Myths in Hong Kong." In C.M. Hall and H. Tucker (Eds.), *Tourism and Postcolonialism: Contested Discourses, Identities and Representations* (pp.153–168). London and New York: Routledge.

Duval, D.T. (2004). "Cultural Tourism in Postcolonial Environments: Negotiating Histories, Ethnicities and Authenticities in St. Vincent, Eastern Caribbean." In C.M. Hall and H. Tucker (Eds.), *Tourism and Postcolonialism: Contested Discourses,*

Identities and Representations (pp. 57–75). London: Routledge.

Echtner, C.M. and Prasad, P. (2003). "The Context of Third World Tourism Marketing." *Annals of Tourism Research*, 30(3): 660–682.

Edensor, T. (1998). *Tourists at the Taj: Performance and Meaning at a Symbolic Site*. London and New York: Routledge.

Errington, F. and Gewertz, D. (1989). "Tourism and Anthropology in a Post-Modern World." *Oceania*, 60: 37–54.

Fisher, D. (2004). "A Colonial Town for Neo-colonial Tourism." In C.M. Hall and H. Tucker (Eds.), *Tourism and Postcolonialism: Contested Discourses, Identities and Representations* (pp. 126–139). London: Routledge.

Gandhi, L. (1998). *Postcolonial Theory: A Critical Introduction*. New York: Columbia University Press.

Hall, C.M. (1998). "Making the Pacific: Globalization, Modernity and Myth." In G. Ringer (Ed.), *Destinations: Cultural Landscapes of Tourism* (pp. 140–153). New York: Routledge.

Hall, C.M. and Tucker, H. (2004a). "Tourism and Postcolonialism: An Introduction." In C.M. Hall and H. Tucker (Eds.), *Tourism and Postcolonialism: Contested Discourses, Identities and Representations* (pp. 1–24). London: Routledge.

Hall, C.M. and Tucker, H. (Eds.), (2004b). *Tourism and Postcolonialism: Contested Discourses, Identities and Representations*. London: Routledge.

Hanson, A. (1989). "The Making of the Maori: Culture Invention and its Logic." *American Anthropologist*, 91(4): 890–902.

Helu-Thaman, K. (1993). "Beyond Hula, Hotels, and Handicrafts: A Pacific Islander's Perspective on Tourism Development." *The Contemporary Pacific*, 5(1): 104–111.

Henderson, J. (2004). "Tourism and British Colonial Heritage in Malaysia and Singapore." In C.M. Hall and H. Tucker (Eds.), *Tourism and Postcolonialism: Contested Discourses, Identities and Representations* (pp. 113–125). London and New York: Routledge.

Hollinshead, K. (1992). "'White' Gaze, 'Red' People—Shadow Visions: The Disidentification of 'Indians' in Cultural Tourism." *Leisure Studies*, 11(1): 43–64.

Hollinshead, K. (1993). "Encounters in Tourism." In M.A. Khan, A. Olsen and T. Var (Eds.), *VNR's Encyclopedia of Hospitality and Tourism* (pp. 636–651). New York: Van Nostrand Reinhold.

Hollinshead, K. (1998a). "Tourism, Hybidity and Ambiguity: The Relevance of Bhabha's 'Third Space' Cultures." *Journal of Leisure Research*, 30(1): 121–156.

Hollinshead, K. (1998b). "Tourism and the Restless Peoples: A Dialectical Inspection of Bhabha's Halfway Populations." *Tourism, Culture and Communication*, 1(1): 49–77.

Hollinshead, K. (2004). "Tourism and New Sense: Worldmaking and the Enunciative Value of Tourism." In C.M. Hall and H. Tucker (Eds.), *Tourism and Postcolonialism: Contested Discourses, Identities and Representations* (pp. 25–42). London and New York: Routledge.

Huggan, G. (2001). *The Postcolonial Exotic: Marketing the Margins*. London and New York: Routledge.

Jackson, R. (2004). "Globalisation and Neo-Colonialist Tourism." In C.M. Hall and H. Tucker (Eds.), *Tourism and Postcolonialism: Contested Discourses, Identities and Representations* (pp. 169–183). London and New York: Routledge.

Kappeler, S. (1986). *The Pornography of Representation*. Minneapolis: University of Minnesota Press.

Kibara, O.N. (1994). "Tourism Development in Kenya: The Government Involvement and Influence." Unpublished masters dissertation, University of Surrey.

Loomba, A. (1998). *Colonialism/Postcolonialism*. London: Routledge.

Marschall, S. (2004). "Commodifying Heritage: Post-Apartheid Monuments and Cultural Tourism in South Africa." In C.M. Hall and H. Tucker (Eds.), *Tourism and Postcolonialism: Contested Discourses, Identities and Representations* (pp. 95–112). London and New York: Routledge.

Matthews, H.G. (1978). *International Tourism: A Political and Social Analysis*. Cambridge: Schenkman Publishing Company.

Meethan, K. (2001). Tourism in Global Society: Place, Culture and Consumption, London: Palgrave.

McClintock, A. (1992). "The Angel of Progress: Pitfalls of the Term 'Post-Colonialism'." *Social Text*, 31/32: 84–98.

McClintock, A. (1995). *Imperial Leather: Race, Gender, and Sexuality in the Colonial Context*. New York: Routledge.

Migot-Adholla, S.E. (1984). "Rural Development Policy and Equality." In J.D. Barkan (Ed.), *Politics and Public Policy in Kenya and Tanzania* (pp. 199–229). Nairobi: Heinemann.

Mishra, V. and Hodge, B. (1991). "What Is Post(-) Colonialism?" *Textual Practice*, 5: 399–414.

Morgan, N. and Pritchard, A. (1998). *Tourism, Promotion and Power: Creating Images, Creating Identities*. Chichester: John Wiley & Sons.

Moore-Gilbert, B. (1997). *Postcolonial Theory: Contexts, Practices, Politics*. London: Verso.

Oglethorpe, R. (1984). "Tourism in Malta: A Crisis of Dependence." *Leisure Studies*, 3(2): 147–161.

Ong, A. (1985). "Industrialisation and Prostitution in Southeast Asia." *Southeast Asia Chronicle*, 96: 2–6.

Opperman, M. (1992). "International Tourism Flows in Malaysia." *Annals of Tourism Research*, 19(3): 482–500.

Opperman, M. and McKinley, S. (1997). "Sexual Imagery in the Marketing of Pacific Tourism Destinations." In M. Opperman (Ed.), *Pacific Rim Tourism* (pp. 117–127). Wallingford: CAB International.

Ortner, S.B. (1989). "Cultural Politics: Religious Activism and Ideological Transformation Among 20th Century Sherpas." *Dialetical Anthropology*, 14: 197–211.

Otto, T. and Verloop, R. (1996). "The Asaro Mudmen: Local Property, Public Culture?" *The Contemporary Pacific*, 8(2): 349–386.

Picard, M. and Wood, R. (1997). *Tourism, Ethnicity and the State in Asian and Pacific Societies*. Honolulu: University of Hawaii Press.

Reimer, G. (1990). "Packaging Dreams: Canadian Tour Operators at Work." *Annals of Tourism Research*, 17(4): 501–512.

Richter, L.K. (1995). "Gender and Race: Neglected Variables in Tourism Research." In R. Butler and D. Pearce (Eds.), *Change in Tourism: People, Places, Processes* (pp. 71–91). London: Routledge.

Said, E.W. (1978). *Orientalism*. New York: Pantheon.

Selwyn, T. (1993). "Peter Pan in South-East Asia: Views from the Brochures." In M. Hitchcock, V.T. King and M.J.G. Parnwell (Eds.), *Tourism in South-East Asia* (pp. 117–137). London and New York: Routledge.

Shaw, G. and Williams, A. (1994). *Critical Issues in Tourism: A Geographical Perspective*. Oxford: Blackwell.

Simmons, B.A. (2004). "Saying the Same Old Things: A Contemporary Travel Discourse and the Popular Magazine Text." In C.M. Hall and H. Tucker (Eds.), *Tourism and Postcolonialism: Contested Discourses, Identities and Representations* (pp. 43–56). London and New York: Routledge.

Sinclair, M.T. (1990). *Tourism Development in Kenya*. Washington, DC: World Bank.

Sindiga, I. (1996). "Domestic Tourism in Kenya." *Annals of Tourism Research*, 23(1): 19–31.

Sindiga, I. (2000). *Tourism and African Development: Change and Challenge of Tourism in Kenya*. Aldershot: Ashgate.

Slemon, S. (1991). "Modernism's Last Post." In I. Adams and H. Tiffin (Eds.), *Past the Last Post*. Hemel Hemstead: HarvesterWheatsheaf.

Spivak, G.C. (1986). "Imperialism and Sexual Difference." *Oxford Literary Review*, 8(1–2): 234–240.

Spivak, G.C. (1987). *In Other Worlds: Essays in Cultural Politics*. London: Methuen.

Spurr, D. (1993). *The Rhetoric of Empire: Colonial Discourse in Journalism, Travel Writing, and Imperial Administration*. Durham, NC: Duke University Press.

Trask, H. (1991). "Natives and Anthropologists: The Colonial Struggle." *The Contemporary Pacific*, 3: 159–167.

Tucker, H. (2003). *Living with Tourism: Negotiating Identities in a Turkish Village*. London: Routledge.

Tucker, H. and Hall, C.M. (2004). "Conclusion." In C.M. Hall and H. Tucker (Eds.), *Tourism and Postcolonialism: Contested Discourses, Identities and Representations* (pp. 184–190). London: Routledge.

Urry, J. (1990). *The Tourist Gaze*. London: Sage.

Ware, V. (1992). *Beyond the Pale: White Women, Racism and History*. London: Verso.

Webb, T. (1994). "Highly Structured Tourist Art: Form and Meaning of the Polynesian Center." *The Contemporary Pacific*, 6(1): 59–85.

Wels, H. (2004). "About Romance and Reality: Popular European Imagery in Postcolonial Tourism in Southern Africa." In C.M. Hall and H. Tucker (Eds.), *Tourism and Postcolonialism: Contested Discourses, Identities and Representations* (pp. 76–94). London and New York: Routledge.

Williams, M. (1993). "An Expansion of the Tourism Life Site Cycle Model: The Case of Minorca (Spain)." *The Journal of Tourism Studies*, 4(2): 24–32.

Williams, P. and Chrisman, L. (1993). "Colonial Discourse and Post-Colonial Theory: An Introduction." In P. Williams and L. Chrisman (Eds.), *Colonial Discourse and Post-Colonial Theory: A Reader* (pp. 1–20). Hemel Hempstead: Harvester Wheatsheaf.

Young, R. (2003). *Postcolonialism: A Very Short Introduction*. Oxford: Oxford University Press.

29

Thanatourism and Its Discontents: An Appraisal of a Decade's Work with Some Future Issues and Directions

Tony Seaton

Thanatourism in Academic Discourse Since 1996

Tourism and death may seem an odd conjunction. It entered tourism discourse as thanatourism in 1996 in a special issue of the *International Journal of Heritage Studies* (IJHS) (Foley and Lennon, 1996a, 1996b). The concept began as a way of addressing a lacuna in the literature of tourism, the existence of a broad range of tourism practices associated with death and disaster that had eluded attention in the substantial literature relating to motivation and tourist typologies. The practices included visits to battlefields, celebrity death sites, graveyards, cemeteries, atrocity and disaster sites, murder locations, memorials, museums of war, torture, and horror.

Lennon and Foley's special issue of IJHS in 1996 brought these previously marginalized tourism practices into focus under the name of "Dark Tourism" or "Thanatourism" (the double naming will be discussed later) with a definition, a brief historical introduction (Seaton, 1996) an overview of their significance and a number of edited case studies.

In the aforementioned special issue thanatourism was defined as:

> ... travel to a location wholly, or partially, motivated by the desire for actual or symbolic encounters with death, particularly, but not exclusively, violent death, which may, to a varying degree be activated by the person-specific features of those whose deaths are its focal objects. (Seaton, 1996: 236)

It was typified as five kinds of behavior.

- Travel to witness public enactments of death (e.g., public executions, "rubbernecking" at accident and disaster scenes).
- Travel to see the sites of mass death (e.g., battlefields) or individual deaths (often, but not always, those of celebrities).

- Travel to internment sites and memorials to the dead (e.g., graveyards, catacombs, crypts, war memorials).
- Travel to view the material evidence, or symbolic representations of death, in locations unconnected with their occurrence (e.g., museums, exhibitions, "chambers of horrors").
- Travel for reenactments or simulation of death, sometimes religious (e.g., Catholic pageants, processions) but also secular (Civil War Society in Britain, and US Civil War enactments). (Seaton, 1996: 237; Seaton, 2000: 578)

Initially the assertion that tourism could be linked to death caused mild shock to academics and lay people alike. How could the "have a nice-day-industry" be implicated in such an apparently macabre theatre of behavior? But later there was a gradual recognition that travel associated with death comprised a rather large field of behavior, and could be an interesting area of study. Thanatourism then began to attract other academics to the field. Over the last 10 years there has been a steady growth of work on the subject. This work has included overview studies of the whole category (Dann, 1998; Lennon and Foley, 2000; Sharpley and Stone, 2009; Wight, 2006). There have also been studies on elements of Thanatourism, including work on:

- battlefield and war tourism (Cooper, 2006; Gordon, 1998; Henderson, 1997, 2000; Knox, 2006; Lloyd, 1998; Ryan, 2007; Seaton, 1999, 2002a; Slade, 2003; Smith, 1996, 1998; Siegenthaler, 2002);
- famous death sites (Alderman, 2002; Blom, 2000; Ryan, 2002);
- punishment, atrocity and Holocaust memorial travel (Ashworth, 1997; Ashworth and Hartmann, 2005; Cole, 2000; Dann, 1998; Lennon and Smith, 2004; Lisle, 2004; Miles, 2002; Strange and Kempa, 2003; Shackley, 2001b; Tunbridge 2005; Williams, 2004; Young, 1993);
- slavery sites in the UK and USA (Seaton, 2001); and
- cemeteries and funerary sites (Seaton, 2002b).

In addition, the field has stimulated a website and attracted an enthusiastic student response that has resulted in several postgraduate research ASNE publication (e.g., Iles 2003, 2006, 2008; Moeller, 2005). In addition, thanatourism has received a significant level of coverage in the mass media (Seaton and Lennon, 2004).

Discontents and Critics

As thanatourism achieved academic currency a number of challenges to, and criticisms of, its initial formulations were mounted. One critique was that some tourism practices were mischaracterized as thanatourism and should not be seen as a desire for encounters associated with death, but rather to stem from other motivations. Slade (2003), on the basis of observations of battlefield sites at Gallipoli, concluded that the reasons Australians and New Zealanders visited them had nothing to do with any motivation to be associated with death and disaster, but were rather to be seen as pilgrimage to a sacred World War I site where national Anzac identity had been first forged. The argument of this article, (entitled, "Gallipoli thanatourism" instead of "Gallipoli non-thanatourism" as one may have expected), does not in fact conflict with definitions of thanatourism. From the start thanatourism was defined as tourism motivated by the desire to visit places that are inherently associated with death, whether or not death is seen to be a principle motivation, or even consciously seen as an element. Moreover, the original formulations of thanatourism made clear that it was not an absolute form, but existed across a continuum of intensity regulated by two circumstances: (1) whether it was the single motivation or existed with others motivations; (2) the extent to which the interest in death was person-centered or generalized, the crucial variable being the extent to which the dead had personal meaning to the traveler. In some cases the dead could be significant others, in other cases they might not be. The fact that fallen Anzacs held a central importance as heroic actors in the grand narrative of nation building did not mean that visiting the sites where they fought and died was not thanatourism. No battlefield visitation could be anything but thanatourism to some extent, since all battle fields involve death, whether or not death is seen as the principal feature of the trip. Thanatourism is always a necessary feature of—even if it is not a sufficient condition for—battlefield tourism. However, as the IJHS discussion made clear, the more differentiated and comprehensive the traveler's knowledge of the dead, the weaker is the pure thanatouristic element. Thus, a battlefield with personal associations will be less purely experienced as a death site than, say, Ground Zero to foreigners with no personal connections to the events of 9/11 (see Photo 29.1).

A more fundamental question posed about thanatourism was whether it was a type of motivation or a collective classification for a genre of sites and attractions—or, to put it another way, whether thanatourism should be seen primarily as a demand-side, or a supply-side, concept. This critique (Sharpley, 2005), has resulted in attempts to distinguish between different kinds of thanatourism. Stone (2006) has produced a typology of thanatourism attractions/sites, grading them

along a darkest-lightest spectrum, using variables such as: authenticity, location, time scale, and purposive orientation as indicators of their place on the spectrum. This is a useful attempt to focus greater attention on qualitative differences between thanatourism phenomena. However, it poses a problem—the semiotic truism that any and all sites are polysemic and do not possess an inherent, essentialist identity that can be fixed to a single meaning whatever the intentions of their creators. For example, a World War I memorial may be seen as a sacred memorial for someone whose family are commemorated, or as an example of monumental design by Edward Lutyens by an architectural visitor. A roadside tree with a wreath around it may to some be a sacred spot where a friend was killed in a car crash; to a road maintenance official from local government, a distracting road hazard to be removed. It is only by introducing

Photo 29.1   Covers for battlefield tours by Thomas Cook & Son in the 1920s.
Source: Thomas Cook & Son.

the perceptions and motivations of the visitor/ onlooker, that one can accommodate differences in meaning. The need is therefore to find a way to integrate both site type and visitor motivation, which may result in quite complex models of thanatourism, if one is to be found that covers the many possible permutations of site type and visitor type.

Third, there has been, and is, a continuing debate over naming. It is unusual for a specialist academic field to come into existence with two names—"Dark Tourism" and "Thanatourism"—that have survived for 10 years. Indeed, it can be argued that two other options—Rojek's (1993) earlier coinage of the terms, "Fatal attractions" and "Black Spots," to designate tourist attractions linking sight seeing and "fatality"—could also be candidates for flagging the field.

These naming disagreements are more than debates about words. They relate to underlying differences in conceptions as to what the phenomenon being named is about, what its contemporary significance is, what it includes and how it relates to history. There are two quite different views. In Lennon and Foley's early work and in Rojek's book the association between fatality and tourism was viewed as a distinctively postmodern phenomenon, which is why these writers sought contemporary-looking names for it. The postmodernist view was particularly foregrounded by Rojek who began his chapter on "Fatal Attractions' with the assertion that:

> Fatality is a striking feature of postmodernism. The "excremental culture" which Kroker and Cook (1986) and Baudrillard negotiate, is choking with mass produced commodities, simulated images and self-negating utopias. Meaning has been replaced with spectacle and sensation dominates. (Rojek, 1993: 136)

Rojek went on to inventory, as examples of postmodern fatal attractions, an eclectic range of sites: Pere La Chaise Cemetery in Paris, Arlington and other national cemeteries, celebrity memorials, Graceland, many literary landscapes (Bronte, Dickens country, etc.), Hollywood necrophiliac halls of fame and theme parks. All of these he associated with "hyperreality"—replicas, simulations, spectacle, and the usual Baudrillardian/ Debordian litany of constructed fantasy and the spectacular that have been identified with the postmodern.

Rojek's account raises a number of issues. First, his selection of examples is puzzling in its eclecticism since it includes heritage sites, literary landscapes, and theme parks that developed at different times under different purposive conditions and by different agencies. It is not clear, for instance, how literary sites such as Haworth Museum and the Bronte country can be closely bracketed with Hollywood theme parks, or how any national war cemeteries resemble Graceland, or how all of them share the same common basis in replica, simulations and spectacle Rojek imputes to postmodern presentations.

More importantly his analysis is radically unhistorical. If fatality is a feature of postmodernism, it is one with a long history that can be exactly traced. Precursors of his replicas, simulations, and spectacles, packaged for public consumption, previously existed in the immense supply of simulated Christian images across Europe, generated by the Catholic Church from the Middle Ages onwards in churches, cathedrals, monasteries.

They can also be found in the vast, ephemeral supply of commercially provided, secular literature, images and artifacts relating to crime and punishment from the seventeenth century onwards. It included illustrated broadside ballads sold to spectators at public executions, and murder and torture museums opened to the public; e.g., Madame Tussauds established in the early nineteenth century, and the Heidelberg Museum of Torture in the early twentieth century (Ichenhauser, n.d.).

Some of Rojek's specific examples have a long history. His citation of Pierre La Chaise as a postmodern tourist attraction ignores the fact that it has always attracted visitors. Like other early cemeteries in Paris, London, and the USA it had its own tourist guide books almost from the time it opened in 1804 (Brown, 1973; Dansel, 1973).

Moreover, Rojek's typology of "Black Spots" and "Fatal Attractions" only really comprise a small part of what both Lennon and Seaton envisage as a much bigger category of phenomena of fatality—not just recent spectacles associated with simulation and images, but both ancient and modernist sites with authentic materiality and substance that have evolved historically within grand narratives (religious, nationalistic, and high cultural) for which postmodernity was supposed to be the death knell. They include: battlefields, historical atrocity sites, martyrdom settings and religious shrines, and national memorials of all sorts commemorating royalty, novelists, poets, politicians, military heroes and unknown soldiers, of which Westminster Abbey in the UK may be seen as a paradigm example.

A brief quotation from a story by the writer Julia Strachey, written 60 years ago, may serve to suggest just how postmodern thanatourism is. It describes a young man reluctantly contemplating a traditional house party in the country he is obliged to attend:

"He falls to thinking that it is the middle of the week, and that therefore the house will be filled with elderly ladies … He begins to picture long, cramped hours spent packed into cars with these ladies in their spotted summer dresses, while they crawl all over the face of the country looking about for barrows, war memorials, beacons and gibbets to visit" (Strachey, 1944: 77). It is difficult to envisage the old ladies in Strachey's story as vanguard flag carriers of the postmodern.

Lennon and Foley share Rojek's postmodern frame of reference in theory. Their early "Dark Tourism" work explicitly invoked postmodernity as a context (Foley and Lennon, 1996b; Lennon and Foley, 2000). However, Lennon's later work (Lennon and Smith 2004, Wight and Lennon, 2007), while intermittently focused on postmodern interpretation methods, is underpinned by a more serious and modernist grand narrative—that of social justice. Its focus is on the geographic selectivity of Jewish Holocaust memorials, and the "significant silences" that exist in relation to the unmemorialized spaces where other groups, gypsies, and homosexuals, were exterminated. This trajectory is implicitly based upon something postmodernist discourse denies—the possibility of establishing non-problematic truth, and belatedly memorializing it.

If the problem with Rojek's term, "fatal attractions" is that the tourism phenomena it comprises are too limited and ill-defined, the problem with the term "dark tourism" is that it is a value judgment, based on an implicit binary contrast with its opposite—a kind of tourism that is "light." This embedded, metaphoric contrast suggests that the connotations of dark tourism are transgressive, morally suspect, and pathological—an agenda around which the mass media, aided and abetted by obliging academics, have sometimes attempted to whip up a moral panic (Seaton and Lennon, 2004). "Light" tourism, conversely, must be good, moral, and normal. This Manichean contrast does not fit the facts disclosed by the wide variety of travel and tourism experiences that comprise death-associated travel. While visiting the homes of UK serial killers like Frederick West or the Yorkshire Ripper may be judged as "dark" by some, a pilgrimage to a Commonwealth War grave that commemorates one's grandfather, or visiting the Taj Mahal, a monumental tribute by a prince to a greatly loved wife, can surely not be.

More recently another term "grief tourism—the act of traveling to the scene of a tragedy or disaster" (www.grief-tourism.com. Accessed March 15, 2008)—has been mooted to define the field of death-related travel. The problem here is its lack of inclusiveness. While being an appropriately solemn term for describing visits to Jewish Holocaust sites and national war memorials, it would not accurately designate more burlesque, entertainment-related settings such as Civil War reenactments, the Chamber of Horrors at Madame Tussauds, and other more commercialized, synthetic attractions, which would fall within the more inclusive concept of thanatourism.

The reasons for preferring thanatourism as a name for the field are, therefore, to avoid the problems just examined—of inclusivity, pejorative association, and postmodern bias present in other terms. There are others that relate to questions about thanatourism's relationship to other social sciences, which will be discussed later.

A Developmental Sketch of Thanatourism

This chapter has so far reexamined the origins, meaning and significance of thana-tourism in academic discourse, and identified problems with the postmodernist definitional frameworks within which it has been treated. This section offers an alternative view of its origins and transformations that suggests that it was a traditional kind of travel that evolved and was shaped by profound shifts in the history of European culture, which still impact today. Specifically it suggests that thanatour-ism as defined in the western tradition was shaped by three key historical discourses: Christianity, as it evolved between c.400 and the 16th century with its unique, doctrinal emphasis on fatality; antiquarianism and the related ideology of national heritage which first emerged in 16th century Europe, and continues to exert considerable impact on tourism today across the world; and Romanticism, a complex and problematic nexus of ideas which evolved from the mid-eighteenth century in Europe, one of whose effects was to influence attitudes and behavior towards death, and expand the desire for travel to places associated with fatality.

The Christian Cult of Death

Thanatourism had its origins in the fatality that was made central to the development of Christianity in western Europe between the 5th and 16th centuries through its emphasis on the crucifixion of Christ, an elaborated cult of saints, and the promotion of pilgrim-age (Brown, 1981; Daniell, 1997). All the major world religions have mythologized and ritualized death, but none made fatality and suffering so central to its basic identity as Christianity in placing the crucifixion of Christ and a cult of martyred saints at the center of its teaching. Its emphasis on fatality and pain was different from the two other main European religions, Judaism and Islam. Neither allowed their followers to make representations of God or the sacred, so their religion was less person-centered and more abstract in its focus on an unknowable deity who was to be obeyed and worshiped, rather than related to as an individual. By contrast, at the heart of Christian myth was the human figure of Christ as personal redeemer, who by his suffering and death took on the burden of the world's sin, and thus made eternal life attainable for mankind.

The crucifixion story produced a religious sensibility among Christians that was dominated by a preoccupation with pain and death, and a disposition to take pilgrimages to sites associated with them. This emphasis on fatality was informally promoted among early Christian communities, but later organized and diffused by the Catholic Church, which shaped and authorized Christian doctrine, liturgy, representation, and the benefits of pilgrimage, all of which made fatality a central focus of belief and religious practice.

Christian Doctrine—The New Testament
The teachings of Christianity, as embodied in the New Testament, are, like all texts, polysemic—capable of many meanings, and being read in different ways by different audiences. The figure of Christ can, and has been, represented in art and literary texts variously as, "Gentle Jesus meek and mild," Jesus as suffering, martyred redeemer, and in Byzantine art, as Pantocritor, the stern faced, all seeing judge of the world. Out of all the many elements of Christ's life that might have been foregrounded—his teachings, miracles, friend-ships, clashes with authority, execution, and Resurrection—early Christianity and, later, medieval Catholic Christianity, and then Protestant religions, all made fatality the key

doctrinal emphasis. This came about through the discursive emphasis on the Crucifixion and the promotion of the Cross as Christianity's identifying symbol which had begun among early Christian communities, was institutionalized in the 4th century when the Emperor Constantine made Christianity the official religion of the Roman Empire. From the 12th century the Cross was commonly placed above the altar as the focal feature of Catholic churches (Daniell, 1997). Christianity was thus the first, and only, world religion to make an instrument of torture and death its corporate logo.

Christian Liturgy

Liturgy comprised the ritual forms of service and worship, prescribed by Christian denominations, Catholic and Protestant, as the way in which believers should express their faith. It was a structured schedule of service forms and observances throughout the year—daily, weekly, monthly—including prayers to be made, psalms to be sung, and biblical readings to be heard.

The cornerstone of Catholic liturgy was and remains the Mass, the symbolic reenactment of Christ's last meal, the Last Supper, before his judicial execution. Lent and Easter were appointed as times to anticipate and remember the Crucifixion. Christ's death was thus at the heart of the medieval religious experience (Daniell, 1997).

This bias to fatality was officially extended by the Church from Christ's death to that of many others through the development of a cult of saints, each with his/her own day or festival (Brown, 1981; Wilson, 1983). In early Christianity these were disciples and immediate associates of Christ but later the ranks of these "very special dead" came to include others famous for their good works or miracles, or as martyrs who had died for the cause, and were nominated as saints by the Church. Dates for celebrating their deaths were specified in martyrologies and Catholic and Protestant Prayer Books as part of the calendar of the Christian year. As Foxe, the great Protestant propagandist declared: "There is no day in the whole year, unto which the number of 5000 martyrs cannot be ascribed, except only the first day of January" (Foxe, c.1880: 15).

Thus the fun concept now known as "holiday" derived from "holy day," the celebration of the deaths of martyr saints.[1]

Crucial to the European development of the cult of saints was the collection and display of relics and ex votos (Bentley, 1985). Relics were the bodies or body parts of saints, while ex votos were artifacts associated with them, particularly clothes and possessions. The possession of them gave status to a church, monastery or cathedral; the more important the saint, the greater the standing of the institution. Relics were also revenue earners since, as the authenticating, material evidence of a saint's presence, they attracted sightseeing pilgrims who, while at a monastery or church, would leave gifts, pay for indulgences, and buy mementoes. So important were relics and ex votos that theft was not uncommon (Geary, 1990), and bodies were sometimes chopped up to allow parts to be distributed at several religious sites (Brown, 1981; Wilson, 1983).

Once an institution had its relics and ex votos, thought and skill went into exhibiting them effectively, as in museums today. Peter Brown has described how presentational techniques were developed for displaying relics to best advantage including the use of elevation, lighting and isolation.

Christian Representation

In addition to doctrinal and liturgical emphasis on fatality, Christianity promoted it in diverse forms of representation, intended not just to depict Christ and the martyr saints, but to encourage reflection on death in the personal lives of the faithful. *Thanatopsis*, meditation on dying and death, was encouraged and supported through a range of textual practices—most directly by sermons and homilies delivered to congregations by the clergy, priesthood, and monastic orders through direct contact with Christian communities.

Reminders of Christian fatality came in other ways: in church designs, which were frequently cruciform in layout; in the naming of churches, which often were those of martyr saints; in paintings that featured images of Christ's agony and saints' martyrdoms on walls and glass windows.

Death was also described and depicted in illuminated manuscripts and, after the invention of printing, in books and graphic art. There were *ars moriendi* texts, printed manuals on how people should best face the approach of dying (O'Connor, 1966) (Photo 29.2). And more bizarre, the *Dance of Death* and the *Danse Macabre*—cartoon drawings, engravings or carvings of Death as a partly fleshed, malevolent skeleton, carrying off people from all walks of life—that could be found in books, on church walls and even decorating bridges (Clark, 1950; Douce, 1896) (Photo 29.3).

Another category of representation was a genre of artifacts called *memento mori*—visual reminders to people that they had to die and

thus the need to have death constantly in mind. This genre included books, small paintings, jewelry depicting skulls and real skulls which were owned by people as contemplative reminders of mortality (Daniell, 1997: 2).

Christian Fatality, Place, and Pilgrimage

Catholicism made locality a key feature of piety through encouraging the practice of pilgrimage in the Middle Ages (Webb, 2000, 2001, 2002). This involved both foreign and domestic travel to places for symbolic encounters with Christianity's significant others—being where Christ and the saints had died, been martyred or interred, or where their relics or ex votos were on display. There were over 150 pilgrimage shrines in England alone. In Europe commercial networks and churches developed along the routes to Compostella del Santiago, Rome, and Jerusalem. People took part in pilgrimage for many reasons: to obtain

Photo 29.2   Frontispiece to a French Ars Moriendi book, 1700. Photo: Tony Seaton.

**Photo 29.3   The Dance of Death, engraved from a medieval picture c. 1820.
Photo: Tony Seaton.**

remission for their sins, to be miraculously cured of disease, to pray for others, and, it has been argued, simply for the break involved in travel. But in most cases the ultimate goal was to make contact with shrines and holy places commemorating the Christian dead, particularly, but not exclusively, dead martyrs to the faith. Before the Papacy assumed monopolistic control over the canonization of saints, there were regional shrines to many revered local and "unofficial" figures that included, in Britain, kings, knights and holy women (Hole, 1954; Finucane, 1977; Webb, 2000, 2001, 2002).

To summarize, Christianity, more than other religions, made fatality central to its identity and ideological practices. Through doctrine, rituals, liturgy, and representations it emphasized suffering and death, which were as comprehensively used to promote Christianity as sex is today used in advertising to sell consumer products. The effect was to produce in Christian populations a pervasive sense of anxiety that could only be relieved by Christian belief and practices, one of which was pilgrimage. It is this legacy that helped to shape the development of thanatourism and its residual effects can still be seen today.

Antiquarianism and the Discovery of Heritage

By the sixteenth century Catholicism's more extreme emphasis on fatality had weakened. The Protestant Reformation challenged and later abolished some of its doctrines, liturgy, and representational forms and ended pilgrimage to religious shrines (Dickens, 1989; Hughes, 1963).

However, even as this happened, another kind of secular fatality emerged as a travel goal, resulting from new cultural developments in the West—antiquarianism and the quest for heritage. This was the pursuit of the past in emerging nation states such as Britain and France through literary study and through travel to identify, record and, where possible, acquire and bring back artifacts from the past. The purposes of antiquarian research were the identification and preservation of historical evidence that could be ordered, constructed, and integrated into a grand narrative supporting notions of evolutionary nationhood and a new concept called national heritage. The antiquarian movement was the first manifestation of the *secular-sacred* in travel, which substituted, for the death sites and relics of Christian figures, the geographical tracking down of national heritage and heritage sites, an elastic category that could include battlefields, death sites of national heroes, ruined monasteries, and castles. Antiquarian discoveries did not just provide evidence of the truth value of the authentic past, but vehicles through which it could be experienced in the present by sightseers.

Seminal British antiquarians included John Leland, William Camden, William Stukely,

John Speed, John Weever, and William Dugdale (Evans, 1947) who traveled round Britain searching out historical documents and recording and describing memorials, epitaphs, burial mounds, effigies that were threatened by the ravages of time. Once the idea took hold it stimulated a cult of tourism among lay populations to the sites the antiquarians had described, as well as to others associated with dead cultural figures— literary, artistic, military, political, religious, communal—claimed as makers, shapers, or charismatic representatives of nationhood. Later still, concepts of heritage and anti-quarianism stimulated the establishment of museums and galleries, the preservation of important buildings and sites, and the inauguration of many kinds of "heritage" organization. All of these developments motivated travel in new ways and expanded the number and kind of places people thought worth visiting. Monasteries, for example, which had been an almost proscribed category of location after the Protestant Reformation, gradually became popular tour-ist targets, seen less as religious institutions than as architectural and cultural monuments of emerging national heritage.

Romanticism and Thanatourism

In the last half of the eighteenth century and through the nineteenth century another emer-gent cultural movement, Romanticism, added to the propensity for secular, death-related travel among those with the time and means to do so. This much debated European phenom-enon was the name given to developments in literary, artistic and philosophical tastes that took place in France, Germany, and Britain, and which had a profound effect on tourism development in Europe (Halsted, 1965; Furst, 1969; Williams, 1976).

For the middle-class populations who were influenced by it, Romanticism had two key aspects. On the one hand, it affected their choice of objects in the external world thought to be worthy of note, reordering priorities of attention to events, people, and places. On the other, it tended to impact upon their subjec-tivity by suggesting characteristic kinds of mental and emotional response to adopt in encountering those objects, events and people. It thus directed people towards what to think about, and ways of thinking and, more especially, *feeling* about them. This duality has been summarized by one com-mentator's typification of Romanticism as, "the cult of feeling and the search for the natural" (Furst, 1969: 51).

The Search for the Natural—A Choice of Objects

Romanticism was a reaction by educated elites—poets such as Wordsworth and Heine, and social philosophers like Rousseau and Thomas Carlyle—to modernity, industrializa-tion and urbanization and the perceived ugli-ness and materialism they produced. These elites effectively became vanguard opinion formers for the emerging middle classes.

Romanticism's goals may be seen as a quest for the Other, modes of experience inverted or different from those of an "everyday" world that was seen as profane and vulgar. It dis-posed people to seek out societies, real, and imagined, that were different from their own culturally or physically, or by virtue of their distance in time from the present. Among cul-tural phenomena that arose from this turning away form the industrial world were: the cult of the child, lauded by artists and writers for their innocence; the cult of the hero or the creative genius in art or literature; the desire for actual encounters or represented encounters through art, fiction, and poetry, with peasant and native communities, seen as simple folk or noble savages (Ellinson, 2001); the elevation of wild or picturesque nature over modern cityscapes as places to commune, versify, paint pictures of or keep holiday journals about (Hussey, 1927; Andrews, 1989); and the cult of the past, par-ticularly the medieval past, which influenced art, architecture, and literature (Charlesworth, 2002; Clark, 1962). And last, but not least, Romanticism stimulated new kinds of fasci-nation with death, the greatest "Other" of all.

The Cult of Feeling—Romantic Subjectivity

In addition to prescribing objects in the external world worthy of encounter, Romanticism inculcated characteristic modes of subjective response to them. The lynchpins of this subjectivity were feeling and emotion, rather than rationality and detachment—which had been dominant modes for cultivated people during the Enlightenment period that immediately preceded Romanticism. The objective order, in short, was replaced by "the principle of subjective reference" (Furst, 1969: 18). Romanticism privileged individualism, the liberated imagination, fresh and authentic responses to the world, and appropriate emotional displays.

Such displays might comprise: transports of delight at the charm of peasant families observed in another country; quasi-religious worship of natural beauty; astonished reverence in the contemplation of great art or literature; and outbursts of pathos and conspicuous mourning before death.

One element in the repertoire of Romantic subjectivity was appreciation of the sublime. The sublime was originally a concept about personal greatness and elevation of mind, associated with the work of the Roman author Longinus, which had persisted and evolved for nearly two millennia (Monk, 1960). In 1757, it was distinctively reformulated by Edmund Burke in a treatise (Burke, 1958), which had a profound influence on Romantic attitudes to art, literature, landscape and, crucially, to tourism. Burke asserted that the sublime was an aesthetic response, pleasure produced by exposure to things that inculcated terror and awe. Sublimity might be the effect of magnitude, impenetrability, or isolation produced by such concepts and phenomena as infinity, darkness, solitude, vacuity and uniformity.

It could also be a vicarious pleasure in pain:

> Whatever is fitted in any sort to excite the ideas of pain, and danger, that is to say, whatever is in any sort terrible, or is conversant about terrible objects, or operates in a manner analogous to terror, is a source of the sublime … The idea of bodily pain, in all the modes and degrees of labor, pain, anguish, torment, is productive of the sublime; and nothing else in this sense can produce it. (Burke, 1958: 13–14)

All these sublime effects could be encountered by travel that revealed untamed nature in crashing waterfalls, ice-bound wastes, dizzying peaks, dangerous seas, frightful chasms, mighty storms, volcanoes, earthquakes; and in human affairs through displays of conspicuous power, ritual pomp and splendor, and in some of the grander memorials to the distant dead.

Romanticism, like the Renaissance three hundred to four hundred years earlier, helped to reconstruct individual subjectivity—how a person felt and what he or she felt, but unlike Renaissance frames of mind and reference which were largely potent among small aristocratic and educated elites, Romanticism permeated down the educational and social scale and affected a broader swathe of people. Its fans were the expanding middle class created during the Industrial Revolution, which provided the first generations of mass tourists in the late eighteenth and nineteenth centuries.

The Past, Death and Dying—The Age of the Beautiful Death and the Terrifying Murder

Many of the distinctive features of Romanticism just described impacted on attitudes to death and travel. Death was a major subject of Romantic art, literature, and travel. Romanticism turned death into sensibility—not so much a religious and moral meditation in the medieval, *memento mori* tradition, as an imaginative dwelling on fatality for aesthetic gratification. It was part of the general imaginative pull of the past, which is, of course, mainly constituted by the dead. Romanticism reclaimed the past, not just for historical research, the building of genealogical trees, the determination of heraldic details of local family histories, the measurements of monastic ruins—all the preoccupations of the antiquarian and gentleman dilettantes—but as a stimulus to more subjective, imaginative feelings. The past was revaluated for contemplation and subjective epiphanies articulated as the romance of Middle Ages, the atmospherics of time-worn ruins (Macaulay, 1953: passim), and the poignancy of the dead commemorated on monument or in epitaph. All became subjects for melancholic travel. Under the influence of Romanticism tourists became great lookers at graves; reflectors in cemeteries such as Campo Santo locations in Naples or Pisa; awestruck sightseers at ruined monasteries such as Tintern, Rievaulx, or Fountains; and visitors of battlefields such as Flodden and Waterloo. Epitaph hunting and brass rubbing became popular from the late eighteenth century onwards and throughout the Victorian period, hobbies that naturally disposed enthusiasts to travel widely to hunt down interesting examples (Seaton, 2002b).

Romanticism created the "age of the beautiful death" in which art and literature aestheticized and sentimentalized dying and death bed scenes and made them into set pieces of stylized and heart-rending emotion. Poets wrote graveyard tributes to the celebrated dead, particularly if they were young, beautiful and talented like Shelley or Keats, in the same way that rock shrines have since grown up to dead musicians. One product of this aestheticization was that gravestone memorials and mausoleums came to be more baroque, florid with marble angels, floral motifs, and heraldic trumpets (Curl, 1972, 1980, 2000, 2002; Robinson, 1996).

Not all kinds of fatality were sentimentalized. One of the offshoots of Romantic sensibility was the gothic frame of mind, which celebrated fatality in more robust ways. This was a literary taste for the morbid and sensational, which had been stimulated during the last half of the eighteenth century in novels by Horace Walpole, Anne Radcliffe, M.G. Lewis, C.R. Maturin, and others. The main ingredients of gothic horror were: a sensational plot which often had innocent young women imprisoned or beset by evil barons or sinister monks attempting to rob

them of their inheritances, or virtue or both; settings in castles, monasteries, old houses, or picturesque ruins with secret passages, hidden rooms, underground dungeons, and other occluded recesses; and storylines involving murder and assassination, dismal incarcerations, torture, ghostly appearances, and hauntings (Davenport-Hines, 1998; Railo, 1926).

Gothic novels often had a very specific geography. Mighall (1999) has shown how the settings of the early ones commonly featured southern European, Catholic countries—southern Italy, Spain, and Portugal. To English Protestant audiences, brought up on Foxe's *Book of Martyrs*, these represented superstition, the Inquisition, treachery, corruption, sin and transgression (Sage, 1988). Later the topography of mid-Victorian horror stories expanded into urban settings in London and Paris, thus "locating terrors and mysteries in criminalized districts in the heart of the modern metropolis" (Mighall, 1999: xiv).

The themes and settings of the gothic novel helped to expand tourism possibilities. Southern Europe came to seem even more "otherly." Castles with dungeons and haunted houses became standard tourist targets, and, at a more popular level, less educated audiences flocked to funfair attractions to take "ghost rides" complete with painted skeletons and open graves painted on their marquees.

Romanticism thus shifted contemplation of death from an essentially religious matter in the public, communal sphere as it had been in the Middle Ages, to the private sphere by focusing not on the moral or religious significance of death, but on its significance in the realm of individual aesthetics—that of personal taste and leisure. It became a discursive field of consumption, a spectator sport like tourism. Heritage, antiquarianism, and Romanticism, which in time became inextricably mixed in the public mind, disposed people to travel to make vicarious contact with death while they were on vacation. The results were that, as religious pilgrimage declined in Protestant countries, new kinds of secular-sacred, sightseeing tours evolved to locations associated

Photo 29.4   The Gothic Tower House and Cemetery built by the eccentric writer, William Beckford in 1820s, now owned by the Landmark Trust and available for holiday renting.
Photo: Tony Seaton.

with national or aesthetic celebrities. Museums came to evolve from simply being "cabinets of curiosities" (collections of miscellaneous, naturally-occurring, physical exhibits—minerals, fossils, stuffed specimens, etc.) and historical and archaeological objects (coins, swords, spears), to providing personalized displays, themed around a few primary ex votos, celebrating the life and death of the talented, the notorious, or the merely well known. A writer's desk, a poet's guitar, the lock of hair of an artist, or the coach of Napoleon could be displayed as Thanatouristic exhibits by entertainment providers like Madame Tussauds (Chapman, 1985) to attract visitors in the same way that a London publican in the 1990s bought an expensive Elvis Presley autograph to have framed in his pub, and the dresses of Princess Diana have been put on display as ex votos of Britain's leading secular, royal saint. This aestheticization of death also resulted in a taste for travel to graveyards, cemeteries (Sears, 1989: 87–121; Seaton, 2002b), and sites where charismatic and canonical figures had died (Hall, 1853), as well as to locations associated

with historical battles, traumas, and disasters (Howitt, 1840).

From the Romantic period, through the Victorian era, and down to this day there was a great expansion of travel which included these thanatouristic elements. Travel books, memoirs and diaries record visits to locations of death and violence, both contemporary and historical, including: castles, prisons, graveyards, battlefields (Seaton, 1996).

Romanticism then engendered two kinds of mind sets: a cult of sensibility and sentimentality that was significantly bound up with responses to death; and a more covert, slightly sadomasochistic mentality, expressing the vicarious pleasures of terror, fostered by the sublime and the gothic (see Photo 29.4).

Summary

The importance of the three cultural forces—Christianity with its focus on fatality, antiquarianism with its project of constructing national heritage out of the "ruins of time," and

Romanticism, with its deep impacts upon individual subjectivity—cannot be underestimated in understanding how thanatourism evolved and modern tourist responses to it today. Modern observers have commented on the surprising and excessive public outbursts of grief and emotionalism associated with Princess Diana's funeral and other occasions of public mourning over the last decade (West, 2004). It may be argued that they are products of a sensibility forged by the three cultural forces here discussed. Christianity engendered a fatality-biased religiosity, focused on saints, that was transferred, by an almost Freudian process of displacement and transference, to new forms of secular–sacred figure. Princess Diana could also be seen as a part of National Heritage in a country such as Britain which, like others, has a tradition of ritualized state funerals and public nationhood displays (Bland, 1986; Wolffe, 2000) which have always attracted crowds and tourists—as they were always intended to. And from Romanticism people have learned the appropriate emotional responses to make to charismatic public figures, particularly when they are young, beautiful and dead.

Thanatourism may thus be seen as a historically evolved kind of motivational programming whose etiology metamorphosed from religious awe to the cult of secular-sacred nationalism and celebrity, responses to which were shaped and accentuated by Romanticism's cult of emotional sensitivity and subjective display. In many instances these produced an aestheticized, often, morbid dwelling on death; in the more gothically influenced subject, a more covert, secret pleasure in terror, violence and the transgressive.

Future Directions in Thanatourism: Issues and Research Agendas

Thanatourism and Thanatology

Thanatourism, or dark tourism, as we have seen, has developed in the field of tourism studies and is conceived as a subset of tourism interest. This has usefully pointed up a province of tourism motivation and attraction previously hardly noted or discussed. However, it may have also have concealed the extent to which thanatourism may be productively explored in relation to other fields of study, and it also inhibits the possible benefits work in thanatourism might bring to other social science disciplines.

One key area is the emergent subdiscipline of the social sciences called thanatology. Thanatology is an interdisciplinary and multidisciplinary social science, whose province is the systematic, cross-cultural, and historical study of death in society. Over the past quarter of a century it has developed as a discrete, legitimate social science subject, carrying no morbid stigma, to be systematically studied and explored within a social, anthropological, literary and historical context, as well as in its more traditional religious and medical aspects. This followed 50 years or more when there was a reaction against Victorian morbidity and sentimentality, provoked probably by the industrial scale and horror of death in two world wars, making post-Romantic dreams and reveries of "beautiful death" seem indulgent and obscene.

The field attracted interest in seminal overviews of death from the 1970s onwards (Aries, 1974, 1981; Curl, 1972 and 2000; Litten, 1991; Morley, 1971).Thanatology's eclectic, multidisciplinary components comprise a wide range of physical and behavioral topics, particularly located in the disciplines of medicine, sociology, anthropology, history, comparative religion, and art history. The topics of this emergent field have since come to include a wide range of physical and behavioral issues that include: the history and anthropology of religious pilgrimage structures and practices (past and present) associated with visiting sacred death sites (Finucane, 1977; Sumption, 1975; Turner, 1974, 1992; Turner and Turner, 1978); the development of saints,' cults and holy relics (Bentley, 1985; Brown, 1981; Charles, 1913; Geary, 1978, 1990; Wilson, 1983); cross cultural funeral customs and practices (Davies, 1997);

comparative notions of death and reward and punishment in the afterlife (McManners, 1981; Morley, 1971); the study of funerary practices, including the development of the commercial funeral industry, its marketing practices, client orientations and disposal technologies (Polson et al., 1962; Emery and Marshall, 1965; Jupp and Gittings, 1999); the history, design and architecture of memorials (Burgess, 1963; Curl, 2002; Esdaile, 1946; Etlin, 1984; Gillon, 1972; Ragon, 1983; Weaver, 1915; Young, 1993); the psychology of death (Kastenbaum and Aisenberg, 1974); the sociology of death (Richardson, 1987); the history of cemeteries and graveyards (Bailey, 1987; Brooks, 1989; Lindley, 1965; Loudon, 1843; Meller, 1985; Sloane, 1991); mourning customs and traditions (Davey, 1889; Puckle, 1926); and prescriptive and homiletic texts on dying (O'Connor, 1966).

All of these elements have connections with thanatourism since they may be the object of the "tourist gaze" abroad and at home. Death has, in fact, historically been a recurrent and fascinating field of observation by writer-travelers of the past who, before the professionalization of the social sciences, were *de facto* amateur anthropologists who described burial and funerary customs, remembrance ceremonies and notions of the afterlife in the countries they visited. Observation of how other cultures handle death can be found in works that stretch from Herodotus to later writer-travelers such as Picart (1727–1733), and the gothic revivalist, William Beckford (1834). Today attitudes and practices associated with death are now seen in thanatology as an indicator of many others associated with life, rather than as an encapsulated field of its own. The concept of morbidity, the notion that any dwelling on death is some kind of pathology, has a very short history, compared to the much longer and more universal assumption that it is an intrinsic, even essential subject, for reflection among the living.

Thanatourism may thus be seen as an important component of thanatology and bringing them together offers opportunity for establishing links between groups of researchers who currently know little of the others' work. And, to return to the debate about naming, the name "thanatourism" most clearly subsumes the subject within this evolving social science stream.

Heritage, Identity, Collective Memory and the Politics of Remembrance

The politics of remembrance are founded on the assumption that there are narrated discourses of history that deeply affect people, groups and nations in their understanding and valuation of their own identity, as well as others' understanding of them, and that therefore control of these discourses is a crucial political issue. These discourses are often enshrined as visitor experiences in thanatourism.

Thanatourism may be seen, in many instances, as travel undertaken to maintain or construct individual identity, however temporarily, through remembrance of people and things past, real or imagined, at locations associated with or dedicated to them. In other instances thanatourism may be seen as travel undertaken to view the constructions of other people's identity in commemorative locations. Over the last 20 years there has been a burgeoning interest in the way such popular and collective memories of identity are constructed and their sociopolitical effects (e.g., Bhabha, 1994; Fowler, 1992; Hobsbawn, 1997; Kirshenblatt-Gimblett, 1998; Lowenthal, 1985, 1996; Slyomovics, 1998).

The effect of this work has been to promote a cultural relativism that has problematized the writing of history (or rather *histories*, as it is increasingly seen) and the way history is transformed and transmitted as heritage. There is now much greater awareness of the institutional biases in commemoration and remembrance—including those relating to who are remembered, when, where and how they are remembered, and why forms of remembrance have changed or should change over time. Critical commentaries are also emerging on how experiences at sites of death, disaster and traumatic memory are mediated by various mimetic forms and processes of representation (Keil, 2005; Young, 1993).

All this work on heritage as remembrance, collective memory, and identity construction offers stimulating and fruitful potential as a basis for the analysis and understanding of thanatourism as a set of geographically specific sites, and also, it is likely, in understanding the responses of different populations who visit them and the management of such sites (Ashworth and Hartmann, 2005).

The Sociology of Thanatourism

Another major research field barely entered is that of theorizing the sociological significance of thanatourism. There are two broad perspectives that may be distinguished in existing academic work—the first is the *sequestration thesis*, and the other the *societal congruence thesis*. The first assumes that thanatourism runs counter to the way that death is treated in society, and the other that the existence of thanatourism is a consistent part of other trends in society.

The sequestration thesis, proposed by Stone and Sharpley (2009) to account for thanatourism, suggests that in the modern era death is hidden away and delegated to specialist trustees in the medical and funeral industries, so that the layman is largely divorced from the processes and consequences of death. Thanatourism is thus seen as a behavioral practice that implicitly confronts the way in which death as a subject is normally silenced in dominant societal ordering. This is not a new idea; indeed it was the starting assumption of Aries' (1974, 1981, 1985) seminal works. Aries argued that attitudes to death in history have changed by a series of transitions from the traditional concept of death as a familiar, uniform and anonymous event to the suppression of death in the modern period (Aries, 1974, 1981). Earlier still the thesis had been developed in Britain by Gorer (1965). His book, a path breaking study of death in society, was based on interviews with bereaved people on experiences of loss, aimed to ventilate issues to do with death and the dying that had been suppressed. His conclusion was, like that of Aries, that death was the modern

taboo. Stone and Sharpley have adopted this view and sought to explain thanatourism as a creative reaction to sequestration.

Such a view seems too narrowly conceived and worth examining further. It makes the assumption that thanatourism is a distinctively modern phenomenon that emerged to compensate for recent societal trends that suppressed death as the great unmentionable, whereas the theme of this chapter has been to show that it is a cultural practice that has existed and evolved over a long period in Europe. Moreover, Rojek's position as discussed earlier assumes that the various examples of tourism and fatality he analyzes are instances of postmodernity and thus are a part of, and consistent with, broader emerging societal trends.

It is possible to argue quite the reverse of Stone and Sharpley's view on the basis of impressionistic evidence. Far from being sequestrated, it can be argued that death has never been more publicly owned and represented than it has been over the last 10–15 years. There are several indicators that death and dying are prominent parts of the contemporary zeitgeist.

The hospice movement, which began at almost the exact moment Gorer published his book in 1964, had the declared aim of allowing the terminally ill and their loved ones to take more ownership of the dying process, making dying a talkable, participatory affair in which medical specialists offered support for families, rather than acted as custodians and trustees. This movement has now expanded greatly and is a national one in the UK.

Similarly, in the past 20 years there has been a tidal shift in funerary practices, allowing family and friends to manage and customize internment services for their loved ones. Examples of idiosyncratic pick-and-mix funerary arrangements now include: bikers' funerals; rock and pop music instead of orthodox hymns in church; biodegradable coffins, and idiosyncratic secular funerals where friends participate by eulogies, speeches and reflections. All these developments reverse the 1950s situation in which death was controlled by the church, the medical profession and the funeral industry.

In addition, there has been the extraordinary expansion of do-it-yourself roadside memorials, originally a practice in Catholic countries, to commemorate road accident deaths, that has expanded so widely in Britain and the USA that local authorities in some regions restrict them in the interests of road safety. This attempt by people to reclaim the streets as personal memorials does not look like sequestration.

In other ways death has become more and more an everyday part of the scene in our times in ways scarcely imaginable in the 1950s and 1960s, and freelance writers and journalists have produced guides extolling the attractions of visiting graveyards and cemeteries (Seaton, 2002b). There is also a burgeoning genre of television programs on natural disasters—volcanic eruptions, tidal waves, asteroid strikes. What passes as history on the History Channel is predominantly violent death, torture, war, and oppression. In the past five years it has been possible to watch on television: features on the progress of horrific chronic and terminal illnesses; suicide from windows during 9/11; disaster documentaries showing the poor dying of famine before our eyes on the news; the victims of serial killers gunned down; and countless instances of bodies filmed at war and terrorism sites. In retrospect it may be argued that it was only for a comparatively short period—no more than a half century or so in the twentieth century—that death was the great sequestered unmentionable.

The truth may be that death is less absent than it has ever been from everyday life, but it is only holidays that provide leisure and thinking space to engage in the reflections that may be precipitated by visits to memorials, churchyards, and heritage sites.

Motivational Research

For a decade academics have commented on the absence of work on thanatourism motivation. Indeed, the regularity with which commentators have observed and regretted the lack of research into thanatourism motivation seems only to have been equaled by their reluctance to redress the situation. There have been few motivational studies that have engaged with tourists in any depth (Stone, 2006), and thus the voice of the visitor has hardly troubled academic research to date.

With such an absence of experiential data on thanatourism consumption, academics are unlikely to achieve any credible theorizing of motivation, nor even know whether one is possible. It is impossible to produce explanations when there is no agreement on what needs to be explained. Case studies based on phenomenological data derived from consumers of different kinds of thanatourism will help to identify the range of main questions that need addressing, formulate hypotheses about them, test the hypotheses, and then to theorize what lies behind them.

Until such work is more developed it is only possible to identify the potential questions that seem worthy of investigation by inductive means. These might include the following: what is thanatourism motivation? Is it a discrete set of impulses, distinct and different from others, or is it a variant of existing ones (e.g., interest in heritage, history, religious experience?). Is thanatourism motivation a trivial or significant force in travel behavior—a main or sole motivation for a trip—or is it a relatively small impulse that might be acted on briefly as a minor trip component? Are the motivations for visiting sites that might be typified as "dark," few or many, homogenous or heterogeneous? Is thanatourism based on a common set of impulses in everyone, or does it vary both within, and between, different populations? What are the cross-cultural differences? Why does it seem to be activated more in tourism spaces than in home environments—if that is the case? What is the role of the tourism "industry" in stimulating curiosity and desire to visit dark sites? Is thanatourism normal or pathological behavior—an issue Madame Tussauds was sufficiently interested in to engage a psychologist to report on when it relaunched its Chambers of Horrors

(Canter, 1996)? How might thanatourism motivation relate to other theories in psychological discourse; e.g., Social and psychological theories of the Other (Seaton, 2009), and Freud's briefly sketched hypothesis of Eros and Thanatos (1922), as basic instincts in human behavior?

It is likely that prototypical work on these issues and others will methodologically adopt qualitative strategies operationalized through focused groups, depth interviews, unobtrusive observations, and diaries, obtained from respondent samples of people narrating specific thanatouristic experiences.

Conclusion

This chapter has set out to review thanatourism in academic discourse, assess it as a historically evolved form in European culture, and to suggest agendas for its study in the future.

It might be appropriate to conclude with the bad news and the good news. The bad news is that there are still many more questions than answers, and there are almost certainly many more still to be asked. The good news is that thanatourism seems to be a field that has caught both the popular and academic imagination and, from the number of people who have expressed a desire to work in it, it should not be too long before the current situation improves as research searchlights are turned up more fully.

Notes

1 To this day in Spain and Italy it is not uncommon in rural towns and villages to see particular holydays observed by carrying blood painted, effigies of Christ or martyrs through the streets in procession. Still more common are the exhibiting of such effigies—some as realistic as Madame Tussaud's celebrities—in glass cases for local people's devotions and the camera opportunity of tourists.

References

Alderman, Derek H. (2002). "Writing on the Graceland Wall: On the Importance of Authorship in Pilgrimage Landscapes." *Tourism Recreation Research*, 27(2): 27–35.

Andrews, Malcolm (1989). *The Search for the Picturesque*. Aldershot, England: Scolar Press.

Aries, Philippe (1974). *Western Attitudes toward Death from the Middle Ages to the Present*. Baltimore, MD: John Hopkins University Press.

Aries, Philippe (1981). *The Hour of Our Death*. New York: Knopf.

Aries, Philippe (1985). *Images of Man and Death*. Cambridge, MA: Harvard University Press.

Ashworth, G.J. (1997). Jewish Culture and Holocaust Tourism. In M. Robinson (Ed.), *Culture and Tourism*. Newcastle: Centre for Tourism Studies.

Ashworth, G. and Hartmann, R. (2005). *Horror and Human Tragedy Revisited: The Management of Sites of Atrocities for Tourism*. New York: Cognizant Communications Corporation.

Bailey, Brian (1987). *Churchyards of England and Wales*. London: Robert Hale.

Bentley, James (1985). *Restless Bones: The Story of Relics*. London: Constable.

Bhabha, H.K. (1994). *The Location of Culture*. London: Routledge.

Bland, Olivia (1986). "*The Royal Way of Death*," Constable, London.

Blom, T. (2000). "Morbid Tourism: A Postmodern Market Niche with an Example from Althorpe." *Norwegian Journal of Geography*, 54: 29–36.

Brooks, Chris (1989). Mortal Remains: The History and Present State of the Victorian and Edwardian Cemetery. Exeter: The Victorian Society and Wheaton.

Brown, Frederick (1973). *Pere Lachaise Elysium as Real Estate*. New York: Viking Press.

Brown, Peter (1981). The Cult of the Saints Its Rise and Function in Latin Christianity. Chicago, IL: University of Chicago Press.

Burgess, Frederick (1963). *English Churchyard Memorials*. London: Lutterworth.

Burke, Edmund (1757/1958). In J.T. Boulton (Ed.), *A Philosophical Enquiry into the Origin of Our Ideas of the Sublime and Beautiful*. London: Routledge and Kegan Paul.

Canter, David (1996). Horror: Continuing Attraction and Common Reactions. London: Madame Tussauds.

Chapman, Pauline (1985). Madame Tussaud's Chamber of Horrors. Two Hundred Years of Crime. London: Constable.

Charles, Mrs. Rundle (1913). Martyrs and Saints of the First Twelve Centuries. Studies from the Lives of the Black Letter Saints of the English Calendar. London: Society for Promoting Christian Knowledge.

Charlesworth, Michael (2002). The Revival. Literary Sources and Documents (3 vols.). Robertsbridge: Helm Information.

Clark, James M. (1950). The Dance of Death in the Middle Ages and the Renaissance. Glasgow: Jackson, Son and Co.

Clark, Kenneth (1962). The Gothic Revival. London: John Murray.

Cole, T. (2000). Selling the Holocaust: From Auschwitz to Schindler, How History is Bought, Packaged and Sold. London: Routledge.

Cooper, M. (2006). "The Pacific War Battlefields: Tourist Attractions or War Memorials?," International Journal of Tourism Research, 8(3): 213–222.

Curl, J.S. (1972). The Victorian Celebration of Death. Newton Abbot: David and Charles.

Curl, J.S. (1980/1993). A Celebration of Death. London: Batsford.

Curl, J.S. (2000). The Victorian Celebration of Death. Stroud: Sutton Publishing.

Curl, J.S. (1980/1993/2002). Death and Architecture. Stroud: Sutton Publishing.

Daniell, Christopher (1997). Death and Burial in Medieval England 1066–1550. London: Routledge.

Dann, G. (1998). "The Dark Side of Tourism." Etudes et Rapports, Série L, Serie Sociology/Psychology/Philosophy/Anthropology (Vol. 14). Aix-en-Provence, France: Centre International de Recherches et d'Etudes Touristiques.

Dann, G. and Seaton, A.V. (Eds.) (2001). Slavery, Contested Heritage and Thanatourism. Binghampton, NY: Haworth Hospitality Press.

Dann, G.S. and Seaton, A. (2001). "Introduction." In G.M.S. Dann and A.V. Seaton (Eds.), Slavery, Contested Heritage and Thanatourism (pp. 1–30). New York: Haworth Hospitality Press.

Dann, G.S. (2005). "Children of the Dark." In G.J. Ashworth and R. Hartmann (Eds.), Human Tragedy and Trauma Revisited: The Management of Atrocity Sites for Tourism. New York: Cognizant.

Dansel, Michael (1973). Au Pere Lachaise, son histoire, ses secrets, ses promenades. Paris: Fayard.

Davenport-Hines, Richard (1998). Gothic 400 Years of Excess, Horror and Ruin. London: Fourth Estate.

Davies, Douglas J. (1997). Death, Ritual and Belief. London: Cassell.

Davey, Richard (1889). A History of Mourning. London: Jay's Regent Street.

Dickens, A.G. (1989). The English Reformation. London: Batsford.

Douce, Francis (1896). Holbein's Dance of Death. London: George Bell and Co.

Ellinson, Ter (2001). The Myth of the Noble Savage. Berkeley and Los Angeles: University of California Press.

Esdaile, Katharine A. (1946). English Church Monuments 1510–1840. London: Batsford.

Etlin, Richard A. (1984). The Architecture of Death. Cambridge, MA: MIT Press.

Evans, Joan (1956). A History of the Society of Antiquaries. London: Oxford.

Ferrari, Giulio (1910). La tomba nell'arte Italiana. Milan: Ulrico Hoepli.

Finucane, Ronald C. (1977). Miracles and Pilgrims: Popular Beliefs in Medieval England. London: Denet and Sone.

Foley, M. and Lennon, J. (1996a). "Editorial: Heart of Darkness." International Journal of Heritage Studies, 2(4): 195–197.

Foley, M. and Lennon, J.J. (1996b). "JFK and a Fascination with Assassination." International Journal of Heritage Studies, 2(4): 210–216.

Fowler, P.J. (1992). The Past in Contemporary Society: Then, Now. London: Routledge.

Foxe, John (c.1880). In Ingram Cobbin (Ed.), Foxe's Book of Martyrs. London: Morgan and Scott.

Freud, Sigmund (1922). Beyond the Pleasure Principle. New York: Boni and Liveright.

Furst, Lilian R. (1969). Romanticism. London: Methuen.

Geary, Patrick J. (1978/1990). Furta Sacra Thefts of Relics in the Central Middle Ages. Princeton, NJ: Princeton University Press.

Gillon, Edmund V. (1972). Victorian Cemetery Art. New York: Dover.

Gordon, B.M. (1998). "Warfare and Tourism. Paris in World War II." Annals of Tourism Research, 25(3): 616–638.

Gorer, Geoffrey (1965). *Death, Grief and Mourning in Contemporary Britain*. London: Cresset Press.

Hall, Mrs. S.C. (1853). *Pilgrimages to English Shrines*. London: Hall, Virtue and Co.

Henderson, Joan C. (1997). "Singapore's Wartime Heritage Attractions." *Journal of Tourism Research*, 8(2): 39–49.

Henderson, Joan C. (2000). "War as a Tourist Attraction: The Case of Vietnam." *International Journal of Tourism Research*, 2(4): 269–280.

Hobsbawn, E. (1997). "Introduction: Inventing Traditions." In E. Hobsbawn and T. Ranger (Eds.), *The Invention of Tradition*. Cambridge: Cambridge University Press.

Hole, Christina (1954). *English Shrines and Sanctuaries*. London: Batsford.

Howitt, William (1840). *Visits to Remarkable Places: Old Halls, Battlefields, and Scenes Illustrative of Striking Passages in English History* (2 vols.). London: Longman, Orme, Brown, Green and Longmans.

Hughes, Philip (1963). *The Reformation in England* (3 vols. in 1). London: Burns and Oates.

Hussey, Christopher (1927). *The Picturesque. Studies in a Point of View*. London: Putnam.

Ichenhauser, J. (compiled) (n.d.). "Illustrated Catalogue of the Original Collection of Instruments of Torture from the Royal Castle of Nuremberg. Lent by the Right Honourable Earl of Shrewsbury and Talbot." No publisher.

Iles, J. (2003). "Death, Leisure and Landscape: British Tourism to the Western Front." In M. Dorrian and G. Rose (Eds.), *Deterritorialisations … Revisioning Landscapes and Politics* (pp. 234–243). London: Black Dog.

Iles, J. (2006). "Recalling the Ghosts of War: Performing Tourism on the Battlefields of the Western Front." *Text and Performance Quarterly*, 26(2): 162–180.

Iles, J. (2008). "Leisure and the Heritage of War: Tourism to the Battlefields of the Western Front." *Journal of Tourism and Cultural Change* (forthcoming).

Kastenbaum, Robert and Aisenberg, Ruth (1974). *The Psychology of Death*. London: Duckworth.

Keil, C. (2005). "Sightseeing in the Mansions of the Dead." *Social and Cultural Geography*, 6(4): 479–494.

Kirshenblatt-Gimblett, B. (1998). *Destination Culture: Tourism, Museums and Heritage*. Berkeley: University of California Press.

Knox, D. (2006). "The Sacralised Landscapes of Glencoe: From Massacre to Mass Tourism, and Back Again." *International Journal of Tourism Research*, 8(3): 185–197.

Kroker, A. and Cook, D. (1986). *The Postmodern Scene: Excremental Culture and Hyper Aesthetics*. New York: St. Martins.

Lennon, J.J. and Foley, M. (2000). *Dark Tourism: The Attraction of Death and Disaster*. London: Cassell.

Lennon, J.J. and Smith, H. (2004). "A Tale of Two Camps: Contrasting Approaches to Interpretation and Commemoration in the Sites at Terezin and Lety, Czech Republic." *Journal of Tourism Recreation Research*, 29(1):15–25.

Lindley, Kenneth (1965). *Of Graves and Epitaphs*. London: Hutchinson.

Lisle, D. (2004). Gazing at Ground Zero: Tourism, Voyeurism and Spectacle. *Journal for Cultural Research*, 8(1): 3–21.

Litten, Julian (1991). *The English Way of Death. The Common Funeral Since 1450*. London: Robert Hale.

Lloyd, David William (1998). *Battlefield Tourism: Pilgrimage and the Commemoration of the Great War in Britain, Australia and Canada 1919–1939*. Oxford: Berg.

Loudon, J.C. (1843/1981). *On the Laying Out, Planting and Managing of Cemeteries*. Redhill: Ivelet Books.

Lowenthal, David (1985). *The Past is Another Country*. Cambridge: Cambridge University Press.

Lowenthal, David (1996). The Heritage Crusade and the Spoils of History. London: Viking.

Macaulay, Rose (1953). *The Pleasure of Ruins*. London: Weidenfeld and Nicholson.

McManners, John (1981). *Death and the Enlightenment. Changing Attitudes to Death Among McNutt, Christians and Unbelievers in Eighteenth Century France*. Oxford: Oxford University Press.

Meller, Hugh (1985). *London Cemeteries*. Godstone: Gregg International.

Mighall, Robert (1999). *A Geography of Victorian Gothic Fiction. Mapping History's Nightmares*. Oxford: Oxford University Press.

Miles, W. (2002). "Auschwitz: Museum Interpretation and Darker Tourism." *Annals of Tourism Research*, 29(4): 1175–1178.

Moeller, Mariecki (2005). "Battlefield Tourism in South Africa with Special Reference to Isandlwana and Rorke's Drift KwaZulu-Nata." Unpublished MPhil thesis, University of Pretoria.

Monk, Samuel H. (1960). *The Sublime*. Ann Arbor: University of Michigan Press.

Morley, John (1971). *Death, Heaven and Victorians*. London: Studio Vista.

O'Connor, Mary Catherine (1966). *The Art of Dying Well: The Development of the Ars Moriendi*. New York: Columbia University Press.

Polson, C.J., Brittain, R.P. and Marshall, T.K.M. (1953/1962). *The Disposal of the Dead*. London: English Universities Press.

Puckle, Bertram (1926). *Funeral Customs: Their Origin and Development*. London: Werner Laurie.

Ragon, Michel (1983). *The Space of Death*. Charlottesville: University Press of Virginia.

Railo, Eino (1926). *The Haunted Castle—A Study of the Elements of English Romanticism*. New York: Humanities Press.

Richardson, Ruth (1987). *Death, Dissection and the Destitute*. London: Routledge and Kegan Paul.

Robinson, David (1996). *Beautiful Death. Art of the Cemetery*. London: Penguin Studio.

Rojek, C. (1993). *Ways of Escape*. Basingstoke: Macmillan.

Ryan, C. (Ed.) (2007). *Battlefield Tourism*. Oxford: Elsevier.

Ryan, Robert (2002). "Standing Where Hitler Fell." *Sunday Times*, December 15: T3.

Sage, Victor (1988). *Horror Fiction in the Protestant Tradition*. New York: St. Martin Press.

Sears, John F. (1989). *Sacred Places: American Tourist Attractions in the Nineteenth Century*. Oxford: Oxford University Press.

Seaton, A.V. (1996). "Guided by the Dark: From Thanatopsis to Thanatourism." *International Journal of Heritage Studies*, 2(4): 234–244.

Seaton, A.V. (1999). "War and Thanatourism: Waterloo 1815–1914." *Annals of Tourism Research*, 26(1): 130–158.

Seaton, A.V. (2000). "Thanatourism." In Jafar Jafari (Ed.), *Encyclopedia of Tourism*. London and New York: Routledge.

Seaton, A.V. (2001). "Sources of Slavery—Destinations of Slavery: The Silences and Disclosures of Slavery Heritage in the UK and US." In G.M.S. Dann, and A.V. Seaton (Eds.), *Slavery, Contested Heritage and Thanatourism* (pp. 107–130). New York: Haworth Hospitality Press.

Seaton, A.V. (2002a). "'Another Weekend Away Looking for Dead Bodies': Battlefield Tourism on the Somme and in Flanders." *Tourism Recreation Research*, 25(3): 63–78.

Seaton, A.V. (2002b). "Thanatourism's Final Frontiers? Visits to Cemeteries, Churchyards and Funerary Sites as Sacred and Secular Pilgrimage." *Tourism Recreation Research*, 27(2): 73–82.

Seaton, A.V. (2009). "Purposeful Otherness: Approaches to the Management of Thanatourism." In R. Sharpley and P. Stone (Eds.), *The Darker Side of Travel: The Theory and Practice of Dark Tourism*. London: Cognizant.

Seaton, A.V. and Lennon, J.J. (2004). "Thanatourism in the Early 21st Century: Moral Panics, Ulterior Motives and Alterior Desires." In T.V. Singh (Ed.), *New Horizons in Tourism. Strange Experiences and Stranger Practices* (pp. 63–82). Wallingford: CABI.

Shackley, Myra (2001a). "Managing Sacred Sites." London: Continuum.

Shackley, M. (2001b). "Potential Futures for Robben Island: Shrine, Museum or Theme Park?" *International Journal of Heritage Studies*, 7(4): 355–363.

Sharpley, R. (2005). "Travels to the Edge of Darkness: Towards a Typology of Dark Tourism." In C. Ryan, S. Page and M. Aicken (Eds.), *Taking Tourism to the Limit: Issues, Concepts and Managerial Perspectives* (pp. 215–226). London: Elsevier.

Sharpley, R. and Stone, P. (2009). *The Darker Side of Travel: The Theory and Practice of Dark Tourism*. London: Cognizant.

Siegenthaler, P. (2002). "Hiroshima and Nagasaki in Japanese Guidebooks." *Annals of Tourism Research*, 29(4): 1111–1137.

Slade, P. (2003). "Gallipoli Thanatourism." *Annals of Tourism Research*, 3(4): 779–794.

Sloane, David Charles (1991). "The Last Great Necessity Cemeteries in American History." Baltimore, MD: John Hopkins University Press.

Slyomovics, Susan (1998). *The Object of Memory: Arab and Jew Narrate the Palestinian Village*. Philadelphia: University of Pennsylvania Press.

Smith, Valene (1998). "War and Tourism: An American Ethnography." *Annals of Tourism Research*, 25(1): 202–207.

Smith, Valene (1996). "War and Its Tourist Attractions." In A. Pizam and Y. Mansfield (Eds.) *Tourism, Crime and International Security Issues* (pp. 247–264). Chichester: Wiley.

Stone, P. (2006). "A Dark Tourism Spectrum: Towards a Typology of Death and Macabre Related Tourist Sites, Attractions and Exhibitions." *Tourism: An Interdisciplinary International Journal*, 54(2): 145–160.

Stone, P.R. and Sharpley, R. (2009). *The Darker Side of Travel: The Theory and Practice of Dark Tourism*.

Strachey, Julia (1944). "An Attack of Indigestion." *New Writing and Daylight* (pp. 77–80). London: Autumn, Hogarth Press.

Strange, C. and Kempa, M. (2003). "Shades of Dark Tourism: Alcatraz and Robben Island." *Annals of Tourism Research*, 30(2): 386–405.

Sumption, Jonathan (1975). *Pilgrimage an Image of Medieval Religion*. London: Faber.

Tunbridge, J. (2005). "Penal Colonies and Tourism with Reference to Robben Island, South Africa: Commodifying the Heritage of Atrocity?" In G. Ashworth and R. Hartmann (Eds.) *Horror and Human Tragedy Revisited: The Management of Sites of Atrocities for Tourism* (pp. 19–40). New York: Cognizant.

Tunbridge, J.E. and Ashworth, G.J. (1996). *Dissonant Heritage: The Management of the Past as a Resource in Conflict*. Chichester: John Wiley.

Turner, V. (1974). "Pilgrimages as Social Processes." In V. Turner (Ed.), *Dramas, Fields and Metaphors. Symbolic Action in Human Society*. Ithaca, NY: Cornell University Press.

Turner, V. (1992). "Death and the Dead in the Pilgrimage Process." In E. Turner, *Blazing the Trail. Way Marks in the Exploration of Symbols*. Tucson: University of Arizona Press.

Turner, V. and Turner, E. (1978). *Image and Pilgrimage in Christian Culture: Anthropological Perspectives*. Oxford: Blackwell.

Weaver, Lawrence (1915). *Memorials and Monuments*. London: Country Life.

West, P. (2004). *Conspicuous Compassion: Why Sometimes It Really Is Cruel To Be Kind*. London: Civitas.

Webb, Diana (2000). *Pilgrimage in Medieval England*. London: Hambledon and London.

Webb, Diana (2001). *Pilgrims and Pilgrimage in the Medieval West*. New York: I.B. Tauris.

Webb, Diana (2002). *Medieval European Pilgrimage*. New York: Palgrave.

Wight, C. (2006). "Philosophical and Methodological Praxes in Dark Tourism: Controversy, Contention and the Evolving Paradigm." *Journal of Vacation Marketing*, 12(2): 119–129.

Wight, C. and Lennon, J. (2007). "Selective Interpretation and Eclectic Human Heritage in Lithuania." *Tourism Management*, 28(2): 519–529.

Williams, P. (2004). "Witnessing Genocide: Vigilance and Remembrance at Tuol Sleng and Choeng Ek." *Holocaust and Genocide Studies*, 18(2): 234–255.

Williams, Raymond (1976). *Keywords. A Vocabulary of Culture and Society*. London: Fontana.

Wilson, Stephen (Ed.) (1983). *Saints and Their Cults. Studies in Religious Sociology, Folklore and History*. Cambridge: Cambridge University Press.

Wolffe, John (2000). *Great Deaths. Grieving, Religion and Nationhood in Victorian and Edwardian Britain*. Oxford: British Academy and the Oxford University Press.

Young, J.E. (1993). *Holocaust Memorials and Meaning: The Texture of Memory*. New Haven, CT: Yale University Press.

30

Tourism and Performance

Tim Edensor

Theorizing Performance

The use of the metaphor of performance in tourism studies can be traced to Dean MacCannell's (1976) seminal assertion that tourism is a quest for an evasive authenticity. MacCannell suggests that tourists, disenchanted by the apparent inauthenticity of their lives, are searching for more "real" experiences, perhaps by visiting non-Western cultures they understand as "traditional." However, they are doomed only to find a "staged authenticity." This form of dramatic production, which typically might be a dance show or craft demonstration, organized by local hosts to satisfy tourist desires, is merely a "front stage" commercial performance that is part of the tourist product they are destined to consume. It may well be, argues MacCannell, that authenticity resides in "backstage" areas where the mundane passage of local life carries on—the home, workplace, or "the place where members of the home team retire between performances to relax and to prepare" (MacCannell, 1976: 92). However, the tourist has no access to, nor is welcome, in such spaces.

While the notion that tourism is a quest for authenticity has been subject to lengthy debate, augmentation and critique in subsequent tourist studies, the important point for the purposes of this discussion is that MacCannell's argument is informed by the sociological work of Erving Goffman. Goffman (1959) contends that the nature of social life is inherently dramatic. He maintains that in their social interactions, people invariably play particular roles in "frontstage" social contexts, driven by an urge for "impression management," removing their masks only in informal, "backstage" regions. Such a notion imagines individuals as strategy-making beings, always calculating how situations might best be engineered to their advantage. Performances are not construed as primarily individualistic or improvisational for there are particular cultural codes that should be followed in order that they are intelligible and convincing. Goffman suggests that people acquire the competence to reproduce recognizable performative conventions through the rehearsal and familiarity with social scripts. His analysis has been enormously influential in broader sociological enquiry, and the ordinary dramas he accounts for certainly seem to describe certain areas of social performance, including some tourist roles. However, they are somewhat reductive, offering a rather impoverished view of human agency and motivation. Goffman conjures up a continually self-reflexive individual, forever jockeying to achieve favorable positions in the company of others. Not only does this suggest that social beings are continually aware of what is happening, always distanced from the interaction of the moment, but it also infers that we are motivated by self-interest in all "front stage" situations, overstressing the importance of instrumentality. MacCannell also reduces the complexity of social interactions and drives in his depiction of tourist encounters and desires, replicating ideas about singular motivations in his assumptions. It is my intention to consider how performance might be a useful metaphor through which to explore dimensions of contemporary tourism by drawing upon a broader spectrum of theoretical influences that account for diverse tourist practices.

Besides Goffman, the most influential theorist of the drama of social life and identity is Judith Butler. Instead of performance, Butler (1993) uses the notion of *performativity* to identify how *gender* and *sex* categories are reproduced by actions, disavowing essentialist notions that either term refers to a pre-discursive or "natural" condition of femininity. By adopting a gamut of attributes assigned as "feminine," for instance, playing with dolls, wearing dresses, homemaking, wearing makeup and sitting "properly," girls and women continually "perform" gender, internalizing and embodying feminine identities through a repetitive iteration which seems to produce unambiguously gendered bodies (Butler, 1993). This is a coproduction involving the participation of parents, siblings, peers, and teachers who support performances that conform to gendered expectations. Most tellingly, what begins as self-conscious childish conformity ends up as unreflexive habit. Accordingly, the repetition of gendered practices makes it far more difficult to interrogate and challenge unreflexive habits but they do provide an identifiable set of cultural norms that can be resisted.

Kevin Hannam (2006) contends that this notion of *performativity*—as opposed to *performance*—is a more suitable concept

to explain tourist practices for it utilizes a more embodied understanding of identity and is also concerned with our involvements with others. Moreover, he notes, it is not a static conception but depends upon being performed over and over again to secure its apparent "common sense" naturalness. Hannam quotes from Catherine Nash, who highlights Butler's emphasis "on practices that cannot adequately be spoken of, that words cannot capture, that texts cannot convey—on forms of experience and movement that are not only or never cognitive" (Nash, 2000: 655). I will discuss how certain unreflexive and habitual enactions make up much of the practices through which people become tourists, but first I will warn of the dangers of overstressing the seemingly automatic reiteration of practical norms.

This foregrounding of identity as an ongoing process is very useful, but to distinguish *performativity* from *performance* is unhelpful for it creates a binary notion where performance is characterized as self-conscious and deliberate, whereas performativity is conceived as reiterative and unreflexive. I have criticized Goffman for the suggestion that social performances are inevitably instrumental and reflexive. Similarly, I think Butlerian accounts overstress the unreflexive in social interaction, which in turn, suggest a *lack* of agency. Both accounts neglect the blurred boundaries between purposive and unreflexive actions. Seemingly self-conscious performances may become "second nature" to the habituated actor, and similarly, unfamiliar surroundings may provoke an acute self-awareness of iterative performances where none had previously been experienced. In short, people tend to move between unreflexive and reflexive states, sometimes self-conscious of their actions, sometimes instrumental, and sometimes engaging in unreflexive habits that seem beyond interrogation. Tourists similarly move between these states, sometimes becoming aware of their performances, at other times comfortably inured to self-questioning in their engagement with tourist procedures.

Perhaps the best way of charting a course through these contrasting notions is to draw upon Pierre Bourdieu's (1984) notion of *habitus*, which is conceived as a form of *practical* reflexivity in which embodied know-how modulates unforeseen events. Accordingly, when we confront unfamiliar events (as tourists as in other realms of social life), we draw upon a practical know how, or what we might call a "feel for the tourist game." A purely self-aware consciousness would minimize performative effectiveness but a disposition towards responding to unfamiliar events and practices is also part of what constitutes the competence of tourists to move across the world and carry out a range of practices.

I want to stress that tourist performances comprise a great range of different enactions in different cultural contexts, spaces, and times. They move between the habitual and the self-aware. They may be improvisational, critical, or carnivalesque. Furthermore, they may be conformist and unreflexive, collective or individual, and indeed may be staged or performed by the tourist industry.

I will now discuss ways in which the habitual performances of tourists can be further conceived and depicted. This is particularly important in view of the tendency to generalize about tourist motivation and conceive tourism as a rupture from everyday practice and space, an extraordinary occasion when people enter a "liminal" realm, or engage in a special search for authenticity. I argue that on the contrary, tourism has become a widespread, protean practice that occurs in mundane settings, everyday routines and home cities as well as in far-flung places (Edensor, 2007).

Tourist Habits and Conventions

Tourism is replete with rigid conventions of its own, habits, and routines that shape the particular practices and experiences of tourists.

Rather than transcending the everyday, most forms of tourism are fashioned by culturally coded escape attempts. Although informed by notions about escaping normativity, tourists carry quotidian habits, and responses with them along with their luggage. Even as it extends across an increasingly vast range of times and places, tourism involves unreflexive, habitual and practical enactions that reflect common sense understandings of how to be a tourist.

John Urry (2002) points out that we are tourists much of the time whether we like it or not, and Franklin and Crang maintain that tourism is part of everyday perception, "A way of seeing and sensing the world with its own kit of technologies, techniques and aesthetic sensibilities and predispositions" (2001: 8). In a spectacular society, bombarded by signs and mediatized spaces, tourism is increasingly part of everyday worlds, saturating the everyday life which it supposedly escapes. Throughout the West and elsewhere, the regeneration of urban economies has involved the development of cultural attractions, part of a rebranding and reimaging which produces a proliferating range of consumption and leisure spaces to attract shoppers, tourists, investors, and would-be middle class inhabitants. Sophisticated retail strategies mix various shopping "experiences" with themed pubs and restaurants, festival marketplaces, amusement parks, museums, heritage attractions, art spaces, spectacles and signature buildings, cultural quarters, and ethnic or gay villages. Increasingly, people belong to spaces where the highlighting of selective cultural and historical attributes is routine. For the workers, inhabitants and shoppers of cities, such sights become mundane but they may also encourage curiosity and a disposition to gaze and consume.

This process is allied to the by now unremarkable globalization of culture in most spheres, introducing products previously unavailable, including music, food, spectacles and fashion, to produce a sort of mundane cosmopolitanism. As Franklin and Crang remark, "most people are now alerted to, and routinely excited by, the flows of global cultural materials all around them" (2001: 8). This penetration of the exotic into everyday lives and banal spaces, and the dense intertextual and interspatial resonances which resound between similarly themed and designed spaces, have the effect of rendering the exotic mundane, and diluting its power to confound normativity. Accordingly, the separate tourist adventure has consequently lost much of its power as a practice through which the everyday might be transcended via a confrontation with "otherness." This is further compounded by the proliferation of occasions for leisure that are now available to increasing numbers of people, at evening, weekly, weekend, monthly, and annual temporal scales, although these leisure opportunities continue to be distributed unequally. So frequently do many people travel that they become habituated to modes of traveling, experiencing, and consuming the world beyond their locales according to a host of mobile consistencies. These include a deep familiarity with air travel, coach tours, guided visits, and gleaning information from travel and tourism literature, as well as staying in hotels, and purchasing souvenirs and craft items. And it must be emphasized that most tourists travel with familiar others—family members or friends—so they reproduce their intimate relationships while mobile or dwelling in particular tourist spaces that serve as a "home-from-home," or what Baerenholdt et al. (2004) call "travelings-in-dwelling" or "dwelling-in-traveling."

The banal ubiquity of tourism calls for analysis which is able to identify the characteristics and formation of unreflexive tourist habits, what Nigel Thrift calls the "mundane everyday practices, that shape the conduct of human beings toward others and themselves at particular sites" (1997: 126–127). The notion of the "everyday" can partly be captured by unreflexive habit that is inscribed on the body. The everyday is a normative unquestioned way of being in the world that makes life comfortable and consistent. Repetitive tourist routines and conventions about how and when to photograph sights, communicate with others

and behave as part of a tour party are akin to everyday work and domestic routines in their unreflexive performance and their tendency to constitute a realm of "common sense," which minimizes unnecessary reflection every time a decision is required and grounds identity—in this case, tourist identity. Tourist habits, like all such rituals, are internalized through rehearsal and become ingrained through interaction with others, so that "cultural community is often established by people together tackling the world around them with familiar maneuvers" (Frykman and Löfgren, 1996: 10–11). In this collective sense, performers are subject to the disciplinary gaze of co-participants and onlookers, and the appropriateness of the performance is equally reliant upon the ability of any audience to share the meaning the actor hopes to transmit. This internal and external surveillance may restrict the scope of performances and help to underscore communal conventions about "appropriate" ways of being a tourist. In aiming for coherence, tourists collectively produce consistency of action and banish ambivalence and ambiguity. Thus, culturally bound technologies of tourism are enmeshed in diverse embodied dispositions towards reproducing the appropriate wearing of the right clothes, moving in the correct style, looking "properly," photographing and recording according to particular conventions, and expressing delight and communicating meaning in the suitable manner. Other touristic dispositions towards the desire to visit particular sites, learn something about "other" cultures or develop the self involve similar unexamined notions about being and becoming a tourist.

Yet habitual performative norms need to be continually enacted to retain their power. The prescriptive conventions and values that inhere in them are rarely disrupted if they are performed unreflexively. An unreflexive disposition characterizes much of tourism. Where this is not the case, where reflexive improvisation and a critical disposition are mobilized, the resultant ambiguity can threaten the sense of well-being that is one of the main aims of tourism—to relax and let go.

Self-conscious concern about the competence and appropriateness of performance engenders an anxiety that is not conducive to having a good time.

Tourism is constituted by an array of techniques and technologies that are mobilized in distinct settings. Thus, when tourists enter particular stages, they are usually informed by preexisting discursive, practical, embodied norms which help to guide their performative orientations. A useful account of the normative performance of tourism is provided by Judith Adler (1989), who shows how travel programs, brochures, accounts and guidebooks are "a means of preparation, aid, documentation and vicarious participation" for tourists. By following the "norms, technologies, institutional arrangements and mythologies" (1989: 1371) which are instantiated in particular places and tours, tourists reconstruct tourism, carrying out the unreflexive and conscious enactions informed by shared "common sense."

Another obvious example of a somewhat repetitive and mundane tourist practice is the staging, framing and taking of photographic snapshots at symbolic attractions. Such photographic practices are part of the common sense understanding about what to do at such sites, and are enmeshed within procedures and techniques of display, storage, and recording. The objects of the photograph and its framing usually follow very precise conventions, often closely reproducing the "classic" views of famous places. For instance, at the Taj Mahal, there are innumerable photographic possibilities involving a plethora of angles and distances. However, for western package tourists the overwhelmingly preferred shot is of the familiar view taken from the entrance, looking down the linear canal which guides the eye to the middle of the monument (Edensor, 1998). Baerenholdt et al. argue that tourist photographs are "scripted by, and acted out, in response to dominant 'tourist gazes' and mythologies that circulate in photo albums and the 'imagescapes' of television, films, magazines and so on" (2004: 70). But not only are such photographs taken to put people in

place, but the staging of family members and friends within the frame also follows conventions of deportment and expression that utilize tourist attractions as "theatres for staging a 'nice' family life" (Baerenholdt et al., 2004: 70). Here, the performance is by and for the family, which presents itself to itself in a remaking of domestic relationships, using a "family gaze" that "revolves around the *production* of social relations rather than the consumption of place" (Baerenholdt et al., 2004: 70).

These normative performances thus draw upon the mundane artifacts of tourism, which are part of the material, spatial, knowledge, and organizational networks that allow tourism to be carried out. The widely available films, disposable cameras, bum bags, postcards, guidebooks, medicaments, and clothes possess the qualities or affordances which facilitate the comfortable enaction of touristic conventions. Equally, such unreflexive endeavors are supported by travel networks from the buses and taxis that convey tourists to attractions. These ensure that performances are not distilled by the unnecessary expenditure of energy. Within these technologies of comfortable mobility, which tend to insulate passengers from the potential epistemological and physical discomfort of the outside world, tourists are able to adopt dispositions of relaxing and looking out onto the world while they are obliged to comport themselves in "suitable" fashion.

These embodied and unreflexive habits extend across all sorts of tourist practices—for instance, backpackers are as likely to be informed by particular cultural conventions as package tourists. They may wander off the "beaten track," or seek apparently unorthodox mystical, drug-enhanced, and other countercultural experiences. Yet they usually rely on *Lonely Planet* and *Rough Guides* to mediate their experience of unfamiliar places and customs, and share practical, aesthetic, and ethical aspects of "backpacker lore," usually wearing "rough and ready" clothing that transmits scorn for fashion, or is local apparel to signify "going native." Their performances often revolve around the transmission and circulation of particular norms around acquiring cultural capital, where, for example, they relate how far off the beaten track they have traveled, the authentic quality of their encounters with "locals," and the degree of material privation they have suffered (Desforges, 1998; Munt, 1994). Moreover, their relative lack of finance induces backpackers to put great emphasis on reflexive pursuits such as journal keeping, and the ability to haggle, to find cheap accommodation and food, and to live "like the locals." These contests to broadcast the cultural capital they believe they acquire through such "authentic" strategies are played out in dramas of competition in the cheap restaurants and hotels, and other sites within the networks of mobility and space they inhabit. Clearly, forms of tourism that purport to disavow "conventional," "conformist" tourists are imbued with their own conventions, their own unreflexive assumptions about what distinguishes them from the "others."

To understand tourism as solely unreflexive, within a discussion of the prevalence of tourism as mundane and habitual, is to compound over-general assumptions about performance. The degree of reflexive awareness mobilized by the performer specified as their level of detachment or involvement influences the range of an actor's repertoire and the scope for improvisation. Thus, one of the sources of tension and contestation in tourist performance is that between unreflexive and reflexive dispositions. These distinctions have been described as between "deep play" (Carlson, 1996: 24), where tourists share performative conventions in unchallenging contexts—often as strategies to minimize disorientation in unfamiliar settings—and enactions that endeavor to test such conventions.

While changing habits is not always easy—given that they are precognitive and affective—where they are over-prescriptive they are potentially subject to challenge, for habits provide an identifiable code against which to react, as younger generations often do. The most obvious challenge to tourist conventions comes from what Feifer (1985)

calls "post-tourists," people who participate in the guided tours, coach parties, and itineraries that characterize much mass tourism but revel in the very inauthenticity of the tourist product and mock the predictable performances expected from tourists. Such challenges are only mildly subversive and seem to exemplify what Goffman calls "role-distance," here expressed as a reflexive awareness of the constructed nature of a role but an unwillingness to challenge it. For instance, post-tourists affect mock astonishment and reverence when they witness a highly symbolic or famous site, or criticize it. Such is the case at the Taj Mahal (Edensor, 1998) where orthodox notions about how the attraction should be gazed upon romantically and beheld with intense seriousness are undermined when visitors refuse to acknowledge the building's beauty but point to the extravagance of its design or exclaim that it was "nothing special." Post-tourists are also apt to perform cynically in front of the camera, pulling ridiculous faces, or posing comically. They may take photographs of objects that appear to exemplify the banality of mass tourism, or conversely might be considered to be entirely non-touristic. Such critical commentary is an increasingly common feature of travel blogs and tourist chat pages on the Internet.

Besides these "post-tourist" performances, sometimes tourists engage in more rebellious performances that refuse to conform to the roles expected of them. This often results from frustration at the limitations that are placed on their time and movement, particularly on highly managed tours. Again, an example from The Taj Mahal highlights this nonconformity with expectations. Before a coach party of English tourists disembarked, they were told by their tour guide that after 30 minutes they were to gather at the exit to the monument so that they could fulfill the day's schedule (so they could visit a marble craft emporium where the guide might reap commission from any tourist purchases). This short stop produced consternation among many in the party, who felt that this was insufficient time to visit what was, after all, the highlight of their weeklong trip to India, and would not allow them enough opportunities to photograph and gaze upon the famous mausoleum. By loud collective protest and a refusal to countenance going to the shop, the tourists were able to gain a small concession from the tour organizers by negotiating an extra half-hour at the site.

Resistance against the directors and choreographers of performance can be a reaction to the over-zealous prescription of roles. However, where performances are more amorphous and open-ended, and scripts and actions are not tightly managed, "There is scope for lying, creative ambiguity, deliberate misdirection ... improvised codings of subversive messages" (Palmer and Jankowiak, 1996: 236). Tourists may deviate from organized tours in ways akin to how, according to Michel de Certeau (1984), pedestrians (temporarily) transform public space and transmit alternative meanings by using "tactics" to reappropriate space.

Yet, as we have seen with backpackers, along with other tourists who endeavor to escape from the itineraries, destinations and procedures of much tourism, this is more easily said than done. It is usually the case that other kinds of performative norms become established. It is true that the expansion of tourism has produced a plethora of tourist destinations and tourist activities that continually expand. Now specialist tourisms might revolve around visits to nuclear power stations (Sullivan, 2004), war zones, European housing estates (Halgreen, 2004), and a host of other unorthodox venues, yet however far off the "beaten track" such ventures stray, the tendency is for performative norms to become instantiated in the routines of travel.

More crucially, however, an over-emphasis on the unreflexive iteration of mundane performances misunderstands the nature of the mundane and the everyday. For everyday life is not merely full of robotic enactions but contains a multitude of other potentialities. The everyday is also "polydimensional: fluid, ambivalent and labile" (Gardiner, 2000: 6). The everyday contains "redemptive moments

that point towards transfigured and liberated social existence," and "transgressive, sensual and incandescent qualities" (Gardiner, 2000: 208). Likewise, Harrison says that "in the everyday enactment of the world there is always immanent potential for new possibilities of life" (2000: 498). This emergent quotidian process is open-ended, fluid and generative, concerns becoming rather than being, is a sensual experiencing and understanding that is "constantly attaching, weaving and disconnecting; constantly mutating and creating" (Harrison, 2000: 502). Thus the immanent experience of the everyday—the daydreams, disruptions, and sensual intrusions—constantly threaten to undermine the structure laid down by habit. Accordingly, the similarity between tourism and the everyday must also allow for a transcendence of the banal. The scope for this transcendence will be examined shortly.

Staging Tourism

It should be apparent that specific performances need a particular stage and audience for their realization and it is to a discussion of the various stages or spaces in which tourist performances occur that I now turn.

To develop my argument that tourism can be conceived as a habitual practice rather than an extraordinary pursuit, I contend that the increasing range of tourist spaces are akin to the "taskscapes" described by Ingold and Kurttila (2000), who argue that the grounding of routine performance is achieved through regular, sensual interaction with familiar space. Here, I will develop the concept of "touristscape" to account for the particular characteristics of tourist stages.

Ingold and Kurttila (2000) distinguish "taskscapes" as everyday spaces that are fostered by the ways in which habits and habitation recreate local and domestic space and render it comfortable and homely, providing an unquestioned backdrop to daily tasks, pleasures, and routine movement. This is the terrain on which quotidian maneuvers and modes of dwelling are unreflexively carried out, a habitat organized to enable continuity and stability, and recreated by regular existential practices. These taskscapes can be likened to the many tourist spaces to which we become accustomed. Similarly, enmeshed in routines, tourists possess a practical, unreflexive knowledge of such spaces; what to do there, where to go, how to look and what to look at. These taken-for-granted spaces are realms in which tourists dwell as "habituated body subjects" (Ingold and Kurttila, 2000: 90–91). There exist constraints and opportunities that inhere in the specific qualities of tourist space and these merge with bodily dispositions that have emerged from routine practices that become embedded over time. Such space is not only understood and experienced cognitively but is approached with what Crouch (2003) calls "lay geographical knowledge," through which the influences of representations and semiotics are melded with sensual, unreflexive, practical knowledge.

The "taskscape" accommodates unreflexive modes of dwelling and of "being-in-the-world," of mundanely organizing and sensing familiar environments. Sensuous knowing is practical, a flexible skill which can adapt to new circumstances and continuously emerges out of an unfixed and improvisatory disposition, which nevertheless is influenced by conventions and traditional practice. Thus, such sensual, knowledgeable practices make space. They are part of the ways in which people inhabit place and come to belong in it.

The coherence of normative tourist performances depends on their being performed in familiar "theaters." Accordingly, different tourist ventures are carried out upon particular stages—on beaches and mountains, in cities, heritage sites, museums, and theme parks. These settings are distinguished by the extent to which they are bounded spaces, whether physically or symbolically, and the degree to which they are organized—or *stage-managed*—to provide and sustain common sense understandings about what activities should take place. A cast of directors, stage-managers, and choreographers support tourist performance, guiding tourists along particular routes and arranging their photographic performances. They maintain stages in an organized state so as to minimize any disruptions, and reinforce collective norms.

Together with the physical and social qualities of tourist space, such stage-management regularizes the particular kinds of performances which occur, the degree to which they are regulated and controlled, the boundaries which typically delimit the scope of enactions, and the potential for improvisation and challenge. Touristscapes may also be cluttered with other actors playing different roles, full of shifting scenes and random events or juxtapositions. To explore these different forms of stage, I have written elsewhere of the distinction between "enclavic" and "heterogeneous" space (Edensor, 1998, 2001).

To exemplify the highly regulated characteristics of serial touristscapes, I will first consider what I have described as "enclavic" tourist spaces. Here I am referring to the resorts, restaurants, hotels, tour buses, and whole network of intersecting spaces which contain familiar amenities including tour operators, health, sports and beauty facilities, shops, banks, and information services. It is in such realms that the comfortable performative habits of tourists are most easily identifiable and the qualities of this highly managed space facilitate such enactions.

These sites, in which tourism is unambiguously the preferred mode of practice, depend, first, upon the extremely tight management of a host of tourist workers to ensure that spatial qualities and modes of social organization are maintained. This is a huge endeavor that is usually overlooked by tourists. However, places retain their meaning and purpose through such endless work. Cleaners, receptionists, and guides participate in stage management, making sure that any activity or artifact or anything else "out of place" is removed so as not to disrupt the normative spatial associations of comfort, convenience, entertainment, relaxation and leisure.

Second, on guided tours, guides direct tourists to look at particular features, deliver potted and highly scripted accounts about selective points of interest, and encourage tourists to take photographs from a limited set of "ideal" vantage points. These tour personnel also choreograph tourists' movements, chaperoning them along prescribed paths, and restraining those who stray. Thus, "appropriate" behavior and normative performative procedures are regulated by these key personnel.

It is also vital that *materialities* should not be neglected, for the understanding of, and engagement with space, does not only emerge out of discursive and representational epistemologies. It is therefore essential to acknowledge the *affordances* of place and space, those qualities that are spatial potentialities, constraining and enabling a range of actions. The surfaces, textures, temperatures, atmospheres, smells, sounds, contours, gradients, and pathways of enclavic tourist space encourage humans—given the limitations and advantages of their normative physical abilities—to follow particular courses of action. They produce an everyday practical orientation dependent upon a multisensory apprehension of place and space. These serial affordances thus inform a practical engagement which becomes part of "second nature" for tourists (Edensor, 2006).

Such spaces are implicitly designed to minimize disorderly experience and cultivate the art of relaxation through a battery of architectural, design and managerial techniques. All harsh sensations are kept to a minimum through the reproduction of modulated soundscapes, tactilities, smells, and scenes. The design of hotel and resort enclaves is typified by the rigorous monitoring of clutter, so that preferred paths are well-maintained, shrubbery pruned, lawns mowed and an aura of spaciousness prevails in which any distracting sights that might intrude from outside are banished. Space is organized to encourage a performative disposition to gaze upon such spectacles and scenes by various techniques. These include the positioning of key features

at the end of uncluttered passages, the installation of information boards and markers, and the installing of benches at preferred spots. The visual predominates and tourists are able to "take possession of objects and environments, often at a distance" (Urry, 2002: 147). Strong smells, loud noises and rough textures are kept at bay as incense wafts through hotel lobbies and scented blooms thrive in their gardens, while soundscapes comprised of the tinkle of fountains and piped music pervade space. An organized smoothness ensures that bodies perform unhindered movement towards destinations and cushioned furniture and air conditioning persuade bodies to relax in habituated fashion. Paths are swept, floors polished, guidance provided and rooms serviced. Despite their spatial homogeneity, the stage scenery typically features a few selective "exotic" items sparsely displayed, providing a gesture to an imagined difference of the world beyond. Yet to keep this world at a safe distance, tall fences are built and security guards patrol the perimeter. As I have stressed, these stages cajole conformist performances by virtue of their organizational and material qualities, yet where tourists contravene these conventions—for instance, where they fail to stick to schedules—they might be upbraided by hotel personnel, and more importantly, by the frosty glare of fellow tourists.

Crucially, these enclavic touristscapes are comprised of interlinked sites that are sewn together on tour itineraries. While movement between these sites is required, typically this takes the form of traveling in a mobile enclave, typically the air-conditioned tour bus, which conveys tourists from hotel to attraction to restaurant to emporium to attraction and back to the hotel. The predictability of these limited spatial explorations over a restricted time, together with the inhabitation of familiar hotels and environments, constitute the banal, satisfyingly predictable ventures typical of much tourism. These are experiences that can be realistically anticipated and enjoyed in comfort. It is vital to acknowledge the mundane pleasures of such tourism, for to impugn the desire for predictability, comfort, convenience, and relaxation in familiar space, seems perverse.

However, these highly regulated stages do provide their own limitations for tourist performance, a characteristic that sometimes results in frustration for those who have come to experience cultural "otherness." For their incorporation into tightly structured tour timetables means they may have very little time to venture beyond the schedule or into the world beyond. Typically, hotel personnel, preoccupied with managing tourist time, develop strategies to keep guests "captive" so that they spend money in the hotel complex or in the associated businesses visited during tours. One tactic is to exaggerate the dangers that might greet tourists outside, a tactic that can lead to dissatisfaction and a desire, even a decision, to transgress this particular stage and venture outside (see Edensor, 1998).

Largely, however, in such locations, tourists themselves prefer to dwell and move within familiar space, and here, the reiteration and direction of "appropriate" tourist performances can disguise the actual contingency of performance and the innumerable performative possibilities that are available. Yet the potential confrontation with difference that tourism can facilitate can stimulate a desire to force oneself to challenge habitual enactions or to experiment by playing unfamiliar roles. While cultural, sensual, and spatial strangeness may render visitors unable to develop any practical sense of how to perform—how to move and comport themselves—it has the potential to provide a stimulating experience in its distinction from the familiar enclave. Other than the mild rebellions and subversions that occur, this may be difficult to carry out in highly organized tourist spaces. But there are other kinds of tourist space where such opportunities are available.

I have drawn a distinction between enclavic and heterogeneous tourist spaces (Edensor, 1998, 2001)—or touristscapes—and by following this schematic distinction we can explore the parameters of tourist performance and the importance of considering the

characteristics of the spatial stages upon which performance occurs.

The most important feature of heterogeneous tourist space is that it is not dominated by a single purpose function as in enclavic tourist space. Furthermore, it also lacks clear boundaries and is regulated according to different imperatives. Heterogeneous tourist space contains tourist facilities as well as work places, schools, meeting and eating places, informal and formal leisure sites, transportation termini, bathing points, political headquarters, offices, administrative centers, places of worship, and temporary and permanent dwellings. These assemblages defy the dichotomies of public and private, and work and leisure. Typically, such spaces are characterized by mild regulation and a labyrinthine structure, enabling the multidirectional flows of different bodies and vehicles and facilitating a wide range of movement. In contrast to a themed or manicured appearance, a bricolage of designs and signs mingle among carefully decorated and unkempt facades. Additionally, distractions and diversions, and a shifting series of juxtapositions, can provide surprising and unique scenes, which interrupt the tourist gaze. In terms of bodily movement, unlike the linear progression experienced on guided tours, in heterogeneous tourist space it is difficult to move in a straight line. Instead tourists must weave around obstacles and be alert to other people, traffic, and animals. This jostling means that there is continuous touching of others and weaving among bodies. The different textures brushed against and underfoot render the body aware of diverse tactile sensations. The "smellscapes" in such spaces may be rich and varied, jumbling together pungent aromas to produce intense "olfactory geographies." Likewise, the combination of noises generated by numerous human activities, animals, forms of transportation, and performed and recorded music, produces a changing symphony of diverse pitches, volumes, and tones. Moreover, these aromas and noises are part of constantly changing soundscapes and smellscapes, in contrast to the regulated sensory and aromatic environments of enclavic tourism. The body must continually confront a more variegated set of sensual stimuli than the one that prevails in enclavic tourist space.

Habituation in such spaces means that the codes of conduct can be quickly learnt. However, if they initially seem entirely alien, they can thwart the practice of tourism. Bereft of fellow tourists carrying out habitual enactions, stage managers, cues, props, and sensual familiarity, such spaces might be devoid of the reference points that facilitate particular orientations and choreographies. In such spaces, some tourists may feel entirely overwhelmed and unable to perform—they lack the competence to engage in tourist practice and, in any case, familiar tourist roles might lack coherence in these settings. Such a situation evokes the "vertigo" described by Caillois wherein perception is temporarily destabilized by a "foregrounding of physical sensation, an awareness of the body set free from the normal structures of control and meaning" (1961: 13), and entry into unregulated and indefinable space. The deliberate foregrounding of the body and the senses, and the dismissal of normative ways of understanding and performing is akin to what Schechner calls "dark play," full of "unsteadiness, slipperiness, porosity, unreliability and ontological riskiness" (1993: 39). This may produce an existential anxiety, acute self-consciousness and an urgent return to familiar space. However, many tourists seek out heterogeneous spaces, reveling in unexpected social encounters and sensual stimuli where constant mental and physical disruption denies habitual tourist experience and performance.

For instance, an example of improvisatory tourist performance is barter, into which many Western tourists to non-Western settings are initiated in their dealings with local traders. The performance of barter has been described by Buie as a sensual as well as economic activity; an "art," "ritual" and "dance of exchange" (1996: 227). It is a dramatic encounter characterized by improvisatory response, including humor, melodrama and irony. The search for "different" experiences implies a desire to extend the roles available in mundane life. Accordingly, there are a growing range of tourist activities which promise an escape from the normative range of performance by promoting "limit experiences" (Rojek, 2000: 151–156). For example, there are an increasing multitude of adventure sports on offer where physical and mental endurance can be tested and bodies jolted out of their usual comportment. There are also rave and dance tourisms where a transcendence of everyday states through movement and drug taking are sought (Saldanha, 2002), as well as forms of sex tourism which involve "testing and challenging routine moral and cultural boundaries" (Rojek, 2000: 152). Not knowing what to think or how to act gives these endeavors their potency by calling upon the resourcefulness of the performer to act according to contingency.

I am not suggesting that these tourist practices do not also follow particular performative codes. For instance, adventure tourism promises risk but is, in fact, saturated with strict forms of safety that effectively minimize danger. But such codes are generally looser and do allow for greater improvisation. However, some more radical forms of tourism take place in settings where there is no tourist infrastructure at all, and thus no performative conventions to follow. Several accounts are exemplary here. Nick Papadimitriou (2006) describes his investigation of Bedfont Court Estate, a colony of derelict smallholdings, at the site designated for Heathrow Airport's Terminal 5, which culminates in his being apprehended by antiterrorist police. The collection edited by Franck and Stevens (2007) features voyages through abandoned and deserted spaces. Alphonso Lingis relates his journey to Antarctica where he becomes absorbed by an egoless communion with nature (Fullagar, 2000). Finally, Valerie Plumwoods's (Cited by Fullagar, 2000) dangerous journey into Australian crocodile territory on a small canoe, which culminates in her becoming the prey of the crocodile, a situation from which she barely escapes with her life.

Dramas Staged for Tourists

I now want to focus upon the increasingly theatrical provision of an enormous diversity of tourist attractions, sites which draw upon dramatic techniques and technologies in producing spectacles, and also rituals which involve the participation of tourists themselves. Such spaces proliferate in everyday settings and expand across all kinds of space, further developing the already theatrical conventions of tourism. I will focus upon "cast members," "traditional" rituals, dramaturgical enactments, themed spaces, and mediatized sites.

It is well known that at the various Disney theme parks, the workers who maintain the running of these playgrounds are called "cast members." Here, these "actors" are trained to perform roles that fit in with their institutional setting and express attributes such as deference, eagerness to please and friendliness, and are required to wear outfits and expressions that harmonize with themed environments. Crucially, these environments are "meaningful settings that tourists consume and tourism employees help produce" (Crang, 1997: 143) and extend beyond theme parks to most tourist venues, including hotels, resorts, guided tours and cruises. Such roles increasingly proliferate in other everyday spaces, in the costumes worn by staff in restaurants and other amenities and depend upon the reiteration of corporate notions of hospitality and service to secure the desired predictability and identity.

Grand traditional rituals, such as the British Trooping of the Color, the Edinburgh Military Tattoo, Independence Day celebrations, religious rituals and historical commemorations abound across the world and as well as embodying and exemplifying prestige and inscribing ideological messages, they are often huge tourist attractions. Such showpiece events are examples of what Hobsbawm and Ranger (1983) term "invented" ceremonies, and typically involve elaborate costumes, colorful pageantry, solemn parades, anthemic music, the strict observation of protocol and precise timetabling. Usually masquerading as time-honored traditions for ideological purposes—and it is this "traditional" element that appeals to tourists—such events tend to be of recent origin. The disciplined forms of conduct and comportment are devised to minimize ambiguity, improvisation, contestation, and mockery, while fixing meaning and identity. These more sober dramas have been supplemented by a host of more convivial, expressive and affective tourist productions.

Many tourist attractions now use their sites theatrically. This often involves the employment of actors to take on particular roles, which may be confined to a particular stage or rove more widely across space. The small dramas that they script and perform also frequently coerce visitors into performing with the paid actors. These stagings are most evident at large scale military reenactments and in the dramas produced in theme parks, such as Universal Studios in Los Angeles and Williamsburg heritage site where actors play historical roles, but they also occur in more modest settings, during local celebrations and at smaller attractions.

In enclavic tourist space, the dearth of any distinctive local context in these somewhat homogeneous "non-places" is often ameliorated by the provision of craft displays, "local" music and dance performances. Typically, versions of local customs are adapted, perhaps "exoticized" for tourists, or made palatable or comprehensible through the adaptation of popular music styles and costumes, and staged in hotel space. For instance, the "traditional" dance of the African origin Creole population of the island of Mauritius, sega dancing, accompanies a folk percussive music which has recently developed to embrace an electronic pop musical form. The dance, originating as a symbolic form of resistance to the brutalities of slavery in Mauritian sugar plantations, has been adapted by hotels to titillate spectators. Political messages and overt sexual expression have been edited from this form. Accompanied by Westernized versions of sega music, locals complain that the meaning of the dance has become cheapened and diluted for tourists, so that Mauritians are now sexualized objects rather than convivial participants in their own dance. Paradoxically however, it has also encouraged the skilful production of new forms of sega music for the Mauritian pop market, and the training of actors in dance and music can be argued to have replenished a rather moribund local cultural practice (Wood, 1998).

Dramas in tourist space frequently involve the participation of tourists themselves, who are required to improvise with the professional actors. The success of the occasion partly depends on the degree to which tourists are able to immerse themselves in the role. For instance, at Quarry Bank Mill, an eighteenth-century cotton mill heritage attraction in Cheshire, besides the displays of social conditions and the working looms, several costumed actors wander around the site, approach visitors and entangle them in dramas and role-play. One such character is the recruitment officer of the mill, dressed in tweeds and with authoritative demeanor, who demands of parents that they encourage their children to work in the factory. The actors imaginatively dramatize the historical prevalence of child labor by encouraging parents to enact a make-believe role, and by playfully imploring that they do become millworkers or encouraging their hostility towards the recruitment officer, parents in turn embroil their children in the drama.

Besides these actual performances in distinct tourist settings, there is an ongoing proliferation of what Gottdiener (1997) calls "themed" spaces in specialized tourist enclaves and in more quotidian spaces. Themed shopping malls, heritage sites, cultural quarters and waterfront attractions, holiday resorts, Las Vegas casinos and theme park attractions produce simulacra of greater or lesser verisimilitude. The themed pubs and cafés of everyday commercial spaces complement these spaces. The dramatic setting provides the stage for tourists to perform particular roles in ways that vary from the ironic to the immersed,

from the self-conscious to the perfunctory. Here the intertwining of everyday media drama and tourism reinforces a network that constitutes a thoroughly dramatized landscape.

These themed spaces frequently rely on mediatized celebrity, fantasy, and fiction; the cultural styles, dramas, characters, narratives, and spectacles purveyed by television, cinema, and computer games. This is clearly evident at theme parks where rides and spectacles tend to be based upon popular films, actors, pop stars, and cartoons. And at a more mundane level we have the globally extensive Planet Hollywood restaurant chain and the Fashion Café, which rely on the reflected allure of celebrity supermodels. This mediatized theming extends to incorporating the branding of whole areas and cities, suggesting they are stages associated with particular dramas and fantasies. For example, a part of the North Yorkshire Moors has been branded *Heartbeat Country*, being the location for the British television comedy drama of that name. And after the Hollywood film *Braveheart*, which depicts William Wallace's 14th-century struggle against English for Scottish independence, the Loch Lomond, Trossachs and Stirling Tourist Board promoted their area as "Braveheart Country."

The mediatized theming and staging of tourist space might seem to epitomize postmodern notions that we are living in a "society of the spectacle," in which signs, disembedded from their cultural context, circulate freely to be depthlessly consumed. Yet the assumption there is a passive consumption of such signs and images ignores the richer cultural meanings produced and consumed in tourism. We might better understand these touristic forms of presenting knowledge and information, along with the other forms of tourist stagings identified above, as a turn away from didactic instruction and authoritative explanations about cultures, histories and places to a more pleasurable, sensual, affective and expressive

556THE SAGE HANDBOOK OF TOURISM STUDIES

way of transmitting, performing and sharing knowledge.

Conclusion: Globalization and Contesting Tourist Performances

I have emphasized that while tourism is replete with unreflexive habits, tourist performance does not involve endless reiteration but rather, like other kinds of social performance, is an interactive and contingent process which succeeds according to the skill of the actors, the context within which it is performed and the way in which it is interpreted by an audience. Even the most disciplinary social performance must be reenacted in different conditions and its reception may be unpredictable. Therefore, meaning can never be exactly reproduced and fixity must be continually strived for. Tourist venues are equally unfixed for places are not reified and fixed stages but are made and refashioned, contested, and transformed through the performances of tourists and the dramatic productions of the tourist industry (Coleman and Crang, 2002).

The instability of place and performance is perhaps particularly well exemplified by tourism, for as it extends globally, it involves the confrontation with a host of different performative conventions, as tourists come across others who carry out practices which contradict and challenge their own embodied and unreflexive ways of doing things. Thus, contrasting performances take place on the same stage, perhaps expressing different dispositions and identities informed by class, gender, and ethnicity. Tourists gaze upon attractions in distinctive styles (Urry, 2002) and there are also multiple ways of walking, communicating and recording impressions. These are, therefore, opportunities to become reflexive about particular habitual performances. As Frykman and Löfgren assert, "In a mobile culture where people constantly meet otherness, habits are brought to the surface, becoming manifest and thereby challenged" (1996: 14).

Equally, however, numerous tourist stages are sites upon which contesting performances are occurring, for at a global level, "performative and counter performative cultures abound" (Rojek, 2000: 17). For example, in the European and North American countryside, there are numerous contestations between tourists who conceive of rural space as appropriate for their own chosen activity. Thus, the same mountainous terrain may be used by walkers, fell runners, mountain bikers, birdwatchers, botanists, and hunters who all enact distinctly different practices. At winter sport resorts, the conflicts between snowboarders and skiers are fierce (Edensor and Richards, 2007). There is no sense then in which tourist performances are homogeneous, static or essentialist, and the globalization of the industry and expansion of venues and practices is likely to ensure that this remains the case.

References

Adler, J. (1989). "Travel as Performed Art." *American Journal of Sociology*, 94: 1366–1391.
Baerenholdt, J., Haldrup, M., Larsen, J. and Urry, J. (2004). *Performing Tourist Places*. Aldershot: Ashgate.
Bourdieu, P. (1984). *Distinction*. London: Routledge.
Buie, S. (1996). "Market as Mandela: The Erotic Space of Commerce." *Organization*, 3: 225–232.
Butler, J. (1993). *Bodies That Matter: The Discursive Limits of Sex*. London: Routledge.
Caillois, R. (1961). *Man, Play and Games*. New York: Free Press.
Carlson, M. (1996). *Performance: A Critical Introduction*. London: Routledge.
Coleman, S. and Crang, M. (Eds.) (2002). *Tourism: Between Place and Performance*. Oxford: Bergahn Books.
Crang, P. (1997). "Performing the Tourist Product." In C. Rojek and J. Urry (Eds.), *Touring Cultures: Transformations of Travel and Theory* (pp. 137–154). London: Routledge.

Crouch, D. (2003). "Spacing, Performing and Becoming: Tangles in the Mundane." *Environment and Planning A*, 35: 1945–1960.

de Certeau, M. (1984). *The Practice of Everyday Life*. Berkeley: University of California Press.

Desforges, L. (1998). "Checking Out the Planet: Global Representations/Local Identities and Youth Travel." In T. Skelton and G. Valentine (Eds.), *Cool Places: Geographies of Youth Cultures* (pp. 175–192). London: Routledge.

Edensor, T. (1998). *Tourists at the Taj*. London: Routledge.

Edensor, T. (2001). "Performing Tourism, Staging Tourism: (Re)producing Tourist Space and Practice." *Tourist Studies*, 1(1): 59–82.

Edensor, T. (2006). "Sensing Tourism." In C. Minca and T. Oakes (Eds.), *Travels in Paradox* (pp. 23–45). London: Rowman and Littlefield.

Edensor, T. (2007). "Mundane Mobilities, Performances and Spaces of Tourism." In *Social and Cultural Geography*.

Edensor, T. and Richards, S. (2007). "Snowboarders vs. Skiers: Contested Choreographies of the Slopes." *Leisure Studies*, 26(1): 97–114.

Feifer, W. (1985). *Going Places*. London: MacMillan.

Franck, K. and Stevens, Q. (Eds.) (2007). *Loose Space: Possibility and Diversity in Urban Life*. London: Routledge.

Franklin, A. and Crang, M. (2001). "The Trouble with Tourism and Travel Theory?" *Tourist Studies*, 1(1): 5–22.

Frykman, J. and Löfgren, O. (Eds.) (1996). "Introduction." In *Forces of Habit: Exploring Everyday Culture*. Lund: Lund University Press.

Fullagar, S. (2000). "Desiring Nature: Identity and Becoming in Narratives of Travel." *Cultural Values*, 4: 58–76.

Gardiner, M. (2000). *Critiques of Everyday Life*. London: Routledge.

Goffman, E. (1959). *The Presentation of Self in Everyday Life*. New York: Doubleday.

Gottdiener, M. (1997). *The Theming of America*. Oxford: Westview Press.

Halgreen, T. (2004). "Tourists in the Concrete Desert." In M. Sheller and J. Urry (Eds.), *Tourism Mobilities: Places to Play, Places in Play* (pp. 143–154). London: Routledge.

Hannam, K. (2006). "Tourism and Development III: Performances, Performativities and Mobilities." *Progress in Development Studies*, 6(3): 243–249.

Harrison, P. (2000). "Making Sense: Embodiment and the Sensibilities of the Everyday." *Environment and Planning D: Society and Space*, 18: 497–517.

Hobsbawm, E. and Ranger, T. (Eds.) (1983). *The Invention of Tradition*. Oxford: Blackwell.

Ingold, T. and Kurttila, T. (2000). "Perceiving the Environment in Finnish Lapland." *Body and Society*, 3–4: 6.

MacCannell, D. (1976). *The Tourist*. London: Macmillan.

Munt, I. (1994). "The 'Other' Postmodern Tourism: Culture, Travel and the New Middle Classes." *Theory Culture and Society*, 11: 101–123.

Nash, C. (2000). "Performativity in Practice: Some Recent Work in Cultural Geography." *Progress in Human Geography*, 24: 653–664.

Palmer, G. and Jankowiak, W. (1996). "Performance and Imagination: Toward an Anthropology of the Spectacular and the Mundane." *Cultural Anthropology*, 11(2): 225–258.

Papadimitriou, N. (2006). "Bedfont Court Estate." In I. Sinclair (Ed.), *London: City of Disappearances* (pp. 612–619). London: Hamish Hamilton.

Rojek, C. (2000). *Leisure and Culture*. London: Macmillan.

Saldanha, A. (2002). "Music Tourism and Factions of Bodies in Goa." *Tourist Studies*, 2(1): 43–62.

Schechner, R. (1993). *The Future of Ritual*. London: Routledge.

Sullivan, K. (2004). "Atomica World: The Place of Nuclear Tourism." In M. Sheller and J. Urry (Eds.), *Tourism Mobilities: Places to Play, Places in Play* (pp. 192–204). London: Routledge.

Thrift, N. (1997). "The Still Point: Resistance, Expressive Embodiment and Dance." In S. Pile and M. Keith (Eds.), *Geographies of Resistance* (pp. 124–151). London: Routledge.

Urry, J. (2002). *The Tourist Gaze* (2nd edition). London: Sage.

Wood, R. (1998). "Tourist Ethnicity: A Brief Itinerary." *Ethnic and Racial Studies*, 21: 218–241.

31

Information Technology: Shaping the Past, Present, and Future of Tourism

Ulrike Gretzel and Daniel R. Fesenmaier

Introduction

Information technology has played a central role in the growth and development of the tourism industry. In the early years of mass global tourism (from the 1950s to the 1970s), computer systems were used to support the internal functions of large operators in the transportation, hotel, and food service sectors. Also, central reservation systems (CRSs) and global distribution systems (GDSs)—Sabre, Amadeus, Galileo, and Worldspan—were developed first by airlines and then by hotel companies to enable travel agencies (and other similar businesses) to access schedule and pricing information and to request reservations for clients (Sheldon, 1997). These businesses became the primary users of travel information systems, thus providing important links between travelers and industry players (World Tourism Organization Business Council [WTOBC], 1999).

During the late 1980s and early 1990s these systems and the information they included were recognized as important elements for tourism product distribution, enabling them to grow and successfully position themselves within the travel industry. Mayros and Werner (1982) and Wiseman (1985) provide a more elaborate description of this development in the travel and tourism industry. An important characteristic of the growth of these systems was the inclusion of detailed information about each customer; even more important was the fact that these networks were proprietary and they were used widely by travel suppliers and agents, thus creating high barriers to entry. As a consequence, the travel industry changed dramatically, placing emphasis on expanding strategic relationships in order to more fully exploit various business opportunities within the travel value chain.

The success of CRSs and GDSs paved the way for the Internet, enabling the travel and tourism industry to quickly exploit its many strengths. Today, the travel and tourism industry is one of the most significant users of Internet technology, which has become one of the most important communication tools for travelers as well as travel and tourism enterprises (Werthner and Klein, 1999). Internet applications and other technological innovations have influenced tourism in a variety of ways and resulted in fundamental changes in industry structures and traveler behaviors. For instance, online reservation and payment options are used by many travel suppliers and consumers and have led to the emergence of tourism as one of the most important e-commerce categories. It can be argued that the primary reason for this rapid adoption of e-commerce in tourism lies in the close fit between the characteristics of tourism products and the capabilities of e-commerce applications. That is, the purchase of tourism-related products and services typically involves the movement of information rather than the physical delivery of goods and many times occurs in an international context and is, therefore, often concluded through credit card payments. Also, the complex and strictly hierarchical tourism distribution system of the pre-Internet period led to enormous information asymmetries and offered little choice for consumers in terms of where or how to acquire tourism products. With the introduction of e-commerce, consumers were not only offered more choices but also were provided easy access to information about the various products. In addition, e-tickets are a direct result of e-commerce initiatives and have tremendously simplified travel, especially business travel. Further, destination management systems are becoming more widespread and promise more extensive e-commerce adoption, thus providing consumers with even greater access to an increasing variety of tourism products and services. Yet, e-commerce adoption and use not only provides better services for consumers but triggers ongoing structural changes in the industry (Werthner and Ricci, 2004). Beyond e-commerce, advances in wireless networks and mobile technologies promise new applications for travel that will spur continuing innovation in the industry and will increasingly influence the experiences travelers have.

This chapter presents an overview of ways in which information technology has shaped and continues to shape various aspects of tourism. More specifically, it discusses the impact of the Internet from both the industry as well as the consumer perspective. The practical implications and developments as well as gaps in theory and research are discussed. The chapter closes with a brief look at the future of information technology in tourism.

Information Technology and the Travel and Tourism Industry

The travel and tourism industry is comprised of all organizations that are involved in the production and distribution of travel and tourism products. It can be viewed as an umbrella industry with a complex distribution chain (see Figure 31.1) containing a set of interrelated businesses, such as transportation companies, accommodation facilities, attractions, catering enterprises, tour operators, travel agents, and providers of recreation and leisure facilities, as well as a multitude of government agencies (Werthner and Klein, 1999).

In contrast to other industries, it is not a physical product but information that moves from suppliers to customers. To respond effectively to the dynamic character of the industry, this information must be able to flow smoothly among consumers, intermediaries, and each of the suppliers involved in serving customer needs. As a result, information technology (IT) has become an almost universal distribution platform for the tourism industry and has emerged as the "info-structure" that supports internal and external processes in tourism organizations (Buhalis, 2003). IT reduces the cost of each transaction by minimizing print, coordination, communication, and

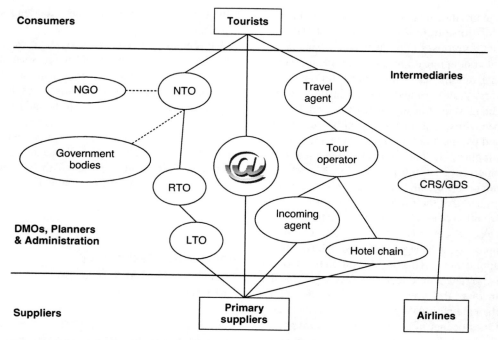

Figure 31.1   Travel and Tourism Industry Value Chain.
Source: Adapted from Werthner and Klein (1999).
Note: NGO=Nongovernmental Organization; NTO=National Tourism Organization;
   RTO=Regional Tourism Organization; LTO=Local Tourism Organization;
   CRS=Central Reservation System; GDS=Global Distribution System.

distribution costs. It also allows short-notice changes, supports one-to-one interaction with the customer, and enables organizations to reach a broad audience (Poon, 1993). Most communications and transactions are now supported by Web-based systems; however, the Internet has not been adopted equally by all tourism sectors. Certain sectors, such as airlines, have been aggressive adopters of technology, using it to help manage and streamline their operations and to gain strategic advantages (Buhalis, 2004; McGuffie, 1994). Especially the low cost carriers have long received a majority of their bookings through their websites, helping them keep distribution and fulfillment costs below those of other airlines. Further, surveys of American convention and visitor bureaus show that essentially every bureau maintains a website, with some offering more advanced marketing and ecommerce capabilities (Wang and

Fesenmaier, 2002). Others, such as the restaurant sector and small hotels, have been less enthusiastic and have only recently begun to take advantage of many of the benefits that the technology can bring (Connolly and Olsen, 1999). Many traditional travel agencies are also lagging behind other sectors in terms of technological adaptation, and it is increasingly evident that experienced consumers are often better informed than professional advisors. Given the way in which information technology is reshaping the structure of both commerce and society in general, its importance to the success of all types of tourism companies can only grow in the future. As a result, tourism companies have changed dramatically the way in which they conduct their business and are under pressure to invest further in new technology in order to maintain their competitive advantage (Buhalis and O'Connor, 2005; Buhalis and Zoge, 2007).

Travel Distribution

Figure 31.1 clearly illustrates the dramatic impact of Internet technology on travel distribution as it enables direct transactions between consumers and primary suppliers by reducing transaction costs and risks tremendously. Such disintermediation in the tourism system clearly empowers smaller suppliers, who were previously not able to obtain and maintain contacts with consumers and handle transactions without the help of intermediaries. At the same time, travel distribution experienced re-intermediation as new intermediaries, such as online travel agencies emerged (Buhalis, 2003; Buhalis and Licata, 2002). While these intermediaries provide great exposure and handle transactions, which is especially important in a global context, their yield management approaches and tight control over inventories have led to increasing dependencies. Several large hotel providers and well-known properties have opted out of this form of distribution and only allow booking from their own websites. Others have established best price guarantees and a number of incentives for those consumers who book directly with them. Auction sites provide yet another platform for distribution, which offers consumers access to discount prices and allows suppliers to shed leftover inventory. Auction models are only possible because IT makes instant updates feasible and reduces coordination costs. The latest addition, in terms of technology-based players in the distribution chain, is meta-mediaries such as Sidestep and Kayak (Park and Gretzel, 2006). They form strategic alliances with suppliers and intermediaries and provide consumers with opportunities to simultaneously search the databases of their partners. The partner site then handles the transaction. Meta-mediaries are empowered by increasingly sophisticated search technology.

Search engines in general play a fundamental role in creating traffic to travel websites. Search has become increasingly important in travel and tourism in that about two-thirds (64%) of online travelers use search engines for travel planning (Travel Industry Association of America, 2005). In addition, the Hitwise US Travel Report shows that search engines account for about 30% of upstream traffic to travel websites (Prescott, 2006). Search engines, through their indexing, matching, and ranking technologies, control what information is available to consumers and how it is presented. Xiang and Fesenmaier (2008) demonstrate that the tourism industry in its complexity and with its nuances in semantics is far from being well represented by search engines. Tourism suppliers and intermediaries, if they want their websites to be accessible through search, have to accommodate search engines and engage in sophisticated search engine optimization strategies and/or search engine advertising.

Dynamic packaging is another technology-based development disrupting established relationships among tourism service providers. Enabled through direct access to inventory databases and semantic web technologies, dynamic packaging involves the assembly of various travel products and service components into one package at the moment of request (Cardoso, 2005; Cardoso and Lange, 2007). Dynamic packaging requires instant access to information, interaction with the consumer, and adaptability. Dynamic packaging applications change the notion of collaboration in tourism as the consumer rather than the providers now drives bundling. They also challenge traditional tour operators in that they will have to increasingly retreat to niche markets not captured by dynamic packaging systems. And they require sophisticated knowledge of constraints and synergies among tourism products (Zach et al., 2008). An additional issue for dynamic packaging is interoperability between systems. With standardization initiatives having mostly failed in tourism (Fodor and Werthner, 2005), the focus has shifted towards solving the problem from a technological point of view, e.g. through semantic technologies and ontology building. The latest trend in IT development and interoperability are so-called Web services (Curbera et al., 2002). Web services are hosted on a company's server and can be used by Web users or other Web applications. Web services allow applications to freely access contents and services and integrate them into their structures. This is especially important for dynamic packaging but Web services are also used in other areas, for instance customer relationship management systems and to allow supplier sites to import and integrate contents from review sites such as TripAdvisor.com.

Tourism Marketing

The above-mentioned technological developments have obvious impacts on power relationships and structural configurations in the tourism industry. They also create new opportunities for value creation and challenge established ways in which services are provided as well as their value per se and likelihood to lead to competitive advantages (Gratzer, Werthner, Winiwarter, 2004). IT has also led to change in the marketing environment of the tourism industry. Website marketing and search engine marketing have become essential components of contemporary tourism marketing. Yet, the degree to which more sophisticated techniques have been implemented remains rather low and innovation in Web marketing is not widespread, at least not among destination marketing organizations in the USA (Zach et al., 2007, 2008).

Destination marketing organizations (DMOs) (see Chapter 24) are particularly affected by technological developments (Gretzel et al., 2006). Their "product" is destination-related information and such information is increasingly provided by other websites; e.g., those of travel agencies, portals, publishers, consumer communities, and even suppliers. Also, destination management systems (Brown, 2004) have been developed to integrate content at the destination-level and to provide a common distribution platform for all providers at the destination. While in many cases these systems are owned and managed by DMOs, private versions of

such systems also exist and could easily take over many functions of DMOs. Thus, DMOs have to constantly adapt their offerings and services to the new realities of tourism marketing. At the same time, their organizational structures often prohibit them from successfully adjusting to technological developments (Yuan et al., 2006). Especially smaller DMOs with limited resources seem to lag behind in terms of successfully integrating new technologies and implementing new marketing approaches (Gretzel and Fesenmaier, 2002). DMOs also face the challenge of increasing pressure on demonstrating accountability. They have yet to establish valid and comprehensive performance measures for their online marketing efforts in order to be able to justify their existence (Gretzel et al., 2006). Finally, emerging technologies often provide opportunities for collaboration within the destination and among destinations in a region. However, technology alone cannot overcome barriers to collaboration and DMOs have to become more and more engaged in partnership building in order to be able to realize the opportunities promised by Web-based collaborative marketing (Wang and Fesenmaier, 2006, 2007).

Most notably and recently, so-called Web 2.0 technologies (Gretzel, 2006), which are based on user-generated content and social networking applications, provide tourism marketers with increasing challenges (Schmallegger and Carson, 2008). Costly branding strategies employed by tourism marketers can easily be undermined by consumer reviews and blogs. These contents are perceived as more credible than marketer-based information and are extremely search engine friendly, thus making it likely that they reach greater rates of exposure and have more impact on consumers (Yoo and Gretzel, 2008). While user-generated contents provide tourism marketers with invaluable information about their consumers, ways to efficiently capture sentiments from dispersed contents have yet to be found and marketers have yet to learn how to respond to comments and seize the opportunities brought about by Web 2.0 applications (O'Connor, 2008). Some tourism marketers have successfully implemented Web 2.0 marketing. The big online travel agencies solicit traveler reviews and ratings. JetBlue Airways asks consumers to submit stories online or visit their touring JetBlue Story Booth to make a recording. Similarly, Sheraton presents consumer stories on its website. Tourism destinations seem to be much more reluctant, often because of their quasigovernmental status, and only a few have started to use consumer-generated content to their advantage. Switzerland Tourism, for instance, has recently implemented a user rating system for hotel properties on their MySwitzerland.com website. Those who have ventured into the world of consumer-generated media seem to be quite successful. IgoUgo reports increases in conversion by 10% for those travel sites that integrate consumer-generated content (Eyefortravel, 2006). Many tourism businesses seem to forget that travelers very often will be looking for other customers' experiences. Given the ease with which previous consumers can now generate their personal evaluations in the form of different media, prospective consumers will find them; if not on the website of the specific brand or destination, then somewhere else. Yet, the use of Web 2.0 technologies is still very limited in the tourism-marketing arena and the interactive, social, and narrative capabilities of the Web remain largely unexplored (Meadows, 2003). Ultimately, tourism marketers need to realize that word of mouth has evolved and that new technologies need to be leveraged to better capture and promote word of mouth (Gruber, 2006).

Information Technology's Role in Shaping Tourism Experiences

Studies by the Travel Industry Association of America (TIA) (2005) indicate that over half (52%) of American travelers use the Internet to search for travel information and/or make reservations. Internet-based technologies have become important drivers of change in consumer behavior. Indeed, Internet technologies have had a profound impact on the way consumers search for tourism information, construct and share tourism experiences, and purchase tourism products and services. In contrast to many consumer goods and services, the consumption of tourism experiences involves often extensive pre- and post-consumption stages, in addition to the actual trip, which itself can spread over several weeks (Jeng and Fesenmaier, 2002; Moutinho, 1987). These stages of the tourism consumption process are typically information-intensive, and Internet technologies have come to play a significant role in supporting consumers throughout this multistage process. The specific ways in which the various technologies are used in the different stages depend on the particular communication and information needs they are expected to serve (see Figure 31.2).

For instance, Internet technologies are used in the pre-consumption phase to obtain information necessary for planning trips, formulate correct expectations, and evaluate, compare, and select alternatives, as well as to communicate with the providers of tourism products and services to prepare or

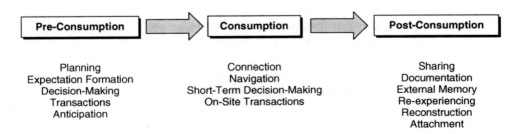

Figure 31.2 Communication and Information Needs in the Three Stages of Tourism Consumption.

execute transactions. In contrast, the functions served by technologies during the actual consumption of tourism experiences are more related to being connected and to obtaining detailed information relevant at a specific place and moment in time. During the post-consumption phase, Internet technologies are used in ways that allow sharing, documenting, storing, and reliving tourism experiences, as well as establishing close relationships with places, attractions, or product/service providers, as in the case of frequent flyer programs. For example, email will typically be used in all stages, but mainly to obtain information or make reservations in the pre-consumption phase, to stay connected with family and friends while traveling, and to share pictures and stories with members of one's travel party or other individuals after concluding a trip.

Pre-Consumption

It is in the initial phase of the tourism consumption process that most of the impacts related to Internet-based technologies are currently experienced. Consumers use the Internet and its diverse applications in this first stage of the tourism experience to gather information, formulate expectations, inform/support their decision-making, and reserve or purchase the various components (transportation, accommodation, etc.) to be consumed during their trips. The challenge in the context of tourism lies in providing consumers with an opportunity for "product trial" before the actual purchase. Tourism products are, in large part, experience-oriented intangible goods (Vogt and Fesenmaier, 1998) that are typically consumed at a place far away from the point of purchase and often cannot be experienced without being consumed in their entirety. Consequently, product trial is usually not available to the potential consumers of tourism products. However, tourism bears many risks because its components are consumed in unfamiliar environments, constitute a significant expenditure for most consumers,

and typically entail high involvement from the part of the consumer. Given the limited opportunity for pre-purchase trial in the context of tourism, virtual tours, with their ability to represent tourism products and services in more realistic and dynamic ways than other promotional materials, play a crucial role in offering rich travel information (Cho et al., 2002). The new generation of 3D applications are virtual worlds such as SecondLife, which have an even greater potential of immersing the user and creating telepresence, the feeling of being transported to and present in the virtual environment (Steuer, 1992). Immersion and telepresence are critical in establishing strong attitudes toward destinations and suppliers (Lee et al., 2008). Several tourism destinations, attractions and service providers already have virtual representations in SecondLife, the most popular and widely used virtual world at the moment, and the number is expected to increase dramatically as it becomes easier and cheaper to create a virtual world presence. Indeed, virtual worlds are seen as important Web 3.0 applications (Hayes, 2006).

Another pillar of Web 3.0 is recommendations and personalization (Kiss, 2008). Travel decision support systems can provide such personalized recommendations. Travel decision support systems (TDSS) are information systems designed to simplify the travel decision-making process and support consumers in the various steps involved in planning trips. Trip planning is a very complex process that consists of a number of decisions, which often condition each other (Dellaert et al., 1998; Jeng and Fesenmaier, 2002; Woodside and MacDonald, 1994). Also, each decision requires different kinds of information; thus, separate information search activities are necessary. This increases the cost of the information search process for the consumer and can often lead to information overload (Good et al., 1999; Hibbard, 1997). The main function of a TDSS is to identify and present certain tourism products and services in accordance with consumer preferences, thus reducing the number of alternatives that the consumer would have to evaluate. The functionality of such systems ranges from more sophisticated search engines and intelligent-agent-supported information retrieval to true recommender systems that enable the consumer to identify destinations or tourism products of interest (Vanhof and Molderez, 1994). The use of a TDSS generally requires specifying preferences such as desired date of travel and preferred activities. In their most advanced form, these systems try to mimic human interactions that could occur between a consumer and a travel agent. In such cases, the TDSS is typically referred to as a travel counseling system (Hruschka and Mazanec, 1990). Current developments in the TDSS area focus on increasing the ability of such systems to capture consumer preferences and adapt information accordingly, as well as to learn from past interactions and support group decision-making (Delgado and Davidson, 2002; Hwang and Fesenmaier, 2001; Loban, 1997; Mitsche, 2001; Ricci and Werthner, 2001). There is also a great need for these systems to become "conversational"; i.e., to be able to judge the willingness of users to provide information and receive recommendations based on the interactions they have with the system (Mirzadeh et al., 2005). Consumers can take advantage of such systems and benefit from the customized information presented to them at various stages in the trip planning process. However, the currently available TDSS versions are still more capable of supporting consumers with a clear understanding of what they desire than helping individuals with only a vague idea of what they are looking for. It is expected that these systems will play an increasingly important role in travel planning as they become more human-centric in design and truly adaptive with respect to the needs of consumers (Gretzel et al., 2006). However, this requires elaborate knowledge of the cognitive and behavioral foundations of travel information search and decision-making in online environments and such knowledge currently exists only in fragments (Fesenmaier et al., 2006).

IT also allows for representation and storage of information needs, preferences, and personal characteristics in so-called user profiles. Information in profiles can be entered by the user or derived through tracking technologies that capture users' behaviors when interacting with a site. These profiles constitute immense opportunities for content to be personalized and often form the basis for recommendations. Consumers can interact with websites through their profiles rather than having to directly specify needs and wants for every interaction. While it is typically assumed that users should not be burdened with profile content creation, elaborate profiles in social networking and movie recommendation sites seem to suggest that users are willing to invest considerable time in establishing profiles. However, users are unlikely to establish such elaborate profiles for every website they visit. It is expected that user profiles will become portable in the near future to be able to capture behaviors across a variety of sites and virtual worlds and allow users to carry over personal information when switching sites (Hayes, 2006). It seems that portable profiles, which store various types of information about the user and can be carried from site to site are particularly important in the context of travel and tourism. Tourism websites face a specific challenge with respect to user profiles in that needs and wants are very much situation-dependent (honeymoon versus business trip) and loyalty is limited in that very often destination choice drives which suppliers will be available, and considerable price differences can lead consumers to book from a website they had never used before. Portable profiles would allow travelers to communicate their personal characteristics and needs to a wide variety of sites and build a behavioral history based on visits to different tourism websites.

Mediated interactions also happen through agent technology (Bradshaw, 1997). Software programs such as bots can be programmed to alert users of changes in their itineraries, search for specific vacation deals, or monitor travel-related auctions. With advances in artificial intelligence, it can be expected that such intelligent agents will become ever more sophisticated and able to act on users' behalves, whether it is for information search or e-commerce purposes. Their promise lies in not only responding to information needs but also anticipating user needs.

In virtual environments, interactions are mediated through avatars. Users increasingly explore content and interact with others through their virtual personas. Avatars are an essential component of a user's identity online and allow for quasi-bodily experiences (Taylor, 2002), which can certainly provide important additional information to users when exploring travel-related contents. Avatars lead to a paradigm shift in communication online in that they allow users to engage in much richer communication including gestures and recently also voice. This can be particularly important in the context of travel information search in that it can provide potential travelers with greater opportunities to interact with, ask questions, and receive instant feedback from travel service providers, destination marketers, intermediaries, or other consumers.

Another type of mediated communication in the pre-consumption phase occurs through online customer support technology. Online customer support is a summary term for Internet technologies that allow consumers to contact the suppliers or distributors of tourism products if additional information or other forms of assistance are needed. Applications that provide consumers with the means to communicate faster and more easily in order to get support are especially important in the context of tourism. First, the special nature of tourism products and services (Kotler et al., 1999) makes them more likely to require additional support. It is very difficult to describe the many experiential aspects of tourism accurately; thus consumers often require further interpretation or more detailed explanations. Also, tourism products and services are usually purchased or at least reserved long before they are consumed, and many things can potentially happen during this extensive period of commitment between travel- and

tourism-related businesses and consumers. Second, geographical and cultural distances between travel and tourism suppliers and consumers render communication through traditional means very difficult. The Internet, on the other hand, provides consumers with fast, easy, and cost-effective ways of contacting the providers of travel and tourism-related goods and services. Technologies of support include "Frequently Asked Questions" sections on websites, online request forms, bulletin boards, Internet phones, email, real-time chat options, and instant messaging applications. These technologies are currently used in very passive ways, which means consumers are required to initiate the contact. However, a growing number of tourism organizations are adopting more proactive approaches to online customer support. They provide consumers with active assistance, either through automatic email updates or by monitoring the behavior of a websites' visitors and offering real-time assistance through instant messaging or chat if they recognize search or click patterns that are typically associated with a need for help, such as seemingly uncoordinated clickstreams. This innovative use of online customer support technologies actively encourages consumers to communicate with customer representatives and has the potential to prevent confusion or misunderstandings instead of following the traditional model of solving problems after they have occurred. This trend is driven by a recognition that personal communication can be more effective in resolving complaints and building customer loyalty and that IT can provide essential means for such personal communication to happen when necessary or desired by the consumer.

In addition, Internet technologies allow individuals to make their thoughts and opinions easily available to a global community of Internet users (Dellarocas, 2003), and a growing number of users actively takes advantage of this opportunity. Such online word of mouth (WOM) or e-WOM serves as important input for other consumers when engaging in information search and decision-making. Word-of-mouth information search is greater in circumstances when a consumer is unfamiliar with a service provider (Chatterjee, 2001), which is often the case for travel-related decisions. Word of mouth, in general, has long been recognized as one of the important external information sources for travel planning (Crotts, 1999; Fodness and Murray, 1997; Hwang et al., 2006; Kotler et al., 1999; Murphy et al., 2007; Snepenger and Snepenger, 1993). For instance, Hanlan and Kelly (2005) found that word of mouth and independent information sources are the key media through which respondents formed their image of an iconic Australian tourist destination. e-WOM differs significantly from its offline form in that it includes many-to-many communication between communicators who do not necessarily share any social ties and that it is much more voluminous (Chatterjee, 2001) and is widely accessible (Schindler and Bickart, 2005). As the use of the Internet for travel planning becomes ever more prevalent, travel decision-making processes will be increasingly influenced by e-WOM. Indeed, a growing use of online travel referrals for the purpose of planning travel has been reported by several travel-related studies (Bonn et al., 1999; MacKay et al., 2005). Further, e-WOM can even have a significant influence on travel-related decisions after they have been made. eMarketer (2007) reports that among travelers who use peer reviews for their hotel booking, 25% of infrequent leisure travelers and 33% of frequent travelers report having changed a hotel stay based on reviews by other consumers.

e-WOM takes on a variety of forms and can occur through email, chat rooms, or other online types of communication (Litvin et al., 2008). Especially user-generated content plays an important role in that it is often created, initiated, circulated, and utilized by consumers to educate each other about products, brands, services, personalities, and issues (Blackshaw and Nazzaro, 2004). Consumer opinion platforms, in particular, have established themselves as important venues for e-WOM (Hennig-Thurau et al., 2004).

Indeed, consumer reviews and ratings are seen as the most accessible and prevalent form of e-WOM (Chatterjee, 2001). As posted reviews are "published" opinions of consumers, they remarkably affect other consumers' decision making. Consumer reviews serve two distinct roles: (1) they provide information about products and services; and (2) they serve as recommendations (Park et al., 2007). Consumer reviews are perceived as particularly influential because they are written from a consumer's personal perspective and, thus, provide an opportunity for indirect experience (Bickart and Schindler, 2001). They are also perceived as more credible than information provided by marketers (Smith et al., 2005). According to Ricci and Wietsma (2006), product reviews, when consulted during a decision making process, have the tendency to augment user's confidence in the decision by offering a feeling of higher objectivity. Furthermore, ratings add an important quantitative dimension to reviews and add convenience and usefulness to review contents. Importantly, consumers tend to rely more on consumer reviews when purchasing high involvement products (Park et al., 2007); since travel is a high involvement product, one can expect extensive use of reviews for travel-related decisions. Indeed, Compete, Inc. (2006) found that nearly 50% of travel purchasers visited a message board, forum, or online community for their online travel purchasing and one in three of these buyers said that consumer reviews helped with their purchase decision. Clearly, online consumer-generated information is taking on an important role in online travelers' decision making.

During Consumption

Internet technologies are used during the actual trip mainly for travelers to stay connected and to obtain en route information if the need arises. The spread of Internet cafés at tourist destinations, the growing number of accommodation establishments offering (often high-speed) Internet connections, and the recent efforts of airlines to provide in-flight Internet access to travelers indicate that a substantial need for these kinds of information and communication links exists. En route Internet access means anywhere-and-anytime availability of tourism-related information for consumers. Therefore, many of the trip planning and information gathering tasks of travelers could shift from pre-consumption to during consumption and make travel much more spontaneous if the Internet becomes more widely available to the traveling public.

Mobile technologies play an increasingly important role in tourism due to their ability to provide travelers with wireless and, thus, instantaneous and pervasive Internet access. Handheld devices such as personal digital assistants (PDAs) and cellular phones supported through a wireless application protocol (WAP), a global system for mobile communication (GSM), and short message service (SMS) allow travelers to take full advantage of the Internet while on the road. More ambitious developments of mobile technology go beyond simple access by providing real-time, location-based services (Eriksson, 2002; Oertel et al., 2002). Empowered by geographical information systems (GIS) and global positioning system technology (GPS) in combination with information available on the Internet, these advanced mobile applications identify the traveler's location in space and the spatial context of this position. This information is then used to generate personalized assistance in the form of location-specific and time-sensitive information. Many advancements related to mobile technologies are spurred by needs that directly arise from information and communication problems encountered during travel. Projects such as CRUMPET— creation of user-friendly mobile services personalized for tourism (Poslad et al., 2002; Zipf, 2002)—and the development of wireless-based tourism infrastructures, for instance the ambient intelligence landscape described by the Information Society Technologies Advisory Group (ISTAG) (2001), are two examples of the many efforts undertaken at the juncture of mobile technology and tourism; yet they represent developments with important implications for the future of IT in tourism.

Information and communication technologies increasingly mediate tourism experiences. Jansson stresses that this "mediatization alters perceptions, of place, distance, sociality, authenticity, and other pre-understandings that frame tourism" (2006: 1). Access to communication technologies changes the travel experience itself in that notions of home and away become blurred (Rosh et al., 2007). Memories of a trip that is not over yet can be instantly shared through the technology and messages from home or work can easily interrupt experiences at the destination (Jansson, 2007). Friends and family at home can follow every move of the traveler if updates are posted online. Internet cafés have become part of the touristic infrastructure and Internet connectivity is an important amenity offered by hotels and sought after by travelers to be able to stay connected while being away. Digital cameras, now very often integrated in mobile technologies, allow for almost unlimited picture taking and instantaneous review of what has been experienced. New media, especially smart phones including tools such as navigation systems, can "eliminate some of the sociocultural friction of touristic mobility" and affect travelers' appropriation of foreign terrains (Jansson, 2007: 13). Technologies also create new opportunities for social interactions. Travelers can connect with other travelers and with locals through social networking tools such as WAYN.com and Couchsurfing.com. Technology also changes the experience at historic sites, attractions and museums in that it is increasingly used for interpretation and allows travelers to be more actively engaged with contents that could even be personalized to fit their needs.

Especially, mixed reality technology can greatly enhance education and social interaction in public spaces such as galleries and museums (Hall et al., 2001).

Post-Consumption

The post-consumption stage in the context of tourism involves treasuring souvenirs, remembering special moments, reliving an experience through photographs, sharing travel stories, and often developing a strong sense of attachment to a specific destination. Internet technologies play a significant role in these post-trip activities and have started to significantly influence memory practices as they relate to tourism.

Virtual communities are an example of Internet applications that provide consumers with support during the post-consumption phase. The term *virtual community* describes a group of people who are connected through computer-mediated communication technologies and share interests and feelings in cyberspace (Rheingold, 1994). Virtual travel communities, then, are communities facilitated by computer-mediated communication that allow members to conduct various types of travel-related tasks, such as obtaining travel information, maintaining connections, finding travel companions, or simply having fun by telling each other interesting travel experiences and stories (Wang et al., 2002). Consumers can use these virtual travel communities to post photographs and stories/testimonials of their trip(s) on the community website, where they serve as information to other consumers. In addition to this purely functional aspect, virtual travel communities offer opportunities for members to fulfill hedonic, psychological, and social needs. Sense of belonging, fun, and self-identification are only a few of the benefits that can be derived from online community membership. In the context of tourism, the most important function virtual travel communities serve is the extension of travel/tourism-related experiences beyond the actual

trip. Used as digital substitutes for traditional photo albums, the digital images uploaded onto community Web pages and discussion boards help recall aspects of trips and assist consumers in constructing memories of vacations. The travel stories and discussions that can be found in such communities mimic real-world storytelling activities typical of this last stage of the tourism consumption process.

Stories play an important role in the recollection of travel experiences, which are usually comprised of many different impressions and emotions. Travelers reconstruct what happened during a trip so that it sounds good as a story to tell to others. They include or omit details or stress certain aspects depending on the needs of their listeners. Thus, a story might change each time it is told, and as the story changes, so does the memory of the travel experience associated with it and possibly also the meaning attributed to it (Tversky and Marsh, 2000). Technology makes this process especially easy in that pictures can be manipulated, contents can be assembled from one's own materials or integrated from other sites, narration and sounds can be easily added, and posted materials can be assigned with different meanings through tags. The process can also be a social one in that others can post additional materials or comments. These activities prolong the travel experience and lead to distinct memories of experiences that might or might not have occurred as they are remembered.

Tourism experiences are an integral part of the identity of individuals and collective memory of families and peer groups and, thus, require sharing. Consequently, consumer-generated media have gained importance beyond the settings of virtual communities. In contrast to traditional conversations about the adventures, fun events, or other types of memorable moments of past trips, communication about travel experiences in blogs, video and photo sharing sites, personal Web pages, and other consumer-generated content sites takes place with an audience that has a very tailored interest in the topic and typically resides outside the boundaries of one's usual social circle. Blogs offer new levels of interactivity and immediacy in broadcasting a story that were not conceivable in the past and have the advantage of closely resembling traditional travel journals, which used to be kept by many travelers. Podcasts and videos add an auditory and visual dimension to travel storytelling. It is now possible to easily record the sounds in addition to the sites and narrate events for the education or entertainment of other consumers. Tagging provides an enormous opportunity to add relevance to consumer-generated stories and to make them even more searchable. Importantly, the information posted by consumers in the course of the post-consumption recollection of the travel experience serves as valid information for consumers in earlier stages, thus closing the loop of the tourism information cycle.

Shih (1998) conceptualizes *bricolage* as an important aspect of experiences in cyberspace. With the advances of virtual worlds and consumer-generated media, consumers will be provided with increasingly sophisticated ways to construct "storyscapes" and to use avatars as virtual storytellers. Also, the convergence of different technologies into smart devices will make it ever more possible and convenient for consumers to record, narrate and post stories while they are on vacation. Mobile technologies are also expected to become more intuitive and supportive of storytelling as well as of social networking. Thus, the lines between *en route* activities and post-consumption behaviors will become ever more blurred in that post-consumption will increasingly happen while still on the trip.

Implications for Tourism Practice and Research

The Internet has had and will continue to have a tremendous impact on the way consumers search for, purchase, consume, and remember tourism experiences. However, the Internet is not the only channel through which consumers obtain information, communicate, or complete transactions. Rather, it is one of many options currently used by tourism consumers. Traditional WOM, for instance, remains the most popular way of gaining access to first-hand knowledge about travel destinations and tourism experiences. Also, travel magazines and movies continue to be significant sources of inspiration. It seems that the concept of the "hybrid" consumer who uses many media and technologies simultaneously (Wind et al., 2002) is especially applicable to tourism. Thus, the Internet has not replaced traditional channels but has placed additional options in the hands of consumers. Nevertheless, many current technology developments aim at convergence and the creation of one channel that can satisfy all information search, transaction, and communication needs and, therefore, this situation might change in the near future. For the tourism industry, the Internet is clearly the biggest opportunity but simultaneously the biggest challenge.

Importantly, however, the Internet changes how people communicate and exchange information. The resulting abundance of information and ease of communication have led to profound changes in consumer attitudes and behavior. What makes new consumers "new" is that they are empowered by the Internet, which provides them with easy and cheap access to various information sources and extended communities (Windham and Orton, 2000). New tourism consumers are well informed, are used to having many choices, expect speed, and use technologies to overcome the physical constraints of bodies and borders (Poon, 1993). Lewis and Bridger (2000) describe the new consumer as being (1) individualistic; (2) involved; (3) independent; and (4) informed. New tourism consumers also exhibit new levels of mobility and needs for creativity and meaning (Gretzel and Jamal, 2007). The Internet is a highly personalized medium and new consumers expect marketers to address and cater to their complex personal preferences. Consequently, new tourism consumers are "in control" and have become important players in the process of creating and shaping brands as well as their own experiences.

New tourism consumers are also very independent in making consumption decisions but, at the same time, like to share stories about their travel experiences with members of different communities. Stories can convey emotional aspects of experiences and product/service qualities that are generally hard to express in writing and, consequently, are rarely included in traditional product descriptions. Storytelling is an important means of creating and maintaining communities (Muniz and O'Guinn, 2000) and Internet technologies greatly facilitate this form of communication and community building among travelers. New travel-oriented communities are brand communities or communities of interest and are imagined, involve limited liability, and focus on a specific consumption practice (Muniz and O'Guinn, 2000; Wang, et al., 2002). Travelers in this networked world are expected to increasingly take advantage of (or contribute) to consumer-generated content—sharing their experiences or advice with others—across the Internet's global community. This will greatly empower consumers and will force travel product suppliers to strive for excellence. It will also challenge grand narratives constructed by the media and large travel companies and will give consumers an opportunity to construct knowledge about a destination or product offering from a great number of diverse sources. In addition, this trend will likely change host–guest interactions as the new consumers increasingly seek contact with the locals through these new forms of networked communication.

It has long been recognized that travel is an experience and tourism is a key part of the "experience industry" (Pine and Gilmore, 1999). However, the role of experience in consumption (including pre-, during, and post-consumption) is only now being considered as one of the foundations for effective marketing. Research efforts have shown that the experiential aspects of products and services provide the starting point for effective marketing (Pine and Gilmore, 1999; O'Sullivan and Spangler, 1998; Schmitt, 1999). This research indicates that experiences are personal "events" that engage the individual in a meaningful way. The core element of travel experiences is the travel activity, whereas the tourism industry plays the part of an experience "facilitator"; importantly, the setting (social or personal) in which activities occur contributes substantially to the nature of the experience. It is suggested that although the experiential aspects of travel are the foundation, the memories that are stored as a result of these experiences are the key to attracting new visitors as well as retaining current ones. Furthermore, it is suggested that stories—the mechanisms for communicating experiences through word of mouth or as "documentaries" of experiences (through articles, film, etc.)—provide the path through which the tourism industry can build and extend markets.

Schmitt (1999) and others have argued that the new consumer evaluates products more on their experiential aspects than on "objective" features such as price and availability and that experiential marketing should focus on the experiential aspects that make the consumption of the product most compelling—that is, the five senses. Effective experiential marketing is sensory and affective. It approaches consumption as a holistic experience and acknowledges that consumers can be either rational or emotional or both at the same time. Whereas traditional marketing is based on consumer behavior, product features, benefits, and quantifiable market segments, an understanding of consumer experiences and the need for personalization drives experiential marketing. New consumers require advertising that is entertaining, stimulating, and at the same time informative. Brands are no longer seen as mere identifiers but become themselves sources of experiences by evoking sensory, affective, creative, and lifestyle-related associations (Schmitt, 1999). Thus, experiential marketing blurs the border between advertising, purchase, and use as it attempts to create a unique shopping experience and lets the new consumer anticipate what the consumption experience will be like.

Clearly, more information on online tourism consumers, their behaviors and their experiences with and through technologies, is needed to inform technology development and marketing practices in tourism. Current tourism research has mostly focused on technology adoption, information search patterns and demographic differences. Studies include various attempts to profile Internet users in terms of demographic and travel behavior-related characteristics (Beldona, 2005; Bonn et al., 1999; Weber and Roehl, 1999), differences in Internet use based on age, gender, geographic location, and cultural differences (Furr et al., 2002; Kim et al., 2007; Lee et al., 2007), its adoption and role as an information source (Jun et al., 2007; MacKay et al., 2005; Pearce and Schott, 2005; Zins, 2007), its credibility (Teichmann and Zins, 2006), resistance to Internet use (Susskind et al., 2003), differences between online travel searchers and bookers (Card et al., 2003), online information search strategies (Pan and Fesenmaier, 2006), perceptions of website feature usefulness and their influence on intentions to visit a destination (Kaplanidou and Vogt, 2006), the influence of Internet skills on Internet perceptions and benefits derived from Internet use for travel planning (Yoo et al., 2006), e-satisfaction (Kim et al., 2006), and the impact of Internet use on image formation (Frias et al., 2008; Seabra et al., 2007). Online experiences have been mostly studied in the context of flow (Skadberg et al., 2005). Only recently have Tussyadiah and Fesenmaier (2007) begun to examine the mediation effects of the Internet on the tourism experience. Similarly, the literature on mobile technology in tourism has mostly focused on adoption and intentions to use (Rasinger et al., 2007). While these studies have greatly informed theory building and tourism management and marketing practice, research gaps are apparent

with respect to consumer experience and use of emerging technologies such as consumer-generated media and virtual worlds as well as the consequences of IT use.

IT creates tremendous opportunities for the tourism industry. However, the effective use of IT remains a substantial challenge for tourism organizations (Gretzel et al., 2000, 2006; Werthner and Klein 1999). It is not enough to document adoption levels. What is needed is a better understanding of the organizational drivers behind IT adoption (Yuan et al., 2006). With IT changing fast, competitive advantages never last long and the industry has to constantly innovate in order to keep up with new developments. Innovation is also central to identifying new value propositions and uses for emerging technologies. Thus, it is important to understand what facilitators, inhibitors, and processes of innovation exist in the tourism industry and within its various elements. While some research is available (e.g., Pikkemaat and Peters, 2005), more insights are needed to inform the industry.

New technologies make collaboration at new levels possible. Such collaboration is extremely important not only for current success in tourism distribution and marketing but also for innovation (Pikkemaat and Weiermair, 2007). Partnership formation is critical to effective marketing, especially in an online context (Wang and Fesenmaier, 2007). Given the specific characteristics of the tourism industry, general studies on collaboration can only inform researchers and practitioners in tourism to some extent. Tourism industry professionals often see the need for partnership and innovation but do not know how to best implement these strategies (Gretzel et al., 2006). Consequently, they need to be better informed through empirical research in this area.

The above only touches upon the many studies that have been conducted in the field of technology and tourism and the myriad of research questions that are related to technology use in tourism. Overviews and analyses of technology-related research in the context of tourism can be found in Buhalis and Law

(2008), Frew (2000), and O'Connor and Murphy (2004). While the field has made substantial progress in the past two decades, new technological developments constantly demand new understandings and insights and make previous research oftentimes obsolete in a very short period of time.

Conclusion

The chapter presented a lot of evidence that the Internet and emerging technologies have had profound impacts on the tourism industry. The following briefly summarizes some expectations for the future role of IT in travel and tourism.

- Travel will continue to be one of the most popular online interests to consumers. This trend will increase in magnitude as travel providers create more effective means with which to communicate the nature of their offerings.
- The Internet and mobile communication devices are increasing the number of electronic connections between customers and the tourism industry. These new technologies will continue to provide an environment for creating relationships, allowing consumers to access information more efficiently, conducting transactions, and interacting electronically with businesses and suppliers.
- The changes in demographic profiles of Internet users over the past decade suggest that the evolving Internet and related systems will ultimately be adopted by the large majority of the traveling public and, therefore, the Internet will be considered the primary source for travel information.
- The demands of travelers, and in particular the purchase process(es) they use, will continue to evolve as consumers of travel products gain more experience and confidence in product purchasing over the Internet. Importantly, conversations among travelers will continue to grow and will increasingly be mediated through network technologies.
- Experience- and emotion-oriented communications will grow in importance as human-centric computing and emotionally intelligent interfaces are offered. These interfaces/systems will incorporate a variety of interpreted information, enabling the systems to recognize the information needs of the user within an emotional-psychological need context, in order to provide supportive interactions and suggestions.
- User-generated media such as blogging, podcasting, pictures, and social networking technologies are expected to play an ever more important role in supporting travel planning activities as well as the construction of memories and extended experiences in the post-consumption phase of travel. It is expected that there will be an increasing need to integrate such applications on tourism and travel websites and there are already applications available which suggest that social networking sites and virtual worlds will merge, offering extremely engaging opportunities for communication, sharing, and online experience.
- As individuals become more mobile and also more reliant on network technologies they will increasingly demand systems that can support their lifestyle during trips. Travelers will expect to be able to enjoy the same level of technology use on the road as they do at home. This means that systems have to become truly portable/wearable, wireless, global, integrated, and smart. Indeed, museums and hotel rooms provide ideal test beds for networked applications such as ambient intelligence due to their limited range of user activities and their relatively small scale. Also, they can potentially serve as catalysts for the adoption of specific technologies as they have the ability to expose applications to a significant number of potential users.

New technologies are being developed continuously and many of these innovations will have significant impacts on tourism. For instance, advances in surface computing (see Perenson, 2007) and increasing reliance on Web service platforms will provide new opportunities for seamless information provision and exchange in the context of tourism. These technological developments are also likely to continue to disrupt existing value chains, lead to the emergence of new players in the tourism industry, and significantly influence consumers' experiences.

References

Beldona, S. (2005). "Cohort Analysis of Online Travel Information Search Behavior: 1995–2000." *Journal of Travel Research*, 44(2): 135–142.

Bickart, B. and Schindler, R.M. (2001). "Internet Forums as Influential Sources of Consumer Information." *Journal of Interactive Marketing*, 15(3): 31–40.

Blackshaw, P. and Nazzaro, M. (2004). "Consumer-Generated-Media (CGM). 101: Word-of-Mouth in the Age of the Web-Fortified Consumer." Retrieved June 3, 2007 from www.nielsenbuzzmetrics.com/whitepapers.asp.

Bonn, M., Furr, H. and Susskind, A. (1999). "Predicting a Behavioral Profile for Pleasure Travelers on the Basis of Internet Use Segmentation." *Journal of Travel Research*, 37(4): 330–340.

Bradshaw, J.M. (1997). *Software Agents*. Cambridge, MA: AAAI Press/MIT Press.

Brown, G. (2004). "Developing a Destination Management System to Act as an Enabler in Sustaining a Competitive Advantage in the (net) Marketplace." In A. Frew (Ed.), *Information and Communication Technologies in Tourism 2004* (pp. 326–336). Vienna: Springer Verlag.

Buhalis, D. (2003). *eTourism: Information Technology for Strategic Tourism Management*. Upper Saddle River, NJ: Financial Times/Prentice Hall.

Buhalis, D. (2004). "eAirlines: Strategic and Tactical Use of ICTs in the Airline Industry." *Information and Management*, 41(7): 805–825.

Buhalis, D. and Law, R. (2008). "Progress in Information Technology and Tourism Management: 20 Years on and 10 Years After the Internet—The State of eTourism Research." *Tourism Management*, 29(4): 609–623.

Buhalis, D. and Licata, M.C. (2002). "The Future eTourism Intermediaries." *Tourism Management*, 23(3): 207–220.

Buhalis, D. and O'Connor, P. (2005). "Information Communication Technology Revolutionizing Tourism." *Tourism Recreation Research*, 30: 7–16.

Buhalis, D. and Zoge, M. (2007). "The Strategic Impact of the Internet on the Tourism Industry."

In M. Sigala, L. Mich and J. Murphy (Eds.), *Information and Communication Technologies in Tourism 2007* (pp. 481–492). Vienna: Springer Verlag.

Card, J.A., Chen, C.-Y. and Cole, S.T. (2003). "Online Travel Products Shopping: Differences Between Shoppers and Nonshoppers." *Journal of Travel Research*, 42(2): 133–139.

Cardoso, J. (2005). *E-Tourism: Creating Dynamic Packages using Semantic Web Processes*. Retrieved April 15, 2008 from www.w3.org/2005/04/FSWS/Submissions/16/paper.html.

Cardoso, J. and Lange, C. (2007). "A Framework for Assessing Strategies and Technologies for Dynamic Packaging Applications in e-Tourism." *Journal of Information Technology and Tourism*, 9(1): 27–44.

Chatterjee, P. (2001). "Online Reviews—Do Consumers Use Them?" In M.C. Gilly and J. Myers-Levy (Eds.), *ACR 2001 Proceedings* (pp. 129–134). Provo, UT: Association for Consumer Research.

Cho, Y., Wang, Y. and Fesenmaier, D.R. (2002). "Searching for Experiences: The Web-Based Virtual Tour in Tourism Marketing." *Journal of Travel & Tourism Marketing*, 12(4): 1–17.

Compete Inc. (2006). "Embracing Consumer Buzz Creates Measurement Challenges for Marketers." Retrieved December 10, 2006 from www.cymfony.com/files/pdf/Compete_Spark_12_06_Embracing_Consumer_Buzz_Creates_Measurement_Challenges.pdf.

Connolly, D. and Olsen, M. (1999). *Hospitality Technology in the New Millennium: Findings of the IH&RA Think-Tanks on Technology*. Paris: International Hotel & Restaurant Association.

Crotts, J.C. (1999). "Consumer Decision-Making and Prepurchase Information Search." In A. Pizam and Y. Masfeld (Eds.), *Consumer Behavior in Travel and Tourism* (pp. 149–168). Binghamton, NY: Haworth Hospitality Press.

Curbera, F., Duftler, M., Khalaf, R., Nagy, W., Mukhi, N. and Weerawarana, S. (2002). "Unraveling the Web Services Web: An Introduction to SOAP, WSDL, and UDDI." *IEEE Internet Computing*, 6(2): 86–93.

Delgado, J. and Davidson, R. (2002). "Knowledge Bases and User Profiling in Travel and Hospitality Recommender Systems." In K. Wöber, A.J. Frew and M. Hitz (Eds.),

Information and Communication Technologies in Tourism 2002 (pp. 1–16). Vienna: Springer-Verlag.

Dellaert, B.G.C., Ettema, D.F. and Lindh, C. (1998). "Multi-Faceted Tourist Travel Decisions: A Constraints-Based Conceptual Framework to Describe Tourists' Sequential Choices of Travel Components." *Tourism Management*, 19(4): 313–320.

Dellarocas, C. (2003). "The Digitization of Word of Mouth: Promise and Challenge of Online Feedback Mechanisms." *Management Science*, 49(10): 1407–1424.

eMarketer (2007). "Niche Sites Invigorate Online Travel." Retrieved April 11, 2007 from www.eMarketer.com.

Eriksson, O. (2002). "Location Based Destination Information for the Mobile Tourist." In K. Wöber, A.J. Frew, and M. Hitz (Eds.), *Information and Communication Technologies in Tourism 2002* (pp. 255–264). Vienna: Springer-Verlag.

Eyefortravel (2006). "Consumer-Generated Media is Becoming More and More Commercialized by the Day." Retrieved May 5, 2006 from www.m-travel.com/news/2006/05/consumergenerat.html.

Fesenmaier, D.R., Werthner, H. and Wöber, K. (2006). *Destination Recommendation Systems: Behavioral Foundations and Applications*. Cambridge, MA: CAB International.

Fodness, D. and Murray, B. (1997). "Tourist Information Search." *Annals of Tourism Research*, 24(3): 503–523.

Fodor, O. and Werthner, H. (2005). "Harmonise: A Step Toward an Interoperable eTourism Marketplace." *International Journal of Electronic Commerce*, 9(2): 11–39.

Frew, A. (2000). "A Critical Analysis of Tourism Information Technology Research." In D. Fesenmaier, S. Klein, and D. Buhalis (Eds.), *Information and Communication Technologies in Tourism 2000* (pp. 39–52). Vienna: Springer.

Frias, D.M., Rodriguez, M.A. and Castaneda, J.A. (2008). "Internet vs. Travel Agencies on Pre-Visit Destination Image Formation: An Information Processing View." *Tourism Management*, 29(1): 163–179.

Furr, H.L., Bonn, M. and Hausman, A. (2002). "A Generational and Geographic Analysis of Internet Travel-Service Usage." *Tourism Analysis*, 6(2): 139–147.

Good, N., Schafer, J.B., Konstan, J., Borchers, A., Sarwar, B., Herlocker, J. and Riedl, J. (1999). "Combining Collaborative Filtering With Personal Agents For Better Recommendations." In J. Hendler, D. Subramanian, R. Uthurusamy and B. Hayes-Roth (Eds.), *Proceedings of the Sixteenth National Conference on Artificial Intelligence and Eleventh Conference on Innovative Applications of Artificial Intelligence* (pp. 439–446). Menlo Park, CA: AAAI Press.

Gratzer, M., Werthner, H. and Winiwarter, W. (2004). "Electronic Business in Tourism." *International Journal of Electronic Business*, 2(5): 450–459.

Gretzel, U. (2006). "Consumer-Generated Content—Trends and Implications for Branding." *eReview of Tourism Research*, 4(3). Retrieved April 1, 2008 from ertr.tamu.edu/commentaries.cfm?articleid=69.

Gretzel, U. and Fesenmaier, D.R. (2002). "The New Realities of Destination Marketing: Integrating Technology, Networks, and Communities into DMO Strategies." *Proceedings of the Annual Conference, Travel and Tourism Research Association, Canadian Chapter*. Edmonton, Alberta.

Gretzel, U., Fesenmaier, D.R., Formica, S. and O'Leary, J.T. (2006). "Searching for the Future: Challenges Faced by Destination Marketing Organizations." *Journal of Travel Research*, 45(2): 116–126.

Gretzel, U., Hwang, Y.-H. and Fesenmaier, D.R. (2006). "A Behavioral Framework for Destination Recommendation Systems Design." In D.R. Fesenmaier, H. Werthner and K. Wöber (Eds.), *Destination Recommendation Systems: Behavioral Foundations and Applications* (pp. 53–64). Cambridge, MA: CAB International.

Gretzel, U. and Jamal, T. (2007). "The Rise of the Creative Tourist Class: Technology, Experience and Mobilities." In F. Dimanche (Ed.), *Tourism, Mobility and Technology, Proceedings of the TTRA Europe Conference* (pp. 22–28). Nice, France, April 23–25, 2007. Borläge, Sweden: Travel and Tourism Research Association Europe Chapter.

Gretzel, U., Yuan, Y. and Fesenmaier, D.R. (2000). "Preparing for the New Economy: Advertising Strategies and Change in Destination Marketing Organizations." *Journal of Travel Research*, 39(2): 146–156.

Gruber, F. (2006). "WOM in the New Social Media Landscape." Retrieved August 9, 2006 from www.imediaconnection.com/content/10533.asp.

Hall, T., Ciolfi, L., Bannon, L., Fraser, M., Benford, S., Bowers, J., Greenhalgh, C., Hellström, S.-O., Izadi, S., Schnädelbach, H. and Flintham, M. (2001). "The Visitor as Virtual Archaeologist: Explorations in Mixed Reality Technology to Enhance Educational and Social Interaction in the Museum." *Proceedings of the 2001 Conference on Virtual Reality, Archaeology and Cultural Heritage, VAST'01* (pp. 91–96). Glyfada, Greece, November 28–30, 2001. New York: ACM Press.

Hanlan, J. and Kelly, S. (2005). "Image Formation, Information Sources and an Iconic Australian Tourist Destination." *Journal of Vacation Marketing*, 11(2): 163–177.

Hayes, G. (2006). "Virtual Worlds, Web 3.0 and Portable Profiles." Retrieved April 29, 2008 from www.personalizemedia.com/index.php/2006/08/27/virtual-worlds-web-30-and-portable-profiles/.

Hennig-Thurau, T., Gwinner, K.P., Walsh, G. and Gremler, D.D. (2004). "Electronic Word-of-Mouth Via Consumer-Opinion Platforms: What Motivates Consumers to Articulate Themselves on the Internet?" *Journal of Interactive Marketing*, 18(1): 38–52.

Hibbard, J. (1997). "Straight Line to Relevant Data." *Information Week*, 657: 21–25.

Hruschka, H. and Mazanec, J. (1990). "Computer-Assisted Travel Counseling." *Annals of Tourism Research*, 17(2): 208–227.

Hwang, Y-H. and Fesenmaier, D.R. (2001). "Collaborative Filtering: Strategies for Travel Destination Bundling." In P. Sheldon, K. Wöber and D.R. Fesenmaier (Eds.), *Information and Communication Technologies in Tourism 2001* (pp. 167–175). Vienna: Springer-Verlag.

Hwang, Y., Gretzel, U., Xiang, Z. and Fesenmaier, D.R. (2006). "Information Search for Travel Decisions." In D. Fesenmaier, H. Werthner and K. Wöber (Eds.), *Destination Recommendation Systems: Behavioral Foundations and Applications* (pp. 3–16). Cambridge, MA: CAB International.

Information Society Technologies Advisory Group (2001). "Scenarios for Ambient Intelligence in 2010." Retrieved December 20, 2002 from ftp://ftp.cordis.lu/pub/ist/docs/istagscenarios2010.pdf.

Jansson, A. (2006). "Specialized Spaces: Touristic Communication in the Age of Hyper-Space-Biased Media." *Working Paper No. 137–06.* Centre for Cultural Research, University of Aarhus. Retrieved April 1, 2008 from www.hum.au.dk/ckulturf/pages/publications/aj/specialized_spaces.html.

Jansson, A. (2007). "A Sense of Tourism: New Media and the Dialectic of Encapsulation/Decapsulation." *Tourist Studies*, 7(1): 5–24.

Jeng, J-M. and Fesenmaier, D.R. (2002). "Conceptualizing the Travel Decision-Making Hierarchy: A Review of Recent Developments." *Tourism Analysis*, 7(1): 15–32.

Jun, S.H., Vogt, C. and MacKay, K. (2007). "Relationship Between Travel Information Search and Travel Product Purchase in Pretrip Contexts." *Journal of Travel Research*, 45(3): 266–274.

Kaplanidou, K. and Vogt, C. (2006). "A Structural Analysis of Destination Travel Intentions as a Function of Web Site Features." *Journal of Travel Research*, 45(2): 204–216.

Kim, D.-Y., Lehto, X.Y. and Morrison, A.M. (2007). "Gender Differences in Online Travel Information Search: Implications for Marketing Communications on the Internet." *Tourism Management*, 28(2): 423–433.

Kim, W.G., Ma, X. and Kim, D. J. (2006). "Determinants of Chinese Hotel Customers' E-Satisfaction and Purchase Intentions." *Tourism Management*, 27(5): 890–900.

Kiss, J. (2008). "Web 3.0 is All about Rank and Recommendation." Retrieved April 17, 2008 from www.guardian.co.uk/media/2008/feb/04/web20?gusrc=rss&feed=media.

Kotler, P., Bowen, J. and Makens, J. (1999). *Marketing for Hospitality and Tourism* (2nd edition.). Upper Saddle River, NJ: Prentice Hall, Inc.

Lee, W., Gretzel, U. and Law, R. (2008). "Quasi-Trial Experiences Through Sensory Information on Destination Websites." Working paper. College Station, TX: Laboratory for Intelligent Systems in Tourism.

Lee, J., Soutar, G. and Daly, T. (2007). "Tourists' Search for Different Types of Information: A Cross-National Study." *Journal of Information Technology & Tourism*, 9(3–4): 165–176.

Lewis, D. and Bridger, D. (2000). *The Soul of the New Consumer*. London: Nicholas Brealey Publishing.

Litvin, S., Goldsmith, R.E. and Pan, B. (2008). "Electronic Word-of-Mouth in Hospitality and Tourism Management." *Tourism Management*, 29(3): 458–468.

Loban, S. (1997). "A Framework for Computer-Assisted Travel Counseling." *Annals of Tourism Research*, 24(4): 813–831.

MacKay, K., McVetty, D. and Vogt, C. (2005). "Web-Based Information Search and Use: Is it the New Tourism Reality? A Preliminary Examination of Visitors to Canada's Four Mountain National Parks." Paper presented at the *Travel & Tourism Research Association Conference-Canada*. Kelowna, BC.

Mayros, V. and Werner, D.M. (1982). *Marketing Information Systems: Design and Applications for Marketers*. Radnor, PA: Chilton Book Company.

McGuffie, J. (1994). "CRS Development in the Hotel Sector." *EIU Travel and Tourism Analyst*, 2: 53–68.

Meadows, M.S. (2003). *Pause & Effect: The Art of Interactive Narrative*. Indianapolis, IN: New Riders.

Mirzadeh, N., Ricci, F. and Bansal, M. (2005). "Feature Selection Methods for Conversational Recommender Systems." In *Proceedings of the 2005 IEEE International Conference on e-Technology, e-Commerce and e-Service (EEE'05)* (pp. 772–777). Washington: IEEE Computer Society.

Mitsche, N. (2001). "Personalized Traveling Counseling System: Providing Decision Support Features for Travelers." In P. Sheldon, K. Wöber, and D.R. Fesenmaier (Eds.), *Information and Communication Technologies in Tourism 2001* (pp.160–166). Vienna: Springer-Verlag.

Moutinho, L. (1987). "Consumer Behavior in Tourism." *European Journal of Marketing*, 21: 2–44.

Muniz, A.M. and O'Guinn, T.C. (2000). Brand Community. *Journal of Consumer Research*, 27: 227–235.

Murphy, L., Moscardo, G. and Benckendorff, P. (2007). "Exploring Word-of-Mouth Influences on Travel Decisions: Friends and Relatives vs. Other Travelers." *International Journal of Consumer Studies*, 31(5): 517–527.

O'Connor, P. (2008). "User-Generated Content and Travel: A Case Study on Tripadvisor.com." In P. O'Connor, W. Höpken and U. Gretzel (Eds.), *Information and Communication Technologies in Tourism 2008* (pp. 35–46). Vienna: Springer Verlag.

O'Connor, P. and Murphy, J. (2004). "Research on Information Technology in the Hospitality Industry." *International Journal of Hospitality Management*, 23(5): 473–484.

Oertel, B., Steinmüller, K. and Kuom, M. (2002). "Mobile Multimedia Services for Tourism." In K. Wöber, A.J. Frew and M. Hitz (Eds.), *Information and Communication Technologies in Tourism 2002* (pp. 265–274). Vienna: Springer-Verlag.

O'Sullivan, E.L. and Spangler, K.J. (1998). *Experience Marketing*. State College, PA: Venture Publishing.

Pan, B. and Fesenmaier, D.R. (2006). "Online Information Search: Vacation Planning Process." *Annals of Tourism Research*, 33(3): 809–832.

Park, D.H., Kim, S. and Han, J. (2007). "The Effects of Consumer Knowledge on Message Processing of Electronic Word of Mouth Via Online Consumer Review." Paper presented at the *ECIS 2007 Conference*. St. Gallen, Switzerland, June 7–9.

Park, D.H., Lee, J. and Han, J. (2007). "The Effect of Online Consumer Reviews on Consumer Purchasing Intention: The Moderating Role of Involvement." *International Journal of Electronic Commerce*, 11(4): 125–148.

Park, Y. and Gretzel, U. (2006). "Evaluation of Emerging Technologies in Tourism: The Case of Travel Search Engines." In M. Hitz, M. Sigala and J. Murphy (Eds.), *Information and Communication Technologies in Tourism 2006* (pp. 371–382). Vienna: Springer Verlag.

Pearce, D.G. and Schott, C. (2005). "Tourism Distribution Channels: The Visitors' Perspective." *Journal of Travel Research*, 44(1): 50–63.

Perenson, M.J. (2007). "Microsoft Debuts 'Minority Report'-Like Surface Computer." *PC World*. Retrieved May 29, 2007 from www.pcworld.com/printable/article/id,132352/printable.html#.

Pikkemaat, B. and Peters, M. (2005). "Towards the Measurement of Innovation—A Pilot

Study in the Small and Medium Sized Hotel Industry." *Journal of Quality Assurance in Hospitality & Tourism*, 6(3/4): 113–128.

Pikkemaat, B. and Weiermair, K. (2007). "Innovation through Cooperation in Destinations: First Results of an Empirical Study in Austria." *Anatolia: An International Journal of Tourism and Hospitality Research*, 18(1): 67–83.

Pine, B.J. and Gilmore, J.H. (1999). *The Experience Economy*. Boston: Harvard Business School Press.

Poon, A. (1993). *Tourism, Technology and Competitive Strategies*. Wallingford: CAB International.

Poslad, S., Laamanen, H., Malaka, R., Nick, A., Buckle, P. and Zipf, A. (2001). "CRUMPET: Creation of User-Friendly Mobile Services Personalized for Tourism." In *Proceedings of 3G 2001*. London: Institution of Electrical Engineers. Retrieved December, 22, 2002, from www.eml.villa-bosch.de/english/homes/zipf/3g-crumpet2001.pdf.

Prescott, L. (2006). *Hitwise US Travel Report*. New York: Hitwise.

Rasinger, J., Fuchs, M. and Höpken, W. (2007). "Information Search with Mobile Tourist Guides: A Survey of Usage Intention." *Information Technology & Tourism*, 9(3/4): 177–194.

Rheingold, H. (1994). "A Slice of Life in My Virtual Community." In L.M. Harasim (Ed.), *Global Networks: Computers and International Communications* (pp. 57–80). Cambridge, MA: MIT Press.

Ricci, F. and Werthner, H. (2001). "Cased-Based Destination Recommendations Over an XML Data Repository." In P. Sheldon, K. Wöber and D.R. Fesenmaier (Eds.), *Information and Communication Technologies in Tourism 2001* (pp. 150–159). Vienna: Springer-Verlag.

Ricci, F. and Wietsma, R. (2006). "Product Reviews in Travel Decision Making." In M. Hitz, M. Sigala, and J. Murphy (Eds.), *Information and Communication Technologies in Tourism 2006* (pp. 296–307). Vienna: Springer.

Rosh White, N. and White, P.B. (2007). "Home and Away: Tourists in a Connected World." *Annals of Tourism Research*, 34(1): 88–104.

Schindler, R.M. and Bickart, B. (2005). "Published 'Word of Mouth': Referable,

Consumer-Generated Information on the Internet." In C.P. Haugtvedt, K.A. Machleit, and R.F. Yalch (Eds.), *Online Consumer Psychology: Understanding and Influencing Consumer Behavior in the Virtual World* (pp. 35–61). Hillsdale, NJ: Lawrence Erlbaum Associates.

Schmallegger, D. and Carson, D. (2008). "Blogs in Tourism: Changing Approaches to Information Exchange." *Journal of Vacation Marketing*, 14(2): 99–110.

Schmidt-Belz, B., Makelainen, M., Nick, A. and Poslad, S. (2002). "Intelligent Brokering of Tourism Services for Mobile Users." In K. Wöber, A.J. Frew and M. Hitz (Eds.), *Information and Communication Technologies in Tourism 2002* (pp. 265–274). Vienna: Springer-Verlag.

Schmitt, B.H. (1999). *Experiential Marketing: How to Get Customers to Sense, Feel, Think, Act, and Relate to Your Company and Brands*. New York: Free Press.

Seabra, C., Abrantes, J.L. and Lages, L.F. (2007). "The Impact of Using Non-Media Information Sources on the Future Use of Mass Media Information Sources: The Mediating Role of Expectations Fulfillment." *Tourism Management*, 28(6): 1541–1554.

Sheldon, P.J. (1997). *Tourism Information Technology*. Wallingford: CAB International.

Shih, C.F. (1998). "Conceptualizing Consumer Experiences in Cyberspace." *European Journal of Marketing*, 32(7/8): 655–663.

Skadberg, Y.X., Skadberg, A.N. and Kimmel, J.R. (2005). "Flow Experience and Its Impact on the Effectiveness of a Tourism Website." *Information Technology & Tourism*, 7(3/4): 147–156.

Smith, D., Menon, S. and Sivakumar, K. (2005). "Online Peer and Editorial Recommendations, Trust, and Choice in Virtual Markets." *Journal of Interactive Marketing*, 19(3): 15–37.

Snepenger, D. and Snepenger, M. (1993). "Information Search by Pleasure Travelers." In M. Kahn, M. Olson and T. Var (Eds.), *Encyclopedia of Hospitality and Tourism* (pp. 830–835). New York: Van Nostrand Reinhold.

Steuer, J. (1992). "Defining Virtual Reality: Dimensions Determining Telepresence." *Journal of Communication*, 42(4): 73–93.

Susskind, A.M., Bonn, M. and Dev, C.S. (2003). "To Look or Book: An Examination of

Consumers' Apprehensiveness toward Internet Use." *Journal of Travel Research*, 41(3): 256–264.

Taylor, T.L. (2002). "Living Digitally: Embodiment in Virtual Worlds." In R. Schroeder (Ed.), *The Social Life of Avatars* (pp. 40–62). London: Springer Verlag.

Teichmann, K. and Zins, A. (2006). "Source Credibility in the Tourist Information Search Behaviour: Comparing the Pre- and Post-Consumption Stage." *Proceedings of the 37th Annual TTRA Conference* (pp. 67–77). Dublin, Ireland, June 18–20.

Travel Industry Association of America (2005). *Travelers' Use of the Internet*. Washington: Travel Industry Association of America.

Tussyadiah, I. and Fesenmaier, D.R. (2007). "Marketing Destinations Through First-Person Stories: A Narrative Structure Analysis." *Proceedings of the 2007 TTRA Annual Conference*. Las Vegas, NV, June 17–20, 2007.

Tversky, B. and Marsh, E.J. (2000). "Biased Retellings of Events Yield Biased Memories." *Cognitive Psychology*, 40: 1–38.

Vanhof, K. and Molderez, I. (1994). "An Advice System for Travel Agents." In W. Schertler, B. Schmid, A. Tjoa, and H. Werthner (Eds.), *Information and Communication Technologies in Tourism 1994* (pp. 126–132). Vienna: Springer-Verlag.

Vogt, C.A. and Fesenmaier, D.R. (1998). "Expanding the Functional Information Search Model." *Annals of Tourism Research*, 25(3): 551–578.

Wang, Y. and Fesenmaier, D.R. (2002). *Assessing Web Marketing Strategies: Approaches, Issues, and implications: A Report on the Results of National Survey of City and County Tourism Organizations in the United States of America*. Champaign, IL: National Laboratory for Tourism and eCommerce, University of Illinois.

Wang, Y. and Fesenmaier, D.R. (2006). "Identifying the Success Factors of Web-Based Marketing Strategy: An Investigation of Convention and Visitors Bureaus in the United States." *Journal of Travel Research*, 44(3): 239–249.

Wang, Y. and Fesenmaier, D.R. (2007). "Collaborative Destination Marketing: A Case Study of Elkhart County, Indiana." *Tourism Management*, 28(3): 863–875.

Wang, Y., Yu, Q. and Fesenmaier, D.R. (2002). "Defining the Virtual Tourist Community: Implications for Tourism Marketing." *Tourism Management*, 23(4): 407–417.

Weber, K. and Roehl, W. (1999). "Profiling People Searching for and Purchasing Travel Products on the World Wide Web." *Journal of Travel Research*, 37(3): 291–298.

Werthner, H. and Klein, S. (1999). *Information Technology and Tourism—A Challenging Relationship*. Vienna: Springer-Verlag.

Werthner, H. and Ricci, F. (2004). "E-Commerce and Tourism." *Communications of the ACM*, 47(12): 101–105.

Wind, Y., Mahajan, R. and Gunther, R. (2002). *Convergence Marketing*. Upper Saddle River, NJ: Prentice Hall.

Windham, L. and Orton, K. (2000). *The Soul of the New Consumer*. New York: Allworth Press.

Wiseman, C. (1985). *Strategy and Computers: Information Systems as Competitive Weapons*. Homewood, IL: Dow Jones–Irwin.

Woodside, A.G. and MacDonald, R. (1994). "General System Framework of Customer Choice Processes of Tourism Services." In V. Gasser and K. Weiermair (Eds.), *Spoilt for Choice. Decision Making Processes and Preference Change of Tourists: Intertemporal and Intercountry Perspectives* (pp. 30–59). Thaur: Kulturverlag.

World Tourism Organization Business Council (1999). *Marketing Tourism Destinations Online*. Madrid: World Tourism Organization Business Council.

Xiang, P. and Fesenmaier, D.R. (2008). "Identifying the Online Tourism Domain: Implications for Search Engine Development for Tourism." In P. O'Connor, W. Höpken, and U. Gretzel (Eds.), *Information and Communication Technologies in Tourism 2008* (pp. 486–496). Vienna: Springer Verlag.

Yoo, K.H. and Gretzel, U. (2008). "Use and Impact of Online Travel Reviews." In P. O'Connor, W. Höpken, and U. Gretzel (Eds.), *Information and Communication Technologies in Tourism 2008* (pp. 35–46). Vienna: Springer Verlag.

Yoo, K.-H., Lee W. and Gretzel, U. (2006). "Role of the Internet in the Travel Planning

Process." *Proceedings of the Annual TTRA Conference*. Dublin, Ireland.

Yuan, Y., Gretzel, U. and Fesenmaier, D.R. (2006). "The Role of Information Technology Use in American Convention and Visitors Bureaus." *Tourism Management*, 27(2): 326–341.

Zach, F., Gretzel U. and Fesenmaier, D.R. (2008). "Tourist Activated Networks: Implications for Dynamic Packaging Systems in Tourism." In P. O'Connor, W. Höpken, and U. Gretzel (Eds.), *Information and Communication Technologies in Tourism 2008* (pp. 198–208). Vienna: Springer Verlag.

Zach, F., Xiang, P. and Fesenmaier, D.R. (2007). "An Assessment of Innovation in Web Marketing: Investigating American Convention and Visitors Bureaus." In M. Sigala, L. Mich and J. Murphy (Eds.), *Information and Communication Technologies in Tourism 2007* (pp. 365–376). Vienna: Springer Verlag.

Zach, F., Xiang, P., Gretzel, U. and Fesenmaier, D.R. (2008). "Innovation in the Web Marketing Programs of American Convention and Visitors Bureaus." Working paper. Philadelphia, PA: National Laboratory for eCommerce in Tourism, Temple University.

Zins, A. (2007). "Exploring Travel Information Search Behavior Beyond Common Frontiers." *Journal of Information Technology & Tourism*, 9(3/4): 149–164.

Zipf, A. (2002). "User-Adaptive Maps for Location-Based Services (LBS) for Tourism." In K.W. Wöber, A.J. Frew, and M. Hitz (Eds.), *Information and Communication Technologies in Tourism* (pp. 329–338). Vienna: Springer Verlag.

32

Global Tourism Business Operations—Theoretical Frameworks and Key Issues

Keith G. Debbage and Suzanne Gallaway

Introduction

It has been nearly two decades since *Tourism Management* published the influential special issue on Tourism and Transnationalism that was guest edited by Go and Ritchie (1990). The central theme of the special issue was the identification of the growing role of transnational corporations (TNCs) in the international tourism industry. One of the most significant findings was that tourism-related TNCs were no longer constrained to just North America and Europe. The broader geographic reach of TNCs was partly explained by the advent of more sophisticated communications technology and the rapid global consolidation of the travel industry.

What is new today is the increasingly complex and fast changing nature of global business operations. Forces of technology, which have facilitated increasingly sophisticated networks of production, are leveling the global competitive playing field. *New York Times* columnist Thomas Friedman has coined the phrase "The world is flat" to capture how fiber optic cable, digital networks, and global production chains have succeeded in flattening the world by permitting collaboration on a global scale. International tourism business operations are no exception to this rule, although the ongoing restructuring of globally oriented tourism companies has recently been supplemented by the rise of networks of flexible specialization; ongoing innovations in telecommunications and information technology; the emergence of strategic alliances; the commodification of place; and the evolution of more sophisticated forms of consumer demand.

Changes in consumer demand and the evolution of increasingly more sophisticated consumer preferences have undoubtedly played substantive roles in reshaping the international tourist product. Franklin and Crang (2001) persuasively argued that complex cultural and social processes shape tourism consumption even in the face of profound global economic restructuring.

The reassertion of the distinctiveness of the locale as a place to invest in has become crucial to these processes of globalization, particularly as the consumer becomes more discerning when choosing a destination. It is now clear that there are existential, experiential, and cultural-political dimensions to international tourism that make it a complex, highly social and political phenomenon.

That said, we argue in this chapter that it is the actual "machinery of production" (e.g., airlines, hotels, cruise ships, and tour operators) that most directly manipulate and facilitate origin–destination tourist flows across the world. Investment capital in tourism is increasingly tied up in international circuits of finance involving some of the most powerful business

Table 32.1   Largest Tourist Business Operations, 2005

Business	Units
Airlines	Passengers (millions)
American	98.1
Southwest	88.5
Delta	86.1
Air France–KLM	69.2
United	68.8
US Airways–America West	64.0
JAL	58.0
Northwest	56.5
Lufthansa	51.3
ANA	49.6
Hotel chains	Rooms
Intercontinental Hotels Group	537,533
Wyndham Worldwide	532,284
Marriott International	499,165
Hilton Hotels Corp.	485,356
Choice Hotels International	481,131
Accor	475,433
Best Western International	315,875
Starwood Hotels & Resorts Worldwide	257,889
Carlson Hospitality Worldwide	147,129
Global Hyatt Corp.	134,296
Cruise ship companies (North American market)	Lower berths
Carnival Cruise Lines	47,908
Royal Caribbean International	45,570
Princess Cruises	28,800
Norwegian Cruise Lines	20,950
Costa Cruise Lines	17,265

Source: *Air Transport World* (2006), *Hotels* (2006), and Cruise Lines International Association (2006).

corporations in the world (Table 32.1). By most accounts, tourism is now one of the largest industries in the world, responsible for nearly one-third of total global service trade in 2004 (World Tourism Organization [WTO], 2005).

The overall purpose of this chapter is to provide a state-of-the-art review of theory and research relating to global tourism business operations. It will be argued that comprehending tourism requires a more critical understanding of how the global tourism production system manipulates and shapes tourist places and destinations at the macroscale. The chapter does not attempt to provide a comprehensive view of all aspects of global tourism business operations nor cover the entire world from a spatial perspective. Instead, the chapter will focus on the most recent research in the field and particular attention will be paid to how the competitive environment influences tourism origin–destination flows, particularly through the airline, lodging, and cruise-ship industries. The chapter will highlight some of the more current conceptual and research-related advances and focus on the thorny issue of how substantive global tourism business operations can impact tourism development processes. We begin the chapter by arguing that a more fundamental understanding of tourism as a supply-side industry is crucial to a better understanding of global tourism business operations.

Global Tourism Systems: Some Supply-Side Concerns

In what has become an academic classic, Britton (1991) provided an intellectual roadmap for those interested in the globalization of tourism capital. Britton argued that tourism is a highly sophisticated production system that explicitly markets and packages places on a global scale and, therefore, is implicated in many of the economic, political, and social issues of current concern to tourism researchers and scholars. These issues include the ongoing debates about the globalization of tourism capital; the creation of new "postmodern" landscapes, such as Las Vegas; the changing role of world cities as places of consumption as well as production; and broader processes of industrial and regional restructuring.

Building on Britton's recommendations, Ioannides and Debbage (1998) have suggested several new research directions for a more informed economic geography of the global tourist industry, including a more rigorous conceptualization of what comprises the tourism production chain; a better appreciation for how the larger competitive environment shapes the global geography of tourism production; and a heightened awareness of the ongoing place and cultural commodification processes at play in the global contemporary economy. Agarwal et al. (2000) echoed the concerns of Ioannides and Debbage (1998) when they argued that the overall understanding of the international geography of tourism business operations is theoretically isolated and threadbare. In an analysis of tourism development in the UK, they found that changes in tourist consumption patterns, changes in the scale and ownership of production through strategic alliances, and changes in the geographical organization of production are all leading to new supply-side structures in the international tourism industry. However, the study of tourism has long been handicapped by an inattention to the supply side of global tourism business operations (Debbage and Ioannides, 2004; Ioannides and Debbage, 1997).

More recently, Judd (2006) has articulately pointed out how the paucity of supply-side research in tourism has resulted in tourism rarely being mentioned by scholars who study globalization and cities. For example, Thomas Friedman (2006) in his book *The World is Flat* does not include a single index reference to tourism even though WTO statistics show that the international tourist industry generated US$524 billion in international tourism receipts in 2003 (World

Tourism Organization, 2005.) Judd argues that part of the problem is that the current definitions of tourism are deficient because they define tourism as a system of consumption rather than production.

> The tourism system cannot logically be a system of consumption unless there are also producers. Producers seek to shape the tourist experience; it does not arise by accident. It is important to study the demographics of tourists and their desires and patterns of consumption. But what tourists want or think they want, and the choices from which they choose, are determined at least as much by those who consciously produce the tourist experience as they are by consumers. (Judd, 2006: 333)

Judd suggests that the concept of commodity chains (or value chains) may be a more appropriate conceptual framework for identifying the organizational structure of global tourism business operations. Although few tourism scholars have attempted to theorize a global commodity chain of tourism, Judd points out that key inputs in any value chain should include: the marketing and image firms that "manufacture" the tourist experience, place infrastructure, and the major tourism providers such as the airlines and hotels. Gathering data to trace the commodity chain may be a daunting task given the conceptual and definitional issues, but Judd suggests that "there is little reason to believe that tourism is inherently more complex than many other economic industries" (2006: 333). He believes that by treating tourism as a coherent system of production, it becomes possible to fully integrate the tourism literature within the broader literature on globalization.

D'Hauteserre objected to Judd's suggestion of utilizing value chains to better understand the tourism supply-side. She suggested that commodity chains reflect a deterministic, static approach that "denies the role of consumers in shaping the chain" (2006: 340). Because Judd's approach underplayed the social relations of production, D'Hauteserre argued that a preferred approach may be to utilize Actor Network Theory (ANT) if we are to successfully "unravel the complex relations that contribute to tourism as an economic activity" (2006: 341). She indicated that ANT is a more appropriate conceptual vehicle for investigating both the complex networks of labor and production processes, and the transformational feedback loops that exist between the production and consumption of tourism.

Although it is good to see robust debate about commodity chains and ANT, a precursor to any discussion about global tourism commodity chains should include an overview of the fundamental global flows of tourism capital—we now turn to a discussion of the recent literature on global tourism capital.

Quantifying Global Flows of Tourism Capital: Issues of Definition and Scale

A clearer understanding of the pattern and scale of global foreign direct investment (FDI) in tourism is crucial if we are to better understand the primary mechanics that drive global tourism business operations. However, not many studies have been conducted focused on FDI flows in the international tourism industry. According to Endo (2006), the lack of research is partly attributable to the industry classification methodology used in conventional FDI statistics, which does not correspond well with the wide range of activities captured by tourism. Endo is an Economic Affairs Officer with the United Nations Conference on Trade and Development (UNCTAD) and is well placed to utilize the extensive UNCTAD database in any analysis of tourism FDI.

Endo attempted to integrate corporate data from the major tourism transnational corporations (TNCs) to supplement FDI tourism data in order to get a clearer picture of global tourism investment flows. She argued that while tourism appears to be a global industry based on origin-destination tourist flows, the reality is that most tourism TNCs are not as global as other industries. She also pointed out that many tourism TNCs take non-equity forms (e.g., leasing,

management contract, and franchising) and, therefore, tend to be underrepresented in FDI statistics—which tend to assume some level of equity investment.

According to Endo, "the market share of the major TNCs in the global hotel industry … is not as dominant as one may think. What they account for is a little less than one-fifth (in 1998) of the world's hotel supply" (2006: 603). Similar trends are reported for the international airline industry, where much of the globalization of airlines takes the form of non-equity based strategic alliance networks such as the Star and One World alliances. According to Endo, although the tourism industry as a whole accounted for US$160 billion in cross-border merger and acquisition deals from 1987 to 2002, this was only 3% of the deals for all industries during the same period.

Endo indicated that much of the tourism FDI has been generated largely within the developed world (i.e., North America, European Union, and Japan.) However, she also suggested that no matter how small global FDI in tourism may be in the lesser developed countries, it is important for third world countries to secure non-equity forms of TNC participation to fully integrate into international tourism networks and attract visitors.

While some progress has been made in our understanding of investment flows in international tourism, others have grappled with the appropriate geographic scale of analysis when analyzing global tourism business operations. In an effort to get a better understanding of the complexities involved in global tourism analysis, Prideaux (2005) proposed a bilateral tourism framework because much international trade continues to be conducted on a nation-to-nation basis despite the shift to regional free trade blocs such as the European Union. According to Prideaux, "bilateral tourism describes the flow of tourists between two countries, irrespective of proximity, and is measured by actual tourists, their percentage as a proportion of inbound and outbound flows, and the state of the tourism balance of payments" (2005: 781). Prideaux suggests that the demand for global business tourism operations at a bilateral scale is likely to be substantively shaped by "factors that include price, personal preferences, destination image, government regulations, personal financial capacity to travel, international political/ military tensions, health epidemics, concerns for personal safety, and fear of crime" (2005: 784). Although Prideaux's conceptualization may be useful when analyzing the pattern of tourist flows between specific country pairs, the bilateral model understates the complex multilateral commodity chains that shape tourist demand on an international scale.

By contrast, Coles and Hall have argued that the 2004 expansion of the European Union (EU) to 25 countries with an economy of US$850 billion has the potential to "precipitate significant new and modified tourist flows" (2005: 52), particularly for global tourist business operations. They identified several key issues that could emerge as major research themes triggered, in part, by the latest round of EU enlargement. First, Coles and Hall encourage tourism researchers to study the connections that exist between evolving tourism development processes in Europe and the EU governance structure. They point out that although tourism has been targeted as a key growth industry by the EU, paradoxically, there is no separate commissioner for tourism. One key implication is that international tourist business operations may be constrained by an inability to successfully lobby the EU for a regulatory environment that facilitates the tourist industry's competitive advantage relative to other industries.

Second, Coles and Hall suggest that EU enlargement has altered the playing field regarding the flow of international tourism capital and labor mobility, effectively producing new "winners and losers" that have the potential to significantly modify the production and consumption of tourism. They argue that these changes may directly impact airline route networks and the locational strategies of the lodging industry throughout the EU and beyond.

At the other end of the research spectrum, Algieri (2006) analyzed the relationships that existed between international tourism specialization and economic growth in small countries. Her analysis suggested that specialization in tourism can be associated with fast economic growth and that cost of living and international airfares are "highly significant factors in determining tourism revenues for the tourism-based economies" (Algieri, 2006: 10). We now turn to a more detailed examination of some of the key issues in specific tourist industries that play a pivotal role in shaping the international tourist product.

Air Transportation and Tourism: Regulatory Reform and Network Economies

One of the most important component parts of any global tourism business operation is the international airline industry. Many significant international tourism destinations, especially in the relatively isolated "pleasure peripheries" of the Caribbean and the South Pacific are highly dependent on international tourist arrivals by air. According to Endo (2006), 80% of tourists now arrive by air when visiting third world destinations. Consequently, the competitive strategies of the airline industry can have profound implications on tourism development processes.

Despite this, most tourism focused books and articles tend to consider air transportation as just one of several component parts of the international tourist industry while the transportation literature rarely addresses the movement of tourists or leisure travel. Consequently, while air transportation frequently acts as the critical link between tourist-generating and tourist-receiving countries, it is usually relegated to a minor place in tourism studies although this is slowly changing (Bieger and Wittmer, 2006; Debbage, 2000, 2002, 2005; Forsyth, 2006; Wheatcroft, 1994).

Recent research has tended to focus on the "peculiar" regulatory regimes of international aviation and their ability to substantially constrain international air transportation operations. For example, Endo (2006) has pointed out that FDI in airlines is small because international regulations largely preclude a majority interest in other rival airlines. The implications of these international regulations for global tourist business operations is substantial and, therefore, this chapter now turns to an overview of the most recent research that has addressed this crucial issue.

According to Chang et al. (2004), one of the most serious barriers to air transportation liberalization is the airline ownership and control restrictions contained in nearly all bilateral Air Service Agreements. Chang et al. argued, "the nationality clauses contained in virtually all bilateral air service agreements (ASAs) have limited the companies designated to provide services to airlines owned and managed by nationals of the respective countries" (2004: 161). Chang et al. then proceeded to provide an overview of how ownership rules have evolved around the world. They pointed out that a free trade area for air transportation between the EU and the USA—the so-called Open Aviation Area (OAA)—has the potential to radically reconfigure global tourism business operations. "A report by The Brattle Group (2002) has estimated that an EU-US open aviation area would generate upwards of 17 million extra passengers, consumer benefits of at least $5 billion a year and would boost employment on both sides of the Atlantic" (Chang et al., 2004: 166). It is widely believed that as economies and industries are becoming more global in scope that multilateral agreements will replace bilateral agreements. Chang et al. make the case that an OAA agreement may serve as model for future multilateral agreements in other regions of the world.

Forsyth (2006) also argued that restrictive international aviation regulations remain a significant constraint on tourism growth, even though it is widely accepted that aviation liberalization has the potential to reduce airfares and stimulate tourism growth. He argued that if aviation policy is a key determinant of the price and availability of air travel then it is also a key determinant of the aggregate pattern of origin–destination tourist flows. Forsyth argued that the economic benefits of international tourism have become "an important driver of aviation policies even where policy makers have not attempted to take a quantitative approach to assess how large the benefits and costs might be" (2006: 8). He illustrated how tourism benefits can be a substantive factor in shaping aviation policy through four case studies that included an analysis of charter airlines and the Spanish tourism boom; low cost carriers in Europe (e.g., EasyJet and Ryan Air); the Qantas-Air New Zealand strategic alliance proposal; and liberalization proposals for the USA–Australia route. He concluded that "while the tourism benefits to a country from aviation liberalization are not likely to be as large as benefits to home country travelers or the costs to home country airlines, they are sufficiently large to tilt the balance of benefits and costs of liberalization in many cases" (Forsyth, 2006: 3).

Bieger and Wittmer (2006) echoed these sentiments and suggested that a coherent airline policy and air access strategy is crucial to the effective strategic development of tourist destinations. They advocated that a systems model approach be utilized to fully analyze the interrelationships that exist between global air transportation networks and tourism. Bieger and Wittmer argued, "the timing and frequency of flights, together with the nature of the airlines offering services, can affect the quality of the tourists arriving" (2006: 43). By analyzing tourism as a complex system of supply and demand points linked by increasingly sophisticated transportation networks, Bieger and Wittmer suggest it becomes possible to see how different business models can shape visitor streams in different ways. For example, they indicated that attraction-based destinations that rely on a mix of business and leisure traffic tended to rely on network carriers, while resort-based destinations with a heavy mix of leisure travelers may be more dependent on low-cost carriers and charter airlines.

Other scholars have questioned the long-term viability of charter airlines in light of the intense competition from scheduled airlines. Buck and Lei analyzed the UK charter airline industry since it is the most competitive and largest in Europe. They found that "the five biggest charter airlines are controlled by the five major tour groups and dominate nearly 90% of charter traffic flown by UK airlines" (2004: 73). According to Buck and Lei, upstream and downstream vertical integration has helped the major tour operators to control the quality of the product and service, and also enabled charter airlines, such as Brittania, to effectively compete on price. They also point out that the charter airlines have also embraced some of the competitive strategies of low cost carriers by developing no-frills subsidiaries, offering more sophisticated yield management pricing strategies, and offering more seats through the Internet. Buck and Lei concluded that charter airlines would continue to play a significant role in the European market particularly for holiday destination markets requiring flights exceeding 2000 kilometers.

Whether the analysis incorporates scheduled airlines or charters, a major trend appears to be the development of multilateral airline-based alliances as a way to circumvent relatively restrictive aviation bilateral agreements. Gudmundsson and Lechner pointed out that "competition between airlines is less a matter of individual firms competing against individual firms but of airline groups against airline groups, or to be more precise—networks against networks" (2006: 153). They suggest that strategic alliance networks allow airlines to "exploit scope and density economies across geographical boundaries" (2006: 153) through a peculiar sort of "coopetition" relationship where airlines simultaneously both compete and cooperate depending on the issue. Gudmundsson and Lechner argue that competition results from the efforts of

airlines to try to fill "structural holes" in the network market.

Rather than focusing on international regulatory regimes or route networks, Alamdari and Mason (2006) provided an overview of the key changes impacting airline distribution costs—which can account for up to 20% of total costs. They suggested that the major US airlines and some European countries have cut costs by simultaneously reducing or eliminating fees to intermediaries such as travel agents and increasing direct ticket sales through the Internet. One of the major implications is that travel agents have been forced to switch their business model from "being agents of the airlines to travel management service providers to travelers" (Alamdari and Mason, 2006: 122). Additionally, they point out that large online agencies—such as Expedia, Orbitz, and Travelocity—have benefited enormously from these changes with a 40% market share of the global online travel market in 2004. Alamdari and Mason indicated that these changes have been more widely embraced in the US where 37% of all tickets are sold online compared to just 16.7% in Europe and 10% in Asia Pacific. They also suggested that these titanic changes in distribution strategies have fundamentally impacted corporate customers, airlines, travel management companies, and global distribution systems in very different ways.

The International Hotel Industry: Globally Oriented Competitive Strategies

According to Milne and Pohlmann, "hotel chains have increased their overall share of global accommodation capacity considerably in recent decades, with the total number of rooms controlled by the world's twenty-five largest companies virtually doubling every decade since the 1970s" (1998: 184). Of course, the larger international hotel chains have attempted to increase profits and market share and this has led to intense global competitive pressures. However, relatively few studies have applied conceptual models to the international hotel sector, with some exceptions to the rule (Dunning and McQueen, 1982; Gannon and Johnson, 1995; Go et al., 1990; Go and Pine, 1995; Littlejohn and Beattie, 1992.) Some of this early research suggested that more stringent decision criteria should be applied in analyzing globally oriented expansion strategies and that international lodging chains should expand their activities through equity sharing, management contracts and franchise agreements (Go et al., 1990.)

Although non-equity arrangements are a key strategy in the international hotel industry, Altinay (2006) has recently suggested that little research has been conducted investigating how international franchise partners are selected. He argued that the decision-making criteria used to select partners should be more clearly understood, since the failure to select the "right" partner could have adverse monetary and strategic impacts on the holding company. Based on a case study of a major international hotel chain, Altinay concluded that there are three important contextual variables that determine how an international hotel chain selects its franchise partners. These included "the strategic context of the organization, different country markets and the nature of the business itself (franchise partnership)" (Altinay, 2006: 126). He argued that although franchising is perceived as a low risk strategy, international franchise negotiations could be difficult and time-consuming. Altinay recommended direct investment or joint venture partnerships as a more efficient expansion mode under certain conditions. He concluded by recommending that more research needed to be conducted in other parts of the world given that his own case study was limited to researching only the European, Middle East and African divisions of a major international hotel chain.

Pan (2005) analyzed the Asian market examining the market structure of various international tourist hotels in Taiwan and the impact of hotel location on profitability. Pan used the Herfindahl-Hirschman Index to facilitate a cross-sectional analysis of market concentration over time. He found that a positive relationship existed between hotel room market concentration and profitability although the strength of this relationship varied by metropolitan market. Pan also suggested that high levels of market concentration in Taiwan may have facilitated collusion and created significant barriers to entry, thus, making it difficult for new entrants to enter the marketplace. He argued that the lack of competition partly explains the high profitability of the major international hotel chains in Taiwan.

Johnson and Vanetti (2005) recently conducted an empirical study of the expansion strategies of international hotel chains in Eastern Central Europe with the goal of disentangling the major locational strategies employed by each chain. They suggested that two major trends included increases in the level of merger/acquisition activity in the international hotel industry and a proliferation of non-equity agreements. Johnson and Vanetti also argued that "in order to attain truly global distribution of brands and properties, non-equity methods through strategic alliances, franchising, and management contracts are the only means of reaching the required size for effective economies of scale and scope" (2005: 1095). These conclusions contradict Altinay's findings, who suggested that a significant equity investment may be more effective in certain situations. Of course, the significant role of non-equity arrangements in Johnson and Vanetti's study may also represent an attempt by the international hotel chains to minimize risk since Eastern Central Europe is still perceived as a risky investment environment.

Johnson and Vanetti also found that the overall perceived competitive strengths of the larger international chains tended to be knowledge of guest needs, strategic planning, and reservation systems. Key locational attributes included the size and nature of the city in which the hotel is located, the infrastructural base of the city, and the perception of the region as a good place to conduct business.

They also pointed out that the smaller chains perceived a competitive disadvantage relative to the larger chains regarding brand name, the ability to form a network of strategic alliances and physical size.

Although it is clear that the international hotel industry has embraced a broad range of responses to the evolving competitive environment of the early twenty-first century, the development of new global partnership agreements and increasingly sophisticated locational strategies appear to be driving forces in the industry. However, the lack of an overarching theoretical framework makes it difficult to place the myriad forces of globalization in context.

Cruise Tourism: Economies of Scale and 'Floating Resorts'

The number of tourism researchers that have studied the international impact of cruise tourism is surprisingly small (Braun et al., 2002; Douglas and Douglas, 2004; Dwyer and Forsyth, 1998; Hall and Braithwaite, 1990; Hobson, 1993; Jaakson, 2004; Weaver, 2005). Even fewer scholars have examined cruise tourism from a global perspective, although Wood (2000) and Dowling (2006) are notable exceptions to the rule.

Key themes in the rapid growth of cruise tourism have been the increased emphasis on both economies of scale and the marketing of ships as "floating resort destinations"—largely in an effort to compete directly with land-based resorts like Las Vegas and Orlando (Wood, 2000). The rapid increases in cruise ship passenger capacity have been made possible because the "big three"—Carnival, Royal Caribbean, and Princess—have been building ever larger "super-sized" ships. In 2006, the 160,000-ton Royal Caribbean *Freedom of the Seas* became the largest cruise ship in the world in terms of volume with 1800 rooms for up to 4375 passengers. Royal Caribbean is also working on a much larger ship, code named Project Genesis, which will measure 220,000 tons

and have a capacity of up to 6400 passengers when it comes into service in 2009.

Given these significant changes, Wood (2000) has argued that the study of cruise tourism represents a new opportunity to better understand the complexities of international tourism and globalization. Wood pointed out that "if economic globalization means the increased mobility of capital and its spatial disembeddedness, cruise ships represent the ultimate in globalization: physically mobile; massive chunks of multinational capital; capable of being "repositioned" anywhere in the world at any time; crewed with labor migrants from up to 50 countries on a single ship, essentially unfettered by national or international regulations" (2000: 352–353). According to Wood, an important example of the influence of globalization in cruise tourism is the way the major cruise ship companies use flags of convenience (FOCs) to circumvent the labor laws, taxes, and maritime regulations of the home country (usually the USA where most of the largest cruise company headquarters are located). Most of the major ships are registered in countries such as Panama, Liberia, and the Bahamas, in part to keep labor costs low and avoid restrictive environmental policies. Additionally, Wood suggests that cruise ships are increasingly offering tourist experiences that are becoming detached from local culture and society as the ship itself becomes the destination and ports of call include "fantasy islands" that are frequently wholly privately owned by the cruise companies.

Unfortunately, little additional research has been conducted on globalization and cruise tourism although Weaver (2005) provided an important contribution in his analysis of cruise tourism and its connections to Ritzer's (1993) McDonaldization thesis (also see Chapter 33 by Wood in this *Handbook*). The central premise of the McDonaldization thesis is that certain key forces of change have facilitated globalization. These forces include the rationalization, standardization, and routinization of production that has been so successfully applied to the US fast-food market. Weaver suggested that Ritzer's thesis of sameness and economies of scale is one way to interpret the "carefully orchestrated nature of "pleasure production" on board super-sized ships (and within other tourism-based environments)" (2005: 348).

Weaver also pointed out that while mass production and mass customization are at the heart of recent changes in the cruise ship industry, the McDonaldization thesis fails to account for the significant product diversity and the enormous range of options available to tourists on board ships like the *Freedom of the Seas*. He argued that the trend towards a post-Fordist style customization of the travel product should not be viewed as a process that is simply subordinate to Ritzer's visions of standardization and sameness. "Instead, McDonaldization and post-Fordist customi-zation should be viewed as processes that influence each other in a reciprocal fashion" (Weaver, 2005: 359). The ongoing debate about broader changes to "post-Fordist" and "postmodern" forms of consumption and pro-duction in the travel industry provide a useful departure point from which to build a broader theoretical framework within which we can place global tourist business operations. We will attempt to develop this broader research agenda in our concluding comments.

Globalized Neo-Fordist Framework?

Although it is now well understood that the international tourist industry is inherently heterogeneous and complex, many of the conventional models of tourism continue to fail to incorporate all the complexities of global tourist business operations into a broader theoretic. Although significant progress has been made in our understanding of how the international production system is shaped by the larger competitive environ-ment, tourism scholars remain unclear about how spaces of tourist consumption connect

back to the global production of tourist space. Part of the problem rests with our limited understanding of the supply-side of tourism, particularly at the global scale.

Some tourism scholars believe that a neo-Fordist framework may have some application in this context. The term Fordist derives its name from Henry Ford's auto-mated assembly line and refers to the mass production of standardized goods that was the dominant form of industrial production for the past century. According to Ioannides and Debbage, "Neo-Fordism refers to the inherent contradiction of increased levels of industrial concentration and increasingly large-scale industrial organizations, while simultaneously implementing increasingly sophisticated, brand, super-segmentation strategies and highly flexible travel-based products" (1998: 116). Super-segmentation has become commonplace in both the lodging and cruise ship industries as global tourist business operations attempt to personalize their travel products through niche marketing, design variations, and adver-tising. The tourist's role is changing from passive consumer to active participant in shaping and creating experiences, both at home and during travel (e.g., downloading interpretive information on a destination or event onto mp3 players to be listened to at home or at the destination, posting accom-modation critiques, travel accounts, and photos and video clips during or after the trip). Increasingly, web-based technologies (including social networking) are being used to directly involve consumers and employees in product development and marketing.[1] By doing so, large tourism TNCs are able to even better "camouflage" their enormous econo-mies of scale and the heavily industrialized and mass-produced nature of their products. The underlying assumption of a neo-Fordist perspective is that it does not assume a radical break from the mass marketing practices of the past but instead assumes a reciprocal rela-tionship, as recently suggested by Weaver (2005). Mass customization is the notion that the holding companies of most global tourist business operations will continue to emphasize large-scale industrial organization and an essentially Fordist *modus operandi* while also offering sophisticated product differentiation. The globalization of finance, labor, capital, technology, and culture facilitates this paradigm as businesses are able to competitively locate materials, manufacturing locations and markets globally and establish cross-linkages for optimal production and sales.

What is less clear about this technologically evolving neo-Fordist picture is which structures and processes are best suited to exploit the "new" geography of global production in the international tourist industry. An increased emphasis on building complex inter-firm strategic alliance networks grounded in a variety of contractual agreements (equity investments, franchises, management contracts) is likely to continue apace, but determining how tourist consumption patterns and new emerging web-based technologies shape the allocation of capital and the production of the tourist "experience" are crucial research questions (see Gretzel and Fesenmaier [Chapter 31] in this *Handbook*). For example, Urry (1990, 1995) has argued that there is a level of "spatial fixity" in the provision of tourist services because the tourist experience has to be produced and consumed at the same location. An improved understanding of how production and consumption interact in the increasingly mobile and technologically influenced local–global spaces is critical to a clearer understanding of what key forces will shape global tourism commodity chains in the future. Although the production and consumption of the tourist experience tend to occur simultaneously, they rarely occur at only one fixed point of supply because of the enormous complexity involved in any given commodity chain and the growing participation of tourists and employees in shaping production–consumption activities and experiences. A crucial research priority here is

better understanding of how technology and the Internet empower consumer and worker participation in both shaping experiences and supply-side services through such online vehicles as trip advisor.com, blogs, prediction markets and social networking tools.

Other emerging issues include better understanding of how climate change issues and the "greening" of global tourism business operations might shape tourist demand and service supply. For example, in early 2008, Virgin Atlantic Airways conducted a successful test flight of a jumbo jet that was partly powered by a biofuel made from babassu nuts and coconut oil as part of a joint project with Boeing and General Electric. Virgin Airlines[2] is exploring ways to minimize the airline's carbon footprint by developing sustainable next-generation oils, while others are exploring innovations in jet engine design to reduce fuel consumption, noise, and pollutants (Wald, 2008). Left unanswered and lagging in research exploration, is the question of whether empowered consumer participation can substantially influence the greening of the travel industry whereby consumers explicitly seek out those more "sustainable" travel products.

What is certain is that global tourist business operations will continue to play a growing role in facilitating origin-destination flows across the world even in an environment where external shocks such as wars, hurricanes, and terrorist attacks have the potential to substantially disrupt tourist activities (Evans and Elphick, 2005.) A good example is the recent competitive strategies of some of the largest US airlines. Even in a post 9/11 era, many US airlines now, ironically, view international markets as a major avenue for profitable growth and a way to avoid the brutal competition and fiscal hardships of the US domestic market. One potential end result of the new emphasis on international flights may be increased tourist volume in the North Atlantic market as a consequence of this new competitive strategy, particularly with the establishment of the USA–EU Open Aviation Area which began in April 2008.

Overall, it is clear that substantial progress has been made in our understanding of global tourist business operations since the publication of the *Tourism Management* journal's special issue on Tourism and Transnationalism in 1990. We remain impressed by, and excited about, the recent efforts of many tourism scholars. However, more work needs to be done. Tourism scholars need to be more actively engaged in supply-side issues and developing broader theoretical frameworks that can help unravel the complexities of the international tourist industry, particularly as they interact with processes of tourist consumption and the social relations of production.

Notes

1 InterContinental Hotels created an online market in Fall 2007 to "harvest and prioritize ideas" from within the hotel's 1000-person technology staff, so that they could tap this "creative class." The winning ideas in this prediction market exercise "in which more than 200 employees participated" were suggestions to improve searching the company's website to locate and book hotel rooms. Two projects have been initiated as a result of this, and the company is contemplating opening up prediction markets to InterContinental customers (Lohr, 2008: 7).

2 "Biofuel, Partly from Nuts, Is Tested on an Airline Flight." *New York Times*, February 25, 2008. Retrieved April 14, 2008 from www.nytimes.com/2008/02/25/business/25virgin.html? pagewanted=print.

References

Agarwal, S., Ball, R., Shaw, G. and Williams, A.M. (2000). "The Geography of Tourism Production: Uneven Disciplinary Development?" *Tourism Geographies*, 2(3): 241–263.

Air Transport World (2006). "World Airline Report: Location, Location, Location." July: 26–37.

Alamdari, F. and Mason, K. (2006). "The Future of Airline Distribution." *Journal of Air Transport Management*, 12(3): 122–134.

Algieri, B. (2006). "International Tourism Specialisation of Small Countries." *International Journal of Tourism Research*, 8(1): 1–12.

Altinay, L. (2006). "Selecting Partners in an International Franchise Organisation." *Hospitality Management*, 25(1): 108–128.

Bieger, T. and Wittmer, A. (2006). "Air Transport and Tourism—Perspectives and Challenges for Destinations, Airlines and Governments." *Journal of Air Transport Management*, 12(1): 40–46.

Braun, B., Xander, J. and White, K. (2002). "The Impact of the Cruise Industry on a Region's Economy: A Case Study of Port Canaveral, Florida." *Tourism Economics*, 8(3): 281–288.

Britton, S.G., (1991). "Tourism, Capital and Place: Towards a Critical Geography of Tourism." *Environment and Planning D: Society and Space*, 9(4): 451–478.

Buck, S. and Lei, Z. (2004). "Charter Airlines: Have They a Future?" *Tourism and Hospitality Research*, 5(1): 72–78.

Chang, Y., Williams, G. and Hsu, C. (2004). "The Evolution of Airline Ownership and Control Provisions." *Journal of Air Transport Management*, 10(3): 161–172.

Coles, T. and Hall, D. (2005). "Tourism and European Union Enlargement. Plus ça Change?" *International Journal of Tourism Research*, 7(2): 51–61.

Cruise Lines International Association (2006). *Cruise Industry Overview*. Fort Lauderdale: CLIA.

Debbage, K. (2000). "Air Transportation and International Tourism: The Regulatory and Infrastructural Constraints of Aviation Bilaterals and Airport Landing Slots." In M. Robinson et al. (Eds.), *Reflections on International Tourism: Management, Marketing and the Political Economy of Travel and Tourism*. Gateshead: Business Education Publishers Ltd.

Debbage, K. (2002). "Airport Runway Slots: Limits to Growth." *Annals of Tourism Research*, 29(4): 933–951.

Debbage, K. (2005). "Airlines, Airports, and International Aviation." In L. Pender and R. Sharpley (Eds.), *The Management of Tourism* (pp. 28–46). London: Sage.

Debbage, K. and Ioannides, D. (2004). "The Cultural Turn? Towards a More Critical Economic Geography of Tourism." In A. Lew,

M. Hall and A.M. Williams (Eds.), *A Companion to Tourism Geography*. Companion to Geography Series (pp. 99–109). Oxford: Blackwell.

D'Hauteserre, A.M. (2006). "A Response to 'Tracing the Commodity Chain of Global Tourism' by Dennis Judd" *Tourism Geographies*, 8(4): 337–342.

Douglas, N. and Douglas, N. (2004). "Cruise Ship Passenger Spending Patterns in Pacific Island Ports." *International Journal of Tourism Research*, 6(4): 251–261.

Dowling, R. (2006). *Cruiseship Tourism*. Cambridge, MA: CABI Publishing.

Dunning, J. and McQueen, M. (1982). "Multinational Corporations in the International Hotel Industry." *Annals of Tourism Research*, 9(1): 69–90.

Dwyer, L. and Forsyth, P. (1998). "Economic Significance of Cruise Tourism." *Annals of Tourism Research*, 25(2): 393–415.

Endo, K. (2006). "Foreign Direct Investment in Tourism—Flows and Volumes." *Tourism Management*, 27(4): 600–614.

Evans, N. and Elphick, S. (2005). "Models of Crisis Management: An Evaluation of their Value for Strategic Planning in the International Travel Industry." *International Journal of Tourism Research*, 7(3): 135–150.

Forsyth, P. (2006). "Martin Kunz Memorial Lecture. Tourism Benefits and Aviation Policy." *Journal of Air Transport Management*, 12(1): 3–13.

Franklin, A. and Crang, M. (2001). "The Trouble with Tourism and Travel Theory?" *Tourist Studies*, 1(1): 5–22.

Friedman, T.L. (2006). *The World is Flat: A Brief History of the Twenty-First Century*. New York: Farrar, Straus and Giroux.

Gannon, J. and Johnson, K. (1995). "The Global Hotel Industry: The Emergence of Continental Hotel Companies." *Progress in Tourism and Hospitality Research*, 1(1): 31–42.

Go, F. and Pine, R. (1995). *Globalization Strategy in the Hotel Industry*. London: Routledge.

Go, F. and Ritchie, J.R.B. (1990). "Tourism and Transnationalism." *Tourism Management*, 11(4): 287–290.

Go, F., Pyo, S.S., Uysal, M. and Mihalik, B.J. (1990). "Decision Criteria for Transnational Hotel Expansion." *Tourism Management*, 11(4): 297–304.

Gudmundsson, S.V. and Lechner, C. (2006). "Multilateral Airline Alliances: Balancing Strategic Constraints and Opportunities." *Journal of Air Transport Management*, 12(3): 153–158.

Hall, A.J. and Braithwaite, R. (1990). "Caribbean Cruise Tourism: A Business of Transnational Partnerships." *Tourism Management*, 11(4): 339–347.

Hobson, J.S. (1993). "Analysis of the US Cruise Line Industry." *Tourism Management*, 14(6): 453–462.

Hotels (2006). "Corporate 300 Rankings." 40(7): 40–52.

Ioannides, D. and Debbage, K. (Eds.) (1998). *The Economic Geography of the Tourist Industry: A Supply-Side Analysis*. New York: Routledge.

Ioannides, D. and Debbage, K. (1997). "Post-Fordism and Flexibility: The Travel Industry Polyglot." *Tourism Management*, 18(4): 229–241.

Jaakson, R. (2004). "Beyond the Tourist Bubble? Cruiseship Passengers in Port." *Annals of Tourism Research*, 31: 44–60.

Johnson, C. and Vanetti, M. (2005). "Locational Strategies of International Hotel Chains." *Annals of Tourism Research*, 32(4): 1077–1099.

Judd, D.R. (2006). "Commentary: Tracing the Commodity Chain of Global Tourism." *Tourism Geographies*, 8(4): 323–336.

Littlejohn, D. and Beattie, R. (1992). "The European Hotel Industry: Corporate Structures and Expansion Activity." *Tourism Management*, 13(1): 27–33.

Lohr, S. (2008). "Betting to Improve the Odds." *New York Times*, April 9 (Special Section on Technology): H1 and H7.

Milne, S. and Pohlmann, C. (1998). "Continuity and Change in the Hotel Sector: Some Evidence from Montreal." In D. Ioannides and K. Debbage (Eds.), *The Economic Geography of the Tourist Industry: A Supply-Side Analysis* (pp. 180–196). London: Routledge.

Pan, C. (2005). "Market Structure and Profitability in the International Tourist Hotel Industry." *Tourism Management*, 26(6): 845–850.

Prideaux, B. (2005). "Factors Affecting Bilateral Tourism Flows" *Annals of Tourism Research*, 32(3): 780–801.

Ritzer, G. (1993). *The McDonaldization of Society: An Investigation into the Changing*

Character of Contemporary Social Life. Newbury Park: Pine Forge Press.

The Brattle Group (2002). *The Economic Impact of an E.U.-U.S. Open Aviation Area*. London: Brattle Group.

Urry, J. (1995). *Consuming Places*. London: Routledge.

Urry, J. (1990). *The Tourist Gaze*. London: Sage.

Wald, M.L. (2008). "A Cleaner, Leaner Jet Age Has Arrived." *New York Times*, April 9: H2.

Weaver, A. (2005). "The McDonaldization Thesis and Cruise Tourism." *Annals of Tourism Research*, 32(2): 346–366.

Wheatcroft, S. (1994). *Aviation and Tourism Policies: Balancing the Benefits*. London: Routledge.

Wood, R. (2000). "Caribbean Cruise Tourism: Globalization at Sea." *Annals of Tourism Research*, 27(2): 345–370.

World Tourist Organization (WTO) (2005). *Tourism Market Trends*. Madrid: WTO.

33

Tourism and International Policy: Neoliberalism and Beyond

R.E. Wood

Introduction

International tourism policy and governance are in a process of transition. Until the early 1990s, international tourism policy was mainly a matter of national policies and bilateral agreements between nations (Edgell, 1990; Hall, 1994). States and intergovernmental organizations were the major players, and reducing government restrictions that limited transportation, travel, and currency exchange constituted their major agenda. Coordinated tourism promotion helped produce what Hall (2001) calls "international regionalism," and tourism provisions were occasionally embedded in broader multilateral agreements such as the Helsinki Accord. Overall, however, as Edgell (1990: xi) put it in his book, *International Tourism Policy*, it was in its "infancy," and focused on tourism primarily as "leisure migration" (Borocz, 1992).

Within a few years, however, Edgell (1995) was hailing the prospect of a "barrier-free future for tourism," thanks to the Uruguay Round of Multilateral Trade Negotiations that for the first time included

services, counting tourism. The General Agreement on Trade in Services (GATS) that resulted from the Uruguay Round was annexed to the Marrakesh Agreement Establishing the World Trade Organization (WTO), which was signed at the conclusion of the Uruguay Round. It came into force on January 1, 1995.[1] Global tourism policy had arrived—some would say, with a vengeance.

GATS was in fact part of a broader, although uneven, process of multilateralization that gave rise to new institutional actors and the emergence of supranational forms of tourism governance, what Cornellissen (2005) calls the *global tourism system*. While this process was driven by a variety of interests and issues, that it reflected at its heart the ideological hegemony of neoliberalism and its corresponding globalization project (Cornellissen, 2008; McMichael, 2000).

Tourism is of course shaped by a much broader array of national, international, and global policies and processes. Tourism's vulnerability to politics and events outside its control is well-documented: September 11, 2001 and the Indian Ocean tsunami of December 26,

2004 come quickly to mind. A broad range of nongovernmental organizations (NGOs) addressing a variety of areas of tourism concern has emerged over the past few decades to challenge many policies and industry practices. Policy debates about tourism today swirl around such issues as sustainability, environmental impact, responsible tourism, equitable development and poverty alleviation, local participation, world heritage, cultural integrity and survival, human trafficking, security, climate change, fair trade, and much more.

While this chapter will touch on several of these issues, its central focus will be on the effort to bring tourism more completely under the regime of neoliberal ideas and institutions, for it is these ideas and institutions that appear to be the ones shaping global tourism policy the most. The relationship of neoliberalism to international policy is complex: a neoliberal world order requires an overarching set of rules and procedures that privilege market forces and restrain government or international policies that offset or interfere with them.[2] Represented most clearly in the various treaties of the WTO, this form of global governance serves mainly to delegitimatize alternative policies and mechanisms and to question the need for them. (This suspicion of international policy apart from that which creates a market-dominant framework may help explain the withdrawal of the USA from the World Tourism Organization and the dismantling of its own national tourism agency in 1996, a year after GATS went into effect.[3]) Hence much of the debate over the implications of GATS for tourism concerns what *other* policies GATS may override or weaken. How broad and deep the impact of GATS will be, however, remains a matter of vigorous debate.

The chapter will therefore begin with GATS as a manifestation of the neoliberal agenda for tourism, examining first its structure and operation, and then the debate over its impact. The subsequent section then argues that one type of tourism—cruise ship tourism—conforms so closely to the neoliberal ideal that it can be seen as a kind of paradigmatic case, providing a glimpse of what a full realization of the neoliberal vision in tourism might mean. Examination of the cruise industry also suggests that this extreme form of neoliberal globalization is provoking a counter-reaction, somewhat along the lines Polanyi (1957) identified in the case of the classical liberal utopian ideal. The final section of this chapter thus provides a brief survey of several attempts to move international tourism policy and global governance beyond neoliberalism and its associated market paradigm. In these efforts we see the emergent outlines of a more comprehensive and balanced tourism policy.

GATS and the Trade in Tourism Services

Tourism has been both a source and a beneficiary of the globalization of services (Fayed and Fletcher, 2002) and now accounts for over one-third of the global services trade (Endo, 2006:1). Indeed, for the world's least developed countries, tourism constitutes over 70% of their service exports (World Tourism Organization 2008). Merchandise trade has been subject to multilateral negotiations and rules for over 50 years, but the coming into force of the GATS in January 1995 marked the first time that trade in services was similarly regulated. The notion that cross-border service transactions should be considered a form of trade and brought under the GATT/WTO trade regime was a highly contentious one at first.[4] In their analysis of how this radically new—and classically neoliberal—idea spread, Drake and Nicolaïdis note: "The shift to a trade discourse [for services] was a revolution in social ontology … It took a fundamental change of mindset to believe that the long-term benefits of trade liberalization could outweigh the substantial adjustment costs and risks involved" (1992: 38).

The WTO considers GATS's contribution to the global trade in services to rest on two main pillars: (1) transparent rules and regulations; and (2) progressive liberalization. The second pillar suggests that any existing version of GATS should be considered only a way-station along a unidirectional journey towards greater economic liberalization. No limits to the process are specified, and no other competing priorities (e.g., sustainability, equitable distribution, etc.) are formally recognized as anything more than temporary.

GATS specifies four different "modes" in the trade of services, which are described below with examples from tourism:

- **Mode 1:** Consumer in one country purchases a service directly from a service provider in another country, e.g., purchasing a tour or a travel insurance policy from a firm in another country.
- **Mode 2:** Consumer travels to another country and purchases services there, e.g., a meal at a restaurant, in that country.
- **Mode 3:** Consumer purchases a service from a foreign service *supplier* who has established a commercial presence in the consumer's country, e.g., hiring consultants from a foreign-owned firm with a local presence to develop a tourism marketing campaign.
- **Mode 4:** A service transaction involving the presence of a *person* from another country, e.g., a foreign manager in a hotel.

GATS distinguishes between 12 core service sectors, one of which is tourism and travel-related services (TTRS).[5] These are divided into 160 subsectors. TTRS is divided into four subsectors: (1) hotels and restaurants; (2) travel agencies and tour operators services; (3) tourist guide services; and (4) other. However, there are numerous subsectors within the 11 other core service sectors that are relevant to tourism.[6] The World Tourism Organization has expressed its unhappiness with GATS's narrow definition of tourism subsectors, which leaves out such key sectors as passenger transportation, computer reservation systems, and the entire cruise ship industry. Several countries, led by the Dominican Republic, have lobbied for a Tourism Annex to GATS to extend the range of coverage and to incorporate developmental and sustainability goals—as well as

"anti-competitive practices" in the air passenger transportation sector—but to no avail so far (Cornelissen, 2008; Dunlop, 2003: 9–11).

The GATS agreement imposes a number of general obligations, including most-favored-nation treatment and transparency, and certain general commitments regarding domestic regulation, monopolies, business practices, and subsidies. Beyond these, each GATS member (generally a country, except for the European Union [EU], which signs as one) may choose to make commitments regarding "market access" and "national treatment" for the four modes of supply for each the subsectors of the 12 sectors. Market access (Article XVI) mainly involves the application of the most-favored-nation principle, which says that any market access granted to one GATS member is automatically granted to all; however, some other limitations on certain types of market access may be scheduled. National treatment (Article XVII) requires that in sectors for which a member has scheduled commitments, foreign and national service suppliers must be treated the same, unless (allowable) exceptions are registered at the outset. The structure of the commitment schedule for TTRS is provided in Table 33.1.

As can be seen, there are 32 possible categories of bindings/restrictions for the TTRS sector alone. If a country wishes to make a full commitment for either market access or national treatment, it enters "none" into its schedule for a specific subsector—meaning that there are no limitations. At the other extreme, "unbound" means that the member wants to remain free to maintain or introduce measures inconsistent with market access or national treatment. In between there are various options; e.g., "Unbound except for . . ." (Council for Trade in Services, 2001). This "bottom-up" system of members choosing to "bind" or leave "unbound" various sectors and subsectors stands in marked contrast with the General Agreement on Tariffs and Trade (GATT) agreements on merchandise trade, which are

Table 33.1   GATS Commitment Schedule for the Tourism and Travel-Related Services (TTRS) Sector

Subsector	Mode	Limitations on Market Access	Limitations on National Treatment
Hotels and	Mode 1		
restaurants	Mode 2		
	Mode 3		
	Mode 4		
Travel agencies and tour	Mode 1		
operators	Mode 2		
	Mode 3		
	Mode 4		
Tourist guide services	Mode 1		
	Mode 2		
	Mode 3		
	Mode 4		
Other	Mode 1		
	Mode 2		
	Mode 3		
	Mode 4		

generally automatically binding on all members.

Tourism in the Age of GATS

With GATS having been in operation for over 10 years now, it might seem that an assessment of its impact in the area of tourism would not be difficult, especially since more WTO members (125) have scheduled commitments in the TTRS sector than in any other. The task is complicated by several different factors, however, as discussed below.

The Standstill Thesis

Tourism was the most liberalized service sector going into the GATS negotiations (Endo, 2006; WTO, 1999). Expectations about tourism's contribution to foreign exchange earnings and perceptions of the need to elicit transnational corporate involvement to attract tourists had already led to significant deregulation and liberalization in the tourism sector. In this context, most members scheduled commitments in TTRS

and other sectors that basically reflected existing practice, rather than increasing the level of economic liberalization. This has given rise to what might be called the *standstill thesis*, which sees GATS as simply reaffirming the *status quo ante*. For example, two WTO economists have argued that "GATS has obviously not yet lived up to ambitious expectations," and that the commitments resulting from the Uruguay Round "apparently have not had significant liberalization effects" (Adlung and Roy, 2005: 1161–1162). Te Velde and Nair similarly conclude: "GATS is scarcely used as a liberalizing tool" (2006: 439).

The standstill thesis, however, misses the significance of binding current levels of liberalization within the framework of GATS and the wider WTO. As Drake and Nicolaïdis note, the application of the discourse of trade to services itself carried important consequences:

The very act of defining services transactions as "trade" established normative presumptions that "free" trade was the yardstick for good policy against which regulations, redefined as nontariff barriers (NTBs), should be measured and justified only exceptionally. Members believing there to be many justifiable exceptions thus had to defend what their counterparts label "protectionism". (1992: 40–41)[7]

In addition to this ideological change, inscribing the current level of liberalization in the tourist sector within the GATS framework carries important practical implications. Countries become subject to WTO procedures for renegotiations and dispute settlements, and must commit to progressive liberalization in the future (Dunlop, 2003: 24; Perrin et al., 2001: 30). Policy flexibility, especially in terms of returning to a lower level of liberalization, is significantly constrained, and policy reversals can prove very costly. Even if the first round of GATS negotiations did not result in much further liberalization, its accomplishment in bringing WTO members into an institutional regime of progressive liberalization of services constituted a major step towards the realization of neoliberal ideals.

Methodological Problems of Assessing GATS' Impact

Since GATS became operative, there have been rapid and substantial changes in the tourism industry, most notably absolute increases in international tourists and significant shifts in their countries of origin and destination; major corporate consolidation in key sectors; and significant increases in levels of tourism foreign direct investment (FDI). The degree to which any of these trends can be directly linked to GATS is much debated, however. One preliminary study of Turkey (Perrin et al., 2001) finds a link between economic liberalization and increased tourist arrivals and FDI in tourism, but notes that Turkey's GATS commitments are significantly less than its actual level of economic liberalization. A comparative study by te Velde and Nair (2006) also finds a positive relationship between the level of GATS commitments and inward FDI in tourism, but concludes that the way countries signal their openness to foreign investment through the ongoing GATS process may be more important than the commitments themselves, and that in any case other factors may

be more important in determining the level of FDI. In a statement that reflects the sense of much of the limited literature on this subject, Smith concurs that "the full impacts of GATS on tourism are impossible to model empirically with current data. There are so many forces affecting international tourism that it is not possible to determine quantitatively the impact of trade liberalization in isolation from other factors" (2007: 128). One might note in this context that the advent of GATS coincided with key technological changes, most notably the explosion of Internet usage, (a greater proportion of tourism purchases are made over the Internet than in any other sector). In addition, bilateral agreements continue to be a major alternative mechanism of liberalization in tourism, particularly with respect to air travel.

Recognizing GATS as one important component among many in an emerging multi-layered system of tourism governance that shifts significant powers both to supranational institutions and to private sector organizations (see Cornelissen, 2005, for a fuller analysis), the subsections below briefly review recent trends in corporate consolidation and FDI in the tourism industry and then look at the issue which most preoccupies the critics of GATS: its relationship to such issues as sustainability and equity.

Tour Operator, Global Distribution Systems, Hotel and Air Transportation Investment and Concentration

The World Tourism Organization's (2002) study, *Tourism in the Age of Alliances, Mergers and Acquisitions*, shows that there was a sharp increase in these different forms of transnational consolidation throughout the 1990s, and that some of the most aggressive expansion and concentration took place after 1995, the year GATS came into effect. Consolidation in the vertically integrated tour operator sector has been particularly striking, with TUI Travel (owned by TUI, formerly Preussag) and Thomas Cook (majority owned by the German retailer, KarstadtQuelle) gobbling up many of their competitors and emerging as the two largest tour operators in the world, especially dominant in the European market.[8] TUI owns roughly 3500 travel agencies, 79 tour operators, over 120 aircraft, 12 hotel brands with 163,000 beds, and 10 cruise liners and a good deal more. It operates in 180 countries and claims over 30 million customers (TUI AG, 2007: 30). With TUI merging with First Choice in 2007 (having already swallowed up the major British tour operator Thomson a few years earlier), and with Thomas Cook merging with MyTravel (formerly Airtours) in the same year, the process of consolidation in the European tour operator industry is clearly an ongoing one.

A similar process of consolidation among an already-small number of key players has occurred among global distribution system (GDS) firms. GDSs are computer and online reservation systems (known originally as computer reservation systems [CRS] when they were developed by various airlines) that operate globally and handle the full range of tourism services. Stepped-up consolidation in recent years has reduced the major GDS players to four: Sabre, Amadeus, Galileo, and Worldspan. Galileo's parent company, Travelport, purchased Worldspan in 2007, reducing the dominant corporate players to three. The top global distribution system companies have been called a "cosy oligopoly" (Dunlop, 2003: 41), as reflected by the launch in 2007 of the Moneydirect joint venture of Amadeus and Sabre to facilitate automated payment processing in the industry. The GDS transnational companies own most major online ticketing and reservations sites.

Outward stocks of FDI in tourism-related sectors (mainly hotels and air transportation) doubled for the UK between 1995 and 2002, almost quadrupled for Germany, and more than doubled for the USA (Endo, 2006: 606). Between 1995 and 1998 alone, 27 major hotel groups were targeted and taken over

(Knowles et al., 2001: 73). While the hotel sector overall is less dominated by transnational capital than the GDS, tour operator, and air transportation sectors, concentration of ownership, leasing, management and/or franchising of four- and five-star hotels is increasing. Reflecting the interconnections between these developments, TUI is today the largest hotelier in Europe.

The negotiations that produced GATS kept most of the major issues involved in air passenger transportation off the table, deferring to the longstanding bilateral-based aviation regime (see Fayed and Westlake, 2002, also Cornelissen, 2005, for further details). This regime, while arguably giving less powerful players more bargaining power than a global multilateral one, nonetheless has moved, under pressure from the USA and its "Open Skies" proposals, towards deregulation and a market-based system (see Debbage and Gallaway [Chapter 32] in this *Handbook* for more on regulatory issues in the air transportation sector). An important milestone was the open skies pact between the USA and the EU, which came into effect in 2008. Parallel to progressive liberalization in GATS, the agreement carries a commitment for a further round of negotiations to extend the liberalization process to issues of foreign investment and voting rights. In the meantime, the airline industry has also moved towards substantially increased concentration, privatization, and, at the level of most individual countries, towards greater foreign ownership and control.

Four airline alliances hold nearly 70% of global market share, with the expectation that just two or three will hold 90% by the year 2010 (Endo, 2006: 605, 612). While this kind of penetration and consolidation has been both praised and criticized, it does lend support to the general claim of critics that GATS reinforces neoliberal-inspired trends already in place (Cornelissen, 2008; Hoad, 2002: 226), primarily benefiting the large transnational enterprises best situated to take advantage of these new opportunities.[9]

Externalities: Environmental and Cultural Concerns

The rationale for tourism public policies in capitalist economies is often made in terms of externalities (Fayos-Solà and Bueno, 2001: 60–61; Johnson and Thomas, 1992: 2). Externalities are costs or benefits that lie outside of the economic exchange that produces them. Tourism development can have positive externalities: nicer places for local people to walk and eat, increased property values for homeowners, a chance to practice one's English (or, increasingly, Chinese), etc. The fact that tourism can have negative externalities, particularly with respect to the environment and local culture, is well-documented in the literature and widely interpreted as evidence of the need for robust policies at both the national and international level. What is new and controversial is the claim that GATS may make developing public policies to deal with these tourism-related concerns more difficult, or in the worst case scenario, impossible.

GATS has been opposed from the start by a broad array of NGOs, political parties, intellectuals, academics, and local activists. Apart from general concerns about democracy and national sovereignty, the broadest array of claims—and literature—focus on health and other public services, most notably education and water. Here the claim has generally been that GATS may be used to challenge, deregulate, and privatize public services, with large profits for a few and adverse consequences for the great majority. Since most tourism services almost everywhere are provided by the private sector, the concerns involving GATS and tourism have focused on somewhat different issues: environmental impact, local participation, and sustainability of tourism (see Plüss and Hochuli [2005] for a detailed NGO analysis of these issues).

There is no reference to environmental protection or sustainability in GATS. Environmental concerns go beyond their neglect in the agreement; there is also widespread suspicion that GATS rules about market access and barriers to trade may provide a basis for challenging efforts to enforce environmental standards. Several studies (e.g., Bendell and Font, 2004; Hoad, 2002) conclude that the wording of GATS is sufficiently ambiguous on key points as to make these concerns at least plausible, and in addition the history of rulings in WTO disputes show a clear bias towards market mechanisms and a presumption that environmental and labor considerations have no place in WTO agreements.

A central theme in the rapidly growing literature on environmental sustainability and tourism is the importance of eliciting local participation in tourism planning, provision, and staffing. Local people are likely to hold important knowledge necessary for sustainable tourism development. They will be much more likely to contribute this knowledge and to help sustain the local environment if they are involved in all phases of tourism development and if they are significant beneficiaries of it (Sofield, 2003). It has become something of a truism in the literature that community participation must be built into tourism development and expansion, and some countries have passed legislation to decentralize decision-making to make this happen.[10] Such measures may very well conflict with a variety of GATS obligations, most notably national treatment. Reservation of employment or business licenses for local people may be construed as discrimination against foreign suppliers or as barriers to trade. Again, the vagueness and ambiguity of the GATS language gives ammunition to both sides, but clearly the expressed concerns do have a reasonable basis.

Such conclusions stand in stark contrast to the WTO's own critique of GATS critics, which dismisses the claims outright by labeling them as at best misunderstandings or at worst deliberate fiction and scare tactics (WTO, 2001). Much of the WTO's rejoinder to its critics revolves around three key assertions: (1) GATS members freely choose what they want to commit to—GATS gives its members a great deal of flexible in deciding what areas it wants to schedule commitments for and what the nature of that commitment will be. (2) GATS does not force or require members to do anything they don't want to do. Neither privatization nor deregulation is required. "Virtually any policy concerns can thus be accommodated within the structure of the Agreement" (Adlung, 2005: 136). (3) Members are allowed to change their minds. Commitments are "voluntary, conditional and temporary" (WTO, 2001: 16).

Again, the issues are complex. But a few points deserve mention:

1   *The freedom to choose can be greatly overstated.* Developing country members can be greatly pressured to schedule commitments, both informally and through the "request and offer" process. Furthermore, the commitment process is extremely complex and few countries have the expertise to understand fully what is involved. As Hoad notes: "Members outline their commitments before they know what the environmental, social or economic implication might be and at no point in the agreement is there reference to sustainability or environmental protection" (2002: 225). In this connection, an instructive GATS case involves the dispute between the USA and Antigua over the latter's online gambling operations. WTO bodies have ruled that some US state laws are in violation of GATS because the USA neglected to exclude gambling from its GATS commitments (Kelly, 2006). An analysis by Krajewski notes:

> The US negotiators may either not have appreciated the different ways in which their schedule could be read. This would highlight the complicated nature of scheduling and the ambiguities it may entail. Alternatively, the US negotiators may have known what they were scheduling but could not imagine that gambling and betting services could one day be traded and communicated so easily through the Internet that an entire new branch of the industry would be built on this. (2005: 446)

If highly-trained and paid US negotiators can make this sort of mistake—and if commitments like this can indeed override state and national laws—"freedom to choose" becomes laden with both ambiguity and consequence, and the exercise of extreme caution in scheduling commitments certainly seems warranted.

2   *Changes need not be "required."* While it is true that GATS does not require deregulation or privatization per se, the obligations entailed in becoming a signer do raise the possibility of challenges, perhaps along the lines of Chapter 11 in the North American Free Trade Agreement (NAFTA), which has led to suits for damages supposedly incurred by foreign companies due to environmental regulation or subsidies to domestic institutions. Certainly the ideological context of progressive liberalization implies deregulation and privatization over time. Language that makes challenges to national policies plausible tends to create a disincentive effect.

3   *Changing course can be very costly.* While it is true that countries can decide to modify their schedule, this opens them to compensatory claims by those affected. The member is required to negotiate an agreement with all members seeking compensation. If this fails, the latter can refer the matter to arbitration. "The modifying Member may not modify or withdraw its commitment until it has made compensatory adjustments in conformity with the findings of the arbitration" (WTO, 1994: 300). Belatedly changing one's mind—even for the best of reasons—can be a long, burdensome, and expensive process.

Neoliberal Globalization at Sea: The Cruise Ship Industry

If we think of neoliberal globalization as being fundamentally about the freedom of capital from territorially-based constraints, unfettered by significant regulation, then one type of tourism does seem to come striking close to the neoliberal utopia: the cruise ship industry. Deterritorialized like no other form of tourism, it also represents an extreme case of escape from meaningful regulation across the full gamut of policy areas: tax, labor, health and safety, consumer rights, and environment. In this sense, as I have suggested elsewhere, cruise tourism can be considered a paradigmatic case of neoliberal globalization which is "at sea" in the additional sense of having an unknown—and potentially dangerous—destination (Wood, 2000, 2006).

In his historical account of the development of the US cruise industry, Garin observes:

In nearly every facet of its operations—in the vast disconnect between its capital base, its labor, and its markets; in the extreme consolidation of its power and wealth; in its relentless appetite for innovation; in its nearly total freedom from a strong governmental hand—the cruise industry is business at its most unfettered. The same quirks of law and history that have enabled it to grow at such a remarkable rate have also given us a glimpse into a possible future in which government has receded almost entirely into the background and society in nearly every aspect is governed by the markets alone. (2005: 10—11)

As Garin's reference to the cruise industry's quirky origins suggest, its growth and shape has only in part been shaped by the neoliberal globalization project. This however tells us something about one basis of that project's success; i.e., its ability to incorporate and build upon preexisting structures, laws, and conventions that may have come into being for other reasons but which collectively help produce neoliberalism's vision of a worldwide market-dominant order, unfettered by all but the minimum-necessary international regulation.

The most central piece of this picture is the flag of convenience (FOC) system. International treaty law specifies that all countries must fly the flag of an internationally recognized state that belongs to the International Maritime Organization (IMO). Ships acquire the nationality of the flag state that registers them, and it is the responsibility of the flag state to certify them and to enforce applicable international regulations. While the system has historical roots going back several centuries (Thuong, 1987), as late as 1940, there were only two flag of convenience states and only 1% of the world's tonnage sailed under their flags (Toh and Phang, 1993: 33). Today, two-thirds of the world's merchant fleet tonnage is registered in FOC states (DeSombre, 2006: 3); roughly the same proportion applies for the cruise ship industry.

FOC-granting states—which include some landlocked states with no navies or merchant marines—largely compete with each other on the basis of low cost and laxity of enforcement of national and international regulations. Since technically cruise ships are floating islands of whatever country whose flag they fly, this means that most cruise ships are largely either unregulated or free from the enforcement of regulation wherever they are. This has given them an enormous economic advantage over their land-based competition which, particularly in the Caribbean, has complained for years about the absence of a level-playing field.

In reality, registering a cruise ship with a FOC state does more than save money and escape regulation. It also helps ensure that a meaningful maritime regulatory regime never comes into existence. This is because ratification of IMO conventions is based on registered tonnage, which gives FOC states dominant power in the organization. Each IMO convention must be ratified by a minimum number of states representing a certain proportion of total vessel tonnage. Since just a few FOC states account for most tonnage, they have able to prevent the ratification of many IMO treaties. Furthermore, under IMO rules, only ratifying countries are subject to a convention that comes into effect. This results in a situation where, even if the cruise companies heed the voluntary and non-monitored International Council of Cruise Lines (ICCL) environmental standards, which call for observance of international environmental regulations, they will still be able to dump just about everything but oil, plastics, and radioactive material in most of the world's oceans, thanks to successful opposition by FOC states to the ratification of more robust regulations.

The biggest cost advantages of FOC involve labor costs and taxation. Spruyt (1994: 51) calculated that for a ship with a 24-member crew, the difference between an all-northern European crew and an all-Chinese crew came to US$698,400 per year. For a single typical cruise ship today with 1000 crew, that difference would be something in the order of US$29 million, not adjusting for inflation. This saving is not simply a matter of different national pay scales. It also reflects the avoidance of national labor regulations, which in most countries would never countenance seven-day working weeks of 60 or more hours or the no-holds-bar tactics employed to avoid labor organizing.

The giant cruise ship companies are incorporated in offshore tax havens and are also able to take advantage of bilateral agreements originally designed to prevent double taxation for nationally-based airlines. For cruise ship companies incorporated in states such as Liberia and Panama and entities such as the Isle of Man, these treaties result not simply in the avoidance of double-taxation, but of single-taxation as well. Florida-based Carnival and Royal Caribbean escape almost all US taxation (Frantz, 1999; Garin, 2005: 199–208; Klein, 2005: 47–86).

This discussion does not exhaust the ways in which the cruise industry is both uniquely deterritorialized and free from regulation, but it should suffice to suggest its unusual proximity to the neoliberal ideal of a global, unfettered market. Not only has the industry maintained its unique freedom from the kinds of oversight and regulation that most other industries have to take for granted, but it has been quite successful in promoting the privatization of global governance insofar as the cruise industry is concerned. It has used memoranda of understanding with local authorities as well as aggressively publicized but unmonitored and unenforced voluntary codes of conduct in such areas as environmental impact and passenger safety to head off calls for regulation from outside (see Klein, 2003, 2005; Wood, 2006, for further details).

As a paradigmatic case of neoliberal globalization, what outcomes and trends do we see in this unique case?

1   Rapid growth. Consistent with the neoliberal emphasis on the objective of economic growth, the cruise industry has for several decades been the fastest-growing major tourism sector, generally increasing at a rate about twice the rate

for the industry as a whole. While the North American market (including the Caribbean) remains predominant, the reach of the industry in terms of both passengers and ports is increasingly global. The industry sets new records for both passengers and profits practically every year.

2   A unique level of industry concentration. No other sector of tourism or arguably any other industry even comes close to the level of corporate concentration in the cruise industry. Three companies, Carnival, Royal Caribbean, and Star, with their numerous subsidiaries, control well over 80% of industry capacity worldwide, and the figure is over 90% in the North American market.

3   An uneven playing field with competing modes of tourism. The cruise industry's avoidance of normal business and labor costs give it an enormous advantage over its land-based competition—something the Caribbean Hotel Organization in particular has complained about bitterly for many years. The industry escapes most corporate taxation and is able to impose wages, labor conditions, and hiring practices that would be illegal on land in most places. So central are FOC-based prerogatives that one highly critical analysis of the environmental effects of the FOC regime nonetheless rejects out of hand the idea of eliminating FOCs because such an action "would be financially devastating to the cruise industry" (Schulkin, 2002: 125).

4   Minimal rule-making combined with minimal enforcement. The structural bases and organization of the industry operates in a variety of ways to limit rule-making across the gamut of policy areas, but particularly in taxation, labor, and environment. Linking ratification to tonnage in the IMO ensures the weakness of maritime regulation. In a sense, the whole system has much the same effect as the WTO, whose function is as much to prevent nationally based regulation as it is to provide a global framework for trade. Furthermore, the IMO does not have the power to enforce its own conventions.

5   The inadequacy of voluntary and privatized environmental governance. Bad publicity from widely publicized pollution prosecutions in the 1990s, combined with increased recognition of the economic payoffs of investment in less-polluting technologies, has led to major investments by the major cruise companies to make their ships less polluting. Since the industry's

voluntary environmental code contains no provision for monitoring, it is hard to know how much previous practices have changed. Even with the modest commitments embodied in the code, however, a steady discharge of environmental violations and subsequent fines by port states has continued to embarrass the industry. Neither the ICCL nor the Cruise Lines International Association (CLIA), which merged in 2006, has done anything when its own members have violated its own code. Studies have clearly shown that when the voluntary memorandum of understanding (MOU) approach is compared to those cases in which port states, mainly Alaska and California, have been aggressive in passing and enforcing their own environmental legislation, violations have decreased in the latter much more than in the former. Furthermore, the cruise companies have shifted their least-polluting ships to those areas with legislative enforcement, leaving their more-polluting ships to serve voluntary MOU areas (Klein, 2003; Schmidt, 2004). It is the position of virtually all environmental organizations that voluntary policies are no substitute for governmental or international regulation (Klein, 2003; Nowlan and Kwan, 2001; Oceans Blue Foundation, 2002; Ocean Conservancy, 2002).

6   A workplace both paramilitary and lawless. Cruise companies are secretive about their workplace operations, and on-site studies by outsiders have been practically nonexistent. The industry likes to point out that workers flock to work on cruise ships from all over the globe, often investing substantial money to get such a coveted job, although there is much evidence of false advertising and outright trickery in many of the recruiting agencies that the industry relies upon. Certainly the capacity to manage concentrated labor forces of 40 or more nationalities is an achievement of broad interest. Still, the evidence that exists highlights many practices that could only exist in such an unregulated setting. For one thing, the application of the basic paramilitary model of shipboard command to the hospitality crew creates a situation of virtually no rights, and much fear, for cruise ship workers. At the same time, there is evidence of diffused lawlessness in such forms as coercive exchange of sexual favors and bribes to keep or get one's job done. This workplace lawlessness may also extend to implicit encouragement to subordinates to violate environmental and other laws in order

to save money and earn bonuses without involving higher management directly. Both racial and ethnic discrimination in hiring and promotion practices are common. There can be little question that the bulk of the cruise ship workforce, however greater the economic advantages over its local options may be, is uniquely without rights or expectations of due process.[11]

Sorting out how much such characteristics of the "unfettered" cruise industry can be generalized as likely outcomes for tourism in a truly neoliberal global order is difficult. Clearly cruise tourism has special characteristics that limit its comparability to other types of tourism. At the very least, however, the cruise industry should function as a cautionary tale about some of the potential dangers of any international tourism policy that tilts too far in the direction of neoliberal assumptions and ideas.

Rebalancing Tourism Policy

As Cornelissen (2008) has observed, the debate about GATS "mirrors predominant discourses on development in tourism scholarship." Some, particularly economists, see economic liberalization as breaking down archaic obstacles to tourism growth and point to generally positive outcomes where it has occurred. Others, especially anthropologists, cultural geographers, and sociologists, identify a broad range (economic, social, and cultural) negative outcomes of market-driven tourism development. Political scientists have tended to take an intermediate position, emphasizing the potential contributions of well-conceived tourism public policies.

These discourses in turn clearly reflect broader ideological positions among both scholars and publics about globalization generally: those who largely celebrate neoliberal globalization, those who harshly criticize it, and those who seek a "third way" (Burns, 2004), some form of alternative globalization that captures its liberating potentialities while institutionalizing environmental, equity, and other important values in global governance (for an excellent discussion of the link between perspectives on globalization and tourism scholarship, see Munar [2007]).

How the issues about GATS raised in the first part of this chapter—and perhaps also how much the analysis of the cruise industry in the second part reveals about the future of tourism—will depend very much on how this larger struggle over the rules and institutions of globalization develops in the twenty-first century. For critics of neoliberalism who see the strength of neoliberal ideology and systemic constraints as likely to block substantive alternatives (e.g., Higgott and Weber, 2005; Hollinshead and Jamal, 2001; Schilcher, 2007), the worst fears about GATS are likely to be realized as goals of sustainable and ProPoor development remain marginalized as the harmless rhetoric of academia and United Nations agencies. Conversely, those who identify with the "transformationalist" position of Held et al. (1999) tend to see globalization processes as more diverse and open-ended, with varying trajectories possible simultaneously. Many who share this perspective see uncritical acceptance of neoliberal (or hyperglobalist, in their language) claims as potentially damaging, and see a need to rebalance the nature of the globalization project. They see the future of both globalization and of tourism as being shaped by the interaction between elite neoliberal strategies and social and political movements from below.

Neoliberal globalization is widely accused of promoting a "race to the bottom," and here recent changes in the flag of convenience regime are instructive. As DeSombre (2006) shows in her book, *Flagging Standards: Globalization and Environmental, Safety, and Labor Regulations at Sea*, a combination of social movements from below and governmental initiatives around the world have produced significant changes in the FOC regime that partly offset this tendency. Under pressure from their citizenry, port

states have used their hitherto-underused powers to inspect, detain, fine, and even ban ships from their ports, in the process helping to shift ship owner self-interest in the direction of better ship maintenance and towards the use of FOC registries that have better reputations for upholding safety and environmental standards. The International Transport Workers Federation has used its global reach to get dock workers in certain ports to refuse to unload or service ships with particularly bad labor standard reputations and in the process has significantly increased the number of ships obtaining "blue certificates" from the union for agreeing to meet minimal labor standards. Such pressures have produced what DeSombre (2006) calls "a race to the middle," as ship owners increasingly look to registries whose reputations will protect their ships from costly delays and sanctions. Because of their enormous size and polluting potential, cruise ships have been targeted in these processes, particularly in Europe and in western coastal US states. Standards have improved, even if they remain well below the levels of IMO conventions (often unratified, as discussed above) and of the International Labor Organization, which in 2006 introduced a new standard-setting convention specifically for maritime workers that has yet to be ratified. The partial success of these efforts, often spearheaded or at least supported by NGOs, shows that some of the destructive tendencies of neoliberal-style rules can be offset by social and governmental activism.

In this context, Cornelissen's (2005) analysis of the global tourism system provides a useful basis for a few concluding comments. A system of global tourism governance is emerging. It is significantly privatized, but it is nonetheless complex and multilayered, with a broad range of actors. GATS is an important piece of it, but there are countervailing forces as well.

Initiatives to rebalance neoliberal tourism policy span a broad spectrum. Some attempt to use market forces to produce non-market ends, as in various efforts to provide voluntary standards and certification schemes, as a "real step towards international and global governance" (Fayos-Solà and Bueno, 2001: 61). Ultimately these rely on consumer awareness and commitment and seem unlikely to transcend niche status, whatever their contribution to specific enterprises or places may be. Two other initiatives (among many interesting ones) that likewise have their limitations, but nonetheless embody potential for deeper structural reform, are the World Heritage Program and Fair Trade in Tourism. Space limitations preclude an in-depth discussion, but a brief indication of what makes them particularly interesting from a policy/governance point of view follows.

World Heritage Program

While successful in terms of its growing coverage, this UNESCO program, which in 2008 included over 850 sites in 141 countries, involves an "often fraught relationship" between its conservation goals and tourism development (Smith, 2003: 109). But from the point of view of international tourism policy, the World Heritage Program does attempt to rebalance neoliberal tourism policy in several significant ways. First, it legitimizes the idea of global heritage and is a good example of the international creation of public goods. Second, it is often explicitly intended to offset the threat of market forces, and thus to provide a counter-balance to them. Third, World Heritage Status (WHS) changes the nature of sovereignty, but in a very different way than the commercialized sovereignty of the "offshore world" (Palan, 2003) that includes flags of convenience and functions to escape oversight and regulation. As Bianchi and Boniface put it, WHS status "implies the sharing of sovereignty over a particular site, which then becomes ostensibly subject to an international framework of policies and regulations pertaining to WHS, with all the ambiguity that this entails" (2002: 80). With no limit on potential additions to the list, this unique sharing of sovereignty

has the capacity to become quite widespread and to provide a model for other efforts to institutionalize global environmental and social standards.[12]

Fair Trade in Tourism

Fair trade in tourism establishes its identity directly in contrast to neoliberal free trade ideals as exemplified in GATS and the failed Multilateral Agreement on Investment. Exposing the implicit normative assumptions in free trade ideology, it asserts the priority of other values in trade. In their valuable exploration of the topic, Cleverdon and Kalisch (2000: 172) see the concept of fair trade "as a mark of distinction for a particular trading process and product," hitherto limited to primary products like coffee. Despite various implementation challenges, fair trade certification principles and practices demonstrate a trenchant critique of free trade and an explicit goal of reshaping international trade policy to reflect a broader range of important values; a number of NGOs such as Tourism Concern[13] have supported the promotion of fair trade certification, as have coffee certifiers such as the Max Havelaar Foundation, the first third-party fair trade coffee certifier in the world (Bacon, 2005). As such, fair trade certification has much in common with ecotourism certification and other similar schemes in tourism that attempt to ensure local benefit and corporate social responsibility in a global marketplace (cf. Littrell and Dickson, 1999).

International Policy and Sustainable Development

From a planning perspective, the growth of international tourism, the emergence of new tourism forms and concerns about sustainability require new considerations in policy making at global, national, regional and local levels. As Francesco Frangialli, the Secretary-General of the World Tourism Organization (UNWTO), said, international tourism needs to be looked at from two perspectives: the immediate one calls for examining safety and security, but the other, longer-term view "is focused on establishing a mode of tourism development that reduces vulnerability, increases sustainability and maximizes the benefits of tourism for the most disadvantaged communities" (2006: 4). The UNWTO thus developed a Global Code of Ethics to guide destination development and travel, consisting of ten articles accompanied by guiding principles (http://www.world-tourism.org/code_ethics/eng.html, accessed May 15, 2008). While these are useful holistic directions, the example of neoliberalism in the cruise sector above shows the need for more than informal policy and self-regulation mechanisms that, as Mowforth and Munt (1998) pointed out, are inadequate for facilitating sustainability and fair practices.

A number of global conventions and planning initiatives have emerged, fortunately, to direct biodiversity conservation and sustainable development. In 1995, the World Tourism Organization and the World Travel and Tourism Council joined with the Earth Council to develop "Agenda 21 for the Travel and Tourism Industry" (WTTC, UNWTO and the Earth Council 1995). Much of the impetus for this came from the 1992 United Nations Conference on Environment and Development in Rio de Janeiro, Brazil. Also known as the Rio Earth Summit, this conference strove to establish guidelines for governments and businesses to engage in sustainable development. The results were encapsulated as Agenda 21 and subsequent initiatives strove to develop implementation guidelines at the local level via Local Agenda 21 (UNEP-ICLEI, 2003). The Convention on Biological Diversity was another outcome of the Rio Earth Summit and established policy goals in line with the Rio discussions on sustainable development; in addition to ecological sustainability, these goals addressed "sustainable use" through economic and social sustainability, particularly focusing on "equitable sharing" in North-South relationships (UNEP, 1999: 1, cited in van der Duim and Caalders, 2002).

While the fair trade in tourism movement and global sustainability initiatives in tourism are in early stages of development, their ideas directly connect with many of the concerns and demands of the alternative globalization movement. Much will depend on the ability of the new social movement and NGOs, such as Tourism Concern, as well as new "alternative" initiatives such as ProPoor tourism and volunteer tourism, to articulate an ethical vision relevant to tourism concerns and capable of rebalancing global tourism policy and governance in light of GATS's neoliberal agenda (see also Wearing and Ponting [Chapter 15] in this *Handbook*). Given what Higgins-Desbiolles (2006) has called "the forgotten power of tourism as a social force," it is possible that the importance of travel and leisure experiences in people's lives will help propel such a vision and agenda.

Notes

1 For more on the WTO General Agreement on Trade in Services, see: http://tcc.export.gov/Trade_Agreements/Exporters_Guides/List_All_Guides/WTO_TradeinServices_Guide.asp. Accessed May 15, 2008.

2 The essence of neoliberalism is its faith in free markets (often referred to as market fundamentalism) and its hostility to state regulation. For more detailed discussions of neoliberalism, whose international face is often called the Washington Consensus, see Stiglitz (2004) and Harvey (2005).

3 Fayos-Solà and Bueno (2001: 45) find the disinterest in global tourism policy "baffling," but note: "In some cases, it seems that the concept of globalization is introduced to justify non-action, or, more specifically, the dismantling of national and international *public* tourism policy. Somehow, the argument goes, the market forces will find a way, and it will be to the benefit of consumers."

4 The World Trade Organization (WTO) succeeded GATT (General Agreement on Trade and Tariffs). This multilateral trading system celebrated its 60th anniversary on January 1, 2008. See the WTO 2007 press release (press/502), December 4, 2007 on the 2007 WTO World Trade Report: http://www.wto.org/english/news_e/pres07_e/pr502_e.htm. Accessed 15 May 08.

5 For Articles 1-XXVI of GATS, see: http://www.wto.org/english/docs_e/legal_e/26-gats_01_e.htm. Accessed May 15, 1998.

6 For more descriptive detail of the tourism-related sections of GATS, see Diamantis and Fayed (2000) and Lee et al. (2002). The World Tourism Organization and the World Travel and Tourism Council have promoted for some time the concept and methodology of the "tourism satellite account," which is designed to capture tourism-related activities in other sectors as part of an overall measure of the size of the tourism sector.

7 An example of this continuing defensiveness may be found in a World Tourism Organization report that, having laid out a general set of policy priorities for preserving sustainability of natural, cultural, and social resources, feels compelled to say: "Rather than protectionism, these efforts should be seen as respect for cultural identities, the preservation of authenticity and the promotion of diversity" (2002: 90).

8 TUI's parent company actually acquired Thomas Cook in 1998, but to get approval from the EU for its take over of Thomson Travel in 2000, it had to agree to sell off Thomas Cook, whose new parent company, Condor and Neckermann Touristik AG, then went on a buying spree of its own, eventually changing its overall name to Thomas Cook.

9 The World Tourism Organization (2002: 73) takes a generally sanguine view of this, particularly in the case of large hotel chains that are seen as attracting other investors, ensuring project viability, creating new business opportunities for smaller companies providing complementary products and services, etc. On the other hand, others (e.g., Cornelissen, 2005: 82–83; Fayed and Fletcher, 2002: 227–228; Knowles et al., 2001: 211–213) express concern about the gradual crowding out of local SMEs (small- and medium-sized enterprises).

10 A number of countries have developed national tourism policies and master plans for tourism. The United Nations World Tourism Organization reported, for instance, that it has completed a Tourism Master Plan for Nigeria that includes policies and implementation strategies aimed at supporting sustainable tourism development up to the year 2010 (Source: UNWTO News, Issue 1/26, 1996: 10).

11 Probably the best overall summary of workplace issues on cruise ships may be found in Garin (2005: ch. 8).

12 While there are criticisms related to the politics of selecting and managing World Heritage Sites as well as of the impacts of sites being "discovered" and impacted by high visitation numbers, the need for multi-stakeholder involvement and local involvement is well demonstrated (see, for instance, Aas et al., 2005).

13 Fair Trade in Tourism: The bulletin of Tourism Concern's Fair Trade in Tourism Network, Issue 3, Winter 2001/Spring 2002. Retrieved May 15, 2008 from http://www.retour.net/Resourcecenter/WebDocuments/documents/TCdocs/Tourism%20Concern%20GATS%20document.pdf.

References

Aas, C., Ladkin, A. and Fletcher, J. (2005). "Stakeholder Collaboration and Heritage Management." *Annals of Tourism Research*, 32(1): 28–48.

Adlung, Rudolf (2005). "The (Modest) Role of the GATS." *Intereconomics*, 40(3): 135–139.

Adlung, Rudolf and Roy, Martin (2005). "Turning Hills into Mountains? Current Commitments Under the General Agreement on Trade in Services and Prospects for Change." *Journal of World Trade*, 39(6): 1161–1194.

Bacon, C. (2005). "Confronting the Coffee Crisis: Can Fair Trade, Organic and Specialty Coffees Reduce Small-Scale Farmer Vulnerability in Northern Nicaragua?" *World Development*, 33(3): 497–511.

Bendell, Jem and Font, Xavier (2004). "Which Tourism Rules? Green Standards and GATS." *Annals of Tourism Research*, 31(1): 139–156.

Bianchi, Raoul and Boniface, Priscilla (2002). "Editorial: The Politics of World Heritage." *International Journal of Heritage Studies*, 8(2): 79–80.

Borocz, Jozsef (1992). "Travel-Capitalism: The Structure of Europe and the Advent of the Tourist." *Comparative Studies in Society and History*, 34(4): 708–741.

Burns, Peter M. (2004). "Tourism Planning: A Third Way?" *Annals of Tourism Research*, 31(1): 24–45.

Cleverdon, Robert and Kalisch, Angela (2000). "Fair Trade in Tourism." *International Journal of Tourism Research*, 2(3): 171–187.

Council for Trade in Services, World Trade Organization (2001). *Guidelines for the Scheduling of Specific Commitments Under the General Agreement on Trade in Services*. Geneva: World Trade Organization.

Cornelissen, Scarlett (2005). *The Global Tourism System: Governance, Development, and Lessons from South Africa*. Aldershot: Ashgate.

Cornelissen, Scarlett (2008). "Tourism and the General Agreement on Trade in Services: Debates,

Progress and Implications for the African Continent." *Tourism Review International*, 12 (in press).

DeSombre, Elizabeth R. (2006). *Flagging Standards: Globalization and Environmental, Safety, and Labor Regulations at Sea*. Cambridge, MA: MIT Press.

Diamantis, Dimitrios and Fayed, Hanna (2000). "The General Agreement on Trade in Services (GATS) and Its Impact on Tourism." *Travel and Tourism Analyst*, 3: 87–99.

Drake, William J, and Nicolaïdis, Kalypso (1992). "Ideas, Interests, and Institutionalization: 'Trade in Services' and the Uruguay Round." *International Organization*, 46: 37–100.

Dunlop, Adam (2003). *Tourism Services Negotiation Issues: Implications for CARIFORUM Countries*. Report for the Caribbean Regional Negotiating Machinery (CRNM).

Edgell, Sr., David L. (1990). *International Tourism Policy*. New York: Van Nostrand Reinhold.

Edgell, Sr., David L. (1995). "A Barrier-Free Future for Tourism?" *Tourism Management*, 16(2): 107–110.

Endo, Kumi (2006). "Foreign Direct Investment in Tourism—Flows and Volumes." *Tourism Management*, 27(4): 600–614.Z

Fayed, Hanna and Fletcher, John (2002). "Globalization of Economic Activity: Issues for Tourism." *Tourism Economics*, 8(2): 207–230.

Fayed, Hanna and Westlake, John (2002). "Globalization of Air Transport: The Challenges of the GATS." *Tourism Economics* 8(4): 431–455.

Fayos-Solà, Eduardo and Bueno, Aurora P. (2001). "Globalization, National Tourism Policy and International Organizations." In Salah Wahab and Chris Cooper (Eds.), *Tourism in the Age of Globalisation* (pp. 45–65). London: Routledge.

Frangialli, Francesco (2006). "The 'Tourism Paradox': Growth in the Midst of Changes." *UNWTONEWS*. Quarterly Magazine of the World Tourism Organization, Year XX, Issue 1. Madrid, Spain: World Tourism Organization.

Frantz, Douglas (1999). "Cruise Lines Profit from Friends in Congress." *New York Times*, February 19.

Garin, Kristoffer A. (2005). *Devils on the Deep Blue Sea: The Dreams, Schemes and Showdowns That Build America's Cruise-Ship Empires*. New York: Viking.

Hall, C.M. (1994). *Tourism and Politics: Policy, Power and Place*. Chichester: John Wiley & Sons.

Hall, C.M. (2001). "Territorial Economic Integration and Globalisation." In Salah Wahab and Chris Cooper (Eds.), *Tourism in the Age of Globalisation* (pp. 22–44). London and New York: Routledge.

Harvey, David (2005). *A Brief History of Neoliberalism*. New York: Oxford University Press.

Held, David, McGrew, A., Goldblatt, D. and Perraton, J. (1999). *Global Transformations: Politics, Economics and Culture*. Stanford, CA: Stanford University Press.

Higgins-Desbiolles, Freya (2006). "More than an 'Industry': The Forgotten Power of Tourism as a Social Force." *Tourism Management*, 27(6): 1192–1208.

Higgott, Richard and Weber, Heloise (2005). "GATS in Context: Development, an Evolving *Lex Mercatoria* and the Doha Agenda." *Review of International Political Economy*, 12(3): 434–455.

Hoad, Darren (2002). "The General Agreement on Trade in Services and the Impact of Trade Liberalisation on Tourism and Sustainability." *Tourism and Hospitality Research*, 4(3): 213–227.

Hollinshead, Keith, and Jamal, Tazim B. (2001). "Delving Into Discourse: Excavating the Inbuilt Power-Logic(s) of Tourism." *Tourism Analysis*, 6(1): 63–73.

Johnson, Peter and Thomas, Barry (1992). "Tourism Research and Policy: An Overview." In Peter Johnson and Barry Thomas (Eds.), *Perspectives on Tourism Policy* (pp. 1–13). London: Mansell.

Kelly, Joseph M. (2006). "Clash in the Caribbean: Antigua and U.S. Dispute Internet Gambling and GATS: An Interview with Joseph M. Kelly." *UNLV Gaming Research and Review Journal*, 10(1): 15–19.

Klein, Ross A. (2003). *The Cruise Industry and Environmental History and Practice: Is a Memorandum of Understanding Effective for Protecting the Environment?* San Francisco and Seattle: Bluewater Network and Ocean Advocates.

Klein, Ross A. (2005). *Cruise Ship Squeeze: The New Pirates of the Seven Seas*. Gabriola Island, BC: New Society Publishers.

Knowles, Tim, Diamantis, D. and El-Mourhabi, J.B. (2001). *The Globalization of Tourism and Hospitality: A Strategic Perspective*. London: Continuum.

Krajewski, Markus (2005). "Playing by the Rules of the Game? Specific Commitments after US—Gambling and Betting and the Current GATS Negotiations." *Legal Issues of Economic Integration*, 32(4): 417–447.

Lee, Misoon, Fayed, Hanna and Fletcher, John (2002). "GATS and Tourism." *Tourism Analysis*, 7(2): 125–137.

Littrell, M.A. and Dickson, M. A. (1999). *Social Responsibility in the Global Market Fair Trade of Cultural Products*. Thousand Oaks, CA: Sage Publications.

McMichael, Philip (2000). *Development and Social Change: A Global Perspective* (2nd edition.). Thousand Oaks, CA: Pine Forge Press.

Mowforth, M. and Munt, I. (1998). *Tourism and Sustainability. New Tourism in the Third World*. London: Routledge.

Munar, Ana Maria (2007). "Rethinking Globalization Theory in Tourism." *Tourism, Culture and Communication*, 7: 99–115.

Nowlan, Linda and Kwan, Ines (2001). "Cruise Control—Regulating Cruise Ship Pollution on the Pacific Coast of Canada." Retrieved July 5, 2005 from http://www.wcel.org/wcelpub/2001/13536.pdf.

Ocean Conservancy. (2002). *Cruise Control: A Report On How Cruise Ships Affect the Marine Environment*. Retrieved September 9, 2002 from http://www.oceanconservancy.org/dynamic/aboutUs/publications/cruiseControl.pdf.

Oceans Blue Foundation (2002). "*Blowing the Whistle" and the Case for Cruise Certification: A Matter of Environmental and Social Justice Under International Law*. Vancouver, BC.

Palan, Ronen (2003). *The Offshore World: Sovereign Markets, Virtual Places, and Nomad Millionaires*. Ithaca, NY: Cornell University Press.

Perrin, Mireille, Juda, N. and Richardson, S. (2001). *Preliminary Assessment of the Environmental and Social Effects of Trade in Tourism*. Gland: World Wide Fund for Nature.

Plüss, Christine, and Hochuli, Marianne (2005). "The WTO General Agreement on Trade in Services (GATS) and Sustainable Tourism in Developing Countries—in Contradiction?" Position paper by the Berne Declaration and the Working Group on Tourism and Development. Berne, Switzerland. Retrieved January 19, 2009 from http://www.evb.ch/cm_data/Tourismus_und_GATS_englisch_2.pdf

Polanyi, Karl (1957). *The Great Transformation*. Boston, MA: Beacon Press.

Schilcher, Daniela (2007). "Growth Versus Equity: The Continuum of Pro-Poor Tourism and Neoliberal Governance." *Current Issues in Tourism*, 10: 166–193.

Schmidt, Kira (2004). *What Works Best, Regulatory or Non-Regulatory Solutions to Cruise Ship Pollution Prevention? The Environmental Perspective*. Retrieved from http://bluewaternetwork.org/reports/rep_ss_cruise_sandiego2.pdf. Accessed on November 12, 2007.

Schulkin, Andrew (2002). "Safe Harbors: Crafting an International Solution to Cruise Ship Pollution." *Georgetown International Environmental Law Review*, 15(1): 105–132.

Smith, Melanie K. (2003). *Issues in Cultural Tourism Studies*. London and New York: Routledge.

Smith, Stephen L.J. (2007). "Duelling Definitions: Challenges and Implications of Conflicting International Concepts of Tourism." In John Tribe and David Airey (Eds.), *Developments in Tourism Research* (pp. 123–136). Oxford: Elsevier.

Sofield, Trevor (2003). *Empowerment for Sustainable Tourism Development*. Amsterdam: Pergamon.

Spruyt, John (1994). *Ship Management*. London: Lloyd's of London Press Ltd.

Stiglitz, Joseph E. (2004). "Post Washington Consensus." *Initiative for Policy Dialogue Working Paper Series*.

te Velde, Dirk Willem and Nair, Swapna (2006). "Foreign Direct Investment, Services Trade Negotiations and Development: The Case of Tourism in the Caribbean." *Development Policy Review*, 24: 437–454.

Thuong, Le T. (1987). "From Flags of Convenience to Captive Ship Registries." *Transportation Journal*, 27(2): 22–34.

Toh, Rex S. and Phang, Sock-Yong (1993). "Quasi-Flag of Convenience Shipping: The Wave of the Future." *Transportation Journal*, 33(2): 31–39.

TUI (2007). *Annual Report*. Hanover: TUI.

UNEP (1999). "Convention on Biodiversity. Development of Approaches and Practices for Sustainable Use of Biological Resources, Including Tourism." *Fourth Meeting of the Subsidiary Body on Scientific, Technical and Technological Advice*. Item 4.8 of the Provisional Agenda. Montreal, Canada, June 21–25, 1999. UNEP/CBD/SBSTTA/4/1Rev.1. Paris: UNEP.

UNEP-ICLEI (2003). *Tourism and Local Agenda 21: The Role of Local Authorities in Sustainable Tourism*. United Nations Environment Programme (UNEP) and International Council for Local Environmental Initiatives (ICLEI). Paris: United Nations Publication (UNEP).

van de Duim, R. and Caalders, J. (2002). "Biodiversity and Tourism: Impacts and Interventions." *Annals of Tourism Research*, 29(3): 743–761.

Wood, Robert E. (2000). "Caribbean Cruise Tourism: Globalization at Sea." *Annals of Tourism Research*, 27(2): 345–370.

Wood, Robert E. (2006). "Cruise Ship Tourism: A Paradigmatic Case of Globalization?" In R.K. Dowling (Ed.), *Cruise Tourism*. Wallingford: CAB International.

World Tourist Organization (2002). *Tourism in the Age of Alliances, Mergers and Acquisitions*. Madrid: World Tourism Organization.

World Tourist Organization (2008). Homepage. Retrieved April 8, 2008 from http://www.unwto.org/index.php.

WTO (1994). *General Agreement on Trade in Services (Annex 1B)*. Geneva: World Trade Organization.

WTO (1999). *The Developmental Impact of Trade Liberalization Under GATS: Informal Note by the Secretariat (Revision)*. World Trade Organization Document Job No. 1748/Rev.1. Geneva: World Trade Organization.

WTO (2001). *GATS—Fact and Fiction*. Geneva: World Trade Organization.

WTTC, UNWTO and the Earth Council (1995). *Agenda 21 for the Travel and Tourism Industry – Towards Environmentally Sustainable Tourism*. World Travel and Tourism Council, World Tourism Organization and The Earth Council, London.

34

Ethical Perspectives: Exploring the Ethical Landscape of Tourism

Mick Smith

Introduction

> The annoyance with the crowd was not that they blocked the ways and obstructed access to different places. What was much more bothersome was their tourist's zeal, their toing and froing, in which one was, without being aware, included, as it threatened to degrade what was just now the element of our experience into an object ready-at-hand for the viewer. No one, however, would like to contest or underestimate the fact that several of them would preserve a serious impression from the temples of the Acropolis for the rest of their journey. (Heidegger, 2005: 42)

This is how Martin Heidegger, one of the key philosophers of the twentieth century, describes his first visit to Greece in 1962. Like many tourists, then and today, he came to see its ancient monuments, including, of course, the Parthenon perched atop the Acropolis in Athens. What seems surprising is that he waited until he was 70 years old to make such a trip when these same places were so closely identified with the Ancient Greek philosophy that formed the center of his entire professional life and thought.

Perhaps, though, this passage also reveals something of the reason for this apparent reluctance to visit, the ways in which he considered the frenetic hustle and bustle associated with tourism might intervene in any attempt to experience these sites *mindfully*. Heidegger worries that tourists' tenuous relations to the places they visit risks reducing them, no matter what their cultural and historic importance, to mere items on a tourist agenda; the once sacred temple of the Parthenon becomes an object whose main purpose is to serve as a backdrop for tourists' photographic records of their travels. Being caught up in the constantly shifting crowd makes it very difficult to bring to mind this place's actual connection with the past. And yet, even so, Heidegger (albeit in a rather supercilious way) admits that some people may still carry away with them more than their photographs, that they will be changed by their cultural experiences.

This passage then begins to raise certain philosophical and ethical questions that go to the heart of tourism practices. Tourism often seems to encourage precisely the kind of superficial relationships that regard people and places *instrumentally*, reducing them to objects valued only as a *means* to serve our more self-interested *ends*. And, as Immanuel Kant (1724–1804) famously argued, using someone (and, we might add, somewhere) for one's own purposes is the antithesis of an ethical relation which should always involve treating others as ends-in-themselves, that is, of being valuable in their own right independently of any use they may be to us (Kant, 1785). This leads to several important questions. Is tourism then inherently unethical? Are some kinds of tourism more ethical than others? How would we even begin to answer such questions and thereby grasp something of both the scope of ethics and the nature of tourism?

Certainly, those who visit Greece in search of sun, sand, or sex seem to be explicitly guided by self-centered instrumental relations to their surroundings, as does the tour operator or hotelier who regards their clients merely as a source of profit. But is this always so, and are those "cultural tourists" who envisage themselves as engaged in far more edifying pursuits as they peruse Athens' ancient ruins actually any more ethical than the hedonistic pleasure seekers on the beach? After all, the images they capture on film often comprise a form of "symbolic capital" (Bourdieu, 1998) a trophy of their exotic travels that they will employ to distinguish themselves from, and elevate themselves above, those back home who are less well traveled—much as flaunting designer sunglasses might have similar symbolical resonances for those who know or care about such things. The cultural tourism that Heidegger witnessed might, from one perspective, be a sign of a supposedly more "refined" taste, but it too risks reducing the Parthenon to a cipher of someone's social standing, a means for gaining kudos, or, perhaps at best, to an educational *resource*, a means for one's own self-improvement. None of these would treat it with the respect that Heidegger thinks it is due, though we should notice that even Heidegger is primarily interested in the acropolis temples because they serve as an experiential opening on a past world, an experience which, he thinks,

mass tourism threatens to "degrade." It is not entirely clear then whether Heidegger's own perspective is ethical, instrumental, or perhaps, a little of both.

The relations between tourism and ethics are then extraordinarily complex, not just because tourism itself encompasses so many heterogeneous purposes and practices, but also because what constitutes an ethical relation is so very difficult to define. For some, ethics (or perhaps morality is a better word here) is simply a matter of following rules or guidelines, of fulfilling one's obligations and duties to fellow citizens or a higher authority, of the application of generally accepted principles, and/or of conforming to tradition or social expectations. The purpose of morality, so understood, is then both normative and regulatory, that is to say it encapsulates, encourages, and enforces, social norms of behavior; it defines currently "acceptable" or "unacceptable" ways of treating others. These kinds of moral rules and principles are often expressed in legalistic frameworks which can be explicitly used to police actions and punish divergence from current behavioral norms as, for example, when drunken tourists are charged with creating a public nuisance. But, despite its importance, this is a depressingly narrow understanding of ethics and one which, if accepted, would tend to reduce it to an uncritical moral conformity with current standards, a kind of when in Rome do as the Romans do.

Ethics has to be so much more than this. The problem with a notion of moral conformity is that it leaves little or no room for ethical interpretation, judgment, or critique and apparently suggests that our ethical responsibilities go no further than simple compliance. But one can easily imagine numerous scenarios where to comply with certain norms might go against our deeply held ethical views, and a morality of this kind can be entirely inadequate for coping with new or unexpected situations where we are challenged to enlarge or change our understandings of what seems appropriate. How, for example, should we respond to situations where the tourist's affluence stands in stark contrast to the grinding poverty experienced by a majority of locals, where our recreational breaks from work depend entirely on others putting in long hours of menial labor, where our holiday activities contribute directly to pollution and environmental degradation, or where they exacerbate the blatant corruption of border officials?

We can, of course, always fall back onto various strategies that mitigate or assuage any guilt we might feel. We can claim, with some justification, that we are not personally responsible for global poverty, that our spending tourist dollars might raise the living standards of some locals, that pollution is often unavoidable, and corruption already endemic. Such strategies attempt to evade, rather than face up to, the ethical quandaries our involvement in tourism engenders but they do also rightly point to the *structural* nature of many ethical problems. That is, they alter and enlarge the range of questions we need to address from (relatively) simple questions about our own *individual* responsibilities as "hosts" or "guests" to the ethical problems and possibilities inherent in tourism itself as a global capitalist enterprise that now plays an increasingly influential role in structuring contemporary social and environmental relations. In this sense the pressing need for a more profound ethical analysis of tourism practices exemplifies the difficulties in locating shifting patterns of ethical responsibility in general. Any ethical analysis worth its salt must address in a critical manner the ways in which responsibilities are defined, determined, and just as often dodged and dispersed by passing the blame onto others. Such understandings cannot be generated in social, political, or environmental, isolation.

The Ethical Turn in Tourism

The recent surge of commercial and academic interest in what Butcher (2003) refers to as the

New Moral Tourism, by which he means those forms of "responsible tourism," "ecotourism" "sustainable tourism," and so on, that define their practices and purposes in contrast to what they regard as the socially and environmentally damaging aspects of mass tourism, might serve to illustrate the complex dynamics and difficulties in apportioning individual and structural responsibilities. These forms of tourism are usually understood as the tourism industries' structural response to consumer pressure from ethically concerned individuals seeking to ameliorate or find alternatives to tourism's more negative impacts. In many ways they appear to present a way of squaring the ethical circle since they offer personal satisfaction to concerned tourists, partly for the very reason that they appear more sensitive to the needs of the human and ecological communities visited.

Butcher (2003) himself though is intensely skeptical of moral tourism's claims for three main reasons, all of which oppose what he terms the "moralization of tourism." First, he regards mass tourism as a vehicle for largely positive and progressive economic and social development—perhaps the main problem many tourist destinations have is too few rather than too many tourists (2003: 61). Second, he thinks that claims about tourism's environmental impacts rest upon a concern with wilderness preservation that only those living in comfortable developed regions can afford to have. Finding new ways to exploit natural resources is a positive, not a negative, aspect of tourism. Third, he objects to the way that tourists are made to feel "guilt in an arena traditionally associated with innocence, fun and a footloose and fancy free attitude" (2003: 139). After all, we go on holiday to escape some of the moral norms we are forced to accept at home. For Butcher, the moralization of tourism is quite literally a form of "guilt tripping" and ethics should have little or no place at all in discussions of tourism.

However, despite Butcher's apparent moral skepticism his arguments actually incorporate fairly typical modern Western presuppositions about the boundaries and roles of ethical relations. His dismissal of environmental ethics and ecotourism in favor of a purely instrumental approach to a natural world he regards as only a means (resource) to be exploited for human ends is a case in point (see below). But what is most interesting in terms of our current concerns is the way he wants to argue that the individual's tourism experience can or should be an ethics free zone, an argument he presents in terms of the need to maintain the tourists' "innocence" in their holiday pleasures, their freedom from guilt inducing associations. His individualistic proposal that tourism "need only be about enjoyment" (2003: 142) is supported by his initial claim that as a structural force tourism development is, after all, generally in everyone's best interests through facilitating social progress—so there is actually nothing to feel guilty about anyway! Ironically, of course, this kind of claim is in no sense ethics free because it involves passing all manner of judgments about whether tourism development is actually better for others. And, even if we do accept that tourism is *generally* a force for positive change, this certainly does not mean that it *never* causes problems about which we can and should be concerned.

From Butcher's perspective the only structural responsibility the tourist industry seems to have is to make sure that the tourist is able to divest themselves of any nagging feelings of individual responsibility—they should just relax and everything including, apparently, their consciences should be looked after. By contrast the New Moral Tourism is, from this perspective, akin to a form of moral Puritanism, whereby the promotion of ethical travel symbolizes the concerns of a select (and relatively privileged) few who want to demonstrate their individual moral superiority over the tourist masses. And, as with historical Puritanism, the proponents of today's New Moral Tourism are also associated with guilt-inducing condemnation of the (in this case tourist) masses for their shallow, conscienceless, enjoyment of worldly pleasures.

Butcher's critique of moral tourism is then rather reminiscent of the historian Thomas Babington Macaulay's remark that Puritans disliked bear-baiting, not because of the pain it gave the bear, but because of the pleasure it gave the spectators (see Thomas, 1984: 157). Those espousing ethical tourism are the modern equivalents of Puritan party poopers on a "moral crusade" (Thomas, 1984: 93) to stop everyone's innocent sporting fun. Here, however, we can easily see that Macaulay's dismissal of puritanical campaigns against bear-baiting only holds so long as we can or do ignore the pain the bear really is in. Similarly Butcher's analysis works only so long as we deny, ignore, or constantly minimize the well-documented structural downsides of tourism developments in favor of business as usual.

Interestingly, even many mainstream tourist businesses claim to recognize this is no longer a viable option. The fact that even a small minority of tourists, and some vocal organizations like Tourism Concern, take the social and environmental repercussions of their holidays seriously has begun to be reflected *structurally* in terms of institutional and corporate responses. Institutionally, for example, the World Tourism Organization (WTO) adopted at its sixth general assembly in 1985 a Tourism Bill of Rights and Tourist Code and has since developed a Global Code of Ethics for Tourism. These codes are still very abstract and much less inclusive than those developed by sectors of the industry more closely involved in promoting forms of ethical tourism (to take just one random example, the Belize Eco-Tourism Association Code of Ethics),[1] but they are, nonetheless, indicative of the spread of ideas of "corporate social responsibility."

Here the idea is that businesses have ethical responsibilities to monitor, evaluate, and if necessary change their activities in terms of their beneficial or detrimental effects on relevant social communities; responsibilities that should go beyond maximizing profits for their shareholders. That being said, theoretical models of corporate social responsibility vary dramatically in terms of the extent to which they actually deem businesses responsible and in terms of the range of so-called "stakeholders" whose interests they include.

Some influential economic and management gurus like Milton Friedman have explicitly argued that businesses should not be constrained by any moral responsibilities at all (Friedman, 1962). Others, who, for example, only emphasize a company's responsibility to its paying customers, clearly do not come close to addressing the wider ethical concerns that form the basis of, say, community-based tourism or ecotourism. Also, as many critics point out, these codes of corporate responsibility (like the WTO guidelines themselves) are almost entirely voluntary and largely lacking in regulatory teeth. They are often promoted on the self-serving (and therefore rather unethical) basis that their adoption might forestall further governmental regulation of the industry and/or that positive public images and community relations are good for profits (Sasseen, 1993). The acid test for any such code would clearly be whether it continues to be applied by the corporation concerned if the responsibilities it implies begin to eat into that corporation's profits.

We might ask then whether codes of conduct and pledges of corporate social responsibility are *solutions* to ethical dilemmas or merely *sticking plasters* that provide only temporary respite from, and perhaps even hide the real extent of, the problems associated with some tourism developments. While many businesses specializing in ethical forms of tourism are clearly committed to implementing their ideals, the fact that profits are almost always the bottom line does engender a rather different form of skepticism about the structural relations between tourism and ethics. Here the key issue is not (as Butcher [2003] suggests) a skepticism about the *need* to moralize the institutional and corporate forces structuring the tourism industry, but about the fact that the industry's actions often

bear little resemblance to their ethical rhetoric. The problem with the moralization of tourism isn't that a few tourist operations might make susceptible individuals feel guilty about their holiday pleasures but that many do their very best to hide any socially or environmentally negative aspects of their trade, using various forms of image management that sometimes includes spurious or exaggerated ethical claims for their businesses (Font and Harris, 2004; Henderson, 2007). Without the existence of strong regulatory frameworks or intimate knowledge of particular business's track records in geographically distant places, individuals are still left having to make judgments about whether to *trust* what tourist operators say.

So, despite corporations, claim to bear responsibility for their actions the question of whether to *trust* what the travel brochure tells us or question what industry derived kite marks and standards actually mean, redistributes at least some responsibility back onto individuals. To what extent can or should we expect corporations to behave ethically given that they too can claim to be constrained by even more powerful structural forces, namely by the competitive markets that form the basis of capitalism as an economic system? The answer to such questions also depends in part on how one envisages corporations, that is to say on whether or not we decide it makes sense to think of a corporation as the kind of thing that can be ethical, be held responsible, or be trusted in the same way that we might think of another individual person.

Indeed, the question of trust provides a useful way of thinking about such issues since it is so closely associated with the notion of ethical responsibility. As Alphonso Lingis (2004) suggests, when traveling we frequently find ourselves in circumstances where we have to decide whether to trust people of whom we know little or nothing; strangers who speak an entirely different language and inhabit a very different culture to our own. In trusting others we place ourselves in potentially vulnerable situations, at the mercy of those others. Another way of saying this is that we give up to them some responsibility for our future well-being. We do so because we somehow make a judgment about their ethical character, their "trustworthiness," their ability and willingness to take that responsibility seriously. In this sense trust is associated with a deeply personal response to another individual, which, of course, is why we feel so hurt if our trust is betrayed. Somehow, on an emotional and interpersonal level, we seem relatively well suited to making such judgments but the question remains as to whether it makes sense to have this same kind of ethical relation to corporations, to hotel chains, airline companies, travel or development agencies, or even governments? Can these supra-individual structures have an ethical character at all?

We need to be clear about what is being asked here. The question of ethical trust is not the same as asking whether one can have confidence in, say, a carrier getting you to your destination on time. Rather, it is whether a structural body like a corporation can be thought of as having the kind of ethical integrity necessary to behave well, even when it is not being overseen and will not directly and financially profit from so behaving. The question of corporate responsibility, at least in an ethical sense, thus seems closely tied to the degree to which we can think of these rather nebulous but very powerful entities, composed of all kinds of economic and material flows, differing layers and forms of managerial structures, geographically dispersed and functionally diverse employees, properties, technologies, and so on, as being like, or alternatively unlike, individual persons.

The very idea that a corporation might be in any sense like a person seems very strange indeed when put in this light. And yet, the idea of developing an internal "corporate culture," or of promoting codes of conduct and corporate responsibility, is in many senses supposed to be analogous to an individual person developing their own ethical character as, say, a good citizen. When a tour operator attempts to present itself as a good "corporate citizen" it also tries to suggest a similar kind of "trustworthiness." Importantly, this image, whether it is lived up to or not, is not so much an attempt to induce guilt as it is an attempt to offer to those who are already ethically concerned a way of both expressing and, perhaps more importantly, *giving up* or *transferring* some of the responsibilities they already feel to this strange quasi-person, the (socially responsible) corporation.

What is odd is how easily we can and do seem to be able to relate to corporations in an ethical light, as *morally* good or bad actors rather than just good or bad service providers. It seems that we anthropomorphize them, that is we understand them as though they actually had the form of another human being. Corporations have themselves encouraged and fought for such recognition as and when it suited their purposes. Over the four hundred years since the emergence of corporations in their modern capitalist forms (the Dutch East Indies Company, usually regarded as the first, was incorporated in 1602), these fictional legal "bodies" have increasingly been granted the kind of sociopolitical standing previously reserved for individual humans. From their inception corporations could, like individuals, own property but, through a series of legal judgments in the nineteenth and twentieth centuries, they have also come to enjoy a broader quasi-human status, for example, being granted protections under both the US Constitution and Bill of Rights. Corporations have been granted legal status as "natural persons," the right to jury trials, to free speech, and in one recent case even attempted to claim that the company's "human [sic] rights" were being infringed under Article 6 of the European Convention (cf. Bendell, 2000). All these claims about corporations ethical "rights" suggest that they are regarded in many ways analogous to (and often legally equivalent to) human individuals, but are they actually ethically equivalent?

Certainly, while corporations seek quasi-human protection under the law in terms of their "rights," and despite the emergence of discourses of corporate social responsibility, they are noticeably less keen on having such responsibilities governmentally and legislatively en-framed. Indeed, a regulatory regime that imposes corporate responsibilities is often portrayed as an impediment to free trade, as introducing competitive disadvantages, as unnecessary red tape and so on. It seems rather bizarre that at a time when individual human beings are finding their lives and their ability to travel increasingly regulated, many continue to emphasize the need for corporate deregulation, especially given the fact that these fictional "bodies" can radically change their composition and ownership over relatively short periods of time and are so much more powerful, influential, and mobile in terms of where they relocate themselves, than most individuals can usually hope to be (Held, 2004; also see Wood [Chapter 33] in this *Handbook*).

Where then does this leave claims of an ethical turn in tourism? Certainly the so-called moralization of tourism raises as many questions as it answers but it clearly needs to be understood in a much wider social, economic, and political context. Tourism cannot possibly be ethics free; it is never *just* about enjoyment. But grasping just how ethics plays out in the complex interactions between individual tourists, host communities, and the different structural scales of tourism enterprises, is extraordinarily complicated because of the variety of different "actors" involved and the myriad ways of dispersing and reallocating responsibilities within an ever-changing matrix of complicated commercial, institutional, and social relations.

Interestingly, while sectors of the industry are clearly trying to respond to the concerns that have arisen from the impacts of socially and environmentally insensitive forms of tourism, and while alternative modes of ethical tourism and codes of conduct continue to

proliferate, there has been relatively little theoretical debate within tourism research about the nature and importance of ethics itself (Smith and Duffy, 2003). Partly this may be because, as Fennell (2006) notes, tourism ethics is a relatively new field and because tourism research in general has not been ethics driven. Thus, while there is no shortage of literature making and disputing ethical claims, these discussions tend to focus on case studies of best practices in, for example, community tourism and ecotourism. They rarely address more fundamental questions about how and why diverse ethical values arise, how ethical responsibilities might come to be recognized, the nature of living a good life in different cultures, or whose ethical values should (and should not) be taken into account. But these are all crucial questions. How then might ethical theories help here?

Ethical Responsibilities and Mobile Individualism

If even our understanding of corporate social responsibilities is, as suggested above, partly dependent upon our making various analogies and links between corporations and human individuals then it seems imperative we think more deeply about the relation between ethics, individualism and tourism. This is especially so since tourism, as a modern industry, is so closely associated with, and dependent upon, modernity's promotion of particular understandings and forms of individualism. As John Urry notes "acting as a tourist is one of the defining characteristics of being modern" (1990: 2) and modern (human) beings are socially, politically, and philosophically, characterized in dominant discourses as autonomous (self-contained) individuals. The kinds of holiday we *choose* are supposed to reflect and exemplify our *self-image*, our travels are meant to give us a sense of *independence* and to be *character forming*, our vacations are understood as sources of *personal* pleasure, and so on. Modern tourism, unlike many forms of travel such as nomadism, pilgrimage (see Sharpley [Chapter 14] in this *Handbook*), or movements of refugees, tends to assume the centrality of an individual capable of exercising their consumer choice, someone who wants to differentiate and/or develop themselves through these choices, and who is more or less driven by egoistic desires for self-gratification.

This kind of understanding of humans, as autonomous, self-interested, individuals able to use their rational abilities to promote their own interests is, of course, the basic model that underlies liberal and neoclassical understandings of economics and politics. This model of human existence is so self-centered that it initially seems difficult to reconcile with any kind of ethics at all. Indeed, some early-modern proponents of this conception, like Thomas Hobbes (1588–1679), simply denied that there was any such thing as genuinely altruistic behavior (Hobbes, 1651). The fact that people often appeared to behave ethically was to be explained either by the fact that they were really trying to curry favor with those who benefited, or was just a consequence of their being afraid of being punished if they behaved badly.

Although this is still a widely held view it is not actually very plausible given the wide variety of activities we engage in that benefit others, often at considerable personal cost.

Most philosophers in the modern Western tradition have sought to develop a rather less two-dimensional view of human nature, one that sees us as motivated by more than greed and fear and gives at least some room for recognizing the role of genuine other-directed ethical concerns (Smith, 1759/2006). There is, however, no denying the pervasive influence of this idea of humans as separate and basically self-interested bundles of personal preferences in competition and conflict with each other.

Many social theorists would argue that this understanding is a product of the particular socioeconomic processes associated with modernity rather than a universal and time-less model of human nature. The suggestion here is that rapid rates of social change, together with the structural diversity that characterizes modern societies (a diversity that tourism itself exemplifies, where everyone has their own specialized roles and functions to perform, as steward, pilot, mechanic, tour guide, agent, hotelier, and so on) leads to a parallel fragmentation of previously communal interests and values. Why? Because individuals who find themselves placed in these very different and shifting roles will experience and relate to the social world in different ways. The successful entrepreneur and the pool attendant are, for example, hardly likely to view inequalities in wealth in the same light.

In ethical terms modern societies tend to differ from many premodern cultures because they no longer possess a common framework of ideas and ideals that the society as a whole can agree on. Even notions of right and wrong are far from settled, as heated debates over issues like the death penalty or abortion exemplify in the USA. Ironically, the only ideals and values that *everyone* might agree on in modern societies seem to be those based on this very same fragmentation of culture, namely that *we are all* (different) *individuals*! It should come as no surprise then that this is precisely the kind of individualist, self-centered understanding of humanity that the two most influential strands of modern ethical theory, "utilitarian" and "deontological" (or rights based) take as the basis for their deliberations.

Individualism and Utilitarianism

Utilitarianism developed as a coherent moral theory in the late eighteenth and early nineteenth centuries under the auspices of influential philosophical figures and social reformers James Mill (1773–1836), his close friend Jeremy Bentham (1748–1832), and his son John Stuart Mill (1806–1873). Bentham (1948) famously argued that, though individuals may gain their pleasures from very different kinds of pursuits, they all, nevertheless, share a common desire to experience as much pleasure and avoid as much pain as they can. Such hedonism is, Bentham claims, the fundamental basis of human nature and he uses this very simple (and many have argued, overly simplistic) understanding of individuals as egoistic pleasure seekers to develop a similarly simple ethical "principle of utility." This states that those actions that tend to increase the overall level of happiness of those concerned (that is, to maximize utility) should be considered good, those that reduce it are bad. This principle applies to individuals, institutions, and governments, explicitly requiring that each should calculate the positive and negative *consequences* of their, actions, policies, and laws.

It is, then, easy to see how the basic idea of Utilitarianism resonates with modernist understandings of individualism, not just in terms of its hedonistic and egoistic presuppositions, but also in recognizing that every individual is both autonomous and potentially different. It makes no attempt to legislate about what should, or should not, make people happy, nor does it try to impose any specific ethical ideals of right and wrong beyond that of the principle of utility itself. This is both one of Utilitarianism's key strengths and its weaknesses. It allows it to be envisaged as a universal, pluralistic, tolerant, and democratic, theoretical system where any one person's pleasures counts for as much as another's. It also enables it to appear in the role of neutral arbiter in social and ethical disputes since it does not take the side of one set of values over another but tries to resolve any conflict through a supposedly disinterested process of rational calculation.

Conversely, Utilitarianism's lack of specific ethical content means that whatever makes people happiest is, consequently deemed *morally* good, a concern that led some of Bentham's early critics to label Utilitarianism a philosophy fit for pigs rather than humans, since pigs appear content even while wallowing in mud.[2] To put this criticism in contemporary terms, if watching daytime soaps on television makes you happier than going to a Shakespeare play, or if building yet another generic theme park creates more pleasure than saving a unique world heritage site or wilderness area, then Bentham's version of Utilitarianism says these are the *right* things to do. This kind of criticism later led John Stuart Mill to distinguish between different *qualities* as well as *quantities* of happiness, although doing so clearly risks reintroducing a hierarchy of supposedly "higher" or "lower" pleasures that undermines Utilitarianism's democratic pretensions (Mill, 1863).

Utilitarian arguments are by far the most common kinds of justification presented in discussions of the rights and wrongs of tourism. Butcher's argument (see above) that mass tourism is to be defended on the grounds that it is generally beneficial itself implicitly presupposes that, in Bentham's words, "the greatest happiness of the greatest number . . . is the measure of right and wrong" (1948: 3). The increased economic prosperity promised by tourist developments frequently overrides any qualms about even the most culturally significant losses to smaller numbers of people. The misery caused to a few families forcibly evicted from their traditional homes to make way for, say, a golf course development (Keefe, 1995), may count for little when calculated against the benefits accruing to the developers, golfers, and other prospective beneficiaries. Unfortunately then, Utilitarianism can seemingly support the most appalling injustices to a minority so long as the aggregate quantity of happiness is increased.

Of course, it is pretty much impossible in practice to measure and compare degrees of (un)happiness (and predicting the consequences of any activity is increasingly difficult the further into the future one goes) so any suggested outcome can always be disputed. But this is precisely where the fact that Utilitarianism shares so many individualistic presuppositions with neoclassical economics often comes into play. It is relatively easy to see how, if we substitute a slightly different understanding of utility, in terms of satisfaction of *personal preferences* rather than *pleasures*, and further argue that such preferences can be measured and determined by consumer choices in terms of dollars spent, then Utilitarianism as an ethical system can be collapsed into a kind of economic cost-benefit analysis. This may explain why some neoliberal economists think that business ethics is largely superfluous since they apparently believe that whatever maximizes economic benefits is effectively morally right (Chwieroth, 2007).

But should we accept the idea that economic wealth is in any sense quantitatively related and directly proportional to happiness? Even on an individual level, once certain basic social requirements are in place, this seems very doubtful. The discrepancy between figures for gross domestic product GDP and people's actual self-reported *quality* of life is widely known (Samuelson, 1995). A parking lot may be a big money earner but its no one's vision of paradise. What is more, the philosophical presuppositions underlying this economic comparison, including the central idea that people are reducible to bundles of consumptive preferences, have been extensively criticized (Sen, 1977; Sen and Williams, 1982). People are not isolated, selfish, and totally autonomous individuals but are intimately involved with and dependent upon each other in many (indeed most) respects. Moreover, simply maximizing total utility is in no sense ethical since some people should not have to lose everything so that others can benefit. What really matters, many would argue, is encouraging a distribution of wealth that might best fulfill the differing needs of all the individuals concerned, while protecting their basic well-being: Discourses of distributive justice and human rights attempt to address just such concerns.

Rights, Responsibilities and Justice

The idea that we all possess basic human rights, whether to life, liberty, property, or the pursuit of happiness is commonplace, though it is often forgotten that these ideas are, in their current form, the relatively recent outcomes of the intense political struggles that accompanied the birth of modern societies. The recognition of many such rights by governments, trans-governmental organizations like the United Nations, and international bodies such as the WTO, might suggest that they are relatively uncontroversial but there is still extensive debate about their basis, extent, and even their usefulness. They are also contested in another sense since, as the case of Guantánamo Bay shows, even governments that make human rights central to their constitutions have ignored them when it serves their perceived interests.

Writing in the period following the restoration of the English monarchy, John Locke (1632–1704) perhaps the most influential early rights theorist, sought to counter the claims of kings to wield absolute power over the lives of their subjects. Locke (1988) argued that people were naturally independent beings free to control their lives and their possessions as they themselves saw fit, a radical claim about political equality that would later find expression in both the American and French revolutions. Natural rights then, prescribe the limits of any state's powers since, on Locke's view, any government's political legitimacy depends entirely upon their respecting and protecting the basic rights of their citizens. Where a state fails to do this then Locke held that the citizens of that state have the moral right to remove it, by force if necessary.

Most contemporary rights theorists think that we have to see the relation between rights and governments rather differently. Rights are not natural, in the Lockean sense that they predate or would exist without their recognition by any government; rather they are actually a product of such social institutions, that is to say, rights only exist *because* they are institutionally recognized as existing. In effect this has meant that rights are recognized through one's belonging, as a citizen, to a particular nation-state. This, of course, makes rights far less politically radical and far more dependent upon those in power, though organizations like the United Nations still see their role as a transnational institution as a protector of individual rights when particular governments fail to do so (this, one might say, is the basis of the United Nations's own claim to legitimacy). Whatever their basis "though" there is no doubt that claims about human rights, and human right abuses, do form a very important part of any ethical evaluation of a country's policies.

Rights claims play out in tourism in a number of very different ways. For example, the well-documented human rights abuses of regimes like the military dictatorship in Myanmar (Burma) (see Pilger, 1998) have led to call for tourism boycotts of such nations. On the other hand, the WTO's Tourism Bill of Rights and Tourism Code (mentioned above) focus primarily on the rights to rest and leisure and the freedom to travel. This, of course, seems more applicable to financially privileged "guests" than it does to potentially oppressed "hosts." Of course, any claim to have human rights for oneself certainly implies that one has corresponding *responsibilities* (in Kant's [1785] terms a "duty") to respect the same rights for other humans, but different people's rights can obviously conflict and it is not clear how such conflicts should be resolved given the supposedly absolute and inviolable nature of rights' claims.

Apart from those cases where basic rights, for example, to life, openly conflict there are many more cases where it is far from clear how far one's rights extend or how

exactly one's rights are being compromised. In such circumstances right holders will always need to either negotiate appropriate outcomes or agree to differ in a way that minimizes the scope for conflicts. This partly explains why the ethical form of liberal individualism underlying rights discourse is also closely associated with ideals of civility (including a willingness to speak and listen to each other) and tolerance (respect for difference). An important ethical question for any tourism development is then, whether it does foster such ideals. Will the development concerned lead to increased understanding between differing cultures, or is it just the agent of a new, though often outwardly more benign, form of value colonialism (Escobar, 1995)?

Claims of a "right to travel" characterize modernity's mobile individualism. Modern societies require people to move to fit constantly changing patterns of work availability but this has ambiguous ethical repercussions. On the one hand, it means that traditional patterns of social life, including tradition based moralities, break down, which is often regarded as a matter of regret. On the other hand, this same process also led to the recognition of people's rights to movement, to not be tied down to one particular place. Thus, in his work entitled Toward *Perpetual Peace: A Philosophical Sketch*, originally published in 1795, Kant argued for "the right to visit foreign lands, the right to hospitality, and 'the right of temporary sojourn'" (Arendt, 1982 : 16). All people, Kant thought, had this right "by virtue of their common possession of the surface of the earth, where, as a globe, they cannot infinitely disperse, and hence must finally tolerate the presence of each other" (Kant, 1963: 103). Such rights, grounded in a notion of necessary global interdependence, were intended to form the basis of a new *cosmopolitan* ideal, a kind of world-citizenship that all might enjoy in addition to the protections offered by their citizenship of individual nation states. Although Kant was obviously not thinking about mass tourism (his concerns were primarily with protecting the rights of those *forced* by circumstance to seek hospitality) he did recognize the ethical problems and possibilities arising from the early stages of processes we now refer to as globalization.

The increasing level of global interconnectivity and breakneck pace of international development and change, exemplified by tourism, make Kant's interests in questions of ethical cosmopolitanism much more pressing today. While the individualism that underlay Kant's theory of rights and responsibilities appears (however misleadingly) historically triumphant, in the sense that, outwardly at least, most nations now espouse versions of liberal democracy, it is equally clear that many nation states are actually relatively powerless in the face of transnational economic trends. For example, they often have relatively little control over the ebbs and flows of tourism which originate outside their national borders. Another concern is that neoliberal economics is by no means as closely tied to liberal individualism as an ethical ideal as many of its historical proponents have maintained. When neoliberal economic forces are allowed to operate without ethical and political regard for others, they generate complex and socially divisive patterns of dependency and resistance. Those living in such circumstances often look to alternative value systems that appear to offer at least some kind of social support and solidarity, no matter how narrowly focused they may be. Kant's cosmopolitan ideal is therefore threatened in many ways, and not least because of the resurgence of ethnic, nationalistic, and religiously based forms of intolerance that make many parts of the world very unhospitable to those with different beliefs and cultures.

Of course, there have been many attempts to link the ethical concerns at the heart of liberal individualism with wider concerns about social justice and thereby ameliorate or limit the economic inequalities generated by capitalism. The most influential recent example is that of John Rawls *A Theory of Justice* (1973). Rawls (1973) sets out from the same all pervasive notion of self-interested, rational, autonomous, individualism to develop a model of justice that will both support certain claims to equal basic human rights for all and yet also allow a certain degree of inequality in terms of the distribution of socioeconomic goods (so long as the lot of everyone, and especially those worst off, are thereby improved). This conception of justice as fairness would, Rawls supposes, be the outcome of a rational discussion if individuals were actually ignorant of (and hence unbiased by) their future position and wealth in any society; for example, if they might end up as either pool attendant or president. If accepted, Rawls's theoretical model certainly provides a basis to criticize those situations where the all the benefits of tourism accrue to some while the problems and risks and are borne by others who benefit least and/or lack protection for their basic rights.

Ingenious as Rawls's model is, it has been widely criticized for simply accepting too many of liberalism's basic assumptions, which means that in many ways it operates as an ideological defense of the status quo while, at best, encouraging the kind of mild reformism that leaves the basic structures that create individual inequalities unaffected (Pateman, 1979; Young, 1990). The individual it imagines making decisions about a just social framework seems an implausibly abstract caricature, entirely lacking in any features that would actually make them different (and hence have different values) from anyone else. Also, since another of Rawls liberal presuppositions is, unsurprisingly, the political centrality of the nation-state, it has trouble coping with problems of transnational globalization, the claims of cosmopolitanism (though see Rawls, 1999), and the internal cultural fragmentation of nations in a world where a wide variety of ethical and ethnic communities cross national borders as temporary residents, refugees, economic migrants, and tourists.

Rawls' work has, at least, generated renewed interest in questions about the fair distribution of goods (distributive justice) and about the extent and nature of citizens' political obligations within liberal democracies. More recent extensions and criticisms of his work have also tried to address the cosmopolitan and multicultural limits of his theory by taking seriously the fact that people's identities, including their moral perspectives, are produced within culturally, ethnically, or religiously, defined communities. Such cultural diversity is, of course, a feature of modern life and one that tourists often travel to experience. The problem is that these same cultural differences can also be a source of friction and conflict. Indeed Will Kymlicka claims that "ethno-cultural conflicts have become the most common source of political violence in the world" (1995: 1).

These conflicts, as in the former Yugoslavia, may seem to impact on tourism only because they make certain destinations, such as Northern Sri Lanka, or Fiji, more dangerous places to travel. However, philosophical debates around multiculturalism also impinge on tourism to the extent that as a global industry it constantly mediates ethno-cultural differences and often plays a major role in eroding, repackaging, or exacerbating such differences. Tourism is, quite rightly, often portrayed as a positive force that breaks down the barriers that hinder cross-cultural understandings. But we still need to ask on what basis these barriers are breached and what respect for another culture's values might entail?

Some of those involved in debates over multiculturalism have argued that we should try to develop a sense of cross-cultural identification that could transcend any particular ethno-cultural values (e.g., Miller, 1989). But, since the whole multicultural debate arises precisely because common grounds are hard to find, this seems to involve trying to change people's cultural identities. This, in turn, begs the question as to what (and whose) values are to be used as the template for any overarching framework. Imagine, as an extreme example, a tribe in the Amazon that wants to avoid all

contact with outsiders. What right have we to argue that they should be more tolerant of tourist intrusions, especially given the appalling history of cultural genocide those espousing modernization have inflicted on such groups, both accidentally (through spreading disease) and purposefully? Do they not actually have a right to be left entirely alone?

While recognizing that there are no clear answers as to how to ensure respect and equality within and between cultural communities, Kymlicka (1995) favors the recognition of minority rights that might offer some protection to specific ways of life so central to people's different sense of identity. Charles Taylor (1991), another key figure in these debates, argues for the importance of a notion of what he terms "deep diversity," that requires us to respect not only diversity itself but diverse ways of negotiating the differences between groups rather than looking for a one size fits all solution.

Kymlicka (1995) and Taylor (1991) alike recognize that a notion of justice has to include respect for others' differences. This insight becomes absolutely central to forms of difference ethics that are sometimes labeled "postmodern," most notably the writings of Emmanuel Levinas (1996). Rather than trying to develop a philosophy that might underpin current political and regulatory frameworks, Levinas' ethics focuses more directly on individual face to face encounters with others. In this sense, Levinas' ethics might be thought less "useful" in terms of providing policy solutions to ethical problems. In another sense, however, he explicitly offers an ethical ideal that provides fundamental insights into the very nature of ethics, which he understands as an ongoing (though always incomplete) task of coming to respect others' differences, a respect that emerges from the experience of wonder that encounters with others generates (see Smith and Duffy, 2003: 109–113).

It is worth reemphasizing the importance of work like Levinas' that tries to speak of ethics *as such* precisely because ethics often gets treated as if it offered a series of formulae that enabled those employing them to determine right and wrong. But this is a fundamental mistake. Ethics is *not* a management tool. Even though utilitarianism may seem close to becoming merely a mathematical calculus it is, more fundamentally, a way of recognizing the social importance of maintaining others' happiness. When this is forgotten it ceases to be ethics and becomes something else entirely, perhaps a moralistic parody of economics. Like all ethical frameworks it offers a way of articulating and communicating certain kinds of concerns, highlighting some aspects of our situation and playing down or excluding others. Different ethical discourses express different concerns and would therefore compose our ethical relations in other ways. This is why there are few definitive answers in ethics, and why it seems so intangible to those who only recognize as real that which can be captured by numbers or procedures. It is also why ethics remains the vital core of any life worth living.

Environmental Ethics and Ecotourism

While Levinas focuses on the ethics of human encounters one very important strand of ethical tourism has been concerned to recognize the wonder and diversity of the non-human world. Ecotourism is lauded because it seems to offer small-scale, sustainable and educative alternatives to environmentally damaging forms of mass tourism (Fennell, 2003). It often provides much needed funds directed primarily to local populations while simultaneously encouraging these populations to value and protect their ecologically diverse heritages. It also takes a wide variety of forms from whale watching and rainforest hikes to much more controversial projects like CAMPFIRE in Zimbabwe, where local communities have benefited from revenues from big game hunting (Smith and Duffy, 2003).

Generally speaking, however, the label ecotourist would be restricted to those who are more concerned to photograph than shoot the creatures they travel to see. These ecotourists are often motivated by ethical concerns in the sense that they wish to conserve some aspect of the environment as an end in itself, rather than merely because that environment might constitute a resource for future generations of humans (Fennell, 2006). Western ethics has, of course, traditionally focused only on human relations, but ecotourism is itself a mark of changing sensibilities and recent philosophical developments have tried to give expression to these forms of ecocentric rather than anthropocentric (human centered) ethical concerns. The Norwegian philosopher Arne Naess (1988) coined the term "deep ecology" for attempts to think of the natural world as being of *intrinsic* rather than merely *instrumental* value. In Naess' view, humans are only one species amongst many, though one with a special ethical responsibility to the Earth's other inhabitants.

Deep ecology is by no means part of the ethical mainstream and many (including many community tourism organizations) continue to argue that we should focus entirely on the human benefits of environmental protection. From this anthropocentric perspective, ecotourism provides a pragmatic solution for certain communities needing tourist dollars but natural environments would be afforded protection only insofar as they continue to contribute to the well-being of these communities. The key question here is whether such an approach is likely to provide any lasting protection for the environment? The obvious downside to such arguments is that whenever tourism incomes fall or it becomes advantageous to the human community to destroy an environment, this would be deemed ethically as well as economically right.

Ecotourism projects that are not sufficiently informed by environmental ethics are also easily transformed into just another form of mass-tourism where nature is confined to small reserves and/or treated as a commodity to be bought and sold. The unique ecologies of the Galapagos Islands, for example, are now seriously threatened by the development of a mass-market version of ecotourism.[3] Indeed, thousands of people have actually moved to the islands just to service this new industry. So while human-centered arguments may fit well with the dominant worldview, those closer to deep ecology might argue this is precisely the kind of narrow thinking that has led to our current environmental crisis (Smith, 2001). We desperately need to develop less exploitative and more sensitive relations to the places and communities (including the ecological communities) we inhabit. It remains to be seen whether tourism can help us do this.

The Sojourn: Authenticity, Ethics and the Inhabitation of Places

After a brief description of Heidegger's own ski-hut in the Black Forest ... there followed a polemical attack on the educated "townspeople" who spend their holidays in the Black Forest to "view" and "enjoy" its beauty objectively—two words that have a contemptuous ring with Heidegger because they denote idle behavior without "access." He claimed that he himself never "viewed" the landscape; rather that it was his "working world" [... it was] the active practice of the caring existence that disclosed the Being of this world. (Löwith, 1994: 32)

Ethics often seems to come back to the development of an appropriately respectful relationship to other people and places. Some aspects of tourism seem to make such relationships problematic. The ecotourist wants to see species in their *natural* habitat, the visitor to Guatemala see *authentic* examples of local culture and crafts. But most tourism experiences are packed into relatively short, intense, visits and consequently tourist experiences also become packaged to suit visitors' time schedules and, often unrealistic, expectations. On a recent visit to Sri Lanka, for example, our party was guided around entirely fake gem mines and craft villages, and the "wildlife" we saw was all too often paraded by us on a lead.

A lot of ink has been spilled in tourism literature over the ethics of "staged authenticity" (see Jamal and Hill, 2002; MacCannell, 1999). Is it simply a form of deception or does it involve an unspoken collusion between hosts and guests in order to fulfill tourists' expectations? Are the performances of supposedly "genuine" traditional dances in the hotel lobby preserving or demeaning local cultures? Is the zoo's presentation of a lion in front of a painted concrete savannah educative, or merely an attempt to make the animal's living quarters seem more expansive than they really are? Do people even care if they see the "real thing"—after all visitors to the famous Neolithic cave paintings at Lascaux tour a concrete replica (Lascaux II) of the, now closed, original, but they still come in their thousands. What would it even mean to speak of the "real" or "authentic" Disney World experience?

It is easy to dismiss these worries altogether (especially if you hold that tourism is just about enjoyment) but they are, nonetheless, important precisely because they tell us something about the kind of relations between peoples and places that tourism promotes. As the quotations beginning this article and this section illustrate, Heidegger suggests that such relations, whether acted out on the acropolis or in the Black Forest, threaten to degrade "the element of our experience into an *object* ready-at-hand for the *viewer*." Tourism, Heidegger claims, makes the world available to us but only superficially, as a series of disconnected objects that are *there for us to view*, in other words, as impassively experienced means to our touristic ends. Think of the tour parties rushing past the masterpieces in the Uffizi Gallery in Florence, crowding together for the briefest moment in front of Botticelli's "Birth of Venus," then moving on to the next "highlight." How do they experience this painting? Are they struck by the beauty of its composition or the bodily form of Venus? Are they moved by it emotionally or do they wonder about it intellectually? Does it come as a revelation, or is it just a "must see," an item on their shopping list of major "attractions"?

To even raise such questions might sound elitist (as indeed, Heidegger often is) but it doesn't have to be so. Heidegger is indicating something about very different kinds of relation to the world. In one we force things, like a work of art or a stretch of woodland, to appear in ways that serve our self-interested purposes. In another we regard things in ways that allow them to disclose something of their otherwise unsuspected dimensions. To "view" is, for Heidegger, to objectify, to see something only in a certain very restricted (and restricting) light, whereby the objects' significance for us is already prescribed. This might be understood in terms of our relations to people as well as things. If I shout at the person behind the airport counter when my plane is delayed, I am viewing them only in their role as a material representative of the airline, not as a person. It might be understandable that I do this, but it is not ethical, because it objectifies them, making them just a target for my anger. By contrast, Heidegger's ethical ideal might be described as a kind of "being-with" others, a concerned involvement, and evolving coexistence, with other people and things that "lets them be" (allows then to exist as who or what they are) rather than imposing my presumptions upon them (Heidegger, 1996).

This kind of involvement, this being-with others, is clearly not facilitated by the toing and froing of many tourist practices; which is not to say that it can never happen. Even a visit to the zoo can, after all, disclose an animal as something much more than a photographic object. In considering a lion's pacing I might come to recognize the distressed existence of another creature. I have an experience of "being-with" the lion, of a concerned involvement with this beast that is more ethical than instrumental. This is not necessarily a matter of having an "authentic" experience (and Heidegger's own view of authenticity is hotly debated), at least in the sense that this meeting takes place in an entirely "artificial" environment. But Heidegger's thought might still help highlight what is, and what is not, *ethically*

important about such questions and about other elements of tourism. What matters ethically, we might say, takes the form of a relation best understood as a "being-with" or "staying-with" others.

What then if we understand ethical tourism in Heidegger's sense as an attempt to open the possibilities of "being-with"/"staying-with" other people or as "being-within"/"staying-within" other places? For Heidegger this relationship of "being-with" was epitomized by his "stays" in the Black Forest hut where he wrote his philosophy—a kind of existence he characterized as "dwelling" (Heidegger, 1971). Dwelling has the connotation of both "a dwelling" (a building that makes a suitable home, like Heidegger's hut) and dwelling as "a practice of living in place" (for example, the daily fetching of drinking water from the well alongside the hut). To dwell somewhere is then to inhabit that place, to live there at peace. Indeed it is no coincidence that Heidegger describes philosophy itself as a form of homesickness, as an intellectual desire to find a way of being at home in the world.

Heidegger thinks that the hustle and bustle of modern societies, and the mobile individualism which characterizes them, makes it extremely difficult to dwell anywhere. Tourism would seem straightforwardly to exacerbate this problem since it seems all about incessant movement. Yet things are, perhaps, not so simple. Some aspects of tourism can also involve a kind of "staying-with," a kind of involvement in another place that appears truly worthwhile, even if it is only temporary. This *staying* of incessant movement might, to use Heidegger's phrase, help "preserve a serious impression" for the rest of our journey through life. The experiences that stay with us might take many forms, a lover's kiss on a beach, a waterfall's spray on our face, our witnessing an act of unspeakable cruelty or of uncalled-for kindness. These moments stay with and within us in ways that are far more profound than the souvenirs and snapshots we carry away. They all, whatever form they take, *bring home to us* the fact that we are not just isolated, self-interested, individuals but beings composed in and through our involvement with a wider world. This relatedness and involvement might also let us reconceive our stay as a sojourn (the title of Heidegger's travelogue) rather than just a trip. A sojourn is a temporary staying-with others and staying-within other places that informs our worldly concerns. (In one sense our entire stay in this world is, at best, only a temporary sojourn.) This is why tourism ethics are important, because they make us mindful of the importance of resisting a worldview which would reduce everything to economic *objects*, commodities to be bought and sold, thereby losing sight of what really matters. This resistance with and on behalf of others is, as has already been suggested, an infinite task, a journey looking for the (ethically) good life.

As a final irony it is worth mentioning that, following his death, Heidegger's hut at Todtnauberg has itself become a travel destination. There is even a Heidegger trail, a three kilometer path set out in 2002 with five large signs that tell the curious about the philosopher's life and work. Is this, we might ask, an ethical form of tourism?

Notes

1 www.bzecotourism.org/ethics.htm. Accessed May 15, 2008.
2 www.utilitarianism.com/biotech.html. Accessed May 15, 2008.
3 See "Sustainable Tourism A Cruel Necessity in the Galapagos," Chris Benson, www.i-to-i.com/sustainable-tourism-a-cruel-necessity-in-the-galapagos.html. Accessed May 15, 2008.

References

Arendt, Hannah (1982). *Lectures on Kant's Political Philosophy*. Chicago, IL: University of Chicago Press.

Bendall, Jem (Ed.) (2000). *Terms for Endearment: Business, NGOs and Sustainable Development*. Sheffield: Greenleaf Publishing Limited.

Bentham, Jeremy (1948). "A Fragment on Government." In W. Harrison (Ed.), *A Fragment on Government and An Introduction to the Principles of Morals and Legislation* (pp. 1–104). Oxford: Blackwell .

Bourdieu, Pierre (1998). *Distinction: A Social Critique of the Judgement of Taste*. London: Routledge.

Butcher, Jim (2003). *The Moralisation of Tourism: Sun, Sand ... and Saving the World?* London: Routledge.

Chwieroth, Jeffrey (2007). "Neoliberal Economists and Capital Account Liberalization in Emerging Markets." *International Organization*, 61(2): 443–463.

Escobar, A. (1995). *Encountering Development: The Making and Unmaking of the Third World*. Princeton, NJ: Princeton University Press.

Fennell, D.A. (2003). *Ecotourism: An Introduction*. London: Routledge.

Fennell, David A. (2006). *Tourism Ethics*. Toronto: Channel View Publications.

Font, Xavier and Harris, Catherine (2004). "Rethinking Standards from Green to Sustainable." *Annals of Tourism Research*, 31(4): 986–1007.

Friedman, Milton (1962). *Capitalism and Freedom*. Chicago, IL: University of Chicago Press.

Henderson, Joan C. (2007). "Corporate Social Responsibility and Tourism: Hotel Companies in Phuket, Thailand, After the Indian Ocean Tsunami." *International Journal of Hospitality Management*, 26(1): 228–239.

Heidegger, Martin (1971). "Building, Dwelling, Thinking." In *Poetry, Language, Thought*. Trans. Albert Hofstadter. New York: Harper & Row.

Heidegger, Martin (1996). *Being and Time*. Trans. Joan Stambaugh. Albany, NY: State University of New York Press.

Heidegger, Martin (2005). *Sojourns: The Journey to Greece*. Albany, NY: State University of New York Press.

Held, David (2004). *A Globalizing World? Culture, Economics, Politics* (2nd edition.). New York: Routledge.

Hobbes, T. (1651). In C.B. Macpherson (Ed.) (1988), *Leviathan*. London: Penguin.

Jamal, Tazim and Hill, Steve (2002). "The Home and the World: (Post)touristic Spaces of (In)authenticity." In G.M.S. Dann (Ed.),

The Tourist as Metaphor of the Social World. Oxford: Oxford University Press.

Kant, Immanuel (1963). *On History.* New York: Bobbs Merrill.

Kant, Immanuel (1795). *Toward Perpetual Peace: A Philosophical Sketch.* Retrieved May 15, 2008 from socsci.colorado.edu/~parisr/ PS4173/Kant.htm.

Kant, Immanuel, (1785). *The Groundwork of the Metaphysics of Morals.* Translated by M. Gregor (Ed.) (1998). Cambridge: Cambridge University Press.

Keefe, J (1995). "Whose Home is it Anyway?" *Tourism in Focus,* 15: 4–16.

Kymlicka, Will (1995). *Multicultural Citizenship.* Oxford: Oxford University Press.

Levinas, Emmanuel (1996). *Basic Philosophical Writings.* Ed. A.T. Peperzak, S. Critchley and R. Bernasconi. Bloomington: Indiana University Press.

Lingis, Alphonso (2004). *Trust.* Minneapolis: University of Minnesota Press.

Locke, John (1988). *Two Treatises of Government* (2nd edition.). Ed. P. Laslett. Cambridge: Cambridge University Press.

Löwith, Karl (1994). *My Life in Germany Before and After 1933.* Chicago: University of Illinois Press.

MacCannell, D. (1999). *The Tourist: A New Theory of the Leisure Class.* Berkeley: University of California Press

Mill, John Stuart (1863). *Utilitarianism* (7th edition., 1879). London: Longmans.

Miller, David (1989). *Market, State and Community: The Foundations of Market Socialism.* Oxford: Oxford University Press.

Naess, Arne (1988). "Identification as a Source of Deep Ecological Attitudes." In Michael Tobias (Ed.), *Deep Ecology* (pp. 256–270). San Marcos, CA: Avant Books.

Pateman, Carole (1979). *The Problem of Political Obligation.* Cambridge: Polity Press.

Pilger, John (1998). *Hidden Agendas.* London: Vintage.

Rawls, John (1973). *A Theory of Justice.* Oxford: Oxford University Press.

Rawls, John (1999). *The Law of Peoples.* Cambridge, MA: Harvard University Press.

Samuelson, Robert J. (1995). *The Good Life and its Discontents: The American Dream in the Age of Entitlement 1945–1995.* London: Vintage.

Sasseen, J. (1993). "Companies Clean Up." *International Management,* 48(8): 30–31.

Sen, Amartya (1977). "Rational Fools: A Critique of the Behavioural Foundations of Economic Theory." *Philosophy and Public Affairs,* 6(3): 317–344.

Sen, Amartya and Williams, Bernard (Eds.) (1982). *Utilitarianism and Beyond.* Cambridge: Cambridge University Press.

Smith, Adam (1759/2006). *The Theory of Moral Sentiments.* London: Dover Publications.

Smith, Mick (2001). *An Ethics of Place: Radical Ecology, Postmodernity, and Social Theory.* New York: State University of New York Press.

Smith, Mick and Duffy, Rosaleen (2003). *The Ethics of Tourism Development.* London: Routledge.

Taylor, Charles (1991). "Shared and Divergent Values." In R. Watts and D. Brown (Eds.), *Options for a New Canada.* Toronto: University of Toronto Press.

Thomas, Keith (1984). *Man and the Natural World.* Harmondsworth: Penguin.

Urry, John (1990). *The Tourist Gaze: Leisure and Travel in Contemporary Societies.* London: Sage Publications.

Young, Iris Marion (1990). *Justice and the Politics of Difference.* Princeton: Princeton University Press.

35

Gender and Tourism Discourses: Advancing the Gender Project in Tourism Studies

Cara Aitchison

Introduction

Gender and, more specifically, women, form an increasingly central focus of the academic tourism gaze in addition to being an established focus of the practiced "tourist gaze" (Urry, 1990). In contrast to early tourism research, which viewed tourism relations from an economic and largely gender-neutral perspective, tourism is now widely recognized as a cultural site and process in which gender identities and difference are represented through exclusionary practices and discourses. Thus, in a world where differences are increasingly marked by patterns of consumption rather than modes of production, the world's largest "industry" has become a key signifier of economic, social and cultural capital formation shaping identities of gender, class, nation, ethnicity, religion, race, disability and the myriad intersections between these identities.

This chapter seeks to map the terrain of gender and tourism studies by outlining the major theoretical perspectives and associated literature that have informed thematic discussions in feminist and gender studies of tourism previously introduced by Swain (1995). The chapter synthesizes, critiques, and develops the growing but fragmented field of gender and tourism research while seeking to offer theoretical insights to produce a critical discourse on gender and tourism studies. In doing so the chapter develops a critique structured to provide an overview of the chronological development of gender and tourism discourses in tourism studies. This chronology charts four distinct phases in the development of gender and tourism discourses: first, *feminist studies in tourism employment*, with research informed by liberal feminist approaches; second, Marxist, radical and socialist feminist critiques of *sex inequality in tourism*; third, poststructural feminist approaches to *gender, tourism and cultural relations*, informed in large part by "the cultural turn" in social science; and, fourth, current calls for *the rematerialization of gender and tourism studies* through social, cultural, and spatial research in which issues of material and structural power, and the mutual relationship between the social and the cultural, are reinserted and reinterpreted into recent cultural-dominated poststructural critiques of gender relations.

To understand how our perspectives on gender and tourism have developed we need to acknowledge the dominant and emergent knowledge formations that have induced changes in these perspectives. With the benefit of over two decades of research on gender and tourism we can now see the project of gender and tourism research as one of accumulation of knowledge, with new knowledge being created and old knowledge reinterpreted as a result of new ways of seeing what Kuhn (1975) referred to as the "particular constellation" of received beliefs within each previously established paradigm. In addition, we can view the project of gender and tourism research as having developed from the seeming coherence of the feminist empiricism of the 1970s and early 1980s to the emancipatory agendas of Marxist, radical and socialist feminism of feminist standpoint theory of the late 1980s and early 1990s, to the fragmentation of poststructural perspectives of the late 1990s and 2000s, through to "rematerialized" critiques as we approach the 2010s.

Thus the gender project in tourism studies can be viewed as having moved from a period of relative internal coherence in the form of the early feminist studies in tourism employment from two decades ago, to a larger and more fragmented set of discourses at the turn of the 21st century where, it could be argued, the breakup of different feminist and gender perspectives has been in danger of fracturing the incomplete project of gender and tourism studies (Aitchison, 2005a). One of the challenges now is to identify ways in which internal coherence in the overall project of gender studies in tourism can be regained without diluting the sophistication and rigor of the feminist and gender research which has developed in

part as a result of the increasingly nuanced perspectives set out in the specific "types" of feminist and gender approaches to tourism research highlighted above. The identification of feminist research according to its perceived epistemological underpinning or methodological approach has been something of a double-edged sword for the gender project in tourism studies. On the one hand, creating distinctions between particular approaches to feminist and gender tourism research has served to reveal the nuances of different research philosophies and practices, together with the commensurate influence on theoretical and political understandings at a micro level, rather than simply offering one homogenous and homogenizing feminist interpretation of the world. On the other hand, however, in creating such fine-grained distinctions and analysis there is a danger of losing site of the overall feminist project and weakening the whole through a focus on the individual parts (Aitchison, 2005b). Moreover, such categories can create rather arbitrary boundaries between frequently overlapping perspectives and such classifications are usually apportioned retrospectively by the readers of feminist research rather than by the writers of the research themselves (Letherby, 2003). For example, subsequent sections of this chapter demonstrate that it is possible to make feminist sense of a range of gendered practices in tourism, including sex tourism for example, from a variety of seemingly competing theoretical perspectives, including Marxist, radical and poststructural feminism.

The chronological critique outlined in this chapter then develops a more detailed evaluation of these contemporary discourses in gender and tourism studies. Here, reference is made to "the social-cultural nexus" (Aitchison, 2003) of gender-power relations in tourism, where power is seen as being produced, legitimated, reproduced and reworked at the interface of social and cultural relations or in the "third space" between material and symbolic power. The concept of the social-cultural nexus both informs, and is informed by, poststructural critiques or what has recently come to be known with the tourism academy as "critical tourism studies" (Ateljevic et al., 2007) that have emanated from the "cultural turn" in social science and by recent sociological, geographical, and cultural studies research that has called for the rematerialization of relations of cultural consumption, including tourism. Within this discussion the chapter pays particular attention to the place of three specific and interrelated concepts in gender and tourism discourses: the gaze, surveillance, and embodiment. Discussions of these concepts synthesize some of the major writings within contemporary gender and tourism studies in addition to highlighting their origins within social, cultural, and spatial theory. In particular, these discussions draw on the work of Urry and Foucault in relation to the gaze and surveillance and recent gender and tourism studies research in relation to embodiment.

While the place of gender in wider economic discourses of structural power in both tourism development and tourism employment is acknowledged, these materialist discourses are somewhat beyond the scope of this chapter and are, in part, addressed elsewhere in this volume. However, as the conclusion of the chapter points out, the future of feminist and gender studies of tourism must lie, at least in part, in recognition of the need for a rematerialization of the poststructural critiques of the early 21st century and for acknowledgement of the continuing economic influences and consequences of social and cultural actions and relations. The future of the gender project in tourism studies, it is argued here, lies in the further development of the growing body of research and literature in tourism studies that engages with tourism as a culturally embodied phenomenon but also as an economically employed force in an increasingly globalized industry.

Mapping the Terrain of Gender and Tourism Studies

Feminist Studies in Tourism Employment

Feminist studies in tourism employment began to be published in the late 1980s and can be seen as a liberal feminist derivative of generic tourism management research where the dominant disciplinary underpinnings were those of economics and employment studies. In spite of some shortcomings relating to theoretical sophistication, this body of research clarified definitions, established sets of empirical data and descriptive statistics, identified areas of sex-inequality and helped to inform equal opportunities agendas. This category or typology of research tends to view "gender as a variable" (Alvesson and Billing, 1997), emphasizes distributive rather than relational data and thus adopts a quantitative rather than qualitative approach with a focus on social roles (Hearn et al., 1989) and macro-level structural power systems rather than micro-level processes. Such research, here termed "liberal feminist," has also acquired a variety of other terms including "feminist empiricism" (Harding, 1986) and "feminist rationalism" (Di Stefano, 1990).

Initially, these feminist studies were undertaken in relation to the hospitality industry rather than the wider tourism sector per se. Guerrier's (1986) study, for example, addressed issues of sex-segregation and sex-role stereotyping by examining the challenges facing women seeking to pursue careers in hotel management. Stockdale defined such occupational sex-segregation, which has a clear relationship to levels of financial remuneration, as "... the jobs that women do are different from those done by men (horizontal segregation) and women work at lower levels than men in the occupational hierarchy (vertical segregation)" (1991: 57). Related research has demonstrated that many service sector industries, including tourism, are "dominated by women but managed by men" (Brockbank and Traves, 1996) where further explanations for the differential pay and conditions experienced by women in service sector work are provided by the concepts of *sex role spillover* and *sex role stereotyping*. Stockdale defines *sex role spillover* as "the assumption that people in particular jobs, and the jobs themselves, have the characteristics of only one gender" (1991: 57). Both sex role spillover and sex role stereotyping of women can have detrimental impacts on their working conditions and career prospects as women may be viewed as committed primarily to the private/domestic sphere and thus less interested than their male peers in pursuing a career (Cockburn, 1985). *Sex role stereotyping*, in reference to decisions made based on preconceptions of character traits or physical differences, can also have a negative impact on women's career progression. Traditionally, appropriate characteristics of a manager are often deemed to be those associated with men such as leadership, objectivity and aggressiveness. Traits conventionally ascribed to women, such as caring and emotion, are often not only considered to be irrelevant to leadership positions but actually detrimental to effective management. Adkins (1994), for example, building on insights from researchers such as Guerrier (1986) and Hearn et al. (1989), provided a detailed and widely cited account of the gendered occupations in the hospitality trade with in-depth ethnographic evidence to complement and supplement the earlier quantitative evidence. This body of comparative research evidence, of both a distributive and relational nature and augmented by research from other services sector industries and organizations including education, health, retail, and financial services, serves to provide an overview of the gendered structure of work, sex role spillover, sex-role stereotyping, and related gender differences in power and pay (Acker, 1994; Cockburn, 1983, 1985, 1991; Hearn et al., 1989; Ledwith and Colgan, 1996; Morley and Walsh, 1995; Savage and Witz, 1992; Walby, 1986, 1997; Wearing 1996; Witz, 1992).

The more specific area of tourism employment has "not been subjected to widespread academic analysis" (Baum, 1994: 259). Thus, there is limited empirical evidence concerning the position of women in tourism. However, studies that have been carried out reveal employment patterns which mirror those in hospitality (Adkins, 1994; Ireland, 1993; Richter, 1994; Sinclair, 1997). Kinnaird and Hall (1994) comment that women fulfill the majority of jobs in tourism, especially those which are poorly paid, low skilled, and part-time. They point out that this situation has been created and supported by gender stereotyping and traditional notions of what constitutes appropriate work for women. Jordan (1997: 532) has presented both distributive and relational findings that illustrate the sex-segregated nature of the tourism industry and the impact of the *sexuality of organization* upon women's careers (Hearn et al., 1989) by concluding "that the majority of the tourism organizations studied do reproduce and rationalize sex segregation." More recently, and depicting a picture of continuing inequality in tourism employment, White et al. concluded that "significant inequalities still exist in the tourism workplace and that bottom-up power mechanisms can override legislative top-down power mechanisms so that women are quiescent and feeling powerless to act" (2005: 37). Such findings serve to shift attention from purely empirical data, reflecting the structural inequalities in the gender division of labor to the cultural experiences of gendered power in tourism employment. Subsequent discourses of gender research in tourism, and poststructural approaches in particular, have enabled these more nuanced insights to be revealed and later sections of this chapter outline ways in which the concept of the social-cultural nexus has helped to frame such research (Aitchison, 2005c).

Thus the empirical studies of gender in tourism management have been useful in mapping sex-segregation, sex-role stereotyping and gendered structures of work and related pay differences between men and women in tourism occupations and employment. Moreover, this body of empirical evidence has provided us with a detailed picture of the employment-related structure of the tourism economy and aspects of the gendered nature of tourism. Its contribution is thus focused on the gendered nature of tourism production rather than tourism consumption or the relationship between production and consumption which has come to form the focus of the majority of more recent gender research in tourism studies, including much of the research referred to in later sections of this chapter.

Feminist Critiques of Sex Inequality in Tourism

Feminist critiques of sex inequality in tourism have been informed by Marxist, radical and socialist feminism. This category or typology of research tends to view gender relations from a feminist "standpoint" and each "feminist standpoint" (Alvesson and Billing, 1997), "standpoint feminism" (Harding, 1986) or "feminist standpoint epistemology" (Letherby, 2003) reflects a particular focus on the locus of power structures or systemic power within society; namely class, gender, or the relationship between the two. Here the emphasis of research may be distributive *and* relational and may employ a mixed methods approach in its analysis of political categories rather than social roles (Hearn et al., 1989).

Marxist feminism locates gender relations within an explanation of economic and class relations. A central tenet of Marxist feminism is that any improvement in women's situation requires economic change as a precondition. The family is seen as propping up capitalist society by providing unpaid domestic work and a reserve army of labor to service its needs. As such, Marxist feminist theory is concerned with examining the material base of women's subordination in both employment and family relations. Although Marxism has been criticized for

failing to address issues of gendered power directly, Marxist feminists emphasize that Marx did refer to both *production* and *reproduction* in his theory of the creation of a surplus value of labor. Within the tourism literature the industry has come to be viewed as an important economic force within global capitalism. Although Marxist critiques are rare, and explicit Marxist feminist critiques are notable by their absence, there is a body of political economy literature within tourism and development studies that is clearly informed by Marxist theory, albeit often seeking to move beyond "the rigid dualisms between structure and agency" (Bianchi, 2003).

In contrast to Marxist feminism, radical feminism views patriarchy rather than class as the cause of women's subordination and oppression. Patriarchy is seen as being present in all structures and processes within society, in both the public and private spheres, preceding all other forms of oppression related to class or "race." With radical feminists asserting that male sexual power is the root of patriarchal power particular attention has been paid to patriarchal constructions of society through sex-role stereotyping, heterosexism and compulsory heterosexuality, the institution of marriage, and practices of pornography, prostitution, rape, sexual abuse of women and children, and other forms of abuse of power including "domestic" violence. Increasingly, radical feminist analyses have begun to inform research into sex tourism and its relationship to child abuse and the trafficking of women, with radical feminist writers such as Enloe (1989) and Jeffreys (1999, 2003) providing some of the earliest research critiquing the political economy of international sex tourism and informing subsequent and more theoretically diverse work by writers such as Kempadoo (2004) and O'Connell Davidson (2005). Indeed, poststructural and postcolonial feminists have also recognized the relationship between sex tourism, "Othering" and the colonial heritage that has informed many of the relationships between current tourist-generating countries and those former colonies now dependent on tourism and frequently marketed in ways which emphasize, eroticize, and exoticize their colonial heritage (O'Connell Davidson, 2001).

Sex tourism provides an interesting illustration of gender-power relations "at work" (and "at play" depending on whether it is viewed from the tourist or sex worker's perspective) and the issue has provoked some of the most animated academic discourses, policy debates and practical strategies in relation to tourism and as responses from tourism theory, policy and practice respectively (Opperman, 1998; Ryan and Hall, 2001; Seabrook, 1996, 2000). Indeed, it is one of the few areas in tourism where academics, policy makers and practitioners are increasingly working together to develop greater understanding to address one of the most serious gendered consequences of tourism. For example, O'Connell Davidson and Sanchez Taylor have amassed a wealth of empirical data and critical analysis relating to the development, experience and impact of sex tourism in countries that have become increasingly dependent on tourism for foreign earnings at the level of the nation and for economic survival at the level of the individual (O'Connell Davidson and Sanchez Taylor, 1996a, 1996b, 1996c, 2001). Here, it is possible to see both economic and sexual inequality at work and thus both Marxist feminist and radical feminist approaches offer insights into the production and reproduction of economic and sexual inequality and through tourism.

O'Connell Davidson (2005), in drawing attention to the unequal economic relations of tourism, implies a kind of inevitability to sex tourism within capitalist and patriarchal global relations when she asserts that:

> ... very few campaigners insist that the industry address questions about the derisory wages paid to hotel workers, or think about how this might contribute to their willingness to accept "bribes" and "tips" for turning a blind eye to the activities of tourists. Nor are we called upon to think about the social costs of tourism, or the fact that profits from tourism are largely repatriated to affluent

> sending countries and so will never "trickle down" to those who pick up tourists' litter, clean their toilets, make their beds, serve their food, and fulfill their sexual fantasies. (O'Connell Davidson, 2005: 138–139)

Linking the two perspectives of Marxist and radical feminism, socialist feminism draws attention to the nexus of Marxist and radical approaches by emphasizing the dual role of capitalism and patriarchy in the continued subordination of women. It has been argued that socialist feminism has been the acceptable face of feminism within academia as it provides a more clearly articulated theoretical and hence academic base than liberal feminism, but is not as unpalatable to a male-dominated establishment as radical feminism (Aitchison, 2003). While Marxist and socialist feminism have a number of features in common, they are separated by the different relationships they identify between class and gender relations. Whereas Marxist feminism emphasizes economic relations over patriarchal relations as the cause of women's oppression, socialist feminism sees both patriarchy and capitalism operating together as a "dual system" of oppression without one system necessarily having primacy over the other.

Poststructural Feminist Approaches to Gender, Tourism and Cultural Relations

The previous two sections have demonstrated that different feminist perspectives focus on what they deem to be the major cause of women's oppression. Liberal feminists are largely concerned with male domination of institutional and employment structures, Marxist feminists are concerned with male domination of economic relations, radical feminists are primarily concerned with male domination of private familial and sexual relations and socialist feminists point to the duality of the social relations of the family and the economic relations of the market as being the cause of women's oppression.

In contrast, poststructural feminism draws our attention to the ways in which cultural relations serve to shape gender relations. Instead of focusing on the political and social manifestations of economic and/or patriarchal oppression of the gender order poststructural feminism seeks to uncover the cultural codes by which such an order is constructed, legitimated, and reproduced. This category or typology of research, often deemed to be either "postmodern" or "poststructural," tends to view gender as a relational concept and construct that is best investigated through qualitative research designed to examine "discourses of power" (Hearn et al., 1989).

Postmodernism and poststructuralism are frequently used interchangeably and it is important to acknowledge that although they are overlapping and mutually informing they are also differentiated by their objects of study. Postmodernism is concerned with the critical study of modernity whereas poststructuralism is concerned with the critical study of the power relations inherent in, and resulting from, the structures and structured order of modernity. Thus postmodernism seeks to deconstruct the meta-narratives and grand theories of modernist society, whereas poststructuralism seeks to reveal the power relations upon which the construction, legitimation, and reproduction of modernist society depends. This difference in object and method of study has resulted in postmodern accounts remaining largely within the realms of the humanities while poststructural critiques have crossed into the social sciences where critical engagement with theories of social, economic and cultural power is already established (Aitchison, 2005a).

Heavily influenced by French philosophy, much of poststructural theory draws on the psychoanalytic, linguistic and cultural theories of male writers. Michel Foucault's theory of discourse and power, Jacques Derrida's theory of *différence* and the psychoanalytic theories of Jacques Lacan have been articulated more recently in feminist poststructural theory by French feminist writers such as Cixous (1983), Kristeva (1969, 1980) and Irigaray (1993) who all combine their feminism with cultural theory, literary criticism, philosophy and psychoanalysis (Moi, 1985, 1986). The deconstruction of language as communicative practice is central to their poststructural critiques, which employ discourse analysis in relation to culture, literature, philosophy, and psychology in reading between the lines of social and cultural relations to identify and make sense of the power relations inherent within these social and cultural processes. For example, Irigaray's work has been highly influential in revealing the patriarchal, phallogocentric, and dualistic nature of language whereby men, masculinity and objects pertaining to maleness become the normal reference point in language and women, femininity and objects pertaining to femaleness become deviant or "the Other" as identified in de Beauvoir's (1949) *The Second Sex*.

Poststructural theory is thus deeply indebted to, although moves beyond, the structural linguistic theories advanced by those proponents of the "structure as construct" thesis outlined above. Whereas Saussure focused on the "structural" nature of language as comprising the relationship between the two components of "the sign," in the form of the signifier (the word, sound or image), and "the signified" (what the word, sound or image comes to *mean* in relation to other signifiers), poststructural theory focuses on the historical specificity of this relationship, its dynamic nature and its embeddedness within relations of power. As Weedon emphasizes, "Once language is understood in terms of competing discourses, competing ways of giving meaning to the world, which imply differences in the organization of social power, then language becomes an important site of political struggle" (1997: 23).

Within the social sciences emerging sub-disciplines, such as the new social and cultural geographies of the 1990s, have reworked earlier geographical perspectives with the sociological analyses of Bourdieu (1984), de

Certeau (1984), Foucault (1977), and others thereby offering insights into the role of cultural capital, productive consumption and the power of surveillance respectively. Thus poststructuralism has also drawn upon theories of "structure as process" and the work of Foucault, examined more closely below, is perhaps the most widely recognized for illustrating the ways in which power is exercised within everyday structures *and* discourses to maintain "regimes of truth."

Within tourism studies, poststructural analyses have developed further critical discourse analysis as utilized within wider social sciences and the humanities with such research leading to both theoretical and methodological innovation in the gender project in tourism studies. Illustrative examples here include research examining the construction and representation of the gendered "Other" in tourism (Aitchison, 2000; Johnston, 2001; Pritchard and Morgan, 2005, 2007), gendered landscapes in tourism (Aitchison, 1999; Aitchison, MacLeod and Shaw, 2000; Pritchard and Morgan, 2000a, 2000b), and gendered images, iconographies tourism brochures and photographs (Edwards, 1996; Morgan and Pritchard, 1998).

The Rematerialization of Gender and Tourism Studies

While acknowledging the positive influence of the "cultural turn" within feminist and gender studies of tourism, a growing body of social science research has cautioned against the wholesale adoption of poststructural approaches to the neglect of structural and material analyses. Here, the concept of the social-cultural nexus is introduced as a theoretical development that has the potential to combine both critical and cultural analyses. Such a framework seeks to accommodate both the material and the symbolic in an integrated analysis that explores the mutually informing nature of social and cultural relations in shaping gender relations (Aitchison, 2003; Bondi,

1992; Letherby, 2003). The rationale for such an approach is that while women and girls still suffer structural oppression within almost all social and cultural arenas, it is inappropriate to discontinue a research tradition that has served feminism well in highlighting the material constraints that women and girls face as part of everyday life, including those produced by, and in relation to, tourism. However, poststructural theory offers additional conceptual rigor with which to interrogate and understand seemingly material constraints. The concept of the social-cultural nexus renders visible the connections between social and cultural relations and their respective material and symbolic representations of power. This way of seeing reveals that sites of exclusion and inequality are often most embedded where the two forms of exclusionary power relations (the material and the symbolic) coexist and mutually reinforce at the nexus of the social and the cultural. Thus the social-cultural nexus is explained as both a site, and a process, of construction, legitimation, reproduction, and a reworking of power relations where power is inherently related to identity (Aitchison, 2005a).

A key question for the gender project in tourism studies is therefore to enquire as to the extent to which systemic economic power (capitalism as revealed and contested by Marxist feminism) and systemic male power (patriarchy as revealed and contested by radical feminism) exist in relation to the production and consumption of tourism and/or the extent to which localized, contextualized, and pluralized power relations exert their influence on gender relations within tourism. This questioning and cautionary note has been signaled by a number of writers in feminist, gender and women's studies across social science (Evans, 2003; Valentine, 2001). As far back as 1992, the social geographer Liz Bondi urged against prioritizing the cultural over the social or the "unharnessing of the symbolic and the sociological" (1992: 166). In addition to stressing the dangers of neglecting the social within social science, including tourism studies, such discussions have emphasized the importance of maintaining the dual influences of the social and the cultural, the material and the symbolic, and the social sciences and the humanities in feminist and gender analyses of tourism as sites, forms and processes which are themselves both social and cultural phenomena.

The Social-Cultural Nexus of Gender-Power Relations in Tourism

This chapter has sought to evaluate the different trajectories of a range of feminist and gender perspectives that have contributed to the gender project in tourism studies. Such an exploration has revealed the neglected interface between the two seemingly polarized perspectives of the social/cultural, material/symbolic, structural/poststructural and, in doing so, has advocated the expansion of our current research horizons by exploring *the social-cultural nexus* of gender relations in tourism. Rather than focusing on either the material *or* the cultural, this chapter summarizes previous calls for feminist and gender research which acknowledges and investigates further the lineage and linkages between structural and poststructural perspectives and the complexities of gendered power inherent in these mutually informing social and cultural relationships (Aitchison, 2003, 2005a, 2006).

The focus of this chapter now turns to the development of a theoretical critique that further integrates material *and* cultural perspectives through a rematerialized poststructural gender project in tourism studies. This accommodation of the social and the cultural is articulated here through the conceptualization of the social-cultural nexus. The social-cultural nexus is explained as both a site and process of construction, legitimation, reproduction, and reworking of gender relations. In this way, the concept engages with structural and poststructural theories to explore the social *and* cultural workings and reworkings of gender-power relations in relations of production, consumption, productive consumption and everyday life. Simultaneously, however, the concept acknowledges the value of materialist analyses of patriarchy and capitalism, or patriarchal capitalism, in shaping the power relations that construct, legitimate, and reproduce gender relations in tourism, often on a global scale. The concept therefore seeks to offer a more critical and comprehensive frame for the exploration of gender relations in tourism at different scales from the global to the local and from the world stage to the body. The final three subsections of this chapter therefore introduce three specific, interrelated and primarily *visual* concepts that have recently captured significant attention within the gender project in tourism studies: the gaze, surveillance and embodiment.

The Gaze, Surveillance and Embodiment: The New Gender Project in Tourism Studies

The concept of the gaze entered the tourism studies lexicon with the publication, in 1990, of Urry's seminal text *The Tourist Gaze*. Influenced by Foucault's writings on the panoptican-like disciplining power of surveillance, the gaze can be viewed as a means of effecting control through regimes of observation where, as in the illustration of the prison's panoptican, the manifest power of observation may be exercised through the threat of its use rather than its actual deployment.

Initially, Urry's work considered the gaze in purely visual terms but, subsequently revised through a series of iterations; he came to see the gaze as a kind of metaphor for the disciplining and embodied power of tourism (Franklin, 2001). Over the last two decades the concept of the tourist gaze has been further developed from its original emphasis on the gaze *of* the tourist *upon* the host or host destination to "the mutual gaze" (Maoz, 2006) *between* tourist and host to "the local gaze" where the tourist—and most specifically the female tourist—is gazed upon by locals as a sexualized and embodied Other (Jordan and Aitchison, 2008).

Although Foucault's work has been widely used in social and cultural studies, including tourism studies' sister fields of leisure and sport studies, it is only relatively recently that it has come to the attention of tourism studies' scholars (Hollinshead, 1999). In relation to the gender project in tourism studies recent published work has employed Foucauldian analysis to critique dominant discourses in tourism research (Wearing and McDonald, 2002), to explore the relationship between power and resistance among women tourists (Jordan and Gibson, 2005), to further examine the concept of Othering referred to earlier (Aitchison, 2000; Aitchison et al., 2000), and within the more established body of tourism research analyzing women's travel writing (Fullagar, 2002). Recent research has also pointed to the differential type of the gaze according to the nature of the tourism space in which the gaze is deployed with "enclavic" tourism spaces of resorts being subject to a greater level of gaze than "heterogeneous" spaces (Edensor, 2000). Jordan and Aitchison (2008), in their research exploring the ways in women tourists perceived themselves to be the objects of the gazes of local male residents in tourist destinations, have argued that the gaze is also gendered, sexualized and embodied.

The concepts of the gaze and surveillance are inextricably linked. Surveillance can take the form of "physical watching" or "digitized surveillance" with the "electronic eye" becoming increasingly prevalent in contemporary "surveillance society" (Lyon, 1993, 2001, 2002). In an era of increasing insecurity and fear of risk relating to violent street crime and terrorism, "the gaze without eyes" (Koskela, 2000) is increasingly seen to focus its attention on men and the commensurate rise in surveillance studies has drawn attention to the role of surveillance in invasions of privacy. But it is when we are at our most mobile and in public

places that we are most the subject of and subjected to surveillance in both electronic and physical form (Lyon, 2002). Indeed, the physical watching of women by men is a common pastime of local men in tourist destinations and creates a gendered, sexualized, and embodied dimension to surveillance (Ateljevic and Hall, 2007; Jordan and Aitchison, 2008).

It is through the process of surveillance that the gaze becomes embodied and tourism, with its emphasis on mobility and the flow of people, provides multiple *sites* for the embodiment of *sight* as the most natural form of surveillance. Yet it is only recently that tourism studies has engaged with and sought to develop discourses of embodiment within the subject field (Johnston, 2001; Pritchard and Morgan, 2000a; Pritchard et al., 2007) and even more recently that such discourses of embodiment have been related to discourses of surveillance (Jordan, 2007). The "embodied turn" in tourism studies has developed in response to the writing out of the body in earlier research where there was a failure to recognize "(Other) bodies and tourism studies" (Johnston, 2001).

This initial call to acknowledge the significance of the gendered body in tourism's multifaceted discourses of power was first heard following the publication of Veijola and Jokinen's "The Body in Tourism" published in *Theory, Culture and Society* in 1994. Feminist research on embodiment has since been complemented and supplemented by wider poststructural work that has sought to engage with the embodied nature of tourism in all its multisensory forms. Recent research exploring embodiment in tourism has thus extended earlier research on performativity (Edensor, 2000), sexuality and homosexuality (Herold et al., 2001; Padilla, 2007a, 2007b) with the dominant discourse of visual embodiment, as developed through the concept of "the tourist gaze," and "embodied surveillance" (Jones and Aitchison, 2007) now being challenged by other forms of embodiment and sensory experience, including taste, touch and smell (Everett, 2008).

Jordan and Aitchison, in concluding their research, state that women, unlike men, are not able to act as anonymous flâneurs in public spaces. Rather, they are highly visible and frequently scrutinized as both the subject and object of the male tourist gaze. Such a gaze is likely to be exercised by a local man or men and is not neutrally deployed but is highly gendered, sexualized and embodied. Thus, while both Foucault and Urry continue to inform the discourse of tourism studies it is also the case that, for many women, the tourist gaze is not the genuinely disembodied or remote surveillant gaze of the tourist as previous research has suggested. Instead, it is ever-present and proximate, highly gendered, sexualized and embodied, and more normally deployed by locals rather than tourists.

Thus, one of the roles of the gender project in tourism studies, and following on from its progression from the descriptive data of liberal feminism to the more complex articulations of a rematerialized poststructuralism, is this kind of disruption of "the givens" of the tourism studies lexicon and cannon such that we can develop a more nuanced and inclusive account of tourism that takes full account of the complexity of gender-power relations. Through illustrative examples such as those outlined above relating to experiences such as the surveillant gaze and sex tourism, it is possible to see a range of power relations at play in constructing, contesting, and reworking gender relations in tourism. No one perspective offers the full picture of gender and power in tourism but, by adopting and adapting a range of perspectives to provide a more integrated and holistic analysis, it is possible to develop a more sophisticated and rigorous analysis of tourism that takes account of economic, patriarchal, and cultural relations of power. Moreover, such an approach offers the scope to reveal the ways in which these different systems and processes of power interact to support each other such that gender-power relations are revealed at the nexus of the material and the symbolic or in "the social and cultural nexus" of gender-power relations. As O'Connell Davidson has written in relation to

those tourists who do not "conform to the dominant stereotype of the "sex tourist":

> They do not go to seedy brothels where women and children are visibly brutalized by brothel keepers. But they will have sex with a local 15 year old if she or he approaches them in a disco, smiles, flirts and dances with them, and offers to come back to their room. And in the morning, if she or he asks for US$10 for the taxi fare home, they will give it, maybe with a little extra just to be kind. They will feel no worse about this interaction, possibly even better, than they will feel about their other interactions with locals—the boy who shines their shoes, the woman or teenager who cleans their room, the small child who washes sand from their feet as they lie on a sun lounger on the beach in exchange for a few coins, the old woman who pleads with her to buy fruit from her, the little beggar child sitting on the pavement outside their hotel. The sex, like the sun, the sand, the drinking, the excess and above all the conspicuous waste (of food, energy, natural resources and time) in places where local people cannot afford to waste anything at all is all part of the tourist experience. It is all part of the "local color," the "party atmosphere," the "exotic beach with a great nightlife" that tourists have been sold, not by "organized child sex tour operators," but by big, respectable, mainstream tourism companies. (O'Connell Davidson, 2005: 138)

Thus, the devil is in the detail of research that can reveal and explain the gender-power relations that exist within tourism; in the intellectual places and research sites visited in what has been termed above "the social-cultural nexus" of structural and cultural relations. The future of the gender project within tourism studies is therefore a challenging one. The key to its success must surely be the transfer and further development of collaborative working across different feminist and gender perspectives and between theory, policy and practice in conversations between academics, NGOs, and tourism producers and consumers.

References

Acker, S. (1994). *Gendered Education*. Buckingham: Open University Press.
Adkins, L. (1994). *Gendered Work: Sexuality, Family and the Labour Market*. Buckingham: Open University Press.

Aitchison, C. (1999). "New Cultural Geographies: The Spatiality of Leisure, Gender and Sexuality." *Leisure Studies*, 18(1): 19–39.

Aitchison, C. (2000). "Poststructural Feminist Theories of Representing Others: A Response to the 'Crisis' in Leisure Studies Discourse." *Leisure Studies*, 19(3): 127–144.

Aitchison, C.C. (2003). *Gender and Leisure: Social and Cultural Perspectives*. London and New York: Routledge.

Aitchison, C.C. (2005a). "Feminist and Gender Perspectives in Tourism Studies: The Social-Cultural Nexus of Critical and Cultural Theories." *Tourist Studies*, 5(3): 207–224.

Aitchison, C.C. (2005b). "Feminist and Gender Perspectives in Leisure and Tourism Research." In B. Ritchie, P. Burns and C. Palmer (Eds.), *Tourism Research Methods: Integrating Theory with Practice* (pp. 21–35). Oxford: CAB International.

Aitchison, C.C. (2005c). "Feminist and Gender Research in Sport and Leisure Management: Understanding the Social-Cultural Nexus of Gender-Power Relations." *Journal of Sport Management*, 19(4): 422–441.

Aitchison, C.C. (2006). "The Critical and the Cultural: Explaining the Divergent Paths of Leisure Studies and Tourism Studies." *Leisure Studies*, 25(4): 417–422.

Aitchison, C.C., MacLeod, N. and Shaw, S. (2000). *Leisure and Tourism Landscapes: Social and Cultural Geographies*. London: Routledge.

Alvesson, M. and Billing, Y.D. (1997). *Understanding Gender and Organizations*. London: Sage Publications.

Ateljevic, I. and Hall, D. (2007). "The Embodiment of the Macho Gaze in South-Eastern Europe: Performing Masculinity and Femininity in Albania and Croatia." In A. Pritchard, N. Morgan, I. Ateljevic and C. Harris (Eds.), *Tourism and Gender: Embodiment, Sensuality and Experience* (pp. 138–157). Wallingford: CAB International.

Ateljevic, I., Pritchard, A. and Morgan, N. (2007). *The Critical Turn in Tourism Studies*. Oxford: Elsevier.

Baum, T (Ed.) (1994). *Human Resource Issues in International Tourism*. Oxford: Butterworth-Heinemann.

de Beauvoir, S. (1949). *The Second Sex*. Harmondsworth: Penguin.

Bianchi, Raoul (2003). "Place and Power in Tourism Development: Tracing the Complex Articulations of Community and Locality." *Pasos: Revista de Turismo Patrimonio Cultural*, 1(1): 13–32.

Bondi, L. (1992). "Gender and Dichotomy." *Progress in Human Geography*, 16(1): 98–104.

Bourdieu, P. (1984). *Distinction: A Social Critique of the Judgement of Taste*. London: Routledge.

Brockbank, A. and Traves, J. (1996). "Career Aspirations—Women Managers and Retailing." In S. Ledwith and F. Colgan (Eds.), *Women in Organisations: Challenging Gender Politics* (pp.78–98). Basingstoke: Macmillan.

de Certeau, M. (1984). *The Practice of Everyday Life*. Berkeley: University of California Press.

Cixous, Helene (1983/1992). "The Laugh of the Medusa." In E. Abel and E.K. Abel (Eds.), *The Signs Reader: Women, Gender and Scholarship*. Chicago, IL: University of Chicago Press.

Cockburn, C. (1983). *Brothers: Male Dominance and Technological Change*. London: Pluto Press.

Cockburn, C. (1985). *Machinery of Dominance: Women, Men and Technical Knowhow*. London: Pluto Press.

Cockburn, C. (1991). *In The Way of Women: Men's Resistance to Sex Equality in Organisations*. Basingstoke: Macmillan.

Edwards, E. (1996). "Postcards: Greetings from Another World." In T. Selwyn (Ed.), *The Tourist Image: Myths and Myth Making in Tourism*. Chichester: Wiley.

Edensor, T. (2000). "Staging Tourism: Tourists as Performers." *Annals of Tourism Research*, 27(2): 322–344.

Evans, M. (2003). *Gender and Social Theory*. Buckingham: Open University Press.

Everett, S. (in press). "Beyond the Visual Gaze? The Pursuit of an Embodied Experience Through Food Tourism." *Tourist Studies*.

Franklin, A. (2001). "The Tourist Gaze and Beyond: An Interview with John Urry." *Tourist Studies*, 1(2): 115–131.

Fullagar, S. (2002). "Narratives of Travel: Desire and the Movement of Subjectivity." *Leisure Studies*, 21(1): 57–74.

Enloe, C. (1989). *Bananas, Beaches and Bases: Making Feminist Sense of International Politics*. London: Pandora.

Foucault, M. (1977). *Discipline and Punish: The Birth of the Prison*. Harmondsworth: Peregrine.

Guerrier, Yvonne (1986). "Hotel Manager—An Unsuitable Job for a Woman?" *Service Industries Journal*, 6(2): 227–239.

Harding, S. (1986). *The Science Question in Feminism*. Buckingham: Open University Press.

Hearn, J., Sheppard, D.L., Tancred-Sherrif, P. and Burrell, G. (1989). *The Sexuality of Organisation*. London: Sage Publications.

Herold, E., Garcia, R. and DeMoya, T. (2001). "Female Tourists and Beach Boys: Romance or Sex Tourism?" *Annals of Tourism Research*, 28(4): 978–997.

Hollinshead, K. (1999). "Surveillance of the Worlds of Tourism: Foucault and the Eye-of-Power." *Tourism Management*, 20(1): 7–23.

Ireland, M. (1993). "Gender and Class Relations in Tourism Employment." *Annals of Tourism Research*, 20(4): 666–684.

Irigaray, L. (1993). *An Ethics of Sexual Difference*. (translated by C. Burke and G. Gill from Irigaray, L. (1984)). *Ethique de la difference sexuelle*). New York: Cornell University Press.

Jeffreys, S. (1999). "Globalizing Sexual Exploitation: Sex Tourism and the Traffic in Women." *Leisure Studies*, 18(3): 179–196.

Jeffreys, S. (2003). "Sex Tourism: Do Women Do It Too?" *Leisure Studies*, 22(3): 223–238.

Johnston, L. (2001). "(Other) Bodies and Tourism Studies." *Annals of Tourism Research*, 28(1): 180–201.

Jones, A. and Aitchison, C.C. (2007). "Triathlon as a Space for Women's Technologies of the Self." In C. Aitchison (Ed.), *Gender, Sport and Identity: Masculinities, Femininities and Sexualities* (pp. 53–73). London: Routledge.

Jordan, F. (1997). "An Occupational Hazard? Sex Segregation in Tourism Employment." *Tourism Management*, 18(8): 525–534.

Jordan, F. (2007). "Life's a Beach and Then We Diet: Critical Discourses of Tourism and the Body." In A. Pritchard, N. Morgan, I. Ateljevic and C. Harris (Eds.), *Tourism and Gender: Embodiment, Sensuality and Experience* (pp. 92–106). Wallingford: CAB International.

Jordan, F. and Aitchison, C.C. (2008). "The Sexualization of the Tourist Gaze: Solo Female Tourists' Experiences of Gendered Power, Surveillance and Embodiment." *Leisure Studies*, 27(3): 329–349.

Jordan, F. and Gibson, H. (2005). "We're not Stupid . . . But We'll Not Stay Home Either." *Tourism Review International*, 9(2): 195–212.

Kempadoo, K. (2004). Sexing the Caribbean: Gender, Race and Sexual Labour. New York: Routledge.

Kinnaird, V. and Hall, D. (1994). *Tourism: A Gender Analysis*. London: Wiley.

Koskela, H. (2000). "'The Gaze without Eyes': Video-Surveillance and the Changing Nature of Urban Space." *Progress in Human Geography*, 24(2): 243–265.

Kristeva, J. (1969). *Séméiôtiké: Recherches pour une Sémanalyse*. Paris: Edition du Seuil. (English translation.)

Kristeva, J. (1980). *Desire in Language: A Semiotic Approach to Literature and Art*. Oxford: Blackwell.

Kuhn, T. (1975). *The Structure of Scientific Revolutions* (second edition). Chicago, IL: University of Chicago Press.

Ledwith, S. and Colgan, F. (1996). *Women in Organisations: Challenging Gender Politics*. Basingstoke: Macmillan.

Letherby, G. (2003). *Feminist Research in Theory and Practice*. Open University Press: Buckingham.

Lyon, D. (1993). *The Electronic Eye: The Rise of Surveillance Society*. Cambridge: Polity Press.

Lyon, D. (2002). "Surveillance Studies: Understanding Visibility, Mobility and the Phonetic Fix." Surveillance and Society, 1(1): 1–7.

Lyon, D. (2001). *Surveillance Society: Monitoring Everyday Life*. Buckingham: Open University Press.

Maoz, D. (2006). "The Mutual Gaze." *Annals of Tourism Research*, 33(1): 221–239.

Moi, T. (1985). *Sexual/Textual Politics: Feminist Literary Theory*. New York: Methuen.

Moi, T. (Ed.) (1986). *The Kristeva Reader*. New York: Columbia University Press.

Morgan, Nigel and Pritchard, Annette (1998). *Tourism Promotion and Power: Creating Images, Creating Identities*. Chichester: Wiley.

Morley, L. and Walsh, V. (Eds.) (1995). *Feminist Academics: Creative Agents for Change*. London: Taylor and Francis.

O'Connell Davidson, J. (2001). "The Sex Tourist, the Expatriate, His Ex-Wife and Her 'Other': The Politics of Loss, Difference and Desire." *Sexualities*, 4(1): 5–24.

O'Connell Davidson, J. (2005). *Children and the Global Sex Trade*. Cambridge: Polity.

O'Connell Davidson, J. and Sanchez Taylor, J. (1996a). *Child Prostitution and Sex Tourism in South Africa*. Bangkok: End Child Prostitution in Asian Tourism.

O'Connell Davidson, J. and Sanchez Taylor, J. (1996b). *Child Prostitution and Sex Tourism in Goa*. Bangkok: End Child Prostitution in Asian Tourism.

O'Connell Davidson, J. and Sanchez Taylor, J. (1996c). *Child Prostitution and Sex Tourism in Costa Rica*. Bangkok: End Child Prostitution in Asian Tourism.

O'Connell Davidson, J. and Sanchez Taylor, J. (2001). *Children in the Sex Trade in the Caribbean*. Stockholm: Save the Children Sweden.

Opperman, M. (Ed.) (1998). *Sex Tourism and Prostitution: Aspects of Leisure, Recreation and Work*. New York: Cognizant Communications.

Padilla, M. (2007a). "'Western Union Daddies' and Their Quest for Authenticity: An Ethnographic Study of the Dominican Gay Sex Tourism Industry." *Journal of Homosexuality*, 53(1): 241–275.

Padilla, M. (2007b). *Caribbean Pleasure Industry: Tourism, Sexuality and AIDS in the Dominican Republic*. Chicago, IL: University of Chicago Press.

Pritchard, Annette and Morgan, Nigel (2000a). "Constructing Tourism Landscapes: Gender, Sexuality and Space." *Tourism Geographies*, 2(2): 115–139.

Pritchard, Annette and Morgan, Nigel (2000a). "Privileging the Male Gaze: Gendered Tourism Landscapes." *Annals of Tourism Research*, 27(3): 883–905.

Pritchard, Annette and Morgan, Nigel (2005). "On Location: Reviewing Bodies of Fashion and Places of Desire." *Tourist Studies*, 5(3): 283–302.

Pritchard, Annette and Morgan, Nigel (2007). "Encountering Scopophillia, Sensuality and Desire: Engendering Tahiti in Travel Magazines." In A. Pritchard, N. Morgan, I. Ateljevic and C. Harris (Eds.), *Tourism, Gender and Embodiment*. Wallingford: CAB International.

Richter, L.K. (1994). "Exploring the Political Role of Gender in Tourism Research." In Theobold, W. (Ed.), *Global Tourism: The Next Decade*. Oxford: Butterworth Heinemann.

Ryan, C. and Hall, M. (2001). *Sex Tourism: Marginal People and Liminalities*. London: Routledge.

Savage, M. and Witz, A. (Eds.) (1992). *Gender and Bureaucracy*. Blackwell: Oxford.

Seabrook, J. (1996). *Travels in the Skin Trade: Tourism and the Sex Industry*. London: Pluto.

Seabrook, J. (2000). *No Hiding Place: Child Sex Tourism and the Role of Extraterritorial Legislation*. London: Zed Books.

Sinclair, T. (1997). *Tourism and Employment*. London: Routledge.

Di Stefano, C. (1990). "Dilemmas of Difference: Feminism, Modernity and Postmodernism." In Nicholson, L. (Ed.), *Feminism/Postmodernism*. London: Routledge.

Stockdale, J.E. (1991). "Sexual Harassment at Work." In J. Firth-Cozens and M.A. West (Eds.), *Women at Work: Psychological and Organizational Perspectives*. Milton Keynes: Open University Press.

Swain, M.B. (1995). "Gender in Tourism." *Annals of Tourism Research*, 22(2): 247–266.

Urry, J. (1990). *The Tourist Gaze: Leisure and Travel in Contemporary Societies*. London: Sage Publications.

Valentine, G. (2001). "Whatever Happened to the Social? Reflections on the "Cultural Turn" in British Human Geography." *Norsk Geografisk Tidsskrift* [*Norwegian Journal of Geography*], 55(3): 166–172.

Veijola, S. and Jokinen, E. (1994). "The Body in Tourism." *Theory, Culture and Society*, 11(3): 125–151.

Walby, S. (1986). *Patriarchy at Work*. Cambridge: Polity.

Walby, S. (1997). *Gender Transformations*. London: Routledge.

Theobold, W. (Ed.) (1998). *Global Tourism: The Next Decade* (2nd edition.). Oxford: Butterworth Heinemann.

Wearing, B. (1996). *Gender: The Pleasure and Pain of Difference*. Melbourne: Longman.

Wearing, S. and McDonald, M. (2002). "The Development of Community-Based Tourism: Re-Thinking the Relationship between Tour Operators and Development Agents as Intermediaries in Rural and Isolated Area Communities." *Journal of Sustainable Tourism*, 10(3): 191–206.

Weedon, C. (1997). *Feminist Practice and Poststructural Theory* (2nd edition.). Oxford: Blackwell.

White, A., Jones, E. and James, D. (2005) "There's a Nasty Smell In The Kitchen! Gender and Power In The Tourism Workplace in Wales." *Tourism, Culture and Communication*, 6(1): 37–49.

Witz, A. (1992). *Professions and Patriarchy*. London: Routledge.

36

Tourism Studies and the New Mobilities Paradigm

Mišela Mavrič and John Urry

Introduction: Why the Need for A New Paradigm?

The history of tourism studies put forward by Graburn and Jafari (1991) and Jafari (1990, 2002) identifies several approaches and topics that were central within particular periods. They explain how before 1930 most research regarding tourism was historical and concerned with tracing the development of particular places or kinds of places. With the development of the car, and later the plane, tourism became principally understood as an economic activity. Analyses were provided of the nature of the industry and the kinds of firms that were typical of the tourism sector. Jafari (1990, 2002) characterizes the 1960s as involving an Advocacy Platform. But by the 1970s the reaction to mass tourism and the one-sided economic argument for tourism raised new questions and concerns of research. These included many noneconomic impacts of tourism, which, aided by a rapidly growing environmental movement in the USA, brought to the fore issues of conservation and carrying capacity (Graburn and Jafari, 1991). This was termed the Cautionary Platform by

Jafari (1990, 2002). As researchers came to understand more fully the impacts of tourism, especially the negative consequences, the 1980s saw a greater focus on examining and recommending less destructive forms of tourism, such as ecotourism, small-scale tourism, and sustainable tourism. Jafari (1990, 2002) called this phase the Adaptancy Platform.

Squire (1994) offers a related account of tourism research in the 1970s and 1980s. The first area of research is the "spatial and economic" cluster that focuses upon tourism as an industry that produces commodities for tourists and considers people as subjects causing various "impacts" upon the local economy, the surrounding environment or the host culture. Squire's second cluster of research, "meaning and values," is concerned with social and cultural impacts, the complex interactions between hosts and guests, images and representations in tourism (1994: 3). Especially important is the study of representations in advertising, photographs, diaries, brochures, film, television, souvenirs, and so on. Various researchers during this early stage of tourism studies drew upon social psychology, sociology, and media studies to propose typologies of people or of motives that either push people to go to certain places or pull them to certain destinations (see Cohen 1972, 1979; Dann 1977, 1981).

Tourism research was much influenced by the cultural turn at the end of 1980s and the beginning of the 1990s. Ateljevic writes that tourism geography up to the 1990s treated tourism "as a discrete economic subsystem existing in isolation from other spheres of social, political and economic life" (2000: 370). But by the mid-1990s, several researchers had started to bridge the gap between tourism, economic geography, and human geography. Scholars explored topics such as "landscaping tourist destinations, highlighting the active role of tourism in the social construction of space through place . . . landscape analysis and travel and mobility" (Ateljevic, 2000: 370–371).

Influenced by feminism and cultural studies, this new trend in tourism studies started raising questions about the body and the senses (Veijola and Jokinen, 1994) and introduced a metaphor of tourist performances which conceptually reached "beyond the passive gaze of the visual towards the embodiment of the acts of production and consumption" (Doorn and Ateljevic, 2005: 17; also see Edensor [Chapter 30] in this *Handbook*). According to Jafari (2002), the 1990s Knowledge-Based Platform represents a holistic, multidisciplinary approach in tourism studies. But despite these useful considerations and good beginnings, tourism studies faces several constraints and is yet to develop a broader framework in order to become effectively "holistic."

Several issues have been identified over the years that the nascent field of tourism studies has been evolving (indeed some may wish to name this field "tourism studies"). First, there is the more general problem of the "economic" approach. Research in tourism (particularly on the business and economics side) has tended to often be "policy led and industry sponsored," resulting in one-sided analyses that serve the industry (Franklin and Crang, 2001: 5). Approaches that address tourism primarily as an economic activity bringing revenue to nation states not only ignore "questions of taste, fashion and identity" (Rojek and Urry, 1997: 2), but also fail to recognize the wider social implications of tourism and the thinking represented by the new mobilities paradigm (NMP) we describe below.

Second, most research presumed that tourism is "a series of discrete, localized events consisting of 'travel, arrival, activity, purchase and departure'" (Franklin and Crang, 2001: 6). In this, tourism seems almost torn out of the context of everyday life or put in opposition to it. Franklin (2004) suggests that tourism has tended to be most commonly explained as a way to escape from the routines of modern life to see/do what can be regarded as extraordinary. Structural (and also motivational) explanations of tourism restrict the understanding of tourism in space (destination) and time (Franklin, 2004; Law and Urry, 2004) and leave little room for understanding tourism as "a significant modality through which transnational modern life is organized" (Franklin, 2004; Franklin and Crang, 2001: 6–7). Similarly, motivational explanations have been criticized for trying to fit tourists into neat typological boxes. Such typologies exemplify problematic social categories and types of people and by doing so, they "deny the subjective reconstruction of tourism by tourists" (Edensor, 2001: 59–60).

Third, in tourism research there is a common division made between production and consumption, as well as between tourists and the places they visit. These two distinctions go together because tourists are often understood as passive consumers of places, goods or views and "the industry" is seen as the producer of places and tourists' experiences. This problem stems from the Cartesian division between subject and object. However, as Ingold (2000) suggests, the environment should be viewed as experienced from within, as people belong to the environment and cannot be seen as simply exogenous to it. As such, they are as much producers as they are consumers of the environment. New approaches since the late 1990s have successfully started to bridge this gap with the metaphor of performance that ascribes tourists an active role in the production of tourist experiences and places (Edensor, 1998), and by showing other social-political relationships (Dann, 1996). However, this is only a partial answer to the production-consumption divide. This metaphor, as we argue below, needs to be understood within a broader framework of mobilities. As Franklin suggests:

> Even a phenomenology of sites that showed a more contested, performative and active set of subjectivities at play, reproduced tourism as a social spatial enclave. But tourism is not just what tourists do at tourist sites, it is also how they came to be created as tourists ... We still need to ask where the desire originates from; how the entire materially heterogeneous network supporting their ability to be tourists came to be the way it is and how tourism orders other objects and people in the world as well as the ordering effects that they in turn create. (2004: 278)

Not surprisingly, Jamal and Kim (2005) lament that not only research in tourism but most social science in the twentieth century deployed either micro- or macro-level analysis. They further suggest that "[t]he micro-macro divide is also a modern artifice of disciplinary interest and methodologies influenced by subject-object dichotomies" (Jamal and Kim, 2005: 67). This divide can be further understood within the two approaches to mobility: the sedentarist and the nomadic.

The main argument of *sedentarist* theories is that authentic human identity, sense of home and stability only exist within certain places (Cresswell, 2002). Furthermore, the notion of place is seen in a static way and only as such can it produce meaning (Tuan, 1977). Consequently, mobility is regarded as a threat to human identity and the authenticity of places, since mobility dilutes the peculiarities of place (Relph, 1976, also

see Urry, 2000: 36). Home and place represent highly ethical notions of commitment, attachment and involvement, and mobility appears as immoral, selfish, and deviant (Cresswell, 2002).

However, the focus of sedentarist theories upon the local and static character of places is problematic for various reasons. First, places are not static and fixed, but as Hetherington (1997) suggests, places should be seen as like ships that can move around within various human and material webs. So places can be "dislocated" since images, thoughts, photographs or memories are on the move, by means of technologies and the moving flows of people. Furthermore, if places become meaningful only when a person establishes his/her roots, then "mobile" or "transitive" places are necessarily depleted of meaning (see Relph [1976] for placelessness; Augé [1995] for non-places; and Bærenholdt et al. [2004] for a critique). By contrast, such mobile places (airports, train stations, etc.) should be seen as nodes where various mobilities or flows intersect. There are various practices of "domesticating" other places (see Ahmed et al., 2003; Bærenholdt et al., 2004: ch. 7) as well as the personalizing of very local spaces while on the move (e.g., using mobile phones or laptops while on the move; see Watts [2008]).

Nomadic metaphysics by contrast represents a global perspective that developed under the influence of the "cultural turn" and as a reaction to sedentarist theories. Its main argument is that nothing is fixed, nothing certain, nothing bounded (neither places nor disciplines). Travel and mobility are manifestations of freedom and sovereignty, mobility is a way to transgress power. The grand narrative of nomadic metaphysics shifts focus from the static to the mobile and disregarded forms of rootedness and meaning, everyday and local mobilities, which can knit together and contribute to multiple mobilities. According to Cresswell (2002: 32), Augé (1995), and Clifford (1997) developed "new mobile ways of thinking" about place, but place in turn became depleted of meaning and identity. Furthermore, many of these nomadic and travel metaphors have been criticized for their masculinist character since they suggest that there is ungrounded and unbounded movement (Skeggs, 2004; Wolff, 1993). Different social categories have very different access to being "on the road" both literally and metaphorically (see Jokinen and Veijola, 1997, on nomadism as masculine).

The New Mobilities Paradigm: Metaphors and Concepts

We now develop the NMP drawing upon the work of one of us (Urry, 2000, 2003, 2007, also see Hall, 2005; Sheller and Urry, 2006). Urry argues that sociology should be reconsidered and formulated anew along the lines of a mobilities framework. He explains that the basis of sociological enquiry had been societies, but due to the rise of multiple mobilities they no longer constitute (if they ever did) an appropriate context for research. He believes that "the material transformations that are remaking the 'social,' especially those diverse mobilities that, through multiple senses, imaginative travel, movements of images and information, virtuality and physical movement, are materially reconstructing the 'social as society' into the 'social as mobility'" (Urry, 2000: 2). Societies should be then understood as systems that are shaped through relations with other such systems. This means that the social is an open system of mobilities (and immobilities) or networks.

Networks are "complex and enduring connections across space and through time between peoples and things" (Urry, 2000: 34). Or, in more abstract terms, networks are "set[s] of interconnected nodes" (Urry, 2003: 9). Networks do not represent vertical hierarchies or structures with a center of power. Their power is dispersed; networks differ in power, and in size that derives from the number of nodes and the density of connections between these nodes (Urry, 2003). We can further distinguish between relatively stable networks or *scapes*, and these enable the movement of unpredictable *flows*. Scapes are complex, enduring and predictable "networks of machines, technologies, organizations, texts and actors that constitute various interconnected nodes along which the flows can be relayed" (Urry, 2000: 35).

This mobilities paradigm consists of a number of further interdependent claims. First, all social relationships involve diverse "connections" often involving physical movement. Social relations are not only fixed or based on propinquity but can exist in various imaginary forms through communication and other mobilities. Second, there are five interdependent "mobilities" that produce social life organized across distance and which form (and re-form) its contours. These are corporeal travel, movement of objects, imaginative travel, virtual travel and communicative travel. Third, physical travel involves lumpy, fragile, aged, gendered, racialized bodies encountering other bodies, objects, and the physical world multi-sensuously. On occasions and for specific periods, face-to-face connections and meetings occur, often as a consequence of extensive movement. Also, distance raises massive problems for states that seek to effect "governmentality" over their intermittently moving populations of lumpy bodies. Furthermore, social life is constituted through various material objects (including "nature" and "technologies") that directly or indirectly move or alternatively block the movement of objects, people, and information (Hollinshead, 1999).

Crucial to analyzing these cultural-political relationships is how the changing environment affords different possibilities of action, movement and belief. It is therefore necessary to analyze the various systems that distribute people, activities, and objects in and through time and space; these various mobility-systems and route-ways often linger over time with a powerful spatial fixity. Mobility systems are based on increasingly expert and alienating forms of knowledge; interdependent systems of "immobile" material worlds, and especially exceptionally immobile platforms (transmitters, roads, garages, stations, aerials, airports, docks) structure mobility experiences through forming *complex* systems (Urry, 2007).

When speaking about mobilities from a global perspective, we may understand them in terms of flows along various scapes. However, when we try to grasp the physical movement of people (as particles or networks within flows) we can also understand this movement as involving various *performances*. Examining people's performances reveals how places are made and how they exist (partially) by what and how people perform within them (Bærenholdt et al., 2004). They "are sedimented practices requiring extensive networks and flows of mobilities in order to stabilize," such as institutionalized narratives, information, networks mediating transportation, social relations, etc. (Bærenholdt et al., 2004: 10). Further, people perform mobilities when they are on the move. Traveling from one location to another should not be regarded as a "dead time that people always try to minimize" but rather as "dwelling-in-motion" (Sheller and Urry, 2006: 213–214).

When discussing performances the NMP recognizes the body as "an affective vehicle through which we sense place and movement, and construct emotional geographies" (Sheller and Urry, 2006: 216). The body, senses and the wish to connect also play an important part in *sociality* (Sheller and Urry, 2006: 216). Even though many long-distance relations can be partially sustained through various communication technologies, Urry argues that in order to "cement" the weak ties, people have to occasionally meet face-to-face, or even body-to-body (2004: 117). Meetings can often be obligatory because of "legal, economic or familiar obligations" or because of "expectations of presence *and* of attention" (Urry, 2004: 118). Meetings can also be "initiated" by objects, activities and special events that necessitate co-presence, or by special places that need to be seen. All these meetings involve some kind of movement and, somehow ironically, the better the technology that, on the one hand enables better distant communication, and on the other hand increases motility, the greater are the obligations to meet (Urry, 2007).

Furthermore these involve various *inequalities*. Ahmed argues that it is through the body and proximity that bodies are characterized as different (2000). The NMP, however, acknowledges more than just "bodily" inequality—it understands diverse and intersecting mobilities as "located in the fast and slow lanes across the globe" (Sheller and Urry, 2006: 207). Economic processes, climate-related disasters and political conflicts continue to create increasingly mobile populations and hybrid resident-tourists. Cross-border migrations, refugees and diasporas, globally situated second-home owners and amenity migrants, regular, short-stay commuters, and longer-stay economic migrants, all contribute to a global landscape characterized by hybridities, postcolonial identities and roots-seeking homelessness (Hollinshead, 1998). Access to mobility is highly uneven. It is necessary to examine "zones of connectivity, centrality and empowerment" on the one hand, and "disconnection, social exclusion, and inaudibility" on the other (Sheller and Urry, 2006: 210). Immobilities (or scapes) enable (but also disable) flows or mobilities to exist. Mobilities and flows are not completely without borders and are influenced by different powers that channel, limit, regulate, or monitor them. In addition, inequality in the midst of mobilities does not only derive from unequal access to mobility. The NMP proposes to turn the question of inequality around. How are mobilities changing systems of values, worldviews and ways of life, and thus creating or uncovering new social exclusions (Bauman, 2000)?

Finally, *technology* is intertwined with mobilities in constituting (expert) systems of immobilities or scapes that enable flows of people, information, words, and images (Internet, mobile telephony) and materials (transportation, postal service). Simmel (1997) shows how punctuality and order in the high mobility metropolis becomes important for enabling interconnected systems to function. Punctuality, the significance of time, and the creation of personal temporalities through the pocket watch are features of modern life intertwined with various technologies. More recently, various technologies are becoming more interwoven with our bodies, enabling us to be connected while on the move. It is, therefore, changing social relations, blurring the distinction between presence and absence, home and away, and enhancing space-time compression. Furthermore, technologies are an essential part of surveillance and inequality. Those in the fast lanes may have better access to advanced technologies or may even have the power to police the access to mobilities. The NMP understands such complex relations of people, materials and technology as hybrid systems (Graham and Marvin, 2001).

The Mobilities Paradigm Offers a New Holistic Logic to Tourism Studies

The NMP opens up a new perspective and opportunity for tourism studies. By considering the social as comprised and created by various intersecting mobilities (and immobilities) or as networks stretching from local to global, the NMP offers an escape from dichotomies (economic–noneconomic, production–consumption, local–global, people–places) that cause problems for tourism research. The NMP brings together the situated and mobile nature of tourism and allows analysis from many (interpersonal, regional, global) perspectives. We now discuss the production–consumption and people–places dichotomies and show how Bærenholdt et al. (2004) make use of the

NMP in order to transcend these problems (see also Coleman and Crang, 2002; Sheller and Urry, 2004).

Destinations are often treated in empirical work as homogeneous entities, bounded localities or containers (Bærenholdt et al., 2004: 29). Research in tourism understood places and the people that visit them as separate. In their attempt to conceptualize tourist phenomena, they focus upon peoples' motives for travel (push and pull motives) to a specific fixed location or upon the impacts upon the environment. The NMP by contrast understands tourism and travel as complex systems of people and places that come into existence through performances, with many such performances also being on the move, as insightfully described in Cresswell's (2006) *On the Move: Mobility in the Modern Western World*. Tourist places are hybrid systems of material and mobile objects, technologies and social relations that are produced, embodied, imagined, memorized and anticipated. Moreover, places are not fixed locations on a map but are better viewed like ships moving around the globe; they travel around as images and memories, and move closer to global centers or further away. In the NMP no place is seen as isolated from influences from outside its geographical borders. All places are in one way or another connected by networks and therefore no place can simply preserve its imagined authenticity. Tourist places come into existence and develop when various mobilities intersect (Sheller and Urry, 2004), and a similar argument may be made for tourist performances, as Edensor provides (see Chapter 30 in this *Handbook*).

The *production* of tourist places or destinations has mostly been associated with the "tourism industry," which mainly deals with marketing and promotion, offers accommodation, transportation, and food, and sometimes creates the built environment or infrastructure. Bærenholdt et al. (2004) suggest that we should not think of industry as a coherent group of organizations with one common goal. It should rather be seen as "industries" or actors forming, creating and deconstructing *networks* (depending on a goal) that range from the local to the global scale. The other "producer" of tourism identified in the tourism literature is the "state" with its laws and development plans for tourism and local authorities which try to implement governmental strategies and control and guide the physical planning within municipalities (Bærenholdt et al., 2004: 24). However, such political and municipal networks may also participate in the webs of "industries." The third, mostly neglected producer of tourism experiences are people themselves, the hosts and especially the guests, who, with their desires, practices, and memories actively transform the spatial practices that the industry and state construct (Lefebvre, 1991).

Bærenholdt et al. (2004) identify various types of networks within and beyond the "destination" itself that contribute to its production. There are *vertical* networks to deliver raw materials and services. They can exist within the local environment but also spread beyond the destination. *Horizontal* networks such as hotel chains mostly exceed the boundaries of the destination. *Marketing* networks are usually organized at the local and regional level. These can involve businesses or other actors such as museums and municipality representatives. *Informal* networks are mostly comprised of local people involved in tourism. Such networks are based on trust and produce social capital among inhabitants. *Political* networks find their meaning in expressing common interests regarding municipal planning and infrastructure or funding. Finally, *networking with tourists* may take many forms, resulting in repeat visitors, direct booking, and visitor participation in cultural events.

This begins to capture the complexities involved in producing tourism. If we think, for example, of marketing and promotion for creating the destination image in the world of mobilities, any clear-cut production roles for the industry or for the state become blurred. The image a destination wishes to portray to its potential visitors has a fluid form. "The industry," writes Arellano, "participates in a real mobilization of the imagination and meaning where tourists, as active interpreters and performers, significantly imagine and reimagine the contours of [places]" (2004: 67). The official representations of businesses, municipalities and states, guidebooks, mass media representations, visitors' photos on the World Wide Web, their mouth-to-mouth promotion of experiences, and other contingent imaginative associations all blur into the images people have of that destination. The complexity of such phenomena calls for a research approach that allows understanding of various intersecting mobilities.

Tourists and their "consumption" of tourist places is at the same time a force that produces tourist places and experiences. "Tourist places are simultaneously places of the *physical environment, embodiment, sociality, memory* and *image*" (Bærenholdt et al., 2004: 32, original emphasis). People are in one way or another producers of these components (Arellano, 2004; Crang, 1997; Crouch, 2000; Crouch et al., 2001). People inhabiting the place historically produce the physical environment as the material component of places. Furthermore, the physical environment on the one hand represents several restrictions, constraints or limitations for tourist's performances (Edensor, 1998). On the other hand, it is also a "playground" for people's imagination, creativity and innovative ways of overcoming such boundaries (de Certeau, 1984). Furthermore, embodiment or "[t]he corporeal approach to place makes it possible to understand places as practiced, produced and performed" (Bærenholdt et al., 2004: 32). In the constant making and remaking of space, bodies are the receptors of sensations and experiences as well as the producers of that space (Edensor, 2000). Various practices that tourists perform are intertwined with technology, such as cameras in photographic performances, with the built environment when strolling in the old town center, with other materials such as food and drink and especially with other people (sociality). Tourist places and tourist experiences are therefore hybrids of material, imagined, and social components.

Tourism research should also examine the affordances of the body and senses by drawing upon literature and analysis from outside the social science field, such as interactional, conversational, and biological analyses (Sheller and Urry, 2006). Furthermore, as with the networks that "produce" places or destinations, the analysis of performances should neither stop at the boundaries of destinations, nor be restricted in time. Examples of the place image or memories are illustrative in that mobilities existing outside of destinations inform people and guide them in their performances; image, imagination, and anticipation are established prior to the arrival to destination; and memories in tangible (photographs, souvenirs) or intangible form last long after departure from destination and mobilize the place.

The following are thus the key features of the NMP:

- People and places are not separate entities but are constantly creating and shaping each other.
- Experiences of people are negotiated through practices or performances.
- Body and senses play a paramount role in tourist experience.
- The co-presence of others plays a significant role in tourist experience.
- Mobility/movement is embodied and is a significant part of the whole experience.
- Places consist of networks of mobilities and immobilities and come to life as and when they intersect.
- Places are not fixed and static but mobile—they can exist in other spaces and temporalities.
- Places are hybrids of the material and the imagined (Anderson, 1983/2006).
- To understand tourism phenomena we need to develop active, mobile methods of research.

Some Implications of 'Mobilities' for Tourism Research

We have attempted to illustrate how the study of tourism has drastically changed over the past 15 years, since Jafari (1990) described the field's evolution in terms of four platforms. We are dealing now with a new paradigm where it is important to understand the world as networks of mobilities and immobilities. Researchers have to tackle a wide variety of new phenomena in the contemporary world, which implies the need for different kinds of "mobile" research methods and techniques. We put forward below some examples of new methodological approaches.

Ethnographic Methods

Ethnographic methods of enquiry provide a good starting point for research. However, classical ethnography needs to be coupled with other methods and techniques to establish a broader, more holistic view. One of the seminal works on extending ethnographic method beyond a single site of observation is Marcus' (1995) multi-sited or mobile ethnography. This "is designed around chains, paths, threads, conjunctions, or juxtapositions of locations in which the ethnographer establishes some form of literal, physical presence, with an explicit, posited logic of association or connection among sites that in fact defines the argument of the ethnography" (Marcus, 1995: 105). Gille and Ó Riain especially argue that ethnography is able to deal with studies of the social life in global conditions "because it does not rely on fixed and comparable units of analysis, as do survey and comparative research" (2002: 273). They argue that place should remain the focus in new ethnographies that try to tackle fluidity, networks, and the global. "Places matter because it is in places that we find the ongoing creation, institutionalization, and contestation of global networks, connections, and borders." (Gille and Ó Riain, 2002: 278).

They particularly discuss how to extend ethnography in space and time. They believe that such extension will involve the use of interviews, history, or tracing networks and decrease the time spent at each site. We explore some of these methods below.

Observation

Observation can most efficiently deal with micro worlds of peoples' interaction with other people, their movement or performances, their interaction with the environment, technology, and so forth. Edensor (2001) for example explores three types of performances stemming from his research at the Taj Mahal (see Edensor, 1998). He divides them into "directed performances," "identity-oriented performances," and "non-conformist tourist performances" that are subdivided into several other groups. Through these performances he explores the nature of guidebooks for tourists, the built environment of destination, the symbolic meaning of places, and control that various powers try to exercise over visitors.

Zukin (2003) presents a kind of "self-reflective" observation. She analyzes her own mobile performances through a narrative of a traveling jug. The jug takes different properties, in different contexts or at least changes from Zukin's perspective. The jug in a Manhattan-shop window represents good European taste, and later in Tuscany these jugs become tourist kitsch. When she develops expertise in jugs, jugs become a collection and a passion that triggers mobile performances and travel for acquiring such jugs. She ends up selling and buying the jugs on an online auctions website. Her narrative highlights two important points. First, the way materials or things travel (as materials and images) take different imaginary forms in different contexts. Second, she highlights the complexity of observation in the world of mobilities that needs to develop appropriate methods.

Mobile observation or "following people" as an observational technique should be, according to Marcus (1995), especially used when dealing with ritual cycles, pilgrimage, and diasporas. The procedure is to follow and to stay with the group of people/subjects. This technique also enables one to understand what happens to subjects of research in other sites or "off-stage," which may be especially useful in migration studies but also in tourism research (Marcus, 1995: 106). Bærenholdt et al. (2004) coupled their mobile observation with interviewing while on the move. Cuthill (2006) developed a "speed interviewing" technique on the move to have a better access to subjects within clubs and bars. Crouch et al. argue that, in order to obtain relevant information about relatedness between tourists and their experiences and practices, a researcher should "'follow' people from their everyday life (through and during which holidays may be constituted and imagined) to their holidays, and back again" and complement such research by in-depth interviewing and participant observation (Crouch et al., 2001: 265). This approach would establish the complexity of a tourist experience that can start well before the arrival at a destination and ends much after the departure.

Cyberethnography

Another kind of observation is that of virtual space or a cyberethnography. This technique explores new hybrid forms of moving people, intertwined with new information technologies, or "interactive travel" (Germann Molz, 2006: 378). It mostly uncovers new forms of communication that enable new social interaction at a distance, altered perception of presence and absence, and even possibilities of surveillance, by analyzing texts, images, and narratives on the World Wide Web. "The concept of interactive travel recognizes that travelers are traveling *with* the Internet as well as *on* it" (Germann Molz, 2006: 378, original emphasis). Germann Molz's (2004) exploration of around-the-world travelers through examining their Web pages analyzes social and cultural meanings, imagination, and understanding of the global that construct traveler's corporeal practices. Technically she analyzed sites by scrupulously reading them, observing the images, clicking on internal and external links to understand their context and navigation, and keeping field notes about each site. The sites in progress (travelers that were on the around-the-world trip during the course of a research study) were observed for a year, subjects were contacted by email or phone, and the researcher even participated in discussion forums and live chats.

Interviews

It should be noted here that, from a practical point of view, following people in this sense may prove to be difficult. A researcher may physically follow a group of people when they are engaged in a relatively open pattern of travel, such as backpackers or other kinds of packaged, organized tourism, but it is impossible to follow a family or a romantic couple on their entire holiday journey. Therefore, we need other techniques to enable us to grasp the nature of their movement and experience. A classical approach would be interviewing either through a survey or through more qualitative interviewing. Another more recent technique is to conduct focus group discussion with subjects.

Time Diaries

An innovative way to gather information on the "mobile" traveler is to ask subjects to keep a time diary. Time diaries have at least a 40-year-long tradition and have been used for uncovering the trends in time use (Gershuny,

2002), changes in time use, leisure, paid, and unpaid work time (Sullivan and Gershuny, 2001), the impact of technology such as the Internet on time use (Gershuny, 2002), and trends in the use of the means of transport (bicycle) (Noble et al., 2000). An in depth "time-space" diary was used in a research by Bærenholdt et al. (2004) to collect data relating to movement, practices and perceptions of tourists at a "moving destination." Such a technique could be used to capture the practices and anticipation prior to a tourist experience, time-space paths taken during a visit, and the organizing of memories after the visit (generally on time and tourism, see Hall, 2005).

Visual and Literary Sources

Poetry, literature, and photography can also be used. Such methods can enable a researcher to grasp the importance and meaning of the "atmosphere of place" (see Degen and Hetherington, 2001, on a place's "hauntings"). Visual and other material represents a broad range of data for research in tourism. On one side, guidebooks, official catalogs, postcards, and souvenirs speak about the "production" side of tourist places. Their materiality and myths that develop around them organize peoples' expectations, perceptions and experiences of place. The other side of such visual material, especially photographs of tourists, represents a rich database for understanding peoples' performances, dreams, images, and especially memories (see Larsen 2005, on family memories). Photographs especially provoke memories of the death of loved ones, the inexorable ageing of the fragile human body and the complex movement of people and relationships as hearts are broken and dreams are shattered. Transient holiday pictures are not simply transient, but rather they "have an enduring after-life ... a vital part of life-stories and spaces of everyday life" (Bærenholdt et al., 2004: 122). Travel is thus more generally about friendship and family life, and hence filled with multiple anticipations and memories of peoples and places.

Digital Recording

When a researcher observes or follows people, he/she can use classical note taking or more technologically mediated recording of data through a digital or a video camera. Crang argues that camera is a research tool that is "socially embedded and closes the gap of representation and practice" (1997: 365). By this, he argues that video produces the most "objective" picture of the tourist experience. Video material can be produced by a researcher, providing "'scientific' material" (Crang, 1997: 368–369) or by tourists. Crang further suggests a technique of video diary as "the potential for allowing tourists a familiar mode of self-expression that highlights the aspect of self-presentation, and allows the confessional exploration of understanding, the recording of activity and motion, the interaction of people as well as what they see, and the enjoyment of each other's company" (1997: 370). New technologies and practices such as mobile phones, navigation systems, digital mapping,[1] the Internet, and so on, represent new possibilities and challenges for researching those "on the move."

Historical Research

Historical research can also be pertinent to understanding mobilities and tourism. One example is Peters' (1996) analysis of mobilities and technologies that historically transformed the social and material world first in the USA. Exploring the changes induced by the emergence of the car he examines not only the changing perception and expectations of the car by its users, but also the changes in lifestyle, built environment (roads, gas stations, fast food restaurants, design of national parks), standardization in the production (food chains), and so forth.

Conclusion

We have explored various ways in which thinking through the lens of "mobilities" provides another paradigm from which to approach the study of tourism. Obviously not all is new here, but the mobilities paradigm does generate a different perspective. Arguably, it also brings tourism theory and research "out of the ghetto." No longer is it the study of exotic places visited by people for very distinct and special periods of time. Rather, tourism should be seen as more continuous with other mobilities—overlapping and interdependent. More generally we have seen how places are dynamic, moving around and not necessarily staying in one "location." Places travel within networks of human and nonhuman agents, of photographs, sand, cameras, cars, souvenirs, paintings, surfboards, and so on. These objects extend what humans are able to do, what performances of place are possible. And the resulting networks swirl around, increasingly fluid-like, changing the fixing of place and bringing unexpected new places "into" play. Tourism studies need to be mobile and networked to keep up with the astonishing transformations of place that the new world dis/order seems to be ushering in.

Notes

1 See Futuresonic. Retrieved November 11, 2006 from 10.futuresonic.com/urban_play/off_the_map_projects.

References

Ahmed, S. (2000). *Strange Encounters: Embodied Others in Postcoloniality*. London: Routledge.

Ahmed, S., Castaneda, C., Fortier, A. and Sheller, M. (2003). *Uprootings/Regroundings: Questions of Home and Migration*. Oxford: Berg.

Anderson, B. (1983/2006). *Imagined Comm-unities*. London and New York: Verso.

Arellano, A. (2004). "Bodies, Spirits and Incas: Performing Machu Picchu." In M. Sheller and J. Urry (Eds.), *Tourism Mobilities: Places to Play, Places in Play* (pp. 67–77). London: Routledge.

Ateljevic, I. (2000). "Circuits of Tourism: Stepping Beyond the 'Production/Consumption' Dichotomy." *Tourism Geographies*, 2(4): 369–388.

Augé, M. (1995). *Non-Places*. London: Verso.

Bauman, Z. (2000). *Liquid Modernity*. Cambridge: Polity.

Bærenholdt, J.O., Haldrup, M., Larsen, J. and Urry, J. (2004). *Performing Tourist Places*. Aldershot: Ashgate.

Clifford, J. (1997). *Routes*. Cambridge, MA: Harvard University Press.

Cohen, E. (1972). "Toward a Sociology of International Tourism." *Social Research*, 39: 164–182.

Cohen, E. (1979). "A Phenomenology of Tourist Experiences." *Sociology*, 13: 179–201.

Coleman, S. and Crang, M. (Eds.) (2002). *Tourism: Between Place and Performance*. Oxford: Berghahn Books.

Crang, M. (1997). "Picturing Practices: Research Through the Tourist Gaze.' *Progress in Human Geography*, 21(3): 359–373.

Cresswell, T. (2002). "Introduction: Theorizing Place." In G. Verstraete and T. Cresswell (Eds.), *Mobilizing Place, Placing Mobility* (pp. 11–32). Amsterdam: Rodopi.

Cresswell, T. (2006). *On the Move: Mobility in the Modern Western World*. London: Routledge.

Crouch, D. (2000). "Places Around Us: Embodied Lay Geographies in Leisure and Tourism." *Leisure Studies*, 19(2): 63–76.

Crouch, D., Aronsson, L. and Wahlstrom, L. (2001). "Tourist Encounters." *Tourist Studies*, 1(3): 253–270.

Cuthill, V. (2006). "Complex Mobilities: Transforming Tourist Places and Service Cultures." PhD thesis, Lancaster University.

Dann. G. (1977). "Anomie, Ego-Enhancement and Tourism." *Annals of Tourism Research*, 4(4): 184–194.

Dann, G. (1981). "Tourist Motivation: An Appraisal." *Annals of Tourism Research*, 8(2): 187–219.

Dann, G. (1996). *The Language of Tourism: A Sociolinguistic Perspective*. Wallingford: CAB International.

de Certeau, M. (1984). The Practices of Everyday Life. Berkeley: University of California Press.

Degen, M. and Hetherington, K. (Eds.) (2001). "Spatial Hauntings." *Space and Culture*, 1–6.

Doorn, S. and Ateljevic, I. (2005). "Tourism Performance as Metaphor: Enacting Backpacker Travel in the Fiji Islands." In A. Jaworski, and A. Pritchard (Eds.), *Discourse, Communication and Tourism* (pp. 173–198). Clevedon: Cromwell Press.

Edensor, T. (1998). *Tourists at the Taj: Performance and Meaning at a Symbolic Site*. London: Routledge.

Edensor, T. (2000). "Walking in the British Countryside: Reflexivity, Embodied Practices and Ways to Escape." *Body and Society*, 6: 81–106.

Edensor, T. (2001). "Performing Tourism, Staging Tourism: (Re)producing Tourist Space and Practice." *Tourist Studies*, 1(1): 59–81.

Franklin, A. and Crang, M.A. (2001). "The Trouble with Tourism and Travel Theory?" *Tourist Studies*, 1(1): 5–22.

Franklin, A. (2004). "Tourism as an Ordering: Towards a New Ontology of Tourism." *Tourist Studies*, 4(3): 277–301.

Germann Molz, J. (2004). "Destination World: Technology, Mobility and Global Belonging in Round-the-World Travel Websites." PhD thesis, Lancaster University.

Germann Molz, J. (2006). "'Watch us Wander': Mobile Surveillance and the Surveillance of Mobility." *Environment and Planning A*, 38: 377–393.

Gershuny, J. (2002). "Social Leisure and Home IT: A Panel Time Diary Approach." *IT & Society*, 1(1): 54–72.

Gille, Z. and Ó Riain, S. (2002). "Global Ethnography." *Annual Review of Sociology*, 28(1): 271–295.

Graburn, N. and Jafari, J. (1991). "Introduction: Tourism Social Science." *Annals of Tourism Research*, 18(1): 1–11.

Graham, S. and Marvin, S. (2001). *Splintering Urbanism*. London: Routledge.

Hall, C.M. (2005). *Tourism: Rethinking the Social Science of Mobility*. Essex: Pearson Prentice Hall.

Hetherington, K. (1997). "In Place of Geometry: The Materiality of Place." In K. Hetherington and R. Munro (Eds.), *Ideas of Difference* (pp. 183–199). Oxford: Blackwell.

Hollinshead, K. (1998). "Tourism, Hybridity and Ambiguity: The Relevance of Bhabha's Third

Space Cultures." *Journal of Leisure Research*, 30(1): 121–156.

Hollinshead, K. (1999). "Surveillance of the Worlds of Tourism: Foucault and the Eye-of-Power." *Tourism Management*, 20(1): 7–23.

Ingold, T. (2000). *The Perception of the Environment: Essays on Livelihood, Dwelling and Skill*. London: Routledge.

Jafari, J. (1990). "Research and Scholarship: The Basis of Tourism Education." *Journal of Tourism Studies*, 1(1): 33–41.

Jafari, J. (2002). "Retracing and Mapping Tourisms Landscape and Knowledge." Retrieved May 22, 2006 from www.fas.harvard.edu/~drclas/publications/revista/Tourism/jafari.html.

Jamal, T. and Kim, H. (2005). "Bridging the Interdisciplinary Divide: Towards an Integrated Framework for Heritage Tourism Research." *Tourist Studies*, 5(1): 55–83.

Jokinen, E. and Veijola, S. (1997). "The Disoriented Tourist: The Figuration of the Tourist in Contemporary Cultural Critique." In C. Rojek and J. Urry (Eds.), *Touring Cultures* (pp. 23–51). London: Routledge.

Larsen, J. (2005). "Families Seen Photographing: The Performativity of Family Photography in Tourism." *Space and Culture*, 8: 416–434.

Law, J. and Urry, J. (2004). "Enacting the Social." *Economy and Society*, 33(3): 390–410.

Lefebvre, H. (1991). *The Production of Space*. Oxford: Blackwell.

Marcus, G.E. (1995). "Ethnography in/of the World System: The Emergence of Multi-Sited Ethnography." *Annual Review of Anthropology*, 24: 95–117.

Noble, B., Dickson, M., Gershuny, J. and Fugeman, D. (2000). "Using Omnibus Survey to Investigate Travel." *Extract from Transport Trends 2000 Edition*. DETR.

Peters, P. (2006). *Time Innovation and Mobilities*. London: Routledge.

Relph, E. (1976). *Place and Placelessness*. London: Pion.

Rojek, C. and Urry, J. (Eds.) (1997). *Touring Cultures*. London: Routledge.

Sheller, M. and Urry, J. (Eds.) (2004). *Tourism Mobilities: Places to Play, Places in Play*. London: Routledge.

Sheller, M. and Urry, J. (2006). "The New Mobilities Paradigm." *Environment and Planning A*, 38(2): 207–226.

Simmel, G. (1997). In D. Frisby and M. Featherstone (Eds.), *Simmel on Culture*: Selected Writings. London: Sage Publications.

Skeggs, B. (2004). *Class, Self, Culture*. London: Routledge.

Squire, S.J. (1994). "Accounting for Cultural Meanings: The Interface Between Geography and Tourism Studies Re-Examined." *Progress in Human Geography*, 18(1): 1–16.

Sullivan, O. and Gershuny, J. (2001). "Cross-National Changes in Time-Use: Some Sociological (Hi)stories Re-Examined." *British Journal of Sociology*, 52(2): 331–347.

Tuan, Y. (1977). *Space and Place: The Perspective of Experience*. Minneapolis: University of Minnesota Press.

Urry, J. (2000). *Sociology Beyond Societies*. London: Routledge.

Urry, J. (2003). *Global Complexity*. Cambridge: Polity Press.

Urry, J. (2004). "Small Worlds and the New 'Social Physics'." *Global Networks*, 4(2): 109–130.

Urry, J. (2007). *Mobilities*. Cambridge: Polity Press.

Veijola, S. and Jokinen, E. (1994). "The Body in Tourism." *Theory, Culture and Society*, 6: 125–151.

Watts, L. (2008). "The Art and Craft of Train Travel." *Journal of Social and Cultural Geography*, 9(6): 711–726.

Wolff, J. (1993). "On the Road Again: Metaphors of Travel in Cultural Criticism." *Cultural Studies*, 7(2): 224–239.

Zukin, S. (2003). "Home Shopping in the Global Marketplace." Paper for the Les sens de mouvement colloque. Cerisy-la-salle. June.

37

Tourism and Languaging

Alison Phipps

Tourism and Languages

Tourism offers a profound and concentrated encounter with other languages. It concentrates global linguistic diversity. Some languages are more "global" than others, and more likely to be offered up in phrase books or tourist language courses than others. The commonsense of the global paradigm is that I will "get further" with English than I will with Chicheŵa. As a tourist I now readily assume that I will be able to "get by" in English, that the world speaks English. A journey from Scotland to Lisbon finds me leafing through my language notebooks from a survival language course I took the year before, talking to my neighbor on the plane, reading over my phrase book, checking in my head and with my mouth whether I've retained anything of the Portuguese I've been learning. I am not alone, other tourists also display signs of foreign language anxiety, and tell of this before and after holidays.

Tourism and languages are inextricably interlinked. While considerable attention has been paid to the discursive construction of tourism and tourist language and discourse, most notably in the work of Graham Dann (1996) but also latterly in, for instance, the

work of Jaworski and Pritchard (2005), very little attention has been paid to the *languages* and *languaging* worlds inhabited by tourists.

Language and discourse are not the same as languages or *languaging*. To tour the world is to move in and out of languages and changing linguistic soundscapes. To do this is not just to learn languages or to speak a language but *to language*. And tourists are *languagers*—they are people who, when brought into relationship with different languages, will have a go, often in broken and fragmentary ways, at communicating and understanding—not just at speaking, but of putting themselves into a position where they can make sense of the foreign language. To do this, tourists, being resourceful, will often prepare themselves for the activities of languaging by investing in tapes, CDs, portable language courses, and phrase books that they use prior to a holiday and which are then packed away in hand baggage and pockets.

The research to date in languages and tourism falls into three categories:

1 Research taking a discourse analytic approach looking inside language for the ways in which tourism constructs and represents worlds in language (Dann, 1996; Jaworski and Pritchard, 2005; Jaworski et al., 2003; Snow, 2004).

2 An applied, model-based approach (Pearce, 2005). Such models purport to offer ways of enabling the tourism industry to deal with the supposed problem of monolingual, monocultural tourists through intercultural training (Baysan, 2001; Leclerc and Martin, 2004; Pearce, 2005).

3 An emergent literature addressing the teaching and training in languages and intercultural communication in the tourism industry (Fighiera and Harmon, 1986; Russell and Leslie, 2004; Winslow, 1997).

In the last three decades discourse analysis— "the study of how stretches of language take on meaning, purpose, and unity for their uses" (Cook, 1994: 1)—has contributed much to the understanding of the social nature of communication, of contexts for speech and interaction, of the negotiations of meaning, and the ways in which social relationships and social identities determine and are determined in and by language. The research undertaken at the University of Cardiff under the auspices of the Leverhulme Language and Global Communication project[1] has gone some way towards documenting the discursive qualities of tourism as a form of global communication. Such analysis helps us understand some of the wide ranging concerns at play in discussions of tourism and language, particularly of macro-level structures, institutions and agencies which aim to protect and legislate on behalf of the rights of peoples, languages and cultures, and on behalf of global capitalism (Urry, 2000).

In recent years attention in the tourism literature has turned in particular to questions of intercultural communication in an attempt to document and model practices which may help with easing the flow of people, their languages and their cultural differences. Several articles have engaged with the question of managing intercultural communication, and of cultural sensitivity with respect to those who work in the tourism industry (Leclerc and Martin, 2004). These articles have argued for the insertion of intercultural training in tourism contexts as part of maximizing the customer experience and

the "take" that accompanies customer satisfaction. The empirical and theoretical research that unpins this new strand of research in the tourism research field is largely aimed at modeling behavior and tourist types according to typologies developed in the 1980s and 1990s by intercultural communication theorists. These models have now also been widely critiqued (Corbett, 2003; Guilherme, 2002; Jack and Phipps, 2005).

Without wishing to prolong a review of the intercultural communication theories, developed largely in the USA at a point in history when consumer capitalism was taking off as a major and revolutionary political project, it may be useful here to highlight some of the key elements and premises of this stand of intercultural communication literature. Much critical ink has been spilled already on the problems inherent in the intercultural projects of Hofstede and Hall (Hall, 1990; Hofstede, 1996), amongst others, and on the difficulties and even the desirability of modeling intercultural and cultural behaviors and of testing for certain behavioral norms. However, the intercultural training industry has been built upon these foundational texts and many training programs have resources based on models and ideas that these researchers produced. It is therefore no surprise that, in tourism contexts, where the key questions that are posed are those of managing diversity to the benefit of the tourism industry and for customer satisfaction, the research chosen to enable this practical work is that of consumer capitalist concerns and the emerging mobilities of global capitalism.

Of course, it is important for those who enjoy the benefits of tourism, from the refreshment it promises to the return on investment, to ensure that all may go smoothly. In the communication challenges posed in tourism, from ordering coffee to attending to medical emergencies, the possession of some key phrases or some awareness of how other cultures do things (in either direction) can considerably help things along. The problem with these models is that they see intercultural communication and language learning as skills to solve problems, rather than as the manner of movement, of encounter, learning and engagement with the world.

I believe that the impulse to help and to communicate well and effectively, to get along with others rather than just to get by, is an important one and one that deserves greater attention than modeling behaviors and responses would suggest. It is therefore my contention that many of the studies of intercultural communication in tourist settings, while addressing issues that are of immediate practical concern, exacerbate the problem by creating intercultural communication, languages and translation to be a problem; one which an industry of technological fixes may then grow to serve, rather than taking a *dwelling* perspective; one which is heavier, messier, and requires time to be taken with languages, places, and people.[2]

It is no surprise, in the supply and demand models that dominate intercultural and linguistic training in the tourism industry, that the languages learned to be spoken *for* tourists are those deemed to be the most welcoming to visitors from the historically colonial countries of the problematically named "First World." It is therefore clear that any intercultural assessment of languages and tourism will need at some point to reflect upon the postcolonial condition of tourism and connections between continuing colonialism and languages practiced under conditions of tourism. In short, it is important to realize that there is something of a political, language economy at work in this field of intercultural analysis. No languages come with innocent histories, rather, they are carriers of cultural legacies and tourists, as language carriers and language makers are themselves embedded in an ongoing process of telling and writing of other cultures and other experiences, in and through languages. Tourism, as a crucial site of intercultural encounter and linguistic endeavor, sustains and resists these language economies, and what Thurlow and Jaworski (2003) more hopefully term the language ecologies of tourism.

These language economies do not equate simply with cultural economies (Anderson, 1991). There are indeed powerful connections between languages and cultures and these are particularly in evidence in tourism; tourist Spanish for Spain, Italian for Italy, French for traveling in France. But of course whereas, as tourists, we expect to find French culture in France and Japanese culture in Japan, the languages, following the former patterns of trade, travel, exploration and colonialism, do not equate with culture in the same way. So one may learn Portuguese for holidays in Portugal, Brazil, Angola, or Macao. Likewise, English will be spoken in many places that are far removed from English culture. Indeed we may find it necessary, in order to reflect on this relation, to speak of the *cultures* of English, of French, or of Portuguese—to avoid the partial and often essentialist aspects that pervade our intercultural imaginations as tourists.

Cultures are not static or simple nor are the actions performed by cultural beings, as tourists or as services, neutral actions. Advice given on what to do and how to do it in tourist language courses, phrase books, tourist guides and in the curricula of hospitality industry degree programs is cultural advice that is ideologically freighted. This political, language economy is not simply confined to languages learned and spoken by tourists. Language of all kinds marks travel writing, travel guides, and travel literature, the stories told of trips taken, of life in the destination. All of these find their way into the communicative syllabi of tourist language courses of all kinds, recast for use in tourism. From the enduring stories that shape the canons of our cultures to backs of tickets, phrase books and the leaflets handed out by tour guides in information booths, we find resources for tourist languages in profusion. It is to the specific example of phrase books that I shall turn to give examples of the ways in which tourists and languages intermingle, but first I wish to introduce a different term, to enable fresh ways of conceptualizing the relationship between languages, language learning and tourists.

Tourism and Languaging

The term "languaging" is one that I have developed together with Mike Gonzalez (Phipps and Gonzalez, 2004). It has been used before in different contexts and at different times in history. It emerged for us out of the process of struggling to find a way of articulating the full, embodied and engaged interaction with the world that comes when we put the languages we are learning into action. We make a distinction between the effort of using languages that one is learning in the classroom contexts with the effort of being a person in that language in the social and material world of everyday interactions. "Languagers," for us, are those people, we may even term them "agents" or "language activists," who engage with the world-in-action, who move in the world in a way that allows the risk of stepping out of one's habitual ways of speaking and attempt to develop different, more relational ways of interacting with the people and phenomena that one encounters in everyday life. "Languagers" use the ways in which they perceive the world to develop new dispositions for poetic action in another language and they are engaged in developing these dispositions so that they become habitual and durable. Languaging, then, is an act of encounter. It is first and foremost about relationships rather than possession of a set of skills. This term, we acknowledge, takes some getting used to. The idea of languaging remains a rather abstract one, unless the interrelationships and sense of process it expresses are exemplified in detail. I therefore turn now to an examination of phrase books and their place in tourism by way of illustration.

Phrase Books

The relationship between tourists and phrase books is at once both complex and banal. Although a multimillion-pound industry paralleling that of the guidebook industry, the way in which the knowledge economies of phrase books is both accessed and used is markedly different. This section will summarize some of the ways in which phrase books are used and how phrase book knowledge is learned. Autoethnographic reflection and examples of translated materials from tourism sites will be used to illustrate how the phrase book rapidly becomes largely redundant. Despite the intimacy of their carriage—in pockets, on iPods®, in handbags—phrase books are social objects with little linguistic, pedagogic value, designed to become one of the most rejected objects in tourist baggage, an item of comic status, entertaining tourists once they begin to language and move beyond the confines of their covers.

For as long as I can remember being able to read I seem to have been fascinated by what I could not read. So there I am, aged 6, sitting with the *Children's Encyclopedia Britannica* my Grandma had won as a Sunday School prize in the box room at my grandparents in Blackburn, Lancashire, trying to learn phrase book French. Aged 11, I was formally allowed to learn at school—French and German. My mum would feed my clearly insatiable passion for languages with second hand phrase books from the charity shop where she volunteered. The books traveled with me when I first went abroad, to France and then Germany on school exchanges, aged 14, and then again aged 15, 16, 17, 18 when I took them with me to university, and then for a year abroad in Germany, to France for a year after graduating, aged 22, and then back home again, and over to Germany to accompany my PhD fieldwork. They arrived in boxes in Birmingham when I got married, and followed me to my first job in Glasgow, moving between the available space on my shelves at home and in the office. Three flat moves later I can safely say that they have never come in handy. Instead they have sat on assorted shelves gathering dust until the next move or necessary journey.

When I began working on an ethnographic project to examine tourist language learning practices as a tourist language learner myself I thought that the phrase books would at last find their purpose. Putting myself in the subject position of a tourist language learner, rather than as a teacher of languages, would surely mean a need to engage with my phrase books. But even then the books remained untouched, somehow irrelevant. This discussion is my autoethnographic attempt to understand why.

The phrase book is as ubiquitous as the guidebook and miniature versions of phrase books can be found in most leading guidebooks. Phrase books, however, more than guidebooks, come in pocket-sized formats. Despite their ubiquity and their intimate format they have barely attracted any critical literature in either modern language studies, in tourism studies or in translation studies. Furthermore, the few studies in applied linguistics that do exist work explicitly within the binary "tourism, bad": "criticism of tourism, good." Proof of the "badness" of phrase books is allied to their pedagogic structure and their commodified form. Clearly, anything sold to tourists can have little going for it, and this misperception continues, despite the considerable efforts of those working in tourism and intercultural studies to expose the assumptions inherent in such knee-jerk assumptions regarding tourism and forms of popular culture over many decades.

The work of any significance in the field of phrase book studies, as I will now call it, relates to a couple of articles on the colonial potential of phrase books in contexts such as Southern Rhodesia, Mozambique, and India, and to a couple of historical articles—one about the sixteenth century translator John Florio, who is claimed by translation scholars as the first phrase book writer; the other examining Wilhelm von Humboldt's language (Dummler, 1998; Franceschini, 2003; Putanec, 1990; Steadman-Jones, 1999).

In translation studies the most comprehensive attempt at theorizing the relationship between translation and tourism as a functional aspect of processes of hegemonic and counter-hegemonic globalization is provided in the work of Michael Cronin (2003). Cronin takes pains to understand the function and ubiquity of a range of translation activities beyond the literary, demonstrating persuasively the need for a considered and careful place for translation in contexts where languages are characterized as minority and where linguistic diversity is threatened. In an article which provides a careful investigation of translation and its accompanying objects, Cronin argues for an understanding of the material production and institutional structures which have supported their creation in terms of time, materials and status, giving weight through their resources to the practice of translation:

> Translations as organized matter, text objects, have depended throughout history for their preservation and transmission on the material organizations of church, army, academy, company, state, or supranational entity, which are socially constituted bodies with the express aim of enduring beyond the present moment, even if their specific temporalities vary widely. (Cronin, 2002b: 3)

To this list I would add the institutions that support the development of tourist language learning. In particular, I would refer to the language schools, tourist language adult education courses, and language holidays which now form a large part of the tourism industry, gaining and giving status through linguistic exchange carefully facilitated by tour operators and through the careful appeal to intercultural and international humanistic goals such as the Oxford International Language College's "Learn Spanish in Spain," and "Learn French while hiking." In *Learning the Arts of Linguistic Survival* (Phipps, 2007) I examined the way in which tourist languages are learned and argued for an understanding of this phenomenon through a dwelling perspective. I examined the phenomenological dimensions of learning to language, to speak from the body and towards others, as opposed to the now standard colonial and postcolonial critiques of linguistic hegemonic forces present in the globalizing contexts today. I was keen to explore the lived, languaging relationship between languages and tourism and to do so autoethnographically.

The accumulations of dust and miles traveled by my collection of phrase books has led me to a particular focus on phrase books as traveling objects, and also as agents interacting with our imagined futures and languages. In short, I am interested to begin exploring the question as to what phrase books might be for. I would add to this, following Cronin's work, some further questions regarding the organization and representation of the human languages. Furthermore, I would also wish to ask some questions regarding the function and purposes of phrase books, in educational, practical, and metaphysical terms; When and how are phrase books actually used and by whom? Cronin maintains that:

> In a properly integrated approach to translation, it is necessary to consider not only the general symbolic system (human language), the specific code (the language translated), the physical support (Stone, papyrus, CD ROM), the means of transmission (Manuscript, printing, digital communication) but also how translations are carried through societies over time by particular groups. (Cronin, 2002b: 3)

Phrase books are carried, intimately. They form part of the hand luggage, like medicines and water, passports, and currency. They are held in the same receptacles as those elements seen to give life. They can also be easily bought in those sanctuaries of safety—the airport shops, on the hither side of the scanner, where only safe goods are available. You will find them in the stationers and newsagents at railway stations and ports—hybrid objects hovering somewhere between the stand with the bestsellers and the stand with the newspapers. As well as coming in the handy pocket book format they can also now be carried in plug-in, cyborg form, on CD ROMs, and iPods®. As such they become emancipatory objects, as theorized by Donna Haraway:

> We are all chimeras, theorized and fabricated hybrids of machine and organism; in short, we are cyborgs.

> The cyborg is our ontology; it gives us our politics. [. . .] The cyborg is resolutely committed to partiality, irony, intimacy, and perversity. (Haraway, 2004: 8)

But more than this, the ubiquity of phrase books make the tourist-cyborgs, in their intimate acts of language carrying, major, if often unwitting carriers of translation, and in ways which have entirely escaped translation and tourism studies to date.

Phrase books appear at transitional moments, moments between walking and riding, or flying, moments in international, or intercultural spaces, where the edge of one language meets the life of another. They are objects for edges and also agents of edges and with edges, edging away at language and transliterating words and morphing letters into new arrangements. Although largely privately used objects they appear on planes and trains, in the odd transitional spaces of airplane seats. All of these aspects—the carried intimacy, the proximity to other survival necessities—water, medicines, lipstick—their status as hand baggage, their appearance and purchase at transitional moments, and their lettered edginess give them a talismanic aura. They make manifest our imaginations of lives to be lived in other contexts. They tell of desire and intent, as well as telling of fear and hope. They are there for the eventuality of an imagined crisis where words may indeed fail us. They represent a small, material manifestation of Beck's Risk Society (1992), where the ready availability of a small pocket-sized phrase book may be all that is needed to help us ensure we escape danger.

But this is not the only material agency we may accord to our phrase books. They also move around in space: from shelves, to bags, to hand baggage, or to breast pocket; getting closer and closer to the body with the nearness of the imagined destination. The prospect of entering a new "languagescape" and of needing not just to learn a language but also to have to language, makes phrase books the ultimate hermeneutic key. Hermes of course was a winged God in Greek mythology and the flying of phrase books from shelves into bags and across continents offers a modern parallel to this myth of understanding and of meaning-making when confronted with the need to imagine interacting with the incomprehensible other.

In moving around in space, phrase books also offer a co-present possibility for moving the body. The body, not the linguistic other, is the ultimate subject of the phrase book. The body needs to learn to move to a different language beat. The phrase books become something of a language wardrobe, from which the language flesh may be re-clothed. It offers the resource for changing the flow of breath, the tap of tongue on teeth, the shape of the lips, and the holding of the body. The edges of letters edge the body into new modes of exhalation and phonetic shape.

And within their pages is the full delight of an epic story: comedy and tragedy in its thrall, and the full eventuality of adventuring life offered up in phrases for the memory. Aristotle sees the epic as needing to encompass reversal, discovery, and calamity, and the dialogues and imagined sketches that fill the pages of the phrase book offer all of these to the reader, as we shall see in the examples to follow. According to Walter Benjamin (1973) there are two kinds of storyteller, the one who stays at home and the one who travels. We might also suggest that there are two kinds of stories: those for home and those for traveling. Travel stories need to reach out, not in. They need to have the confidence of what Benjamin (1973), in *The Task of the Translator,* terms their interlinearity. In short, the epic stories of the phrase book are already translations, devised as travel epics and written out as such, however formulaic the publishing or series style might be. These are not stories written in one language for the contexts that grew that language, rather, they speak with two voices, of the human condition as it may be experienced and understood. They speak already with two voices, to two language audiences, of reversal, discovery and calamity. To use Michael Cronin's (2002a) terms here, they

are both one with the earth and one with the birds.

As epic tourist dramas the scripted imagined events may be both comic and tragic. Indeed, as my opening epigraph shows, they are used by comedians because of their often ridiculous, comic examples of chaos and human folly. Ionesco used phrase books as an inspiration for his absurdist comedy *La Cantatrice Chauve* for instance. All of human life is here, acted out in role plays, short scripted dialogues, and dramas. Beyond this, however, a different meta-drama is enacted in the phrase books for they also trouble the power relations that a majority language enacts vis-à-vis one of a supposed minority status (Cronin, 2003). As such we may see phrase books working in the interstices of national and world language power to trouble, to ridicule, to help, and to change—if and when they are used.

Phrase books, then, are not just repositories for the epic stories told for the benefit of those who stay at home. They are already translators of stories. More than this, however, they are also transliterations of stories. They are interlinear translations for those who would read their words, the literature in other languages, but before they translate they transliterate the words so that they may be spoken, languaged, and understood. This is a key difference from other parallel texts used in teaching situations, or even from language textbooks which rarely transliterate. Languaging, is for me, a key term here as it makes a distinction between language learning as a structured activity based in and around the classroom, and the embodiment of the language being learned in the whole social world, the speaking from the body and the effort, even humility that this social act requires.

Learning from a Phrase Book

The following two examples are taken from two of the phrase books I used myself on holiday, autoethnographically. I was keen to try out phrase book learning in the contexts for which they were designed. With a holiday planned walking the hills of northern Scotland, and another trip to Malawi in the offing, I had two interesting, and somewhat unusual languages to play with. These are not the most obvious of tourist languages, to be sure, but both languages position themselves in the phrase book market with products aimed at tourists like me.[3]

Both books used had similarities and differences in structure, but differences in presentation were marked. More standardized phrase book publishers, such as Harraps, Lonely Planet, Langenscheidt, Rough Guide, and Berlitz, standardize their presentation of languages, evening out culture differences and inserting tips for travelers into the phrase books themselves, to make up a hybrid of guidebook and phrase book. In the case of my two different guides it is fair to say that the epic purpose of language learning was very apparent in the serious postcolonial, yet obviously colonialized approach to language learning and to an anthropological scholarship worn very much on its Malawian context. In the Gaelic context, we were in the opposite world, in the world of the strip cartoon. Here language is presented as part of comic holiday fun, but linked to Romance, not to trial.

In both guides we find a common structure, beginning with rules for pronunciation and moving through aspects of life, such as greetings, food, dress, shopping, dancing, help, and into scripts for dialogue for different eventualities. "Local color" comes through palpably in the language, with phrases that already take on a metonymic hue with tourism being foregrounded, especially around greeting, meeting, and eating. It would be easy to dismiss these aspects as unimportant, but as I argued in *Learning the Arts of Linguistic Survival* (Phipps, 2007), the focus on these crucial aspects of the social bond and of what Williams (2000) terms the miracle of neighborliness, gets to the heart of intercultural life and the ways in

which it may be lived in the present age. If we cannot meet, greet and eat with the other, as neighbors, then the social bond breaks and social life enters dangerous and precarious times. Courtesy is crucial for all the reasons outlined famously by Goffman (1969) in *The Presentation of Self in Everyday Life*. It represents face work—the effort of courtesy as seen in facial expression—that is done in real time presence of the other. Phrase books are objects designed for easing this vital work between human beings. Their presence in touristic encounters means they can be called upon to aid the flow of social life.

The extracts in Figures 37.1 and 37.2, from two minority language, tourist phrase books, are examples of primary source material and act as a basis for the discussion of the representations and expectations.

Using Phrase Books

In the context of considering my own non-usage of phrase books I am apparently not the only one who, in interactions with others, and in situations where a phrase book would indeed serve, leaves the book firmly in the bag or pocket. If others use phrase books then it is as I do: when traveling, in transition, in train, or in airplane seats. Or they are used privately? Do users secretly bone up on words and phrases once out of the context, for somehow, it does not do to be found at study. It is rare indeed that phrase books are resorted to for help in communicative interaction. Gesturing and pointing are the first recourse, when other languages already held with some degree of poise, in the body, will no longer do. As such, phrase books are one of the most rejected objects, packed intimately yet strangely unused.

In their overall architecture and structure, phrase books may be seen as epic translations that show their workings out and their stage directions. They carry with them a good deal of instruction, often presented in brackets or italics, with explanations as to

Chichewa for Tourists
By M.V.B. Mangoche; revised by Egidio H. Mpanga (1990)

A Phrase Book
- "Introduction
- General Grammatical Observations
- General Greetings
- Courtesy, Relationships, Beliefs
- Numerals, Currency, Weights and Measures
- Directions, Times and Seasons
- Various Scenes, Sample Dialogues
- Selected Words and Expressions" (p. 3)

Epic Purpose
"The purpose of this note book is not to teach Chichewa. Rather it is to help those English speaking visitors who come to Malawi and who would wish to add a little more to their happiness during such visits by occasionally conversing with the people in their own tongue." (p. 6)

General Grammatical Observations
"All vowels in Chichewa are open and are pronounced as in the following English Words" (p. 7).
"Chichewa is a concordial language. This means that all words in the sentence take prefixes, infixes or suffixes according to rules of concordial agreement between nouns and pronouns with other parts of speech." (p. 9)

Script for General Greetings
- "Moni bambo (Greetings sir), Moni mai (Greetings madam), Moni agogo (Greetings old lady/ granny)
- Zikomo (Good day)
- Kodi muli bwanji?
- Ndili bwino
- Sindili bwino
- Zikomo, Pitani bwino." (p. 14)

Some Anthropology
"The Achewa are both matri-linear and matri-local. The family is so extended that for most foreigners some of the relationships are very remote, while to the Achewa these are real and impose on individual members certain obligations which must be honored.
When addressing people by their clan name it is *courteous (my emphasis)* to prefix 'A' to the clan name. The honorific 'A' should be written disjunctively." (p. 19)

Scripts:
- "Traveling by Car
- Tabwerani (Come here please)
- Ndatchona m'matope (I am stuck in the mud)
- Kankhani (Push hard)
- Imani (Stop)
- Ndatopa (I am tired)
- Ziko mo ndapita (Thank you, Good bye, I'm off)" (p. 26)

**Figure 37.1   Extract from *Chiche wa Guide for Tourists* Phrase Book.
Source: Mangoche and Mpanga (1990).**

how grammatical or pronunciation aspects of the language actually work (Figures 37.1 and 37.2). Throughout there is a sense that the phrase book, as with the guidebook, will stand in for the hired guide or the hired interpreter or translator (Cronin, 2000); books and words, in place of the people. Ghostly books, kept on shelves, bags, and in pockets, intimate yet disembodied, made small, mobile, and ready to come alive in the body and speech of another, parasitic upon their carriers for their speech.

In their organization it can also be noted that phrase books aim not at literacy, though they are clearly initial objects grounded in literacy, but they push hard through phonetic

Gaelic: Na Leasain

- "Latha math (la-a-mah) Good day
- Failte (Faal tche) Welcome
- Latha math duhut fhein (la a nah ghoot heyn) Good day to you too (reply)
- Ciamar a tha thu?
- Tha gu math, tapadh leat.
- An aimsir: The Weather
- Madainn mhath (mad-in vah) good morning
- Grian (gree –an) (sun)
- Traigh (traa ee) beach
- Tha e breagha (its fine)
- Tha an t-usige anb an-drasada (its raining just now)" (p. 15)
- 'Aig A' Cheilidh (At the Ceilidh)
- Uisge Beatha (Whisky)
- Chan urrainn dhomh-sa dannsa ach is urrainn dhutosa pogadh (you can't dance but you can kiss)" (p. 48)

Figure 37.2 Extract from *Gaelic for Tourists Phrase Book*.

Source: Ó Baoill (1997).

script and transliterations, for transmission as speech. In short, the goal of the phrase book is not literacy in learning the language. This is incidental and lesser. Rather, their goal is languaging. As such one of the organizing principles of the phrase book is the presence of strips of speech and idealized dialogue. Indeed, we might say, following Habermas (1984), that phrase books offer an example of ideal speech situations, in which help will be forthcoming, speech understood unequivocally and where the ending will, despite the many possible trials, have a happy ending.

Walter Ong has famously made a distinction between oral and literate cultures. Writing for the 1980s he develops an argument which replaces notions of primitive or civilized culture with a different opposition, that of orality and literacy, and stresses the primacy of orality:

> Orality is not an ideal, and never was . . . . Oral cultures today value their oral traditions and agonize over the loss of these traditions, but *I have never encountered or heard of an oral culture that does not want to achieve literacy as soon as possible.* (Ong, 1982: 172, emphasis added)

The desire for education, the straining to be able to enter the mobile worlds of literacy are captured neatly here for us to consider. Ong's arguments have been influential though not uncontested. Ingold in particular has argued persuasively for a different conception of writing and literacy, not as part of a binary divide, which enacts other divides inherent in the notion of culture, but as a graphism, a skilled practice which transmutes language and gives it mobility. Writing and literacy practices, Ingold argues, are inscribed, they do not transcribe, they provide a graphic counterpart to speech (Ingold, 2000, 2007).

This view of literacy and writing helps to make some sense of the paradox I identified in my work on, with, and as a tourist language learner, described fully in *Learning the Arts of Linguistic Survival* (Phipps, 2007). For throughout this work, and in all my years of teaching languages, I have never encountered or heard of a tourist language learner who does not want to achieve oral fluency as soon as possible. Phrase books, as objects of and for literacy in tourist languages, in Ong's (1982) terms, represent the achievement of a cultural goal. Those who buy them, carry them, and work to use a different language to their habitual ones when on holiday are not doing so in order to write more wonderful phrase books. They are aiming to reach a degree of fluency as soon as is possible. This may not be fluency in the sense of being able to converse easily, but it is a degree of fluency desired with even just a few phrases; in particular those for the meeting, the greeting, and eating.

What this points to here is yet another instance of the many reversals, and new habits tourists imagine themselves acquiring, and often also acquire, through time spent on holiday. The type of reversal at work here is not one of age to youth, affluence to frugality, north to south, or heat to cold. It is one which reverses the strong technocratic literacies of high modern societies. It undoes the hegemonic status of English and opens a space for other worlds to be imagined using other words—not in writing, but in face-to-face contact and in speech. It requires the graphing of language—writing, literacy, for much of its communication. Phrase books push in the opposite direction, into the body so that speech—translated and transliterated—is bodied forth in face-to-face encounters.

The fact that phrase books are rarely used in face-to-face contexts underscores this wider point about the push from literacy into orality in tourist languaging. The dramatic metaphor is helpful again here, for in this context, we find gesturing, mime, movement of the body, pointing and hand shapings are present. Merleau-Ponty's (2002) considerable thesis on the *Phenomenology of Perception* sees the person, or agent, as a being-in-the-world, as an embodied presence. Rather than an objectivized view of languages as external to the human body, or as part of the realm of cognition, Merleau-Ponty's work enables us to understand the ways in which the human body and its movement are language, not disassociated from gesture or speech production.

> The analysis of speech and expression brings home to us the enigmatic nature of our own body . . . It has been observed that speech or gesture transfigure the body, but no more was said on the subject than that they develop or disclose another power, that of thought or soul. The fact was overlooked that, in order to express it, the body must in the last analysis become the thought or intention that it signifies for us. It is the body which points out, and speaks. (Merleau-Ponty, 2002: 229–230)

Even if not used in context, the presence of sections on pronunciation and phonetics which often give detailed instructions as to the position of the tongue, the voicing or not of consonants, etc., enables the body to read of how it may speak. Often the transliterations and pronunciation guides are highly normative, reverting to so-called standard forms rather than varieties, though variation is present in some of the examples of sounds that may not actually occur in the source language.

The matter cannot just be left there though, neat as the reversal may be. A further

practice, a literacy practice, needs to be taken into account here. Holiday note books, as with ethnographers' note books, become alternative sites for the inscription of useful phrases. To these accrue scraps of paper, notes of vocabulary, transliterations, words, additional phrases. The bought book, the book which may only rarely be used, is remade through dictionaries and through the tourist's work at the language, written out for themselves as personal language, not scripted but scrappy, not tidy dialogue but postcards to the self, language charms for the journey, all still prompting the body to language, to speech. The fear with a phrase book is that if the other speaks, the answer will not be as scripted. Language behavior may script in the classroom but not in the real world of languaging.

Epic Scripts

As epic scripts, reversing relations between host and guest, majority and minority language powers, between oral and literacy phrase books encompass stories of the whole of human frailty, and survival. Through them language becomes a distanciated epic event. It becomes an occasion to practice for moral challenge, confrontation with difference and most persistently, for courtesy (Brecht, 1967). In their dramatic, even tragic hues, the scripts act as a magic charm or talisman, protecting from imagined harm, already enacting the worst scenarios and showing happy ends and ways of reaching a resolution. As comic scripts they represent the ridiculous, metonymic, or improbable. They pay their dues to the learner in comic narrative, written out and learned before use. They suggest the kinds of stories that may be recounted at a later date, or become the stories themselves. More than this, however, and continuing to draw on Brechtian understandings of the potential of the Epic, such scripts enable an engagement with difference so as to enact a pedagogic, even didactic transformation in their audience. Brecht describes the potential of epic scripts thus: The Epic arouses capacity for action, forces decisions to be taken, we are made to face up to something, brought to the point of recognition, we study, the human being is alterable and able to alter, a process, eyes on the course—not on the finish (cited in Willett, 1964: 37). The contexts in which these epics are enacted are contexts changed by different aspects of varied forms of globalization. Translation moves language around in books and in bodies, crossing the borders of languages, crossing the borders when language lives and is embodied. The lack of interest in phrase books in academic literature, even in the field of modern languages, applied linguistics, and tourism studies is perhaps not surprising, given the way in which translators in general are commonly rendered invisible (Venuti, 1995), given the gendered nature of much translation as women's work (Simon, 1996) and given the association of much translation with function and manual. The phrase book enacts a prior connection between translators and the technical tourist environment they inhabit (Cronin, 2003). This connection is unpracticed in phrase book users, by definition. It is therefore both comic and potentially tragic. Mostly there is very little relationship between the tourist and the language of phrase books. The languaging relationship is more usually with alternatives: dictionaries, representations, phonetics, and grammar. When the tourist makes the effort—meets, greets and eats in a different language—with or without the help of the phrase book talisman then the tourist body becomes a carrier for newly languaged relationships with other people and objects.

Conclusion

Languaging and translation in tourism are always intercultural work, the work needing to be done as part of the work of dwelling in intercultural worlds. The intensity of interlingual/intercultural tourist worlds manifests itself in material objects such as phrase books, alongside other translation supports such as tourist language classes, language holidays, bilingual menus, and a tourism and hospitality industry that acknowledges and actively trains its employees to be good linguistic hosts. Perhaps most acutely, in the tourist context, we see enacted the persistence of diversity that Forsdick (2005) writes of so persuasively. This diversity is scripted in the phrase book as a symbol of the same, as a symbol of a hoped-for courtesy carried by tourists who, as languaging tourists, must be understood as major carriers of translation and transliteration as well as both the subjects and objects of translation.

There is no simple way of understanding or describing the relationships between languages, language-objects (such as the phrase books exemplified here) and languaging tourists—those making a real effort to work with the foreign languages however they may be encountered. The traditional work on language, discourse and communication in tourism is important and offers a genuine contribution to understanding the construction of tourism, but it does not offer ways of understanding the multilingual and plurilingual contexts, objects and behaviors present in tourist life. For this, as I have shown using the example of the phrase book in this chapter, we need to work to understand how and where languages are present in tourism, to engage with the paradoxes present and to suggest different ways of understanding the language networks and activities which form intimate experiences for tourists. Furthermore, tourism researchers in this area must address the phenomenological, bodily experience and encounter of the tourist with the touristic world through linguistic media such as the guidebook, phrase book, and other texts.

Notes

1 Retrieved May 10, 2008 from www.global.cf. ac.uk.

2 As the existential philosopher Heidegger (1971: 228) expressed it, to dwell is to inhabit "the poetic," to experience the world poetically and to live in a place meaningfully and resolutely. To *dwell* is to become at home even under the homelessness of modernity.

3 As a fluent speaker of other languages and a keen linguist I encountered one of the key fallacies about language learning: that it is easier to speak other languages once you have familiarity with one or two different languages already. This is a fallacy from the point of view of knowledge of new languages. Any ease comes with regard to the process of learning and the depth and intensity of the relationship in question that the language symbolizes, not with the language itself, at least not unless there is a close relationship, as say between Spanish and Portuguese, or Irish and Scottish Gaelic.

References

Anderson, B. (1991). *Imagined Communities: Reflections on the Origin and Spread of Nationalism*. London: Verso.

Baysan, K. (2001). "Perceptions of the Environmental Impacts of Tourism: A Comparative Study of the Attitudes of German, Russian and Turkish Tourists in Kemer, Antalya." *Tourism Geographies*, 3(2): 218–235.

Beck, U. (1992). *Risk Society: Towards a New Modernity*. London: Sage Publications.

Benjamin, W. (1973). *Illuminations*. London: Fontana.

Brecht, B. (1967). *Gesammelte Werke*. Frankfurt am Main: Suhrkamp.

Cook, G. (1994). *Discourse and Literature: The Interplay of Form and Mind*. Oxford: Oxford University Press.

Corbett, J. (2003). *An Intercultural Approach to English Language Teaching*. Clevedon: Multilingual Matters.

Cronin, M. (2000). *Across the Lines: Travel, Language and Translation*. Cork: Cork University Press.

Cronin, M. (2002a). "'Thou Shalt be One with the Birds': Translation, Connexity and the New Global Order." *Language and Intercultural Communication*, 2(2): 86–95.

Cronin, M. (2002b). "Babel's Standing Stones: Language, Translation and the Exosomatic." *Crossings*, 2(1): 1–7.

Cronin, M. (2003). *Translation and Globalization*. London and New York: Routledge.

Dann, G. (1996). *The Language of Tourism: A Sociolinguistic Perspective*. Wallingford: CAB International.

Dummler, C. (1998). "Las anotaciones de Wilhelm von Humboldt sobre algunas lenguas indigenas de la Nueva Granada: las gramaticas betoi y mosca (chibcha)." *Forma y Funcion*, 11: 121–134.

Fighiera, C. and Harmon, L. (1986). "Le Probleme des Languages dans le Tourisme." *Documents sur l'Esperanto*, 21: 1–24.

Forsdick, C. (2005). *Travel in Twentieth Century French and Francophone Cultures: The Persistence of Diversity*. Oxford: Oxford University Press.

Franceschini, R. (2003). "Das Bild des Italienischen in früheren Jahrhunderten: Spuren in Dialogbüchern des 16–18. Jahrhunderts." *Italienisch*, 50: 70–83.

Goffman, E. (1969). *The Presentation of Self in Everyday Life*. London: Allen Lane.

Guilherme, M. (2002). *Critical Citizens for an Intercultural World*. Clevedon: Multilingual Matters.

Habermas, J. (1984). *The Theory of Communicative Action: Reason and the Rationalization of Society*. Boston, MA: Beacon Press.

Hall, E.T. and Hall, M.R. (1990). *Understanding Cultural Differences: Germans, French and Americans*. Yarmouth: Intercultural Press.

Haraway, D. (2004). *The Haraway Reader*. London: Routledge.

Heidegger, M. (1971). *Poetry, Language, Thought*. New York: Harper Colophon Books.

Hofstede, G. (1996). *Cultures and Organizations, Software of the Mind: Intercultural Cooperation and its Importance for Survival*. New York: McGraw-Hill.

Ingold, T. (2000). *The Perception of the Environment: Essays in Livelihood, Dwelling and Skill*. London: Routledge.

Ingold, T. (2007). *Lines: A Brief History*. London: Routledge.

Jack, G. and Phipps, A. (2005). *Tourism and Intercultural Exchange: Why Tourism Matters*. Clevedon: Channel View.

Jaworski, A. and Pritchard, A. (2005). *Discourse, Communication and Tourism*. Clevedon: Channel View.

Jaworski, A., Thurlow, C. and Lawson, S. (2003). "The Uses and Representations of Local Languages in Tourist Destinations: A View from British TV Holiday Programmes." *Language Awareness*, 12(1): 5–29.

Leclerc, D. and Martin, J.N. (2004). "Tour Guide Communication Competence: French, German and American Tourists' Perceptions." *International Journal of Intercultural Relations*, 28(3/4): 181–200.

Mangoche, M.V.B. and Mpanga, Egidio H. (1999). Chichewa Guide for Tourists. Blantyre, Malawi: Dzukua Publishing.

Merleau-Ponty, M. (2002). *Phenomenology of Perception*. London: Routledge.

Ó Baoill, C. (1997). *Gaelic is Fun*. Stornoway: Acair.

Ong, W. (1982). *Orality and Literacy*. London: Routledge.

Pearce, P. (2005). *Tourist Behaviour: Themes and Conceptual Schemes*. Clevedon: Channel View.

Phipps, A. (2007). *Learning the Arts of Linguistic Survival: Languaging, Tourism, Life*. Clevedon: Channel View.

Phipps, A. and Gonzalez, M. (2004). *Modern Languages: Learning and Teaching in an Intercultural Field*. London: Sage Publications.

Putanec, V. (1990). "Poliglotni ar.-perz.-grc.-srp. i ar.-perz.-grc.-hrv. rukopisni konverzacijski prirucnici s konca 15.st na porti u Carigradu." *Rasprave Zavoda za jezik*, 16: 237–244.

Russell, H. and Leslie, D. (2004). "Foreign Languages and the Health of UK Tourism." *International Journal of Contemporary Hospitality Management*, 16(2): 136–138.

Simon, S. (1996). *Gender in Translation: Cultural Identity and the Politics of Transmission*. London: Routledge.

Snow, P. (2004). "Tourism and Small-Language Persistence in a Panamanian Creole Village." *International Journal of the Sociology of Language*, 166: 113–129.

Steadman-Jones, R. (1999). "Learning Urdu in the Late Eighteenth and Early Nineteenth Centuries: Dialogues and Familiar Phrases." In D. Cram, Andrew Robert and Elke Nowak (Eds.), *History of Linguistics 1996* (Volume 1: Traditions in Linguistics Worldwide) (pp. 165–174). Amsterdam: John Benjamins.

Thurlow, C. and Jaworski, A. (2003). "Communicating a Global Reach: Inflight Magazines as a Globalizing Genre in Tourism." *Journal of Sociolinguistics*, 7(4): 579–606.

Venuti, L. (1995). *The Translator's Invisibility: A History of Translation*. London and New York: Routledge.

Willett, J. (1964). *Brecht on Theatre: The Development of an Aesthetic*. London: Methuen.

Williams, R. (2000). *On Christian Theology*. Oxford: Blackwell.

Winslow, J.D. (1997). "Languages and Tourism: Raising the Standards." *Linguist*, 36(4): 94–98.

38

Methodologies and Methods

G.R. Jennings

Introduction

Methodologies and methods cannot be discussed without first considering their meanings along with the related term paradigm. Why the latter term? Because paradigms serve to inform both methodologies and methods used in tourism studies (as well as broadly in the social sciences). First, the meaning of methodologies is founded on the definition of its singular form: a methodology. A methodology "is a model, which entails theoretical principles as well as a framework that provides guidelines about how research is done in the context of a particular paradigm" (Sarantakos, 1998: 32). Second, methods are defined as "the tools or instruments employed by researchers to gather empirical evidence or to analyze data" (Sarantakos, 1998: 32). Third, a paradigm is a particular view of the way the world operates (Kuhn, 1962) or "guides action" (Guba, 1990: 17) and is associated with four frames: ontology, epistemology, methodology, and axiology (Guba, 1990; Guba and Lincoln, 2005). Drawing on the work of Guba and Lincoln (2005), each is briefly described in turn. Ontology is the study of the nature of reality (what entities exist, how they are related, etc.). Epistemology is the study of knowledge (the necessary and

sufficient conditions of knowledge, knowledge as justified true belief).[1] Methodology, as already noted, is a set of guidelines for conducting research. Axiology is the study of values and ethics (the nature, criteria, and justifications of values; e.g., studying the principles of aesthetics/ethics and justification of aesthetic/ethical values).[2]

There are a number of different interpretations of the term paradigm. Masterman (1970), for example, identifies 21 interpretations in Kuhn's work. Specifically within tourism studies, the term is used in differing ways by different people (Dann, 1997). Debates have also arisen within the social sciences regarding Kuhn's intended "meaning(s)" (see Hill and Eckberg, 1981; Ritzer, 1981). Despite the passage of time, interpretation of what a "paradigm" is and means remains manifold. Discussions regarding "paradigms" continue in tourism studies (and other social sciences) and draw upon Thomas Kuhn's (1962, 1970, 1996) writings[3] (see, for example, Dann, 1997; Echtner and Jamal, 1997; Wearing et al., 2005). I have provided the previously stated meaning of a paradigm as well as methodology and methods as working definitions so that the work of this chapter may progress. I do this with the same intent in mind as Guba (1990: 17) so we can reshape their meaning(s) as "our understanding of [their] many implications improves."

The purpose of this chapter is to situate methodologies and methods as they relate to tourism within broader discourses of paradigms that may and do inform tourism research. The chapter commences with an overview of the suite of paradigms that may inform tourism studies research and, by association, its methodologies and methods. Next, the chapter provides an historical snapshot of tourism history to highlight the consequences of this history with regard to paradigms as well as to methodologies and methods. The snapshot focuses particularly on perspectives/platforms, planning and development processes evident in tourism studies and praxis. The chapter then briefly touches on paradigmatic debates. Following this, the chapter then takes a critical lens to consideration of methodologies and methods before concluding with reflections of future directions and a research agenda.

Paradigms, Methodologies, and Methods

The suite of paradigms that inform methodologies and methods, from which tourism studies researchers may draw (and have drawn from) is varied. Within the extant tourism studies literature, the suite includes: positivism, post/ positivism, critical realism, pragmatism, chaos and complexity theory, critical theory orientation, constructivism/interpretivism, postmodernism, and participatory paradigms. See Table 38.1 for an overview of these. The table distinguishes the differing positioning of each paradigm with respect to its origins, related terms, focus, ontological, epistemological, methodological and axiological frames, and examples of relevant discussion and/or examples of each of the paradigms.

Disputes exist in the extant literature as to whether some of the "paradigms" presented in the table are paradigms in their own right or innovations or perspectives of existing

paradigms (see Jennings, 2001, 2005; Sarantakos, 1998). Various positions are held amongst tourism studies as well as in the social sciences regarding the categorizing of paradigms. Broadly, in the social sciences, Denzin and Lincoln (2005b: 183), for example, describe four: positivism, postpositivism, constructivism, and participatory views. These are further complemented by the following perspectives: cultural studies, critical race theory, feminism, and queer theory (Denzin and Lincoln, 2005b). Alternatively, Guba and Lincoln (2005) outline five: positivism, postpositivism, critical theory, constructivism, and participatory views. Variously in their discourse, Guba and Lincoln refer to postmodern paradigms (constructivism and postmodernist critical theory). Additionally, the tables that they use to complement their text merge positivism and postpositivism together under the same rubric on a number of criteria, thereby emphasizing perceived commensurability between the two framings. Contemporaneously and in addition to their earlier clustering, Denzin and Lincoln (2005a: 24) specify the following as interpretive paradigms/theories: positivist/ postpositivist, constructivist, feminist, ethnic, Marxist, cultural studies, and queer theory. Another paradigmatic framing drawn from tourism studies identifies three paradigms: scientific positivism, interpretive method, critical theory (Tribe, 2001). While still another uses two frames: positivism and postpositivism; wherein interpretive paradigms are subsumed into post-positivistic framings, and "postpositivism" here refers specifically to the period after positivism, despite issues of (in)commensurability perceived by some in such a twofold framing (see Downward and Mearman's [2004] discussion of Davies [2003]; also see Gale and Beeftink, 2005). Subsequently, Table 38.1 has been constructed to demonstrate those paradigms distinguishable in tourism studies discourses and literature by their reoccurring nature. No doubt, Table 38.1 will contribute to further debate with regard to what has paradigmatically been "left in"

Table 38.1   Overview of Paradigms that Inform Tourism Research

Related Paradigms	Positivism	Postpositivism	Critical Realism	Pragmatism (Mixed Methods)
Origins	Founded in the hard/natural sciences (Naturwissenschaften)	Founded upon principles of hard/natural sciences (Naturwissenschaften)	Founded upon the principles of hard/natural sciences (Naturwissenschaften)	Founded in human (social) sciences (Geisteswissenschaften)
Synonyms and/or related terms	Empiricism Realism Naïve realism Objectivism, foundationalism, representationalism	New realism (Note: developed as a response to critique of positivism.)	Described as a midpoint between realism and relativism.	Transformative-emancipatory paradigm
Focus	Explanation (Erklären) Realism Objectivism	Explanation (Erklären) Realism Objectivism	Explanation (Erklären) Realism Objectivism	Research "question" focus dictates the emphasis on explanation (Erklären) or Understanding (Verstenhen) or both
Ontology (world view of nature of reality)	Truths and laws are universal	Truths are fallible and a product of historical and social contexts	Truths are fallible and a product of historical and social contexts	"What works" in the external reality
Epistemology (science of knowledge; "relationship between researcher and that which is to be known")	Objective	Objective—acknowledges potential for researcher bias	Objective—acknowledges potential for researcher bias	Ability to solve problems Objective and subjective
Methodology (guidelines for conducting research)	Quantitative	Quantitative (use of mixed methods)	Quantitative Inclusion of mixed methods	Mixed methods Triangulation Compatibility of methods thesis
Axiology (study of ethics and values)	Value free Extrinsic purpose of research project	Essays to be value free Extrinsic purpose of research project	Essays to be value free Extrinsic purpose of research project Consideration of emancipatory role of research	Essays to be value free Extrinsic purpose of research project Consideration of emancipatory role of research May have elements of value laden
Discussion and/or tourism text examples	Examples are manifold and exist in early journal publications	See Journal of Travel Research, particularly early editions	Bhasker (1978, 1982, 1986, 1990) Harré (1981, 1986) Gale and Botterill (2005) Downward (2005)	Tashakkori and Teddlie (1998) Parsini (2005) Parsini (2006) Morgan (2007)

Notes: This table was developed from texts presented in Denzin and Lincoln's (1994, 2000, 2005) editions of The SAGE Handbook of Qualitative Research, particularly the work of Denzin and Lincoln (2000), Lincoln and Guba (2000), Schwandt (2000) and Guba and Lincoln (1994) as well as Guba's (1990) text entitled The Paradigm Dialog and Jennings' (2001 text, Tourism Research, Jennings (2004, 2007a), Tashakkori and Teddlie (1998), and their (2003) edited volume, Handbook of Mixed Methods in Social and Behavioral Research, and Powell (2001). The German terms used in this table are drawn from the writings of Dilthey (1833–1911). Readers who are unfamiliar with terms used in this table are referred to the sources noted herein.

Chaos and Complexity Theory Orientation	Critical Theory	Social Constructivism	Postmodern	Participatory
Funded in hard/natural sciences (*Geisteswissenschaften*)	Founded in human (social) sciences (*Geisteswissenschaften*)	Founded in human (social) sciences (*Geisteswissenschaften*)	Founded in human (social) sciences (*Geisteswissenschaften*)	Founded in human (social) sciences (*Geisteswissenschaften*)
	A number of types: Marxist/socialist Postpositivist Postmodern critical theorists	Interpretivism Constructivism Constructionism	Ludic postmodernism Oppositional postmodernism Critical postmodernism	Cooperative inquiry Participatory action research Action inquiry Appreciative Inquiry
Explanation (*Erklären*) Understanding (*Verstenhen*)	Understanding (*Verstenhen*) *Praxis* (change) Historical realism Perspectivism Interpretivism Intentionalism	Understanding (*Verstenhen*) Relativism Perspectivism Interpretivism Intentionalism	Relativism Perspectivism	Understanding (*Verstenhen*) Experience & meaning Relativism Perspectivism Interpretivism Intentionalism Phenomenology
Systems are complex, nonlinear dynamic ever changing and unpredictable Chaotic and disordered Self organizing	Socio-historical realities Realities reflective of power relations	Multiple perspectives/ realities	Multiple realities No privileging of position. Skepticism towards truth and -isms	Realities collectively constructed via interactions between self-other
Objective and subjective	Subjective-objective unless postpositivist critical theory (objective)	Intersubjective	Relativism	Embodied and situated, reflexive Hermeneutic
Open systems and descriptive algorithms Metaphors	Qualitative Some quantitative	Qualitative	Qualitative	Qualitative Quantitative Mixed method
Essays to be value free	Value laden. Intrinsic focus of research projects Political agendas Emancipatory Transformative	Value laden Intrinsic focus of the research project	Skeptical of emancipation and trans-formation Continuous deconstruction process	Value laden Transformation
Gleick (1987) Byrne (1998) McKercher (1999) Faulkner and Russell (2003) Russell (2006)	Kincheloe and McLaren (2005) Fox (2007) Chambers (2007) Tribe (2007)	Berger and Luckman (1981) Gurney and Humphreys (2006) O'Gorman (2005) Jennings (1999)	Lyotard (1999) Gubrium and Holstein (2003) Pitman (2004) Urry (1990, 2002) Rojeck and Urry (1997)	Lewin (1948) Bennett (2004) Darcy (2006) Westwood (2007)

and/or "out." Such debate is welcomed as it signals "maturity of the field" (Ritchie et al., 2005; see Tribe, 2004 regarding differing viewpoints and field ability to engage in dialogue).

Framing the History of Tourism Research

Initial epistemological pursuits with regard to knowledge building enterprises in tourism research focused primarily on patterns of travel and economic impacts, which were closely aligned with the view that tourism was a panacea for economic development and growth, and associated with the platform of boosterism. Over time, this economic emphasis has remained a core theme of tourism research along with related growth of tourism research within business and marketing framings (see Echtner and Jamal, 1997; Tribe, 1997, 2004). Alternate emphases, which drew more broadly on other social sciences and environmental sciences disciplinary framings, were able to gain only limited currency. Such social and environmental science framings emphasized tourism phenomena as complex, multimodal, multisector, multi-participant phenomena with multiple stakeholder (human and nonhuman) interactions, interrelationships, and interconnectivities. Business framings in the 2000s are starting to embrace similar holistic framings.

Due to the informing perspectives of tourism studies, planning traditions, and key informing paradigms, a number of perspectives with regard to tourism studies have also framed the foci of tourism research. See Table 38.2.[4] Towards the end of the twentieth and into the twenty-first centuries, aided by greater inclusion of social and environmental sciences into tourism research and studies, other paradigms commenced broadening and informing research in tourism studies. These paradigms include interpretive social sciences, critical theory orientation, and participatory

action research. Researchers had been drawing on these paradigms previously, but they were not mainstream agendas then. The history of tourism research had established and reified the hegemonic principles of touristic inquiry and epistemological domains as being post/positivistic in nature.

As Table 38.2 demonstrates, there has been a shift in the type of platform informing tourism studies, the associated planning traditions, the complementary research paradigms, and related research undertaken. While the table looks like some of the frames, platforms, traditions, paradigms, and types of research are mutually exclusive, there are overlaps between frames. In presenting the table, the emphasis has been on identifying the key elements operating at any one time; especially within "western" frameworks. As the global landscape continues to change due to the differing distribution of knowledge economies, electronic communications, and the impacts of globalization, the spread of tourism and tourists, it must be recognized that various nations in the 2000s and 2010s may be situated in differing frames in Table 38.2 and subsequently not necessarily in real time chronological order.

To reiterate, the history of tourism research and disciplinary-related inquiries of tourism phenomena, described here as "tourism studies," is one that has been grounded in the hard sciences, in scientific inquiry informed by positivism and postpositivism (including that branch of postpostivism described as critical realism).[5] Alternate approaches, such as those informed by interpretive social sciences, critical theory orientation, and participatory action research tended to be marginalized or pushed into other disciplinary areas, where such paradigmatic approaches were accepted in order to gain voice, representation, and publication. Against this hegemonic positioning of post/positivism, counter-discourses emerged as demonstrated in Table 38.2. These alternate discourses emerged as the perspectives informing tourism studies and related planning positions shifted from advocacy, boosterism, and economic traditions to sustainable, decommodified, and ethical platforms; as well as various incorporations of other platforms and complementary planning approaches.

Methodologies and Methods: A Critical Lens

Returning to an earlier comment regarding what has been left out of tourism research, it should be clear by now that this relates directly to its background historical hegemony. An examination of research and discussion in this area leads to the identification of at least five alternate agendas, issues, and themes that have been emerging to challenge the dominant discourses and entrenched narratives of the past: acceptance of diversity in paradigmatic approach, quality of works undertaken as research enterprises, shifting efforts away from paradigmatic debates, critical and reflexive methodological dialogue, and alternatives to western-centric research pedagogy and praxis. Each of these is discussed below.

Acceptance of Diversity in Paradigmatic Approach

Until the late twentieth century, tourism research, organizations, structures, and various stakeholders reified positivism's and postpositivism's hegemonic position as the orthodox approach to engaging in tourism studies and research (Jennings, 2001; Reid and Andereck, 1989; Ryan, 1997). Seaton (1996), McKercher, (2002), and Tribe (2004) have variously commented with regard to the gatekeeping roles associated with people and their institutional and professional roles related to knowledge "creation" and "innovation" in tourism studies. Examples of such gatekeepers and their roles include journal editors, reviewers, academic publishers being able to dictate topics and directions (though the rise of the Internet has facilitated

online journals, discussion groups, blog sites and other ways of distributing knowledge). Echoing a similar perspective, Ryan has commented that reviewers of journals "tend to work within restricted and conservative guidelines of orthodox research" and that "orthodoxies are not commonly queried in journal articles" (2005: 12). Contemporaneously, Goeldner (2005: 48) noted that the *Journal of Travel Research* had an early "policy" of privileging publication of quantitative research to "aid in the development of the field" and thereby instituted development of a post/ positivistic agenda.

The acceptance of post/positivist orthodoxy or *hegemony* meant that ontological and epistemological discussion with regard to the conduct of tourism research was absent in many research texts, such as journals, conference proceedings, and graduate research reports. Post/positivism was legitimized through the "institutions" of research training praxes, publication outlets, and professional organizations (Hall, 2004; Jennings, 2001, 2007a; Tribe, 2004). Subsequently, post/positivistic research approaches were accepted as "the norm"—the orthodoxy and hegemonic status quo. Additionally, explication of research processes was assumed as taken-for-granted knowledge, implicit and/or tacit knowledge. Alternate approaches, if accepted for publication, were required to give detailed information on research methodology and methods/processes; or were marginalized and relegated to other publishing outlets to achieve currency. The term *hegemony* is therefore fitting to this situation, and is used in the Gramscian (1971) sense with regard to the domination of one class/ group over another. Such domination is achieved by "controlling" the nature and substance of cultural practices and socializing institutions, in this instance, tourism studies research cultures, practices, praxis, professional governance systems, and publication outlets.

New voices, new journals and new stakeholders are now arriving to challenge

Table 38.2 Overview of Historical Perspectives Influencing the Development of Tourism Studies and Tourism Research[a]

Predominant Time Frame	Informing Perspective of Tourism Studies	Planning Traditions	Key Informing Research Paradigms Reified via Tourism Journals and Publication Outlets, as well as Emergent (explicitly stated) Paradigms and "Perspectives" Appearing in the Same	Foci of Research Undertaken and Methodologies Used[b]
1950s	Advocacy platform	Boosterism Economic tradition	Positivism and post/positivism	Visitor arrivals, economic contributions Forecasting tourism demand. *Primarily, quantitative methods of data collection and interpretation*
1960s Late 1960s	Advocacy platform Cautionary platform	Boosterism Economic tradition	Positivism and post/positivism	As above
1970s	Cautionary platform	*Physical/spatial approach* *Community oriented tourism planning* Economic tradition Boosterism	Positivism and post/positivism	Economic impacts, market analysis, visitor motivations, Environmental impact assessments Social impact assessments Cultural impact assessments Production and consumption of goods, services, and experiences *Quantitative mixed methods, qualitative methodologies, and methods*
1980s Late 1980s	Adaptancy platform Knowledge-based platform	*Sustainable approach* Community oriented tourism planning Physical/spatial approach Economic tradition Boosterism	Positivism and post/positivism *Interpretivism/constructivism/ phenomenology* *Critical theory orientation* *Postmodernism*	As above
1990s	Knowledge-based platform	Sustainable approach Community based tourism planning Physical/spatial approach Economic tradition Boosterism	Positivism and post/positivism Interpretivism/constructivism/ phenomenology Critical theory orientation *Participatory action research* *Critical realism* *"Feminist perspectives"* *Chaos and complexity theory*	As above Growth in qualitative and mixed methodologies *Increasing attention to embodied experience, narrative, textual analysis*

2000s	Sustainable tourism platform[c] Decommodified research platform	Sustainable approach Community based tourism planning Physical/spatial approach Economic tradition Boosterism	Positivism and post/positivism "Critical realism" Interpretivism/constructivism/ phenomenology Critical theory orientation "Feminist perspectives" Postmodernism "Pragmatism" Participatory action research "Gender studies" "Cultural Studies" "Queer theory" "Ethnic Studies" Indigenous paradigms[d] Virtual paradigm[e]	As above *Growth in indigenous and cross-cultural methodologies* *Increasing attention to rectifying "othering" and "silencing"* *of perspectives inherent in traditional research agendas* *Increasing criticality with regard to researcher reflexivity,* *reciprocity, voice, audience, time, and space*
2010s	Ethics platform		Positivism and post/positivism "Critical realism" "Pragmatism" Interpretivism/constructivism/ phenomenology Critical theory orientation "Feminist perspectives" "Gender studies" "Cultural Studies" "Queer theory" "Ethnic Studies" Indigenous paradigms Participatory action research Virtual paradigm *Mobilities paradigm[f]* *New perspectives and paradigms*	As above

Continued

Table 38.2 Overview of Historical Perspectives Influencing the Development of Tourism Studies and Tourism Research *(Continued)*

Predominant Time Frame	Informing Perspective of Tourism Studies	Planning Traditions	Key Informing Research Paradigms Reified via Tourism Journals and Publication Outlets, as well as Emergent (explicitly stated) Paradigms and "Perspectives" Appearing in the Same	Foci of Research Undertaken and Methodologies Used
Beyond 2020			As above	As above
				Growth in new foci and methodologies

Sources: Getz (1986, 1987); Hall (1995, 1998); Jafari (1990, 2001); Kensbock (2007); Macbeth (2005); Uysal (2004); Weaver and Oppermann (2000); Wearing, et al. (2006); Xiao and Smith (2006); Yolles (1998).

Notes:

Emergent paradigms and perspectives are italicized

[a] Readers who are unfamiliar with terms used in this table are referred to the sources noted herein.

[b] With regard to shifts in paradigms and a growing use of qualitative research in tourism studies, Denzin and Lincoln's (2005: 1–32) identification of "moments" in North American qualitative research provide a comparative similarity: (1) 1900s–early 1940s—traditional period (objective research); (2) 1945–1970s—modernist phase (formalizing of qualitative research); (3) 1970–1986—blurred genres (a broad suite of paradigms and methods); (4) mid-1980s—crisis of representation (reflexivity with greater consideration of "gender, class, and race," search for "new models" of research); (5) blurred between mid-1980s–1995—postmodern period ("tales from the field," issues of "other," the silenced given voice, subjective researcher poses, participatory research, localized theory building); (6) 1995–2000—postexperimental inquiry (blurring between scientific qualitative writing and narrative genres as well as representations beyond text-based formats); (7) 2000–2004—methodologically contested period (informed by conflicts and tensions from the previous moments); (8) 2005–the future (responding to evidence-based social research and . . .).

[c] Sharpley (2000) notes that sustainable tourism has been referred to as an "adaptive paradigm" and links to the work of Hunter (1997).

[d] Indigenist and indigenous paradigms have been used here in a generic sense to capture three perspectives and standpoints: indigenous standpoint, indigenist research, and indigenous research conducted by non-indigenist researchers. Indigenist standpoint theory "enables Indigenous researchers to speak from their own cultural standpoint, assist in cultural maintenance and present their own epistemological 'truth' in an attempt to produce a more inclusive and therefore more complex form of knowledge" (Foley, 2005, online document). Indigenist research is "the body of knowledge by Indigenous scholars in relation to research methodological approaches" (Rigney, 2001: 1). Indigenous research conducted by non-indigenist researchers is research undertaken by researchers who do not identify with the indigenist peoples providing the indigenous context for the research.

[e] See Yolles (1998) for discussion on virtual paradigms.

[f] Refer to Mavric and Urrys' [Chapter 36]) in this *SAGE Handbook.*

the status quo. While journals like *Annals of Tourism Research* have consistently fostered interdisciplinary research, avenues for more nontraditional research and critique are being provided by a number of younger journals, such as *Current Issues in Tourism*, *Tourist Studies*, and *Journal of Tourism and Cultural Change*. Bramwell and Lane, in the course of reflecting on the *Journal of Sustainable Tourism*, advocated that "ST [sustainable tourism] research must encourage diversity and new approaches and perspectives, and it must strenuously avoid creating rigid orthodoxies that go unchallenged" (2005: 60). This, however, has been more difficult to achieve until more recently, due to the hegemony that has been in place since the inception of "tourism studies."

Quality of Works Undertaken as Tourism Research Enterprises

While "quality" is an elusive term to define (Jennings, 2006); critiques of the quality of tourism research, paradigmatic applications, methodologies and methods persevere. According to Botterill (2001), the underpinning principles of the paradigms that inform tourism research have rarely been made explicit, including the hegemonic paradigm of positivism. Weed (2005) similarly decries the lack of attention to epistemology and methodology regarding quantitative and qualitative research in tourism related journal articles. Earlier, and more critically, Dann et al. (1988: 4) had commented that "'research' often falls into one of the following three categories: theoretical discourse without empirical foundation; descriptive essays which assemble a collection of impressionistic and anecdotal material; and data analyses devoid of theoretical content." Approximately a decade later, Seaton (1997) professed that research training routinely emphasized verification over explanations (and was grounded in post/positivism roots). Continuing into the 2000s, Cooper reflected that in the 1980s, "tourism

research [was] bedevilled [sic] by conceptual weakness and fuzziness;" lacked focus, was "descriptive, often based on one-off case studies, specific destinations or problems," and "concerned with measurement" (2003: 1). The situation he asserted was still applicable to tourism in the 2000s.

The hegemony and practices of tourism research, however, are changing, as demonstrated, for example, in the work of Ayikoru and Tribe (2007), Heimtun (2007), and Small et al. (2007), among others now too numerous to list. Quality remains an elusive parameter, but it is worthy of attention with respect to both quality of "research" and how this is reflected through the ranking and rating of tourism journals. Amid the recent debates on journal ranking and rating, Jamal et al. (2008) argue for differentiating journals by *scope*, *influence*, *relevance*, and *quality*. But they warn, too, that "ascertaining the items that delineate quality in tourism research is a politically charged task—active involvement of the scientific community in tourism studies ... is crucial to the process of developing and legitimizing ranking/rating innovations" (Jamal et al., 2008: 75).

Shifting Efforts Away from Paradigmatic Debates

Initially paradigmatic discourses related to tourism research tended to bifurcate into discourses associated with which paradigm was better than the other and why. Focus on the relative merits of each with regard to the tourism phenomenon being studied tended to disappear into the background as the foreground concentrated on privileging one paradigmatic view over another. As a consequence, dualistic positioning framed debates, that is, post/positivistic and interpretive/phenomenological/constructivist positioning. This duality emphasized explanation (*Erklären*) and "realism" (post/positivism) on the former, and understanding (*Verstehen*) and "relativism" (interpretive/phenomenological/

constructivist) on the latter (Guba, 1990; Guba and Lincoln, 1994; 2005; Lincoln and Guba, 2000). The use of such a duality has been critiqued by tourism writers affiliated with critical realism (Downward and Mearman, 2004; Gale and Botterill, 2005), and by proponents of pragmatism (Johnson and Onwuegbuzie, 2004; Pansiri, 2005, 2006). It has also been countered by chaos theory and complexity theory (Byrne, 1998; Gleick, 1987; McKercher, 1999). Towards the end of the twentieth century, tolerance towards alternate viewpoints has fostered contemporaneous growth in the number of researchers familiar with alternative approaches, and able to conduct, supervise and review research outside of orthodox mainstream post/positivist agendas.

The lessening of debate and shift towards greater acceptance of paradigmatic and related methodological diversity in tourism studies has lagged behind other social science areas. Bramwell and Lane, for example, commented that "[w]hile radical views in the social sciences were arguably at their height in the 1970s, the burgeoning of research in the tourism field did not occur until the 1980s and 1990s" (2006: 2). An earlier proponent of alternative paradigmatic processes was Cohen (1979, 1984, 1988). Advocates of counterapproaches to the dominant hegemony of post/positivism and quantitative methodologies, in support of critical and interpretive approaches as well as qualitative methodologies, include Aitchison (1999, 2005), Hollinshead (1994, 1996), Jamal and Hollinshead (2001), Jamal and Everett (2004), Jamal and Lee (2003), and Jennings (2001, 2003, 2007a, 2007b). Duijnhoven and Roessingh (2006) discuss the introduction of ethnographic studies in tourism research, noting the first being reported around the 1960s. Initially, as these alternative research methodologies and methods are explored and gain legitimacy, a learning curve is in process and "quality" will tend to vary as Miles observed early on, saying "[t]he most serious and central

difficulty in the use of qualitative data is that methods of analysis are not well formulated" (1979: 591). In the early 2000s, Mehmetoglu (2004) suggested that this was still the case.

Denzin and Lincoln (2000, 2005a) and Geertz (1983, 1988) identified and forecast a blurring of genres. In tourism studies, such blurring has occurred and research has finally taken a turn and shifted away from debating paradigms to exploring alternate approaches and engaging in critical reflections with regard to the conduct of research in tourism studies.

Critical and Reflexive Methodological Dialogue

Critiques regarding the methodologies and methods used in tourism studies exist. Walle (1997), Riley and Love (2000), and Mehmetoglu (2004) previously identified a predilection of tourism studies towards quantitative methodologies (derived from positivism). Botterill (2001), Davies (2003), and Ryan (1997) proffer a similar viewpoint on positivist traditions, which may be constraining interpretive capabilities of tourism phenomena. Similar comments have been made with regard to hospitality studies (Lynch, 2005; O'Gorman, 2005; Taylor and Edgar, 1999; Wood, 1999). Jones stated that "UK hospitality research, both qualitatively and quantitatively, is at best static or even in decline" and that "groups of hospitality academics might" do well to publish their "research manifestos" in a way that "would articulate their philosophy of science" (2004: 42–43).

Shifts towards qualitative methodologies and research have been identified by Botterill et al. (2003), Dann and Phillips (2001), and Goodson and Phillimore (2004). Tourism studies literature has advanced a "critical turn" akin to Denzin and Lincoln's (2005a) "crisis of representation" moment and its associated research agendas. Tourism studies and research is demonstrating greater reflexivity and greater consideration of "gender, class and race," as well as searches for "new models" of research (see commentaries by Cooper, 2002; Tribe, 2005; and the edited work by Ateljevic et al., 2007). While a duality has been framed around quantitative/ qualitative methodologies of conducting research (see Jennings, 2001), Phillimore and Goodson's (2004) edited work represented a growing acceptance of qualitative research within tourism. The work also served as a marker that qualitative research had come of its time as a mainstream agenda due to its marketability for publishers. It is unfortunate that at the time the editors in their own writings did not engage with the Denzin and Lincoln (2000) *The Handbook of Qualitative Research* instead of relying on one of three (1998) volumes generated out of the first *Handbook* edition (1994). Had they done so, they would have been able to have advanced a qualitative agenda related to axiology, where social situatedness, reflexivity, audience, voice, reciprocity, and values are key elements of the (critical) interpretive researcher's tool kit.

Mixed Methods

In the late 1990s and early 2000s, qualitative and quantitative agendas have been challenged by the use of (methodological) "triangulation" in tourism research studies, particularly using mixed methods (generally quantitative followed by qualitative methods) in research projects/agendas. Mixed methods tend to be associated with pragmatism and critical realism (Tashakkori and Teddlie, 1998, 2003). Supporters of pragmatism within tourism studies include Pansiri (2005, 2006), while Botterill (2000, 2001) and Gale and Botterill (2005) provide discourses related to critical realism.

In practice, the mixing of methodologies is generally applied at different phases of research designs, particularly, before, after, and at times concurrently (for further information see Brannen, 1992; Creswell, 2003; Tashakkori and Teddlie, 1998, 2003). In reflecting on mixed methods, another debate

emerges with regard to the commensurability/incommensurability of paradigmatic framings—ontology, epistemology, methodology and axiology (see Jennings, 2004; Teddlie and Tashakkori, 2003). Tourism researchers who articulate issues related to the incommensurability of methods because of paradigmatic framing tend to draw on the works of Guba and Lincoln (1994, 2005), Lincoln and Guba (2000) as well as Denzin and Lincoln (1994, 2000, 2005). A number of researchers advocate for "triangulating" quantitative and qualitative research (Davies, 2003). Davies acknowledges that "the problem of complementarity may be less acute in the case of mixing methods but may present serious philosophical obstacles when mixing paradigms" (2003: 104).

Alternatives to Western-Centric Research Pedagogy and Praxis

Until the latter half of the twentieth century, considerations of indigenous and cultural approaches with regard to tourism research were strongly marginalized. Part of this was due to a mainstream absence of reflexivity with regard to readjusting privileging of western or developed world viewpoints and associated paradigmatic worldviews with regard to ontology, epistemology, methodology, and axiology (see commentary by Aitchison, 1999; Bishop, 2005; Dann et al., 1988; Jennings, 2003, 2007a, 2007b; Kobasic, 1996). In the main, tourism and hospitality research agendas have tended to be constructed using western epistemologies as lenses; these same have been used to "design" and (re)interpret tourism and hospitality phenomena and experiences to others outside western contexts (Jennings, 2003, 2007a, 2007b). Such western research practices have been strongly critiqued outside the tourism literature (Bourke, 1995; Foley, 2003; Ivanitz, 1999; Scheurich, 1997; Stanfield II, 1994) and portrayed as imperialist or colonialist (Bourdieu, 1990; Laclau, 1990; Smith 2005). Smith has explicitly argued for "decolonizing methodologies" and iterated a need for indigenous methodologies, since:

> Indigenous methodologies tend to approach cultural protocols, values and behaviours as an integral part of methodology. They are factors to be built in to research explicitly, to be thought about reflexively, to be declared openly as part of the research design, to be discussed as part of the final results of a study and to be disseminated back to the people in culturally appropriate ways and in a language that can be understood. (1999: 15)

With specific regard to tourism studies, the following critiques have emerged. Berno (1996) identified a silencing in tourism research, specifically, that tourism researchers have ignored tourism phenomena outside western understanding of social and cultural constructions. Echtner has emphasized that researchers need to be aware of the cultural boundedness of sign systems and that their meanings, which are derived from social conventions in one culture, need to be considered through "integrated multicultural studies" (1999: 55). Sofield (2000) has criticized the use of etic viewpoints when interpreting differing cultural realties. Earlier, Dann et al. (1988) had lamented that "[d]espite earlier calls by Cohen (1979b) for tourist research to be 'emic, processual, contextual and time based,' few researchers have managed to compare two tourist settings or to study difference in two tourism cultures." Berno (1996), Bricker and Kerstetter (2006), Hollinshead (1992), Lee (2001), Schaper et al., (2007), Urry (1996), and the edited work of Butler and Hinch (1996), also recognized and iterated that cultural differences need to be incorporated in research designs (see Gurung, 2008 for a recent discussion). Kuokkanen (2003) has similarly stated the need for hospitality to recognize indigenous epistemologies. Pearce voiced similar sentiments, saying that "[t]he promise of a special kind of contribution to theoretical tourism innovation in research from the Asia Pacific region [for example] lies in the cultural traditions of the researchers' own countries" (2004: 66).

Such commentaries resonate with earlier critiques by Urry (1990, 1996, 2002) that twentieth-century social research demonstrated a propensity for research to be framed using essentially etic approaches and omitted acknowledgement of space, time, societal, and cultural differences. More recently, Tribe also iterated the need for an appreciation of diversity "across time and place so that different cultural ensembles sustain different recipes for truth and knowledge" (2006: 361) and for this to infuse tourism research. The coming of time (and marketability) of alternate positions, to western and developed world paradigmatic views as mainstream agenda, has been recognized in various extant tourism studies literature. The recently published social sciences publication *Handbook of Critical and Indigenous Methodologies* (2008), edited by Denzin, Lincoln, and Smith, may provide a useful reference source for continued growth in indigenous research and indigenist perspectives.

Conclusion

In the past, positivism and postpositivism have been major paradigms of influence in tourism studies and by association have served to privilege quantitative research methodologies and methods. This privileging was orchestrated by the historical development of tourism studies from its roots in an advocacy perspective and planning traditions situated in boosterism and economic traditions. Over time, institutionalizing processes such as research training, professional associations, and publication outlets served to reify post/positivism's hegemony. In the latter quarter of the twentieth century, counter-discourses and debates, which had previously emerged in the 1980s from environmentally and socially situated framings, started to challenge the orthodoxy of tourism as solely a business-focused phenomena to be understood primarily from post/positivist agendas. Other paradigmatic views gained sway and included: critical realism, pragmatism, chaos and complexity theory, critical theory orientation, constructivism/interpretivism, postmodernism, and participatory paradigms. These framings brought with them contrary paradigmatic foci including qualitative and mixed methods methodologies.

At the turn of the twentieth century, in conjunction with the unstable and unexpected times and shifts in geopolitics that mark the start of the twenty-first century, recognition has grown that western ontologies and epistemologies are only one way of knowing and (re)interpreting the world. There are other world-views. Relatedly, tourism and hospitality researchers need to reexamine the continued replication and dominance of western-centric perspectives in theoretical, epistemological, methodological and axiological aspects of travel and tourism research. Such ethnocentric perspectives do not enable researchers to "understand" tourism phenomena from other views, standpoints and experiences. These "other" perspectives have different frames and are equally important. These frames include indigenous onotologies, epistemologies, methodologies and axiologies, which are manifold. More innovative and radical approaches are needed, as well as sharing and dialogue among varying ontological, epistemological, methodological, and axiological perspectives, in order to develop new and novel ways of understanding the phenomena which is tourism. For tourism and hospitality research to be more effective in the current and future world contexts, researchers need to:

- be familiar and competent in a range of theoretical research paradigms including those that use emic as well as etic perspectives;
- question "taken for granted" meanings and assumptions contained in western hegemonic research project design and implementation;
- develop research constructs based on indigenous, intra-, inter-, and cross-cultural, as well as nonwestern ontologies and epistemologies;
- support, incorporate, and use indigenous, intra-, inter-, and cross-cultural, as well as nonwestern methodologies;
- take into account indigenous, intra-, inter-, and cross-cultural, as well as nonwestern axiologies where this does not generate moral dilemmas for researchers;

- develop and use intra-, inter-, and cross-cultural communication skills;
- engage in longitudinal studies;
- engage in intracultural, intercultural, cross-cultural, cross-national research; as well as
- participate in research, which focuses on local, regional, national and international "boundaries." (Jennings, 2007b, developed from Jennings, 2003, 2006, 2007a)

Recommendations such as these will serve to advance tourism research agendas that are cognizant of the varying ways that the touristic worlds may be viewed paradigmatically through the specific consideration, incorporation and development of differing ontological, epistemological, methodological, and axiological viewpoints.

Notes

1 The Stanford Encyclopedia of Philosophy online provides excellent entries on ontology and epistemology. See, for instance, plato.stanford.edu/entries/epistemology. Accessed May 17, 2008.

2 For more on this branch of philosophy, see philosophy.lander.edu/intro/introbook2.1/x924.html. Accessed May 17, 2008.

3 Kuhn proffers that a paradigm is constituted of "accepted examples of actual scientific practice ... from which spring particular coherent traditions of scientific research" (1970, 10). The later 1997 edition of Kuhn's 1970 text differs by the inclusion of a newer index.

4 In this table, the decommodified research paradigm of Wearing et al. (2005) has been added, albeit that Butcher (2006) argues that the framing of an ecocentric over humanist positions is spurious.

5 Critical realism also appears in Table 38.1 as a paradigm.

References

Aitchison, C.C. (1999). "New Cultural Geographies: The Spatiality of Leisure, Gender and Sexuality." *Leisure Studies*, 18(1): 19–39.

Aitchison, C.C. (2005). "Feminist and Gender Perspectives in Leisure and Tourism Research." In B.W. Ritchie, P. Burns and C. Palmer (Eds.),

Tourism Research Methods: Integrating Theory with Practice (ch. 3). Oxfordshire: CABI Publishing.

Ateljevic, I., Morgan, N. and Pritchard, A. (Eds.) (2007). The Critical Turn in Tourism Studies: Innovative Research Methodologies. Amsterdam: Elsevier.

Ayikoru, M. and Tribe, J. (2007). "Enhancing the Interpretive and Critical Approaches to Tourism Education Enquiry Through Discursive Analysis." In I. Ateljevic, N. Morgan and A. Pritchard (Eds.), The Critical Turn in Tourism Studies: Innovative Research Methodologies (pp. 279–292). Amsterdam: Elsevier.

Bennet, J. (2004). Indigenous Entrepreneurship, Social Capital and Tourism Enterprise Development: Lessons from Cape York. Unpublished PhD Thesis. LaTrobe University, Australia.

Berger, P.L. and Luckman, T. (1981). The Social Construction of Reality. Harmondsworth: Penguin Books.

Berno, T. (1996). "Cross-Cultural Research Methods: Content or Context? A Cook Island Example." In R. Butler and T. Hinch (Eds.), Tourism and Indigenous Peoples (pp. 376–395). London: International Thomson Business Press.

Bhasker, R. (1978). A Realist Theory of Science (2nd edition). Brighton: Harvester.

Bhasker, R. (1982). "Emergence, Explanation and Emancipation." In P. Secord (Ed.), Explaining Social Behavior: Consciousness, Behavior and Social Structure (pp. 275–310). Beverley Hills: Sage Publications.

Bhasker, R. (1986). Scientific Realism and Human Emancipation. London: Verso.

Bhasker, R. (Ed.) (1990). Harré and his Critics. Oxford: Blackwell.

Bishop, R. (2005). Freeing Ourselves from Neocolonial Domination in Research: A Kaupapa Māori Approach to Creating Knowledge. In N.K. Denzin and Y.S. Lincoln (Eds.), Handbook of Qualitative Research (2nd edition.) (pp. 109–138). Thousand Oaks, CA: Sage Publications.

Botterill, D. (2000). "Chapter 10: Social Scientific Ways of Knowing Hospitality." In C. Lashley and A. Morrison (Eds.), Search of Hospitality: Theoretical Perspectives and Debates (pp. 177–196). Oxford: Butterworth-Heinemann.

Botterill, D. (2001). "The Epistemology of a Set of Tourism Studies." Leisure Studies, 20(3): 199–214.

Botterill, D., Gale, T. and Haven, C. (2002). "A Survey of Doctoral Theses Accepted by Universities in the UK and Ireland for Studies Related to Tourism 1990–1999." Tourist Studies, 2(3): 283–311.

Bourdieu, P. (1990). The Logic of Practice. Trans. R. Nice. Cambridge: Polity Press.

Bourke, E. (1995). "Dilemmas of Integrity and Knowledge: Protocol in Aboriginal Research." Paper presented at the Indigenous Research Ethics. Townsville, Australia, September.

Bramwell, B. and Lane, B. (2005). "From Niche to General Relevance? Sustainable Tourism, Research and the Role of Tourism Journals." Journal of Tourism Studies, 16(2): 52–62.

Bramwell, B. and Lane, B. (2006). "Editorial: Policy Relevance and Sustainable Tourism Research: Liberal, Radical and Post-Structuralist Perspectives." Journal of Sustainable Tourism, 14(1): 1–5.

Brannen, J. (Ed.) (1992). Mixing Methods: Qualitative and Quantitative Research. Averbury: Aldershot.

Bricker, K.S. and Kerstetter, D. (2006). "Saravanua ni naua: Exploring Sense of Place in the Rural Highlands of Fiji." In G.R. Jennings and N. Nickerson (Eds.), Quality Tourism Experiences (pp. 99–111). Burlington, MA: Elsevier.

Butcher, J. (2006). "A Response to Building a Decommodified Research Paradigm in Tourism: The Contribution of NGOs'. By Stephen Wearing, Matthew McDonald and Jess Ponting. Journal of Sustainable Tourism, 13(5) 2005: 424–455." Journal of Sustainable Tourism, 14(3): 307–310.

Butler, R. and Hinch, T. (Eds.) (1996). Tourism and Indigenous Peoples. London: International Thomson Business Press.

Byrne, D. (1998). Complexity Theory and the Social Sciences: An Introduction. London: Routledge.

Chambers, D. (2007). "Interrogating the 'Critical' in Critical Approaches to Tourism Research." In I. Ateljevic, N. Morgan and A. Pritchard (Eds.), The Critical Turn in Tourism Studies: Innovative Research Methodologies (pp. 105–119). Amsterdam: Elsevier.

Cohen, E. (1979). "Rethinking the Sociology of Tourism." Annals of Tourism Research, 6(1): 18–35.

Cohen, E. (1984). "The Sociology of Tourism: Approaches, Issues and Findings." Annual Review of Sociology, 10: 373–392.

Cohen, E. (1988). "Traditions in the Qualitative Sociology of Tourism." *Annals of Tourism Research*, 15(1): 29–46.

Cooper, C.P. (2002). "Tourism Research, Social Capital and Commercialisation Agendas." In E. Arola, J. Karkkainen and M. Siitari (Eds.), *Tourism Industry and Education Symposium 2*. Jyvaskyla, Finland, May 16–18, 2002.

Cooper, C. (2003). "Progress in Tourism Research." In C. Cooper (Ed.), *Classic Reviews in Tourism*. Aspects of Tourism Series, Number 3. Clevedon: Channel View Press.

Creswell, J.W. (2003). *Research Design: Qualitative, Quantitative, and Mixed Methods Approaches* (2nd edition.). Thousand Oaks, CA: Sage Publications.

Dann, G. (1997). "Paradigms in Tourism Research." Research Notes and Reports. *Annals of Tourism Research*, 24(2): 472–474.

Dann, G. and Phillps, J. (2001). "Qualitative Tourism Research in the Late Twentieth Century and Beyond." In B. Faulkner, G. Moscardo and E. Laws (Eds.), *Tourism in the Twenty-First Century: Reflections on Experience*. London: Continuum.

Dann, G., Nash, D. and Pearce, P. (1988). Methodology in Tourism Research. *Annals of Tourism Research*, 15(1): 1–28.

Darcy, S. (2006). *Setting a Research Agenda for Accessible Tourism*. Technical Report. Australia: CRC for Sustainable Tourism.

Davies, B. (2003). "The Role of Quantitative and Qualitative Research in Industrial Studies of Tourism." *International Journal of Tourism Research*, 5(2): 97–111.

Denzin, N.K. and Lincoln, Y.S. (1994). "Introduction: Entering the Field of Qualitative Research" In N.K. Denzin and Y.S. Lincoln, (Eds.), *Handbook of Qualitative Research* (1st edition.) (pp. 1–17). Thousand Oaks, CA: Sage Publications.

Denzin, N.K. and Lincoln, Y.S. (Eds.) (1998). *The Landscape of Qualitative Research: Theoretical Issues*. Thousand Oaks, CA: Sage Publications.

Denzin, N.K. and Lincoln, Y.S. (2000). "Introduction: The Discipline and Practice of Qualitative Research." In N.K. Denzin and Y.S. Lincoln, (Eds.), *Handbook of Qualitative Research* (2nd edition.) (pp. 1–28). Thousand Oaks, CA: Sage Publications.

Denzin, N.K. and Lincoln, Y.S. (2005a). "Introduction: The Discipline and Practice of Qualitative Research." In N.K. Denzin and Y.S. Lincoln, (Eds.), *The SAGE Handbook of Qualitative Research* (3rd edition.) (pp. 1–32). Thousand Oaks, CA: Sage Publications.

Denzin, N.K. and Lincoln, Y.S. (2005b). "Paradigms and Perspectives in Contention." In N.K. Denzin and Y.S. Lincoln (Eds.), *The SAGE Handbook of Qualitative Research* (3rd edition.) (pp. 183–190). Thousand Oaks, CA: Sage Publications.

Denzin, N.K., Lincoln, Y.S. and Smith, L.T. (Eds.) (2008). *Handbook of Critical and Indigenous Methodologies*. Thousand Oaks, CA: Sage Publications.

Downward, P. (2005). "Critical (Realist). Reflection on Policy and Management Research in Sport, Tourism and Sports Tourism." *European Sport Management Quarterly*, 5(3): 303–320.

Downward, P. and Mearman, A. (2004). "On Tourism and Hospitality Management Research: A Critical Realist Proposal." *Tourism and Hospitality Planning and Development*, 1(2): 107–122.

Duijnhoven, H. and Roessingh, C. (2006). "The Tourist with a Hidden Agenda? Shifting Roles in the Field of Tourism Research." *International Journal of Tourism Research*, 8(2): 115–126.

Echtner, C. and Jamal, T. (1997). "The Disciplinary Dilemma of Tourism Studies." *Annals of Tourism Research*, 24(4): 868–883.

Echtner, C.M. (1999). "The Semiotic Paradigm: Implications for Tourism Research." *Tourism Management*, 20(1): 47–57.

Faulkner, B. and R. Russell (2003). "Chaos and Complexity in Tourism: In Search of a New Perspective." In L. Fredline, L. Jago and C. Cooper (Eds.), *Progressing Tourism Research—Bill Faulkner* (pp. 205–219). Clevedon: Channel View.

Foley, D. (2003). "Indigenous Epistemology and Indigenous Standpoint Theory." *Social Alternatives*, 22(1): 44–52.

Foley, D. (2005). "A Search for a More Complex Truth in Academia: Indigenous Standpoint." Abstract of Paper presented at the *Third International Conference on New Directions in Humanities, Humanities Conference 2005*. University of Cambridge, UK, August 2–5. Retrieved March 4, 2005 from h05.cgpublisher.com/proposals/333/index_html.

Fox, K. (2007). "Critical Theory and Katrina." *City*, 11(1): 81–99.

Gale, T. and Beeftink, K. (2005). "Exploring the Differences between Positivistic and Post-Positivistic Philosophy: An Interpretivistic

Case Study of Tourist Expectations and Satisfaction." *2005 Northeastern Recreation Research Symposium*. Bolten Landing, NY: US Forest Service, Northeastern Research Station.

Gale, T. and Botterill, D. (2005). "A Realist Agenda for Tourist Studies, or Why Destination Areas Really Rise and Fall in Popularity." *Tourist Studies*, 5(2): 151–174.

Geertz, C. (1983). *Local Knowledge: Further Essays in Interpretive Anthropology*. London: Fontana.

Geertz, C. (1988). *Works and Lives: The Anthropologist as Author*. Cambridge: Polity.

Getz, D. (1986). "Models of Tourism Planning Towards Integration of Theory and Practice." *Tourism Management*, 7(1): 21–32.

Getz, D. (1987). "Tourism Planning and Research: Traditions, Models and Futures." Paper presented at *The Australian Travel Research Workshop*. Bunbury, Western Australia, November 5–6.

Gleick, J. (1987). *Chaos: Making a New Science*. New York: Penguin.

Goeldner, C.R. (2005). "Reflections on the Historic Role of Journals in Shaping Tourism Knowledge." *Journal of Tourism Studies*, 16(2): 44–51.

Goodson, L. and Phillimore, J. (2004). "The Inquiry Paradigm in Qualitative Tourism Research. In Goodson, L. and J. Phillimore (Eds.), *Qualitative Research in Tourism: Ontologies, Epistemologies and Method-ologies* (pp. 30–45). London: Routledge.

Gramsci, A. (1971). *Selections from the Prison Notebooks of Antonio Gramsci*. Ed. and transcribed Q. Hoare and G. Nowell Smith. London: Lawrence and Wishart.

Guba, E. (1990). "The Alternative Paradigm Dialog." In E. Guba (Ed.), *The Paradigm Dialog* (pp. 17–27). Newbury Park: Sage Publications.

Guba, E.G. and Lincoln, Y.S. (1994). "Competing Paradigms in Qualitative Research." In N.K. Denzin and Y.S. Lincoln (Eds.), *Handbook of Qualitative Research*. Thousand Oaks, CA: Sage Publications.

Guba, E.G. and Lincoln, Y.S. (2005). "Paradigmatic Controversies, Contradictions, and Emerging Confluences." In N.K. Denzin and Y.S. Lincoln (Eds.), *The SAGE Handbook of Qualitative Research* (3rd edition.)

(pp. 191–216). Thousand Oaks, CA: Sage Publications.

Gubrium, J.F. and Holstein, J.A.. (2003). "Post-modern Sensibilities." In J.F. Gubrium and J.A. Holstein (Eds.), *Postmodern Interviewing* (pp. 3–18). Thousand Oaks, CA: Sage Publications.

Gurney, P.M. and Humphreys, M. (2006). "Consuming Responsibility: The Search for Value at Laskarina Holidays." *Journal of Business Ethics*, 64: 83–100.

Gurung, H.B. (2008). "Fusioning." PhD thesis, Griffith University.

Hall, C.M. (1998). *Introduction to Tourism: Development, Dimensions and Issues* (3rd edition.). South Melbourne: Longman.

Hall, C.M. (1995). *Introduction to Tourism in Australia: Impacts, Planning and Development* (2nd edition.). South Melbourne: Longman.

Hall, C.M. (2004). "Reflexivity and Tourism Research: Situating Myself and/with Others." In J. Phillimore and L. Goodson (Eds.), *Qualitative Research in Tourism: Ontologies, Epistemologies and Methodologies* (pp. 137–155). London: Routledge.

Harré, R. (1981). "The Positive-Empiricist Approach and its Alternative." In P. Reason and J. Rowan, (Eds.), *Human Inquiry: A Sourcebook of New Paradigm Research* (pp. 3–17) Chichester: Wiley.

Harré, R. (1986). *Varieties of Realism: A Rationale for the Natural Sciences*. Oxford: Blackwell.

Heimtun, B. (2007). "From Principles to Practices in Feminist Tourism Research: A Call for Greater Use of the Survey Method and the Solicited Diary." In I. Ateljevic, N. Morgan and A. Pritchard (Eds.), *The Critical Turn in Tourism Studies: Innovative Research Methodologies* (pp. 245–259). Amsterdam: Elsevier.

Hill, L. Jr. and Eckberg, D.L. (1981). "Clarifying Confusions about Paradigms: A Reply to Ritzer." *American Sociological Review*, 46(2): 248–252.

Hollinshead, K. (1992). "'White' Gaze, 'Red' People-Shadow Visions: The Disidentification of 'Indians' in Cultural Tourism." *Leisure Studies*, 11(1): 43–64.

Hollinshead, K. (1994). "The Truth about Texas: A Naturalistic Study of the Construction of Heritage." Paper presented to the conference *Tourism: The State of the Art*. University of Strathclyde, Scotland, July 10–14, 1994.

Hollinshead, K. (1996). "The Tourism Researcher as Bricoleur: The New Wealth and Diversity in Qualitative Inquiry." *Tourism Analysis*, 1: 67–74.

Hollinshead, K. (2004). "A Primer in Ontological Craft." In J. Phillimore and L. Goodson (Eds.), *Qualitative Research in Tourism: Ontologies, Epistemologies and Methodologies* (pp. 63–82). London: Routledge.

Hunter, C. (1997). "Sustainable Tourism as an Adaptive Paradigm." *Annals of Tourism Research*, 24(4): 850–867.

Ivanitz, M. (1999). "Culture, Ethics, and Participatory Methodology in Cross-Cultural Research." *Australian Aboriginal Studies*, 2: 46–58.

Jafari, J. (1990). "Research and Scholarship. The Basis of Tourism Education." *Journal of Tourism Studies*, 1(1): 33–41.

Jafari, J. (2001). "The Scientification of Tourism." In V. Smith and M. Brent (Eds.) *Hosts and Guests Revisited: Tourism Issues of the 21st Century* (pp. 28–41). Elmsford: Cognizant Communications.

Jamal, T. and Everett, J. (2004). "Resisting Rationalisation in the Natural and Academic Life-World: Critical Tourism Research or Hermeneutic Charity?" *Current Issues in Tourism*, 7(1): 1–19.

Jamal, T. and Hollinshead, K. (2001). "Tourism and the Forbidden Zone: The Underserved Power of Qualitative Inquiry." *Tourism Management*, 22(1): 63–82.

Jamal, T. and Lee, J.-H. (2003). "Integrating Micro-Macro Approaches to Tourist Motivations: Toward an Interdisciplinary Theory." *Tourism Analysis*, 8(1): 47–59.

Jamal, T., Smith, B. and Watson, E. (2008). "Rankings, Ratings and Relevance of Tourism Journals: Interdisciplinary Challenges and Insights." *Tourism Management*, 29(1): 66–78.

Jennings, G.R. (1999). *Voyages from the Centre to the Margins: An Ethnography of Long Term Ocean Cruisers*. Unpublished PhD thesis. Murdoch, Australia: Murdoch University.

Jennings, G.R. (2001). *Tourism Research*. Brisbane: John Wiley & Sons.

Jennings, G.R. (2003). "Tourism Research: Theoretical Paradigms and Accountability." *Targeted Research: The Gateway to Accountability: TTRA 34th Annual Conference Proceedings* [CD Rom]. St Louis, MO, June 15–18.

Jennings, G.R. (2004). "Business Research, Examples of Theoretical Paradigms that Inform." *Encyclopedia of Social Measurement* (pp. 211–217). San Diego, CA: Academic Press.

Jennings, G.R. (2005). "Interviewing—A Focus on Qualitative Techniques." In B.W. Ritchie, P. Burns, and C. Palmer (Eds.), *Tourism Research Methods: Integrating Theory and Practice* (pp. 99–117). London: CAB International Tourism/Leisure Series.

Jennings, G.R. (2006). "Quality Tourism Experiences—An Introduction." In G.R. Jennings and N. Nickerson (Eds.), *Quality Tourism Experiences* (pp.1–21). Burlington, MA: Elsevier.

Jennings, G.R. (2007a). "Advances in Tourism Research: Theoretical Paradigms and Accountability." In A. Matias, P. Nijkamp and P. Neto (Eds.), *Advances in Modern Tourism Research, Economic Perspectives* (pp. 9–35). Heidelberg: Springer, Physica-Verlag.

Jennings, G.R. (2007b). "Tourism Perspectives Towards 'Regional Development and Asia's Values'." Paper presented at *Dong-Eui University*. Busan, South Korea, October 22–23.

Johnson, R.B. and Onwuegbuzie, A.J. (2004). "Mixed Methods Research: A Research Paradigm Whose Time Has Come." *Educational Researcher*, 33(7): 14–26.

Jones, P. (2004). "Finding the Hospitality Industry? Or Finding Hospitality Schools of Thought." *Journal of Hospitality, Leisure, Sport and Tourism Education*, 3(1): 33–45.

Kensbock, S. (2007). "A Grounded Theory of Tourism Entrepreneurs' Understanding of Sustainable Tourism." BA (Hons) dissertation, Griffith University, Australia.

Kincheloe, J.L. and McLaren, P. (2005). "Rethinking Critical Theory and Qualitative Research." In N.K. Denzin and Y.S. Lincoln (Eds.), *The SAGE Handbook of Qualitative Research* (3rd edition.) (pp. 303–342). Thousand Oaks, CA: Sage Publications.

Kobasic, A. (1996). "Level and Dissemination of Academic Findings about Tourism." *Turizam*, 44(7–8): 169–181.

Kuhn, T.S. (1962). *The Structure of Scientific Revolutions* (1st edition.). Chicago, IL: University of Chicago Press.

Kuhn, T.S. (1970). *The Structure of Scientific Revolutions* (2nd edition.). Chicago, IL: University of Chicago Press.

Kuhn, T.S. (1996). *The Structure of Scientific Revolutions* (3rd edition.). Chicago, IL: University of Chicago Press.

Kuokkanen, R. (2003). "Toward a New Relation of Hospitality in the Academy." *American Indian Quarterly*, 27(1&2): 267–295.

Laclau, E. (1990). *New Reflections on the Revolution of Our Time*. London: Verso.

Lee, Y.S. (2001). "Tourist Gaze: Universal Concept?" *Tourism, Culture and Communication*, 3(2), 93–99.

Lewin, K. (1948). "Action Research and Minority Problems." In K. Lewin (Ed.), *Resolving Social Conflicts*. New York: Harper and Row.

Lincoln, Y.S. and Guba, E.G. (2000). "Paradigmatic Controversies, Contradictions, and Emerging Confluences." In N.K. Denzin and Y.S. Lincoln (Eds.), *Handbook of Qualitative Research* (2nd edition.) (pp. 163–188). Thousand Oaks, CA: Sage Publications.

Lynch, P.A. (2005). "Sociological Impressionism in a Hospitality Context." *Annals of Tourism Research*, 32(3): 527–548.

Lyotard, J.–F. (1999). "The Postmodern Condition: A Report on Knowledge." Trans. G. Bennington and B. Massumi. Foreword F. Jameson. *Theory and History of Literature, 10*. Minneapolis: University of Minnesota Press.

Macbeth, J. (2005). "Towards an Ethics Platform for Tourism." *Annals of Tourism Research*, 32(4): 962–984.

Masterman, M. (1970). "The Nature of a Paradigm." In I. Lakatos and A. Musgrave (Eds.), *Criticism and the Growth of Knowledge* (pp. 59–89). Cambridge: Cambridge University.

McKercher, B. (1999). "A Chaos Approach to Tourism." *Tourism Management*, 20(4): 425–434.

McKercher, B. (2002). "Privileges and Responsibilities of Being a Referee." *Annals of Tourism Research*, 29(30): 856–859.

Mehmetoglu, M. (2004). "Quantitative or Qualitative? A Content Analysis of Nordic Research in Tourism and Hospitality." *Scandinavian Journal of Hospitality and Tourism*, 4(3): 176–190.

Miles, M.B. (1979). "Qualitative Data as an Attractive Nuisance: The Problem of Analysis." *Administrative Science Quarterly*, 24: 590–601.

Morgan D.L. (2007). "Paradigms Lost and Pragmatism Regained." *Journal of Mixed Methods Research*, 1(1): 48–76.

O'Gorman, K.D. (2005). "Modern Hospitality: Lessons from the Past." *Journal of Hospitality and Tourism Management*, 12(2): 141–151.

Pansiri, J. (2005). "Pragmatism: A Methodological Approach to Researching Strategic Alliances in Tourism." *Tourism and Hospitality Planning and Development*, 2(3): 191–206.

Pansiri, J. (2006). "Doing Tourism Research Using the Pragmatism Paradigm: An Empirical Example." *Tourism Hospitality Planning and Development*, 3(3): 223–240.

Pearce, P.L. (2004). "Theoretical Innovation in Asia Pacific Tourism Research." *Asia Pacific Journal of Tourism Research*, 9(1): 58–70.

Phillimore, J. and Goodson, L. (2004). "Progress in Qualitative Research in Tourism: Epistemology, Ontology and Methodology." In J. Phillimore and L. Goodson (Eds.), *Qualitative Research in Tourism: Ontologies, Epistemologies and Methodologies* (pp. 3–29). London: Routledge.

Pitman, T. (2004). "Postmodernity, Post-Tourism and Postmodern Irony: Juan Villoro's *Palmeras de la brisa rapida*, and the Possibility of a Postmodern Travel-Chronicle." *Bulletin of Spanish Studies*, LXXI(1): 77–97.

Powell, T.C. (2001). "Competitive Advantage: Logical and Philosophical Considerations." *Strategic Management Journal*, 22(9): 875–888.

Reid, L. and Andereck, K. (1989). "Statistical Analyses Use in Tourism Research." *Journal of Travel Research*, 28(2): 21–24.

Rigney, L.-I. (2001). "A First Perspective of Indigenous Australian Participation in Science: Framing Indigenous Research towards Indigenous Australian Intellectual Sovereignty." *Kaurna Higher Education Journal*, 7: 1–13.

Riley, R.W. and Love, L.L. (2000). "The State of Qualitative Tourism Research." *Annals of Tourism Research*, 27(1): 164–187.

Ritchie, B.W., Burns, P. and Palmer, C. (2005). *Tourism Research Methods: Integrating Theory with Practice*. Wallingford: CABI.

Ritzer, G. (1981). "Paradigm Analysis in Sociology: Clarifying the Issues." *American Sociological Review*, 46(2): 245–248.

Rojek, C. and Urry, J. (1997). *Touring Cultures: Transformations of Travel and Theory.* London: Routledge.

Russell, R. (2006). "Chaos Theory and Its Application to the TALC Model." In R.W. Butler (Ed.), *The Tourism Area Life Cycle 2: Conceptual and Theoretical Issues* (Chapter 10). Clevedon: Channel View Publications.

Russell, R. and Faulkner, B. (2003). "Movers and Shakers: Chaos Makers in Tourism Development." In L. Fredline, L. Jago and C. Cooper (Eds.), *Progressing Tourism Research—Bill Faulkner* (pp. 220–243).Clevedon Channel View

Ryan, C. (1997). "Tourism: A Mature Discipline?" *Pacific Tourism Review*, 1(1): 3–5.

Ryan, C. (2005). "Authors and Editors—Getting Published: Context and Policy—An Editor's View." *The Journal of Tourism Studies*, 16(2): 6–13.

Sarantakos, S. (1998). *Social Research* (2nd edition.). South Melbourne: Macmillan Education.

Schaper, M. Carlsen, J. and Jennings, G.R. (2007). "Reflections on Researching Indigenous Enterprises." In J. Buutljens (Ed.), *Striving for Sustainability: Case Studies in Indigenous Tourism* (pp. 37–66). Lismore: Southern Cross University Press.

Scheurich, J.J. (1997). *Research Methods in the Postmodern.* London: Falmer Press.

Schwandt, T.A. (2000). "Three Epistemological Stances for Qualitative Inquiry: Interpretivism, Hermeneutics, and Social Constructionism." In N.K. Denzin and Y.S. Lincoln, (Eds.), *Handbook of Qualitative Research* (2nd edition) (pp. 189–213). Thousand Oaks, CA: Sage Publications.

Seaton, A.V. (1996). "Blowing the Whistle on Tourism Referees." *Tourism Management*, 17(6): 397–399.

Seaton, A.V. (1997). "Unobtrusive Observational Measures as a Quality Extension of Visitor Surveys at Festivals and Events: Mass Observation Revisited." *Journal of Travel Research*, 35(4): 25–30.

Sharpley, R. (2000). "Tourism and Sustainable Development: Exploring the Theoretical Divide." *Journal of Sustainable Tourism* 8(1): 1–19.

Small, J., Cadman, K., Friend, L., Gannon, S., Ingleton, C., Kutroulis, G., McCormack, C., Mitchell, P., Onyx, J., O'Regan, K. and Rocco, S. (2007). "Unresolved Power for Feminist Researchers Employing Memory-Work." In I. Ateljevic, N. Morgan and A. Pritchard (Eds.), *The Critical Turn in Tourism Studies: Innovative Research Methodologies* (pp. 261–278). Amsterdam: Elsevier.

Smith, L.T. (2005). "On Tricky Ground: Researching the Native in the Age of Uncertainty." In N.K. Denzin and Y.S. Lincoln (Eds.), *The SAGE Handbook of Qualitative Research* (3rd edition.) (pp. 85–107). Thousand Oaks, CA: Sage Publications.

Smith, L.T. (1999). *Decolonizing Methodologies— Research and Indigenous Peoples.* London: Zed Books.

Sofield, T.H.B. (2000). "Re-Thinking and Re-Conceptualising Social and Cultural Issues of Tourism Development in South and East Asia." Institute for Sustainability and Technology Policy, Case Study. Murdoch University, Australia. Retrieved May 29, 2008 from www. ecotonline.org/Pages/downloads/ Re-thinking%20and%20re-conceptualising%20social%20and%20cultural%20 issues%20of%20toutism%20develoopment%20in%20South%20and%20 South%20East%20Asia..pdf.

Stanfield II, J.H. (1994). "Ethnic Modelling in Qualitative Research." In N.K. Denzin and Y.S. Lincoln (Eds.), *Handbook of Qualitative Research* (1st edition.) (pp. 175–188). Newbury Park, CA: Sage Publications.

Tashakkori, A. and Teddlie, C. (1998). "Mixed Methodology: Combining Qualitative and Quantitative Approaches." *Applied Social Science Research Methods Series* (Volume 46). Thousand Oaks, CA: Sage Publications.

Tashakkori, A. and Teddlie, C. (2003). *Handbook of Mixed Methods in Social and Behavioral Research.* Thousand Oaks, CA: Sage Publications.

Taylor, S. and Edgar, D. (1999). "Lacuna or Lost Cause? Some Reflections on Hospitality Management Research." In B. Brotherton (Ed.), *The Handbook of Contemporary Hospitality Management Research* (pp. 19–38). Chichester: Wiley.

Teddlie, C. and Tashakkori, A. (2003). "Major Issues and Controversies in the Use of Mixed Methods in the Social Sciences." In A. Tashakkori and C. Teddlie (Eds.), *Handbook of Mixed Methods in Social and Behavioral Research.* Thousand Oaks, CA: Sage Publications.

Tribe, J. (1997). "The Indiscipline of Tourism." *Annals of Tourism Research*, 24(3): 638–657.

Tribe, J. (2001). "Research Paradigms and the Tourism Curriculum." *Journal of Travel Research*, 39(4): 442–448.

Tribe, J. (2004). "Knowing about Tourism: Epistemological Issues." In J. Phillimore and L. Goodson (Eds.), *Qualitative Research in Tourism: Ontologies, Epistemologies and Methodologies* (pp. 46–62). London: Routledge.

Tribe, J. (2005). "New Tourism Research." *Tourism Recreation Research*, 30(2): 5–8.

Tribe, J. (2006). "The Truth about Tourism." *Annals of Tourism Research*, 33(2): 360–381.

Tribe, J. (2007). "Critical Tourism: Rules and Resistance." In I. Ateljevic, N. Morgan and A. Pritchard (Eds.), *The Critical Turn in Tourism Studies: Innovative Research Methodologies* (pp. 29–39). Elsevier: Advances in Tourism Research.

Urry, J. (1990). *The Tourist Gaze, Leisure and Travel in Contemporary Societies*. London: Sage Publications.

Urry, J. (1996). Sociology of Time and Space. In B.S. Turner (Ed.), *The Blackwell Companion to Social Theory* (pp. 369–395). Oxford: Blackwell.

Urry, J. (2002). *The Tourist Gaze* (2nd edition.). London: Sage Publications.

Uysal, M. (2004). "Advancement in Computing: Implications for Tourism and Hospitality." *Scandinavian Journal of Hospitality and Tourism*, 4(3): 208–224.

Walle, A.H. (1997). Quantitative Versus Qualitative Tourism Research. *Annals of Tourism*, 24(3): 524–536.

Wearing, S., McDonald, M. and Ponting, J. (2005). "Building a Decommodified Research Paradigm in Tourism: The Contribution of NGOs." *Journal of Sustainable Tourism*, 13(5): 424–439.

Weaver, D. and M. Oppermann. (2000). *Tourism Management* (1st edition). Brisbane: John Wiley & Sons.

Weed, M. (2005). "Sports Tourism, Theory and Method—Concepts, Issues and Epistemologies." *European Sport Management Quarterly*, 5(3): 229–242.

Westwood, S. (2007). "What Lies Beneath? Using Creative, Projective and Participatory Techniques in Qualitative Tourism Inquiry." In I. Ateljevic, N. Morgan and A. Pritchard (Eds.), *The Critical Turn in Tourism Studies: Innovative Research Methodologies* (pp. 293–316). Amsterdam: Elsevier.

Wood, R. (1999). "Traditional and Alternative Research Philosophies." In B. Brotherton (Ed.), *The Handbook of Contemporary Hospitality Management Research* (pp. 3–18). Chichester: John Wiley & Sons.

Xiao, H. and Smith, S.L.J. (2006). "The Making of Tourism Research: Insights from a Social Sciences Journal." *Annals of Tourism Research*, 33(2): 490–507.

Yolles, M. (1998). "A Cybernetic Exploration of Methodological Complementarism." *Kybernetes*, 27(5): 527–542.

Conclusions: Tourism Studies—Past Omissions, Emergent Challenges

Mike Robinson and Tazim Jamal

From Order to Chaos?

The end of a substantive volume such as this inevitably invites reflection and a certain degree of reflexivity. The achievement of amassing such a range of contributions, valuable as they are, leave no room for complacency. So, while recognizing and drawing from the value and diversity of our authors, in this final chapter we reflect upon the expansive issues that are still to be addressed in tourism studies and some of the challenges that will be faced by all engaged in tackling them.

Picking up on the themes of the introductory chapter, the purpose of studying tourism is primarily to gain a deeper understanding of a highly complex phenomenon which increasingly touches the lives and environments of millions. Studying tourism, and the hopefully worthwhile contribution of this *Handbook*, is an attempt to provide some order and structure to the understandings of the complexities of modern tourism. One of the great paradoxes of tourism is the apparent disjuncture between the simple pleasures and enjoyment experienced by the tourist, and the complex web of structures, arrangements, relationships and histories which are brought together to produce these intensive moments of experience. Of course, what are cited as "simple" moments of individual enjoyment belie further complexities stretching well into the realms of psychoanalysis.

Complexity (from the Latin, *complexus*), means something which is "entwined," which implies two or more components which are joined or connected in such a way that it becomes difficult to separate them. It is easy to see that even the most basic and straightforward articulation of tourism as a process or simple system involves the core components of travel, accommodation, services, facilities, attractions, sites, and structures of the destination. In addition to related economic systems are the ecological, social, and political systems that are intricately interwoven into the above. Thus exists a duality between elements that are in themselves distinct entities and yet, at the same time are connected. As more elements are identified then more connections can also be identified. The notion of distinction implies diversity and variety so that within complexity each element is different and does different things. The notion of connection however, points to constraints, relations, and varying degrees of dependence and interdependence, in that knowing of one element provides insight into the workings of others.

Some early interpretations of tourism reflected this latter approach, tending to *model* tourism as a connected system that, while useful in ordering the emergence of a range of different elements, was often remote from the peoples who actually practiced and experienced tourism. Similarly, significant works in anthropology and sociology very much focused upon the tourist—ever the most complex of figures—often neglecting the elements, structures and other systems that comprise the "tourism system." The tourist while very much connected to a larger "system," is, in a sense, seen as hyper-distinct, difficult to predict and capable of disrupting order. These two strands of analysis have largely been maintained over the past 30 years and have run parallel to one another. This parallel progression is discernible in the previous chapters, with overlapping moments as shown in discussions of performative spaces and situated, embodied encounters.

The multilayered complexity of tourism is exacerbated by the sheer rates of changes that have, and are taking place. The scholars we have featured in this *Handbook*, will have already moved their research and their critical thinking onto new pastures and already there are many more books, papers, and reports in the world, all directed to tourism, or connected with tourism in various ways. As tourism continues to develop its complexity as a social practice and as part of the international structures of business and policy, it is increasingly important that we understand the fullest extent of the processes and possibilities at all of its stages and scales. At some point the complexities of tourism can seem to morph in a chaotic mass, and yet this promises much for those communities committed to the study of tourism in that it

opens up a myriad and seemingly endless range of opportunities for research.

The complexities of tourism spill over into the *doing* of research, raising a number of challenges. These fall in two broad but related categories. The first relates to the work still needing to be conducted in the field of tourism studies. The second and perhaps the more problematic set of ongoing challenges cuts deep into wider debates on epistemologies, pedagogic practices, and the structures of learning; it relates to the *doing* of tourism studies and to the ways in which we can construct, interpret and disseminate our understandings of tourism.

Mind the Gaps

In the process of assembling a reference volume such as this *Handbook of Tourism Studies*, while attention is necessarily focused on what is included, there is also an ever-present reflection regarding what is not being included. The contributors to this volume have between them covered a substantive part of the tourism studies horizon, but it appears effectively to be an endless horizon. The authors of this handbook are all too well aware of this and the limitations that each has had to work with, in his or her contribution, have impacted upon the volume as a whole. Omissions can be explained through the practicalities of assemblage, while priorities have been shaped by what we have deemed to be core areas of concern. Of greater importance are the genuine knowledge gaps that are still to be filled by tourism researchers. What we present here are our thoughts on these gaps in the hope that they will stimulate interest and action among the research community.

The so-called "cultural turn" within tourism studies has been welcome and continues to provide a fertile and critical zone for research. The cultural practice and performance of tourism, together with its analytical overlays relating to gender, the body, race, ethnicity, and class, and informed by poststructuralist perspectives and critical theory, are now well championed in the academy. Much has already been achieved in this vein with regard to leisure studies (Rojek et al., 2007), though there still appears to be a surprising lack of communication between the two fields.

Within the encompass of the cultural turn, an important area which would benefit from deeper interrogation is that of communication. Here, existing complexity and the rapid rates of change have created somewhat of a vacuum in tourism studies. While there is much in the way of studies with regard to *representation* and *production*, as well as the more operational aspects of marketing, there are still questions to be addressed with regard to the circulation of knowledges which not only inform decision making, but which play out through all parts of tourist experience. The impacts of the rapidly changing terrain of tourism, technology and travel have been discussed in the *Handbook*. Weblogs and websites have rapidly become standard ways of communicating with and between tourists, while also acting as a (re)depository for tourist-generated experiences and stories. As noted, the mobile phone and digital camera technologies continue to revolutionize the ways in which the tourist engages with the world, how risks are differentiated, and how tourists and hosts interact. This broad topic would benefit from genuine linkages between scholars who understand the technologies, the politics of cross-cultural communications and who can undertake ethnographies of technology use, as tourists continue to be plugged into wider communicative networks.

A challenge to tourism researchers who would engage with the cultural is also to direct attention and rigor of method and theoretical application to the structures and management of international tourism. Arguably, this is one of the most significant gaps in our collective understanding of tourism. International hotel and resort development, airline routes and global alignments and transnational tour operators are the essential hardware for global tourism and are frequently, if anecdotally, implicated in the more critically applied literature on tourism's environmental and social impacts. And yet, little is actually known about them in terms of how and why they work in the way they do. Who are these corporate players and how do they interface with governments, regulators, one another? Additionally, what are the roles of multilateral institutions and international nonprofit organizations in global governance (Duffield, 2001; O'Brien, 2000)? Rather traditional political economies of international tourism have made important contributions in drawing attention to their role, but still we have scant understanding of them. Reasons for this vary but do include not being able to get good access to data (which is sometimes protected for commercial reasons). Those who do undertake research on this topic tend to be already engaged with management studies or economics, but there appears to be unwillingness on the part of some academics to recognize the realities of international finance and trade as having anything to do with tourism or tourists. What may be very productive, if not always easy, is if more anthropologists, sociologists, cultural theorists and the like could turn their attention on these organizations (in both public and private sectors) and the people who own, manage and negotiate for them.

The eclipse of the "journey" and the "experience" of traveling, as proffered by the likes of Boorstin (1987) and Fussell (1980), have been largely dismissed as nostalgic reminiscences broadly in line with a position of "anti-tourism," or, more precisely, against a particular stereotype of the non-discerning and strictly hedonistic tourist. There remains a persistent tourist-traveler tension in contemporary tourism studies which surfaces from time to time, but the argument still holds sway that the processes and experiences of traveling and touring have been considerably downplayed. While they have certainly been compressed, the processes of travel and tourist movements have never evaporated, merely changed, and yet they have not been particularly well addressed in the study of tourism, which has long been dominated by a destination-centric approach. Environmental externalities such as increasing concern for carbon emissions, rising global oil prices, the introduction (and potential demise) of low cost airlines, threats of terrorism, and the growth of "backpacking" and "volunteer tourism," all continue to impact upon not only the type, duration and destination of the journey, but also on the experience the tourist has on that journey. Understanding this experience in the light of the changing contexts of travel and transportation, global economies of movement, and how tourists make sense of a world in motion is something that requires further research. Again, it implies a dual approach linking understandings of structural changes to those of individual tourist reactions to, and experiences of, them, and of understanding tourism in the context of other reasons for mobility such as migration.

In part, the above suggestions seek to draw together the two dominant parallel tracks of tourism studies in order that each may benefit from the other's capacities and approaches. This is happening in other fields where anthropologists have fruitfully engaged with organizations, and likewise researchers in management have adopted a variety of critical cultural approaches to the study of various business activities and hospitality practices. The fact that this has not happened so widely in tourism may relate to issues of rapid change and corporate sensitivities, and arguably a lack of sustained research interest in the sector.

Time Frames, Space Frames, Conceptual Frames

Tourism as essentially a project of the modern world has been captured as such with the emphases very much upon understanding tourism within the here and now. The study of tourism is essentially a fixed affair; its fixidity relating to both time and space. Many case studies focusing on the impacts of tourism, for instance, involve the setting of parameters—geographical, historical, sociocultural, etc. At one level, for the researcher, this is driven by pure necessity in terms of the pragmatics of time and resources, and also disciplinary capacities. At another level, the notion of discrete research boundaries fails to capture the dynamic(s) of tourism. This is something more substantive than the elaboration of trends and the extrapolation of data and scenarios, and refers to the ways in which tourism—in the ways that it is organized, structured and practiced—*moves* through societies in the context of wider systems of being. A number of *Handbook* chapters offer insights into this phenomenon.

Historians have a lot of offer the field of tourism studies. Walton (2005), while noting the differences in the research style and communication used, makes a powerful case for the role of the historian in assisting in understanding the processes and dynamics of tourism. However, historians clearly work within boundaries, temporal and spatial. An ethos of working within discrete periods still dominates and this is reflected in the chronological banding of histories of tourism. Within this, certain periods have attracted more attention than others. Notably, histories of tourism of the recent modern period remain relatively rare, as compared with say works that examine the "Grand Tour" of the eighteenth century. Arguably, as tourism has developed so swiftly in the past 30 years or so, it may well be that historians have not caught up with the *rate* of change, or maybe the great developments of mass charter tourism of the 1960s and 1970s take the historian too close to the present? These are rhetorical questions and are intended to stimulate further reflection.

Histories of tourism are also mainly culturally distinctive, reflecting the specific circumstances from which tourism has emerged. Understandings of British tourism histories have been supplied by the likes of Berghoff et al. (2002), Inglis (2000), Ousby (1990), and Towner (1996). Histories of tourism in the United States have been provided by Rothman (1998), Sears (1998) and Rugh (2008); Australia (White, 2005), and Germany (Koshar, 2000). More generic histories such a Lofgren (1999) are still very much predicated on looking at tourism within the context of the developed (and largely Anglophone) "West." In the ferment of globalization, with its notions of flows and, in dealing with tourism, which has long been part of the mechanics of globalization, it is indeed ironic that studies are still tied to the idea of nation states. So here too there are spatial boundaries interplaying with temporal and cultural ones. While such boundaries are understandable, and perhaps necessary, they nevertheless appear to prevent us from a deeper understanding of the flows and dynamics of tourism which, as well as being identified conceptually, are also experienced ourselves as tourists. History is not singled out here by way of criticism but as an indicator of the boundaries researchers learn and work within. Geographical approaches to tourism, and others too, similarly reflect a set of ontological and epistemological boundaries that, it is argued, fall short in elaborating the linkages, flows and dynamics of tourism. On the one hand, it is important to maintain depth in understanding the specificities of tourism. On the other hand it raises a series of questions. In the example of historians of tourism as used above, how can we draw out common threads from a range of historical studies to better understand the phenomenon of tourism? How do we activate the links between discrete and compartmentalized studies of the past with the realities of the contemporary? Similarly, how can we better examine not only tourism in a particular place, but also with regard to a place's wider relations with the rest of world in both the real and imagined sense? Are we destined to understand tourism in a partial way? And

critically, whose role is it to move beyond the conventional boundaries we work to as researchers and who does the "joining-up" process?

Rudy Koshar (2000) reflects on the possibilities surrounding the sheer amount of information and material available to the historian of tourism. Koshar's point can be widened to the study of tourism generally as the touch of tourism is increasingly felt around the globe and at many different levels; the sheer diversity of topics for PhD studies on tourism is testimony to this (Bao, 2002; Botterill, Haven and Gale, 2002; Meyer-Arendt and Justice, 2002). Koshar, too, identifies the gaps in knowledge still to be tackled by researchers and highlights the absence of some form of general framework. He argues that this should not necessitate the generation of some grand narrative of tourism, but rather it should point to:

> the need to offer a set of more general conceptual markers that will bring organization into a field that is at present dispersed and without direction. These markers do not (and could not) add up to a comprehensive and definitive history or a general explanatory model, but rather to a set of useful heuristic constellations, whose relationship with one another remains to be elucidated. (Koshar 2000: 13)

A narrow interpretation of such words could infer the consolidation of a tourism studies discipline in a way that effectively closes down the very possibilities of cross-fertilization between the existing disciplinary approaches. A more productive interpretation is one in which emphasis is given to exploring the linkages and synergies between disciplines and the ways in which they have directed their attention to the global dynamics of tourism. Further to the cross-disciplinary collaboration that many handbook authors have also encouraged, critical research attention is needed to address the intricate interrelationships within and between various systems, spaces and patterns of consumption, in addition to modes of production. A study of culinary tourism at the destination level, for instance, might also attempt to situate the discourse of food and consumption in the wider context of food production, transportation and sustainability. Jamal et al. (2003) argue that it is important to understand how the *globality* of tourism is constructed, negotiated and hence open to creative reworking at the level of both self and society—in other words, to critically examine the discourse and sociology of globalization (Yearley, 1996), and examine closely the practices that shape the use and management of natural and cultural spaces for tourism. These spaces include natural and built environments like museums (see, for instance, Hall, 1997; Kirshenblatt-Gimblett, 1998). A useful critical approach has been to examine these spaces in terms of mediated processes of "production" and "consumption," as several handbook chapters have illustrated. Increasingly important also is addressing the distribution of costs and benefits within and between various groups, noting not only related issues of environmental justice but also cultural justice and the meaning of cultural sustainability within the complexities of transnational identities and mobilities discussed in this *Handbook* (Camargo et al., 2007).

Crossing Disciplinary Boundaries?

As reflected to some extent in this volume, the study of tourism is primarily undertaken from a range of disciplinary perspectives, or more accurately, a range of perspectives that span the more traditionally conceived disciplines such as sociology and economics to the more emergent disciplines of cultural studies and fields such as gender studies. Each chapter offers a "state-of-the-art" reflection on tourism from a particular perspective, though each also acknowledges, explicitly and implicitly, that the study of tourism comes under no particular domain but untidily works with blurred boundaries.

The undoubted purpose of any handbook is to allow specialists and, to some extent, non-specialists, to access the latest knowledge and state-of-the-art thinking and perspectives on a particular subject. Invariably, for readers this will involve some "dipping-in" and "dipping-out" of chapters, themes, and topics. However, we also hope that readers will make the effort to read the complete set of chapters in all the sections. This is a formidable request, which requires precious time, serious reflection, and a modicum of courage.

The questions posed earlier generate a genuine set of challenges to researchers from all disciplines and cut into long standing issues relating to the nature of interdisciplinarity as opposed to the multidisciplinary conventions reflected in this volume. Understanding site specifics, moments of change, and techniques, are all highly valued, but how can these be woven together and theoretically exceeded to reflect the hyper-complexities of a flowing, global phenomenon such as tourism? And the supplementary question again arises as to *who* is able to do this? Despite the realities and multilayered experiences of tourism, our research apparatus and research culture is still heavily loaded toward national interests and disciplinary traditions. As Fuller (2003) suggests, in the academic environment, interdisciplinarity is a high-risk undertaking for researchers. Undertaking a full-scale reconstruction of academic disciplines to account for global and complex realities such as tourism is unnecessary. Instead, and what appears to work well, is to keep attention away from structural change and direct it toward cultural change effected through the enactment of creative multidisciplinary partnerships, projects, and social spaces in which academics can freely explore and exchange ideas and approaches. This implies openness and willingness to move, periodically at least outside of disciplinary comfort zones and "traditional" curricula.

As various *Handbook* chapters demonstrate, critical cultural studies are being introduced into tourism studies, but one has still to step into other disciplines like geography, sociology or cultural anthropology, in order to explore various strands of critical inquiry and classic/contemporary theorists relevant to the tourism topic of interest. Returning to the field of tourism *studies* and applying these "other" perspectives opens up possibilities for interdisciplinary theory building and a more critical reflexive researcher (or practitioner) who can approach the wide diversity of topics in tourism critically yet thoughtfully. No matter whether it is wine tourism, retail, shopping, second homes, resort growth, or one of the topics addressed in this *Handbook*—religion and spirituality, volunteer tourism, special events, theme parks, national parks, thanatourism, urban destinations or cruising at sea, global tourism system or the management and marketing of local destinations—a critical, yet reflexive researcher is an imperative participant in tourism and tourism studies.

Location, Translocation and Translation

As mentioned in the Introduction of this volume, a majority of the world does not practice tourism though is probably affected by it. The great drivers of tourism have come from the developed nations of the North and West of the globe (with some notable exceptions such as Australia and Japan, etc.), so it is hardly surprising that the study of tourism has emerged from the nations that practice, and essentially control, tourism. As Bruner and Kirschenblatt-Gimblett (1994) demonstrated in their work on the ways by which the Masai dress for tourists, tourism is scripted (in this case by the tour operator), increasingly at a distance. The local and the global are increasingly linked and the relations which are exhibited in tourism are

shaped by both the immediate (such as an incident of terrorism or a natural disaster), and the gradual, and often imperceptible, playing out of longer histories (colonial relations, trade, exchange relationships, etc.) and narratives—real and imagined. Studies of tourism increasingly need to adopt an approach which situates an activity or a location within the nexus of the immediate and long term, the near and the distant and, the real and the imagined.

The patterns and flows of international tourism are themselves changing however, and relations between places are being reconfigured and in some cases, reversed. Powerful countries such as China and India are increasingly developing outbound tourism sectors, together with related infrastructures to underpin these, which includes educational and research capacities. This raises exciting prospects for extending understandings of tourism amongst scholars already engaged and immersed in the study of tourism in the developed world. However, we need more involvement from scholars from the developing world to share their insights and perspectives on tourism, in order to break the binaries of "us" studying "them." Moving beyond a first world analysis of tourism presents the obvious challenge of working outside the dominant languages of tourism studies. But this is more than an issue of language. It poses major questions regarding the (in)commensurability between intellectual traditions: Do all our understandings of tourism need to make reference to the critical Euro-rooted traditions? Can the developed world accept a system of tourism that is rooted in different sets of values, needs, wants and aesthetic preferences which is different to its own? Can the developed world *learn* of tourism with reference to interpretive systems and local cosmologies from the developing world? The well-cited case of Bhutan's bold subversion of modernist notions of progress through growth (which undergirds notions such as GDP and GNP) to aim for sustainable development and GNH (Gross National Happiness) is one of many such instances worth exploring for "other" perspectives.[1]

These are ethical questions which extend into the policymaking world. Increasingly such questions are being addressed with regard to the major sustainability and development debates. While the linguistic and postmodern turns of the twentieth century have encouraged social scientists to engage in epistemological debates such as that of the social construction of science and nature (Cronon, 1996), "nature" (the biophysical world) itself still appears to be taken as a simple given in tourism research. What sort of nature is being represented in the destination sites, whose construction is it and how it is communicated, are infrequently questioned among scholars in tourism studies. What do we sustain in terms of constructs such as "nature," and built and intangible "heritage" for instance? Or rather, *whose* constructs are allowed to participate in the debate? Such questions imply not only deeper understandings of the wider contexts of tourism with respect to shifts in worldviews, but they also imply a process of translation, whereby attempts are made to gain entry to and understand different worldviews.

The central point is that despite the fact that notions of flows, currents, and mobilities that have emerged over recent years and which have provided helpful frameworks for seeing tourism as something constantly moving along axes of space and time (see for instance Appadurai, 1996; Bauman, 1998; Bhabha, 1994; Hannerz, 1996; Sheller and Urry, 2004, 2006), our approaches to investigating tourism still generally remain fixed in specific and static *frames*. What we suggest is required are approaches that look more to notions of sequencing where the linkages and overlaps in tourism are able to be tracked and made explicit, through research in tourism which is (1) coordinated, cognizant of globalities, and the realities of tourism, (2) longitudinal, cumulative, and capable of being translated and transposed across disciplinary and cultural boundaries into local, regional, national, and transnational policy arenas, as well as ethically conducted and directed. These are ambitious targets for those engaged in the study of tourism but targets that are appropriate for such a dynamic and world changing phenomenon.

Notes

1 See, for instance, "The 10th Plan will be GNH-oriented," *Bhutan Observer*, April 4, 2008. Online at www.bhutanobserver.bt/2008/bhutan-news/04/the-10th-plan-will-be-gnh-oriented.html. Accessed June 23, 2008.

References

Appadurai, A. (1996). *Modernity at Large—Cultural Dimensions of Globalization*. Minneapolis: University of Minnesota Press.

Bao, J. (2002). "Tourism Geography as the Subject of Doctoral Dissertations in China, 1989–2000." *Tourism Geographies*, 4: 148–152.

Bauman, Z. (1998). *Globalization: The Human Consequences*. New York: Columbia University Press.

Berghoff, H., Korte, B., Schneider, R. and Harvie, C. (2002). *The Making of Modern Tourism: The Cultural History of the British Experience, 1600–2000*. London: Palgrave.

Bhabha, H.K. (1994). *The Location of Culture*. London: Routledge.

Boorstin, D.J. (1987). *The Image, A Guide to Pseudo Events in America*. New York: Atheneum.

Botterill, D., Haven, C. and Gale, T. (2002). "A Survey of Doctoral Theses Accepted by Universities in the UK and Ireland for Studies of Tourism, 1990–1999." *Tourist Studies* 2(3): 283–311.

Bruner, E.M. and Kirshenblatt-Gimblett, B. (1994). "Maasai on the Lawn: Tourism Realism in East Africa." *Cultural Anthropology*, 9(2): 435–470.

Camargo, B., Lane, K. and Jamal, T. (2007). "Environmental Justice and Sustainable

Tourism: The Missing Cultural Link." *The George Wright Society Forum*, 24(3): 70–80.

Cronon, W. (Ed.) (1996). *Uncommon Ground: Rethinking the Human Place in Nature*. New York: Norton.

Duffield, Mark (2001). *Global Governance and the New Wars: The Merging of Development and Security*. London: Zed.

Fuller, S. (2003). "Interdisciplinarity. The Loss of the Heroic Vision in the Marketplace of Ideas." Paper presented at the *Rethinking Interdisciplinarity—Emergent Issues Conference*, (Moderators, Heintz, C., Sperber, D. and Origgi, G.). Retrieved June 11, 2008 from www.interdisciplines.org/interdisciplinarity/papers/3

Fussell, P. (1980). *Abroad: British Literary Travelling Between the Wars*. Oxford: Oxford University Press.

Hall, S. (Ed.) (1997). *Representation: Cultural Representation and Signifying Practices*. London: Sage Publications.

Hannerz, U. (1996). *Transnational Connections*. London: Routledge.

Inglis, F. (2000). *The Delicious History of the Holiday*. London: Routledge.

Jamal, T., Everett, J. and Dann, G.M. (2003). "Ecological Rationalization and Performative Resistance in Natural Area Destinations." *Tourist Studies*, 3(2): 143–169.

Kirshenblatt-Gimblett, B. (1998). *Destination Cultures: Tourism, Museums, and Heritage*. Berkeley: University of California Press.

Koshar, R. (2000). *German Travel Cultures*. Oxford: Berg.

Lofgren, O. (1999). *On Holiday: A History of Vacationing*. Berkeley: University of California Press.

Meyer-Arendt, K. and Justice, C. (2002). "Tourism as the Subject of North American Doctoral Dissertations, 1987–2000." *Annals of Tourism Research*, 29(4): 1171–1174.

O'Brien, R., Goetz, A.M., Scholte, J.A. and Williams, M. (2000). *Contesting Global Governance: Multilateral Economic Institutions and Global Social Movements*. Cambridge: Cambridge University Press.

Ousby, I. (1990). *The Englishman's England: Taste, Travel and the Rise of Tourism*. Cambridge: Cambridge University Press.

Rojek, C. and Urry, J. (Eds.) (1997). *Touring Cultures: Transformations of Travel and Theory*. London: Routledge.

Rojek, C., Veal, A.J. and Shaw, S.M. (2007). *A Handbook of Leisure Studies*. London: Palgrave Macmillan.

Rothman, H.K. (1998). *Devil's Bargains: Tourism in the Twentieth-Century American West*. Lawrence: University Press of Kansas.

Rugh, S.S. (2008). *Are We There Yet?: The Golden Age of American Family Holidays*. Lawrence: University Press of Kansas.

Sears, J.F. (1998). *Sacred Places: American Tourist Attractions in the Nineteenth Century*. Amherst: University of Massachusetts Press.

Sheller, M. and Urry, J. (2004). *Tourism Mobilities: Places to Stay, Places in Play*. London: Routledge.

Sheller, M. and Urry, J. (2006). "The New Mobilities Paradigm." *Environment and Planning A*, 38(2): 207–226.

Towner, J. (1996). *An Historical Geography of Recreation and Tourism in the Western World*. Chichester: John Wiley & Sons.

Walton, J.K. (2005). *Histories of Tourism: Representation, Identity, and Conflict*. Clevedon: Channel View Press.

White, R. (2005). On Holidays: *A History of Getting Away in Australia*. North Melbourne, Australia: Pluto Press.

Yearley, S. (1996). *Sociology, Environmentalism, Globalization*. London: Sage Publications.

INDEX